A-Z

LONDON
Street Atlas

Geographers' A-Z Map Company Ltd.

D0435631

Geographers' A-Z Map Company Ltd.

Fairfield Road, Borough Green, Sevenoaks, Kent TN15 8PP
Telephone : 01732 781000 (Enquiries & Trade Sales)
          01732 783422 (Retail Sales)

www.a-zmaps.co.uk

The publishers are deeply grateful for the ready co-operation and valuable help
given to them in the production of this atlas. They would like to record their
obligation to: The Engineers and Surveyors Departments and Planning Offices
of all the Local Authorities covered in this atlas, The Department for Transport,
Highways Agency, Transport for London, The Post Office, Police Authorities,
Fire Brigades, Taxi Drivers, Members of the Public.

Printed and bound in the United Kingdom by Polestar Wheatons Ltd., Exeter.

An AtoZ Publication

CONTENTS

REFERENCE

Motorway	**M1**
A Road	**A2**
Under Construction	
Proposed	
B Road	**B408**
Dual Carriageway	
One-way	
Traffic flow on A Roads is indicated by a heavy line on the driver's left.	
Junction Name	**MARBLE ARCH**
Restricted Access	
Pedestrianized Road	
Track & Footpath	
Residential Walkway	
Congestion Charging Zone	
Superscale pages only	
Railway	Tunnel
Stations:	Level Crossing
National Rail Network	
Docklands Light Railway	**DLR**
Underground Station ● ⊖	is the registered trade mark of Transport for London
Croydon Tramlink	Tunnel
The boarding of Tramlink trams at stops may be limited to a single direction, indicated by the arrow.	Stop
Map Continuation	**62**
	Large Scale Map Pages **160**
National Grid Reference	⁵30

Built-up Area	BANK STREET
House Numbers A & B Roads only	51 19 48 22
Car Park Selected	**P**
Church or Chapel	†
Fire Station	■
Hospital	**H**
Information Centre	**i**
Park & Ride	Bromley **P+**
Police Station	▲
Post Office	★
River Bus Stop	**R**
Toilet	▽
with facilities for the Disabled	▽
Disabled facilities only	▽
Educational Establishment	
Hospital or Hospice etc.	
Industrial Building	
Leisure or Recreational Facility	
Place of Interest	
Public Building	
Shopping Centre or Market	
Other Selected Buildings	

SCALE

Map Pages 4-19
1:11,000 5¾ inches to 1 Mile

0	⅛	¼

0	100	200	300	400	500 Metres

14.62cm to 1 mile 9.1cm to 1 km

Map Pages 20-173
1:22,000 2.88 inches to 1 Mile

0	¼	½

0	250	500	750 Metres	1 Kilometre

7.31cm to 1 mile 4.55cm to 1 km

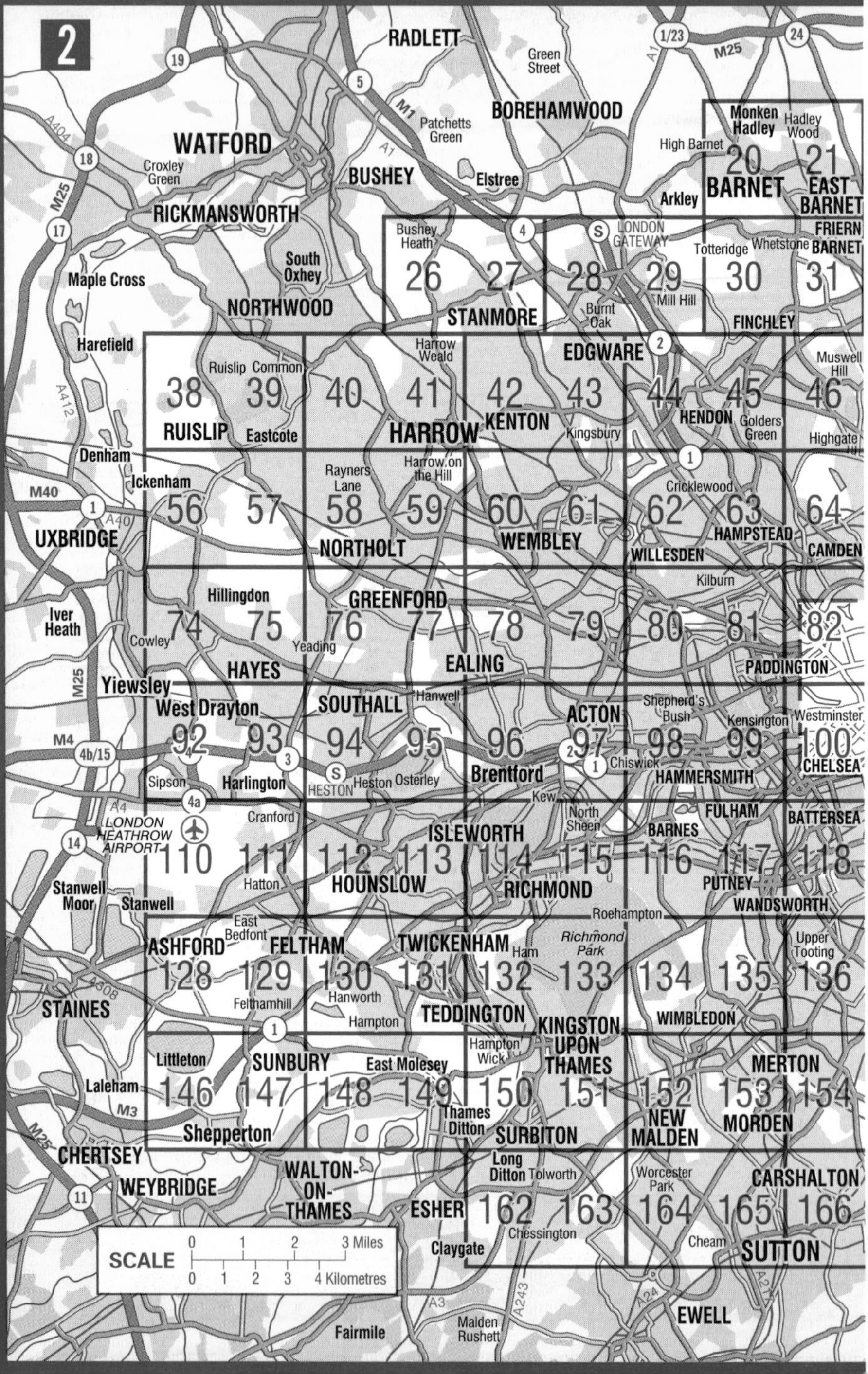

2

RADLETT

Green Street

M25 1/23 24

WATFORD
Croxley Green
Patchetts Green
BOREHAMWOOD
High Barnet
Monken Hadley Hadley Wood
BARNET 20 21 **EAST BARNET**

BUSHEY
Elstree
Arkley

RICKMANSWORTH
Bushey Heath 4
LONDON GATEWAY S
FRIERN BARNET

Maple Cross
South Oxhey
26 27 28 29 30 31
Totteridge Whetstone
STANMORE
Burnt Oak
Mill Hill
FINCHLEY

NORTHWOOD

Harefield
Harrow Weald
EDGWARE 2
Muswell Hill

38 39 40 41 42 43 44 45 46
Ruislip Common
RUISLIP Eastcote
HARROW KENTON
Kingsbury
HENDON Golders Green
Highgate

Denham
M40
Ickenham
Rayners Lane
Harrow on the Hill
Cricklewood

56 57 58 59 60 61 62 63 64
UXBRIDGE
NORTHOLT
WEMBLEY
WILLESDEN
HAMPSTEAD
CAMDEN

Iver Heath
Hillingdon
GREENFORD
Kilburn

74 75 76 77 78 79 80 81 82
Cowley
Yeading
EALING
PADDINGTON

Yiewsley
HAYES
Hanwell
Shepherd's Bush
Kensington
Westminster

West Drayton
SOUTHALL
ACTON
100
92 93 94 95 96 97 98 99
M4 4b/15
Sipson Harlington
HESTON S Heston Osterley
Chiswick
HAMMERSMITH
CHELSEA

Brentford
Kew
FULHAM
BATTERSEA

LONDON HEATHROW AIRPORT
Cranford
North Sheen
BARNES

14
110 111 112 113 114 115 116 117 118
Stanwell Moor Stanwell
Hatton
HOUNSLOW
ISLEWORTH
RICHMOND
PUTNEY
WANDSWORTH

East Bedfont
Roehampton
Upper Tooting

ASHFORD FELTHAM
TWICKENHAM Ham
Richmond Park
128 129 130 131 132 133 134 135 136
STAINES
Felthamhill
Hanworth
Hampton
TEDDINGTON
KINGSTON UPON THAMES
WIMBLEDON

Littleton
SUNBURY
East Molesey
Hampton Wick
MERTON
146 147 148 149 150 151 152 153 154
Laleham
M3
Shepperton
Thames Ditton
SURBITON
NEW MALDEN
MORDEN

CHERTSEY
WEYBRIDGE
WALTON-ON-THAMES
Long Ditton Tolworth
Worcester Park
CARSHALTON

11
ESHER
162 163 164 165 166
Claygate
Chessington
Cheam
SUTTON

SCALE 0 1 2 3 Miles
0 1 2 3 4 Kilometres

Fairmile
Malden Rushett
EWELL

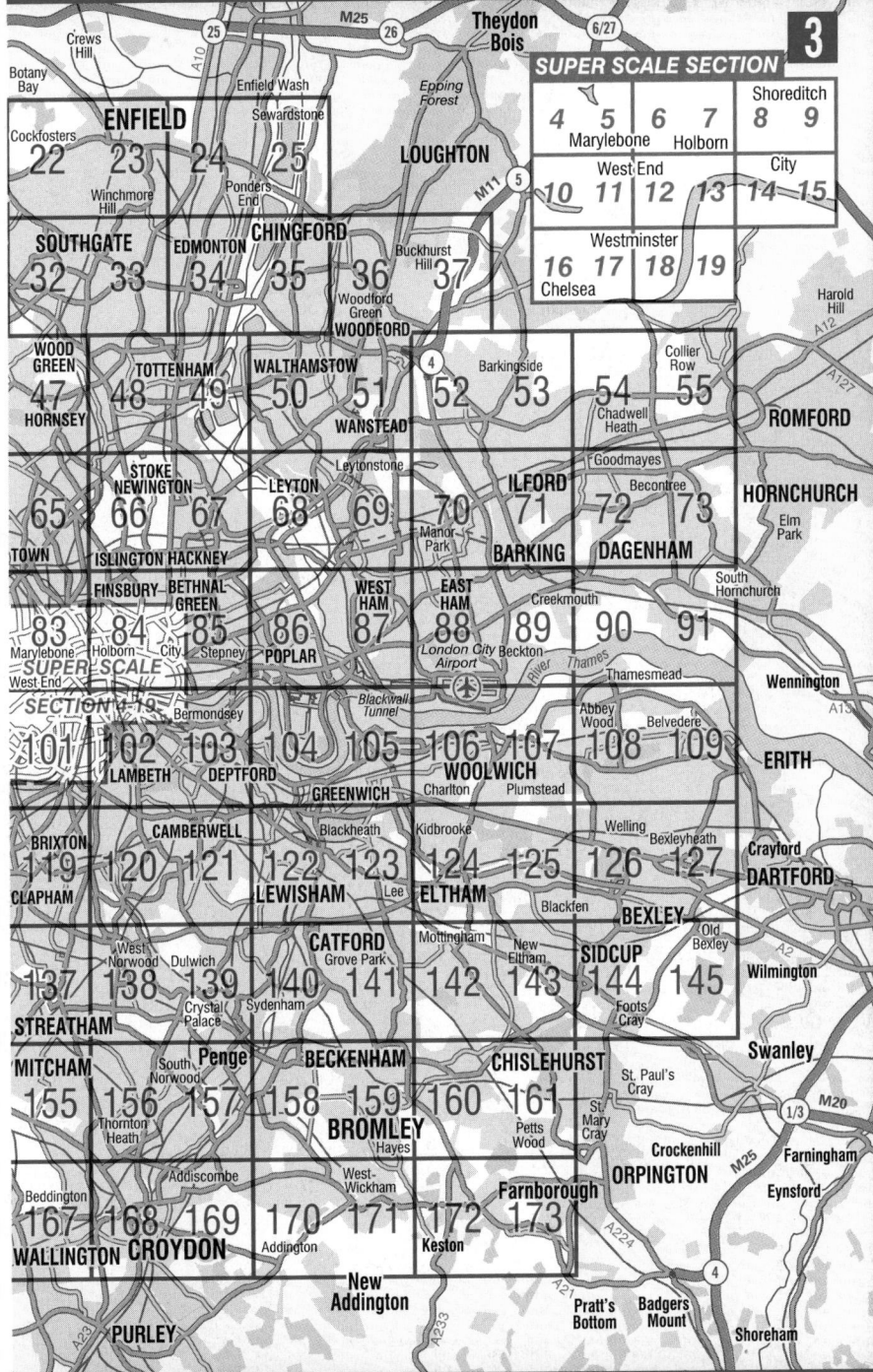
SUPER SCALE SECTION
4 5 6 7 8 9
Marylebone
Holborn
Shoreditch
West End
City
10 11 12 13 14 15
Westminster
16 17 18 19
Chelsea
ENFIELD
22 23 24 25
SOUTHGATE
EDMONTON
CHINGFORD
32 33 34 35 36 37
WOODFORD
WOOD GREEN
TOTTENHAM
WALTHAMSTOW
47 48 49 50 51 52 53 54 55
HORNSEY
WANSTEAD
ROMFORD
STOKE NEWINGTON
LEYTON
ILFORD
65 66 67 68 69 70 71 72 73
HORNCHURCH
ISLINGTON
HACKNEY
BARKING
DAGENHAM
FINSBURY
BETHNAL GREEN
WEST HAM
EAST HAM
83 84 85 86 87 88 89 90 91
POPLAR
SUPER SCALE SECTION 4-19
101 102 103 104 105 106 107 108 109
LAMBETH
DEPTFORD
GREENWICH
WOOLWICH
ERITH
BRIXTON
CAMBERWELL
119 120 121 122 123 124 125 126 127
CLAPHAM
LEWISHAM
ELTHAM
DARTFORD
BEXLEY
CATFORD
SIDCUP
137 138 139 140 141 142 143 144 145
STREATHAM
MITCHAM
BECKENHAM
CHISLEHURST
155 156 157 158 159 160 161
BROMLEY
ORPINGTON
167 168 169 170 171 172 173
WALLINGTON
CROYDON
PURLEY
Theydon Bois
LOUGHTON
Crews Hill
Botany Bay
Cockfosters
Enfield Wash
Sewardstone
Epping Forest
Winchmore Hill
Ponders End
Buckhurst Hill
Woodford Green
Barkingside
Collier Row
Harold Hill
Chadwell Heath
Goodmayes
Becontree
Leytonstone
Manor Park
Elm Park
South Hornchurch
Creekmouth
Marylebone
Holborn
City
Stepney
London City Airport
Beckton
River Thames
Thamesmead
Wennington
Bermondsey
Blackwall Tunnel
Abbey Wood
Belvedere
Charlton
Plumstead
Blackheath
Kidbrooke
Welling
Bexleyheath
Crayford
Lee
Blackfen
Mottingham
Old Bexley
West Norwood
Dulwich
Grove Park
New Eltham
Wilmington
Crystal Palace
Sydenham
Foots Cray
Swanley
Penge
South Norwood
St. Paul's Cray
Thornton Heath
Hayes
Petts Wood
St. Mary Cray
Crockenhill
Farningham
Addiscombe
West Wickham
Farnborough
Eynsford
Beddington
Addington
Keston
New Addington
Pratt's Bottom
Badgers Mount
Shoreham
M25
M11
M20
A10
A12
A127
A13
A2
A224
A21
A233
A23
25
26
6/27
5
4
1/3
TOWN

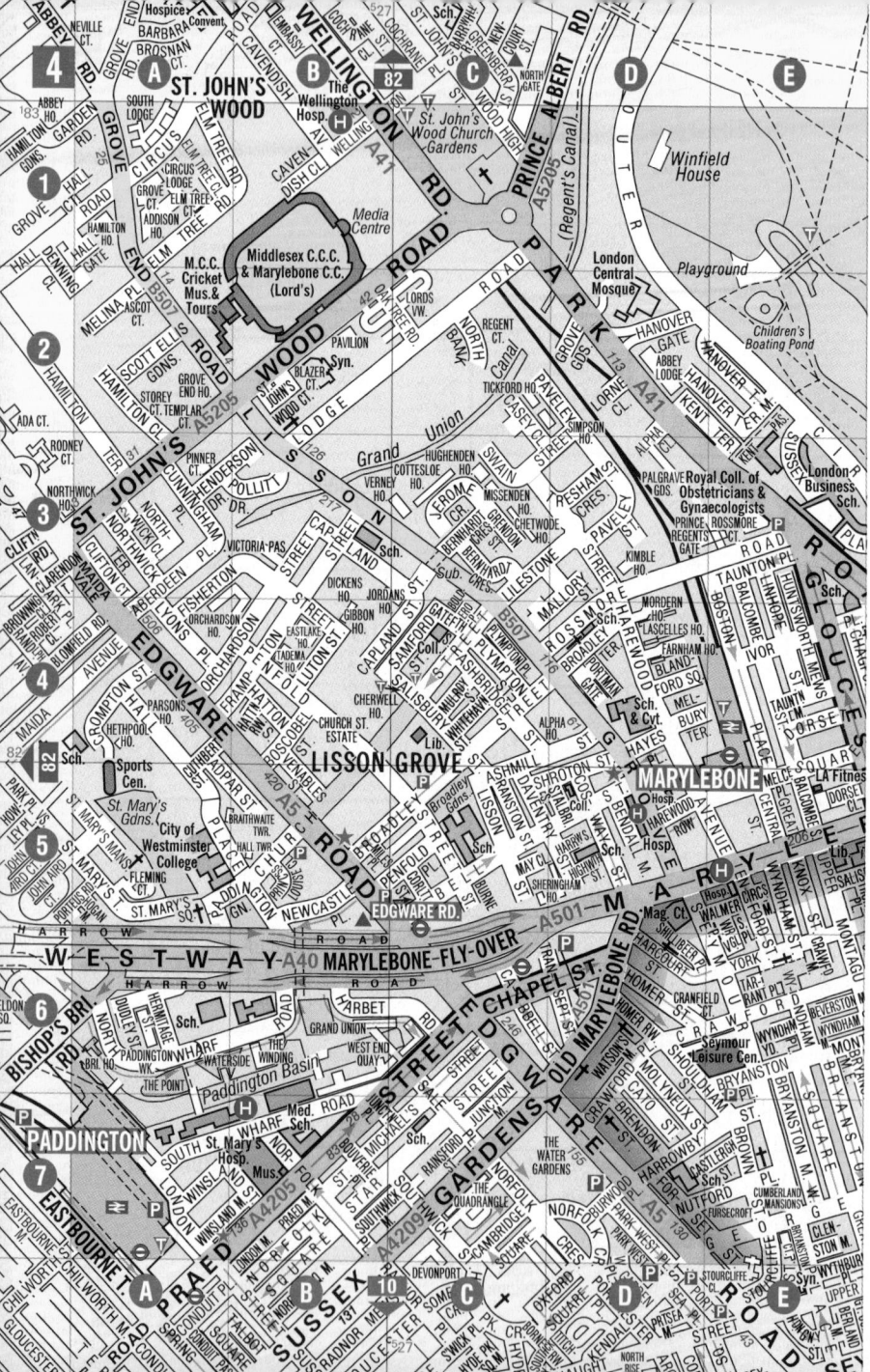
4
A
B
C
D
E
1
2
3
4
5
6
7
82
10
ST. JOHN'S WOOD
LISSON GROVE
MARYLEBONE
PADDINGTON
EDGWARE RD.
ABBEY RD.
NEVILLE CT.
Hospice
Convent
BARBARA
BROSNAN CT.
GROVE END RD.
CAVENDISH
EMBASSY CT.
WELLINGTON
COCHRANE
ST. JOHN'S
BARRWHILL
GREENBERRY
NEW COURT ST.
PRINCE ALBERT RD.
NORTH GATE
OUTER CIRCLE
Winfield House
ABBEY HO.
HAMILTON GARDEN
SOUTH LODGE
CIRCUS
ELM TREE RD.
ELM TREE CL.
CIRCUS LODGE
GROVE CT.
ADDISON HO.
The Wellington Hosp.
St. John's Wood Church Gardens
CAVENDISH CL.
WELLINGTON RD.
A41
A5205
(Regent's Canal)
HAMILTON GDNS.
GROVE HALL CT.
HAMILTON HO.
HALL GATE
DENNING CL.
Media Centre
Middlesex C.C.C. & Marylebone C.C. (Lord's)
M.C.C. Cricket Mus.& Tours
London Central Mosque
Playground
Children's Boating Pond
MELINA PL.
ASCOT CT.
B507
LORDS VW.
OAK TREE RD.
PAVILION
BLAZER CT.
Syn.
NORTH BANK
REGENT CT.
HANOVER GATE
ABBEY LODGE
HANOVER TER.
HANOVER TER. M.
KENT TER.
SCOTT ELLIS GDNS.
GROVE END HO.
HAMILTON CL.
STOREY CT.
TEMPLAR CT.
ST. JOHN'S WOOD CT.
LODGE ROAD
TICKFORD HO.
GROVE GDS.
LORNE CL.
PAVELEY
CASEY CL.
SIMPSON HO.
ALPHA CL.
SUSSEX PL.
London Business Sch.
ADA CT.
RODNEY CT.
HAMILTON TER.
PINNER CT.
HENDERSON DR.
POLLITT DR.
CUNNINGHAM PL.
Grand Union Canal
HUGHENDEN HO.
COTTESLOE HO.
VERNEY HO.
SWAIN STREET
JEROME CR.
MISSENDEN HO.
RESHAM CRES.
PALGRAVE GDS.
Royal Coll. of Obstetricians & Gynaecologists
NORTHWICK HO.
ST. JOHN'S WOOD ROAD
NORTHWICK CL.
NORTHWICK TER.
CLIFTON CT.
CLIFTON RD.
VICTORIA PAS.
CAPLAND STREET
Sch.
BERNHARDT CRES.
GRENDON ST.
CHETWODE HO.
PAVELEY ST.
PRINCE REGENTS GATE
ROSSMORE CT.
ROSSMORE ROAD
GLOUCESTER PL.
KIMBLE HO.
TAUNTON PL.
BALCOMBE ST.
LINHOPE ST.
HUNTSWORTH MEWS
MAIDA VALE
CLARENDON
LANARK PL.
ROBERT CL.
BROWNING CL.
RANDOLPH AV.
BLOMFIELD RD.
ABERDEEN PL.
LYONS PL.
FISHERTON
ORCHARDSON HO.
ORCHARDSON
DICKENS HO.
JORDANS HO.
GIBBON HO.
EASTLAKE HO.
TADEMA HO.
LUTON ST.
CAPLAND ST.
SAMFORD ST.
GATEFORTH ST.
Coll.
PLYMPTON ST.
ASHBRIDGE ST.
LILESTONE ST.
MALLORY ST.
MORDEN HO.
LASCELLES HO.
HAREWOOD
BROADLEY TER.
BOSTON PL.
IVOR PL.
MAIDA AVENUE
EDGWARE ROAD
CROMPTON ST.
HALL PL.
PARSONS HO.
FRAMPTON ST.
PENFOLD ST.
HATTON ST.
MULROY HO.
WHITEHAVEN ST.
SALISBURY ST.
PORTMAN GATE
BLANDFORD SQ.
MELBURY TER.
FARNHAM HO.
TAUNTON M.
DORSET SQUARE
HETHPOOL HO.
BOSCOBEL ST.
CHERWELL HO.
CHURCH ST. ESTATE
Lib.
ALPHA HO.
Sch. & Cvt.
HAYES PL.
Sports Cen.
St. Mary's Gdns.
CUTHBERT ST.
ADPAR ST.
VENABLES ST.
BROADLEY STREET
Broadley Gdns.
ASHMILL ST.
LISSON ST.
SHROTON ST.
DAVENTRY ST.
STALBRIDGE ST.
COSWAY ST.
BENDALL M.
Hosp.
HAREWOOD ROW
HAREWOOD AVENUE
MELCOMBE PL.
CENTRAL ST.
GREAT CENTRAL
BALCOMBE ST.
LA Fitness
DORSET CL.
PARK PL. VS.
HOWLEY PL.
ST. MARY'S MANS.
BRAITHWAITE TWR.
HALL TWR.
City of Westminster College
PADDINGTON GN.
CHURCH ST.
PRINCE LOUISE CL.
MILES PL.
PENFOLD PL.
CORLETT ST.
BELL ST.
BURNE ST.
RANSTON ST.
MAY CL.
HARROWBY ST.
HIGHWITH ST.
SHERINGHAM HO.
Sch.
MARYLEBONE ROAD
KNOX ST.
UPPER
Lib.
JOHN AIRD CT.
FLEMING CT.
ST. MARY'S SQ.
ST. MARY'S ST.
PORTEUS RD.
HOGAN M.
NEWCASTLE PL.
HARROW ROAD
WESTWAY
A40
MARYLEBONE FLY-OVER
A501
Mag. Ct.
WALMER PL.
SHILLIBEER PL.
WYNDHAM ST.
CIRCUS M.
SEYMOUR PL.
YORK ST.
CRAWFORD M.
MONTAGU
TRANSEPT ST.
CHAPEL ST.
HARCOURT ST.
TARRANT PL.
CRAWFORD ST.
BEVERSTON M.
WYNDHAM PL.
WYNDHAM YD.
HELDON SQ.
BISHOP'S BRI. RD.
NORTH WHARF
DUDLEY ST.
HERMITAGE ST.
Sch.
HARBET RD.
CABBELL ST.
EDGWARE ROAD
OLD MARYLEBONE RD
HOMER ST.
HOMER RW.
CRANFIELD CT.
PADDINGTON WHARF
GRAND UNION
WEST END QUAY
WATERSIDE
THE WINDING
THE POINT
BRI. HO.
PADDINGTON WK.
Paddington Basin
SALE PL.
STREET
JUNCTION M.
WATSON'S M.
CRAWFORD PL.
MOLYNEUX ST.
SHOULDHAM ST.
Seymour Leisure Cen.
BRYANSTON PL.
BRYANSTON ST.
BRYANSTON SQUARE
BRYANSTON M. W.
BRYANSTON M. E.
SOUTH WHARF ROAD
Med. Sch.
St. Mary's Hosp.
Mus.
NORFOLK PL.
SOUTH
EDGWARE
CATO ST.
BRENDON ST.
HARROWBY ST.
BROWN ST.
STREET
SUSSEX GARDENS
THE WATER GARDENS
CASTLEREAGH ST.
Sch.
CUMBERLAND MANSIONS
PADDINGTON
EASTBOURNE T.
LONDON ST.
WINSLAND ST.
WINSLAND M.
A4205
BOUVERIE PL.
ST. MICHAEL'S
Sch.
RAINSFORD ST.
SOUTHWICK PL.
THE QUADRANGLE
NORFOLK CRES.
BURWOOD PL.
PARK WEST PL.
NUTFORD PL.
FURSECROFT
CLENSTON M.
A5
EASTBOURNE M.
CHILWORTH ST.
CHILWORTH M.
PRAED ST.
LONDON M.
PRAED M.
NORFOLK SQUARE
STAR ST.
SOUTHWICK M.
A4209
CAMBRIDGE SQUARE
NORFOLK CRES.
PORTSEA PL.
SEYMOUR
STOURCLIFFE ST.
STOURCLIFFE CL.
BRYANSTON CT.
Syn.
WYTHBURN
UPPER
GLOUCESTER
CONDUIT PL.
SPRING ST.
TALBOT SQUARE
SUSSEX
RADNOR M.
DEVONPORT
SOMERS CR.
HYDE PK. CR.
OXFORD SQUARE
KENDAL ST.
CONNAUGHT
STREET
PORTSEA M.
BERLAND M.
NORTH RISE
ROAD

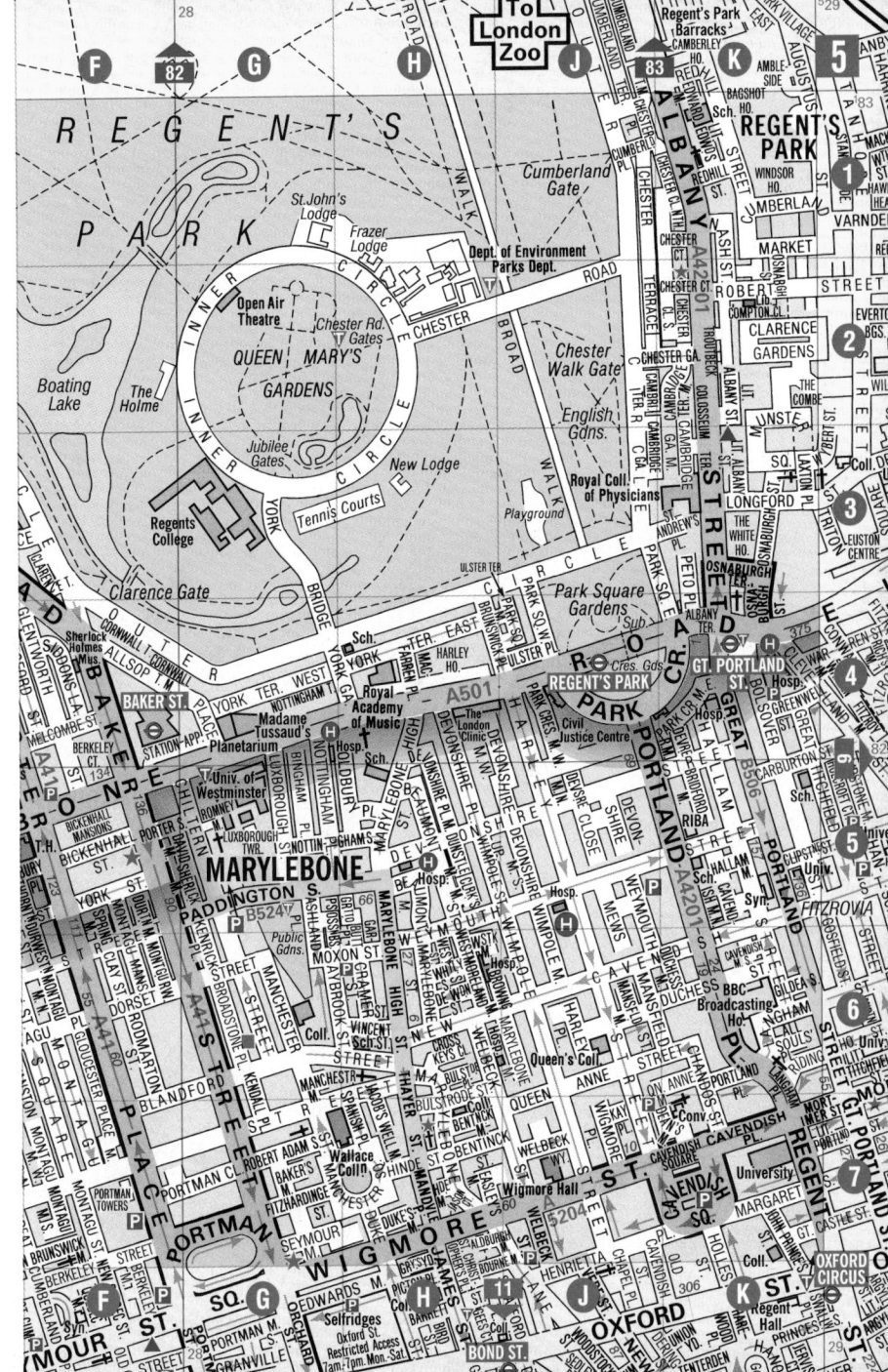
28
F
82
G
H
To London Zoo
J
83
K
5
Regent's Park Barracks
REGENT'S PARK
Cumberland Gate
St.John's Lodge
Frazer Lodge
Dept. of Environment Parks Dept.
INNER CIRCLE
Open Air Theatre
Chester Rd. Gates
QUEEN MARY'S GARDENS
CHESTER ROAD
BROAD WALK
Chester Walk Gate
English Gdns.
Boating Lake
The Holme
Jubilee Gates
New Lodge
Tennis Courts
Playground
Royal Coll. of Physicians
Regents College
YORK BRIDGE
Clarence Gate
OUTER CIRCLE
Park Square Gardens
ALBANY STREET
A4201
CLARENCE GARDENS
MUNSTER SQ.
CUMBERLAND MARKET
ROBERT STREET
LONGFORD
THE WHITE HO.
EUSTON CENTRE
Sherlock Holmes Mus.
BAKER ST.
BAKER STREET
Madame Tussaud's
Planetarium
Royal Academy of Music
The London Clinic
A501
MARYLEBONE ROAD
REGENT'S PARK
GT. PORTLAND ST.
PARK CRESCENT
Civil Justice Centre
Univ. of Westminster
MARYLEBONE
RIBA
HARLEY STREET
PORTLAND PLACE
DEVONSHIRE CLOSE
WEYMOUTH MEWS
WIMPOLE STREET
MARYLEBONE HIGH ST.
PADDINGTON ST.
Public Gdns.
MOXON ST.
NEW CAVENDISH STREET
BBC Broadcasting Ho.
FITZROVIA
GREAT PORTLAND STREET
QUEEN ANNE STREET
Queen's Coll.
MONTAGU SQUARE
GLOUCESTER PLACE
A41
BAKER STREET
BLANDFORD ST.
MANCHESTER SQ.
Wallace Colln
Wigmore Hall
WIGMORE ST.
A5204
CAVENDISH SQ.
University
MARGARET ST.
REGENT ST.
PORTMAN SQ.
PORTMAN TOWERS
SEYMOUR ST.
Selfridges
Oxford St. Restricted Access 7am.-7pm. Mon.-Sat.
11
BOND ST.
OXFORD ST.
OXFORD CIRCUS
Regent Hall
1
2
3
4
5
6
7
29

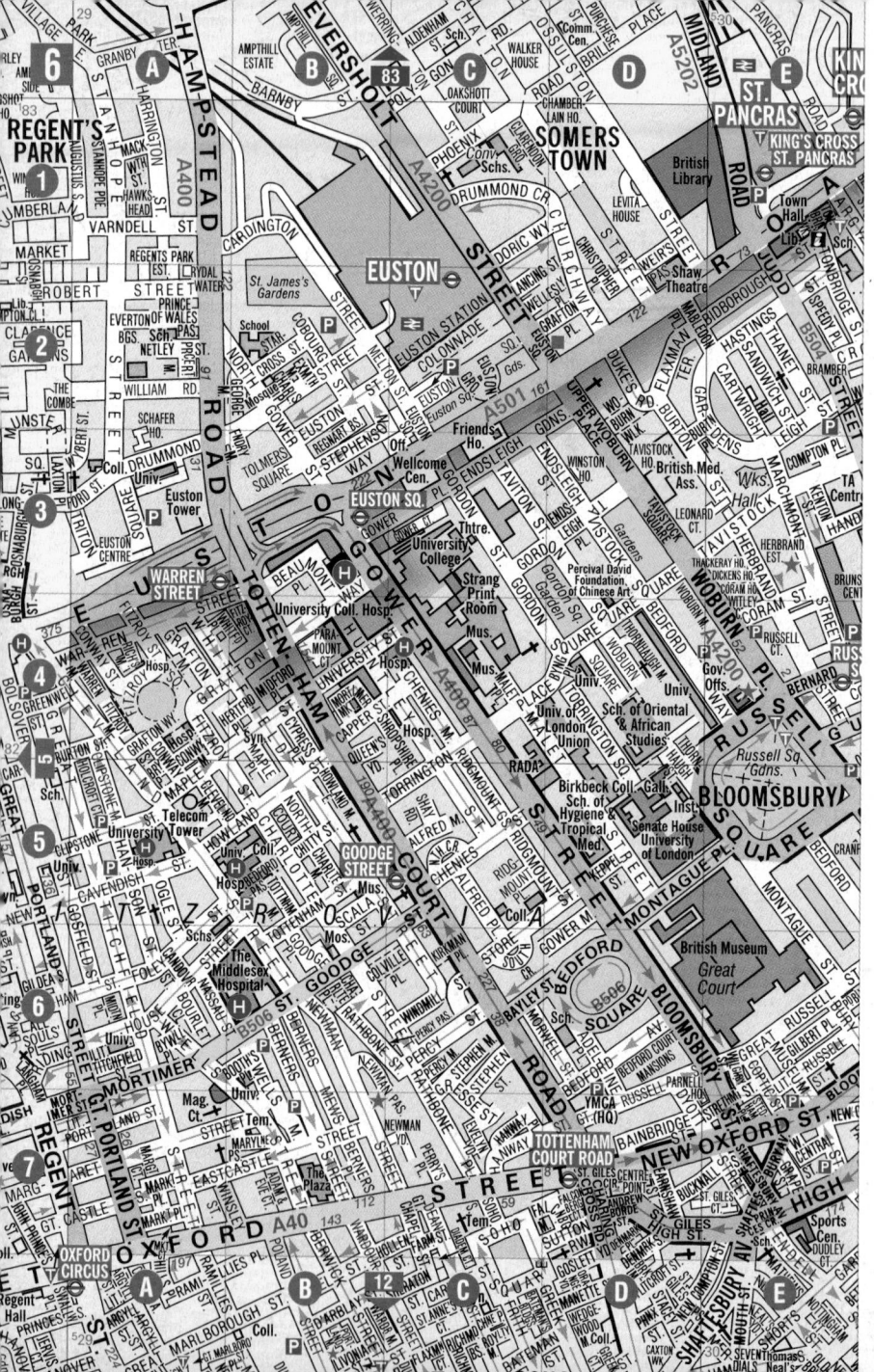

6
A
B
C
D
E
83
REGENT'S PARK
SOMERS TOWN
British Library
ST. PANCRAS
KING'S CROSS ST. PANCRAS
EUSTON
EUSTON SQ.
WARREN STREET
GOODGE STREET
TOTTENHAM COURT ROAD
OXFORD CIRCUS
BLOOMSBURY
FITZROVIA
EUSTON ROAD
HAMPSTEAD ROAD
EVERSHOLT STREET
MIDLAND ROAD
TOTTENHAM COURT ROAD
GOWER STREET
BLOOMSBURY STREET
WOBURN PL.
RUSSELL SQUARE
BEDFORD SQUARE
NEW OXFORD ST.
OXFORD STREET
GREAT PORTLAND STREET
GT. PORTLAND ST.
REGENT ST.
HIGH ST.
SHAFTESBURY AV.
CHARING CROSS RD.
SOHO SQUARE
ST. GILES CIRCUS
CENTRE POINT
St. James's Gardens
University College
Strang Print Room
University Coll. Hosp.
Percival David Foundation of Chinese Art
Gordon Sq. Garden
Tavistock Square Gardens
Russell Sq. Gdns.
British Museum
Great Court
Senate House University of London
Birkbeck Coll.
Sch. of Hygiene & Tropical Med.
Sch. of Oriental & African Studies
Univ. of London Union
Telecom Tower
The Middlesex Hospital
Euston Tower
Wellcome Cen.
Friends Ho.
British Med. Ass.
Shaw Theatre
Town Hall
YMCA (HQ)
The Plaza
A400
A4200
A501
A5202
A40
B506
B504
1
2
3
4
5
6
7
12
5

7
8
83
84
13
PENTONVILLE ROAD
A501
KING'S CROSS THAMESLINK
KING'S CROSS
GRAY'S INN ROAD
A5200
SWINTON ST.
ACTON ST.
ST. PANCRAS
ARGYLE SQUARE
CALEDONIA ST.
YORK WAY
BIRKENHEAD ST.
CHAD'S PL.
BRITANNIA ST.
LEEKE ST.
London Inst.
Hosp.
WHARTON ST.
GREAT PERCY ST.
PERCY CIR.
PRIDEAUX PL.
Holford Gds.
MYDDELTON SQUARE
AMWELL ST.
CLAREMONT SQ.
Covered Res.
The Angel Centre
ST. JOHN ST.
Dame Alice Owen's Coll.
Sadler's Wells
ARLINGTON WY.
MYDDELTON PAS.
NEW RIVER HEAD
SPA GREEN ESTATE
TUNBRIDGE HO.
LLOYD'S RW.
THE HYDRA BUILDING
ROSEBERY AVENUE
A401
GREEN Family Records Cen.
JOSEPH TROTTER CL.
FINSBURY ESTATE
MICHAEL CLIFFE HO.
SKINNER ST.
B502
Spa Fields Open Space
CORPORATION ROW
London Metropolitan Archives
NORTHAMPTON RD.
EXMOUTH MKT.
ROSOMAN ST.
FARRINGDON ROAD
A201
KING'S CROSS ROAD
Post Office Mount Pleasant
CLERKENWELL
CLERKENWELL GN.
CLERKENWELL CL.
SEKFORDE ST.
ST. JAMES'S WLK.
CALTHORPE ST.
PHOENIX PL.
MOUNT PLEASANT
WESTMINSTER Kingsway Coll.
St. George's Gdns.
HEATHCOTE ST.
MECKLENBURGH SQ.
Mecklenburgh Sq. Gds.
The Foundling Museum
The Wolfson Assessment Cen.
The Eastman Dental Hosp. & Institute
St. Andrew's Gds.
BRUNSWICK SQ.
Coram's Fields
HUNTER ST.
GUILFORD ST.
LANSDOWNE TER.
DOUGHTY ST.
Dickens Ho.
ITN
JOHN ST.
ROGER ST.
NORTHINGTON ST.
Great Ormond Street Hosp. for Children
The National Hosp.
QUEEN SQUARE
GT. ORMOND ST.
CHANCELLORS CT.
LAMB'S CONDUIT ST.
Budd. Cen.
CLERKENWELL ROAD
A5201
HATTON GARDEN
BOURNE ESTATE
PORTPOOL LA.
Liby.
Gray's Inn Gdns.
Gray's Inn
THEOBALD'S ROAD
SOUTHAMPTON ROW
RED LION SQUARE
PRINCETON ST.
BEDFORD ROW
GREVILLE ST.
BALDWIN'S GDS.
Islamic Cen.
LEATHER LANE
SAFFRON HILL
BLEEDING HRT YD.
VIADUCT BS.
CHARTERHOUSE ST.
CHANCERY LA.
HOLBORN
HIGH HOLBORN
HOLBORN CIR.
HOLBORN VIADUCT
A40
A4
A4200
B400
B402
B521
Min. Offs.
Mus.
Lincoln's Inn Liby.
Lincoln's Inn Hall
HOLBORN Lincoln's Inn Fields
Land Registry Off.
Royal Coll. of Surgeons
CHANCERY LANE
FETTER LA.
NEW FETTER LA.
KINGSWAY
King's College Library
Royal Courts of Justice
Temple Bar
FLEET ST.
SHOE LA.
ST. BRIDE ST.
FARRINGDON ST.
Freemasons Hall
GT. QUEEN ST.
LONG ACRE
DRURY LANE
PORTUGAL ST.
CAREY ST.
CLEMENT'S INN
Sch.
Coll.

8
A
B
C
D
E
84
14
1
2
3
4
5
6
7
The Angel Centre
CITY ROAD
GOSWELL ROAD
Fitness First
Dame Alice Owen Bldg.
Coll.
Sadler's Wells
ROSEBERY AV.
SPA GREEN ESTATE
TUNBRIDGE HO.
LLOYD'S RW.
Sch.
Family Records Cen.
MYDDLETON SQ.
WHISKIN ST.
JOSEPH TROTTER CL.
FINSBURY ESTATE
MICHAEL CLIFFE HO.
SKINNER ST.
Spa Fields Open Space
London Metropolitan Archives
ST. JOHN STREET
B501
RAWSTORNE ST.
WYNYATT ST.
SPENCER ST.
The City University
(King's Annexe)
NORTHAMPTON SQ.
WYCLIF ST.
BRUNSWICK CLOSE EST.
Kings Bldg.
PERCIVAL ST.
Lib.
WAKLEY ST.
PEREGRINE HO.
City Road Basin
Wenlock Basin
WENLOCK RD.
A501
MICAWBER ST.
HERDESS
WALK
NILE ST.
MURRAY
SHEPHERDS PL.
Crusoe Ho. Sch.
CATHERWOOD CT.
EBENEZER ST.
Moorfields Eye Hosp.
MORELAND ST.
Moreland Prim. Sch.
MACCLESFIELD RD.
KING SQ.
CENTRAL ST.
DINGLEY RD.
IRONMONGER ROW
Baths
GALWAY ST.
CAYTON ST.
GUINNESS CT.
PEERLESS ST.
BALDWIN ST.
ST. LUKE'S ESTATE
OLD STREET
LEVER STREET
B502
SEWARD ST.
TELFER HO.
FINSBURY
Leisure Cen.
RADNOR ST.
ST. LUKE'S
BUNHILL ROW
B144
A5201
OLD STREET
MITCHELL ST.
WHITECROSS
GOLDEN LANE
FEATHERSTONE ST.
Bunhill Flds. Burial Grd.
Health Club
TA Cen.
HAC Ground
A1
GOSWELL ROAD
ALDERSGATE ST.
PEAR TREE ST.
Spts. Cen.
Halls
Schs.
COMPTON ST.
BREWERY SQ.
GREAT SUTTON ST.
CLERKENWELL ROAD
CLERKENWELL GN.
St.John's Ga.
Charterhouse
The Medical Coll. of St. Bartholomew's Hospital
CHARTERHOUSE SQ.
BARBICAN
BEECH STREET
CHISWELL STREET
THE BREWERY
ROPEMAKER ST.
Leis. Cen.
GOLDEN LANE ESTATE
FORTUNE ST.
Park
Sch.
Hlth. Cen.
St. John's Gardens
FARRINGDON
FARRINGDON RD.
A201
COWCROSS ST.
CHARTERHOUSE STREET
Central Markets
SMITHFIELD
WEST SMITHFIELD
LONG LA.
CLOTH FAIR
BARBICAN
Sch.
Arts Cen.
Lib.
Coll.
LAUDERDALE TWR.
SHAKESPEARE TWR.
CROMWELL TWR.
BRITANNIC TOWER
MOORGATE
NEW UNION ST.
FORE ST.
Ironmongers Hall
Museum
LONDON WALL
A1211
HOSIER LA.
COCK LA.
HOLBORN
HOLBORN CIR.
CITY THAMESLINK
Mus.
St. Bartholomew's Hospital
LITTLE BRITAIN
KING EDWARD ST.
A40
Park
British Telecom Cen.
ST. MARTIN'S LE-GRAND
GRESHAM ST.
ALDERMANBURY
BASINGHALL ST.
Guildhall
Clock Mus.
Lib.
COLEMAN ST.
MOORGATE
LOTHBURY
FARRINGDON ST.
V'DUCT
NEWGATE ST.
Old Bailey
FLEET BUILDING
SHOE LA.
Liby.
ST. BRIDE ST.
NEW BRIDGE ST.
Stock Ex.
ST. PAUL'S
PATERNOSTER SQ.
Chapter Ho.
St. Paul's Cathedral
Sch.
Bank of England Offs.
CHEAPSIDE
POULTRY
WATLING ST.
LUDGATE HILL
LUDGATE CIRCUS
PILGRIM ST.
Bank of England

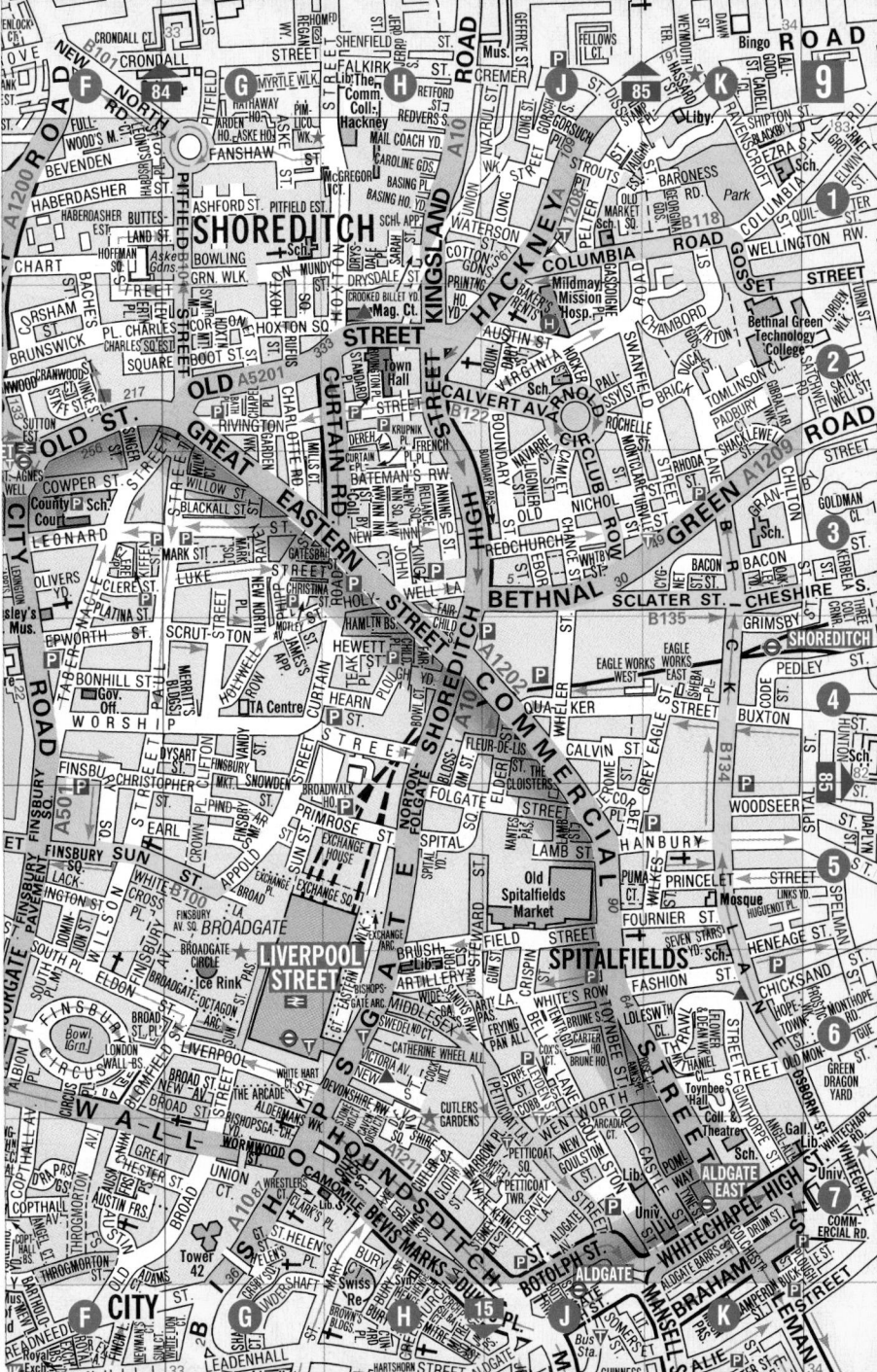

9
84
85
15
33
34
F
G
H
J
K
1
2
3
4
5
6
7
SHOREDITCH
SPITALFIELDS
BROADGATE
CITY
LIVERPOOL STREET
SHOREDITCH
ALDGATE
ALDGATE EAST
OLD ST.
CITY ROAD
NEW NORTH RD.
CRONDALL ST.
CRONDALL CT.
SHENFIELD ST.
FALKIRK ST.
CREMER ST.
FELLOWS CT.
MYRTLE WLK.
FANSHAW ST.
BEVENDEN ST.
HABERDASHER ST.
PITFIELD ST.
ASHFORD ST.
PITFIELD EST.
KINGSLAND ROAD
HACKNEY ROAD
COLUMBIA ROAD
WELLINGTON RW.
GOSSET STREET
BARONESS RD.
Park
Bethnal Green Technology College
HOXTON SQ.
HOXTON STREET
OLD STREET
CHARLES SQUARE
BRUNSWICK
CORSHAM ST.
CHART ST.
BOWLING GRN. WLK.
Mag. Ct.
Town Hall
CURTAIN RD.
GREAT EASTERN STREET
RIVINGTON ST.
CALVERT AV.
ARNOLD CIR.
BOUNDARY ST.
VIRGINIA RD.
SWANFIELD ST.
BRICK LANE
BETHNAL GREEN ROAD
REDCHURCH ST.
SCLATER ST.
CHESHIRE ST.
GRIMSBY ST.
PEDLEY ST.
BUXTON ST.
WOODSEER ST.
HANBURY ST.
PRINCELET STREET
FOURNIER ST.
FASHION ST.
WHITE'S ROW
SHOREDITCH HIGH STREET
COMMERCIAL STREET
QUAKER STREET
CALVIN ST.
FOLGATE STREET
ELDER ST.
THE CLOISTERS
LAMB ST.
Old Spitalfields Market
BISHOPSGATE
LEONARD ST.
WORSHIP ST.
BONHILL ST.
EPWORTH ST.
FINSBURY SQ.
FINSBURY PAVEMENT
SUN ST.
APPOLD ST.
PRIMROSE ST.
EXCHANGE HOUSE
EXCHANGE SQ.
BROADGATE CIRCLE
Ice Rink
FINSBURY CIRCUS
LONDON WALL
LIVERPOOL ST.
OLD BROAD ST.
WORMWOOD ST.
CAMOMILE ST.
HOUNDSDITCH
BEVIS MARKS
ST. HELEN'S PL.
UNDERSHAFT
Tower 42
Swiss Re
LEADENHALL
THROGMORTON ST.
COPTHALL AV.
MOORGATE
MIDDLESEX ST.
ARTILLERY LA.
BRUSHFIELD STREET
WENTWORTH ST.
TOYNBEE ST.
GOULSTON ST.
OLD CASTLE ST.
PETTICOAT SQ.
PETTICOAT TWR.
CUTLERS GARDENS
DEVONSHIRE RW.
WHITECHAPEL HIGH ST.
BOTOLPH ST.
ALDGATE BARS
BRAHAM ST.
LEMAN STREET
MANSELL ST.
ALIE ST.
OSBORN ST.
OLD MONTAGUE STREET
GREEN DRAGON YARD
CHICKSAND ST.
HENEAGE ST.
SPELMAN ST.
Toynbee Hall
Mosque
Bus Sta.
Hackney Comm. Coll.
Mildmay Mission Hosp.
County Court
Gov. Off.
TA Centre
Bowl. Grn.
Bingo
A10
A1200
A5201
A501
A1202
A1209
A1208
A1211
B101
B104
B100
B118
B122
B135
B134

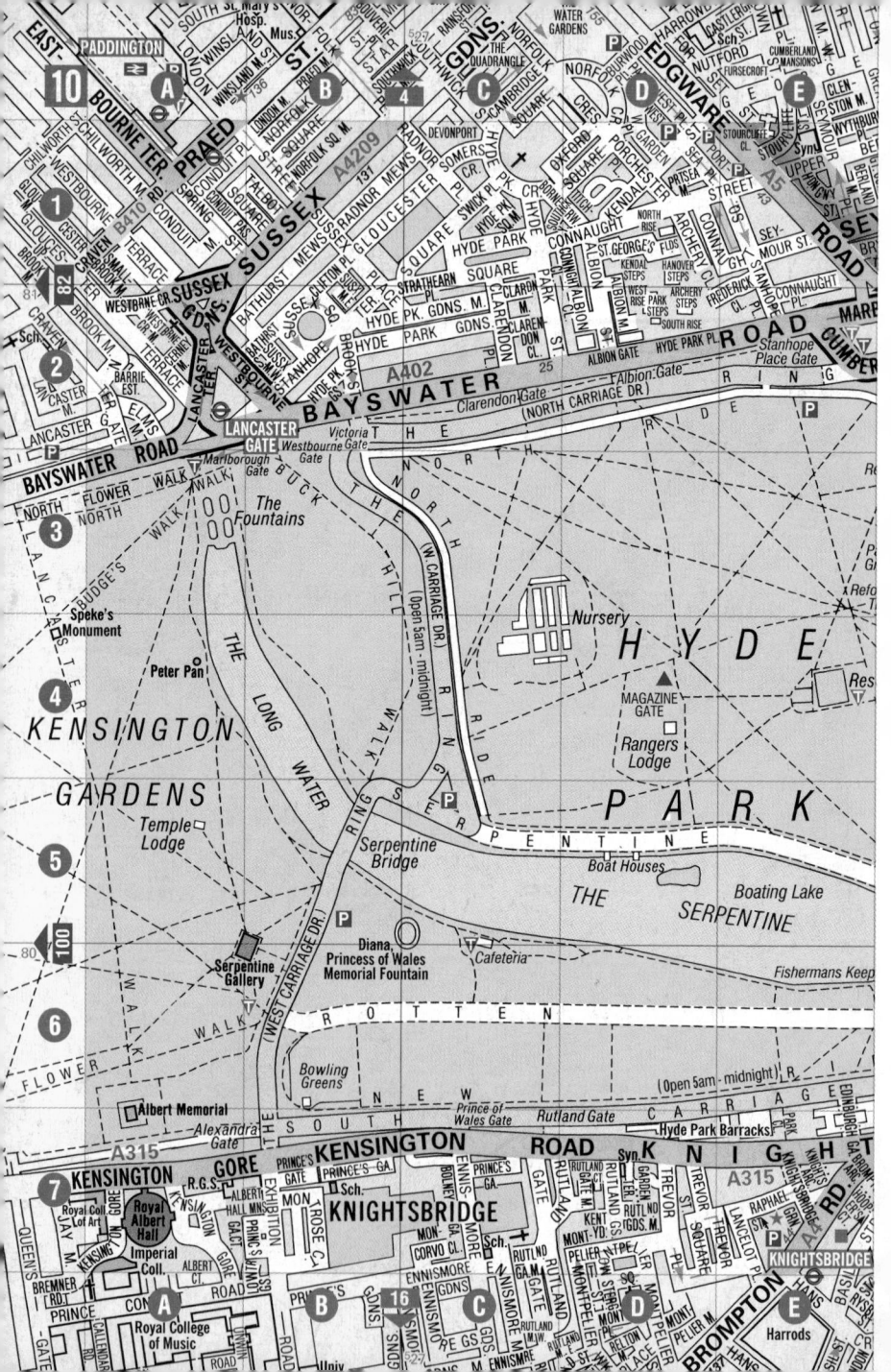

10
PADDINGTON
A
B
C
D
E
1
2
3
4
5
6
7
EAST-BOURNE TER.
PRAED
SUSSEX
A4209
B410
SUSSEX GDNS.
WESTBOURNE ST.
LANCASTER TER.
LANCASTER GATE
BAYSWATER ROAD
A402
EDGWARE ROAD
A5
SEYMOUR ST.
CONNAUGHT SQUARE
HYDE PARK SQUARE
HYDE PARK GDNS.
HYDE PARK PL.
ALBION GATE
Stanhope Place Gate
Albion Gate
Clarendon Gate
Victoria Gate
Westbourne Gate
Marlborough Gate
THE RING
THE NORTH RIDE
NORTH CARRIAGE DR.
BUCK HILL WALK
The Fountains
Speke's Monument
Peter Pan
KENSINGTON GARDENS
THE LONG WATER
Temple Lodge
Serpentine Bridge
Nursery
HYDE PARK
MAGAZINE GATE
Rangers Lodge
SERPENTINE RD.
Boat Houses
THE SERPENTINE
Boating Lake
Serpentine Gallery
Diana, Princess of Wales Memorial Fountain
Cafeteria
Fishermans Keep
ROTTEN ROW
Bowling Greens
(Open 5am - midnight)
WEST CARRIAGE DR.
SOUTH CARRIAGE DR.
Prince of Wales Gate
Rutland Gate
Hyde Park Barracks
Albert Memorial
Alexandra Gate
A315
KENSINGTON GORE
KENSINGTON ROAD
KNIGHTSBRIDGE
Royal Albert Hall
Royal Coll. of Art
Imperial Coll.
Royal College of Music
PRINCE'S GATE
ENNISMORE GDNS.
RUTLAND GATE
MONTPELIER SQ.
TREVOR SQUARE
BROMPTON RD.
Harrods
82
100
16

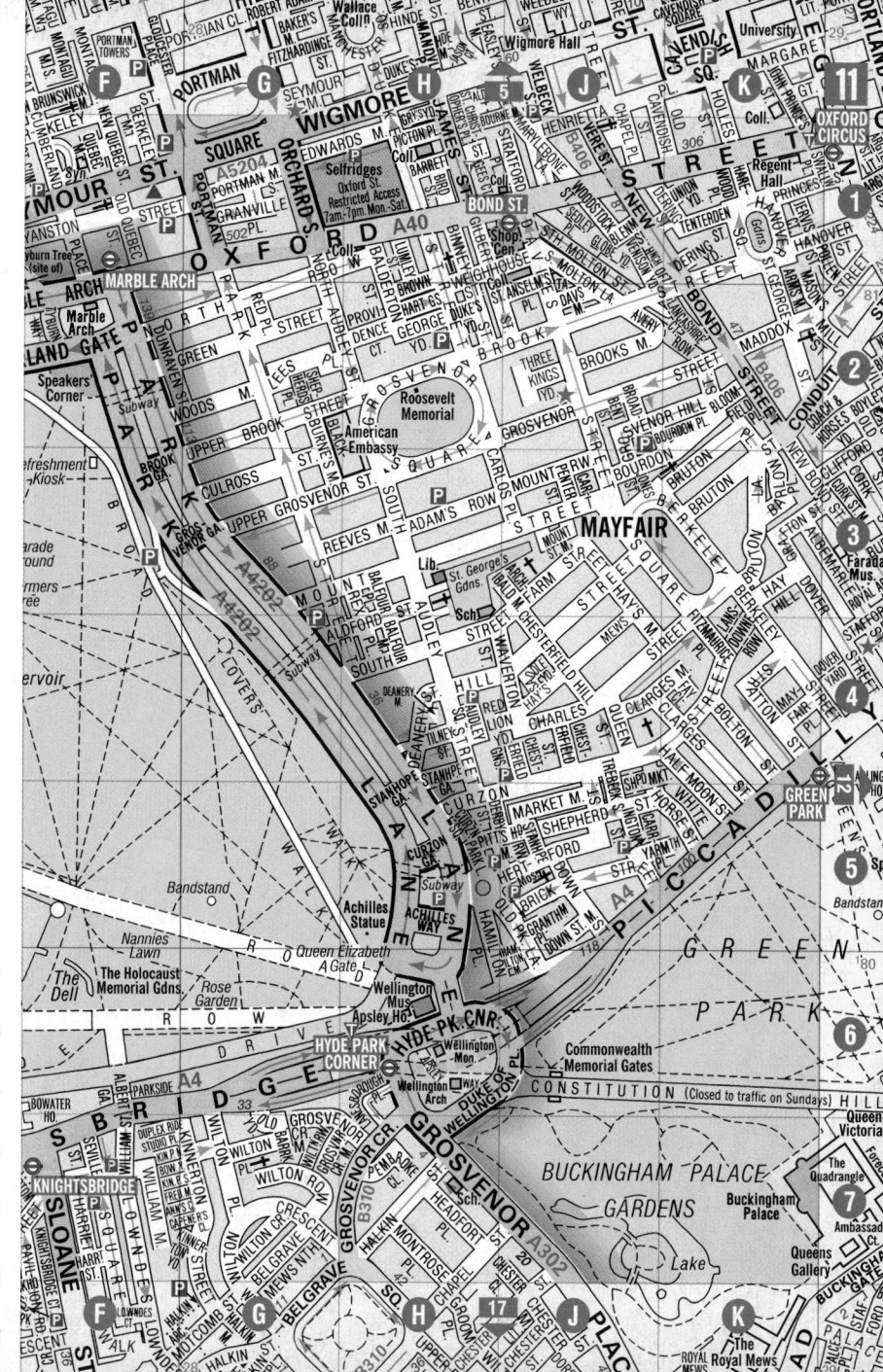

F
G
H
J
K
11
1
2
3
4
5
6
7
12
17
OXFORD CIRCUS
University
Wigmore Hall
Wallace Coll.
CAVENDISH SQ.
PORTMAN SQUARE
WIGMORE ST.
Selfridges
Oxford St. Restricted Access 7am-7pm. Mon.-Sat.
OXFORD ST.
A40
A5204
B406
BOND ST.
MARBLE ARCH
Tyburn Tree (site of)
Marble Arch
Speakers' Corner
Refreshment Kiosk
NEW BOND STREET
REGENT STREET
Regent Hall
HANOVER SQ.
St. George's Gdns.
NORTH AUDLEY ST.
SOUTH AUDLEY ST.
GROSVENOR SQUARE
Roosevelt Memorial
American Embassy
BROOK STREET
UPPER BROOK ST.
UPPER GROSVENOR ST.
MOUNT STREET
MAYFAIR
BERKELEY SQUARE
CONDUIT ST.
BRUTON ST.
Faraday Mus.
PARK LANE
A4202
Subway
GREEN PARK
PICCADILLY
A4
CURZON ST.
SHEPHERD MARKET
HALF MOON ST.
CLARGES ST.
Achilles Statue
Bandstand
Nannies Lawn
The Dell
The Holocaust Memorial Gdns.
Rose Garden
Queen Elizabeth Gate
Wellington Mus.
Apsley Ho.
HYDE PK. CNR.
HYDE PARK CORNER
Wellington Mon.
Wellington Arch
Commonwealth Memorial Gates
CONSTITUTION HILL (Closed to traffic on Sundays)
ROTTEN ROW
KNIGHTSBRIDGE
SLOANE ST.
LOWNDES SQUARE
WILTON CRESCENT
BELGRAVE SQ.
GROSVENOR PLACE
A302
BUCKINGHAM PALACE GARDENS
Lake
Buckingham Palace
The Quadrangle
Queen Victoria
Queens Gallery
The Royal Mews
ROYAL MEWS
BUCKINGHAM GATE

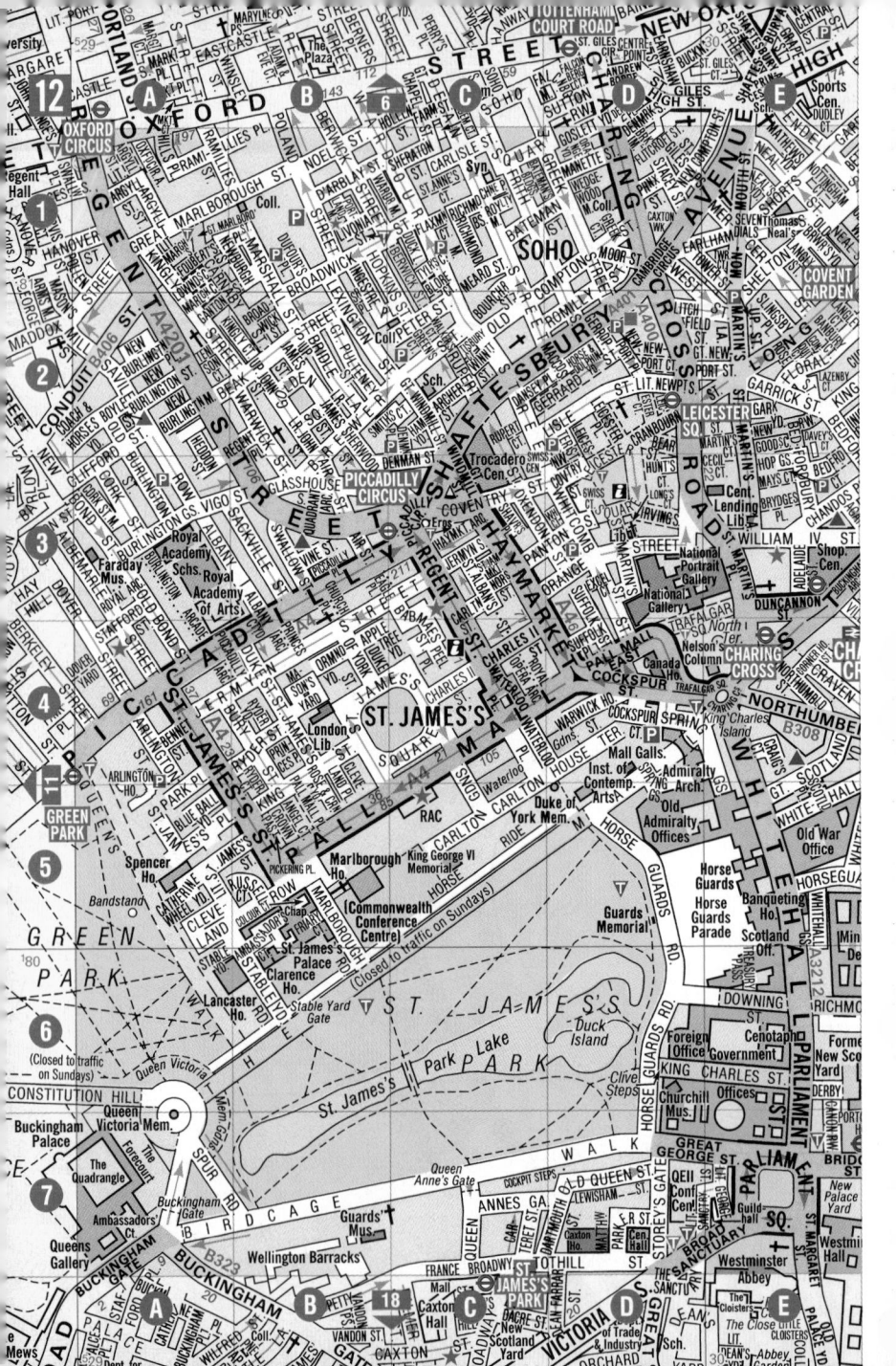

12
A
B
C
D
E
1
2
3
4
5
6
7
OXFORD CIRCUS
OXFORD
TOTTENHAM COURT ROAD
NEW OXFORD
STREET
HIGH
ST. GILES
CENTRE POINT
The Plaza
SOHO
SQUARE
Regent Hall
REGENT
STREET
GREAT MARLBOROUGH ST.
BROADWICK
CARNABY
BERWICK
WARDOUR
DEAN
FRITH
GREEK
CHARING
CROSS
ROAD
SHAFTESBURY
AVENUE
SEVEN DIALS
Thomas Neal's
COVENT GARDEN
LONG
GARRICK ST.
LEICESTER SQ.
Trocadero Cen.
PICCADILLY CIRCUS
PICCADILLY
HAYMARKET
COVENTRY ST.
GLASSHOUSE
VIGO ST.
SACKVILLE
ALBANY
Royal Academy Schs.
Royal Academy of Arts
Faraday Mus.
DOVER
BERKELEY
ALBEMARLE
JERMYN
ST. JAMES'S
ST. JAMES'S SQUARE
London Lib.
PALL MALL
PALL MALL EAST
National Portrait Gallery
National Gallery
TRAFALGAR SQ.
Nelson's Column
Canada Ho.
CHARING CROSS
COCKSPUR ST.
NORTHUMBERLAND
WHITEHALL
STRAND
WILLIAM IV ST.
DUNCANNON
Cent. Lending Lib.
RAC
Waterloo
Duke of York Mem.
Inst. of Contemp. Arts
Mall Galls.
Admiralty Arch
Old Admiralty Offices
Old War Office
Horse Guards
Horse Guards Parade
Banqueting Ho.
Scotland Off.
Spencer Ho.
Bandstand
GREEN PARK
Marlborough Ho.
King George VI Memorial
(Commonwealth Conference Centre)
St. James's Palace
Clarence Ho.
Lancaster Ho.
Stable Yard Gate
(Closed to traffic on Sundays)
ST. JAMES'S PARK
Lake
Duck Island
Guards Memorial
Clive Steps
DOWNING ST.
Foreign Office
Cenotaph
Government Offices
KING CHARLES ST.
Churchill Mus.
PARLIAMENT ST.
PARLIAMENT SQ.
New Palace Yard
Westminster Hall
Westminster Abbey
The Cloisters
The Close
Guildhall
QEII Conf. Cen.
GREAT GEORGE ST.
STOREY'S GATE
HORSE GUARDS RD.
CONSTITUTION HILL
Queen Victoria Mem.
Buckingham Palace
The Quadrangle
The Forecourt
Ambassadors' Ct.
Queens Gallery
Buckingham Gate
Queen Anne's Gate
COCKPIT STEPS
OLD QUEEN ST.
BIRDCAGE WALK
Guards' Mus.
Wellington Barracks
BUCKINGHAM GATE
BUCKINGHAM
Caxton Hall
BROADWAY
ST. JAMES'S PARK
New Scotland Yard
VICTORIA
Dept. of Trade & Industry
TOTHILL ST.
THE SANCTUARY
CAXTON
18
11
6

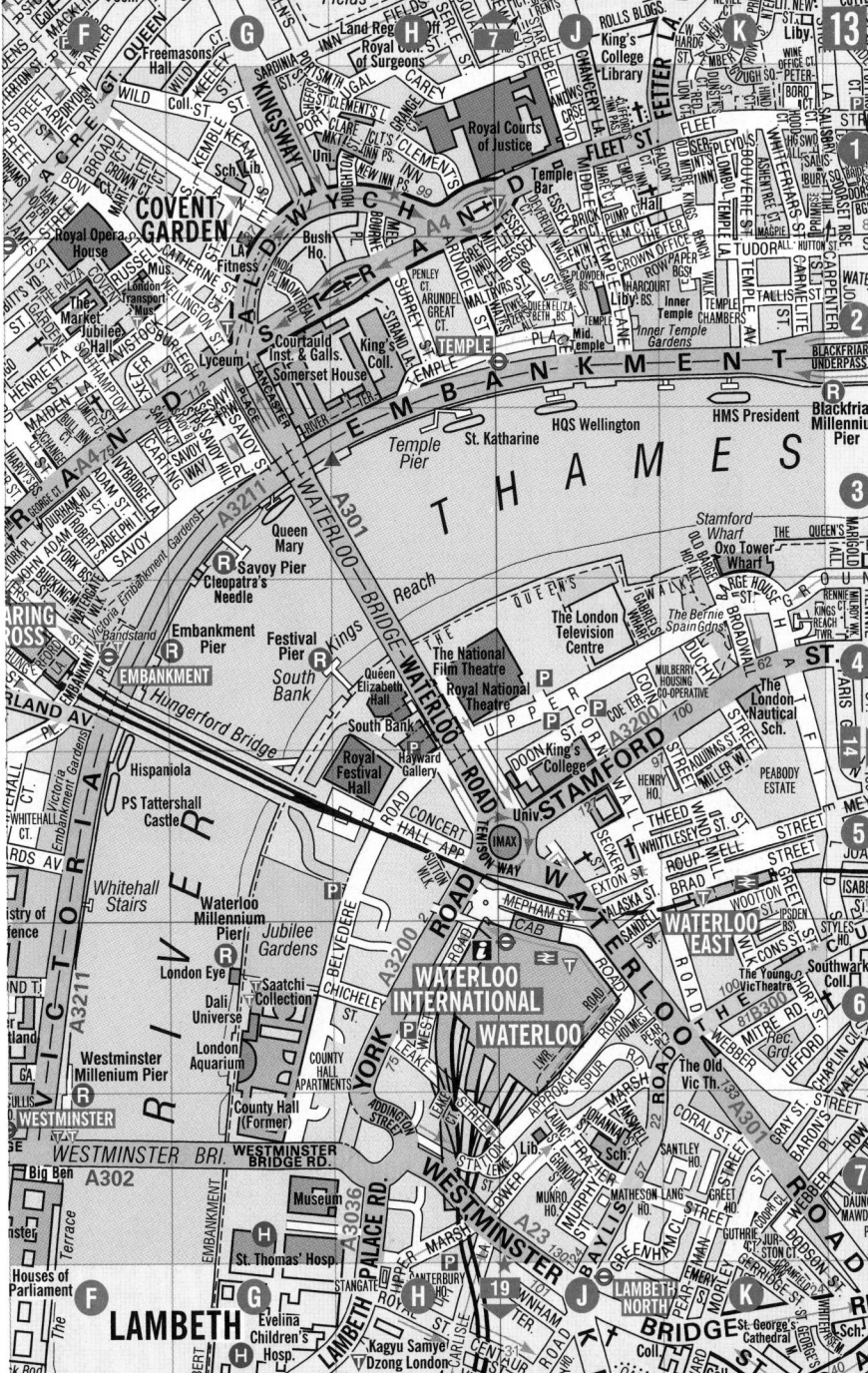
13
14
7
19
F
G
H
J
K
1
2
3
4
5
6
7
COVENT GARDEN
Royal Opera House
The Market
Jubilee Hall
London Transport Mus.
Lyceum
Freemasons' Hall
Lincoln's Inn Fields
Land Registry Off.
Royal Coll. of Surgeons
King's College Library
Royal Courts of Justice
Temple Bar
FLEET ST.
ALDWYCH
STRAND
KINGSWAY
Bush Ho.
Courtauld Inst. & Galls.
Somerset House
King's Coll.
TEMPLE
Inner Temple
Inner Temple Gardens
Mid. Temple
EMBANKMENT
BLACKFRIARS UNDERPASS
Blackfriars Millennium Pier
HMS President
HQS Wellington
St. Katharine
Temple Pier
THAMES
Queen Mary
Savoy Pier
Cleopatra's Needle
Victoria Embankment Gardens
Embankment Pier
Festival Pier
South Bank
Kings Reach
Stamford Wharf
Oxo Tower Wharf
The London Television Centre
The Bernie Spain Gdns.
The National Film Theatre
Royal National Theatre
Queen Elizabeth Hall
South Bank
Hayward Gallery
Royal Festival Hall
King's College
STAMFORD ST.
The London Nautical Sch.
PEABODY ESTATE
Hungerford Bridge
WATERLOO BRIDGE
WATERLOO ROAD
A301
A3200
A3211
A4
Hispaniola
PS Tattershall Castle
RIVER
Whitehall Stairs
Waterloo Millennium Pier
Jubilee Gardens
London Eye
Saatchi Collection
Dali Universe
London Aquarium
Westminster Millenium Pier
County Hall (Former)
COUNTY HALL APARTMENTS
IMAX
WATERLOO INTERNATIONAL
WATERLOO
WATERLOO EAST
Southwark Coll.
The Young Vic Theatre
The Old Vic Th.
VICTORIA EMBANKMENT
WESTMINSTER
WESTMINSTER BRI.
WESTMINSTER BRIDGE RD.
A302
Big Ben
Houses of Parliament
Museum
St. Thomas' Hosp.
LAMBETH
Evelina Children's Hosp.
Kagyu Samye Dzong London
LAMBETH NORTH
St. George's Cathedral
YORK ROAD
LAMBETH PALACE RD.
A3036
A23
BAYLIS
BRIDGE

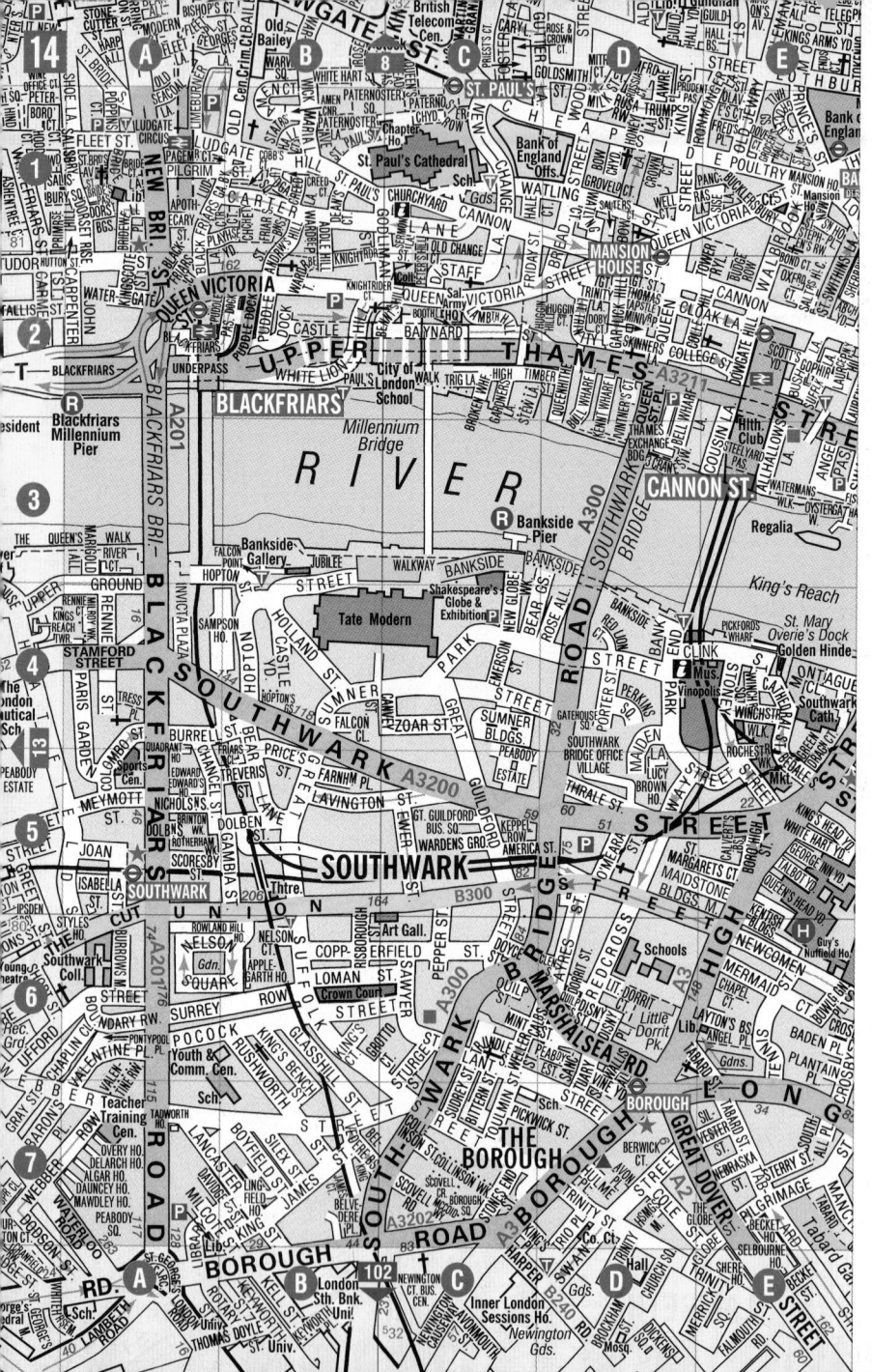

14
A
B
C
D
E
1
2
3
4
5
6
7
8
13
102
Old Bailey
British Telecom Cen.
ST. PAUL'S
St. Paul's Cathedral
Bank of England Offs.
Bank of England
CHEAPSIDE
POULTRY
MANSION HOUSE
QUEEN VICTORIA ST.
CANNON ST.
LUDGATE HILL
LUDGATE CIRCUS
FLEET ST.
NEW BRI. ST.
BLACKFRIARS
UNDERPASS
UPPER THAMES STREET
City of London School
Blackfriars Millennium Pier
Millennium Bridge
RIVER
Bankside Pier
Bankside Gallery
Tate Modern
Shakespeare's Globe & Exhibition
King's Reach
St. Mary Overie's Dock
Golden Hinde
CLINK STREET
Mus. Vinopolis
Southwark Cath.
Regalia
CANNON ST.
SOUTHWARK BRIDGE
A300
A3211
A3200
A201
B300
A3
A2
A3202
B240
BLACKFRIARS BRI.
BLACKFRIARS ROAD
SOUTHWARK STREET
SOUTHWARK
UNION STREET
THE CUT
Southwark Coll.
NELSON SQUARE
Art Gall.
COPPERFIELD ST.
Crown Court
SURREY ROW
Youth & Comm. Cen.
Teacher Training Cen.
SOUTHWARK BRIDGE ROAD
MARSHALSEA RD.
Little Dorrit Pk.
BOROUGH HIGH STREET
BOROUGH
THE BOROUGH
LONG LANE
GREAT DOVER STREET
BOROUGH ROAD
LAMBETH ROAD
London Sth. Bnk. Uni.
Inner London Sessions Ho.
Newington Gds.
Schools
Guy's Nuffield Ho.
Tabard Ga

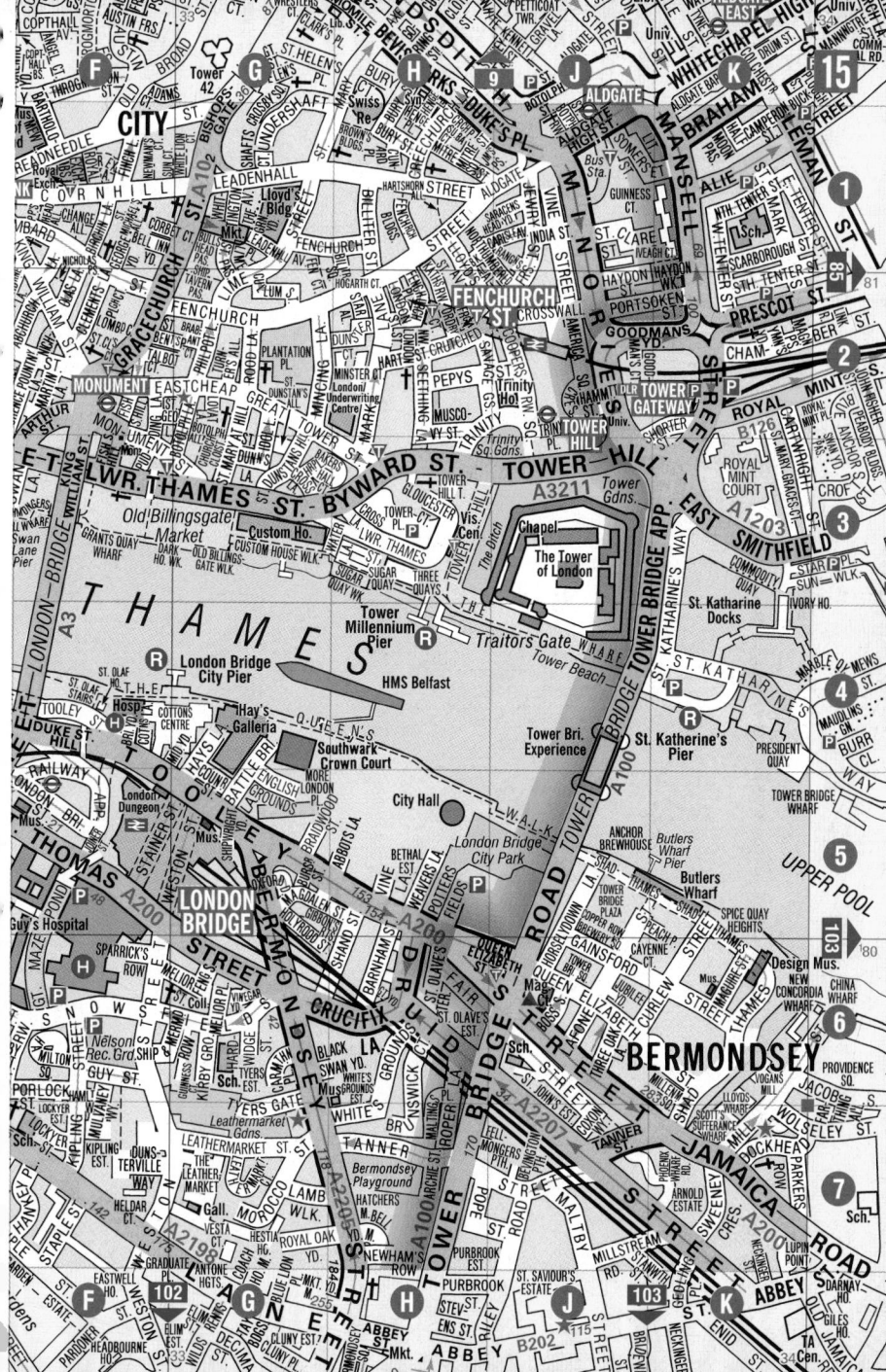

15
CITY
Tower 42
LEADENHALL
CORNHILL
Lloyd's Bldg
Swiss Re
FENCHURCH
ALDGATE
ALDGATE EAST
WHITECHAPEL HIGH ST.
MANSELL
MINORIES
LEMAN STREET
PRESCOT ST.
ROYAL MINT ST.
FENCHURCH ST.
GRACECHURCH ST.
MONUMENT
EASTCHEAP
GREAT TOWER ST.
LWR. THAMES ST.
BYWARD ST.
TOWER HILL
TOWER GATEWAY
A3211
Custom Ho.
Old Billingsgate Market
The Tower of London
Chapel
Traitors Gate
Tower Beach
Tower Millennium Pier
THAMES
London Bridge City Pier
HMS Belfast
Hay's Galleria
Southwark Crown Court
City Hall
London Bridge City Park
Tower Bri. Experience
St. Katherine's Pier
St. Katharine Docks
EAST SMITHFIELD
A1203
TOWER BRIDGE APP.
TOWER BRIDGE ROAD
A100
TOOLEY ST.
LONDON BRIDGE
LONDON BRIDGE
A3
London Dungeon
Guy's Hospital
ST. THOMAS ST.
A200
BERMONDSEY ST.
CRUCIFIX LA.
DRUID ST.
Leathermarket Gdns.
Bermondsey Playground
LONG LANE
A2198
A2206
A2207
Butlers Wharf
UPPER POOL
Design Mus.
BERMONDSEY
JAMAICA ROAD
ABBEY ST.
85
103
102
9
F G H J K
1 2 3 4 5 6 7

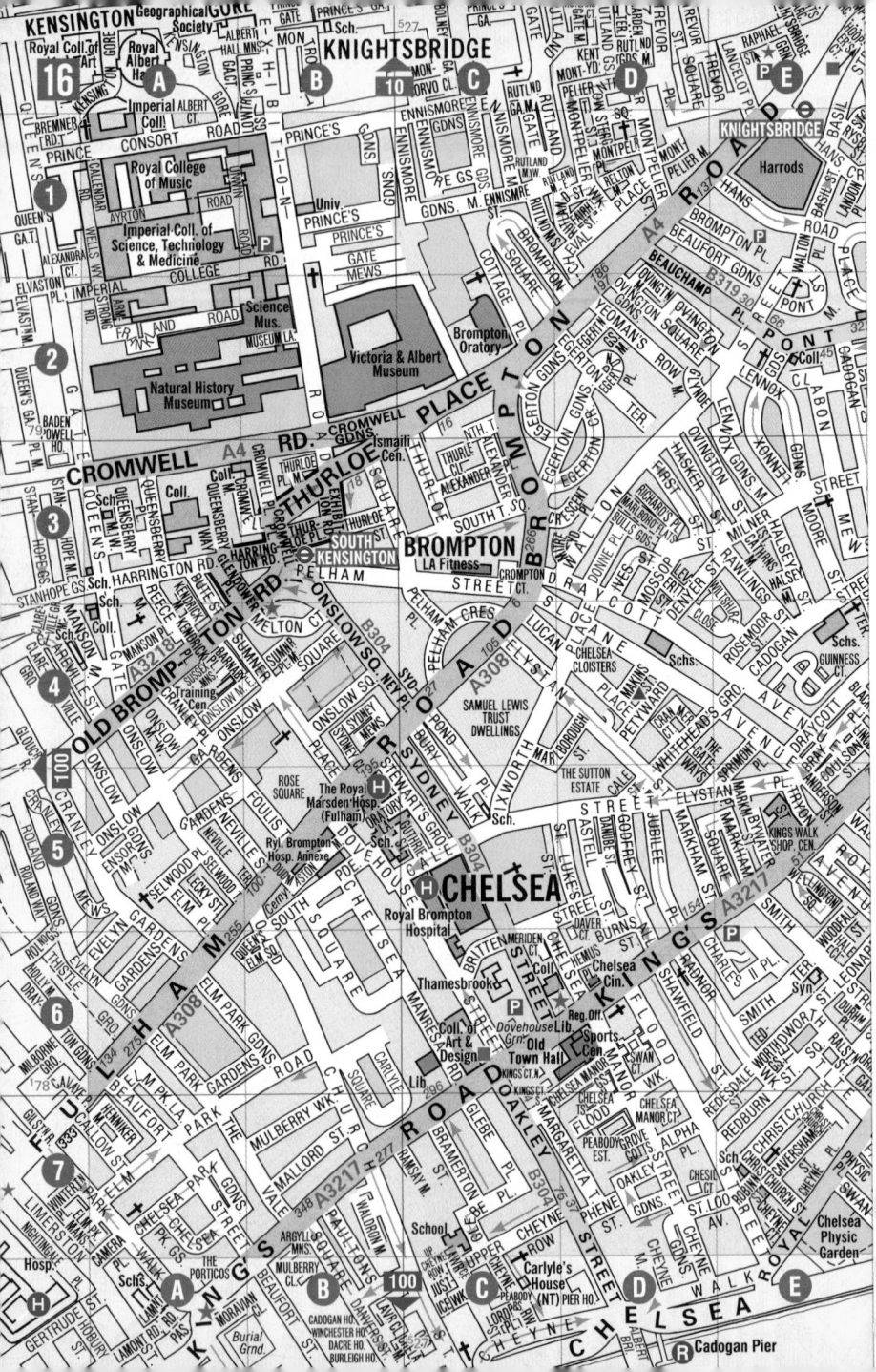

16
KENSINGTON
Geographical Society
GORE
Royal Coll. of Art
Royal Albert Hall
A
B
C
D
E
1
2
3
4
5
6
7
KNIGHTSBRIDGE
10
KNIGHTSBRIDGE
Harrods
Imperial Coll.
ALBERT CT.
PRINCE CONSORT ROAD
Royal College of Music
Imperial Coll. of Science, Technology & Medicine
IMPERIAL COLLEGE RD.
Science Mus.
Natural History Museum
Victoria & Albert Museum
Brompton Oratory
Univ.
PRINCE'S GDNS.
PRINCE'S GATE MEWS
ENNISMORE GDNS.
MONTPELIER SQ.
BROMPTON SQUARE
BROMPTON ROAD
A4
BEAUCHAMP PL.
B319
OVINGTON SQUARE
YEOMAN'S ROW
EGERTON GDNS.
EGERTON CR.
EGERTON TER.
PONT ST.
LENNOX GDNS.
CADOGAN
CROMWELL RD.
CROMWELL GDNS.
CROMWELL PLACE
THURLOE PLACE
THURLOE SQUARE
Ismaili Cen.
ALEXANDER SQ.
SOUTH T. SQ.
BROMPTON
LA Fitness
SOUTH KENSINGTON
PELHAM STREET
PELHAM CRES.
HARRINGTON RD.
QUEEN'S GATE
QUEENSBERRY PL.
STANHOPE GS.
OLD BROMPTON RD.
A3218
ONSLOW SQUARE
ONSLOW GARDENS
SYDNEY PL.
B304
FULHAM ROAD
A308
DRAYCOTT PLACE
SLOANE AVENUE
ELYSTAN PL.
ELYSTAN ST.
CHELSEA CLOISTERS
SAMUEL LEWIS TRUST DWELLINGS
IXWORTH PL.
THE SUTTON ESTATE
MARLBOROUGH ST.
WALTON ST.
MILNER ST.
HALSEY ST.
ROSEMOOR ST.
GUINNESS CT.
Schs.
KINGS WALK SHOP. CEN.
ROSE SQUARE
The Royal Marsden Hosp. (Fulham)
Ryl. Brompton Hosp. Annexe
SYDNEY STREET
CHELSEA
Royal Brompton Hospital
Thamesbrook
Coll. of Art & Design
Dovehouse Grn.
Old Town Hall
Sports Cen.
Chelsea Cin.
Reg. Off.
Lib.
JUBILEE PL.
MARKHAM SQUARE
SMITH ST.
KING'S ROAD
A3217
CHELSEA SQUARE
MANRESA RD.
ELM PARK GDNS.
EVELYN GARDENS
CRANLEY GARDENS
MULBERRY WK.
MALLORD ST.
CHURCH ST.
OAKLEY STREET
GLEBE PL.
OLD CHURCH ST.
FLOOD ST.
SHAWFIELD ST.
CHELSEA MANOR ST.
PEABODY EST.
ST. LOO AV.
TITE ST.
ROYAL HOSPITAL RD.
CHRISTCHURCH ST.
Chelsea Physic Garden
CHEYNE WALK
CHELSEA EMBANKMENT
Cadogan Pier
Carlyle's House (NT)
PIER HO.
School
100
Hosp.
Schs.
THE PORTICOS
BEAUFORT ST.
MORAVIAN CL.
Burial Grnd.
CADOGAN HO.
WINCHESTER HO.
DACRE HO.
BURLEIGH HO.

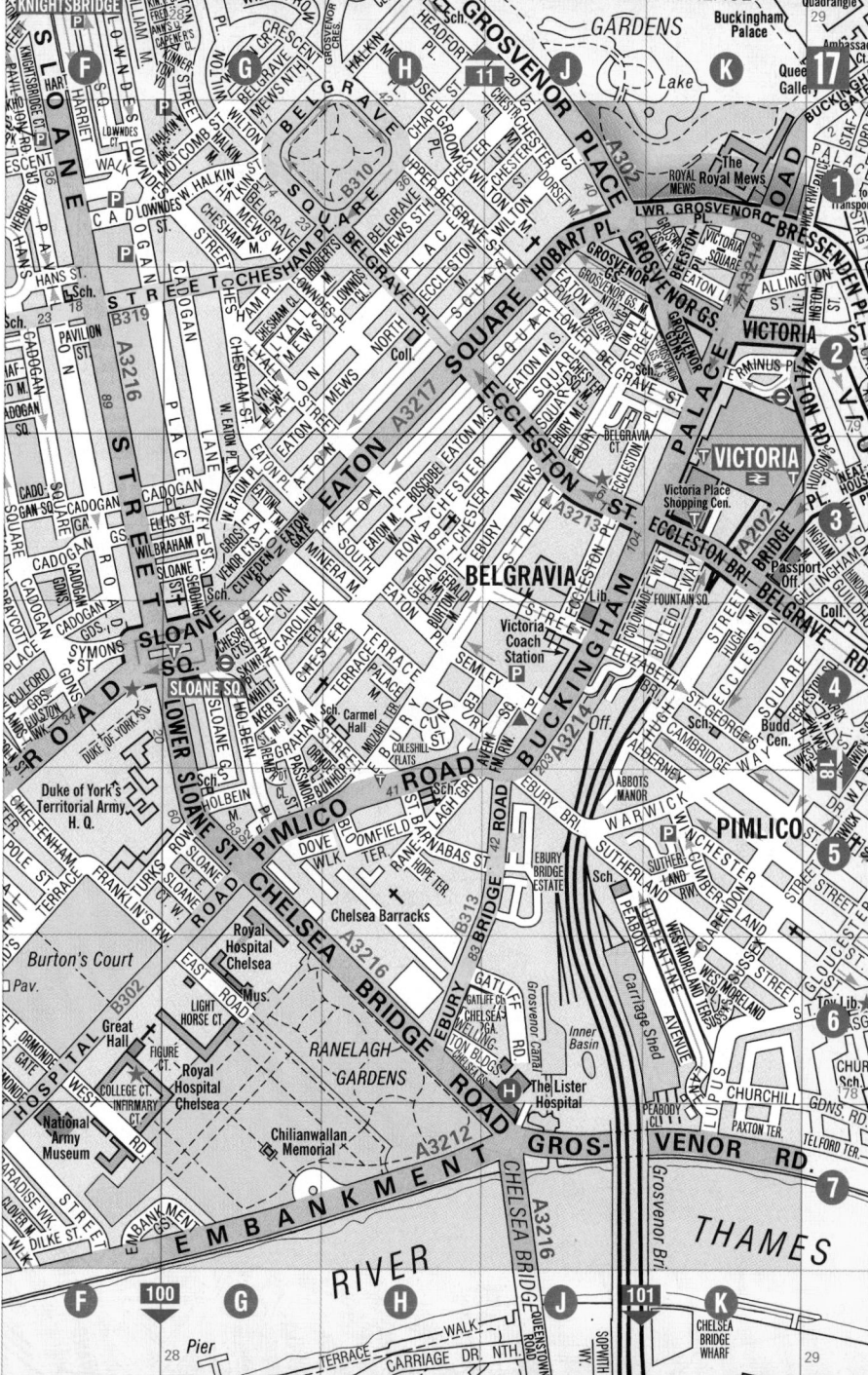

KNIGHTSBRIDGE
BUCKINGHAM PALACE GARDENS
Buckingham Palace
Quadrangle
Ambassador Ct.
Queen's Gallery
17
Lake
The Royal Mews
ROYAL MEWS
GROSVENOR PLACE
A302
BELGRAVE SQUARE
B310
SLOANE STREET
A3216
B319
CHESHAM PL.
CHESHAM ST.
CADOGAN PLACE
CADOGAN SQUARE
CADOGAN GDNS.
LOWNDES SQ.
LOWNDES ST.
MOTCOMB ST.
W. HALKIN ST.
HALKIN ST.
WILTON CRESCENT
WILTON PL.
GROSVENOR CRES.
HEADFORT PL.
UPPER BELGRAVE ST.
BELGRAVE PL.
CHESTER SQUARE
WILTON ST.
HOBART PL.
LWR. GROSVENOR PL.
BRESSENDEN PL.
VICTORIA SQUARE
GROSVENOR GDNS.
A3214
ALLINGTON ST.
VICTORIA ST.
TERMINUS PL.
VICTORIA
Victoria Place Shopping Cen.
A202
EATON SQUARE
A3217
EATON PL.
EATON TERRACE
ECCLESTON ST.
A3213
ECCLESTON PL.
BELGRAVIA
ELIZABETH ST.
CHESTER ROW
EBURY ST.
BUCKINGHAM PALACE ROAD
Victoria Coach Station
ECCLESTON BRI.
BELGRAVE RD.
Passport Off.
ECCLESTON SQUARE
ST. GEORGE'S DRIVE
CAMBRIDGE ST.
WARWICK WAY
PIMLICO
Budd. Cen.
18
ELIZABETH BRI.
EBURY BRI.
ABBOTS MANOR
SLOANE SQ.
SYMONS ST.
DUKE OF YORK SQ.
Duke of York's Territorial Army H. Q.
HOLBEIN PL.
LOWER SLOANE ST.
PIMLICO ROAD
GRAHAM TERRACE
Carmel Hall
COLESHILL FLATS
SEMLEY PL.
EBURY SQ.
AVERY FM. RW.
CHELSEA BRIDGE ROAD
A3216
BOURNE ST.
CHELTENHAM TERRACE
FRANKLIN'S RW.
TURKS ROW
Burton's Court
B302
ROYAL HOSPITAL ROAD
Royal Hospital Chelsea
Mus.
EAST ROAD
LIGHT HORSE CT.
Great Hall
FIGURÉ CT.
COLLEGE CT.
INFIRMARY CT.
National Army Museum
WEST RD.
Chelsea Barracks
B313
EBURY BRIDGE ROAD
EBURY BRIDGE ESTATE
GATLIFF RD.
Grosvenor Canal
Inner Basin
The Lister Hospital
RANELAGH GARDENS
Chilianwallan Memorial
A3212
CHELSEA EMBANKMENT
GROSVENOR RD.
Carriage Shed
SUTHERLAND ST.
WINCHESTER ST.
CUMBERLAND ST.
CLARENDON ST.
WESTMORELAND TER.
SUSSEX STREET
GLOUCESTER ST.
Toy Lib.
CHURCHILL GDNS. RD.
PAXTON TER.
TELFORD TER.
LUPUS ST.
PEABODY AVENUE
TURPENTINE LANE
PEABODY CL.
Grosvenor Bri.
CHELSEA BRIDGE
THAMES
RIVER
DILKE ST.
PARADISE WK.
EMBANKMENT GDS.
100
101
Pier
CARRIAGE DR. NTH.
QUEENSTOWN ROAD
SOPWITH WY.
CHELSEA BRIDGE WHARF
F
G
H
J
K
1
2
3
4
5
6
7
28
29

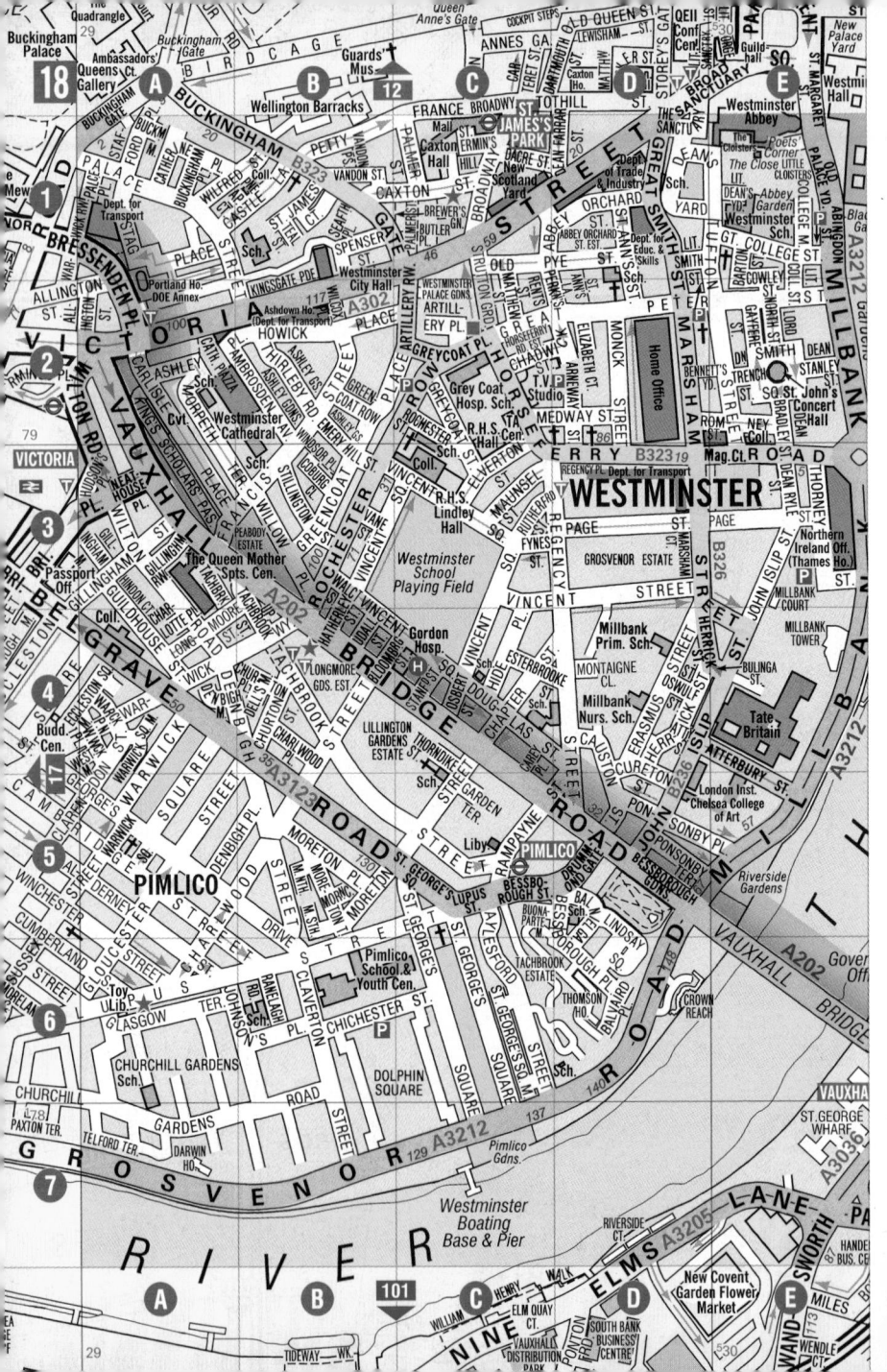

18
Buckingham Palace
Queens Gallery
Ambassadors' Ct.
Buckingham Gate
Queen Anne's Gate
BIRDCAGE
Guards' Mus.
12
Wellington Barracks
COCKPIT STEPS
OLD QUEEN ST.
ANNES GA.
LEWISHAM ST.
QEII Conf. Cen.
Guild-hall
New Palace Yard
Westminster Hall
BROAD SANCTUARY
THE SANCTUARY
Westminster Abbey
The Cloisters
Poets' Corner
The Close
LITTLE CLOISTERS
Abbey Garden
Westminster Sch.
DEAN'S YARD
GT. COLLEGE ST.
COWLEY
BARTON
ABINGDON
MILLBANK
A3212
BUCKINGHAM GATE
BUCKINGHAM
PALACE
STAFFORD PL.
CATHERINE PL.
WILFRED ST.
CASTLE LA.
ST. JAMES CT.
SEAFTH PL.
Dept. for Transport
BRESSENDEN PL.
PLACE
STAG
Sch.
Portland Ho. DOE Annex
KINGSGATE PDE.
Westminster City Hall
ALLINGTON ST.
VICTORIA
STREET
A302
Ashdown Ho. (Dept. for Transport)
PETTY FRANCE
BROADWY
ST. JAMES'S PARK
Caxton Hall
CAXTON ST.
BREWER'S GN.
BUTLER PL.
New Scotland Yard
TOTHILL ST.
DEAN FARRAR ST.
Dept. of Trade & Industry
GREAT SMITH ST.
ABBEY ORCHARD ST.
ABBEY ORCHARD ST. EST.
OLD PYE ST.
Dept. for Educ. & Skills
WESTMINSTER PALACE GDNS.
ARTILLERY PL.
ARTILLERY RW.
PETER ST.
GREAT PETER ST.
Home Office
MARSHAM ST.
SMITH SQ.
St. John's Concert Hall
DEAN STANLEY ST.
HOWICK PL.
GREYCOAT PL.
Grey Coat Hosp. Sch.
ROCHESTER ROW
CHADWICK ST.
T.V. Studio
MEDWAY ST.
ELIZABETH CT.
MONCK STREET
ARNEWAY
HORSEFERRY ROAD
B323
Dept. for Transport
REGENCY PL.
Mag. Ct.
WESTMINSTER
THORNEY ST.
DEAN RYLE ST.
PAGE ST.
R.H.S. Hall
R.H.S. Lindley Hall
VINCENT SQ.
Westminster School Playing Field
ASHLEY PL.
CARLISLE PL.
Cvt.
Westminster Cathedral
AMBROSDEN AV.
THIRLEBY RD.
MORPETH TER.
FRANCIS ST.
WILLOW PL.
VICTORIA
WILTON RD.
VAUXHALL BRIDGE ROAD
A202
HUDSON'S PL.
NEATHOUSE PL.
Passport Off.
KING'S SCHOLARS PAS.
PEABODY ESTATE
The Queen Mother Spts. Cen.
GILLINGHAM ST.
Coll.
BELGRAVE ROAD
GUILDHOUSE ST.
ECCLESTON SQ.
WARWICK WAY
WARWICK SQ.
Budd. Cen.
17
TACHBROOK ST.
LONGMORE GDS. EST.
Gordon Hosp.
STANFORD ST.
CHAPTER ST.
FYNES ST.
GROSVENOR ESTATE
REGENCY ST.
VINCENT STREET
Millbank Prim. Sch.
MONTAIGNE CL.
Millbank Nurs. Sch.
ERASMUS ST.
HERRICK ST.
JOHN ISLIP ST.
Northern Ireland Off. (Thames Ho.)
MILLBANK COURT
MILLBANK TOWER
BULINGA ST.
Tate Britain
ATTERBURY ST.
London Inst. Chelsea College of Art
CURETON ST.
PONSONBY PL.
PONSONBY TER.
JOHN ISLIP ST.
Riverside Gardens
LILLINGTON GARDENS ESTATE
THORNDIKE ST.
GARDEN TER.
A3123
ST. GEORGE'S DRIVE
CHURTON ST.
CHARLWOOD PL.
DENBIGH PL.
DENBIGH STREET
CAMBRIDGE STREET
PIMLICO
MORETON PL.
MORETON TER.
LUPUS ST.
ST. GEORGE'S SQ.
RAMPAYNE ST.
PIMLICO
DRUMMOND GATE
BESSBOROUGH ST.
BESSBOROUGH GDNS.
LINDSAY SQ.
TACHBROOK ESTATE
BUONAPARTE M.
THOMSON HO.
BALVAIRD PL.
CROWN REACH
VAUXHALL BRIDGE
A202
Pimlico School & Youth Cen.
CLAVERTON ST.
CHICHESTER ST.
JOHNSON'S PL.
GLASGOW TER.
Toy Lib.
CHURCHILL GARDENS
DOLPHIN SQUARE
AYLESFORD ST.
ST. GEORGE'S SQUARE
WINCHESTER ST.
CUMBERLAND ST.
SUSSEX STREET
GLOUCESTER STREET
ALDERNEY STREET
CLAREDON ST.
CHURCHILL GARDENS ROAD
PAXTON TER.
TELFORD TER.
DARWIN HO.
GROSVENOR ROAD
A3212
Pimlico Gdns.
Westminster Boating Base & Pier
RIVER
VAUXHALL
ST. GEORGE WHARF
A3036
RIVERSIDE CT.
NINE ELMS LANE
A3205
HENRY WALK
New Covent Garden Flower Market
WANDSWORTH
MILES
WENDLE CT.
ELM QUAY CT.
WILLIAM
VAUXHALL DISTRIBUTION PARK
PONTON RD.
SOUTH BANK BUSINESS CENTRE
TIDEWAY WK.
101
A B C D E
1 2 3 4 5 6 7
29
79

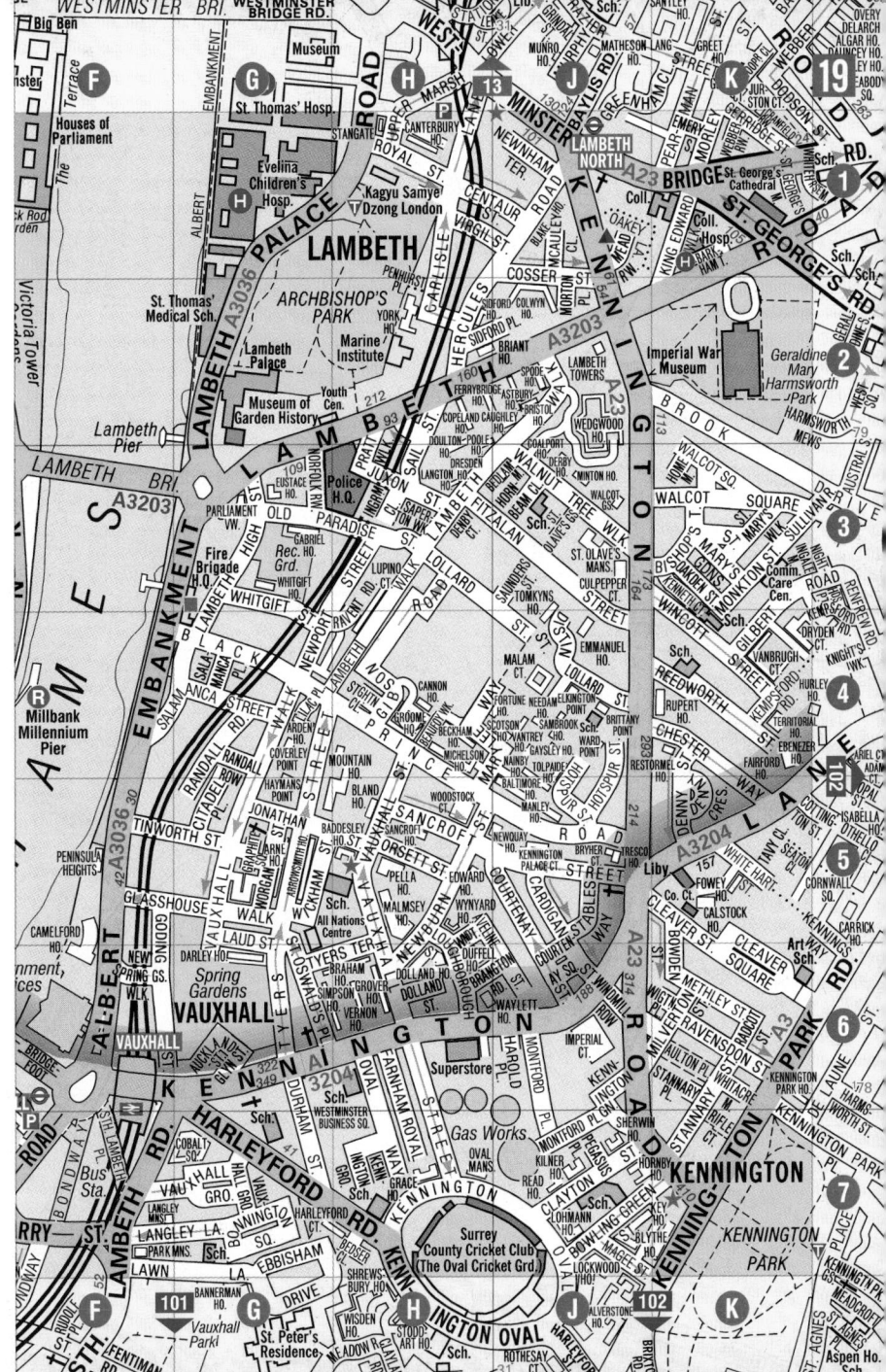

19
LAMBETH
ARCHBISHOP'S PARK
Lambeth Palace
Museum of Garden History
Houses of Parliament
St. Thomas' Hosp.
Evelina Children's Hosp.
St. Thomas' Medical Sch.
Imperial War Museum
Geraldine Mary Harmsworth Park
St. George's Cathedral
LAMBETH NORTH
Lambeth Pier
Millbank Millennium Pier
Fire Brigade H.Q.
Police H.Q.
Spring Gardens
VAUXHALL
KENNINGTON
KENNINGTON PARK
Surrey County Cricket Club (The Oval Cricket Grd.)
Gas Works
Superstore
Vauxhall Park
St. Peter's Residence
LAMBETH PALACE ROAD
LAMBETH BRIDGE
ALBERT EMBANKMENT
KENNINGTON ROAD
KENNINGTON LANE
KENNINGTON PARK RD.
HARLEYFORD RD.
KENNINGTON OVAL
ST. GEORGE'S RD.
WESTMINSTER BRIDGE RD.
LAMBETH WALK
BLACK PRINCE ROAD
101
102
13

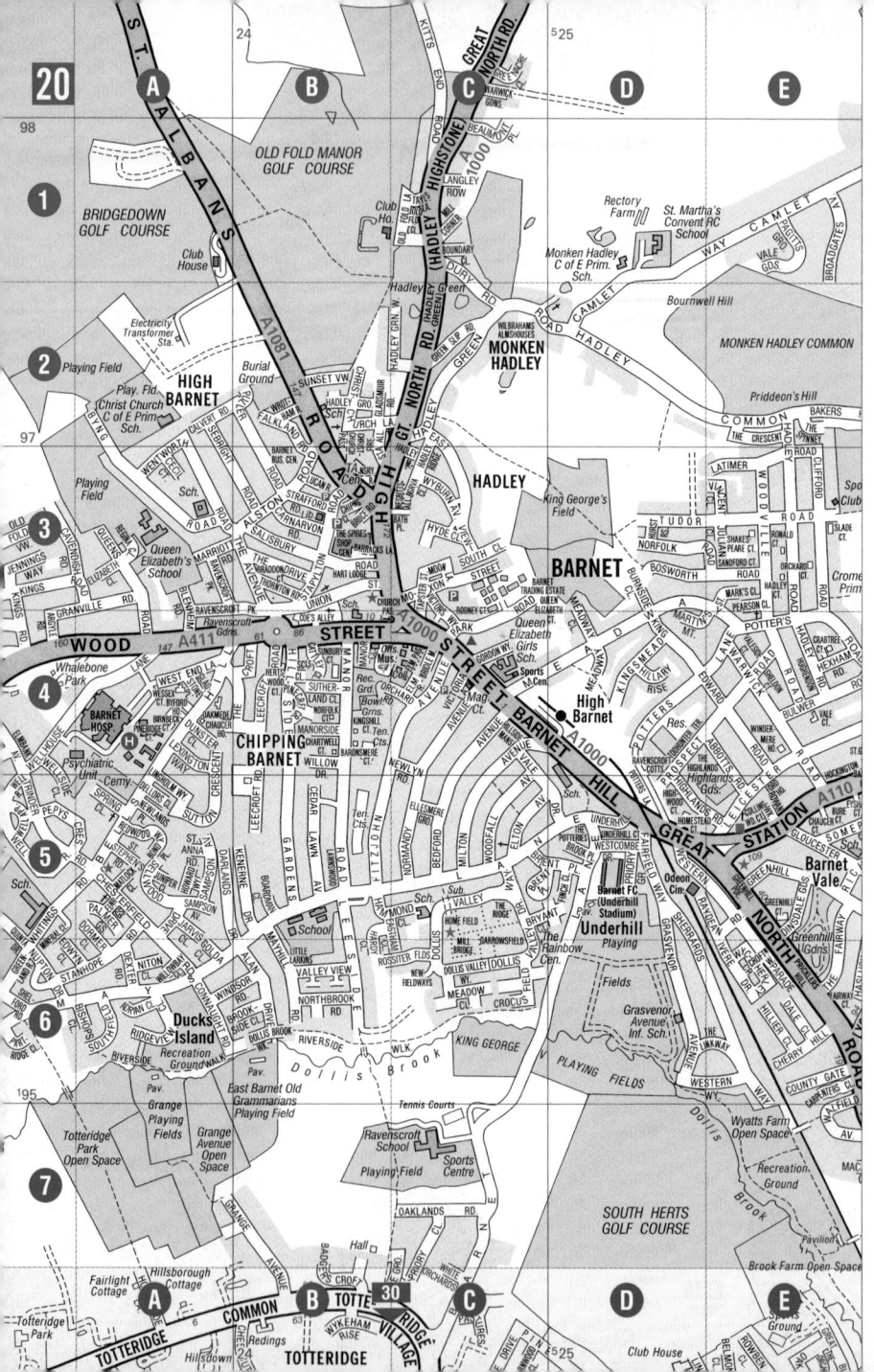
20
A
B
C
D
E
1
2
3
4
5
6
7
24
525
98
97
195
30
ST. ALBANS ROAD
A1081
OLD FOLD MANOR GOLF COURSE
BRIDGEDOWN GOLF COURSE
Club House
Club Ho.
GREAT NORTH RD.
HIGHSTONE (HADLEY HIGHSTONE)
A1000
GT. NORTH RD. (HADLEY GREEN)
KITTS END ROAD
WARWICK GDNS.
BEAUMONT PL.
LANGLEY ROW
MILL CORNER
BOUNDARY CL.
DURY RD.
Hadley Green
Rectory Farm
St. Martha's Convent RC School
Monken Hadley C of E Prim. Sch.
CAMLET WAY
CAMLET ROAD
HADLEY ROAD
VALE GDS.
BROADGATES AV.
Bournwell Hill
MONKEN HADLEY COMMON
MONKEN HADLEY
WILBRAHAMS ALMSHOUSES
GREEN SLIP RD.
Priddeon's Hill
COMMON
BAKERS
THE CRESCENT
THE SPINNEY
Electricity Transformer Sta.
Playing Field
HIGH BARNET
Burial Ground
SUNSET VW.
Play. Fld.
Christ Church C of E Prim. Sch.
BYNG RD.
CALVERT RD.
SEBRIGHT ROAD
WENTWORTH RD.
CECIL CT.
FALKLAND RD.
HAM RD.
BARNET BUS. CEN.
LUCAN RD.
HADLEY GRO.
GLADSMUIR RD.
HADLEY GRN. W.
HIGH STREET
HADLEY
King George's Field
Sch.
ALSTON ROAD
STRAFFORD RD.
CARNARVON RD.
SALISBURY
THE SPIRES SHOP. CEN.
BARRACKS LA.
BATH PL.
WYBURN AV.
HYDE CL.
VIEW
SOUTH CL.
OLD FOLD VW.
JENNINGS WAY
CAVENDISH ROAD
QUEENS RD.
ELIZABETH CL.
Queen Elizabeth's School
MARRIOTT RD.
RAVENSCROFT PK.
THE AVENUE
BRADDON DRIVE
THORNTON RD.
STAPYLTON ROAD
HART LODGE
UNION ST.
MOON ST.
TAPSTER ST.
STREET
ROONEY CT.
BARNET
BARNET TRADING ESTATE
QUEEN ELIZABETH CT.
MEADWAY
TUDOR ROAD
NORFOLK
BOSWORTH ROAD
LATIMER
WOODVILLE ROAD
CLIFFORD
SLADE CT.
KINGS RD.
GRANVILLE RD.
BLENHEIM RD.
ARGYLE
Ravenscroft Gdns.
COE'S ALLEY
CHURCH PAS.
WOOD STREET
A411
Whalebone Park
WEST END LA.
LANE
Queen Elizabeth Girls Sch.
GORDON WY.
PARK
Sports Cen.
High Barnet
BARNET HILL
A1000
KINGSMEAD
HILLARY RISE
EDWARD
WARWICK
LANE
MARK'S CL.
PEARSON CL.
POTTER'S
CRABTREE CT.
HEXHAM RD.
BULWER
VALE CT.
BARNET HOSP.
Psychiatric Unit
Cemy.
CHIPPING BARNET
LEECROFT RD.
MANORSIDE
WILLOW DR.
NEWLYN RD.
ELLESMERE GRO.
BEDFORD
MILTON AVENUE
WOODFALL AV.
ELTON AV.
VALE AV.
Mus.
Rec. Grd.
Bowl. Grns.
Ten. Cts.
POTTERS
Res.
PROSPECT
Highlands Gds.
ABBOTTS RD.
LEICESTER
A110
STATION
GREAT NORTH ROAD
WINDERMERE RD.
HOCKINGTON
WELLHOUSE LA.
WELLSIDE CL.
PEPYS CRES.
SPRING CL.
DUNSTER
LEXINGTON WAY
SUTTON CRESCENT
LINGHOLM WY.
DELLORS CL.
NEWLANDS
REDWOOD
ST. STEPHEN'S RD.
CHESTERFIELD
JUNIPER
SAMPSON AV.
DARLANDS
KENERNE DR.
BOARDMAN
GARDENS
CEDAR LAWN AV.
LAWNSWOOD ROAD
FITZJOHN
NORMANDY
LEES SIDE
UNDERHILL
WESTCOMBE
THE POTTERIES
BRENT PL.
FINCH CL.
PRIORY GR.
FAIRFIELD WAY
WESTERN
Barnet FC (Underhill Stadium)
Underhill Playing Fields
Odeon Cin.
GREENHILL
Barnet Vale
GLOUCESTER
Greenhill Gdns.
THE FAIRWAY
Sch.
WHITINGS
EDWYN CL.
DORMER CL.
PALMER
STANHOPE
DEXTER RD.
NITON CL.
JARVIS
GOLDA
WILLOWBANK
CONNAUGHT RD.
WINDSOR
ALAN DR.
MAYHILL RD.
School
VALLEY VIEW
NORTHBROOK RD.
HAMMOND CL.
ROSSITER FLDS.
NEW FIELDWAYS
DOLLIS VALLEY WY.
DOLLIS
MEADOW CL.
CROCUS
BRYANT CL.
VALLEY DR.
The Rainbow Cen.
SHERRARDS
GRASVENOR AVENUE
Grasvenor Avenue Inf. Sch.
THE LINKWAY
RAYDEAN
IVERE DR.
HILLIER CL.
DALE CL.
CHERRY HILL
COUNTY GATE
WALFIELD AV.
BISHOPS
SOUTHFIELD
RIDGEVIEW
Ducks Island Recreation Ground
RIVERSIDE WALK
DOLLIS BROOK WK.
Dollis Brook
KING GEORGE PLAYING FIELDS
WESTERN WAY
Wyatts Farm Open Space
Recreation Ground
Pav.
East Barnet Old Grammarians Playing Field
Grange Playing Fields
Grange Avenue Open Space
Totteridge Park Open Space
Tennis Courts
Ravenscroft School
Playing Field
Sports Centre
SOUTH HERTS GOLF COURSE
Pavilion
Brook Farm Open Space
OAKLANDS RD.
PRIORY CL.
WHITE ORCHARDS
GRANGE AVENUE
Hall
BADGERS CROFT
Fairlight Cottage
Hillsborough Cottage
Totteridge Park
TOTTERIDGE COMMON
Redings
WYKEHAM RISE
TOTTERIDGE VILLAGE
TOTTERIDGE
Hillsdown
Sports Ground
Club House

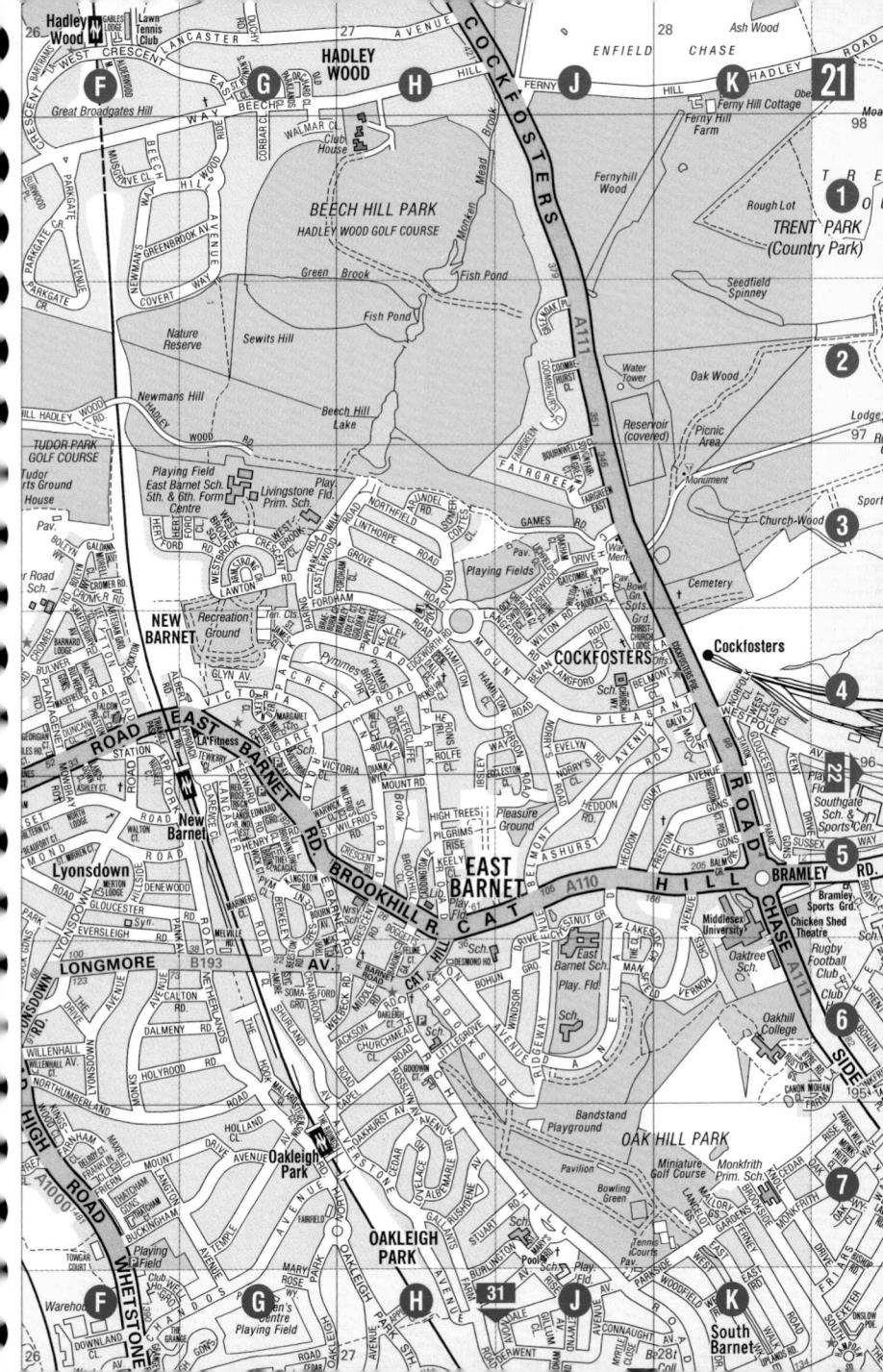

21
22
31
Hadley Wood
HADLEY WOOD
ENFIELD CHASE
Ash Wood
Ferny Hill Cottage
Ferny Hill Farm
Fernyhill Wood
Rough Lot
TRENT PARK
(Country Park)
Seedfield Spinney
BEECH HILL PARK
HADLEY WOOD GOLF COURSE
Great Broadgates Hill
Green Brook
Fish Pond
Nature Reserve
Sewits Hill
Newmans Hill
Beech Hill Lake
Water Tower
Oak Wood
Reservoir (covered)
Picnic Area
Monument
TUDOR PARK GOLF COURSE
Playing Field
East Barnet Sch. 5th. & 6th. Form Centre
Livingstone Prim. Sch.
Church Wood
Cemetery
Playing Fields
NEW BARNET
Recreation Ground
COCKFOSTERS
Cockfosters
New Barnet
Lyonsdown
Pleasure Ground
EAST BARNET
Middlesex University
Oaktree Sch.
Bramley Sports Grd.
Chicken Shed Theatre
Rugby Football Club
Southgate Sch. & Sports Cen.
Oakhill College
East Barnet Sch.
Bandstand
Playground
OAK HILL PARK
Miniature Golf Course
Monkfrith Prim. Sch.
Pavilion
Bowling Green
Oakleigh Park
OAKLEIGH PARK
South Barnet
COCKFOSTERS ROAD
A111
A110
A1000
B193
CAT HILL
BROOKHILL RD.
EAST BARNET RD.
LONGMORE AV.
HIGH ROAD
WHETSTONE
CHASE SIDE
BRAMLEY RD.
HADLEY WOOD RD.
FERNY HILL

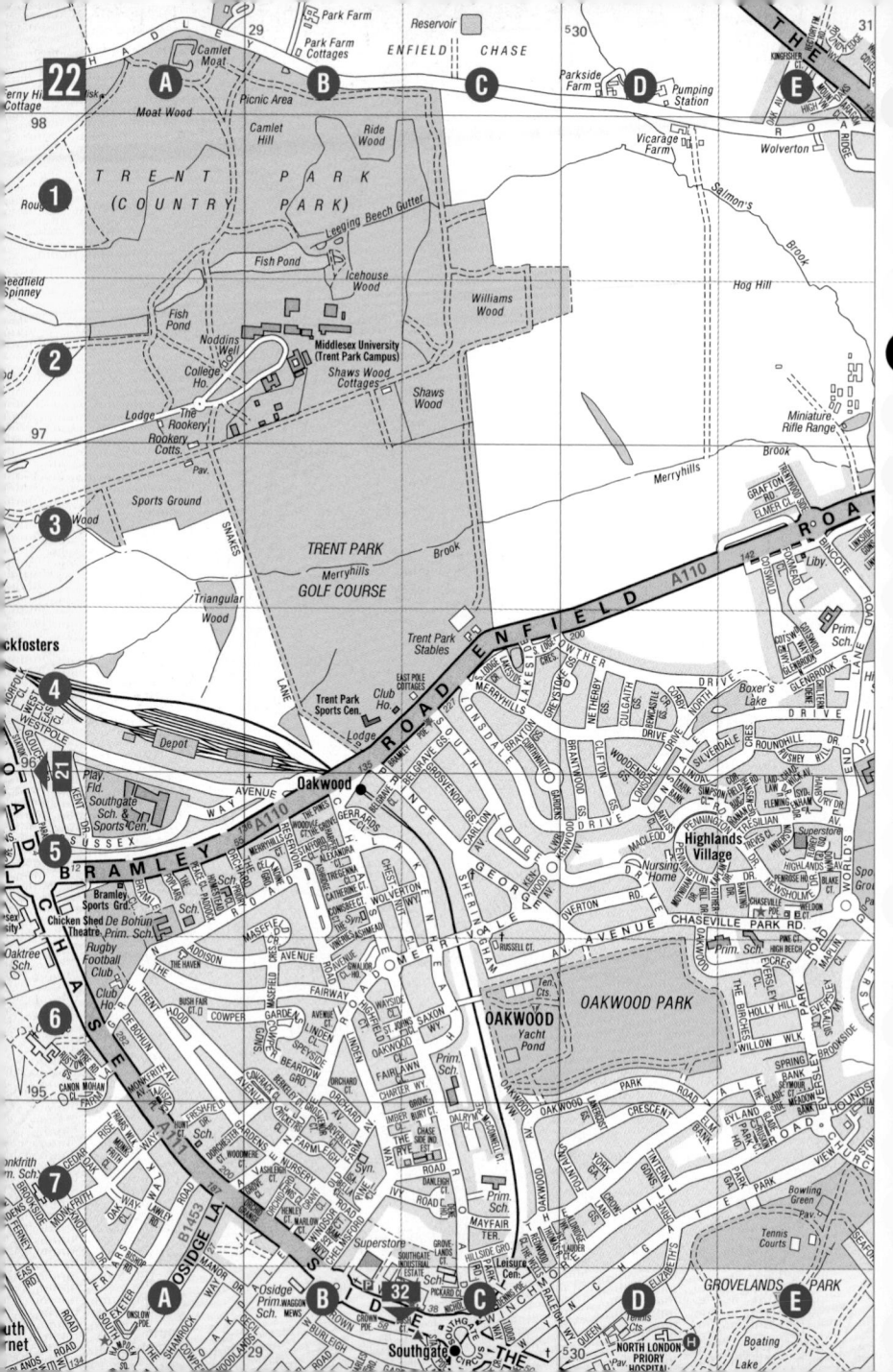22
Park Farm
Park Farm Cottages
Reservoir
ENFIELD CHASE
Camlet Moat
Moat Wood
Picnic Area
Parkside Farm
Pumping Station
Vicarage Farm
Wolverton
Camlet Hill
Ride Wood
TRENT PARK (COUNTRY PARK)
Leeging Beech Gutter
Salmon's Brook
Fish Pond
Icehouse Wood
Williams Wood
Hog Hill
Middlesex University (Trent Park Campus)
Noddins Well
College Ho.
Shaws Wood Cottages
Shaws Wood
Lodge
The Rookery
Rookery Cotts.
Pav.
Miniature Rifle Range
Merryhills Brook
Sports Ground
SNAKES LANE
TRENT PARK GOLF COURSE
Triangular Wood
Trent Park Stables
Trent Park Sports Cen.
Club Ho.
EAST POLE COTTAGES
Lodge
ENFIELD ROAD A110
Depot
Oakwood
Play. Fld.
Southgate Sch. & Sports Cen.
BRAMLEY ROAD A110
Bramley Sports Grd.
Chicken Shed Theatre
De Bohun Prim. Sch.
Rugby Football Club
Oaktree Sch.
Highlands Village
Nursing Home
Boxer's Lake
Prim. Sch.
Liby.
Superstore
OAKWOOD PARK
OAKWOOD
Yacht Pond
Ten. Cts.
CHASE SIDE A111
OSIDGE LA. B1453
Osidge Prim. Sch.
Superstore
SOUTHGATE INDUSTRIAL ESTATE
Leisure Cen.
Southgate
GROVELANDS PARK
Bowling Green
Tennis Courts
Boating Lake
NORTH LONDON PRIORY HOSPITAL
21
32

23
24
33
FORTY HILL
CEMETERY
CHASE FARM HOSPITAL
KING'S OAK BMI HOSP.
Gordon Hill
Chase Side
Sports Ground
St. Michael's Cen.
Chace Com. Sch. & Spts. Cen.
Lavender Prim. Sch.
Enfield Grammar School (Lower)
ENFIELD TOWN
Enfield Sch.
Civic Cen.
ENFIELD
Enfield Chase
Enfield Town
Chase Green
Town Park
New River (old course)
World's End
ENFIELD GOLF COURSE
Club House
Moat
Salmon's Brook
GRANGE PARK
Grange Park
Grange Park Prim. Sch.
BUSH HILL PARK GOLF COURSE
Bush Hill
BUSH HILL PARK
Bush Hill Park
Cricket Ground
WINCHMORE HILL
Winchmore Hill
Hounsden Gutter
The Paulin Ground
Tennis & Squash Club
RIDGEWAY
SLADES HILL
WINDMILL HILL
CHURCH ST.
SOUTHBURY ROAD
CECIL ROAD
LONDON ROAD
BAKER STREET
SILVER STREET
PARSONAGE LANE
CHURCHBURY LANE
LANCASTER ROAD
GORDON HILL
CHASE SIDE
LAVENDER HILL
GREEN LANES
RIDGE AV.
VILLAGE RD.
PARK AV.
CHURCH ST.
WAGON ROAD
CAMBRIDGE RD.
A1005
A110
A105
B154
1
2
3
4
5
6
7
F
G
H
J
K

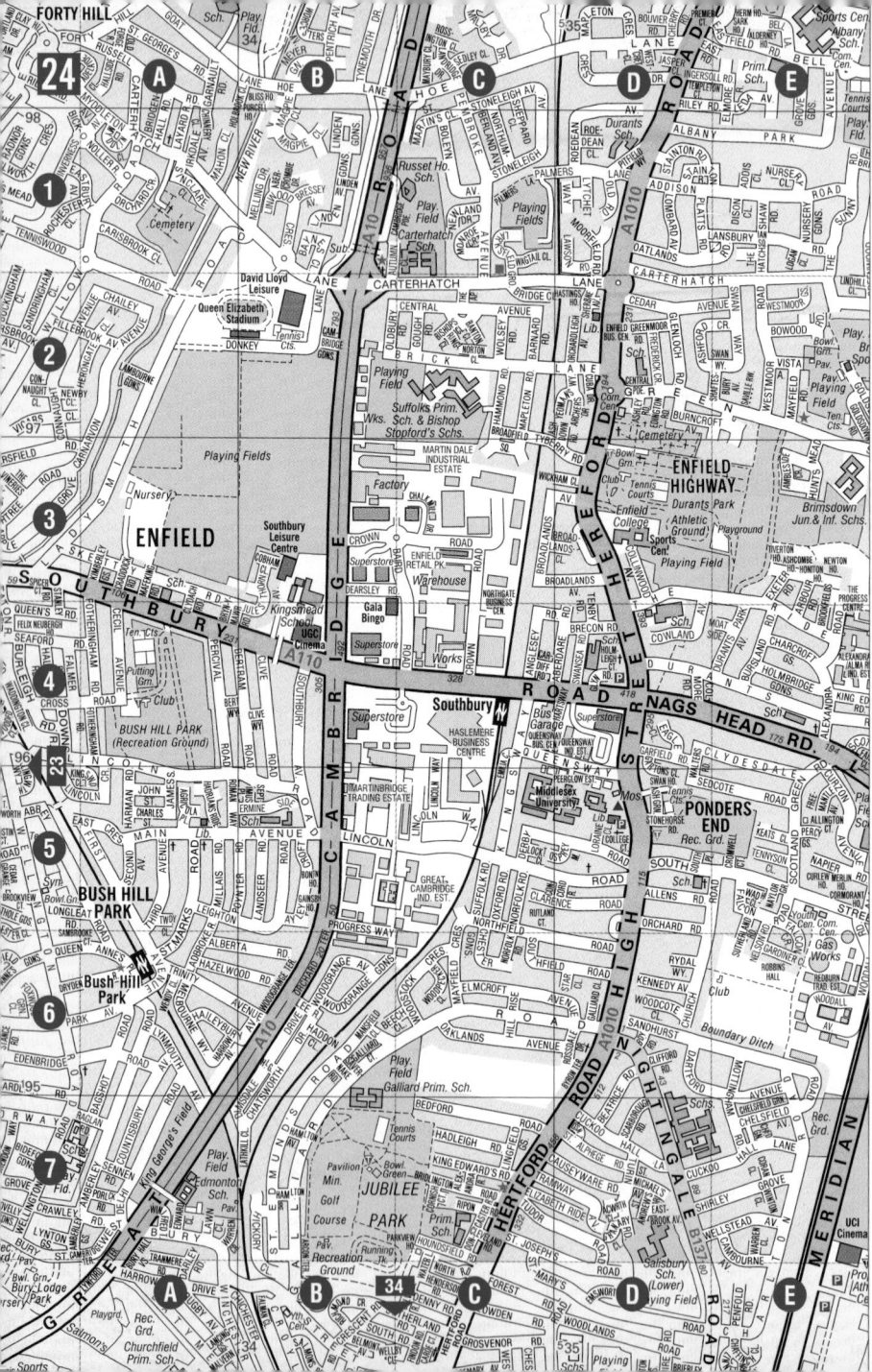
FORTY HILL
A
B
C
D
E
1
2
3
4
5
6
7
98
97
96
95
23
34
ENFIELD
ENFIELD HIGHWAY
PONDERS END
BUSH HILL PARK
Bush Hill Park
David Lloyd Leisure
Queen Elizabeth Stadium
Southbury Leisure Centre
Kingsmead School
UGC Cinema
Gala Bingo
Southbury
HASLEMERE BUSINESS CENTRE
MARTIN DALE INDUSTRIAL ESTATE
ENFIELD RETAIL PK.
NORTHGATE BUSINESS CEN.
MARTINBRIDGE TRADING ESTATE
GREAT CAMBRIDGE IND. EST.
Middlesex University
Suffolks Prim. Sch. & Bishop Stopford's Schs.
Russet Ho. Sch.
Carterhatch Sch.
Durants Sch.
Enfield College
Durants Park Athletic Ground
Brimsdown Jun.& Inf. Schs.
BUSH HILL PARK (Recreation Ground)
JUBILEE PARK
Galliard Prim. Sch.
Edmonton Sch.
Salisbury Sch. (Lower)
Churchfield Prim. Sch.
Bury Lodge Park
UCI Cinema
Albany Sch.
Sports Cen.
Playing Fields
Cemetery
Boundary Ditch
Gas Works
King George's Field
SOUTHBURY ROAD
CARTERHATCH LANE
HOE LANE
HERTFORD ROAD
HIGH STREET
NAGS HEAD RD.
GREAT CAMBRIDGE ROAD
NIGHTINGALE ROAD
MERIDIAN
LINCOLN ROAD
QUEENSWAY
SOUTH STREET
ALBANY PARK AVENUE
DURANTS ROAD
A10
A110
A1010
B137

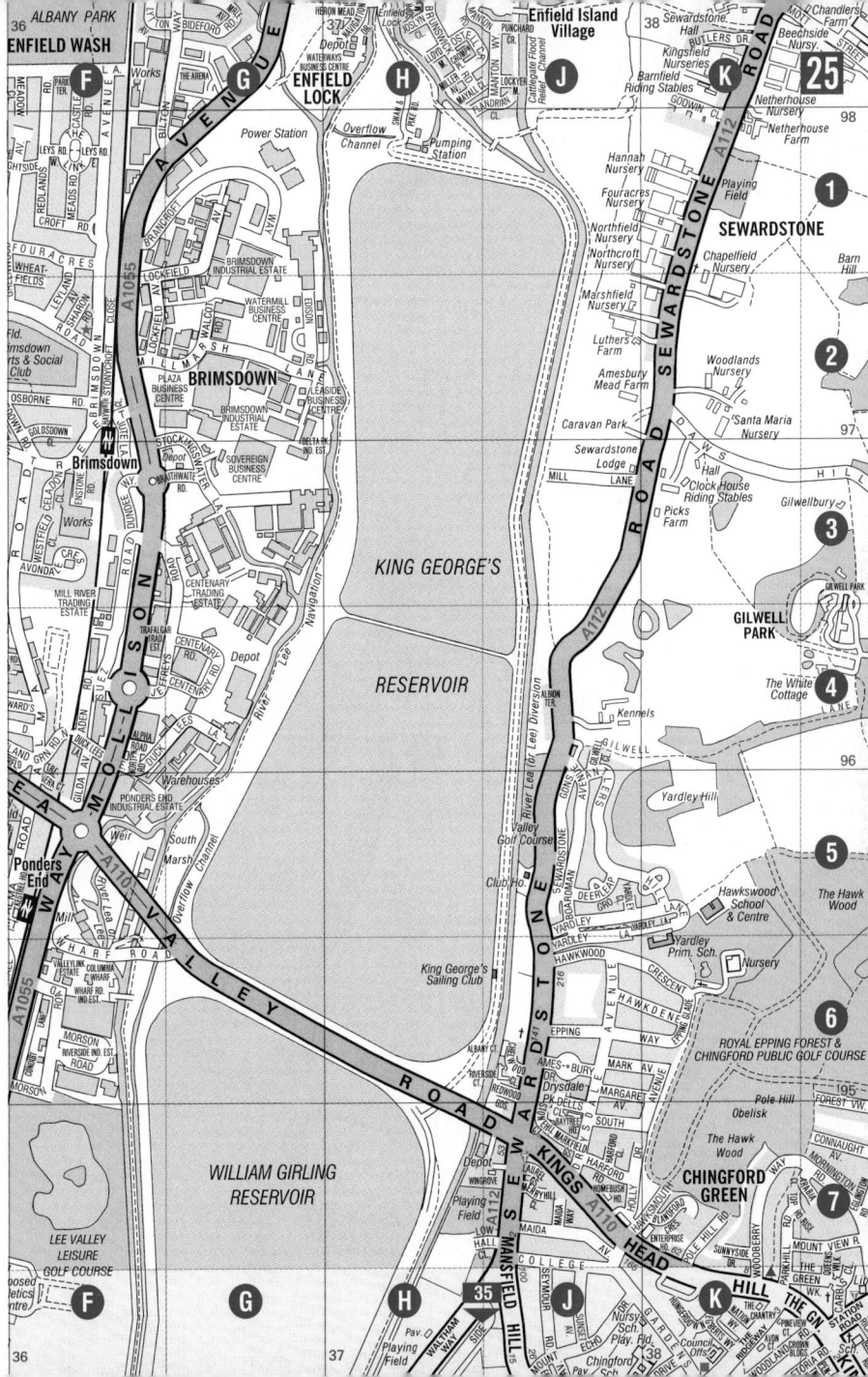

ALBANY PARK
ENFIELD WASH
Works
THE ARENA
BIDEFORD
HERON MEAD
NAVIGATION DR.
Enfield Lock
Depot
WATERWAYS BUSINESS CENTRE
ENFIELD LOCK
Enfield Island Village
Cattlegate Flood Relief Channel
Sewardstone Hall
BUTLERS DR.
Kingsfield Nurseries
Barnfield Riding Stables
Chandlers Farm
Beechside Nursy.
MOTT STREET
Netherhouse Nursery
Netherhouse Farm
GODWIN CL.
Power Station
Overflow Channel
SWAN & PIKE RD.
Pumping Station
FLANDRIAN CL.
LOCKYER M.
MANTON WY.
PUNCHARD CR.
AVENUE
A1055
BRANCROFT WAY
LOCKFIELD AV.
BRIMSDOWN INDUSTRIAL ESTATE
WATERMILL BUSINESS CENTRE
WALCOT RD.
EDISON RD.
MILLMARSH LANE
BRIMSDOWN
PLAZA BUSINESS CENTRE
LEASIDE BUSINESS CENTRE
BRIMSDOWN INDUSTRIAL ESTATE
DELTA PK. IND. EST.
STOCKINGSWATER LA.
Depot
BRAITHWAITE RD.
SOVEREIGN BUSINESS CENTRE
DUNDEE WY.
CENTENARY TRADING ESTATE
TRAFALGAR TRAD. EST.
CENTENARY RD.
JEFFREYS RD.
Depot
DUCK LEES LA.
ALPHA ROAD
Warehouses
PONDERS END INDUSTRIAL ESTATE
River Lee Navigation
MOLLISON
Weir
South Marsh
Overflow Channel
MEADOW CL.
PARK TER.
THE CASTLE
THE LINK
LEYS RD.
REDLANDS RD.
MEADS RD.
CROFT RD.
FOURACRES
WHEATFIELDS
LEYLAND AV.
SHARON RD.
Fld.
Brimsdown Sports & Social Club
BRIMSDOWN AVENUE
STONYCROFT CLOSE
HAYWRTH CL.
JUTE LA.
OSBORNE RD.
GOLDSDOWN CL.
Brimsdown
CELADON CL.
ENSTONE RD.
WESTFIELD CL.
Works
AVONDALE CRES.
MILL RIVER TRADING ESTATE
ADEN RD.
SUEZ RD.
DUCK LEES LA.
GILDA AV.
ALMA RD.
Ponders End
WAY
A110
VALLEY
WHARF ROAD
River Lea
Mill
VALLEYLINK ESTATE
COLUMBIA WHARF
WHARF RD. IND. EST.
MORSON ROAD
RIVERSIDE IND. EST.
MORSON
CONDUIT LANE
A1055
KING GEORGE'S
RESERVOIR
River Lea (or Lee) Diversion
Valley Golf Course
Club Ho.
King George's Sailing Club
WILLIAM GIRLING RESERVOIR
LEE VALLEY LEISURE GOLF COURSE
ROAD
KINGS HEAD
Hannah Nursery
Fouracres Nursery
Northfield Nursery
Northcroft Nursery
Marshfield Nursery
Luthers Farm
Amesbury Mead Farm
Caravan Park
Sewardstone Lodge
MILL LANE
SEWARDSTONE ROAD
A112
Playing Field
SEWARDSTONE
Chapelfield Nursery
Barn Hill
Woodlands Nursery
Santa Maria Nursery
DAWS HILL
Hall
Clock House Riding Stables
Picks Farm
Gilwellbury
GILWELL PARK
GILWELL PARK
The White Cottage
LANE
ALBION TER.
Kennels
GILWELL
GILWELL CL.
Yardley Hill
SEWARDSTONE GDNS.
Hawkswood School & Centre
The Hawk Wood
DEERLEAP GRO.
BOARDMAN
YARDLEY LANE
YARDLEY LA.
Yardley Prim. Sch.
Nursery
HAWKWOOD CRESCENT
HAWKDENE
EPPING WAY
EPPING GLADE
ROYAL EPPING FOREST & CHINGFORD PUBLIC GOLF COURSE
AMESBURY DR.
MARK AV.
Drysdale Pk.
MARGARET AV.
DELLS CLS.
SOUTH
DRYSDALE AV.
HARFORD CL.
HARFORD RD
HOMEBUSH HO.
HOLLY DR.
Pole Hill Obelisk
FOREST VW.
The Hawk Wood
CONNAUGHT AV.
MORNINGTON RD.
EGLINTON
CHINGFORD GREEN
HAWKSMOUTH
BLANDFORD CRES.
ENTERPRISE HO.
POLE HILL RD.
WOODBERRY WAY
TOP HO. RISE
MOUNT VIEW R
ALBANY CT.
RIVERSIDE CT.
REDWOOD GDS.
Depot
WINGROVE
Playing Field
LAUREL
MERRYHILL CL.
MAIDA WAY
MAIDA AV.
LOW HALL CL.
MANSFIELD HILL
COLLEGE
SEYMOUR RD.
SUNNYSIDE DR.
PARKHILL RD.
QUEENS WLK.
THE GREEN
THE GREEN WK.
HILL
THE GN.
STATION ROAD
Lib.
HUNGERDOWN
EGBERTS WY
NATION WY
THE CHANTRY
THE RIDGEWAY
AVON CT.
PINEVIEW CT.
CROWN BLDGS.
WOODLAND
VICTORIA RD.
Council Offs.
Nursy. Sch.
Play. Fld.
ECHO
SUNSET AV.
GARDENS
DRIVE
Chingford Sch.
MOUNT
Pav.
Playing Field
WALTHAM WAY
SIDE
35
F
G
H
J
K
1
2
3
4
5
6
7
36
37
38
98
97
96
195

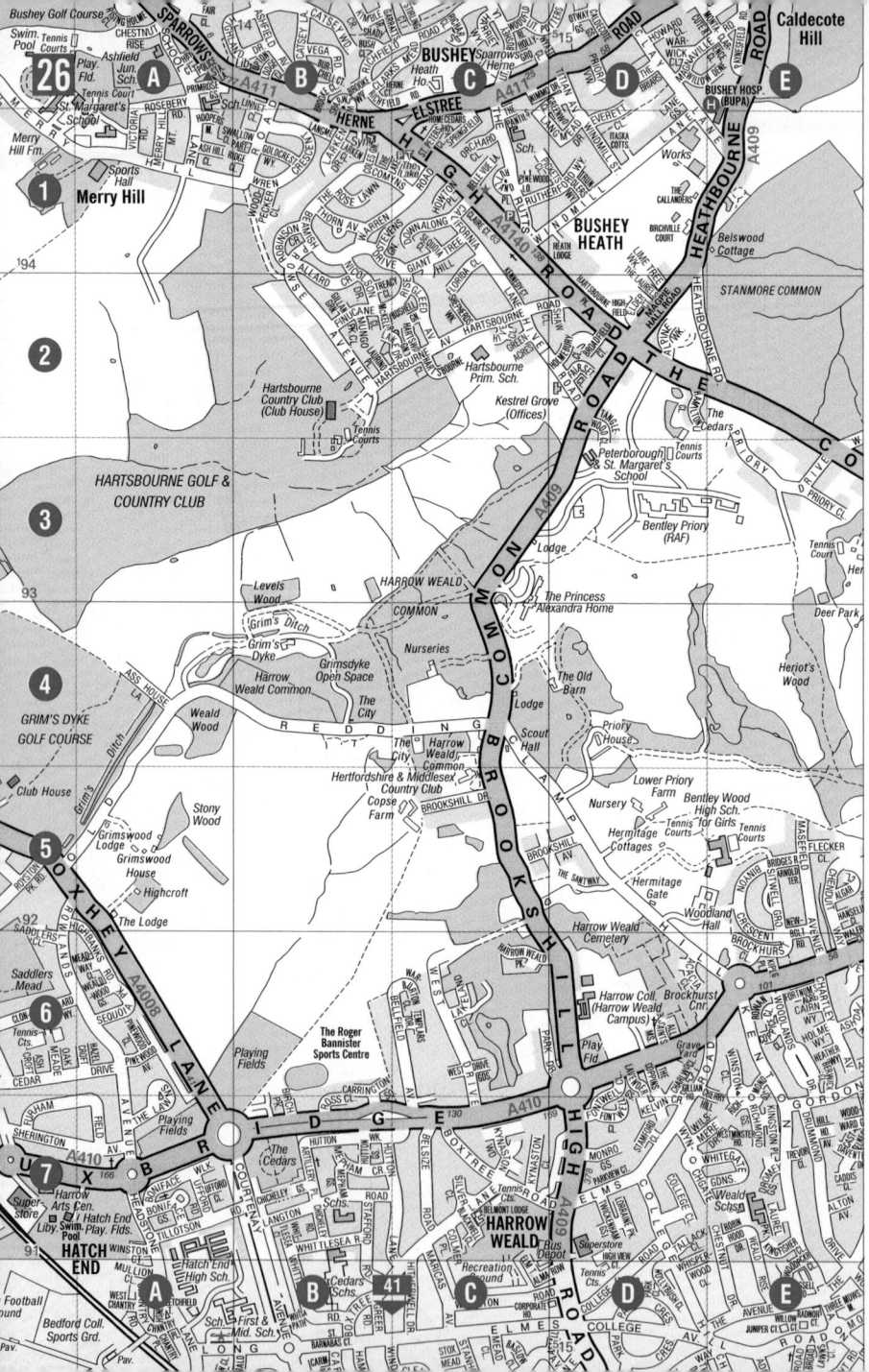
26
A
B
C
D
E
1
2
3
4
5
6
7
Bushey Golf Course
Swim. Pool
Tennis Courts
Play. Fld.
Ashfield Jun. Sch.
Tennis Court
St. Margaret's School
Merry Hill Fm.
Sports Hall
Merry Hill
SPARROWS HERNE
BUSHEY
Heath Ho.
A411
HERNE
ELSTREE
Sch.
Works
THE CALLANDERS
BIRCHVILLE COURT
BUSHEY HOSP. (BUPA)
Caldecote Hill
HEATHBOURNE ROAD
A409
Belswood Cottage
STANMORE COMMON
BUSHEY HEATH
HEATH LODGE
HIGH ROAD
A4140
HARTSBOURNE AV.
Hartsbourne Prim. Sch.
Hartsbourne Country Club (Club House)
Tennis Courts
Kestrel Grove (Offices)
THE COMMON
The Cedars
Tennis Courts
PRIORY DRIVE
PRIORY CL.
Peterborough & St. Margaret's School
HARTSBOURNE GOLF & COUNTRY CLUB
Bentley Priory (RAF)
Lodge
Tennis Court
COMMON ROAD
Levels Wood
HARROW WEALD COMMON
The Princess Alexandra Home
Deer Park
Grim's Ditch
Grim's Dyke
Nurseries
Harrow Weald Common
Grimsdyke Open Space
The City
The Old Barn
Heriot's Wood
GRIM'S DYKE GOLF COURSE
Weald Wood
REDDING
Lodge
Scout Hall
Priory House
The City
Harrow Weald Common
Hertfordshire & Middlesex Country Club
Copse Farm
BROOKSHILL DR.
Lower Priory Farm
Club House
Stony Wood
Nursery
Bentley Wood High Sch. for Girls
Tennis Courts
Hermitage Cottages
Grimswood Lodge
Grimswood House
BROOKSHILL AV.
THE SANTWAY
Hermitage Gate
Highcroft
The Lodge
Woodland Hall
Harrow Weald Cemetery
BROOKSHILL
OXHEY LANE
A4008
Saddlers Mead
HARROW WEALD PK.
Harrow Coll. (Harrow Weald Campus)
Brockhurst Cnr.
Tennis Cts.
The Roger Bannister Sports Centre
Playing Fields
Play. Fld.
Grave Yard
KENTON ROAD
Playing Fields
UXBRIDGE ROAD
A410
The Cedars
Harrow Arts Cen.
Super-store
Liby.
Swim. Pool
Hatch End Play. Flds.
HATCH END
Hatch End High Sch.
Cedars Schs.
Schs.
41
HARROW WEALD
Bus Depot
Recreation Ground
Superstore
Tennis Cts.
Weald Schs.
Football Ground
Bedford Coll. Sports Grd.
Sch.
First & Mid. Sch.
Pav.
LONG ELMES
COLLEGE AV.
HIGH ROAD

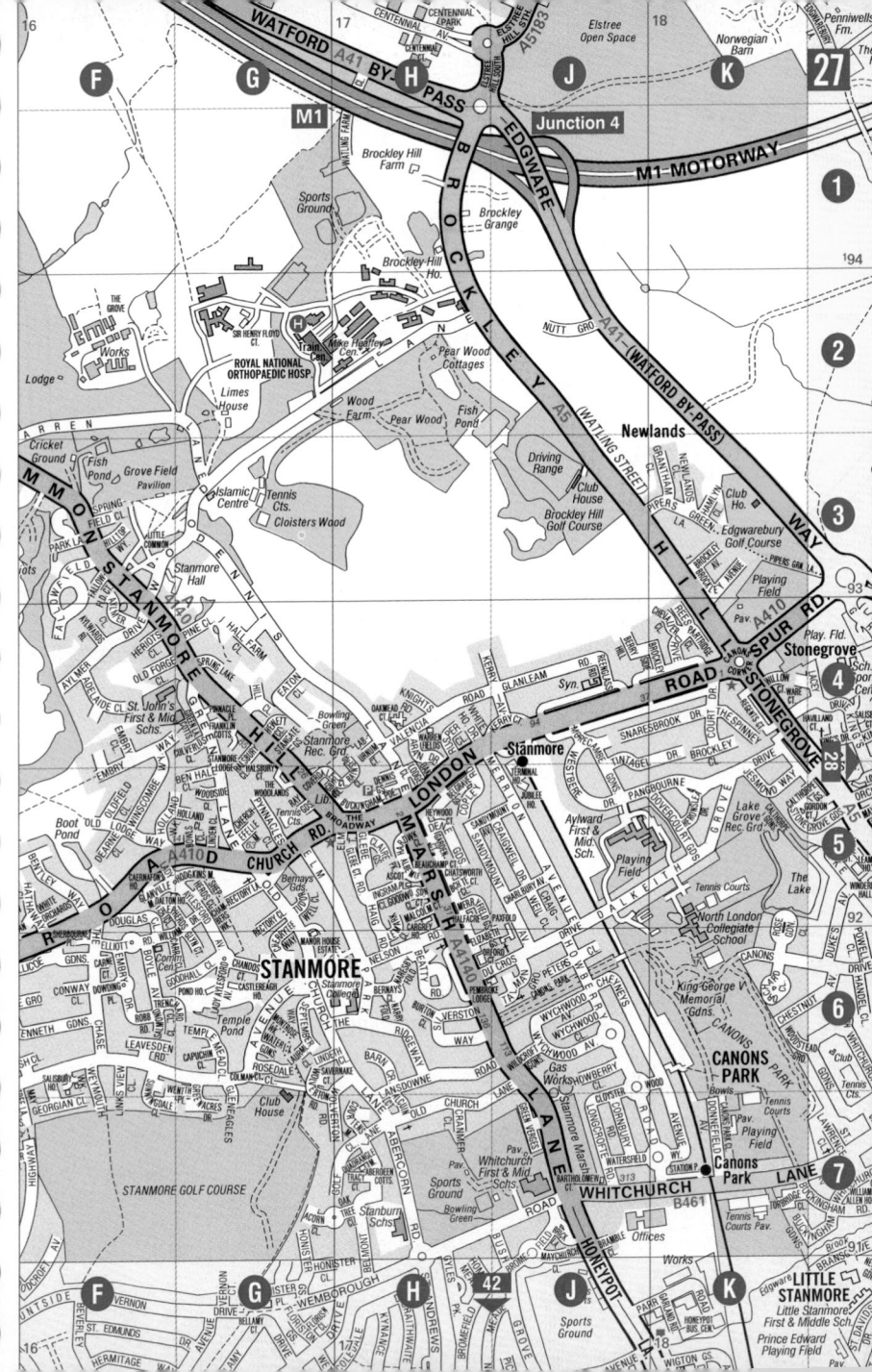

16
17
18
WATFORD BY-PASS
A41
CENTENNIAL PARK
CENTENNIAL AV.
ELSTREE HILL SOUTH
A5183
Elstree Open Space
Penniwells Fm.
Norwegian Barn
27
F
G
H
J
K
M1
Junction 4
EDGWARE
BROCKLEY
M1-MOTORWAY
WATLING FARM
Brockley Hill Farm
Sports Ground
Brockley Grange
Brockley Hill Ho.
1
2
3
4
5
6
7
194
93
92
THE GROVE
Works
Lodge
SIR HENRY FLOYD CT.
ROYAL NATIONAL ORTHOPAEDIC HOSP.
Train. Cen.
Mike Heaffey Cen.
Pear Wood Cottages
Limes House
Wood Farm
Pear Wood
Fish Pond
NUTT GRO.
A41 (WATFORD BY-PASS)
A5 (WATLING STREET)
Newlands
Driving Range
Club House
Brockley Hill Golf Course
GRANTHAM CL.
NEWLANDS CL.
PIPERS GREEN LA.
Club Ho.
Edgwarebury Golf Course
Playing Field
WAY
Cricket Ground
Fish Pond
Grove Field Pavilion
Islamic Centre
Tennis Cts.
Cloisters Wood
SPRINGFIELD CL.
HILLTOP WY.
LITTLE COMMON
PARK LA.
Stanmore Hall
DENNIS LANE
STANMORE
A4140
A410
SPUR RD.
Play. Fld.
Stonegrove
Sch. & Sports Cen.
GLANLEAM RD.
KERRY AV.
KNIGHTS RD.
Syn.
ROAD
CANONS CORNER
STONEGROVE
OLD FORGE
HERIOTS CL.
PINE CL.
AYLMER DRIVE
ADELAIDE CL.
St. John's First & Mid. Schs.
Bowling Green
Stanmore Rec. Grd.
EMBRY WAY
OLDFIELD CL.
WINSCOMBE WAY
HOLLAND
LONDON
Stanmore
SNARESBROOK DR.
TINTAGEL DR.
BROCKLEY CL.
THE SPINNEY
JESMOND WAY
28
PANGBOURNE DR.
DOVERCOURT GDS.
Lake Grove Rec. Grd.
Boot Pond
THE BROADWAY
CHURCH RD.
MARSH
Aylward First & Mid. Sch.
Playing Field
Tennis Courts
DALKEITH GROVE
The Lake
North London Collegiate School
BENTLEY WAY
DOUGLAS CL.
ROAD
STANMORE
Stanmore College
NELSON RD.
BEATTY RD.
King George V Memorial Gdns.
CANONS PARK
Temple Pond
THE RIDGEWAY
SILVERSTON WAY
WYCHWOOD AV.
Gas Works
Club House
LANSDOWNE ROAD
CHURCH LANE
Stanmore Marsh
STANMORE GOLF COURSE
Whitchurch First & Mid. Schs.
Sports Ground
Bowling Green
Stanburn Schs.
WHITCHURCH LANE
B461
Canons Park
Tennis Courts
Playing Field
Offices
Works
HONEYPOT LANE
LITTLE STANMORE
Little Stanmore First & Middle Sch.
Prince Edward Playing Field
42
WEMBOROUGH RD.
VERNON DRIVE
Sports Ground

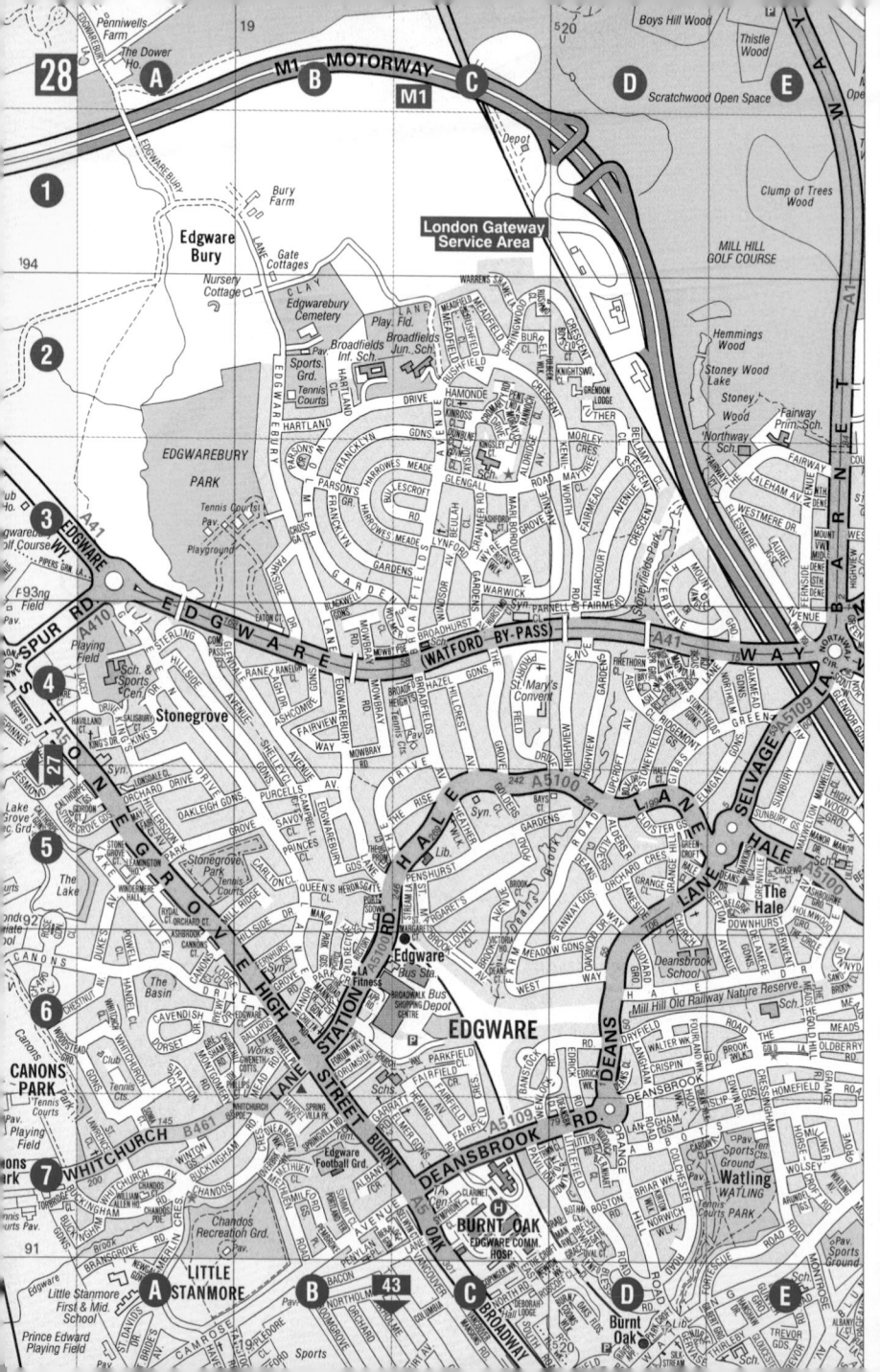

28
M1 MOTORWAY
Edgware Bury
London Gateway Service Area
Scratchwood Open Space
MILL HILL GOLF COURSE
EDGWAREBURY PARK
Edgwarebury Cemetery
EDGWARE WAY (WATFORD BY-PASS)
Stonegrove
STONEGROVE
HIGH STREET
STATION RD.
HALE LANE
DEANS LANE
DEANSBROOK RD.
SELVAGE LANE
BARNET WAY
Edgware
EDGWARE
The Hale
Deansbrook School
Mill Hill Old Railway Nature Reserve
BURNT OAK
EDGWARE COMM. HOSP.
CANONS PARK
WHITCHURCH LANE
Chandos Recreation Grd.
LITTLE STANMORE
Little Stanmore First & Mid. School
Prince Edward Playing Field
Watling
WATLING PARK
Burnt Oak
BROADWAY
27
43

29
30
44
Junction 2
F
G
H
J
K
1
2
3
4
5
6
7
21
22
23
91
92
93
94
Hyver Manor
Barnet Gate Wood
Gravel Pit Wood
Tanglewood
Moat Mount Open Space
HENDON WOOD LANE
B552
BARNET GATE LANE
MAYS LA.
Allendale
Brent Lodge Farm
Dollis Brook
Hendon Wood Lane Open Space
Sports Ground
Pav.
Fairlight Cottage
Totteridge Park
Abattoir
St. Edward's College
TOTTERIDGE COMMON
A5109
MOAT MOUNT OPEN SPACE
The Shrubbery
Moat Mount Camp Site
Leg of Mutton Pond
Mote End Farm
Mote Mount
Nut Wood
White Lodge
Boundary House
Farmleigh
Oak Lodge
Totteridge Common
Ellern Mede Nursing Home
Ellern Mede Farm
Tennis Courts
Mill Hill High Sch.
Club House
Playing Field
Beech Wood
Highwood Park
The Barn
Highwood Ho.
Hendon Park
CLARK'S LANE
CROWN CL.
HIGHWOOD HILL
TOTTERIDGE
The Lynch House
Fairlawn
Highwood
Highwood Hill
Highwood Hill Cottage
Holcombe Dale
Folly Brook
Holcombe Hill
Pool
Playing Field
Riding School
Folly Farm
Sports Ground Cricket Club
MARSH LANE
RAMILLIES
WORCESTER
NORBURY GRO.
GLENWOOD RD.
THE LINCOLNS
ABBEY VIEW
LAWRENCE GDS.
THE REDDINGS
REDDINGS CL.
SUNNYFIELD
BRABOURNE HGTS.
AUSTELL GDS.
GARDENS
TRETAWN PK.
UPHILL RD.
St. Mary's Abbey
The Mill Field
Belmont Sch.
Belmont Farm
MILLERS CL.
Lawrence Green
APEX CORNER
WATFORD WAY
A1
M1 MOTORWAY
Cemetery
Sports Ground
Nursery
Pav.
Burtonhole Farm
St. Paul's C of E Prim. Sch.
Tennis Courts
CHALET ESTATE
DRAPERS' COTTAGE HOMES
St. Joseph's RC College
LAWRENCE
SHAKESPEARE RD.
MILTON RD.
TAYLORSMEAD
TENNYSON RD.
B1461
HAMMERS LANE
Leisure Cen.
Spts. Grd.
Mill Hill School
MARSHALL ESTATE
Ten. Cts.
KINGSHEAD HO.
THE RIDGEWAY
St. Vincent's School
St. Vincent's Convent
Medical Research Laboratory
Works
ST. VINCENTS LA.
BURTONHOLE LA.
Oakfield House
St. Vincent's RC Prim. Sch.
Wentworth Hall
Drivers Hill
The Mount Sch.
Play. Fld.
HIGH ST.
MILESPIT HILL
GROVE
VINERIES BANK
HOLLIES END
Tennis Court
Ridgeway Ho.
Pavilion
Burton Bank
School Park
Arrandene Open Space
Featherstone Hill
Playground
MILL HILL
Playing Field
VICTORIA RD.
ALBERT RD.
WILTSHIRE
BIRKBECK RD.
BYRON RD.
MARION RD.
DAWS LANE
WILLS GROVE
WISE LANE
WINTER-STOKE GS.
Sub.
Garden Centre
WEYMOUTH AV.
NEWCOMBE
Hall
Sch.
GOODWYN
MONTEREY PL. SHOPPING CEN.
CLARENCE CT.
MILL HILL CIRCUS
THE BROADWAY
HARTLEY AV.
FLOWER LANE
Lib.
Univ.
STANHOPE GDNS.
SYLVAN AV.
WISTERIA CL.
OAKLODGE WAY
COURTGATE CL.
PARK CL.
WOODLAND WAY
(BARNET BY-PASS)
Pav.
Tennis Courts
Cricket Ground
MILL HILL PARK
Watch Tower House
AVENUE
RUSHDEN GDNS.
MILL HILL CEMETERY
MELDEX CL.
WOODCOTE
ENGEL PARK
BITTACY HILL
BITTACY RISE
Bittacy Hill P
Ten. Cts.
LANE WISE
LANE
BUNNS LANE
Mill Hill Broadway
GRANARD BUS. CEN.
Lyndhurst Park
LYNDHURST AV.
ROAD
WOODCROFT AV.
Woodcroft Park
Sports Ground
Pavilion
GRAHAME PARK WAY
M1
MILL HILL IND. EST.
MILL HILL PARK
PENTAVIA RETAIL PK.
THE RISE
PARKSIDE
HOLMDENE AV.
GLENMERE AV.
HILLSIDE GRO.
COPTHALL GDNS.
COPTHALL DR.
Ten. Cts.
GRENFELL CT.
FEATHERSTONE RD.
BROOKFIELD AV.
BROOKFIELD CRES.
MOORLANDS AV.
HOLLAND CT.
TUDOR CT.
Playing Field
Copthall Sch. & Sports Cen.
PAGE ST.
PURSLEY RD.
Playing Field
Chase Lodge
Powerleague Soccer Cen.
Dollis Jun. & Inf. Schs.
SANDERS LANE
BITTACY
SALCOMBE
MORETON
GRANTS CL.
TAVISTOCK
ASHLEY LANE
ABERDARE GDNS.
Club House
Tennis Courts
Copthall Swimming Pool
Barnet Copthall Stadium
Rugby Club
Pav.
ROWLANDS
COLENSO
LONGFIELD AVENUE
THE WLK.
HENDON GOLF COURSE
BARNET COPTHALL SPORTS CENTRE
Pavilion
High Sch.
PAGE
WAY
CHADBURY CT.
Play. Fld.
Tennis Cts.
Barnet Coll.
Sub.
Grahame Park
HEYWOOD
MEAD
CLAYTON FIELD
LONG FIELD
GREAT FIELD
CORNER MEAD
SOUTH MEAD
BROOKLEA CL.
LARCH GN.
PARKLEA CL.
SOUTH GN.
GOLDBEATERS
MOSTYN RD.
MAPLE GDNS.
STORKSMEAD RD.
GROVE
DEANSBROOK

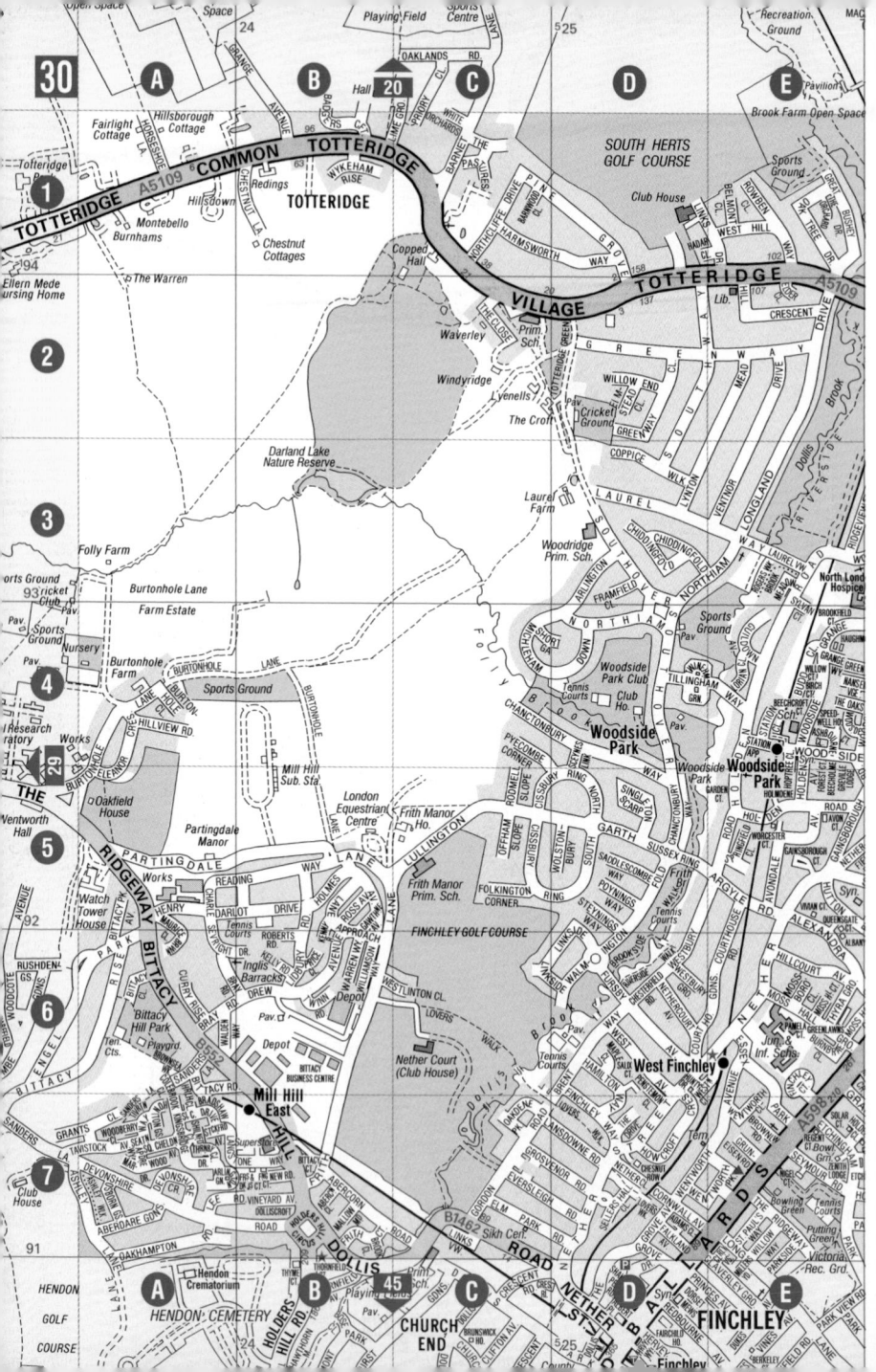
A
B
C
D
E
1
2
3
4
5
6
7
20
29
45
24
25
96
94
93
92
91
Playing Field
Sports Centre
Recreation Ground
Pavilion
Brook Farm Open Space
OAKLANDS RD.
Hall
Fairlight Cottage
Hillsborough Cottage
TOTTERIDGE COMMON
TOTTERIDGE
A5109
Totteridge Park
Redings
Hillsdown
Montebello
Burnhams
WYKEHAM RISE
Chestnut Cottages
The Warren
Ellern Mede Nursing Home
SOUTH HERTS GOLF COURSE
Club House
Sports Ground
WEST HILL
Copped Hall
HARMSWORTH WAY
TOTTERIDGE VILLAGE
Lib.
CRESCENT
Waverley
Prim. Sch.
GREENWAY
Windyridge
Lyenells
The Croft
Cricket Ground
Darland Lake Nature Reserve
COPPICE WLK
LAUREL WAY
Laurel Farm
Woodridge Prim. Sch.
Dollis Brook
Folly Farm
Burtonhole Lane Farm Estate
Sports Ground
Cricket Club
Nursery
Burtonhole Farm
BURTONHOLE LANE
Folly Brook
North London Hospice
Woodside Park Club
Tennis Courts
Club Ho.
Woodside Park
Works
HILLVIEW RD.
Mill Hill Sub. Sta.
London Equestrian Centre
Frith Manor Ho.
Oakfield House
Wentworth Hall
Partingdale Manor
PARTINGDALE LANE
LULLINGTON GARTH
SUSSEX RING
Works
Watch Tower House
Frith Manor Prim. Sch.
FINCHLEY GOLF COURSE
Inglis Barracks
Depot
RIDGEWAY
BITTACY HILL
B552
Bittacy Hill Park
Playgrd.
Depot
BITTACY BUSINESS CENTRE
Nether Court (Club House)
West Finchley
Jun. & Inf. Schs.
Mill Hill East
Superstore
A598
BALLARDS LANE
Club House
Bowling Green
Tennis Courts
Putting Green
Victoria Rec. Grd.
B1462
Sikh Cen.
DOLLIS ROAD
NETHER ST.
Hendon Crematorium
HENDON GOLF COURSE
HENDON CEMETERY
CHURCH END
FINCHLEY
Playing Fields
HOLDERS HILL RD.

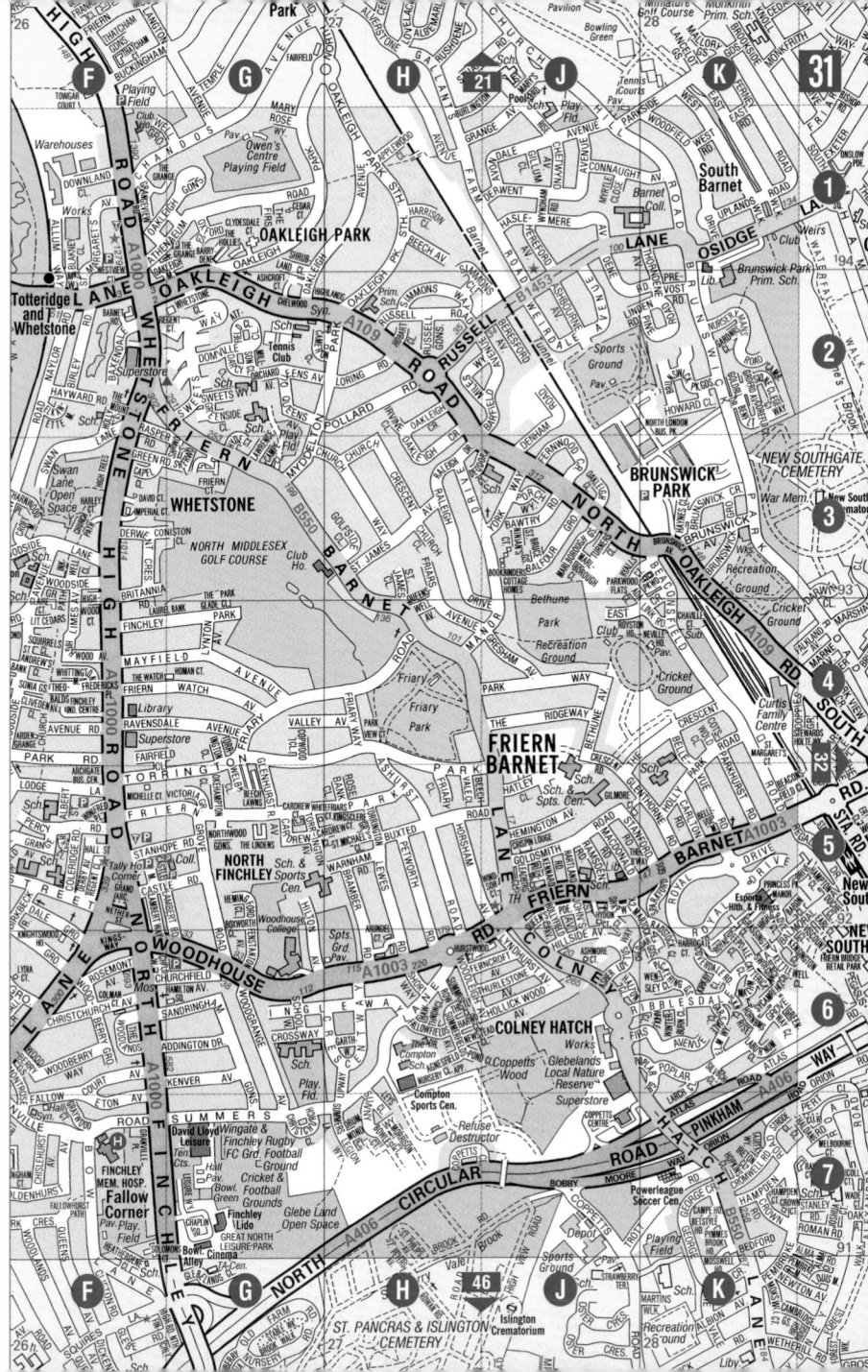

31
21
46
32
F
G
H
J
K
1
2
3
4
5
6
7
OAKLEIGH PARK
South Barnet
Totteridge and Whetstone
WHETSTONE
NORTH MIDDLESEX GOLF COURSE
BRUNSWICK PARK
NEW SOUTHGATE CEMETERY
FRIERN BARNET
NORTH FINCHLEY
COLNEY HATCH
Fallow Corner
Friary Park
Bethune Park Recreation Ground
Glebelands Local Nature Reserve
Coppetts Wood
Glebe Land Open Space
Owen's Centre Playing Field
ST. PANCRAS & ISLINGTON CEMETERY
Islington Crematorium
FINCHLEY MEM. HOSP.
Barnet Coll.
Woodhouse College
Compton Sports Cen.
David Lloyd Leisure
Wingate & Finchley Rugby FC Grd. Football Ground
Cricket & Football Grounds
Finchley Lido
GREAT NORTH LEISURE PARK
Powerleague Soccer Cen.
Curtis Family Centre
Esporta Hlth. & Fitness
Brunswick Park Prim. Sch.
Tennis Club
Tally Ho Corner
HIGH ROAD
WHETSTONE HIGH ROAD
OAKLEIGH ROAD NORTH
OAKLEIGH RD SOUTH
RUSSELL ROAD
FRIERN BARNET LANE
FRIERN BARNET ROAD
FRIERN BARNET RD.
WOODHOUSE RD.
COLNEY HATCH LANE
NORTH CIRCULAR ROAD
PINKHAM WAY
ATLAS ROAD
BOBBY MOORE WAY
OSIDGE LANE
BRUNSWICK PARK ROAD
TORRINGTON PARK
BALLARDS LANE
A1000
A109
A1003
A406
B550
B1453

32
22
31
47
A
B
C
D
E
1
2
3
4
5
6
7
SOUTHGATE
OSIDGE
NEW SOUTHGATE
GROVELANDS PARK
ARNOS PARK
NEW SOUTHGATE CEMETERY
New Southgate Crematorium
NORTH LONDON PRIORY HOSPITAL
Southgate College
Southgate Cricket Club Ground
Broomfield Park
Palmers Green
Bowes Park
Bounds Green
Arnos Grove
Southgate
New Southgate
MUSWELL HILL GOLF COURSE
Hollickwood Park
Scout Park
CLOCKHOUSE JUNCTION
Boating Lake
Pitch & Putt Course
Sports Grd.
Playing Fields
Cemetery
FRIERN BRIDGE RETAIL PARK
Esporta Hlth. & Fitness
Curtis Family Centre
Durnsford Spts. Cen.
CHASE SIDE
THE BOURNE
HIGH STREET
CANNON HILL
ALDERMANS HILL
WATERFALL RD.
BOWES RD.
TELFORD RD.
BOUNDS GREEN RD.
GREEN LANES
DURNSFORD RD.
PINKHAM WAY
FRIERN BARNET RD.
STATION RD.
OAKLEIGH RD. STH.
HAMPDEN WAY
POWYS LA.
WILMER WY.
A111
A1004
A1003
A1110
A406
A109
B1453
B1452
B106
A105

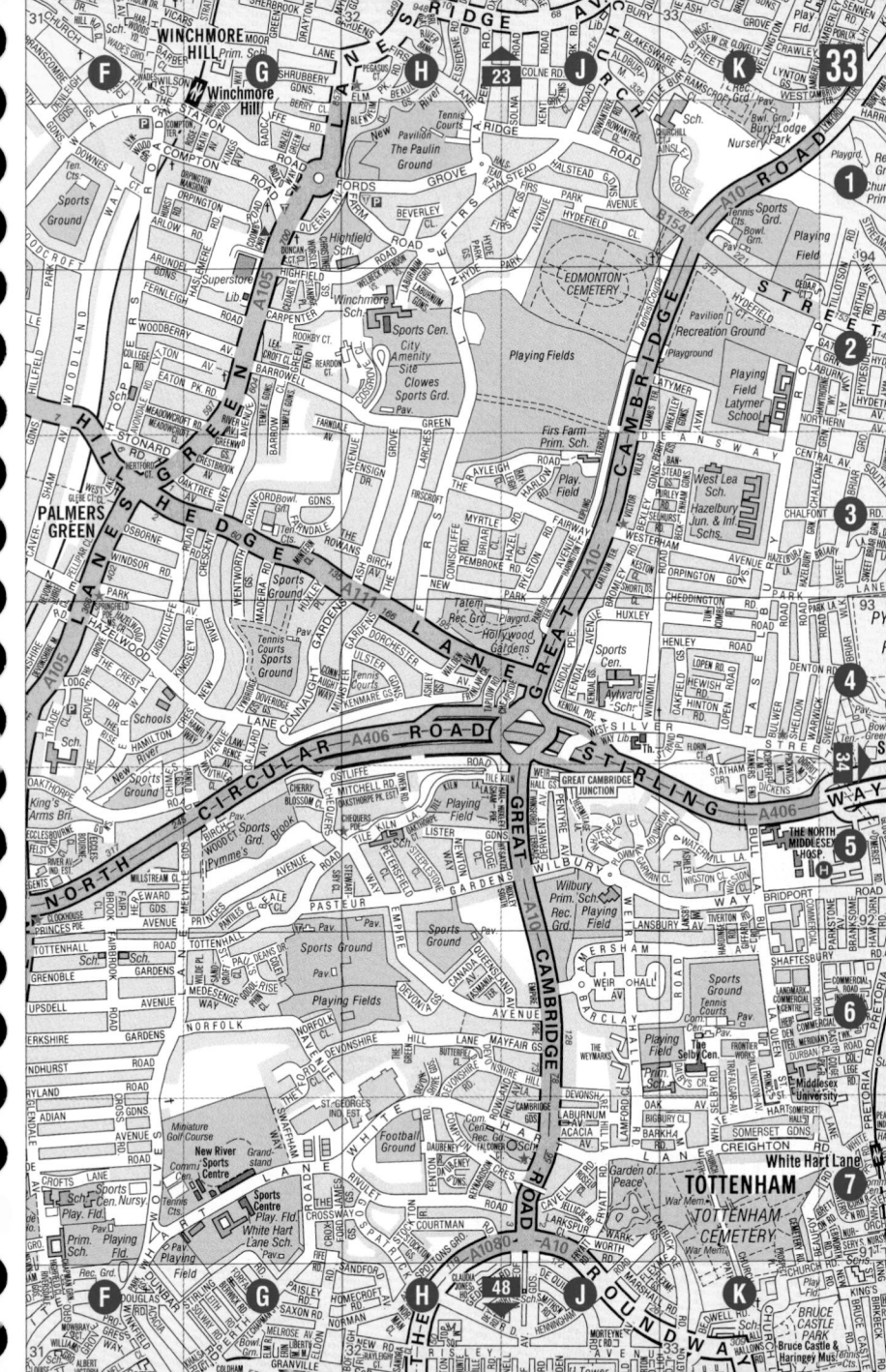
33
WINCHMORE HILL
Winchmore Hill
PALMERS GREEN
TOTTENHAM
White Hart Lane
23
48
34
F
G
H
J
K
1
2
3
4
5
6
7
31
32
33
The Paulin Ground
Highfield Sch.
Superstore
Winchmore Sch.
Sports Cen.
City Amenity Site
Clowes Sports Grd.
Playing Fields
EDMONTON CEMETERY
Recreation Ground
Playing Field Latymer School
Firs Farm Prim. Sch.
Play. Field
West Lea Sch.
Hazelbury Jun. & Inf. Schs.
Tatem Rec. Grd.
Hollywood Gardens
Sports Ground
Aylward Sch.
GREAT CAMBRIDGE JUNCTION
THE NORTH MIDDLESEX HOSP.
Wilbury Prim. Sch.
Playing Field
Pymme's Brook
Sports Grd.
Miniature Golf Course
New River Sports Centre
Football Ground
White Hart Lane Sch.
Garden of Peace
TOTTENHAM CEMETERY
Middlesex University
The Selby Cen.
BRUCE CASTLE PARK
Bruce Castle & Haringey Mus.
Bury Lodge Park
Nursery
Schools
King's Arms Bri.
ST. GEORGES IND. EST.
NORTH CIRCULAR ROAD
A406
GREAT CAMBRIDGE ROAD
A10
A105
A111
A1080
B154
GREEN LANES
HEDGE LANE
SILVER STREET
STERLING WAY
THE ROUNDWAY
WHITE HART LANE
HERTFORD ROAD
FIRS LANE
CHURCH STREET
BURY STREET
HASELBURY ROAD
HYDE PARK AVENUE
DEANSWAY
WILBURY WAY
BARCLAY AVENUE
CREIGHTON RD.
COMPTON ROAD
ORPINGTON RD.
FERNLEIGH ROAD
WOODBERRY AV.
CARPENTER GDNS.
TOTTENHALL ROAD
DEVONSHIRE HILL LANE
PASTEUR GARDENS
PRINCES AVENUE
NORFOLK AVENUE
MEDESENGE WAY
GRENOBLE GARDENS
UPSDELL AVENUE
RIVULET RD.
COURTMAN ROAD
FIRS PARK AVENUE
HALSTEAD ROAD
LATYMER WAY
NORTHERN AV.
CENTRAL AV.
CHALFONT RD.
HUXLEY ROAD
HENLEY ROAD
OSBORNE RD.
WINDSOR RD.
HAZELWOOD LANE

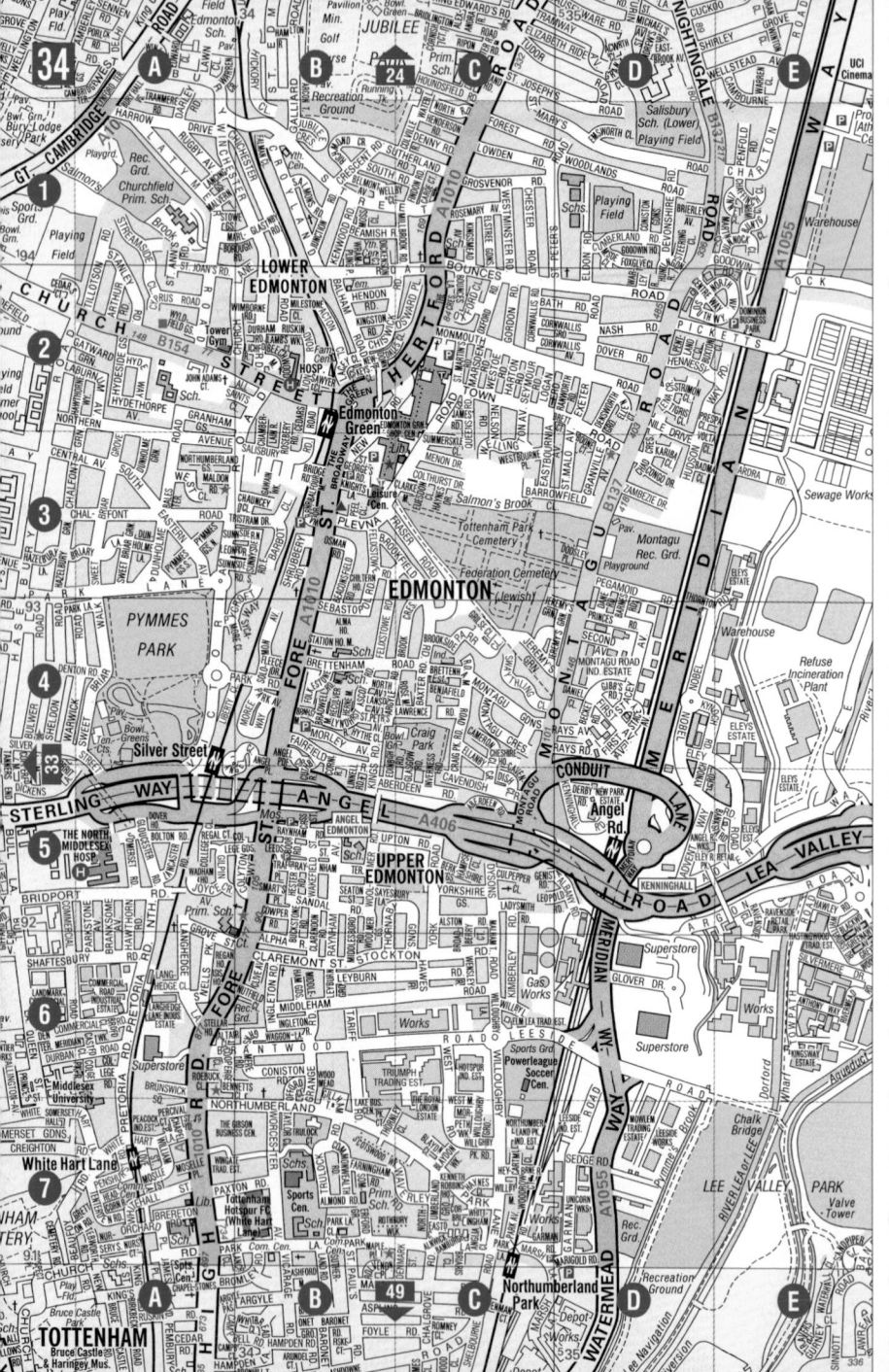

34
A
B
C
D
E
24
1
2
3
4
5
6
7
33
49
JUBILEE
LOWER EDMONTON
EDMONTON
UPPER EDMONTON
TOTTENHAM
Edmonton Green
Silver Street
White Hart Lane
Angel Rd.
Northumberland Park
PYMMES PARK
Tottenham Park Cemetery
Federation Cemetery (Jewish)
Montagu Rec. Grd.
Salmon's Brook
Recreation Ground
Playing Field
Churchfield Prim. Sch.
Salisbury Sch. (Lower) Playing Field
THE NORTH MIDDLESEX HOSP.
Middlesex University
Tottenham Hotspur FC (White Hart Lane)
Sports Cen.
Craig Park
Powerleague Soccer Cen.
TRIUMPH TRADING EST.
Gas Works
Superstore
Works
Warehouse
Sewage Works
Refuse Incineration Plant
ELEYS ESTATE
UCI Cinema
LEE VALLEY PARK
Chalk Bridge
Valve Tower
Lee Navigation
Bruce Castle Park
Bruce Castle & Haringey Mus.
GT. CAMBRIDGE RD.
A10
CHURCH STREET
B154
HERTFORD ROAD
A1010
FORE ST.
HIGH RD.
MONTAGU ROAD
B137
MERIDIAN WAY
A1055
WATERMEAD WAY
NIGHTINGALE ROAD
STERLING WAY
ANGEL RD.
A406
CONDUIT LANE
LEA VALLEY ROAD
ADVENT WAY
LEESIDE ROAD
NORTHUMBERLAND PARK
PICKETTS LOCK LANE
BOUNCES ROAD
PARK LANE
SILVER STREET
VICTORIA RD.
BRANTWOOD ROAD
NORTHUMBERLAND
WILLOUGHBY LANE
PRETORIA RD.
FOREST RD.
LATYMER RD.

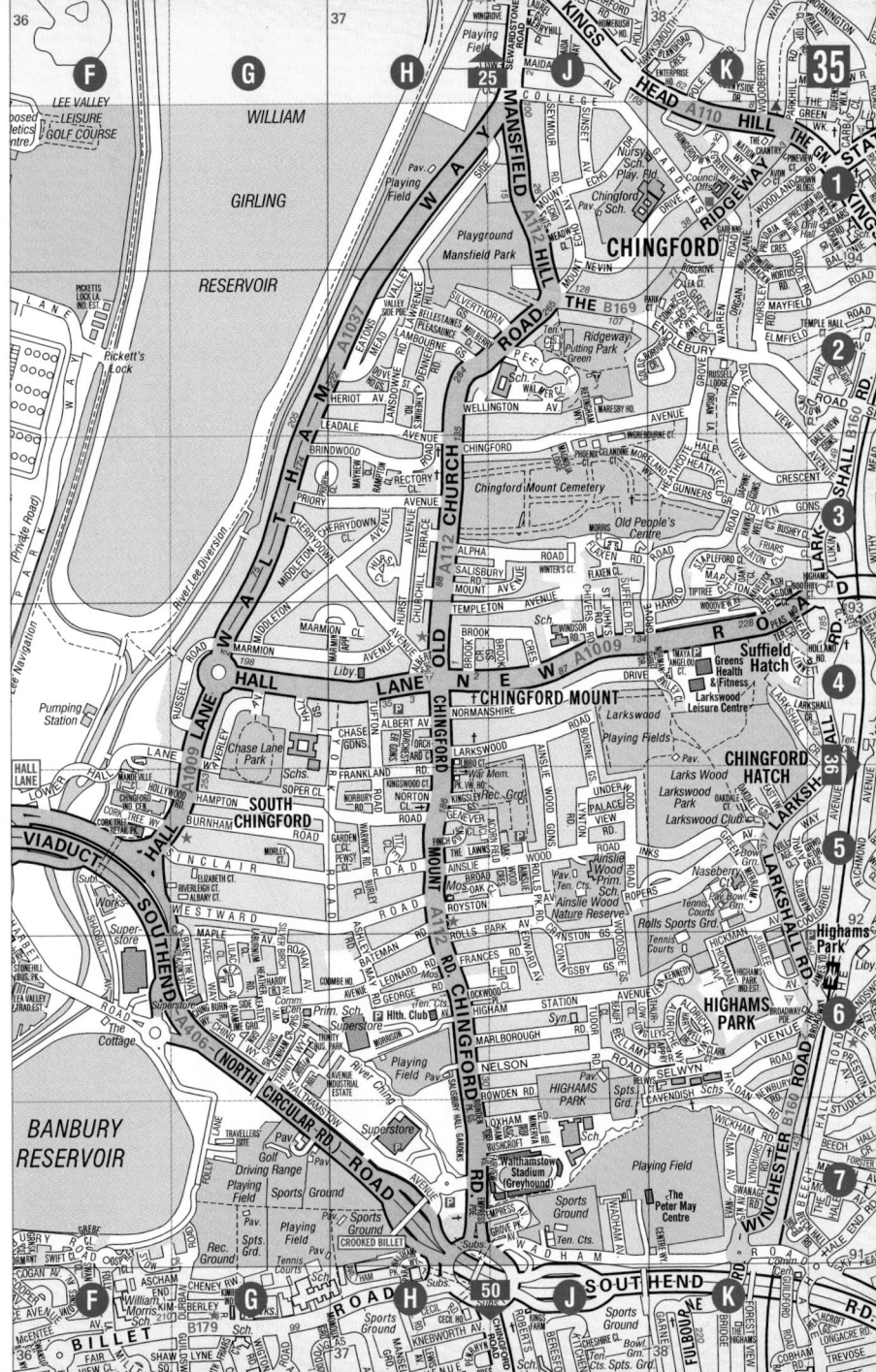
35
CHINGFORD
SOUTH CHINGFORD
CHINGFORD MOUNT
CHINGFORD HATCH
HIGHAMS PARK
WILLIAM GIRLING RESERVOIR
BANBURY RESERVOIR
LEE VALLEY LEISURE GOLF COURSE
Chingford Mount Cemetery
Larkswood Playing Fields
Walthamstow Stadium (Greyhound)
The Peter May Centre
Mansfield Park
Ridgeway Park
Chase Lane Park
Rolls Sports Grd.
Ainslie Wood Nature Reserve
CROOKED BILLET
25
36
50

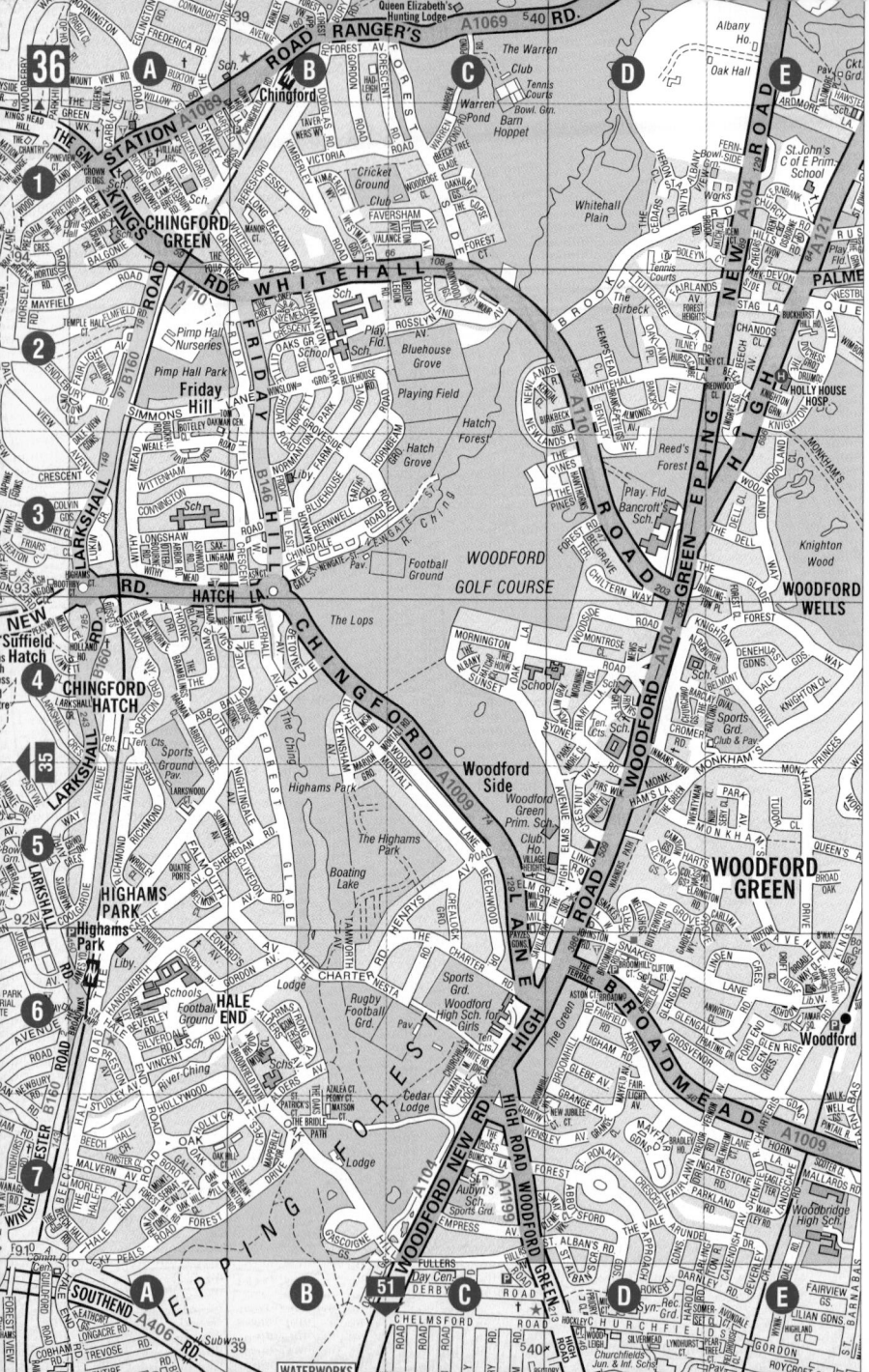

36
A
B
C
D
E
1
2
3
4
5
6
7
Queen Elizabeth's Hunting Lodge
RANGER'S RD.
A1069
Chingford
The Warren Club
Tennis Courts
Warren Pond
Bowl. Grn.
Barn Hoppet
Albany Ho.
Oak Hall
STATION ROAD
KINGS HEAD HILL
THE GN
CHINGFORD GREEN
KINGS ROAD
Cricket Ground Club
Whitehall Plain
St.John's C of E Prim. School
WHITEHALL RD.
A110
Pimp Hall Nurseries
Pimp Hall Park
Friday Hill
FRIDAY HILL
B146
Bluehouse Grove
Playing Field
Hatch Forest
Hatch Grove
The Birbeck
Reed's Forest
HOLLY HOUSE HOSP.
EPPING NEW ROAD
A104
A121
HIGH ROAD
Bancroft's Sch.
Knighton Wood
WOODFORD GOLF COURSE
WOODFORD WELLS
LARKSHALL ROAD
B160
HATCH LA.
CHINGFORD LANE
A1009
Football Ground
The Lops
NEW RD.
Suffield Hatch
CHINGFORD HATCH
35
Sports Ground
Highams Park
The Highams Park
Boating Lake
Woodford Side
Woodford Green Prim. Sch.
WOODFORD GREEN
HIGHAMS PARK
Highams Park
Schools
Football Ground
HALE END
Rugby Football Grd.
Sports Grd. Woodford High Sch. for Girls
BROADMEAD ROAD
Woodford
EPPING FOREST
Cedar Lodge
Lodge
WOODFORD NEW RD.
HIGH ROAD WOODFORD GREEN
A1199
St. Aubyn's Sch.
Woodbridge High Sch.
SOUTHEND RD.
A406
51
Day Cen.
CHURCHFIELDS
Churchfields Jun. & Inf. Schs.
WATERWORKS
39
540

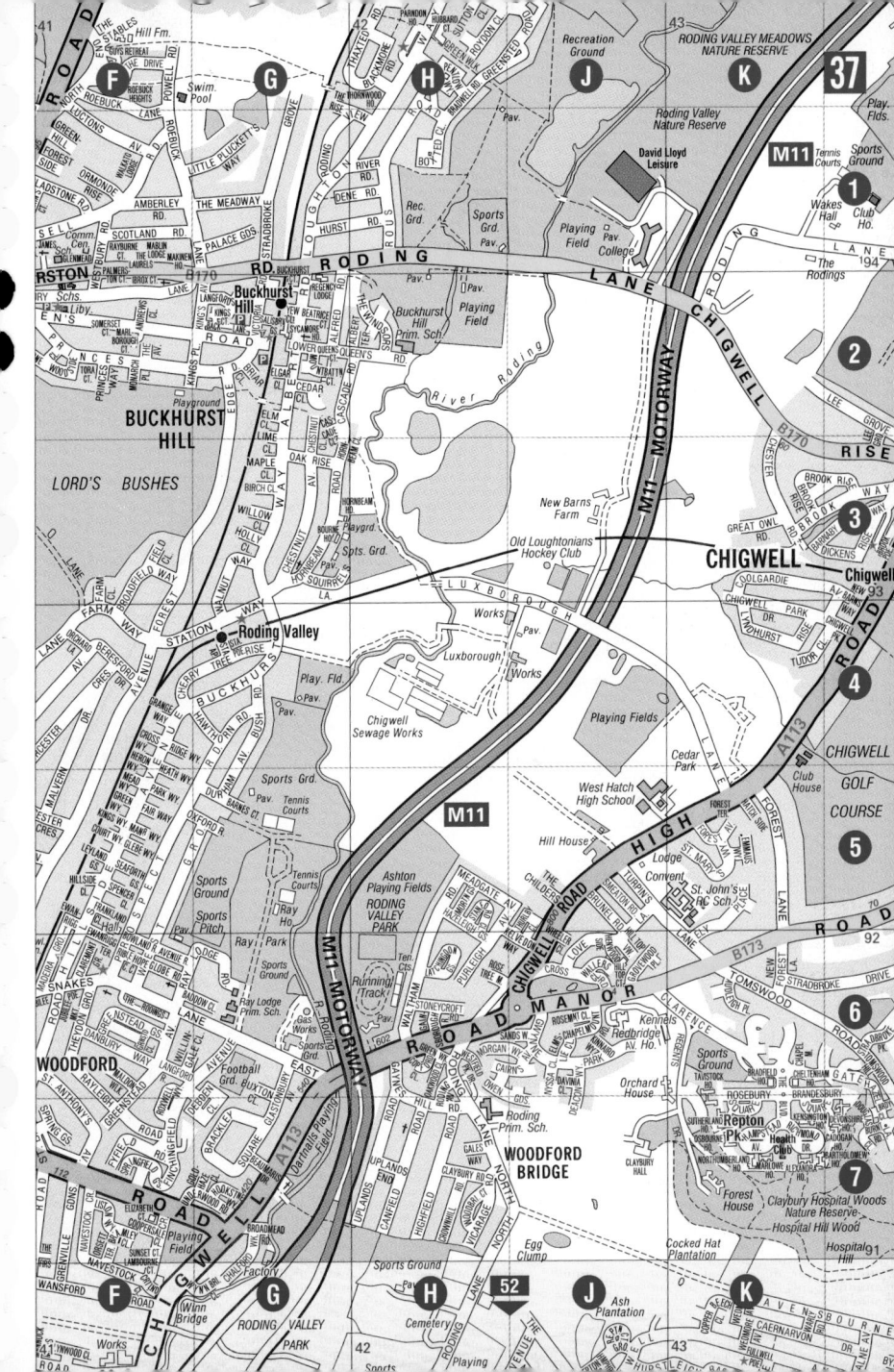

37
Recreation Ground
RODING VALLEY MEADOWS NATURE RESERVE
Roding Valley Nature Reserve
David Lloyd Leisure
Play. Flds.
Sports Ground
Tennis Courts
M11
Wakes Hall
Club Ho.
Playing Field
College
Rec. Grd.
Sports Grd.
RODING LANE
The Rodings
CHIGWELL
B170
LEE GROVE
RISE
BROOK RISE
BROOK WAY
GREAT OWL RD.
DICKENS RISE
CHIGWELL
Chigwell
COOLGARDIE AV.
CHIGWELL PARK DR.
LYNDHURST RISE
TUDOR CL.
ROAD
A113
CHIGWELL GOLF COURSE
Club House
M11 MOTORWAY
New Barns Farm
Old Loughtonians Hockey Club
LUXBOROUGH LA.
Works
Luxborough
Playing Fields
Chigwell Sewage Works
Cedar Park
West Hatch High School
Hill House
HIGH ROAD
Lodge
Convent
St. John's RC Sch.
MANOR ROAD
B173
TOMSWOOD ROAD
STRADBROKE DRIVE
Kennels
Redbridge Av. Ho.
Orchard House
Sports Ground
Repton Pk
Health Club
Forest House
Claybury Hospital Woods Nature Reserve
Hospital Hill Wood
Hospital Hill
Cocked Hat Plantation
Egg Clump
Ash Plantation
CAERNARVON DR.
AVENSBOURNE
WOODFORD BRIDGE
Roding Prim. Sch.
Ashton Playing Fields
RODING VALLEY PARK
Running Track
Gas Works
Sports Grd.
Ray Park
Sports Ground
Ray Ho.
Tennis Courts
Ray Lodge Prim. Sch.
Sports Ground
Sports Pitch
Football Grd.
Darnalls Playing Field
WOODFORD
SNAKES LANE
CHIGWELL ROAD
Playing Field
Factory
Winn Bridge
RODING VALLEY PARK
Cemetery
Sports Ground
Works
52
Sports Grd.
Tennis Courts
Play. Fld.
Roding Valley
STATION WAY
BUCKHURST WAY
LORD'S BUSHES
BUCKHURST HILL
Playground
Buckhurst Hill
Buckhurst Hill Prim. Sch.
Playing Field
River Roding
QUEEN'S RD.
PRINCES WAY
ROAD
Liby.
Schs.
RODING RD.
B170
SCOTLAND RD.
AMBERLEY RD.
THE MEADWAY
PALACE GDS.
Swim. Pool
Hill Fm.
ROEBUCK LANE
LOUGHTON WAY
RIVER RD.
DENE RD.
HURST RD.
Pav.
F G H J K
1 2 3 4 5 6 7
41 42 43
194 93 92 91 70

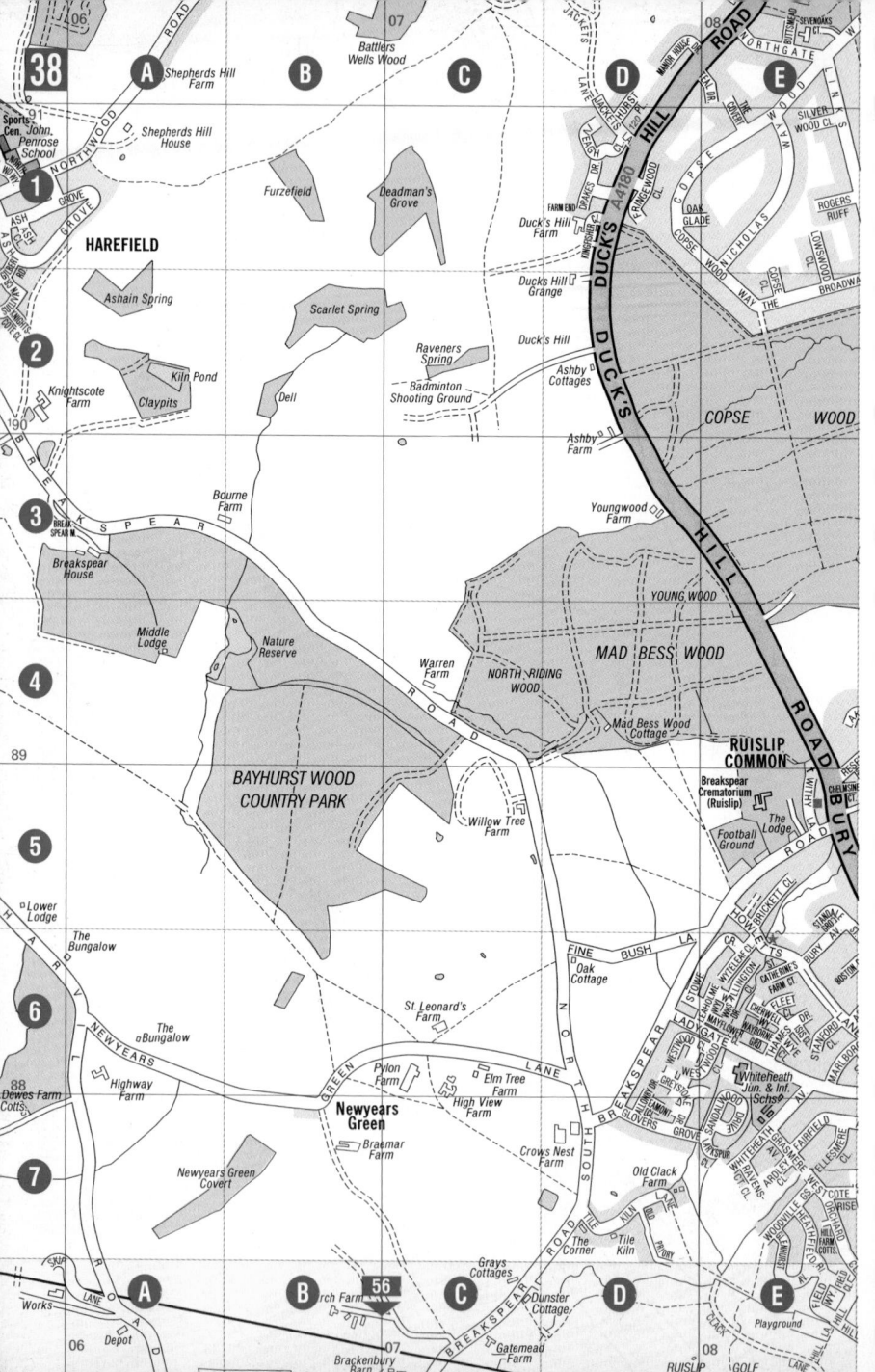

38
HAREFIELD
Shepherds Hill Farm
Shepherds Hill House
Battlers Wells Wood
John Penrose School
Sports Cen.
Furzefield
Deadman's Grove
Ashain Spring
Scarlet Spring
Kiln Pond
Claypits
Knightscote Farm
Dell
Raveners Spring
Badminton Shooting Ground
Duck's Hill Farm
Ducks Hill Grange
Duck's Hill
Ashby Cottages
Ashby Farm
DUCK'S HILL ROAD
A4180
COPSE WOOD
Youngwood Farm
YOUNG WOOD
MAD BESS WOOD
NORTH RIDING WOOD
Mad Bess Wood Cottage
RUISLIP COMMON
Breakspear Crematorium (Ruislip)
The Lodge
Football Ground
Bourne Farm
BREAKSPEAR ROAD
Breakspear House
Middle Lodge
Nature Reserve
Warren Farm
BAYHURST WOOD COUNTRY PARK
Willow Tree Farm
FINE BUSH LA.
Oak Cottage
St. Leonard's Farm
Lower Lodge
The Bungalow
HARVIL ROAD
NEWYEARS GREEN LANE
Highway Farm
Dewes Farm Cotts.
Pylon Farm
Elm Tree Farm
High View Farm
Newyears Green
Braemar Farm
Crows Nest Farm
Newyears Green Covert
Old Clack Farm
TILE KILN LANE
The Corner
Tile Kiln
Grays Cottages
Dunster Cottage
Gatemead Farm
Brackenbury Barn
Works
Depot
SKIP LANE
56
Playground
RUISLIP GOLF
BREAKSPEAR ROAD SOUTH
BREAKSPEAR ROAD NORTH
Whiteheath Jun. & Inf. Schs
LADYGATE LA.
BURY ST.

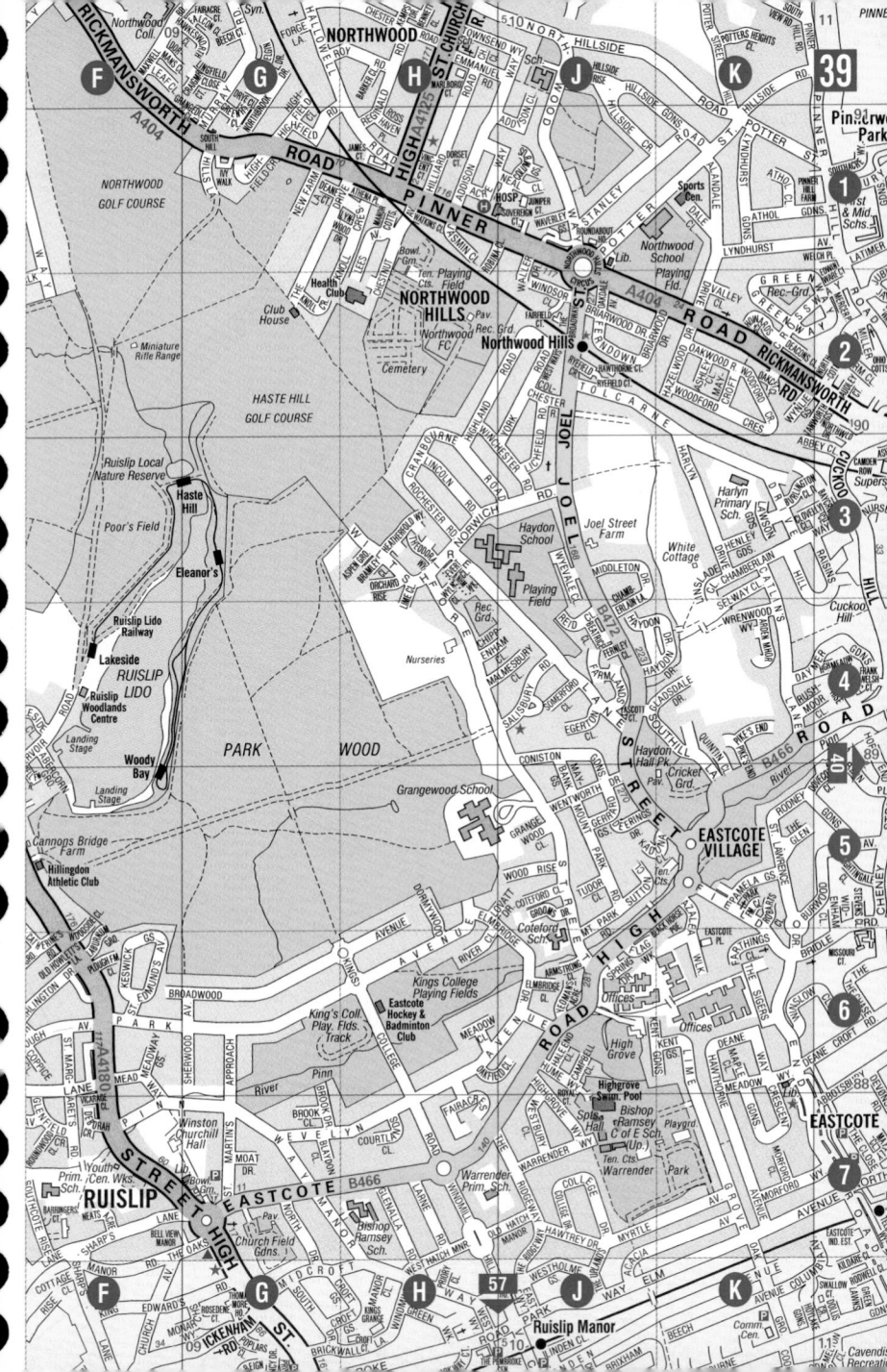

40
PINNER HILL GOLF COURSE
Pinnerwood Park
First & Mid. Schs.
PINNER GREEN
Montesole Play. Flds.
UXBRIDGE ROAD
A404
RICKMANSWORTH ROAD
HATCH END
Rugby Football Ground
PINNER PARK
Pinner Park Farm
Tennis Courts
GEORGE V AVENUE
Paine's Br.
Cemetery
Little Common
Innellan Ho. Sch.
Superstore
Pinner
Pinner Village Hall
Pinner Memorial Park
West Lodge Schs.
PINNER
Reddiford Sch.
Nower Hill
Pinner New Cemetery
Nower Hill High Sch.
Woodlands Open Space
North Harrow
Yeading Brook Open Space
Cuckoo Hill
B466
HIGH RD.
CUCKOO HILL
Pinner Village Gardens (Rec. Grd.)
The Croft
Play. Fld.
Cannon Lane First & Mid. Schs.
Heathfield Sch.
Longfield Schs.
Streamside Rec. Grd.
EASTCOTE
Eastcote
Roxborough Rough
Roxbourne Park
Playground
Rayners Lane
RAYNERS LANE
ALEXANDRA AV.
IMPERIAL
A4090
A410
Rayners La. Junc.
Sports Ground
Cavendish Recreation
39
58

41
26
42
59
F
G
H
J
K
1
2
3
4
5
6
7
14
16
91
90
89
88
HARROW WEALD
Hatch End High Sch.
Cedars Schs.
First & Mid. Sch.
Headstone Lane
Headstone Lane Sports Grd.
Pinner Pk. Schs.
Salvatorian Coll.
Belmont First & Mid. Schs.
WEALDSTONE
Recreation Ground
Harrow Leisure Centre
Harrow Driving Cycling and Road Safety Cen.
Harrow Crown Court
The Cliveden Cen.
Sports Ground
Open Air Theatre
Headstone Manor
Harrow Museum & Heritage Cen.
Headstone Manor Recreation Ground
Yeading Brook
Harrow & Wealdstone
Civic Centre
HEADSTONE
GREENHILL
Harrow Recreation Ground
Harrow Cemetery
Superstore
Gala Bingo
NORTH HARROW
West Harrow
Vaughan Schs.
WEST HARROW
Harrow-on-the-Hill
Bus Sta.
St. Ann's Shopping Cen.
The Grove Open Space
HARROW
HARROW HILL GOLF COURSE
Miniature Rifle Range
Playing Fields
Whitmore High Sch.
Whitmore Sports Cen.
Cricket Ground
Harrow Sch.
Music Sch.
Harrow School Playing Fields
A409
A404
A4005
A312
B457
HIGH ROAD
STATION ROAD
ST. GEORGE GANGE WAY
GREENHILL ROAD
LOWLANDS RD.
KENTON RD.
BESSBOROUGH RD.
PINNER ROAD
HARROW VIEW
HEADSTONE LANE
LONG ELMES
COLLEGE AV.
WEALD LANE
PINNER PARK AV.
HEADSTONE GARDENS
HEADSTONE DRIVE
SHEEPCOTE RD.
WATFORD RD.
WHITMORE ROAD

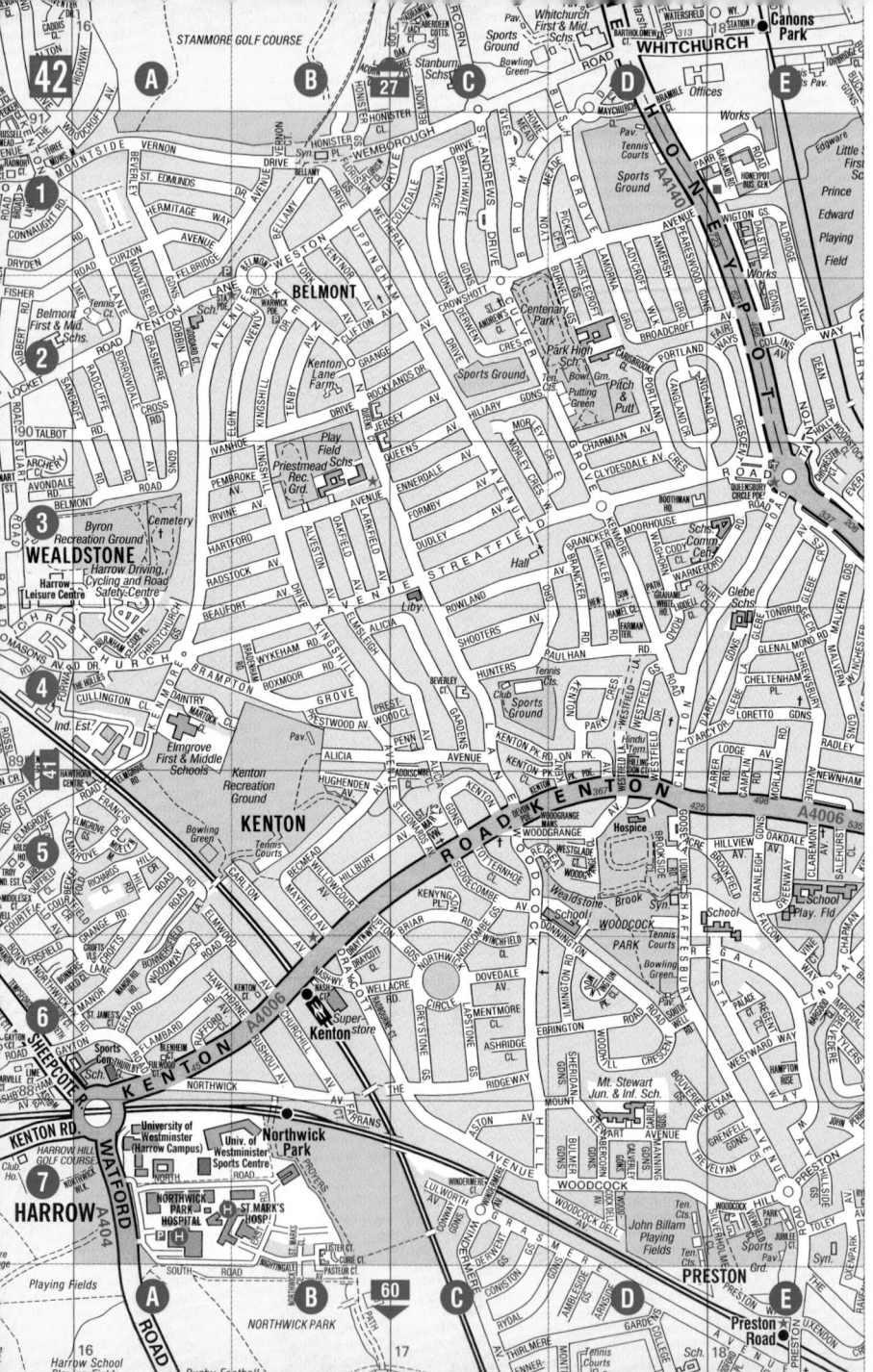

42
27
41
60
STANMORE GOLF COURSE
WHITCHURCH
Canons Park
BELMONT
WEALDSTONE
Byron Recreation Ground
Cemetery
Harrow Leisure Centre
Harrow Driving, Cycling and Road Safety Centre
Centenary Park
Park High Sch.
Sports Ground
Kenton Recreation Ground
KENTON
Elmgrove First & Middle Schools
Priestmead Rec. Grd.
Play Field Schs.
Kenton Lane Farm
Belmont First & Mid. Schs.
Prince Edward Playing Field
Hospice
Wealdstone Brook
WOODCOCK PARK
Glebe Schs.
Kenton
Superstore
Northwick Park
University of Westminster (Harrow Campus)
Univ. of Westminster Sports Centre
NORTHWICK PARK HOSPITAL
ST. MARK'S HOSP.
HARROW HILL GOLF COURSE
HARROW
Playing Fields
NORTHWICK PARK
Mt. Stewart Jun. & Inf. Sch.
John Billam Playing Fields
PRESTON
Preston Road
KENTON ROAD
A4006
A4140
A404
WATFORD ROAD
HONEYPOT LANE
Harrow School Playing Fields
16
17
18

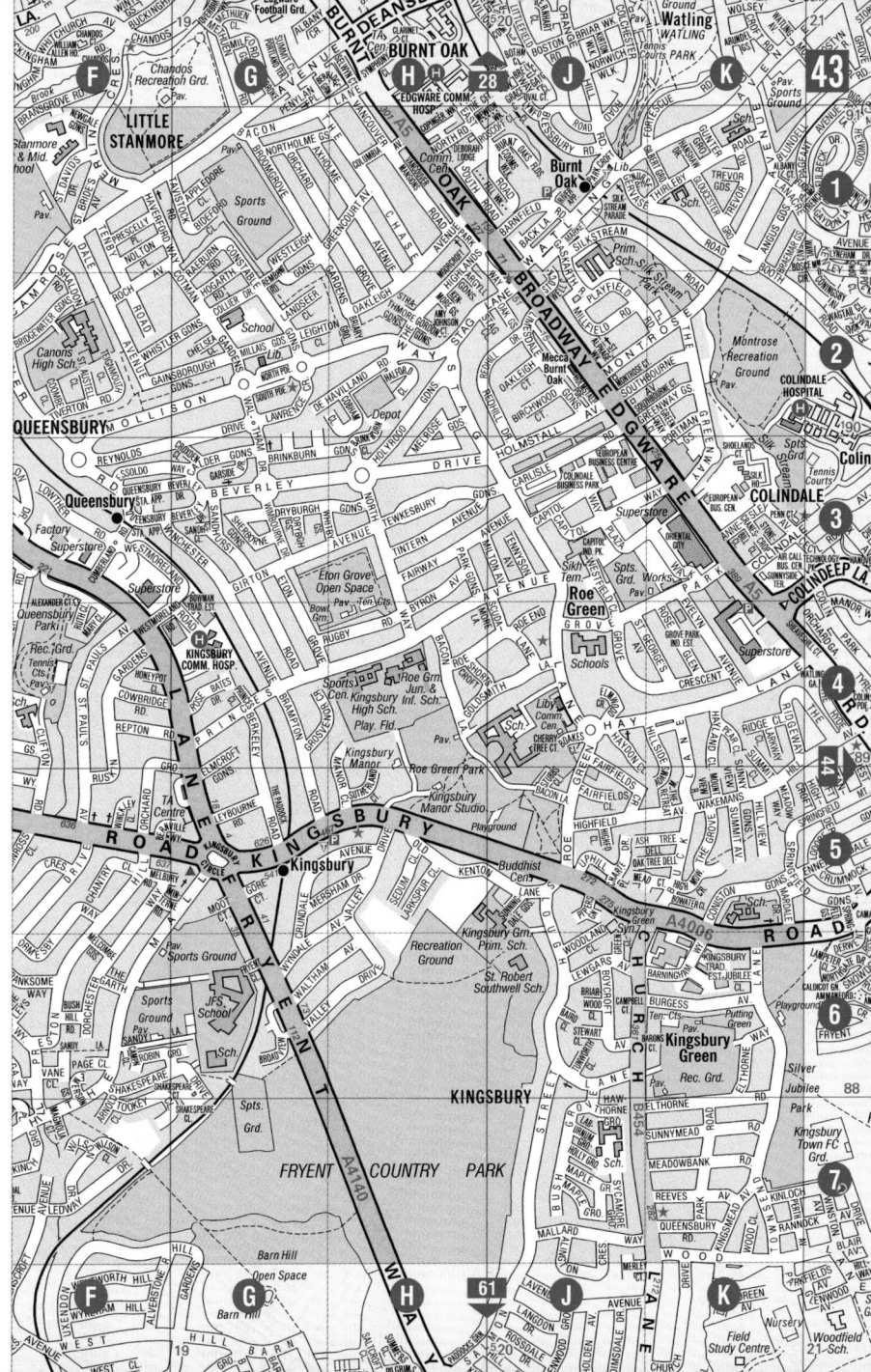

BURNT OAK
EDGWARE COMM. HOSP.
28
Chandos Recreation Grd.
LITTLE STANMORE
Stanmore & Mid. School
Watling
WATLING
Tennis Courts PARK
Burnt Oak
Sports Ground
Canons High Sch.
QUEENSBURY
Queensbury
Factory
Superstore
Queensbury Park
Rec. Grd.
KINGSBURY COMM. HOSP.
Eton Grove Open Space
Kingsbury High Sch. Play. Fld.
Roe Grn Jun. & Inf. Sch.
Sports Cen.
Roe Green
Roe Green Park
Kingsbury Manor
Kingsbury Manor Studio
Playground
Mecca Burnt Oak
Montrose Recreation Ground
COLINDALE HOSPITAL
Colindale
COLINDALE
EUROPEAN BUSINESS CENTRE
COLINDALE BUSINESS PARK
ORIENTAL CITY
Sikh Tem.
Schools
Liby. Comm. Cen.
44
Kingsbury
Buddhist Cen.
Kingsbury Green Syn.
TA Centre
Sports Ground
JFS School
Recreation Ground
Kingsbury Grn. Prim. Sch.
St. Robert Southwell Sch.
KINGSBURY
Kingsbury Green Rec. Grd.
Silver Jubilee Park
Kingsbury Town FC Grd.
FRYENT COUNTRY PARK
Barn Hill Open Space
Barn Hill
61
Field Study Centre
Nursery
Woodfield Sch.
BROADWAY
EDGWARE
KINGSBURY ROAD
FRYENT WAY
A4140
A4006
A5
B454
CHURCH LANE
COLINDEEP LA.
STAG LANE
HONEYPOT LANE
ROE GREEN

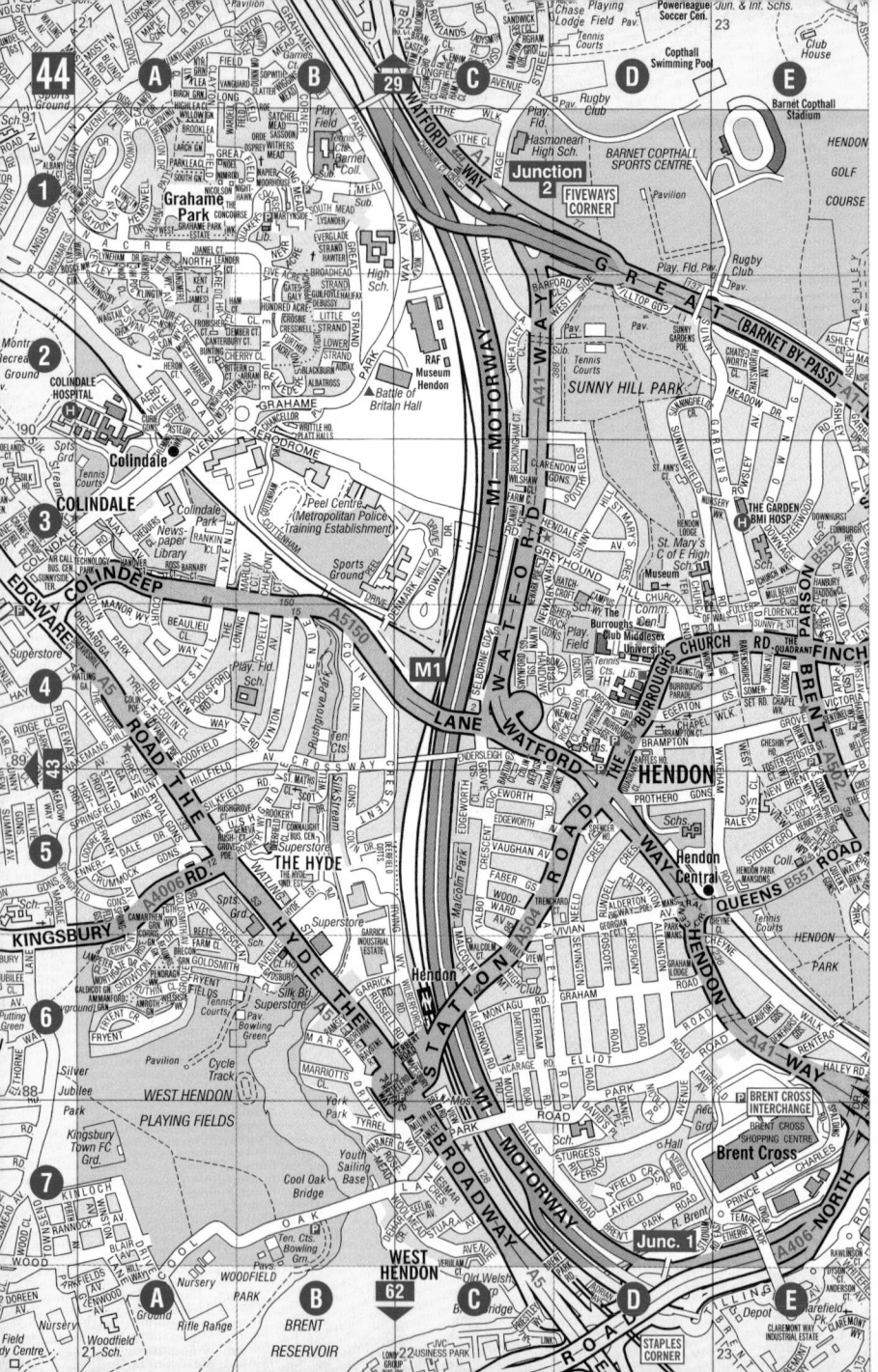

44
A
B
C
D
E
1
2
3
4
5
6
7
29
43
62
Powerleague Soccer Cen.
Jun. & Inf. Schs.
Chase Lodge
Playing Field
Club House
Copthall Swimming Pool
Barnet Copthall Stadium
Rugby Club
Hasmonean High Sch.
BARNET COPTHALL SPORTS CENTRE
HENDON GOLF COURSE
Junction 2
FIVEWAYS CORNER
Pavilion
GREAT
(BARNET BY-PASS)
WATFORD WAY
SUNNY HILL PARK
Tennis Courts
Grahame Park
Barnet Coll.
High Sch.
RAF Museum Hendon
Battle of Britain Hall
COLINDALE HOSPITAL
Colindale
COLINDALE
Newspaper Library
Colindale Park
Peel Centre (Metropolitan Police Training Establishment)
Sports Ground
GRAHAME PARK WAY
AERODROME
M1 MOTORWAY
A41 WATFORD WAY
THE GARDEN BMI HOSP
St. Mary's C of E High Sch.
Museum
The Burroughs
Middlesex University
HENDON
Hendon Central
QUEENS ROAD
HENDON PARK
CHURCH RD.
BRENT ST.
COLINDEEP LANE
A5150
M1
EDGWARE ROAD
THE HYDE
Rushgrove Park
Silk Stream
THE HYDE
Superstore
GARRICK INDUSTRIAL ESTATE
KINGSBURY RD.
A4006
STATION ROAD
A504
Malcolm Park
Hendon
WEST HENDON PLAYING FIELDS
Silver Jubilee Park
Kingsbury Town FC Grd.
Cycle Track
Youth Sailing Base
Cool Oak Bridge
York Park
BROADWAY
COOL OAK LANE
WEST HENDON
BRENT RESERVOIR
Rifle Range
WOODFIELD PARK
BRENT CROSS INTERCHANGE
BRENT CROSS SHOPPING CENTRE
Brent Cross
Junc. 1
NORTH CIRCULAR ROAD
A406
STAPLES CORNER
CLAREMONT WAY INDUSTRIAL ESTATE
A41 HENDON WAY
Woodfield Sch.

45
F
G
H
J
K
30
FINCHLEY
Hendon Crematorium
HENDON CEMETERY
DOLLIS
ROAD
NETHER
Playing Fields
CHURCH END
Finchley Central
BALLARDS
LANE
A598
B552
B1462
HENDON GOLF COURSE
Holders Hill
Windsor Open Space
College
Avenue House Grounds
Sports Ground
EAST END ROAD
A504
HENDON
College Farm
REGENTS PARK
St. Marylebone Crematorium
ST. MARYLEBONE CEMETERY
Christ's College
NORTH CIRCULAR
A406
A1
HENLYS CORNER
FALLODEN
FINCHLEY ROAD
Mutton Brook
Bowl Grn.
Monastery
Little Wood
Big Wood
Willifred Green
Temple Fortune
Princes Park
Jewish Cemetery
Golders Green Crematorium
GOLDERS GREEN
Brent Cross
A502
Superstores
Sports Cen.
HENDON WAY
A41
Works
Golders Green
HAMPSTEAD
HEATH
NORTH END RD
63
46
1
2
3
4
5
6
7
24
25
26
88
89
90
91

46
31
45
64
A
B
C
D
E
1
2
3
4
5
6
7
27
28
26
90
89
88
NORTH CIRCULAR ROAD
A406
HIGH RD. NTH. FINCHLEY
A1000
HIGH ROAD
EAST FINCHLEY
EAST END ROAD
A504
FORTIS GREEN
GREAT NORTH RD.
LYTTELTON ROAD
A1
AYLMER ROAD
ARCHWAY ROAD
NORTH HILL
B519
HAMPSTEAD LANE
B550
MUSWELL HILL
COLNEY HATCH LANE
SOUTHWOOD LANE
FINCHLEY MEM. HOSP.
Fallow Corner
Play. Fld.
Cricket & Football Grounds
Glebe Land Open Space
Bowl. Alley
Cinema
GREAT NORTH LEISURE PARK
Powerleague Soccer Cen.
Sports Ground
Playing Field
Islington Crematorium
Strawberry Vale Brook
ST. PANCRAS & ISLINGTON CEM.
Muswell Hill Spts. Grd.
COLDFALL WOOD
Coldfall Prim. Sch.
Recreation Ground
Martin Jun. & Inf. School
Fortismere Sch.
Our Lady of Muswell RC Prim. Sch.
St. Marylebone Crem.
ST. MARYLEBONE CEMETERY
Oak Lodge Sch.
EAST FINCHLEY
ABBOTS GARDENS
East Finchley
FORTIS GREEN
ST. LUKE'S WOODSIDE HOSP.
Cherry Tree Wood Rec. Grd.
St. James CE Prim. Sch.
HIGHGATE WOOD
Stormont Lawn Tennis & Squash Club
HAMPSTEAD GARDEN SUBURB
Playing Fields
HIGHGATE GOLF COURSE
Club House
HIGHGATE
HIGHGATE HOSPITAL
HAMPSTEAD GOLF COURSE
Bunkers Hill
HAMPSTEAD HEATH
Turners Wood
Mallinson Sports Centre
Highgate School Playing Field
Sports Ground
North Wood
Visitor Cen.
Kenwood House
Ken Wood Towers Farm
ATHLONE HOUSE
The Spaniards
Yth. Hostel
Nursery

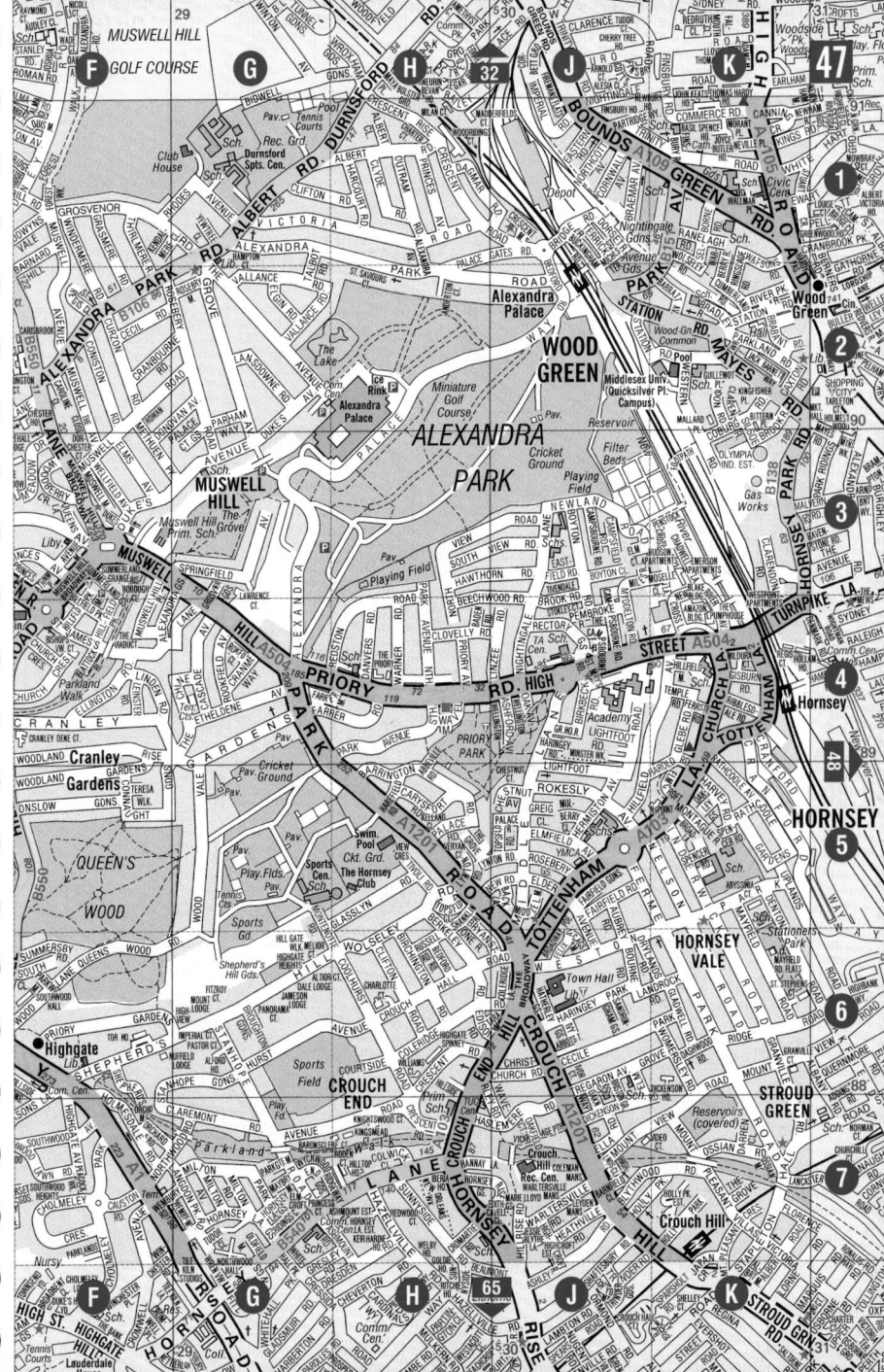

29
30
31
MUSWELL HILL
GOLF COURSE
F
G
H
J
K
32
47
48
65
88
89
90
1
2
3
4
5
6
7
Club House
Durnsford Spts. Cen.
DURNSFORD RD.
ALBERT RD.
ALEXANDRA PARK RD.
B106
B550
ALEXANDRA
GROSVENOR
WINDERMERE
GRASMERE
THIRLMERE
RHODES AVENUE
VICTORIA ROAD
ALEXANDRA PARK ROAD
PALACE GATES RD.
VALLANCE RD.
ST. SAVIOURS
TALBOT RD.
ELGIN RD.
CLIFTON RD.
ALBERT RD.
HARCOURT RD.
CLYDE
OUTRAM
PRINCES
CRESCENT
DAGMAR
CRESCENT RISE
Rec. Grd.
Tennis Courts
Pool
BOUNDS GREEN RD.
A109
BOUNDS GREEN RD.
NIGHTINGALE
FINSBURY RD.
COMMERCE RD.
CLARENCE
SIDNEY RD.
HIGH ROAD
A105
Wood Green
Civic Cen.
Depot
Nightingale Gdns
Avenue Gds.
PARK AV.
B151
STATION RD.
RANELAGH
LORDSHIP LANE
Lib.
Cin.
SHOPPING CITY
WOOD GREEN
Alexandra Palace
Ice Rink
The Lake
Com. Cen.
Miniature Golf Course
ALEXANDRA PARK
Cricket Ground
Playing Field
Reservoir
Filter Beds
Middlesex Univ. (Quicksilver Pl. Campus)
Pool
Sch.
Wood Grn. Common
MAYES RD.
WESTERN RD.
OLYMPIA IND. EST.
Gas Works
B138
HORNSEY PARK RD.
TURNPIKE LA.
ALEXANDRA PALACE WAY
DUKE'S AVENUE
MUSWELL HILL
The Grove
Muswell Hill Prim. Sch.
Liby.
MUSWELL HILL
A504
SPRINGFIELD
MUSWELL HILL BROADWAY
MUSWELL AVENUE
CONISTON
CURZON
CECIL RD.
ROSEBERY RD.
CRANBOURNE RD.
GROVE AV.
LANSDOWNE RD.
METHUEN PK.
ELMS AV.
PARHAM WAY
Playing Field
NEWLAND ROAD
SOUTH VIEW RD.
HAWTHORN RD.
BEECHWOOD RD.
CLOVELLY RD.
PRIORY RD.
HIGH STREET
A504
PRIORY PARK
PARK AVENUE
REDSTON RD.
DANVERS RD.
NIGHTINGALE
RECTORY GDS.
TA Cen.
Academy
LIGHTFOOT RD.
ROKESLY
CHURCH LA.
TOTTENHAM LA.
Hornsey
HORNSEY
New River
CRANFORD WAY
A103
TOTTENHAM LA.
HERMISTON AV.
NELSON RD.
FERME PARK RD.
Sch.
CRANLEY GARDENS
Cranley Gardens
WOODLAND RISE
ONSLOW GDNS.
QUEEN'S WOOD
B550
Cricket Ground
Pav.
Swim. Pool
Ckt. Grd.
Sports Cen.
The Hornsey Club
Play. Flds.
Tennis Cts.
Sports Gd.
Shepherd's Hill Gds.
PARK ROAD
A1201
WOLSELEY RD.
Town Hall
Lib.
THE BROADWAY
CROUCH END HILL
HORNSEY VALE
Stationers Park
HORNSEY VALE
QUEENS WOOD RD.
SHEPHERD'S HILL
Highgate
Lib.
STANHOPE GDNS.
Sports Field
CROUCH END
Play. Fd.
Parkland Walk
AVENUE
CROUCH END HILL
A103
HORNSEY LANE
B540
Comm. Hornsey Cen.
CROUCH HILL
A1201
Crouch Hill
Rec. Cen.
Reservoirs (covered)
STROUD GREEN
STROUD GREEN RD.
Sch.
ARCHWAY RD.
A1
HIGHGATE
HIGH ST.
HIGHGATE HILL
Lauderdale House
Tennis Courts
HORNSEY RISE
HORNSEY ROAD
Comm. Cen.
CHOLMELEY CRES.
Nursy.
WHITEHALL PK.
CHEVERTON RD.
HAZELLVILLE RD.

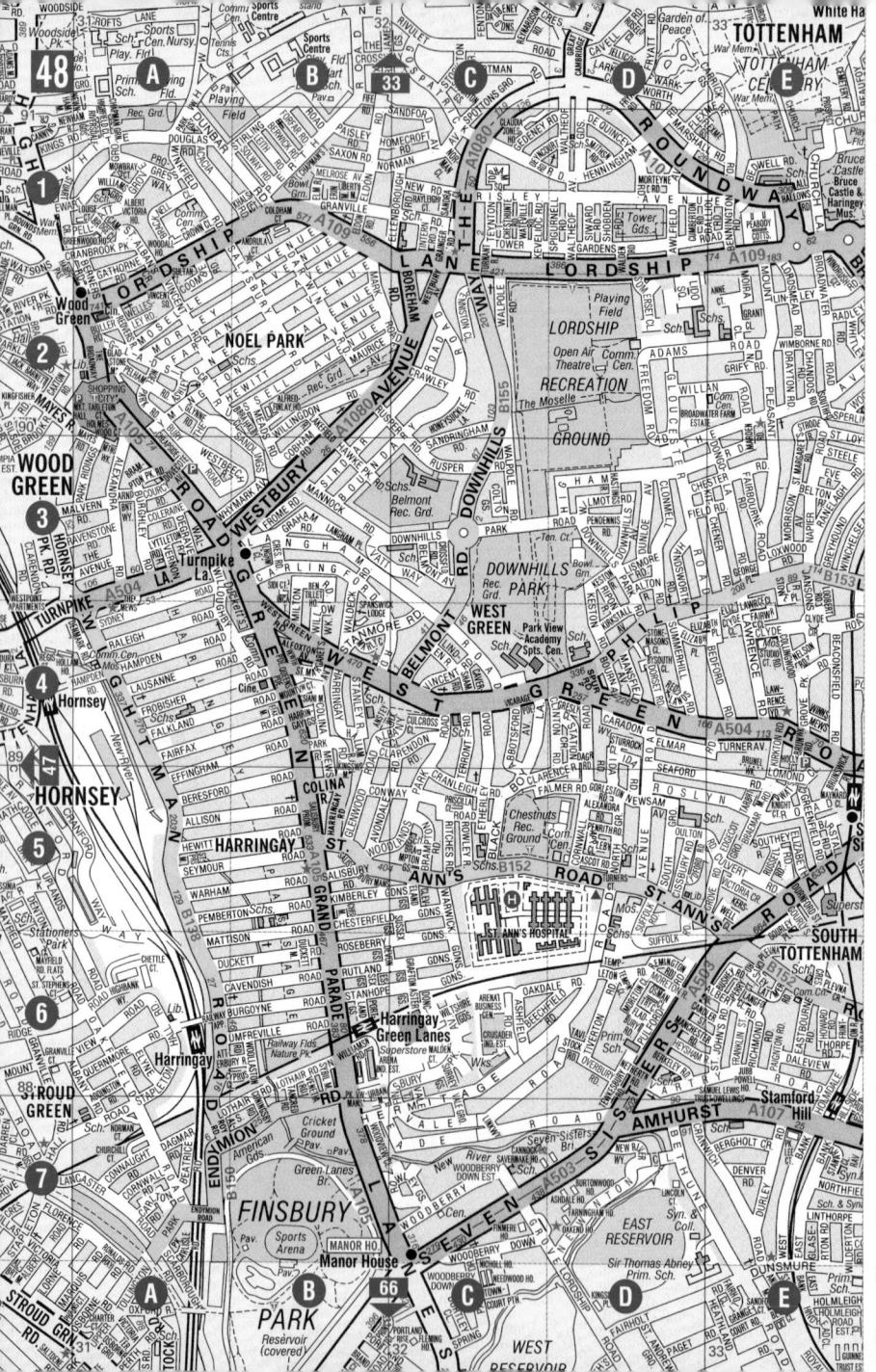

48
33
TOTTENHAM
TOTTENHAM CEMETERY
Bruce Castle & Haringey Mus.
ROUNDWAY
LORDSHIP LANE
A109
THE AVENUE
A1080
WOOD GREEN
Wood Green
NOEL PARK
LORDSHIP RECREATION GROUND
Open Air Theatre
The Moselle
BROADWATER FARM ESTATE
DOWNHILLS WAY
B155
DOWNHILLS PARK
Belmont Rec. Grd.
WEST GREEN
Park View Academy Spts. Cen.
WEST GREEN ROAD
A504
PHILIP LANE
B153
WESTBURY AVENUE
Turnpike La.
TURNPIKE LA.
HORNSEY
Hornsey
47
WIGHTMAN ROAD
GREEN LANES
HARRINGAY
Harringay
Harringay Green Lanes
GRAND PARADE
A105
ST. ANN'S ROAD
B152
ST. ANN'S HOSPITAL
Chestnuts Rec. Ground
SOUTH TOTTENHAM
A503
SEVEN SISTERS ROAD
AMHURST
A107
Stamford Hill
STROUD GREEN
STROUD GRN. RD.
Stationers Park
B138
B150
ENDYMION ROAD
FINSBURY PARK
Sports Arena
MANOR HO.
Manor House
Cricket Ground
American Gds.
Green Lanes Br.
New River
Seven Sisters Bri.
EAST RESERVOIR
Sir Thomas Abney Prim. Sch.
WEST RESERVOIR
Reservoir (covered)
66
32
A
B
C
D
E
1
2
3
4
5
6
7

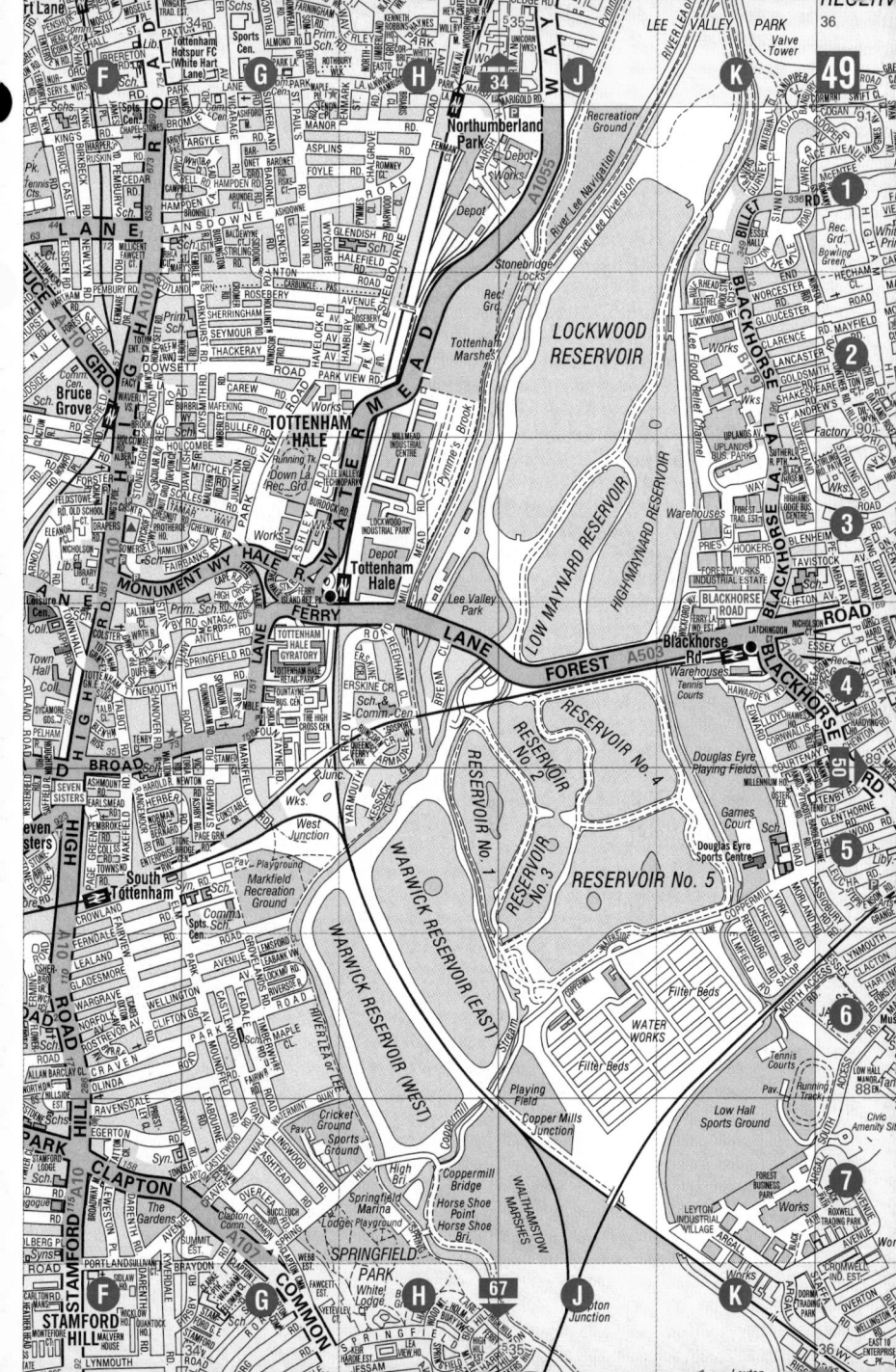
49
36
F
G
H
J
K
1
2
3
4
5
6
7
34
50
67
LEE VALLEY PARK
Valve Tower
Tottenham Hotspur FC (White Hart Lane)
Sports Cen.
Northumberland Park
Recreation Ground
River Lee Navigation
River Lee Diversion
Stonebridge Locks
LOCKWOOD RESERVOIR
Tottenham Marshes
Lee Flood Relief Channel
Bruce Grove
TOTTENHAM HALE
MILLMEAD INDUSTRIAL CENTRE
Pymme's Brook
LOW MAYNARD RESERVOIR
HIGH MAYNARD RESERVOIR
Tottenham Hale
Lee Valley Park
FERRY LANE
FOREST ROAD
A503
Blackhorse Rd.
BLACKHORSE ROAD
BLACKHORSE LA.
BLACKHORSE RD.
TOTTENHAM HALE GYRATORY
MONUMENT WY
HIGH RD.
BROAD LANE
SEVEN SISTERS
Seven Sisters
South Tottenham
RESERVOIR No. 1
RESERVOIR No. 2
RESERVOIR No. 3
RESERVOIR No. 4
RESERVOIR No. 5
WARWICK RESERVOIR (EAST)
WARWICK RESERVOIR (WEST)
Douglas Eyre Playing Fields
Douglas Eyre Sports Centre
Games Court
West Junction
Markfield Recreation Ground
Filter Beds
WATER WORKS
Playing Field
Copper Mills Junction
Low Hall Sports Ground
Civic Amenity Site
LEYTON INDUSTRIAL VILLAGE
FOREST BUSINESS PARK
ROXWELL TRADING PARK
Cricket Ground
Sports Ground
Springfield Marina
Coppermill Bridge
Horse Shoe Point
Horse Shoe Bri.
WALTHAMSTOW MARSHES
SPRINGFIELD PARK
Clapton Junction
STAMFORD HILL
CLAPTON COMMON
A107
A10
A1055
A1010
A1006
B179
WATERMEAD WAY
CLAPTON
STAMFORD HILL

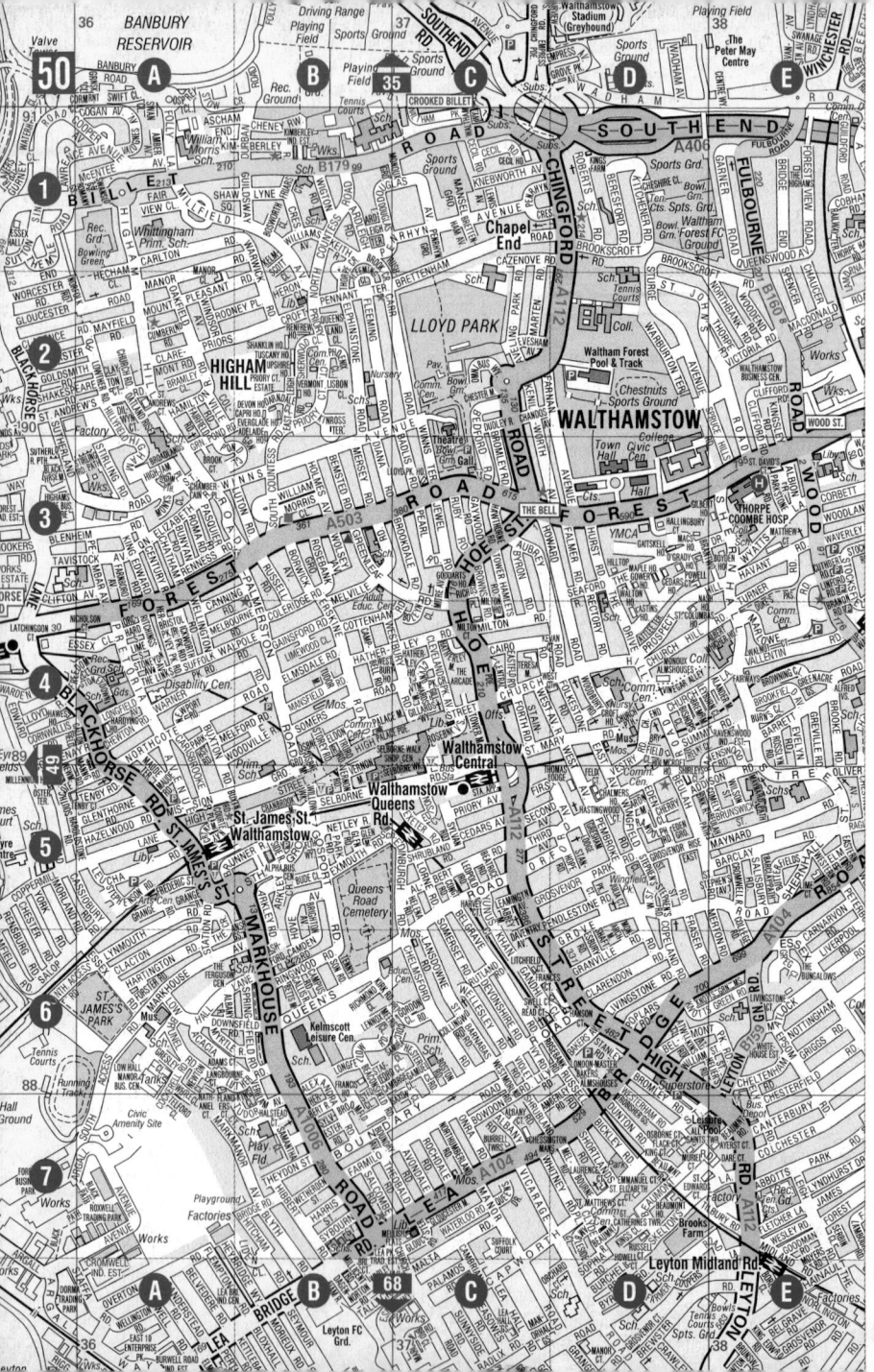

50
BANBURY RESERVOIR
Valve Tower
Driving Range
Playing Field
Sports Ground
35
Walthamstow Stadium (Greyhound)
Playing Field
The Peter May Centre
Rec. Ground
Tennis Courts
CROOKED BILLET
SOUTHEND RD
BILLET ROAD
B179
SOUTHEND ROAD
A406
William Morris Sch.
Whittingham Prim. Sch.
Rec. Grd.
Bowling Green
Chapel End
CHINGFORD ROAD
A112
Waltham Forest FC Ground
FULBOURNE ROAD
B160
LLOYD PARK
HIGHAM HILL
Waltham Forest Pool & Track
Chestnuts Sports Ground
WALTHAMSTOW
Town Hall
Civic Cen.
College
Theatre
BLACKHORSE LANE
FOREST ROAD
A503
THE BELL
THORPE COOMBE HOSP.
YMCA
HOE ST.
WOOD ST.
Disability Cen.
Walthamstow Central
Walthamstow Queens Rd.
St. James St. Walthamstow
BLACKHORSE RD.
ST. JAMES'S ST.
MARKHOUSE ROAD
Queens Road Cemetery
HIGH STREET
Kelmscott Leisure Cen.
ST. JAMES'S PARK
Tennis Courts
Running Track
Hall Ground
Civic Amenity Site
Playground
Factories
Works
ROXWELL TRADING PARK
CROMWELL IND. EST.
A1006
LEA BRIDGE ROAD
A104
ESSEX RD.
A104
B159
Superstore
Leisure Pool
Bus Depot
Brooks Farm
Leyton Midland Rd.
LEYTON RD.
Leyton FC Grd.
68
49
36
37
38
A
B
C
D
E
1
2
3
4
5
6
7

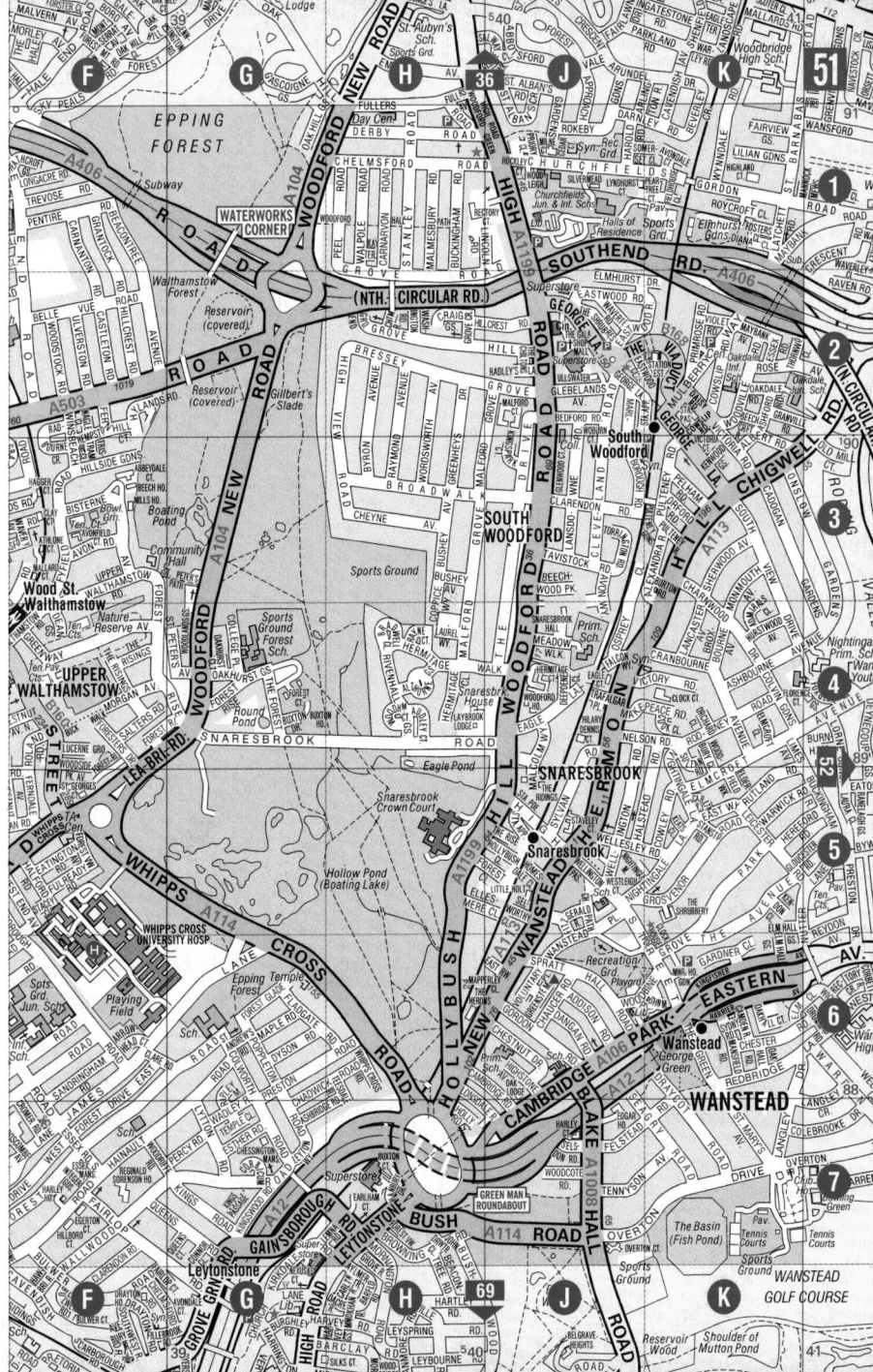

51
36
52
69
F
G
H
J
K
1
2
3
4
5
6
7
540
41
39
91
88
89
190
EPPING FOREST
A406
NORTH CIRCULAR RD.
SOUTHEND RD.
WATERWORKS CORNER
WOODFORD NEW ROAD
A104
HIGH ROAD WOODFORD GREEN
A1199
Walthamstow Forest
Reservoir (covered)
A503
FOREST ROAD
Gilbert's Slade
Boating Pond
Community Hall
Wood St. Walthamstow
UPPER WALTHAMSTOW
Nature Reserve
Sports Ground Forest Sch.
Round Pond
SNARESBROOK ROAD
Eagle Pond
Snaresbrook Crown Court
Hollow Pond (Boating Lake)
WHIPPS CROSS ROAD
A114
WHIPPS CROSS UNIVERSITY HOSP.
Epping Forest
Playing Field
LEA BRI. RD.
B160
Sports Ground
SOUTH WOODFORD
South Woodford
CHURCHFIELDS
Churchfields Jun. & Inf. Schs.
Halls of Residence
Sports Grd.
Superstore
GEORGE LA.
B168
THE VIADUCT
CHIGWELL RD.
A113
Oakdale Inf. Sch.
Oakdale Jun. Sch.
Nightingale Prim. Sch.
SNARESBROOK
Snaresbrook
Snaresbrk. House
HOLLYBUSH HILL
WOODFORD ROAD
WANSTEAD
Wanstead
George Green
Recreation Grd.
CAMBRIDGE PARK
A106
EASTERN AV.
A12
BLAKE HALL ROAD
A1008
GREEN MAN ROUNDABOUT
BUSH ROAD
Leytonstone
HIGH ROAD
GAINSBOROUGH RD.
LEYTONSTONE RD.
The Basin (Fish Pond)
Tennis Courts
Sports Ground
WANSTEAD GOLF COURSE
Reservoir Wood
Shoulder of Mutton Pond
Woodbridge High Sch.
Elmhurst Gdns.
St. Aubyn's Sch.
Sports Grd.
Fullers Day Cen.

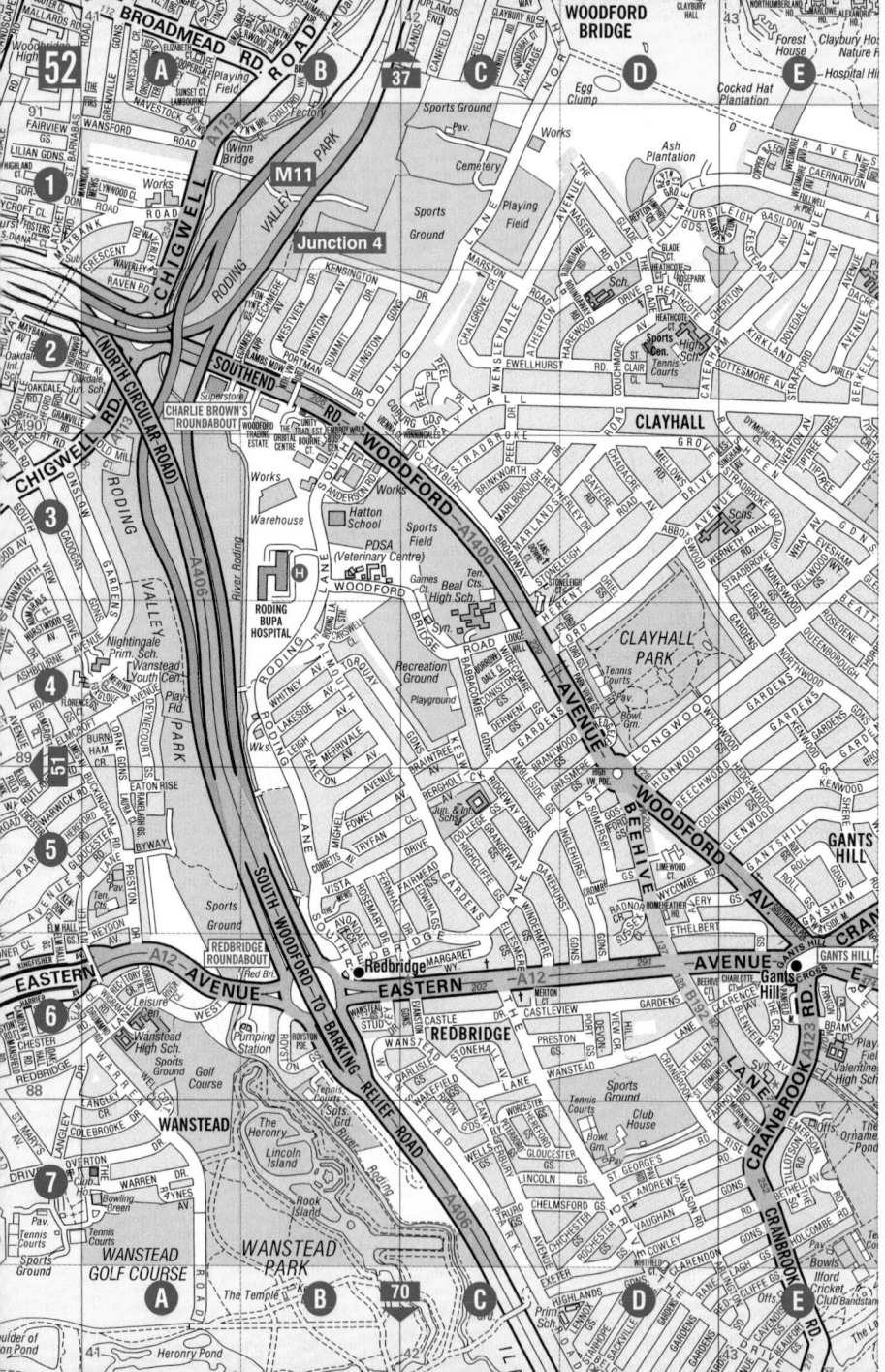

52
37
51
70
A
B
C
D
E
1
2
3
4
5
6
7
41
42
43
91
90
89
88
WOODFORD BRIDGE
BROADMEAD RD.
ROAD
CHIGWELL
Playing Field
Factory
Winn Bridge
M11
Junction 4
RODING VALLEY PARK
Sports Ground
Cemetery
Works
Egg Clump
Ash Plantation
Cocked Hat Plantation
Forest House
Claybury Hospital Nature Reserve
Hospital Hill
CLAYBURY HALL
SOUTHEND RD.
CHARLIE BROWN'S ROUNDABOUT
Superstore
WOODFORD TRADING ESTATE
(NORTH CIRCULAR ROAD)
CHIGWELL RD.
A113
A406
A1400
A12
A123
B192
WOODFORD AVENUE
CLAYHALL
CLAYHALL PARK
Tennis Courts
Pav.
Bowl. Grn.
Sports Cen.
High Sch.
Sch.
Schs.
Hatton School
Sports Field
PDSA (Veterinary Centre)
RODING BUPA HOSPITAL
Beal High Sch.
Recreation Ground
Playground
Warehouse
River Roding
Nightingale Prim. Sch.
Wanstead Youth Cen.
Jun. & Inf. Schs.
BEEHIVE LANE
GANTS HILL
Gants Hill
REDBRIDGE ROUNDABOUT
Redbridge
EASTERN AVENUE
REDBRIDGE
SOUTH WOODFORD TO BARKING RELIEF ROAD
Pumping Station
Leisure Cen.
Wanstead High Sch.
Golf Course
WANSTEAD
The Heronry
Lincoln Island
Rook Island
WANSTEAD PARK
WANSTEAD GOLF COURSE
The Temple
Heronry Pond
Club House
Bowling Green
CRANBROOK RD.
Valentines High Sch.
Ilford Cricket Club
Bowls
Prim. Sch.
Offs.
Syn.

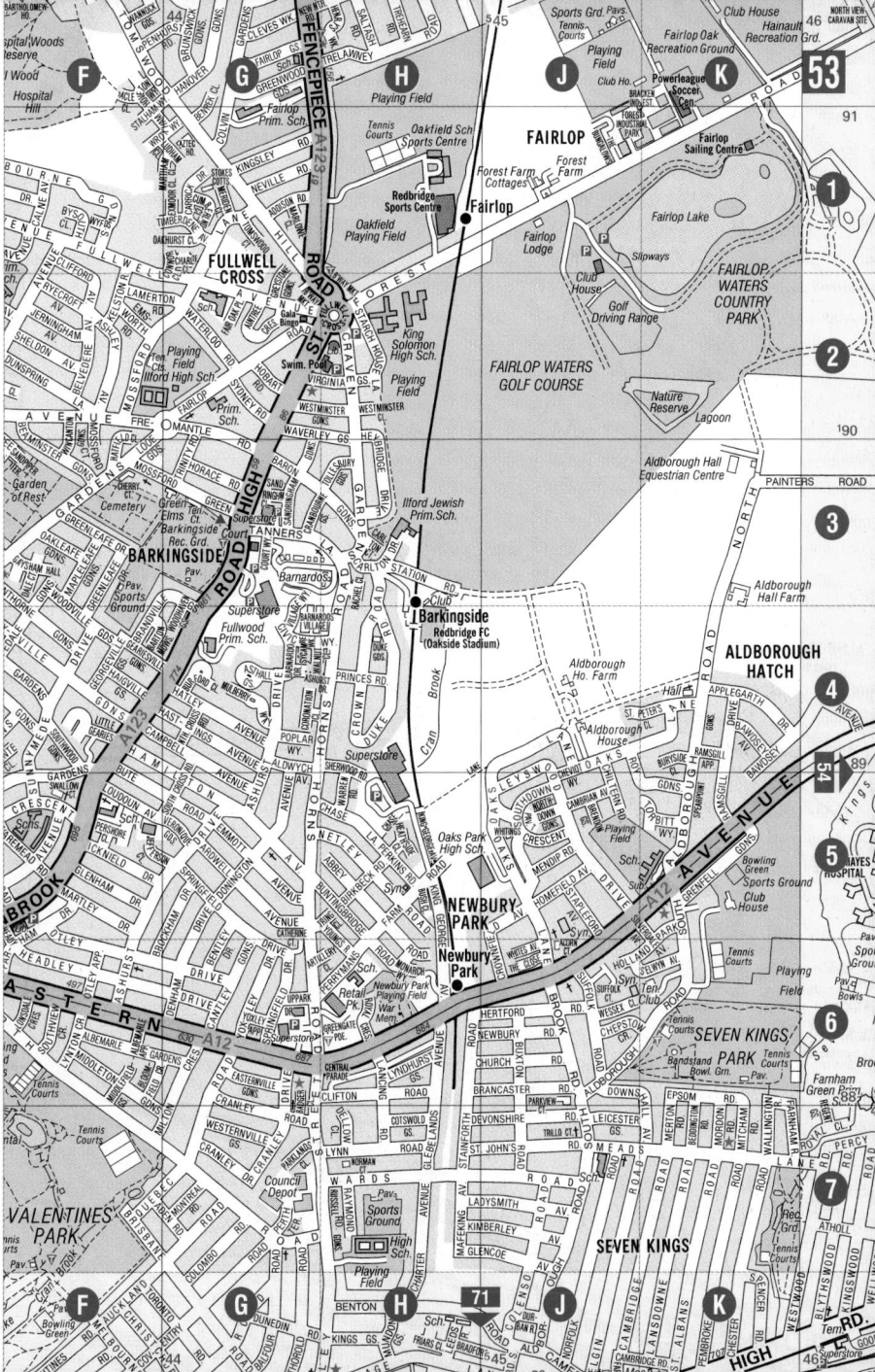

53
F
G
H
J
K
1
2
3
4
5
6
7
44
46
545
91
190
89
54
71
88
FAIRLOP
FULLWELL CROSS
BARKINGSIDE
ALDBOROUGH HATCH
NEWBURY PARK
SEVEN KINGS
FENCEPIECE ROAD
A123
HIGH ROAD
EASTERN AVENUE
A12
Fairlop
Barkingside
Newbury Park
Hospital Woods Reserve
Hospital Hill
Fairlop Prim. Sch.
Playing Field
Oakfield Sch. Sports Centre
Redbridge Sports Centre
Oakfield Playing Field
Forest Farm Cottages
Forest Farm
Fairlop Lodge
Club House
Golf Driving Range
Fairlop Lake
Slipways
FAIRLOP WATERS COUNTRY PARK
Fairlop Sailing Centre
Fairlop Oak Recreation Ground
Powerleague Soccer Cen.
Hainault Recreation Grd.
Sports Grd.
Tennis Courts
NORTH VIEW CARAVAN SITE
King Solomon High Sch.
FAIRLOP WATERS GOLF COURSE
Nature Reserve
Lagoon
Aldborough Hall Equestrian Centre
PAINTERS ROAD
Aldborough Hall Farm
Ilford Jewish Prim.Sch.
Redbridge FC (Oakside Stadium)
Aldborough Ho. Farm
Aldborough House
Cran Brook
Playing Field Ilford High Sch.
Gala Bingo
Swim. Pool
Garden of Rest
Cemetery
Barkingside Rec. Grd.
Superstore
Barnardos
Pav. Sports Ground
Fullwood Prim. Sch.
Oaks Park High Sch.
Bowling Green
Sports Ground
Council Depot
Sports Ground
High Sch.
VALENTINES PARK
SEVEN KINGS PARK
Bandstand
Bowl. Grn.
Farnham Green Prim. Sch.
Newbury Park Playing Field
War Mem.
Retail Pk.
CENTRAL PARADE

54
A
B
C
D
E
46
47
48
1
2
3
4
5
6
7
Club House
Hainault Rec. Grd.
NORTH VIEW CARAVAN SITE
FOREST ROAD
HAINAULT
WHALEBONE
A1112
91
Fairlop Sailing Centre
FAIRLOP WATERS COUNTRY PARK
FAIRLOP WATERS
Seven Kings Water
Hainault Works
Farm Cottages
Hainault Farm
Marks Gate
Furze Cottage
Furze House Farm
190
PAINTERS ROAD
NORTH
Aldborough Hall Farm
ALDBOROUGH HATCH
Red House Farm
Hainault House
BILLET ROAD
Willow Farm
Playing Field
Little Heath Sch.
Sports Ground
Chadwell Heath Cemetery
Jun. Sch.
Comm. Cen.
Infant Sch.
LANE
NORTH
EASTERN AVENUE
A12
AVENUE EAST
53
89
KING GEORGE HOSPITAL
North Residence
South Residence
Nursery
Redbridge College
Ethel Davis Sch.
Grove Prim. Sch.
LITTLE HEATH
GOODMAYES HOSPITAL
Sports Ground
Club House
Tennis Courts
Playing Field
Pav.
Bowls
Brookside
SEVEN KINGS PARK
Farnham Green Prim. Sch.
88
The Chadwell Centre
ST. CHAD'S PARK
Playground
Playgrd.
CHADWELL HEATH
WHALEBONE LA.
HIGH ROAD
A118
B177
BARLEY LANE
Playing Field
Factory
Sch.
Prim. Sch.
Play. Fld.
Rec. Grd.
Works
GROVE FARM RETAIL PK.
Mecca Bingo
Chadwell Heath
Works
Warehouse
MIRRAVALE TRADING EST.
CHADWELL HEATH INDUSTRIAL PARK
72
GOODMAYES RETAIL PARK
Superstore
Goodmayes
Play. Field
Mayfield Sch. Coll.
HIGH ROAD
GOODMAYES AV.
FRESHWATER ROAD
SELINAS LANE

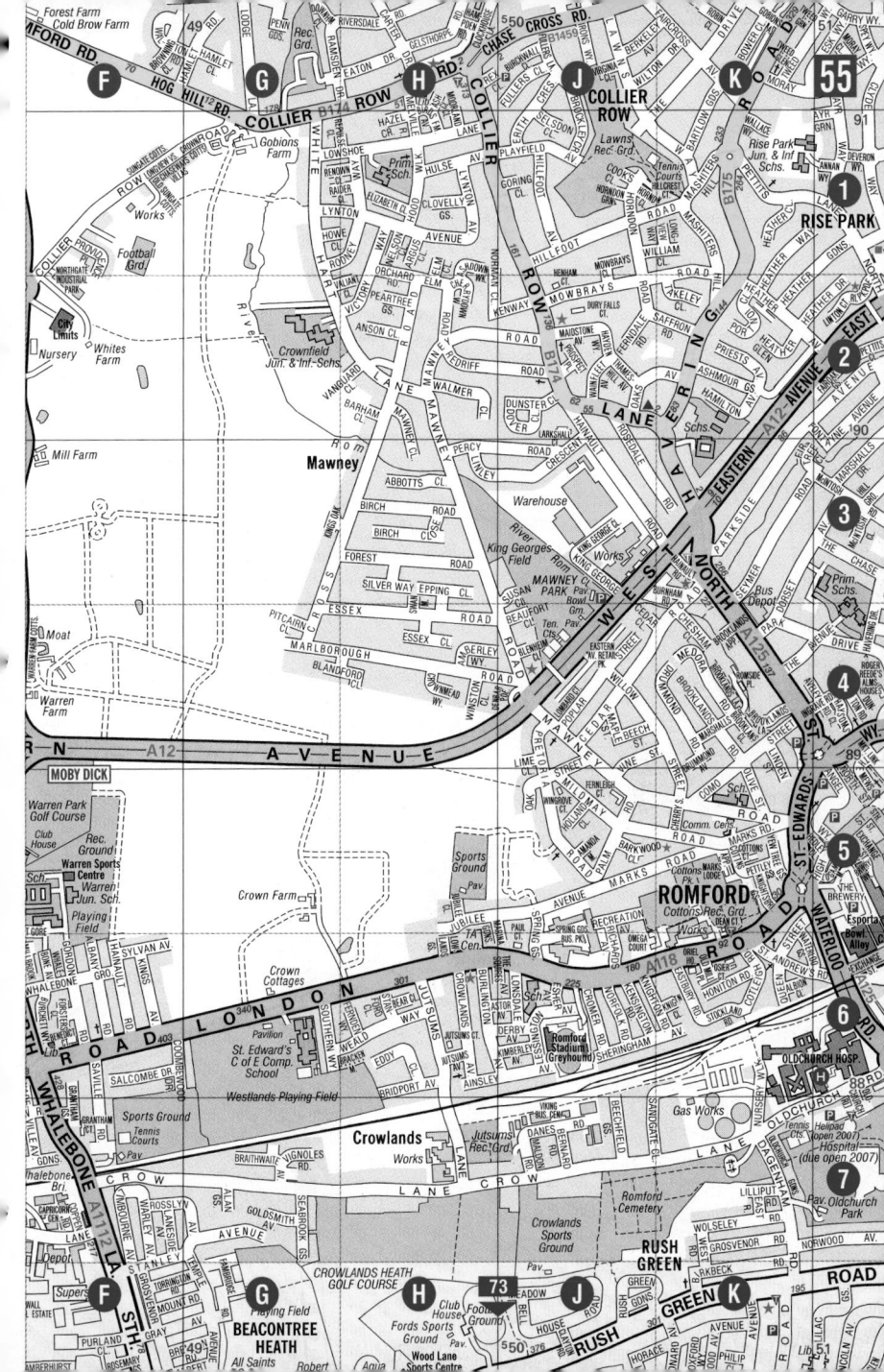

55
Forest Farm
Cold Brow Farm
HOG HILL RD.
COLLIER ROW RD.
CHASE CROSS RD.
COLLIER ROW
Gobions Farm
Lawns Rec. Grd.
Rise Park Jun. & Inf. Schs.
RISE PARK
Works
Football Grd.
NORTHGATE INDUSTRIAL PARK
City Limits
Nursery
Whites Farm
Crownfield Jun. & Inf. Schs.
Mill Farm
Mawney
River Rom
King Georges Field
Warehouse
MAWNEY PARK
EASTERN AVENUE
WEST
NORTH
HAVERING
Bus Depot
Prim. Schs.
ROGER REEDE'S ALMS HOUSES
Moat
Warren Farm
A12
MOBY DICK
Warren Park Golf Course
Club House
Rec. Ground
Warren Sports Centre
Warren Jun. Sch.
Playing Field
Sports Ground
Crown Farm
Crown Cottages
ROMFORD
Cottons Rec. Grd.
Esporta
Bowl. Alley
LONDON ROAD
A118
Pavilion
St. Edward's C of E Comp. School
Westlands Playing Field
Romford Stadium (Greyhound)
OLDCHURCH HOSP.
Gas Works
Tennis Courts
Helipad (open 2007)
Hospital (due open 2007)
Crowlands
Jutsums Rec. Grd.
CROW LANE
WHALEBONE LA.
A1112
Romford Cemetery
Crowlands Sports Ground
Oldchurch Park
RUSH GREEN
RUSH GREEN ROAD
CROWLANDS HEATH GOLF COURSE
73
Playing Field
BEACONTREE HEATH
Club House
Football Ground
Fords Sports Ground
Wood Lane Sports Centre
All Saints

56
A
B
C
D
E
38
74
06
07
08
87
86
85
1
2
3
4
5
6
7
Newyears Green Covert
Old Clack Farm
The Corner
Kiln
Grays Cottages
Research Farm
Dunster Cottage
Works
Depot
Gatemead Farm
Brackenbury Barn
Moat
Copthall Covert
RUISLIP GOLF COURSE
WEST RUISLIP
Golf Driving Range
Playground
Club Ho.
West Ruislip
Club House
Harvil Farm
Copthall Farm
Playing Field
Cricket Ground
Pav.
Sch.
UXBRIDGE GOLF COURSE
HARVIL ROAD
BREAKSPEAR ROAD
SOUTH
HIGH ROAD
ICKENHAM
B467
GREEN ACRES AVENUE
THREE OAKS CL.
SWAKELEYS ROAD
HIGHFIELD DR.
COPTHALL RD.
HOYLAKE CRES.
BUSHEY RD.
CHARLES CURRAN HO.
Compass Theatre & Arts Cen.
Community Cl.
Lib.
Ickenham
GLEBE AV.
LONG LANE
B466
River Pinn
Tennis Courts
Bowling Green
Harrington House
Swakeleys Sports Ground
The Clump
Common Plantation
Play. Fld.
Vyners School
Weatherlys Covert
SWAKELEYS ROUNDABOUT
A40
WESTERN AVENUE
Fray's Farm
Fray's Bri.
HAREFIELD RD.
B467
Sports Ground
Park Wood
The Doway Martyrs Sch.
Long Lane Farm
Ickenham Manor
Play. Flds.
Moat
Clare House
Hillingdon Ski Centre
Ski Slope
Uxbridge Common
Bowling Green
Cricket Ground
Uxbridge Athletic Track
Playing Field
Hillingdon
HILLINGDON CIRCUS
Motel
Freezeland Covert
Canal Feeder
Hillingdon House Farm Showground
Uxbridge College
UXBRIDGE
Prim. Sch.
Superstore
York Ho.
B483
TA Centre
RAF Uxbridge Track
HILLINGDON COURT PARK
Rec. Grd.
Play. Fld.
Playgrd.
American Community School
RAF STATION
Sports Ground
Tennis Courts
Bowling Green
Halls
Schs.
Civic Cen.
HILLINGDON ROAD
A437
Convent
Playground
GRANVILLE
RICHMOND ROAD
MERTON AVENUE
HERCIES ROAD
SWEETCROFT
HONEYCROFT HILL
PARKWAY
GROSVENOR
WINDSOR

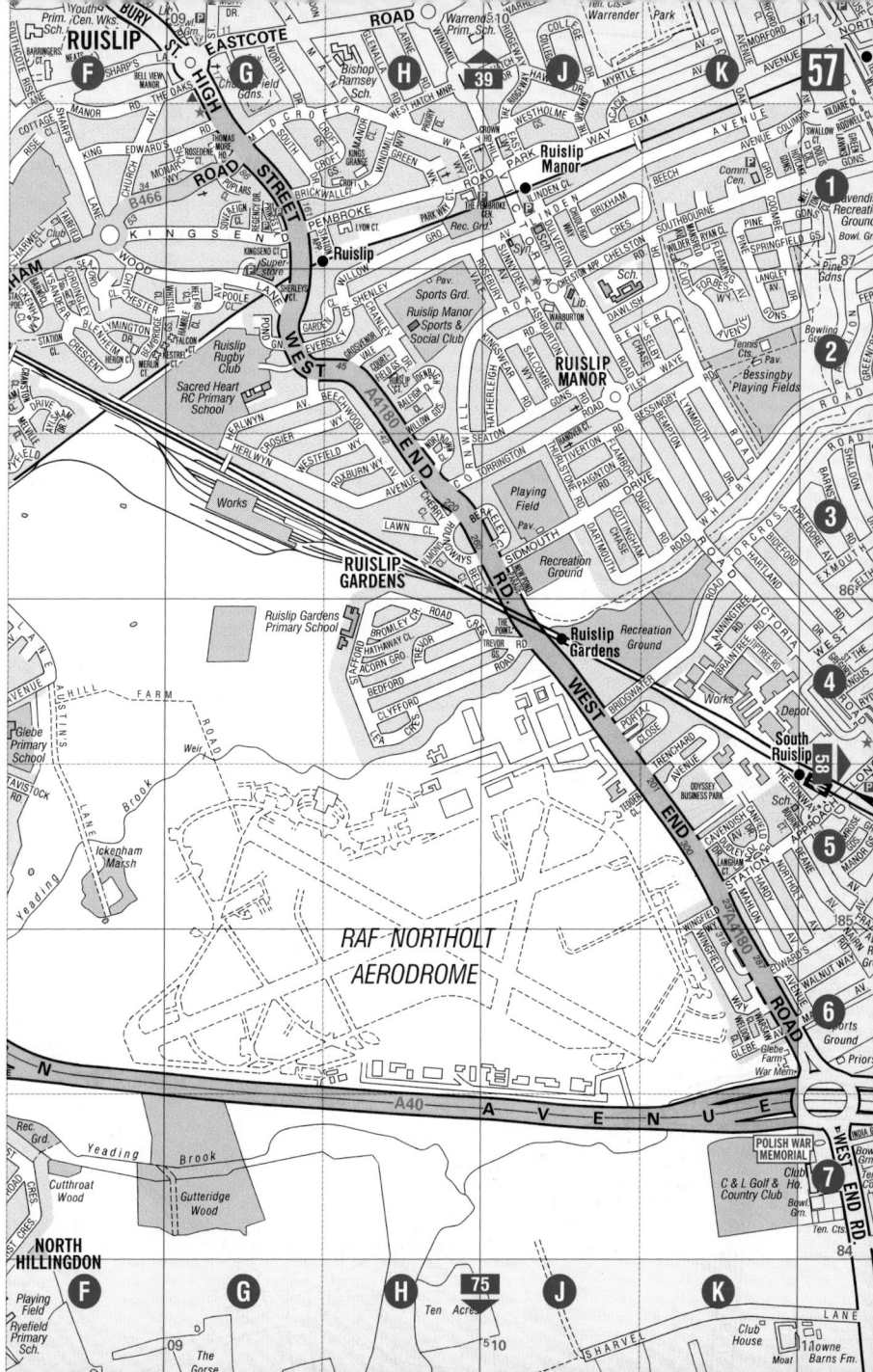
57
RUISLIP
RUISLIP MANOR
Ruislip Manor
Ruislip
RUISLIP GARDENS
Ruislip Gardens
South Ruislip
NORTH HILLINGDON
RAF NORTHOLT AERODROME
HIGH STREET
WEST END RD.
WEST END ROAD
A4180
A40
AVENUE
B466
KINGSEND
EASTCOTE ROAD
PARK WAY
VICTORIA ROAD
Bishop Ramsey Sch.
Warrender Prim. Sch.
Warrender Park
Ruislip Rugby Club
Sacred Heart RC Primary School
Ruislip Manor Sports & Social Club
Sports Grd.
Playing Field
Recreation Ground
Ruislip Gardens Primary School
Bessingby Playing Fields
Comm. Cen.
Works
Depot
ODYSSEY BUSINESS PARK
Ickenham Marsh
Yeading Brook
Glebe Primary School
Cutthroat Wood
Gutteridge Wood
POLISH WAR MEMORIAL
C & L Golf & Country Club
Ten Acres
The Gorse
Ryefield Primary Sch.
Towne Barns Fm.
SHARVEL LANE
39
58
75
F
G
H
J
K
1
2
3
4
5
6
7

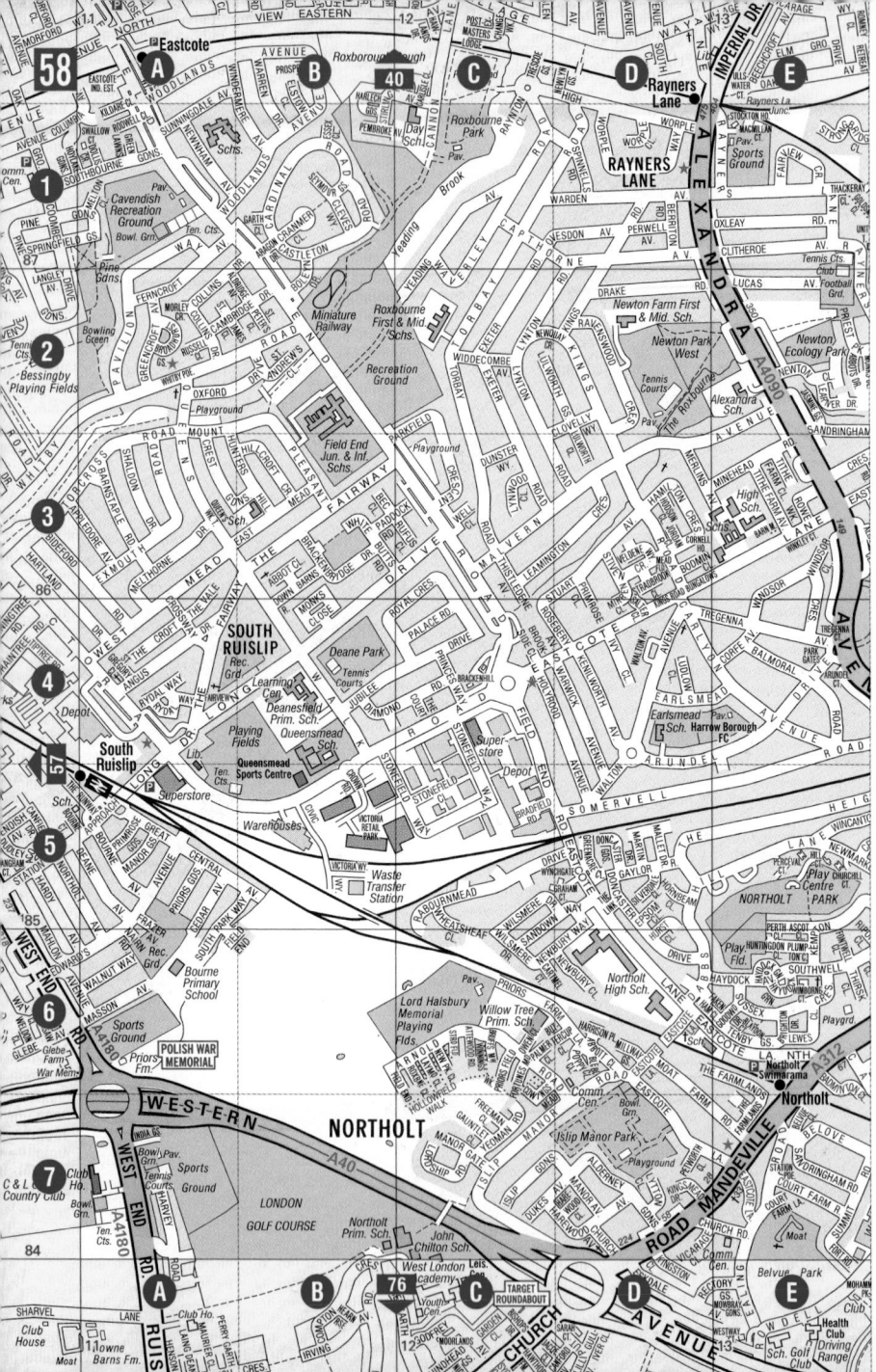
58
40
57
76
A
B
C
D
E
1
2
3
4
5
6
7
87
86
85
84
Eastcote
Rayners Lane
RAYNERS LANE
SOUTH RUISLIP
South Ruislip
NORTHOLT
Northolt
Cavendish Recreation Ground
Bessingby Playing Fields
Roxbourne Park
Miniature Railway
Roxbourne First & Mid. Schs.
Recreation Ground
Field End Jun. & Inf. Schs.
Deane Park
Deanesfield Prim. Sch.
Queensmead Sch.
Queensmead Sports Centre
Newton Farm First & Mid. Sch.
Newton Park West
Newton Ecology Park
Alexandra Sch.
High Sch.
Earlsmead Sch.
Harrow Borough FC
Victoria Retail Park
Waste Transfer Station
Bourne Primary School
POLISH WAR MEMORIAL
Lord Halsbury Memorial Playing Flds.
Willow Tree Prim. Sch.
Northolt High Sch.
NORTHOLT PARK
Islip Manor Park
LONDON GOLF COURSE
Northolt Prim. Sch.
John Chilton Sch.
West London Academy
TARGET ROUNDABOUT
Belvue Park
Northolt Swimarama
C & L Country Club
WESTERN
A40
A4180
A4090
A312
ALEXANDRA
MANDEVILLE
ROAD
WEST END
CHURCH
AVENUE
EASTCOTE
LONG DR.
VICTORIA RD.
FIELD END RD.
SOMERVELL
ARUNDEL ROAD

WEST HARROW
HARROW
F
G
H
J
K
41
The Grove Open Space
Miniature Rifle Range
Playing Fields
WHITMORE
Whitmore High Sch.
Whitmore Sports Cen.
Cricket Ground
Harrow School
Music Sch.
Parade Grd.
Tennis Cts.
1
Harrow School Playing Fields
HARROW ON THE HILL
School Lake
Grange Schs.
LOWER RD.
BESSBOROUGH RD.
A312
B457
ROXETH HILL
ROXETH
Superstore
Cricket Ground
Kennet End
2
ST. ANDREW'S AT HARROW
THE CLEMENTINE CHURCHILL BMI HOSPITAL
Burial Ground
South Harrow
SUDBURY HILL
SUDBURY COURT DR.
A4127
A4005
3
Schools
Cemetery
Orley Farm Sch.
Playing Fld.
Playing Fields
Toll Gate
Roxeth Rec. Grd.
Harrow Ckt. Club
SOUTH HARROW
Welldon Park First Sch.
ALEXANDRA PARK
NORTHOLT ROAD
4
Sudbury Hill Harrow
Sudbury Hill Play. Flds.
Northolt Pk.
Sudbury Hill
David Lloyd Leisure
Ealing Northern Sports Centre
60
Wood End
5
WHITTON AV. WEST
A4090
AVENUE
WHITTON AV. EAST
Prim. Sch.
Jun. Sch.
Play. Fld.
Inf. Sch.
Liby.
PETT'S HILL
HORSENDEN LA. NORTH
Radio Station
Greenford Green
Horsenden Primary Sch.
6
Factory
Bowling Green
Pavilion
GREENFORD
A4127
BERKELEY FIELDS
Warehouses
GRAND UNION CANAL
(PADDINGTON BRANCH)
Lyon's Dock
Works
Youth & Comm. Cen.
Horsenden Hill Rec. Grd.
7
Nature Reserve
Warehouses
GREENFORD INDUSTRIAL ESTATE
Depot
Greenford
77
Sports Ground
Oldfield Rec. Grd.
Perivale Wood Local Nature Reserve
Mosque

HARROW
60
42
59
78
A
B
C
D
E
1
2
3
4
5
6
7
16
17
18
87
86
185
84
NORTHWICK PARK HOSPITAL
ST. MARK'S HOSP.
Playing Fields
NORTHWICK PARK
Harrow School Playing Fields
Rugby Football Grounds
Harrow School Farm
WATFORD ROAD
A404
SOUTH ROAD
NORVAL RD.
ABBOTTS DRIVE
NORTH WEMBLEY
Byron Ct. Prim. Sch.
South Kenton
WINDERMERE AV.
GRASMERE AV.
WOODCOCK
John Billam Playing Fields
Sports Ground
Preston Road
PRESTON
PRESTON ROAD
Preston Park Recreation Ground
Tennis Courts
Playground
CARLTON AV.
EAST LANE
A4088
North Wembley
SUDBURY COURT DRIVE
A4127
SUDBURY COURT
Elmwood Pk.
Vale Farm Sports Ground
Vale Farm Sports Centre
East Lane Pavilion Rugby Football Grd.
Wembley FC (Vale Farm)
East La. Theatre Club
Play. Fld. Wembley High Tech. Coll.
Rec. Grd.
Train. Cen.
EAST LANE BUSINESS PARK
WEMBLEY COMMERCIAL CENTRE
Sports Grd.
Wembley Manor Jun. & Inf. Sch.
KING EDWARD VII PARK
Bowl. Grns.
Prim. Sch.
HARROW ROAD
A4005
Butler's Grn.
SUDBURY
Maybank Open Space
Sudbury & Harrow Road
BARHAM PARK
Library
Sudbury Hill Play. Flds.
WHITTON AVENUE
A4090
Sudbury Town
BRIDGEWATER ROAD
HARROW RD. HIGH RD.
A404
Wembley Central
WEMBLEY (MATS) HOSP.
EALING ROAD
A4089
Horsenden Wood
Club House
HORSENDEN HILL GOLF COURSE
Horsenden Hill
SUDBURY GOLF COURSE
Alperton Cemetery
One Tree Hill Rec. Grd.
Hindu Tem.
Alperton Sch.
Spts. Cen.
Alperton
Bus Garage
GRAND UNION CANAL (PADDINGTON BRANCH)
Moat
Horsenden Farm
HORSENDEN LANE
PERIVALE
Perivale Wood Local Nature Reserve
Comm. Centre
Lib.
Govt. Training Cen.
Wks.
Warehouse
PHOENIX TRAD. EST.
ABERCORN COMMERCIAL CEN.

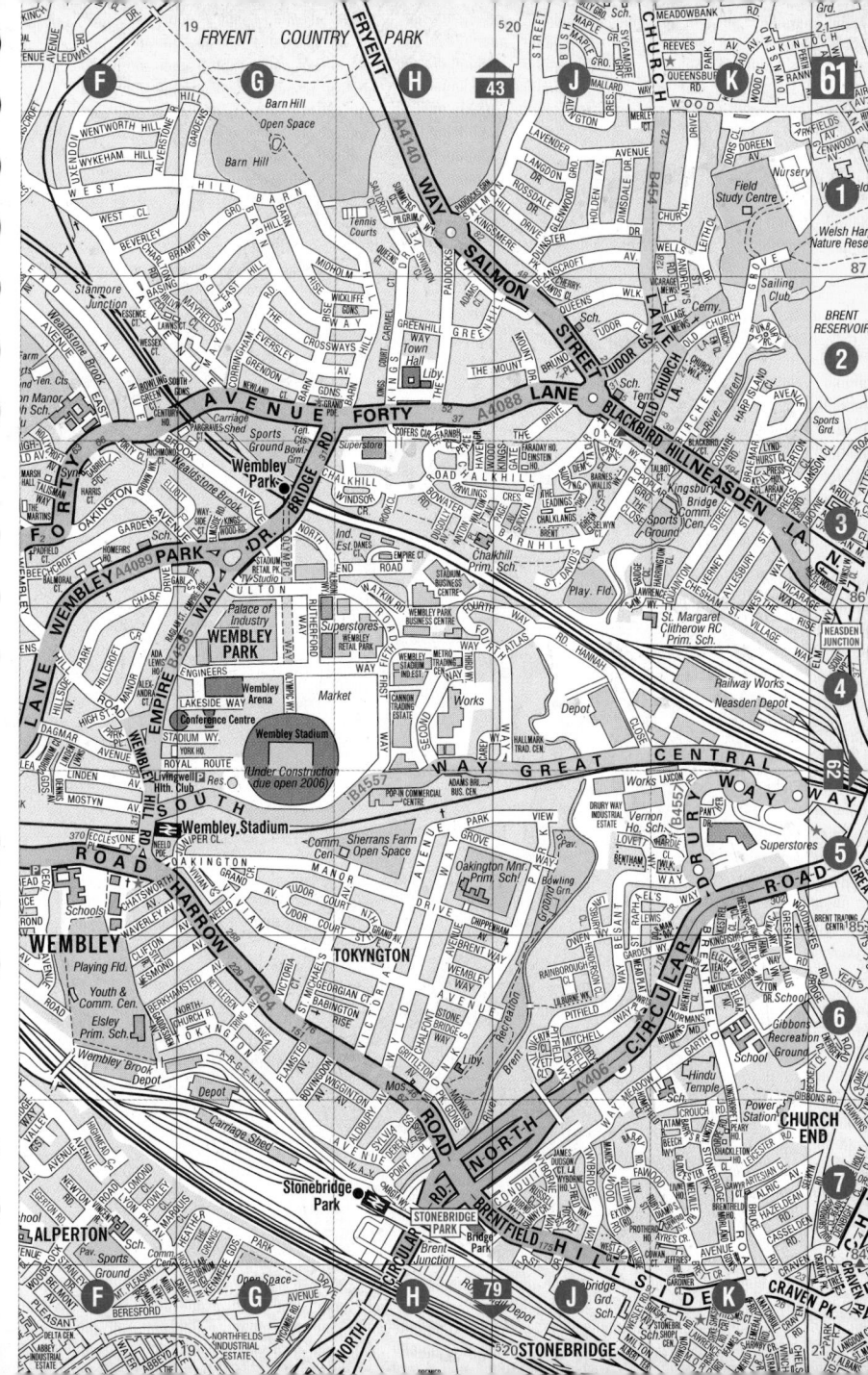

61
43
FRYENT COUNTRY PARK
Barn Hill Open Space
Barn Hill
FRYENT WAY
A4140
SALMON STREET
CHURCH LANE
B454
Field Study Centre
Nursery
Welsh Harp Nature Reserve
Sailing Club
BRENT RESERVOIR
Tennis Courts
Town Hall
Liby.
FORTY AVENUE
FORTY LANE
A4088
BLACKBIRD HILL
NEASDEN LA.
OLD CHURCH LA.
Cemy.
Stanmore Junction
Wealdstone Brook
Carriage Shed
Sports Ground
Superstore
Wembley Park
BRIDGE RD.
CHALKHILL ROAD
Chalkhill Prim. Sch.
Kingsbury Bridge Comm. Cen.
Sports Ground
Play. Fld.
St. Margaret Clitherow RC Prim. Sch.
NEASDEN JUNCTION
WEMBLEY PARK DR.
A4089
Ind. Est.
Palace of Industry
WEMBLEY PARK
Superstores
WEMBLEY RETAIL PARK
WEMBLEY PARK BUSINESS CENTRE
Railway Works
Neasden Depot
Depot
EMPIRE WAY
B4565
Wembley Arena
Conference Centre
Market
Works
Wembley Stadium
(Under Construction due open 2006)
GREAT CENTRAL WAY
B4557
62
SOUTH WAY
Wembley Stadium
Livingwell Hlth. Club
DRURY WAY
Superstores
Sherrans Farm Open Space
Comm. Cen.
Oakington Mnr. Prim. Sch.
Bowling Grn.
Vernon Ho. Sch.
ROAD
HARROW ROAD
A404
WEMBLEY
Schools
Playing Fld.
Youth & Comm. Cen.
Elsley Prim. Sch.
TOKYNGTON
Brent Recreation Ground
NORTH CIRCULAR ROAD
A406
Wembley Brook Depot
Depot
Carriage Shed
Liby.
Hindu Temple
Gibbons Recreation Ground
School
Power Station
CHURCH END
Stonebridge Park
STONEBRIDGE PARK
Bridge Park
Brent Junction
BRENTFIELD
HILLSIDE
ALPERTON
Sports Ground
Open Space
79
Depot
STONEBRIDGE
NORTHFIELDS INDUSTRIAL ESTATE
CRAVEN PK.
F G H J K
1 2 3 4 5 6 7

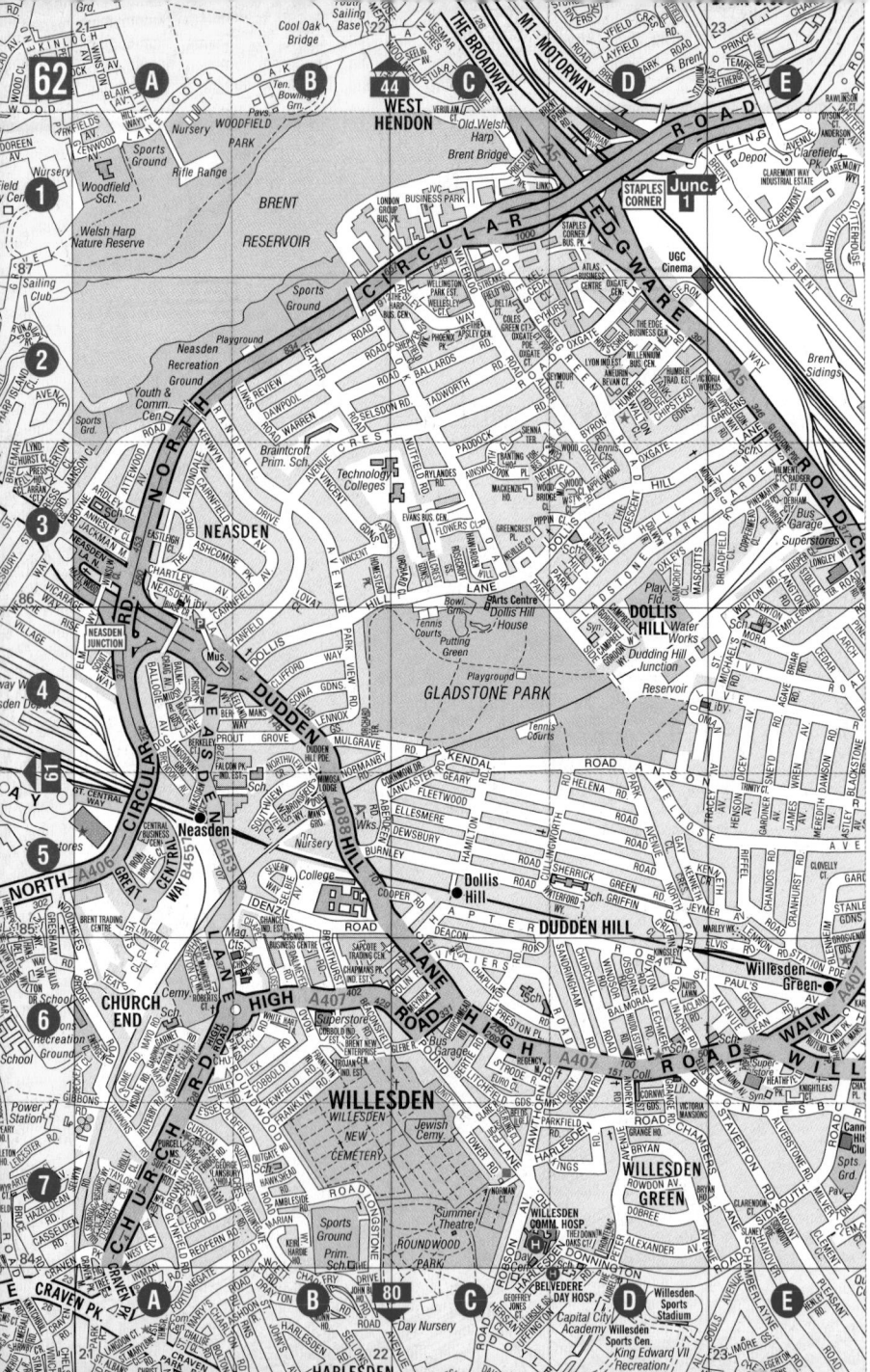
44
61
80
A
B
C
D
E
1
2
3
4
5
6
7
21
22
23
87
86
85
84
WEST HENDON
Cool Oak Bridge
Youth Sailing Base
COOL OAK LANE
WOODFIELD PARK
Woodfield Sch.
Sports Ground
Nursery
Rifle Range
Welsh Harp Nature Reserve
BRENT RESERVOIR
Sailing Club
Old Welsh Harp
Brent Bridge
THE BROADWAY
M1 MOTORWAY
NORTH CIRCULAR ROAD
EDGWARE ROAD
A5
STAPLES CORNER
Junc. 1
STAPLES CORNER BUS. PK.
CLAREMONT WAY INDUSTRIAL ESTATE
Clarefield Pk.
Depot
UGC Cinema
Brent Sidings
R. Brent
PRINCE
TEMPELHOF
LAYFIELD CRES.
LAYFIELD RD.
JVC BUSINESS PARK
LONDON GROUP BUS. PK.
ATLAS BUSINESS CENTRE
OXGATE CEN.
THE EDGE BUSINESS CEN.
MILLENNIUM BUS. CEN.
HUMBER TRAD. EST.
VICTORIA WORKS
WELLINGTON PARK EST.
WELLESLEY CT.
THE HARP BUS. CEN.
PHOENIX PK.
APSLEY CEN.
Sports Ground
Playground
Neasden Recreation Ground
Youth & Comm. Cen.
Sports Grd.
NEASDEN
NEASDEN JUNCTION
Neasden
Mus.
Braintcroft Prim. Sch.
Technology Colleges
EVANS BUS. CEN.
HEATHER
REVIEW
DAWPOOL
WARREN
LINKS
SELSDON RD.
BALLARDS
TADWORTH
PADDOCK
NUTFIELD RD.
RYLANDES RD.
OXGATE
OXGATE GARDENS
DOLLIS HILL
DOLLIS HILL LANE
DOLLIS HILL AVENUE
GLADSTONE PARK
GLADSTONE PARK GARDENS
Arts Centre
Dollis Hill House
Bowl. Grn.
Tennis Courts
Putting Green
Playground
Play. Fld.
Water Works
Dudding Hill Junction
Reservoir
Bus Garage
Superstores
DUDDEN HILL
DUDDEN HILL LANE
A4088
KENDAL
ANSON ROAD
MELROSE AVENUE
MULGRAVE RD.
NORMANBY RD.
PROUT GROVE
FLEETWOOD
ELLESMERE
DEWSBURY
BURNLEY
COOPER RD.
CHAPTER ROAD
DEACON RD.
VILLIERS RD.
Dollis Hill
College
Nursery
GREAT CENTRAL WAY
B4551
B453
A406
NORTH CIRCULAR RD.
BRENT TRADING CENTRE
CENTRAL BUSINESS CEN.
CHURCH END
CHURCH ROAD
NEASDEN LANE
HIGH ROAD
A407
Superstore
Bus Garage
WILLESDEN
WILLESDEN NEW CEMETERY
Jewish Cemy.
Cemy.
Mag. Cts.
Sports Ground
Summer Theatre
ROUNDWOOD PARK
Prim. Sch.
Willesden Green
WILLESDEN GREEN
WALM LANE
WILLESDEN LANE
BRONDESBURY PARK
WILLESDEN COMM. HOSP.
BELVEDERE DAY HOSP.
Day Cen.
Capital City Academy
Willesden Sports Stadium
Willesden Sports Cen.
King Edward VII Recreation
Day Nursery
HARLESDEN
HARLESDEN RD.
DONNINGTON
CRAVEN PK.
Power Station
Recreation Ground
School
Coll.
Lib.
Liby.
Syn.
CHAMBERLAYNE
Spts. Grd.

63
HAMPSTEAD
HEATH
GOLDERS GREEN
Golders Green
NORTH END ROAD
A502
HENDON WAY
A41
FINCHLEY ROAD
Clitterhouse Recreation Ground
Hendon FC
CRICKLEWOOD
Cricklewood
CRICKLEWOOD BROADWAY
CRICKLEWOOD LANE
A407
CHILD'S HILL
CHILDS HILL PARK
GOLDERS HILL PARK
Leg of Mutton Pond
West Heath
Jack Straws Castle
WEST HEATH ROAD
PLATT'S LANE
FORTUNE GREEN ROAD
Fortune Green
Hampstead Cemetery
Sports Ground
Hampstead School
WEST HAMPSTEAD
West Hampstead
West Hampstead Thameslink
Finchley Rd. & Frognal
SHOOT UP HILL
BROADWAY
A5
CHICHELE RD.
WALM LANE
WILLESDEN LANE
A4003
Kilburn
KILBURN HIGH RD.
Brondesbury
BRONDESBURY
BRONDESBURY PARK
Brondesbury Park
Willesden Lane Cemetery
KILBURN
WEST END LANE
B510
B520
IVERSON RD.
MILL LANE
SOUTH HAMPSTEAD
BELSIZE ROAD
ABBEY RD.
B509
Camden Arts Cen.
45
64
81
F
G
H
J
K
1
2
3
4
5
6
7
24
25
26

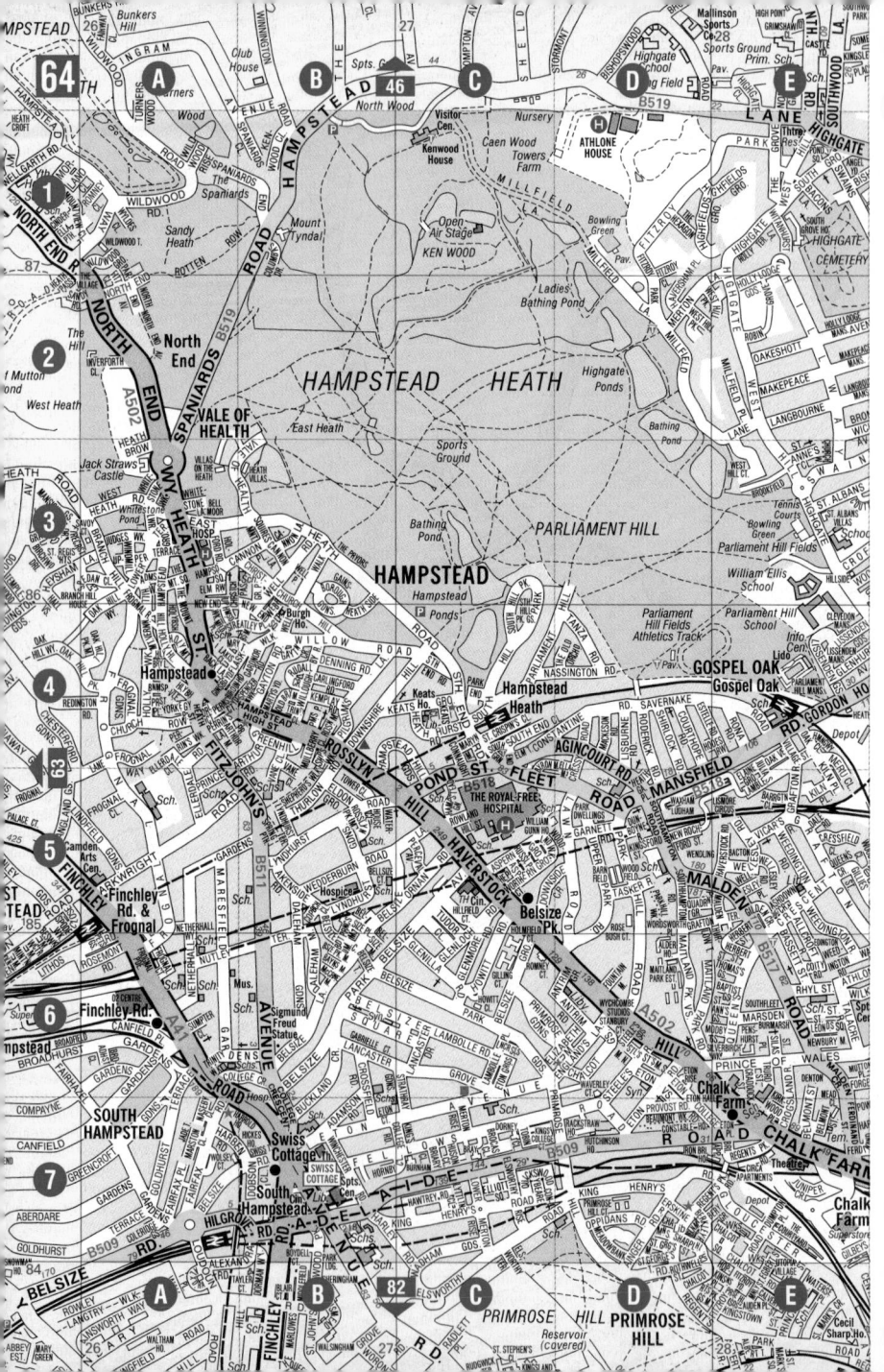

HAMPSTEAD HEATH
HAMPSTEAD
PARLIAMENT HILL
GOSPEL OAK
Gospel Oak
Hampstead Heath
Hampstead
North End
VALE OF HEALTH
SOUTH HAMPSTEAD
South Hampstead
Swiss Cottage
Finchley Rd. & Frognal
Finchley Rd.
Belsize Pk.
Chalk Farm
PRIMROSE HILL
ATHLONE HOUSE
Kenwood House
Visitor Cen.
Caen Wood Towers Farm
North Wood
Nursery
Highgate School
Mallinson Sports Cen.
Sports Ground
Prim. Sch.
Club House
Turners Wood
The Spaniards
Sandy Heath
Mount Tyndal
Open Air Stage
KEN WOOD
Ladies' Bathing Pond
Highgate Ponds
Bathing Pond
Bowling Green
Pav.
East Heath
Sports Ground
West Heath
The Hill
Jack Straws Castle
Whitestone Pond
Hampstead Ponds
Burgh Ho.
Keats Ho.
Parliament Hill Fields Athletics Track
Parliament Hill Fields
Parliament Hill School
William Ellis School
Tennis Courts
Lido
Info. Cen.
HIGHGATE CEMETERY
THE ROYAL FREE HOSPITAL
Camden Arts Cen.
Sigmund Freud Statue
Mus.
Hospice
Depot
Superstore
Theatre
Reservoir (covered)
Cecil Sharp Ho.
HAMPSTEAD ROAD
SPANIARDS ROAD
NORTH END
NORTH END RD.
HEATH ST.
FITZJOHN'S AVENUE
ROSSLYN HILL
HAVERSTOCK HILL
POND ST.
FLEET ROAD
AGINCOURT RD.
MANSFIELD ROAD
GORDON HO. RD.
MALDEN ROAD
CHALK FARM RD.
FINCHLEY ROAD
ADELAIDE ROAD
AVENUE ROAD
BELSIZE PARK
BELSIZE AVENUE
ETON AVENUE
PRIMROSE HILL RD.
ELSWORTHY
HIGHGATE WEST HILL
MILLFIELD LA.
HAMPSTEAD LANE
HIGHGATE
A502
A41
B519
B518
B517
B511
B509
A B C D E
1 2 3 4 5 6 7

46
63
82

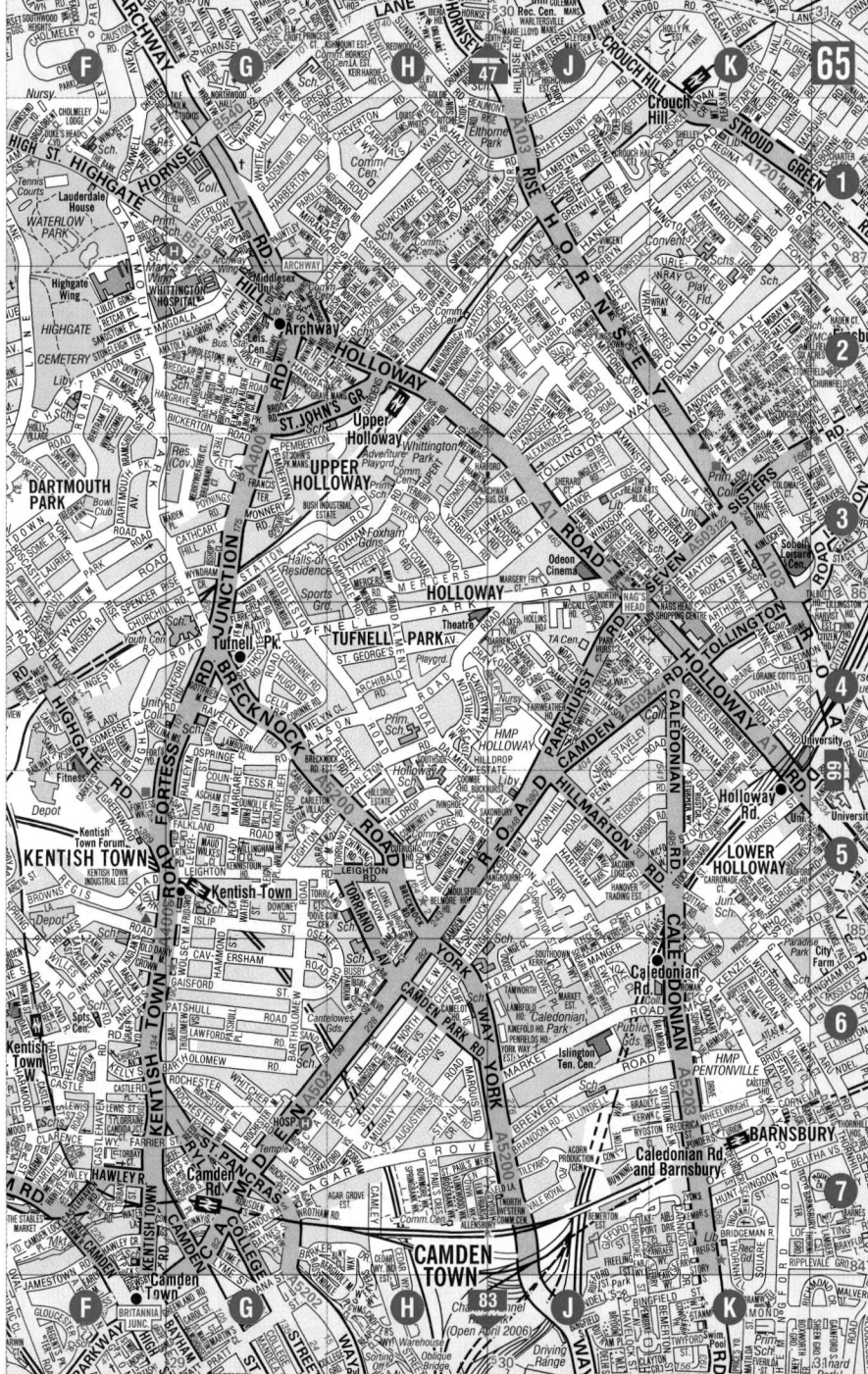

65
47
F
G
H
J
K
1
2
3
4
5
6
7
99
83
HIGHGATE
HIGHGATE CEMETERY
Lauderdale House
WATERLOW PARK
WHITTINGTON HOSPITAL
Highgate Wing
Archway
HOLLOWAY
UPPER HOLLOWAY
Upper Holloway
DARTMOUTH PARK
Crouch Hill
Finsbury
Whittington Park
Elthorne Park
Odeon Cinema
NAG'S HEAD
Sobell Leisure Cen.
Tufnell Pk.
TUFNELL PARK
HMP HOLLOWAY
Holloway Rd.
LOWER HOLLOWAY
KENTISH TOWN
Kentish Town
Kentish Town W.
Caledonian Rd.
Caledonian Park
HMP PENTONVILLE
Islington Ten. Cen.
BARNSBURY
Caledonian Rd. and Barnsbury
CAMDEN TOWN
Camden Town
Camden Rd.
BRITANNIA JUNC.
City Farm
Paradise Park
JUNCTION RD.
ARCHWAY RD.
HORNSEY RISE
HORNSEY RD.
HOLLOWAY RD.
CAMDEN RD.
YORK WAY
CALEDONIAN RD.
BRECKNOCK RD.
KENTISH TOWN RD.
FORTESS RD.
HIGHGATE RD.
SEVEN SISTERS RD.
STROUD GREEN RD.
CROUCH HILL
CAMDEN PARK RD.
ST. PANCRAS WAY
AGAR GROVE
PARKWAY
(Open April 2006)
Driving Range

A
B
C
D
E
1
2
3
4
5
6
7
48
65
84
FINSBURY PARK
Reservoir (covered)
Sports Arena
Manor House
MANOR HO.
Green Lanes Br.
WEST RESERVOIR
West Reservoir Centre
The Castle Climbing Cen.
EAST RESERVOIR
Sir Thomas Abney Prim. Sch.
FINSBURY PARK
Finsbury Park
Rowans Complex
BROWNSWOOD PARK
CLISSOLD PARK
Clissold Ho.
Council Offices
Tennis Courts
Bowl. Grn.
Paddling Pool
Clissold Leisure Cen.
ABNEY PARK CEMETERY
STOKE NEWINGTON
STOKE NEWINGTON CHURCH
Old Peoples Home
BIRCHMORE HALL
Isledon Village
Gillespie Local Park
Arsenal
Arsenal FC (Highbury Stadium)
Arsenal Stadium (Due Open 2006)
Drayton Park
HIGHBURY
HIGHBURY FIELDS
Highbury Pool
Highbury & Islington
HIGHBURY CNR.
Canonbury
CANONBURY
Dalston Kingsland
KINGSLAND
BARNSBURY
City Farm
Paradise Park
ISLINGTON
PO Depot
Essex Rd.
Bingo
DE BEAUVOIR TOWN
Kingsland Basin
SEVEN SISTERS RD.
BLACKSTOCK RD.
GREEN LANES
LORDSHIP PARK
MANOR RD
STOKE NEWINGTON CHURCH ST.
HIGHBURY PARK
HIGHBURY GROVE
ST. PAUL'S RD.
BALLS POND RD
CANONBURY RD.
UPPER ST.
HOLLOWAY RD.
LIVERPOOL RD.
NEW NTH. RD
ESSEX RD.
ALBION RD.
NEWINGTON GRN. RD.
KINGSLAND RD.
STROUD GREEN RD.
HORNSEY RD.
TOLLINGTON
BROWNSWOOD RD.
A503
A105
A1201
A1199
A104
A1200
A103
A1
A10
B105
B104
B515

67
49
85
68
F
G
H
J
K
1
2
3
4
5
6
7
STAMFORD HILL
Stoke Newington
UPPER CLAPTON
Clapton
LOWER CLAPTON
HACKNEY DOWNS
Hackney Downs
SHACKLEWELL
HOMERTON
Homerton
LEA BRIDGE
HACKNEY
London Fields
DALSTON
SOUTH HACKNEY
SPRINGFIELD PARK
Springfield Marina
Horse Shoe Point
Coppermill Bridge
WALTHAMSTOW MARSHES
Clapton Junction
Leyton Marshes
Lea Bridge Riding Sch.
Playing Field
Lee Valley Ice Centre
Filter Beds
Middlesex Filter Beds Nature Reserve
NORTH MILLFIELDS Recreation Ground
South Millfields Rec. Grd.
SOUTH MILL FIELDS
HOMERTON UNIVERSITY HOSPITAL
Rectory Road
Hackney Cen.
Mossbourne Community Academy
Stormont House Sch.
LONDON FIELDS
WELL STREET COMMON
Victoria Fountain
Royal Gate East
Bandstand
Leyton Industrial Village
Forest Business Park
UPPER CLAPTON ROAD
LOWER CLAPTON ROAD
LEA BRIDGE ROAD
HOMERTON HIGH ST.
STOKE NEWINGTON HIGH ST.
STOKE NEWINGTON RD.
KINGSLAND HIGH S.
MARE STREET
GRAHAM ROAD
DALSTON LA.
AMHURST RD.
PEMBURY RD.
QUEENSBRIDGE RD.
WELL ST.
CASSLAND RD.
VICTORIA PARK ROAD
NORTHWOLD RD.
RECTORY ROAD
STAMFORD HILL
WICK RD.
MORNING LANE
A10
A107
A104
A102
A106
A1207
B111
B113
B108
34
35
36
84
85
86
87

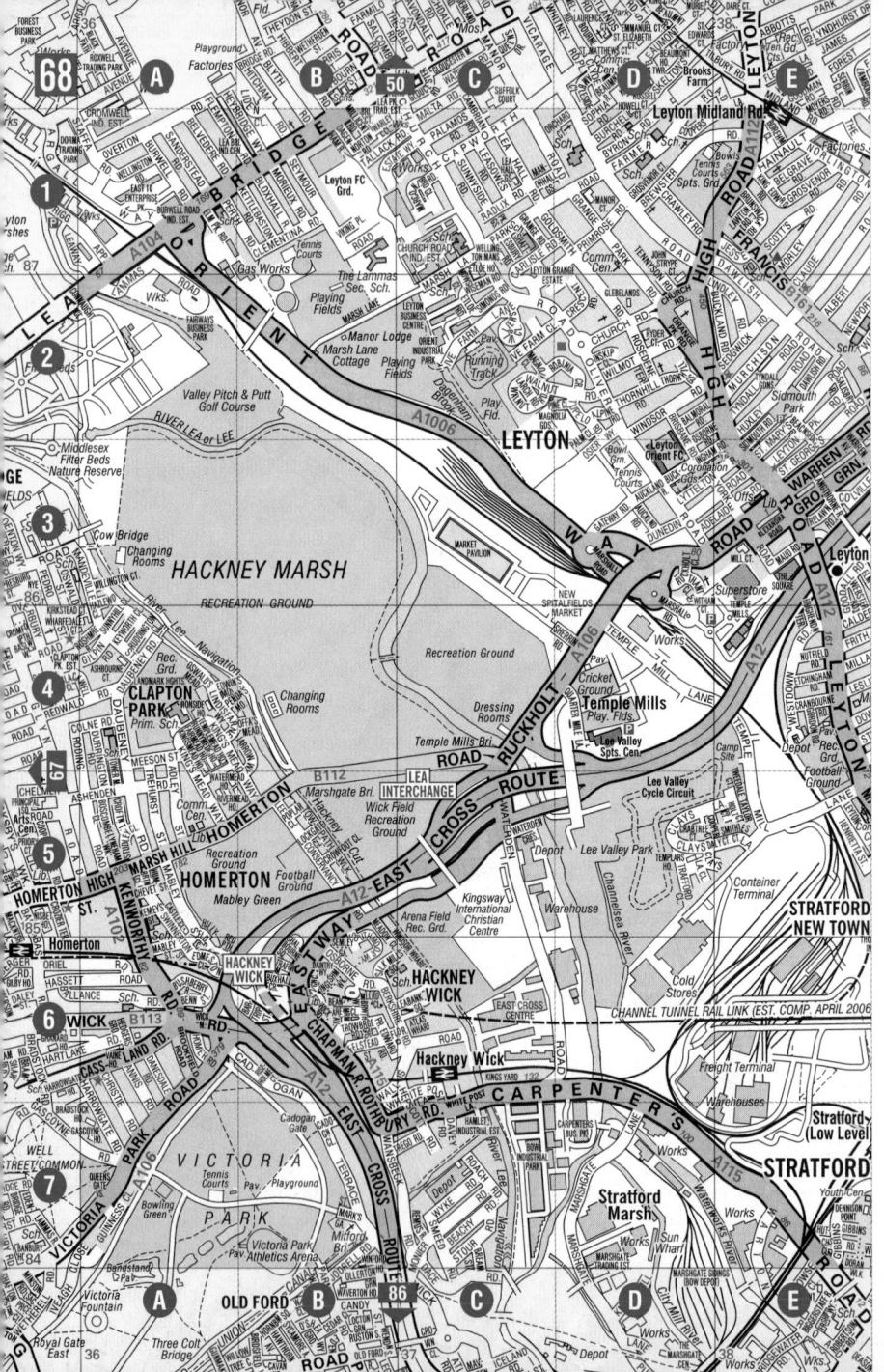

A
B
C
D
E
1
2
3
4
5
6
7
50
67
86
36
37
38
87
86
85
84
LEYTON
HACKNEY MARSH
RECREATION GROUND
CLAPTON PARK
HOMERTON
HACKNEY WICK
OLD FORD
STRATFORD
STRATFORD NEW TOWN
Stratford Marsh
Temple Mills
Leyton Midland Rd.
Leyton
Homerton
Hackney Wick
Stratford (Low Level)
LEA BRIDGE ROAD
ORIENT WAY
A104
A1006
A106
A12
A112
A115
A102
B112
B113
B161
EAST CROSS ROUTE
RUCKHOLT ROAD
HOMERTON ROAD
MARSH HILL
HOMERTON HIGH ST.
KENWORTHY RD.
WICK RD.
CASSLAND RD.
VICTORIA PARK ROAD
CARPENTER'S RD.
HIGH ROAD LEYTON
FRANCIS RD.
WARREN RD.
TEMPLE MILL LANE
CHAPMAN R.
ROTHBURY RD.
LEA INTERCHANGE
HACKNEY WICK
Leyton FC Grd.
Leyton Orient FC
Valley Pitch & Putt Golf Course
RIVER LEA or LEE
Middlesex Filter Beds Nature Reserve
Cow Bridge
Changing Rooms
River Lee Navigation
Recreation Ground
Dressing Rooms
Temple Mills Bri.
Marshgate Bri.
Wick Field Recreation Ground
Hackney Cut
Lee Valley Spts. Cen.
Lee Valley Cycle Circuit
Lee Valley Park
Camp Site
Container Terminal
Channelsea River
Warehouse
Depot
Kingsway International Christian Centre
Arena Field Rec. Grd.
CHANNEL TUNNEL RAIL LINK (EST. COMP. APRIL 2006
Freight Terminal
Warehouses
Cold Stores
EAST CROSS CENTRE
Manor Lodge
Marsh Lane Cottage
Playing Fields
The Lammas Sec. Sch.
Gas Works
MARKET PAVILION
NEW SPITALFIELDS MARKET
Superstore
Running Track
Sidmouth Park
Brooks Farm
VICTORIA PARK
Victoria Park Athletics Arena
Victoria Fountain
Royal Gate East
Three Colt Bridge
Cadogan Gate
Mabley Green
Football Ground
Bowling Green
Tennis Courts
Playground
Bandstand
WELL STREET COMMON
Mitford Bri.
MARSHGATE TRADING EST.
MARSHGATE SIDINGS (BOW DEPOT)
Sun Wharf
City Mill River
Waterworks River
CARPENTERS BUS. PK.
BOW INDUSTRIAL PARK
HAMLET INDUSTRIAL EST.
Youth Cen.

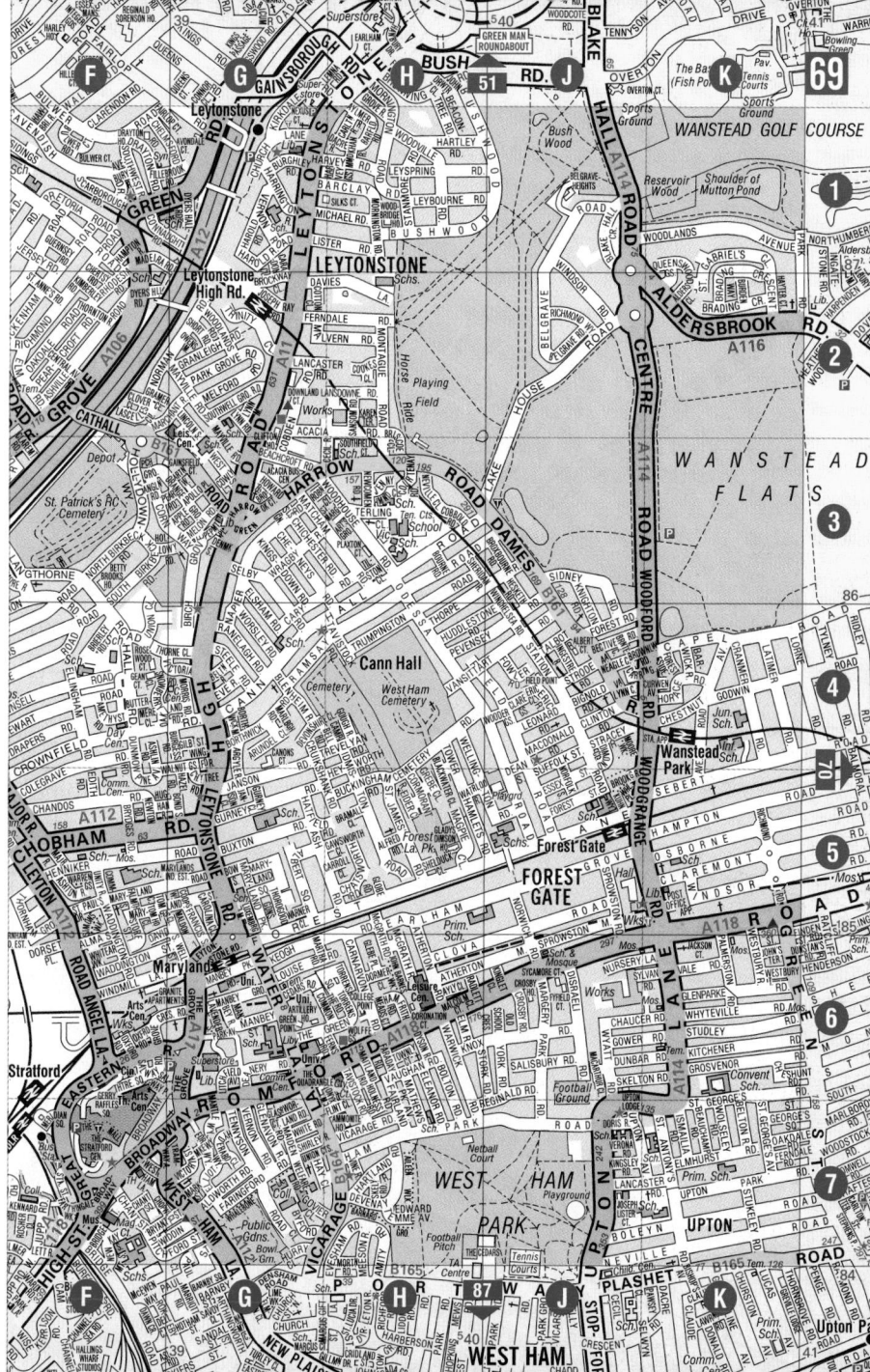

69
70
51
87
F
G
H
J
K
1
2
3
4
5
6
7
GREEN MAN ROUNDABOUT
BUSH RD.
Leytonstone
Leytonstone High Rd.
LEYTONSTONE
LEYTONSTONE RD.
HIGH RD. LEYTONSTONE
HARROW ROAD
WANSTEAD GOLF COURSE
Reservoir Wood
Shoulder of Mutton Pond
The Basin (Fish Pond)
Sports Ground
Bush Wood
ALDERSBROOK RD.
A116
A114
A11
A12
A106
A112
A118
B161
B164
B165
HOLLY TREE RD.
WANSTEAD FLATS
Playing Field
Horse Ride
LAKE HOUSE ROAD
CENTRE ROAD
WOODFORD ROAD
DAMES ROAD
St. Patrick's RC Cemetery
Cann Hall
West Ham Cemetery
Wanstead Park
Forest Gate
FOREST GATE
Maryland
Stratford
ROMFORD ROAD
WATER LANE
CHOBHAM RD.
LEYTON ROAD
ANGEL LA.
GREAT EASTERN RD.
BROADWAY
WEST HAM LA.
VICARAGE LA.
WEST HAM PARK
Netball Court
Playground
Football Pitch
Tennis Courts
Football Ground
UPTON LANE
WOODGRANGE RD.
GREEN STREET
UPTON
PORTWAY
PLASHET ROAD
WEST HAM
Upton Park

70
52
69
88
WANSTEAD PARK
WANSTEAD GOLF COURSE
The Temple
Keepers Lodge
Heronry Pond
Perch Pond
Rook Island
Sewage Works
WANSTEAD FLATS
ALDERSBROOK
ALDERSBROOK ROAD
A116
Aldersbrook Prim. Sch.
NORTHUMBERLAND AVENUE
WANSTEAD PARK AVENUE
CITY OF LONDON CEMETERY
City of London Crematorium
ILFORD GOLF COURSE
River Roding
Alders Brook
SOUTH WOODFORD TO BARKING RELIEF ROAD
A406
CRANBROOK
Ilford Cricket Club
Bowls
Cranbrook Coll.
Ilford
A123
THE MANOR PARK CEMETERY
Manor Park Crem.
MANOR PARK
Manor Park
FOREST DRIVE
A117
ROMFORD ROAD
A118
Woodgrange Park
Woodgrange Park Cemetery
HIGH STREET NORTH
LITTLE ILFORD LANE
LITTLE ILFORD
Little Ilford Park
NORTH CIRCULAR ROAD
PLASHET
Jewish Cemetery
PLASHET PARK
The Shrewsbury Cen.
East Ham
B165
B167
B109
GREEN STREET
KATHERINE ROAD
PLASHET GROVE
EAST AV.
BROWNING ROAD
WALLEND
Sports Ground
Gasholder
Running Track
Playing Field
Depot
Upton Park
UPTON PARK
PLASHET RD.
BARKING RD.
RON LEIGHTON
SOUTH WOODFORD

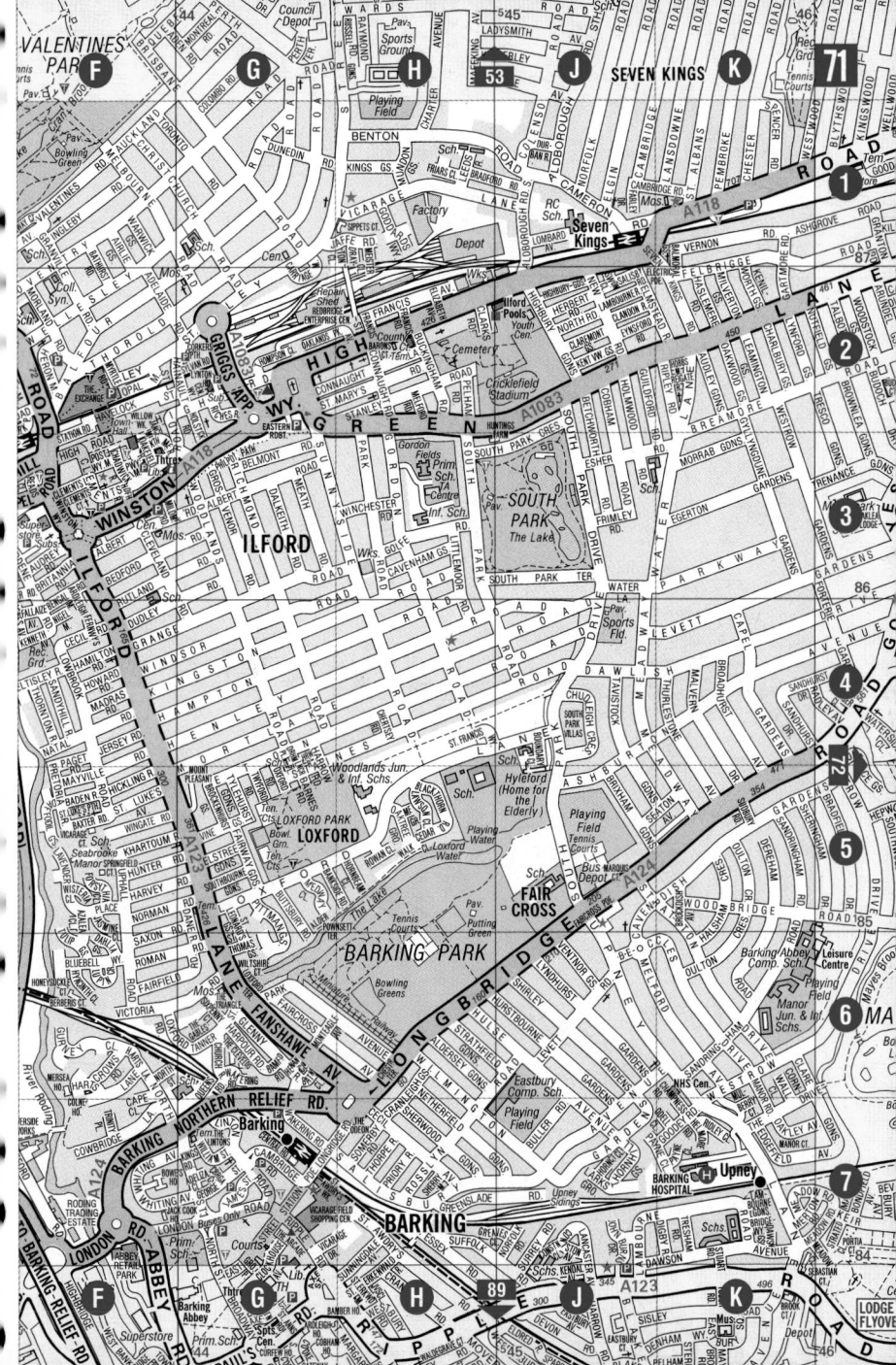

71
53
72
89
F
G
H
J
K
1
2
3
4
5
6
7
VALENTINES PARK
SEVEN KINGS
Seven Kings
ILFORD
SOUTH PARK
The Lake
LOXFORD
LOXFORD PARK
BARKING PARK
FAIR CROSS
BARKING
Barking
Upney
BARKING HOSPITAL
Ilford Pools
Cricklefield Stadium
Cemetery
Factory
Depot
Playing Field
Sports Ground
Council Depot
Woodlands Jun. & Inf. Schs.
Hyleford (Home for the Elderly)
Barking Abbey Comp. Sch.
Leisure Centre
Manor Jun. & Inf. Schs.
Eastbury Comp. Sch.
Barking Abbey
VICARAGE FIELD SHOPPING CEN.
RODING TRADING ESTATE
ABBEY RETAIL PARK
LODGE FLYOVER
HIGH ROAD
GREEN LANE
HIGH RD.
ILFORD LANE
LONGBRIDGE ROAD
FANSHAWE AV.
BARKING NORTHERN RELIEF RD.
BARKING RELIEF RD.
RIPPLE RD.
LONDON RD.
ABBEY RD.
WINSTON WY.
GRIGGS APP.
A118
A1083
A123
A124

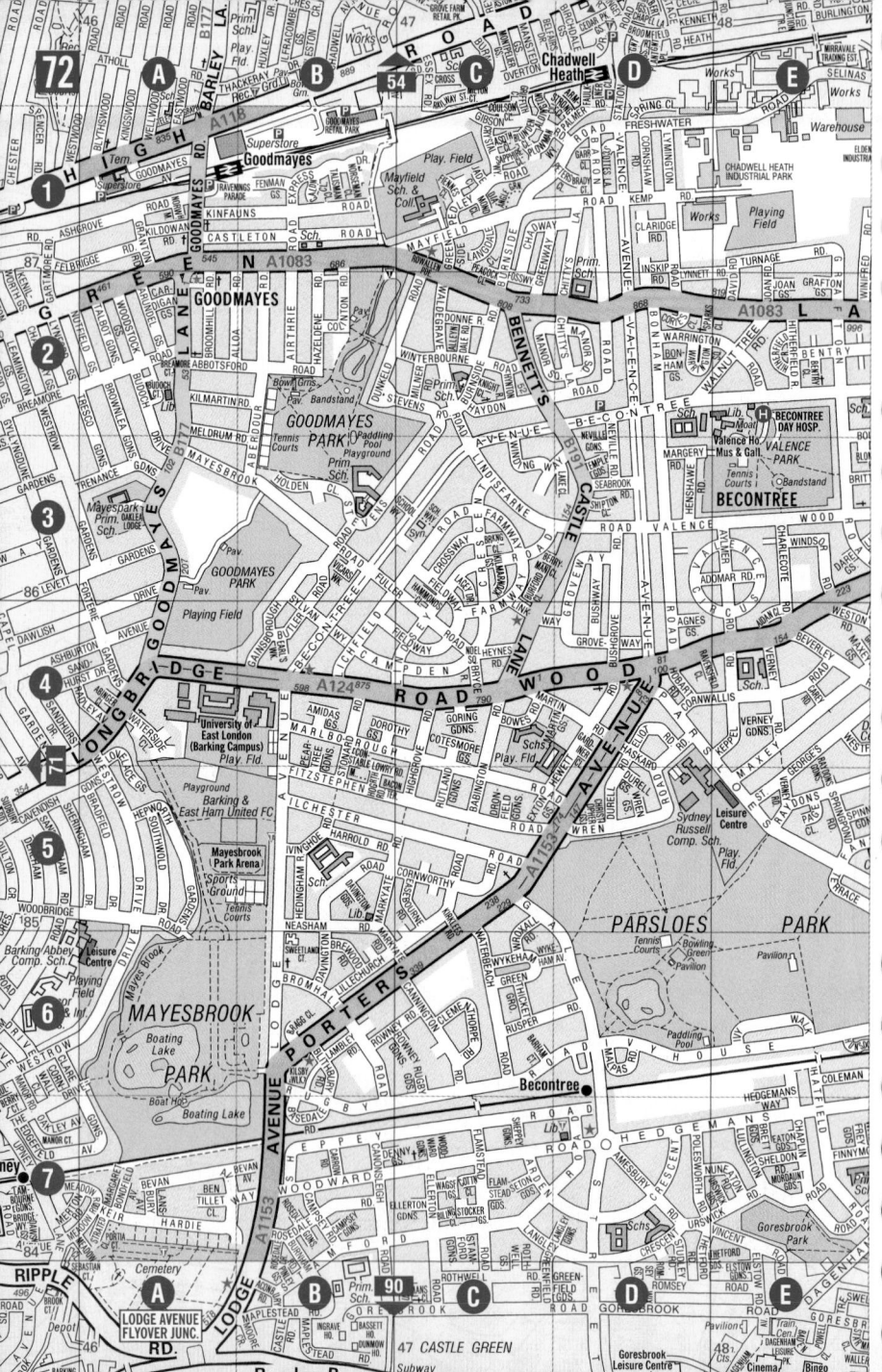
72
54
71
90
HIGH ROAD
A118
Goodmayes
Superstore
GOODMAYES RETAIL PARK
Chadwell Heath
CHADWELL HEATH INDUSTRIAL PARK
GROVE FARM RETAIL PK
MIRRAVALE TRADING EST.
Warehouse
Works
Play. Field
Mayfield Sch. & Coll.
Playing Field
GREEN LANE
A1083
GOODMAYES
GOODMAYES LANE
B177
BARLEY LA.
GOODMAYES PARK
Paddling Pool
Playground
Tennis Courts
Bandstand
Bowl. Grns.
Prim. Sch.
Mayespark Prim. Sch.
MAYESBROOK
BENNETT'S CASTLE LANE
B191
BECONTREE AVENUE
VALENCE AVENUE
VALENCE CIRCUS
BECONTREE DAY HOSP.
Valence Ho. Mus & Gall.
VALENCE PARK
BECONTREE
LONGBRIDGE ROAD
WOOD LANE
A124
University of East London (Barking Campus)
Play. Fld.
Barking & East Ham United FC
Mayesbrook Park Arena
Sports Ground
Tennis Courts
Sydney Russell Comp. Sch.
Leisure Centre
PARSLOES PARK
Bowling Green
Pavilion
Paddling Pool
MAYESBROOK PARK
Boating Lake
Boat Ho.
Barking Abbey Comp. Sch.
Leisure Centre
Playing Field
PORTERS AVENUE
A1153
LODGE AVENUE
Becontree
HEDGEMANS ROAD
IVY HOUSE ROAD
RUGBY ROAD
SHEPPEY ROAD
WOODWARD ROAD
Cemetery
RIPPLE RD.
LODGE AVENUE FLYOVER JUNC.
GORESBROOK ROAD
47 CASTLE GREEN
Goresbrook Park
Goresbrook Leisure Centre
DAGENHAM
Cinema
Bingo
Subway

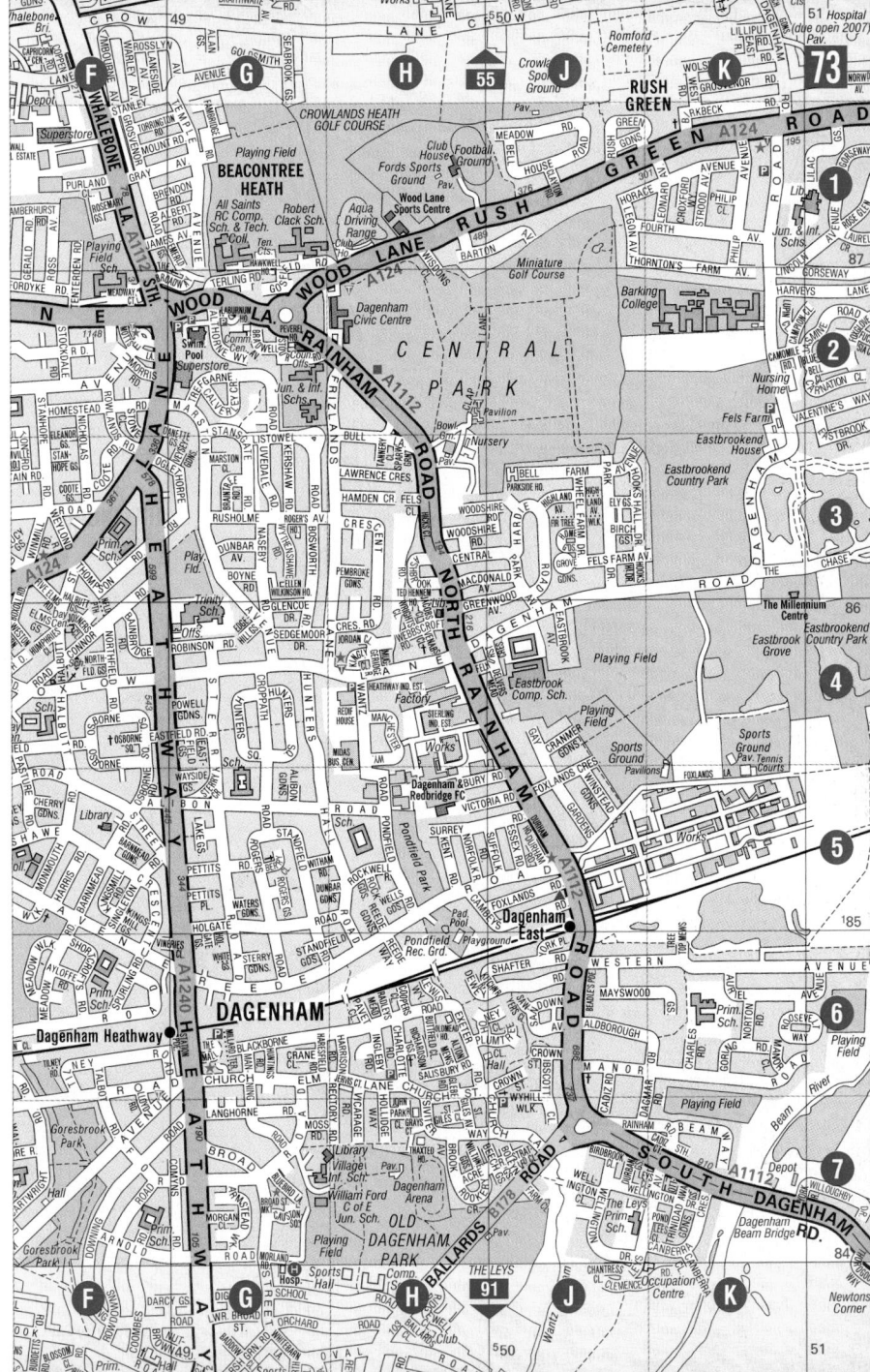

73
55
91
RUSH GREEN
Romford Cemetery
Crowlands Heath Golf Course
Crowlands Sports Ground
BEACONTREE HEATH
Playing Field
All Saints RC Comp. Sch. & Tech. Coll.
Robert Clack Sch.
Fords Sports Ground
Football Ground
Club House
Wood Lane Sports Centre
Aqua Driving Range
Miniature Golf Course
Barking College
Dagenham Civic Centre
CENTRAL PARK
Pavilion
Nursery
Swim. Pool
Superstore
Jun. & Inf. Schs.
Eastbrookend House
Eastbrookend Country Park
Fels Farm
Nursing Home
The Millennium Centre
Eastbrook Grove
Eastbrook Comp. Sch.
Playing Field
Sports Ground
Pavilions
Tennis Courts
Trinity Sch.
Library
Works
Factory
Dagenham & Redbridge FC
Pondfield Park
Pondfield Rec. Grd.
Playground
Dagenham East
DAGENHAM
Dagenham Heathway
Goresbrook Park
Village Inf. Sch.
William Ford C of E Jun. Sch.
Dagenham Arena
OLD DAGENHAM PARK
Sports Hall
Hosp.
Occupation Centre
The Leys Prim. Sch.
Dagenham Beam Bridge
Newtons Corner
Beam River
Depot
ROAD
RUSH GREEN ROAD
WOOD LANE
RAINHAM ROAD NORTH
RAINHAM ROAD SOUTH
DAGENHAM RD.
BALLARDS ROAD
HEATHWAY
WHALEBONE LA.
A124
A1112
A1240
B178
THE LEYS
Newtons Corner

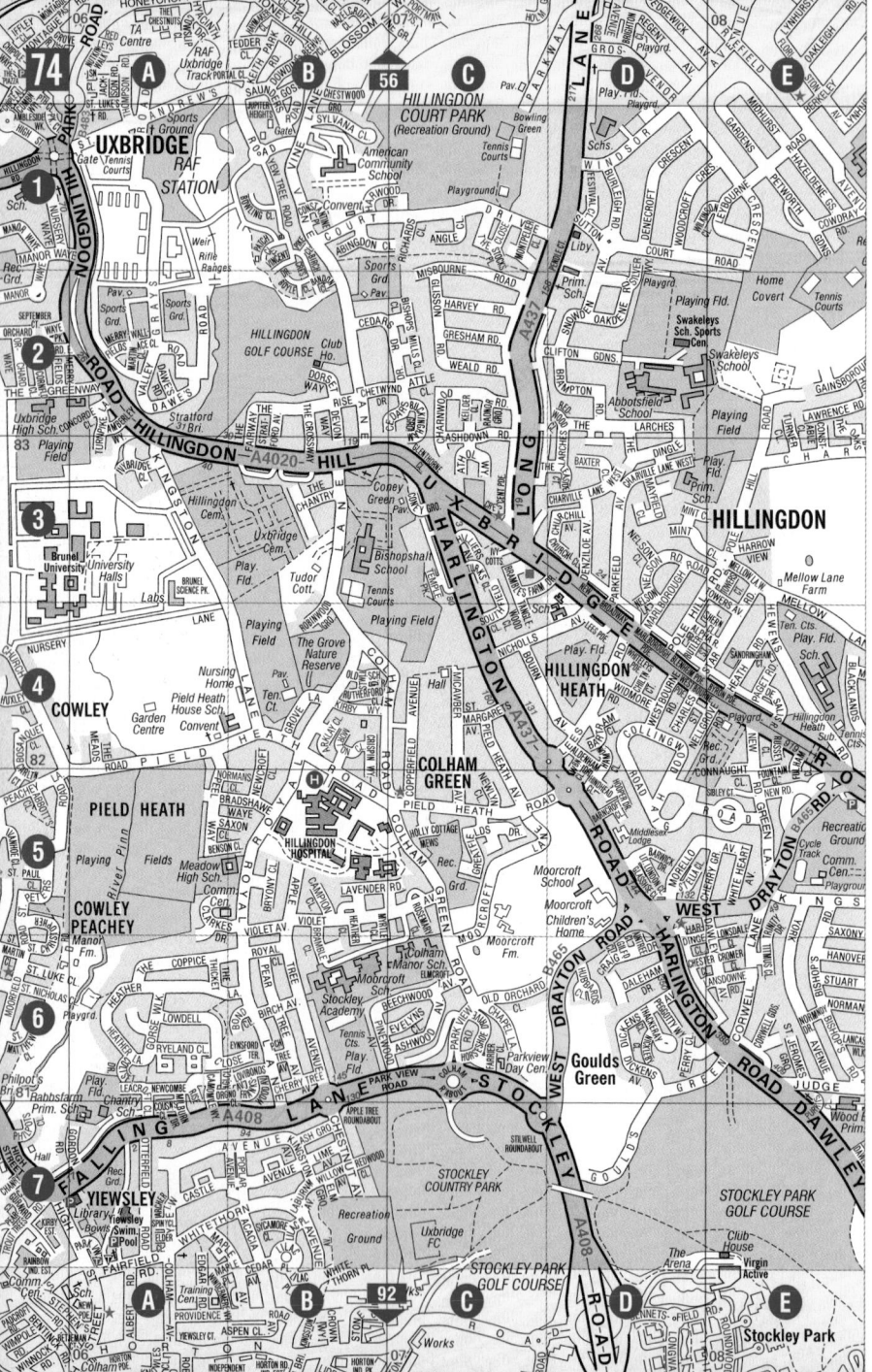

74
56
92
UXBRIDGE
RAF STATION
HILLINGDON COURT PARK (Recreation Ground)
American Community School
HILLINGDON GOLF COURSE
HILLINGDON
HILLINGDON HEATH
COLHAM GREEN
COWLEY
PIELD HEATH
COWLEY PEACHEY
YIEWSLEY
WEST DRAYTON
Goulds Green
STOCKLEY COUNTRY PARK
STOCKLEY PARK GOLF COURSE
Stockley Park
Brunel University
University Halls
BRUNEL SCIENCE PK.
Uxbridge High Sch.
Hillingdon Cem.
Uxbridge Cem.
Bishopshalt School
The Grove Nature Reserve
HILLINGDON HOSPITAL
Meadow High Sch.
Stockley Academy
Moorcroft School
Moorcroft Children's Home
Swakeleys School
Abbotsfield School
Swakeleys Sch. Sports Cen.
Hillingdon Heath
Uxbridge FC
Virgin Active
HILLINGDON ROAD
HILLINGDON HILL
A4020
UXBRIDGE ROAD
LONG LANE
A437
HARLINGTON ROAD
FALLING LANE
A408
STOCKLEY ROAD
WEST DRAYTON ROAD
B465
DAWLEY ROAD
PIELD HEATH ROAD
COLHAM GREEN ROAD
ROYAL LANE
KINGSTON LANE

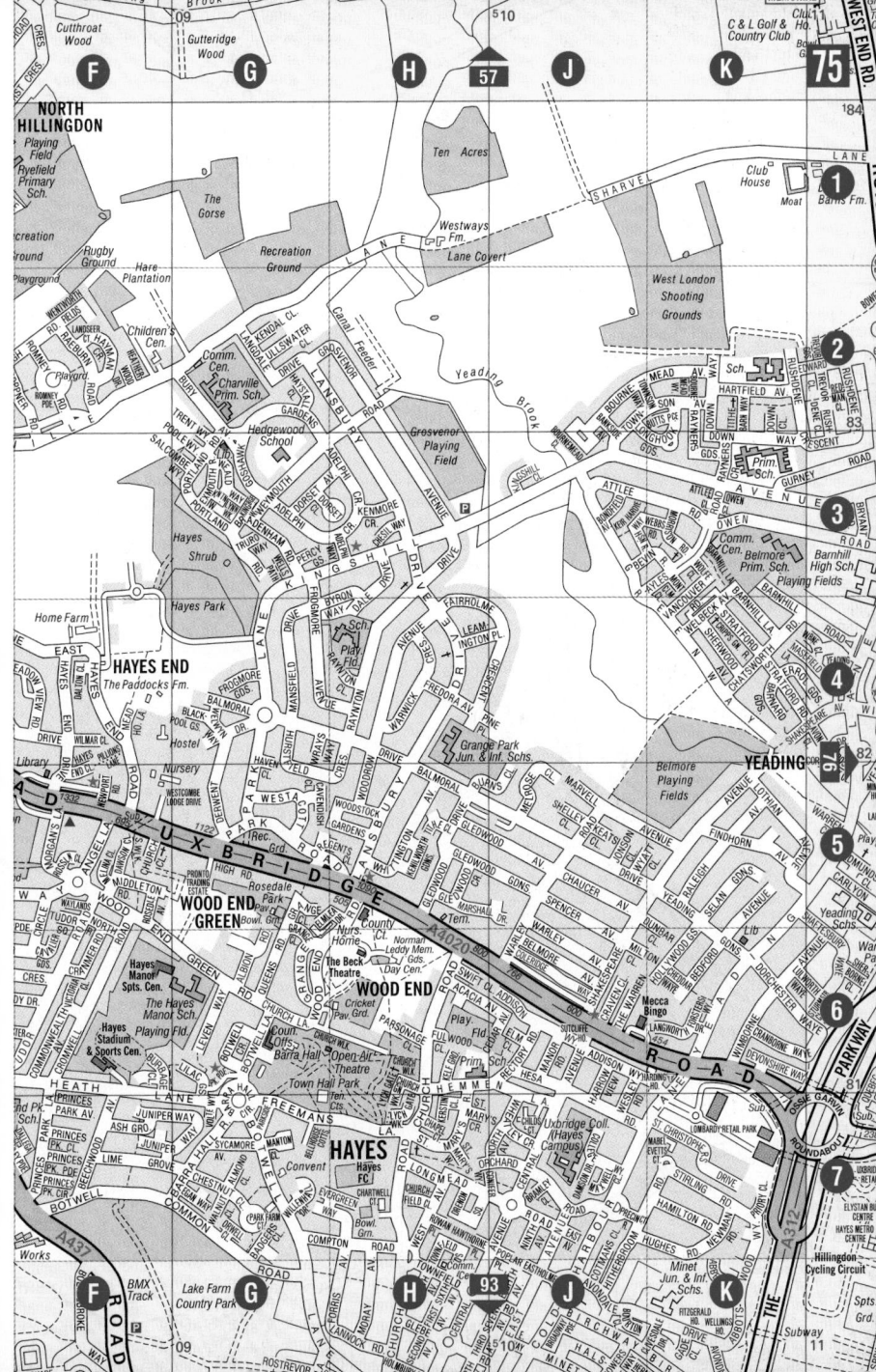

Cutthroat Wood
Gutteridge Wood
Brook
C & L Golf & Country Club
WEST END RD.
57
F
G
H
J
K
NORTH HILLINGDON
Playing Field
Ryefield Primary Sch.
Recreation Ground
Rugby Ground
Playground
Hare Plantation
The Gorse
Recreation Ground
Ten Acres
Westways Fm.
Lane Covert
SHARVEL LANE
Club House
Moat
Barns Fm.
West London Shooting Grounds
Canal Feeder
Yeading Brook
Children's Cen.
Comm. Cen.
Charville Prim. Sch.
Hedgewood School
Grosvenor Playing Field
LANSBURY DRIVE
KINGSHILL DRIVE
KINGSHILL AVENUE
ATTLEE ROAD
OWEN ROAD
GURNEY ROAD
Comm. Cen.
Belmore Prim. Sch.
Barnhill High Sch. Playing Fields
Prim. Sch.
Sch.
HARTFIELD AV.
DOWN WAY
RUSHDENE CRESCENT
Hayes Shrub
Hayes Park
Home Farm
HAYES END
The Paddocks Fm.
Hostel
Nursery
Library
Play. Fld.
Grange Park Jun. & Inf. Schs.
Belmore Playing Fields
YEADING
76
Sch.
UXBRIDGE ROAD
A4020
Rec. Grd.
Rosedale Park
PRONTO TRADING ESTATE
WOOD END GREEN
County Ct.
Nurs. Home
Norman Leddy Mem. Gds.
Day Cen.
The Beck Theatre
WOOD END
Cricket Grd.
Play. Fld.
Prim. Sch.
Hayes Manor Spts. Cen.
The Hayes Manor Sch. Playing Fld.
Hayes Stadium & Sports Cen.
Coun. Offs.
Barra Hall
Open-Air Theatre
Town Hall Park
Ten. Cts.
HEATH LANE
FREEMANS LA.
HAYES
Convent
Hayes FC
Uxbridge Coll. (Hayes Campus)
Mecca Bingo
Lib
Yeading Schs.
LOMBARDY RETAIL PARK
OSSIE GARVIN ROUNDABOUT
PARKWAY
THE PARKWAY
A312
UXBRIDGE RETAIL
ELYSTAN BUS. CENTRE
HAYES METRO CENTRE
Hillingdon Cycling Circuit
Spts. Grd.
Minet Jun. & Inf. Schs.
FITZGERALD HO.
WELLINGS HO.
A437
Works
BMX Track
Lake Farm Country Park
COMPTON ROAD
93
Subway
1
2
3
4
5
6
7

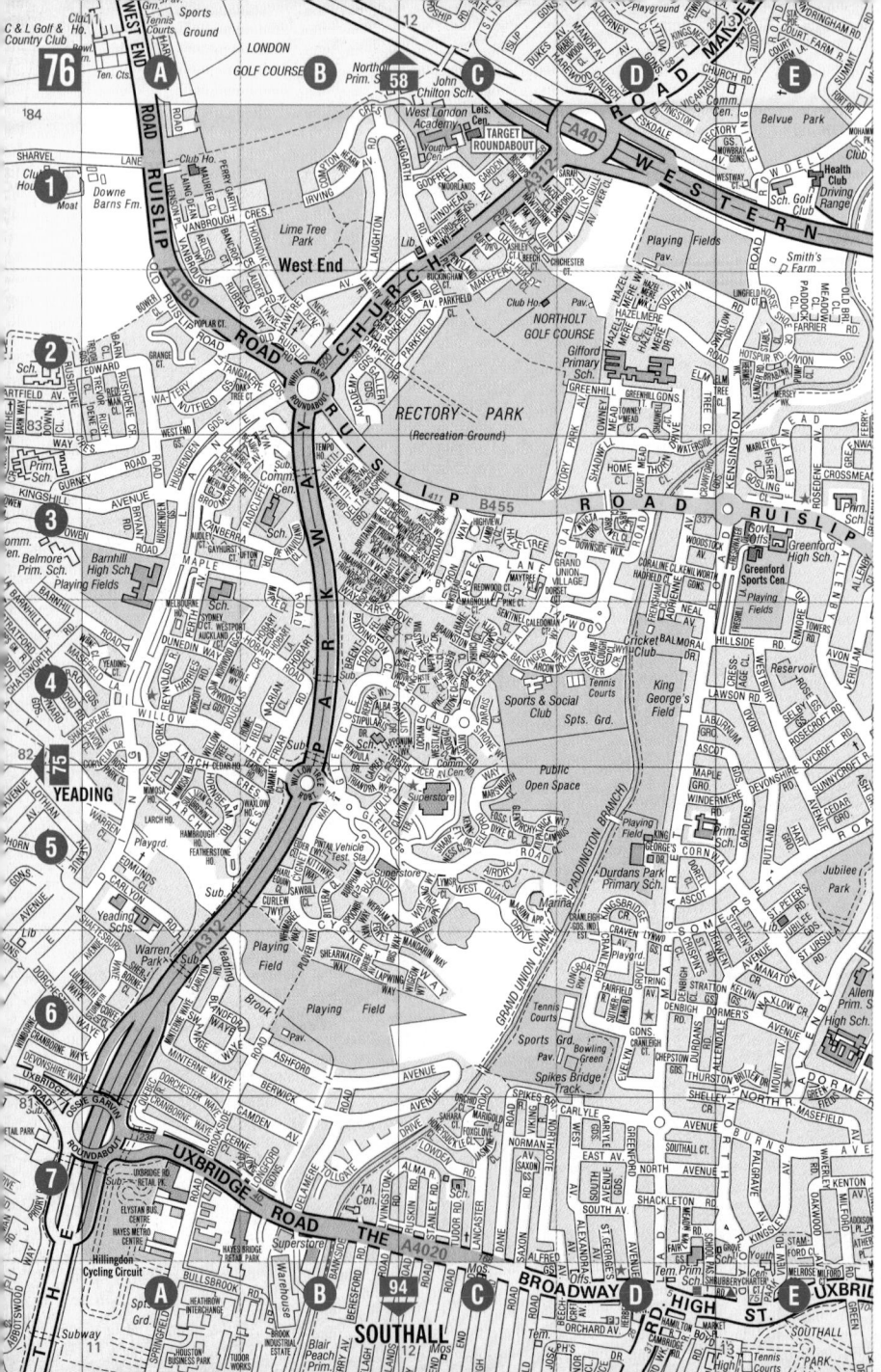

76
58
75
94
A
B
C
D
E
1
2
3
4
5
6
7
WEST END ROAD
RUISLIP ROAD
A4180
C & L Golf & Country Club
Sports Ground
LONDON GOLF COURSE
Northolt Prim. Sch.
John Chilton Sch.
West London Academy
Leis. Cen.
TARGET ROUNDABOUT
A40
WESTERN
MANDEVILLE ROAD
Belvue Park
Health Club
Sch. Golf Club
Driving Range
SHARVEL LANE
Downe Barns Fm.
Moat
Lime Tree Park
West End
CHURCH ROAD
A312
Playing Fields
Smith's Farm
NORTHOLT GOLF COURSE
Gifford Primary Sch.
WHITE HART ROUNDABOUT
RECTORY PARK
(Recreation Ground)
PARKWAY
B455
RUISLIP ROAD
KENSINGTON ROAD
Greenford High Sch.
Greenford Sports Cen.
KINGSHILL AVENUE
Belmore Prim. Sch.
Barnhill High Sch.
Playing Fields
GRAND UNION VILLAGE
Cricket Club
King George's Field
Sports & Social Club
Tennis Courts
Reservoir
WILLOW TREE ROBT.
YEADING
Superstore
Public Open Space
GRAND UNION CANAL (PADDINGTON BRANCH)
Durdans Park Primary Sch.
Jubilee Park
Marina
Yeading Schs.
Warren Park
Playing Field
Brook
Spikes Bridge Track
Sports Grd.
Bowling Green
OSSIE GARVIN ROUNDABOUT
UXBRIDGE ROAD
THE BROADWAY
A4020
Hillingdon Cycling Circuit
Superstore
Warehouse
HAYES BRIDGE RETAIL PARK
UXBRIDGE RD. RETAIL PK.
SOUTHALL
HIGH ST.
UXBRIDGE

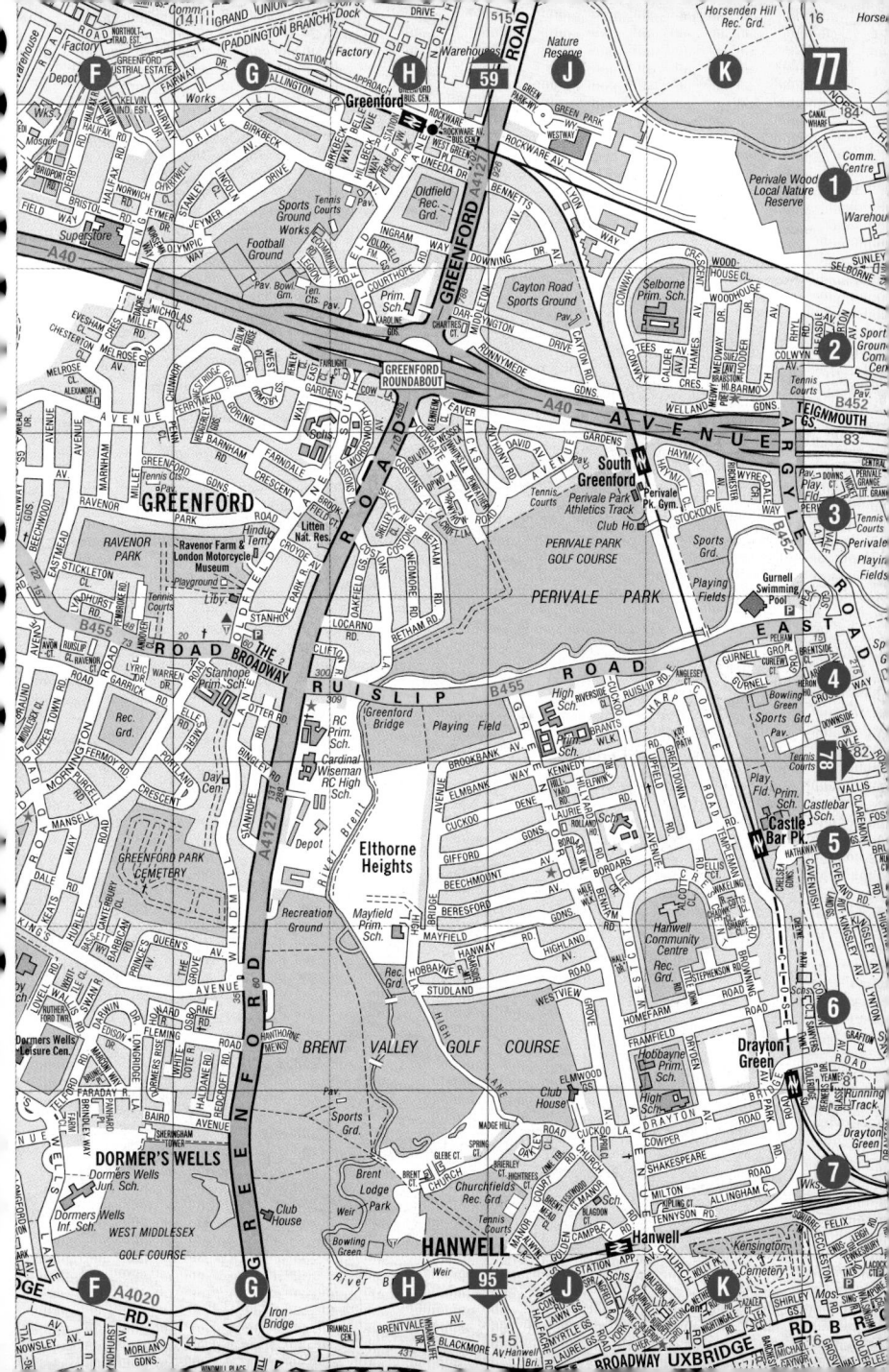

77
78
59
95
F
G
H
J
K
1
2
3
4
5
6
7
GREENFORD
HANWELL
DORMER'S WELLS
Elthorne Heights
Greenford
South Greenford
Castle Bar Pk.
Drayton Green
Hanwell
GRAND UNION
(PADDINGTON BRANCH)
Lyon's Dock
Horsenden Hill Rec. Grd.
Nature Reserve
Perivale Wood Local Nature Reserve
GREENFORD INDUSTRIAL ESTATE
NORTHOLT TRAD. EST.
KELVIN IND. EST.
Superstore
Mosque
Oldfield Rec. Grd.
Sports Ground Works
Football Ground
Cayton Road Sports Ground
Selborne Prim. Sch.
GREENFORD ROUNDABOUT
A40
A4127
A4020
B455
B452
GREENFORD ROAD
RUISLIP ROAD
WESTERN AVENUE
ARGYLE ROAD
EAST ROAD
THE BROADWAY
OLDFIELD LANE
GREENFORD AVENUE
RAVENOR PARK
Ravenor Farm & London Motorcycle Museum
Litten Nat. Res.
Hindu Tem.
Stanhope Prim. Sch.
PERIVALE PARK GOLF COURSE
PERIVALE PARK
Perivale Park Athletics Track
Perivale Pk. Gym.
Gurnell Swimming Pool
Sports Grd.
Playing Fields
Greenford Bridge
Playing Field
High Sch.
Prim. Sch.
RC Prim. Sch.
Cardinal Wiseman RC High Sch.
Depot
River Brent
GREENFORD PARK CEMETERY
Recreation Ground
Mayfield Prim. Sch.
Hanwell Community Centre
Rec. Grd.
Hobbayne Prim. Sch.
BRENT VALLEY GOLF COURSE
Club House
Dormers Wells Leisure Cen.
Dormers Wells Jun. Sch.
Dormers Wells Inf. Sch.
WEST MIDDLESEX GOLF COURSE
Brent Lodge Park
Churchfields Rec. Grd.
Bowling Green
Iron Bridge
Kensington Cemetery
Running Track
UXBRIDGE ROAD
BROADWAY

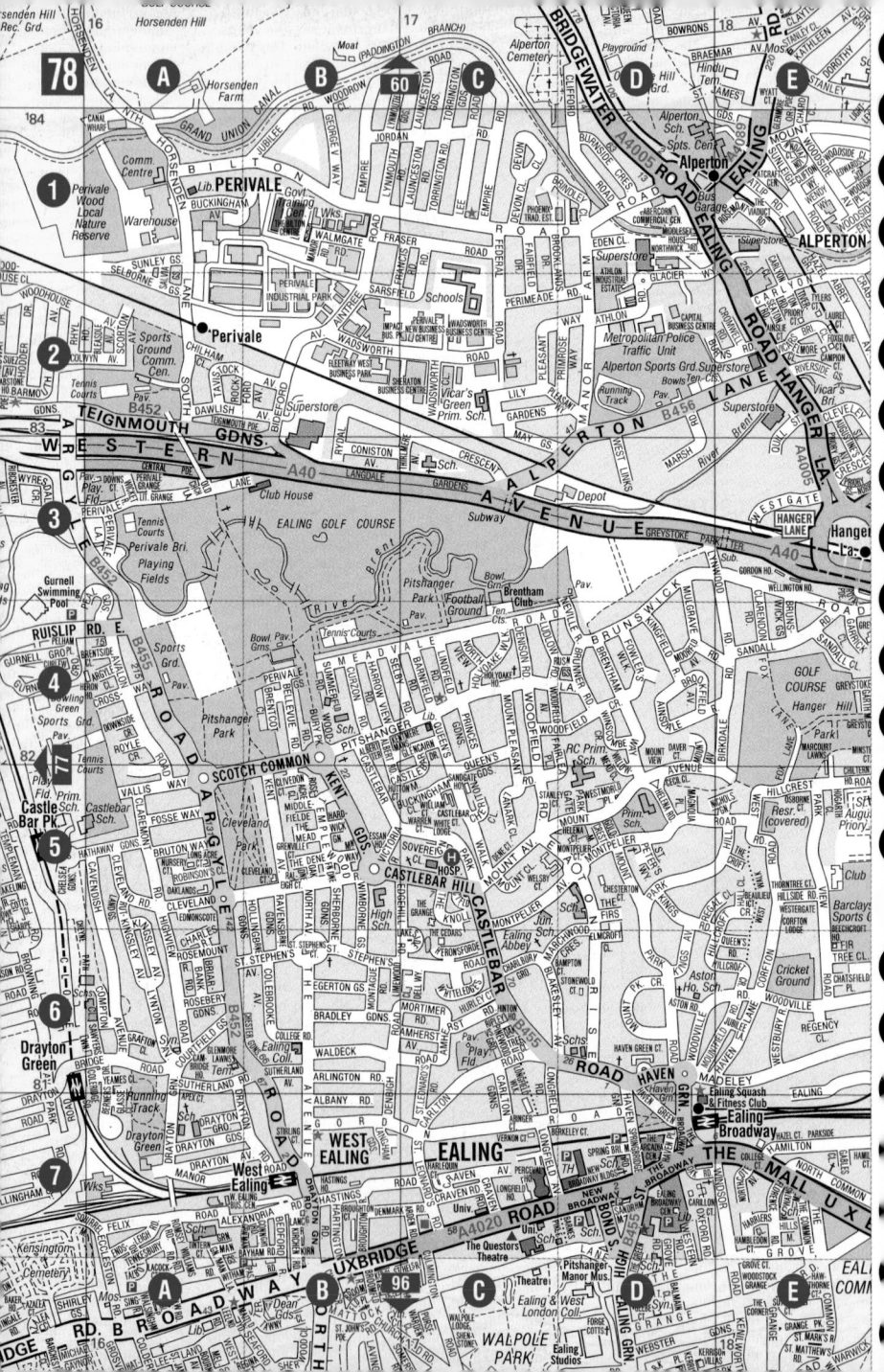

78
A
B
C
D
E
1
2
3
4
5
6
7
60
77
96
PERIVALE
Perivale
Perivale Wood Local Nature Reserve
Horsenden Hill
Horsenden Farm
GRAND UNION CANAL
(PADDINGTON BRANCH)
Alperton Cemetery
Alperton
ALPERTON
WESTERN AVENUE
ALPERTON LANE
EALING ROAD
HANGER LANE
Hanger La.
BRIDGEWATER ROAD
Metropolitan Police Traffic Unit
Alperton Sports Grd.
EALING GOLF COURSE
Pitshanger Park
Brentham Club
Gurnell Swimming Pool
RUISLIP RD. E.
ARGYLE ROAD
SCOTCH COMMON
CASTLEBAR HILL
CASTLEBAR ROAD
Castle Bar Pk.
Drayton Green
WEST EALING
West Ealing
EALING
Ealing Broadway
HAVEN GRN.
THE MALL
UXBRIDGE ROAD
BROADWAY
The Questors Theatre
Pitshanger Manor Mus.
Ealing & West London Coll.
WALPOLE PARK
Ealing Studios
Kensington Cemetery
Ealing Squash & Fitness Club
Ealing Abbey
Cleveland Park
Hanger Hill
GOLF COURSE
Cricket Ground
A40
A4005
A4020
B452
B455
B456

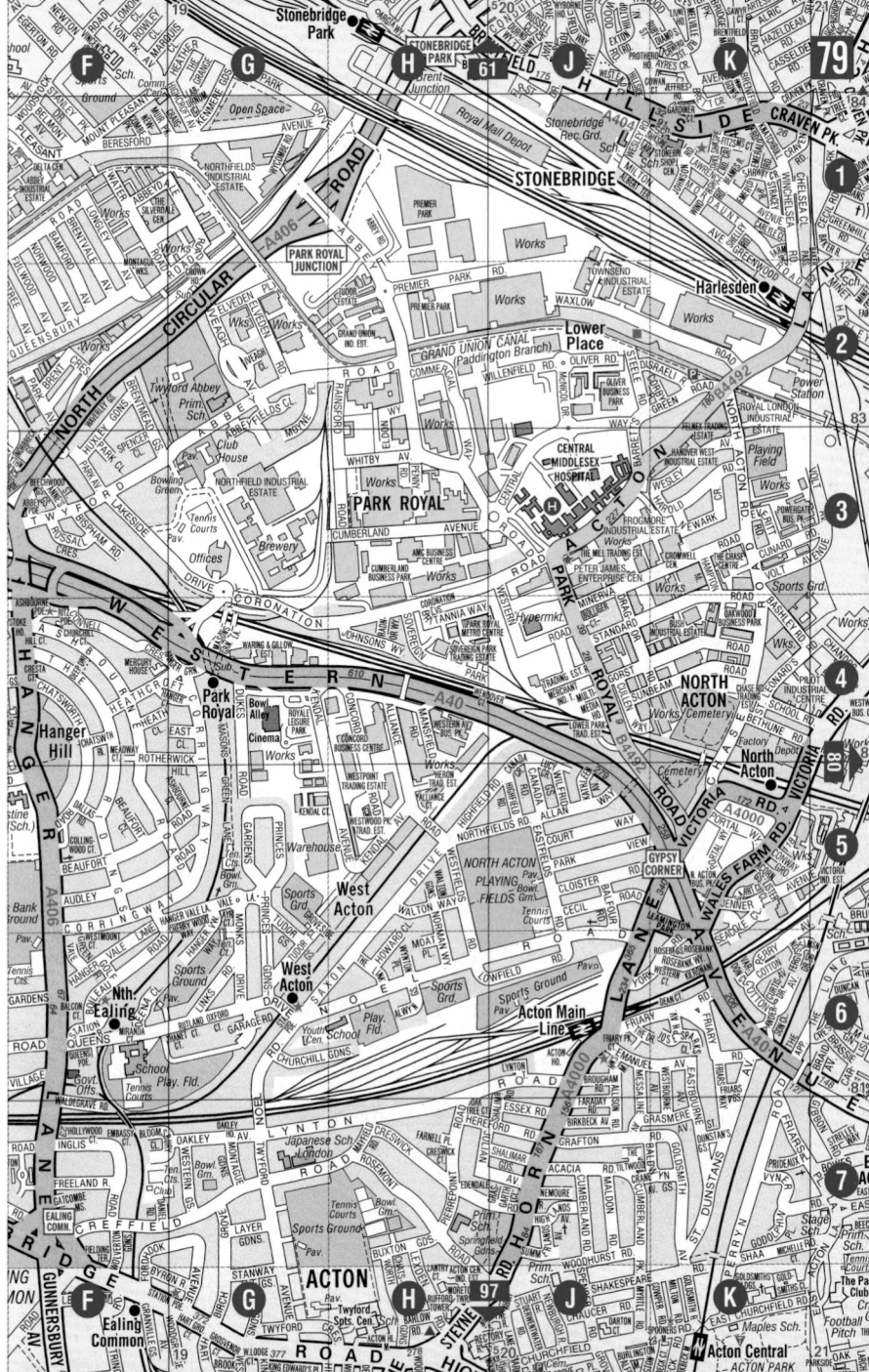

79
Stonebridge Park
STONEBRIDGE PARK
61
Brent Junction
Royal Mail Depot
Stonebridge Rec. Grd.
STONEBRIDGE
HILLSIDE
CRAVEN PK.
NORTHFIELDS INDUSTRIAL ESTATE
PREMIER PARK
PARK ROYAL JUNCTION
NORTH CIRCULAR ROAD
A406
A404
Harlesden
TOWNSEND INDUSTRIAL ESTATE
Lower Place
GRAND UNION CANAL (Paddington Branch)
Twyford Abbey Prim. Sch.
OLIVER BUSINESS PARK
CENTRAL MIDDLESEX HOSPITAL
ROYAL LONDON INDUSTRIAL ESTATE
Power Station
PARK ROYAL
Brewery
Offices
FROGMORE INDUSTRIAL ESTATE
ACTON LANE
B4492
PARK ROYAL ROAD
WESTERN AVENUE
A40
Park Royal
Hanger Hill
Bowl. Alley
Cinema
NORTH ACTON
Cemetery
North Acton
A4000
VICTORIA RD.
GYPSY CORNER
NORTH ACTON PLAYING FIELDS
West Acton
Sports Ground
Acton Main Line
Nth. Ealing
EALING COMN.
Japanese Sch. London
ACTON
Twyford Spts. Cen.
Ealing Common
Acton Central
ACTON PARK
97
HORN LANE
HANGER LANE
GUNNERSBURY AV.
EAST ACTON
The Park Club
Football Pitch
Maples Sch.
F G H J K
1 2 3 4 5 6 7
19
520
21
80
82
83
84
81

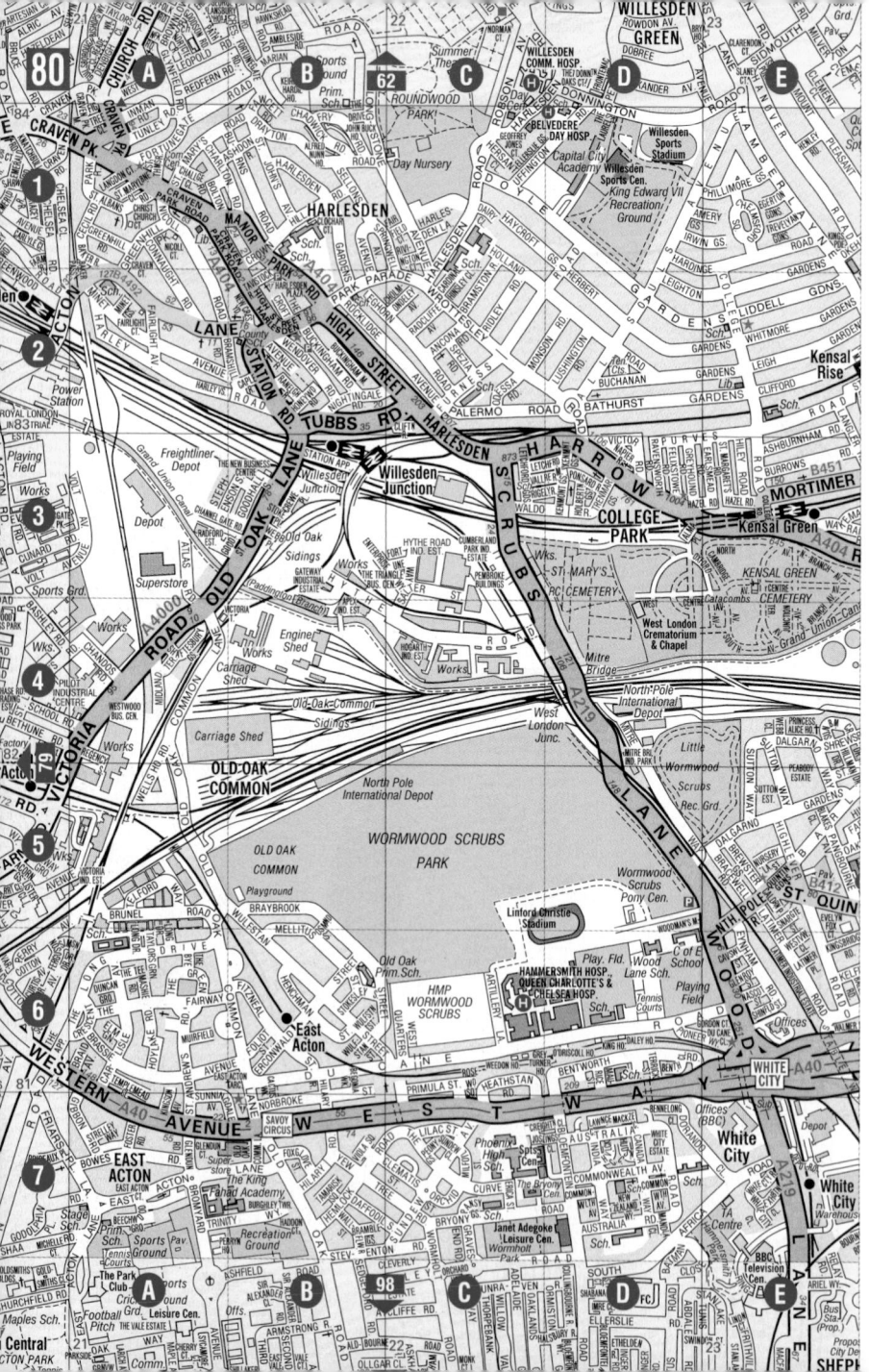
80
62
98
79
A
B
C
D
E
1
2
3
4
5
6
7
WILLESDEN GREEN
HARLESDEN
Roundwood Park
Willesden Comm. Hosp.
Belvedere Day Hosp.
Willesden Sports Stadium
Willesden Sports Cen.
Capital City Academy
King Edward VII Recreation Ground
Day Nursery
Kensal Rise
Kensal Green
COLLEGE PARK
Kensal Green Cemetery
St. Mary's RC Cemetery
West London Crematorium & Chapel
Willesden Junction
Freightliner Depot
Grand Union Canal
Power Station
Superstore
Old Oak Sidings
Hythe Road Ind. Est.
Cumberland Park Ind. Estate
Pembroke Buildings
Engine Shed
Carriage Shed
Old Oak Common Sidings
North Pole International Depot
West London Junc.
Mitre Bridge
OLD OAK COMMON
WORMWOOD SCRUBS PARK
Little Wormwood Scrubs Rec. Grd.
Wormwood Scrubs Pony Cen.
Linford Christie Stadium
Hammersmith Hosp., Queen Charlotte's & Chelsea Hosp.
HMP Wormwood Scrubs
Old Oak Prim. Sch.
Wood Lane Sch.
East Acton
EAST ACTON
WHITE CITY
White City
Offices (BBC)
BBC Television Cen.
Phoenix High Sch.
Janet Adegoke Leisure Cen.
Wormholt Park
Hammersmith Park
The King Fahad Academy
Recreation Ground
Sports Ground
North Acton
Central Acton Park
Acton
CRAVEN PK.
MANOR PARK RD.
HIGH STREET
HARLESDEN RD.
TUBBS RD.
STATION RD.
OLD OAK LANE
A4000
ROAD
VICTORIA
SCRUBS LANE
A219
HARROW ROAD
A404
MORTIMER
B451
WESTERN AVENUE
A40
WESTWAY
WOOD LANE
DU CANE ROAD
OLD OAK COMMON LANE
AUSTRALIA RD.
COMMONWEALTH AV.
ST. QUINTIN
B412
BATHURST GARDENS
PALERMO ROAD
CHAMBERLAYNE ROAD
LIDDELL GDNS.
DONNINGTON ROAD
DOYLE GARDENS
HARLESDEN GARDENS
PARK PARADE
ACTON LANE
B4492
SAVOY CIRCUS
WELLS HO. RD.
NORTH POLE RD.
LATIMER RD.

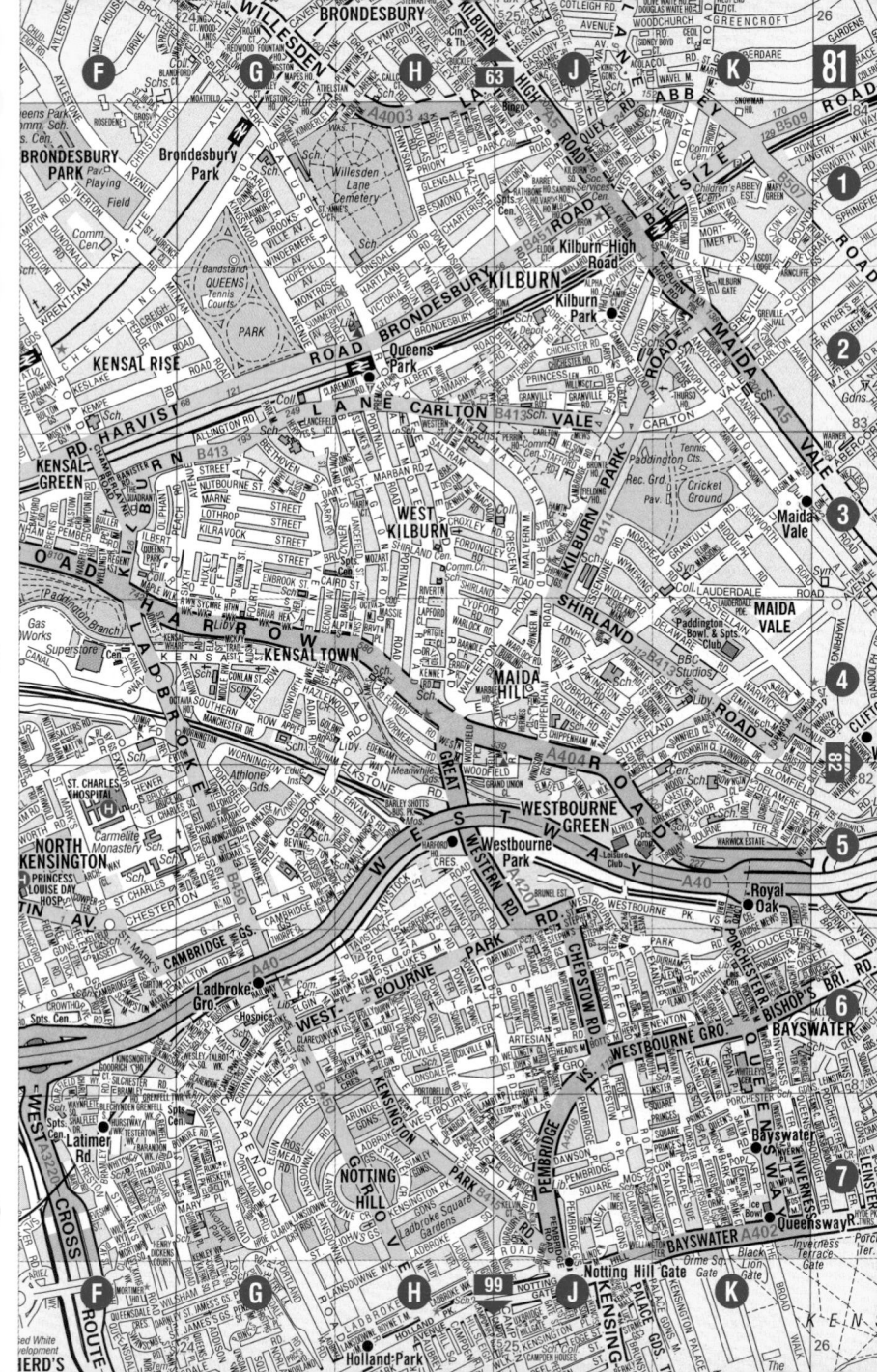
BRONDESBURY
WILLESDEN
KILBURN
63
F
G
H
J
K
1
2
3
4
5
6
7
BRONDESBURY PARK
Brondesbury Park
Willesden Lane Cemetery
Queens Park Comm. Sch.
Playing Field
QUEENS PARK
Tennis Courts
Bandstand
KILBURN
Kilburn High Road
Kilburn Park
Queens Park
KENSAL RISE
KENSAL GREEN
HARVIST RD.
CARLTON VALE
MAIDA VALE
Maida Vale
ABBEY ROAD
BELSIZE ROAD
KILBURN PARK ROAD
SHIRLAND ROAD
Paddington Rec. Grd.
Cricket Ground
Paddington Bowl. & Spts. Club
BBC Studios
WEST KILBURN
KENSAL TOWN
HARROW ROAD
LADBROKE GROVE
MAIDA HILL
WESTBOURNE GREEN
Westbourne Park
WESTWAY
GREAT WESTERN RD.
Gas Works
Superstore
Paddington Branch
GRAND UNION CANAL
Athlone Gds.
ST. CHARLES HOSPITAL
Carmelite Monastery
NORTH KENSINGTON
PRINCESS LOUISE DAY HOSP.
CHESTERTON
CAMBRIDGE GS.
Ladbroke Gro.
Latimer Rd.
Hospice
WESTBOURNE PARK ROAD
CHEPSTOW RD.
WESTBOURNE GRO.
Royal Oak
BAYSWATER
BISHOP'S BRI. RD.
QUEENSWAY
Bayswater
Queensway
Ice Bowl
NOTTING HILL
Ladbroke Square Gardens
PEMBRIDGE
KENSINGTON PARK RD.
BAYSWATER ROAD
Notting Hill Gate
Holland Park
Orme Sq. Gate
Black Lion Gate
Inverness Terrace Gate
WEST CROSS ROUTE
A40
A404
A5
A3220
A402
B413
B450
82
99
24
25
26

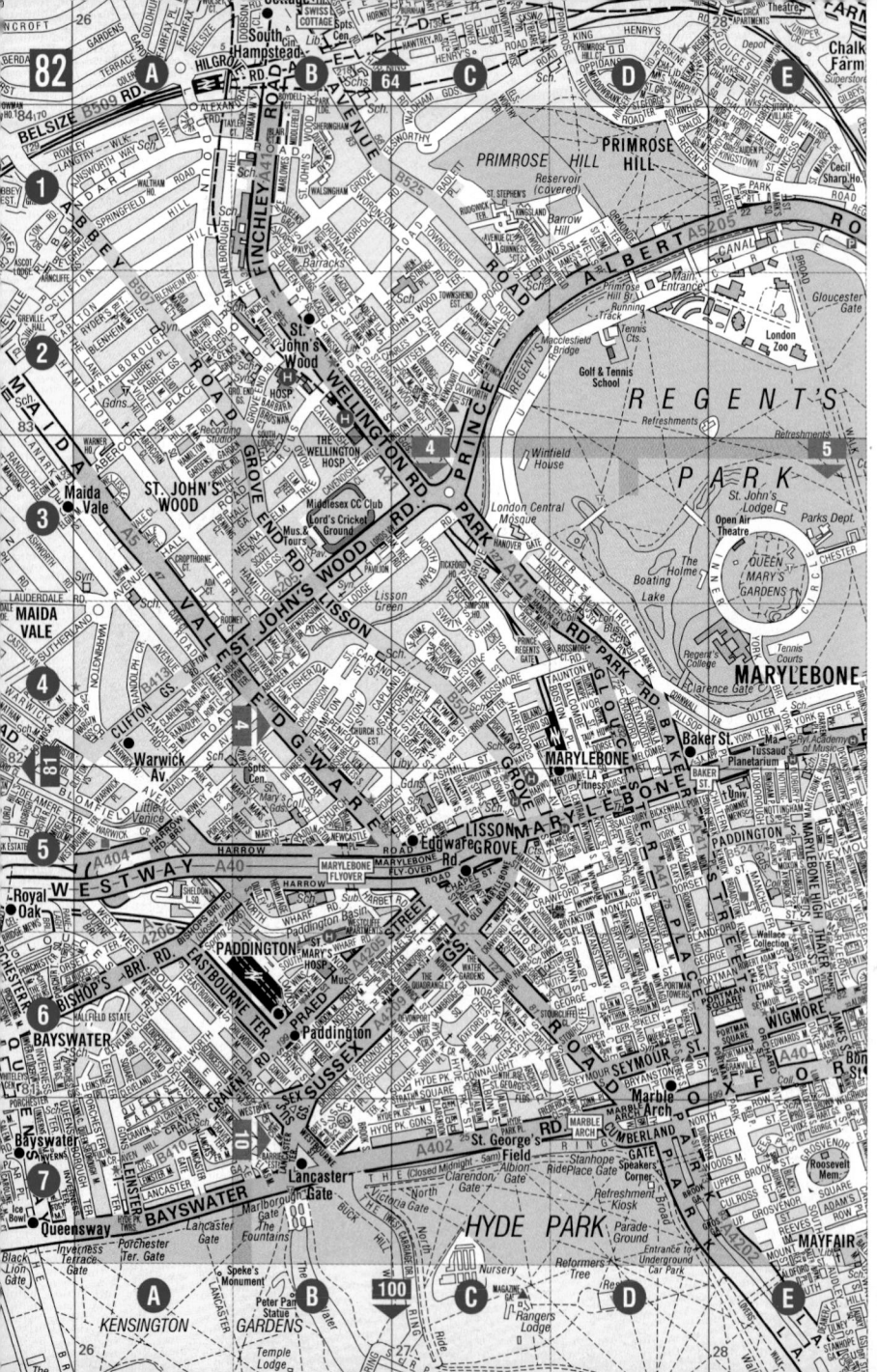

64
4
5
81
4
10
100
A
B
C
D
E
1
2
3
4
5
6
7
South Hampstead
SWISS COTTAGE
Chalk Farm
PRIMROSE HILL
PRIMROSE HILL
Reservoir (covered)
Barrow Hill
BELSIZE RD.
FINCHLEY ROAD
AVENUE
ABBEY ROAD
ALBERT ROAD
PRINCE ALBERT ROAD
St. John's Wood
WELLINGTON RD.
THE WELLINGTON HOSP
Barracks
ST. JOHN'S WOOD
Middlesex CC Club
Lord's Cricket Ground
Mus.& Tours
GROVE END RD.
ST. JOHN'S WOOD RD.
LISSON
Lisson Green
Maida Vale
MAIDA VALE
MAIDA VALE
EDGWARE
Warwick Av.
Little Venice
London Zoo
Golf & Tennis School
REGENT'S PARK
Winfield House
London Central Mosque
Open Air Theatre
QUEEN MARY'S GARDENS
Boating Lake
The Holme
Regent's College
Tennis Courts
St. John's Lodge
Parks Dept.
Clarence Gate
MARYLEBONE
Baker St.
MARYLEBONE
Ma. Tussaud's
Planetarium
Ryl. Academy of Music
Wallace Collection
PADDINGTON ST.
MARYLEBONE HIGH ST.
LISSON GROVE
Edgware Rd.
WESTWAY A40
HARROW ROAD
MARYLEBONE FLYOVER
Paddington Basin
PADDINGTON
ST. MARY'S HOSP
Paddington
PRAED
SUSSEX GARDENS
EASTBOURNE TER.
BISHOP'S BRI. RD.
Royal Oak
BAYSWATER
Bayswater
Queensway
BAYSWATER
Lancaster Gate
Marble Arch
MARBLE ARCH
OXFORD
EDGWARE ROAD
SEYMOUR
PARK LANE
WIGMORE
PORTMAN SQUARE
UPPER BROOK
GROSVENOR
Roosevelt Mem.
MAYFAIR
HYDE PARK
St. George's Field
Speakers' Corner
Stanhope Gate
Refreshment Kiosk
Parade Ground
Reformers Tree
Nursery
Rangers Lodge
Speke's Monument
Peter Pan Statue
The Fountains
Marlborough Gate
Victoria Gate
KENSINGTON GARDENS
Temple Lodge
Porchester Ter. Gate
Black Lion Gate
Inverness Terrace Gate
Lancaster Gate
26
27
28

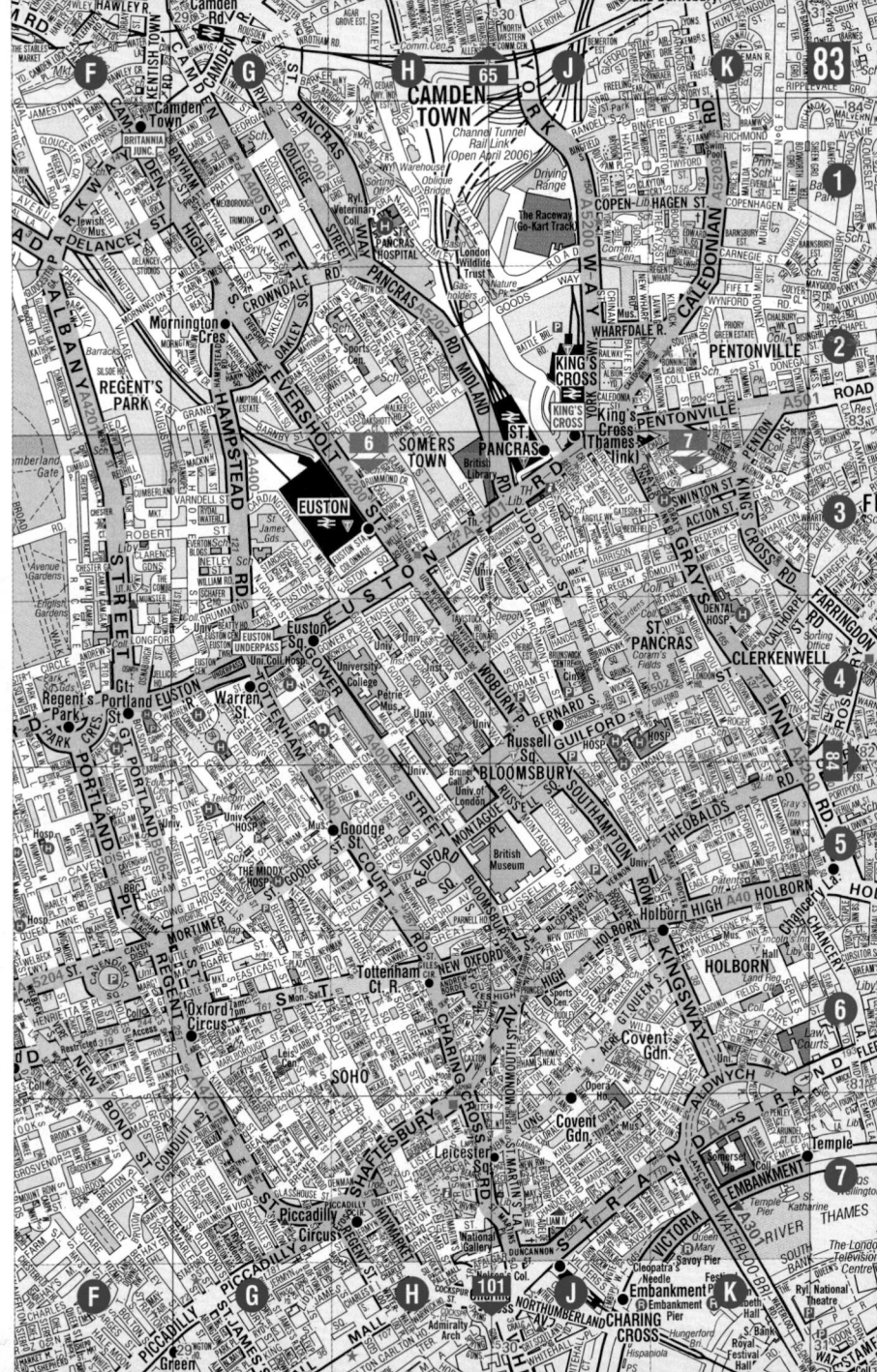

83
F
G
H
J
K
65
1
2
3
4
5
6
7
84
101
6
7
CAMDEN TOWN
Camden Town
Camden Rd.
BRITANNIA JUNC.
KENTISH TOWN RD.
CAMDEN ST.
PARKWAY
DELANCEY ST.
ALBANY ST.
PANCRAS WAY
COLLEGE ST.
CROWNDALE RD.
Channel Tunnel Rail Link (Open April 2006)
Driving Range
The Raceway (Go-Kart Track)
London Wildlife Trust
COPENHAGEN ST.
CALEDONIAN RD.
YORK WAY
A5200
PENTONVILLE
PENTONVILLE ROAD
A501
WHARFDALE R.
KING'S CROSS
King's Cross (Thameslink)
ST. PANCRAS
SOMERS TOWN
British Library
MIDLAND RD.
Mornington Cres.
REGENT'S PARK
HAMPSTEAD RD.
EVERSHOLT ST.
EUSTON
EUSTON RD.
Euston Sq.
EUSTON UNDERPASS
Warren St.
Regent's Park
Gt. Portland St.
ST. PANCRAS
CLERKENWELL
GRAY'S INN RD.
KING'S CROSS RD.
FARRINGDON RD.
Coram's Fields
Russell Sq.
BLOOMSBURY
GUILFORD ST.
BERNARD S.
WOBURN PL.
University College
Petrie Mus.
GOWER ST.
TOTTENHAM CT. RD.
Goodge St.
British Museum
THE MIDDX. HOSP.
PORTLAND PL.
GT. PORTLAND ST.
THEOBALDS RD.
SOUTHAMPTON ROW
Holborn
HIGH HOLBORN
A40
HOLBORN
KINGSWAY
Chancery La.
Tottenham Ct. R.
NEW OXFORD ST.
Oxford Circus
REGENT ST.
SOHO
SHAFTESBURY AV.
CHARING CROSS RD.
Covent Gdn.
Opera Ho.
Leicester Sq.
Piccadilly Circus
PICCADILLY
HAYMARKET
National Gallery
Nelson's Col.
Admiralty Arch
MALL
STRAND
ALDWYCH
Law Courts
Temple
Somerset Ho.
EMBANKMENT
VICTORIA EMBANKMENT
WATERLOO BRI.
Savoy Pier
Cleopatra's Needle
Embankment
Embankment Pier
CHARING CROSS
Hungerford Bri.
RIVER THAMES
Royal Festival Hall
Ryl. National Theatre
The London Television Centre
SOUTH BANK
NEW BOND ST.
CONDUIT ST.
MORTIMER ST.
CAVENDISH SQ.
GROSVENOR ST.
Green Pk.

84
A
B
C
D
E
66
102
83
7
8
9
1
2
3
4
5
6
7
ISLINGTON
Essex Rd.
DE BEAUVOIR TOWN
Angel
PENTONVILLE RD.
FINSBURY
HOXTON
SHOREDITCH
CLERKENWELL
ST. LUKE'S
Old Street
Farringdon
Barbican
Moorgate
LIVERPOOL ST.
City Thameslink
St. Paul's
Bank
Mansion Ho.
Monument
Temple
BLACKFRIARS
SOUTHWARK
CANNON STREET
FENCHURCH ST.
CITY
UPPER STREET
CITY ROAD
GOSWELL RD.
NEW NORTH RD.
ST. JOHN ST.
FARRINGDON RD.
CLERKENWELL RD.
HOLBORN
HOLBORN VIADUCT
CHEAPSIDE
LONDON WALL
BISHOPSGATE
UPPER THAMES STREET
LOWER THAMES ST.
VICTORIA EMB.
STRAND
FLEET ST.
SOUTHWARK BRI.
LONDON BR.
BLACKFRIARS RD.
RIVER THAMES
Charterhouse
Barbican Arts Centre
Tate Modern
Millennium Bridge
Blackfriars Millennium Pier
Bankside Pier
London Bri. City Pier
Tower Millennium Pier
Law Courts
The Temple
St. Paul's Cath.
Lloyds' Bdg
Tower 42
Finsbury Circus
Britannia Centre
Shoreditch Park
Regent's Canal
City Road Basin
Barnard Park
A501
A5201
A1
A10
A1211
A3211
A3
A300
A5200
A201
B100
B144
B501
B502
B515

DALSTON
London Fields
SOUTH HACKNEY
Victoria Fountain
Royal Gate East
VICTORIA PARK
Skew Bridge
Crown Ga. East
Crown Gate West
Gore Gate
St. Agnes Gate
Bonner Hall Bri.
HAGGERSTON
Haggerston
Football Pitch
City Farm
Cambridge Heath
BISHOP'S
Town Hall
GLOBE TOWN
MEATH GDNS.
Warehouses
Suttons Wharf
MILE END
Halls of Residence
MILE END HOSPITAL
Queen Mary University of London
Bethnal Green
BETHNAL GREEN
Shoreditch
SPITALFIELDS
Old Spitalfields Mkt.
Whitechapel
ROYAL LONDON HOSP.
Stepney Green
STEPNEY
Stepney Grn. Pk.
RATCLIFF
Aldgate East
Aldgate
WHITECHAPEL
Tower Gateway
Tower Hill
TOWER HILL
The Tower of London
Tower Beach
St. Katharine's Pier
St. Katharine Docks
Tower Hotel
Shadwell
SHADWELL
Shadwell Basin
King Edward Mem. Park
Shadwell Dock Stairs
RIVER THAMES
ROTHERHITHE TUNNEL
Pelican Stairs
New Crane Stairs
Wapping
John Orwell Sports Cen.
Printing Works
Brussels Wharf
Globe Stairs
Bellamy's Wharf
Aldermans Stairs
COMMERCIAL ROAD
WHITECHAPEL RD.
MILE END RD.
CAMBRIDGE HEATH RD.
CABLE ST.
THE HIGHWAY
EAST SMITHFIELD
VICTORIA PARK RD.
GROVE RD.
BETHNAL GRN. RD.
OLD FORD RD.
ROMAN RD.
MARE ST.
COMMERCIAL ST.
NEW RD.
CANNON ST. RD.
MANSELL ST.
LEMAN ST.
MINORIES
A1208
A1209
A107
A1205
A11
A13
A1203
A1202
A101
A100
B108
B118
B119
B127
B134
B135
B140
B126
F
G
H
J
K
1
2
3
4
5
6
7
67
69
86
15
103
DLR

86
SOUTH HACKNEY
A
B
C
D
E
68
37
38
36
Stratford Marsh
STRATFORD
VICTORIA PARK
Victoria Fountain
Victoria Park Athletics Arena
OLD FORD
Three Colt Bridge
Skew Bridge
Crown Gate East
Crown Gate West
Pudding Mill Lane
OLD FORD
BOW INTERCHANGE
BOW
Bow Church
Bow Rd.
Grove Hall Park
GLOBE TOWN
MILE END
MILE END HOSPITAL
Queen Mary University of London
Mile End
ST. CLEMENT'S HOSPITAL
TOWER HAMLETS CEMETERY
BROMLEY
Bromley-by-Bow
ST. ANDREW'S HOSP.
Devons Rd.
BOW COMMON
Three Mills Green
Three Mills
Superstore
85
82
83
84
Mile End Stadium
Shandy Park
Gas Works
Ragged Sch. Mus.
Go-Kart Track
RATCLIFF
LIMEHOUSE
Bartlett Park
Langdon Park
Limehouse
Limehouse Basin
Westferry
POPLAR
All Saints
Poplar
West India Quay
Canary Wharf
Billingsgate Fish Market
WEST INDIA DOCKS
The Mus. in Docklands
Ratcliff Cross Stairs
RIVER THAMES
LIMEHOUSE REACH
Globe Stairs
Pageant Stairs
Ordnance Wharf
Canary Wharf Pier
Columbia Wharf
Hilton Docklands Pier
WESTFERRY CIRCUS
104
BLACKWALL BASIN
1
2
3
4
5
6
7
A12
A11
A13
A1205
A1261
A1203
B140
B118
B135

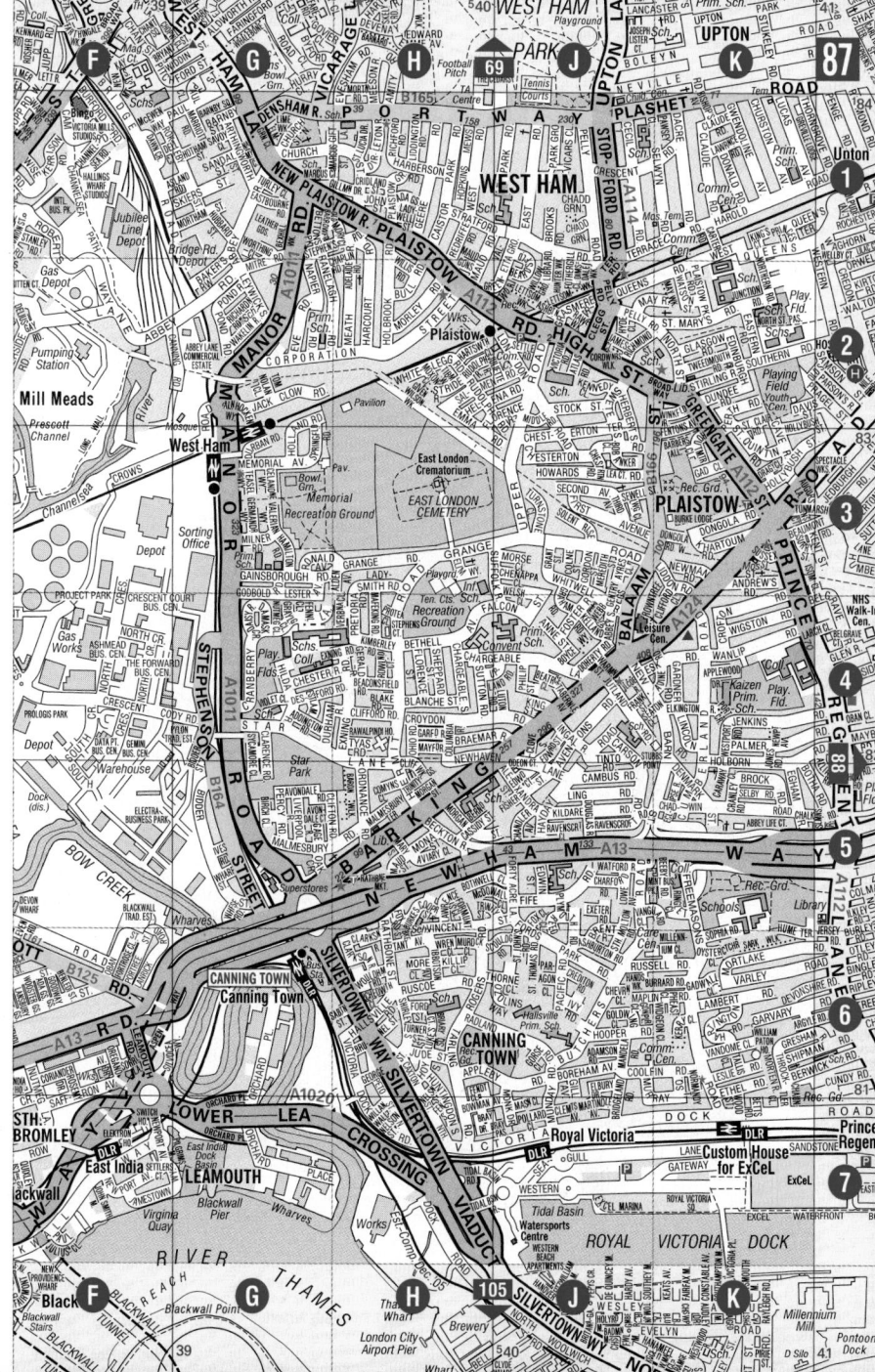
WEST HAM
PARK
69
UPTON
PLASHET
PORTWAY
WEST HAM
NEW PLAISTOW RD.
PLAISTOW RD.
HIGH ST.
GREENGATE ST.
UPTON LA.
STOPFORD RD.
Mill Meads
Prescott Channel
Channelsea
Pumping Station
Gas Depot
Jubilee Line Depot
Bridge Rd. Depot
ABBEY LANE COMMERCIAL ESTATE
West Ham
Plaistow
MANOR RD.
MANOR ROAD
CORPORATION
East London Crematorium
EAST LONDON CEMETERY
Memorial Recreation Ground
Sorting Office
Depot
Gas Works
PROJECT PARK
CRESCENT COURT BUS. CEN.
ASHMEAD BUS. CEN.
THE FORWARD BUS. CEN.
PROLOGIS PARK
Warehouse
ELECTRA BUSINESS PARK
BOW CREEK
Recreation Ground
PLAISTOW
BALAAM ST.
PRINCE REGENT LANE
BARKING RD.
NEWHAM WAY
Star Park
STEPHENSON STREET
Superstores
Wharves
BLACKWALL TRAD. EST.
CANNING TOWN
Canning Town
CANNING TOWN
SILVERTOWN WAY
LOWER LEA CROSSING
LEAMOUTH
East India
STH. BROMLEY
Blackwall
Virginia Quay
Blackwall Pier
RIVER THAMES
Blackwall Point
Royal Victoria
Custom House for ExCeL
Prince Regent
ExCeL
Tidal Basin
Watersports Centre
ROYAL VICTORIA DOCK
SILVERTOWN VIADUCT
London City Airport Pier
Brewery
Millennium Mill
Pontoon Dock
105
SILVERTOWN WY.
NORTH WOOLWICH
88
Schools
Library
Rec. Grd.
Hallsville Prim. Sch.
NHS Walk-In Cen.
Leisure Cen.
Playing Field Youth Cen.
Kaizen Prim. Sch.

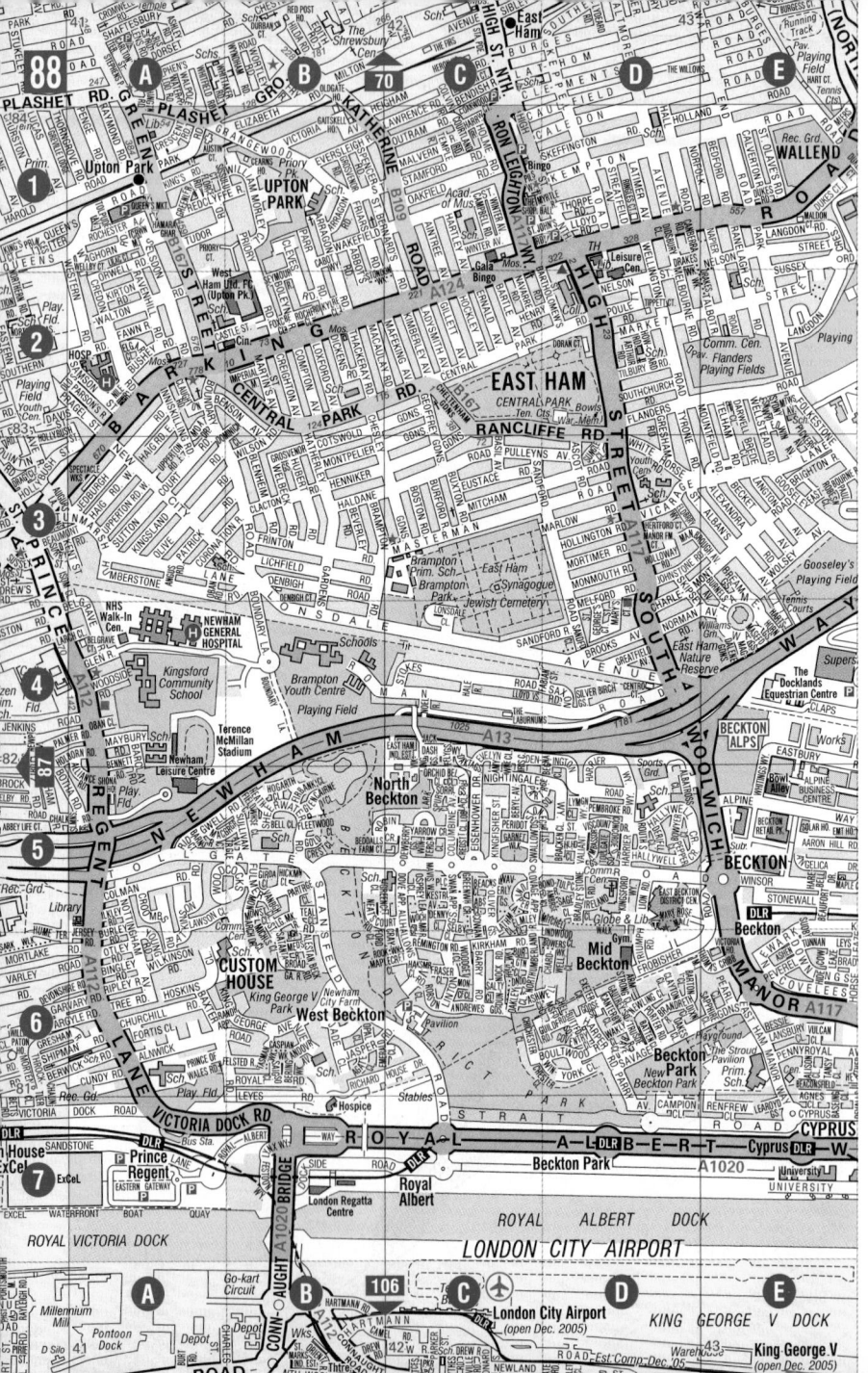

A
B
C
D
E
1
2
3
4
5
6
7
70
87
106
PLASHET RD.
PLASHET GRO.
GREEN STREET
KATHERINE ROAD
B109
HIGH ST. NTH.
RON LEIGHTON WY.
A117
East Ham
Upton Park
UPTON PARK
WALLEND
BARKING ROAD
A124
CENTRAL PARK RD.
B167
EAST HAM
CENTRAL PARK
RANCLIFFE RD.
HIGH STREET SOUTH
West Ham Utd. FC (Upton Pk.)
Gala Bingo
Leisure Cen.
Comm. Cen.
Flanders Playing Fields
Brampton Prim. Sch.
Brampton Park
East Ham Synagogue
Jewish Cemetery
NHS Walk-In Cen.
NEWHAM GENERAL HOSPITAL
Kingsford Community School
Brampton Youth Centre
Playing Field
East Ham Nature Reserve
Gooseley's Playing Field
The Docklands Equestrian Centre
BECKTON ALPS
NEWHAM WAY
A13
Terence McMillan Stadium
Newham Leisure Centre
North Beckton
WOOLWICH MANOR WAY
REGENT LANE
A112
PRINCE REGENT
TOLLGATE RD.
BECKTON
Beckton
Mid Beckton
CUSTOM HOUSE
King George V Park
West Beckton
Newham City Farm
Beckton Park
New Beckton Park
Hospice
Stables
VICTORIA DOCK RD.
ROYAL ALBERT WAY
CYPRUS
Cyprus
Prince Regent
Royal Albert
Beckton Park
A1020
University
ExCeL
London Regatta Centre
ROYAL VICTORIA DOCK
ROYAL ALBERT DOCK
LONDON CITY AIRPORT
CONNAUGHT BRIDGE
Go-kart Circuit
Millennium Mill
Pontoon Dock
London City Airport (open Dec. 2005)
KING GEORGE V DOCK
King George V (open Dec. 2005)

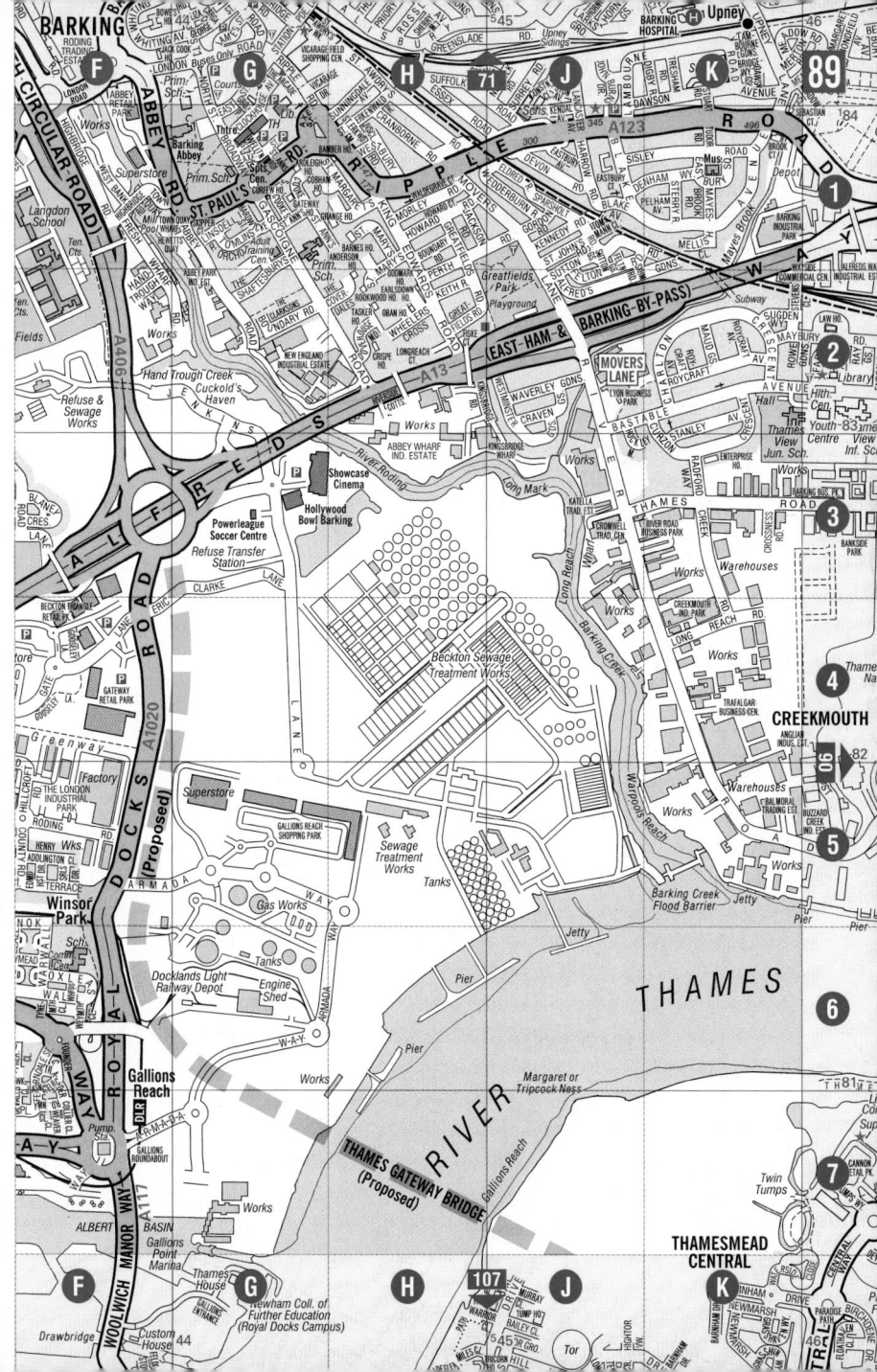

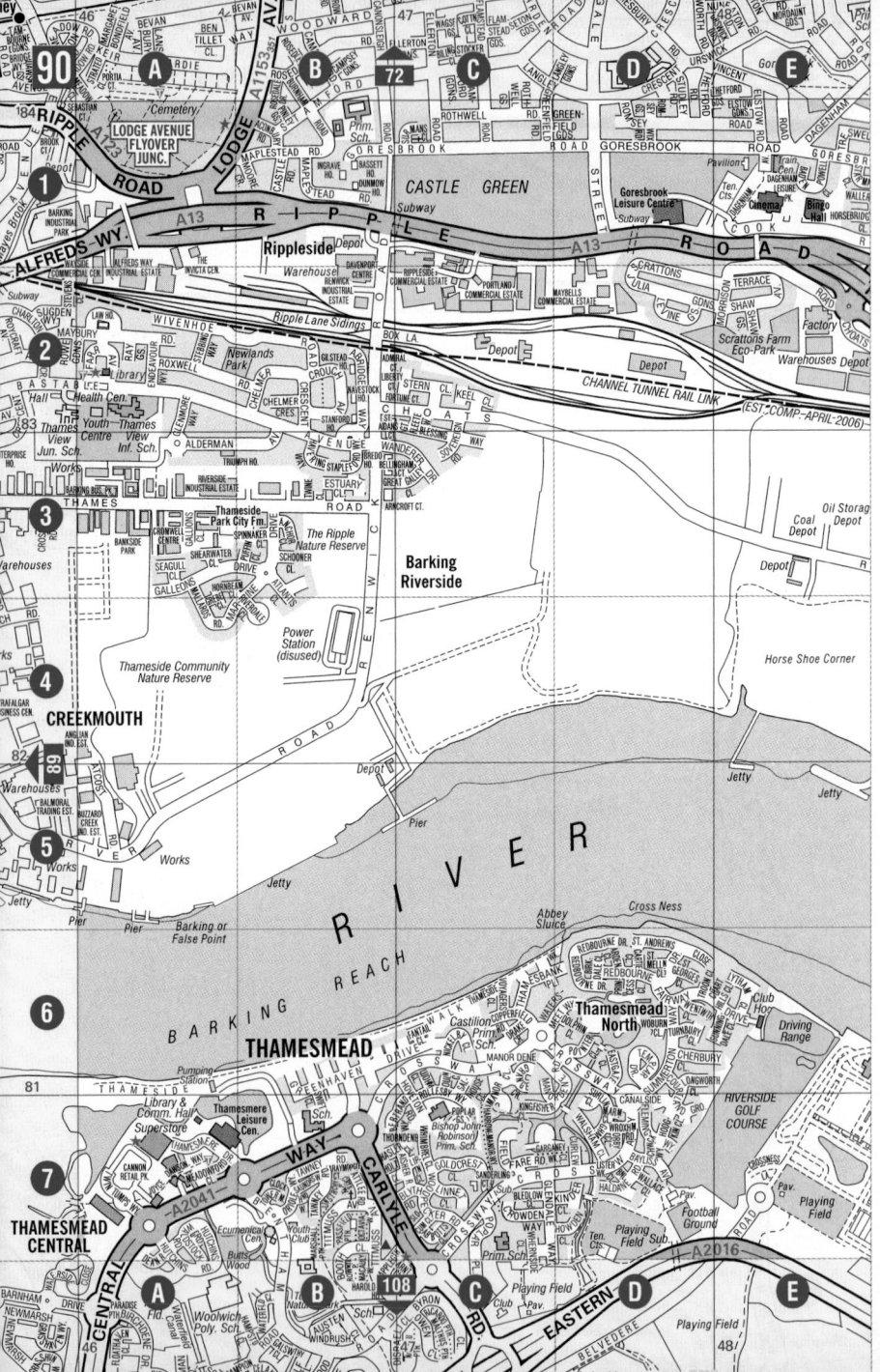

90
72
89
108
A
B
C
D
E
1
2
3
4
5
6
7
46
47
48
184
83
82
81
LODGE AVENUE FLYOVER JUNC.
Cemetery
RIPPLE ROAD
LODGE AV.
A1153
A123
A13
RIPPLE ROAD
ALFREDS WY.
BARKING INDUSTRIAL PARK
WAYSIDE COMMERCIAL CEN.
ALFREDS WAY INDUSTRIAL ESTATE
THE INVICTA CEN.
Rippleside
Depot
Warehouse
DAVENPORT CENTRE
RENWICK INDUSTRIAL ESTATE
RIPPLESIDE COMMERCIAL ESTATE
PORTLAND COMMERCIAL ESTATE
MAYBELLS COMMERCIAL ESTATE
Subway
CASTLE GREEN
GORESBROOK ROAD
WOODWARD RD.
STAMFORD RD.
ROTHWELL RD.
MAPLESTEAD RD.
Prim. Sch.
Goresbrook Leisure Centre
Pavilion
Train. Cen.
DAGENHAM LEISURE PK.
Cinema
Bingo Hall
Ten. Cts.
COOK
HORSEBRIDGE
SCRATTONS TERRACE
MORRISON
SHAW AV.
LEVINE GDNS.
Factory
Scrattons Farm Eco-Park
Warehouses
Depot
Ripple Lane Sidings
BOX LA.
CHANNEL TUNNEL RAIL LINK
(EST. COMP. APRIL 2006)
WIVENHOE RD.
ROXWELL
Newlands Park
Library
BASTABLE
Hall
Health Cen.
Youth Centre
Thames View Inf. Sch.
Thames View Jun. Sch.
ALDERMAN
TRIUMPH HO.
Works
RIVERSIDE INDUSTRIAL ESTATE
BARKING BUS. PK.
THAMES ROAD
CHOATS
ESTUARY CL.
RENWICK ROAD
Thameside Park City Fm.
The Ripple Nature Reserve
BANKSIDE PARK
CROMWELL CENTRE
Barking Riverside
Power Station (disused)
Thameside Community Nature Reserve
Warehouses
CREEKMOUTH
ANGLIAN IND. EST.
BALMORAL TRADING EST.
BUZZARD CREEK IND. EST.
RIVER RD.
Works
Jetty
Pier
Depot
Barking or False Point
Coal Depot
Oil Storage Depot
Horse Shoe Corner
RIVER
BARKING REACH
Abbey Sluice
Cross Ness
THAMESMEAD
Thamesmead North
Castilion Prim. Sch.
Club Ho.
Driving Range
RIVERSIDE GOLF COURSE
CROSSWAY
Pumping Station
THAMESIDE
Library & Comm. Hall
Superstore
Thamesmere Leisure Cen.
CANNON RETAIL PK.
WAY
A2041
CARLYLE
THAMESMEAD CENTRAL
Ecumenical Cen.
Youth Club
Butts Wood
Bishop John Robinson Prim. Sch.
Sch.
Prim. Sch.
Football Ground
Playing Field
Playing Field
Pav.
Ten. Cts.
A2016
EASTERN
Playing Field
Woolwich Poly. Sch.
Waterfield Canal
CENTRAL
BARNHAM DRIVE
NEWMARSH
BELVEDERE
Playing Field
Club

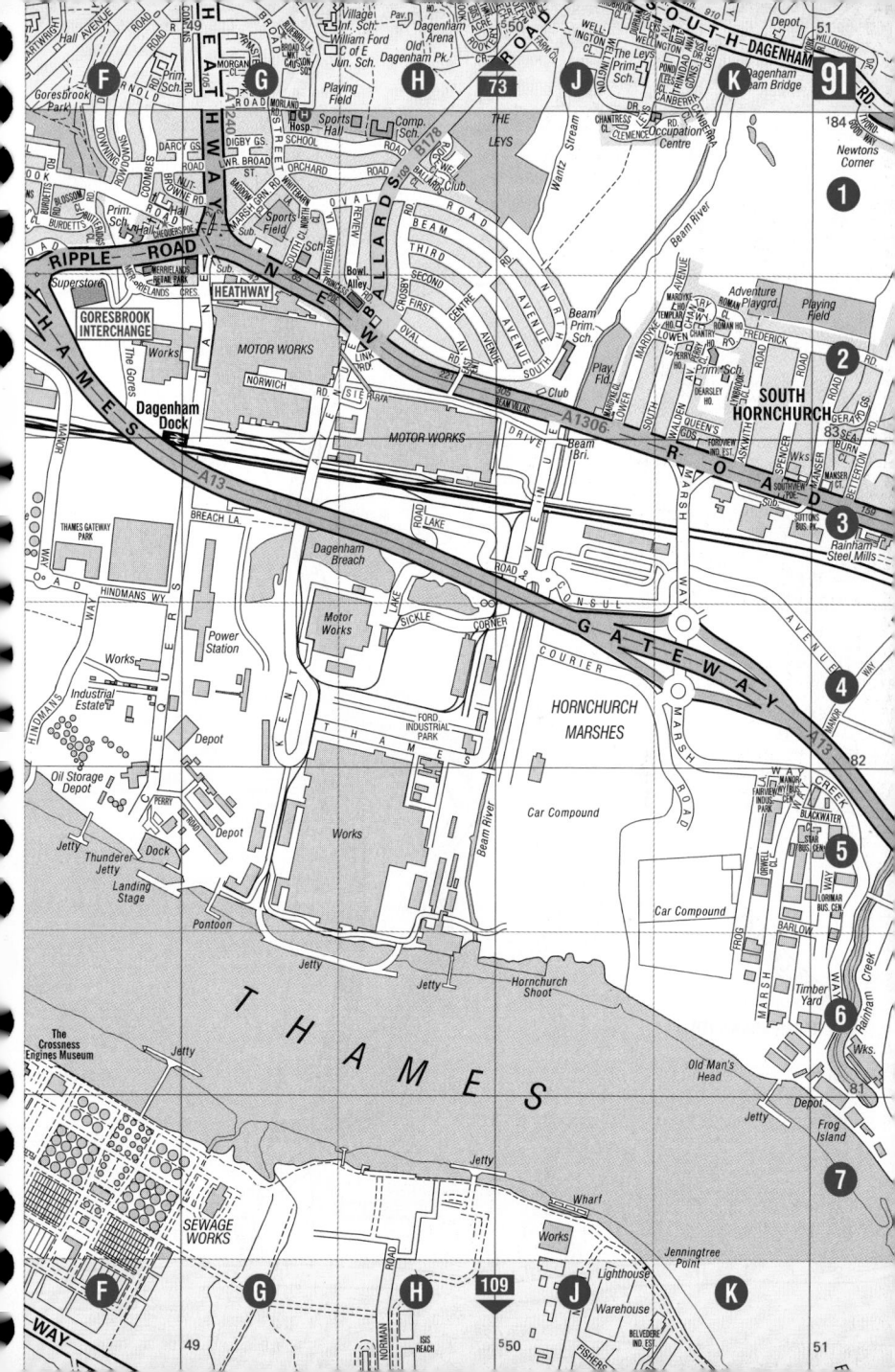

91
73
109
F
G
H
J
K
1
2
3
4
5
6
7
49
550
51
184
83
82
81
SOUTH DAGENHAM
RIPPLE ROAD
HEATHWAY
A1240
BALLARDS
B178
A1306
A13
THAMES
GATEWAY
GORESBROOK INTERCHANGE
Superstore
Dagenham Dock
MOTOR WORKS
Motor Works
Power Station
Dagenham Breach
FORD INDUSTRIAL PARK
HORNCHURCH MARSHES
Car Compound
SOUTH HORNCHURCH
Rainham Steel Mills
Newtons Corner
Dagenham Beam Bridge
Occupation Centre
THE LEYS
Wantz Stream
Beam River
Beam Prim. Sch.
Adventure Playgrd.
Playing Field
Old Dagenham Pk.
Dagenham Arena
Village Inf. Sch.
William Ford C of E Jun. Sch.
Goresbrook Park
Oil Storage Depot
Industrial Estate
THAMES GATEWAY PARK
Thunderer Jetty
Landing Stage
Pontoon
Hornchurch Shoot
Old Man's Head
Frog Island
Rainham Creek
Timber Yard
The Crossness Engines Museum
SEWAGE WORKS
Jenningtree Point
Lighthouse
Warehouse
BELVEDERE IND. EST.
ISIS REACH
Wharf

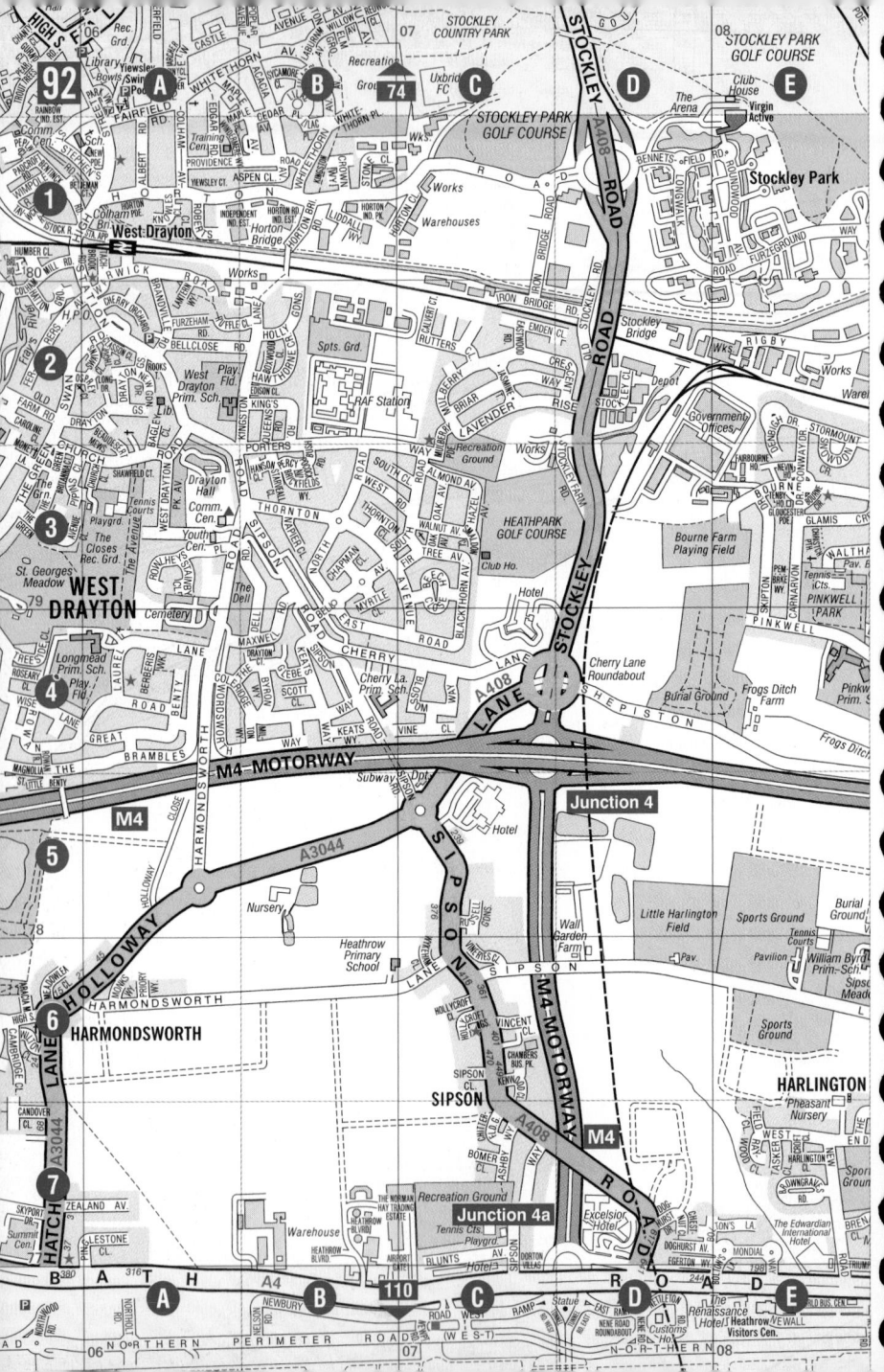
92
74
110
WEST DRAYTON
HARMONDSWORTH
SIPSON
HARLINGTON
Stockley Park
STOCKLEY COUNTRY PARK
STOCKLEY PARK GOLF COURSE
West Drayton
Horton Bridge
Stockley Bridge
RAF Station
Spts. Grd.
Government Offices
HEATHPARK GOLF COURSE
Club Ho.
Bourne Farm Playing Field
PINKWELL PARK
Cherry Lane Roundabout
Cherry La. Prim. Sch.
Burial Ground
Frogs Ditch Farm
M4 MOTORWAY
Junction 4
Junction 4a
A408
A3044
A4
STOCKLEY ROAD
HOLLOWAY LANE
SIPSON ROAD
SIPSON LANE
HARMONDSWORTH LANE
HORTON ROAD
BATH ROAD
NORTHERN PERIMETER ROAD
CHERRY LANE
SHEPISTON LANE
Little Harlington Field
Sports Ground
Wall Garden Farm
Heathrow Primary School
Nursery
Recreation Ground
Warehouse
Excelsior Hotel
The Edwardian International Hotel
The Renaissance Hotel
Heathrow Visitors Cen.
Customs Ho.
West Drayton Prim. Sch.
Longmead Prim. Sch.
St. Georges Meadow
The Closes Rec. Grd.
Drayton Hall
Cemetery
The Dell
Uxbridge FC
Virgin Active
The Arena
Club House
Pheasant Nursery
William Byrd Prim. Sch.
Pinkwell Prim. Sch.
Tennis Cts.
Pavilion
Hotel
Works
Warehouses
Depot
Yiewsley Swimming Pool
Library
06
07
08
77
78
79
80
A
B
C
D
E
1
2
3
4
5
6
7

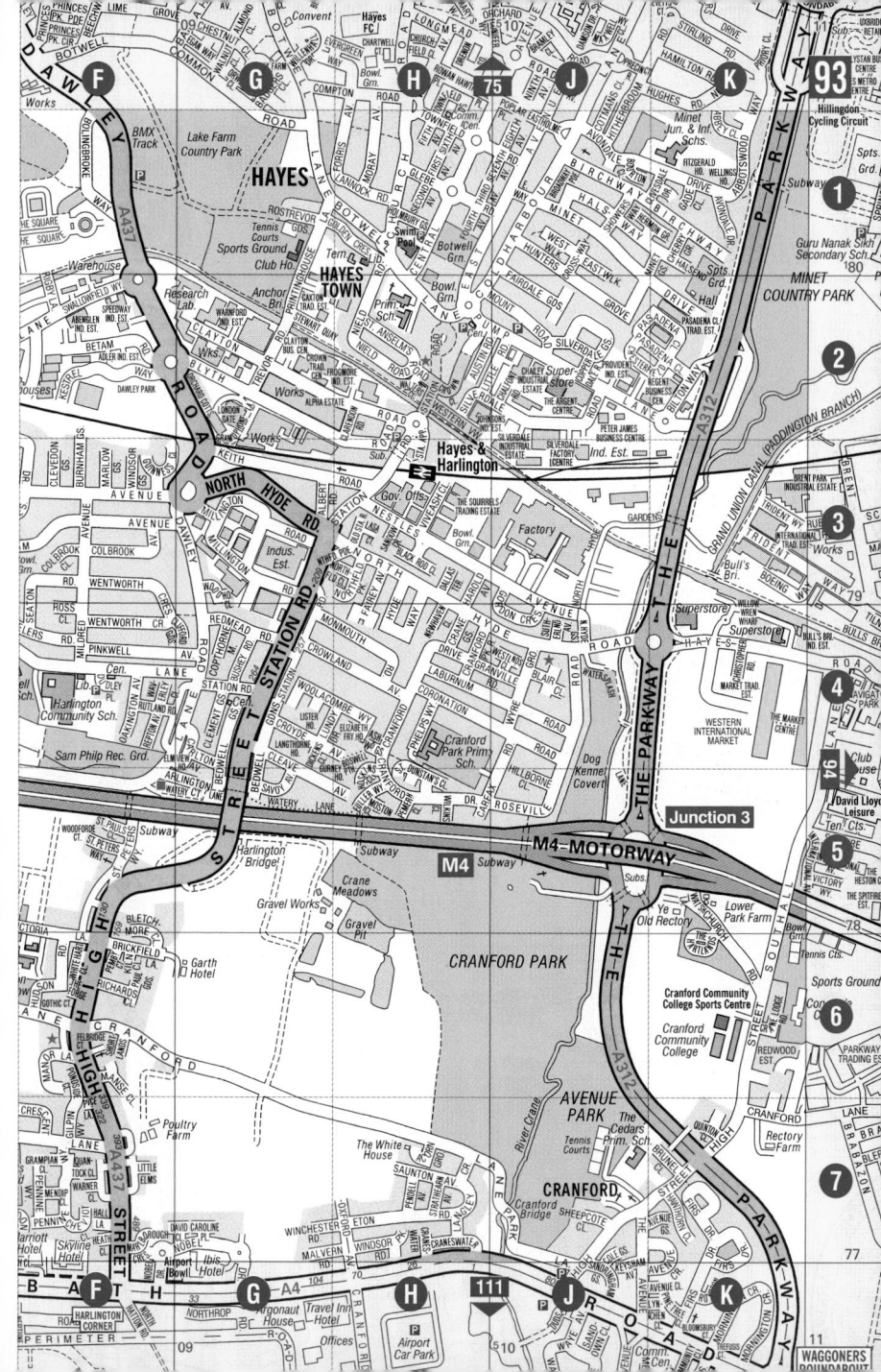

93
75
94
111
F
G
H
J
K
1
2
3
4
5
6
7
HAYES
HAYES TOWN
Hayes & Harlington
Hayes FC
Lake Farm Country Park
BMX Track
Convent
Hillingdon Cycling Circuit
Minet Jun. & Inf. Schs.
MINET COUNTRY PARK
Guru Nanak Sikh Secondary Sch.
Botwell Grn.
Swim Pool
Sports Ground
Club Ho.
Research Lab.
Anchor Bri.
Warehouse
Works
DAWLEY PARK
Gov. Offs.
Factory
Indus. Est.
Superstore
WESTERN INTERNATIONAL MARKET
THE MARKET CENTRE
GRAND UNION CANAL (PADDINGTON BRANCH)
Bull's Bri.
Junction 3
M4 MOTORWAY
M4
Subway
Harlington Bridge
Crane Meadows
Gravel Works
Gravel Pit
CRANFORD PARK
Dog Kennel Covert
Ye Old Rectory
Lower Park Farm
Cranford Community College Sports Centre
Cranford Community College
AVENUE PARK
The Cedars Prim. Sch.
CRANFORD
Cranford Bridge
River Crane
Rectory Farm
Garth Hotel
Poultry Farm
The White House
Harlington Community Sch.
Sam Philp Rec. Grd.
Cranford Park Prim. Sch.
David Lloyd Leisure
Skyline Hotel
Marriott Hotel
Airport Bowl
Ibis Hotel
Argonaut House
Travel Inn Hotel
Airport Car Park
Offices
HARLINGTON CORNER
WAGGONERS ROUNDABOUT
THE PARKWAY
A312
A437
A4
BATH ROAD
DAWLEY ROAD
NORTH HYDE RD.
STATION RD.
HIGH STREET
HAYES ROAD
PERIMETER ROAD

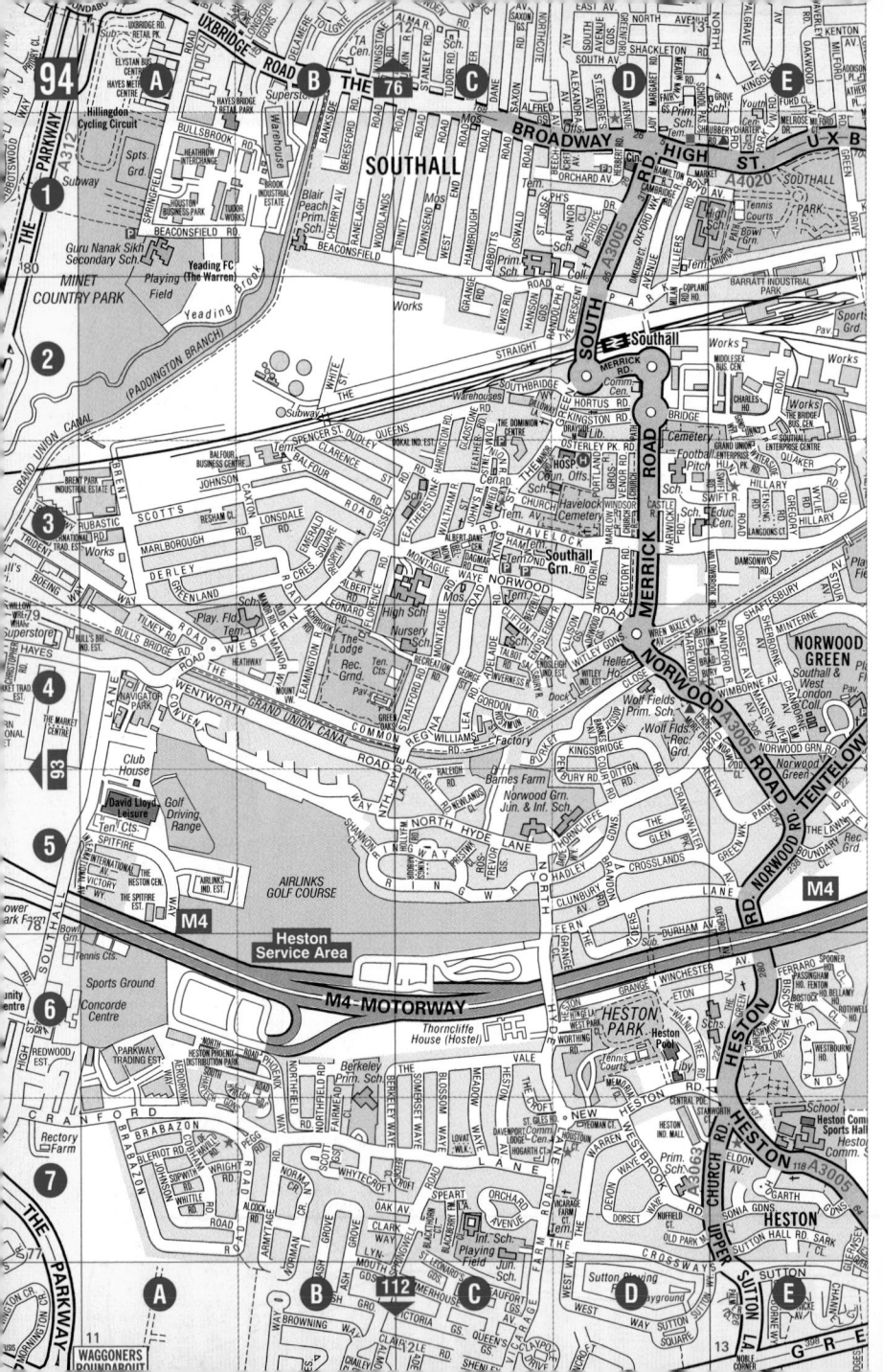
94
76
93
112
SOUTHALL
NORWOOD GREEN
HESTON
HESTON PARK
M4
M4-MOTORWAY
Heston Service Area
AIRLINKS GOLF COURSE
MINET COUNTRY PARK
GRAND UNION CANAL
(PADDINGTON BRANCH)
Yeading Brook
Hillingdon Cycling Circuit
Guru Nanak Sikh Secondary Sch.
Yeading FC (The Warren)
UXBRIDGE ROAD
THE BROADWAY
HIGH ST.
A4020
A3005
A3063
A312
THE PARKWAY
SOUTH RD.
MERRICK ROAD
NORWOOD ROAD
TENTELOW
NORTH HYDE LANE
WESTERN ROAD
HAVELOCK RD.
BEACONSFIELD RD.
THE STRAIGHT
CRANFORD
SOUTHALL PARK
Southall
Havelock Cemetery
Southall Grn.
Heston Pool
David Lloyd Leisure
Golf Driving Range
Sports Ground
Concorde Centre
Thorncliffe House (Hostel)
Sutton Playing Fields
BARRATT INDUSTRIAL PARK
PARKWAY TRADING EST.
Heston Comm. Sports Hall
WAGGONERS ROUNDABOUT
A
B
C
D
E
1
2
3
4
5
6
7
11
12
13

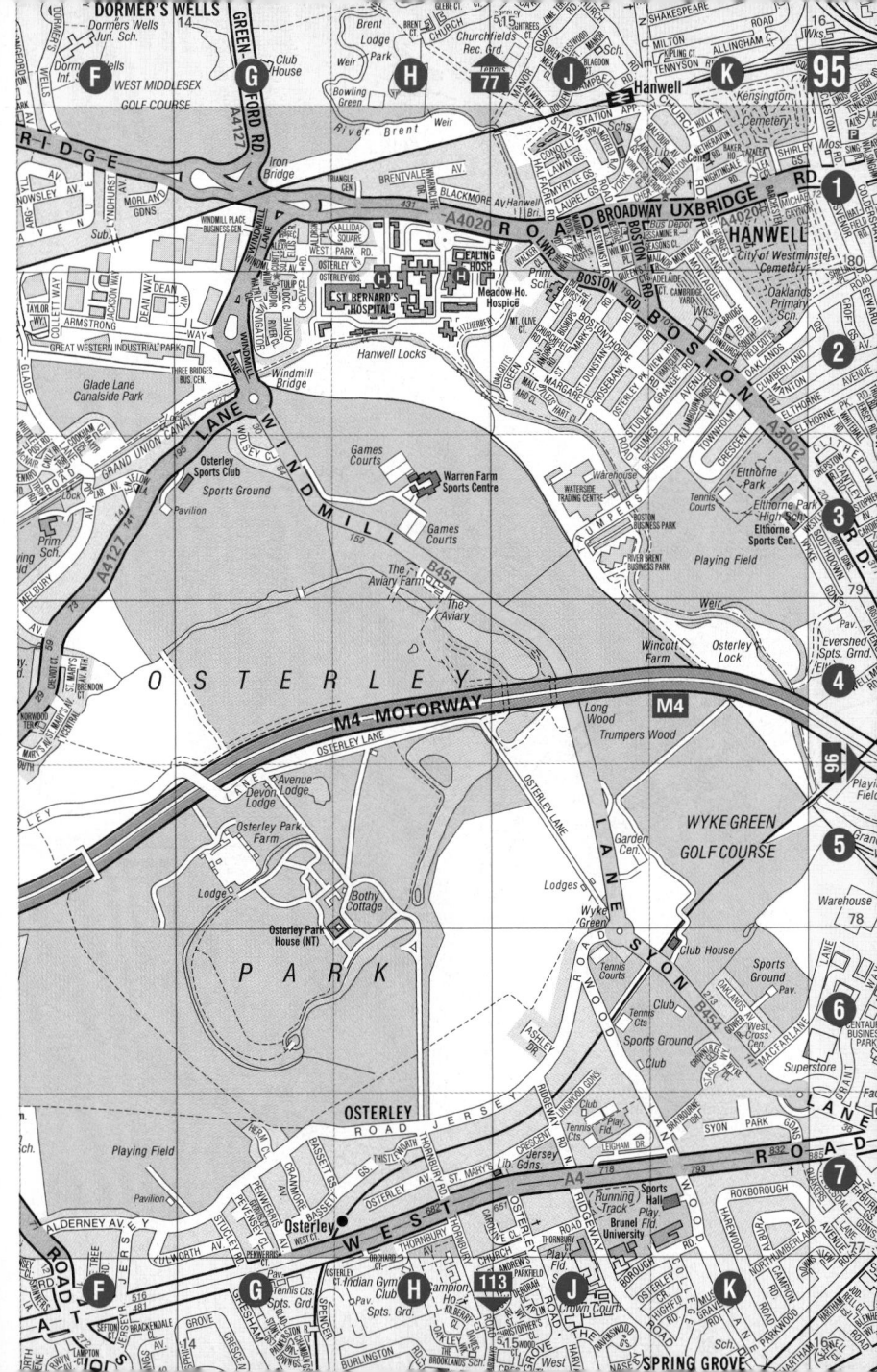
95
DORMER'S WELLS
Dormers Wells Jun. Sch.
Dormers Wells Inf. Sch.
WEST MIDDLESEX GOLF COURSE
GREENFORD RD.
A4127
Club House
Brent Lodge Park
Weir
Bowling Green
River Brent
Churchfields Rec. Grd.
77
Hanwell
Kensington Cemetery
Iron Bridge
UXBRIDGE RD.
BROADWAY
A4020
HANWELL
City of Westminster Cemetery
Oaklands Primary Sch.
BLACKMORE AV.
BRENTVALE AV.
WINDMILL PLACE BUSINESS CEN.
EALING HOSP.
ST. BERNARD'S HOSPITAL
Meadow Ho. Hospice
BOSTON RD.
A3002
GREAT WESTERN INDUSTRIAL PARK
THREE BRIDGES BUS. CEN.
Glade Lane Canalside Park
Windmill Bridge
Hanwell Locks
GRAND UNION CANAL
Osterley Sports Club
Sports Ground
Pavilion
Games Courts
Warren Farm Sports Centre
WINDMILL LANE
B454
The Aviary Farm
The Aviary
WATERSIDE TRADING CENTRE
BOSTON BUSINESS PARK
RIVER BRENT BUSINESS PARK
TRUMPERS WAY
Elthorne Park
Elthorne Park High Sch.
Elthorne Sports Cen.
Playing Field
Weir
Osterley Lock
Wincott Farm
Evershed Spts. Grnd.
OSTERLEY
M4 MOTORWAY
M4
Long Wood
Trumpers Wood
96
OSTERLEY LANE
Avenue Lodge
Devon Lodge
Osterley Park Farm
WYKE GREEN GOLF COURSE
Garden Cen.
Lodge
Lodges
Bothy Cottage
Osterley Park House (NT)
Wyke Green
PARK
SYON LANE
Club House
Tennis Courts
Sports Ground
Warehouse
Superstore
Sports Hall
Running Track
Brunel University
Crown Court
OSTERLEY
JERSEY ROAD
Playing Field
Pavilion
Osterley
GREAT WEST ROAD
A4
113
Indian Gym Club
Campion Ho.
SPRING GROVE
F
G
H
J
K
1
2
3
4
5
6
7

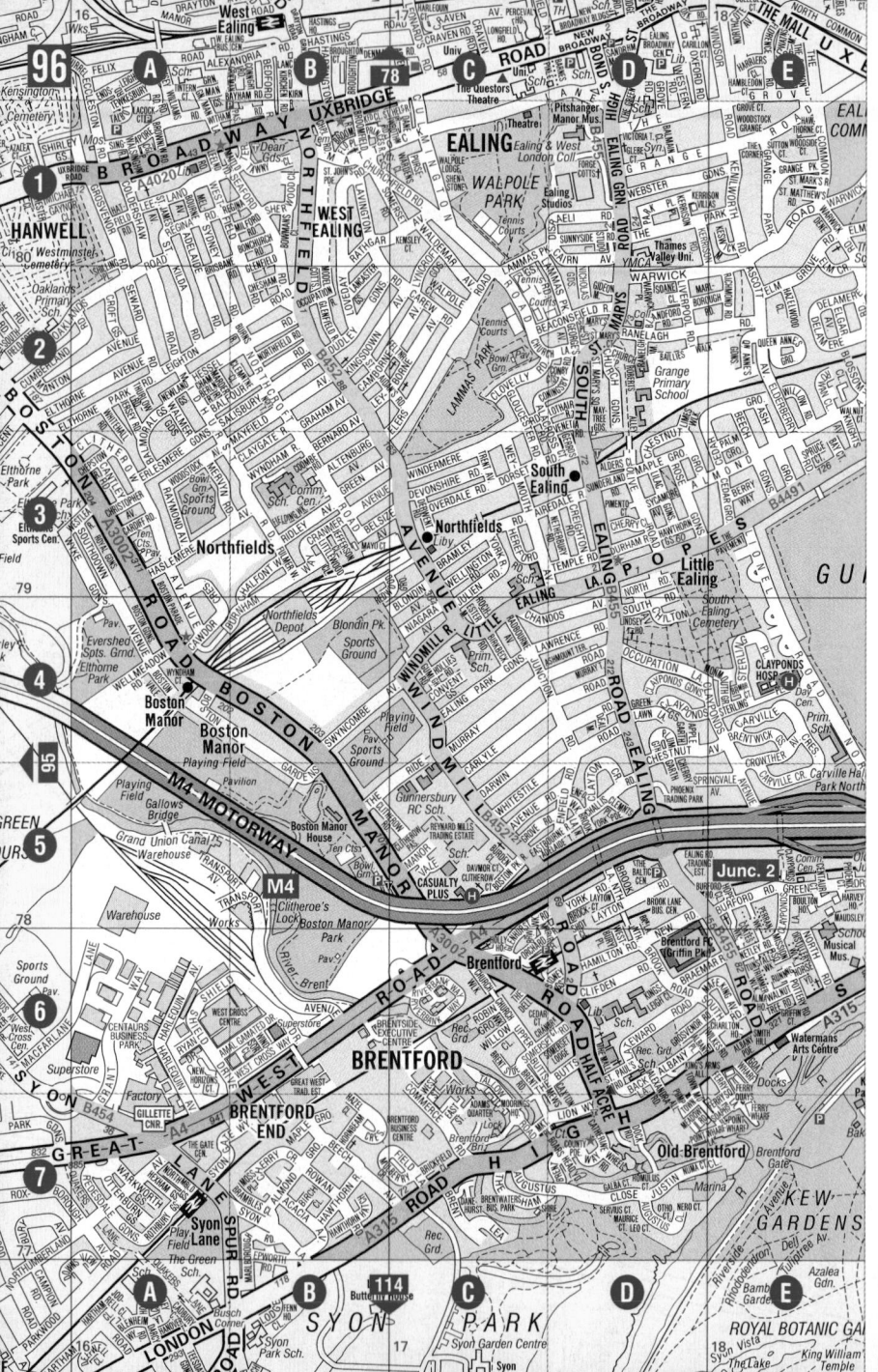

96
78
95
114
West Ealing
EALING
WEST EALING
HANWELL
Northfields
South Ealing
Little Ealing
Boston Manor
BRENTFORD
BRENTFORD END
Old Brentford
Brentford
Syon Lane
SYON PARK
KEW GARDENS
ROYAL BOTANIC GA
UXBRIDGE ROAD
BROADWAY
NORTHFIELD AVENUE
BOSTON ROAD
BOSTON MANOR ROAD
M4 MOTORWAY
GREAT WEST ROAD
HIGH ROAD
SOUTH EALING ROAD
ST. MARYS ROAD
POPES LA.
WINDMILL ROAD
HALF ACRE
SYON LANE
LONDON ROAD
WALPOLE PARK
LAMMAS PARK
Junc. 2
Pitshanger Manor Mus.
The Questors Theatre
Ealing Studios
Thames Valley Uni.
Grange Primary School
Northfields Depot
Blondin Pk.
South Ealing Cemetery
Gunnersbury RC Sch.
Boston Manor House
Boston Manor Park
Grand Union Canal
River Brent
Brentford FC (Griffin Pk.)
Watermans Arts Centre
Musical Mus.
CLAYPONDS HOSP.
CASUALTY PLUS
Kensington Cemetery
Westminster Cemetery
Syon Garden Centre
Butterfly House
Syon Park Sch.
King William Temple
The Lake
Syon Vista
A4020
A3002
B452
B455
B4491
B454
A315
A4
M4

97
EAST ACTON
F
G
H
J
K
79
ACTON
Ealing Common
EALING COMN.
GUNNERSBURY LANE
A406
A4020
HIGH ST.
THE VALE
STEYNE RD.
HORN LA.
Acton Central
ACTON PARK
Maples Sch.
The Park Club
Acton & W. London Coll.
Reynolds Sports Cen.
Acton High Sch.
Twyford Spts. Cen.
Popefield Playing Flds.
Southfields Rec. Grd.
SOUTHFIELD
B491
B490
A4000
Acton Town
SOUTH ACTON
South Acton
ACTON GREEN
BEDFORD PARK
THE AVENUE
SOUTH PARADE
B409
GUNNERSBURY PARK
Museum
Boating Lake
Nurseries
Bowling Green
Miniature Golf Course
Refreshment Pavilion
Tennis Courts
PARK
Potomac (Fish Pond)
Kensington Cemetery
Kew East Junc.
Acton Sports Club
Works
GUNNERSBURY
CHISWICK PARK
Esporta Health & Fitness
Chiswick Pk.
Acton Grn. Comn.
Chiswick Common
Nature Res.
Gunnersby Junc.
CHISWICK HIGH RD.
A315
M4
M4 MOTORWAY
A4
CHISWICK RBT.
Gunnersbury
HEATHFIELD TER.
A3000
98
TURNHAM GREEN
Kew Bridge
Brentford Fountain Leis. Cen.
Steam Mus.
WELLESLEY
KEW BRIDGE
A205
Junc.1
GT. WEST RD.
CEDARS RD.
ELLESMERE RD.
HOGARTH LANE
CHISWICK
Strand on the Green
Kew Pier
Oliver's Island
Brentford Ait
Botanical Library
Kew Green
Kew Gardens Gallery
Main Gate
Orangery
Alpine Ho.
Princess of Wales Conservatory
KEW
KEW GREEN
MORTLAKE RD.
A307
Seven Sisters Walk
Plants & People Exhibition
Palm House
The Pond
Rose Garden
Victoria Ga.
Temple of Bellona
Cumberland Ga.
KEW GARDENS RD.
Kew Gds.
Public Record Office
Nature Reserve
Chiswick House
Cricket Ground
Temple
Sports Hall
ALEXANDRA AV.
A316
Chiswick
Chiswick Cemetery
BURLINGTON LANE
GREAT CHERTSEY RD.
GROVE PARK
Sports Ground
115
1
2
3
4
5
6
7

98
80
97
116
EAST ACTON
A
B
C
D
E
1
2
3
4
5
6
7
The King Fahad Academy
Recreation Ground
Janet Adegoke Leisure Cen.
Wormholt Park
BBC Television Centre
QPR FC
White City
Sports Ground
The Park Club
Cricket Ground
Football Pitch
Leisure Cen.
THE VALE ESTATE
ACTON PARK
ACTON PARK ESTATE
THE VALE
UXBRIDGE ROAD
A4020
Shepherd's Bush
SHEPHERD'S BUSH
A219
Wendell Park
Cathnor Park
Goldhawk Rd.
A402
B408
GOLDHAWK RD.
SOUTHFIELD RD.
BEDFORD PARK
B491
Ravenscourt Park
Adventure Playground
RAVENSCOURT PARK HOSP.
PADDENSWICK RD.
Turnham Green
Stamford Brook
Ravenscourt Park
Hammersmith
Lyric Theatre
CHISWICK HIGH RD.
A315
KING ST.
CHISWICK LA.
A316
GREAT WEST ROAD
A4
HAMMERSMITH
Homefield Recreation Ground
Hammersmith Pier
Furnival Gdns.
St. Pauls School
Playing Field
Chiswick Eyot
Chiswick Lodge
Brewery
Swedish Sch.
Riverside Studios
HAMMERSMITH BRI.
Apollo
HOGARTH LA.
HOGARTH RBT.
TURNHAM GREEN
CHISWICK
Chiswick House
Temple
BURLINGTON LA.
Church Wharf
Corney Reach
Chiswick Pier
Nature Reserve
The Harrodian Sch.
Castelnau
A306
CASTELNAU
B350
LONSDALE
LONDON WETLAND CENTRE
Peter Scott Visitor Centre
Riverside Recreation Ground
Sports Ground
RIVER THAMES
Blakes Wharves
Barn Elms
21
22
23

99
NOTTING HILL
KENSINGTON
Notting Hill Gate
KENSINGTON GARDENS
The Orangery
Round Pond
Kensington Palace
Palace Gate
KENSINGTON RD.
Holland Park
HOLLAND PARK
King George VI Memorial Youth Hostel
Holland Ho.
Theatre
Cricket Field
Commonwealth Inst.
Art Gallery & Mus.
Town Hall
High St. Kensington
Shepherd's Bush
HOLLAND PARK
Kensington Olympia
Olympia
Brook Green
HAMMERSMITH
WEST KENSINGTON
West Kensington
Barons Court
Hammersmith Cemetery
The Queen's Club
CHARING CROSS HOSP.
EARL'S COURT
Earl's Court
Earls Court Exhibition Building
EMPRESS STATE BUILDING
Gibbs Green School
West Brompton
Brompton Cemetery
WEST BROMPTON
Gloucester Rd.
SOUTH KENSINGTON
100
Chelsea FC (Stamford Bridge)
Fulham Broadway
FULHAM BROADWAY
Fulham Pools
Fulham Cemetery
FULHAM
WALHAM GREEN
Eel Brook Common
Gas Works
SANDS END
81
117
HOLLAND PARK AVENUE
NOTTING HILL GATE
HOLLAND ROAD
KENSINGTON HIGH STREET
KENSINGTON ROAD
CROMWELL ROAD
HAMMERSMITH ROAD
TALGARTH ROAD
WEST CROMWELL ROAD
NORTH END ROAD
OLD BROMPTON ROAD
LILLIE ROAD
DAWES ROAD
FULHAM PALACE ROAD
FULHAM ROAD
KING'S RD.
EARL'S COURT ROAD
WARWICK ROAD
REDCLIFFE GDNS.
FINBOROUGH RD.
GLOUCESTER RD.
A3220
A402
A315
A4
A4204
B405
A219
A3218
A3219
A304
A308
B317
F
G
H
J
K
1
2
3
4
5
6
7

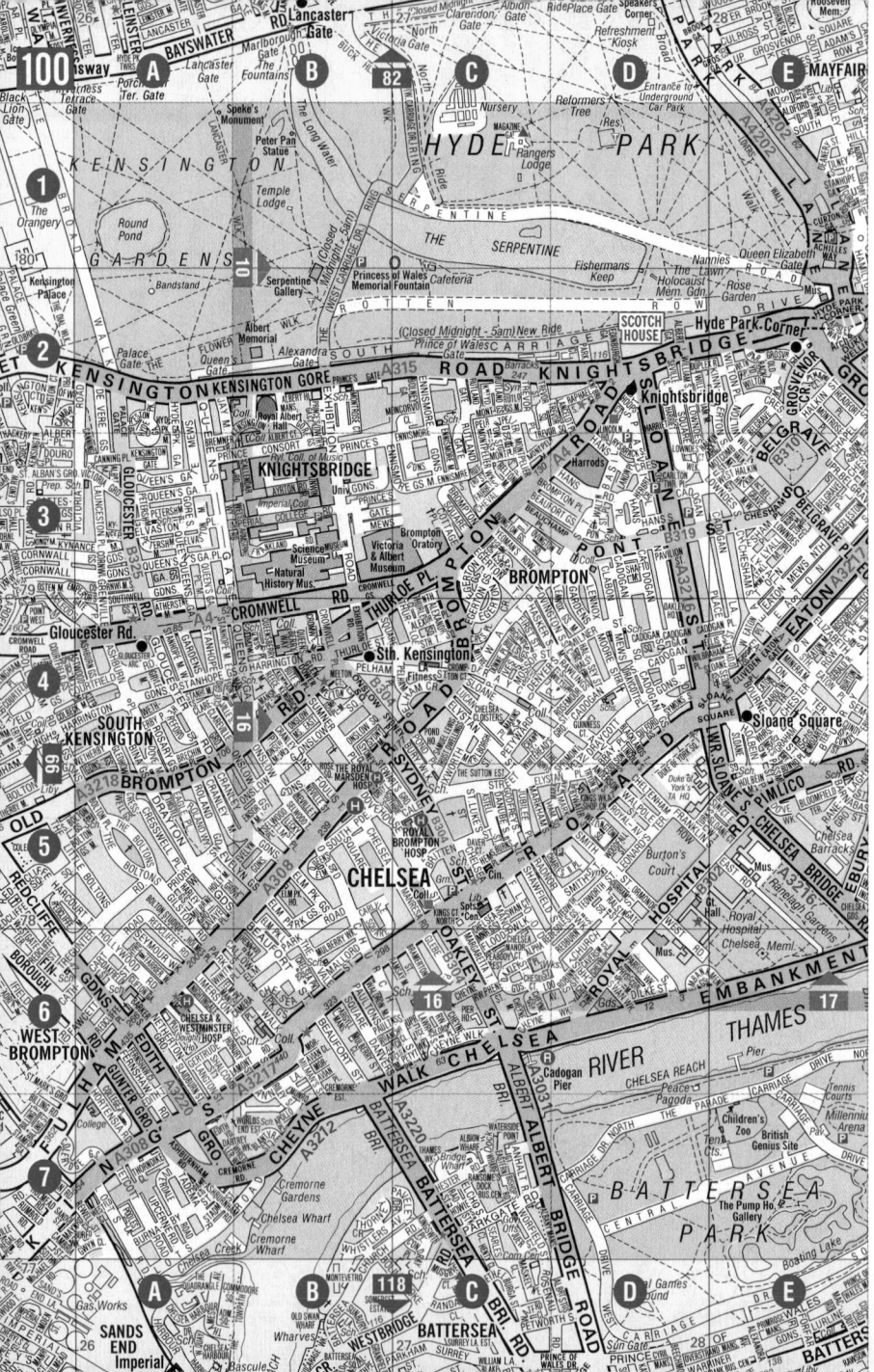

100
82
A
B
C
D
E
1
2
3
4
5
6
7
Lancaster Gate
BAYSWATER RD.
Speakers' Corner
Marlborough Gate
Lancaster Gate
The Fountains
Victoria Gate
Clarendon Gate
Albion Gate
Ride
Place Gate
Refreshment Kiosk
Broad Walk
Porchester Ter. Gate
Black Lion Gate
Speke's Monument
Peter Pan Statue
The Long Water
Nursery
Reformers Tree
Entrance to Underground Car Park
MAYFAIR
HYDE PARK
KENSINGTON GARDENS
Rangers Lodge
Temple Lodge
The Orangery
Round Pond
SERPENTINE
THE SERPENTINE
Fishermans Keep
Nannies
Queen Elizabeth Gate
The Lawn
Holocaust Mem. Gdn.
Rose Garden
ROTTEN ROW
Kensington Palace
Bandstand
Serpentine Gallery
Princess of Wales Memorial Fountain
Cafeteria
(Closed Midnight - 5am)
(Closed Midnight - 5am) New Ride
Albert Memorial
Queen's Gate
Alexandra Gate
Palace Gate
Prince of Wales Gate
SOUTH CARRIAGE DRIVE
SCOTCH HOUSE
Hyde Park Corner
KENSINGTON GORE
KENSINGTON ROAD
KNIGHTSBRIDGE
A315
Royal Albert Hall
Rly. Coll. of Music
PRINCE CONSORT RD.
KNIGHTSBRIDGE
Imperial Coll.
Science Museum
Natural History Mus.
Victoria & Albert Museum
Brompton Oratory
Knightsbridge
Harrods
BELGRAVE SQ.
GROSVENOR CR.
BROMPTON ROAD
BROMPTON
PONT ST.
B319
SLOANE ST.
GLOUCESTER RD.
B325
CROMWELL RD.
A4
THURLOE PL.
Gloucester Rd.
Sth. Kensington
SOUTH KENSINGTON
99
16
A3218
BROMPTON RD.
Sloane Square
EATON SQ.
PIMLICO RD.
CHELSEA BRIDGE RD.
A3216
CHELSEA
Chelsea Barracks
Burton's Court
Duke of York's TA HQ
Royal Hospital Chelsea
Ranelagh Gardens
ROYAL HOSPITAL RD.
B302
THE ROYAL MARSDEN HOSP.
ROYAL BROMPTON HOSP.
SYDNEY ST.
B304
KING'S ROAD
A308
OLD BROMPTON RD.
REDCLIFFE GDNS.
THE BOLTONS
WEST BROMPTON
FULHAM RD.
CHELSEA & WESTMINSTER HOSP.
EDITH GRO.
A3220
A3217
CHEYNE WALK
CHELSEA EMBANKMENT
17
THAMES
RIVER
Cadogan Pier
CHELSEA REACH
Pier
Peace Pagoda
CARRIAGE DRIVE NORTH
Children's Zoo
British Genius Site
Tennis Courts
Millennium Arena
BATTERSEA PARK
The Pump Ho. Gallery
Boating Lake
CENTRAL AVENUE
ALBERT BRIDGE
ALBERT BRIDGE ROAD
A3031
BATTERSEA BRI.
BATTERSEA BRI. RD.
A3212
Cremorne Gardens
Chelsea Wharf
Cremorne Wharf
Chelsea Creek
Gas Works
SANDS END
Imperial
Wharves
118
WESTBRIDGE
BATTERSEA
PARKGATE RD.
PRINCE OF WALES DR.
Sun Gate
College

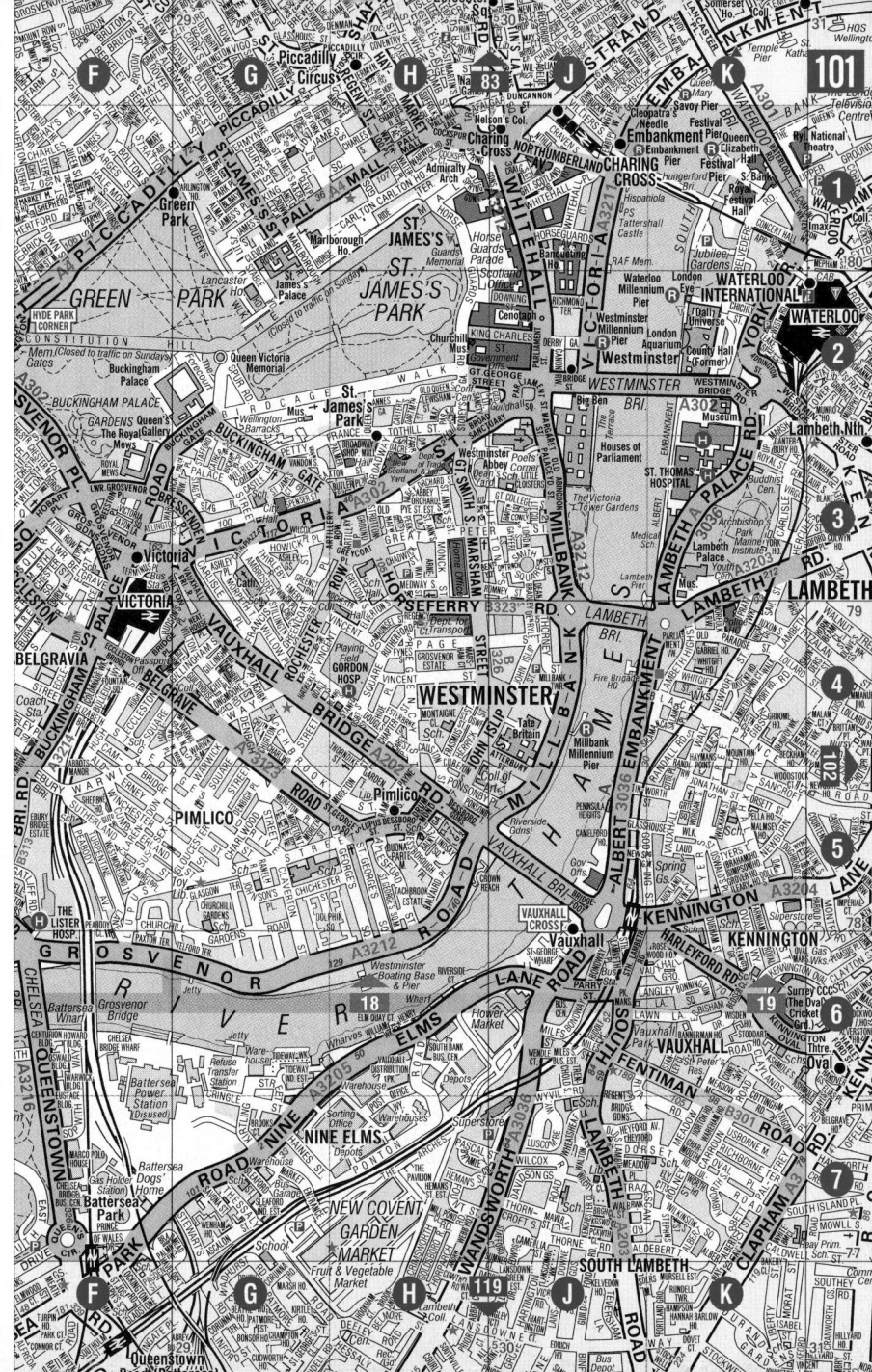
101
F
G
H
J
K
1
2
3
4
5
6
7
83
18
19
102
119
29
30
31
PICCADILLY
Piccadilly Circus
Green Park
GREEN PARK
HYDE PARK CORNER
CONSTITUTION HILL
Buckingham Palace
BUCKINGHAM PALACE GARDENS
Queen's Gallery
The Royal Mews
Queen Victoria Memorial
ST. JAMES'S PARK
St. James's Palace
Marlborough Ho.
Lancaster Ho.
PALL MALL
THE MALL
Admiralty Arch
Charing Cross
CHARING CROSS
Nelson's Col.
Horse Guards Parade
Scotland Office
Cenotaph
WHITEHALL
Banqueting Ho.
Embankment
Embankment Pier
Cleopatra's Needle
Hungerford Bri.
Festival Pier
Queen Elizabeth Hall
Royal Festival Hall
Rtl. National Theatre
Imax
WATERLOO INTERNATIONAL
WATERLOO
London Eye
Waterloo Millennium Pier
Westminster Millennium Pier
London Aquarium
County Hall (Former)
Westminster
WESTMINSTER BRIDGE
Big Ben
Houses of Parliament
Museum
ST. THOMAS' HOSPITAL
Westminster Abbey
The Victoria Tower Gardens
Lambeth Palace
LAMBETH
LAMBETH BRI.
Victoria
VICTORIA
VICTORIA ST.
BELGRAVIA
Playing Field
GORDON HOSP.
WESTMINSTER
Tate Britain
Millbank Millennium Pier
Coll. of Art
PIMLICO
Pimlico
Vauxhall
VAUXHALL CROSS
VAUXHALL BRI.
VAUXHALL
KENNINGTON
Surrey CCC (The Oval) Cricket Grd.
Oval
THE LISTER HOSP.
GROSVENOR ROAD
RIVER
Grosvenor Bridge
Westminster Boating Base & Pier
Battersea Power Station (Disused)
NINE ELMS
NEW COVENT GARDEN MARKET
Fruit & Vegetable Market
Battersea Park
Battersea Dogs' Home
SOUTH LAMBETH
Queenstown
WANDSWORTH ROAD
CLAPHAM RD.
SOUTH LAMBETH ROAD
ALBERT EMBANKMENT
MILLBANK
KENNINGTON LANE

102
EMBANKMENT
RIVER THAMES
BLACKFRIARS
Millennium Bridge
Blackfriars Millennium Pier
HQS Wellington
HMS President
Bankside Pier
84
CANNON STREET
LOWER THAMES ST.
BYWARD ST.
The London Television Centre
Ryl. National Theatre
Tate Modern
Golden Hinde
LONDON BRIDGE HOSP.
London Bri. City Pier
HMS Belfast
Tower Millennium Pier
City Hall
SOUTHWARK
STAMFORD ST.
SOUTHWARK ST.
UPPER GROUND
Peabody Estate
LONDON BRI.
TOOLEY ST.
THE BOROUGH
GUY'S HOSP.
Vinopolis
Southwark
UNION ST.
Waterloo East
THE CUT
WATERLOO INTERNATIONAL
WATERLOO
WATERLOO RD.
BLACKFRIARS RD.
SOUTHWARK BRIDGE RD.
BOROUGH HIGH ST.
LONG LA.
BERMONDSEY ST.
DRUID ST.
TOWER BRIDGE RD.
Borough
GREAT DOVER ST.
BOROUGH RD.
LONDON RD.
Lambeth Nth.
WESTMINSTER BRI. RD.
ST. GEORGE'S CIRCUS
ST. GEORGE'S RD.
LAMBETH RD.
Imperial War Mus.
Geraldine Mary Harmsworth Park
NEWINGTON
NEWINGTON CAUSEWAY
Elephant & Castle
ELEPHANT & CASTLE
NEW KENT RD.
BRICKLAYER'S ARMS
LAMBETH
BROOK DRIVE
KENNINGTON RD.
KENNINGTON LANE
KENNINGTON PARK RD.
Kennington
WALWORTH RD.
WALWORTH
EAST ST.
OLD KENT RD.
101
19
14
15
Burgess Park
BURGESS PARK
ALBANY RD.
KENNINGTON
Surrey CCC (The Oval Cricket Grd.)
Oval
CAMBERWELL NEW RD.
CAMBERWELL RD.
SOUTHAMPTON WAY
BRIXTON RD.
CLAPHAM RD.
120
CAMBERWELL GREEN
PECKHAM
A
B
C
D
E
1
2
3
4
5
6
7

Tower Hill
TOWER HILL
The Tower of London
St. Katharine's Pier
Tower Hotel
SHADWELL
Shadwell
King Edward Mem. Park
Shadwell Dock Stairs
THAMES
Wapping
WAPPING
Wapping Old Stairs
Wapping New Stairs
Wapping Dock Stairs
RIVER
UPPER POOL
LOWER POOL
BERMONDSEY
Cherry Garden Pier
King's Stairs
Cumberland Wharf
Rotherhithe
ROTHERHITHE
ROTHERHITHE TUNNEL
A101
Canada Water
Surrey Quays
Bermondsey
South Bermondsey
Millwall FC (The Den)
Lewisham Lions Cen.
Waste Transfer Station
Southwark Pk. Sports Cen. Track
SOUTHWARK PARK
JAMAICA ROAD
TOWER BRI. ROAD
A100
JAMAICA STREET
A2207
ABBEY ST.
B202
SOUTHWARK PARK RD.
A200
LOWER RD.
REDRIFF RD.
A2202
SALTER RD.
BRUNEL RD.
TUNNEL APP.
LOWER ROTHERHITHE NEW RD.
PLOUGH WY.
B206
EVELYN STREET
ROTHERHITHE NEW RD.
A2208
RAYMOUTH RD.
A2206
ROLLS RD.
B204
CATLIN ST.
DUNTON RD.
B203
OLD KENT ROAD
A2
TRAFALGAR AV.
SUMNER ROAD
B215
PECKHAM PARK RD.
B216
PECKHAM HILL ST.
PECKHAM HIGH ST.
QUEEN'S ROAD
NEW CROSS RD.
NEW CROSS GATE
New Cross Gate
Queens Rd (Peckham)
TRUNDLEYS RD.
B207
SURREY CANAL ROAD
ILDERTON RD.
PENARTH ST.
ORMSIDE ST.
HATCHAM PK. RD.
POMEROY ST.
KENDER ST.
Brimmington Pk.
Paterson Pk.
Leisure Cen.
Superstore
85
15
104
121
F
G
H
J
K
1
2
3
4
5
6
7

A
B
C
D
E
1
2
3
4
5
6
7
86
103
122
LIMEHOUSE REACH
RIVER THAMES
GREENWICH REACH
ISLE OF DOGS
POPLAR
Poplar
West India Quay
Billingsgate Fish Market
Canary Wharf
WEST INDIA DOCKS
Heron Quays
South Quay
Canary Wharf Pier
Hilton Docklands Pier
Durand's Wharf
Surrey Docks Farm
Barnards Wharf
Greenland Pier
Watersports Cen.
SOUTH DOCK
GREENLAND DOCK
Ecological Park
Stave Hill
Sports Cen.
Printing Works
Bowl. Alley & Gala Bingo
SALTER ROAD
PLOUGH WAY
EVELYN STREET
DEPTFORD PARK
Pepys Park
CONVOY'S WHARF
WESTFERRY ROAD
MARSH WALL
Docklands Sailing Cen.
MILLWALL OUTER DOCK
MILLWALL
MILLWALL INNER DOCK
Crossharbour & London Arena
CUBITT TOWN
Mudchute Farm
MUDCHUTE PARK
Mudchute
Island Gds.
MILLWALL PARK
MANCHESTER ROAD
Masthouse Terrace Pier
Greenwich Pier
Cutty Sark for Maritime Greenwich
DEPTFORD
CREEK ROAD
DEPTFORD CHURCH ST.
Deptford
Greenwich
New Cross
New Cross Gate
NEW CROSS RD.
NEW CROSS
Goldsmiths' Coll.
GREENWICH HIGH RD.
BLACKHEATH RD.
BLACKHEATH HILL
ROYAL HILL
A2
A200
A206
A1206
A1261
A2202
B205
B206
B207
B208
DLR

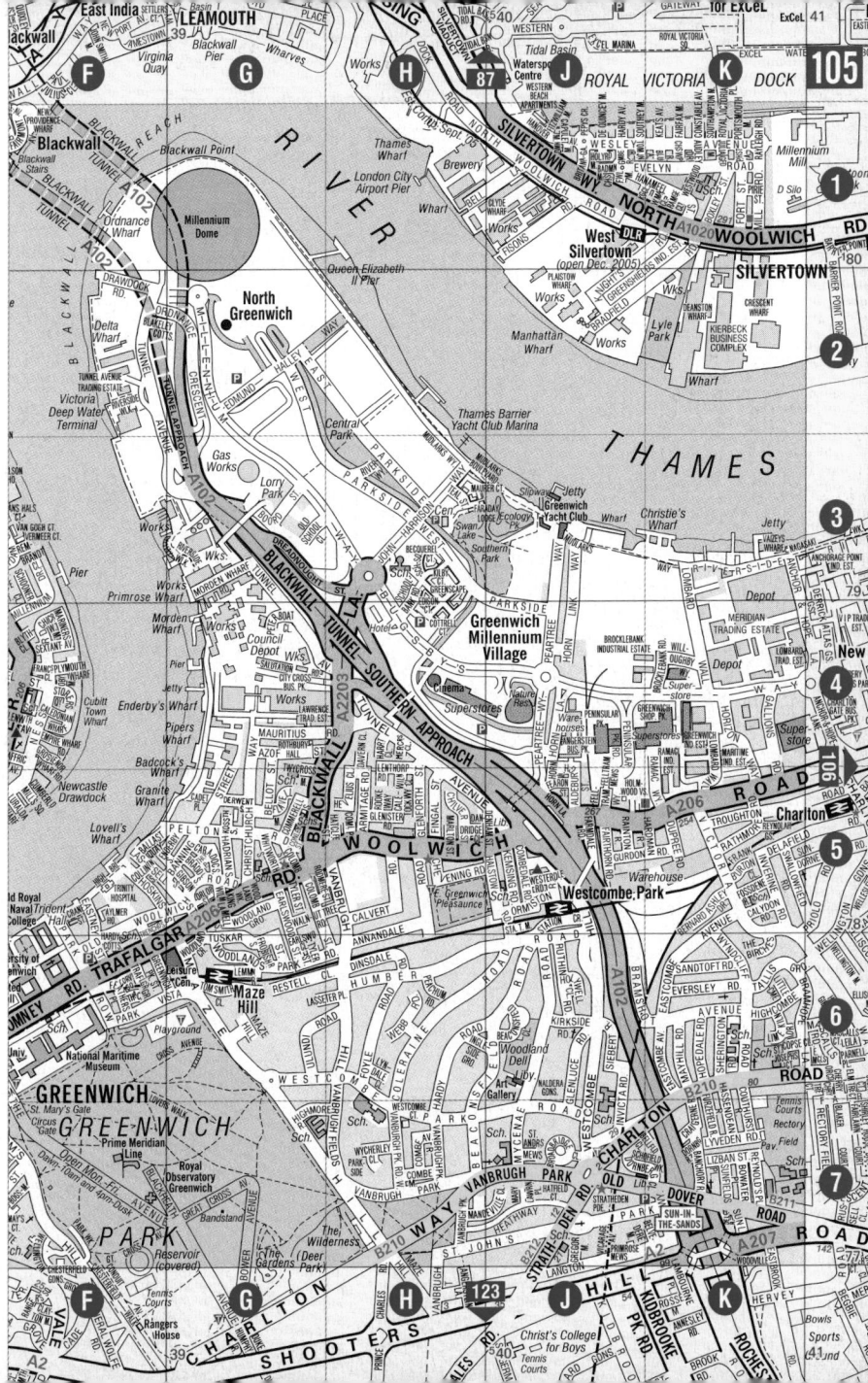
East India
LEAMOUTH
Blackwall
Virginia Quay
Blackwall Pier
Wharves
Works
for ExCeL
ExCeL
41
ROYAL VICTORIA DOCK
Tidal Basin
Watersports Centre
WESTERN
87
F
G
H
J
K
RIVER
THAMES
BLACKWALL REACH
Blackwall Point
Blackwall Stairs
BLACKWALL TUNNEL
A102
Ordnance Wharf
Millennium Dome
North Greenwich
Thames Wharf
London City Airport Pier
Brewery
Wharf
Queen Elizabeth II Pier
Est. Comp. Sept. '05
SILVERTOWN WY.
NORTH WOOLWICH RD.
NORTH WOOLWICH ROAD
A1020
West Silvertown
(open Dec. 2005)
SILVERTOWN
Millennium Mills
D Silo
1
Works
Manhattan Wharf
Lyle Park
KIERBECK BUSINESS COMPLEX
CRESCENT WHARF
Wharf
2
DRAWDOCK RD.
Delta Wharf
TUNNEL AVENUE
TUNNEL AVENUE TRADING ESTATE
Victoria Deep Water Terminal
TUNNEL APPROACH
MILLENNIUM WAY
EDMUND HALLEY WAY
Central Park
Thames Barrier Yacht Club Marina
Gas Works
Lorry Park
PARKSIDE
Greenwich Yacht Club
Ecology Pk.
Swan Lake
Southern Park
Christie's Wharf
Jetty
3
Slipway
RIVERSIDE
Depot
MERIDIAN TRADING ESTATE
New C
4
Works
Pier
Primrose Wharf
Morden Wharf
Council Depot
Wks.
DREADNOUGHT ST.
JOHN HARRISON WAY
BLACKWALL TUNNEL SOUTHERN APPROACH
A2203
Greenwich Millennium Village
Hotel
Cinema
Superstores
Nature Res.
BROCKLEBANK INDUSTRIAL ESTATE
Super-store
Depot
Pier
Jetty
Enderby's Wharf
Cubitt Town Wharf
Pipers Wharf
Badcock's Wharf
Granite Wharf
Lovell's Wharf
Newcastle Drawdock
BLACKWALL LA.
WOOLWICH ROAD
A206
106
Charlton
5
Westcombe Park
Warehouse
Old Royal Naval College
Trident Hall
TRAFALGAR RD.
ROMNEY RD.
Leisure Cen.
Maze Hill
E. Greenwich Pleasaunce
Playground
National Maritime Museum
GREENWICH
GREENWICH PARK
St. Mary's Gate
Circus Gate
Prime Meridian Line
Royal Observatory Greenwich
Open Mon.-Fri. Dawn-10am and 4pm-Dusk
Bandstand
Reservoir (covered)
The Gardens
The Wilderness (Deer Park)
Woodland Dell
Art Gallery
6
CHARLTON ROAD
B210
Tennis Courts
Rectory Field
7
VANBRUGH PARK
B212
A2
SUN-IN-THE-SANDS
A207
SHOOTERS HILL
KIDBROOKE PK. RD.
123
Christ's College for Boys
Tennis Courts
Rangers House
Tennis Courts
CHARLTON WAY
Bowls
Sports Ground
A102

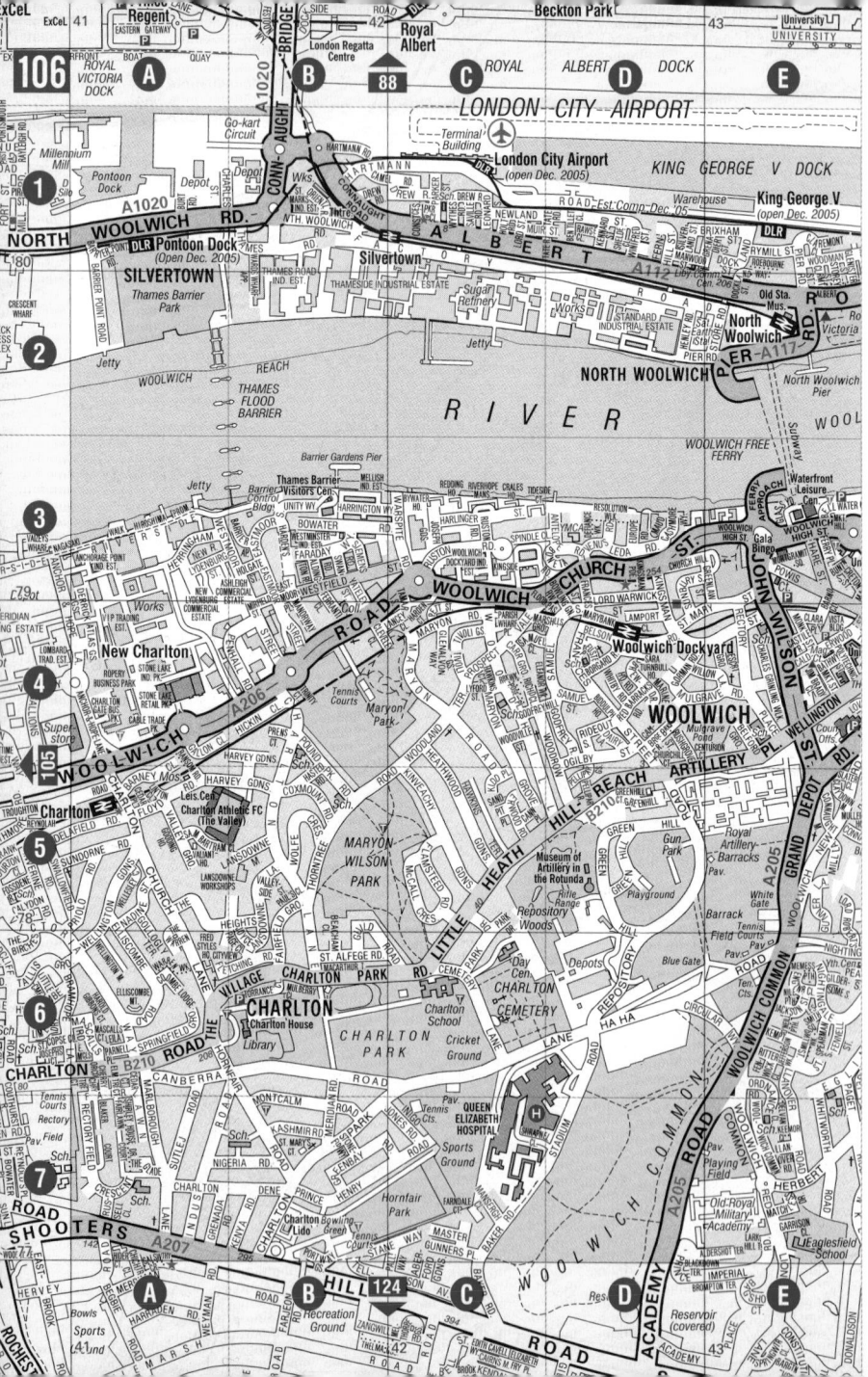
106
88
105
124
A
B
C
D
E
1
2
3
4
5
6
7
41
42
43
80
79
78
77
ExCeL
Prince Regent
Royal Albert
Beckton Park
University
London Regatta Centre
ROYAL VICTORIA DOCK
ROYAL ALBERT DOCK
LONDON CITY AIRPORT
Terminal Building
London City Airport (open Dec. 2005)
KING GEORGE V DOCK
King George V (open Dec. 2005)
Millennium Mill
Pontoon Dock
Go-kart Circuit
CONNAUGHT BRIDGE
A1020
NORTH WOOLWICH RD.
Pontoon Dock (Open Dec. 2005)
SILVERTOWN
Thames Barrier Park
Silvertown
THAMESIDE INDUSTRIAL ESTATE
Sugar Refinery
ALBERT ROAD
A112
FACTORY ROAD
STANDARD INDUSTRIAL ESTATE
North Woolwich
Old Sta. Mus.
NORTH WOOLWICH
PIER RD.
A117
North Woolwich Pier
WOOLWICH REACH
THAMES FLOOD BARRIER
RIVER
WOOLWICH FREE FERRY
Subway
Barrier Gardens Pier
Thames Barrier Visitors Cen.
Waterfront Leisure Cen.
Gala Bingo
WOOLWICH HIGH ST.
WOOLWICH CHURCH ST.
WOOLWICH ROAD
A206
Woolwich Dockyard
New Charlton
JOHN WILSON ST.
WOOLWICH
Maryon Park
MARYON WILSON PARK
Charlton
Charlton Athletic FC (The Valley)
CHARLTON CHURCH LANE
LITTLE HEATH
HILL REACH
ARTILLERY PL.
WELLINGTON
B210
Museum of Artillery in the Rotunda
Repository Woods
Gun Park
Royal Artillery Barracks
GRAND DEPOT RD.
A205
CHARLTON PARK RD.
THE VILLAGE
CHARLTON
Charlton House
Library
Charlton School
CHARLTON PARK
Cricket Ground
CHARLTON CEMETERY
HA HA ROAD
QUEEN ELIZABETH HOSPITAL
WOOLWICH COMMON
Sports Ground
Hornfair Park
Charlton Lido
Old Royal Military Academy
Eaglesfield School
CHARLTON ROAD
SHOOTERS HILL ROAD
A207
Recreation Ground
Reservoir (covered)
ACADEMY ROAD

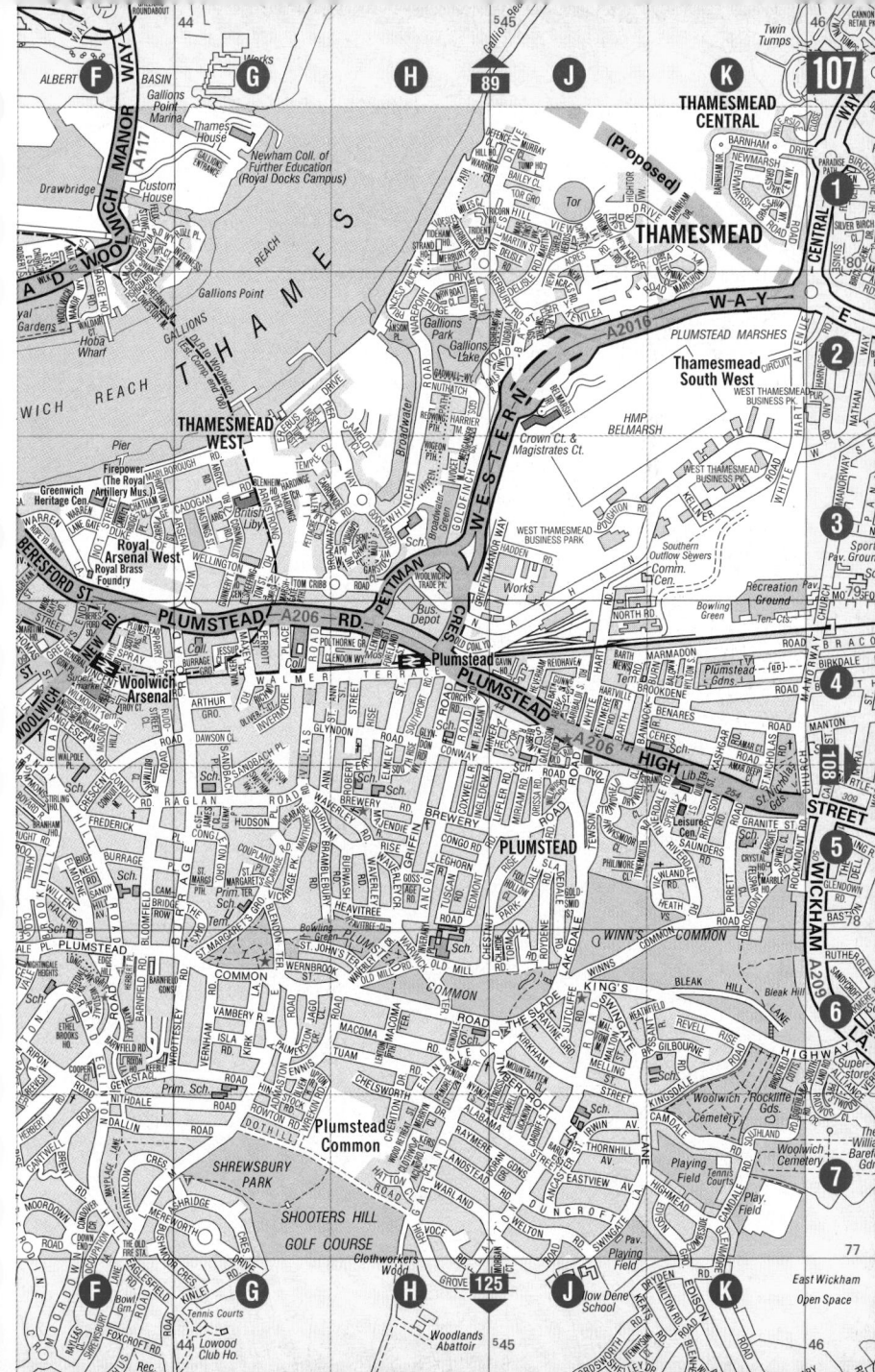
F
G
H
J
K
89
125
108
1
2
3
4
5
6
7
44
545
46
77
78
79
80
THAMESMEAD CENTRAL
THAMESMEAD
Thamesmead South West
THAMESMEAD WEST
(Proposed)
THAMES
GALLIONS REACH
WOOLWICH REACH
ALBERT BASIN
Gallions Point Marina
Thames House
Newham Coll. of Further Education (Royal Docks Campus)
Drawbridge
Custom House
Gallions Point
Hoba Wharf
Pier
Firepower (The Royal Artillery Mus.)
Greenwich Heritage Cen.
Royal Arsenal West
Royal Brass Foundry
British Liby.
Gallions Park
Gallions Lake
Broadwater
Broadwater Green
HMP BELMARSH
Crown Ct. & Magistrates Ct.
PLUMSTEAD MARSHES
WEST THAMESMEAD BUSINESS PK.
WEST THAMESMEAD BUSINESS PARK
Southern Outflow Sewers
Comm. Cen.
Works
Recreation Ground
Bowling Green
Sports Pav. Ground
Bus Depot
WOOLWICH TRADE PK.
Plumstead
Woolwich Arsenal
Plumstead Gdns.
Lib.
Leisure Cen.
St. Nicholas Gds.
PLUMSTEAD
WINN'S COMMON
PLUMSTEAD COMMON
Bleak Hill
Woolwich Cemetery
Rockliffe Gds.
Playing Field
Tennis Courts
Play. Field
Super-store
The William Barefoot Gdn.
Plumstead Common
SHREWSBURY PARK
SHOOTERS HILL GOLF COURSE
Clothworkers Wood
Woodlands Abattoir
Tennis Courts
Lowood Club Ho.
Bowl. Grn.
Pav. Playing Field
East Wickham Open Space
WOOLWICH MANOR WAY
A117
WESTERN WAY
A2016
CENTRAL WAY
PLUMSTEAD RD.
A206
BERESFORD ST.
PLUMSTEAD HIGH STREET
WICKHAM LA.
A209
PETTMAN CRES.
GRIFFIN MANOR WAY
HARTSLOCK DRIVE
NATHAN WAY
WALMER TERRACE
MANORWAY
BRACONDALE RD.
BLEAK HILL LANE
HIGHWAY
KING'S HIGHWAY
SWINGATE LANE
DUNCROFT
GARLAND RD.
EGLINTON HILL
BURRAGE RD.
CONDUIT RD.
RAGLAN RD.
BREWERY RD.
WAVERLEY RD.
GLYNDON RD.
CONWAY RD.
VICARAGE PK.
GENESTA RD.
NITHDALE RD.
DALLIN RD.
WERNBROOK ST.
WOOLWICH NEW RD.
WOOLWICH RD.

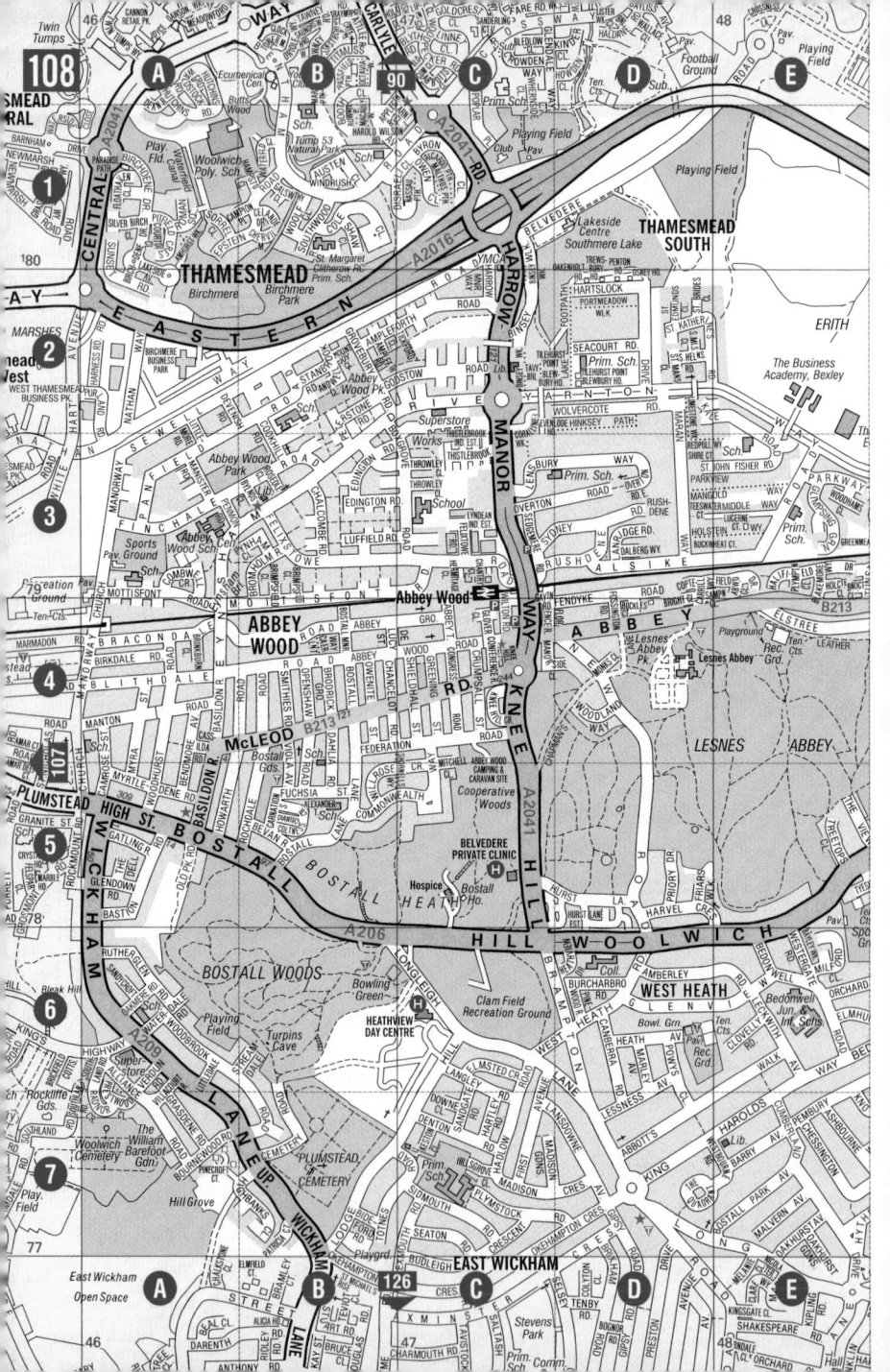
108
THAMESMEAD
THAMESMEAD SOUTH
ABBEY WOOD
WEST HEATH
EAST WICKHAM
ERITH
LESNES ABBEY
BOSTALL WOODS
BOSTALL HEATH
EASTERN WAY
HARROW MANOR WAY
KNEE HILL
McLEOD RD.
PLUMSTEAD HIGH ST.
BOSTALL HILL
WOOLWICH ROAD
WICKHAM LANE
CENTRAL WAY
ABBEY ROAD
ALSIKE ROAD
YARNTON WAY
BELVEDERE
BRAMPTON ROAD
LONG LANE
KING HAROLDS WAY
AXMINSTER CRES.
LODGE HILL
Abbey Wood
Woolwich Poly. Sch.
Lakeside Centre
Southmere Lake
Birchmere Park
The Business Academy, Bexley
Lesnes Abbey
Cooperative Woods
BELVEDERE PRIVATE CLINIC
Hospice
Bostall Ho.
Clam Field Recreation Ground
HEATHVIEW DAY CENTRE
Bowling Green
Turpins Cave
PLUMSTEAD CEMETERY
Woolwich Cemetery
The William Barefoot Gdn.
Hill Grove
East Wickham Open Space
Stevens Park
Rockliffe Gds.
Bleak Hill
Sports Ground
Playing Field
Football Ground
Tump 53 Natural Park
ABBEY WOOD CAMPING & CARAVAN SITE
Bedonwell Jun. & Inf. Schs.
A2041
A2016
A206
A209
B213
90
107
126
46
47
48
180
79
78
77
A
B
C
D
E
1
2
3
4
5
6
7

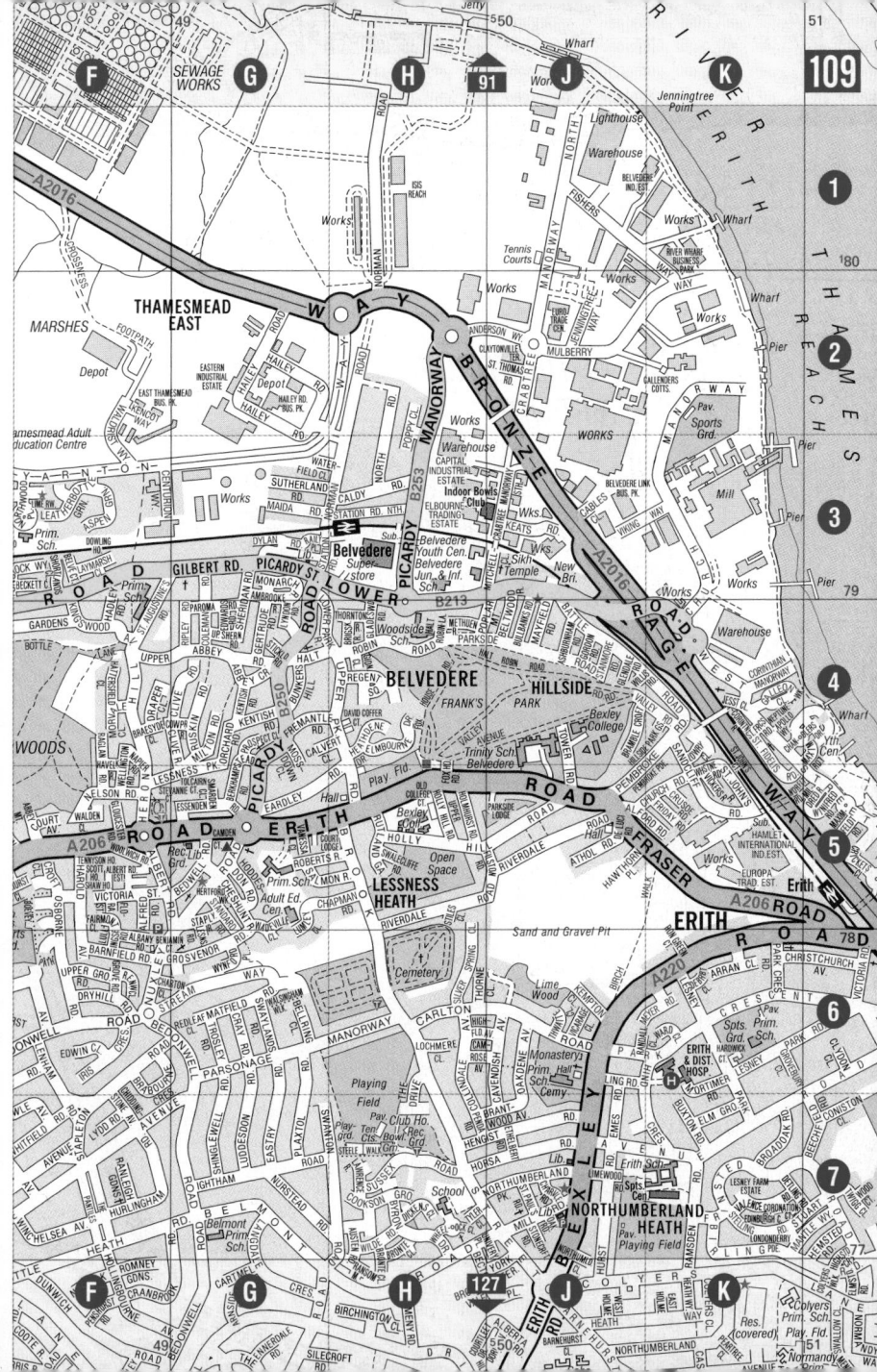

109
49
550
51
F
G
H
J
K
91
127
1
2
3
4
5
6
7
180
79
78
77
RIVER THAMES
ERITH REACH
SEWAGE WORKS
Jetty
Wharf
Jenningtree Point
Lighthouse
Warehouse
BELVEDERE IND. EST.
Works
ISIS REACH
Tennis Courts
RIVER WHARF BUSINESS PARK
Pier
Mill
A2016
WAY
BRONZE
THAMESMEAD EAST
MARSHES
FOOTPATH
Depot
EASTERN INDUSTRIAL ESTATE
EAST THAMESMEAD BUS. PK.
HAILEY RD. BUS. PK.
Thamesmead Adult Education Centre
CROSSNESS
NORMAN ROAD
ANDERSON WY.
CLAYTONVILLE TER.
ST. THOMAS RD.
CRABTREE
MULBERRY
EURO TRADE CEN.
JENNINGTREE WAY
CALLENDERS COTTS.
MANORWAY
Sports Grd.
Pav.
WORKS
CAPITAL INDUSTRIAL ESTATE
Indoor Bowls Club
ELBOURNE TRADING ESTATE
BELVEDERE LINK BUS. PK.
CABLES CL.
VIKING WAY
YARNTON WAY
SUTHERLAND RD.
CALDY RD.
MAIDA RD.
STATION RD. NTH.
Belvedere Superstore
Belvedere Youth Cen.
Belvedere Jun. & Inf. Sch.
Sikh Temple
New Bri.
B253
B213
B250
PICARDY
PICARDY ST.
LOWER ROAD
GILBERT RD.
Prim. Sch.
ROAD
A206
ERITH ROAD
FRASER ROAD
RAGE ROAD
WEST STREET
BELVEDERE
HILLSIDE
FRANK'S PARK
Woodside Sch.
Bexley College
Trinity Sch. Belvedere
Play. Fld.
Open Space
LESSNESS HEATH
Prim. Sch.
Adult Ed. Cen.
Cemetery
Sand and Gravel Pit
ERITH
Erith
HAMLET INTERNATIONAL IND. EST.
EUROPA TRAD. EST.
A220
CRESCENT
PARK CRES.
CHRISTCHURCH AV.
Lime Wood
Monastery Prim. Sch.
Cemy.
ERITH & DIST. HOSP.
Spts. Grd.
Playing Field
Club Ho.
Rec. Grd.
Erith Sch.
Spts. Cen.
NORTHUMBERLAND HEATH
Playing Field
LESNEY FARM ESTATE
Belmont Prim. Sch.
School
Lib.
BEXLEY ROAD
COLYERS LANE
Res. (covered)
Colyers Prim. Sch.
Play. Fld.
WOODS
BEDONWELL ROAD
MANORWAY
CARLTON ROAD
PARSONAGE
HEATH
BELMONT
NORTHUMBERLAND

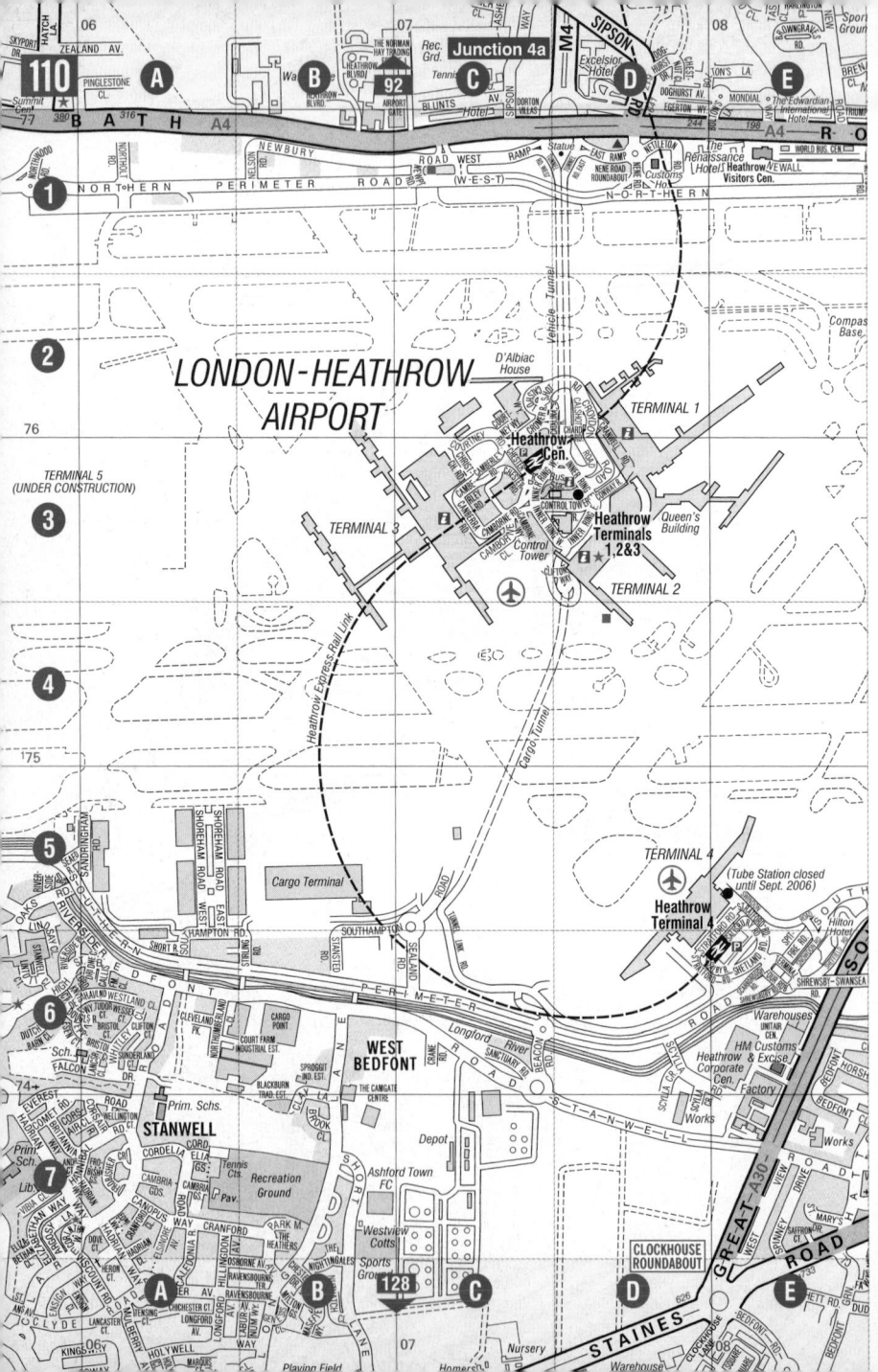

110
92
128
Junction 4a
LONDON-HEATHROW AIRPORT
TERMINAL 1
TERMINAL 2
TERMINAL 3
TERMINAL 4
TERMINAL 5 (UNDER CONSTRUCTION)
Heathrow Cen.
Heathrow Terminals 1,2&3
Heathrow Terminal 4
(Tube Station closed until Sept. 2006)
D'Albiac House
Queen's Building
Control Tower
Compass Base
Vehicle Tunnel
Cargo Tunnel
Heathrow Express Rail Link
Cargo Terminal
NORTHERN PERIMETER ROAD
SOUTHERN PERIMETER ROAD
BATH ROAD
A4
M4
SIPSON RD.
Excelsior Hotel
The Edwardian International Hotel
The Renaissance Hotel
Heathrow Visitors Cen.
Customs Ho.
NENE ROAD ROUNDABOUT
Statue
EAST RAMP
NEWALL
WORLD BUS. CEN.
THE NORMAN HAY TRADING
HEATHROW BLVD.
AIRPORT GATE
BLUNTS AV.
Rec. Grd.
Tennis
Hotel
DORTON VILLAS
PINGLESTONE CL.
ZEALAND AV.
HATCH LA.
SKYPORT DR.
Summit Cen.
NORTHWOOD RD.
NORTHOLT RD.
NEWBURY
NELSON RD.
SHOREHAM ROAD WEST
SHOREHAM ROAD EAST
SANDRINGHAM RD.
SOUTHAMPTON RD.
STIRLING RD.
STANSTED RD.
SEALAND RD.
TUNNEL LINK RD.
BEDFONT ROAD
WEST BEDFONT
Longford River
BEACON RD.
SANCTUARY RD.
STANWELL ROAD
STANWELL
Prim. Schs.
Recreation Ground
Tennis Cts.
Pav.
Ashford Town FC
Depot
Westview Cotts.
Sports Ground
Nursery
Playing Field
Homers
Warehouse
CLOCKHOUSE ROUNDABOUT
STAINES ROAD
GREAT WEST ROAD
A30
Warehouses
HM Customs & Excise
Heathrow Corporate Cen.
Factory
Works
Scylla Works
Hilton Hotel
SHREWSBURY ROAD
CLEVELAND PK.
COURT FARM INDUSTRIAL EST.
CARGO POINT
SPROGGIT IND. EST.
BLACKBURN TRAD. EST.
THE CAMGATE CENTRE
CLAY LANE
BROOK CL.
SHORT LANE
CRANE RD.
CORDELIA RD.
CAMBRIA GDS.
CANOPUS WAY
CRANFORD
CALEDONIA RD.
HILLINGDON AV.
OSBORNE AV.
RAVENSBOURNE AV.
LONGFORD AV.
HOLYWELL WAY
CLYDE ROAD
ELIZABETHAN WAY
FALCON DR.
EVEREST ROAD
COMET RD.
HADRIAN WAY
Prim. Sch.
Lib.
A B C D E
1 2 3 4 5 6 7
06 07 08
76 175 74

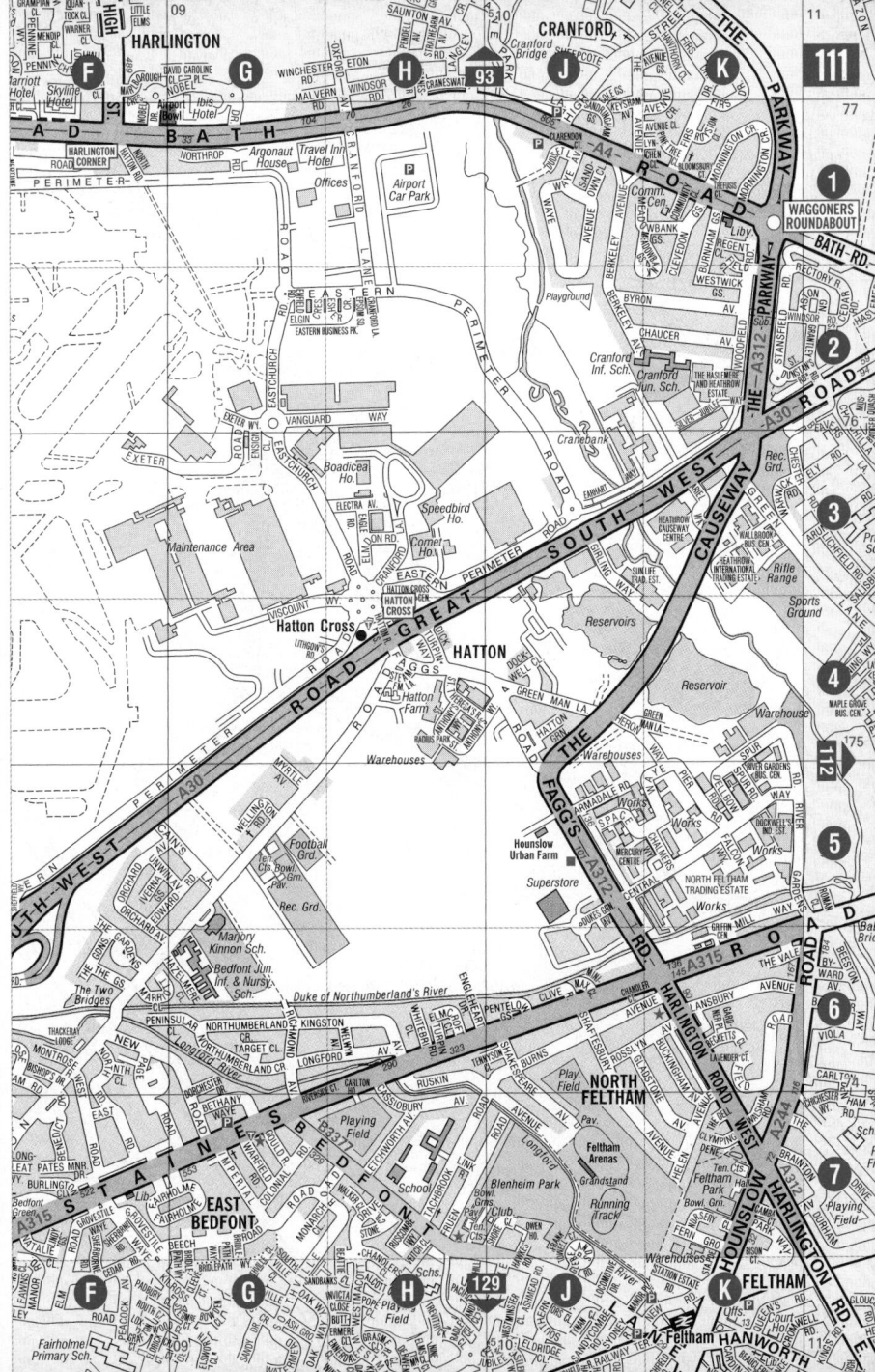

111
09
10
11
77
HARLINGTON
CRANFORD
Cranford Bridge
HATTON
NORTH FELTHAM
EAST BEDFONT
FELTHAM
HANWORTH
Hatton Cross
F
G
H
J
K
1
2
3
4
5
6
7
93
112
129
175
BATH ROAD
A4 ROAD
THE PARKWAY
A312
WAGGONERS ROUNDABOUT
GREAT SOUTH WEST ROAD
A30
PERIMETER ROAD
EASTERN PERIMETER ROAD
THE CAUSEWAY
FAGG'S ROAD
STAINES ROAD
A315
BEDFONT ROAD
B3377
HARLINGTON ROAD WEST
HARLINGTON ROAD EAST
HOUNSLOW ROAD
A244
CRANFORD LANE
EASTCHURCH ROAD
VANGUARD WAY
HIGH STREET
Marriott Hotel
Skyline Hotel
Ibis Hotel
Airport Bowl
Argonaut House
Travel Inn Hotel
Offices
Airport Car Park
HARLINGTON CORNER
EASTERN BUSINESS PK.
Maintenance Area
Boadicea Ho.
Speedbird Ho.
Comet Ho.
HATTON CROSS
Playground
Cranford Inf. Sch.
Cranford Jun. Sch.
Cranebank
Comm. Cen.
Liby.
HEATHROW CAUSEWAY CENTRE
HEATHROW INTERNATIONAL TRADING ESTATE
SUN LIFE TRAD. EST.
Reservoirs
Reservoir
Rifle Range
Sports Ground
Rec. Grd.
Warehouse
Warehouses
Hatton Farm
MAPLE GROVE BUS. CEN.
RIVER GARDENS BUS. CEN.
DOCKWELL'S IND. EST.
Works
MERCURY CENTRE
NORTH FELTHAM TRADING ESTATE
Hounslow Urban Farm
Superstore
GRIFFIN CEN.
Football Grd.
Ten. Cts. Bowl. Grn.
Pav.
Rec. Grd.
Marjory Kinnon Sch.
Bedfont Jun. Inf. & Nursy. Sch.
The Two Bridges
Duke of Northumberland's River
Longford River
Playing Field
School
Play Field
Feltham Arenas
Grandstand
Running Track
Blenheim Park
Club.
Feltham Park
Bowl. Grn.
Sch.
Schs.
Lib.
Bedfont Green
Fairholme Primary Sch.
STATION ESTATE
Feltham
Court Ho.
Offs.

112
94
111
130
A
B
C
D
E
1
2
3
4
5
6
7
THE PARKWAY
A312
WAGGONERS ROUNDABOUT
HENLYS ROUNDABOUT
BATH RD.
A4
A30
GT. SOUTH WEST RD.
GREAT WEST ROAD
HESTON
Sutton Playing Field
SUTTON LA.
A3063
Lampton School
Civic Centre
LAMPTON PARK
Hounslow West
BATH ROAD
A3006
Beaversfield Park
HOUNSLOW WEST
Cavalry Barracks
Playing Field
BEAVERS LANE
PROLOGIS PARK
Rifle Range
Sports Ground
Warehouse
Sports Ground
Cemetery
SUTTON LANE
WELLINGTON RD. NTH.
BULSTRODE AVENUE
ROAD
St. Mark's RC Sch.
Gala Bingo
A315
STAINES RD.
CAMBRIDGE
CENTRAL PARK ESTATE
Superstore
Club Ho.
Heath Nurseries
Training Centre
WELLINGTON ROAD SOUTH
Mosque
The Heathland School
HOUNSLOW HEATH GOLF COURSE
HOUNSLOW HEATH NATURE RESERVE
Baber Bridge
Weir
NORTH FELTHAM
A244
HOUNSLOW RD.
River Crane
A314
HANWORTH ROAD
NELSON ROAD
Comm. Cen.
Hounslow Cemy.
HEATHROW GATEWAY
Bridge Farm Nursery
Cemetery
MILL FARM BUSINESS PARK
South West Middlesex Crematorium
HARLINGTON ROAD EAST
HANWORTH
Playing Field
Heathfield Jun. & Inf. Schs.

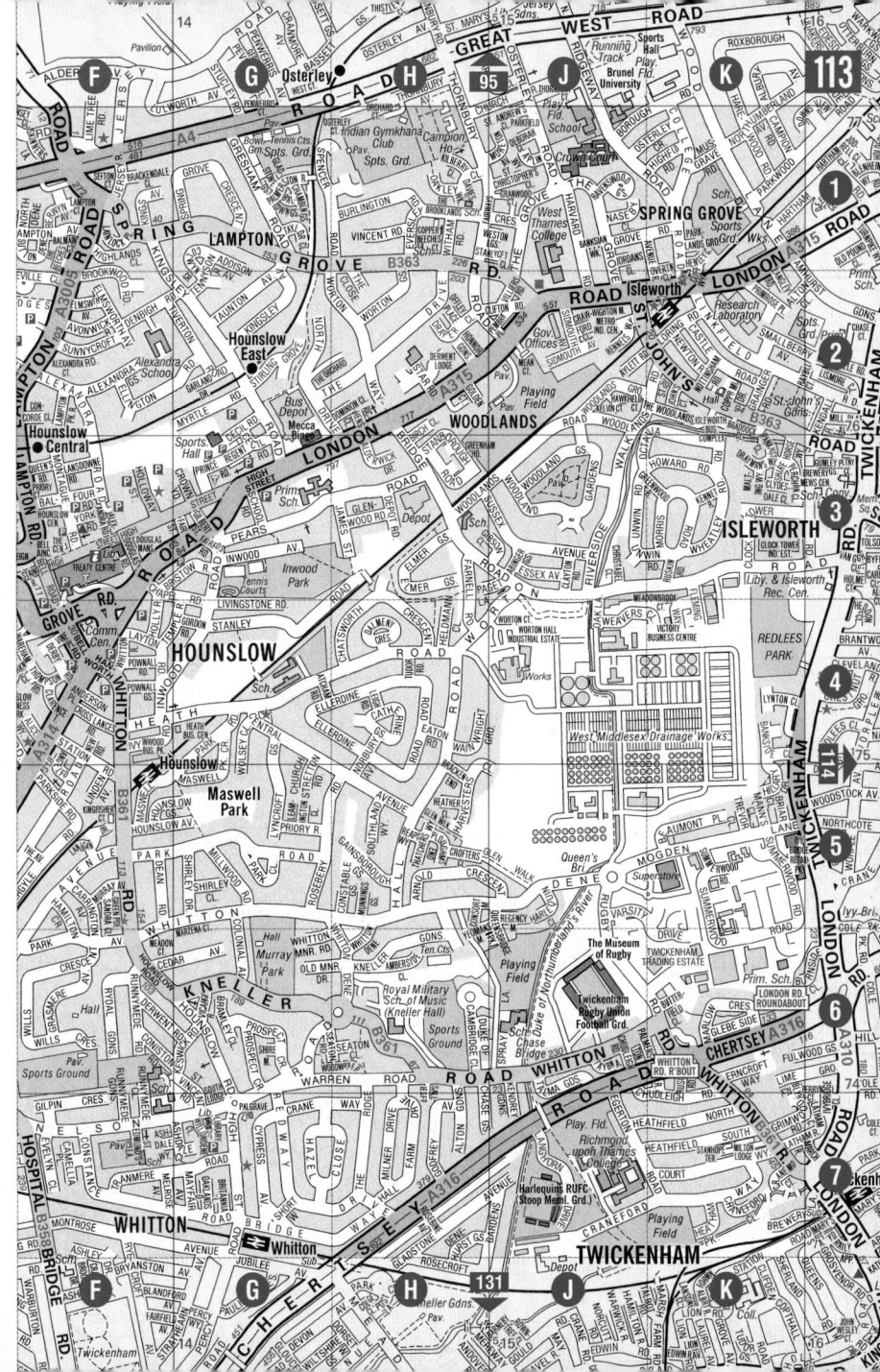
113
95
114
131
F
G
H
J
K
1
2
3
4
5
6
7
14
15
16
GREAT WEST ROAD
A4
Osterley
Running Track
Sports Hall
Play. Fld.
Brunel University
Indian Gymkhana Club
Spts. Grd.
Campion Ho.
Crown Court
LAMPTON
SPRING GROVE
Spring Grove Sports Grd.
LAMPTON GROVE RD.
B363
West Thames College
Isleworth
LONDON ROAD
A315
Research Laboratory
Hounslow East
Alexandra School
Gov. Offices
Playing Field
ST. JOHN'S RD.
St. John's Gdns.
Bus Depot
Mecca Bingo
WOODLANDS
Hounslow Central
Sports Hall
HIGH STREET
Prim. Sch.
Depot
ISLEWORTH
TWICKENHAM ROAD
CLOCK TOWER IND. EST.
Liby. & Isleworth Rec. Cen.
TREATY CENTRE
Inwood Park
Tennis Courts
LIVINGSTONE RD.
Comm. Cen.
HOUNSLOW
WORTON HALL INDUSTRIAL ESTATE
Works
VICTORY BUSINESS CENTRE
REDLEES PARK
West Middlesex Drainage Works
Hounslow
Maswell Park
A314
B361
HOUNSLOW AV.
Queen's Bri.
MOGDEN
Superstore
Duke of Northumberland's River
The Museum of Rugby
TWICKENHAM TRADING ESTATE
Twickenham Rugby Union Football Grd.
Prim. Sch.
LONDON RD. ROUNDABOUT
A310
Murray Park
Royal Military Sch. of Music (Kneller Hall)
Sports Ground
Playing Field
KNELLER
WHITTON RD. R'BOUT
WHITTON ROAD
CHERTSEY A316
Sports Ground
Richmond upon Thames College
Harlequins RUFC (Stoop Meml. Grd.)
Play. Fld.
HOSPITAL BRIDGE RD.
B358
WHITTON
Whitton
TWICKENHAM
Playing Field
Depot
Kneller Gdns.
Coll.
Twickenham

A
B
C
D
E
1
2
3
4
5
6
7
96
113
132
SYON LA.
Syon Lane
Play Field
The Green Sch.
SPUR RD.
B454
Busch Corner
A315
LONDON ROAD
SYON PARK
London Butterfly House
Syon Garden Centre
Syon House
Syon Park Sch.
DUKE OF NORTHUMBERLAND ESTATE
RIVER THAMES
Syon Reach
Isleworth Ferry Gate (Closed)
KEW
ROYAL BOTANIC GARDENS
Rhododendron Dell
Bamboo Garden
Azalea Gdn.
Syon Vista
The Lake
King William's Temple
Arboretum
Water Lily Pond
Evolution House
Temperate House
Cedar Vista
Conservation Area
Queen Charlotte's Cottage
King's Steps Gate
Japanese Gateway & Landscape
Pavilion Restaurant
Pagoda
OLD DEER PARK
ROYAL MID-SURREY GOLF COURSE
King's Observatory
Royal Mid-Surrey Golf Club
Richmond Athletic Ground
Rugby Grd.
Grand Stand
London Welsh RUFC
Cricket Grd.
Bowling Green
Tennis Courts
Pools on the Park
Obelisk
Old Deer Park Recreation Ground
Richmond Lock
WEST MIDDLESEX UNIVERSITY HOSP.
Cemetery
TWICKENHAM RD.
A310
ST. JOHN'S RD.
B363
Old Isleworth
Isleworth Ait
SOUTH ST.
RICHMOND RD.
A3004
Nazareth Ho.
ISLEWORTH
REDLEES PARK
Brunel Univ.
ST. MARGARETS RD.
Pleasure Gdns.
ST MARGARETS
THE AVENUE
TWICKENHAM ROAD
A316
RICHMOND
Richmond Green
Richmond
Corporation Island
PETERSHAM RD.
A307
RICHMOND HILL
B321
Terrace Gardens
Terrace Fld.
Richmond Univ.
Royal Star & Garter Home
Petersham Common
LONDON RD. ROUNDABOUT
CHERTSEY RD.
Moor Mead Bridge
Cole Park
Moor Mead Gd.
St. Margarets
ST. MARGARETS R'BOUT
CROWN RD.
RICHMOND RD.
A305
MARBLE HILL PARK
Marble Hill House
Glover's Island
Buccleugh Gdns.
Petersham Meadows
Petersham Farm
Twickenham
Orleans Ho. Gallery
Orleans Gdns.
Foot Ferry
WARREN
TWICKENHAM
RIVER THAMES
PETERSHAM ROAD
STAR & GARTER HILL
Sports Grd.
The German Sch. London

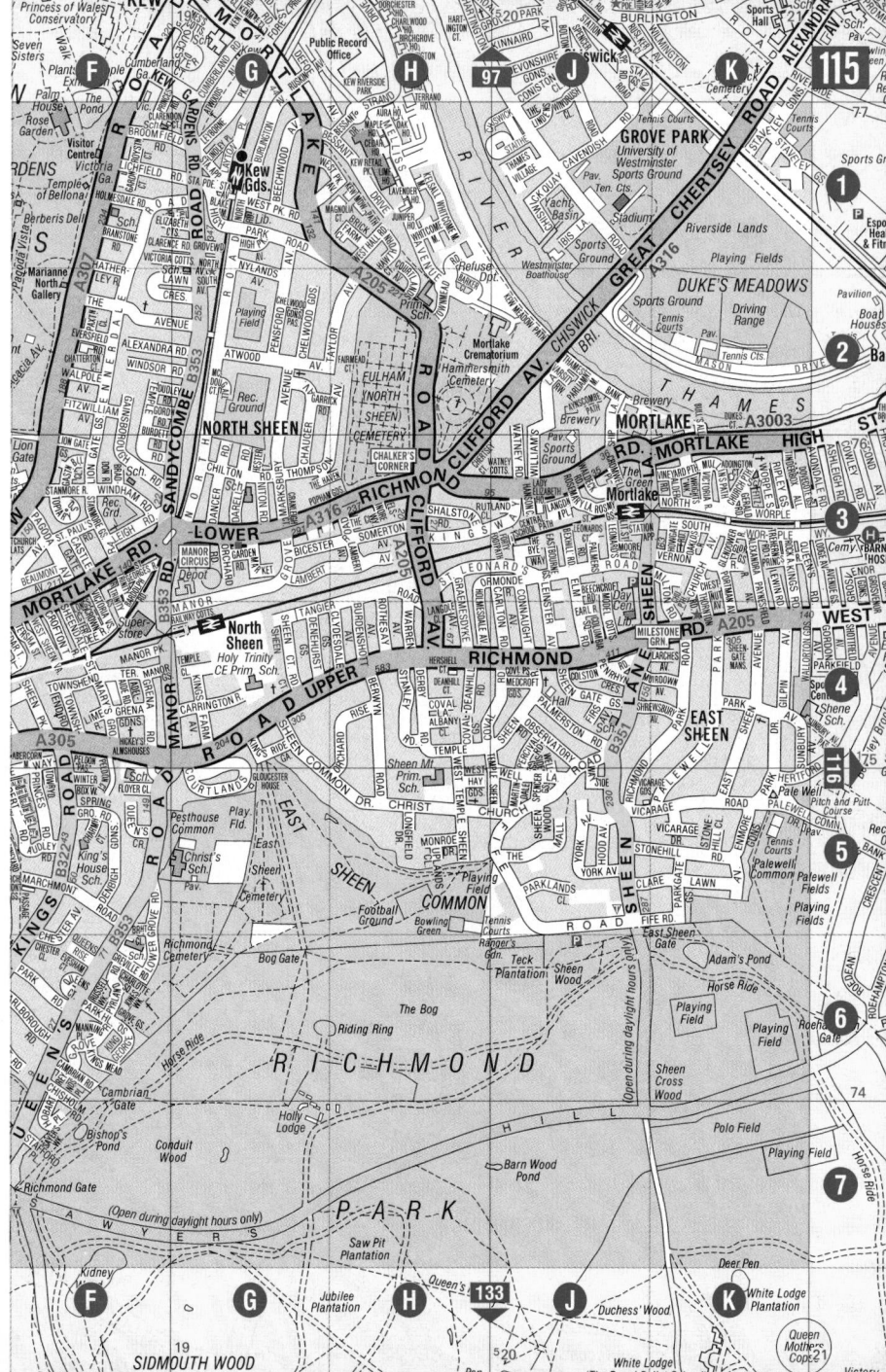

Princess of Wales Conservatory
Seven Sisters
Palm House
Rose Garden
The Pond
Visitor Centre
Victoria Ga.
Temple of Bellona
Berberis Dell
Pagoda Vista
Marianne North Gallery
Cumberland Ga.
KEW GARDENS RD.
KEW RD.
A307
Kew Gds.
MORTLAKE RD.
Public Record Office
KEW RIVERSIDE PARK
STRAND
RIVER THAMES
97
Chiswick
BURLINGTON
GROVE PARK
University of Westminster Sports Ground
Stadium
Riverside Lands
Playing Fields
Yacht Basin
Sports Ground
Westminster Boathouse
DUKE'S MEADOWS
Driving Range
Tennis Courts
Pavilion
Boat Houses
Sports Hall
Cemetery
ALEXANDRA AV.
GREAT CHERTSEY ROAD
A316
CHISWICK BRI.
CLIFFORD AV.
Refuse Dpt.
Mortlake Crematorium
Hammersmith Cemetery
FULHAM (NORTH SHEEN) CEMETERY
CHALKER'S CORNER
Playing Field
Rec. Ground
NORTH SHEEN
SANDYCOMBE ROAD
B353
RICHMOND
CLIFFORD ROAD
A205
MORTLAKE
Brewery
MORTLAKE HIGH ST
A3003
The Green
Mortlake
Pav. Sports Ground
LOWER MORTLAKE RD.
MANOR CIRCUS
Depot
Superstore
North Sheen
Holy Trinity CE Prim. Sch.
MANOR ROAD
UPPER RICHMOND ROAD
A305
SHEEN LANE
B351
EAST SHEEN
WEST
Shene Sch.
116
Sheen Mt Prim. Sch.
CHRIST CHURCH ROAD
Pesthouse Common
Christ's Sch.
East Sheen Cemetery
Richmond Cemetery
SHEEN COMMON
Football Ground
Bowling Green
Tennis Courts
Ranger's Gdn.
Teck Plantation
Sheen Wood
East Sheen Gate
Adam's Pond
Horse Ride
Playing Field
Roehampton Gate
Palewell Common
Palewell Fields
Playing Fields
Pitch and Putt Course
Bog Gate
The Bog
Riding Ring
RICHMOND PARK
(Open during daylight hours only)
Sheen Cross Wood
Cambrian Gate
Holly Lodge
Bishop's Pond
Conduit Wood
Barn Wood Pond
Polo Field
Playing Field
Richmond Gate
SAWYERS HILL
Saw Pit Plantation
Kidney Wood
Queen's Ride
Jubilee Plantation
133
Duchess' Wood
Deer Pen
White Lodge Plantation
Queen Mothers Copse
SIDMOUTH WOOD
White Lodge (The Royal Ballet School)
F
G
H
J
K
1
2
3
4
5
6
7

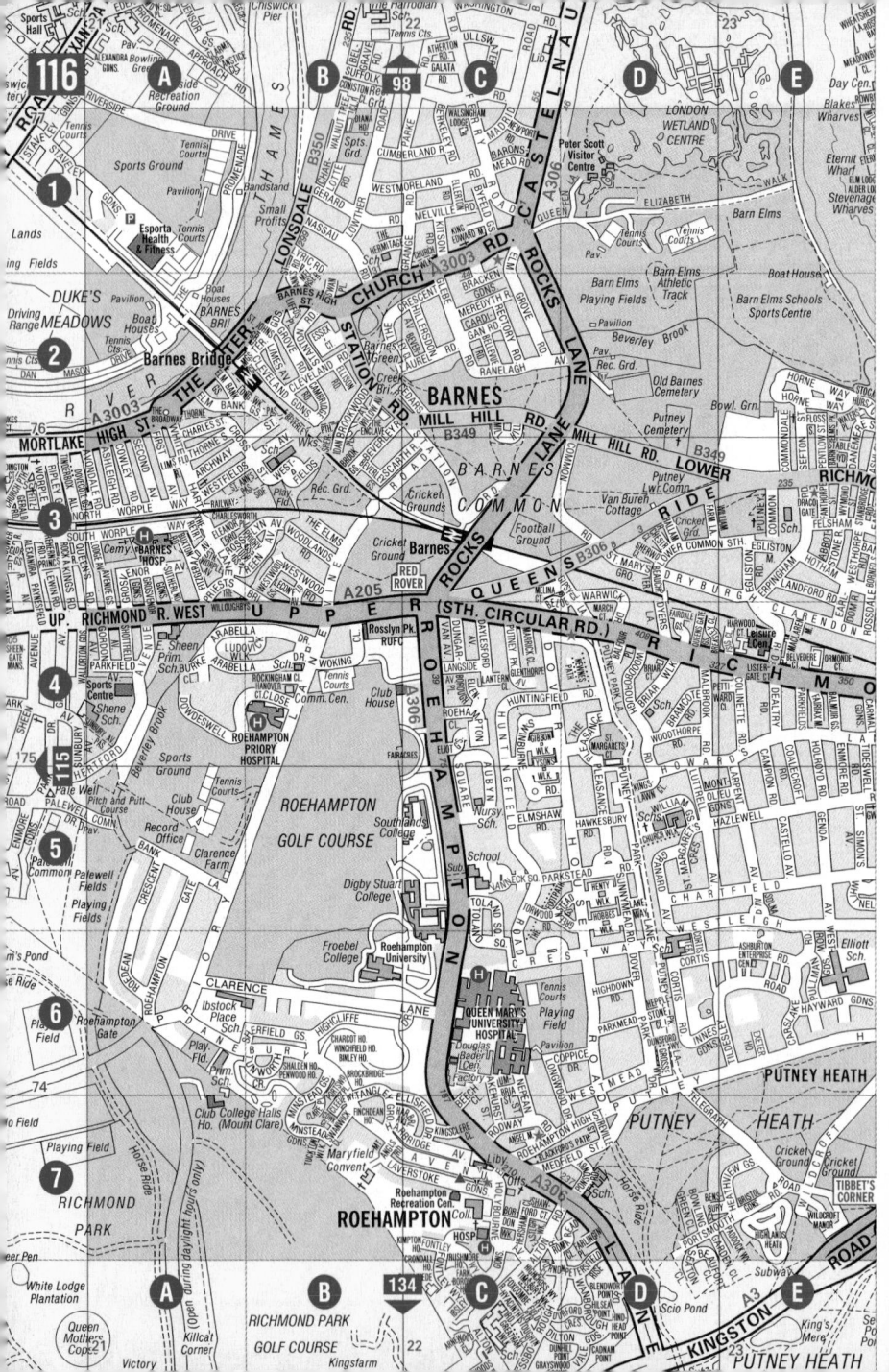

116
A
B
C
D
E
98
134
115
22
23
1
2
3
4
5
6
7
Sports Hall
Chiswick Pier
Riverside Recreation Ground
Sports Ground
Tennis Courts
Pavilion
Esporta Health & Fitness
Bandstand
Small Profits
THAMES
RIVER
DUKE'S MEADOWS
Driving Range
Boat Houses
Barnes Bridge
BARNES BRIDGE
MORTLAKE HIGH ST.
A3003
THE TERRACE
LONSDALE RD.
CHURCH RD.
CASTELNAU
ROCKS LANE
STATION RD.
BARNES
Barnes Green
MILL HILL RD.
B349
BARNES COMMON
Cricket Grounds
Cricket Ground
Barnes
RED ROVER
A205
UPPER RICHMOND R. WEST
UP. RICHMOND
(STH. CIRCULAR RD.)
QUEENS RIDE
B306
ROEHAMPTON LANE
A306
Rosslyn Pk. RUFC
Club House
BARNES HOSP.
Cemy.
Sports Centre
Shene Sch.
E. Sheen Prim. Sch.
ROEHAMPTON PRIORY HOSPITAL
Beverley Brook
Sports Ground
Record Office
Clarence Farm
ROEHAMPTON GOLF COURSE
Southlands College
Digby Stuart College
Froebel College
Roehampton University
QUEEN MARY'S UNIVERSITY HOSPITAL
Douglas Bader Cen.
Ibstock Place Sch.
Roehampton Gate
Palewell Common
Palewell Fields
Playing Fields
Pitch and Putt Course
LONDON WETLAND CENTRE
Peter Scott Visitor Centre
Barn Elms
Barn Elms Athletic Track
Barn Elms Playing Fields
Barn Elms Schools Sports Centre
Boat House
Beverley Brook
Old Barnes Cemetery
Putney Cemetery
Bowl. Grn.
Putney Lwr. Comn.
Van Buren Cottage
Football Ground
LOWER RICHMOND
RICHMOND
Leisure Cen.
Blakes Wharves
Eternit Wharf
Stevenage Wharves
Day Cen.
PUTNEY HEATH
Cricket Ground
TIBBET'S CORNER
Scio Pond
King's Mere
KINGSTON ROAD
A3
Subway
PUTNEY HIGH ST.
ROEHAMPTON HIGH ST.
Horse Ride
Maryfield Convent
Club College Halls Ho. (Mount Clare)
Roehampton Recreation Cen.
ROEHAMPTON
RICHMOND PARK
Playing Field
White Lodge Plantation
Queen Mothers Copse
(Open during daylight hours only)
Killcat Corner
RICHMOND PARK GOLF COURSE
Kingsfarm
Victory

117
F
G
H
J
K
1
2
3
4
5
6
7
99
135
118
FULHAM
Fulham Cemetery
Fulham FC (Craven Cottage)
Fulham Palace
Moat Garden
The Warren Playground
BISHOP'S PARK
RIVER
THAMES
WALHAM GREEN
Eel Brook Common
Parsons Grn.
PARSONS GRN.
SANDS END
Gas Works
SOUTH PARK
HURLINGHAM PARK
Hurlingham Stadium
Running Track
Hurlingham
The Hurlingham Club
Ckt. Grd.
Swim. Pool
Putney Bri.
Putney Pier
Wharves
Hurlingham Wharf
Trinidad Wharf
Jetties
Jetty
River Wandle
Solid Waste Transfer Station
Fitness Club
Wandsworth Town
WANDSWORTH GYRATORY
WANDSWORTH PARK
PUTNEY
Putney
Odeon Cin.
PUTNEY EXCHANGE SHOP. CEN.
East Putney
WANDSWORTH
County Ct.
Brewery
Mus.
WEST HILL
ROYAL HOSP. FOR NEURO-DISABILITY
King George's Park
Rec. Cen.
Works
Playing Fld.
Mosque
Saint Cecilia's
SOUTHFIELDS
Southfields
Play. Fields
Southfields Comm. Coll.
Mecca Bingo
FULHAM PALACE RD.
FULHAM RD.
NEW KINGS RD.
WANDSWORTH BRIDGE RD.
PUTNEY BRIDGE
PUTNEY HIGH ST.
PUTNEY HILL
WANDSWORTH BRIDGE
ARMOURY WAY
WANDSWORTH HIGH ST. EAST
GARRATT LA.
BUCKHOLD RD.
MERTON ROAD
WEST HILL
PUTNEY HEATH LA.
TIBBET'S RIDE
WIMBLEDON PARK SIDE
A219
A304
A308
A217
A3209
A205
A3
A218
B306

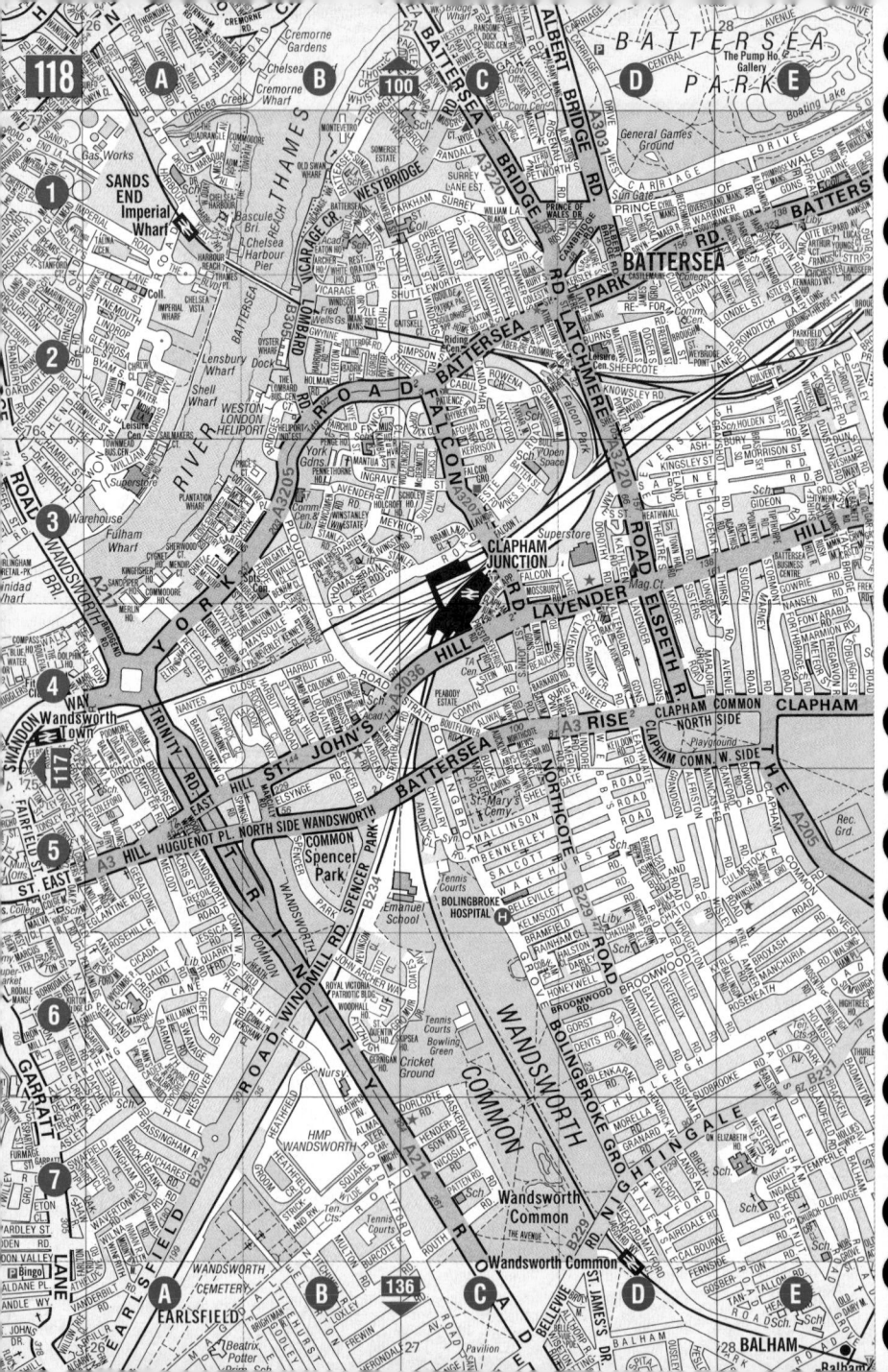
118
100
117
136
A
B
C
D
E
1
2
3
4
5
6
7
26
27
28
BATTERSEA PARK
The Pump Ho. Gallery
Boating Lake
General Games Ground
Cremorne Gardens
Cremorne Wharf
Chelsea Creek
Gas Works
SANDS END
Imperial Wharf
Bascule Bri.
Chelsea Harbour Pier
RIVER THAMES
Lensbury Wharf
Shell Wharf
WESTON LONDON HELIPORT
Fulham Wharf
Warehouse
Superstore
Leisure Cen.
BATTERSEA
CLAPHAM JUNCTION
Falcon Park
Open Space
York Gdns.
PEABODY ESTATE
St. Mary's Cemy.
Tennis Courts
BOLINGBROKE HOSPITAL
Emanuel School
Spencer Park
Cricket Ground
Bowling Green
HMP WANDSWORTH
Wandsworth Common
WANDSWORTH CEMETERY
EARLSFIELD
Wandsworth Town
BALHAM
Rec. Grd.
Playground
ALBERT BRIDGE RD.
BATTERSEA BRIDGE RD.
BATTERSEA PARK RD.
LATCHMERE RD.
FALCON RD.
LAVENDER HILL
ST. JOHN'S HILL
BATTERSEA RISE
CLAPHAM COMMON NORTH SIDE
CLAPHAM COMMON WEST SIDE
NORTHCOTE RD.
BOLINGBROKE GRO.
NIGHTINGALE LA.
TRINITY RD.
WANDSWORTH COMMON
WINDMILL RD.
YORK RD.
WANDSWORTH BRI.
EAST HILL
GARRATT LANE
EARLSFIELD RD.
ELSPETH R.
WESTBRIDGE RD.
A3
A3205
A3220
A3031
A3036
A3207
A214
A205
A217
B305
B229
B231
B234

NEW COVENT GARDEN MARKET
Fruit & Vegetable Market
Battersea Dogs' Home
Battersea Park
Queenstown Road (Battersea)
SOUTH LAMBETH
Stockwell
STOCKWELL
Angell Town
Larkhall Park
Heathbrook Park
Wandsworth Rd.
Clapham High St.
Clapham North
LAMBETH HOSPITAL
CLAPHAM
Clapham Comm.
CLAPHAM COMMON
BRIXTON
CLAPHAM PARK
HMP BRIXTON
Windmill Gdns.
Sports Ground
Clapham Sth.
Eagle Pond
Mount Pond
Long Pond
Bandstand
QUEENSTOWN RD.
WANDSWORTH ROAD
CLAPHAM ROAD
STOCKWELL ROAD
SOUTH LAMBETH RD.
CLAPHAM HIGH ST.
ACRE LANE
BEDFORD RD.
KING'S AVENUE
BRIXTON HILL
POYNDERS RD.
CAVENDISH RD.
CLAPHAM COMMON SOUTH SIDE
CLAPHAM COMMON NORTH SIDE
LONG RD.
CLAPHAM PARK RD.
ATKINS RD.
STREATHAM PL.
CHRISTCHURCH RD.
BALHAM HIGH ROAD
BALHAM HILL
A3
A24
A23
A205
A2217
A3036
B221
101
120
137
F G H J K
1 2 3 4 5 6 7

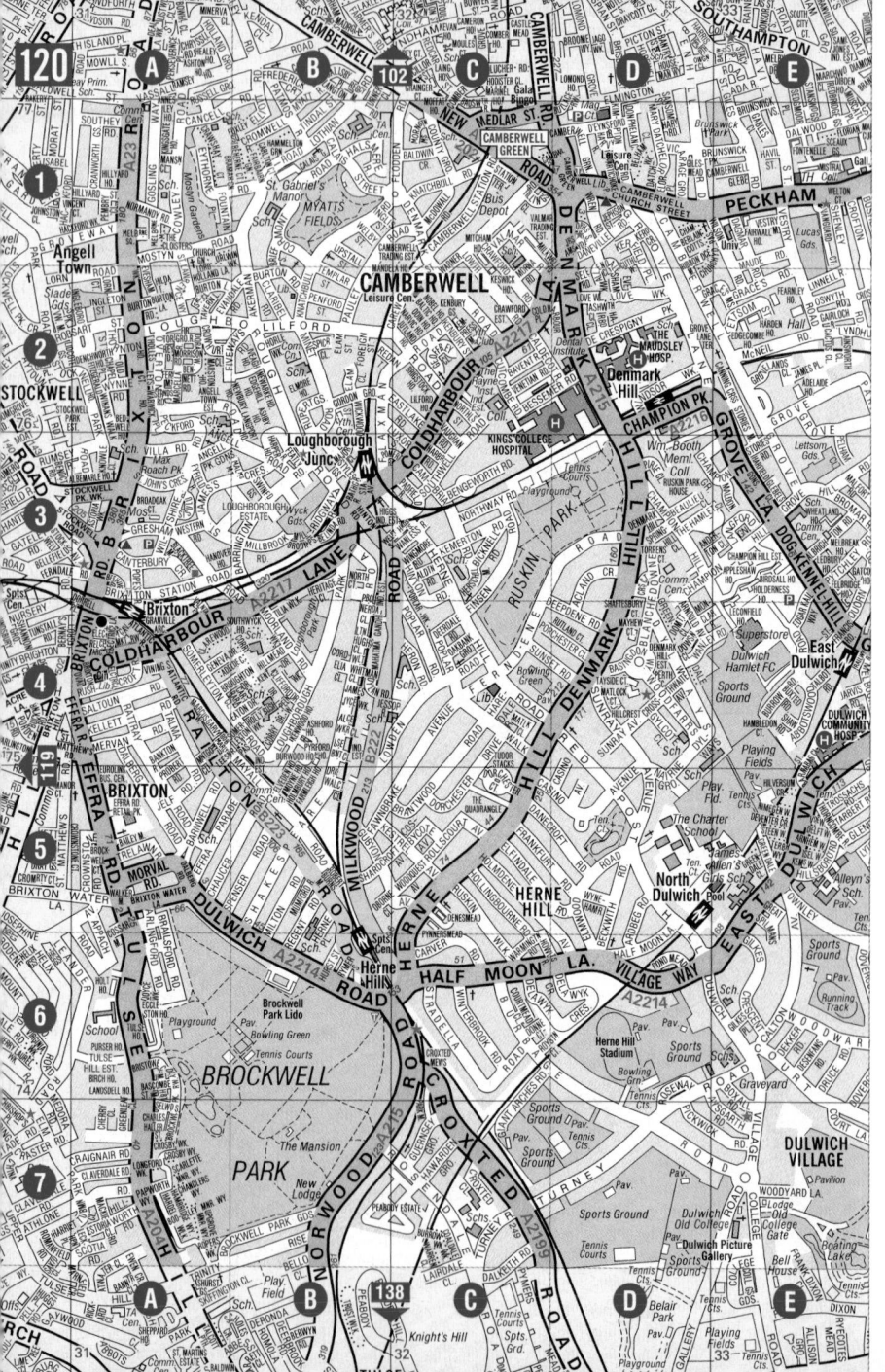
A
B
C
D
E
1
2
3
4
5
6
7
102
119
138
CAMBERWELL
CAMBERWELL GREEN
CAMBERWELL CHURCH STREET
CAMBERWELL NEW RD.
NEW MEDLAR ST.
PECKHAM
SOUTHAMPTON
Angell Town
STOCKWELL
BRIXTON
Brixton
COLDHARBOUR
COLDHARBOUR LANE
A2217
LOUGHBOROUGH
Loughborough Junc.
MYATTS FIELDS
St. Gabriel's Manor
DENMARK HILL
Denmark Hill
CHAMPION PK.
A2216
A215
KINGS COLLEGE HOSPITAL
THE MAUDSLEY HOSP.
RUSKIN PARK
Wm. Booth Meml. Coll.
GROVE LA.
DOG KENNEL HILL
East Dulwich
Dulwich Hamlet FC
Sports Ground
Superstore
DULWICH COMMUNITY HOSP.
MILKWOOD ROAD
B222
RAILTON ROAD
B223
EFFRA RD.
A23
BRIXTON HILL
BRIXTON WATER LA.
DULWICH ROAD
A2214
HERNE HILL
Herne Hill
HALF MOON LA.
VILLAGE WAY
EAST DULWICH
North Dulwich
The Charter School
James Allen's Girls Sch.
Alleyn's Sch.
BROCKWELL PARK
Brockwell Park Lido
The Mansion
New Lodge
Playground
Bowling Green
Tennis Courts
TULSE HILL
A204
NORWOOD ROAD
CROXTED ROAD
A2199
TURNEY ROAD
Herne Hill Stadium
DULWICH VILLAGE
Dulwich Old College
Dulwich Picture Gallery
Belair Park
Knight's Hill
BROCKWELL PARK GDS.
Sports Ground
Running Track
Boating Lake
31
32
33

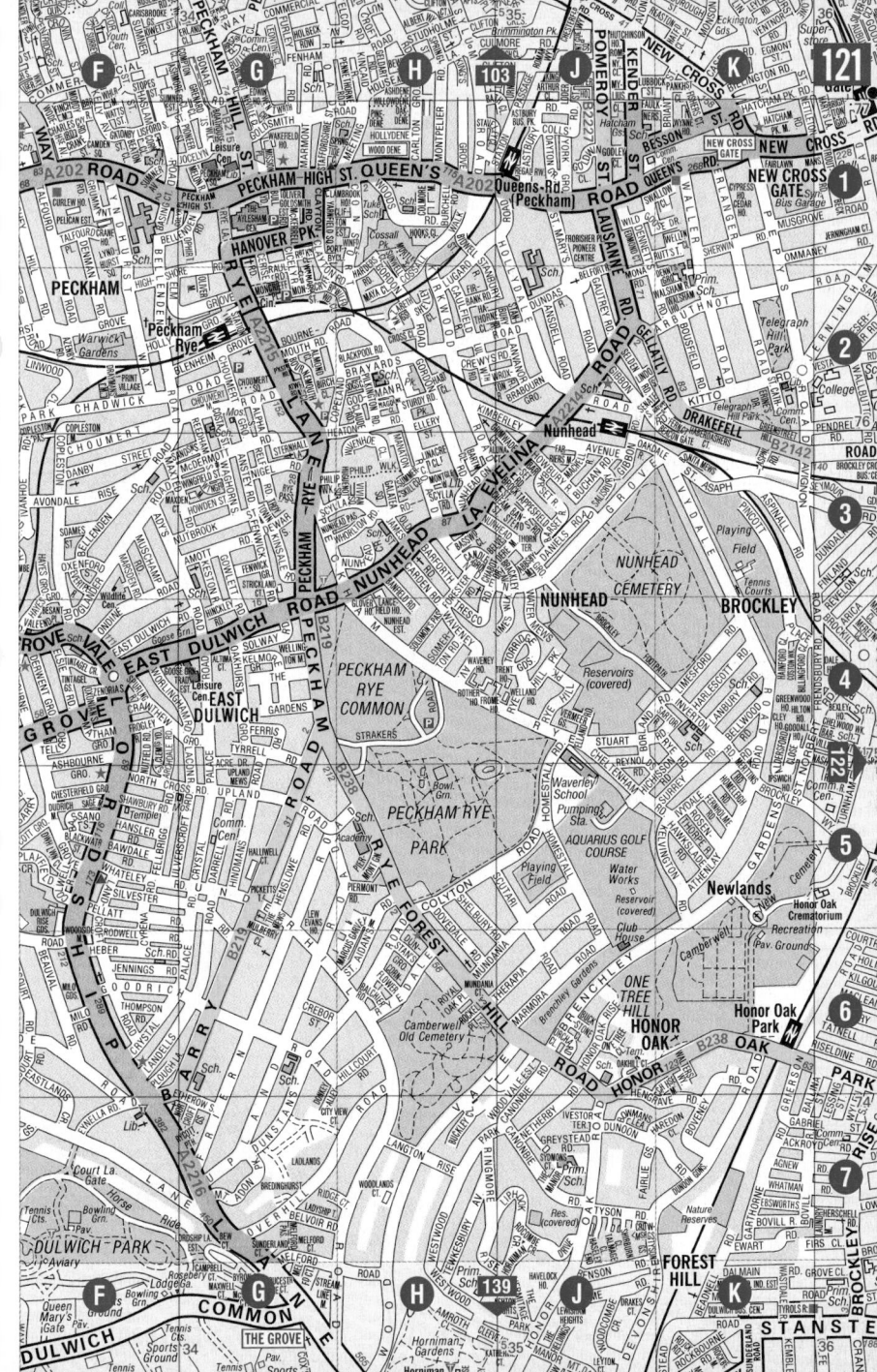

121
103
122
139
F
G
H
J
K
1
2
3
4
5
6
7
34
35
36
PECKHAM
NUNHEAD
BROCKLEY
EAST DULWICH
NEW CROSS GATE
HONOR OAK
FOREST HILL
Newlands
Peckham Rye
Nunhead
Queens Rd. (Peckham)
Honor Oak Park
New Cross Gate
PECKHAM HIGH ST.
QUEEN'S ROAD
NEW CROSS RD.
A202
A2215
A2214
A2216
B238
B219
B2142
B2227
RYE LANE
PECKHAM RYE
EVELINA RD.
NUNHEAD LA.
EAST DULWICH ROAD
GROVE VALE
LORDSHIP LANE
DULWICH COMMON
FOREST HILL ROAD
HONOR OAK ROAD
BRENCHLEY GARDENS
PECKHAM RYE COMMON
PECKHAM RYE PARK
NUNHEAD CEMETERY
Camberwell Old Cemetery
Camberwell New Cemetery
Honor Oak Crematorium
Telegraph Hill Park
Warwick Gardens
DULWICH PARK
Horniman Gardens
AQUARIUS GOLF COURSE
ONE TREE HILL
Reservoirs (covered)
Water Works
Playing Field
Tennis Courts
Nature Reserves
Recreation Ground
Waverley School
Pumping Sta.
Leisure Cen.
Bus Garage
Super-store
THE GROVE
THE AYLESHAM CEN.
HANOVER PK.

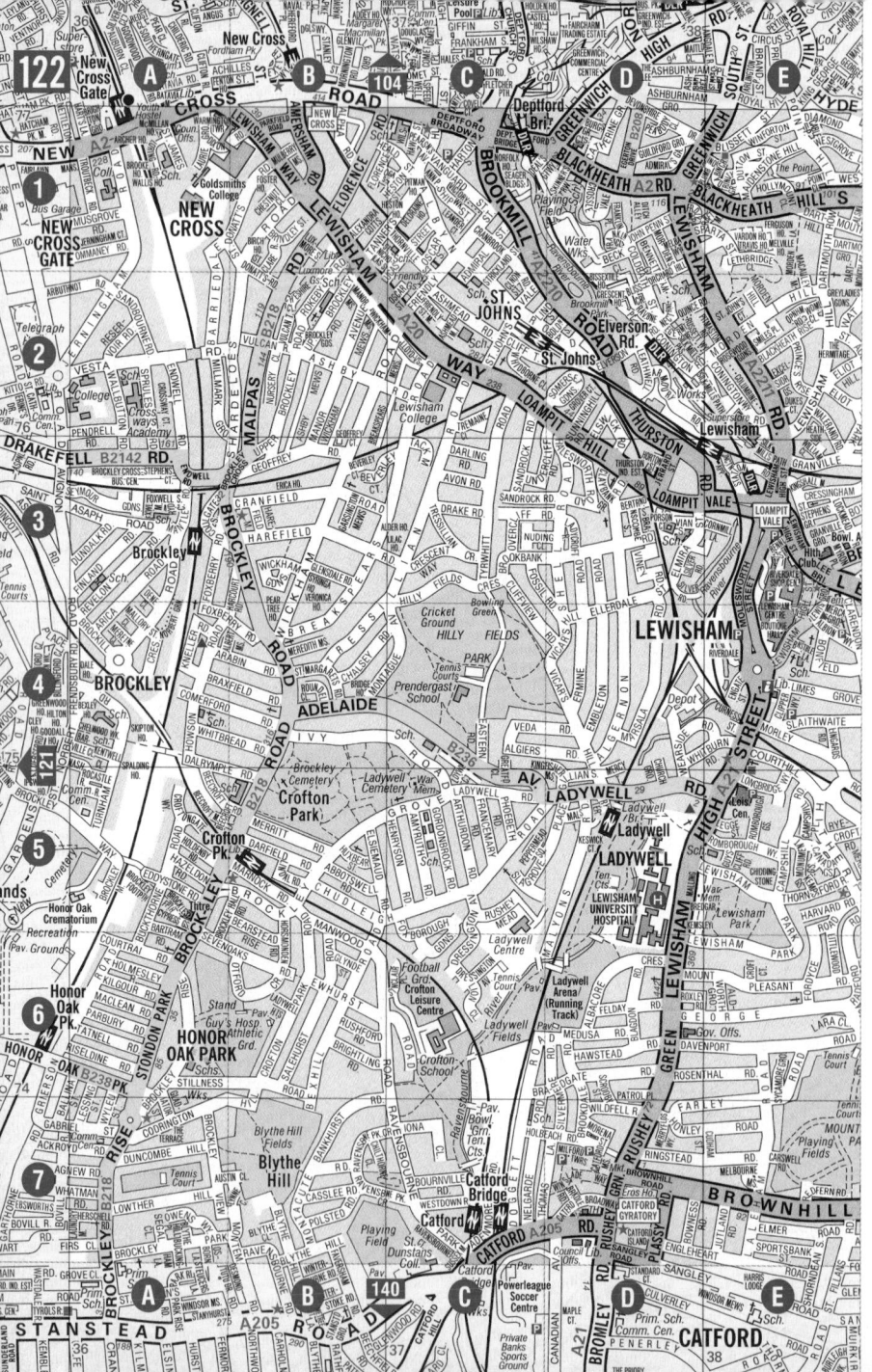

122
104
121
140
A
B
C
D
E
1
2
3
4
5
6
7
New Cross Gate
New Cross
NEW CROSS
NEW CROSS GATE
NEW CROSS ROAD
A2
Goldsmiths College
LEWISHAM WAY
AMERSHAM WAY
DEPTFORD BROADWAY
Deptford Bri.
Deptford Bridge
BROOKMILL ROAD
GREENWICH HIGH RD.
BLACKHEATH RD.
BLACKHEATH HILL
LEWISHAM RD.
GREENWICH SOUTH ST.
ROYAL HILL
ST. JOHNS
St. Johns
Elverson Rd.
LOAMPIT WAY
LOAMPIT HILL
LOAMPIT VALE
THURSTON RD.
Lewisham
LEWISHAM
Lewisham College
MALPAS RD.
DRAKEFELL RD.
B2142
BROCKLEY
Brockley
BROCKLEY ROAD
B218
Telegraph
Crossways Academy
HILLY FIELDS
Cricket Ground
Prendergast School
ADELAIDE AV.
IVY RD.
LADYWELL RD.
Ladywell
LADYWELL
LEWISHAM UNIVERSITY HOSPITAL
Brockley Cemetery
Ladywell Cemetery
Crofton Park
Crofton Pk.
HONOR OAK PARK
Honor Oak Pk.
Honor Oak Crematorium
STONDON PARK
BROCKLEY RISE
Blythe Hill Fields
Blythe Hill
Crofton Leisure Centre
Ladywell Arena (Running Track)
Ladywell Fields
Ladywell Centre
LEWISHAM HIGH STREET
A21
LEWISHAM PARK
Lewisham Park
RUSHEY GREEN
Catford Bridge
Catford
CATFORD
CATFORD GYRATORY
CATFORD RD.
A205
BROWNHILL RD.
STANSTEAD ROAD
Powerleague Soccer Centre
Private Banks Sports Ground
BROMLEY RD.
Playing Field
Playing Fields
Gov. Offs.

123
F
G
H
J
K
1
2
3
4
5
6
7
124
141
105
GREENWICH PARK
Royal Observatory Greenwich
Reservoir (covered)
The Wilderness
The Gardens
(Deer Park)
Rangers House
VANBRUGH PARK
OLD DOVER ROAD
SUN-IN-THE-SANDS
SHOOTERS HILL
CHARLTON ROAD
A2
B210
B212
A2213
A20
A205
A2212
B220
BLACK HEATH
Blackheath Vale
Christ's College for Boys
Morden College (Almshouses)
ROCHESTER WAY RELIEF ROAD
KIDBROOKE PARK ROAD
PRINCE OF WALES RD.
PRINCE CHARLES ROAD
BLACKHEATH
Blackheath
Hollyhedge Ho.
College
Concert Halls
Kidbrooke Nature
Thomas Tallis Sch.
Kidbrooke
BLACKHEATH PARK
Sports Ground
David Lloyd Leis.
Golf Driving Range
Quaggy River
Sutcliffe Pk. Athletics Track
SUTCLIFFE PARK
LEE HIGH ROAD
BELMONT HILL
ELTHAM ROAD
Manor House Gdns.
Manor Park
LEE
Brindishe Prim. Sch.
BURNT ASH RD.
BURNT ASH HILL
Horn Park
Colfes Sch.
Playing Field
Lee
Hither Green
HITHER GREEN
WESTHORNE AVENUE
SIDCUP ROAD
ST. MILDREDS ROAD
BARING ROAD
Horn Park Prim. Sch.
Hither Green Sidings
MOTTINGHAM

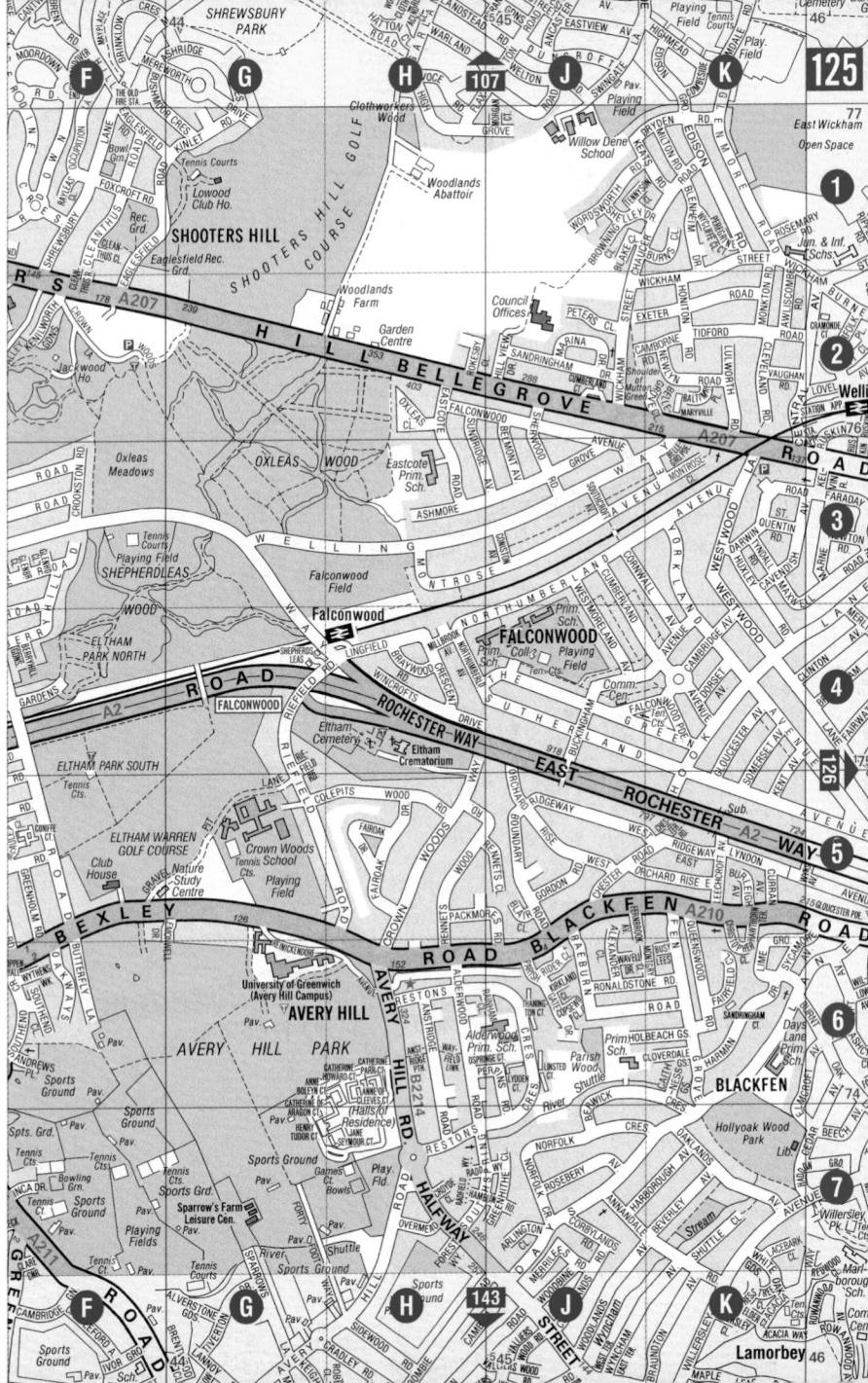

125
107
126
143
F
G
H
J
K
1
2
3
4
5
6
7
SHREWSBURY PARK
SHOOTERS HILL
Clothworkers Wood
SHOOTERS HILL GOLF COURSE
Woodlands Abattoir
Willow Dene School
East Wickham Open Space
Rosemary Jun. & Inf. Schs.
Lowood Club Ho.
Eaglesfield Rec. Grd.
Rec. Grd.
Tennis Courts
Woodlands Farm
Garden Centre
Council Offices
Jackwood Ho.
SHOOTERS HILL ROAD
A207
BELLEGROVE ROAD
Welling
Oxleas Meadows
OXLEAS WOOD
Eastcote Prim. Sch.
WELLING WAY
Falconwood Field
Falconwood
Playing Field
SHEPHERDLEAS WOOD
ELTHAM PARK NORTH
FALCONWOOD
Prim. Sch.
Coll.
Playing Field
Comm. Cen.
A2
ROCHESTER WAY
EAST ROCHESTER WAY
Eltham Cemetery
Eltham Crematorium
ELTHAM PARK SOUTH
ELTHAM WARREN GOLF COURSE
Club House
Nature Study Centre
Crown Woods School
Playing Field
BEXLEY ROAD
BLACKFEN ROAD
A210
University of Greenwich (Avery Hill Campus)
AVERY HILL
AVERY HILL PARK
AVERY HILL RD.
B2214
Halls of Residence
Alderwood Prim. Sch.
Parish Wood
Prim. Sch.
River Shuttle
BLACKFEN
Days Lane Prim. Sch.
Hollyoak Wood Park
Sports Ground
Sports Grd.
Spts. Grd.
Tennis Cts.
Bowling Grn.
Playing Fields
Sparrow's Farm Leisure Cen.
Play. Fld.
Games Ct. Bowls
HALFWAY STREET
A211
Willersley Pk.
Marlborough Sch.
Comm. Cen.
Lamorbey
DAY'S LANE

A
B
C
D
E
1
2
3
4
5
6
7
46
47
48
77
76
75
74
108
125
144
East Wickham Open Space
Hill Grove
PLUMSTEAD CEMETERY
EAST WICKHAM
WELLING
Welling
Welling Corner
WELLING HIGH ST.
PARK VIEW RD.
CROOK LOG
BELLEGROVE RD.
UPPER WICKHAM LA.
A209
A207
A221
A2
A210
B2210
ROCHESTER WAY
EAST ROCHESTER WAY
BLACKFEN ROAD
BLACKFEN
DANSON ROAD
DANSON PARK
THE LAKE
The Mansion
Danson Water Sports Centre
DANSON INTERCHANGE
DANSON UNDERPASS
Bexley Grammar Sch.
Playing Field
Erith & Belvedere FC
Welling United FC
Bexleyheath Sports Club
Sports Grd.
Tennis Courts
Pitch & Putt
Bowl. Grns.
Splashworld
Crook Log Prim. Sch.
UPTON CENTRE
Upton
Red House
Bexleyheath
STATION
Brampton Prim. Sch.
Stevens Park
BEXLEYHEATH GOLF COURSE
PENHILL PARK
PENHILL RD.
Blendon
BLENDON RD.
BRIDGEN RD.
Bridgen
Bexley Park Wood
Blackfen Sch. for Girls
Sherwood Park Prim. Sch.
SIDCUP GOLF COURSE
Marlborough Park
Marlborough Sch.
Lamorbey
Lamorbey Park
Chatsworth Inf. Sch.
Willersley Pk.
Days Lane Prim. Sch.
Hook La Prim. Sch.
Hurst Prim. Sch.
HURST RD.
Rec. Grd.
River Shuttle
Riverside Wlk.
Welling Sch.
Westbrooke Sch.
The Danson Cen.
Theatre
Crook Lodge Spts. Cen.
War Mem.

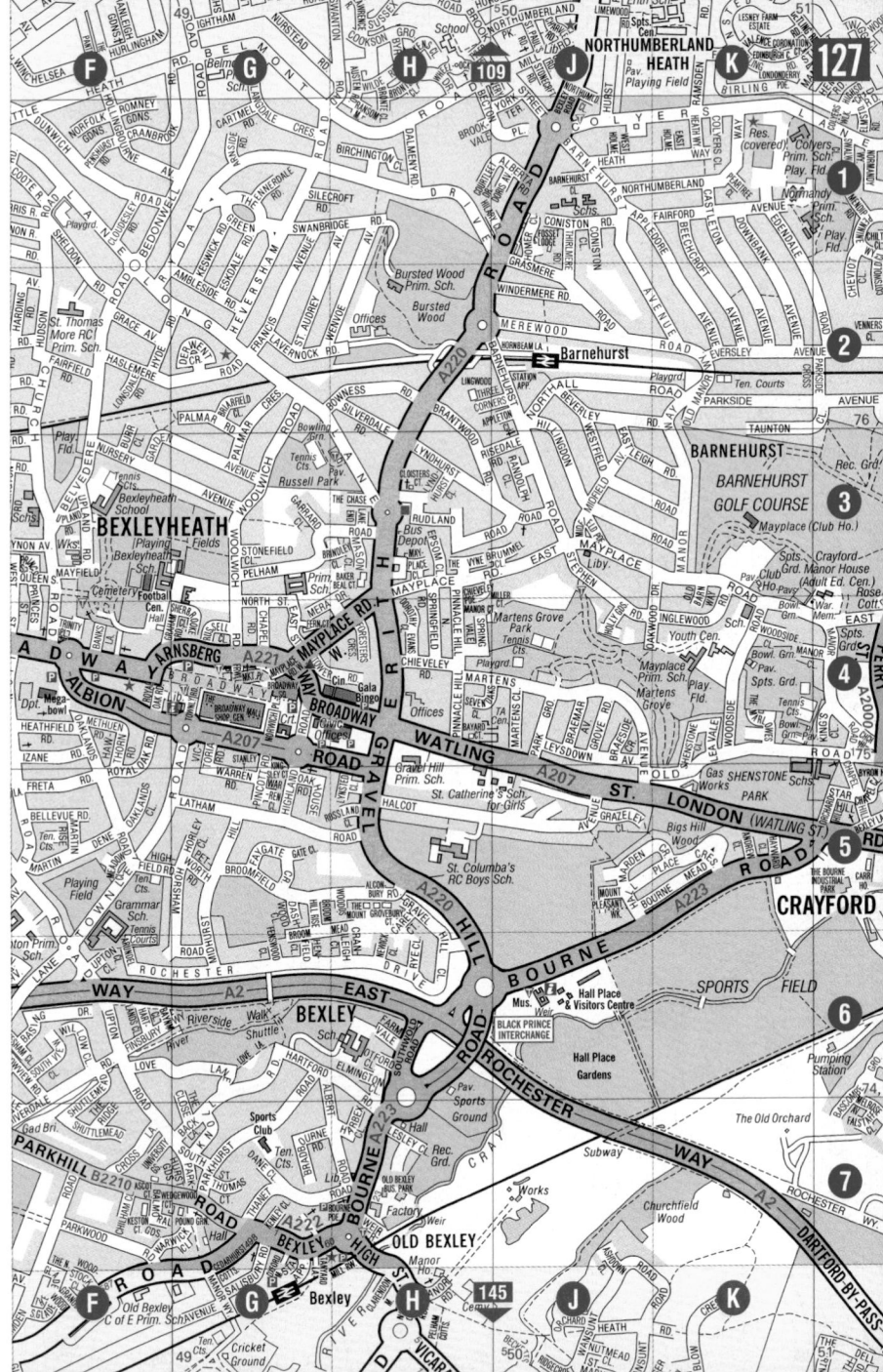
F
G
H
J
K
109
NORTHUMBERLAND HEATH
Erith Sch.
Pav. Playing Field
LESNEY FARM ESTATE
1
2
3
4
5
6
7
BELMONT
COLYERS
Res. (covered)
Colyers Prim. Sch.
Play. Fld.
Normandy Prim. Sch.
BARNEHURST
NORTHUMBERLAND
Bursted Wood Prim. Sch.
Bursted Wood
MEREWOOD
Barnehurst
Ten. Courts
A220
St. Thomas More RC Prim. Sch.
BARNEHURST GOLF COURSE
Mayplace (Club Ho.)
Crayford Manor House (Adult Ed. Cen.)
Bowling Grn.
Russell Park
Bexleyheath School
BEXLEYHEATH
Playing Fields
Bexleyheath Sch.
Cemetery
Football Cen.
Bus Depot
Liby.
Martens Grove Park
Mayplace Prim. Sch.
Martens Grove
Youth Cen.
A221
ARNSBERG WAY
MAYPLACE RD.
BROADWAY
Mega-bowl
THE BROADWAY SHOP. CEN.
Cin.
Gala Bingo
Civic Offices
ALBION
A207
WATLING
Gravel Hill Prim. Sch.
St. Catherine's Sch. for Girls
GRAVEL
SHENSTONE PARK
Gas Works
LONDON (WATLING ST.)
Bigs Hill Wood
St. Columba's RC Boys Sch.
A220 HILL
A223
BOURNE
THE BOURNE INDUSTRIAL PARK
CRAYFORD
A2000
Playing Field
Grammar Sch.
Tennis Courts
ROCHESTER
A2
EAST
WAY
BEXLEY
Riverside Walk
Shuttle River
Mus.
Hall Place & Visitors Centre
BLACK PRINCE INTERCHANGE
Hall Place Gardens
SPORTS FIELD
Pumping Station
ROCHESTER WAY
Sports Club
Pav. Sports Ground
Rec. Grd.
CRAY
The Old Orchard
Subway
PARKHILL
B2210
A222
Works
Churchfield Wood
DARTFORD-BY-PASS
OLD BEXLEY
Factory
Weir
Manor Ho.
Bexley
Old Bexley C of E Prim. Sch.
145
Cemy.
Cricket Ground

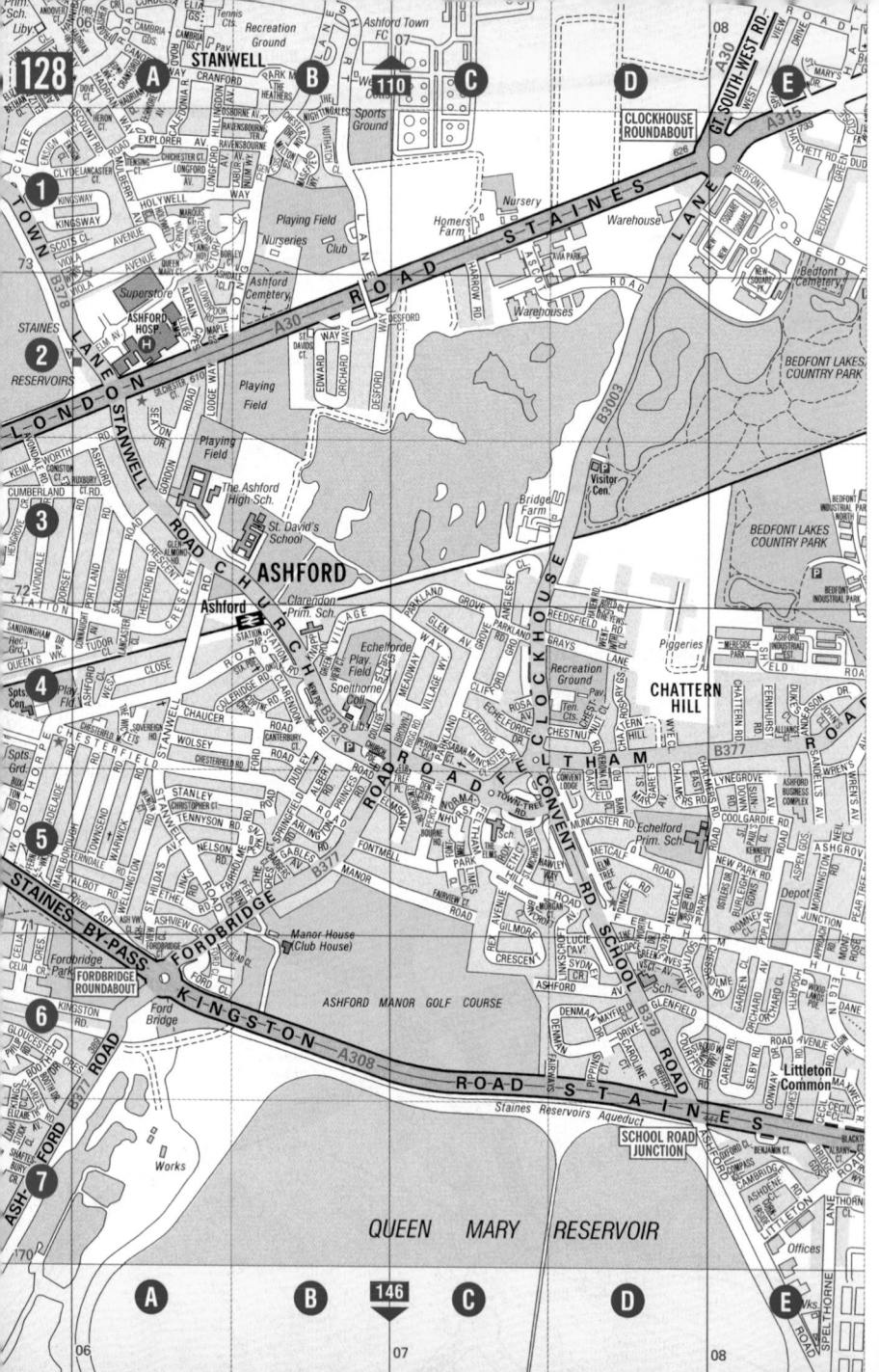
128
STANWELL
ASHFORD
CHATTERN HILL
Littleton Common
Recreation Ground
Ashford Town FC
110
146
Sports Ground
Playing Field
Nurseries
Club
Nursery
Homers Farm
Warehouse
Warehouses
Ashford Cemetery
Superstore
ASHFORD HOSP.
STAINES RESERVOIRS
CLOCKHOUSE ROUNDABOUT
BEDFONT LAKES COUNTRY PARK
Bedfont Cemetery
Visitor Cen.
Bridge Farm
The Ashford High Sch.
St. David's School
Clarendon Prim. Sch.
Ashford
Echelforde Play. Field
Spelthorne Coll.
Piggeries
ASHFORD INDUSTRIAL EST.
BEDFONT INDUSTRIAL PARK
ASHFORD BUSINESS COMPLEX
Echelford Prim. Sch.
Depot
Manor House (Club House)
ASHFORD MANOR GOLF COURSE
Fordbridge Park
FORDBRIDGE ROUNDABOUT
Ford Bridge
Works
Staines Reservoirs Aqueduct
SCHOOL ROAD JUNCTION
QUEEN MARY RESERVOIR
Offices
LONDON ROAD
STAINES ROAD
STAINES-BY-PASS
KINGSTON ROAD
FELTHAM ROAD
CHURCH ROAD
STANWELL ROAD
CLOCKHOUSE LANE
CONVENT RD
SCHOOL ROAD
GT. SOUTH-WEST RD.
A30
A315
A308
B377
B378
B3003
A
B
C
D
E
1
2
3
4
5
6
7
06
07
08
70
71
72
73

129
EAST BEDFONT
Fairholme Primary Sch.
Playing Field
Industrial Est.
Edward Pauling Prim. Sch.
Vineyard Nurseries
HM Young Offenders Institution Feltham
LOWER FELTHAM
Grosvenor Park
FELTHAM
Ordnance Depot
Sports Ground
Feltham Hill Jun. & Inf. Schs.
Cemetery
Croft Farm
Garden Centre
Rugby Football Ground
FELTHAMHILL
Playing Field
Kenyngton Manor Prim. Sch.
Sports Ground
Laboratories
Spelthorne Jun. & Inf. Schs.
King George's Fld.
ASHFORD COMMON
SUNBURY COMMON
Library
Junc.1
M3 MOTORWAY
SUNBURY CROSS
Sunbury
Kempton Park
KEMPTON PARK RACECOURSE
Grandstand
Depot
Stables
Warehouse
Works
Filter Beds
Pumping Station
Club Ho.
Running Track
Blenheim Pk.
Feltham
Gala Bingo
Bowl Alley
Cinema
Super-store
ASHFORD ROAD
CHERTSEY ROAD
HIGH STREET
HANWORTH RD.
HARLINGTON ROAD
BEDFONT LANE
STAINES ROAD
STAINES ROAD WEST
COUNTRY WAY
SNAKEY LANE
HOUNSLOW ROAD
111
130
147

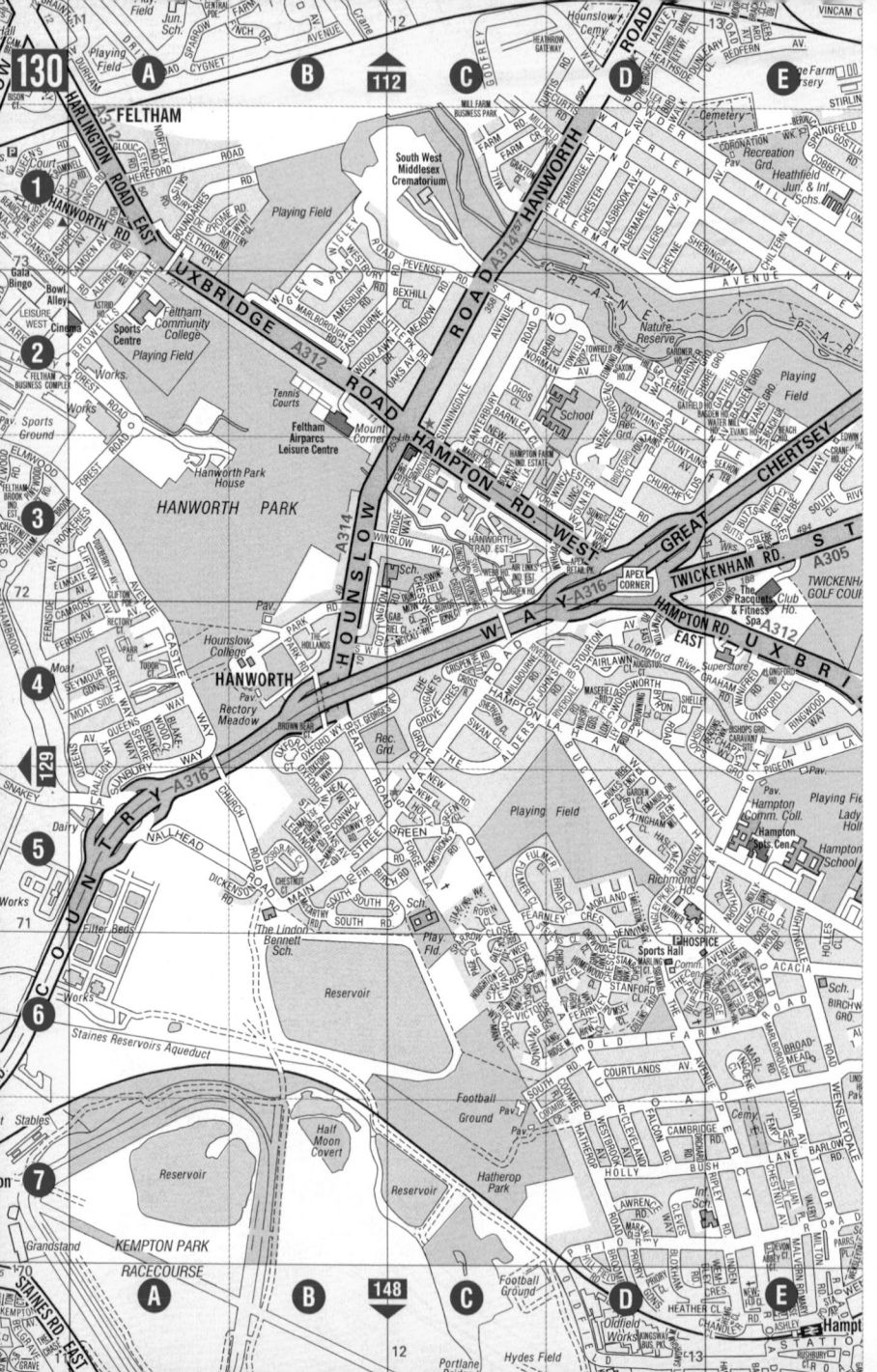

130
112
129
148
A
B
C
D
E
1
2
3
4
5
6
7
FELTHAM
HARLINGTON ROAD EAST
A312
UXBRIDGE ROAD
HANWORTH RD.
HANWORTH ROAD
A314
HOUNSLOW ROAD
HAMPTON RD. WEST
COUNTRY WAY
A316
GREAT CHERTSEY
TWICKENHAM RD.
A305
HAMPTON RD. EAST
APEX CORNER
South West Middlesex Crematorium
Hounslow Cemy.
Playing Field
Feltham Community College
Sports Centre
Feltham Airparcs Leisure Centre
Tennis Courts
Mount Corner
Hanworth Park House
HANWORTH PARK
Hounslow College
HANWORTH
Rectory Meadow
Gala Bingo
Bowl. Alley
Cinema
LEISURE WEST
FELTHAM BUSINESS COMPLEX
Works
Sports Ground
Mill Farm Business Park
Heathrow Gateway
Cemetery
Recreation Grd.
Heathfield Jun. & Inf. Schs.
Nature Reserve
School
Hampton Farm Ind. Estate
Hanworth Trad. Est.
Air Links Ind. Est.
Apex Retail Pk.
The Racquets & Fitness Spa
Club Ho.
TWICKENHAM GOLF COURSE
Superstore
Longford River
Bishops Gro. Caravant Site
Playing Field
Hampton Comm. Coll.
Hampton Spts. Cen.
Hampton School
Rec. Grd.
Filter Beds
Reservoir
The Lindon Bennett Sch.
Play. Fld.
Richmond Ho.
HOSPICE
Sports Hall
Comm. Cen.
Staines Reservoirs Aqueduct
Football Ground
Half Moon Covert
Hatherop Park
KEMPTON PARK RACECOURSE
Grandstand
Stables
Oldfield Works
Hydes Field
Portlane Bridge
STAINES RD. EAST
Inf. Sch.
Cemy.
Dairy
Moat
SUNBURY WAY
SNAKEY LA.
CASTLE WAY
NALLHEAD
DICKENSON RD.
MAIN STREET
OAK AVENUE
BUCKINGHAM ROAD
HAMPTON LA.
RECTORY GROVE
PERCY ROAD
OLD FARM ROAD
ACACIA ROAD
PRIORY ROAD
OLDFIELD RD.
STATION RD.
WAVERLEY AV.
POWDER MILL
CRANE PARK
SAXON AVENUE
FOUNTAINS AV.
CHURCHFIELDS AV.
WINSLOW WAY
SWIFT RD.
BEAR ROAD
COURTLANDS AV.
CAMBRIDGE RD.
HOLLY BUSH LANE

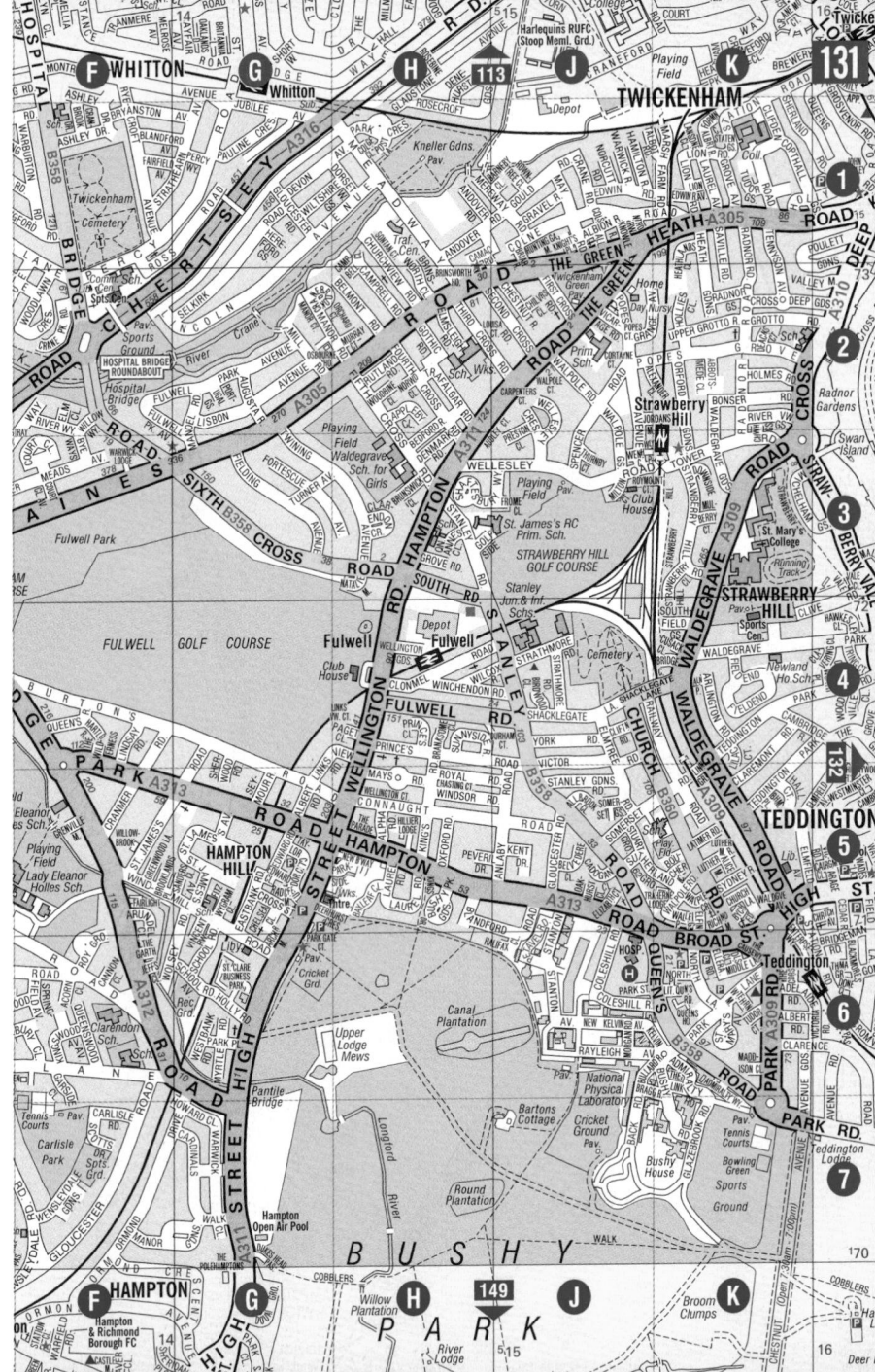

131
113
132
149
F
G
H
J
K
1
2
3
4
5
6
7
14
15
16
170
WHITTON
Whitton
Harlequins RUFC (Stoop Meml. Grd.)
TWICKENHAM
Twickenham Cemetery
Kneller Gdns.
Playing Field
Depot
Coll.
HOSPITAL BRIDGE ROUNDABOUT
Hospital Bridge
Sports Ground
River Crane
Traf. Cen.
Twickenham Green
Home
Day Nursy.
Prim. Sch.
Radnor Gardens
Swan Island
Strawberry Hill
Playing Field Waldegrave Sch. for Girls
St. James's RC Prim. Sch.
STRAWBERRY HILL GOLF COURSE
St. Mary's College
Running Track
STRAWBERRY HILL
Sports Cen.
Fulwell Park
FULWELL GOLF COURSE
Fulwell
Club House
Depot
Stanley Jun.& Inf. Schs.
Cemetery
Newland Ho.Sch.
TEDDINGTON
Lady Eleanor Holles Sch.
HAMPTON HILL
Thtre.
Cricket Grd.
Upper Lodge Mews
Canal Plantation
Hosp.
Teddington
Clarendon Sch.
Pantile Bridge
National Physical Laboratory
Bartons Cottage
Cricket Ground
Bushy House
Tennis Courts
Bowling Green
Sports Ground
Teddington Lodge
Carlisle Park
Spts. Grd.
Round Plantation
Longford River
Hampton Open Air Pool
BUSHY PARK
Willow Plantation
Broom Clumps
River Lodge
HAMPTON
Hampton & Richmond Borough FC
CHERTSEY ROAD
HAMPTON ROAD
STAINES ROAD
SIXTH CROSS ROAD
THE GREEN
HEATH ROAD
WALDEGRAVE ROAD
CROSS DEEP
STRAWBERRY VALE
WELLINGTON ROAD
FULWELL RD.
HAMPTON ROAD
PARK ROAD
STANLEY ROAD
CHURCH ROAD
BROAD ST.
HIGH ST.
QUEEN'S ROAD
PARK RD.
HIGH STREET
CHESTNUT AVENUE
A305
A310
A311
A312
A313
A316
A309
B358
B360
(Open 7:30am-7:00pm)

114
131
150
A
B
C
D
E
1
2
3
4
5
6
7
16
17
18
Twickenham
HOSP
MARBLE HILL PARK
Marble Hill House
Orleans Ho. Gallery
Glover's Island
Petersham Meadows
Petersham Farm
Royal Star & Garter Home
Petersham Common
STAR & GARTER HILL
B353
RIVER THAMES
Foot Ferry
Orleans Gdns.
Theatre
Baths
EEL PIE ISLAND
TWICKENHAM
HEATH RD.
DEEP
KING ST.
YORK ST.
RICHMOND RD.
A305 RD.
LONDON RD.
Sports Grd.
The German Sch. London
Polo Ground
The Russell Prim. Sch.
Strathmore Sch.
PETERSHAM
PETERSHAM PARK
Ham House
Playing Field
Tennis Cts.
Club
Miniature Rifle Range
Ham Riverside Lands
Nature Reserve
Cross Deep
Radnor Gardens
Swan Island
Thames Young Mariners Base
Ham Fields
The Copse
MEADLANDS DR.
BUCKINGHAM RD.
SANDY LANE
Grey Court School
Playing Field
Convent
SUDBROOK PARK
Sudbrook Park (Club Ho.)
The Wilderness
RICHMOND GOLF COURSE
HAM COMMON
HAM GATE
B352
HAM
Meadlands Prim. Sch.
C of E Prim. Sch.
Ham Green
THE CASSEL HOSP.
UPPER HAM RD.
PETERSHAM RD.
A307
RICHMOND ROAD
St. Mary's College
Running Track
STRAWBERRY HILL
Sports Cen.
WALDEGRAVE
STRAWBERRY VALE
TWICKENHAM RD.
A310
Ham Riverside Lands
Teddington Locks
Rec. Gd.
Teddington Studios
Teddington Weir
Sports Ground
Lensbury Club
ST. GEORGE'S INDUSTRIAL ESTATE
YMCA Sports Grd.
Trowlock Island
The Tiffin Girls' Sch.
Fern Hill Prim. Sch.
TEDDINGTON
Pool
A313
HIGH STREET
Arts Cen.
Athletic Ground
Teddington
Teddington Sch. & Sports Cen.
Recreation Ground
Collis Prim. Sch.
Sch.
KINGSTON ROAD
Steven's Eyot
Canbury
The Avenue Centre (Coll.)
KINGSTON UPON THAMES
HAMPTON WICK
Hampton Wick
UP. TEDDINGTON RD.
Teddington Lodge
PARK RD.
SANDY LANE
B358
BUSHY PARK
Hawthorn Lodge
Warren Plantation
Half Moon Plantation
Thatched Cottage
Deer Pen
Leg-of-Mutton
Superstore
Mosque
COMM

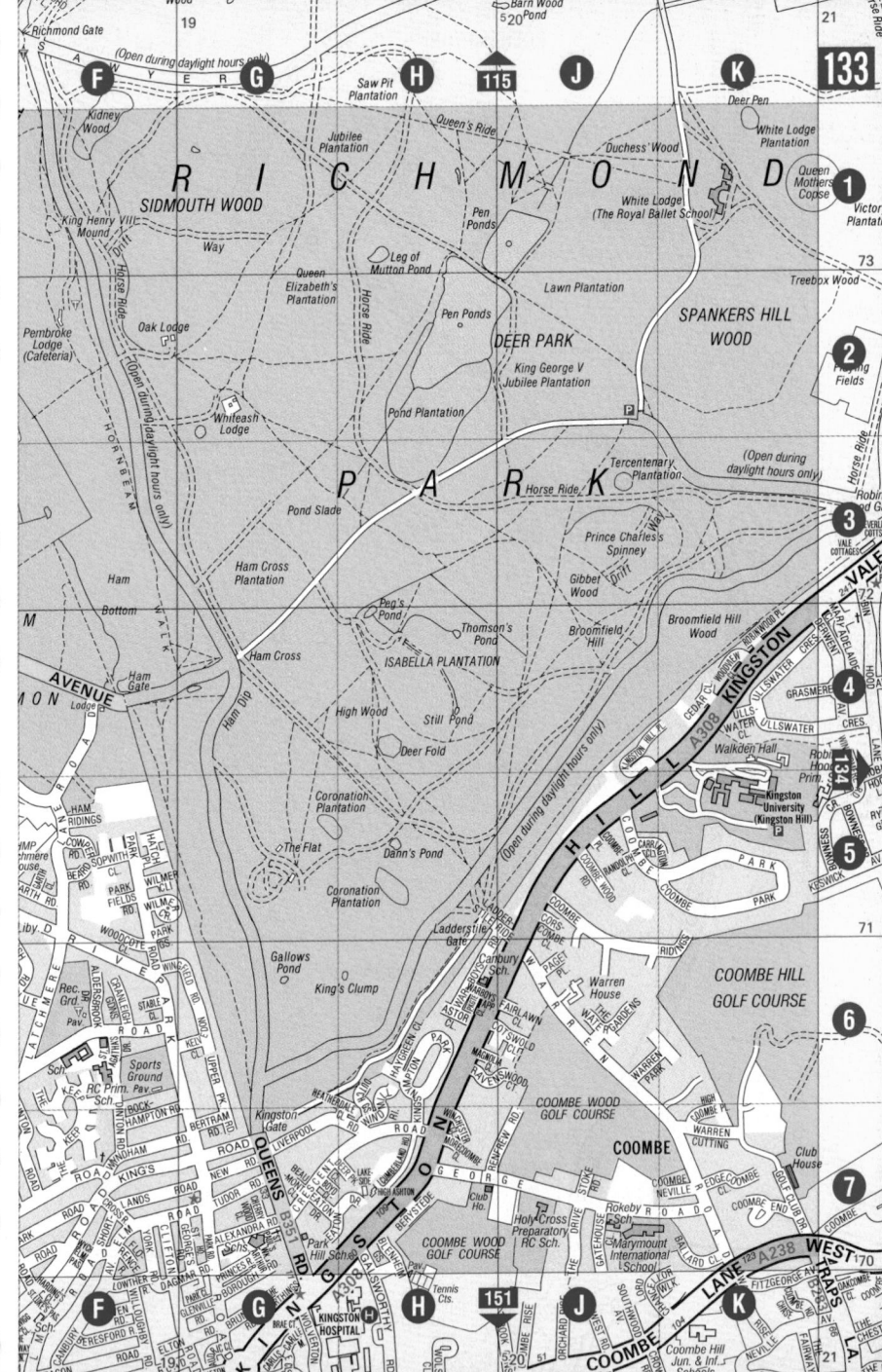

133

F   G   H   J   K

19   520   Barn Wood Pond   21

Richmond Gate   Deer Pen

Kidney Wood   Saw Pit Plantation   115   White Lodge Plantation

Jubilee Plantation   Queen's Ride   Duchess' Wood

R I C H M O N D   Queen Mothers Copse   **1**

SIDMOUTH WOOD   Pen Ponds   White Lodge (The Royal Ballet School)   Victory Plantation

King Henry VIII Mound   Way   Queen Elizabeth's Plantation   Leg of Mutton Pond   Lawn Plantation   Treebox Wood   73

Oak Lodge   Pen Ponds   SPANKERS HILL WOOD

Pembroke Lodge (Cafeteria)   DEER PARK   **2** Playing Fields

Whiteash Lodge   King George V Jubilee Plantation   Pond Plantation

(Open during daylight hours only)   Robin Hood Gate   **3** VALE   VERLEY COTTS   VALE COTTAGES

P A R K   Pond Slade   Horse Ride   Tercentenary Plantation   (Open during daylight hours only)

Ham Cross Plantation   Prince Charles's Spinney   Broomfield Hill Wood   KINGSTON

Ham   Peg's Pond   Gibbet Wood   Broomfield Hill   GRASMERE   **4**

Bottom   Thomson's Pond   ULLSWATER CL   ULLSWATER

Ham Cross   ISABELLA PLANTATION   Walkden Hall   Robin Hood Prim.   **134**

AVENUE   Ham Gate   Ham Lodge   High Wood   Still Pond   Kingston University (Kingston Hill)   **5** RYDAL GDNS   KESWICK AV

Ham Dip   Deer Fold   PARK

Coronation Plantation   (Open during daylight hours only)

HAM RIDINGS   The Flat   Dann's Pond   COOMBE HILL GOLF COURSE   **6**

Coronation Plantation   Ladderstile Gate   Canbury Sch.   Warren House   WARREN

Gallows Pond   King's Clump   Astor Ct.   FAIRLAWN   COTSWOLD   THE WILDERNESS

Sports Ground   Kingston Gate   COOMBE WOOD GOLF COURSE   WARREN CUTTING   Club House   **7**

Liverpool   Park Hill School   COOMBE   WEST   170

Queens Rd   B351   ROAD   Holy Cross Preparatory RC Sch.   Rokeby Sch.   ROAD   A238 LANE   TRAPS

COOMBE WOOD GOLF COURSE   Marymount International School   GATEHOUSE   COOMBE   21

F   G   Kingston Hospital   H   Tennis Cts.   151   J   K   Coombe Hill Jun. & Inf. Schools

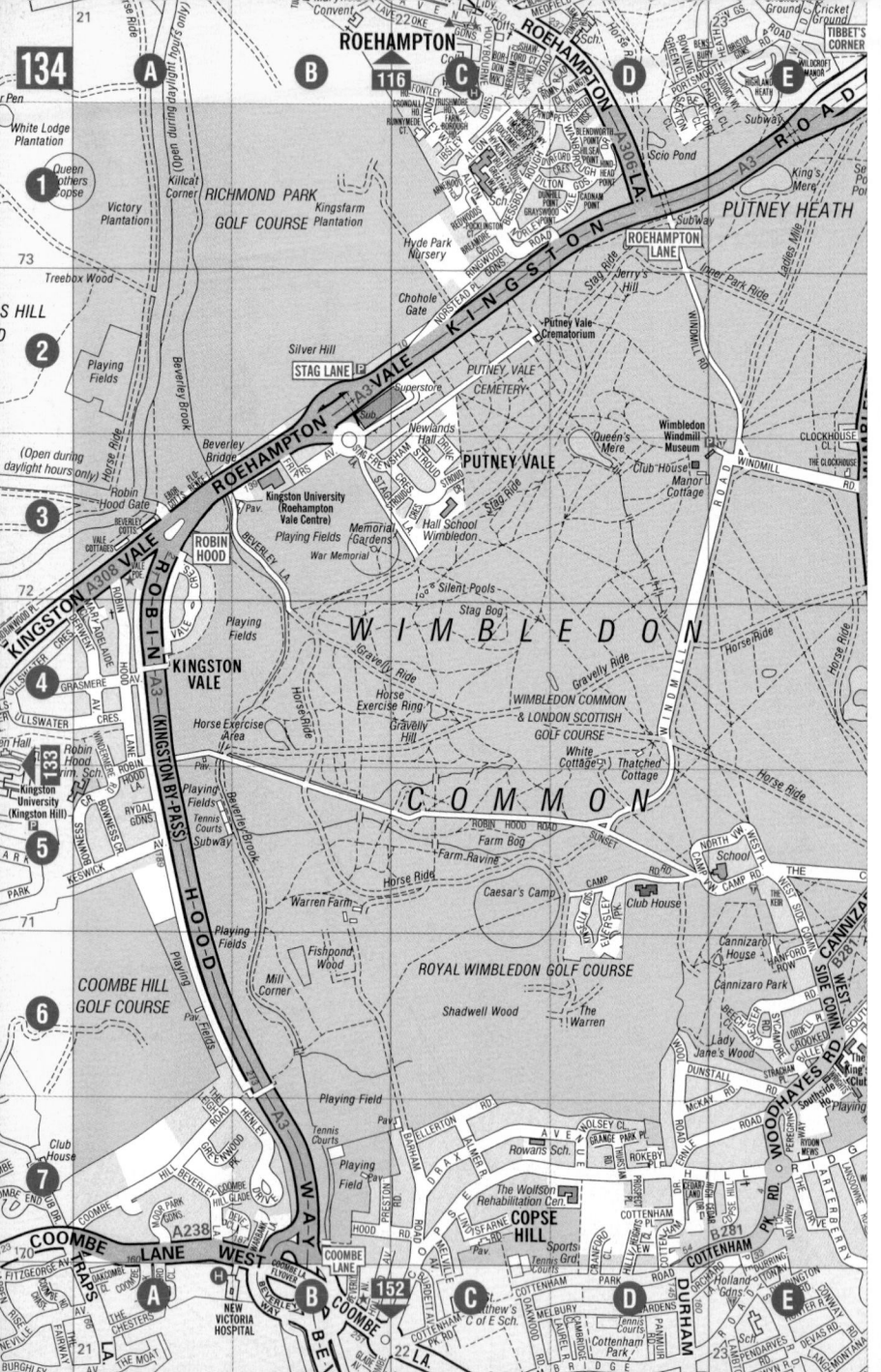

134
ROEHAMPTON
116
133
152
RICHMOND PARK
GOLF COURSE
Kingsfarm Plantation
Killcat Corner
Victory Plantation
Queen Mothers Copse
White Lodge Plantation
Treebox Wood
Playing Fields
Beverley Brook
Horse Ride
(Open during daylight hours only)
Robin Hood Gate
Beverley Bridge
ROEHAMPTON VALE
KINGSTON ROAD
A3
A306
A308
Silver Hill
STAG LANE
Chohole Gate
Hyde Park Nursery
Superstore
Putney Vale Crematorium
PUTNEY VALE CEMETERY
PUTNEY VALE
Kingston University (Roehampton Vale Centre)
Memorial Gardens
War Memorial
Hall School Wimbledon
ROBIN HOOD
ROBIN HOOD WAY (KINGSTON BY-PASS)
KINGSTON VALE
PUTNEY HEATH
Scio Pond
King's Mere
ROEHAMPTON LANE
Jerry's Hill
Inner Park Ride
Ladies Mile
TIBBET'S CORNER
Wimbledon Windmill Museum
Club House
Manor Cottage
Queen's Mere
Stag Ride
Silent Pools
Stag Bog
WIMBLEDON
COMMON
Gravelly Ride
Horse Exercise Ring
Gravelly Hill
Horse Exercise Area
WIMBLEDON COMMON & LONDON SCOTTISH GOLF COURSE
White Cottage
Thatched Cottage
Robin Hood Prim. Sch.
Kingston University (Kingston Hill)
ROBIN HOOD ROAD
Farm Bog
Farm Ravine
Caesar's Camp
Warren Farm
Fishpond Wood
Mill Corner
ROYAL WIMBLEDON GOLF COURSE
Shadwell Wood
The Warren
Cannizaro House
Cannizaro Park
Lady Jane's Wood
COOMBE HILL GOLF COURSE
Playing Field
Tennis Courts
Rowans Sch.
The Wolfson Rehabilitation Cen.
COPSE HILL
Sports Grd.
COOMBE LANE WEST
A238
COOMBE LANE
NEW VICTORIA HOSPITAL
St. Matthew's C of E Sch.
COTTENHAM PARK ROAD
DURHAM ROAD
B281
Cottenham Park
Holland Gdns.
WOODHAYES RD.
WINDMILL RD.

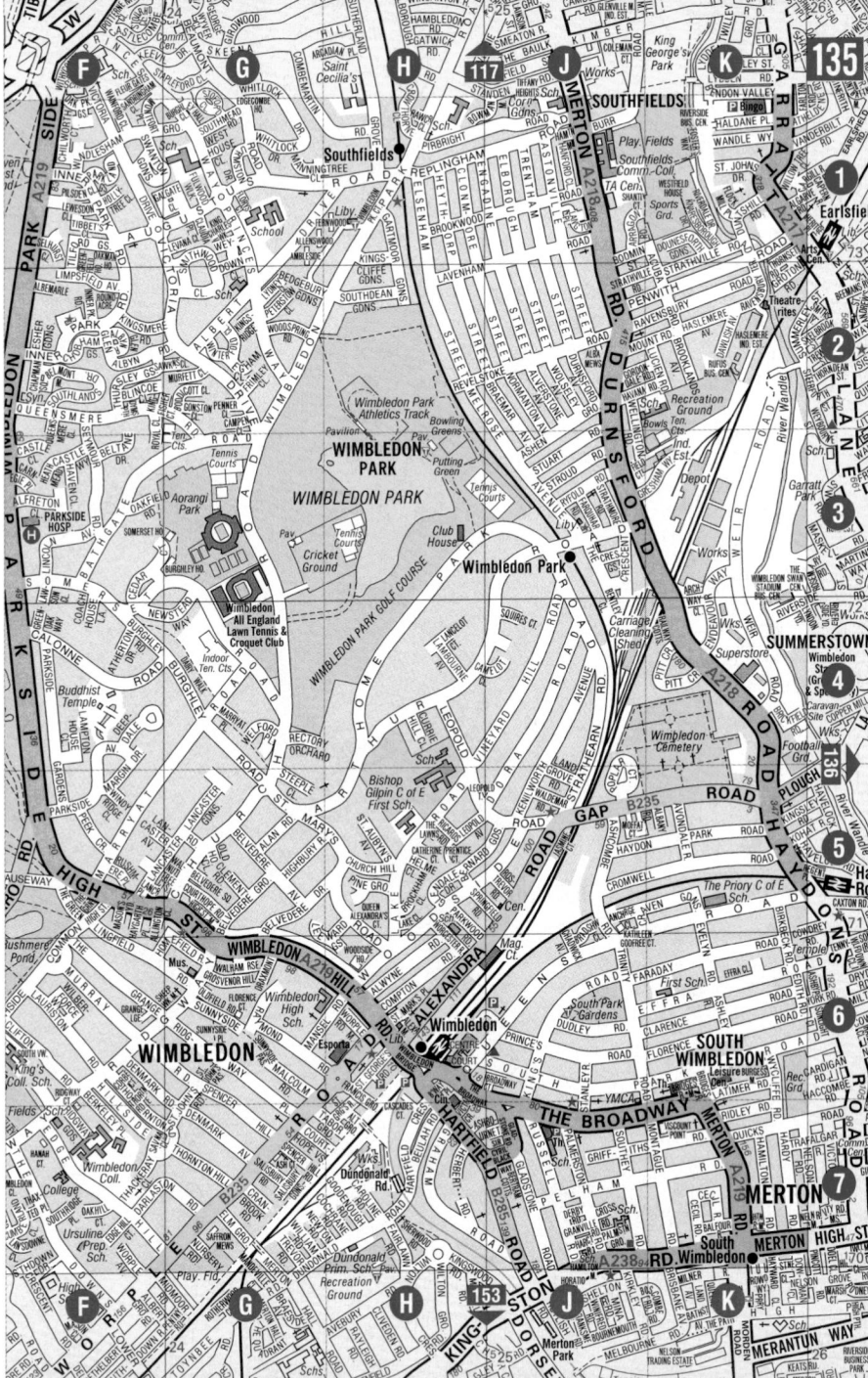

F
G
H
J
K
117
SOUTHFIELDS
Southfields
King George's Park
Earlsfield
1
2
3
4
5
6
7
WIMBLEDON PARK
Wimbledon Park Athletics Track
Bowling Greens
Putting Green
Tennis Courts
Cricket Ground
Club House
WIMBLEDON PARK GOLF COURSE
Wimbledon Park
Aorangi Park
Wimbledon All England Lawn Tennis & Croquet Club
Indoor Ten. Cts.
PARKSIDE HOSP.
Buddhist Temple
Wimbledon Cemetery
Carriage Cleaning Shed
Superstore
SUMMERSTOWN
Wimbledon Stadium
Caravan Site
Football Grd.
136
River Wandle
Garratt Park
Recreation Ground
Depot
Works
Bishop Gilpin C of E First Sch.
The Priory C of E Sch.
South Park Gardens
SOUTH WIMBLEDON
Leisure Cen.
Haydons Road
Wimbledon
WIMBLEDON
Wimbledon High Sch.
Rushmere Pond
King's Coll. Sch.
Wimbledon Coll.
Ursuline Prep. Sch.
Dundonald Rd.
Dundonald Prim. Sch.
Recreation Ground
153
MERTON
South Wimbledon
Merton Park
MERTON HIGH ST.
MERANTUN WAY
THE BROADWAY
WIMBLEDON HILL RD.
HIGH ST.
PARKSIDE
WIMBLEDON PARK SIDE
DURNSFORD RD.
MERTON RD.
GARRATT LANE
HAYDONS ROAD
PLOUGH LA.
GAP ROAD
ALEXANDRA RD.
HARTFIELD RD.
KINGSTON RD.
WORPLE RD.
A219
A218
A217
A238
B235
B285

A
B
C
D
E
1
2
3
4
5
6
7
118
154
135
Wandsworth Common
Wandsworth Common
EARLSFIELD
Earlsfield
WANDSWORTH CEMETERY
Mecca Bingo
Theatres
Arts Cen.
Beatrix Potter Prim. Sch.
Spts. Grd.
Bowling Green
Sports Ground
Playing Field
Pavilion
The Joan Bicknell Centre
THE CENTRAL LONDON GOLF COURSE
SPRINGFIELD UNIVERSITY HOSPITAL
Cottage Day Hospital
Burntwood School
Garratt Green
Garratt Park
River Wandle
BALHAM
Tooting Bec
Tooting Bec
UPPER TOOTING
Playing Field
STREATHAM CEMETERY
SUMMERSTOWN
Wimbledon Stadium (Greyhound & Speedway)
Lambeth Crematorium
LAMBETH CEMETERY
Superstores
Football Grd.
Haydons Road
TOOTING
Tooting Leisure Cen.
Tooting Gardens
ST. GEORGE'S HOSPITAL
Tooting Broadway
Gala Bingo
Mosque
Professional Centre
TOOTING GRAVENEY
Wandle Meadow Nature Park
Garfield Prim. Sch.
Rec. Grd.
Wandle Park
Colliers Wood
COLLIER'S WOOD
Play Fld.
MERTON
Superstore
Cemetery
Tooting
River Graveney
Edenvale Open Space
FIGGE'S MARSH
Tamworth Rec. Grd.
Lavender Park
Colour Ho. Th.
RIVERSIDE BUSINESS PARK
BURNTWOOD LANE
GARRATT LANE
TRINITY ROAD
UPPER TOOTING ROAD
BALHAM HIGH ROAD
TOOTING HIGH ST.
MITCHAM ROAD
LONDON ROAD
MERTON HIGH STREET
HAYDONS ROAD
PLOUGH LANE
SUMMERSTOWN
COLLIERS WOOD HIGH STREET
STREATHAM
ST. JAMES'S DR.
BELLEVUE RD.
A24
A214
A217
A218
A24
B229
B234
B235
B237
B241
MERANTUN WAY
TOOTING BEC ROAD
RECTORY LANE
LONGLEY ROAD
ROBINSON ROAD
KENLOR ROAD

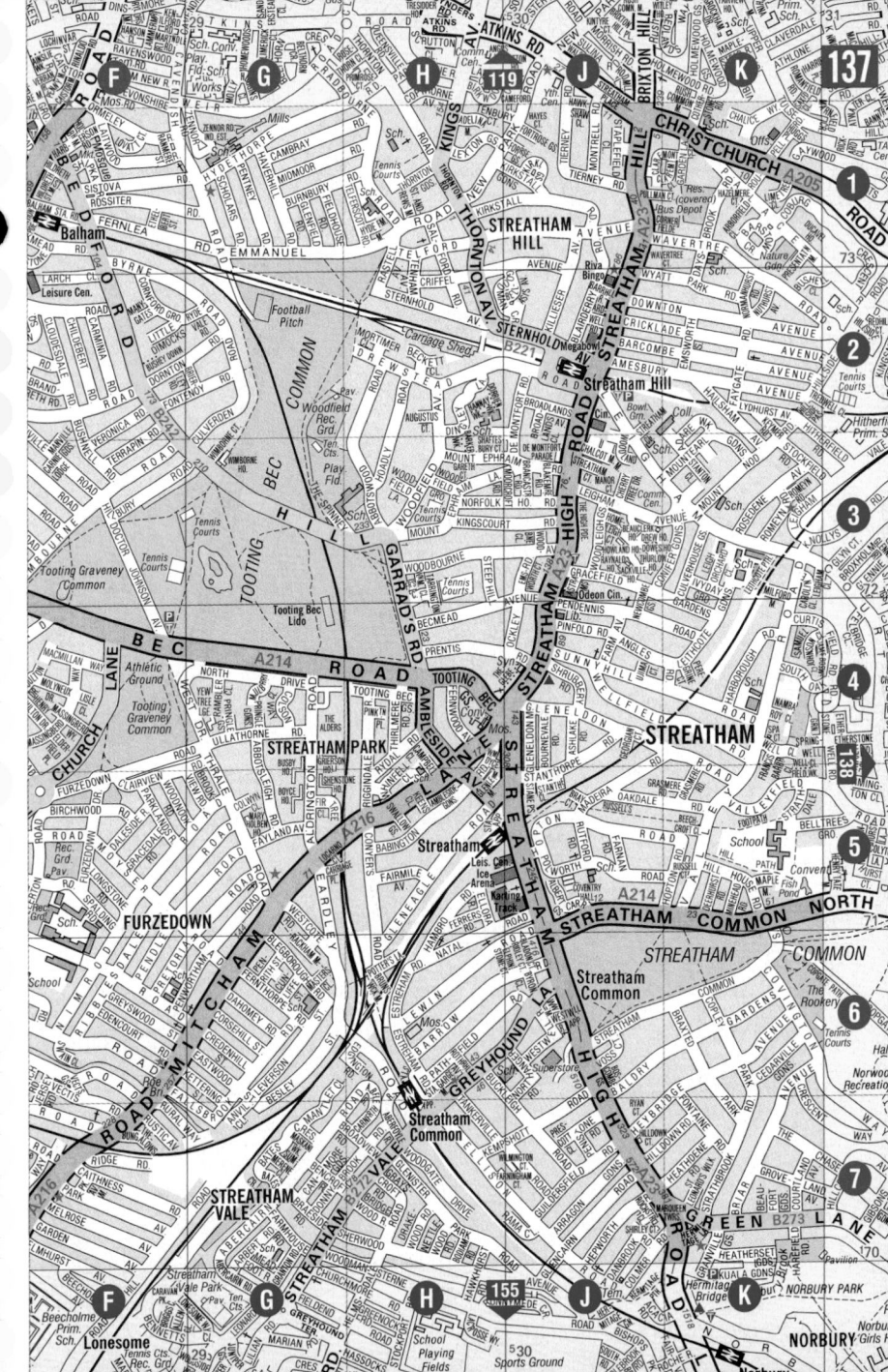
137
F
G
H
J
K
1
2
3
4
5
6
7
119
138
155
ATKINS RD.
CHRISTCHURCH
ROAD
A205
BRIXTON HILL
STREATHAM HILL
Balham
BEDFORD
ROAD
FERNLEA
RD.
EMMANUEL
BYRNE
Leisure Cen.
Football Pitch
COMMON
Woodfield Rec. Grd.
Carriage Shed
STERNHOLD
B221
AV.
Megabowl
Streatham Hill
THORNTON AV.
KINGS AV.
STREATHAM HIGH ROAD
A23
Riva Bingo
Bus Depot
Res. (covered)
Nature Gdn.
WAVERTREE
WYATT PARK RD.
DOWNTON
CRICKLADE AVENUE
BARCOMBE AVENUE
AMESBURY AVENUE
Tennis Courts
TOOTING BEC
HILL
TOOTING
Tennis Courts
Tooting Graveney Common
Tooting Bec Lido
BEC ROAD
A214
GARRAD'S RD.
TOOTING BEC GS.
Athletic Ground
Tooting Graveney Common
CHURCH LANE
STREATHAM PARK
AMBLESIDE AV.
A216
Streatham
Leis. Cen.
Ice Arena
Karting Track
STREATHAM
Odeon Cin.
Lib.
School
Convent
Fish Pond
STREATHAM COMMON NORTH
STREATHAM
COMMON
Streatham Common
The Rookery
Tennis Courts
Norwood Recreation
FURZEDOWN
MITCHAM ROAD
GREYHOUND LA.
Superstore
Streatham Common
STREATHAM VALE
B272
STREATHAM HIGH ROAD
A23
GREEN LANE
B273
NORBURY PARK
Hermitage Bridge
Pavilion
NORBURY
Norbury Girls High
Streatham Vale Park
Beecholme Prim. Sch.
Lonesome
Tennis Cts. Rec. Grd.
School Playing Fields
Sports Ground
5 30
29
31
73
72
71
70

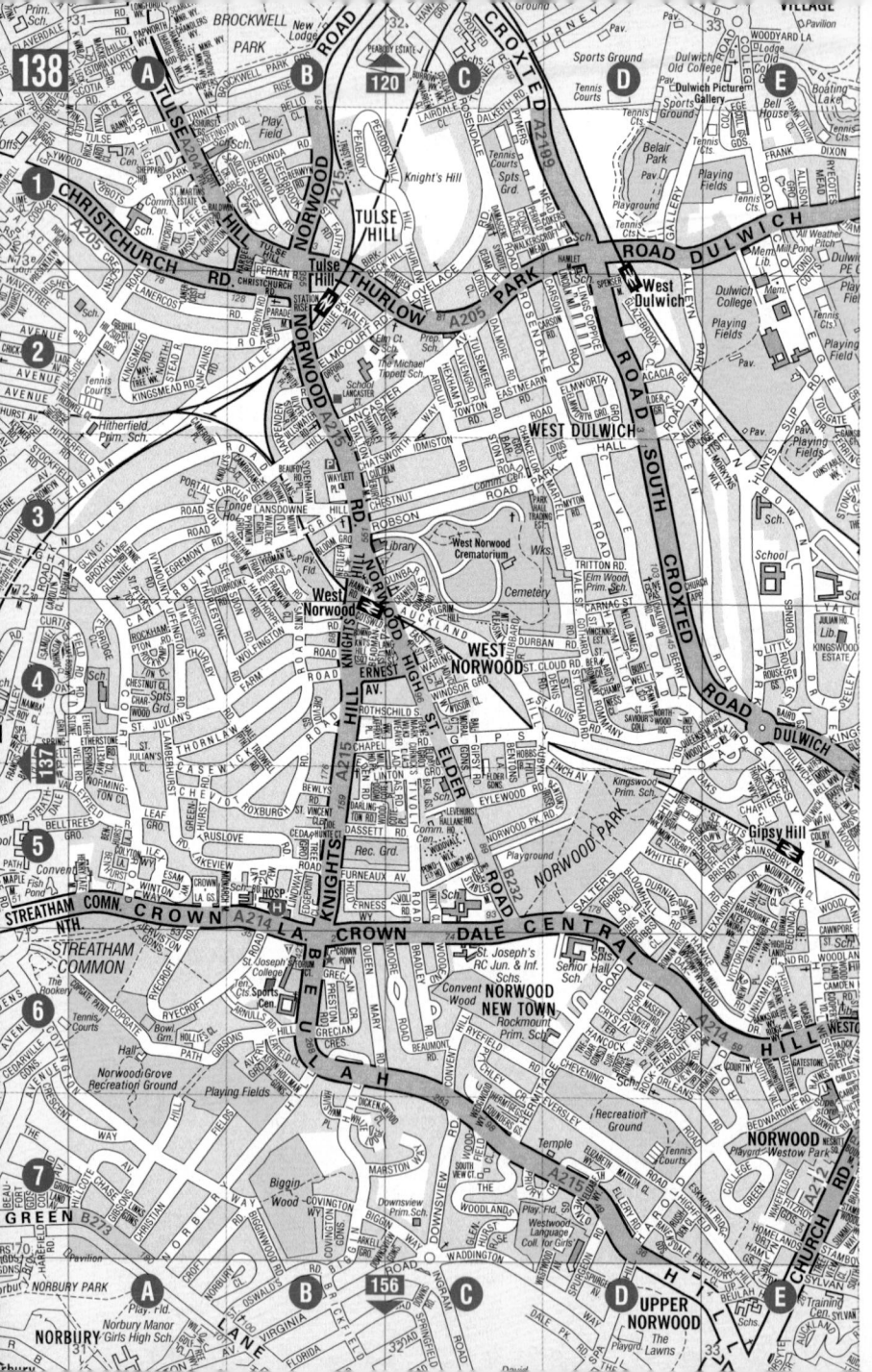

138
A
B
C
D
E
1
2
3
4
5
6
7
120
137
156
BROCKWELL PARK
New Lodge
Sports Ground
Dulwich Old College
Dulwich Picture Gallery
Boating Lake
Bell House
Belair Park
Knight's Hill
TULSE HILL
Tulse Hill
West Dulwich
WEST DULWICH
Dulwich College
Playing Fields
CHRISTCHURCH RD.
THURLOW PARK
ROAD DULWICH
CROXTED ROAD
SOUTH CROXTED ROAD
NORWOOD ROAD
NORWOOD RD.
TULSE HILL
The Michael Tippett Sch.
Hitherfield Prim. Sch.
West Norwood Crematorium
Cemetery
West Norwood
WEST NORWOOD
KNIGHTS HILL
NORWOOD HIGH ST.
GIPSY ROAD
ELDER ROAD
Kingswood Prim. Sch.
NORWOOD PARK
Gipsy Hill
KINGSWOOD ESTATE
STREATHAM COMN. NTH.
CROWN LA.
CROWN DALE
CENTRAL HILL
WESTOW HILL
STREATHAM COMMON
The Rookery
St. Joseph's College
St. Joseph's RC Jun. & Inf. Schs.
Convent Wood
NORWOOD NEW TOWN
Rockmount Prim. Sch.
Senior Sch.
Norwood Grove Recreation Ground
Playing Fields
BEULAH HILL
Recreation Ground
Temple
NORWOOD
Westow Park
CHURCH RD.
Biggin Wood
Downsview Prim. Sch.
Westwood Language Coll. for Girls
NORBURY PARK
Norbury Manor Girls High Sch.
NORBURY
NORBURY HILL
GREEN LANE
UPPER NORWOOD
The Lawns

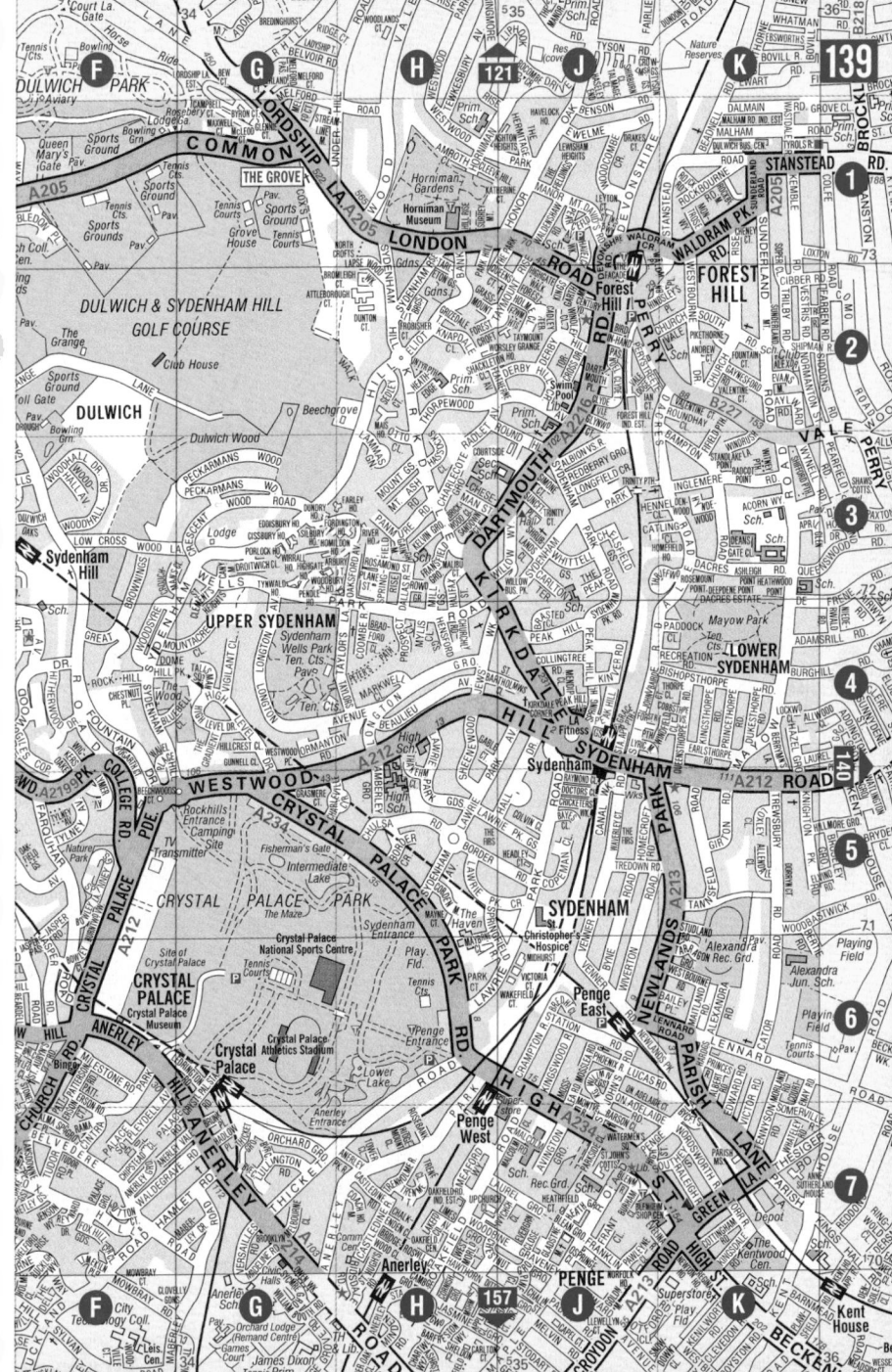
F
G
H
J
K
121
DULWICH PARK
Aviary
Court La. Gate
Horse Ride
Tennis Cts.
Bowling Grn.
Queen Mary's Gate
Sports Ground
Rosebery Lodge Ga.
COMMON
LORDSHIP LA.
A205
THE GROVE
Sports Ground
Sports Grounds
Tennis Cts.
Pav.
Grove House
Tennis Courts
LONDON ROAD
Horniman Gardens
Horniman Museum
Prim. Sch.
DULWICH & SYDENHAM HILL GOLF COURSE
The Grange
Club House
Sports Ground
Toll Gate
DULWICH
Bowling Grn.
Beechgrove
Dulwich Wood
PECKARMANS WOOD
WOOD ROAD
LOW CROSS WOOD LA.
Sydenham Hill
Lodge
UPPER SYDENHAM
Sydenham Wells Park Ten. Cts.
Ten. Cts.
WESTWOOD
CRYSTAL PALACE PARK
A234
A212
A2199
COLLEGE RD.
PDE.
Rockhills Entrance Camping Site
TV Transmitter
Fisherman's Gate
Intermediate Lake
CRYSTAL PALACE PARK
The Maze
Sydenham Entrance
Play. Fld.
Crystal Palace National Sports Centre
Site of Crystal Palace
Tennis Courts
Tennis Cts.
CRYSTAL PALACE
Crystal Palace Museum
Crystal Palace Athletics Stadium
Crystal Palace
Penge Entrance
Lower Lake
Anerley Entrance
ANERLEY HILL
ANERLEY RD.
CHURCH RD.
Bingo
Penge West
HIGH ST.
A234
Anerley
PENGE
157
City Technology Coll.
Leis. Cen.
Anerley Sch.
Orchard Lodge (Remand Centre)
Games Court
James Dixon Prim.
Comm. Cen.
Superstore
Rec. Grd.
Sch.
FOREST HILL
Forest Hill
WALDRAM PK.
STANSTEAD RD.
A205
PERRY VALE
B227
DARTMOUTH RD.
A2216
KIRKDALE
Swim. Pool
Prim. Sch.
Sec. Sch.
Mayow Park
LOWER SYDENHAM
Ten. Cts.
SYDENHAM RD.
A212
140
Sydenham
LA Fitness
SYDENHAM
St. Christopher's Hospice
Penge East
NEWLANDS PARK
A213
Alexandra Rec. Grd.
Playing Field
Alexandra Jun. Sch.
Tennis Courts
PARISH LANE
Kentwood Cen.
Depot
Kent House
Superstore
Play Fld.
CROYDON ROAD
BECKENHAM
Nature Reserves
BROCKLEY
FORMER FACADE
The Haven
The Wood
1
2
3
4
5
6
7
34
35
36

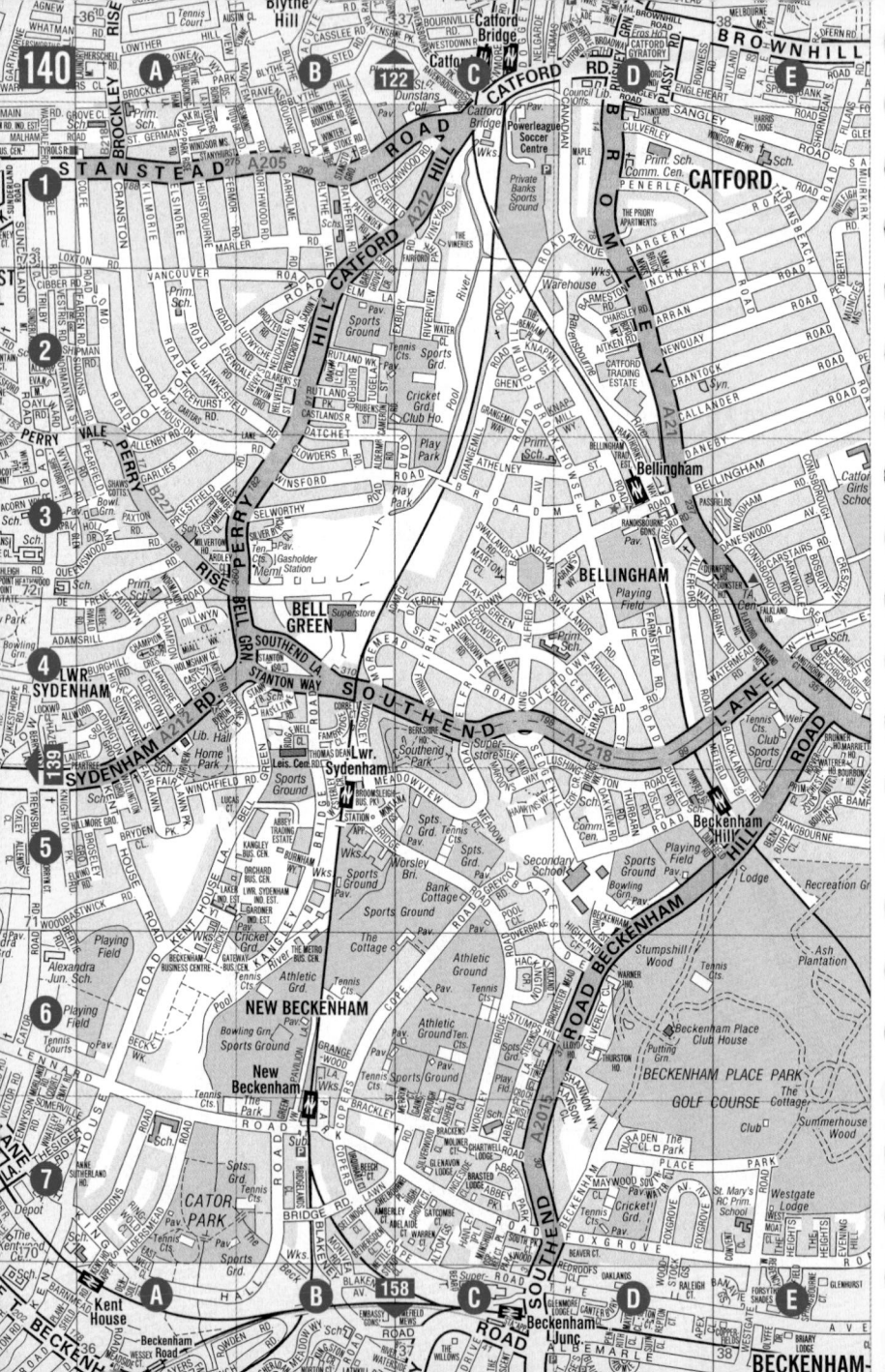

140
122
158
139
36
37
38
A
B
C
D
E
1
2
3
4
5
6
7
Blythe Hill
Catford Bridge
Catford
CATFORD
CATFORD RD.
CATFORD GYRATORY
BROWNHILL ROAD
STANSTEAD ROAD
A205
A21
A212
B218
B227
A2218
A2015
CATFORD HILL
BROMLEY ROAD
PERRY HILL
PERRY VALE
PERRY RISE
BELL GRN.
BELL GREEN
Superstore
SOUTHEND LANE
SYDENHAM RD.
LWR. SYDENHAM
Lwr. Sydenham
Bellingham
BELLINGHAM
Playing Field
Powerleague Soccer Centre
Private Banks Sports Ground
Gasholder Station
Sports Ground
Cricket Grd. Club Ho.
Play Park
Southend Park
Beckenham Hill
BECKENHAM HILL ROAD
Secondary School
Stumpshill Wood
Ash Plantation
Recreation Gr
Beckenham Place Club House
BECKENHAM PLACE PARK
GOLF COURSE
Summerhouse Wood
Westgate Lodge
NEW BECKENHAM
New Beckenham
CATOR PARK
Kent House
Beckenham Road
Beckenham Junc.
SOUTHEND ROAD
Alexandra Jun. Sch.
Athletic Ground
Bank Cottage
Worsley Bri.
Catford Girls School
BROMLEY RD.
Home Park
Lib. Hall
Leis. Cen.

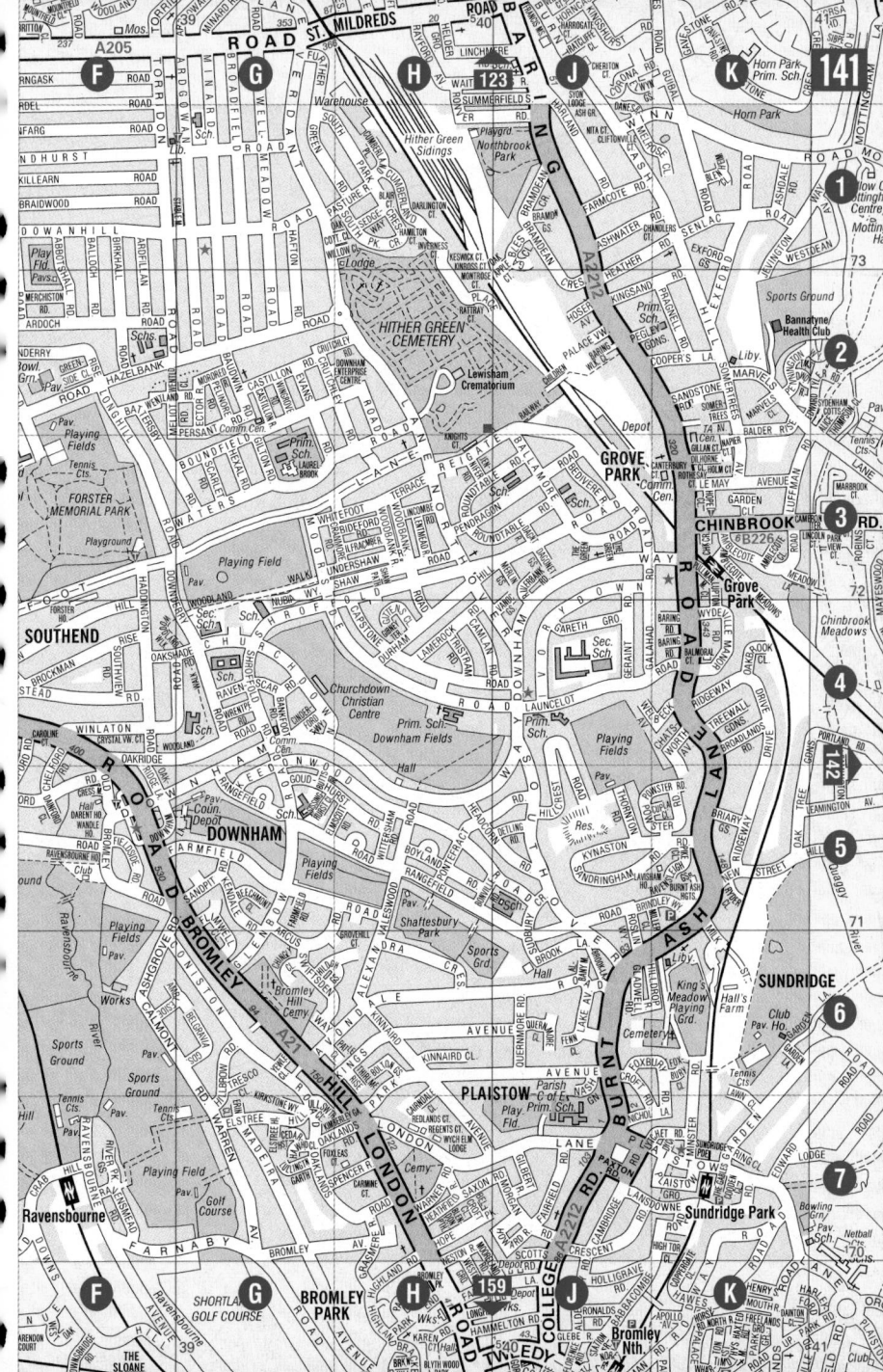
141
123
142
159
A205
A2212
A21
B226
ST. MILDREDS ROAD
Hither Green Sidings
Northbrook Park
HITHER GREEN CEMETERY
Lewisham Crematorium
Horn Park
Horn Park Prim. Sch.
Sports Ground
Bannatyne Health Club
GROVE PARK
Grove Park
CHINBROOK RD.
Chinbrook Meadows
FORSTER MEMORIAL PARK
Playing Field
SOUTHEND
Churchdown Christian Centre
Downham Fields
DOWNHAM
Shaftesbury Park
Bromley Hill Cemy.
SUNDRIDGE
King's Meadow Playing Grd.
Hall's Farm
PLAISTOW
Sundridge Park
Ravensbourne
SHORTLANDS GOLF COURSE
BROMLEY PARK
Bromley Nth.
BROMLEY ROAD
LONDON HILL
BURNT ASH LANE
COLLEGE RD.
THE SLOANE

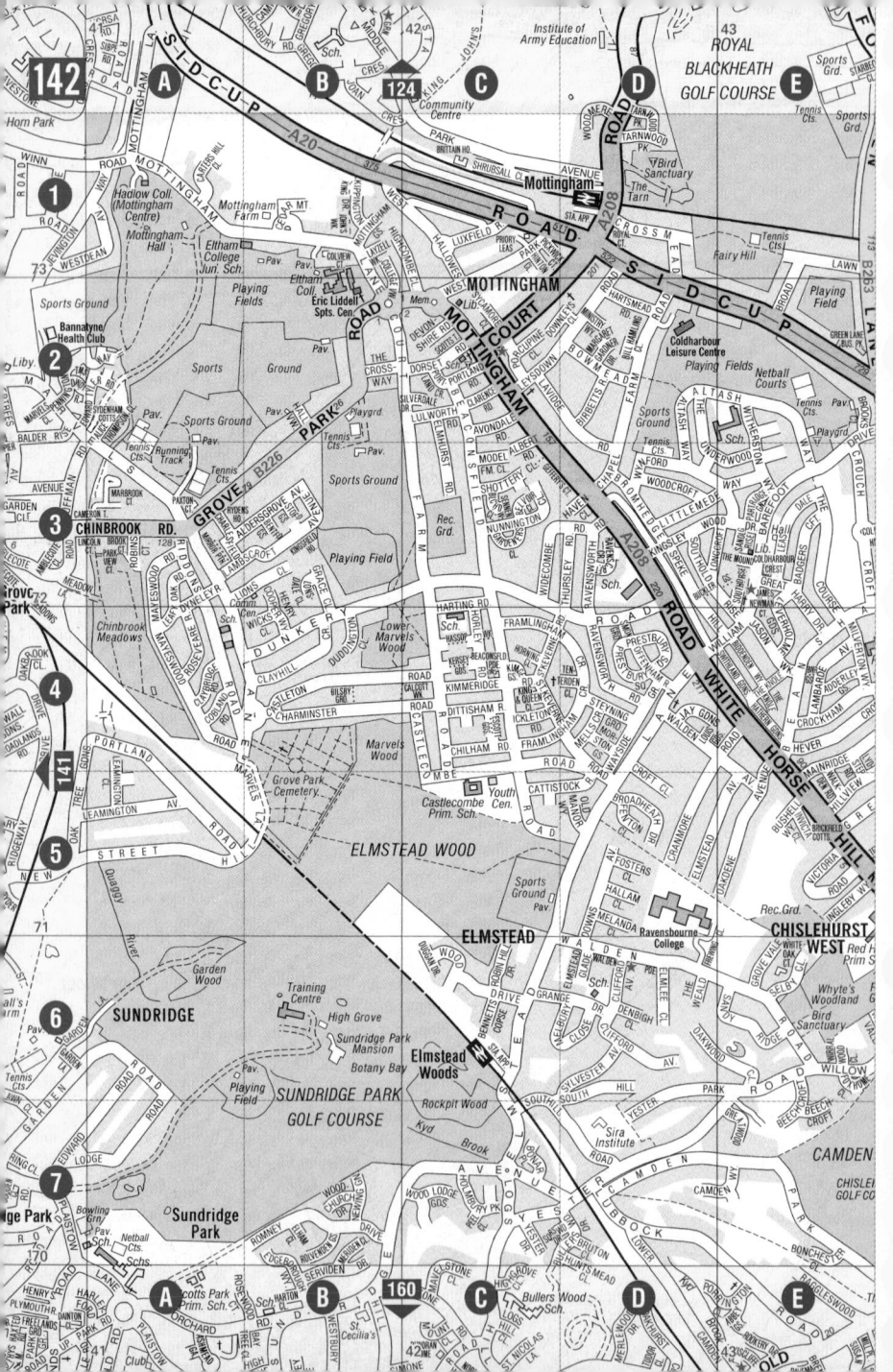

142
A
B
C
D
E
124
160
141
1
2
3
4
5
6
7
SIDCUP ROAD
A20
Institute of Army Education
ROYAL BLACKHEATH GOLF COURSE
Sports Grd.
Tennis Cts.
Community Centre
Mottingham
MOTTINGHAM
Bird Sanctuary
The Tarn
Fairy Hill
Hadlow Coll. (Mottingham Centre)
Mottingham Hall
Mottingham Farm
Eltham College Jun. Sch.
Eltham Coll.
Eric Liddell Spts. Cen.
Playing Fields
Sports Ground
Bannatyne Health Club
Liby.
Sports Ground
Running Track
GROVE PARK ROAD
B226
A208
MOTTINGHAM ROAD
COURT ROAD
Coldharbour Leisure Centre
Playing Fields
Netball Courts
Playing Field
B263
CHINBROOK RD.
Rec. Grd.
Playing Field
Lower Marvels Wood
Chinbrook Meadows
Grove Park
Marvels Wood
Grove Park Cemetery
Castlecombe Prim. Sch.
Youth Cen.
ELMSTEAD WOOD
Sports Ground
WHITE HORSE HILL
Ravensbourne College
ELMSTEAD
CHISLEHURST WEST
Rec.Grd.
Red Hill Prim Sch.
Whyte's Woodland
Bird Sanctuary
Garden Wood
SUNDRIDGE
Training Centre
High Grove
Sundridge Park Mansion
Botany Bay
Elmstead Woods
Quaggy River
Playing Field
SUNDRIDGE PARK GOLF COURSE
Rockpit Wood
Kyd Brook
Sira Institute
CAMDEN
CHISLEHURST GOLF COURSE
Sundridge Park
Bowling Grn.
Netball Cts.
Scotts Park Prim. Sch.
St. Cecilia's
Bullers Wood Sch.
NEW STREET HILL
WALDEN ROAD
LUBBOCK ROAD
CAMDEN PARK ROAD
WILLOW GROVE
SOUTHILL ROAD

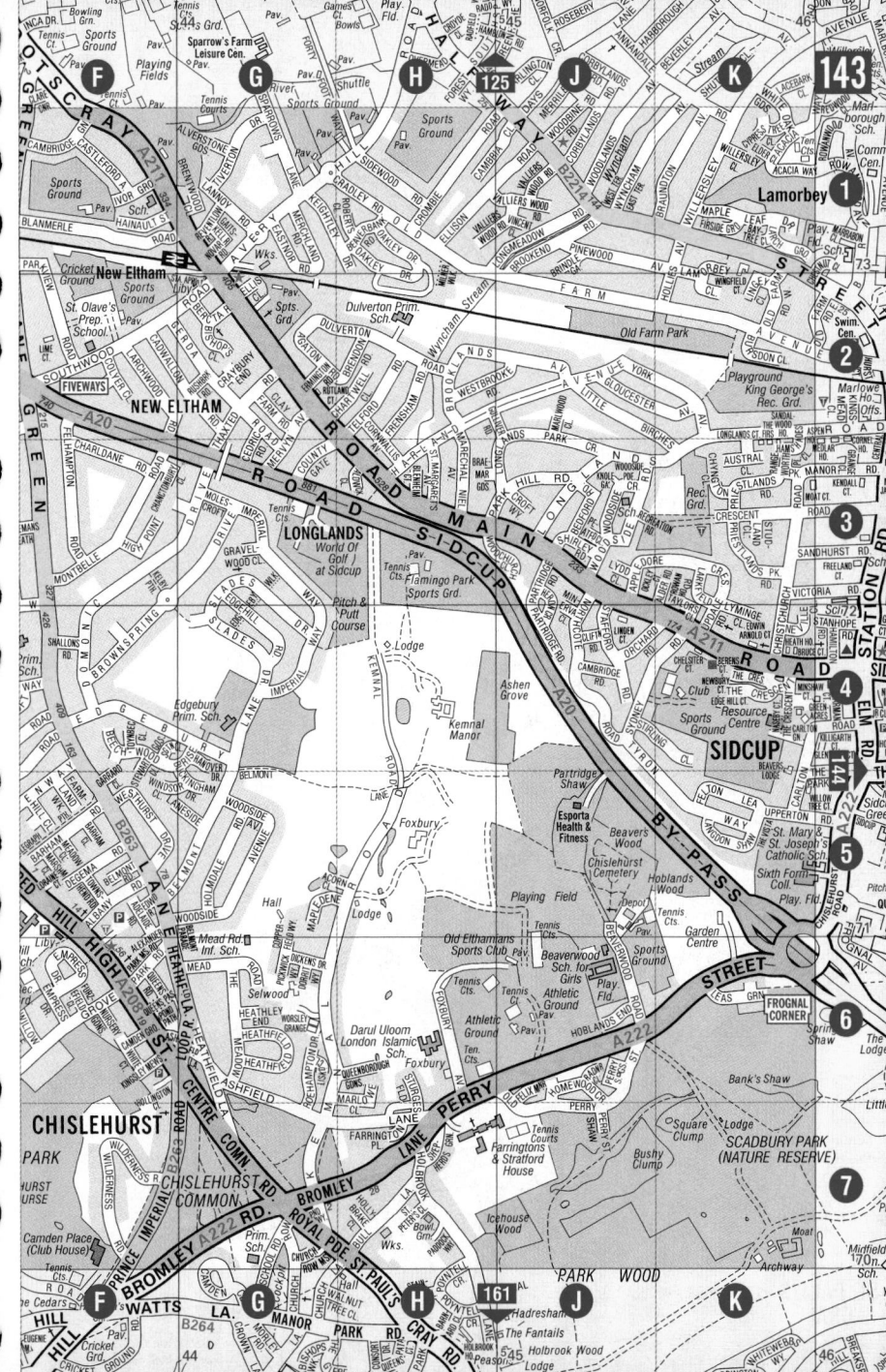

143
125
144
161
F
G
H
J
K
1
2
3
4
5
6
7
Lamorbey
New Eltham
NEW ELTHAM
FIVEWAYS
LONGLANDS
World Of Golf at Sidcup
SIDCUP
CHISLEHURST
CHISLEHURST COMMON
FROGNAL CORNER
SCADBURY PARK (NATURE RESERVE)
Sparrow's Farm Leisure Cen.
Sports Ground
Playing Fields
Cricket Ground
St. Olave's Prep. School
Dulverton Prim. Sch.
Old Farm Park
Playground
King George's Rec. Grd.
Flamingo Park Sports Grd.
Pitch & Putt Course
Edgebury Prim. Sch.
Kemnal Manor
Ashen Grove
Foxbury
Partridge Shaw
Esporta Health & Fitness
Beaver's Wood
Chislehurst Cemetery
Hoblands Wood
Playing Field
Garden Centre
Old Elthamians Sports Club
Beaverwood Sch. for Girls
Athletic Ground
Darul Uloom London Islamic Sch.
Mead Rd. Inf. Sch.
Farringtons & Stratford House
Icehouse Wood
Bushy Clump
Square Clump
Bank's Shaw
Camden Place (Club House)
St. Mary & St. Joseph's Catholic Sch.
Sixth Form Coll.
Resource Centre
Marlborough Sch.
Swim. Cen.
PARK WOOD
Holbrook Wood
The Fantails
Hadresham
SIDCUP ROAD
MAIN ROAD
SIDCUP BY-PASS
MAIN ROAD
HALFWAY STREET
STATION RD.
PERRY STREET
BROMLEY LANE
BROMLEY RD.
CHISLEHURST RD.
CENTRE COMN RD.
ROYAL PDE.
WATTS LA.
MANOR PARK RD.
CRAY RD.
A20
A211
A222
A208
B263
B264
B2214

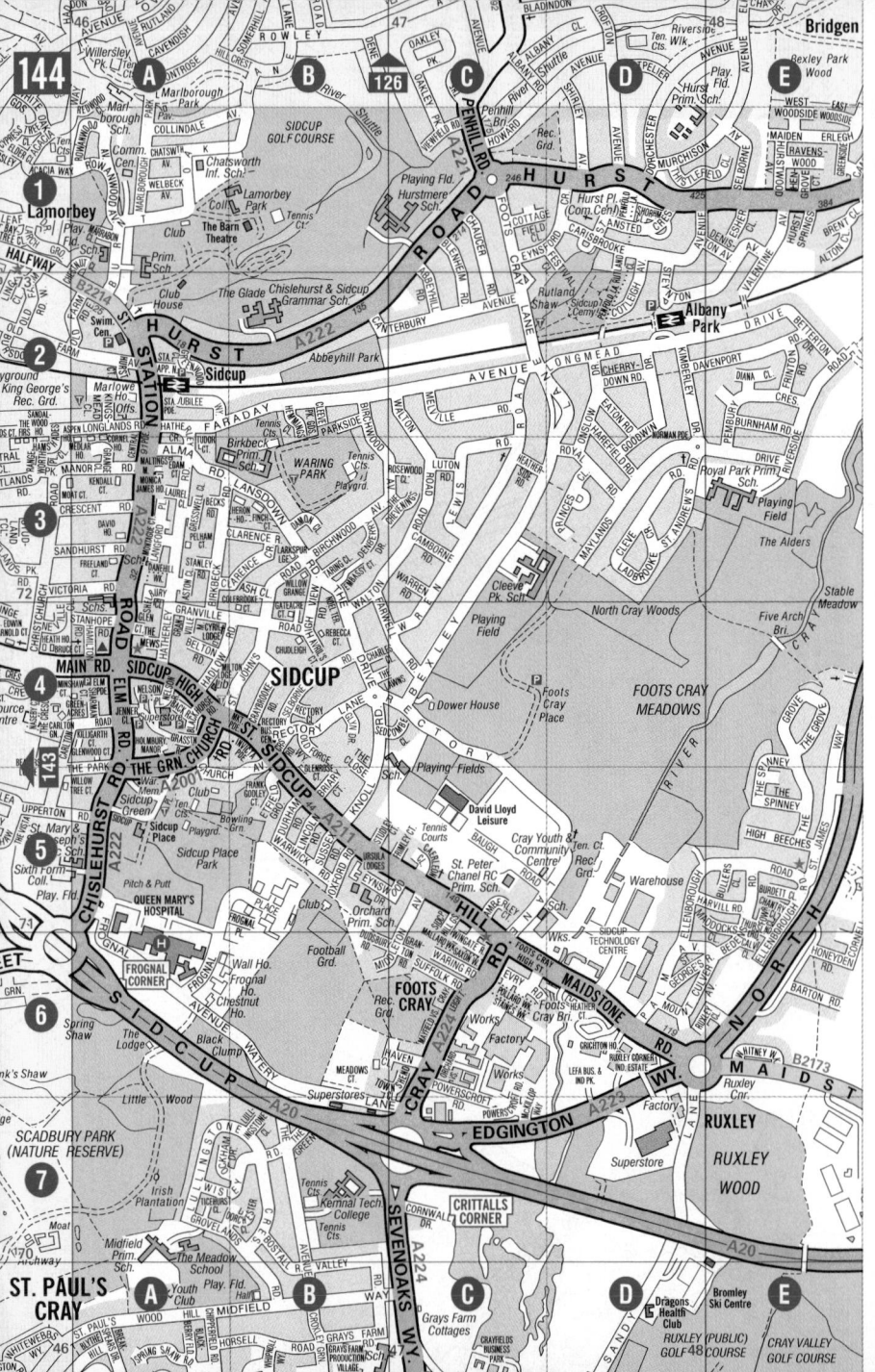

144
126
143
A
B
C
D
E
1
2
3
4
5
6
7
46
47
48
Bridgen
Bexley Park Wood
Lamorbey
HALFWAY
Willersley Pk.
Marlborough Park
Marlborough Sch.
SIDCUP GOLF COURSE
River Shuttle
Chatsworth Inf. Sch.
Lamorbey Park
The Barn Theatre
Club
Prim. Sch.
Club House
The Glade
Chislehurst & Sidcup Grammar Sch.
Swim. Cen.
Playing Fld. Hurstmere Sch.
PENHILL RD.
A221
HURST ROAD
A222
HURST
Rec. Grd.
Hurst Prim. Sch.
Play. Fld.
Riverside
Hurst Pl. (Com. Cen.)
Rutland Shaw
Sidcup Cemy.
Albany Park
Abbeyhill Park
Sidcup
King George's Rec. Grd.
Marlowe Ho. Offs.
STATION ROAD
B2214
ST.
LONGMEAD
AVENUE
DRIVE
Birkbeck Prim. Sch.
WARING PARK
Tennis Cts.
Playgrd.
Royal Park Prim. Sch.
Playing Field
The Alders
Cleeve Pk. Sch.
North Cray Woods
Playing Field
Stable Meadow
Five Arch Bri.
FOOTS CRAY MEADOWS
Foots Cray Place
Dower House
SIDCUP
MAIN RD.
SIDCUP HIGH ST.
THE GRN.
CHURCH
Superstore
Holmbury Manor
The Mews
RECTORY LANE
A2001
A211
Playing Fields
David Lloyd Leisure
Cray Youth & Community Centre
Rec. Grd.
Warehouse
St. Peter Chanel RC Prim. Sch.
Sidcup Green
Sidcup Place
Sidcup Place Park
War Mem.
Bowling Grn.
St. Mary & St. Joseph's Sch.
Sixth Form Coll.
Play. Fld.
Pitch & Putt
QUEEN MARY'S HOSPITAL
CHISLEHURST RD
FROGNAL CORNER
Wall Ho.
Frognal Ho.
Chestnut Ho.
Football Grd.
Orchard Prim. Sch.
Club
HILL RD.
MAIDSTONE RD.
SIDCUP TECHNOLOGY CENTRE
FOOTS CRAY
Rec. Grd.
Foots Cray Bri.
Works
Factory
A224
LEFA BUS. & IND PK.
RUXLEY CORNER IND. ESTATE
NORTH CRAY
B2173
MAIDSTONE
Ruxley Cnr.
RUXLEY
RUXLEY WOOD
Factory
Superstore
EDGINGTON WY.
A223
SIDCUP BY-PASS
A20
Spring Shaw
The Lodge
Black Clump
Little Wood
SCADBURY PARK (NATURE RESERVE)
Irish Plantation
Moat
Archway
Midfield Prim. Sch.
The Meadow School
Play. Fld.
Youth Club
Kemnal Tech. College
Tennis Cts.
CRITTALLS CORNER
SEVENOAKS WY.
Grays Farm Cottages
CRAYFIELDS BUSINESS PARK
Dragons Health Club
Bromley Ski Centre
RUXLEY (PUBLIC) GOLF COURSE
CRAY VALLEY GOLF COURSE
ST. PAUL'S CRAY
MIDFIELD WAY
WOOD HILL
GRAYS FARM RD.

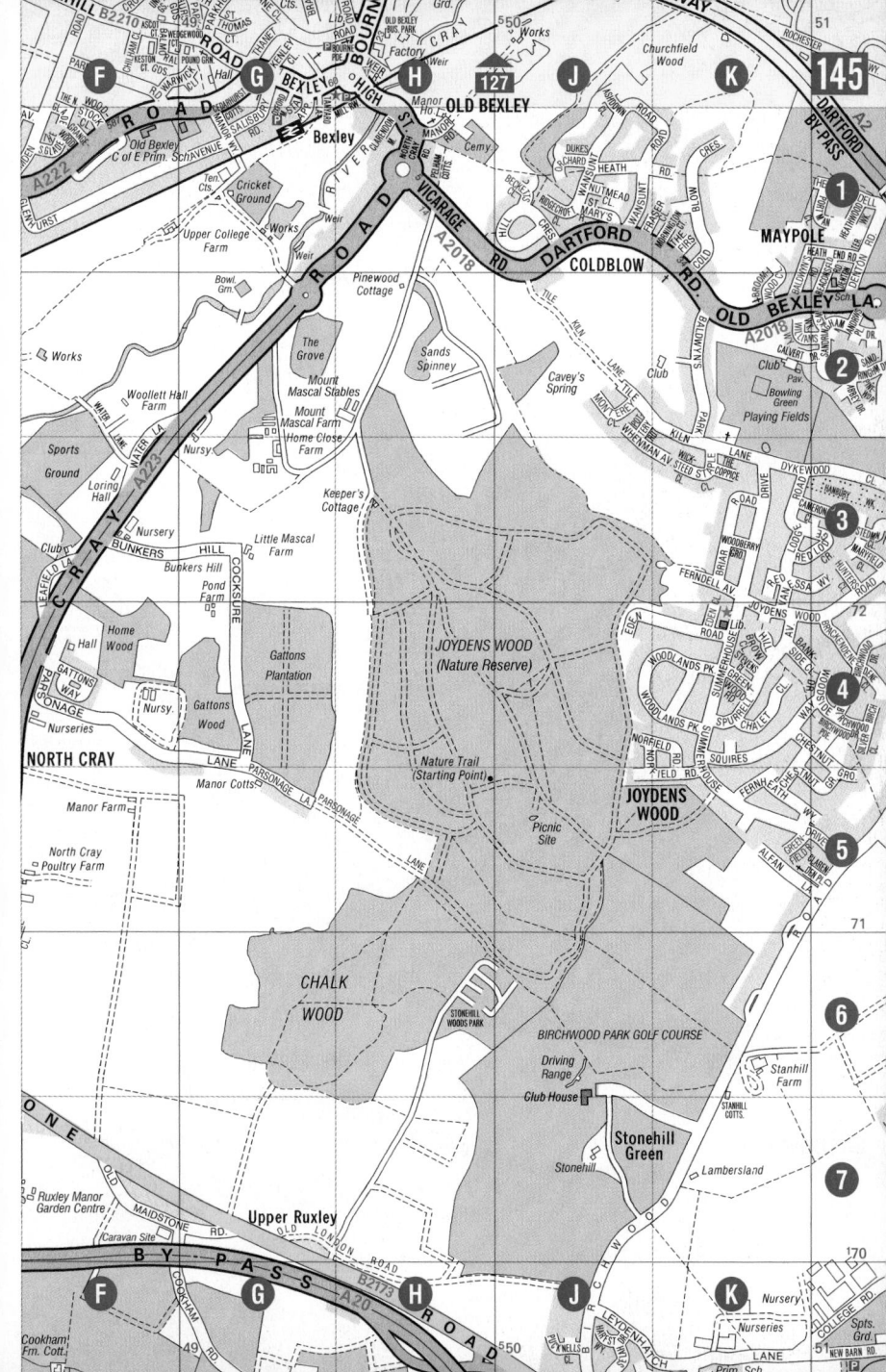

145
127
OLD BEXLEY
Bexley
MAYPOLE
COLDBLOW
JOYDENS WOOD
(Nature Reserve)
JOYDENS WOOD
NORTH CRAY
CHALK WOOD
BIRCHWOOD PARK GOLF COURSE
Stonehill Green
Upper Ruxley
DARTFORD RD.
VICARAGE RD.
CRAY ROAD
OLD BEXLEY LA.
DARTFORD BY-PASS
MAIDSTONE RD.
BY-PASS
Churchfield Wood
Cricket Ground
Upper College Farm
Pinewood Cottage
The Grove
Sands Spinney
Cavey's Spring
Mount Mascal Stables
Mount Mascal Farm
Home Close Farm
Woollett Hall Farm
Sports Ground
Loring Hall
Keeper's Cottage
Little Mascal Farm
Bunkers Hill
Pond Farm
Home Wood
Gattons Plantation
Gattons Wood
Nature Trail (Starting Point)
Picnic Site
Manor Farm
North Cray Poultry Farm
Stonehill Woods Park
Driving Range
Club House
Stonehill
Stanhill Farm
Lambersland
Ruxley Manor Garden Centre
Caravan Site
Cookham Fm. Cott.
Nurseries
Playing Fields
Bowling Green

A **B** ⌂ **128** **C** **D** **E**

1

QUEEN MARY

Pumping Station

RESERVOIR

Round

2

Copse

69

CHARLTON

Manor Farm

3

STUDIOS
Shepperton Film Studios

River

ROAD The Green
Old Manor Ho. M. LITTLETON
Littleton Fm.
Play Fld.

NEW

LITTLETON

Driving Range

Club Ho

Laleham Nurseries

SHEPPERTON B376 RD.

Nurseries

Squire's Bridge

ASH
ROAD

SHEPPERTON GREEN

SUNBURY GOLF

Rec. Grd.

4

68

LALEHAM

Rec. Grd.

Staines Road Farm

Nurseries

B376

Shepperton

SHEPPERTON BUSINESS PK.

5

Works

Gravel Pit

Saxon Prim. Sch. Play. Fld.

Pool End

SHEPPERTON GREEN

Prim. Sch

6

M3-MOTORWAY
M3

Playing Field

SHEPPERTON

Rec. Grd.

Play. Fld. Halliford Sch.

67

CHERTSEY

B375 ROAD RENFREE WAY RUSSELL

Lords Bri.
Pav.

HIGH B376

7

DUMSEY EYOT

Riversleigh Farm

The Range

Mead Farm

Cemetery

War Close
Cricket Ground
Cem Tery

Las Palmas Estate

RIVER THAMES

A **B** **C** **D** Desborough Sailing Club **E**

DESBOROUGH ISLAND

06 Chertsey Meads   07   08

DOCKETT MOORINGS
DOCKETT EDDY

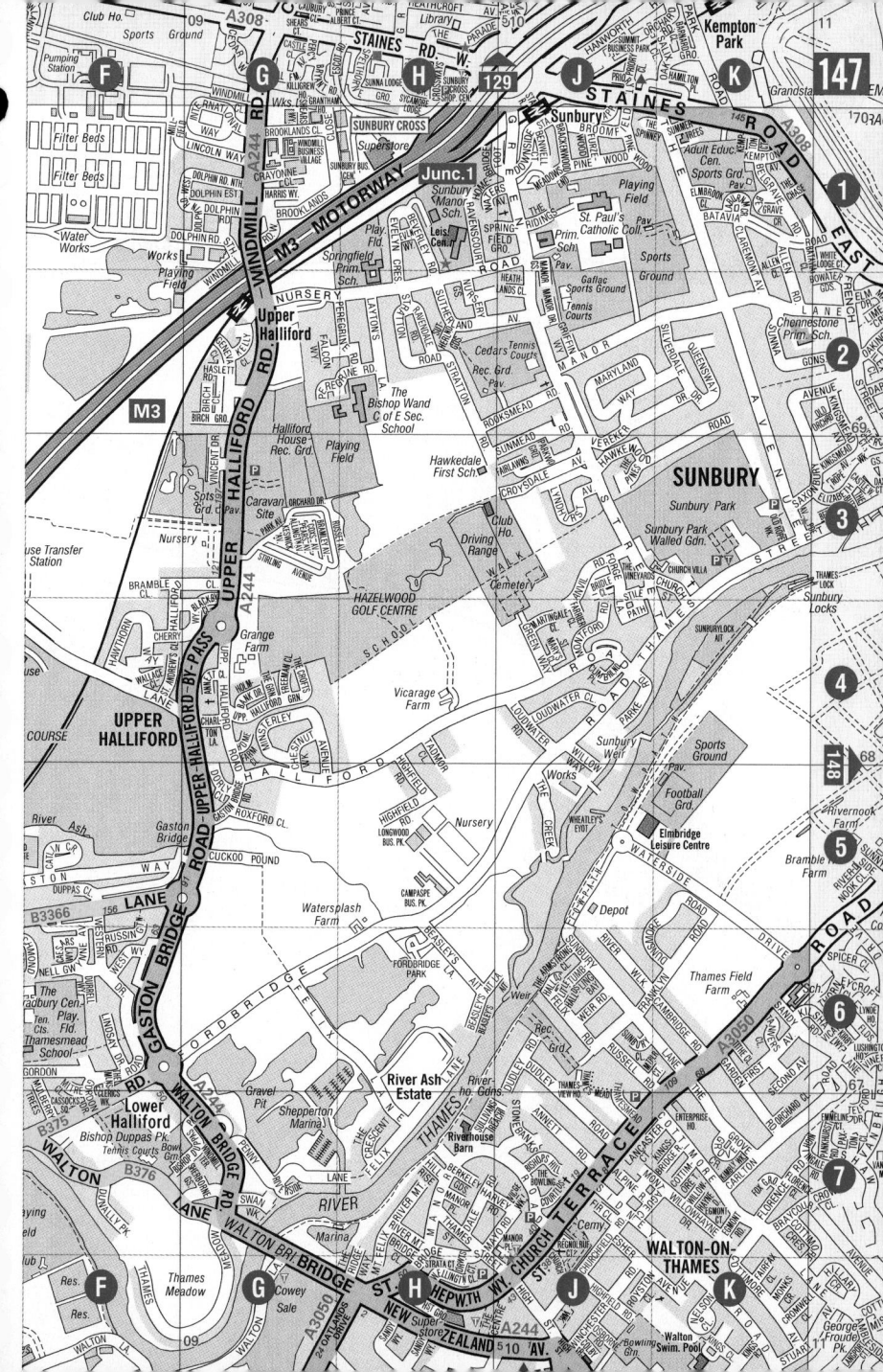

147
Kempton Park
Grandstand
STAINES ROAD EAST
A308
STAINES RD. W.
129
Junc.1
M3 MOTORWAY
M3
Sunbury
SUNBURY CROSS
Superstore
Sunbury Cross Shop. Cen.
Sunbury Bus. Cen.
Windmill Business Village
Brooklands Cl.
Crayonne Cl.
Harris Wy.
Brooklands
Lincoln Way
International Way
Dolphin Rd.
Dolphin Est.
Water Works
Filter Beds
Pumping Station
Sports Ground
Club Ho.
Works
Playing Field
WINDMILL RD.
A244
Upper Halliford
UPPER HALLIFORD RD.
UPPER HALLIFORD-BY-PASS
UPPER HALLIFORD
Nursery
Spelthorne Gro.
Sunna Lodge
Sycamore Lodge
Killigrew Ho.
Shears Ct.
Grantham Ho.
Library
The Parade
Heathcroft Av.
Hanworth Rd.
Summit Business Park
Priory Cl.
Orchard Rd.
Barnard Gro.
Hamilton Pl.
Park Road
Adult Educ. Cen.
Sports Grd.
Kempton Av.
Belgrave Cr.
The Chase
Batavia Rd.
Elmbrook Cl.
Laburnum Cr.
Claremont Av.
Allen Cl.
White Lodge Cl.
Bowater Gds.
French St.
Chennestone Prim. Sch.
Sunna Gdns.
Avenue
Kingsmead Av.
Old Orchard
Saxonbury Av.
Rope Wk.
Elizabeth Gdns.
Castle Wk.
Play. Fld.
Springfield Prim. Sch.
Sunbury Manor Sch.
Leis. Cen.
Evelyn Cres.
Beverley Rd.
Ravenscourt
Springfield Gro.
Springfield Road
Home Wood
Waters Av.
Green St.
Downside
Benwell Ct.
Brackenwood
Broomfield
Furze
Pine Wood
The Spinney
Summer Trees
The Avenue
Meadows End
The Ridings
Playing Field
St. Paul's Catholic Coll.
Prim. Sch.
Sports Ground
Gaflac Sports Ground
Tennis Courts
Heathlands Cl.
Nursery Gs.
Manor Dr.
Griffin Wy.
Nursery Rd.
Peregrine Rd.
Falcon Wy.
Layton's La.
Stratton Rd.
Ravendale Rd.
Sutherland Av.
Cedars Rec. Grd.
Tennis Courts
Manor Lane
Maryland Way
Silverdale Dr.
Queensway Dr.
The Bishop Wand C of E Sec. School
Halliford House Rec. Grd.
Playing Field
Rooksmead Rd.
Sunmead Rd.
Parkwood Gro.
Fairlawns
Vereker Rd.
Hawkewood Rd.
The Pines
Croysdale Av.
Lyndhurst Av.
Hawkedale First Sch.
SUNBURY
Sunbury Park
Sunbury Park Walled Gdn.
Old Rope Wk.
Church Villa
Thames St.
Thames Lock
Sunbury Locks
Sunbury Lock Ait
Club Ho.
Driving Range
Walk
Cemetery
Hazelwood Golf Centre
School
Forge La.
The Vineyards
Church St.
Stile Path
Anvil Rd.
Bridle Cl.
Farrier Cl.
Martingale Cl.
Green Way
Montford Rd.
Cumberland Pl.
Loudwater Cl.
Loudwater Rd.
Parke Rd.
Vincent Dr.
Spts Grd.
Pav.
Caravan Site
Orchard Dr.
Park Av.
Stirling Avenue
Bramble Cl.
Bramley Av.
Russet Av.
Grange Farm
Hawthorn Way
Cherry Way
Wallace Cl.
St. Andrew's Cl.
Halliford Cl.
Blackby Wy.
Charlton La.
Minsterley Av.
Chestnut Wk.
Holmbank Dr.
Freeman Cl.
The Crofts
Halliford Grn.
Vicarage Farm
Halliford Road
Highfield Cl.
Highfield Rd.
Tadmor Cl.
Longwood Bus. Pk.
Nursery
Willow Way
Sunbury Weir
Works
The Creek
Wheatley's Eyot
Sports Ground
Football Grd.
Elmbridge Leisure Centre
Waterside Drive
Towpath
Depot
Dunsmore Road
Thames Field Farm
Road
148
Rivernook Farm
Bramble Farm
Course
Use Transfer Station
River Ash
Gaston Bridge
Cuckoo Pound
Roxford Cl.
Dorly Cl.
Gaston Bridge Rd.
Duppas Cl.
Lane
B3366
Russington Rd.
Western Av.
West Wy.
Nell Gwynne Av.
Durrell Wy.
The Bradbury Cen.
Play. Fld.
Ten. Cts.
Thamesmead School
Lindsay Dr.
Gordon Rd.
GASTON BRIDGE RD.
Watersplash Farm
Campaspe Bus. Pk.
Fordbridge Park
Fordbridge Rd.
Felix La.
Beasley's La.
Beasley's Ait
Weir
River Ash Estate
Gravel Pit
Shepperton Marina
The Crescent
Riverside
Thames
River
Riverhouse Barn
River-ho. Gdns.
Rec. Grd.
Lower Halliford
Bishop Duppas Pk.
Tennis Courts
Bowl. Grn.
B375
B376
WALTON LANE
WALTON BRIDGE RD.
Penny La.
Swan Wk.
Walton Bri.
BRIDGE ST.
A3050
Marina
Thames Meadow
Meadow
Cowey Sale
Res.
Oatlands Drive
New Zealand Av.
Superstore
Hepworth Wy.
Church St.
A244
High St.
Manor Pl.
Thames St.
Manor Rd.
Berkeley Gds.
Harvey Rd.
Mayo Rd.
Dudley Rd.
Thameside
Stonebanks
Bishops Hill
The Bowling
Annett Rd.
Sunbury Lane
Russell Rd.
Cambridge Rd.
Franklyn
River Wlk.
Weir Rd.
TERRACE
A3050
Cottimore La.
Kings Bridge
Mont Ague
Willowhayne Dr.
Egmont
Grove
Carlton
Cemy.
Sidney Rd.
Walton-on-Thames
Fir Cl.
Churchfield
Esher
Royston Av.
Highfield Rd.
Winchester
Osborne
Bowling Grn.
Walton Swim. Pool
Nelson Cl.
Kings Rd.
Thames Field Farm
Sch.
Spicer Cl.
Thorneycroft
First Av.
Second Av.
Tanners Cl.
Garden Cl.
Orchard Cl.
Sandy La.
Florence
Fox Gro.
Braycourt
Cottimore Cres.
Fairfax Cl.
Monks Cr.
Cromwell
Hillary Cr.
George Froude Pk.
Emmeline Ct.
Pankhurst
Lushington
F
G
H
J
K
1
2
3
4
5
6
7
09
10
11
67
68
69
70

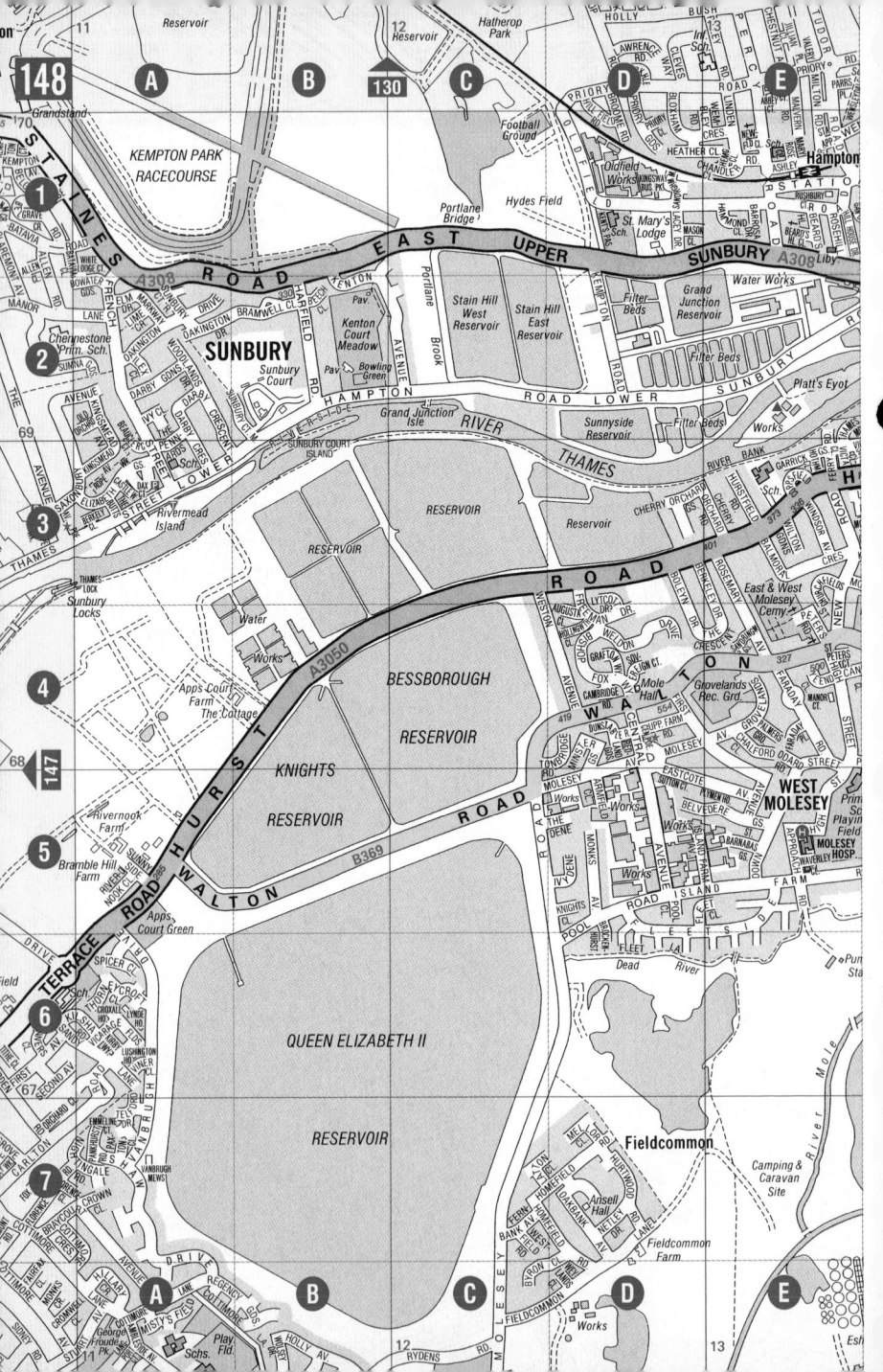
148
130
147
A
B
C
D
E
1
2
3
4
5
6
7
11
12
13
Reservoir
Hatherop Park
Grandstand
KEMPTON PARK RACECOURSE
Football Ground
Oldfield Works
Hydes Field
Portlane Bridge
St. Mary's Lodge
Hampton
UPPER SUNBURY ROAD EAST
A308
Water Works
Filter Beds
Grand Junction Reservoir
Stain Hill West Reservoir
Stain Hill East Reservoir
Kenton Court Meadow
Bowling Green
SUNBURY
Sunbury Court
Chennestone Prim. Sch.
Portlane Brook
LOWER SUNBURY ROAD
HAMPTON
Platt's Eyot
Works
Sunnyside Reservoir
Grand Junction Isle
RIVER THAMES
SUNBURY COURT ISLAND
Rivermead Island
THAMES LOCK
Sunbury Locks
RESERVOIR
Reservoir
Water Works
Apps Court Farm
The Cottage
A3050
HURST ROAD
BESSBOROUGH RESERVOIR
KNIGHTS RESERVOIR
East & West Molesey Cemy.
Grovelands Rec. Grd.
Mole Hall
WALTON ROAD
B369
WEST MOLESEY
MOLESEY HOSP.
Rivernook Farm
Bramble Hill Farm
Apps Court Green
TERRACE ROAD
QUEEN ELIZABETH II RESERVOIR
Dead River
Fieldcommon
Ansell Hall
Fieldcommon Farm
Camping & Caravan Site
River Mole
George Froude Pk.
Schs.
Play. Fld.
MOLESEY ROAD
FIELDCOMMON LANE
RYDENS RD.

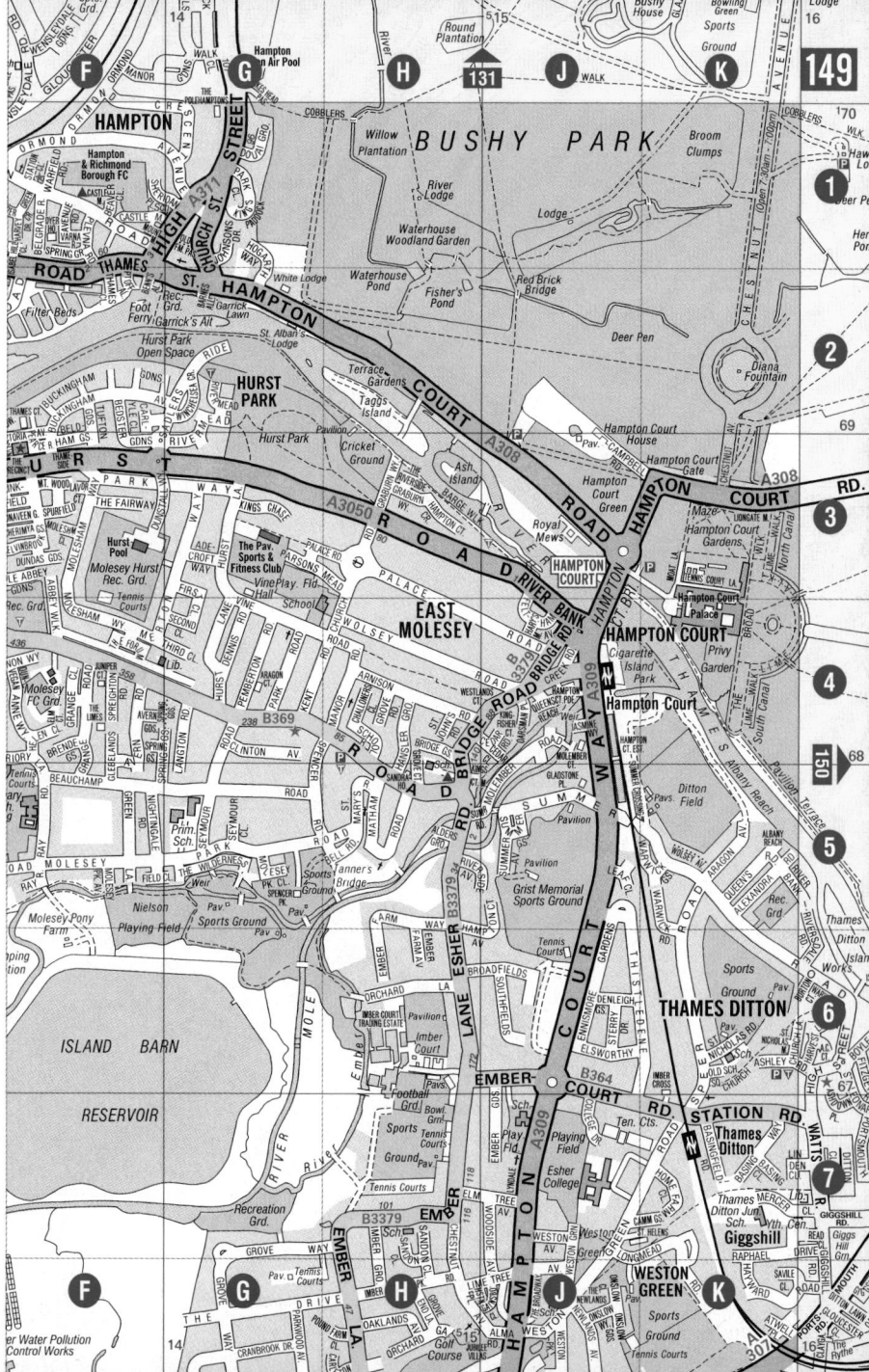
149
131
150
F
G
H
J
K
1
2
3
4
5
6
7
14
15
16
170
69
68
67
HAMPTON
Hampton Open Air Pool
Hampton & Richmond Borough FC
BUSHY PARK
Round Plantation
Bushy House
Sports Ground
Willow Plantation
Broom Clumps
River Lodge
Lodge
Waterhouse Woodland Garden
Waterhouse Pond
Fisher's Pond
Red Brick Bridge
White Lodge
Deer Pen
Diana Fountain
CHESTNUT AVENUE
(Open 7:30am - 7:00pm)
COBBLERS WALK
HIGH STREET
A311
CHURCH ST.
THAMES ST.
ROAD
HAMPTON COURT ROAD
A308
Filter Beds
Foot Ferry
Garrick's Ait
Garrick Lawn
Rec. Grd.
Hurst Park Open Space
St. Alban's Lodge
Terrace Gardens
Taggs Island
HURST PARK
Hurst Park
Pavilion
Cricket Ground
Ash Island
Hampton Court House
Hampton Court Gate
Hampton Court Green
Royal Mews
HAMPTON COURT
Maze
Hampton Court Gardens
Hampton Court Palace
Privy Garden
North Canal
South Canal
Albany Reach
Pavilion Terrace
HURST ROAD
A3050
Hurst Pool
Molesey Hurst Rec. Grd.
The Pav. Sports & Fitness Club
Vine Hall
Play. Fld.
School
EAST MOLESEY
PALACE ROAD
WOLSEY ROAD
RIVER BANK
B369
BRIDGE ROAD
B3379
A309
Cigarette Island Park
Hampton Court
Molesey FC Grd.
Lib.
Prim. Sch.
Sch.
Tennis Courts
Ditton Field
Pavs.
SUMMER ROAD
Pavilion
Grist Memorial Sports Ground
Tanners Bridge
Sports Ground
Nielson Playing Field
Molesey Pony Farm
Weir
ISLAND BARN RESERVOIR
RIVER MOLE
River Ember
IMBER COURT TRADING ESTATE
Imber Court
Football Grd.
Bowl. Grn.
Sports Ground
Recreation Grd.
ESHER LANE
HAMPTON COURT WAY
EMBER COURT RD.
B364
STATION RD.
THAMES DITTON
Thames Ditton
Sports Ground
Thames Ditton Works
Rec. Grd.
Esher College
Playing Field
Thames Ditton Jun. Sch.
Yth. Cen.
Giggshill
WESTON GREEN
Sports Ground
Golf Course
Tennis Courts
Water Pollution Control Works
A307

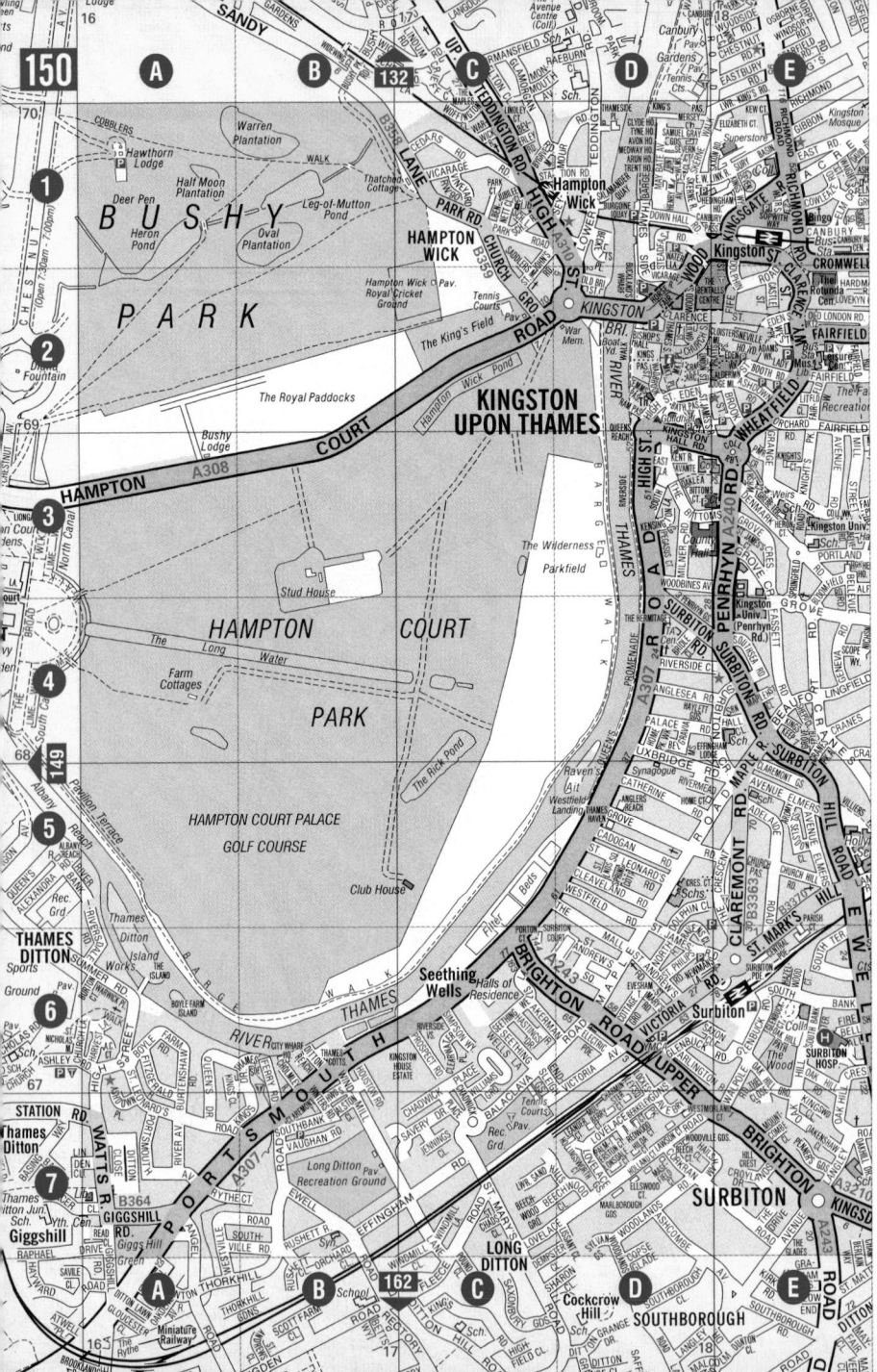

150
BUSHY PARK
HAMPTON COURT PARK
HAMPTON WICK
KINGSTON UPON THAMES
SURBITON
THAMES DITTON
LONG DITTON
SOUTHBOROUGH
Seething Wells
Hampton Wick
Kingston
Surbiton
Thames Ditton
Giggshill
Cockcrow Hill
HAMPTON COURT PALACE GOLF COURSE
The Royal Paddocks
The King's Field
The Long Water
The Wilderness
Parkfield
Stud House
Club House
Farm Cottages
Bushy Lodge
Hawthorn Lodge
Warren Plantation
Half Moon Plantation
Oval Plantation
Leg-of-Mutton Pond
Heron Pond
Deer Pen
Diana Fountain
Thatched Cottage
The Rick Pond
Hampton Wick Pond
Hampton Wick Royal Cricket Ground
Raven's Ait
Westfield Landing
Thames Ditton Island
Boyle Farm Island
Long Ditton Recreation Ground
Kingston House Estate
Halls of Residence
Filter Beds
HAMPTON COURT ROAD
A308
PORTSMOUTH ROAD
A307
BRIGHTON ROAD
A243
UPPER BRIGHTON ROAD
RIVER THAMES
THAMES
BARGE WALK
QUEEN'S PROMENADE
PENRHYN RD.
A240
CLAREMONT RD.
B3363
SURBITON HILL ROAD
EWELL ROAD
RICHMOND ROAD
KINGSTON BRI.
HIGH ST.
A310
TEDDINGTON RD.
B358
B359
B364
B3370
A3210
SANDY LANE
SANDY GARDENS
CHESTNUT AV.
(Open 7:30am - 7:00pm)
Superstore
Kingston Mosque
The Bentalls Centre
The Rotunda Cen.
Leisure Cen.
Kingston Univ.
Kingston Univ. (Penrhyn Rd.)
County Hall
SURBITON HOSP.
Synagogue
Miniature Railway
Sports Ground
132
149
162
A B C D E
1 2 3 4 5 6 7

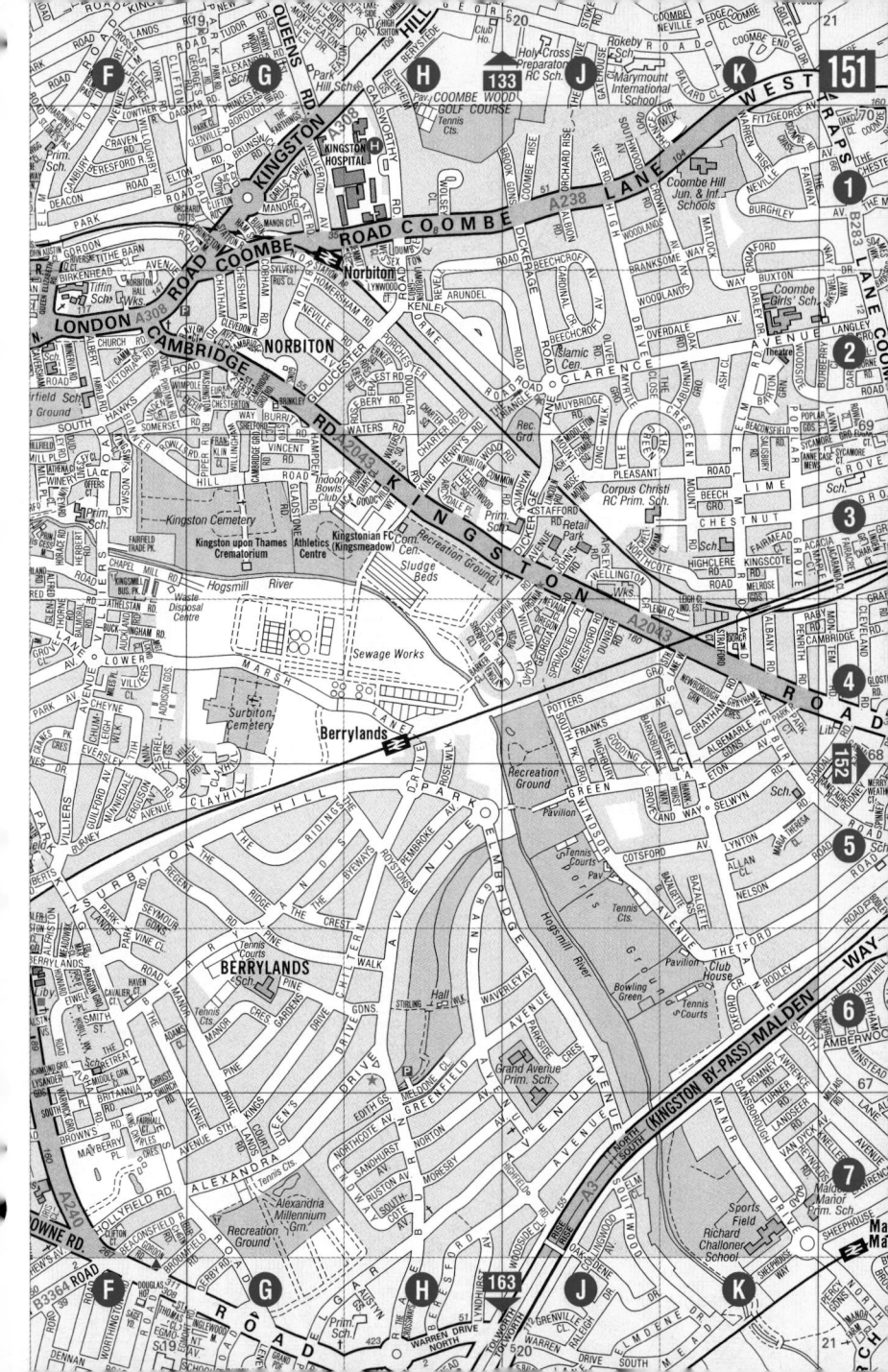

151
133
152
163
F
G
H
J
K
1
2
3
4
5
6
7
Holy Cross Preparatory RC Sch.
Rokeby Sch.
Marymount International School
COOMBE WOOD GOLF COURSE
Park Hill Sch.
KINGSTON HOSPITAL
Coombe Hill Jun. & Inf. Schools
Coombe Girls' Sch.
KINGSTON HILL
QUEENS RD.
A308
A238
COOMBE LANE WEST
TRAPS LANE
B283
COOMBE ROAD
LONDON ROAD
CAMBRIDGE RD
A2043
KINGSTON ROAD
Norbiton
NORBITON
Tiffin Sch.
Islamic Cen.
Rec. Grd.
CLARENCE AVENUE
Corpus Christi RC Prim. Sch.
Retail Park
Kingston Cemetery
Kingston upon Thames Crematorium
Athletics Centre
Kingstonian FC (Kingsmeadow)
Indoor Bowls Club
Recreation Ground
Sludge Beds
Hogsmill River
Waste Disposal Centre
Sewage Works
Surbiton Cemetery
MARSH LANE
Berrylands
BERRYLANDS
PARK AVENUE
Recreation Ground
Pavilion
Tennis Courts
Sports Ground
Club House
Bowling Green
Hall
Grand Avenue Prim. Sch.
ELMBRIDGE AVENUE
KINGSTON BY-PASS
A3
MALDEN WAY
Sports Field
Richard Challoner School
Malden Manor Prim. Sch.
Alexandria Millennium Grn.
Recreation Ground
ALEXANDRA DRIVE
HOLLYFIELD RD.
A240
B3364
WARREN DRIVE NORTH
TOLWORTH
Prim. Sch.

COOMBE LA. WEST
COOMBE LANE
COOMBE LA. FLYOVER
134
NEW VICTORIA HOSPITAL
The Wolfson Rehabilitation Cen.
COPSE HILL
Sports Grd.
Tennis Courts
COTTENHAM PARK ROAD
COTTENHAM
St. Matthew's C of E Sch.
MELBURY GARDENS
Cottenham Park
COTTENHAM PARK
DURHAM ROAD
B281
Holland Gdns.
Sch.
Wimbledon College Playing Fields
Pav.
COOMBE
A238
BEVERLEY
A3
(KINGSTON BY-PASS)
MALDEN
GOLF COURSE
Coombe Brook
Club House
Sports Ground
Club Ho.
Beverley Brook
Tennis Courts
Sports Ground
Civil Service Sports Ground
Raynes Park Sports Ground
Tennis Bowling Green
WORPLE RD.
Raynes Park
RAINBOW IND. EST.
A298
PRINCE GEO PLAYING
Coombe Girls' Sch.
TRAPS LANE
COOMBE LANE
B283
BURGHLEY AV.
THE FAIRWAY
NEVILLE
THE CHESTERS
THE MOAT
Sch.
New Malden
ROAD
HIGH
ST.
DUKES
MALDEN HILL
THE MOUNT
BEVERLEY PARK
Golf Driving Range
Pavilion
Emanuel School Playing Field
Blagdon House
Sports Cen.
Raynes Pk. High Sch.
Superstore
Alliance Sports Ground
BUSHEY ROAD
WEST BARNES LANE
GRAND DRIVE
B279
RAYNES PARK
Spts. Grd
Football Grd.
NEW MALDEN
Com. Cen. Sch.
The Malden Cen.
The Crescent
B282
BURLINGTON
SHANNON CORNER
SHANNON COMMERCIAL CEN.
Superstore
SHANNON CNR. RETAIL PK.
KINGSTON RD.
FOUNTAIN ROUNDABOUT
MALDEN RD.
A2043
Lib.
151
Sch.
WEST BARNES
CROSSWAY
Motspur Park
Lib.
Beverley Sch.
MALDEN JUNC.
The Study Sch.
(KINGSTON BY-PASS)
MALDEN
University of London Athletic Ground
Running Track
Pav.
Sports Ground
Tennis Cts.
Old Blues Rugby Football Grd.
King's Coll. Sch. Sports Grd.
St. John Fisher RC Prim. Sch.
North East Surrey Crematorium
MORDEN CEMETERY
Bowling Green
Putting Green
The Sir Joseph Hood Memorial Playing Fields
BBC Sports Ground
MOTSPUR PARK
Gas Works
Beverley Brook
Playing Fields
Green Lane Prim. Sch.
Merton & Sutton Joint Cemetery
Refuse Destructor
ASM Ten. Cen.
Hall
MANOR PARK
Bowling Green
Pav.
Malden Manor Prim. Sch.
Malden Manor
OLD MALDEN
CHURCH ROAD
164
Malden Green
Worcester Park
Tennis Courts
Mayflower Park
CANTERBURY HALL
(Under Construction)
Rec. Grd.
A B C D E
1 2 3 4 5 6 7
21 22 23

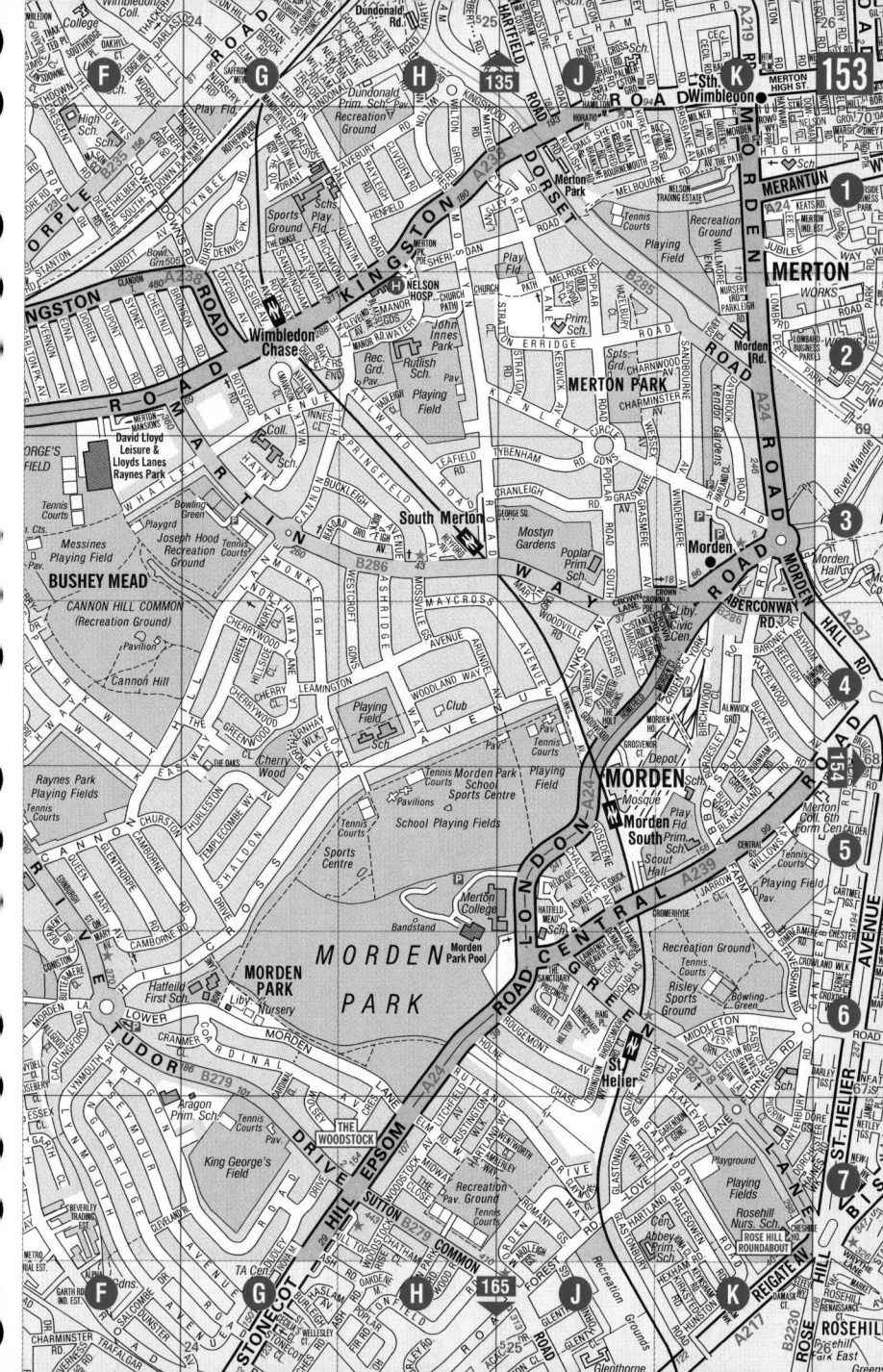

153
135
154
165
F
G
H
J
K
1
2
3
4
5
6
7
24
25
26
68
69
70
MERTON
MERTON PARK
MORDEN
BUSHEY MEAD
MORDEN PARK
ROSEHILL
Wimbledon Chase
South Merton
Sth. Wimbledon
Merton Park
Morden Rd.
Morden
Morden South
St. Helier
KINGSTON ROAD
MARTIN WAY
LONDON ROAD
CENTRAL ROAD
EPSOM ROAD
STONECOT HILL
TUDOR DRIVE
GREEN LANE
MORDEN ROAD
DORSET ROAD
WORPLE ROAD
HARTFIELD ROAD
MORDEN HALL RD.
ST. HELIER AVENUE
SUTTON COMMON RD.
LOWER MORDEN LA.
HILLCROSS AV.
ROSE HILL
A24
A238
A239
A217
A219
A297
B235
B278
B279
B285
B286
B2230
NELSON HOSP.
David Lloyd Leisure & Lloyds Lanes Raynes Park
Messines Playing Field
Joseph Hood Recreation Ground
CANNON HILL COMMON (Recreation Ground)
Cannon Hill
Raynes Park Playing Fields
Morden Park School Sports Centre
School Playing Fields
Merton College
Morden Park Pool
Mostyn Gardens
John Innes Park
Rutlish Sch.
Kendor Gardens
Morden Hall
River Wandle
Recreation Ground
Risley Sports Ground
Rosehill Nurs. Sch.
King George's Field
Aragon Prim. Sch.
Hatfeild First Sch.
Abbey Prim. Sch.
Merton Coll. 6th Form Cen.
THE WOODSTOCK
ROSE HILL ROUNDABOUT
NELSON TRADING ESTATE
MERTON IND. EST.
LOMBARD BUSINESS PARK
BEVERLEY TRADING EST.
GARTH RD. IND. EST.

154
136
153
166
MERTON
MITCHAM
ST. HELIER
ROSEHILL
BEDDINGTON CORNER
MORDEN HALL PARK
Morden Hall
Morden Cottage
Morden Lodge
Phipps Bridge
Belgrave Wlk.
Ravensbury Park
River Wandle
Deen City Farm
Lavender Park
Mitcham
Mitcham Junction
Tooting & Mitcham United FC (Imperial Fields)
Watermeads
Poulter Park
Bishopsford House
Bishopsford Comm. Sch.
Moreton Green
Sutton Arena Leisure Centre
St. Helier Open Space
The Canons Leisure Centre & Lib.
Cricket Green
Beehive Bridge
Blue Houses Bridge
Cranmer Bri.
Willow Lane Bri.
Mill Green
Nature Reserves
Superstore
Colour Ho. Th.
MERANTUN WAY
WESTERN ROAD
LONDON ROAD
STREATHAM ROAD
MORDEN HALL RD.
MORDEN ROAD
ST. HELIER AVENUE
BISHOPSFORD ROAD
CARSHALTON ROAD
CRICKET GRN.
MADEIRA RD.
CRANMER RD.
COMMONSIDE WEST
ROSE HILL ROUNDABOUT
A24
A217
A236
A239
A297
A216
A237
A2392

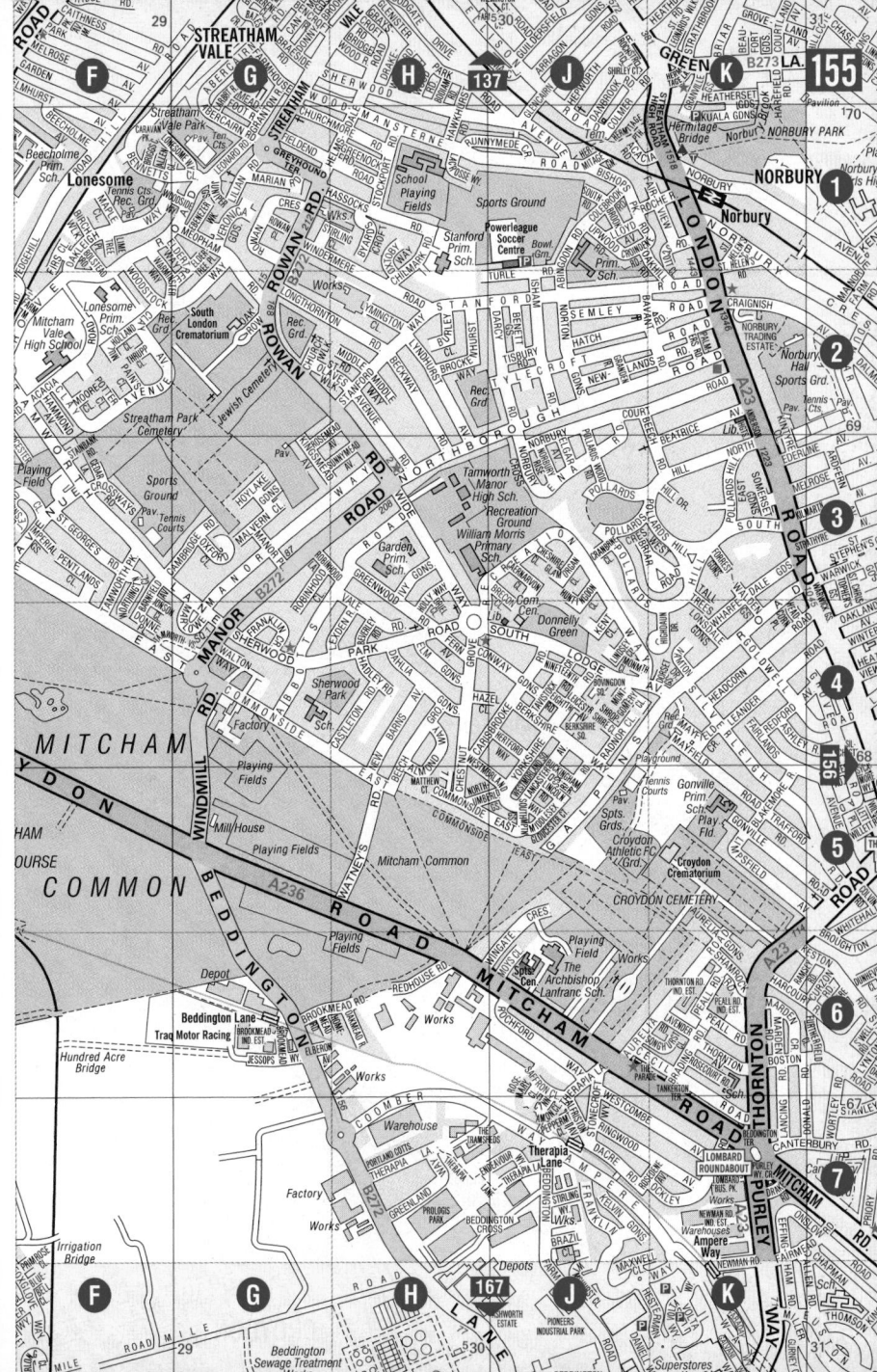
STREATHAM VALE
Streatham Vale Park
Lonesome
Beecholme Prim. Sch.
Lonesome Prim. Sch.
Mitcham Vale High School
South London Crematorium
Jewish Cemetery
Streatham Park Cemetery
Sports Ground
School Playing Fields
Powerleague Soccer Centre
Stanford Prim. Sch.
NORBURY
Norbury
NORBURY PARK
Hermitage Bridge
NORBURY TRADING ESTATE
Norbury Hall Sports Grd.
Tamworth Manor High Sch.
Recreation Ground
William Morris Primary Sch.
Garden Prim. Sch.
Donnelly Green
Sherwood Park Sch.
MITCHAM COMMON
Mitcham Common
Playing Fields
Mill House
Gonville Prim. Sch.
Croydon Athletic FC Grd.
Croydon Crematorium
CROYDON CEMETERY
The Archbishop Lanfranc Sch.
Beddington Lane
Traq Motor Racing
Hundred Acre Bridge
Irrigation Bridge
Therapia Lane
PROLOGIS PARK
BEDDINGTON CROSS
Ampere Way
LOMBARD ROUNDABOUT
Beddington Sewage Treatment
PIONEERS INDUSTRIAL PARK
Superstores
LONDON ROAD
MITCHAM ROAD
ROWAN RD.
MANOR ROAD
WINDMILL RD.
BEDDINGTON LANE
THORNTON ROAD
PURLEY WAY
A23
A236
B272
B273
137
156
167
F G H J K
1 2 3 4 5 6 7
29 30 31

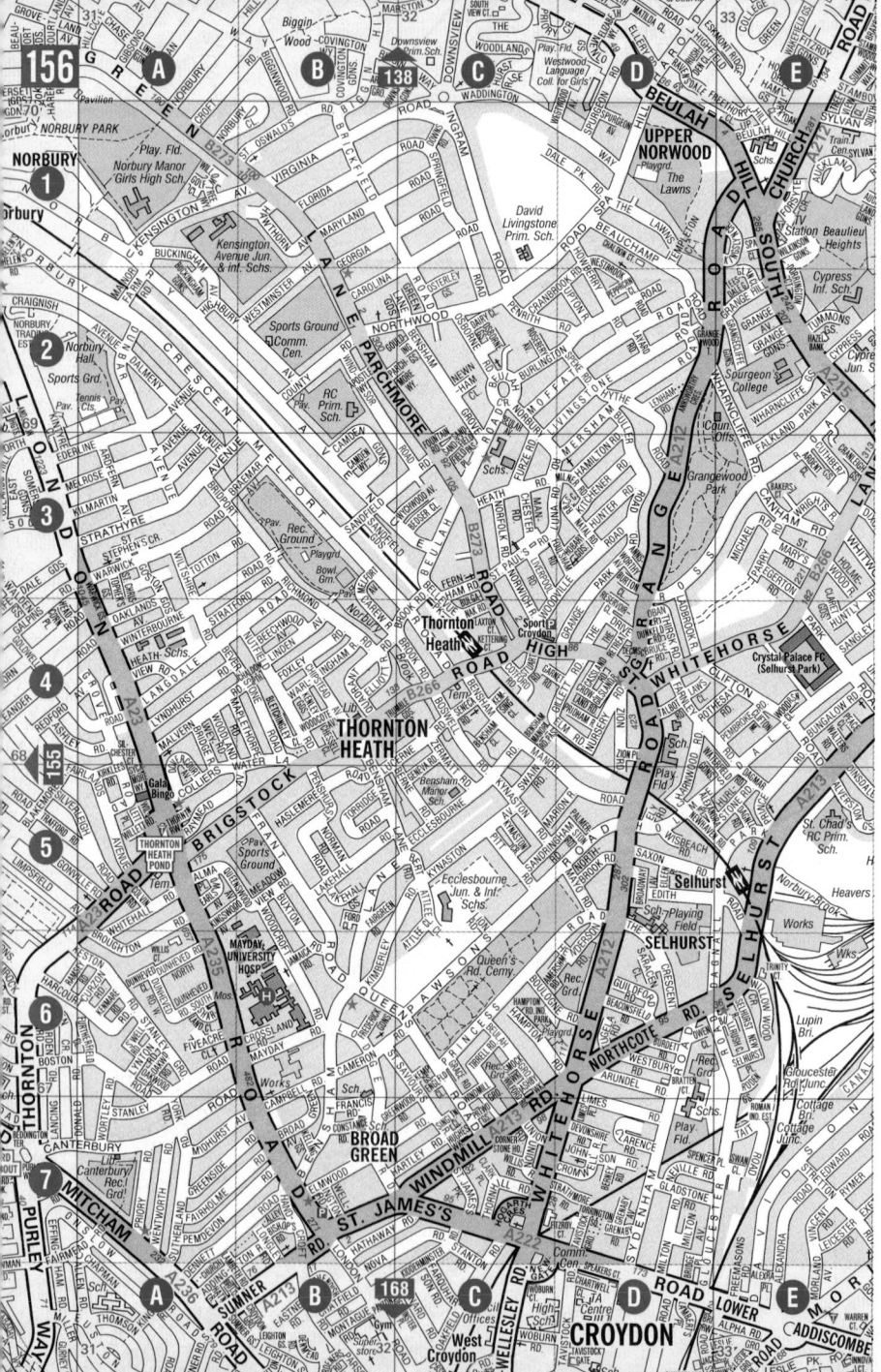

156
A
B
C
D
E
138
155
168
1
2
3
4
5
6
7
NORBURY
NORBURY PARK
Norbury Manor Girls High Sch.
Play. Fld.
Kensington Avenue Jun. & Inf. Schs.
Sports Ground
Comm. Cen.
RC Prim. Sch.
Norbury Hall
Sports Grd.
Rec. Ground
Playgrd
Bowl. Grn.
UPPER NORWOOD
The Lawns
David Livingstone Prim. Sch.
Westwood Language Coll. for Girls'
Downsview Prim. Sch.
Biggin Wood
Spurgeon's College
Cypress Inf. Sch.
TV Station
Beaulieu Heights
Grangewood Park
Coun. Offs.
Thornton Heath
THORNTON HEATH
Sport Croydon
Crystal Palace FC (Selhurst Park)
Bensham Manor Sch.
Ecclesbourne Jun. & Inf. Schs.
Queen's Rd. Cemy.
MAYDAY UNIVERSITY HOSP
THORNTON HEATH POND
Gala Bingo
Selhurst
SELHURST
Playing Field
St. Chad's RC Prim. Sch.
Works
Norbury Brook
Heavers
Lupin Bri.
Gloucester Rd. Junc.
Cottage Bri.
Cottage Junc.
BROAD GREEN
Canterbury Rec. Grd.
CROYDON
West Croydon
GREEN LANE
PARCHMORE ROAD
BRIGSTOCK ROAD
LONDON ROAD
MELFORT AVENUE
CRESCENT
WHITEHORSE ROAD
WHITEHORSE LANE
HIGH ROAD
BEULAH HILL
GRANGE ROAD
SELHURST ROAD
ST. JAMES'S RD.
WINDMILL RD.
NORTHCOTE RD.
MITCHAM ROAD
SUMNER ROAD
PURLEY WAY
LOWER ADDISCOMBE ROAD
PAWSONS ROAD
QUEENS ROAD
A23
A212
A213
A215
A222
A235
A236
B266
B273

157
139
169
158
F
G
H
J
K
1
2
3
4
5
6
7
34
35
36
67
68
69
70
Anerley
PENGE
Kent House
ANERLEY
Harris City Technology Coll.
Orchard Lodge (Remand Centre)
James Dixon Prim. Sch.
Orchard School Sports Centre
Playing Field
Bowling Green
Tennis Courts
South Norwood Lake
Athletic Grounds
Bromley Junction
SOUTH NORWOOD
Stanley Hall
Birkbeck
Beckenham Crematorium
Harrington Rd.
Blind Corner
Pitch & Putt Course
SOUTH NORWOOD COUNTRY PARK
ELMERS END
Elmers End
Superstore
Avenue Road
Norwood Junc.
Recreation Ground
South Norwood Country Park Visitors Cen.
Croydon Sports Arena
Croydon FC Grd.
Ryelands Prim. Sch.
Arena
Croydon Golf Driving Range
CHAFFINCH BUSINESS PARK
Monks Orchard Prim. Sch.
Long Lane Wood
Bird Sanctuary
Glade Wood
WOODSIDE
Brickfields Mdw.
Woodside
Blackhorse La.
Ashburton Park
Library
Ashburton Playing Fields
Ashburton High Sch.
SHIRLEY OAKS BMI HOSPITAL
Shirley Oaks
Addiscombe
Davidson Primary Sch.
Training Cen.
CROYDON ROAD
ELMERS END ROAD
PENGE ROAD
ANERLEY ROAD
LONG LANE
PORTLAND ROAD
SPRING LANE
SHIRLEY ROAD
ADDISCOMBE ROAD
WOODSIDE GREEN
SOUTH NORWOOD HILL
HIGH STREET
BECKENHAM ROAD
A213
A214
A215
A222
A234
B243

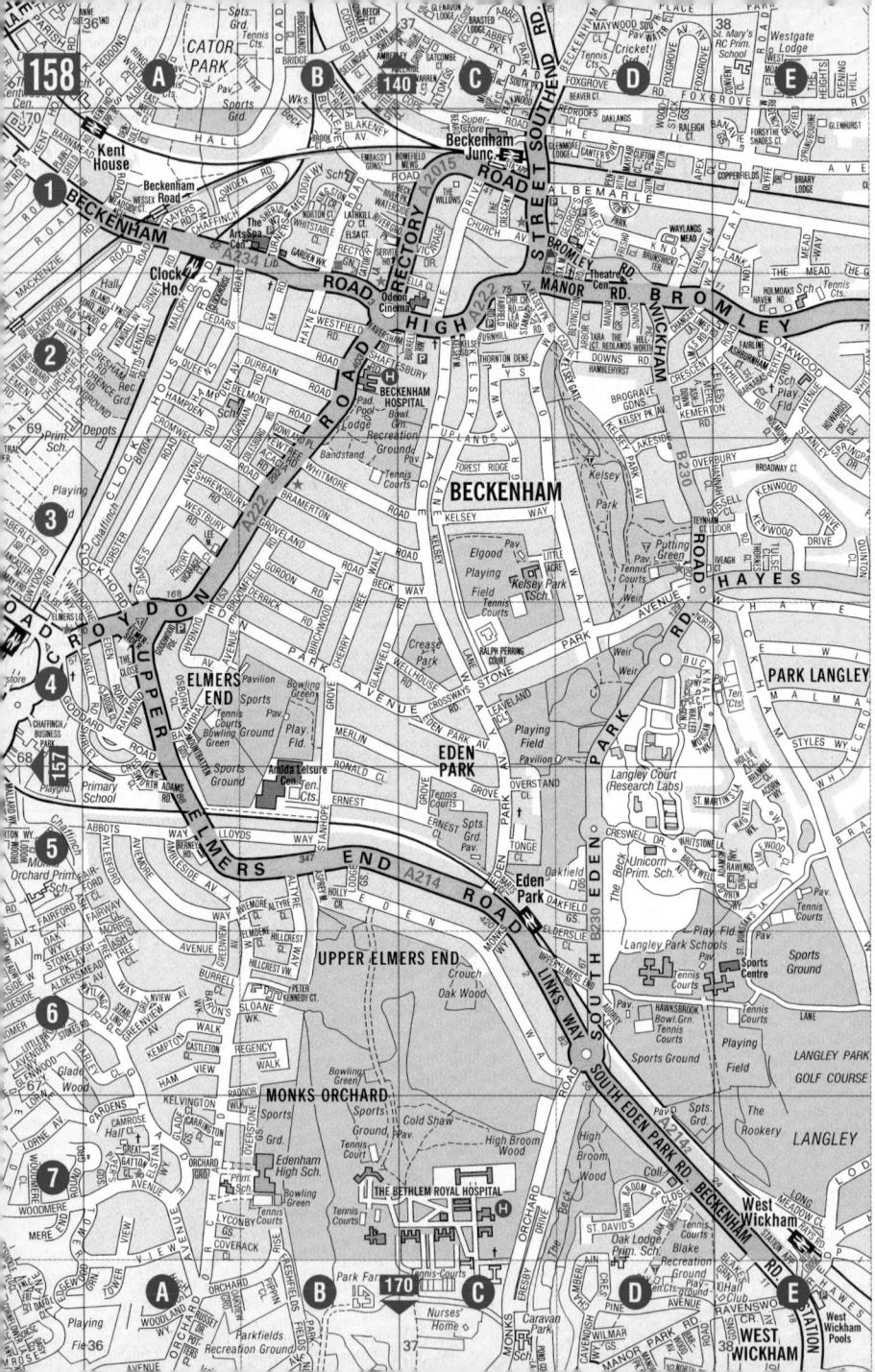

A
B
C
D
E
1
2
3
4
5
6
7
36
37
38
140
157
170
CATOR PARK
Sports Grd.
Kent House
Beckenham Road
BECKENHAM ROAD
Beckenham Junc.
SOUTHEND ROAD
HIGH STREET
ALBEMARLE RD.
FOXGROVE RD.
MANOR RD.
BROMLEY RD.
RECTORY ROAD
A2015
A234
A222
A214
B230
The Spa
Arts Cen.
Clock Ho.
Odeon Cinema
BECKENHAM HOSPITAL
Recreation Ground
Bandstand
BECKENHAM
Kelsey Park
Elgood Playing Field
Kelsey Park Sch.
Putting Green
WICKHAM ROAD
HAYES LANE
PARK LANGLEY
CROYDON ROAD
UPPER ELMERS END
ELMERS END
Sports Ground
Bowling Green
Amida Leisure Cen.
Primary School
Crease Park
EDEN PARK
Eden Park
Playing Field
EDEN PARK AVENUE
STONE PARK AVENUE
SOUTH EDEN PARK RD.
ELMERS END ROAD
Langley Court (Research Labs)
Langley Park Schools
Sports Centre
Unicorn Prim. Sch.
LANGLEY PARK GOLF COURSE
LANGLEY
The Rookery
Crouch Oak Wood
MONKS ORCHARD
Edenham High Sch.
High Broom Wood
THE BETHLEM ROYAL HOSPITAL
Cold Shaw
Glade Wood
Monks Orchard Prim. Sch.
Oak Lodge Prim. Sch.
Blake Recreation Ground
Parkfields Recreation Ground
Nurses' Home
Caravan Park
West Wickham
WEST WICKHAM
West Wickham Pools

F
G
H
J
K
1
2
3
4
5
6
7
39
40
41
141
160
171
Ravensbourne
Sundridge Park
SHORTLANDS GOLF COURSE
BROMLEY PARK
THE SLOANE HOSP.
Playing Field
Golf Course
FARNABY RD.
LONDON RD.
A21
TWEEDY RD.
COLLEGE RD.
Bromley Nth.
BECKENHAM LANE
WIDMORE RD.
A222
KENTISH WAY
Bishop Challoner Sch.
Shortlands
Martin's Hill
Rec. Grd. Queen's Mead
Queens Gdn.
THE GLADES SHOPPING CENTRE
Churchill Theatre
Leisure Cen.
BROMLEY
Bromley Civic Centre
Moat
Bromley South
SHORTLANDS
MASONS HILL
B228
B251
B265
B2212
WESTMORELAND ROAD
HAYES ROAD
HAYES LANE
PICKHURST LANE
South Hill Wood Rec. Grnd
The Ravensbourne Sch.
Hayesford
Weir
Cricket Ground
Bromley FC Ground
Fishers Wood
Ravensbourne
NORMAN PARK
Norman Park Athletics Track
Bromley (Oct. to Jan.)
Cupola Wood
Recreation Ground
Pickhurst Jun. & Inf. Schs.
Pickhurst Green
PARK
HAYES
Hayes Street Farm
Brook Wood
Sports Ground
Sports Grounds
Tennis Courts
Hayes Prim. Sch.
Hayes

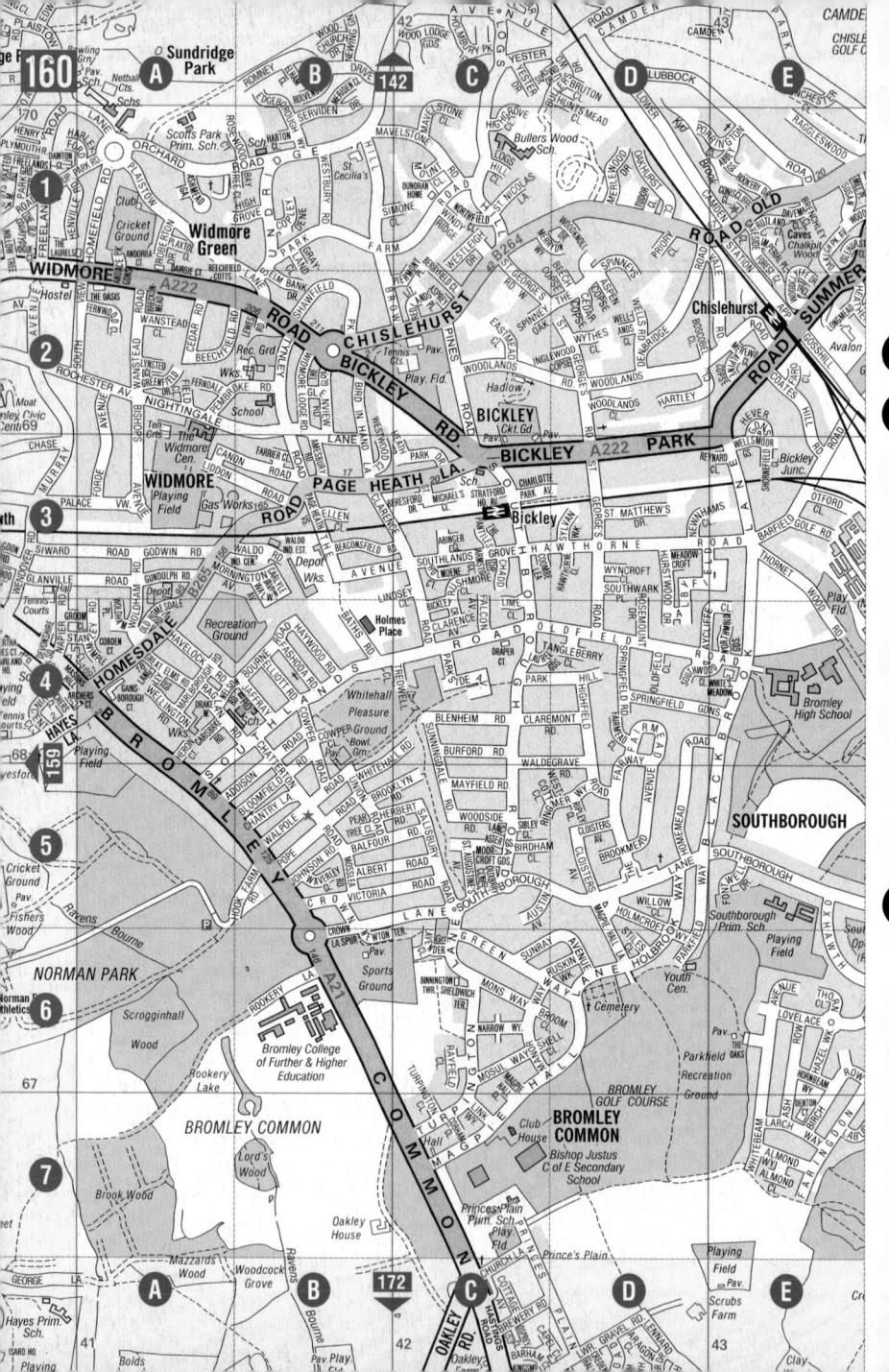
Sundridge Park
142
A
B
C
D
E
1
2
3
4
5
6
7
Scotts Park Prim. Sch.
Bullers Wood Sch.
St. Cecilia's
Widmore Green
Cricket Ground
WIDMORE
WIDMORE ROAD
A222
CHISLEHURST ROAD
B264
BICKLEY RD.
BICKLEY PARK
BICKLEY
Ckt. Gd.
Bickley
Chislehurst
OLD ROAD
SUMMER
Caves
Chalkpit Wood
Avalon
Bickley Junc.
Hadlow
WOODLANDS RD.
ST. GEORGE'S RD.
PAGE HEATH LA.
Play. Fld.
The Widmore Cen.
WIDMORE
Playing Field
Gas Works
School
NIGHTINGALE LANE
PALACE VW.
HAWTHORNE ROAD
OLDFIELD ROAD
Recreation Ground
Holmes Place
Depot Wks.
HOMESDALE ROAD
B265
Whitehall Pleasure Ground
BROMLEY COMMON
A21
BLACKBROOK LANE
Bromley High School
SOUTHBOROUGH
SOUTHBOROUGH LANE
Southborough Prim. Sch.
Playing Field
Youth Cen.
Cemetery
Parkfield Recreation Ground
BROMLEY GOLF COURSE
BROMLEY COMMON
Club House
Bishop Justus C of E Secondary School
Princes Plain Prim. Sch.
Prince's Plain
Oakley House
NORMAN PARK
Scrogginhall Wood
Bromley College of Further & Higher Education
Sports Ground
Rookery Lake
Lord's Wood
Brook Wood
Mazzards Wood
Woodcock Grove
Ravens Bourne
Fishers Wood
Cricket Ground
Hayes Prim. Sch.
Scrubs Farm
159
172
OAKLEY RD.
41
42
43
67
68
69
170

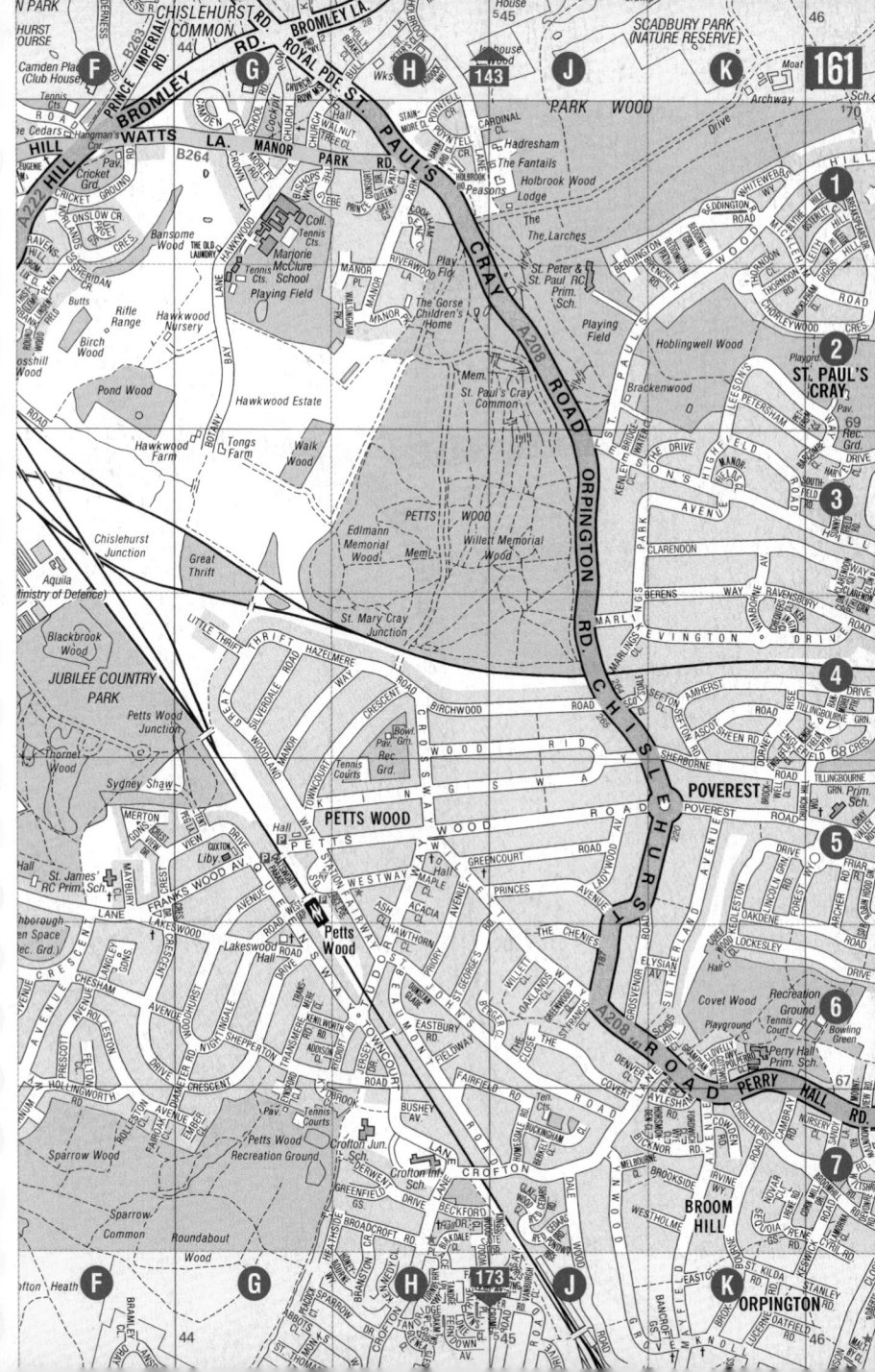
143
173
F
G
H
J
K
1
2
3
4
5
6
7
44
45
46
CHISLEHURST COMMON
SCADBURY PARK (NATURE RESERVE)
PARK WOOD
Camden Place (Club House)
BROMLEY RD.
BROMLEY LA.
ROYAL PDE.
PRINCE IMPERIAL RD.
CHISLEHURST RD.
HILL
WATTS LA.
MANOR PARK RD.
B264
B263
A222
A208
ST. PAUL'S CRAY ROAD
ORPINGTON RD.
CHISLEHURST ROAD
PERRY HALL RD.
Hangman's Cnr.
Cricket Grd.
Pav.
CRICKET GROUND
ONSLOW CR.
Bansome Wood
THE OLD LAUNDRY
Coll.
Tennis Cts.
Marjorie McClure School
Playing Field
Butts
Rifle Range
Hawkwood Nursery
Birch Wood
Pond Wood
Hawkwood Estate
Hawkwood Farm
Tongs Farm
Walk Wood
Hadresham
The Fantails
Holbrook Wood
Peasons
Lodge
The Larches
St. Peter & St. Paul RC Prim. Sch.
Playing Field
Hoblingwell Wood
Brackenwood
ST. PAUL'S CRAY
Rec. Grd.
Play Fld.
The Gorse Children's Home
Mem.
St. Paul's Cray Common
PETTS WOOD
Edlmann Memorial Wood
Willett Memorial Wood
Chislehurst Junction
Great Thrift
Aquila
Ministry of Defence
St. Mary Cray Junction
Blackbrook Wood
JUBILEE COUNTRY PARK
Petts Wood Junction
Thornet Wood
Sydney Shaw
POVEREST
PETTS WOOD
Petts Wood
Liby.
St. James' RC Prim. Sch.
Lakeswood Hall
Bowl. Grn.
Rec. Grd.
Tennis Courts
Covet Wood
Recreation Ground
Tennis Court
Bowling Green
Playground
Perry Hall Prim. Sch.
Sparrow Wood
Petts Wood Recreation Ground
Crofton Jun. Sch.
Crofton Inf. Sch.
Sparrow Common
Roundabout Wood
BROOM HILL
ORPINGTON
Crofton Heath

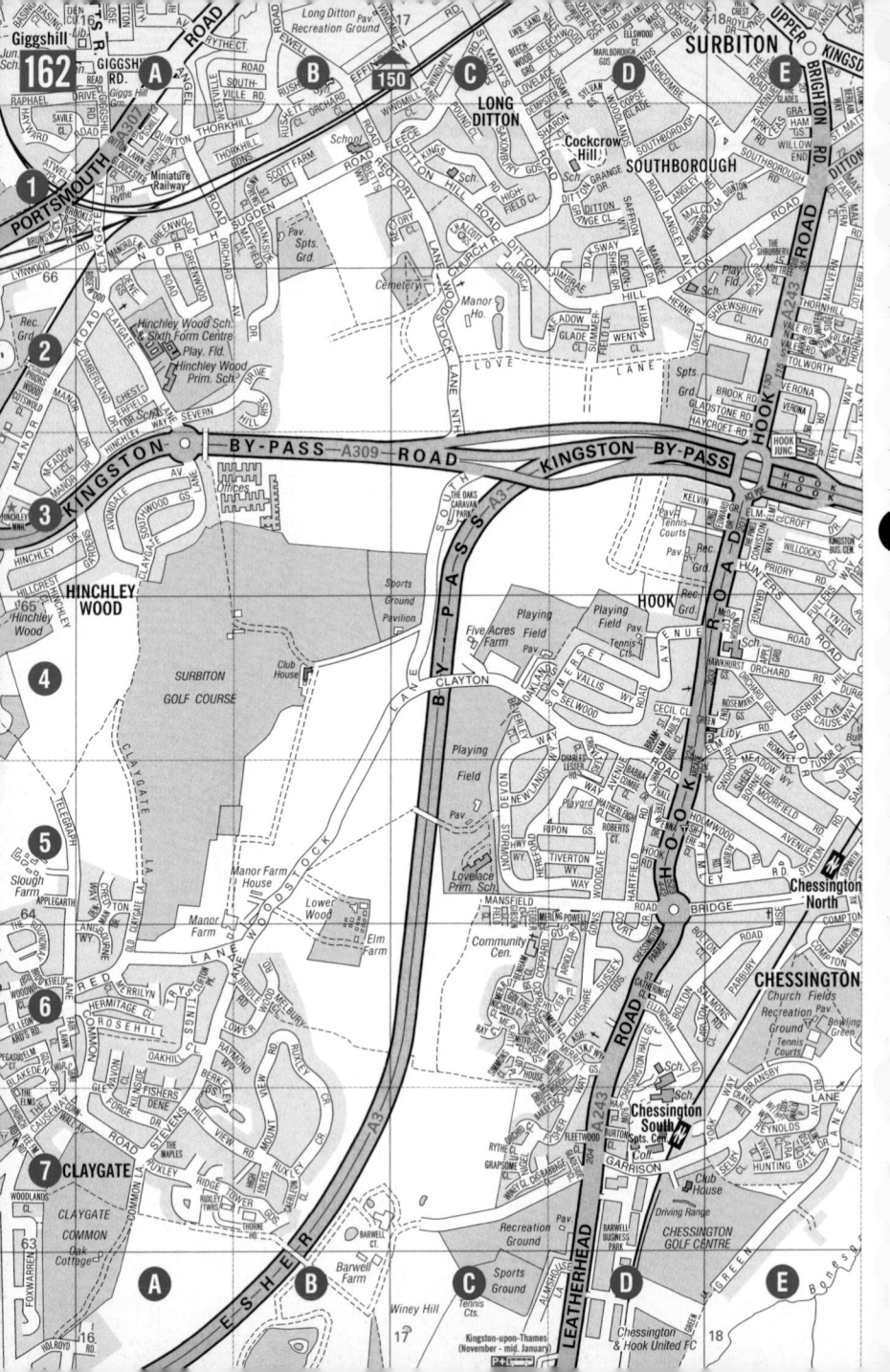

162
150
Giggshill
SURBITON
LONG DITTON
Cockcrow Hill
SOUTHBOROUGH
HINCHLEY WOOD
HOOK
CHESSINGTON
CLAYGATE
Chessington North
Chessington South
Long Ditton Recreation Ground
Miniature Railway
Hinchley Wood Sch. & Sixth Form Centre
Hinchley Wood Prim. Sch.
SURBITON GOLF COURSE
Club House
Sports Ground Pavilion
Five Acres Farm
Playing Field
Manor Farm House
Manor Farm
Lower Wood
Elm Farm
Slough Farm
CLAYGATE COMMON
Oak Cottage
Barwell Farm
Winey Hill
Recreation Ground
Sports Ground
CHESSINGTON GOLF CENTRE
Driving Range
Chessington & Hook United FC
Church Fields Recreation Ground
Lovelace Prim. Sch.
Community Cen.
Cemetery
Manor Ho.
KINGSTON BY-PASS
BY-PASS A309 ROAD
PORTSMOUTH ROAD
A307
A3
ESHER
A243
HOOK ROAD
LEATHERHEAD ROAD
LOVE LANE
Kingston-upon-Thames (November - mid. January)
A B C D E
1 2 3 4 5 6 7
16 17 18
63 64 65 66

163
151
164
Malden Manor
Tolworth
TOLWORTH
TOLWORTH JUNCTION
TOLWORTH HOSP.
WEST EWELL
HORTON COUNTRY PARK
A240
A3
B3364
B284
B2200
KINGSTON ROAD
CHESSINGTON ROAD
RUXLEY LANE
(KINGSTON BY-PASS)
HOOK RD.
Alexandria Millennium Grn.
Recreation Ground
Richard Challoner School
Playing Field
Tennis Courts
Nursery
Maori Sports Ground
Community Centre
Knollmead Prim. Sch.
Sports Ground
Riverhill
Cricket Ground
Linden Bridge Sch. & Spring Cen.
Government Offices
King George's Field Playing Field
Corinthian Casuals FC Grd.
Club
Tolworth Court Bridge
Tolworth Rec. Cen.
Four Oaks Centre
Buckland Inf. Sch.
Moor Lane Jun. Sch.
Hogsmill River
Youth Cen.
Comm. Cen.
Riverview C of E Prim. Sch.
Dragons Hlth. Club
Epsom & Ewell High Sch.
West Ewell Inf. Sch.
Butcher's Grove
Castle Hill
HORTON PARK GOLF & COUNTRY CLUB
Club Ho.
Driving Range
Hook Arena
North Farm Cottage
Gt. Wood
Sports Grd.
St. Ebba's Farm Cottage
Cemetery
ST. EBBA'S
F
G
H
J
K
1
2
3
4
5
6
7
19
20
21

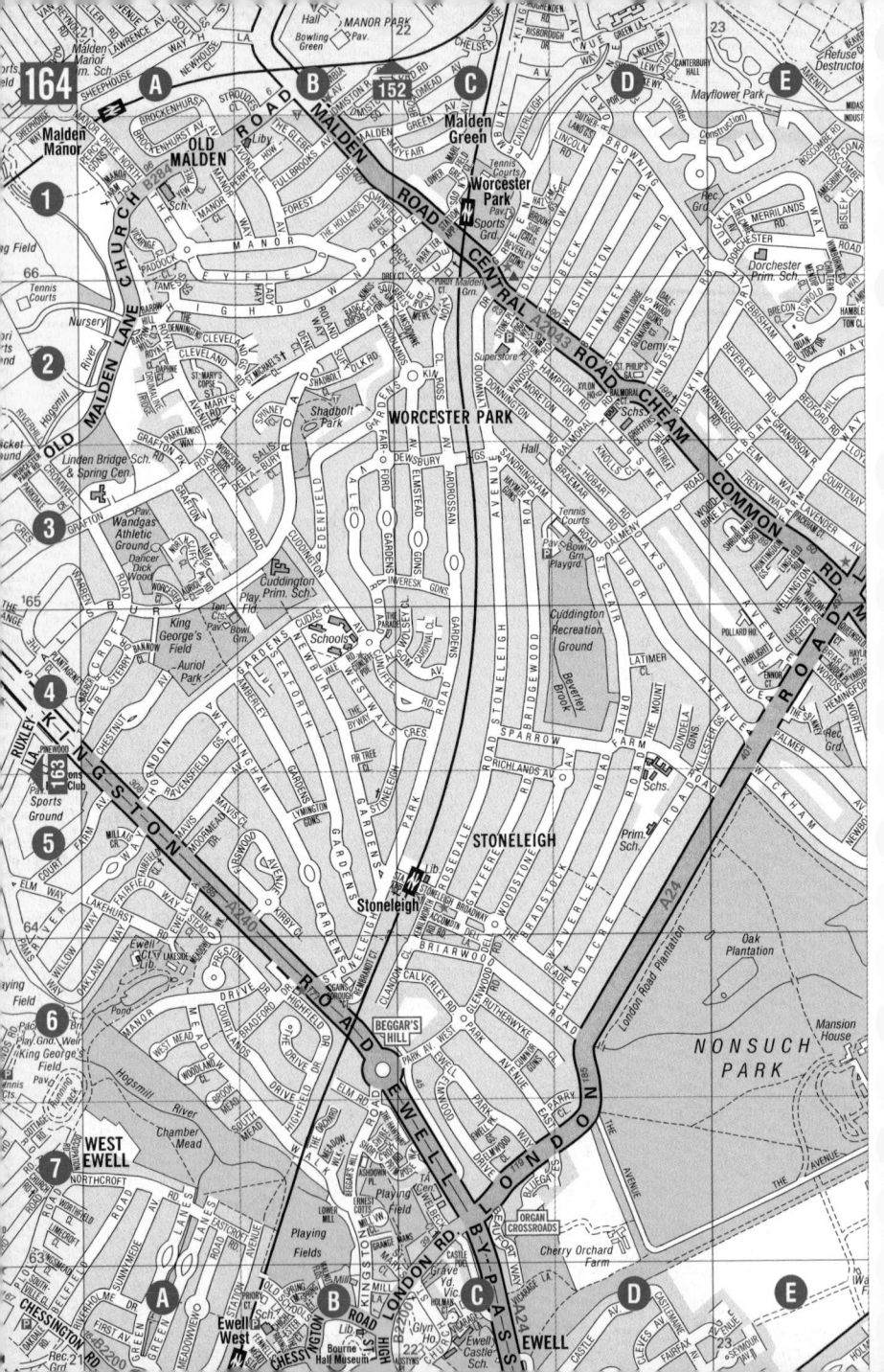
164
152
163
A
B
C
D
E
1
2
3
4
5
6
7
21
22
23
66
165
64
63
Malden Manor
OLD MALDEN
MANOR PARK
Malden Green
Worcester Park
WORCESTER PARK
STONELEIGH
Stoneleigh
WEST EWELL
Ewell West
EWELL
BEGGAR'S HILL
ORGAN CROSSROADS
NONSUCH PARK
Mansion House
Oak Plantation
London Road Plantation
Cherry Orchard Farm
Mayflower Park
Refuse Destructor
Dorchester Prim. Sch.
Linden Bridge Sch. & Spring Cen.
Wandgas Athletic Ground
Dancer Dick Wood
Cuddington Prim. Sch.
King George's Field
Auriol Park
Shadbolt Park
Cuddington Recreation Ground
Beverley Brook
Hogsmill River
Chamber Mead
Playing Fields
Bourne Hall Museum
Glyn Ho.
Ewell Castle Sch.
Sports Ground
Superstore
Cemy.
Schools
Prim. Sch.
MALDEN ROAD
CENTRAL ROAD
CHEAM COMMON ROAD
LONDON ROAD
KINGSTON ROAD
EWELL BY-PASS
OLD MALDEN LANE
CHURCH ROAD
CHESSINGTON RD
A2043
A240
A24
B284
B2200

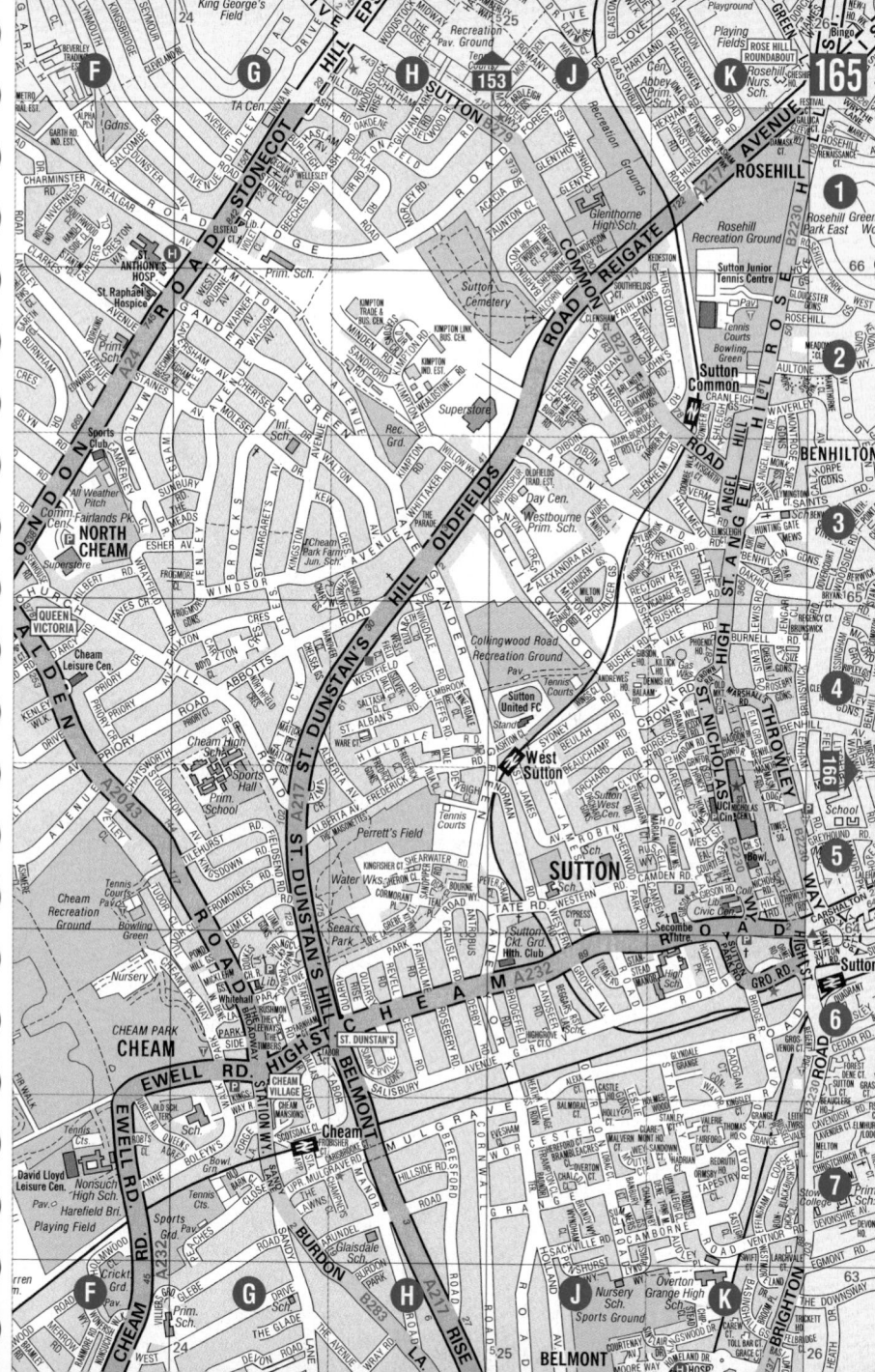
165
153
166
F
G
H
J
K
1
2
3
4
5
6
7
24
25
26
ROSEHILL
BENHILTON
NORTH CHEAM
CHEAM
SUTTON
BELMONT
West Sutton
Sutton Common
Sutton
Cheam
STONECOT HILL
LONDON ROAD
MALDEN ROAD
ST. DUNSTAN'S HILL
OLDFIELDS ROAD
REIGATE AVENUE
COMMON ROAD
ST. NICHOLAS WAY
ANGEL HILL
ROSE HILL
HIGH ST.
THROWLEY WAY
CHEAM ROAD
EWELL RD.
BELMONT RISE
BURDON LA.
BRIGHTON ROAD
MULGRAVE ROAD
SUTTON COMMON ROAD
GANDER GREEN LANE
COLLINGWOOD ROAD
CAMBORNE ROAD
A24
A217
A232
A2043
A217
B279
B2230
B283
King George's Field
Recreation Ground
Sutton Cemetery
Glenthorne High Sch.
Rosehill Recreation Ground
Sutton Junior Tennis Centre
Superstore
Collingwood Road Recreation Ground
Sutton United FC
Westbourne Prim. Sch.
ST. ANTHONY'S HOSP.
St. Raphael's Hospice
QUEEN VICTORIA
Cheam Leisure Cen.
Cheam High Sch.
Perrett's Field
Water Wks.
Seears Park
Cheam Recreation Ground
CHEAM PARK
CHEAM VILLAGE
ST. DUNSTAN'S
Sutton Ckt. Grd. Hlth. Club
Secombe Thtre.
Civic Cen.
UCI Cin.
David Lloyd Leisure Cen.
Nonsuch High Sch.
Harefield Bri. Playing Field
Glaisdale Sch.
Overton Grange High Sch.
Nursery Sch.
Sports Ground
ROSE HILL ROUNDABOUT
Rosehill Park East
Stow College

166
154
165
A
B
C
D
E
1
2
3
4
5
6
7
BEDDINGTON CORNER
ROSEHILL
Rosehill Park East
Greenshaw Wood
St. Helier Open Space
Sutton Arena Leisure Centre
Running Track
ST. HELIER HOSPITAL
QUEEN MARY'S HOSPITAL FOR CHILDREN
Nature Reserves
Comm Hall
BENHILTON
THE WRYTHE
HACKBRIDGE
FELNEX TRADING ESTATE
Wilderness Island
Wandle Bri.
Royston Park
Rushy Meadow Prim. Sch.
Muschamp Prim. Sch.
Sports Cen.
Carshalton Athletic FC
Wrythe Rec. Grd.
Playing Field
Carshalton
Carshalton Coll.
Westcroft Leisure Cen.
The Grove
Council Offices
Studio Thtre
Heritage Cen.
Eco Cen.
St. Philomena's School
CARSHALTON
Benhill Rec. Grd.
Manor Park
SUTTON
Sutton
The Frying Pan
Hogpit Pond
CARSHALTON PARK
CARSHALTON WAR MEMORIAL HOSP.
Carshalton Beeches
Stanley Pk. Rec. Grd.
High Sch.
Play. Fld.
Little Holland Ho.
Stowford College
Resrs (covered)
Tennis Cts.
CARSHALTON ON THE HILL
CARSHALTON BEECHES
WRYTHE LANE
NORTH ST.
HIGH ST.
CARSHALTON ROAD
RUSKIN ROAD
PARK LA.
ERSKINE ROAD
BEECHES AV.
BRIGHTON ROAD
HACKBRIDGE RD.
B278
B277
B271
B2230
A232

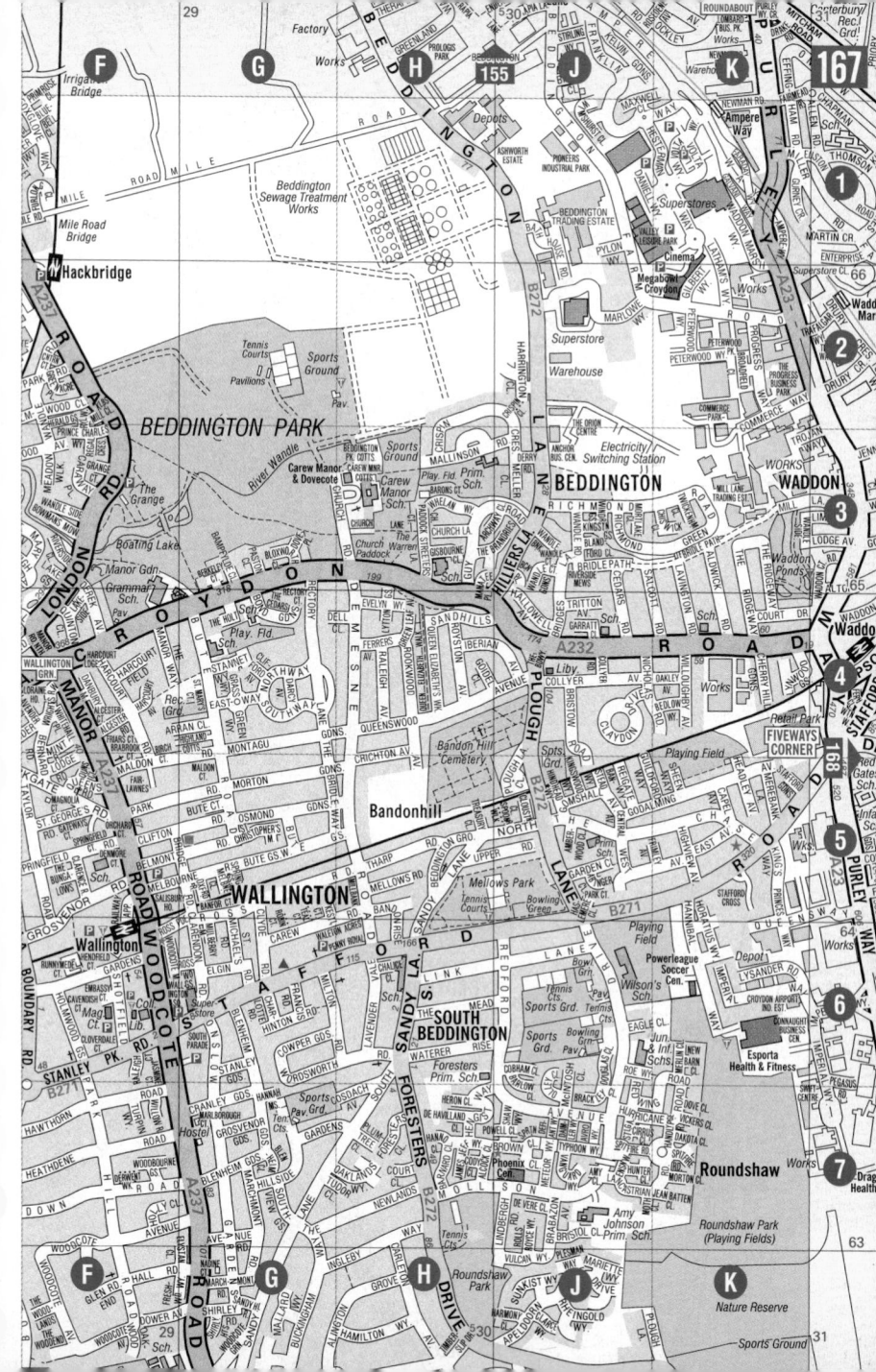

167
155
168
29
30
31
F
G
H
J
K
1
2
3
4
5
6
7
63
64
65
66
Irrigation Bridge
Mile Road Bridge
MILE ROAD
Hackbridge
Factory
Works
PROLOGIS PARK
Depots
ASHWORTH ESTATE
PIONEERS INDUSTRIAL PARK
Beddington Sewage Treatment Works
BEDDINGTON TRADING ESTATE
VALLEY LEISURE PARK
Cinema
Megabowl Croydon
Superstores
Superstore
Warehouse
Ampere Way
PURLEY WAY
A23
A237
B272
B271
A232
LONDON ROAD
BEDDINGTON LANE
BEDDINGTON PARK
Tennis Courts
Pavilions
Sports Ground
Pav.
River Wandle
The Grange
Boating Lake
Manor Gdn.
Grammar Sch.
Carew Manor & Dovecote
Carew Manor Sch.
Church Paddock
The Warren
THE ORION CENTRE
ANCHOR BUS. CEN.
Electricity Switching Station
BEDDINGTON
WADDON
Waddon Ponds
Waddon
Waddon Marsh
MILL LANE TRADING EST.
THE PROGRESS BUSINESS PARK
COMMERCE WAY
COMMERCE PARK
CROYDON ROAD
Retail Park
FIVEWAYS CORNER
Playing Field
Bandon Hill Cemetery
Bandonhill
PLOUGH LANE
Liby.
Works
WALLINGTON
Wallington
MANOR ROAD
WOODCOTE ROAD
STAFFORD ROAD
Mellows Park
Tennis Courts
Bowling Green
SOUTH BEDDINGTON
SANDY LA. S.
Foresters Prim. Sch.
FORESTERS DRIVE
Sports Grd.
Powerleague Soccer Cen.
Wilson's Sch.
Roundshaw
Esporta Health & Fitness
CROYDON AIRPORT IND. EST.
CONNAUGHT BUSINESS CEN.
Phoenix Cen.
Amy Johnson Prim. Sch.
Roundshaw Park (Playing Fields)
Roundshaw Park
Nature Reserve
Sports Ground
STANLEY PK. RD.
BOUNDARY RD.
Hostel
Coll.
Lib.
Super-store
SOUTH PARADE
Mag. Ct.
Sch.

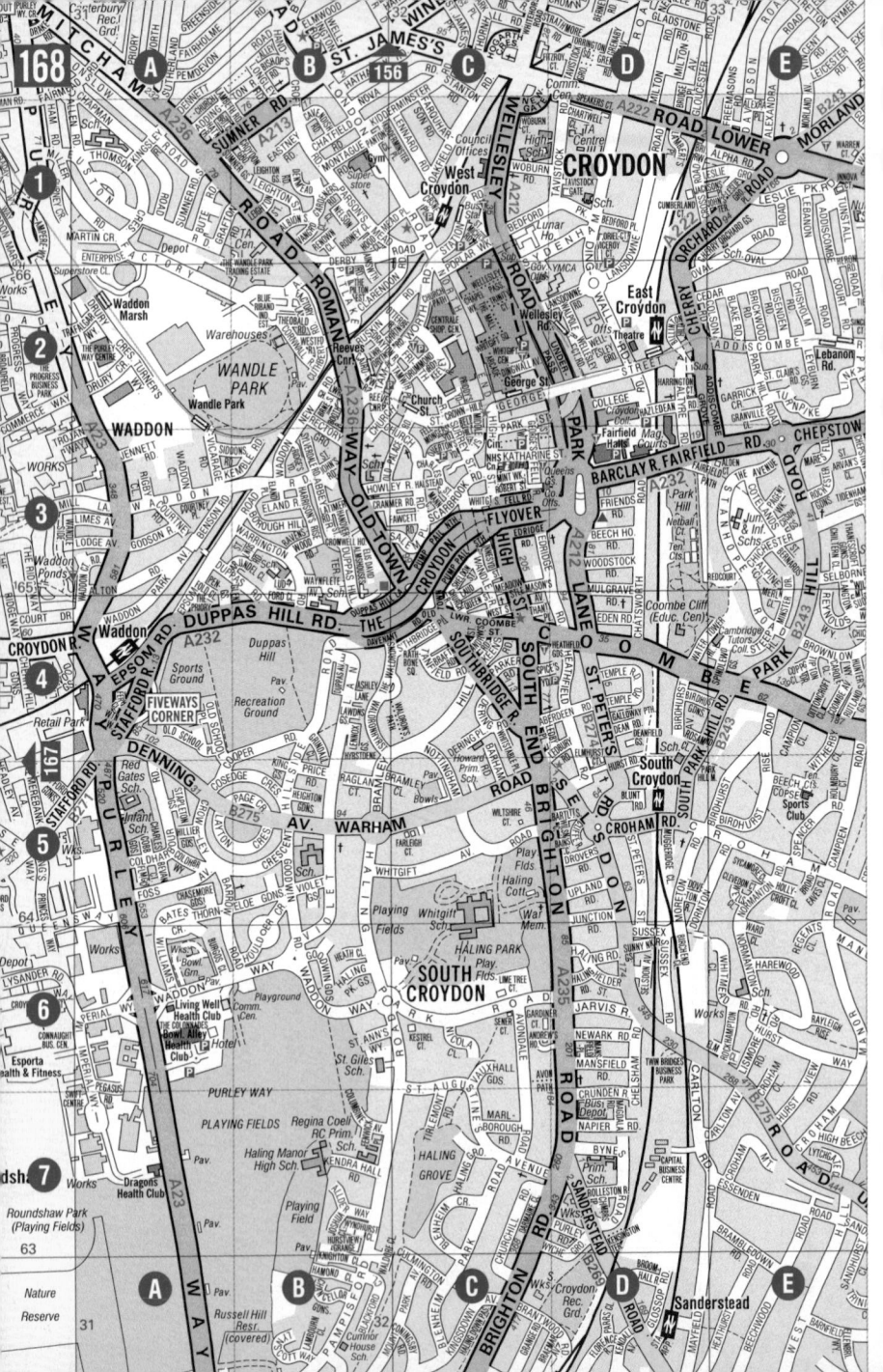

168
156
167
A
B
C
D
E
1
2
3
4
5
6
7
CROYDON
SOUTH CROYDON
WADDON
West Croydon
East Croydon
South Croydon
Waddon
Sanderstead
Waddon Marsh
WANDLE PARK
Wandle Park
Duppas Hill
Sports Ground
Recreation Ground
FIVEWAYS CORNER
Reeves Cnr.
Church St.
George St.
Wellesley Rd.
Lebanon Rd.
Fairfield Halls
Croydon Coll.
Mag. Courts
Theatre
Council Offices
Lunar Ho.
YMCA
Coombe Cliff (Educ. Cen)
Cambridge Tutors Coll.
Park Hill
Whitgift Sch.
Playing Fields
HALING PARK Play. Flds.
HALING GROVE
PURLEY WAY
PLAYING FIELDS
Regina Coeli RC Prim. Sch.
Haling Manor High Sch.
St. Giles Sch.
Living Well Health Club
Bowl. Alley Health Club
Esporta Health & Fitness
Dragons Health Club
Roundshaw Park (Playing Fields)
Nature Reserve
Russell Hill Resr. (covered)
Croydon Rec. Grd.
Cumnor House Sch.
Sports Club
Retail Park
Warehouses
Depot
Works
THE PROGRESS BUSINESS PARK
THE PURLEY WAY CENTRE
TWIN BRIDGES BUSINESS PARK
CAPITAL BUSINESS CENTRE
CONNAUGHT BUS. CEN.
Waddon Ponds
MITCHAM ROAD
ROMAN WAY
OLD TOWN
DUPPAS HILL RD.
THE CROYDON FLYOVER
PURLEY WAY
BRIGHTON ROAD
SOUTH END
HIGH ST.
PARK LANE
COOMBE ROAD
PARK HILL RD.
SELSDON ROAD
CROHAM ROAD
DENNING AV.
WARHAM ROAD
WADDON WAY
HALING PARK ROAD
SANDERSTEAD ROAD
WELLESLEY ROAD
LOWER ADDISCOMBE ROAD
CHERRY ORCHARD ROAD
ADDISCOMBE ROAD
BARCLAY R. FAIRFIELD RD.
CHEPSTOW ROAD
ST. JAMES'S ROAD
SUMNER RD.
STAFFORD RD.
EPSOM RD.
A23
A232
A235
A236
A212
A213
A222
B243
B269
B271
B274
B275

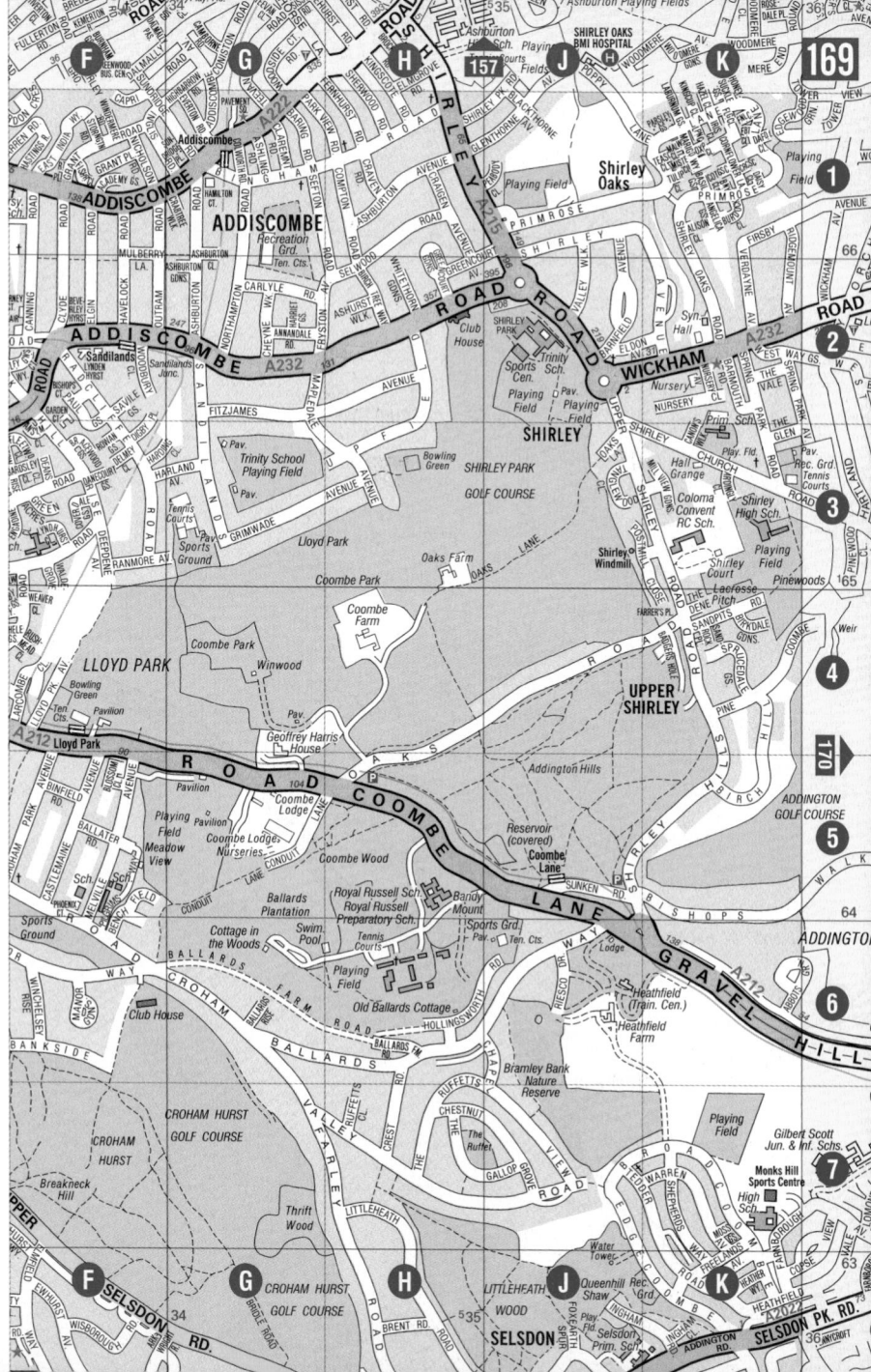

F
G
H
J
K
1
2
3
4
5
6
7
157
170
ADDISCOMBE
SHIRLEY
Shirley Oaks
UPPER SHIRLEY
LLOYD PARK
ADDINGTON
SELSDON
Addiscombe
Sandilands
Lloyd Park
SHIRLEY OAKS BMI HOSPITAL
Ashburton Playing Fields
ADDISCOMBE ROAD
A222
A232
A215
A212
A2022
SHIRLEY ROAD
WICKHAM ROAD
COOMBE ROAD
COOMBE LANE
GRAVEL HILL
SELSDON RD.
SELSDON PK. RD.
ADDINGTON RD.
Recreation Grd.
Trinity School Playing Field
SHIRLEY PARK GOLF COURSE
Lloyd Park
Coombe Park
Oaks Farm
Coombe Farm
Winwood
Geoffrey Harris House
Coombe Lodge
Coombe Lodge Nurseries
Coombe Wood
Ballards Plantation
Royal Russell Sch.
Royal Russell Preparatory Sch.
Bandy Mount
Cottage in the Woods
Old Ballards Cottage
Addington Hills
Reservoir (covered)
Coombe Lane
Shirley Windmill
Coloma Convent RC Sch.
Shirley High Sch.
Shirley Court
Lacrosse Pitch
Pinewoods
Weir
ADDINGTON GOLF COURSE
Heathfield (Train. Cen.)
Heathfield Farm
Bramley Bank Nature Reserve
The Ruffet
CROHAM HURST GOLF COURSE
CROHAM HURST
Breakneck Hill
Thrift Wood
LITTLEHEATH WOOD
Queenhill Shaw
Water Tower
Selsdon Prim. Sch.
Gilbert Scott Jun. & Inf. Schs.
Monks Hill Sports Centre
High Sch.
Club House
Sports Ground
Meadow View
Playing Field
Trinity Sch.
Sports Cen.
Syn. Hall
Nursery
Prim. Sch.
Hall Grange
Rec. Grd.
Tennis Courts
34
35
36
63
64
65
66

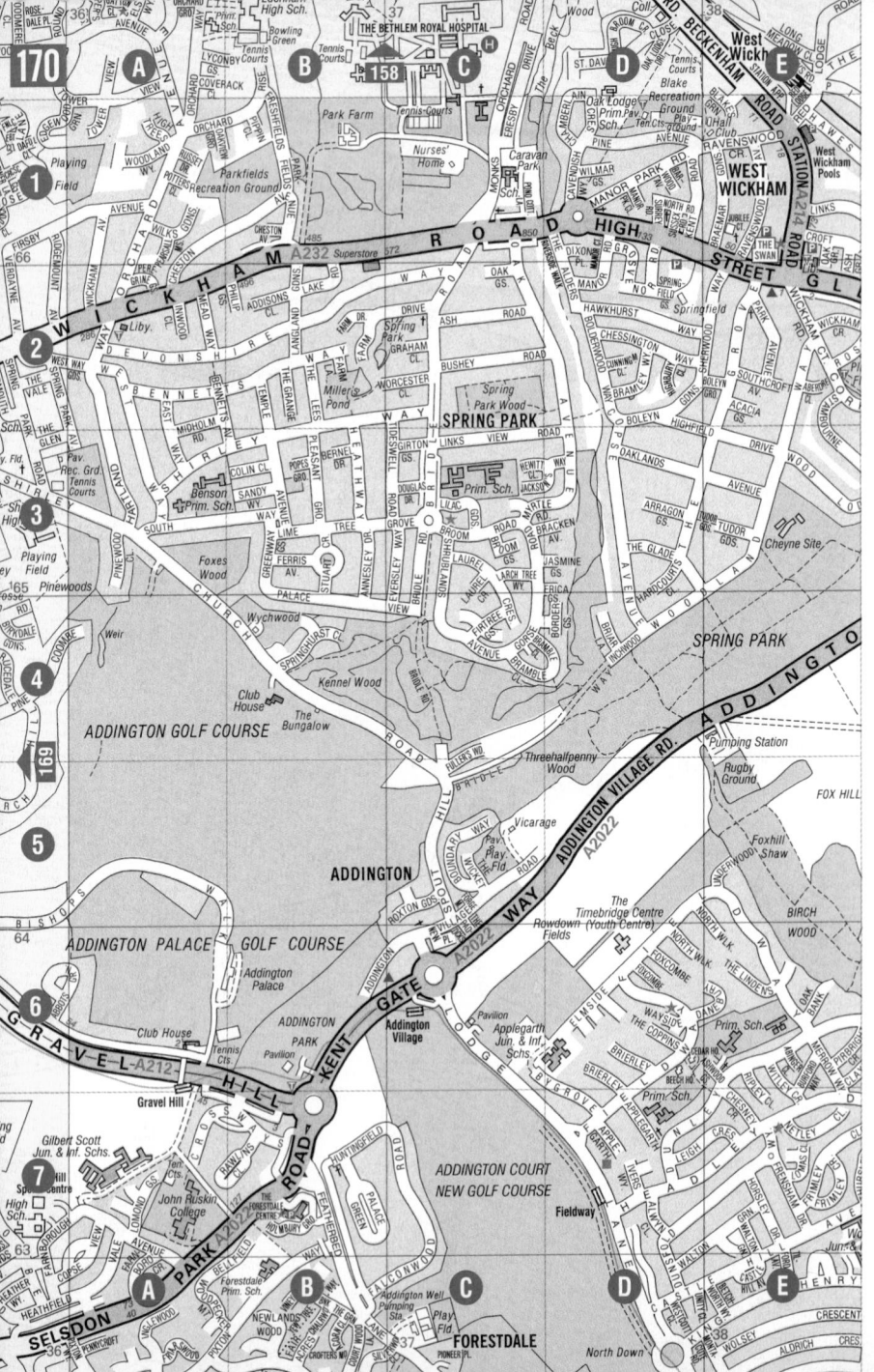
A
B
C
D
E
1
2
3
4
5
6
7
158
169
THE BETHLEM ROYAL HOSPITAL
Langley Park High Sch.
Bowling Green
Tennis Courts
Park Farm
Nurses' Home
Tennis Courts
Caravan Park
Sch.
Oak Lodge Prim. Sch.
Blake Recreation Ground
Play-ground
West Wickham
West Wickham Pools
WEST WICKHAM
THE SWAN
Playing Field
Parkfields Recreation Ground
Superstore
WICKHAM ROAD
A232
HIGH STREET
A214
STATION ROAD
Liby.
Spring Park
Miller's Pond
Spring Park Wood
SPRING PARK
Prim. Sch.
Benson Prim. Sch.
Springfield
Cheyne Site
Foxes Wood
Playing Field
Pinewoods
Wychwood
Weir
Kennel Wood
Club House
The Bungalow
ADDINGTON GOLF COURSE
SPRING PARK
Threehalfpenny Wood
Pumping Station
Rugby Ground
FOX HILL
Foxhill Shaw
BIRCH WOOD
Vicarage
Pav. Play. Fld
ADDINGTON
ADDINGTON VILLAGE RD.
ADDINGTON WAY
A2022
The Timebridge Centre (Youth Centre)
Rowdown Fields
ADDINGTON PALACE GOLF COURSE
Addington Palace
Club House
Tennis Cts.
ADDINGTON PARK
Pavilion
Addington Village
KENT GATE WAY
Applegarth Jun. & Inf. Schs.
Prim. Sch.
Prim. Sch.
GRAVEL HILL
A212
Gravel Hill
Gilbert Scott Jun. & Inf. Schs.
John Ruskin College
ADDINGTON COURT NEW GOLF COURSE
Fieldway
PARK ROAD
SELSDON
Forestdale Prim. Sch.
NEWLANDS WOOD
Addington Well Pumping Sta.
Play. Fld.
FORESTDALE
North Down
Wood
The Beck
SHIRLEY CHURCH ROAD
BISHOPS WALK
LODGE LANE
KING HENRY'S DRIVE
CRESCENT
WOLSEY CRES.
ALDRICH CRES.
36
37
38
63
64
65
66

171
HAYES
CONEY HALL
HAYES COMMON
NASH
NEW ADDINGTON
159
172

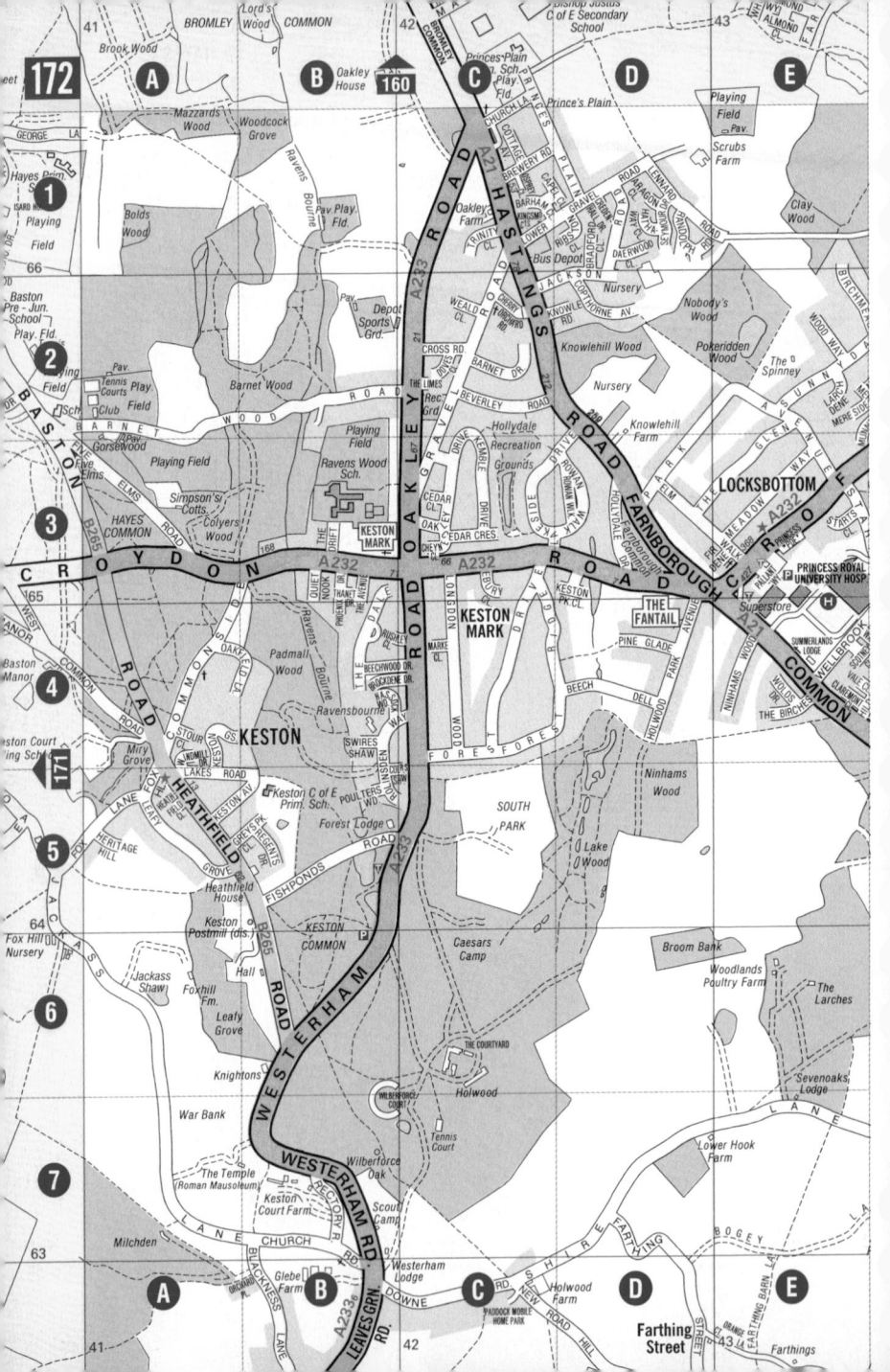

172
160
171
BROMLEY COMMON
Lord's Wood
Brook Wood
Oakley House
Princes Plain Prim. Sch.
Bishop Justus C of E Secondary School
Prince's Plain
Mazzards Wood
Woodcock Grove
GEORGE LA.
Hayes Prim. Sch.
Playing Field
Scrubs Farm
Ravens Bourne
Bolds Wood
Oakley Farm
Clay Wood
Bus Depot
Nursery
Nobody's Wood
Baston Pre-Jun. School
Depot Sports Grd.
Knowlehill Wood
Pokeridden Wood
The Spinney
Barnet Wood
BARNET WOOD ROAD
Tennis Courts
Club
Gorsewood
Rec. Grd.
Hollydale Recreation Grounds
Knowlehill Farm
Ravens Wood Sch.
LOCKSBOTTOM
Five Elms
Simpson's Cotts.
Colyers Wood
HAYES COMMON
KESTON MARK
CROYDON ROAD
FARNBOROUGH COMMON
A232
A233
A21
B265
PRINCESS ROYAL UNIVERSITY HOSP.
Superstore
THE FANTAIL
Farnborough Common
Padmall Wood
Ravensbourne
Baston Manor
KESTON
Miry Grove
Keston C of E Prim. Sch.
Forest Lodge
SOUTH PARK
Ninhams Wood
Lake Wood
Heathfield House
Keston Postmill (dis.)
KESTON COMMON
Caesars Camp
Fox Hill Nursery
Jackass Shaw
Foxhill Fm.
Hall
Leafy Grove
Broom Bank
Woodlands Poultry Farm
The Larches
THE COURTYARD
Holwood
Knightons
War Bank
WILBERFORCE COURT
Tennis Court
Sevenoaks Lodge
Wilberforce Oak
Lower Hook Farm
The Temple (Roman Mausoleum)
Keston Court Farm
Scout Camp
Milchden
Westerham Lodge
Glebe Farm
Holwood Farm
PADDOCK MOBILE HOME PARK
Farthing Street
Farthings
WESTERHAM ROAD
WESTERHAM RD.
OAKLEY ROAD
HASTINGS ROAD
HEATHFIELD ROAD
LANE CHURCH RD.
DOWNE RD.
SHIRE LANE
BOGEY LA.
FARTHING STREET
LEAVES GRN. RD.

173
161
Sparrow Wood
Recreation Ground
Sparrow Common
Roundabout Wood
Crofton Heath
Crofton Inf. Sch.
BROOM HILL
ORPINGTON
Orpington
Civic Halls
CROFTON
A232
CROFTON ROAD
STATION ROAD
SEVENOAKS ROAD
A223
Gumping Common
Darrick Wood Pool
Darrick Wood Sec. Sch.
Sports Centre
Darrick Wood
Darrick Wood Jun. & Inf. Schs.
Farnborough Pav.
Recreation Ground
Tennis Courts
Newstead Wood
Newstead Wood Sch. for Girls
Play. Fld.
Playing Field
Tubbenden Jun. & Inf. Schools
Prim. Sch.
Ontario Centre
Hospice
ORPINGTON HOSPITAL
Rec. Grd.
Bassetts Cen.
FARNBOROUGH HILL
THE GREEN
HIGH STREET FARNBOROUGH
B2158
A21
Scouts Hall
FARNBOROUGH
Club Pav.
Sports Ground
Farnborough Prim. Sch.
The Manse
The Green
WARREN ROAD
SEVENOAKS RD.
Glentrammon Rec. Grd.
Mill Hill
Church Field Plantation
OLD LANE
Ramus Wood
GREEN STREET GREEN
Cocksett Plantation
Cocksett Hill
The Lodge
High Elms Nature Cen.
Woodpiece
HIGH ELMS COUNTRY PARK
Whitelands Wood
Chelsfield Hall
SHIRE LANE
North End Farm
North End Farm Cotts
Blacklands
Club House
The Rookery
High Elms Clockhouse
HIGH ELMS GOLF COURSE
HIGH ELMS ROAD
NORTH END LANE
Rec. Grd.
Rounds Wood
SEVENOAKS ROAD
F
G
H
J
K
1
2
3
4
5
6
7
44
545
46
63
64
65
66

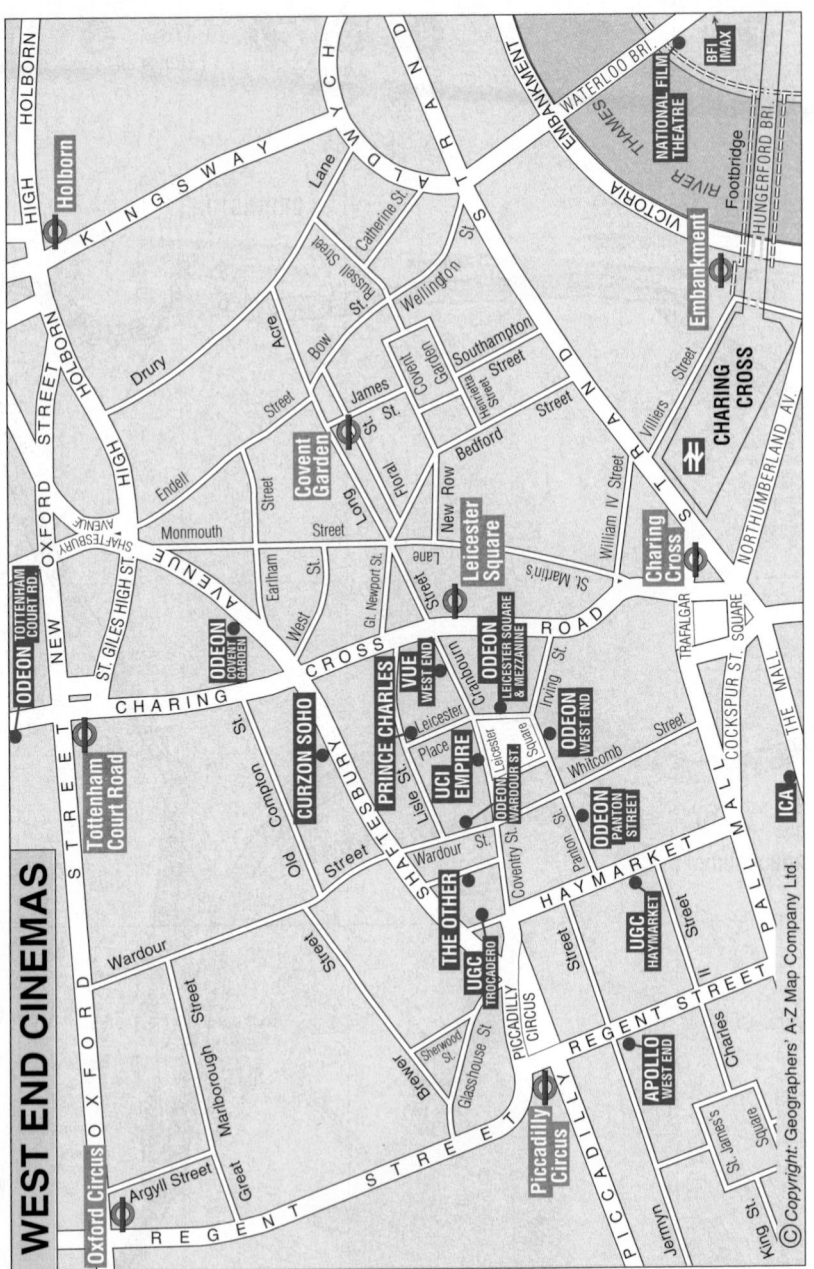

WEST END CINEMAS

Oxford Circus ⊖

Tottenham Court Road ⊖

Holborn ⊖

Covent Garden ⊖

Leicester Square ⊖

Embankment ⊖

Charing Cross ⊖

Piccadilly Circus ⊖

ODEON

ODEON COVENT GARDEN

CURZON SOHO

PRINCE CHARLES

VUE WEST END

ODEON LEICESTER SQUARE & MEZZANINE

ODEON WEST END

UCI EMPIRE

ODEON LEICESTER SQUARE

THE OTHER

UGC TROCADERO

ODEON PANTON STREET

UGC HAYMARKET

APOLLO WEST END

ICA

BFI IMAX

NATIONAL FILM THEATRE

CHARING CROSS

© Copyright: Geographers' A-Z Map Company Ltd.

174

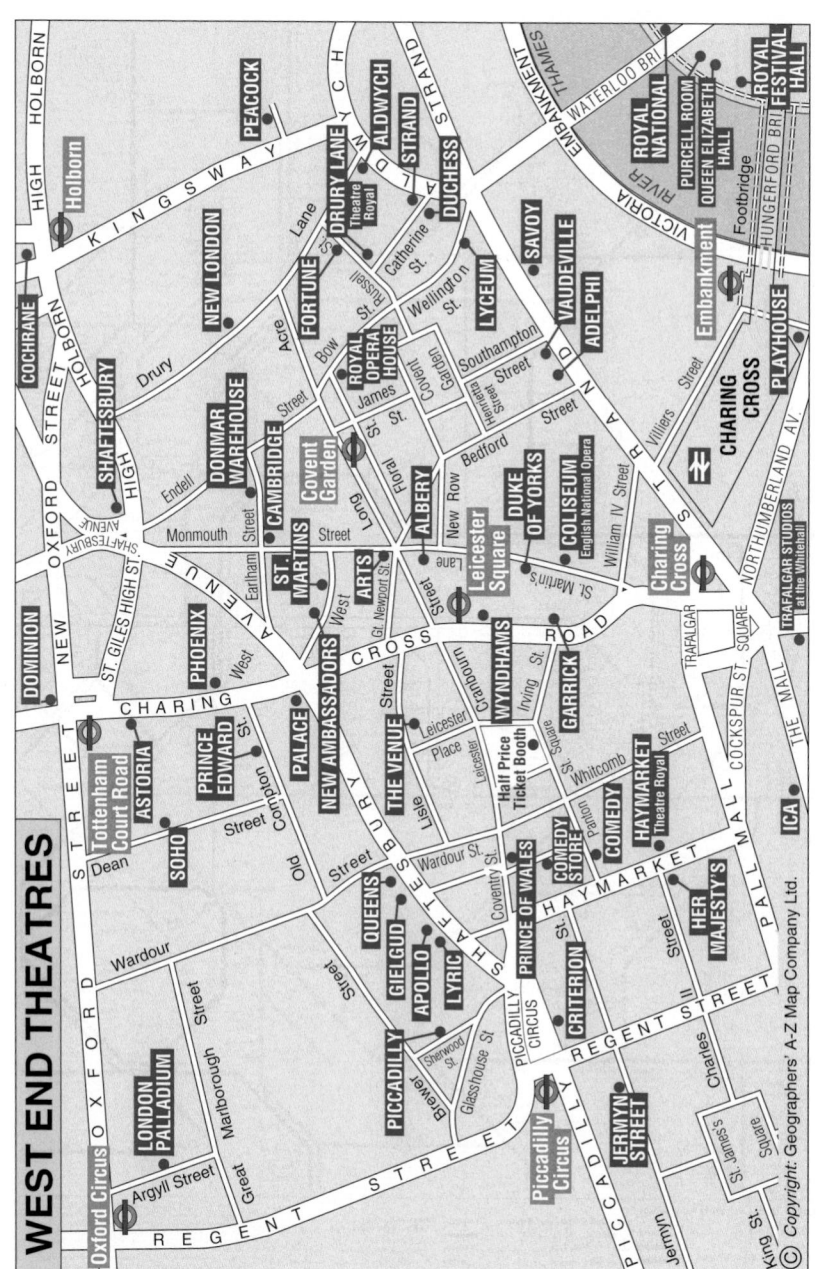
WEST END THEATRES
DOMINION
COCHRANE
Holborn
Oxford Circus
Tottenham Court Road
LONDON PALLADIUM
ASTORIA
SOHO
SHAFTESBURY
PHOENIX
PRINCE EDWARD
DONMAR WAREHOUSE
NEW LONDON
PEACOCK
CAMBRIDGE
ST. MARTINS
PALACE
NEW AMBASSADORS
Covent Garden
FORTUNE
DRURY LANE Theatre Royal
ALDWYCH
STRAND
ROYAL OPERA HOUSE
ARTS
QUEENS
PICCADILLY
GIELGUD
APOLLO
LYRIC
THE VENUE
ALBERY
DUCHESS
LYCEUM
Leicester Square
WYNDHAMS
Half Price Ticket Booth
PRINCE OF WALES
Piccadilly Circus
DUKE OF YORKS
SAVOY
VAUDEVILLE
GARRICK
COMEDY STORE
CRITERION
COLISEUM English National Opera
ADELPHI
COMEDY
JERMYN STREET
HAYMARKET Theatre Royal
ROYAL NATIONAL
Charing Cross
PURCELL ROOM
QUEEN ELIZABETH HALL
HER MAJESTY'S
Embankment
CHARING CROSS
ROYAL FESTIVAL HALL
PLAYHOUSE
ICA
TRAFALGAR STUDIOS at the Whitehall
OXFORD STREET
NEW OXFORD STREET
HIGH HOLBORN
KINGSWAY
ALDWYCH
STRAND
CHARING CROSS ROAD
SHAFTESBURY AVENUE
REGENT STREET
PICCADILLY
HAYMARKET
PALL MALL
THE MALL
VICTORIA EMBANKMENT
NORTHUMBERLAND AV.
TRAFALGAR SQUARE
RIVER THAMES
WATERLOO BRI.
HUNGERFORD BRI.
Footbridge
© Copyright: Geographers' A-Z Map Company Ltd.

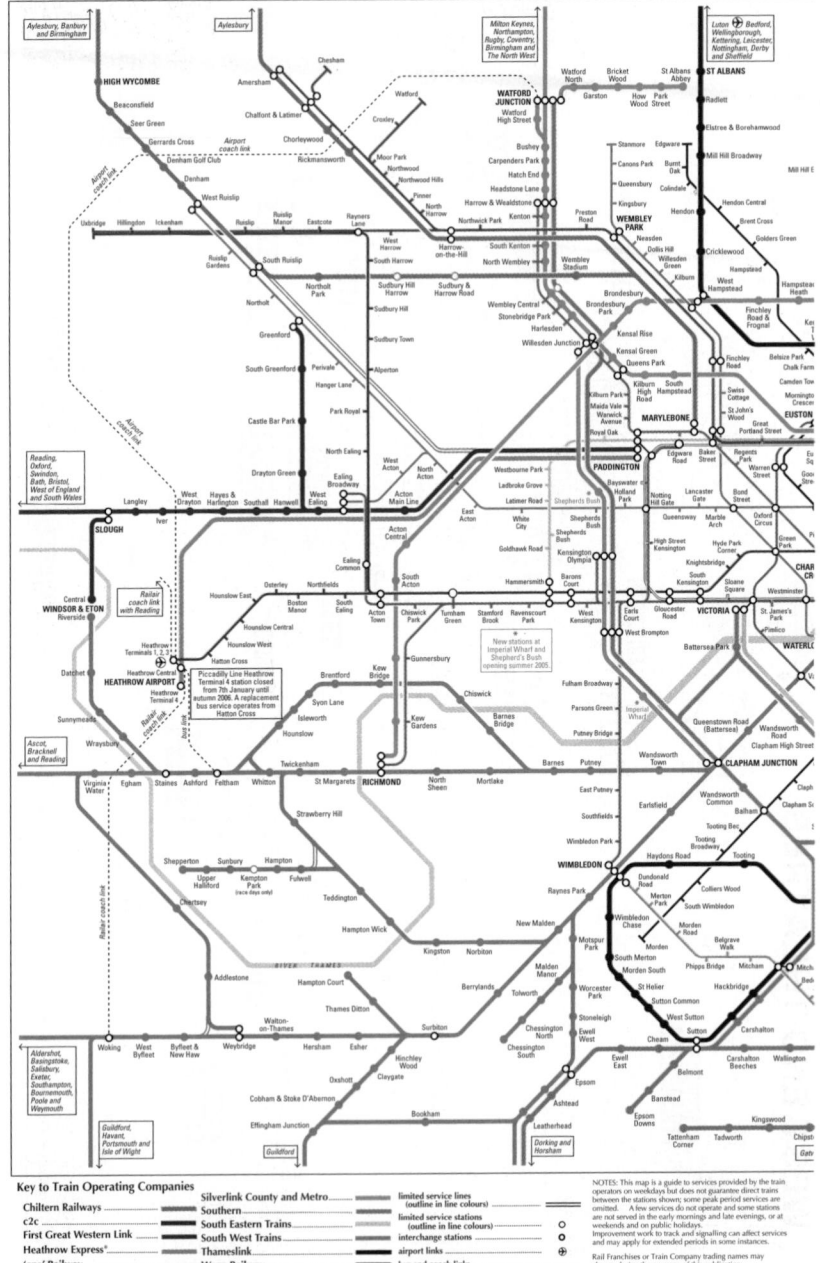

Key to Train Operating Companies

Chiltern Railways	Silverlink County and Metro	limited service lines (outline in line colours)
c2c	Southern	limited service stations (outline in line colours)
First Great Western Link	South Eastern Trains	interchange stations
Heathrow Express*	South West Trains	airport links
'one' Railway	Thameslink	bus and coach links
	Wagn Railway	

NOTES: This map is a guide to services provided by the train operators on weekdays but does not guarantee direct trains between the stations shown; some peak period services are omitted. A few services do not operate and some stations are not served in the early mornings and late evenings, or at weekends and on public holidays.
Improvement work to track and signalling can affect services and may apply for extended periods in some instances.

Rail Franchises or Train Company trading names may change during the currency of this publication.

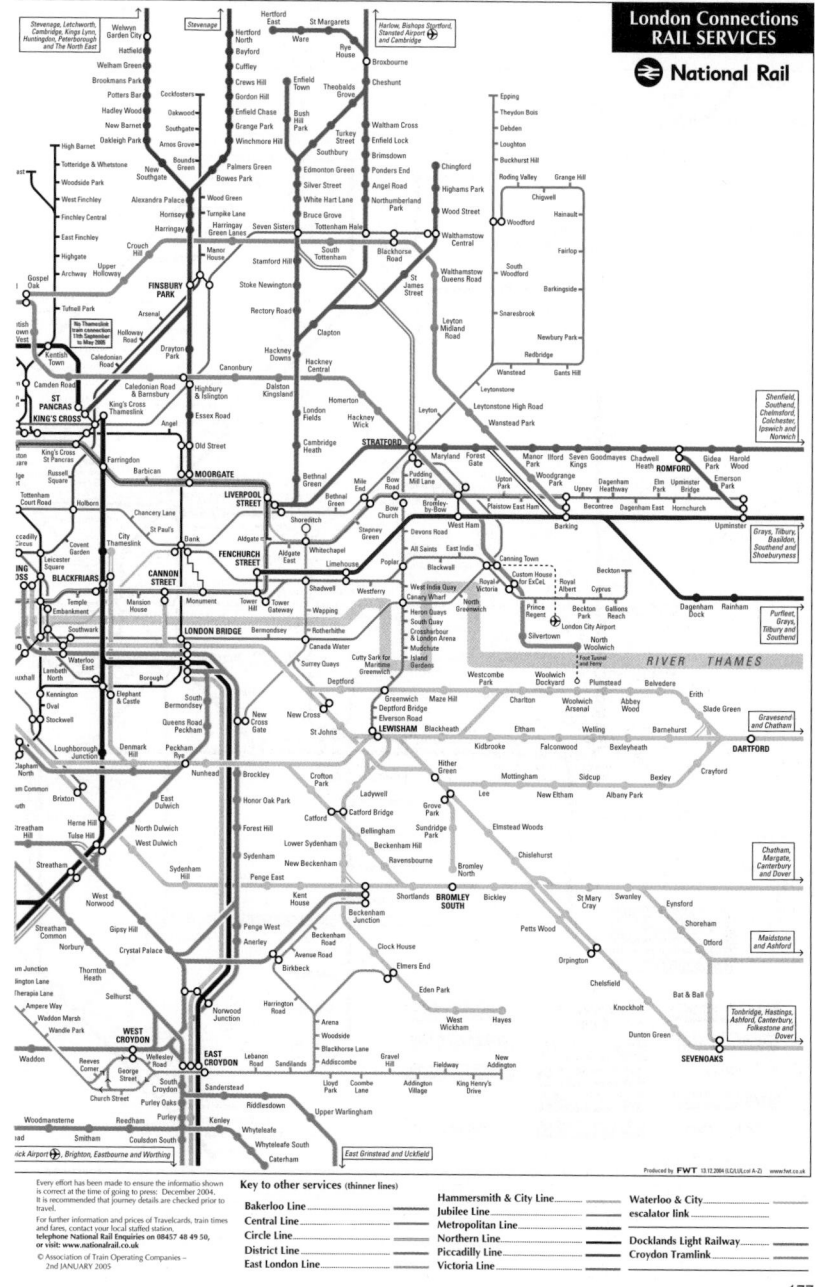

Every effort has been made to ensure the information shown is correct at the time of going to press: December 2004. It is recommended that journey details are checked prior to travel.

For further information and prices of Travelcards, train times and fares, contact your local staffed station. **telephone** National Rail enquiries on 08457 48 49 50, or visit: www.nationalrail.co.uk

© Association of Train Operating Companies – 2nd JANUARY 2005

Produced by **FWT** 13.12.2004 (G/L/L)(col A-Z) www.fwt.co.uk

Key to other services (thinner lines)

Bakerloo Line ....
Central Line ....
Circle Line ....
District Line ....
East London Line ....

Hammersmith & City Line ....
Jubilee Line ....
Metropolitan Line ....
Northern Line ....
Piccadilly Line ....
Victoria Line ....

Waterloo & City ....
escalator link ....

Docklands Light Railway ....
Croydon Tramlink ....

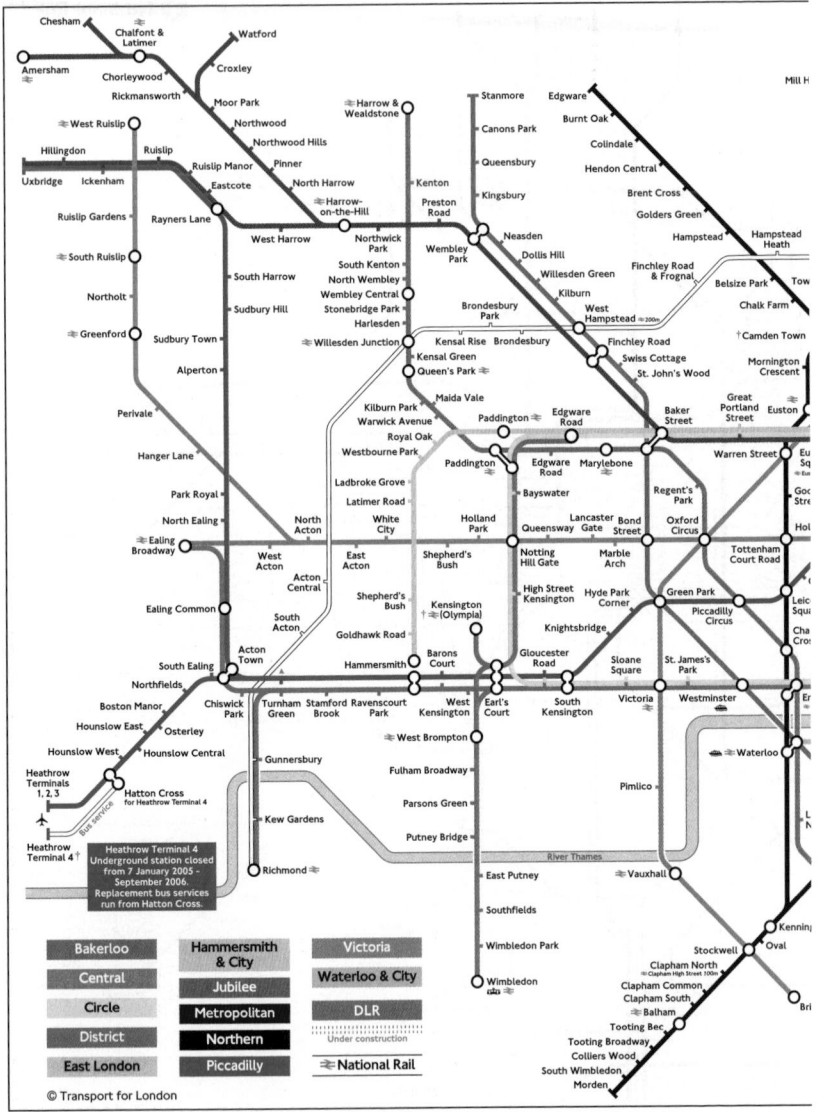
Chesham
Chalfont & Latimer
Watford
Amersham
Chorleywood
Croxley
Rickmansworth
Moor Park
Northwood
Northwood Hills
Pinner
North Harrow
Harrow-on-the-Hill
West Ruislip
Hillingdon
Ruislip
Ruislip Manor
Eastcote
Uxbridge
Ickenham
Ruislip Gardens
Rayners Lane
West Harrow
South Ruislip
Northolt
Greenford
Perivale
Hanger Lane
South Harrow
Sudbury Hill
Sudbury Town
Alperton
Park Royal
North Ealing
Ealing Broadway
West Acton
North Acton
Acton Central
South Acton
Ealing Common
South Ealing
Acton Town
Northfields
Boston Manor
Hounslow East
Osterley
Hounslow West
Hounslow Central
Heathrow Terminals 1, 2, 3
Hatton Cross
for Heathrow Terminal 4
Bus service
Heathrow Terminal 4
Heathrow Terminal 4 Underground station closed from 7 January 2005 - September 2006. Replacement bus services run from Hatton Cross.
Chiswick Park
Turnham Green
Stamford Brook
Ravenscourt Park
Gunnersbury
Kew Gardens
Richmond
Harrow & Wealdstone
Kenton
Preston Road
Northwick Park
South Kenton
North Wembley
Wembley Central
Stonebridge Park
Harlesden
Willesden Junction
Kensal Green
Queen's Park
Kilburn Park
Maida Vale
Warwick Avenue
Royal Oak
Westbourne Park
Ladbroke Grove
Latimer Road
White City
East Acton
Shepherd's Bush
Goldhawk Road
Hammersmith
Barons Court
West Kensington
Kensington (Olympia)
Earl's Court
West Brompton
Fulham Broadway
Parsons Green
Putney Bridge
East Putney
Southfields
Wimbledon Park
Wimbledon
Stanmore
Canons Park
Queensbury
Kingsbury
Wembley Park
Neasden
Dollis Hill
Willesden Green
Kilburn
Brondesbury Park
Kensal Rise
Brondesbury
West Hampstead
200m
Finchley Road
Swiss Cottage
St. John's Wood
Edgware
Burnt Oak
Colindale
Hendon Central
Brent Cross
Golders Green
Hampstead
Hampstead Heath
Finchley Road & Frognal
Belsize Park
Chalk Farm
Camden Town
Mornington Crescent
Euston
Great Portland Street
Warren Street
Baker Street
Paddington
Edgware Road
Marylebone
Bayswater
Regent's Park
Holland Park
Queensway
Lancaster Gate
Bond Street
Oxford Circus
Notting Hill Gate
Marble Arch
Tottenham Court Road
High Street Kensington
Hyde Park Corner
Green Park
Piccadilly Circus
Knightsbridge
Gloucester Road
South Kensington
Sloane Square
Victoria
St. James's Park
Westminster
Waterloo
Pimlico
River Thames
Vauxhall
Stockwell
Oval
Clapham North
Clapham High Street 100m
Clapham Common
Clapham South
Balham
Tooting Bec
Tooting Broadway
Colliers Wood
South Wimbledon
Morden
Bakerloo
Central
Circle
District
East London
Hammersmith & City
Jubilee
Metropolitan
Northern
Piccadilly
Victoria
Waterloo & City
DLR
Under construction
National Rail
© Transport for London

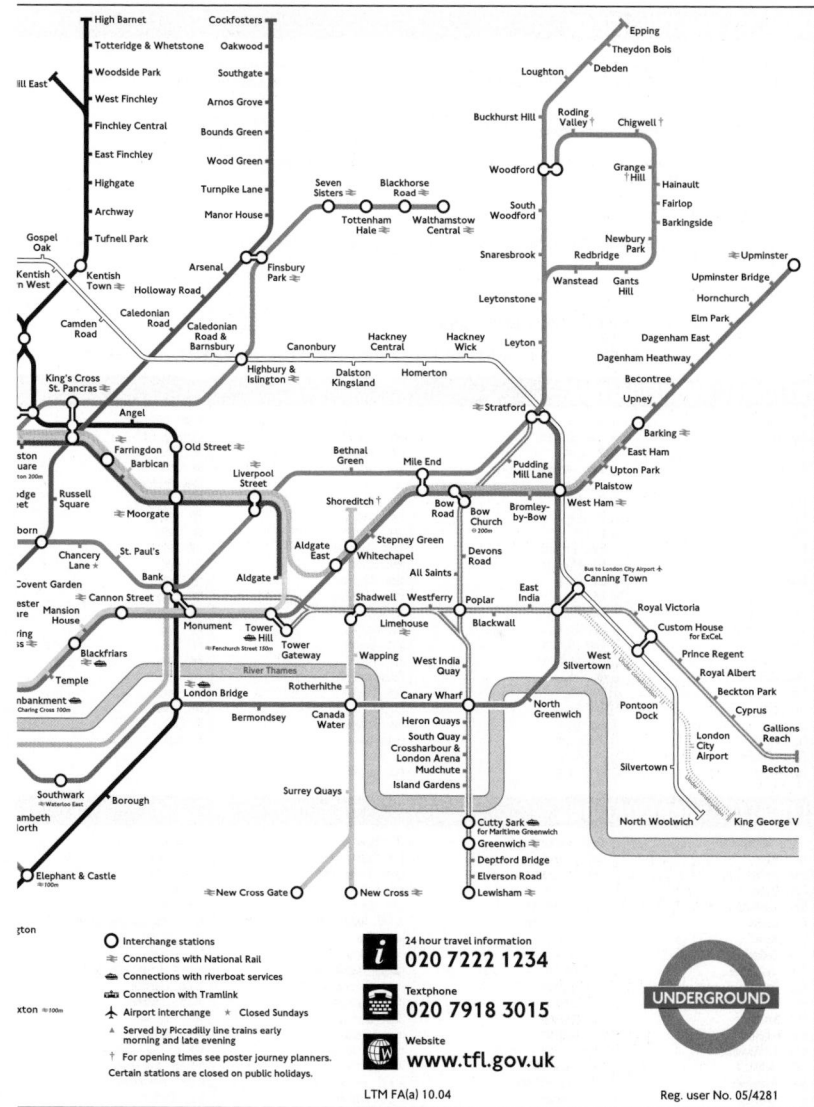

Interchange stations
⇌ Connections with National Rail
🚢 Connections with riverboat services
🚃 Connection with Tramlink
✈ Airport interchange   ★ Closed Sundays
▲ Served by Piccadilly line trains early morning and late evening
† For opening times see poster journey planners.
Certain stations are closed on public holidays.

24 hour travel information
020 7222 1234

Textphone
020 7918 3015

Website
www.tfl.gov.uk

UNDERGROUND

LTM FA(a) 10.04

Reg. user No. 05/4281

INDEX

Including Streets, Places & Areas, Industrial Estates, Selected Flats & Walkways,
Junction Names and Selected Places of Interest.

HOW TO USE THIS INDEX

1. Each street name is followed by its Postcode District (or, if outside the London Postcodes, by its Locality Abbreviation(s)), and then by its map reference;
   e.g. **Abbeville Rd.** SW4 . . . .6G **119** is in the SW4 Postcode District and is to be found in square 6G on page **119**. The page number being shown in bold type.

2. A strict alphabetical order is followed in which Av., Rd., St., etc. (though abbreviated) are read in full and as part of the street name;
   e.g. **Abbeyhill Rd.** appears after **Abbey Gro.** but before **Abbey Ho.**

3. Streets and a selection of flats and walkways too small to be shown on the maps, appear in the index with the thoroughfare to which it is connected shown in brackets;
   e.g. **Abady Ho.** SW1 . . . .3D **18** (off Page St.)

4. Addresses that are in more than one part are referred to as not continuous.

5. Places and areas are shown in the index in **BLUE TYPE** and the map reference is to the actual map square in which the town centre or area is located and not to the place name shown on the map;
   e.g. **ABBEY WOOD** 4C **108**

6. An example of a selected place of interest is Alexander Fleming Mus. 7B **4**

7. Junction names are shown in the index in **BOLD CAPITAL TYPE; e.g. ALDGATE** 6F **85**

8. Map references for entries that appear on large scale pages **4-19** are shown first, with small scale map references shown in brackets; e.g. **Abbey Orchard St.** SW1 . . . .1C **18** (3H **101**)

GENERAL ABBREVIATIONS

All. : Alley	**Cott.** : Cottage	**Ind.** : Industrial	**Prom.** : Promenade
App. : Approach	**Cotts.** : Cottages	**Info.** : Information	**Quad.** : Quadrant
Arc. : Arcade	**Ct.** : Court	**Intl.** : International	**Ri.** : Rise
Av. : Avenue	**Cres.** : Crescent	**Junc.** : Junction	**Rd.** : Road
Bk. : Back	**Cft.** : Croft	**La.** : Lane	**Rdbt.** : Roundabout
Blvd. : Boulevard	**Dpt.** : Depot	**Lit.** : Little	**Shop.** : Shopping
Bri. : Bridge	**Dr.** : Drive	**Lwr.** : Lower	**Sth.** : South
B'way. : Broadway	**E.** : East	**Mnr.** : Manor	**Sq.** : Square
Bldg. : Building	**Emb.** : Embankment	**Mans.** : Mansions	**Sta.** : Station
Bldgs. : Buildings	**Ent.** : Enterprise	**Mkt.** : Market	**St.** : Street
Bungs. : Bungalows	**Est.** : Estate	**Mdw.** : Meadow	**Ter.** : Terrace
Bus. : Business	**Fld.** : Field	**Mdws.** : Meadows	**Twr.** : Tower
Cvn. : Caravan	**Flds.** : Fields	**M.** : Mews	**Trad.** : Trading
C'way. : Causeway	**Gdn.** : Garden	**Mt.** : Mount	**Up.** : Upper
Cen. : Centre	**Gdns.** : Gardens	**Mus.** : Museum	**Va.** : Vale
Chu. : Church	**Gth.** : Garth	**Nth.** : North	**Vw.** : View
Chyd. : Churchyard	**Ga.** : Gate	**Pal.** : Palace	**Vs.** : Villas
Circ. : Circle	**Gt.** : Great	**Pde.** : Parade	**Vis.** : Visitors
Cir. : Circus	**Grn.** : Green	**Pk.** : Park	**Wlk.** : Walk
Cl. : Close	**Gro.** : Grove	**Pas.** : Passage	**W.** : West
Coll. : College	**Hgts.** : Heights	**Pav.** : Pavilion	**Yd.** : Yard
Comn. : Common	**Ho.** : House	**Pl.** : Place	
Cnr. : Corner	**Ho's.** : Houses	**Pct.** : Precinct	

LOCALITY ABBREVIATIONS

Addtn : **Addington**	Chess : **Chessington**	Esh : **Esher**	Ilf : **Ilford**
Ark : **Arkley**	Chig : **Chigwell**	Ewe : **Ewell**	Isle : **Isleworth**
Ashf : **Ashford**	Chst : **Chislehurst**	Farnb : **Farnborough**	Kent : **Kenton**
Avel : **Aveley**	Clay : **Claygate**	Felt : **Feltham**	Kes : **Keston**
Bans : **Banstead**	Cockf : **Cockfosters**	G'frd : **Greenford**	Kew : **Kew**
Bark : **Barking**	Col R : **Collier Row**	Had W : **Hadley Wood**	King T : **Kingston Upon Thames**
Barn : **Barnet**	Cowl : **Cowley**	Ham : **Ham**	Lale : **Laleham**
Beck : **Beckenham**	Cran : **Cranford**	Hamp : **Hampton**	Lon : **London**
Bedd : **Beddington**	Cray : **Crayford**	Hamp H : **Hampton Hill**	H'row A : **London Heathrow Airport**
Bedf : **Bedfont**	Croy : **Croydon**	Hamp W : **Hampton Wick**	Lough : **Loughton**
Belv : **Belvedere**	Cud : **Cudham**	Hanw : **Hanworth**	Mawney : **Mawney**
Bexl : **Bexley**	Dag : **Dagenham**	Hare : **Harefield**	Mitc : **Mitcham**
Bex : **Bexleyheath**	Dart : **Dartford**	Harl : **Harlington**	Mord : **Morden**
Bore : **Borehamwood**	Downe : **Downe**	Harm : **Harmondsworth**	New Ad : **New Addington**
Bford : **Brentford**	E Barn : **East Barnet**	Harr : **Harrow**	New Bar : **New Barnet**
Brim : **Brimsdown**	E Mos : **East Molesey**	Hrw W : **Harrow Weald**	N Mald : **New Malden**
Brom : **Bromley**	Eastc : **Eastcote**	H End : **Hatch End**	N'olt : **Northolt**
Buck H : **Buckhurst Hill**	Edg : **Edgware**	Have B : **Havering-Atte-Bower**	Nwood : **Northwood**
Bush : **Bushey**	Els : **Elstree**	Hayes : **Hayes**	Orp : **Orpington**
Bushy : **Bushy Heath**	Enf : **Enfield**	Hers : **Hersham**	Pet W : **Petts Wood**
Cars : **Carshalton**	Enf H : **Enfield Highway**	Hest : **Heston**	Pinn : **Pinner**
Chad H : **Chadwell Heath**	Enf L : **Enfield Lock**	Hil : **Hillingdon**	Pond E : **Ponders End**
Cheam : **Cheam**	Enf W : **Enfield Wash**	Hin W : **Hinchley Wood**	Prat B : **Pratts Bottom**
Chels : **Chelsfield**	Eps : **Epsom**	Houn : **Hounslow**	Purl : **Purley**
Chert : **Chertsey**	Erith : **Erith**	Ick : **Ickenham**	Rain : **Rainham**

Rich : **Richmond**
Rom : **Romford**
Ruis : **Ruislip**
Rush G : **Rush Green**
St M Cry : **St Mary Cray**
St P : **St Pauls Cray**
Sand : **Sanderstead**
Sels : **Selsdon**
Shep : **Shepperton**
Sidc : **Sidcup**
Sip : **Sipson**
S'hall : **Southall**
S Croy : **South Croydon**
Staines : **Staines**
Stan : **Stanmore**
Stanw : **Stanwell**
Stock P : **Stockley Park**
Sun : **Sunbury**
Surb : **Surbiton**
Sutt : **Sutton**
Swan : **Swanley**
Tedd : **Teddington**
T Ditt : **Thames Ditton**
Thor H : **Thornton Heath**
Twick : **Twickenham**
Uxb : **Uxbridge**
Wadd : **Waddon**
Wall : **Wallington**
Walt C : **Waltham Cross**
Walt T : **Walton-on-Thames**
W'stone : **Wealdstone**
Well : **Welling**
Wemb : **Wembley**
Wenn : **Wennington**
W Dray : **West Drayton**
W Mole : **West Molesey**
W W'ck : **West Wickham**
Weyb : **Weybridge**
Whit : **Whitton**
Wfd G : **Woodford Green**
Wor Pk : **Worcester Park**
Yead : **Yeading**
Yiew : **Yiewsley**

O2 Cen. NW3 6A **64**
198 Gallery *6B 120*
(off Railton Rd.)

A

Aaron Hill Rd. E6 5E **88**
Abady Ho. *SW1* *3D 18*
(off Page St.)
Abberley M. SW4 3F **119**
Abbess Cl. E6 5C **88**
SW2 1B **138**
Abbeville M. SW4 4H **119**
Abbeville Rd. N8 5H **47**
SW4 6G **119**
Abbey Av. HA0: Wemb 2E **78**
Abbey Bus. Cen. SW8 1G **119**
Abbey Cl. E5 4G **67**
HA5: Pinn 3K **39**
SW8 1H **119**
UB3: Hayes 1K **93**
UB5: N'olt 3D **76**
Abbey Ct. *NW8* *2A 82*
(off Abbey Rd.)
SE17 *5C 102*
(off Macleod St.)
TW12: Hamp 7E **130**
Abbey Cres. DA17: Belv 4G **109**
Abbeydale Ct. E17 3F **51**
UB1: S'hall *6F 77*
(off Dormers Ri.)
Abbeydale Rd. HA0: Wemb 1F **79**
Abbey Dr. DA2: Bexl 2K **145**
SW17 5E **136**
Abbey Est. NW8 1K **81**
Abbeyfield Cl. CR4: Mitc 2C **154**
Abbeyfield Est. SE16 4J **103**
Abbeyfield Rd. SE16 4J **103**
(not continuous)
Abbeyfields Cl. NW10 2G **79**
Abbey Gdns. BR7: Chst 1E **160**
NW8 2A **82**
SE16 4G **103**
W6 6G **99**
Abbey Gro. SE2 4B **108**
Abbeyhill Rd. DA15: Sidc 2C **144**
Abbey Ho. *E15* *2G 87*
(off Baker's Row)
NW8 1A **4**
Abbey Ind. Est. CR4: Mitc 5D **154**
HA0: Wemb 1F **79**
Abbey La. BR3: Beck 7C **140**
E15 2E **86**
Abbey La. Commercial Est. E15 2G **87**
Abbey Life Ct. E16 5K **87**
Abbey Lodge NW8 2D **4**
Abbey M. E17 5C **50**
Abbey Mt. DA17: Belv 5F **109**
Abbey Orchard St.
SW1 1C **18** (3H **101**)
Abbey Orchard St. Est.
SW1 1D **18** (3H **101**)
(not continuous)
Abbey Pde. *SW19* *7A 136*
(off Merton High St.)
W5 3F **79**
Abbey Pk. BR3: Beck 7C **140**
Abbey Pk. Ind. Est. IG11: Bark 2G **89**
Abbey Retail Pk. IG11: Bark 7F **71**
Abbey Rd. CR0: Croy 3B **168**
DA7: Bex 4E **126**
DA17: Belv 4D **108**
E15 2F **87**
EN1: Enf 5K **23**
IG2: Ilf 5H **53**
IG11: Bark 1F **89**
NW6 7K **63**
NW8 1A **4** (1K **81**)
NW10 1H **79**
SW19 7A **136**
Abbey Sports Cen. 1G **89**
Abbey St. E13 4J **87**
SE1 7H **15** (3F **103**)
Abbey Ter. SE2 4C **108**
Abbey Trad. Est. SE26 5B **140**
Abbey Vw. NW7 3G **29**
Abbey Wlk. KT8: W Mole 3F **149**
Abbey Wharf Ind. Est.
IG11: Bark 3H **89**
ABBEY WOOD 4C **108**
Abbey Wood Camping & Cvn. Site
SE2 4C **108**
Abbey Wood Rd. SE2 4B **108**
Abbot Cl. HA4: Ruis 3B **58**
Abbot Ct. *SW8* *7J 101*
(off Hartington Rd.)
Abbot Ho. *E14* *7D 86*
(off Smythe St.)
Abbotsbury Cl. E15 2E **86**
W14 2G **99**
Abbotsbury Gdns. HA5: Eastc 7A **40**
Abbotsbury M. SE15 3J **121**
Abbotsbury Rd. BR2: Hayes 2H **171**
SM4: Mord 5K **153**
W14 2G **99**
Abbots Cl. BR5: Farnb 1G **173**
Abbots Dr. HA2: Harr 2E **58**
Abbotsford Av. N15 4C **48**
Abbotsford Gdns. IG8: Wfd G 7D **36**
Abbotsford Rd. IG3: Ilf 2A **72**
Abbots Gdns. N2 4B **46**
Abbots Grn. CR0: Addtn 6K **169**
Abbotshade Rd. SE16 1K **103**
Abbotshall Av. N14 3B **32**
Abbotshall Rd. SE6 1F **141**
Abbot's Ho. *W14* *3H 99*
(off St Mary Abbots Ter.)
Abbots La. SE1 5H **15** (1E **102**)
Abbotsleigh Cl. SM2: Sutt 7K **165**
Abbotsleigh Rd. SW16 4G **137**
Abbots Mnr. SW1 5J **17** (4F **101**)
Abbots Mead TW10: Ham 4D **132**
Abbotsmede Cl.
TW1: Twick 2K **131**
Abbots Pk. SW2 1A **138**
Abbot's Pl. NW6 1K **81**
Abbots Rd. E6 1B **88**
HA8: Edg 7D **28**
Abbots Ter. N8 6J **47**
Abbotstone Rd. SW15 3E **116**
Abbot St. E8 6F **67**
Abbots Wlk. W8 3K **99**
Abbots Way BR3: Beck 5A **158**
Abbotswell Rd. SE4 5B **122**
Abbotswood Cl. DA17: Belv 3E **108**
Abbotswood Gdns. IG5: Ilf 3D **52**
Abbotswood Rd. SE22 4E **120**
SW16 3H **137**
Abbotswood Way UB3: Hayes 1K **93**
Abbott Av. SW20 1F **153**
Abbott Cl. TW12: Hamp 6C **130**
UB5: N'olt 6D **58**
Abbott Rd. E14 5E **86**
(not continuous)
Abbotts Cl. N1 6C **66**
RM7: Mawney 3H **55**
SE28 7C **90**
UB8: Cowl 5A **74**
Abbotts Cres. E4 4A **36**
EN2: Enf 2G **23**
Abbotts Dr. HA0: Wemb 2B **60**
Abbotts Ho. *SW1* *6C 18*
(off Aylesford St.)
Abbotts Pk. Rd. E10 7E **50**
Abbotts Rd. CR4: Mitc 4G **155**
(not continuous)
EN5: New Bar 4E **20**
SM3: Cheam 4G **165**
UB1: S'hall 1C **94**
Abbott's Wlk. DA7: Bex 7D **108**
Abbotts Wharf *E14* *6C 86*
(off Stainsby Pl.)
Abchurch La. EC4 2F **15** (7D **84**)
(not continuous)
Abchurch Yd. EC4 2E **14** (7D **84**)
Abdale Rd. W12 1D **98**
Abel Ho. *SE11* *7K 19*
(off Kennington Rd.)
Abenglen Ind. Est.
UB3: Hayes 2F **93**
Aberavon Rd. E3 3A **86**
Abercairn Rd. SW16 7G **137**
Aberconway Rd. SM4: Mord 4K **153**
Abercorn Cl. NW7 7B **30**
NW8 3A **82**
Abercorn Commercial Cen.
HA0: Wemb 1D **78**
Abercorn Cres. HA2: Harr 1F **59**
Abercorn Gdns. HA3: Kent 7D **42**
RM6: Chad H 6B **54**
Abercorn Gro. HA4: Ruis 4F **39**
Abercorn Ho. *SE10* *7D 104*
(off Tarves Way)
Abercorn Mans. *NW8* *2A 82*
(off Abercorn Pl.)
Abercorn M. TW10: Rich 4F **115**
Abercorn Pl. NW8 3A **82**
Abercorn Rd. HA7: Stan 7H **27**
NW7 7B **30**
Abercorn Way SE1 5G **103**
Abercrombie Dr. EN1: Enf 1B **24**
Abercrombie St. SW11 2C **118**
Aberdale Ct. *SE16* *2K 103*
(off Garter Way)
Aberdare Cl. BR4: W W'ck 2E **170**
Aberdare Gdns. NW6 7K **63**
NW7 7A **30**
Aberdare Rd. EN3: Pond E 4D **24**
Aberdeen Cotts. HA7: Stan 7H **27**
Aberdeen Ct. *W9* *4A 4*
(off Maida Va.)
Aberdeen La. N5 5C **66**
Aberdeen Mans. *WC1* *3E 6*
(off Kenton St.)
Aberdeen Pde. *N18* *5C 34*
(off Aberdeen Rd.)
N18 *5C 34*
(off Montagu Rd.)
Aberdeen Pk. N5 5C **66**
Aberdeen Pl. NW8 4A **4** (4B **82**)
Aberdeen Rd. CR0: Croy 4C **168**
HA3: W'stone 2K **41**
N5 4C **66**
N18 5B **34**
(not continuous)
NW10 5B **62**
Aberdeen Sq. E14 1B **104**
Aberdeen Ter. SE3 2F **123**
Aberdeen Wharf *E1* *1H 103*
(off Wapping High St.)
Aberdour Rd. IG3: Ilf 3B **72**
Aberdour St. SE1 4E **102**
Aberfeldy Ho. SE5 7B **102**
(not continuous)
Aberfeldy St. E14 5E **86**
(not continuous)
Aberford Gdns. SE18 1C **124**
Aberfoyle Rd. SW16 6H **137**
(not continuous)
Abergeldie Rd. SE12 6K **123**
Abernethy Rd. SE13 4G **123**
Abersham Rd. E8 5F **67**
Abery St. SE18 4J **107**
Abingdon *W14* *4H 99*
(off Kensington Village)
Abingdon Cl. NW1 6H **65**
SE1 *4F 103*
(off Bushwood Dr.)
SW19 6A **136**
UB10: Hil 1B **74**
Abingdon Ct. *W8* *3J 99*
(off Abingdon Vs.)
Abingdon Gdns. W8 3J **99**
Abingdon Ho. *E2* *3J 9*
(off Boundary St.)
Abingdon Lodge *BR2: Brom* *2H 159*
(off Beckenham La.)
W8 3J **99**
Abingdon Rd. N3 2A **46**
SW16 2J **155**
W8 3J **99**
Abingdon St. SW1 1E **18** (3J **101**)
Abingdon Vs. W8 3J **99**
Abinger Cl. BR1: Brom 3C **160**
CR0: New Ad 6E **170**
IG11: Bark 4A **72**
SM6: Wall 5J **167**
Abinger Ct. *SM6: Wall* *5J 167*
(off Abinger Cl.)
W5 7C **78**
Abinger Gdns. TW7: Isle 3J **113**
Abinger Gro. SE8 6B **104**
Abinger Ho. *SE1* *7E 14*
(off Gt. Dover St.)

Adelphi Ct.—Albert Bri.

Adelphi Ct. E8 .... 7F 67
(off Celandine Dr.)
SE16 .... 2K 103
(off Garter Way)
W4 .... 6K 97
Adelphi Cres. UB4: Hayes 3G 75
Adelphi Ter.
WC2 .... 3F 13 (7J 83)
Adelphi Theatre 3F 13
(off Strand)
Adelphi Way UB4: Hayes 3H 75
Adeney Cl. W6 .... 6F 99
Aden Gro. N16 .... 4D 66
Aden Ho. E1 .... 5K 85
(off Duckett St.)
Adenmore Rd. SE6 .... 7C 122
Aden Rd. EN3: Brim 4F 25
IG1: Ilf 7G 53
Aden Ter. N16 .... 4D 66
Adeyfield Ho. EC1 .... 2F 9
(off Cranwood St.)
Adie Rd. W6 .... 3E 98
Adine Rd. E13 .... 4K 87
Adler Ind. Est. UB3: Hayes 2F 93
Adler St. E1 .... 6G 85
Adley St. E5 .... 5A 68
Adlington Cl. N18 .... 5J 33
Admaston Rd. SE18 .... 7G 107
Admiral Ct. IG11: Bark 2B 90
SM5: Cars 1C 166
SW10 .... 1A 118
(off Admiral Sq.)
W1 .... 6G 5
(off Blandford St.)
Admiral Ho. SW1 .... 3B 18
(off Willow Pl.)
TW11: Tedd 4A 132
Admiral Hyson Ind. Est. SE16 .... 5H 103
Admiral M. W10 .... 4F 81
Admiral Pl. SE16 .... 1A 104
Admirals Cl. E18 .... 4K 51
Admirals Ct. E6 .... 6F 89
(off Trader Rd.)
SE1 .... 5J 15
(off Horselydown La.)
Admiral Seymour Rd. SE9 .... 4D 124
Admiral's Ga. SE10 .... 1D 122
Admiral Sq. SW10 .... 1A 118
Admiral St. SE8 .... 2C 122
Admirals Wlk. NW3 .... 3A 64
Admirals Way E14 .... 2C 104
Admiralty Arch 4D 12 (1H 101)
Admiralty Cl. SE8 .... 7C 104
Admiralty Rd. TW11: Tedd 6K 131
Admiralty Way TW11: Tedd 6K 131
Admiral Wlk. W9 .... 5J 81
Adolf St. SE6 .... 4D 140
Adolphus Rd. N4 .... 2B 66
Adolphus St. SE8 .... 7B 104
Adomar Rd. RM8: Dag 3D 72
Adpar St. W2 .... 5A 4 (5B 82)
Adrian Av. NW2 .... 1D 62
Adrian Boult Ho. E2 .... 3H 85
(off Mansford St.)
Adrian Cl. EN5: Barn 6A 20
Adrian Ho. N1 .... 1K 83
(off Barnsbury Est.)
SW8 .... 7J 101
(off Wyvil Rd.)
Adrian M. SW10 .... 6K 99
Adriatic Bldg. E14 .... 7A 86
(off Horseferry Rd.)
Adriatic Ho. E1 .... 4K 85
(off Ernest St.)
Adrienne Av. UB1: S'hall 4D 76
Adron Ho. SE16 .... 4J 103
(off Millender Wlk.)
Adstock Ho. N1 .... 7B 66
(off Sutton Est., The)
Advance Rd. SE27 .... 4C 138
Adventure Kingdom 2K 159
Adventurers Ct. E14 .... 7F 87
(off Newport Av.)
Advent Way N18 .... 5D 34
Adys Lawn NW2 .... 6D 62
Ady's Rd. SE15 .... 3F 121
Aegean Apartments E16 .... 7J 87
(off Western Gateway)
Aegon Ho. E14 .... 3D 104
(off Lanark Sq.)
Aerodrome Rd. NW4 .... 2B 44
NW9 .... 2B 44
Aerodrome Way TW5: Hest 6A 94
Aeroville NW9 .... 2A 44
Affleck St. N1 .... 1G 7 (2K 83)
Afghan Rd. SW11 .... 2C 118
Afsil Ho. EC1 .... 6K 7
(off Viaduct Bldgs.)
Aftab Ter. E1 .... 4H 85
(off Tent St.)
Agamemnon Rd. NW6 .... 4H 63
Agar Cl. KT6: Surb 2F 163
Agar Gro. NW1 .... 7G 65
Agar Gro. Est. NW1 .... 7H 65
Agar Ho. KT1: King T 3E 150
(off Denmark Rd.)
Agar Pl. NW1 .... 7G 65
Agar St. WC2 .... 3E 12 (7J 83)
Agate Cl. E16 .... 6B 88
Agate Rd. W6 .... 3E 98
Agatha Cl. E1 .... 1H 103
Agaton Rd. SE9 .... 2G 143
Agave Rd. NW2 .... 4E 62
Agdon St. EC1 .... 3A 8 (4B 84)
Agincourt Rd. NW3 .... 4D 64
Agnes Av. IG1: Ilf 4E 70
Agnes Cl. E6 .... 7E 88
Agnesfield Cl. N12 .... 6H 31
Agnes Gdns. RM8: Dag 4D 72
Agnes Ho. W11 .... 7F 81
(off St Ann's Rd.)
Agnes Rd. W3 .... 1B 98
Agnes St. E14 .... 6B 86
Agnew Rd. SE23 .... 7K 121
Agricola Pl. EN1: Enf 5A 24
Aidan Cl. RM8: Dag 4E 72
Aigburth Mans. SW9 .... 7A 102
(off Mowll St.)
Aileen Wlk. E15 .... 7H 69
Ailsa Av. TW1: Twick 5A 114
Ailsa Ho. E16 .... 7E 88
(off University Way)
Ailsa Rd. TW1: Twick 5B 114
Ailsa St. E14 .... 5E 86
Ainger M. NW3 .... 7D 64
(off Ainger Rd., not continuous)
Ainger Rd. NW3 .... 7D 64
Ainsdale NW1 .... 1A 6
(off Harrington St.)
Ainsdale Cl. BR6: Orp 1H 173
Ainsdale Cres. HA5: Pinn 3E 40
Ainsdale Dr. SE1 .... 5G 103
Ainsdale Rd. W5 .... 4D 78
Ainsley Av. RM7: Rom 6H 55
Ainsley Cl. N9 .... 1K 33
Ainsley St. E2 .... 3H 85
Ainslie Ct. HA0: Wemb 2E 78
Ainslie Wlk. SW12 .... 7F 119
Ainslie Wood Cres. E4 .... 5J 35
Ainslie Wood Gdns. E4 .... 4J 35
Ainslie Wood Nature Reserve 5J 35
Ainslie Wood Rd. E4 .... 5H 35
Ainsty Est. SE16 .... 2K 103
Ainsty St. SE16 .... 2J 103
Ainsworth Cl. NW2 .... 3C 62
SE15 .... 2E 120
Ainsworth Ho. NW8 .... 1K 81
(off Ainsworth Way)
Ainsworth Rd. CR0: Croy 1B 168
E9 .... 7J 67
Ainsworth Way NW8 .... 1A 82
Aintree Av. E6 .... 1C 88
Aintree Cl. UB8: Hil 6D 74
Aintree Cres. IG6: Ilf 2G 53
Aintree Est. SW6 .... 7G 99
(off Aintree St.)
Aintree Rd. UB6: G'frd 2B 78
Aintree St. SW6 .... 7G 99
Airbourne Ho. SM6: Wall 4G 167
(off Maldon Rd.)
Air Call Bus. Cen.
NW9 .... 3K 43
Aird Ho. SE1 .... 3C 102
(off Rockingham St.)
Airdrie Cl. N1 .... 7K 65
UB4: Yead 5C 76
Airedale Av. W4 .... 4B 98
Airedale Av. Sth. W4 .... 5B 98
Airedale Rd. SW12 .... 7D 118
W5 .... 3C 96
Airlie Gdns. IG1: Ilf 1F 71
W8 .... 1J 99
Air Links Ind. Est.
TW13: Hanw 3C 130
Airlinks Ind. Est. TW5: Cran 5A 94
Air Pk. Way TW13: Felt 2K 129
Airport Bowl 1F 111
Airport Ga. UB7: Sip 7B 92
Air St. W1 .... 3B 12 (7G 83)
Airthrie Rd. IG3: Ilf 2B 72
Aisgill Av. W14 .... 5H 99
(not continuous)
Aisher Rd. SE28 .... 7C 90
Aislibie Rd. SE12 .... 4G 123
Aiten Pl. W6 .... 4C 98
Aithan Ho. E14 .... 6B 86
(off Copenhagen Pl.)
Aitken Cl. CR4: Mitc 7D 154
E8 .... 1G 85
Aitken Rd. SE6 .... 2D 140
Ajax Av. NW9 .... 3A 44
Ajax Ho. E2 .... 2H 85
(off Old Bethnal Grn. Rd.)
Ajax Rd. NW6 .... 4H 63
Akabusi Cl. CR0: Croy 6G 157
Akbar Ho. E14 .... 4D 104
(off Cahir St.)
Akehurst St. SW15 .... 6C 116
Akenside Rd. NW3 .... 5B 64
Akerman Rd. KT6: Surb 6C 150
SW9 .... 2B 120
Akintaro Ho. SE8 .... 6B 104
(off Alverton St.)
Alabama St. SE18 .... 7H 107
Alacross Rd. W5 .... 2C 96
Alamaro Lodge SE10 .... 3H 105
Alandale Dr. HA5: Pinn 1K 39
Aland Ct. SE16 .... 3A 104
Alander M. E17 .... 4E 50
Alan Dr. EN5: Barn 6B 20
Alan Gdns. RM7: Rush G 7G 55
Alan Hocken Way E15 .... 2G 87
Alan Preece Ct. NW6 .... 7F 63
Alan Rd. SW19 .... 5G 135
Alanthus Cl. SE12 .... 6J 123
Alaska Bldgs. SE1 .... 4E 102
Alaska St. SE1 .... 5J 13 (1A 102)
Alastor Ho. E14 .... 3E 104
(off Strattondale Ho.)
Alba Cl. UB4: Yead 4B 76
Albacore Cres. SE13 .... 6D 122
Alba Gdns. NW11 .... 6G 45
Albain Cres. TW15: Ashf 2A 128
Alba M. SW18 .... 2J 135
Alban Highwalk EC2 .... 7D 8
(not continuous)
Albany N12 .... 6E 30
W1 .... 3A 12 (7G 83)
Albany, The IG8: Wfd G 4C 36
Albany Cl. DA5: Bexl 7C 126
N15 .... 4B 48
SW14 .... 4H 115
UB10: Ick 5C 56
Albany Ct. E4 .... 6H 25
(Chingford)
E4 .... 5G 35
(South Chingford)
E10 .... 7C 50
HA8: Edg 1K 43
NW8 .... 1A 4
(off Abbey Rd.)
NW10 .... 3D 80
(off Trenmar Gdns.)
TW15: Ashf 7E 128
Albany Courtyard W1 .... 3B 12 (7G 83)
Albany Cres. HA8: Edg 7B 28
Albany Mans. SW11 .... 7C 100
Albany M. BR1: Brom 6J 141
KT2: King T 6D 132
N1 .... 7A 66
SE5 .... 6C 102
SM1: Sutt 5K 165
Albany Pde. TW8: Bford 6E 96
Albany Pk. Av. EN3: Enf W 1D 24
Albany Pk. Rd. KT2: King T 6D 132
Albany Pas. TW10: Rich 5E 114
Albany Pl. N7 .... 4A 66
TW8: Bford 6D 96
Albany Reach KT7: T Ditt 5K 149
Albany Rd. BR7: Chst 5F 143
DA5: Bexl 7C 126
DA17: Belv 6F 109
E10 .... 7C 50
E12 .... 4B 70
E17 .... 6A 50
KT3: N Mald 4K 151
N4 .... 6A 48
N18 .... 5D 34
RM6: Chad H 6F 55
SE5 .... 6D 102
SW19 .... 5K 135
TW8: Bford 6D 96
TW10: Rich 5F 115
W13 .... 7B 78
Albany St. NW1 .... 1K 5 (2F 83)
Albany Ter. NW1 .... 4K 5
TW10: Rich 5F 115
(off Albany Pas.)
Albany Vw. IG9: Buck H 1D 36
Alba Pl. W11 .... 6H 81
Albatross NW9 .... 2B 44
Albatross Cl. E6 .... 5D 88
Albatross St. SE18 .... 7J 107
Albatross Way SE16 .... 2K 103
Albemarle SW19 .... 2F 135
Albemarle App. IG2: Ilf 6F 53
Albemarle Av. TW2: Whit 1D 130
Albemarle Gdns. IG2: Ilf 6F 53
KT3: N Mald 4K 151
Albemarle Ho. SE8 .... 4B 104
(off Foreshore)
SW9 .... 3A 120
Albemarle Pk. BR3: Beck 1D 158
HA7: Stan 5H 27
Albemarle Rd. BR3: Beck 1D 158
EN4: E Barn 7H 21
Albemarle St. W1 .... 3K 11 (7F 83)
Albemarle Way EC1 .... 4A 8 (4B 84)
Alberon Gdns. NW11 .... 4H 45
Alberta Av. SM1: Sutt 4G 165
Alberta Est. SE17 .... 5B 102
(off Alberta St.)
Alberta Ho. E14 .... 1E 104
(off Gaselee St.)
Alberta Rd. DA8: Erith 1J 127
EN1: Enf 6A 24
Alberta St. SE17 .... 5B 102
Albert Av. E4 .... 4H 35
SW8 .... 7K 101
Albert Barnes Ho. SE1 .... 3C 102
(off New Kent Rd.)
Albert Bigg Point E15 .... 2E 86
(off Godfrey St.)
Albert Bri. SW8 .... 7D 16 (7C 100)

Albert Bri. Rd. SW11 ... 7C 100
Albert Carr Gdns.
SW16 ... 5J 137
Albert Cl. E9 ... 1H 85
N22 ... 1H 47
Albert Cotts. *E1* ... *5G 85*
(off Deal St.)
Albert Ct. E7 ... 4J 69
SW7 ... 7A 10 (3B 100)
Albert Ct. Ga. *SW7* ... *7E 10*
(off Knightsbridge)
Albert Cres. E4 ... 4H 35
Albert Dane Cen. UB2: S'hall ... 3C 94
Albert Dr. SW19 ... 2G 135
Albert Emb. SE1 ... 1G 19 (3K 101)
(Lambeth Pal. Rd.)
SE1 ... 6F 19 (5J 101)
(Vauxhall Bri.)
Albert Gdns. E1 ... 6K 85
Albert Ga. SW1 ... 6F 11 (2D 100)
Albert Gray Ho. *SW10* ... *7B 100*
(off Worlds End Est.)
Albert Gro. SW20 ... 1F 153
Albert Hall Mans.
SW7 ... 7A 10 (2B 100)
(not continuous)
Albert Ho. *E18* ... *3K 51*
(off Albert Rd.)
SE28 ... *2G 107*
(off Erebus Dr.)
Albert Mans. *CR0: Croy* ... *1D 168*
(off Lansdowne Rd.)
Albert Memorial ... 7A 10 (2B 100)
Albert M. *E14* ... *7A 86*
(off Northey St.)
N4 ... 1K 65
SE4 ... 4A 122
W8 ... 3A 100
Albert Pal. Mans. *SW11* ... *1F 119*
(off Lurline Gdns.)
Albert Pl. N3 ... 1J 45
N17 ... 3F 49
W8 ... 3K 99
Albert Rd. BR2: Brom ... 5B 160
CR4: Mitc ... 3D 154
DA5: Bexl ... 6G 127
DA17: Belv ... 5F 109
E10 ... 2E 68
E16 ... 1C 106
E17 ... 5C 50
E18 ... 3K 51
EN4: E Barn ... 4F 21
HA2: Harr ... 3G 41
IG1: Ilf ... 3F 71
IG9: Buck H ... 2G 37
KT1: King T ... 2F 151
KT3: N Mald ... 4B 152
N4 ... 1K 65
N15 ... 6E 48
N22 ... 1G 47
NW4 ... 4F 45
NW6 ... 2H 81
NW7 ... 5G 29
RM8: Dag ... 1G 73
SE9 ... 3C 142
SE20 ... 6K 139
SE25 ... 4G 157
SM1: Sutt ... 5B 166
TW1: Twick ... 1K 131
TW3: Houn ... 4E 112
TW10: Rich ... 5E 114
TW11: Tedd ... 6K 131
TW12: Hamp H ... 5G 131
TW15: Ashf ... 5B 128
UB2: S'hall ... 3B 94
UB3: Hayes ... 3G 93
UB7: Yiew ... 1A 92
W5 ... 4B 78
Albert Rd. Est. DA17: Belv ... 5F 109
Albert Sleet Ct. *N9* ... *3C 34*
(off Colthurst Dr.)
Albert Sq. E15 ... 5G 69
SW8 ... 7K 101
Albert Starr Ho. *SE8* ... *4K 103*
(off Bush Rd.)
Albert St. N12 ... 5F 31
NW1 ... 1F 83
Albert Studios SW11 ... 1D 118
Albert Ter. IG9: Buck H ... 2H 37
NW1 ... 1E 82
NW10 ... 1J 79
W5 ... 4B 78
W6 ... *5C 98*
(off Beavor La.)
Albert Ter. M. NW1 ... 1E 82
Albert Victoria Ho. N22 ... 1A 48
Albert Wlk. E16 ... 2E 106
Albert Way SE15 ... 7H 103
Albert Westcott Ho.
SE17 ... 5B 102
Albert Whicher Ho. E17 ... 4E 50
Albert Yd. SE19 ... 6E 138
Albery Ct. *E8* ... *7F 67*
(off Middleton Rd.)
Albery Theatre ... *2E 12*
(off St Martin's La.)
Albion Av. N10 ... 1E 46
SW8 ... 2H 119
Albion Bldgs. *N1* ... *2J 83*
(off Albion Yd.)
Albion Cl. RM7: Rom ... 6K 55
W2 ... 2D 10 (7C 82)
Albion Ct. SM2: Sutt ... 7B 166
W6 ... *4D 98*
(off Albion Pl.)
Albion Dr. E8 ... 7F 67
Albion Est. SE16 ... 2K 103
Albion Gdns. W6 ... 4D 98
Albion Ga. W2 ... 2D 10
(not continuous)
Albion Gro. N16 ... 4E 66
Albion Ho. *E16* ... *1F 107*
(off Church St.)
SE8 ... *7C 104*
(off Watsons St.)
Albion M. N1 ... 1A 84
W2 ... 2D 10 (7C 82)
W6 ... 4D 98
Albion Pde. N16 ... 4D 66
Albion Pl. EC1 ... 5A 8 (5B 84)
EC2 ... 6F 9 (5D 84)
SE25 ... 3G 157
W6 ... 4D 98
Albion Rd. DA6: Bex ... 4F 127
E17 ... 3E 50
KT2: King T ... 1J 151
N16 ... 4D 66
N17 ... 2G 49
SM2: Sutt ... 6B 166
TW2: Twick ... 1J 131
TW3: Houn ... 4E 112
UB3: Hayes ... 6G 75
Albion Sq. E8 ... 7F 67
(not continuous)
Albion St. CR0: Croy ... 1B 168
SE16 ... 2J 103
W2 ... 1D 10 (6C 82)
Albion Ter. E4 ... 4J 25
E8 ... 7F 67
Albion Vs. Rd. SE26 ... 3J 139
Albion Wlk. *N1* ... *2J 83*
(off York Way)
Albion Way EC1 ... 6C 8 (5C 84)
HA9: Wemb ... 3G 61
SE13 ... 4E 122
Albion Wharf SW11 ... 7C 100
Albion Yd. E1 ... 5H 85
N1 ... 2J 83
Albon Ho. *SW18* ... *6K 117*
(off Neville Gill Cl.)
Albrighton Rd. SE22 ... 3E 120
Albuhera Cl. EN2: Enf ... 1F 23
Albury Av. DA7: Bex ... 2E 126
TW7: Isle ... 7K 95
Albury Cl. TW12: Hamp ... 6F 131
Albury Ct. *CR2: S Croy* ... *4C 168*
(off Tanfield Rd.)
CR4: Mitc ... 2B 154
SM1: Sutt ... 4A 166
UB5: Yead ... *3A 76*
(off Canberra Dr.)
Albury Dr. HA5: Pinn ... 1A 40 & 1C 40
Albury Ho. *SE1* ... *7B 14*
(off Boyfield St.)
Albury M. E12 ... 2A 70
Albury Rd. KT9: Chess ... 5E 162
Albury St. SE8 ... 6C 104
Albyfield BR1: Brom ... 4D 160
Albyn Rd. SE8 ... 1C 122
Alcester Ct. SM6: Wall ... 4F 167
Alcester Cres. E5 ... 2H 67
Alcester Rd. SM6: Wall ... 4F 167
Alcock Cl. SM6: Wall ... 7H 167
Alcock Rd. TW5: Hest ... 7B 94
Alconbury DA6: Bex ... 5H 127
Alconbury Rd. E5 ... 2G 67
Alcorn Cl. SM3: Sutt ... 2J 165
Alcott Cl. TW14: Felt ... 1H 129
W7 ... 5K 77
Alcuin Ct. HA7: Stan ... 7H 27
Aldam Pl. N16 ... 2F 67
Aldborough Ct. *IG2: Ilf* ... *5K 53*
(off Aldborough Rd. Nth.)
ALDBOROUGH HATCH ... 4K 53
Aldborough Rd. RM10: Dag ... 6J 73
Aldborough Rd. Nth. IG2: Ilf ... 5K 53
Aldborough Rd. Sth. IG3: Ilf ... 1J 71
Aldbourne Rd. W12 ... 1B 98
(not continuous)
Aldbridge St. SE17 ... 5E 102
Aldburgh M. W1 ... 7H 5 (6E 82)
(not continuous)
Aldbury Av. HA9: Wemb ... 7H 61
Aldbury Ho. *SW3* ... *5C 16*
(off Marlborough St.)
Aldbury M. N9 ... 7J 23
Aldebert Ter. SW8 ... 7J 101
Aldeburgh Cl. E5 ... 2H 67
Aldeburgh Pl. IG8: Wfd G ... 4D 36
SE10 ... *4J 105*
(off Aldeburgh St.)
Aldeburgh St. SE10 ... 5J 105
Alden Av. E15 ... 3H 87
Alden Ct. CR0: Croy ... 3E 168
Aldenham Dr. UB8: Hil ... 4D 74
Aldenham Ho. *NW1* ... *1B 6*
(off Aldenham St.)
Aldenham St. NW1 ... 1C 6 (2G 83)
Alden Ho. *E8* ... *1H 85*
(off Duncan Rd.)
Aldensley Rd. W6 ... 3D 98
Alderbrook Rd. SW12 ... 6F 119
Alderbury Rd. SW13 ... 6C 98
Alder Cl. SE15 ... 6F 103
Alder Gro. NW2 ... 2C 62
Aldergrove Gdns. TW3: Houn ... 2C 112
Alder Ho. NW3 ... 6D 64
SE4 ... 3C 122
SE15 ... *6F 103*
(off Cator St.)
Alder Lodge SW6 ... 1E 116
Alderman Av. IG11: Bark ... 3A 90
Aldermanbury EC2 ... 7D 8 (6C 84)
Aldermanbury Sq. EC2 ... 6D 8 (5C 84)
Alderman Judge Mall
KT1: King T ... 2E 150
Aldermans Hill N13 ... 4D 32
Aldermans Wlk. EC2 ... 6G 9 (5E 84)
Aldermary Rd. BR1: Brom ... 1J 159
Alder M. N19 ... 2G 65
Aldermoor Rd. SE6 ... 3B 140
Alderney Av. TW5: Hest, Isle ... 7F 95
Alderney Gdns. UB5: N'olt ... 7D 58
Alderney Ho. EN3: Enf W ... 1E 24
N1 ... *6C 66*
(off Arran Wlk.)
Alderney Rd. E1 ... 4K 85
Alderney St. SW1 ... 4K 17 (4F 101)
Alder Rd. DA14: Sidc ... 3K 143
SW14 ... 3K 115
Alders, The BR4: W W'ck ... 1D 170
N21 ... 6F 23
SW16 ... 4G 137
TW5: Hest ... 6D 94
TW13: Hanw ... 4C 130
Alders Av. IG8: Wfd G ... 6B 36
ALDERSBROOK ... 2K 69
Aldersbrook Av. EN1: Enf ... 2K 23
Aldersbrook Dr.
KT2: King T ... 6F 133
Aldersbrook La. E12 ... 3D 70
Aldersbrook Rd. E11 ... 2K 69
E12 ... 2K 69
Alders Cl. E11 ... 2K 69
HA8: Edg ... 5D 28
W5 ... 3D 96
Aldersey Gdns. IG11: Bark ... 6H 71
Aldersford Cl. SE4 ... 5K 121
Aldersgate St. EC1 ... 5C 8 (5C 84)
Alders Gro. KT8: E Mos ... 5H 149
Aldersgrove Av. SE9 ... 3B 142
Aldershot Rd. NW6 ... 1H 81
Aldershot Ter. SE18 ... 7E 106
Aldersmead Av. CR0: Croy ... 6K 157
Aldersmead Rd. BR3: Beck ... 7A 140
Alderson Pl. UB2: S'hall ... 1G 95
Alderson St. W10 ... 4G 81
Alders Rd. HA8: Edg ... 5D 28
Alderton Cl. NW10 ... 3K 61
Alderton Ct. *KT8: W Mole* ... *4D 148*
(off Walton Rd.)
Alderton Cres. NW4 ... 5D 44
Alderton Rd. CR0: Croy ... 7F 157
SE24 ... 3C 120
Alderton Way NW4 ... 5D 44
Alderville Rd. SW6 ... 2H 117
Alder Wlk. IG1: Ilf ... 5G 71
Alderwick Ct. *N7* ... *6K 65*
(off Cornelia St.)
Alderwick Dr. TW3: Houn ... 3H 113
Alderwood M. EN4: Had W ... 1F 21
Alderwood Rd. SE9 ... 6H 125
Aldford Ho. *W1* ... *4G 11*
(off Park St.)
Aldford St. W1 ... 4H 11 (1E 100)
ALDGATE ... 6F 85
Aldgate *E1* ... *7J 9*
(off Whitechapel High St.)
EC3 ... 1H 15 (6E 84)
Aldgate Av. E1 ... 7J 9 (6F 85)
Aldgate Barrs E1 ... 7K 9
Aldgate High St. EC3 ... 1J 15 (6F 85)
Aldgate Triangle *E1* ... *6G 85*
(off Coke St.)
Aldham Ho. *SE14* ... *2B 122*
(off Malpas Rd.)
Aldine Ct. *W12* ... *2E 98*
(off Aldine St.)
Aldine Pl. W12 ... 2E 98
Aldine St. W12 ... 2E 98
Aldington Cl. RM8: Dag ... 1C 72
Aldington Ct. *E8* ... *7G 67*
(off London Flds. W. Side)
Aldington Rd. SE18 ... 3B 106
Aldis M. SW17 ... 5C 136
Aldis St. SW17 ... 5C 136
Aldred Rd. NW6 ... 5J 63
Aldren Rd. SW17 ... 3A 136
Aldrich Cres. CR0: New Ad ... 7E 170
Aldriche Way E4 ... 6K 35
Aldrich Gdns. SM3: Cheam ... 3H 165
Aldrich Ter. SW18 ... 2A 136
Aldrick Ho. *N1* ... *1K 83*
(off Barnsbury Est.)

Aldridge Av. HA4: Ruis 5K 39
HA7: Stan 1E 42
HA8: Edg 3C 28
Aldridge Ri. KT3: N Mald 7A 152
Aldridge Rd. Vs. W11 5H 81
Aldridge Wlk. N14 7D 22
Aldrington Rd. SW16 5G 137
Aldsworth Cl. W9 4K 81
Aldwick Cl. SE9 3H 143
Aldwick Rd. CR0: Bedd 3K 167
Aldworth Gro. SE13 6E 122
Aldworth Rd. E15 7G 69
Aldwych WC2 2G 13 (6K 83)
Aldwych Av. IG6: Ilf 4G 53
Aldwych Ct. *E8* 7F 67
(off Middleton Rd.)
Aldwych Theatre 1G 13
(off Aldwych)
Aldwyn Ho. *SW8* 7J 101
(off Davidson Gdns.)
Alers Rd. DA6: Bex 5D 126
Alesia Cl. N22 7D 32
Alestan Beck Rd.
E16 6B 88
Alexa Ct. SM2: Sutt 6J 165
W8 4J 99
Alexander Av. NW10 7D 62
Alexander Cl. BR2: Hayes 1J 171
DA15: Sidc 5J 125
EN4: E Barn 4G 21
TW2: Twick 2J 131
UB2: S'hall 1G 95
Alexander Ct. BR3: Beck 1F 159
HA7: Stan 3F 43
Alexander Evans M. SE23 2K 139
Alexander Fleming Mus. 7B 4
Alexander Ho. *E14* 3C 104
(off Tiller Rd.)
KT2: King T 1E 150
(off Seven Kings Way)
Alexander M. W2 6K 81
Alexander Pl.
SW7 3C 16 (4C 100)
Alexander Rd. BR7: Chst 6F 143
DA7: Bex 2D 126
N19 3J 65
Alexander Sq. SW3 3C 16 (4C 100)
Alexander St. W2 6J 81
Alexander Studios
SW11 4B 118
(off Haydon Way)
Alexander Ter. SE2 5B 108
Alexandra Av. HA2: Harr 1D 58
N22 1H 47
SM1: Sutt 3J 165
SW11 1E 118
UB1: S'hall 7D 76
W4 7K 97
Alexandra Cl. HA2: Harr 3E 58
SE8 6B 104
TW15: Ashf 7F 129
Alexandra Cotts. SE14 1B 122
Alexandra Ct. HA9: Wemb 4F 61
N14 5B 22
SW7 1A 16
TW3: Houn 2F 113
TW15: Ashf 6F 129
UB6: G'frd 2F 77
W2 7K 81
(off Moscow Rd.)
W9 4A 82
(off Maida Va.)
Alexandra Cres. BR1: Brom 6H 141
Alexandra Dr. KT5: Surb 7G 151
SE19 5E 138
Alexandra Gdns. N10 4F 47
SM5: Cars 7E 166
TW3: Houn 2F 113
W4 7A 98
Alexandra Gro. N4 1B 66
N12 5E 30
Alexandra Ho. *E16* 1K 105
(off Wesley Av.)
IG8: Ilf 7K 37
W6 5E 98
(off Queen Caroline St.)
Alexandra Mans. *SW3* 7A 16
(off King's Rd.)
Alexandra M. N2 3D 46
SW19 6H 135
Alexandra National Ho. N4 1B 66
Alexandra Palace 2H 47
Alexandra Pal. Way N22 4G 47
Alexandra Pde. HA2: Harr 4F 59
Alexandra Pk. Rd. N10 2F 47
N22 1G 47
Alexandra Pl. CR0: Croy 1E 168
NW8 1A 82
SE25 5D 156
Alexandra Rd. CR0: Croy 1E 168
CR4: Mitc 7C 136
E6 3E 88
E10 3E 68
E17 6B 50
E18 3K 51
EN3: Pond E 4E 24
KT2: King T 7G 133
KT7: T Ditt 5K 149
N8 3A 48
N9 7C 24
N10 7A 32
N15 5D 48
NW4 4F 45
NW8 1A 82
RM6: Chad H 6E 54
SE26 6K 139
SW14 3K 115
SW19 6H 135
TW1: Twick 6C 114
TW3: Houn 2F 113
TW8: Bford 6D 96
TW9: Kew 2F 115
TW15: Ashf 7F 129
W4 2K 97
Alexandra Rd. Ind. Est.
EN3: Pond E 4E 24
Alexandra Sq. SM4: Mord 5J 153
Alexandra St. E16 5J 87
SE14 7A 104
Alexandra Ter. *E14* 5D 104
(off Westferry Rd.)
Alexandra Wlk. SE19 5E 138
Alexandra Yd. E9 1K 85
Alexandria Rd. W13 7A 78
Alexis St. SE16 4G 103
Alfan La. DA2: Dart 5K 145
Alfearn Rd. E5 4J 67
Alford Ct. *N1* 1D 8
(off Shepherdess Wlk., not continuous)
Alford Grn. CR0: New Ad 6F 171
Alford Ho. N6 6G 47
Alford Pl. N1 1D 8 (2C 84)
Alford Rd. DA8: Erith 5J 109
Alfoxton Av. N15 4B 48
Alfreda St. SW11 1F 119
Alfred Cl. W4 4K 97
Alfred Finlay Ho. N22 2B 48
Alfred Gdns. UB1: S'hall 7C 76
Alfred Ho. *E9* 5A 68
(off Homerton Rd.)
E12 7C 70
(off Tennyson Av.)
Alfred M. W1 5C 6 (5H 83)
Alfred Nunn Ho. NW10 1B 80
Alfred Pl. WC1 5C 6 (5H 83)
Alfred Prior Ho. E12 4E 70
Alfred Rd. DA17: Belv 5F 109
E15 5H 69
IG9: Buck H 2G 37
KT1: King T 3E 150
SE25 5G 157
SM1: Sutt 5A 166
Alfred Rd. TW13: Felt 2A 130
W2 5J 81
W3 1J 97
Alfred's Gdns. IG11: Bark 2J 89
Alfred St. E3 3B 86
Alfreds Way IG11: Bark 3F 89
Alfreds Way Ind. Est. IG11: Bark 1A 90
Alfred Vs. E17 4E 50
Alfreton Cl. SW19 3F 135
Alfriston KT5: Surb 6F 151
Alfriston Av. CR0: Croy 7J 155
HA2: Harr 6E 40
Alfriston Cl. KT5: Surb 5F 151
Alfriston Rd. SW11 5D 118
Algar Cl. HA7: Stan 5E 26
TW7: Isle 3A 114
Algar Ho. SE1 7A 14
Algar Rd. TW7: Isle 3A 114
Algarve Rd. SW18 1K 135
Algernon Rd. NW4 6C 44
NW6 1J 81
SE13 4D 122
Algiers Rd. SE13 4C 122
Alibon Gdns. RM10: Dag 5G 73
Alibon Rd. RM9: Dag 5F 73
RM10: Dag 5G 73
Alice Cl. *EN5: New Bar* 4F 21
(off Station App.)
Alice Gilliatt Ct. *W14* 6H 99
(off Star Rd.)
Alice La. E3 1B 86
Alice M. TW11: Tedd 5K 131
Alice Owen Technology Cen.
EC1 1A 8
(off Goswell Rd.)
Alice Shepherd Ho. *E14* 2E 104
(off Manchester Rd.)
Alice St. SE1 3E 102
(Decima St.)
SE1 3E 102
(Rothsay St.)
Alice Thompson Cl. SE12 2A 142
Alice Walker Cl. SE24 4B 120
Alice Way TW3: Houn 4F 113
Alicia Av. HA3: Kent 4B 42
Alicia Cl. HA3: Kent 4C 42
Alicia Gdns. HA3: Kent 4B 42
Alicia Ho. DA16: Well 1B 126
Alie St. E1 1K 15 (6F 85)
Alington Cres. NW9 7J 43
Alington Gro. SM6: Wall 7G 167
Alison Cl. CR0: Croy 1K 169
E6 6E 88
Alison Ct. SE1 5G 103
Aliwal M. SW11 4C 118
Aliwal Rd. SW11 4C 118
Alkerden Rd. W4 5A 98
Alkham Rd. N16 2F 67
Allan Barclay Cl. N15 6F 49
Allan Cl. KT3: N Mald 5K 151
Allandale Av. N3 3G 45
Allanson Ct. *E10* 2C 68
(off Leyton Grange Est.)
Allan Way W3 5J 79
Allard Cres. WD23: Bushy 1B 26
Allard Gdns. SW4 5H 119
Allardyce St. SW4 4K 119
Allbrook Cl. TW11: Tedd 5J 131
Allcott Ho. *W12* 6D 80
(off Du Cane Rd.)
Allcroft Rd. NW5 5E 64
Allder Way CR2: S Croy 7B 168
Allenby Cl. UB6: G'frd 3E 76
Allenby Rd. SE23 3A 140
SE28 3G 107
UB1: S'hall 3E 76
Allen Cl. CR4: Mitc 1F 155
TW16: Sun 1K 147
Allen Ct. *E17* 6C 50
(off Yunus Khan Cl.)
UB6: G'frd 5K 59
Allendale Av. UB1: S'hall 6E 76
Allendale Cl. SE5 2D 120
SE26 5K 139
Allendale Rd. UB6: G'frd 6B 60
Allen Edwards Dr. SW8 1J 119
Allenford Ho. *SW15* 6B 116
(off Tunworth Cres.)
Allen Rd. BR3: Beck 2K 157
CR0: Croy 1A 168
E3 2B 86
N16 4E 66
TW16: Sun 1K 147
Allensbury Pl. NW1 7H 65
Allens Rd. EN3: Pond E 5D 24
Allen St. W8 3J 99
Allenswood SW19 1G 135
Allenswood Rd. SE9 3C 124
Allerford Ct. HA2: Harr 5G 41
Allerford Rd. SE6 3D 140
Allerton Ho. *N1* 1E 8
(off Fairbank Est.)
Allerton Rd. N16 2C 66
Allerton St. N1 1E 8 (3D 84)
Allerton Wlk. N7 2K 65
Allestree Rd. SW6 7G 99
Alleyn Cres. SE21 2D 138
Alleyndale Rd. RM8: Dag 2C 72
Alleyn Ho. *SE1* 3D 102
(off Burbage Cl.)
Alleyn Pk. SE21 2D 138
UB2: S'hall 5E 94
Alleyn Rd. SE21 3D 138
Alley Way UB8: Uxb 7A 56
Allfarthing La. SW18 6K 117
Allgood Cl. SM4: Mord 6F 153
Allgood St. E2 1K 9 (2F 85)
Allhallows La. EC4 3E 14 (7D 84)
All Hallows Rd. N17 1E 48
Allhallows Rd. E6 5C 88
Alliance Cl. HA0: Wemb 4D 60
Alliance Ct. TW15: Ashf 4E 128
W3 5H 79
Alliance Rd. E13 5A 88
SE18 6A 108
W3 4H 79
Allied Ind. Est. W3 2A 98
Allied Way W3 2A 98
Allingham Cl. W7 7K 77
Allingham M. *N1* 2C 84
(off Allingham St.)
Allingham St. N1 2C 84
Allington Av. N17 6K 33
TW17: Shep 3G 147
Allington Cl. SW19 5F 135
UB6: G'frd 7G 59
Allington Ct. EN3: Pond E 5E 24
(not continuous)
SW1 2K 17
(off Allington St.)
SW8 2G 119
Allington Rd. BR6: Orp 2H 173
HA2: Harr 5G 41
NW4 5D 44
W10 3G 81
Allington St. SW1 2K 17 (3F 101)
Allison Cl. SE10 1E 122
Allison Gro. SE21 1E 138
Allison Rd. N8 5A 48
W3 6J 79
Alliston Ho. *E2* 2K 9
(off Gibraltar Wlk.)
Allitsen Rd. NW8 2C 82
(not continuous)
All Nations Ho. *E8* 7H 67
(off Martello St.)
Allnutt Way SW4 5H 119
Alloa Rd. IG3: Ilf 2A 72
SE8 5K 103
Allom Ho. *W11* 7G 81
(off Clarendon Rd.)
Allonby Dr. HA4: Ruis 7D 38

Amesbury Rd. BR1: Brom 3B **160**
RM9: Dag 7D **72**
TW13: Felt 2B **130**
Amesbury Twr. SW8 2G **119**
Ames Cotts. *E14* *5A 86*
(off Maroon St.)
Ames Ho. *E2* *2K 85*
(off Mace St.)
Amethyst Cl. N11 7C **32**
Amethyst Ct. *BR6: Chels* *5J 173*
(off Farnborough Hill)
Amethyst Rd. E15 4F **69**
AMF Bowling 3E **122**
Amherst Av. W13 6C **78**
Amherst Dr. BR5: St M Cry 4K **161**
Amherst Gdns. *W13* *6C 78*
(off Amherst Rd.)
Amherst Ho. *SE16* *2K 103*
(off Wolfe Cres.)
Amherst Rd. W13 6C **78**
Amhurst Gdns. TW7: Isle 2A **114**
Amhurst Pde. *N16* *7F 49*
(off Amhurst Pk.)
Amhurst Pk. N16 7D **48**
Amhurst Pas. E8 4G **67**
Amhurst Rd. E8 5H **67**
N16 4F **67**
Amhurst Ter. E8 4G **67**
Amhurst Wlk. SE28 1A **108**
Amias Ho. *EC1* *3C 8*
(off Central St.)
Amida Leisure Cen. 5B **158**
Amidas Gdns. RM8: Dag 4B **72**
Amiel St. E1 4J **85**
Amies St. SW11 3D **118**
Amigo Ho. *SE1* *1K 19*
(off Morley St.)
Amina Way SE16 3G **103**
Amis Av. KT19: Ewe 6H **163**
Amity Gro. SW20 1D **152**
Amity Rd. E15 7H **69**
Ammanford Grn. NW9 6A **44**
Ammonite Ho. E15 7H **69**
Amner Rd. SW11 6E **118**
Amor Rd. W6 3E **98**
Amory Ho. *N1* *1K 83*
(off Barnsbury Est.)
Amott Rd. SE15 3G **121**
Amoy Pl. E14 7C **86**
(not continuous)
Ampere Way CR0: Wadd 7J **155**
Ampleforth Rd. SE2 2B **108**
Ampthill Est. NW1 1B **6** (2G **83**)
Ampthill Sq. NW1 1B **6** (2G **83**)
Ampton Pl. WC1 2G **7** (3K **83**)
Ampton St. WC1 2G **7** (3K **83**)
Amroth Cl. SE23 1H **139**
Amroth Grn. NW9 6A **44**
Amstel Ct. *SE15* *7F 103*
(off Garnies Cl.)
Amsterdam Rd. E14 3E **104**
Amundsen Ct. *E14* *5C 104*
(off Napier Av.)
Amunsden Ho. *NW10* *7K 61*
(off Stonebridge Pk.)
Amwell Cl. EN2: Enf 5J **23**
Amwell Ct. Est. N4 2C **66**
Amwell St. EC1 1J **7** (3A **84**)
Amyand Cotts. TW1: Twick 6B **114**
Amyand La. TW1: Twick 7B **114**
Amyand Pk. Gdns. TW1: Twick 7B **114**
Amyand Pk. Rd. TW1: Twick 7A **114**
Amy Cl. SM6: Wall 7J **167**
Amy Johnson Ct. HA8: Edg 2H **43**
Amyruth Rd. SE4 5C **122**
Amy Warne Cl. E6 4C **88**
Anatola Rd. N19 2G **65**
Ancaster Cres. KT3: N Mald 6C **152**
Ancaster M. BR3: Beck 3K **157**
Ancaster Rd. BR3: Beck 3K **157**
Ancaster St. SE18 7J **107**
Anchor SW18 4K **117**
Anchorage Cl. SW19 5J **135**
Anchorage Ho. *E14* *7F 87*
(off Clove Cres.)
Anchorage Point *E14* *2B 104*
(off Cuba St.)
Anchorage Point Ind. Est.
SE7 3A **106**
Anchor & Hope La. SE7 3K **105**
Anchor Brewhouse
SE1 5J **15** (1F **103**)
Anchor Bus. Cen. CR0: Bedd 3J **167**
Anchor Cl. IG11: Bark 3B **90**
Anchor Ct. EN1: Enf 5K **23**
SW1 *4C 18*
(off Vauxhall Bri. Rd.)
Anchor Ho. *E16* *5H 87*
(off Barking Rd.)
E16 *6A 88*
(off Prince Regent La.)
EC1 *3C 8*
(off Old St.)
Anchor M. SW12 6F **119**
Anchor Retail Pk. E1 4J **85**
Anchor Rd. E12 2B **70**
Anchor St. SE16 4H **103**
Anchor Ter. E1 4J **85**
Anchor Wharf *E3* *5D 86*
(off Yeo St.)
Anchor Yd. EC1 3D **8** (4C **84**)
Ancill Cl. W6 6G **99**
Ancona Rd. NW10 2C **80**
SE18 5H **107**
Andace Pk. Gdns. BR1: Brom 2A **160**
Andalus Rd. SW9 3J **119**
Andaman Ho. *E1* *5A 86*
(off Duckett St.)
Ander Cl. HA0: Wemb 4D **60**
Anderson Cl. N21 5E **22**
SM3: Sutt 1J **165**
W3 6K **79**
Anderson Ct. NW2 1E **62**
Anderson Dr. TW15: Ashf 4E **128**
Anderson Hgts. SW16 2K **155**
Anderson Ho. *E14* *7E 86*
(off Woolmore St.)
IG11: Bark 1H **89**
SW17 5B **136**
W12 *6D 80*
(off Du Cane Rd.)
Anderson Pl. TW3: Houn 4F **113**
Anderson Rd. E9 6K **67**
IG8: Wfd G 3B **52**
Anderson Sq. *N1* *1B 84*
(off Gaskin St.)
Anderson St. SW3 5E **16** (5D **100**)
Anderson Way DA17: Belv 2H **109**
Anderton Cl. SE5 3D **120**
Anderton Ct. N22 2H **47**
Andorra Ct. BR1: Brom 1A **160**
Andover Av. E16 6B **88**
Andover Cl. TW14: Felt 1H **129**
UB6: G'frd 4F **77**
Andover Ct. TW19: Stanw 7A **110**
Andover Pl. NW6 2K **81**
Andover Rd. BR6: Orp 1H **173**
N7 2K **65**
TW2: Twick 1H **131**
Andoversford Ct. *SE15* *6E 102*
(off Bibury Cl.)
Andreck Ct. *BR3: Beck* *2E 158*
(off Crescent Rd.)
Andre St. E8 5G **67**
Andrew Borde St. WC2 7D **6** (6H **83**)
Andrew Cl. DA1: Cray 5K **127**
Andrew Ct. SE23 2K **139**
Andrewes Gdns. E6 6C **88**
Andrewes Highwalk EC2 6D **8**
Andrewes Ho. EC2 6D **8**
SM1: Sutt 4J **165**
Andrew Pl. SW8 7H **101**
Andrew Reed Ho. *SW18* *7G 117*
(off Linstead Way)
Andrews Cl. HA1: Harr 7H **41**
IG9: Buck H 2F **37**
KT4: Wor Pk 2F **165**
Andrews Crosse WC2 1J **13**
Andrews Ho. CR2: S Croy 6C **168**
NW3 *7D 64*
(off Fellows Rd.)
Andrews Pl. DA2: Bexl 2K **145**
SE9 6F **125**
Andrew's Rd. E8 1H **85**
Andrew St. E14 6E **86**
Andrews Wlk. SE17 6B **102**
Andringham Lodge *BR1: Brom* *1K 159*
(off Palace Gro.)
Andrula Ct. N22 1B **48**
Andwell Cl. SE2 2B **108**
ANERLEY 2H **157**
Anerley Gro. SE19 7F **139**
Anerley Hill SE19 6F **139**
Anerley Pk. SE20 7G **139**
Anerley Pk. Rd. SE20 7H **139**
Anerley Rd. SE19 7G **139**
SE20 7G **139**
Anerley Sta. Rd. SE20 1H **157**
Anerley Va. SE19 7F **139**
Aneurin Bevan Ct. NW2 2D **62**
Aneurin Bevan Ho. N11 7C **32**
Anfield Cl. SW12 7G **119**
ANGEL 2A **84**
Angela Davies Ind. Est. SE24 4B **120**
Angel All. E1 7K **9**
Angel Cen., The N1 1K **7**
Angel Cl. N18 5A **34**
Angel Cnr. Pde. N18 4B **34**
Angel Ct. EC2 7F **9** (6D **84**)
SW1 5B **12** (1G **101**)
ANGEL EDMONTON JUNC. 5B **34**
Angelfield TW3: Houn 4F **113**
Angel Ga. EC1 1B **8** (3B **84**)
(not continuous)
Angel Hill SM1: Sutt 3K **165**
(not continuous)
Angel Hill Dr. SM1: Sutt 3K **165**
Angelica Cl. UB7: Yiew 6A **74**
Angelica Dr. E6 5E **88**
Angelica Gdns. CR0: Croy 1K **169**
Angelina Ho. *SE15* *1G 121*
(off Goldsmith Rd.)
Angelis Apartments *N1* *1B 8*
(off Graham St.)
Angel La. E15 6F **69**
UB3: Hayes 5F **75**
Angell Pk. Gdns. SW9 3A **120**
Angell Rd. SW9 3A **120**
ANGELL TOWN 1A **120**
Angell Town Est. SW9 2A **120**
Angel M. E1 7H **85**
N1 2A **84**
SW15 7C **116**
Angel Pas. EC4 3E **14** (7D **84**)
Angel Pl. N18 4B **34**
SE1 6E **14** (2D **102**)
Angel Rd. HA1: Harr 6J **41**
KT7: T Ditt 7A **150**
N18 5B **34**
Angel Rd. Works N18 5D **34**
Angel Sq. EC1 2B **84**
Angel St. EC1 7C **8** (6C **84**)
Angel Wlk. W6 4E **98**
Angel Way RM1: Rom 5K **55**
Angel Yd. N6 1E **64**
Angerstein Bus. Pk. SE10 4J **105**
Angerstein La. SE3 1H **123**
Anglebury *W2* *6J 81*
(off Talbot Rd.)
Angle Cl. UB10: Hil 1C **74**
Angle Grn. RM8: Dag 1C **72**
Anglers, The *KT1: King T* *3D 150*
(off High St.)
Anglers Cl. TW10: Ham 4C **132**
Angler's La. NW5 6F **65**
Anglers Reach KT6: Surb 5D **150**
Anglesea Av. SE18 4F **107**
Anglesea Ho. *KT1: King T* *4D 150*
(off Anglesea Rd.)
Anglesea M. SE18 4F **107**
Anglesea Rd. KT1: King T 4D **150**
SE18 4F **107**
Anglesea Ter. W6 3D **98**
Anglesey Cl. TW15: Ashf 3C **128**
Anglesey Ct. W7 4K **77**
Anglesey Ct. Rd. SM5: Cars 6E **166**
Anglesey Gdns. SM5: Cars 6E **166**
Anglesey Ho. *E14* *6C 86*
(off Lindfield St.)
Anglesey Rd. EN3: Pond E 4C **24**
Anglesmede Cres. HA5: Pinn 3E **40**
Anglesmede Way HA5: Pinn 3E **40**
Angles Rd. SW16 4J **137**
Anglia Cl. N17 7C **34**
Anglia Ct. *RM8: Dag* *1D 72*
(off Spring Cl.)
Anglia Ho. *E14* *6A 86*
(off Salmon La.)
Anglian Ind. Est. IG11: Bark 4K **89**
Anglian Rd. E11 3F **69**
Anglia Wlk. *E6* *1E 88*
(off Napier Rd.)
Anglo Rd. E3 2B **86**
Angrave Ct. *E8* *1F 85*
(off Scriven St.)
Angrave Pas. E8 1F **85**
Angus Cl. KT9: Chess 5G **163**
Angus Dr. HA4: Ruis 4A **58**
Angus Gdns. NW9 1K **43**
Angus Ho. SW2 7H **119**
Angus Rd. E13 3A **88**
Angus St. SE14 7A **104**
Anhalt Rd. SW11 7C **100**
Ankerdine Cres. SE18 7F **107**
Anlaby Rd. TW11: Tedd 5J **131**
Anley Rd. W14 2F **99**
Anmersh Gro. HA7: Stan 1D **42**
Annabel Cl. E14 6D **86**
Anna Cl. E8 1F **85**
Annandale Gro. UB10: Ick 3E **56**
Annandale Rd. CR0: Croy 2G **169**
DA15: Sidc 7J **125**
SE10 6H **105**
W4 5A **98**
Anna Neagle Cl. E7 4J **69**
Annan Way RM1: Rom 1K **55**
Anne Boleyn Ct. SE9 6G **125**
Anne Boleyn's Wlk. KT2: King T 5E **132**
SM3: Cheam 7F **165**
Anne Case M. KT3: N Mald 3K **151**
Anne Compton M. SE12 7H **123**
Anne Goodman Ho. *E1* *6J 85*
(off Jubilee St.)
Anne of Cleeves Ct. SE9 6H **125**
Annesley Av. NW9 3K **43**
Annesley Cl. NW10 3A **62**
Annesley Dr. CR0: Croy 3B **170**
Annesley Ho. SW9 1A **120**
Annesley Rd. SE3 1K **123**
Annesley Wlk. N19 2G **65**
Anne St. E13 4J **87**
Anne Sutherland Ho. BR3: Beck 7A **140**
Annett Cl. TW17: Shep 4G **147**
Annette Cl. HA3: W'stone 2J **41**
Annette Cres. N1 7C **66**
Annette Rd. N7 3K **65**
(not continuous)
Annett Rd. KT12: Walt T 7J **147**
Anne Way KT8: W Mole 4F **149**
Annie Besant Cl. E3 1B **86**
Annie Taylor Ho. *E12* *4E 70*
(off Walton Rd.)
Anning St. EC2 3H **9** (4E **84**)
Annington Rd. N2 3D **46**

Archway M.—Arthur Ct.

Archway M. *SW15* 4G **117**
(off Putney Bri. Rd.)
Archway Rd. N6 6E **46**
N19 6E **46**
Archway St. SW13 3A **116**
Arcola St. E8 5F **67**
Arcola Theatre 4F 67
Arcon Dr. UB5: Yead 4C **76**
Arcon Ter. N9 7B **24**
Arctic St. NW5 5F **65**
Arcus Rd. BR1: Brom 6G **141**
Ardbeg Rd. SE24 5D **120**
Arden Cl. HA1: Harr 3H **59**
SE28 6D **90**
Arden Ct. Gdns. N2 6B **46**
Arden Cres. E14 4C **104**
RM9: Dag 7C **72**
Arden Est. N1 2E **84**
Arden Grange N12 4F **31**
Arden Gro. BR6: Farnb 4F **173**
Arden Ho. N1 1G **9**
SE11 4G **19**
SW9 2J **119**
(off Grantham Rd.)
Arden M. E17 5D **50**
Arden Mhor HA5: Eastc 4K **39**
Arden Rd. N3 3H **45**
W13 7C **78**
Ardent Cl. SE25 3E **156**
Ardent Ho. *E3* 2A **86**
(off Roman Rd.)
Ardfern Av. SW16 3A **156**
Ardfillan Rd. SE6 1F **141**
Ardgowan Rd. SE6 7G **123**
Ardilaun Rd. N5 4C **66**
Ardingly Cl. CR0: Croy 3K **169**
Ardleigh Gdns. SM3: Sutt 7J **153**
Ardleigh Ho. IG11: Bark 1G **89**
Ardleigh M. IG1: Ilf 3F **71**
Ardleigh Rd. E17 1B **50**
N1 6E **66**
Ardleigh Ter. E17 1B **50**
Ardley Cl. HA4: Ruis 7E **38**
NW10 3A **62**
SE6 3A **140**
Ardlui Rd. SE27 2C **138**
Ardmay Gdns. KT6: Surb 5E **150**
Ardmere Rd. SE13 6F **123**
Ardmore La. IG9: Buck H 1E **36**
Ardmore Pl. IG9: Buck H 1E **36**
Ardoch Rd. SE6 2F **141**
Ardra Rd. N9 3E **34**
Ardrossan Gdns. KT4: Wor Pk 3C **164**
Ardshiel Cl. SW15 3F **117**
Ardwell Av. IG6: Ilf 5G **53**
Ardwell Rd. SW2 2J **137**
Ardwick Rd. NW2 4J **63**
Arena, The EN3: Enf L 1G **25**
Arena Bus. Cen. N4 6C **48**
Arena Ind. Est. N4 6B **48**
Ares Ct. *E14* 4C **104**
(off Homer Dr.)
Arethusa Ho. *E14* 4C **104**
(off Cahir St.)
Argali Ho. *DA18: Erith* 3E **108**
(off Kale Rd.)
Argall Av. E10 7K **49**
Argall Way E10 1K **67**
Argenta Way HA9: Wemb 6G **61**
NW10 7H **61**
Argent Cen., The UB3: Hayes 2J **93**
Argent Ct. KT6: Chess 3G **163**
Argon M. SW6 7J **99**
Argon Rd. N18 5D **34**
Argos Ct. *SW9* 1A **120**
(off Caldwell St.)
Argos Ho. *E2* 2H **85**
(off Old Bethnal Grn. Rd.)
Argosy Ho. SE8 4A **104**
Argosy La. TW19: Stanw 7A **110**
Argus Cl. RM7: Mawney 1H **55**
Argus Way UB5: N'olt 3C **76**
Argyle Av. TW3: Houn 6E **112**
(not continuous)
Argyle Cl. W13 4A **78**
Argyle Ho. E14 3E **104**
Argyle Pas. N17 1F **49**
Argyle Pl. W6 4D **98**
Argyle Rd. E1 4K **85**
E15 4G **69**
E16 6K **87**
EN5: Barn 4A **20**
HA2: Harr 6F **41**
IG1: Ilf 2E **70**
N12 5E **30**
N17 1G **49**
N18 4B **34**
TW3: Houn 5F **113**
UB6: G'frd 3K **77**
W13 5A **78**
Argyle Sq. WC1 1F **7** (3J **83**)
Argyle St. WC1 1E **6** (3J **83**)
Argyle Wlk. WC1 3J **83**
Argyle Way SE16 5G **103**
Argyll Av. UB1: S'hall 1F **95**
Argyll Cl. SW9 3K **119**
Argyll Gdns. HA8: Edg 2H **43**
Argyll Mans. SW3 7B **16** (6B **100**)
W14 4G **99**
(off Hammersmith Rd.)
Argyll Rd. SE18 3G **107**
W8 2J **99**
Argyll St. W1 1A **12** (6G **83**)
Arica Ho. *SE16* 3H **103**
(off Slippers Pl.)
Arica Rd. SE4 4A **122**
Ariel Ct. SE11 4K **19** (4B **102**)
Ariel Rd. NW6 6J **63**
Ariel Way TW4: Houn 3K **111**
W12 1E **98**
Aristotle Rd. SW4 3H **119**
Ark, The *W6* 5F **99**
(off Talgarth Rd.)
Arkell Gro. SE19 7B **138**
Arkindale Rd. SE6 3E **140**
Arklay Cl. UB8: Hil 4B **74**
Arkley Cres. E17 5B **50**
Arkley Rd. E17 5B **50**
Arklow Ho. SE17 6D **102**
Arklow M. KT6: Surb 2E **162**
Arklow Rd. SE14 6B **104**
Arklow Rd. Trad. Est. SE8 6A **104**
Arkwright Ho. *SW2* 7J **119**
(off Streatham Pl.)
Arkwright Rd. CR2: Sand 7F **169**
NW3 5A **64**
Arlesey Cl. SW15 5G **117**
Arlesford Rd. SW9 3J **119**
Arlingford Rd. SW2 5A **120**
Arlington N12 3D **30**
Arlington Av. N1 1C **84**
(not continuous)
Arlington Cl. DA15: Sidc 7J **125**
SE13 5F **123**
SM1: Sutt 2J **165**
TW1: Twick 6C **114**
Arlington Ct. UB3: Harl 5G **93**
W3 2H **97**
(off Mill Hill Rd.)
Arlington Dr. HA4: Ruis 6F **39**
SM5: Cars 2D **166**
Arlington Gdns. IG1: Ilf 1E **70**
W4 5J **97**
Arlington Grn. NW7 7A **30**
Arlington Ho. *EC1* 1K **7**
(off Arlington Way)
SE8 6B **104**
(off Evelyn St.)
SW1 4A **12** (1G **101**)
TW9: Kew 7H **97**
W12 1D **98**
(off Tunis Rd.)
Arlington Lodge SW2 4K **119**
Arlington M. TW1: Twick 6B **114**
Arlington Pk. Mans. *W4* 5J **97**
(off Sutton La. Nth.)
Arlington Pas. TW11: Tedd 4K **131**
Arlington Pl. SE10 7E **104**
Arlington Rd. IG8: Wfd G 1J **51**
KT6: Surb 6D **150**
N14 2A **32**
NW1 1F **83**
TW1: Twick 6C **114**
TW10: Ham 2D **132**
TW11: Tedd 4K **131**
TW15: Ashf 5B **128**
W13 6B **78**
Arlington Sq. N1 1C **84**
Arlington St. SW1 4A **12** (1G **101**)
Arlington Way EC1 1K **7** (3A **84**)
Arliss Ho. HA1: Harr 5K **41**
Arliss Way UB5: N'olt 1A **76**
Arlow Rd. N21 1F **33**
Armada Ct. SE8 6C **104**
Armadale Cl. N17 4H **49**
Armadale Rd. SW6 7J **99**
TW14: Felt 5J **111**
Armada St. *SE8* 6C **104**
(off McMillan St.)
Armada Way E6 5F **89**
(Gallions Reach Shop. Pk.)
E6 7F **89**
(Woolwich Mnr. Way)
Armagh Rd. E3 1B **86**
Armfield Cl. KT8: W Mole 5D **148**
Armfield Cres. CR4: Mitc 2D **154**
Armfield Rd. EN2: Enf 1J **23**
Arminger Rd. W12 1D **98**
Armistice Gdns. SE25 3G **157**
Armitage Rd. NW11 1G **63**
SE10 5H **105**
Armour Cl. N7 6K **65**
Armoury Rd. SE8 2D **122**
Armoury Way SW18 5J **117**
Armsby Ho. *E1* 5J **85**
(off Stepney Way)
Armstead Wlk. RM10: Dag 7G **73**
Armstrong Av. IG8: Wfd G 6B **36**
Armstrong Cl. BR1: Brom 3C **160**
E6 6D **88**
HA5: Eastc 6J **39**
KT12: Walt T 6J **147**
RM8: Dag 7D **54**
Armstrong Cres. EN4: Cockf 3G **21**
Armstrong Rd. SE18 3G **107**
SW7 2A **16** (3B **100**)
TW13: Hanw 5C **130**
W3 1B **98**
Armstrong Way UB2: S'hall 2F **95**
Armytage Rd. TW5: Hest 7B **94**
Arnal Cres. SW18 7G **117**
Arncliffe NW6 2K **81**
Arncliffe Cl. N11 6K **31**
Arncroft Ct. IG11: Bark 3B **90**
Arndale Wlk. SW18 5K **117**
Arne Gro. BR6: Orp 3K **173**
Arne Ho. SE11 5G **19**
Arne St. WC2 1F **13** (6J **83**)
Arnett Sq. E4 6G **35**
Arne Wlk. SE3 4H **123**
Arneways Av. RM6: Chad H 3D **54**
Arneway St. SW1 2D **18** (3H **101**)
Arnewood Cl. SW15 1C **134**
Arneys La. CR4: Mitc 6E **154**
Arngask Rd. SE6 7F **123**
Arnhem Pl. E14 3C **104**
Arnhem Way SE22 5E **120**
Arnhem Wharf E14 3B **104**
Arnison Rd. KT8: E Mos 4H **149**
Arnold Bennett Way N8 3A **48**
Arnold Cir. E2 2J **9** (3F **85**)
Arnold Cl. HA3: Kent 7F **43**
Arnold Ct. N22 7D **32**
Arnold Cres. TW7: Isle 5H **113**
Arnold Dr. KT9: Chess 6D **162**
Arnold Est. SE1 7K **15** (2F **103**)
(not continuous)
Arnold Gdns. N13 5G **33**
Arnold Ho. *SE3* 7A **106**
(off Shooters Hill Rd.)
SE17 5B **102**
(off Doddington Gro.)
Arnold Mans. *W14* 6H **99**
(off Queen's Club Gdns.)
Arnold Rd. E3 3C **86**
N15 3F **49**
RM9: Dag 7F **73**
SW17 7D **136**
UB5: N'olt 6C **58**
Arnold Ter. HA7: Stan 5E **26**
Arnos Gro. N14 4C **32**
Arnos Gro. Ct.
N11 5B **32**
(off Palmer's Rd.)
Arnos Rd. N11 5B **32**
Arnos Swimming Pool 5C 32
Arnot Ho. *SE5* 7C **102**
(off Comber Gro.)
Arnott Cl. SE28 1C **108**
W4 4K **97**
Arnould Av. SE5 4D **120**
Arnsberg Way DA6: Bex 4F **127**
DA7: Bex 4F **127**
Arnside Gdns. HA9: Wemb 1D **60**
Arnside Rd. DA7: Bex 1G **127**
Arnside St. SE17 6D **102**
Arnulf St. SE6 4D **140**
Arnulls Rd. SW16 6B **138**
Arodene Rd. SW2 6K **119**
Arosa Rd. TW1: Twick 6D **114**
(not continuous)
Arpley Sq. *SE20* 7J **139**
(off High St.)
Arragon Gdns. BR4: W W'ck 3D **170**
SW16 7J **137**
Arragon Rd. E6 1B **88**
SW18 1J **135**
TW1: Twick 7A **114**
Arran Cl. DA8: Erith 6K **109**
SM6: Wall 4F **167**
Arran Ct. NW9 2B **44**
NW10 3K **61**
Arran Dr. E12 1B **70**
Arran Ho. *E14* 1E **104**
(off Raleana Rd.)
Arran M. W5 1F **97**
Arran Rd. SE6 2D **140**
Arran Wlk. N1 7C **66**
Arras Av. SM4: Mord 5A **154**
Arrol Ho. SE1 3C **102**
Arrol Rd. BR3: Beck 3J **157**
Arrow Ct. *SW5* 4J **99**
(off W. Cromwell Rd.)
Arrowhead Ct. E11 6F **51**
Arrow Rd. E3 3D **86**
Arrowscout Wlk. UB5: N'olt 3C **76**
Arrows Ho. *SE15* 7J **103**
(off Clifton Way)
Arrowsmith Ho.
SE11 5G **19**
Arsenal FC 3B 66
Arsenal Rd. SE9 2D **124**
Arsenal Way SE18 3G **107**
Artemis Ct. *E14* 4C **104**
(off Homer Dr.)
Arterberry Rd. SW20 7E **134**
Artesian Cl. NW10 7K **61**
Artesian Gro. EN5: New Bar 4F **21**
Artesian Rd. W2 6J **81**
Artesian Wlk. E11 3G **69**
Arthingworth St. E15 1G **87**
Arthur Ct. *CR0: Croy* 3E **168**
(off Fairfield Path)
SW11 1E **118**

Arthur Ct.—Ash Gro.

Arthur Ct. *W2* .6K 81
(off Queensway)
W10 .6F 81
(off Silchester Rd.)
Arthur Deakin Ho. *E1* .5K 9
(off Hunton St.)
Arthurdon Rd. SE4 .5C 122
Arthur Gro. SE18 .4G 107
Arthur Henderson Ho.
SW6 .2H 117
(off Fulham Rd.)
Arthur Horsley Wlk. *E7* .5H 69
(off Twr. Hamlets Rd.)
Arthur Rd. E6 .2D 88
KT2: King T .7G 133
KT3: N Mald .5D 152
N7 .4K 65
N9 .2A 34
RM6: Chad H .6C 54
SW19 .5H 135
Arthur St. EC4 .2F 15 (7D 84)
Artichoke Hill E1 .7H 85
Artichoke M. *SE5* .1D 120
(off Artichoke Pl.)
Artichoke Pl. SE5 .1D 120
Artillery Cl. IG2: Ilf .6G 53
Artillery Ho. E15 .6G 69
SE18 .5E 106
(off Connaught M.)
Artillery La. E1 .6H 9 (5E 84)
W12 .6C 80
Artillery Pas. E1 .6J 9
Artillery Pl. HA3: Hrw W .7B 26
SE18 .5D 106
SW1 .2C 18 (3H 101)
Artillery Row SW1 .2C 18 (3G 101)
Artillery Sq. *SE18* .3F 107
(off No 1 St.)
Artington Cl. BR6: Farnb .4G 173
Artisan Cl. E6 .6F 89
Artisan Ct. E8 .6G 67
Artisan M. *NW10* .3F 81
(off Warfield Rd.)
Artisan Quarter *NW10* .3F 81
(off Wellington Rd.)
Artizan St. E1 .7J 9
Arts Theatre .2E 12
(off St Martin's St.)
Arun Ct. SE25 .5G 157
Arundale *KT1: King T* .4D 150
(off Anglesea Rd.)
Arundel Av. SM4: Mord .4H 153
Arundel Bldgs. *SE1* .3E 102
(off Swan Mead)
Arundel Cl. CR0: Wadd .3B 168
DA5: Bexl .6F 127
E15 .4G 69
SW11 .5C 118
TW12: Hamp H .5F 131
Arundel Ct. BR2: Brom .2G 159
HA2: Harr .4E 58
N12 .6H 31
N17 .1G 49
SE16 .5H 103
(off Varcoe Rd.)
SW3 .5D 16
(off Jubilee Pl.)
SW13 .6D 98
(off Arundel Ter.)
Arundel Dr. HA2: Harr .4D 58
IG8: Wfd G .7D 36
Arundel Gdns. HA8: Edg .7E 28
IG3: Ilf .2A 72
N21 .1F 33
W11 .7H 81
Arundel Gt. Ct. WC2 .2H 13 (7K 83)
Arundel Gro. N16 .5E 66
Arundel Ho. *CR0: Croy* .5D 168
(off Heathfield Rd.)
W3 .2H 97
(off Park Rd. Nth.)
Arundel Mans. *SW6* .1H 117
(off Kelvedon Rd.)
Arundel Pl. N1 .6A 66
Arundel Rd. CR0: Croy .6D 156
EN4: Cockf .3H 21
KT1: King T .2H 151
SM2: Cheam .7H 165
TW4: Houn .3A 112
Arundel Sq. N7 .6A 66
Arundel St. WC2 .2H 13 (7K 83)
Arundel Ter.
SW13 .6D 98
Arun Ho. KT2: King T .1D 150
Arvon Rd. N5 .5A 66
(not continuous)
Asa Ct. UB3: Harl .3H 93
Asbridge Ct. *W6* .3D 98
(off Dalling Rd.)
Ascalon Ho. *SW8* .7G 101
(off Thessaly Rd.)
Ascalon St. SW8 .7G 101
Ascham Dr. E4 .7J 35
Ascham End E17 .1A 50
Ascham St. NW5 .5G 65
Aschurch Rd. CR0: Croy .7F 157
Ascot Cl. UB5: N'olt .5E 58
Ascot Ct. DA5: Bexl .7F 127
NW8 .2A 4
Ascot Gdns. UB1: S'hall .4D 76
Ascot Ho. NW1 .1K 5
W9 .4J 81
(off Harrow Rd.)
Ascot Lodge NW6 .1K 81
Ascot Pl. HA7: Stan .5H 27
Ascot Rd. BR5: St M Cry .4K 161
E6 .3D 88
N15 .5D 48
N18 .4B 34
SW17 .6E 136
TW14: Bedf .1C 128
Ascott Av. W5 .2E 96
Ascott Cl. HA5: Eastc .4J 39
Ashanti M. E8 .5J 67
Ashbee Ho. *E2* .3J 85
(off Portman Pl.)
Ashbourne Av. DA7: Bex .7E 108
E18 .4K 51
HA2: Harr .2H 59
N20 .2J 31
NW11 .5H 45
Ashbourne Cl. N12 .4E 30
W5 .5G 79
Ashbourne Ct. E5 .4A 68
N12 .4E 30
(off Ashbourne Cl.)
Ashbourne Gro. NW7 .5E 28
SE22 .4F 121
W4 .5A 98
Ashbourne Pde. NW11 .4H 45
W5 .4F 79
Ashbourne Ri. BR6: Orp .4H 173
Ashbourne Rd. CR4: Mitc .7E 136
W5 .4F 79
Ashbourne Ter. SW19 .7H 135
Ashbourne Way NW11 .4H 45
Ashbridge Rd. E11 .7G 51
Ashbridge St. NW8 .4C 4 (4C 82)
Ashbrook HA8: Edg .6A 28
Ashbrook Rd. N19 .1H 65
RM10: Dag .3H 73
Ashburn Gdns. SW7 .4A 100
Ashburnham Av. HA1: Harr .6K 41
Ashburnham Cl. N2 .3B 46
Ashburnham Ct. BR3: Beck .2E 158
Ashburnham Gdns. HA1: Harr .6K 41
Ashburnham Gro. SE10 .7D 104
Ashburnham Mans. *SW10* .7A 100
(off Ashburnham Rd.)
Ashburnham Pl. SE10 .7D 104
Ashburnham Retreat
SE10 .7D 104
Ashburnham Rd. DA17: Belv .4J 109
NW10 .3E 80
SW10 .7A 100
TW10: Ham .3B 132
Ashburnham Twr. *SW10* .7B 100
(off Worlds End Est.)
Ashburn Pl. SW7 .4A 100
Ashburton Av. CR0: Croy .1H 169
IG3: Ilf .5J 71
Ashburton Cl. CR0: Croy .1G 169
Ashburton Ent. Cen.
SW15 .6E 116
Ashburton Gdns. CR0: Croy .2G 169
Ashburton Gro. N7 .4A 66
Ashburton Ho. *W9* .4H 81
(off Fernhead Rd.)
Ashburton Memorial Homes
CR0: Croy .7H 157
Ashburton Rd. CR0: Croy .2G 169
E16 .6J 87
HA4: Ruis .2J 57
Ashburton Ter. E13 .2J 87
Ashbury Dr. UB10: Ick .3D 56
Ashbury Gdns. RM6: Chad H .5D 54
Ashbury Pl. SW19 .6A 136
Ashbury Rd. SW11 .3D 118
Ashby Av. KT9: Chess .6G 163
Ashby Ct. *NW8* .3B 4
(off Pollitt Dr.)
Ashby Gro. N1 .7C 66
(not continuous)
Ashby Ho. *N1* .7C 66
(off Essex Rd.)
SW9 .2B 120
Ashby M. SE4 .2B 122
SW2 .5J 119
(off Prague Pl.)
Ashby Rd. N15 .5G 49
SE4 .2B 122
Ashby St. EC1 .2B 8 (3B 84)
Ashby Wlk. CR0: Croy .6C 156
Ashby Way UB7: Sip .7C 92
Ashchurch Gro. W12 .3C 98
Ashchurch Pk. Vs. W12 .3C 98
Ashchurch Ter. W12 .3C 98
Ash Cl. BR5: Pet W .5H 161
DA14: Sidc .3B 144
HA7: Stan .6F 27
HA8: Edg .4D 28
KT3: N Mald .2K 151
RM5: Col R .1H 55
SE20 .2J 157
SM5: Cars .2D 166
UB9: Hare .1A 38
Ashcombe Av. KT6: Surb .7D 150
Ashcombe Gdns. HA8: Edg .4B 28
Ashcombe Ho. EN3: Pond E .3E 24
Ashcombe Pk. NW2 .3A 62
Ashcombe Rd. SM5: Cars .6E 166
SW19 .5J 135
Ashcombe Sq. KT3: N Mald .3J 151
Ashcombe St. SW6 .2K 117
Ash Ct. KT19: Ewe .4J 163
SW19 .7G 135
Ash Cft. HA5: H End .6A 26
Ashcroft N14 .2C 32
Ashcroft Av. DA15: Sidc .6A 126
Ashcroft Ct. N20 .2G 31
Ashcroft Cres. DA15: Sidc .6A 126
Ashcroft Ho. *SW8* .1G 119
(off Wadhurst Rd.)
Ashcroft Rd. KT9: Chess .3F 163
Ashcroft Sq. W6 .4E 98
Ashcroft Theatre .3D 168
(in Fairfield Halls)
Ashdale Cl. TW2: Whit .7G 113
TW19: Stanw .2A 128
Ashdale Gro. HA7: Stan .6E 26
Ashdale Ho. N4 .7D 48
Ashdale Rd. SE12 .1K 141
Ashdale Way TW2: Whit .7F 113
Ashdene HA5: Pinn .3A 40
SE15 .7H 103
Ashdene Cl. TW15: Ashf .7E 128
Ashdon Cl. IG8: Wfd G .6E 36
Ashdon Rd. NW10 .1B 80
Ashdown *W13* .5B 78
(off Clivedon Ct.)
Ashdown Cl. BR3: Beck .2D 158
DA5: Bexl .7J 127
Ashdown Ct. SM2: Sutt .6A 166
Ashdown Cres. NW5 .5E 64
Ashdowne Ct. N17 .1G 49
Ashdown Ho. SW1 .2B 18
Ashdown Pl. KT7: T Ditt .7A 150
KT17: Ewe .7B 164
Ashdown Rd. EN3: Enf H .2D 24
KT1: King T .2E 150
UB10: Hil .2C 74
Ashdown Wlk. *E14* .4C 104
(off Copeland Dr.)
RM7: Mawney .1H 55
Ashdown Way SW17 .2E 136
Ashe Ho. TW1: Twick .6D 114
Ashen E6 .6E 88
Ashenden *SE17* .4C 102
(off Deacon Way)
Ashenden Rd. E5 .5A 68
Ashen Gro. SW19 .3J 135
Ashentree Ct. EC4 .1K 13
Asher Loftus Way N11 .6J 31
Asher Way E1 .7G 85
Ashfield Av. TW13: Felt .1K 129
WD23: Bush .1B 26
Ashfield Cl. BR3: Beck .7C 140
TW10: Ham .1E 132
Ashfield Ct. *SW9* .2J 119
(off Clapham Rd.)
Ashfield Ho. *W14* .5H 99
(off W. Cromwell Rd.)
Ashfield La. BR7: Chst .6F 143
(not continuous)
Ashfield Pde. N14 .1C 32
Ashfield Rd. N4 .6C 48
N14 .3B 32
W3 .1B 98
Ashfield St. E1 .5H 85
Ashfield Yd. E1 .5J 85
ASHFORD .4B 128
Ashford Av. N8 .4J 47
TW15: Ashf .6D 128
UB4: Yead .6B 76
Ashford Bus. Complex TW15: Ashf .5E 128
Ashford Cl. E17 .6B 50
TW15: Ashf .4A 128
ASHFORD COMMON .7F 129
Ashford Ct. HA8: Edg .3C 28
NW2 .4F 63
Ashford Cres. EN3: Enf H .2D 24
TW15: Ashf .3A 128
Ashford Ho. SE8 .6B 104
SW9 .4B 120
Ashford Ind. Est. TW15: Ashf .4E 128
Ashford M. N17 .1G 49
Ashford Pas. NW2 .4F 63
Ashford Rd. E6 .7E 70
E18 .2K 51
NW2 .4F 63
TW13: Felt .4F 129
TW15: Ashf .7E 128
TW18: Lale, Staines .7A 128
Ashford Sports Cen. .4A 128
Ashford St. N1 .1G 9 (3E 84)
Ash Gro. BR4: W W'ck .2E 170
E8 .1H 85
(not continuous)
EN1: Enf .7K 23
HA0: Wemb .4A 60
N13 .3H 33
NW2 .4F 63
SE12 .1J 141
SE20 .2J 157

Ash Gro.—Atherstone M.

Ash Gro. TW5: Hest 1B 112
TW14: Felt 1G 129
UB1: S'hall 5E 76
UB3: Hayes 7F 75
UB7: Yiew 7B 74
UB9: Hare 1A 38
W5 2E 96
Ashgrove Ct. W9 5J 81
(off Elmfield Way)
Ashgrove Ho. SW1 5D 18
(off Lindsay Sq.)
Ashgrove Rd. BR1: Brom 6F 141
IG3: Ilf 1K 71
TW15: Ashf 5E 128
Ash Hill Cl. WD23: Bush 1A 26
Ash Hill Dr. HA5: Pinn 3A 40
Ash Ho. E14 2E 104
(off E. Ferry Rd.)
SE1 4F 103
(off Longfield Est.)
W10 4G 81
(off Heather Wlk.)
Ashingdon Cl. E4 3K 35
Ashington Ho. E1 4H 85
(off Barnsley St.)
Ashington Rd. SW6 2H 117
Ashlake Rd. SW16 4J 137
Ashland Pl. W1 5G 5 (5E 82)
Ashlar Pl. SE18 4F 107
Ashleigh Commercial Est.
SE7 3A 106
Ashleigh Ct. N14 7B 22
W5 4D 96
(off Murray Rd.)
Ashleigh Gdns. SM1: Sutt 2K 165
Ashleigh Point SE23 3K 139
Ashleigh Rd. SE20 3H 157
SW14 3A 116
Ashley Av. IG6: Ilf 2F 53
SM4: Mord 5J 153
Ashley Cl. HA5: Pinn 2K 39
NW4 2E 44
Ashley Ct. EN5: New Bar 5F 21
NW4 2E 44
NW9 2B 44
(off Guilfoyle)
SW1 2A 18
(off Morpeth Ter.)
UB5: N'olt 1C 76
Ashley Cres. N22 2A 48
SW11 3E 118
Ashley Dr. TW2: Whit 7F 113
TW7: Isle 6J 95
Ashley Gdns. BR6: Orp 5J 173
HA9: Wemb 2E 60
N13 4H 33
SW1 2B 18 (3G 101)
(not continuous)
TW10: Ham 2D 132
Ashley La. CR0: Wadd 4B 168
NW4 7K 29
Ashley Pl. SW1 2A 18 (3G 101)
(not continuous)
Ashley Rd. CR7: Thor H 4K 155
E4 6H 35
E7 7A 70
EN3: Enf H 2D 24
KT7: T Ditt 6K 149
N17 3G 49
N19 1J 65
SW19 6K 135
TW9: Rich 3E 114
TW12: Hamp 1E 148
Ashley Wlk. NW7 7A 30
Ashling Rd. CR0: Croy 1G 169
Ashlin Rd. E15 4F 69
Ash Lodge TW16: Sun 7H 129
(off Forest Dr.)
Ashlone Rd. SW15 3E 116
Ashlyns Way KT9: Chess 6D 162
Ashmead N14 5B 22
Ashmead Bus. Cen. E16 4F 87
Ashmead Ga. BR1: Brom 1A 160
Ashmead Ho. E9 5A 68
(off Homerton Rd.)
Ashmead M. SE8 2C 122
Ashmead Rd. SE8 2C 122
TW14: Felt 1J 129
Ashmere Av. BR3: Beck 2F 159
Ashmere Cl. SM3: Cheam 5F 165
Ashmere Gro. SW2 4J 119
Ash M. NW5 5G 65
Ashmill St. NW1 5C 4 (5C 82)
Ashmole Pl. SW8 6K 101
(not continuous)
Ashmole St. SW8 6K 101
Ashmore NW1 7H 65
(off Agar Gro.)
Ashmore Cl. SE15 7F 103
Ashmore Ct. N11 6J 31
TW5: Hest 6E 94
Ashmore Gro. DA16: Well 3H 125
Ashmore Ho. W14 3G 99
(off Russell Rd.)
Ashmore Rd. W9 2H 81
Ashmount Est. N19 7H 47
Ashmount Rd. N15 5F 49
N19 7G 47
Ashmount Ter. W5 4D 96
Ashmour Gdns. RM1: Rom 2K 55
Ashneal Gdns. HA1: Harr 3H 59
Ashness Gdns. UB6: G'frd 6B 60
Ashness Rd. SW11 5D 118
Ashpark Ho. E14 6B 86
(off Norbiton Rd.)
Ashridge Cl. HA3: Kent 6C 42
Ashridge Ct. N14 5B 22
UB1: S'hall 6G 77
(off Redcroft Rd.)
Ashridge Cres. SE18 7G 107
Ashridge Gdns. HA5: Pinn 4C 40
N13 5C 32
Ashridge Way SM4: Mord 3H 153
TW16: Sun 6J 129
Ash Rd. BR6: Chels 7K 173
CR0: Croy 2C 170
E15 5G 69
SM3: Sutt 7G 153
TW17: Shep 4C 146
Ash Row BR2: Brom 7E 160
Ashtead Rd. E5 7G 49
Ashton Cl. SM1: Sutt 4J 165
Ashton Ct. E4 3B 36
HA1: Harr 3K 59
Ashton Gdns. RM6: Chad H 6E 54
TW4: Houn 4D 112
Ashton Hgts. SE23 1J 139
Ashton Ho. SW9 7A 102
Ashton Rd. E15 5F 69
Ashton St. E14 7E 86
Ashtree Av. CR4: Mitc 2B 154
Ash Tree Cl. CR0: Croy 6A 158
KT6: Surb 2E 162
Ashtree Cl. BR6: Farnb 4F 173
Ash Tree Ct. TW15: Ashf 5D 128
(off Feltham Hill Rd.)
Ash Tree Dell NW9 5J 43
Ash Tree Ho. SE5 7C 102
(off Pitman St.)
Ash Tree Way CR0: Croy 5K 157
Ashurst Cl. SE20 1H 157
Ashurst Dr. IG2: Ilf 6F 53
IG6: Ilf 5G 53
(Hamilton Av.)
IG6: Ilf 4G 53
(Horns Rd.)
TW17: Shep 5A 146
Ashurst Gdns. SW2 1A 138
Ashurst Rd. EN4: Cockf 5J 21
N12 5H 31
Ashurst Wlk. CR0: Croy 2H 169
Ashvale Rd. SW17 5D 136
Ash Vw. Cl. TW15: Ashf 6A 128
Ashview Gdns. TW15: Ashf 5A 128
Ashville Rd. E11 2F 69
Ash Wlk. HA0: Wemb 4C 60
Ashwater Rd. SE12 1J 141
Ashway Cen., The KT2: King T 1E 150
Ashwell Cl. E6 6C 88
Ashwell Ct. TW15: Ashf 2A 128
Ashwin St. E8 6F 67
Ashwood Av. UB8: Hil 6C 74
Ashwood Gdns. CR0: New Ad 6E 170
UB3: Harl 4H 93
Ashwood Ho. NW4 4E 44
(off Harmony Way)
Ashwood Rd. E4 3A 36
Ashworth Cl. SE5 2D 120
Ashworth Est. CR0: Bedd 1J 167
Ashworth Mans. W9 3K 81
(off Elgin Av.)
Ashworth Rd. W9 3K 81
Aske Ho. N1 1G 9
(not continuous)
Asker Ho. N7 4J 65
Askern Cl. DA6: Bex 4D 126
Aske St. N1 1G 9 (3E 84)
Askew Cres. W12 2B 98
Askew Est. W12 1B 98
(off Uxbridge Rd.)
Askew Rd. W12 2B 98
Askham Ct. W12 1C 98
Askham Rd. W12 1C 98
Askill Dr. SW15 5G 117
Askwith Rd. RM13: Rain 3K 91
Asland Rd. E15 1G 87
Aslett St. SW18 7K 117
Asmara Rd. NW2 5G 63
Asmuns Hill NW11 5J 45
Asmuns Pl. NW11 5H 45
Asolando Dr. SE17 4C 102
Aspect Ct. E14 2E 104
(off Manchester Rd.)
Aspen Cl. N19 2G 65
UB7: Yiew 1B 92
W5 2F 97
Aspen Copse BR1: Brom 2D 160
Aspen Dr. HA0: Wemb 3A 60
Aspen Gdns. CR4: Mitc 5E 154
TW15: Ashf 5E 128
W6 5D 98
Aspen Grn. DA18: Erith 3F 109
Aspen Gro. HA5: Eastc 3H 39
Aspen Ho. DA15: Sidc 3A 144
SE15 6J 103
(off Sharratt St.)
Aspen La. UB5: N'olt 3C 76
Aspenlea Rd. W6 6F 99
Aspen Lodge W8 3K 99
(off Abbots Wlk.)
Aspen Way E14 7D 86
TW13: Felt 3K 129
Aspern Gro. NW3 5C 64
Aspinall Rd. SE4 3K 121
(not continuous)
Aspinden Rd. SE16 4H 103
Aspire Training Cen. 2G 27
Aspley Rd. SW18 5K 117
Asplins Rd. N17 1G 49
Asprey M. BR3: Beck 5B 158
Asprey Pl. BR1: Brom 2C 160
Asquith Cl. RM8: Dag 1C 72
Assam St. E1 6G 85
(off White Chu. La.)
Assata M. N1 6B 66
Assembly Pas. E1 5J 85
Assembly Wlk. SM5: Cars 7C 154
Ass Ho. La. HA3: Hrw W 4A 26
Association Gallery, The 3G 9
(off Leonard St.)
Astall Cl. HA3: Hrw W 1J 41
Astbury Bus. Pk. SE15 1J 121
Astbury Ho. SE11 2J 19
Astbury Rd. SE15 1J 121
Astell St. SW3 5D 16 (5C 100)
Aste St. E14 2E 104
Astey's Row N1 7C 66
Asthall Gdns. IG6: Ilf 4G 53
Astins Ho. E17 4D 50
Astleham Rd. TW17: Shep 3A 146
Astle St. SW11 2E 118
Astley Av. NW2 5E 62
Astley Ho. SE1 5F 103
(off Rowcross St.)
SW13 6D 98
(off Wyatt Dr.)
W2 5J 81
(off Alfred Rd.)
Aston Av. HA3: Kent 7C 42
Aston Cl. DA14: Sidc 3A 144
Aston Ct. IG8: Wfd G 6D 36
Aston Grn. TW4: Cran 2A 112
Aston Ho. SW8 1H 119
W11 7H 81
(off Westbourne Gro.)
Aston M. RM6: Chad H 7C 54
Aston Pl. SW16 6B 138
Aston Rd. SW20 2E 152
W5 6D 78
Aston St. E14 5A 86
Aston Ter. SW12 6F 119
Astonville St. SW18 1J 135
Astor Av. RM7: Rom 6J 55
Astor Cl. KT2: King T 6H 133
Astor Ct. E16 6A 88
(off Ripley Rd.)
SW6 7A 100
(off Maynard Cl.)
Astoria, The 7D 6
(off Falconberg M.)
Astoria Ct. E8 7F 67
(off Queensbridge Rd.)
Astoria Mans. SW16 3J 137
Astoria Wlk. SW9 3A 120
Astra Ho. SE14 6B 104
(off Arklow Rd.)
Astrid Ho. TW13: Felt 2A 130
Astrop M. W6 3E 98
Astrop Ter. W6 2E 98
Astwood M. SW7 4A 100
Asylum Rd. SE15 7H 103
Atalanta St. SW6 7F 99
Atbara Rd. TW11: Tedd 6B 132
Atcham Rd. TW3: Houn 4G 113
Atcost Rd. IG11: Bark 5A 90
Atcraft Cen. HA0: Wemb 1E 78
Atheldene Rd. SW18 1K 135
Athelney St. SE6 3C 140
Athelstane Gro. E3 2B 86
Athelstane M. N4 1A 66
Athelstan Gdns. NW6 7G 63
Athelstan Ho. KT1: King T 4F 151
(off Athelstan Rd.)
Athelstan Rd. KT1: King T 4F 151
Athelstone Rd. HA3: W'stone 2H 41
Athena Cl. HA2: Harr 2H 59
KT1: King T 3F 151
Athenaeum Ct. N5 4C 66
Athenaeum Pl. N10 3F 47
Athenaeum Rd. N20 1F 31
Athena Pl. HA6: Nwood 1H 39
Athene Pl. EC4 7K 7
(off St Andrew St.)
Athenia Ho. E14 6F 87
(off Blair St.)
Athenlay Rd. SE15 5K 121
Athens Gdns. W9 4J 81
(off Harrow Rd.)
Atherden Rd. E5 4J 67
Atherfold Rd. SW9 3J 119
Atherley Way TW4: Houn 7D 112
Atherstone Ct. W2 5K 81
(off Delamere Ter.)
Atherstone M. SW7 4A 100

Atherton Dr. SW19 4F **135**
Atherton Hgts. HA0: Wemb 7C **60**
Atherton Leisure Cen. 6H **69**
Atherton M. E7 6H **69**
Atherton Pl. HA2: Harr 3H **41**
UB1: S'hall 7E **76**
Atherton Rd. E7 6H **69**
IG5: Ilf 2C **52**
SW13 7C **98**
Atherton St. SW11 2C **118**
Athlone Cl. E5 5H **67**
Athlone Ct. E17 3F **51**
Athlone Ho. *E1* *6J* ***85***
(off Sidney St.)
Athlone Rd. SW2 7K **119**
Athlone St. NW5 6E **64**
Athlon Ind. Est. HA0: Wemb 1D **78**
Athlon Rd. HA0: Wemb 2D **78**
Athol Cl. HA5: Pinn 1K **39**
Athole Gdns. EN1: Enf 5K **23**
Athol Gdns. HA5: Pinn 1K **39**
Atholl Ho. *W9* *3A* ***82***
(off Maida Va.)
Atholl Rd. IG3: Ilf 7A **54**
Athol Rd. DA8: Erith 5J **109**
Athol Sq. E14 6E **86**
Athol Way UB10: Hil 3C **74**
Atkin Bldg. *WC1* *5H* ***7***
(off Raymond Bldgs.)
Atkins Dr. BR4: W W'ck 2F **171**
Atkinson Cl. BR6: Chels 5K **173**
Atkinson Ct. *E10* *7D* ***50***
(off Kings Cl.)
Atkinson Ho. *E2* *2G* ***85***
(off Pritchards Rd.)
E13 *4H* ***87***
(off Sutton Rd.)
SE17 *4D* ***102***
(off Catesby St.)
Atkinson Rd. E16 5A **88**
Atkins Rd. E10 6D **50**
SW12 7G **119**
Atlanta Ho. *SE16* *3A* ***104***
(off Brunswick Quay)
Atlantic Ct. *E14* *7F* ***87***
(off Jamestown Way)
Atlantic Ho. *E1* *5A* ***86***
(off Harford St.)
Atlantic Rd. SW9 4A **120**
Atlantic Wharf E1 7K **85**
Atlantis Cl. IG11: Bark 3B **90**
Atlas Bus. Cen. NW2 1D **62**
Atlas Gdns. SE7 4A **106**
Atlas M. E8 6F **67**
N7 6K **65**
Atlas Rd. E13 2J **87**
HA9: Wemb 4J **61**
N11 7K **31**
NW10 3A **80**
Atlas Wharf E9 6C **68**
Atley Rd. E3 1C **86**
Atlip Rd. HA0: Wemb 1E **78**
Atney Rd. SW15 4G **117**
Atrium Apartments *N1* *1D* ***84***
(off Felton St.)
Atterbury Rd. N4 6A **48**
Atterbury St. SW1 4D **18** (4J **101**)
Attewood Av. NW10 3A **62**
Attewood Rd. UB5: N'olt 6C **58**
Attfield Cl. N20 2G **31**
Attfield Ct. *KT1: King T* *2F* ***151***
(off Albert Rd.)
Attilburgh Ho. *SE1* *7J* ***15***
(off Abbey St.)
Attleborough Ct. SE23 2G **139**
Attle Cl. UB10: Hil 2C **74**
Attlee Cl. CR7: Thor H 5C **156**
UB4: Yead 3K **75**
Attlee Rd. SE28 7B **90**
UB4: Yead 3J **75**
Attlee Ter. E17 4D **50**
Attneave St. WC1 2J **7** (3A **84**)
Atwater Cl. SW2 1A **138**
Atwell Cl. E10 6D **50**
Atwell Pl. KT7: T Ditt 7K **149**
Atwell Rd. SE15 2G **121**
Atwood Av. TW9: Kew 2G **115**
Atwood Ho. *W14* *4H* ***99***
(off Beckford Cl.)
Atwood Rd. W6 4D **98**
Atwoods All. TW9: Kew 1G **115**
Aubert Ct. N5 4B **66**
Aubert Pk. N5 4B **66**
Aubert Rd. N5 4B **66**
Aubrey Beardsley Ho. *SW1* *4B* ***18***
(off Vauxhall Bri. Rd.)
Aubrey Mans. *NW1* *5C* ***4***
(off Lisson St.)
Aubrey Moore Point *E15* *2E* ***86***
(off Abbey La.)
Aubrey Pl. NW8 2A **82**
Aubrey Rd. E17 3C **50**
N8 5J **47**
W8 1H **99**
Aubrey Wlk. W8 1H **99**
Auburn Cl. SE14 7A **104**
Aubyn Hill SE27 4C **138**
Aubyn Sq. SW15 5C **116**
Auckland Cl. SE19 1F **157**
Auckland Ct. UB4: Yead 4A **76**
Auckland Gdns. SE19 1E **156**
Auckland Hill SE27 4C **138**
Auckland Ho. *W12* *7D* ***80***
(off White City Est.)
Auckland Ri. SE19 1E **156**
Auckland Rd. E10 3D **68**
IG1: Ilf 1F **71**
KT1: King T 4F **151**
SE19 1F **157**
SW11 4C **118**
Auckland St. SE11 6G **19** (5K **101**)
Audax NW9 2B **44**
Auden Pl. NW1 1E **82**
(not continuous)
SM3: Cheam 4E **164**
Audleigh Pl. IG7: Chig 6K **37**
Audley Cl. N10 7A **32**
SW11 3E **118**
Audley Ct. E18 4H **51**
HA5: Pinn 2A **40**
TW2: Twick 3H **131**
UB5: Yead 3A **76**
Audley Dr. E16 1K **105**
Audley Gdns. IG3: Ilf 2K **71**
Audley Pl. SM2: Sutt 7K **165**
Audley Rd. EN2: Enf 2G **23**
NW4 5C **44**
TW10: Rich 5F **115**
W5 5F **79**
Audley Sq. W1 4H **11** (1E **100**)
Audrey Cl. BR3: Beck 6D **158**
Audrey Gdns. HA0: Wemb 2B **60**
Audrey Rd. IG1: Ilf 3F **71**
Audrey St. E2 2G **85**
Audric Cl. KT2: King T 1G **151**
Augurs La. E13 3K **87**
Augusta Cl. KT8: W Mole 4D **148**
Augusta Rd. TW2: Twick 2G **131**
Augusta St. E14 6D **86**
Augustine Rd. HA3: Hrw W 1F **41**
W14 3F **99**
Augustus Cl. TW8: Bford 7C **96**
W12 2D **98**
Augustus Ct. SW16 2H **137**
TW13: Hanw 4D **130**
Augustus Ho. *NW1* *1A* ***6***
(off Augustus St.)
Augustus La. BR6: Orp 2K **173**
Augustus Rd. SW19 1F **135**
Augustus St. NW1 1K **5** (2F **83**)
Aultone Way SM1: Sutt 2K **165**
SM5: Cars 3D **166**
Aultone Yd. Ind. Est. SM5: Cars 3D **166**
Aulton Pl. SE11 6K **19** (5A **102**)
Aura Ho. TW9: Kew 1H **115**
Aurelia Gdns. CR0: Croy 5K **155**
Aurelia Rd. CR0: Croy 6J **155**
Auriel Av. RM10: Dag 6K **73**
Auriga M. N1 5D **66**
Auriol Cl. KT4: Wor Pk 3A **164**
Auriol Dr. UB6: G'frd 7H **59**
UB10: Hil 6C **56**
Auriol Ho. *W12* *1D* ***98***
(off Ellerslie Rd.)
Auriol Pk. Rd. KT4: Wor Pk 3A **164**
Auriol Rd. W14 4G **99**
Aurora Bldg. *E14* *1E* ***104***
(off Blackwall Way)
Aurora Ho. *E14* *6D* ***86***
(off Kerbey St.)
Austell Gdns. NW7 3F **29**
Austell Hgts. *NW7* *3F* ***29***
(off Austell Gdns.)
Austen Cl. SE28 1B **108**
Austen Ho. *NW6* *3J* ***81***
(off Cambridge Rd.)
Austen Rd. DA8: Erith 7H **109**
HA2: Harr 2F **59**
Austin Av. BR2: Brom 5C **160**
Austin Cl. SE23 7A **122**
TW1: Twick 5C **114**
Austin Ct. E6 1A **88**
EN1: Enf 5K **23**
SE15 *3G* ***121***
(off Philip Wlk.)
Austin Friars EC2 7F **9** (6D **84**)
(not continuous)
Austin Friars Pas. EC2 7F **9**
Austin Friars Sq. EC2 7F **9**
Austin Ho. *SE14* *7B* ***104***
(off Achilles St.)
Austin Rd. SW11 1E **118**
UB3: Hayes 2H **93**
Austin's La. HA4: Ruis 4F **57**
UB10: Ick 3E **56**
Austin St. E2 2J **9** (3F **85**)
Austin Ter. *SE1* *1K* ***19***
(off Morley St.)
Austral Cl. DA15: Sidc 3K **143**
Australian War Memorial *6H* ***11***
(off Duke of Wellington Pl.)
Australia Rd. W12 7D **80**
Austral St. SE11 3K **19** (4B **102**)
Austyn Gdns. KT5: Surb 1H **163**
Austyns Pl. KT17: Ewe 7C **164**
Autumn Cl. EN1: Enf 1B **24**
SW19 6A **136**
Autumn Lodge *CR0: Croy* *4E* ***168***
(off South Pk. Hill Rd.)
Autumn St. E3 1C **86**
Avalon Cl. EN2: Enf 2F **23**
SW20 2G **153**
W13 5A **78**
Avalon Rd. SW6 1K **117**
W13 4A **78**
Avante KT1: King T 3D **150**
Avard Gdns. BR6: Farnb 4G **173**
Avarn Rd. SW17 6D **136**
Avebury Ct. *N1* *1D* ***84***
(off Imber St.)
Avebury Pk. KT6: Surb 7D **150**
Avebury Rd. BR6: Orp 3H **173**
E11 1F **69**
SW19 1H **153**
Avebury St. N1 1D **84**
Aveley Mans. *IG11: Bark* *7F* ***71***
(off Whiting Av.)
Aveley Rd. RM1: Rom 4K **55**
Aveline St. SE11 5H **19** (5A **102**)
Aveling Pk. Rd. E17 2C **50**
Ave Maria La. EC4 1B **14** (6B **84**)
Avenell Mans. N5 4B **66**
Avenell Rd. N5 3B **66**
Avenfield Ho. *W1* *2F* ***11***
(off Park La.)
Avening Rd. SW18 7J **117**
Avening Ter. SW18 7J **117**
Avenons Rd. E13 4J **87**
Avenue, The BR1: Brom 3B **160**
BR2: Kes 4B **172**
BR3: Beck 1D **158**
(not continuous)
BR4: W W'ck 7G **159**
BR5: St P 7B **144**
BR6: Orp 2K **173**
CR0: Croy 3E **168**
DA5: Bexl 7D **126**
E4 6A **36**
E11 6K **51**
EN5: Barn 3B **20**
HA3: Hrw W 1K **41**
HA5: Pinn 6D **40**
HA9: Wemb 1E **60**
IG9: Buck H 2F **37**
KT4: Wor Pk 2B **164**
KT5: Surb 6F **151**
KT17: Ewe 7D **164**
N3 2J **45**
N8 3A **48**
N10 2G **47**
N11 5A **32**
N17 3D **48**
NW6 1F **81**
RM1: Rom 4K **55**
SE10 7F **105**
SM2: Cheam 7G **165**
SM3: Cheam 7E **164**
SM5: Cars 7E **166**
SW4 5E **118**
SW18 7C **118**
TW1: Twick 5B **114**
TW3: Houn 5F **113**
TW5: Cran 7J **93**
TW9: Kew 2F **115**
TW12: Hamp 6D **130**
TW16: Sun 1K **147**
UB10: Ick 4C **56**
W4 3A **98**
W13 6B **78**
Avenue Cl. N14 6B **22**
NW8 1C **82**
TW5: Cran 1K **111**
UB7: W Dray 3A **92**
Avenue Ct. N14 6B **22**
NW2 3H **63**
SW3 *4E* ***16***
(off Draycott Av.)
Avenue Cres. TW5: Cran 1K **111**
W3 2H **97**
Avenue Elmers KT6: Surb 5E **150**
Avenue Gdns. SE25 2G **157**
SW14 3A **116**
TW5: Cran 7K **93**
TW11: Tedd 7K **131**
W3 2H **97**
Avenue Ho. *NW8* *2C* ***82***
(off Allitsen Rd.)
NW10 *2D* ***80***
(off All Souls Av.)
Avenue Ind. Est. E4 6G **35**
Avenue Lodge *NW8* *7B* ***64***
(off Avenue Rd.)
Avenue Mans. *NW3* *5K* ***63***
(off Finchley Rd.)
Avenue M. N10 3F **47**
Avenue Pde. N21 7J **23**
TW16: Sun 3K **147**
Avenue Pk. Rd. SE27 2B **138**
Avenue Rd. BR3: Beck 2K **157**
DA7: Bex 3E **126**
DA8: Erith 7J **109**
DA17: Belv, Erith 4J **109**
E7 4K **69**
HA5: Pinn 3C **40**

Avenue Rd.—Bailey Pl.

Avenue Rd. IG8: Wfd G 6F 37
KT1: King T 3E 150
KT3: N Mald 4A 152
N6 7G 47
N12 4F 31
N14 7B 22
N15 5D 48
NW3 7B 64
NW8 7B 64
NW10 2B 80
RM6: Chad H 7B 54
SE20 1J 157
SE25 2F 157
SM6: Wall 7G 167
SW16 2H 155
SW20 2D 152
TW7: Isle 1K 113
TW8: Bford 5C 96
TW11: Tedd 7A 132
TW12: Hamp 1F 149
TW13: Felt 3H 129
UB1: S'hall 1D 94
W3 2H 97
Avenue Sth. KT5: Surb 7G 151
Avenue Ter. KT3: N Mald 3J 151
Averil Gro. SW16 6B 138
Averill St. W6 6F 99
Avern Gdns. KT8: W Mole 4F 149
Avern Rd. KT8: W Mole 4F 149
Avery Farm Row SW1 4J 17 (4E 100)
Avery Gdns. IG2: Ilf 5D 52
AVERY HILL 6H 125
Avery Hill Rd. SE9 6H 125
Avery Row W1 2J 11 (7F 83)
Avia Pk. TW14: Bedf 1D 128
Aviary Cl. E16 5H 87
Aviemore Cl. BR3: Beck 5B 158
Aviemore Way BR3: Beck 5A 158
Avignon Rd. SE4 3K 121
Avington Ct. *SE1 4E 102*
(off Old Kent Rd.)
Avington Gro. SE20 7J 139
Avion Cres. NW9 1C 44
Avis Sq. E1 6K 85
Avoca Rd. SW17 4E 136
Avocet Cl. SE1 5G 103
Avocet M. SE28 3H 107
Avon Cl. KT4: Wor Pk 2C 164
SM1: Sutt 4A 166
UB4: Yead 4A 76
Avon Ct. E4 1K 35
IG9: Buck H 1E 36
N12 5E 30
SW15 5G 117
UB6: G'frd 4F 77
W9 5J 81
(off Elmfield Way)
Avondale Av. EN4: E Barn 1J 31
KT4: Wor Pk 1B 164
KT10: Hin W 3A 162
N12 5E 30
NW2 3A 62
Avondale Ct. E11 1G 69
E16 5G 87
E18 1K 51
SM2: Sutt 7A 166
(off Brighton Rd.)
Avondale Cres. EN3: Enf H 3F 25
IG4: Ilf 5B 52
Avondale Dr. UB3: Hayes 1J 93
Avondale Gdns. TW4: Houn 5D 112
Avondale Ho. *SE1 5G 103*
(off Avondale Sq.)
Avondale Pk. Gdns. W11 7G 81
Avondale Pk. Rd. W11 7G 81
Avondale Pavement SE1 5G 103
Avondale Ri. SE15 3F 121
Avondale Rd. BR1: Brom 6G 141
CR2: S Croy 6C 168
DA16: Well 2C 126
E16 5G 87
Avondale Rd. E17 7C 50
HA3: W'stone 3K 41
N3 1A 46
N13 2F 33
N15 5B 48
SE9 2C 142
SW14 3A 116
SW19 5K 135
TW15: Ashf 3A 128
Avondale Sq. SE1 5G 103
Avonfield Ct. E17 3F 51
Avon Ho. KT2: King T 1D 150
W8 3J 99
(off Allen St.)
W14 4H 99
(off Kensington Village)
Avonhurst Ho. NW2 7G 63
Avonley Rd. SE14 7J 103
Avon M. HA5: H End 1D 40
Avonmore Gdns. W14 4H 99
Avonmore Pl. W14 4G 99
Avonmore Rd. W14 4G 99
Avonmouth St. SE1 7C 14 (3C 102)
Avon Path CR2: S Croy 6C 168
Avon Pl. SE1 7D 14 (2C 102)
Avon Rd. E17 3F 51
SE4 3C 122
TW16: Sun 7H 129
UB6: G'frd 4E 76
Avonstowe Cl. BR6: Farnb 3G 173
Avon Way E18 3J 51
Avonwick Rd. TW3: Houn 2F 113
Avril Way E4 5K 35
Avro Ho. *SW8 7F 101*
(off Havelock Ter.)
Avro Way SM6: Wall 7J 167
Awlfield Av. N17 1D 48
Awliscombe Rd. DA16: Well 2K 125
Axe St. IG11: Bark 1G 89
(not continuous)
Axholme Av. HA8: Edg 1G 43
Axiom Apartments *BR2: Brom 4K 159*
(off Masons Hill)
Axminster Cres. DA16: Well 1C 126
Axminster Rd. N7 3J 65
Aybrook St. W1 6G 5 (5E 82)
Aycliffe Cl. BR1: Brom 4D 160
Aycliffe Rd. W12 1C 98
Ayerst Ct. E10 7E 50
Aylands Cl. HA9: Wemb 2E 60
Aylesbury Cl. E7 6H 69
Aylesbury Ct. SM1: Sutt 3A 166
Aylesbury Ho. *SE15 6G 103*
(off Friary Est.)
Aylesbury Rd. BR2: Brom 3J 159
SE17 5D 102
Aylesbury St. EC1 4A 8 (4B 84)
NW10 3K 61
Aylesford Av. BR3: Beck 5A 158
Aylesford Ho. *SE1 7F 15*
(off Long La.)
Aylesford St. SW1 5C 18 (5H 101)
Aylesham Cen., The SE15 1G 121
Aylesham Cl. NW7 7H 29
Aylesham Rd. BR6: Orp 7K 161
Ayles Rd. UB4: Yead 3K 75
Aylestone Av. NW6 7F 63
Aylett Rd. SE25 4H 157
TW7: Isle 2J 113
Ayley Cft. EN1: Enf 5B 24
Ayliffe Cl. KT1: King T 2G 151
Aylmer Cl. HA7: Stan 4F 27
Aylmer Ct. N2 5D 46
Aylmer Dr. HA7: Stan 4F 27
Aylmer Ho. SE10 5F 105
Aylmer Pde. N2 5D 46
Aylmer Rd. E11 1H 69
N2 5C 46
RM8: Dag 3E 72
W12 2B 98
Ayloffe Rd. RM9: Dag 6F 73
Aylsham Dr. UB10: Ick 2E 56
Aylton Est. SE16 2J 103
Aylward Rd. SE23 2K 139
SW20 2H 153
Aylward School Sports Cen. 4J 33
Aylwards Ri. HA7: Stan 4F 27
Aylward St. E1 6J 85
(Jamaica St.)
E1 6J 85
(Jubilee St.)
Aylwin Est. SE1 3E 102
Aynhoe Mans. *W14 4F 99*
(off Aynhoe Rd.)
Aynhoe Rd. W14 4F 99
Aynscombe Path SW14 2J 115
Ayr Ct. W3 5G 79
Ayres Cl. E13 3J 87
Ayres Cres. NW10 7K 61
Ayres St. SE1 6D 14 (2C 102)
Ayr Grn. RM1: Rom 1K 55
Ayrsome Rd. N16 3E 66
Ayrton Gould Ho. *E2 3K 85*
(off Roman Rd.)
Ayrton Rd. SW7 1A 16 (3B 100)
Ayr Way RM1: Rom 1K 55
Aysgarth Ct. SM1: Sutt 3K 165
Aysgarth Rd. SE21 7E 120
Ayshford Ho. *E2 3H 85*
(off Viaduct St.)
Ayston Ho. *SE16 4K 103*
(off Plough Way)
Ayton Ho. *SE5 7D 102*
(off Edmund St.)
Aytoun Pl. SW9 2K 119
Aytoun Rd. SW9 2K 119
Azalea Cl. IG1: Ilf 5F 71
W7 1K 95
Azalea Ct. IG8: Wfd G 6B 36
W7 1K 95
Azalea Ho. *SE14 7B 104*
(off Achilles St.)
Azalea Wlk. HA5: Eastc 5K 39
Azania M. NW5 6F 65
Azenby Rd. SE15 2F 121
Azof St. SE10 4G 105
Azov Ho. *E1 4A 86*
(off Commodore St.)
Aztec Ho. IG6: Ilf 1G 53
Azure Ho. *E2 3G 85*
(off Buckfast St.)

B

Baalbec Rd. N5 5B 66
Babbacombe Cl. KT9: Chess 5D 162
Babbacombe Gdns. IG4: Ilf 4C 52
Babbacombe Rd. BR1: Brom 1J 159
Baber Bri. Cvn. Site
TW14: Felt 5A 112
Baber Dr. TW14: Felt 6A 112
Babington Ct. WC1 5G 7
Babington Ho. *SE1 6D 14*
(off Disney St.)
Babington Ri. HA9: Wemb 6G 61
Babington Rd. NW4 4D 44
RM8: Dag 5C 72
SW16 5H 137
Babmaes St. SW1 3C 12 (7H 83)
Bacchus Wlk. *N1 2E 84*
(off Regan Way)
Bache's St. N1 1F 9 (3D 84)
Back All. EC3 1H 15
Bk. Church La. E1 6G 85
Back Hill EC1 4K 7 (4A 84)
Backhouse Pl. SE17 4E 102
Back La. DA5: Bexl 7G 127
HA8: Edg 1J 43
IG9: Buck H 2G 37
N8 5J 47
NW3 4A 64
Back La. RM6: Chad H 7D 54
TW8: Bford 6D 96
TW10: Ham 3C 132
Backley Gdns. SE25 6G 157
Back Passage *EC1 5B 8*
(off Long La.)
Back Rd. DA14: Sidc 4A 144
TW11: Tedd 7J 131
Bacon Gro. SE1 3F 103
Bacon La. HA8: Edg 1G 43
NW9 4H 43
(not continuous)
Bacon's College Sports Cen. 1A 104
Bacons La. N6 1E 64
Bacon St. E1 3K 9 (4F 85)
E2 3K 9 (4F 85)
Bacon Ter. RM8: Dag 5B 72
Bacton NW5 5E 64
Bacton St. E2 3J 85
Baddeley Ho. *KT8: W Mole 5E 148*
(off Down St.)
Baddesley Ho. SE11 5H 19
Baddow Cl. IG8: Wfd G 6F 37
RM10: Dag 1G 91
Baddow Wlk. *N1 1C 84*
(off New Nth. Rd.)
Baden Pl. SE1 6E 14 (2D 102)
Baden Powell Cl. KT6: Surb 2F 163
RM9: Dag 1E 90
Baden Powell Ho. *DA17: Belv 3G 109*
(off Ambrooke Rd.)
SW7 2A 16
Baden Rd. IG1: Ilf 5F 71
N8 4H 47
Badger Cl. IG2: Ilf 6G 53
TW4: Houn 3A 112
TW13: Felt 3K 129
Badger Ct. NW2 3E 62
Badgers Cl. EN2: Enf 3G 23
HA1: Harr 6H 41
TW15: Ashf 5B 128
UB3: Hayes 7G 75
Badgers Copse BR6: Orp 2K 173
KT4: Wor Pk 2B 164
Badgers Cft. N20 7B 20
SE9 3E 142
Badgers Hole CR0: Croy 4K 169
Badgers Wlk. KT3: N Mald 2A 152
Badlis Rd. E17 3C 50
Badma Cl. N9 3D 34
Badminton Cl. HA1: Harr 4J 41
UB5: N'olt 6E 58
Badminton M. E16 1J 105
Badminton Rd. SW12 6E 118
Badric Ct. SW11 2B 118
Badsworth Rd. SE5 1C 120
Baffin Way E14 1E 104
Bagley Cl. UB7: W Dray 2A 92
Bagley's La. SW6 1K 117
Bagleys Spring RM6: Chad H 4E 54
Bagnigge Ho. *WC1 2J 7*
(off Margery St.)
Bagshot Ct. SE18 1E 124
Bagshot Ho. NW1 1K 5
Bagshot Rd. EN1: Enf 7A 24
Bagshot St. SE17 5E 102
Baildon *E2 2J 85*
(off Cyprus St.)
Baildon St. SE8 7B 104
Bailey Cl. E4 4K 35
N11 7C 32
SE28 1J 107
Bailey Cotts. *E14 5A 86*
(off Maroon St.)
Bailey Cres. KT9: Chess 7C 162
Bailey Ho. *SW10 7K 99*
(off Coleridge Gdns.)
Bailey M. SW2 5A 120
W4 6H 97
(off Hervert Gdns.)
Bailey Pl. SE26 6K 139

Baillies Wlk.—Bankside Rd.

Baillies Wlk. W5 2D 96
Bainbridge Cl. TW10: Ham 5E 132
Bainbridge Rd. RM9: Dag 4F 73
Bainbridge St. WC1 7D 6 (6H 83)
Baines Cl. CR2: S Croy 5D 168
Baird Av. UB1: S'hall 7F 77
Baird Cl. E10 1C 68
NW9 6J 43
Baird Gdns. SE19 4E 138
Baird Ho. W12 7D 80
(off White City Est.)
Baird Memorial Cotts. N14 2C 32
(off Balaams La.)
Baird Rd. EN1: Enf 3C 24
Baird St. EC1 3D 8 (4C 84)
Bairny Wood App. IG8: Wfd G 6E 36
Baizdon Rd. SE3 2G 123
Baker Beal Ct. DA7: Bex 3H 127
Baker Ho. W7 1K 95
WC1 4F 7
(off Colonnade)
Baker La. CR4: Mitc 2E 154
Baker Pas. NW10 1A 80
Baker Rd. NW10 1A 80
SE18 7C 106
Bakers Av. E17 6D 50
Bakers Ct. SE25 3E 156
Bakers End SW20 2G 153
Baker's Fld. N7 4J 65
Bakers Gdns. SM5: Cars 2C 166
Bakers Hall Ct. EC3 3G 15
Bakers Hill E5 1J 67
EN5: New Bar 2E 20
Bakers Ho. W5 7D 78
(off Grove, The)
Bakers La. N6 6D 46
Bakers M. BR6: Chels 6K 173
W1 7G 5 (6E 82)
Bakers Pas. NW3 4A 64
(off Heath St.)
Baker's Rents E2 2J 9 (3F 85)
Baker's Row E15 2G 87
EC1 4J 7 (4A 84)
BAKER STREET 5D 82
Baker St. EN1: Enf 3J 23
NW1 4F 5 (4D 82)
W1 5F 5 (4D 82)
Baker's Yd. EC1 4J 7
Bakery Cl. SW9 7K 101
Bakery M. KT6: Surb 1G 163
Bakery Path HA8: Edg 6C 28
(off St Margaret's Rd.)
Bakery Pl. SW11 4D 118
Bakewell Way KT3: N Mald 2A 152
Balaam Ho. SM1: Sutt 4J 165
Balaam Leisure Cen. 4J 87
Balaams La. N14 2C 32
Balaam St. E13 4J 87
Balaclava Rd. KT6: Surb 7C 150
SE1 4F 103
Bala Grn. NW9 6A 44
(off Ruthin Cl.)
Balcaskie Rd. SE9 5D 124
Balchen Rd. SE3 2B 124
Balchier Rd. SE22 6H 121
Balcombe Cl. DA6: Bex 4D 126
Balcombe Ho. NW1 3E 4
(off Taunton Pl.)
Balcombe St. NW1 3E 4 (4D 82)
Balcon Ct. W5 6F 79
Balcorne St. E9 7J 67
Balder Ri. SE12 2K 141
Balderton Flats W1 1H 11
(off Balderton St.)
Balderton St. W1 1H 11 (6E 82)
Baldewyne Ct. N17 1G 49
Baldock St. E3 2D 86
Baldrey Ho. SE10 5H 105
(off Blackwall La.)
Baldry Gdns. SW16 6J 137
Baldwin Cres. SE5 1C 120
Baldwin Gdns. TW3: Houn 1G 113
Baldwin Ho. SW2 1A 138
Baldwins Gdns. EC1 5J 7 (5A 84)
Baldwin St. EC1 2E 8 (3D 84)
Baldwin Ter. N1 2C 84
Baldwyn Gdns. W3 7K 79
Baldwyn's Pk. DA5: Bexl 2K 145
Baldwyn's Rd. DA5: Bexl 2K 145
Balearic Apartments E16 7J 87
(off Western Gateway)
Bale Rd. E1 5A 86
Bales Ter. N9 3A 34
Balfern Gro. W4 5A 98
Balfern St. SW11 2C 118
Balfe St. N1 2J 83
Balfour Av. W7 1K 95
Balfour Bus. Cen. UB2: S'hall 3A 94
Balfour Gro. N20 3J 31
Balfour Ho. W10 5F 81
(off St Charles Sq.)
Balfour M. N9 3B 34
W1 4H 11 (1E 100)
Balfour Pl. SW15 4D 116
W1 3H 11 (7E 82)
Balfour Rd. BR2: Brom 5B 160
HA1: Harr 5H 41
IG1: Ilf 2F 71
N5 4C 66
SE25 5G 157
SM5: Cars 7D 166
SW19 7K 135
TW3: Houn 3F 113
UB2: S'hall 3B 94
W3 5J 79
W13 2A 96
Balfour St. SE17 4D 102
Balfour Ter. N3 2K 45
Balfron Twr. E14 6E 86
Balgonie Rd. E4 1A 36
Balgowan Cl. KT3: N Mald 5A 152
Balgowan Rd. BR3: Beck 3A 158
Balgowan St. SE18 4K 107
BALHAM 1E 136
Balham Continental Mkt.
SW12 1F 137
(off Shipka Rd.)
Balham Gro. SW12 7E 118
Balham High Rd. SW12 3E 136
SW17 3E 136
Balham Hill SW12 7F 119
Balham Leisure Cen. 2F 137
Balham New Rd. SW12 7F 119
Balham Pk. Rd. SW12 1D 136
Balham Rd. N9 2B 34
Balham Sta. Rd. SW12 1F 137
Balin Ho. SE1 6E 14
(off Long La.)
Balkan Wlk. E1 7H 85
Balladier Wlk. E14 5D 86
Ballamore Rd. BR1: Brom 3J 141
Ballance Rd. E9 6K 67
Ballantine St. SW18 4A 118
Ballantrae Ho. NW2 4H 63
Ballard Cl. KT2: King T 7K 133
Ballard Ho. SE10 6D 104
(off Thames St.)
Ballards Cl. RM10: Dag 1H 91
Ballards Farm Rd. CR0: Croy 6G 169
CR2: S Croy 6G 169
Ballards La. N3 1J 45
N12 1J 45
Ballards M. HA8: Edg 6B 28
Ballards Ri. CR2: Sels 6G 169
Ballards Rd. NW2 2C 62
RM10: Dag 2H 91
Ballards Way CR2: Sels 6G 169
Ballast Quay SE10 5F 105
Ballater Rd. CR2: S Croy 5F 169
SW2 4J 119
Ball Ct. EC3 1F 15
(off Cornhill)
Ballina St. SE23 7K 121
Ballin Ct. E14 2E 104
(off Stewart St.)
Ballingdon Rd. SW11 6E 118
Ballinger Way UB5: Yead 4C 76
Balliol Av. E4 4B 36
Balliol Rd. DA16: Well 2B 126
N17 1E 48
W10 6E 80
Balloch Rd. SE6 1F 141
Ballogie Av. NW10 4A 62
Ballow Cl. SE5 7E 102
Balls Pond Pl. N1 6D 66
Balls Pond Rd. N1 6D 66
Balmain Cl. W5 1D 96
Balmain Ct. TW3: Houn 1F 113
Balmain Lodge KT5: Surb 4E 150
(off Cranes Pk. Av.)
Balman Ho. SE16 4K 103
(off Rotherhithe New Rd.)
Balmer Rd. E3 2B 86
Balmes Rd. N1 1D 84
Balmoral Apartments W2 6C 4
(off Praed St.)
Balmoral Av. BR3: Beck 4A 158
N11 6K 31
Balmoral Cl. SW15 6F 117
Balmoral Ct. BR3: Beck 1E 158
(off Avenue, The)
HA9: Wemb 3F 61
KT4: Wor Pk 2D 164
SE12 4K 141
SE16 1K 103
(off King & Queen Wharf)
SE17 5D 102
(off Lytham St.)
SE27 4C 138
SM2: Sutt 7J 165
Balmoral Cres. KT8: W Mole 3E 148
Balmoral Dr. UB1: S'hall 4D 76
UB4: Hayes 4G 75
Balmoral Gdns. DA5: Bexl 7F 127
IG3: Ilf 1K 71
W13 3A 96
Balmoral Gro. N7 6K 65
Balmoral Ho. E14 3D 104
(off Lanark Sq.)
E16 1K 105
(off Keats Av.)
W14 4G 99
(off Windsor Way)
Balmoral M. W12 3B 98
Balmoral Rd. E7 4A 70
E10 2D 68
HA2: Harr 4E 58
KT1: King T 4F 151
KT4: Wor Pk 3D 164
NW2 6D 62
Balmoral Trad. Est. IG11: Bark 5K 89
Balmore Cl. E14 6E 86
Balmore Cres. EN4: Cockf 5K 21
Balmore St. N19 2F 65
Balmuir Gdns. SW15 4E 116
Balnacraig Av. NW10 4A 62
Balniel Ga. SW1 5D 18 (5H 101)
Balsam Ho. E14 7D 86
(off E. India Dock Rd.)
Baltic Apartments E16 7J 87
(off Western Gateway)
Baltic Cen., The TW8: Bford 5D 96
Baltic Cl. SW19 7B 136
Baltic Ct. SE16 2K 103
Baltic Ho. SE5 2C 120
Baltic Pl. N1 1E 84
Baltic St. E. EC1 4C 8 (4C 84)
Baltic St. W. EC1 4C 8 (4C 84)
Baltimore Ho. SE11 5J 19
Baltimore Pl. DA16: Well 2K 125
Balvaird Pl. SW1 6D 18 (5H 101)
Balvernie Gro. SW18 7H 117
Balvernie M. SW18 7J 117
Bamber Ho. IG11: Bark 1H 89
Bamber Rd. SE15 1F 121
Bamborough Gdns. W12 2E 98
Bamburgh N17 7C 34
Bamford Av. HA0: Wemb 1F 79
Bamford Ct. E15 5D 68
(off Clays La.)
Bamford Rd. BR1: Brom 5E 140
IG11: Bark 6G 71
Bampfylde Cl. SM6: Wall 3G 167
Bampton Ct. W5 6D 78
Bampton Dr. NW7 7H 29
Bampton Rd. SE23 3K 139
Banavie Gdns. BR3: Beck 1E 158
Banbury Cl. EN2: Enf 1G 23
Banbury Ct. SM2: Sutt 7J 165
WC2 2E 12
Banbury Ho. E9 7K 67
Banbury Rd. E9 7K 67
E17 7E 34
Banbury St. SW11 2C 118
Banbury Wlk. UB5: N'olt 2E 76
(off Brabazon Rd.)
Banchory Rd. SE3 7K 105
Bancroft Av. IG9: Buck H 2D 36
N2 5C 46
Bancroft Cl. TW15: Ashf 5C 128
Bancroft Ct. SW8 7J 101
(off Allen Edwards Dr.)
UB5: N'olt 1A 76
Bancroft Gdns. BR6: Orp 1K 173
HA3: Hrw W 1G 41
Bancroft Ho. E1 4J 85
(off Cephas St.)
Bancroft Rd. E1 3J 85
HA3: Hrw W 2G 41
Bandon Cl. UB10: Uxb 2B 74
BANDONHILL 5H 167
Bandon Ri. SM6: Wall 5H 167
Banfield Rd. SE15 3H 121
Banfor Ct. SM6: Wall 5G 167
Bangalore St. SW15 3E 116
Bangor Cl. UB5: N'olt 5F 59
Banim St. W6 4D 98
Banister Ho. E9 5K 67
SW8 1G 119
(off Wadhurst Rd.)
W10 3G 81
(off Bruckner St.)
Banister M. NW6 7K 63
Banister Rd. W10 3F 81
Bank, The N6 1F 65
Bank Av. CR4: Mitc 2B 154
Bank Bldgs. E4 6A 36
(off Avenue, The)
Bank End SE1 4D 14 (1C 102)
Bankfoot Rd. BR1: Brom 4G 141
Bankhurst Rd. SE6 7B 122
Bank La. KT2: King T 7E 132
SW15 5A 116
Bank M. SM1: Sutt 6A 166
Bank of England 1E 14 (6D 84)
Bank of England Mus. 1F 15
Bank of England Offices EC4 1C 14
Banks Ho. SE1 3C 102
(off Rockingham St.)
Banksian Wlk. TW7: Isle 1J 113
Banksia Rd. N18 5E 34
Bankside CR2: S Croy 6F 169
EN2: Enf 1G 23
SE1 3C 14 (7C 84)
(not continuous)
UB1: S'hall 1B 94
Bankside Art Gallery 3B 14 (7B 84)
Bankside Av. UB5: Yead 2J 75
Bankside Cl. DA5: Bexl 4K 145
SM5: Cars 6C 166
TW7: Isle 4K 113
Bankside Dr. KT7: T Ditt 1B 162
Bankside Pk. IG11: Bark 3A 90
Bankside Rd. IG1: Ilf 5G 71

Bankside Way—Barningham Way

Bankside Way SE19 6E 138
Banks La. DA6: Bex 4F 127
Bank St. E14 1D 104
Banks Way E12 4E 70
Bankton Rd. SW2 4A 120
Bankwell Rd. SE13 4G 123
Bannatyne's Health Club
Chingford 6H 35
Grove Park 2K 141
Bannerman Ho. SW8 7G 19 (6K 101)
Banner St. EC1 4D 8 (4C 84)
Banning St. SE10 5G 105
Bannister Cl. SW2 1A 138
UB6: G'frd 5H 59
Bannister Ho. SE14 6K 103
(off John Williams Cl.)
Bannockburn Rd. SE18 4J 107
Bannow Cl. KT19: Ewe 4A 164
Banqueting House 5E 12 (1J 101)
Banstead Gdns. N9 3K 33
Banstead Rd. SM5: Cars 7B 166
Banstead Rd. Sth. SM2: Sutt 7B 166
Banstead St. SE15 3J 121
Banstead Way SM6: Wall 5J 167
Banstock Rd. HA8: Edg 6C 28
Banting Dr. N21 5E 22
Banting Ho. NW2 3C 62
Bantock Ho. W10 3G 81
(off Third Av.)
Banton Cl. EN1: Enf 2C 24
Bantry Ho. E1 4K 85
(off Ernest St.)
Bantry St. SE5 7D 102
Banwell Rd. DA5: Bexl 6D 126
Banyard Rd. SE16 3H 103
Baptist Gdns. NW5 6E 64
Barandon Rd. W11 7F 81
(off Grenfell Rd.)
Barandon Wlk. W11 7F 81
Barbanel Ho. E1 4J 85
(off Cephas St.)
Barbara Brosnan Ct.
NW8 1A 4 (2B 82)
Barbara Cl. TW17: Shep 5D 146
Barbara Hucklesby Cl. N22 2B 48
Barbauld Rd. N16 3E 66
Barber Beaumont Ho. E1 3K 85
(off Bancroft Rd.)
Barber Cl. N21 7F 23
Barbers All. E13 3K 87
Barbers Rd. E15 2D 86
Barbican Arts Cen. 5D 8 (5C 84)
Barbican Cinema 5D 8
(in Arts Cen.)
Barbican Rd. UB6: G'frd 6F 77
Barbican Theatre 5D 8
(off Silk St.)
Barbican Trade Cen. EC1 5D 8
(off Beech St.)
Barb M. W6 3E 98
Barbon All. EC2 7H 9
(off Houndsditch)
Barbon Cl. WC1 5F 7 (5K 83)
Barbot Cl. N9 3B 34
Barchard St. SW18 5K 117
Barchester Cl. W7 1K 95
Barchester Rd. HA3: Hrw W 2H 41
Barchester St. E14 5D 86
Barclay Cl. SW6 7J 99
Barclay Ho. E9 7J 67
(off Well St.)
Barclay Oval IG8: Wfd G 4D 36
Barclay Path E17 5E 50
Barclay Rd. CR0: Croy 3D 168
E11 1H 69
(not continuous)
E13 4A 88
E17 5E 50
N18 6J 33
SW6 7J 99
Barcombe Av. SW2 2J 137
Barcombe Cl. BR5: St P 3K 161
Bardell Ho. SE1 7K 15
(off Parkers Row)
Barden St. SE18 7J 107
Bardfield Av.
RM6: Chad H 3D 54
Bardney Rd. SM4: Mord 4K 153
Bardolph Rd. N7 4J 65
TW9: Rich 3F 115
Bard Rd. W10 7F 81
Bardsey Pl. E1 4J 85
(off Mile End Rd.)
Bardsey Wlk. N1 6C 66
(off Douglas Rd. Nth.)
Bardsley Cl. CR0: Croy 3F 169
Bardsley Ho. SE10 6E 104
(off Bardsley La.)
Bardsley La. SE10 6E 104
Barents Ho. E1 4K 85
(off White Horse La.)
Barfett St. W10 4H 81
Barfield Av. N20 2J 31
Barfield Rd. BR1: Brom 3E 160
E11 1H 69
Barfleur La. SE8 4B 104
Barford Cl. NW4 2C 44
Barford St. N1 1A 84
Barforth Rd. SE15 3H 121
Barfreston Way SE20 1H 157
Bargate Cl. KT3: N Mald 7C 152
SE18 5K 107
Barge Ho. Rd. E16 2F 107
Barge Ho. St. SE1 4K 13 (1A 102)
Bargery Rd. SE6 1D 140
Barge Wlk. KT1: Hamp W 3D 150
KT8: E Mos 3H 149
Bargrove Cl. SE20 7G 139
Bargrove Cres. SE6 2B 140
Barham Cl. BR2: Brom 1C 172
BR7: Chst 5F 143
HA0: Wemb 6B 60
RM7: Mawney 2H 55
Barham Ct. CR2: S Croy 4C 168
(off Barham Rd.)
Barham Ho. SE17 5E 102
(off Kinglake St.)
Barham Rd. BR7: Chst 5F 143
CR2: S Croy 4C 168
SW20 7C 134
Baring Cl. SE12 2J 141
Baring Ho. E14 6C 86
(off Canton St.)
Baring Rd. CR0: Croy 1G 169
EN4: Cockf 4G 21
SE12 7J 123
Baring St. N1 1D 84
Barker Cl. HA6: Nwood 1H 39
KT3: N Mald 4H 151
TW9: Rich 2H 115
Barker Dr. NW1 7G 65
Barker M. SW4 4F 119
Barkers Arc. W8 2K 99
Barker St. SW10 6A 100
Barker Wlk. SW16 3H 137
Barkham Rd. N17 7J 33
Barkham Ter. SE1 1K 19
BARKING 7G 71
Barking Abbey 1G 89
Barking Abbey School Leisure Cen. 6A 72
Barking Bus. Pk. IG11: Bark 3A 90
Barking Ind. Pk. IG11: Bark 1K 89
Barking Northern Relief Rd.
IG11: Bark 7F 71
BARKING RIVERSIDE 3C 90
Barking Rd. E6 2A 88
E13 5H 87
E16 5H 87
(not continuous)
BARKINGSIDE 3G 53
Bark Pl. W2 7K 81
Barkston Gdns. SW5 4K 99
Barkway Ct. N4 2C 66
(off Queen's Dr.)
Barkwith Ho. SE14 6K 103
(off Cold Blow La.)
Barkwood Cl. RM7: Rom 5J 55
Barkworth Rd. SE16 5H 103
Barlborough St. SE14 7K 103
Barlby Gdns. W10 4F 81
Barlby Rd. W10 5E 80
Barleycorn Way E14 7B 86
Barleyfields Cl. RM6: Chad H 6B 54
Barley La. IG3: Ilf 7A 54
RM6: Chad H 4B 54
Barley Mow Pas. EC1 5B 8
W4 5K 97
Barleymow Way TW17: Shep 4C 146
Barley Shotts Bus. Pk. W10 5H 81
Barling NW1 6F 65
(off Castlehaven Rd.)
Barlings Ho. SE4 4K 121
(off Frendsbury Rd.)
Barlow Cl. SM6: Wall 6J 167
Barlow Dr. SE18 1C 124
Barlow Ho. N1 1E 8
(off Fairbank Est.)
SE16 4H 103
(off Rennie Est.)
W11 7G 81
(off Walmer Rd.)
Barlow Pl. W1 3K 11 (7F 83)
Barlow Rd. NW6 6H 63
TW12: Hamp 7E 130
W3 1H 97
Barlow St. SE17 4D 102
Barlow Way RM13: Rain 5K 91
Barmeston Rd. SE6 2D 140
Barmor Cl. HA2: Harr 2F 41
Barmouth Av. UB6: G'frd 2K 77
Barmouth Rd. CR0: Croy 2K 169
SW18 6A 118
Barnabas Ct. EN2 4F 23
Barnabas Rd. E9 5K 67
Barnaby Cl. HA2: Harr 2G 59
Barnaby Ct. NW9 3A 44
SE16 2G 103
(off Scott Lidgett Cres.)
Barnaby Pl. SW7 4A 16
Barnaby Way IG7: Chig 3K 37
Barnard Cl. BR7: Chst 1H 161
SE18 4E 106
SM6: Wall 7H 167
TW16: Sun 7K 129
Barnard Gdns. KT3: N Mald 4C 152
UB4: Yead 4K 75
Barnard Gro. E15 7H 69
Barnard Hill N10 1F 47
Barnard Ho. E2 3H 85
(off Ellsworth St.)
Barnard Lodge EN5: New Bar 4F 21
W9 5J 81
(off Admiral Wlk.)
Barnard M. SW11 4C 118
Barnardo Dr. IG6: Ilf 4G 53
Barnardo Gdns. E1 7K 85
Barnardo St. E1 6K 85
Barnardos Village IG6: Ilf 4G 53
Barnard Rd. CR4: Mitc 3E 154
EN1: Enf 2C 24
SW11 4C 118
Barnards Ho. SE16 2B 104
(off Wyatt Cl.)
Barnard's Inn EC1 6J 7
Barnbrough NW1 1G 83
(off Camden St.)
Barnby Sq. E15 1G 87
Barnby St. E15 1G 87
NW1 1B 6 (2G 83)
Barn Cl. NW5 5H 65
(off Torriano Av.)
TW15: Ashf 5D 128
UB5: Yead 2A 76
Barn Cres. HA7: Stan 6H 27
Barncroft Cl. UB8: Hil 5D 74
Barneby Cl. TW2: Twick 1J 131
BARNEHURST 3J 127
Barnehurst Av. DA7: Bex 1J 127
DA8: Erith 1J 127
Barnehurst Cl. DA8: Erith 1J 127
Barnehurst Rd. DA7: Bex 2J 127
Barn Elms Athletic Track 2D 116
Barn Elms Pk. SW15 3E 116
BARNES 2B 116
Barnes All. TW12: Hamp 2G 149
Barnes Av. SW13 7C 98
UB2: S'hall 4D 94
Barnes Cl. E12 4B 70
Barnes Ct. E16 5A 88
EN5: New Bar 4E 20
IG8: Buck H, Wfd G 5G 37
N1 7A 66
Barnes End KT3: N Mald 5C 152
Barnes High St. SW13 2B 116
Barnes Ho. E2 2J 85
(off Wadeson St.)
IG11: Bark 1H 89
SE14 6K 103
(off John Williams Cl.)
Barnes Pikle W5 7D 78
Barnes Rd. IG1: Ilf 5G 71
N18 4D 34
Barnes St. E14 6A 86
Barnes Ter. SE8 5B 104
Barnes Wallis Ct. HA9: Wemb 3J 61
BARNET 3B 20
Barnet Bus. Cen. EN5: Barn 3B 20
Barnet By-Pass NW7 6G 29
Barnet Copthall Stadium 7K 29
Barnet Dr. BR2: Brom 2C 172
Barnet FC 5D 20
Barnet Ga. La. EN5: Ark 1H 29
Barnet Gro. E2 1K 9 (3G 85)
Barnet Hill EN5: Barn 4C 20
Barnet Ho. N20 2F 31
Barnet La. EN5: Barn 1C 30
N20 1C 30
Barnet Mus. 4B 20
Barnet Trad. Est. EN5: Barn 3C 20
Barnetts Ct. HA2: Harr 3F 59
Barnett St. E1 6H 85
BARNET VALE 5E 20
Barnet Way NW7: Bore, Lon 3E 28
Barnet Wood Rd. BR2: Brom 2A 172
Barney Cl. SE7 5A 106
Barn Fld. NW3 5D 64
Barnfield KT3: N Mald 6A 152
Barnfield Av. CR0: Croy 2J 169
CR4: Mitc 4F 155
KT2: King T 4D 132
Barnfield Cl. N4 7J 47
SW17 3B 136
Barnfield Gdns. KT2: King T 4E 132
SE18 6F 107
Barnfield Pl. E14 4C 104
Barnfield Rd. CR2: Sand 7E 168
DA17: Belv 6F 109
HA8: Edg 1J 43
SE18 6F 107
(not continuous)
W5 4C 78
Barnfield Wood Cl. BR3: Beck 6F 159
Barnfield Wood Rd. BR3: Beck 6F 159
Barnham Dr. SE28 1K 107
(not continuous)
Barnham Rd. UB6: G'frd 3G 77
Barnham St. SE1 6H 15 (2E 102)
Barn Hill HA9: Wemb 1G 61
Barnhill HA5: Eastc 5A 40
Barnhill Av. BR2: Brom 5H 159
Barnhill La. UB4: Yead 3K 75
Barnhill Rd. HA9: Wemb 3J 61
UB4: Yead 3K 75
Barningham Way NW9 6K 43

Bath Ct.—Beauclerc Rd.

Bath Ct. EC1 4J 7
SE26 3G 139
(off Droitwich Cl.)
Bathgate Rd. SW19 3F 135
Bath Gro. E2 2G 85
(off Horatio St.)
Bath Ho. E2 4G 85
(off Ramsey St.)
SE1 3C 102
(off Bath Ter.)
Bath Ho. Rd.
CR0: Bedd 1J 167
Bath Pas. KT1: King T 2D 150
Bath Pl. EC2 2G 9 (3E 84)
EN5: Barn 3C 20
W6 5E 98
(off Peabody Est.)
Bath Rd. E7 6B 70
N9 2C 34
RM6: Chad H 6E 54
TW3: Houn 2B 112
TW4: Houn 2B 112
TW5: Cran 1G 111
TW6: H'row A 1G 111
UB3: Harl 1G 111
UB7: Harm, Sip 1A 110
W4 4A 98
Baths App. SW6 7H 99
Baths Rd. BR2: Brom 4B 160
Bath St. EC1 2D 8 (3C 84)
Bath Ter. SE1 3C 102
Bathurst Av. SW19 1K 153
Bathurst Gdns. NW10 2D 80
Bathurst Ho. W12 7D 80
(off White City Est.)
Bathurst M. W2 2B 10 (6B 82)
Bathurst Rd. IG1: Ilf 1F 71
Bathurst St. W2 2B 10 (7B 82)
Bathway SE18 4E 106
Batley Cl. CR4: Mitc 7D 154
Batley Pl. N16 3F 67
Batley Rd. EN2: Enf 1H 23
N16 3F 67
Batman Cl. W12 1D 98
Batoum Gdns. W6 3E 98
Batson Ho. E1 6G 85
(off Fairclough St.)
Batson St. W12 2C 98
Batsworth Rd. CR4: Mitc 3B 154
Battenberg Wlk. SE19 6E 138
Batten Cl. E6 6D 88
Batten Cotts. E14 5A 86
(off Maroon St.)
Batten Ho. SW4 5G 119
W10 3G 81
(off Third Av.)
Batten St. SW11 3C 118
Battersby Rd. SE6 2F 141
BATTERSEA 1E 118
Battersea Bri. SW11 7B 100
Battersea Bri. Rd. SW11 7C 100
Battersea Bus. Cen. SW11 3E 118
Battersea Chu. Rd. SW11 1B 118
Battersea High St. SW11 1B 118
(not continuous)
Battersea Pk. 7D 100
Battersea Pk. Children's Zoo 7E 100
Battersea Pk. Equestrian Cen. 2C 118
Battersea Pk. Rd. SW8 1E 118
SW11 2C 118
Battersea Ri. SW11 5C 118
Battersea Sports Cen. 3B 118
Battersea Sq. SW11 1B 118
Battery Rd. SE28 2J 107
Battishill St. N1 7B 66
Battlebridge Ct. N1 2J 83
(off Wharfdale Rd.)
Battle Bri. La. SE1 5G 15 (1E 102)
Battle Bri. Rd. NW1 2J 83
Battle Cl. SW19 6A 136
Battledean Rd. N5 5B 66
Battle Ho. SE15 6G 103
(off Haymerle Rd.)
Battle Rd. DA8: Erith 4J 109
DA17: Belv, Erith 4J 109
Batty St. E1 6G 85
Baudwin Rd. SE6 2G 141
Baugh Rd. DA14: Sidc 5C 144
Baulk, The SW18 7J 117
Bavant Rd. SW16 2J 155
Bavaria Rd. N19 2J 65
(not continuous)
Bavdene M. NW4 4D 44
(off Burroughs, The)
Bavent Rd. SE5 2C 120
Bawdale Rd. SE22 5F 121
Bawdsey Av. IG2: Ilf 4K 53
Bawtree Rd. SE14 7A 104
Bawtry Rd. N20 3J 31
Baxendale N20 2F 31
Baxendale St. E2 3G 85
Baxter Cl. UB2: S'hall 3F 95
UB10: Hil 3D 74
Baxter Rd. E16 6A 88
IG1: Ilf 5F 71
N1 6D 66
N18 4C 34
Bayard Ct. DA6: Bex 4H 127
Bay Ct. E1 4K 85
(off Frimley Way)
W5 3E 96
Baycroft Cl. HA5: Eastc 3A 40
Baydon Ct. BR2: Brom 3H 159
Bayer Ho. EC1 4C 8
(off Golden La. Est.)
Bayes Cl. SE26 5J 139
Bayes Ct. NW3 7D 64
(off Primrose Hill Rd.)
Bayfield Ho. SE4 4K 121
(off Coston Wlk.)
Bayfield Rd. SE9 4B 124
Bayford M. E8 7H 67
(off Bayford St.)
Bayford Rd. NW10 3F 81
Bayford St. E8 7H 67
Bayford St. Bus. Cen. E8 7H 67
(off Sidworth St.)
Baygrove M. KT1: Hamp W 1C 150
Bayham Pl. NW1 1G 83
Bayham Rd. SM4: Mord 4K 153
W4 3K 97
W13 7B 78
Bayham St. NW1 1G 83
Bayhurst Wood Country Pk. 5B 38
Bayleaf Cl. TW12: Hamp H 5H 131
Bayley St. WC1 6C 6 (5H 83)
Bayley Wlk. SE2 6E 108
Baylis M. TW1: Twick 7A 114
Baylis Rd. SE1 7J 13 (2A 102)
Bayliss Av. SE28 7D 90
Bayliss Cl. N21 5D 22
Bayne Cl. E6 6D 88
Baynes Cl. EN1: Enf 1B 24
Baynes M. NW3 6B 64
Baynes St. NW1 7G 65
Baynham Cl. DA5: Bexl 6F 127
Bayonne Rd. W6 6G 99
Bays Ct. HA8: Edg 5C 28
Bayshill Ri. UB5: N'olt 6F 59
Bayston Rd. N16 3F 67
BAYSWATER 7A 82
Bayswater Rd. W2 3A 10 (7K 81)
Baythorne St. E3 5B 86
Bayton Ct. E8 7G 67
(off Lansdowne Dr.)
Bay Tree Cl. BR1: Brom 1B 160
Baytree Cl. DA15: Sidc 1K 143
Baytree Ct. SW2 4K 119
Baytree Ho. E4 7J 25
Baytree Rd. SW2 4K 119
Bazalgette Cl. KT3: N Mald 5K 151
Bazalgette Gdns. KT3: N Mald 5K 151
Bazalgette Ho. NW8 3B 4
(off Orchardson St.)
Bazeley Ho. SE1 7A 14
(off Library St.)
Bazely St. E14 7E 86
Bazile Rd. N21 6F 23
BBC Broadcasting House 6K 5 (5F 83)
BBC Television Cen. 7E 80
BBC Worldwide 6E 80
(off Wood La.)
Beacham Cl. SE7 5B 106
Beachborough Rd. BR1: Brom 4E 140
Beachcroft Rd. E11 3G 69
Beachcroft Way N19 1H 65
Beach Gro. TW13: Hanw 2E 130
Beach Ho. SW5 5J 99
(off Philbeach Gdns.)
TW13: Hanw 2E 130
Beachy Rd. E3 7C 68
Beacon Bingo Hall 4F 63
Beacon Cl. UB8: Uxb 5A 56
Beacon Ga. SE14 3K 121
Beacon Gro. SM5: Cars 4E 166
Beacon Hill N7 5J 65
Beacon Ho. E14 5D 104
(off Burrells Wharf Sq.)
SE5 7E 102
(off Southampton Way)
Beacon Pl. CR0: Bedd 3J 167
Beacon Rd. SE13 6F 123
TW6: H'row A 6C 110
Beacons Cl. E6 5C 88
Beaconsfield Cl. N11 5K 31
SE3 6J 105
W4 5J 97
Beaconsfield Pde. SE9 4C 142
Beaconsfield Rd. BR1: Brom 3B 160
CR0: Croy 6D 156
DA5: Bexl 2K 145
E10 2E 68
E16 4H 87
E17 6B 50
KT3: N Mald 2K 151
KT5: Surb 7F 151
N9 3B 34
N11 3K 31
N15 4E 48
NW10 6B 62
SE3 7H 105
SE9 2C 142
SE17 5D 102
TW1: Twick 6B 114
UB1: S'hall 1B 94
UB4: Yead 1A 94
W4 3K 97
W5 2C 96
Beaconsfield Ter. RM6: Chad H 6D 54
Beaconsfield Ter. Rd. W14 3G 99
Beaconsfield Wlk. E6 6E 88
SW6 1H 117
Beacontree Av. E17 1F 51
BEACONTREE HEATH 1G 73
Beacontree Rd. E11 1H 69
Beadle's Pde. RM10: Dag 6J 73
Beadlow Cl. SM5: Cars 6B 154
Beadman Pl. SE27 4B 138
Beadman St. SE27 4B 138
Beadnell Rd. SE23 1K 139
Beadon Rd. BR2: Brom 4J 159
W6 4E 98
Beaford Gro. SW20 3G 153
Beagle Cl. TW13: Felt 4K 129
Beak St. W1 2B 12 (7G 83)
Beal Cl. DA16: Well 1A 126
Beale Cl. N13 5G 33
Beale Pl. E3 2B 86
Beale Rd. E3 1B 86
Beal Rd. IG1: Ilf 2E 70
Beam Av. RM10: Dag 1H 91
Beames Rd. NW10 1K 79
Beaminster Gdns. IG6: Ilf 2F 53
Beaminster Ho. SW8 7K 101
(off Dorset Rd.)
Beamish Dr. WD23: Bushy 1B 26
Beamish Ho. SE16 4H 103
(off Rennie Est.)
Beamish Rd. N9 1B 34
Beam Vs. RM9: Dag 2J 91
Beamway RM10: Dag 7K 73
Beanacre Cl. E9 6B 68
Bean Rd. DA6: Bex 4D 126
Beanshaw SE9 4E 142
Beansland Gro. RM6: Chad H 2E 54
Bear All. EC4 7A 8 (6B 84)
Bear Cl. RM7: Rom 6H 55
Beardell St. SE19 6F 139
Beardow Gro. N14 6B 22
Beard Rd. KT2: King T 5F 133
Beardsfield E13 2J 87
Beard's Hill TW12: Hamp 1E 148
Beard's Hill Cl. TW12: Hamp 1E 148
Beardsley Ter. RM8: Dag 5B 72
(off Fitzstephen Rd.)
Beardsley Way W3 2K 97
Beard's Rd. TW15: Ashf 6G 129
Bearfield Rd. KT2: King T 7E 132
Bear Gdns. SE1 4C 14 (1C 102)
Bear La. SE1 4B 14 (1B 102)
Bear Rd. TW13: Hanw 4B 130
Bearstead Ri. SE4 5B 122
Bearsted Ter. BR3: Beck 1C 158
Bear St. WC2 2D 12 (7H 83)
Beasley's Ait TW16: Sun 6H 147
Beasley's Ait La. TW16: Sun 6H 147
Beaton Cl. SE15 1F 121
Beatrice Av. HA9: Wemb 5E 60
SW16 3K 155
Beatrice Cl. E13 4J 87
HA5: Eastc 4J 39
Beatrice Ct. IG9: Buck H 2G 37
Beatrice Ho. W6 5E 98
(off Queen Caroline St.)
Beatrice Pl. W8 3K 99
Beatrice Rd. E17 5C 50
N4 7A 48
N9 7D 24
SE1 4G 103
TW10: Rich 5F 115
UB1: S'hall 1D 94
Beatrix Ho. SW5 5K 99
(off Old Brompton Rd.)
Beatson Wlk. SE16 1A 104
(not continuous)
Beattie Cl. TW14: Felt 7H 111
Beattie Ho. SW8 1G 119
Beattock Ri. N10 4F 47
Beatty Ho. E14 2C 104
(off Admirals Way)
NW1 3A 6
(off Drummond St.)
SW1 6B 18
(off Dolphin Sq.)
Beatty Rd. HA7: Stan 6H 27
N16 4E 66
Beatty St. NW1 2G 83
Beattyville Gdns. IG6: Ilf 4E 52
Beauchamp Cl. W4 3J 97
Beauchamp Ct. EN5: Barn 4C 20
(off Victors Way)
HA7: Stan 5H 27
Beauchamp Pl. SW3 1D 16 (3C 100)
Beauchamp Rd. E7 7K 69
KT8: E Mos 5F 149
KT8: W Mole 5F 149
SE19 1D 156
SM1: Sutt 4J 165
SW11 4C 118
TW1: Twick 7A 114
Beauchamp St. EC1 6J 7 (5A 84)
Beauchamp Ter. SW15 3D 116
Beauclerc Ct. TW16: Sun 2A 148
Beauclerc Rd. W6 3D 98

Beauclere Ho.—Bedster Gdns.

Beauclere Ho. SM2: Sutt . . . 7A **166**
Beauclerk Cl. TW13: Felt . . . 1K **129**
Beauclerk Ho. SW16 . . . 3J **137**
Beaudesert M. UB7: W Dray . . . 2A **92**
Beaufort E6 . . . 5E **88**
Beaufort Av. HA3: Kent . . . 4A **42**
Beaufort Cl. E4 . . . 6J **35**
RM7: Mawney . . . 4J **55**
SW15 . . . 7D **116**
W5 . . . 5F **79**
Beaufort Ct. *E14* . . . *2C* ***104***
(off Admirals Way)
EN5: New Bar . . . 5F **21**
N11 . . . *5A* ***32***
(off Limes Av., The)
SW6 . . . 6J **99**
TW10: Ham . . . 4C **132**
Beaufort Dr. NW11 . . . 4J **45**
Beaufort Gdns. IG1: Ilf . . . 1E **70**
NW4 . . . 6E **44**
SW3 . . . 1D **16** (3C **100**)
SW16 . . . 7K **137**
TW5: Hest . . . 1C **112**
Beaufort Ho. *E16* . . . *1K* ***105***
(off Fairfax M.)
SW1 . . . *6C* ***18***
(off Aylesford St.)
Beaufort M. SW6 . . . 6H **99**
Beaufort Pk. NW11 . . . 4J **45**
Beaufort Rd. HA4: Ruis . . . 2F **57**
KT1: King T . . . 4E **150**
TW1: Twick . . . 7C **114**
TW10: Ham . . . 4C **132**
W5 . . . 5F **79**
Beaufort St. SW3 . . . 7A **16** (6B **100**)
Beaufort Ter. *E14* . . . *5E* ***104***
(off Ferry St.)
Beaufort Way KT17: Ewe . . . 7C **164**
Beaufoy Ho. SE27 . . . 3B **138**
SW8 . . . *7K* ***101***
(off Rita Rd.)
Beaufoy Rd. N17 . . . 7K **33**
Beaufoy Wlk. SE11 . . . 4H **19** (4K **101**)
Beaulieu Av. E16 . . . 1K **105**
SE26 . . . 4H **139**
Beaulieu Cl. CR4: Mitc . . . 1E **154**
NW9 . . . 4A **44**
SE5 . . . 3D **120**
TW1: Twick . . . 6D **114**
TW4: Houn . . . 5D **112**
Beaulieu Ct. W5 . . . 5E **78**
Beaulieu Dr. HA5: Pinn . . . 6B **40**
Beaulieu Gdns. N21 . . . 7H **23**
Beaulieu Lodge *E14* . . . *3F* ***105***
(off Schooner Cl.)
Beaulieu Pl. W4 . . . 3J **97**
Beaumanor Gdns. SE9 . . . 4E **142**
Beaumaris Dr. IG8: Wfd G . . . 7G **37**
Beaumaris Grn. NW9 . . . 6A **44**
Beaumaris Twr. *W3* . . . *2H* ***97***
(off Park Rd. Nth.)
Beaumont *W14* . . . *4H* ***99***
(off Kensington Village)
Beaumont Av. HA0: Wemb . . . 5C **60**
HA2: Harr . . . 6F **41**
TW9: Rich . . . 3F **115**
W14 . . . 5H **99**
Beaumont Bldgs. *WC2* . . . *1F* ***13***
(off Martlett Ct.)
Beaumont Cl. KT2: King T . . . 7G **133**
Beaumont Ct. E1 . . . 3A **86**
E5 . . . 3H **67**
HA0: Wemb . . . 5C **60**
NW9 . . . *2B* ***44***
(off Cherry Cl.)
W1 . . . *5H* ***5***
(off Beaumont St.)
W4 . . . 5J **97**
Beaumont Cres. W14 . . . 5H **99**
Beaumont Dr. TW15: Ashf . . . 5F **129**
Beaumont Gdns. NW3 . . . 3J **63**
Beaumont Gro. E1 . . . 4K **85**
Beaumont Ho. E10 . . . 7D **50**
E15 . . . *1H* ***87***
(off John St.)
Beaumont Lodge *E8* . . . *6G* ***67***
(off Greenwood Rd.)
Beaumont M. HA5: Pinn . . . 3C **40**
W1 . . . 5H **5** (5E **82**)
Beaumont Pl. EN5: Barn . . . 1C **20**
TW7: Isle . . . 5K **113**
W1 . . . 3B **6** (4G **83**)
Beaumont Ri. N19 . . . 1H **65**
Beaumont Rd.
BR5: Pet W . . . 6H **161**
E10 . . . 7D **50**
(not continuous)
E13 . . . 3K **87**
SE19 . . . 6C **138**
SW19 . . . 7G **117**
W4 . . . 3J **97**
Beaumont Sq. E1 . . . 5K **85**
Beaumont St. W1 . . . 5H **5** (5E **82**)
Beaumont Ter. *SE13* . . . *7G* ***123***
(off Wellmeadow Rd.)
Beaumont Wlk. NW3 . . . 7D **64**
Beauvais Ter. UB5: Yead . . . 3B **76**
Beauvale *NW1* . . . *7E* ***64***
(off Ferdinand St.)
Beauval Rd. SE22 . . . 6F **121**
Beaux Arts Bldg., The N7 . . . 3J **65**
Beaverbank Rd. SE9 . . . 1H **143**
Beaver Cl. SE20 . . . 7G **139**
SM4: Mord . . . 7E **152**
TW12: Hamp . . . 1F **149**
Beaver Ct. BR3: Beck . . . 7D **140**
Beaver Gro. UB5: N'olt . . . 3C **76**
Beavers Cres. TW4: Houn . . . 4A **112**
Beavers La. TW4: Houn . . . 2A **112**
Beavers La. Campsite TW4: Houn . . . 4B **112**
Beavers Lodge DA14: Sidc . . . 4K **143**
Beaverwood Rd. BR7: Chst . . . 5J **143**
Beavor Gro. *W6* . . . *5C* ***98***
(off Beavor La.)
Beavor La. W6 . . . 5C **98**
Bebbington Rd. SE18 . . . 4J **107**
Beblets Cl. BR6: Chels . . . 5K **173**
Beccles Dr. IG11: Bark . . . 6J **71**
Beccles St. E14 . . . 6B **86**
Bec Cl. HA4: Ruis . . . 3B **58**
Bechervaise Ct. *E10* . . . *1D* ***68***
(off Leyton Grange Est.)
Bechtel Ho. *W6* . . . *4F* ***99***
(off Hammersmith Rd.)
Beck Cl. SE13 . . . 1D **122**
Beck Ct. BR3: Beck . . . 3K **157**
BECKENHAM . . . 1C 158
Beckenham Bus. Cen. BR3: Beck . . . 6A **140**
Beckenham Crematorium
BR3: Beck . . . 3J **157**
Beckenham Gdns. N9 . . . 3K **33**
Beckenham Gro. BR2: Brom . . . 2F **159**
Beckenham Hill Est. BR3: Beck . . . 5D **140**
Beckenham Hill Rd.
BR3: Beck, Lon . . . 6D **140**
SE6 . . . 6D **140**
Beckenham La. BR2: Brom . . . 2G **159**
Beckenham Pl. Pk. BR3: Beck . . . 7D **140**
Beckenham Rd. BR3: Beck . . . 1K **157**
BR4: W W'ck . . . 7D **158**
Beckenham Theatre Cen., The . . . 2D 158
Beckers, The N16 . . . 4G **67**
Becket Av. E6 . . . 3E **88**
Becket Cl. SE25 . . . 6G **157**
SW19 . . . *1K* ***153***
(off High Path)
Becket Fold HA1: Harr . . . 5K **41**
Becket Ho. *E16* . . . *1K* ***105***
(off Constable Av.)
SE1 . . . 7E **14**
Becket Rd. N18 . . . 4D **34**
Becket St. SE1 . . . 7E **14** (3D **102**)
Beckett Cl. DA17: Belv . . . 3F **109**
NW10 . . . 6A **62**
SW16 . . . 2H **137**
Beckett Ho. *E1* . . . *5J* ***85***
(off Jubilee St.)
SW9 . . . 2J **119**
Becketts Cl. BR6: Orp . . . 3K **173**
DA5: Bexl . . . 1J **145**
TW14: Felt . . . 6K **111**
Becketts Ho. IG1: Ilf . . . 3E **70**
Becketts Pl. KT1: Hamp W . . . 1D **150**
Beckett Wlk. BR3: Beck . . . 6A **140**
Beckfoot *NW1* . . . *1B* ***6***
(off Ampthill Est.)
Beckford Cl. W14 . . . 4H **99**
Beckford Dr. BR5: Orp . . . 7H **161**
Beckford Ho. N16 . . . 5E **66**
Beckford Pl. SE17 . . . 5C **102**
Beckford Rd. CR0: Croy . . . 6F **157**
Beckham Ho. SE11 . . . 4H **19** (4K **101**)
Beck La. BR3: Beck . . . 3K **157**
Becklow Gdns. *W12* . . . *2C* ***98***
(off Becklow Rd.)
Becklow M. *W12* . . . *2C* ***98***
(off Becklow Rd.)
Becklow Rd. W12 . . . 2B **98**
(not continuous)
Beck River Pk. BR3: Beck . . . 1C **158**
Beck Rd. CR4: Mitc . . . 6D **154**
E8 . . . 1H **85**
Becks Rd. DA14: Sidc . . . 3A **144**
Beck Theatre, The . . . 6H 75
BECKTON . . . 5E 88
BECKTON ALPS . . . 4D 88
BECKTON PARK . . . 6D 88
Beckton Retail Pk. E6 . . . 5E **88**
Beckton Rd. E16 . . . 5H **87**
Beckton Triangle Retail Pk. E6 . . . 4F **89**
Beck Way BR3: Beck . . . 3B **158**
Beckway Rd. SW16 . . . 2H **155**
Beckway St. SE17 . . . 4E **102**
(not continuous)
Beckwith Ho. *E2* . . . *2H* ***85***
(off Wadeson St.)
Beckwith Rd. SE24 . . . 5D **120**
Beclands Rd. SW17 . . . 6E **136**
Becmead Av. HA3: Kent . . . 5B **42**
SW16 . . . 4H **137**
Becondale Rd. SE19 . . . 5E **138**
BECONTREE . . . 4D 72
Becontree Av. RM8: Dag . . . 4B **72**
Becquerel Ct. SE10 . . . 3H **105**
Bective Pl. SW15 . . . 4H **117**
Bective Rd. E7 . . . 4J **69**
SW15 . . . 4H **117**
Becton Pl. DA8: Erith . . . 7H **109**
Bedale Rd. EN2: Enf . . . 1H **23**
Bedale St. SE1 . . . 5E **14** (1D **102**)
Beddalls Farm Ct. E6 . . . 5B **88**
BEDDINGTON . . . 4J 167
BEDDINGTON CORNER . . . 7E 154
Beddington Cross CR0: Bedd . . . 7H **155**
Beddington Farm Rd. CR0: Bedd . . . 7J **155**
Beddington Gdns. SM5: Cars . . . 6E **166**
SM6: Wall . . . 6E **166**
Beddington Grn. BR5: St P . . . 1K **161**
Beddington Gro. SM6: Wall . . . 5H **167**
Beddington La. CR0: Croy . . . 5G **155**
Beddington Pk. . . . 2F 167
Beddington Pk. Cotts. SM6: Bedd . . . 3H **167**
Beddington Path BR5: St P . . . 1K **161**
Beddington Rd. BR5: St P . . . 2J **161**
IG3: Ilf . . . 7K **53**
Beddington Ter. CR0: Croy . . . 7K **155**
Beddington Trad. Est. CR0: Bedd . . . 1J **167**
Bede Cl. HA5: Pinn . . . 1B **40**
Bedefield WC1 . . . 2F **7** (3J **83**)
Bede Ho. *SE4* . . . *1B* ***122***
(off Clare Rd.)
Bedens Rd. DA14: Sidc . . . 6E **144**
Bede Rd. RM6: Chad H . . . 6C **54**
Bedfont Cl. CR4: Mitc . . . 2E **154**
TW14: Bedf . . . 6E **110**
Bedfont Grn. Cl. TW14: Bedf . . . 1E **128**
Bedfont Ind. Pk. TW15: Ashf . . . 3E **128**
Bedfont Ind. Pk. Nth. TW15: Ashf . . . 3E **128**
Bedfont Lakes Country Pk. . . . 2E 128
Bedfont Lakes Country Pk. Vis. Cen. . . . 3D 128
Bedfont La. TW13: Felt . . . 7G **111**
TW14: Felt . . . 7G **111**
Bedfont Rd. TW13: Felt . . . 1E **128**
TW14: Bedf . . . 1E **128**
TW19: Stanw . . . 6A **110**
Bedford Av. EN5: Barn . . . 5C **20**
UB4: Yead . . . 6K **75**
WC1 . . . 6D **6** (5H **83**)
Bedfordbury WC2 . . . 2E **12** (7J **83**)
Bedford Cl. N10 . . . 7K **31**
W4 . . . 6A **98**
Bedford Cnr. *W4* . . . *4A* ***98***
(off South Pde.)
Bedford Ct. *CR0: Croy* . . . *1C* ***168***
(off Tavistock Rd.)
WC2 . . . 3E **12** (7J **83**)
(not continuous)
Bedford Ct. Mans. WC1 . . . 6D **6**
Bedford Gdns. W8 . . . 1J **99**
Bedford Hill SW12 . . . 1F **137**
SW16 . . . 1F **137**
Bedford Ho. *SW4* . . . *4J* ***119***
(off Solon New Rd. Est.)
Bedford M. N2 . . . 3C **46**
SE6 . . . 2D **140**
BEDFORD PARK . . . 3K 97
Bedford Pk. CR0: Croy . . . 1C **168**
Bedford Pk. Cnr. W4 . . . 4A **98**
Bedford Pk. Mans. W4 . . . 4K **97**
Bedford Pas. *SW6* . . . *7G* ***99***
(off Dawes Rd.)
W1 . . . 5B **6** (5G **83**)
Bedford Pl. CR0: Croy . . . 1D **168**
WC1 . . . 5E **6** (5J **83**)
Bedford Rd. DA15: Sidc . . . 3J **143**
E6 . . . 1E **88**
E17 . . . 2C **50**
E18 . . . 2J **51**
HA1: Harr . . . 6G **41**
HA4: Ruis . . . 4H **57**
IG1: Ilf . . . 3F **71**
KT4: Wor Pk . . . 2E **164**
N2 . . . 3C **46**
N8 . . . 6H **47**
N9 . . . 7C **24**
N15 . . . 4E **48**
N22 . . . 2J **47**
NW7 . . . 2F **29**
SW4 . . . 4J **119**
TW2: Twick . . . 3H **131**
W4 . . . 3K **97**
W13 . . . 7B **78**
Bedford Row WC1 . . . 5H **7** (5K **83**)
Bedford Sq. WC1 . . . 6D **6** (5H **83**)
Bedford St. WC2 . . . 2E **12** (7J **83**)
Bedford Ter. SM2: Sutt . . . 6A **166**
SW2 . . . 5J **119**
Bedford Way WC1 . . . 4D **6** (4H **83**)
Bedgebury Gdns. SW19 . . . 2G **135**
Bedgebury Rd. SE9 . . . 4B **124**
Bedivere Rd. BR1: Brom . . . 3J **141**
Bedlam M. SE11 . . . 3J **19**
Bedlow Way CR0: Bedd . . . 4K **167**
Bedmond Ho. *SW3* . . . *5C* ***16***
(off Ixworth Pl.)
Bedonwell Rd.
DA7: Belv, Erith, Bex . . . 6F **109**
DA17: Belv . . . 6E **108**
SE2 . . . 6E **108**
Bedser Cl. CR7: Thor H . . . 3C **156**
SE11 . . . 7H **19** (6K **101**)
Bedser Dr. UB6: G'frd . . . 5H **59**
Bedster Gdns. KT8: W Mole . . . 2F **149**

Bedwardine Rd. SE19 7E **138**
Bedwell Ct. *RM6: Chad H* *7D* ***54***
(off Broomfield Rd.)
Bedwell Gdns. UB3: Harl 5G **93**
(not continuous)
Bedwell Ho. SW9 2A **120**
Bedwell Rd. DA17: Belv 5G **109**
N17 1E **48**
Beeby Rd. E16 5K **87**
Beech Av. DA15: Sidc 7A **126**
HA4: Ruis 1K **57**
IG9: Buck H 2E **36**
N20 1H **31**
TW8: Bford 7B **96**
W3 1A **98**
Beech Cl. N9 6B **24**
SE8 6C **104**
SM5: Cars 2D **166**
SW15 7C **116**
SW19 6E **134**
TW15: Ashf 5F **129**
TW16: Sun 2B **148**
UB7: W Dray 3C **92**
Beech Copse BR1: Brom 1D **160**
CR2: S Croy 5E **168**
Beech Ct. *BR1: Brom* *1H* ***159***
(off Blyth Rd.)
BR3: Beck 7B **140**
HA6: Nwood 1G **39**
IG1: Ilf *3E* ***70***
(off Riverdene Rd.)
KT6: Surb 7D **150**
UB5: N'olt 1C **76**
W9 *5J* ***81***
(off Elmfield Way)
Beech Cres. Ct. N5 4B **66**
Beechcroft BR7: Chst 7E **142**
Beechcroft Av. DA7: Bex 1K **127**
HA2: Harr 7E **40**
KT3: N Mald 1J **151**
NW11 7H **45**
UB1: S'hall 1D **94**
Beechcroft Cl. BR6: Orp 4H **173**
SW16 5K **137**
TW5: Hest 7C **94**
Beechcroft Ct. N12 4E **30**
NW11 *7H* ***45***
(off Beechcroft Av.)
Beechcroft Gdns. HA9: Wemb 3F **61**
Beechcroft Ho. W5 5E **78**
Beechcroft Lodge SM2: Sutt 7A **166**
Beechcroft Rd. BR6: Orp 4H **173**
E18 2K **51**
KT9: Chess 3F **163**
SW14 3J **115**
SW17 2C **136**
Beechdale N21 2E **32**
Beechdale Rd. SW2 6K **119**
Beech Dell BR2: Kes 4D **172**
Beechdene *SE15* *1H* ***121***
(off Carlton Gro.)
Beech Dr. N2 2D **46**
Beechen Cliff Way TW7: Isle 2K **113**
Beechen Gro. HA5: Pinn 3D **40**
Beechen Pl. SE23 2K **139**
Beeches, The *CR2: S Croy* *5D* ***168***
(off Blunt Rd.)
E12 7C **70**
TW3: Houn 1F **113**
Beeches Av. SM5: Cars 7C **166**
Beeches Cl. SE20 1J **157**
Beeches Rd. SM3: Sutt 1G **165**
SW17 3C **136**
Beeches Wlk. SM5: Cars 7B **166**
Beechey Ho. *E1* *1H* ***103***
(off Watts St.)
Beechfield Cotts. BR1: Brom 1A **160**
Beechfield Ct. *CR2: S Croy* *4C* ***168***
(off Bramley Hill)
Beechfield Gdns.
RM7: Rush G 7J **55**
Beechfield Rd. BR1: Brom 2A **160**
DA8: Erith 7K **109**
N4 6C **48**
SE6 1B **140**
Beech Gdns. *EC2* *5C* ***8***
(off Beech St.)
RM10: Dag 7J **73**
W5 2E **96**
Beech Gro. CR4: Mitc 5H **155**
(not continuous)
KT3: N Mald 3K **151**
Beech Hall Cres. E4 7A **36**
Beech Hall Rd. E4 7K **35**
Beech Haven Ct.
DA1: Cray *5K* ***127***
(off London Rd.)
Beech Hill EN4: Had W 1G **21**
Beech Hill Av. EN4: Had W 1F **21**
Beechhill Rd. SE9 5E **124**
Beech Ho. CR0: New Ad 6D **170**
E17 3F **51**
SE16 *2J* ***103***
(off Ainsty Est.)
Beech Ho. Rd. CR0: Croy 3D **168**
Beech La. IG9: Buck H 2E **36**
Beech Lawns N12 5G **31**
Beechmont Cl. BR1: Brom 5G **141**
Beechmore Gdns. SM3: Cheam 2F **165**
Beechmore Rd. SW11 1D **118**
Beechmount Av. W7 5H **77**
Beecholme N12 5E **30**
Beecholme Av. CR4: Mitc 1F **155**
Beecholme Est. E5 3H **67**
Beech Rd. N11 6D **32**
SW16 2J **155**
TW14: Bedf 7G **111**
Beechrow TW10: Ham 4E **132**
Beech St. EC2 5C **8** (5C **84**)
RM7: Rom 4J **55**
Beech Tree Cl. HA7: Stan 5H **27**
N1 7A **66**
Beech Tree Glade E4 1C **36**
Beech Tree Pl. SM1: Sutt 5K **165**
Beechvale Cl. N12 5H **31**
Beech Wlk. NW7 6F **29**
Beech Way NW10 7K **61**
TW2: Twick 3E **130**
Beechway DA5: Bexl 6D **126**
Beechwood Av. BR6: Chels 5J **173**
CR7: Thor H 4B **156**
HA2: Harr 3F **59**
HA4: Ruis 2H **57**
N3 3H **45**
TW9: Kew 1G **115**
TW16: Sun 6J **129**
UB3: Hayes 7F **75**
UB6: G'frd 3F **77**
UB8: Hil 6C **74**
Beechwood Circ. HA2: Harr 3F **59**
Beechwood Cl. KT6: Surb 7C **150**
N2 *4D* ***46***
(off Western Rd.)
NW7 5F **29**
Beechwood Ct. SM5: Cars 4D **166**
TW16: Sun 6J **129**
W4 6K **97**
Beechwood Cres. DA7: Bex 3D **126**
Beechwood Dr. BR2: Kes 4B **172**
IG8: Wfd G 5C **36**
Beechwood Gdns.
HA2: Harr 3F **59**
IG5: Ilf 5D **52**
NW10 3F **79**
Beechwood Gro. KT6: Surb 7C **150**
W3 7A **80**
Beechwood Hall N3 3H **45**
Beechwood Ho. *E2* *2G* ***85***
(off Teale St.)
Beechwood M. N9 2B **34**
Beechwood Pk. E18 3J **51**
Beechwood Ri. BR7: Chst 4F **143**
Beechwood Rd. CR2: Sand 7E **168**
E8 6F **67**
N8 4H **47**
Beechwoods Ct. SE19 5F **139**
Beechworth NW6 7G **63**
Beechworth Cl. NW3 2J **63**
Beecroft La. SE4 5A **122**
Beecroft M. SE4 5A **122**
Beecroft Rd. SE4 5A **122**
Beehive Cl. E8 7F **67**
UB10: Uxb 7B **56**
Beehive Ct. IG1: Ilf 6D **52**
Beehive La. IG1: Ilf 5D **52**
IG4: Ilf 5D **52**
Beehive Pl. SW9 3A **120**
Beeken Dene BR6: Farnb 4G **173**
Beeleigh Rd. SM4: Mord 4K **153**
Beemans Row SW18 2A **136**
Bee Pas. *EC3* *1G* ***15***
(off Lime St.)
Beeston Cl. E8 5G **67**
Beeston Ho. *SE1* *3D* ***102***
(off Burbage Cl.)
Beeston Pl. SW1 1K **17** (3F **101**)
Beeston Rd. EN4: E Barn 6G **21**
Beeston Way TW14: Felt 6A **112**
Beethoven St. W10 3G **81**
Beeton Cl. HA5: H End 1E **40**
Begbie Rd. SE3 1A **124**
BEGGAR'S HILL **6B 164**
Beggar's Hill KT17: Ewe 7B **164**
Beggars Roost La. SM1: Sutt 6J **165**
Begonia Cl. E6 5D **88**
Begonia Pl. TW12: Hamp 6E **130**
Begonia Wlk. W12 6B **80**
Beira St. SW12 7F **119**
Bekesbourne St. E14 6A **86**
Belcroft Cl. BR1: Brom 7H **141**
Beldanes Lodge NW10 7C **62**
Beldham Gdns. KT8: W Mole 2F **149**
Belfairs Dr. RM6: Chad H 7C **54**
Belfast Rd. N16 2F **67**
SE25 4H **157**
Belfield Rd. KT19: Ewe 7K **163**
Belfont Wlk. N7 4J **65**
(not continuous)
Belford Gro. SE18 4E **106**
Belford Ho. E8 1F **85**
Belfort Rd. SE15 2J **121**
Belfry Cl. SE16 5H **103**
Belfry Rd. E12 2B **70**
Belgrade Rd. N16 4E **66**
TW12: Hamp 1F **149**
Belgrave Cl. N14 5B **22**
NW7 5E **28**
W3 2H **97**
Belgrave Ct. *E2* *2H* ***85***
(off Temple St.)
E13 4A **88**
E14 *7B* ***86***
(off Westferry Cir.)
SW8 *7G* ***101***
(off Ascalon St.)
W4 5J **97**
Belgrave Cres. TW16: Sun 1K **147**
Belgrave Gdns. HA7: Stan 5H **27**
N14 5C **22**
NW8 1K **81**
Belgrave Hgts. E11 1J **69**
Belgrave Ho. SW9 7A **102**
Belgrave M. Nth.
SW1 7G **11** (2E **100**)
Belgrave M. Sth.
SW1 1H **17** (3E **100**)
Belgrave M. W. SW1 1G **17** (3E **100**)
Belgrave Pl. SW1 1H **17** (3E **100**)
Belgrave Rd. CR4: Mitc 3B **154**
E10 1E **68**
E11 2J **69**
E13 4A **88**
E17 5C **50**
Belgrave Rd. IG1: Ilf 1D **70**
SE25 4F **157**
SW1 4K **17** (4F **101**)
SW13 7B **98**
TW4: Houn 3D **112**
TW16: Sun 1K **147**
Belgrave Sq. SW1 1G **17** (3E **100**)
Belgrave St. E1 5K **85**
Belgrave Ter. IG8: Wfd G 3D **36**
Belgrave Wlk. CR4: Mitc 3B **154**
Belgrave Yd. SW1 2J **17**
BELGRAVIA **2H 17 (3E 100)**
Belgravia Cl. EN5: Barn 3C **20**
Belgravia Ct. SW1 2J **17**
Belgravia Gdns. BR1: Brom 6G **141**
Belgravia Ho. *SW1* *1G* ***17***
(off Halkin Pl.)
SW4 6H **119**
Belgravia M. KT1: King T 4D **150**
Belgravia Workshops *N19* *2J* ***65***
(off Marlborough Rd.)
Belgrove St. WC1 1F **7** (3J **83**)
Belham Wlk. SE5 1D **120**
Belinda Rd. SW9 3B **120**
Belitha Vs. N1 7K **65**
BELL, THE **3C 50**
Bella Best Ho. *W1* *5K* ***17***
(off Westmoreland Ter.)
Bellamy Cl. E14 2C **104**
HA8: Edg 2D **28**
UB10: Ick 3C **56**
W14 5H **99**
Bellamy Ct. HA7: Stan 1B **42**
Bellamy Dr. HA7: Stan 1B **42**
Bellamy Ho. SW17 4B **136**
TW5: Hest 6E **94**
Bellamy Rd. E4 6J **35**
EN2: Enf 2J **23**
Bellamy's Ct. *SE16* *1K* ***103***
(off Abbotshade Rd.)
Bellamy St. SW12 7F **119**
Bel La. TW13: Hanw 3C **130**
Bellasis Av. SW2 2J **137**
Bell Av. UB7: W Dray 4B **92**
Bell Cl. HA4: Ruis 3H **57**
HA5: Pinn 2A **40**
Bellclose Rd. UB7: W Dray 2A **92**
Bell Ct. NW4 4E **44**
Bell Dr. SW18 7G **117**
Bellefields Rd. SW9 3K **119**
Bellegrove Cl. DA16: Well 2K **125**
Bellegrove Pde. DA16: Well 3K **125**
Bellegrove Rd. DA16: Well 2H **125**
Bellenden Rd. SE15 1F **121**
Bellermine Cl. SE28 1K **107**
Bellestaines Pleasaunce E4 2H **35**
Belleville Rd. SW11 5C **118**
Belle Vue UB6: G'frd 1H **77**
Belle Vue Est. NW4 4F **45**
Bellevue La. WD23: Bushy 1C **26**
Bellevue M. N11 5K **31**
Bellevue Pde. SW17 1D **136**
Bellevue Pk. CR7: Thor H 3C **156**
Bellevue Pl. E1 4J **85**
Belle Vue Rd. E17 2F **51**
NW4 4E **44**
Bellevue Rd. DA6: Bex 5F **127**
KT1: King T 3E **150**
(not continuous)
N11 4K **31**
SW13 2C **116**
SW17 1C **136**
W13 4B **78**
Bellew St. SW17 3A **136**
Bell Farm Av. RM10: Dag 3J **73**
Bellfield CR0: Sels 7A **170**
Bellfield Av. HA3: Hrw W 6C **26**
Bellfield Cl. SE3 7J **105**
Bellflower Cl. E6 5C **88**
Bell Gdns. *E10* *1C* ***68***
(off Church Rd.)

Bellgate M. NW5 . . . . . 4F **65**
BELL GREEN 4A **140**
Bell Grn. SE26 . . . . . 4B **140**
Bell Grn. La. SE26 . . . . . 5B **140**
Bell Hill CR0: Croy 2C **168**
Bell Ho. HA9: Wemb 3E **60**
SE10 . . . . . *6E* ***104***
(off Haddo St.)
Bellhouse Cotts. UB3: Hayes 7G **75**
Bell Ho. Rd. RM7: Rush G 1J **73**
Bellina M. NW5 . . . . . 4F **65**
Bell Ind. Est. W4 . . . . . 4J **97**
BELLINGHAM 3C **140**
Bellingham *N17* *7C* ***34***
(off Park La.)
Bellingham Ct. IG11: Bark 3B **90**
Bellingham Grn. SE6 . . . . . 3C **140**
Bellingham Rd. SE6 . . . . . 3D **140**
Bellingham Trad. Est.
SE6 . . . . . 3D **140**
Bell Inn Yd. EC3 . . . . . 1F **15** (6D **84**)
Bell Junc. TW3: Houn 3F **113**
Bell La. E1 . . . . . 6J **9** (5F **85**)
E16 . . . . . 1H **105**
EN3: Enf H, Enf W 1E **24**
HA9: Wemb 2D **60**
NW4 . . . . . 4F **45**
TW1: Twick 1A **132**
Bellmaker Ct. E3 . . . . . 5C **86**
Bell Mdw. SE19 . . . . . 5E **138**
Bell Moor *NW3* *3A* ***64***
(off E. Heath Rd.)
Bello Cl. SE24 . . . . . 7B **120**
Bellot Gdns. *SE10* *5G* ***105***
(off Bellot St.)
Bellot St. SE10 . . . . . 5G **105**
Bellring Cl. DA17: Belv 6G **109**
Bell Rd. EN1: Enf 1J **23**
KT8: E Mos 5H **149**
TW3: Houn 3F **113**
Bells All. SW6 . . . . . 2J **117**
Bells Hill EN5: Barn 5A **20**
Bellsize Ct. NW3 . . . . . 5B **64**
Bell St. NW1 . . . . . 5C **4** (5C **82**)
SE18 . . . . . 1C **124**
Belltrees Gro. SW16 . . . . . 5K **137**
Bell Vw. Mnr. HA4: Ruis 7F **39**
Bell Water Ga. SE18 . . . . . 3E **106**
Bell Wharf La. EC4 . . . . . 3D **14** (7C **84**)
Bellwood Rd. SE15 . . . . . 4K **121**
Bell Yd. WC2 . . . . . 1J **13** (6A **84**)
Bell Yd. M. SE1 . . . . . 7H **15** (2E **102**)
Belmarsh Rd. SE28 . . . . . 2J **107**
BELMONT
Harrow 2A **42**
Sutton 7J **165**
Belmont Av. DA16: Well 2J **125**
EN4: Cockf 5J **21**
HA0: Wemb 1F **79**
KT3: N Mald 5C **152**
N9 . . . . . 1B **34**
N13 . . . . . 5E **32**
N17 . . . . . 3C **48**
UB2: S'hall 3C **94**
Belmont Circ. HA3: Kent 1B **42**
Belmont Cl. E4 . . . . . 5A **36**
EN4: Cockf 4J **21**
IG8: Wfd G 4E **36**
N20 . . . . . 1E **30**
SW4 . . . . . 3G **119**
UB8: Uxb 6A **56**
Belmont Ct. N5 . . . . . 4C **66**
NW11 . . . . . 5H **45**
Belmont Gro. SE13 . . . . . 3F **123**
W4 . . . . . 4K **97**
Belmont Hall Ct. SE13 . . . . . 3F **123**
Belmont Hill SE13 . . . . . 3E **122**
Belmont La. BR7: Chst 5G **143**
(not continuous)
HA7: Stan 1C **42**
Belmont Lodge HA3: Hrw W 7C **26**
Belmont M. SW19 . . . . . 2F **135**
Belmont Pde. BR7: Chst 5G **143**
NW11 . . . . . 5H **45**
Belmont Pk. SE13 . . . . . 4F **123**
Belmont Pk. Cl.
SE13 . . . . . 4G **123**
Belmont Pk. Rd. E10 . . . . . 6D **50**
Belmont Ri. SM2: Sutt 6H **165**
Belmont Rd. BR3: Beck 2A **158**
BR7: Chst 5F **143**
DA8: Erith 7G **109**
HA3: W'stone 3K **41**
IG1: Ilf 3G **71**
N15 . . . . . 4C **48**
N17 . . . . . 4C **48**
SE25 . . . . . 5H **157**
SM6: Wall 5F **167**
SW4 . . . . . 3G **119**
TW2: Twick 2H **131**
UB8: Uxb 7A **56**
W4 . . . . . 4K **97**
Belmont St. NW1 . . . . . 7E **64**
Belmont Ter. W4 . . . . . 4K **97**
Belmore Av. UB4: Hayes 6J **75**
Belmore Ho. N7 . . . . . 5H **65**
Belmore La. N7 . . . . . 5H **65**
Belmore St. SW8 . . . . . 1H **119**
Beloe Cl. SW15 . . . . . 4C **116**
Belsham St. E9 . . . . . 6J **67**
Belsize Av. N13 . . . . . 6E **32**
NW3 . . . . . 6B **64**
W13 . . . . . 3B **96**
Belsize Ct. Garages *NW3* *5B* ***64***
(off Belsize La.)
Belsize Cres. NW3 . . . . . 5B **64**
Belsize Gdns. SM1: Sutt 4K **165**
Belsize Gro. NW3 . . . . . 6C **64**
Belsize La. NW3 . . . . . 6B **64**
Belsize M. NW3 . . . . . 6B **64**
Belsize Pk. NW3 . . . . . 6B **64**
Belsize Pk. Gdns. NW3 . . . . . 6B **64**
Belsize Pk. M. NW3 . . . . . 6B **64**
Belsize Pl. NW3 . . . . . 5B **64**
Belsize Rd. HA3: Hrw W 7C **26**
NW6 . . . . . 1K **81**
Belsize Sq. NW3 . . . . . 6B **64**
Belsize Ter. NW3 . . . . . 6B **64**
Belson Rd. SE18 . . . . . 4D **106**
Beltane Dr. SW19 . . . . . 3F **135**
Belthorn Cres. SW12 . . . . . 7G **119**
Belton Rd. DA14: Sidc 4A **144**
E7 . . . . . 7K **69**
E11 . . . . . 4G **69**
N17 . . . . . 3E **48**
NW2 . . . . . 6C **62**
Belton Way E3 . . . . . 5C **86**
Beltran Rd. SW6 . . . . . 2K **117**
Beltwood Rd. DA17: Belv 4J **109**
BELVEDERE 3G **109**
Belvedere, The *SW10* *1A* ***118***
(off Chelsea Harbour)
Belvedere Av. IG5: Ilf 2F **53**
SW19 . . . . . 5G **135**
Belvedere Bldgs. SE1 . . . . . 7B **14** (2B **102**)
Belvedere Cl. TW11: Tedd 5J **131**
Belvedere Ct. DA17: Belv 3F **109**
N1 . . . . . *1E* ***84***
(off De Beauvoir Cres.)
N2 . . . . . 5B **46**
NW2 . . . . . *6F* ***63***
(off Willesden La.)
SW15 . . . . . 4E **116**
Belvedere Dr. SW19 . . . . . 5G **135**
Belvedere Gdns. KT8: W Mole 5D **148**
Belvedere Gro. SW19 . . . . . 5G **135**
Belvedere Ind. Est. DA17: Belv 1J **109**
Belvedere Link Bus. Pk. DA8: Erith 3J **109**
Belvedere M. SE3 . . . . . 7K **105**
SE15 . . . . . 3J **121**
Belvedere Pl. SE1 . . . . . 7B **14** (2B **102**)
SW2 . . . . . 4K **119**
Belvedere Rd. DA7: Bex 3F **127**
E10 . . . . . 1A **68**
SE1 . . . . . 6H **13** (1K **101**)
SE2 . . . . . 1C **108**
SE19 . . . . . 7F **139**
W7 . . . . . 3K **95**
Belvedere Sq. SW19 . . . . . 5G **135**
Belvedere Strand NW9 . . . . . 2B **44**
Belvedere Way HA3: Kent 6E **42**
Belvoir Cl. SE9 . . . . . 3C **142**
Belvoir Rd. SE22 . . . . . 7G **121**
Belvue Bus. Cen. UB5: N'olt 7F **59**
Belvue Cl. UB5: N'olt 7E **58**
Belvue Rd. UB5: N'olt 7E **58**
Bembridge Cl. NW6 . . . . . 7G **63**
Bembridge Gdns. HA4: Ruis 2F **57**
Bembridge Ho. *SE8* *4B* ***104***
(off Longshore)
SW18 . . . . . *6K* ***117***
(off Iron Mill Rd.)
Bemersyde Point *E13* *3K* ***87***
(off Dongola Rd. W.)
Bemerton Est. N1 . . . . . 7J **65**
Bemerton St. N1 . . . . . 1K **83**
Bemish Rd. SW15 . . . . . 3F **117**
Bempton Dr. HA4: Ruis 2K **57**
Bemsted Rd. E17 . . . . . 3B **50**
Benares Rd. SE18 . . . . . 4K **107**
Benbow Ct. *W6* *3E* ***98***
(off Benbow Rd.)
Benbow Ho. *SE8* *6C* ***104***
(off Benbow St.)
Benbow Rd. W6 . . . . . 3D **98**
Benbow St. SE8 . . . . . 6C **104**
Benbury Cl. BR1: Brom 5E **140**
Bence Ho. *SE8* *4A* ***104***
(off Rainsborough Av.)
Bench, The TW10: Ham 3C **132**
Bench Fld. CR2: S Croy 6F **169**
Bencroft Rd. SW16 . . . . . 7G **137**
Bencurtis Pk. BR4: W W'ck 3F **171**
Bendall M. NW1 . . . . . 5D **4**
Bendemeer Rd. SW15 . . . . . 3F **117**
Benden Ho. *SE13* *5E* ***122***
(off Monument Gdns.)
Bendish Point *SE28* *2G* ***107***
(off Erebus Dr.)
Bendish Rd. E6 . . . . . 7C **70**
Bendmore Av. SE2 . . . . . 5A **108**
Bendon Valley SW18 . . . . . 7K **117**
Benedict Cl. BR6: Orp 3J **173**
DA17: Belv 3E **108**
Benedict Ct. RM6: Chad H 6F **55**
Benedict Dr. TW14: Bedf 7F **111**
Benedict Rd. CR4: Mitc 3B **154**
SW9 . . . . . 3K **119**
Benedict Way N2 . . . . . 3A **46**
Benedict Wharf CR4: Mitc 3C **154**
Benenden Grn. BR2: Brom 5J **159**
Benett Gdns. SW16 . . . . . 2J **155**
Ben Ezra Ct. *SE17* *4C* ***102***
(off Asolando Dr.)
Benfleet Cl. SM1: Sutt 3A **166**
Benfleet Ct. E8 . . . . . 1F **85**
Benfleet Way N11 . . . . . 2K **31**
Bengal Ct. *EC3* *1F* ***15***
(off Birchin La.)
Bengal Ho. *E1* *5K* ***85***
(off Duckett St.)
Bengal Rd. IG1: Ilf 4F **71**
Bengarth Dr. HA3: Hrw W 2H **41**
Bengarth Rd. UB5: N'olt 1C **76**
Bengeo Gdns. RM6: Chad H 6C **54**
Bengeworth Rd. HA1: Harr 2A **60**
SE5 . . . . . 3C **120**
Ben Hale Cl. HA7: Stan 5G **27**
Benham Cl. KT9: Chess 6C **162**
SW11 . . . . . 3B **118**
Benham Gdns. TW4: Houn 5D **112**
Benham Ho. *SW10* *7K* ***99***
(off Coleridge Gdns.)
Benham Rd. W7 . . . . . 5J **77**
Benham's Pl. NW3 . . . . . 4A **64**
Benhill Av. SM1: Sutt 4K **165**
(not continuous)
Benhill Rd. SE5 . . . . . 7D **102**
SM1: Sutt 3A **166**
Benhill Wood Rd. SM1: Sutt 3A **166**
BENHILTON 2K **165**
Benhilton Gdns. SM1: Sutt 3K **165**
Benhurst Ct. SW16 . . . . . 5A **138**
Benhurst La. SW16 . . . . . 5A **138**
Benin St. SE13 . . . . . 7F **123**
Benjafield Cl. N18 . . . . . 4C **34**
Benjamin Cl. E8 . . . . . 1G **85**
Benjamin Ct. DA17: Belv 6F **109**
TW15: Ashf 7E **128**
Benjamin Franklin House *4E* *12*
(off Craven St.)
Benjamin St. EC1 . . . . . 5A **8** (5B **84**)
Ben Jonson Ct. N1 . . . . . 2E **84**
Ben Jonson Ho. EC2 . . . . . 5D **8**
Ben Jonson Pl. EC2 . . . . . 5D **8**
Ben Jonson Rd. E1 . . . . . 5K **85**
Benledi St. E14 . . . . . 6F **87**
Benlow Works *UB3: Hayes* *2H* ***93***
(off Silverdale Rd.)
Bennelong Cl. W12 . . . . . 7D **80**
Bennerley Rd. SW11 . . . . . 5C **118**
Bennets Fld. Rd. UB11: Stock P 1D **92**
Bennet's Hill EC4 . . . . . 2B **14** (7C **84**)
Bennet St. SW1 . . . . . 4A **12** (1G **101**)
Bennett Cl. DA16: Well 2A **126**
HA6: Nwood 1H **39**
KT1: Hamp W 1C **150**
Bennett Ct. N7 . . . . . 3K **65**
Bennett Gro. SE13 . . . . . 1D **122**
Bennett Ho. *SW1* *3D* ***18***
(off Page St.)
Bennett Pk. SE3 . . . . . 3H **123**
Bennett Rd. E13 . . . . . 4A **88**
N16 . . . . . 4E **66**
RM6: Chad H 6E **54**
SW9 . . . . . 2A **120**
Bennetts Av. CR0: Croy 2A **170**
UB6: G'frd 1J **77**
Bennett's Castle La. RM8: Dag 2C **72**
Bennetts Cl. CR4: Mitc 1F **155**
N17 . . . . . 6A **34**
Bennetts Copse BR7: Chst 6C **142**
Bennetts Courtyard SW19 . . . . . 1A **154**
Bennett St. W4 . . . . . 6A **98**
Bennetts Way CR0: Croy 2A **170**
Bennett's Yd. SW1 . . . . . 2D **18** (3H **101**)
Benningholme Rd. HA8: Edg 6F **29**
Bennington Rd. IG8: Wfd G 7B **36**
N17 . . . . . 1E **48**
Benn's All. TW12: Hamp 2F **149**
Benn St. E9 . . . . . 6A **68**
Benns Wlk. *TW9: Rich* *4E* ***114***
(off Michelsdale Dr.)
Benrek Cl. IG6: Ilf 1G **53**
Bensbury Cl. SW15 . . . . . 7D **116**
Bensham Cl. CR7: Thor H 4C **156**
Bensham Gro. CR7: Thor H 2C **156**
Bensham La. CR0: Croy 7B **156**
CR7: Thor H 5B **156**
Bensham Mnr. Rd. CR7: Thor H 4C **156**
Bensham Mnr. Rd. Pas.
CR7: Thor H 4C **156**
Bensley Cl. N11 . . . . . 5J **31**
Ben Smith Way SE16 . . . . . 3G **103**
Benson Av. E6 . . . . . 2A **88**
Benson Cl. TW3: Houn 4E **112**
UB8: Hil 5A **74**
Benson Ho. *E2* *3J* ***9***
(off Ligonier St.)
SE1 . . . . . *5K* ***13***
(off Hatfields)
Benson Quay E1 . . . . . 7J **85**
Benson Rd. CR0: Wadd 3A **168**
SE23 . . . . . 1J **139**

Bentalls Cen., The KT1: King T 2D **150**
Bentfield Gdns. SE9 . . . . 3B **142**
Benthal Rd. N16 . . . . 2G **67**
Bentham Ct. *N1* *7C* ***66***
(off Ecclesbourne Rd.)
Bentham Ho. *SE1* *3D* ***102***
(off Falmouth Rd.)
Bentham Rd. E9 . . . . 6K **67**
SE28 . . . . 7B **90**
Bentham Wlk. NW10 . . . . 5J **61**
Ben Tillet Cl. E16 . . . . 1D **106**
IG11: Bark 7A **72**
Ben Tillet Ho. N15 . . . . 3B **48**
Bentinck Cl. NW8 . . . . 2C **82**
Bentinck Ho. *W12* *7D* ***80***
(off White City Est.)
Bentinck M. W1 . . . . 7H **5** (6E **82**)
Bentinck Rd. UB7: Yiew 1A **92**
Bentinck St. W1 . . . . 7H **5** (6E **82**)
Bentley Cl. SW19 . . . . 3J **135**
Bentley Ct. *SE13* *4E* ***122***
(off Whitburn Rd.)
Bentley Dr. IG2: Ilf 6G **53**
NW2 . . . . 3H **63**
Bentley Ho. *SE5* *1E* ***120***
(off Peckham Rd.)
Bentley M. EN1: Enf 6J **23**
Bentley Rd. N1 . . . . 6E **66**
Bentley Way HA7: Stan 5F **27**
IG8: Buck H, Wfd G 2D **36**
Benton Rd. IG1: Ilf 1H **71**
Bentons La. SE27 . . . . 4C **138**
Benton's Ri. SE27 . . . . 5D **138**
Bentry Cl. RM8: Dag 2E **72**
Bentry Rd. RM8: Dag 2E **72**
Bentworth Ct. *E2* *3K* ***9***
(off Granby St.)
Bentworth Rd. W12 . . . . 6D **80**
Benville Ho. *SW8* *7K* ***101***
(off Oval Pl.)
Benwell Ct. TW16: Sun 1J **147**
Benwell Rd. N7 . . . . 4A **66**
Benwick Cl. SE16 . . . . 4H **103**
Benwood Ct. SM1: Sutt 3A **166**
Benworth St. E3 . . . . 3B **86**
Benyon Ct. *N1* *1E* ***84***
(off De Beauvoir Est.)
Benyon Ho. *EC1* *1K* ***7***
(off Myddelton Pas.)
Benyon Rd. N1 . . . . 1D **84**
Berberis Ct. IG1: Ilf 6F **71**
Berberis Ho. *E3* *5C* ***86***
(off Gale St.)
Berberis Wlk. UB7: W Dray 4A **92**
Berber Pl. E14 . . . . 7C **86**
Berber Rd. SW11 . . . . 5D **118**
Berberry Cl. HA8: Edg 4D **28**
Bercta Rd. SE9 . . . . 2G **143**
Berenger Twr. *SW10* *7B* ***100***
(off Worlds End Est.)
Berenger Wlk. *SW10* *7B* ***100***
(off Worlds End Est.)
Berens Ct. DA14: Sidc 4K **143**
Berens Rd. NW10 . . . . 3F **81**
Berens Way BR7: Chst 3K **161**
Beresford Av. HA0: Wemb 1F **79**
KT5: Surb 1H **163**
N20 . . . . 2J **31**
TW1: Twick 6C **114**
W7 . . . . 5H **77**
Beresford Dr. BR1: Brom 3C **160**
IG8: Wfd G 4F **37**
Beresford Gdns. EN1: Enf 4K **23**
RM6: Chad H 5E **54**
TW4: Houn 5D **112**
Beresford Rd. E4 . . . . 1B **36**
E17 . . . . 1D **50**
HA1: Harr 5H **41**
KT2: King T 1F **151**
KT3: N Mald 4J **151**
N2 . . . . 3C **46**
Beresford Rd. N5 . . . . 5D **66**
N8 . . . . 5A **48**
SM2: Sutt 7H **165**
UB1: S'hall 1B **94**
Beresford Sq. SE18 . . . . 4F **107**
Beresford St. SE18 . . . . 3F **107**
Beresford Ter. N5 . . . . 5C **66**
Berestede Rd. W6 . . . . 5B **98**
Bere St. E1 . . . . 7K **85**
Bergen Ho. *SE5* *2C* ***120***
(off Carew St.)
Bergen Sq. SE16 . . . . 3A **104**
Berger Cl. BR5: Pet W 6H **161**
Berger Rd. E9 . . . . 6K **67**
Berghem M. W14 . . . . 3F **99**
Bergholt Av. IG4: Ilf 5C **52**
Bergholt Cres. N16 . . . . 7E **48**
Bergholt M. NW1 . . . . 7G **65**
Berglen Ct. E14 . . . . 6A **86**
Bering Sq. E14 . . . . 5C **104**
Bering Wlk. E16 . . . . 6B **88**
Berisford M. SW18 . . . . 6A **118**
Berkeley Av. DA7: Bex 1D **126**
IG5: Ilf 2E **52**
RM5: Col R 1J **55**
TW4: Cran 2J **111**
UB6: G'frd 6H **59**
(not continuous)
Berkeley Cl. BR5: Pet W 7J **161**
HA4: Ruis 3J **57**
KT2: King T 7E **132**
Berkeley Ct. *CR0: Croy* *4D* ***168***
(off Coombe Rd.)
KT6: Surb 7D **150**
N3 . . . . 1K **45**
N14 . . . . 6B **22**
NW1 . . . . 4F **5**
NW10 . . . . 4A **62**
NW11 . . . . *7H* ***45***
(off Ravenscroft Av.)
SM6: Wall 3G **167**
W5 . . . . *7C* ***78***
(off Gordon Rd.)
Berkeley Cres. EN4: E Barn 5G **21**
Berkeley Dr. KT8: W Mole 3D **148**
Berkeley Gdns. KT10: Clay 6A **162**
KT12: Walt T 7H **147**
N21 . . . . 7J **23**
W8 . . . . 1J **99**
Berkeley Ho. *SE8* *5B* ***104***
(off Grove St.)
TW8: Bford *6D* ***96***
(off Albany Rd.)
Berkeley M. W1 . . . . 1F **11** (6D **82**)
Berkeley Pl. SW19 . . . . 6F **135**
Berkeley Rd. E12 . . . . 5C **70**
N8 . . . . 5H **47**
N15 . . . . 6D **48**
NW9 . . . . 4G **43**
SW13 . . . . 1C **116**
UB10: Hil 7E **56**
Berkeley Sq. W1 . . . . 3K **11** (7F **83**)
Berkeley St. W1 . . . . 3K **11** (7F **83**)
Berkeley Twr. *E14* *1B* ***104***
(off Westferry Cir.)
Berkeley Wlk. *N7* *2K* ***65***
(off Durham Rd.)
Berkeley Waye TW5: Hest 6B **94**
Berkely Cl. TW16: Sun 3A **148**
Berkhampstead Rd. DA17: Belv 5G **109**
Berkhamsted Av. HA9: Wemb 6F **61**
Berkley Cl. *TW2: Twick* *3J* ***131***
(off Wellesley Rd.)
Berkley Gro. NW1 . . . . 7E **64**
Berkley Rd. NW1 . . . . 7D **64**
Berkshire Ct. *W7* *4K* ***77***
(off Copley Cl.)
Berkshire Gdns. N13 . . . . 6F **33**
N18 . . . . 5C **34**
Berkshire Ho. SE6 . . . . 4C **140**
Berkshire Rd. E9 . . . . 6B **68**
Berkshire Sq. CR4: Mitc 4J **155**
Berkshire Way CR4: Mitc 4J **155**
Bermans Way NW10 . . . . 4A **62**
BERMONDSEY 7K **15** (2G **103**)
Bermondsey Sq. SE1 . . . . 7H **15** (3E **102**)
Bermondsey St. SE1 . . . . 5G **15** (1E **102**)
Bermondsey Trad. Est.
SE16 . . . . 5J **103**
Bermondsey Wall E. SE16 . . . . 2G **103**
Bermondsey Wall W.
SE16 . . . . 6K **15** (2G **103**)
Bernal Cl. SE28 . . . . 7D **90**
Bernard Angell Ho. *SE10* *6F* ***105***
(off Trafalgar Rd.)
Bernard Ashley Dr. SE7 . . . . 5K **105**
Bernard Av. W13 . . . . 3B **96**
Bernard Cassidy St. E16 . . . . 5H **87**
Bernard Gdns. SW19 . . . . 5H **135**
Bernard Mans. *WC1* *4E* ***6***
(off Bernard St.)
Bernard Rd. N15 . . . . 5F **49**
RM7: Rush G 7J **55**
SM6: Wall 4F **167**
Bernard Shaw Ct. *NW1* *7G* ***65***
(off St Pancras Way)
Bernard St. WC1 . . . . 4E **6** (4J **83**)
Bernard Sunley Ho. *SW9* *7A* ***102***
(off Sth. Island Pl.)
Bernays Cl. HA7: Stan 6H **27**
Bernays Gro. SW9 . . . . 4K **119**
Bernel Dr. CR0: Croy 3B **170**
Berne Rd. CR7: Thor H 5C **156**
Berners Dr. W13 . . . . 7A **78**
Berners Ho. *N1* *2A* ***84***
(off Barnsbury Est.)
Berners M. W1 . . . . 6B **6** (5G **83**)
Berners Pl. W1 . . . . 7B **6** (6G **83**)
Berners Rd. N1 . . . . 1B **84**
N22 . . . . 1A **48**
Berners St. W1 . . . . 6B **6** (5G **83**)
Berner Ter. *E1* *6G* ***85***
(off Fairclough St.)
Berney Ho. BR3: Beck 5A **158**
Berney Rd. CR0: Croy 7D **156**
Bernhardt Cres. NW8 . . . . 3C **4** (4C **82**)
Bernhart Cl. HA8: Edg 7D **28**
Bernville Way HA3: Kent 5F **43**
Bernwell Rd. E4 . . . . 3B **36**
Berridge Grn. HA8: Edg 7B **28**
Berridge M. NW6 . . . . 5J **63**
Berridge Rd. SE19 . . . . 5D **138**
Berriman Rd. N7 . . . . 3K **65**
Berriton Rd. HA2: Harr 1D **58**
Berrybank Cl. E4 . . . . 2K **35**
Berry Cl. N21 . . . . 1G **33**
RM10: Dag 5G **73**
Berry Cotts. *E14* *6A* ***86***
(off Maroon St.)
Berry Ct. TW4: Houn 5D **112**
Berrydale Rd. UB4: Yead 4C **76**
Berryfield Cl. BR1: Brom 1C **160**
E17 . . . . 4D **50**
Berryfield Rd. SE17 . . . . 5B **102**
Berry Hill HA7: Stan 4J **27**
Berryhill SE9 . . . . 4F **125**
Berryhill Gdns. SE9 . . . . 4F **125**
Berry Ho. *E1* *4H* ***85***
(off Headlam St.)
BERRYLANDS 6G **151**
Berrylands KT5: Surb 6F **151**
SW20 . . . . 3E **152**
Berrylands Rd. KT5: Surb 6F **151**
Berry La. SE21 . . . . 4D **138**
Berryman Cl. RM8: Dag 3C **72**
Berryman's La. SE26 . . . . 4K **139**
Berrymead Gdns. W3 . . . . 1J **97**
Berrymede Rd. W4 . . . . 3K **97**
Berry Pl. EC1 . . . . 2B **8** (3B **84**)
Berry St. EC1 . . . . 3B **8** (4B **84**)
Berry Way W5 . . . . 3E **96**
Bertal Rd. SW17 . . . . 4B **136**
Bertha Hollamby Ct. *DA14: Sidc* *5C* ***144***
(off Sidcup Hill)
Bertha James Ct. BR2: Brom 4K **159**
Berthons Gdns. *E17* *5F* ***51***
(off Wood St.)
Berthon St. SE8 . . . . 7C **104**
Bertie Rd. NW10 . . . . 6C **62**
SE26 . . . . 6K **139**
Bertram Cotts. SW19 . . . . 7J **135**
Bertram Rd. EN1: Enf 4B **24**
KT2: King T 7G **133**
NW4 . . . . 6C **44**
Bertram St. N19 . . . . 2F **65**
Bertrand Ho. *SW16* *3J* ***137***
(off Leigham Av.)
Bertrand St. SE13 . . . . 3D **122**
Bertrand Way SE28 . . . . 7B **90**
Bert Rd. CR7: Thor H 5C **156**
Bert Way EN1: Enf 4A **24**
Berwick Av. UB4: Yead 6B **76**
Berwick Cl. HA7: Stan 6E **26**
TW2: Whit 1E **130**
Berwick Ct. SE1 . . . . 7D **14**
Berwick Cres. DA15: Sidc 7J **125**
Berwick Gdns. SM1: Sutt 3A **166**
Berwick Ho. N2 . . . . 2B **46**
Berwick Rd. DA16: Well 1B **126**
E16 . . . . 6K **87**
N22 . . . . 1B **48**
Berwick St. W1 . . . . 7B **6** (6G **83**)
Berwick Way BR6: Orp 1K **173**
Berwyn Av. TW3: Houn 1F **113**
Berwyn Rd. SE24 . . . . 1B **138**
TW10: Rich 4H **115**
Beryl Av. E6 . . . . 5C **88**
Beryl Ho. *SE18* *5K* ***107***
(off Spinel Cl.)
Beryl Rd. W6 . . . . 5F **99**
Berystede KT2: King T 7H **133**
Besant Cl. NW2 . . . . 3G **63**
Besant Ct. N1 . . . . 5D **66**
SE28 . . . . *1B* ***108***
(off Titmuss Av.)
Besant Ho. *NW8* *1A* ***82***
(off Boundary Rd.)
Besant Pl. SE22 . . . . 4F **121**
Besant Rd. NW2 . . . . 4G **63**
Besant Wlk. N7 . . . . 2K **65**
Besant Way NW10 . . . . 5J **61**
Besford Ho. *E2* *2G* ***85***
(off Pritchard's Rd.)
Besley St. SW16 . . . . 6G **137**
Bessant Dr. TW9: Kew 1G **115**
Bessborough Gdns.
SW1 . . . . 5D **18** (5H **101**)
Bessborough Pl.
SW1 . . . . 5D **18** (5H **101**)
Bessborough Rd. HA1: Harr 1H **59**
SW15 . . . . 1C **134**
Bessborough St.
SW1 . . . . 5C **18** (5H **101**)
Bessemer Ct. *NW1* *7G* ***65***
(off Rochester Sq.)
Bessemer Pk. Ind. Est. SE24 . . . . 4B **120**
Bessemer Rd. SE5 . . . . 2C **120**
Bessie Lansbury Cl. E6 . . . . 6E **88**
Bessingby Rd. HA4: Ruis 2K **57**
Bessingham Wlk. *SE4* *4K* ***121***
(off Aldersford Cl.)
Besson St. SE14 . . . . 1J **121**
Bessy St. E2 . . . . 3J **85**
Bestwood St. *SE8* *4K* ***103***
(off Rotherhithe New Rd.)
Beswick M. NW6 . . . . 6K **63**
Betam Rd. UB3: Hayes 2F **93**
Beta Pl. SW4 . . . . 4K **119**
Betchworth Cl. SM1: Sutt 5B **166**
Betchworth Rd. IG3: Ilf 2J **71**
Betchworth Way CR0: New Ad 7E **170**
Bethal Est. SE1 . . . . 5H **15**
Betham Rd. UB6: G'frd 3H **77**

Bethany Waye TW14: Bedf . . . 7G **111**
Bethecar Rd. HA1: Harr . . . 5J **41**
Bethel Cl. NW4 . . . 5F **45**
Bethell Av. E16 . . . 4H **87**
IG1: Ilf . . . 7E **52**
Bethel Rd. DA16: Well . . . 3C **126**
Bethersden Cl.
BR3: Beck . . . 7B **140**
Bethersden Ho. *SE17* . . . *5E* ***102***
(off Kinglake St.)
Bethlehem Ho. *E14* . . . *7B* ***86***
(off Limehouse C'way.)
BETHNAL GREEN . . . 3H 85
Bethnal Green Cen. for Sports & Performing Arts . . . 3F 85
Bethnal Green Mus. of Childhood . . . 3J 85
Bethnal Grn. Rd. E1 . . . 3J **9** (4F **85**)
E2 . . . 3K **9** (4F **85**)
Bethune Av. N11 . . . 4J **31**
Bethune Cl. N16 . . . 1E **66**
Bethune Rd. N16 . . . 7D **48**
NW10 . . . 4K **79**
Bethwin Rd. SE5 . . . 7B **102**
Betjeman Cl. HA5: Pinn . . . 4E **40**
Betjeman Ct. UB7: Yiew . . . 1A **92**
Betony Cl. CR0: Croy . . . 1K **169**
Betoyne Av. E4 . . . 4B **36**
Betsham Ho. *SE1* . . . *6E* ***14***
(off Newcomen St.)
Betstyle Cir. N11 . . . 4A **32**
Betstyle Ho. N10 . . . 7K **31**
Betstyle Rd. N11 . . . 4A **32**
Betterton Dr. DA14: Sidc . . . 2E **144**
Betterton Ho. *WC2* . . . *1F* ***13***
(off Betterton St.)
Betterton Rd. RM13: Rain . . . 3K **91**
Betterton St. WC2 . . . 1E **12** (6J **83**)
Bettons Pk. E15 . . . 1G **87**
Bettridge Rd. SW6 . . . 2H **117**
Betts Cl. BR3: Beck . . . 2A **158**
Betts Ho. *E1* . . . *7H* ***85***
(off Betts St.)
Betts M. E17 . . . 6B **50**
Betts Rd. E16 . . . 7K **87**
Betts St. E1 . . . 7H **85**
Betts Way KT6: Surb . . . 1B **162**
SE20 . . . 1H **157**
Betty Brooks Ho. E11 . . . 3F **69**
Betty May Gray Ho.
E14 . . . *4E* ***104***
(off Pier St.)
Beulah Av. CR7: Thor H . . . 2C **156**
Beulah Cl. HA8: Edg . . . 3C **28**
Beulah Cres. CR7: Thor H . . . 2C **156**
Beulah Gro. CR0: Croy . . . 6C **156**
Beulah Hill SE19 . . . 6B **138**
Beulah Path E17 . . . 5E **50**
Beulah Rd. CR7: Thor H . . . 3C **156**
E17 . . . 5D **50**
SM1: Sutt . . . 4J **165**
SW19 . . . 7H **135**
Bevan Av. IG11: Bark . . . 7A **72**
Bevan Ct. CR0: Wadd . . . 5A **168**
Bevan Ho. TW1: Twick . . . 6D **114**
WC1 . . . *5F* ***7***
(off Boswell St.)
Bevan Rd. EN4: Cockf . . . 4J **21**
SE2 . . . 5B **108**
Bevan St. N1 . . . 1C **84**
Bev Callender Cl.
SW8 . . . 3F **119**
Bevenden St. N1 . . . 1F **9** (3D **84**)
Bevercote Wlk. *DA17: Belv* . . . *6F* ***109***
(off Osborne Rd.)
Beveree Stadium . . . 1F 149
Beveridge Ct. *SE28* . . . *7B* ***90***
(off Saunders Way)
Beveridge Rd. NW10 . . . 7A **62**
Beverley Av. DA15: Sidc . . . 7K **125**
SW20 . . . 1B **152**
TW4: Houn . . . 4D **112**
Beverley Cl. EN1: Enf . . . 4K **23**
KT9: Chess . . . 4C **162**
N21 . . . 1H **33**
SW11 . . . 4B **118**
SW13 . . . 2C **116**
Beverley Cotts. SW15 . . . 3A **134**
Beverley Ct. HA2: Harr . . . 3H **41**
HA3: Kent . . . 4C **42**
N2 . . . *4D* ***46***
(off Western Rd.)
N14 . . . 7B **22**
SE4 . . . 3B **122**
(not continuous)
TW4: Houn . . . 4D **112**
W4 . . . 5J **97**
Beverley Cres. IG8: Wfd G . . . 1K **51**
Beverley Dr. HA8: Edg . . . 3G **43**
Beverley Gdns. HA7: Stan . . . 1A **42**
HA9: Wemb . . . 1F **61**
KT4: Wor Pk . . . 1C **164**
NW11 . . . 7G **45**
SW13 . . . 3B **116**
Beverley Ho. *BR1: Brom* . . . *5F* ***141***
(off Brangbourne Rd.)
Beverley Hyrst CR0: Croy . . . 2F **169**
Beverley La. KT2: King T . . . 7A **134**
SW15 . . . 3B **134**
Beverley M. E4 . . . 6A **36**
Beverley Path SW13 . . . 2B **116**
Beverley Rd. BR2: Brom . . . 2C **172**
CR4: Mitc . . . 4H **155**
DA7: Bex . . . 2J **127**
E4 . . . 6A **36**
E6 . . . 3B **88**
HA4: Ruis . . . 2J **57**
KT1: Hamp W . . . 1C **150**
KT3: N Mald . . . 4C **152**
KT4: Wor Pk . . . 2E **164**
RM9: Dag . . . 4E **72**
SE20 . . . 2H **157**
SW13 . . . 3B **116**
TW16: Sun . . . 1H **147**
UB2: S'hall . . . 4C **94**
W4 . . . 5B **98**
Beverley Trad. Est. SM4: Mord . . . 7F **153**
Beverley Way SW20 . . . 1B **152**
Beversbrook Rd. N19 . . . 3H **65**
Beverstone Rd. CR7: Thor H . . . 4A **156**
SW2 . . . 5K **119**
Beverston M. W1 . . . 6E **4**
Bevill Allen Cl. SW17 . . . 5D **136**
Bevill Cl. SE25 . . . 3G **157**
Bevin Cl. SE16 . . . 1A **104**
Bevin Ct. WC1 . . . 1H **7** (3K **83**)
Bevington Path SE1 . . . 7J **15**
Bevington Rd. BR3: Beck . . . 2D **158**
W10 . . . 5G **81**
Bevington St. SE16 . . . 2G **103**
Bevin Ho. *E2* . . . *3J* ***85***
(off Butler St.)
Bevin Rd. UB4: Yead . . . 3J **75**
Bevin Sq. SW17 . . . 3D **136**
Bevin Way WC1 . . . 1J **7** (2A **84**)
Bevis Marks EC3 . . . 7H **9** (6E **84**)
Bewcastle Gdns.
EN2: Enf . . . 4D **22**
Bew Ct. SE22 . . . 7G **121**
Bewdley St. N1 . . . 7A **66**
Bewick M. SE15 . . . 7H **103**
Bewick St. SW8 . . . 2F **119**
Bewley Ho. *E1* . . . *7H* ***85***
(off Bewley St.)
Bewley St. E1 . . . 7J **85**
SW19 . . . 6A **136**
Bewlys Rd. SE27 . . . 5B **138**
Bexhill Cl. TW13: Felt . . . 2C **130**
Bexhill Rd. N11 . . . 5C **32**
SE4 . . . 6B **122**
SW14 . . . 3J **115**
Bexhill Wlk. E15 . . . 1G **87**
BEXLEY . . . 7G **127**
Bexley Gdns. N9 . . . 3J **33**
RM6: Chad H . . . 5B **54**
BEXLEYHEATH . . . 4F **127**
Bexleyheath Sports Club . . . 3C 126
Bexley High St.
DA5: Bexl . . . 7G **127**
Bexley Ho. SE4 . . . 4A **122**
Bexley La. DA1: Cray . . . 5K **127**
DA14: Sidc . . . 4C **144**
Bexley Lawn Tennis & Squash Club . . . 7G 127
Bexley Mus. . . . 6J 127
Bexley Music & Dance Cen. . . . *4A 144*
(off Station Rd.)
Bexley Rd. DA8: Erith . . . 7J **109**
SE9 . . . 5F **125**
Beynon Rd. SM5: Cars . . . 5D **166**
Bianca Rd. SE15 . . . 6G **103**
Bibsworth Rd. N3 . . . 2H **45**
Bibury Cl. SE15 . . . 6E **102**
(not continuous)
Bicester Rd. TW9: Rich . . . 3G **115**
Bickenhall Mans. W1 . . . 5F **5**
(not continuous)
Bickenhall St. W1 . . . 5F **5** (5D **82**)
Bickersteth Rd. SW17 . . . 6D **136**
Bickerton Rd. N19 . . . 2G **65**
BICKLEY . . . 3C 160
Bickley Cres. BR1: Brom . . . 4C **160**
Bickley Pk. Rd. BR1: Brom . . . 3C **160**
Bickley Rd. BR1: Brom . . . 2B **160**
E10 . . . 7D **50**
Bickley St. SW17 . . . 5C **136**
Bicknell Ho. *E1* . . . *6G* ***85***
(off Ellen St.)
Bicknell Rd. SE5 . . . 3C **120**
Bicknoller Rd. EN1: Enf . . . 1K **23**
Bicknor Rd. BR6: Orp . . . 7J **161**
Bidborough Cl. BR2: Brom . . . 5H **159**
Bidborough St. WC1 . . . 2E **6** (3J **83**)
Biddenden Way SE9 . . . 4E **142**
Biddenham Ho. *SE16* . . . *4K* ***103***
(off Plough Way)
Bidder St. E16 . . . 4G **87**
(not continuous)
Biddesden Ho. *SW3* . . . *4E* ***16***
(off Cadogan St.)
Biddestone Rd. N7 . . . 4K **65**
Biddulph Ho. SE18 . . . 4D **106**
Biddulph Mans. *W9* . . . *3K* ***81***
(off Elgin Av.)
Biddulph Rd. W9 . . . 3K **81**
Bideford Av. UB6: G'frd . . . 2B **78**
Bideford Cl. HA8: Edg . . . 1G **43**
TW13: Hanw . . . 3D **130**
Bideford Gdns. EN1: Enf . . . 7K **23**
Bideford Rd. BR1: Brom . . . 3H **141**
DA16: Well . . . 7B **108**
EN3: Enf L . . . 1G **25**
HA4: Ruis . . . 3K **57**
Bidwell Gdns. N11 . . . 7B **32**
Bidwell St. SE15 . . . 1H **121**
Big Ben . . . 7F 13 (2J 101)
Bigbury Cl. N17 . . . 7J **33**
Biggerstaff Rd. E15 . . . 1E **86**
Biggerstaff St. N4 . . . 2A **66**
Biggin Av. CR4: Mitc . . . 1D **154**
Biggin Hill SE19 . . . 1B **156**
Biggin Hill Cl. KT2: King T . . . 5C **132**
Biggin Way SE19 . . . 7B **138**
Bigginwood Rd. SW16 . . . 7B **138**
Biggs Row SW15 . . . 3F **117**
Big Hill E5 . . . 1H **67**
Bigland St. E1 . . . 6H **85**
Bignell Rd. SE18 . . . 5F **107**
Bignold Rd. E7 . . . 4J **69**
Bigwood Ct. NW11 . . . 5K **45**
Bigwood Rd. NW11 . . . 5K **45**
Bilberry Ho. *E3* . . . *5C* ***86***
(off Watts Gro.)
Billet Cl. RM6: Chad H . . . 3D **54**
Billet Rd. E17 . . . 1K **49**
RM6: Chad H . . . 3B **54**
Billets Hart Cl. W7 . . . 2J **95**
Bill Hamling Cl.
SE9 . . . 2D **142**
Billing Cl. RM9: Dag . . . 7C **72**
Billingford Cl. SE4 . . . 4K **121**
Billing Ho. *E1* . . . *6K* ***85***
(off Bower St.)
Billingley *NW1* . . . *1G* ***83***
(off Pratt St.)
Billing Pl. SW10 . . . 7K **99**
Billing Rd. SW10 . . . 7K **99**
Billingsgate Fish Market . . . 1D 104
Billing St. SW10 . . . 7K **99**
Billington M. *W3* . . . *1H* ***97***
(off High St.)
Billington Rd. SE14 . . . 7K **103**
Billinton Hill CR0: Croy . . . 2D **168**
Billiter Sq. EC3 . . . 1H **15**
Billiter St. EC3 . . . 1H **15** (6E **84**)
Bill Nicholson Way
N17 . . . *7A* ***34***
(off High Rd.)
Billockby Cl. KT9: Chess . . . 6F **163**
Billson St. E14 . . . 4E **104**
Bilsby Gro. SE9 . . . 4B **142**
Bilsby Lodge *HA9: Wemb* . . . *3J* ***61***
(off Chalklands)
Bilton Cen., The UB6: G'frd . . . 1B **78**
Bilton Rd. UB6: G'frd . . . 1A **78**
Bilton Towers *W1* . . . *1F* ***11***
(off Gt. Cumberland Pl.)
Bilton Way EN3: Enf L . . . 1F **25**
UB3: Hayes . . . 2K **93**
Bina Gdns. SW5 . . . 4A **100**
Binbrook Ho. *W10* . . . *5E* ***80***
(off Sutton Way)
Bincote Rd. EN2: Enf . . . 3E **22**
Binden Rd. W12 . . . 3B **98**
Bindon Grn. SM4: Mord . . . 4K **153**
Binfield Rd. CR2: S Croy . . . 5F **169**
SW4 . . . 1J **119**
Bingfield St. N1 . . . 1J **83**
(not continuous)
Bingham Ct. *N1* . . . *7B* ***66***
(off Halton Rd.)
Bingham Pl. W1 . . . 5G **5** (5E **82**)
Bingham Rd. CR0: Croy . . . 1G **169**
Bingham St. N1 . . . 6D **66**
Bingley Rd. E16 . . . 6A **88**
TW16: Sun . . . 7J **129**
UB6: G'frd . . . 4G **77**
Binley Ho. SW15 . . . 6B **116**
Binney St. W1 . . . 1H **11** (6E **82**)
Binnie Ct. *SE10* . . . *7D* ***104***
(off Greenwich High Rd.)
Binnie Ho. *SE1* . . . *3C* ***102***
(off Bath Ter.)
Binnington Twr. BR2: Brom . . . 6C **160**
Binns Rd. W4 . . . 5A **98**
Binns Ter. W4 . . . 5A **98**
Binsey Wlk. SE2 . . . 2C **108**
(not continuous)
Binstead Cl. UB4: Yead . . . 5C **76**
Binyon Cres. HA7: Stan . . . 5E **26**
Birbetts Rd. SE9 . . . 2D **142**
Bircham Path *SE4* . . . *4K* ***121***
(off Aldersford Cl.)
Birchanger Rd. SE25 . . . 5G **157**
Birch Av. N13 . . . 3H **33**
UB7: Yiew . . . 6B **74**
Birch Cl. E16 . . . 5G **87**
IG9: Buck H . . . 3G **37**
N19 . . . 2G **65**
RM7: Mawney . . . 3H **55**
SE15 . . . 2G **121**
TW3: Houn . . . 2H **113**
TW8: Bford . . . 7B **96**
TW11: Tedd . . . 5A **132**
TW17: Shep . . . 2G **147**

Birch Ct.—Blackheath Vale

Birch Ct. N12 4E 30
RM6: Chad H 6C 54
SM1: Sutt 4A 166
SM6: Wall 4F 167
Birch Cres. UB10: Uxb 1B 74
Birchdale Gdns.
RM6: Chad H 7D 54
Birchdale Rd. E7 5A 70
Birchdene Dr. SE28 1A 108
Birchen Cl. NW9 2K 61
Birchend Cl. CR2: S Croy 6D 168
Birchen Gro. NW9 2K 61
Birches, The *BR2: Brom* *4H 159*
(off Durham Rd.)
BR6: Farnb 4E 172
E12 4C 70
N21 6E 22
SE7 6K 105
TW4: Houn 7D 112
Birches Cl. CR4: Mitc 3D 154
HA5: Pinn 5C 40
Birchfield Ho. *E14* *7C 86*
(off Birchfield St.)
Birchfield St. E14 7C 86
Birch Gdns. RM10: Dag 3J 73
Birch Grn. NW9 7F 29
Birch Gro. DA16: Well 4A 126
E11 4G 69
SE12 7H 123
TW17: Shep 2G 147
W3 1G 97
Birchgrove Ho. TW9: Kew 7H 97
Birch Hill CR0: Croy 5K 169
Birch Ho. *N22* *1A 48*
(off Acacia Rd.)
SE14 1B 122
SW2 *6A 120*
(off Tulse Hill)
W10 *4G 81*
(off Droop St.)
Birchington Cl. DA7: Bex 1H 127
Birchington Ct. *NW6* *1K 81*
(off W. End La.)
Birchington Ho. E5 5H 67
Birchington Rd. KT5: Surb 7F 151
N8 6H 47
NW6 1J 81
Birchin La. EC3 1F 15 (6D 84)
Birchlands Av. SW12 7D 118
Birchmead BR6: Farnb 2E 172
Birchmead Av. HA5: Pinn 4A 40
Birchmere Bus. Pk. SE28 2A 108
Birchmere Lodge *SE16* *5H 103*
(off Sherwood Gdns.)
Birchmere Row SE3 2H 123
Birchmore Hall N5 3C 66
Birchmore Wlk. N5 3C 66
Birch Pk. HA3: Hrw W 7B 26
Birch Rd. RM7: Mawney 3H 55
TW13: Hanw 5B 130
Birch Row BR2: Brom 7E 160
Birch Tree Av. BR4: W W'ck 5H 171
Birch Tree Way CR0: Croy 2H 169
Birch Va. Ct. *NW8* *3B 4*
(off Pollitt Dr.)
Birchville Ct. WD23: Bushy 1D 26
Birch Wlk. CR4: Mitc 1F 155
DA8: Erith 6J 109
Birchway UB3: Hayes 1J 93
Birchwood Av. BR3: Beck 4B 158
DA14: Sidc 2B 144
N10 3E 46
SM6: Wall 3E 166
Birchwood Cl. SM4: Mord 4K 153
Birchwood Ct. HA8: Edg 2J 43
N13 5G 33
Birchwood Dr. DA2: Dart 4K 145
NW3 3K 63
Birchwood Gro.
TW12: Hamp 6E 130
Birchwood Pde. DA2: Dart 4K 145
Birchwood Rd. BR5: Pet W 4H 161
DA2: Dart 7J 145
SW17 5F 137
Birdbrook Cl. RM10: Dag 7J 73
Birdbrook Ho. *N1* *7C 66*
(off Popham Rd.)
Birdbrook Rd. SE3 4A 124
Birdcage Wlk. SW1 7A 12 (2G 101)
Birdham Cl. BR1: Brom 5C 160
Birdhurst Av. CR2: S Croy 4D 168
Birdhurst Gdns. CR2: S Croy 4D 168
Birdhurst Ri. CR2: S Croy 5E 168
Birdhurst Rd. CR2: S Croy 5E 168
SW18 5A 118
SW19 6C 136
Bird in Bush BMX Track *7H 103*
(off Bird in Bush Rd.)
Bird in Bush Rd. SE15 7G 103
Bird in Hand La. BR1: Brom 2B 160
Bird-in-Hand Pas. SE23 2J 139
Bird in Hand Path *CR0: Croy* *7D 156*
(off Sydenham Rd.)
Bird in Hand Yd. *NW3* *4A 64*
(off Holly Bush Va.)
NW3 4A 64
(Perrin's Ct.)
Birdlip Cl. SE15 6E 102
Birdsall Ho. SE5 3E 120
Birds Farm Av. RM5: Col R 1H 55
Birdsfield La. E3 1B 86
Bird St. W1 1H 11 (6E 82)
Bird Wlk. TW2: Whit 1D 130
Birdwood Cl. TW11: Tedd 4J 131
Birkbeck Av. UB6: G'frd 1G 77
W3 7J 79
Birkbeck College 5D 6
Birkbeck Ct. W3 1K 97
Birkbeck Gdns. IG8: Wfd G 2D 36
Birkbeck Gro. W3 2K 97
Birkbeck Hill SE21 1B 138
Birkbeck M. E8 5F 67
W3 1K 97
Birkbeck Pl. SE21 2C 138
Birkbeck Rd. BR3: Beck 2J 157
DA14: Sidc 3A 144
E8 5F 67
EN2: Enf 1J 23
IG2: Ilf 5H 53
N8 4J 47
N12 5F 31
N17 1F 49
NW7 5G 29
RM7: Rush G 1K 73
SW19 5K 135
W3 1K 97
W5 4C 96
Birkbeck St. E2 3H 85
Birkbeck Way UB6: G'frd 1H 77
Birkdale Av. HA5: Pinn 3E 40
Birkdale Cl. BR6: Orp 7H 161
SE16 5H 103
SE28 6D 90
Birkdale Ct. *UB1: S'hall* *6G 77*
(off Redcroft Rd.)
Birkdale Gdns. CR0: Croy 4K 169
Birkdale Rd. SE2 4A 108
W5 4E 78
Birkenhead Av. KT2: King T 2F 151
Birkenhead St. WC1 1F 7 (3J 83)
Birkhall Rd. SE6 1F 141
Birkwood Cl. SW12 7H 119
Birley Lodge *NW8* *2B 82*
(off Acacia Rd.)
Birley Rd. N20 2F 31
Birley St. SW11 2E 118
Birling Rd. DA8: Erith 7K 109
Birnam Rd. N4 2K 65
Birnbeck Ct. EN5: Barn 4A 20
NW11 5H 45
Birrell Ho. *SW9* *2K 119*
(off Stockwell Rd.)
Birse Cres. NW10 3A 62
Birstall Rd. N15 5E 48
Biscay Ho. *E1* *4K 85*
(off Mile End Rd.)
Biscayne Av. E14 1F 105
Biscay Rd. W6 5F 99
Biscoe Cl. TW5: Hest 6E 94
Biscoe Way SE13 3F 123
Biscott Ho. E3 4D 86
Bisenden Rd. CR0: Croy 2E 168
Bisham Cl. SM5: Cars 1D 166
Bisham Gdns. N6 1E 64
Bishop Butt Cl. BR6: Orp 3K 173
Bishop Ct. TW9: Rich 3E 114
Bishop Duppas Pk. TW17: Shep 7G 147
Bishop Fox Way KT8: W Mole 4D 148
Bishopgate Chu. Yd. EC2 5E 84
Bishop Ken Rd. HA3: W'stone 2K 41
Bishop King's Rd. W14 4G 99
Bishop Rd. N14 7A 22
Bishops Av. BR1: Brom 2A 160
E13 1K 87
RM6: Chad H 6C 54
SW6 2F 117
Bishops Av., The N2 7B 46
Bishop's Bri. Rd. W2 6A 4 (6K 81)
Bishops Cl. E17 4D 50
EN1: Enf 2C 24
EN5: Barn 6A 20
N19 3G 65
SE9 2G 143
SM1: Sutt 3J 165
TW10: Ham 3D 132
UB10: Hil 2C 74
W4 5J 97
Bishops Ct. CR0: Croy 2F 169
EC4 7A 8
HA0: Wemb 4B 60
W2 *6K 81*
(off Bishop's Bri. Rd.)
WC2 7J 7
Bishopsdale Ho. *NW6* *1J 81*
(off Kilburn Va.)
Bishops Dr. TW14: Bedf 6F 111
UB5: N'olt 1C 76
Bishopsford Rd. SM4: Mord 7A 154
Bishopsgate EC2 1G 15 (6E 84)
Bishopsgate Arc. EC2 6H 9
Bishopsgate Institute & Libraries *6H 9*
(off Bishopsgate)
Bishops Grn. *BR1: Brom* *1A 160*
(off Up. Park Rd.)
Bishops Gro. N2 6C 46
TW12: Hamp 4D 130
Bishops Gro. Cvn. Site
TW12: Hamp 4E 130
Bishop's Hall KT1: King T 2D 150
Bishops Hill KT12: Walt T 7J 147
Bishops Ho. *SW8* *7J 101*
(off Sth. Lambeth Rd.)
Bishop's Mans. SW6 2F 117
(not continuous)
Bishops Mead *SE5* *7C 102*
(off Camberwell Rd.)
Bishops Pk. Rd. SW6 2F 117
SW16 1J 155
Bishops Pl. SM1: Sutt 5A 166
Bishops Rd. CR0: Croy 7B 156
N6 6E 46
SW6 1G 117
SW11 7C 100
UB3: Hayes 6E 74
W7 2J 95
Bishop's Ter. SE11 3K 19 (4A 102)
Bishopsthorpe Rd. SE26 4K 139
Bishop St. N1 1C 84
Bishops Vw. Ct. N10 4F 47
Bishops Wlk. BR7: Chst 1G 161
CR0: Addtn 5K 169
HA5: Pinn 3C 40
Bishop's Way E2 2H 85
Bishops Wood Almshouses *E5* *4H 67*
(off Lwr. Clapton Rd.)
Bishopswood Rd. N6 7D 46
Bishop Way NW10 7A 62
Bishop Wilfred Wood Cl.
SE15 2G 121
Bishop Wilfred Wood Ct.
E13 *2A 88*
(off Pragel St.)
Bisley Cl. KT4: Wor Pk 1E 164
Bison Ct. TW14: Felt 7K 111
Bispham Rd. NW10 3F 79
Bissextile Ho. SE13 2D 122
Bisson Rd. E15 2E 86
Bisterne Av. E17 3F 51
Bittacy Bus. Cen. NW7 6B 30
Bittacy Cl. NW7 6A 30
Bittacy Ct. NW7 7B 30
Bittacy Hill NW7 6A 30
Bittacy Pk. Av. NW7 5A 30
Bittacy Ri. NW7 6K 29
Bittacy Rd. NW7 6A 30
Bittern Cl. UB4: Yead 5B 76
Bittern Ct. NW9 2A 44
SE8 6C 104
Bittern Ho. *SE1* *7C 14*
(off Gt. Suffolk St.)
Bittern Pl. N22 2K 47
Bittern St. SE1 7C 14 (2C 102)
Bittoms, The KT1: King T 3D 150
(not continuous)
Bittoms Ct. KT1: King T 3D 150
Bixley Cl. UB2: S'hall 4D 94
Blackall St. EC2 3G 9 (4E 84)
Blackberry Cl. TW17: Shep 4G 147
Blackberry Farm Cl. TW5: Hest 7C 94
Blackberry Fld. BR5: St P 7A 144
Blackbird Ct. NW9 3K 61
Blackbird Hill NW9 2J 61
Blackbird Yd. E2 1K 9 (3F 85)
Blackborne Rd. RM10: Dag 6G 73
Black Boy La. N15 5C 48
Blackbrook La. BR1: Brom 5D 160
BR2: Brom 5D 160
Blackburn NW9 2B 44
Blackburne's M. W1 2G 11 (7E 82)
Blackburn Rd. NW6 6K 63
Blackburn Trad. Est. TW19: Stanw 6B 110
Blackbush Av. RM6: Chad H 5D 54
Blackbush Cl. SM2: Sutt 7K 165
Blackdown Cl. N2 2A 46
Blackdown Ter. SE18 1D 124
Blackett St. SW15 3F 117
Black Fan Cl. EN2: Enf 1H 23
BLACKFEN 7A 126
Blackfen Pde. DA15: Sidc 6A 126
Blackfen Rd. DA15: Sidc 5J 125
Blackford Cl. CR2: S Croy 7B 168
Blackford's Path SW15 7C 116
Blackfriars Bri. SE1 3A 14 (7B 84)
Blackfriars Ct. EC4 2A 14
Black Friars La. EC4 2A 14 (6B 84)
(not continuous)
Blackfriars Pas. EC4 2A 14 (7B 84)
Blackfriars Rd. SE1 4A 14 (2B 102)
Blackfriars Underpass
EC4 2A 14 (7A 84)
Black Gates HA5: Pinn 3D 40
BLACKHEATH 2H 123
Blackheath Av. SE10 7F 105
Blackheath Bus. Est. *SE10* *1E 122*
(off Blackheath Hill)
Blackheath Concert Halls 3H 123
Blackheath Gro. SE3 2H 123
Blackheath Hill SE10 1E 122
BLACKHEATH PARK 4J 123
Blackheath Pk. SE3 3H 123
Blackheath Ri. SE13 2E 122
(not continuous)
Blackheath Rd. SE10 1D 122
BLACKHEATH VALE 2H 123

Blackheath Va.—Blithdale Rd.

Blackheath Va. SE3 .... 2G 123
Blackheath Village SE3 .... 2H 123
Black Horse Ct. SE1 .... 3D 102
(off Gt. Dover St.)
Blackhorse La. CR0: Croy 7G 157
E17 .... 2K 49
Blackhorse M. E17 .... 3K 49
Black Horse Pde. HA5: Eastc 5K 39
BLACKHORSE ROAD 4K 49
Blackhorse Rd. DA14: Sidc 4A 144
E17 .... 4K 49
SE8 .... 6A 104
Blacklands Dr. UB4: Hayes 4E 74
Blacklands Rd. SE6 .... 4E 140
Blacklands Ter. SW3 .... 4E 16 (4D 100)
Black Lion La. W6 .... 4C 98
Black Lion M. W6 .... 4C 98
Blackmans Yd. E2 .... 3K 9
(off Grimsby St.)
Blackmore Av. UB1: S'hall 1H 95
Blackmore Ho. N1 .... 1K 83
(off Barnsbury Est.)
Blackmore Rd. IG9: Buck H 1H 37
Blackmore's Gro. TW11: Tedd 6A 132
Blackmore Twr. W3 .... 3J 97
(off Stanley Rd.)
Blackness La. BR2: Kes 7B 172
Black Path E10 .... 7A 50
Blackpool Gdns. UB4: Hayes 4G 75
Blackpool Rd. SE15 .... 2H 121
BLACK PRINCE INTERCHANGE 6H 127
Black Prince Rd. SE1 .... 4G 19 (4K 101)
SE11 .... 4G 19 (4K 101)
Black Rod Cl. UB3: Hayes 3H 93
Blackshaw Rd. SW17 .... 4A 136
Blacksmiths Cl. RM6: Chad H 6C 54
Blacksmiths Ho. E17 .... 4C 50
(off Gillards M.)
Blacks Rd. W6 .... 5E 98
Blackstock M. N4 .... 2B 66
Blackstock Rd. N4 .... 2B 66
N5 .... 3B 66
Blackstone Est. E8 .... 7G 67
Blackstone Ho. SW1 .... 6A 18
(off Churchill Gdns.)
Blackstone Rd. NW2 .... 5E 62
Black Swan Yd. SE1 .... 6H 15 (2E 102)
Blackthorn Av. UB7: W Dray 4C 92
Blackthorn Ct. E11 .... 4F 69
(off Hall Rd.)
TW5: Hest 7C 94
Blackthorne Av. CR0: Croy 1J 169
Blackthorne Ct. SE15 .... 7F 103
(off Cator St.)
TW15: Ashf 7E 128
UB1: S'hall 1F 95
(off Dormer's Wells La.)
Blackthorne Dr. E4 .... 4A 36
Blackthorn Gro. DA7: Bex 3E 126
Blackthorn Rd. IG1: Ilf 5H 71
Blackthorn St. E3 .... 4C 86
Blacktree M. SW9 .... 3A 120
BLACKWALL 1E 104
Blackwall La. SE10 .... 5G 105
Blackwall Trad. Est. E14 .... 5F 87
Blackwall Tunnel E14 .... 1F 105
(not continuous)
Blackwall Tunnel App. E14 .... 6E 86
Blackwall Tunnel Northern App.
E3 .... 2C 86
E14 .... 2C 86
Blackwall Tunnel Southern App.
SE10 .... 3G 105
Blackwall Way E14 .... 1E 104
Blackwater Cl. E7 .... 4H 69
RM13: Rain 5K 91
Blackwater Ho. NW8 .... 5B 4
(off Church St.)
Blackwater St. SE22 .... 5F 121
Blackwell Cl. E5 .... 4K 67
HA3: Hrw W 7C 26
Blackwell Gdns. HA8: Edg 4B 28
Blackwell Ho. SW4 .... 6H 119
Blackwood Av. N18 .... 5E 34
Blackwood Ho. E1 .... 4H 85
(off Collingwood St.)
Blackwood St. SE17 .... 5D 102
Blade M. SW15 .... 4H 117
Bladen Ho. E1 .... 6K 85
(off Dunelm St.)
Blades Ct. SW15 .... 4H 117
W6 .... 5D 98
(off Lower Mall)
Blades Ho. SE11 .... 7J 19
(off Kennington Oval)
Bladindon Dr. DA5: Bexl 7C 126
Bladon Ct. SW16 .... 6J 137
Bladon Gdns. HA2: Harr 6F 41
Blagdens Cl. N14 .... 2C 32
Blagdens La. N14 .... 2B 32
Blagdon Ct. W7 .... 7J 77
Blagdon Rd. KT3: N Mald 4B 152
(not continuous)
SE13 .... 6D 122
Blagdon Wlk. TW11: Tedd 6C 132
Blagrove Rd. W10 .... 5G 81
Blair Av. NW9 .... 7A 44
Blair Cl. DA15: Sidc 5J 125
N1 .... 6C 66
UB3: Harl 4J 93
Blair Ct. BR3: Beck 1D 158
NW8 .... 1B 82
SE6 .... 1H 141
Blairderry Rd. SW2 .... 2J 137
Blairgowrie Ct. E14 .... 6F 87
(off Blair St.)
Blair Ho. SW9 .... 2K 119
Blair St. E14 .... 6E 86
Blake Av. IG11: Bark 1J 89
Blake Bldg. N8 .... 3K 47
Blake Cl. DA16: Well 1J 125
SM5: Cars 1C 166
Blake Ct. N21 .... 5E 22
NW6 .... 3J 81
(off Malvern Rd.)
SE16 .... 5H 103
(off Stubbs Dr.)
Blakeden Dr. KT10: Clay 6A 162
Blake Gdns. SW6 .... 1K 117
Blake Hall Cres. E11 .... 1J 69
Blake Hall Rd. E11 .... 7J 51
Blakehall Rd. SM5: Cars 6D 166
Blake Ho. E14 .... 2C 104
(off Admirals Way)
SE1 .... 1J 19 (3A 102)
SE8 .... 6C 104
(off New King St.)
Blakeley Cotts. SE10 .... 2F 105
Blake M. TW9: Kew 1G 115
Blakemore Rd. CR7: Thor H 5K 155
SW16 .... 3J 137
Blakemore Way DA17: Belv 3E 108
Blakeney Av. BR3: Beck 1B 158
Blakeney Cl. E8 .... 5G 67
NW1 .... 7H 65
Blakeney Rd. BR3: Beck 7B 140
Blakenham Rd. SW17 .... 4D 136
Blaker Ct. SE7 .... 7A 106
(not continuous)
Blake Rd. CR0: Croy 2E 168
CR4: Mitc 3C 154
E16 .... 4H 87
N11 .... 7B 32
Blaker Rd. E15 .... 2E 86
Blakes Av. KT3: N Mald 5B 152
Blakes Cl. W10 .... 5E 80
Blake's Grn. BR4: W W'ck 1E 170
Blakes La. KT3: N Mald 5B 152
Blakesley Av. W5 .... 6C 78
Blakesley Wlk. SW20 .... 2H 153
Blake's Rd. SE15 .... 7E 102
Blakes Ter. KT3: N Mald 5C 152
Blakesware Gdns. N9 .... 7J 23
Blakewood Cl. TW13: Hanw 4A 130
Blakewood Ct. SE20 .... 7H 139
(off Anerley Pk.)
Blakney Cl. N20 .... 1F 31
Blanchard Cl. SE9 .... 3C 142
Blanchard Ho. TW1: Twick 6D 114
(off Clevedon Rd.)
Blanchard Way E8 .... 6G 67
Blanch Cl. SE15 .... 7J 103
Blanchedowne SE5 .... 4D 120
Blanche St. E16 .... 4H 87
Blanchland Rd. SM4: Mord 5K 153
Blandfield Rd. SW12 .... 7E 118
Blandford Av. BR3: Beck 2A 158
TW2: Whit 1F 131
Blandford Cl. CR0: Bedd 3J 167
N2 .... 4A 46
RM7: Mawney 4G 55
Blandford Ct. N1 .... 7E 66
(off St Peter's Way)
NW6 .... 7F 63
Blandford Cres. E4 .... 7K 25
Blandford Ho. SW8 .... 7K 101
(off Richborne Ter.)
Blandford Rd. BR3: Beck 3J 157
TW11: Tedd 5H 131
UB2: S'hall 4E 94
W4 .... 3A 98
W5 .... 2D 96
Blandford Sq. NW1 .... 4D 4 (4C 82)
Blandford St. W1 .... 7F 5 (6D 82)
Blandford Waye UB4: Yead 6A 76
Bland Ho. SE11 .... 5H 19
Bland St. SE9 .... 4B 124
Blaney Cres. E6 .... 3F 89
Blanmerle Rd. SE9 .... 1F 143
Blann Cl. SE9 .... 6B 124
Blantyre St. SW10 .... 7B 100
Blantyre Twr. SW10 .... 7B 100
(off Blantyre St.)
Blantyre Wlk. SW10 .... 7B 100
(off Worlds End Est.)
Blashford NW3 .... 7D 64
(off Adelaide Rd.)
Blashford St. SE13 .... 7F 123
Blasker Wlk. E14 .... 5D 104
Blawith Rd. HA1: Harr 4J 41
Blaxland Ho. W12 .... 7D 80
(off White City Est.)
Blaydon Cl. HA4: Ruis 7G 39
N17 .... 7C 34
Blaydon Ct. UB5: N'olt 6E 58
Blaydon Wlk. N17 .... 7C 34
Blazer Ct. NW8 .... 2B 4
Bleak Hill La. SE18 .... 6K 107
Blean Gro. SE20 .... 7J 139
Bleasdale Av. UB6: G'frd 2A 78
Blechynden Ho. W10 .... 6F 81
(off Kingsdown Cl.)
Blechynden St. W10 .... 7F 81
Bledlow Cl. SE28 .... 7C 90
Bledlow Ho. NW8 .... 4B 4
(off Capland St.)
Bledlow Ri. UB6: G'frd 2G 77
Bleeding Heart Yd. EC1 .... 6K 7
Blegborough Rd. SW16 .... 6G 137
Blemundsbury WC1 .... 5G 7
(off Dombey St.)
BLENDON 6D 126
Blendon Dr. DA5: Bexl 6D 126
Blendon Path BR1: Brom 7H 141
Blendon Rd. DA5: Bexl 6D 126
Blendon Row SE17 .... 4D 102
(off Townley St.)
Blendon Ter. SE18 .... 5G 107
Blendworth Point SW15 .... 1D 134
Blenheim Av. IG2: Ilf 6E 52
Blenheim Bus. Cen.
CR4: Mitc 2D 154
(off London Rd.)
Blenheim Cl. N21 .... 1H 33
RM7: Mawney 4J 55
SE12 .... 1K 141
SM6: Wall 7G 167
SW20 .... 3E 152
UB6: G'frd 2H 77
Blenheim Ct. BR2: Brom 4H 159
DA14: Sidc 3H 143
HA3: Kent 6A 42
IG8: Wfd G 7E 36
N19 .... 2J 65
SE16 .... 1K 103
(off King & Queen Wharf)
SM2: Sutt 6A 166
Blenheim Cres. CR2: S Croy 7C 168
HA4: Ruis 2F 57
W11 .... 7G 81
Blenheim Dr. DA16: Well 1K 125
Blenheim Gdns. HA9: Wemb 3E 60
KT2: King T 7H 133
NW2 .... 6E 62
SM6: Wall 6G 167
SW2 .... 6K 119
Blenheim Gro. SE15 .... 2G 121
Blenheim Ho. E16 .... 1K 105
(off Constable Av.)
SE18 .... 3G 107
TW3: Houn 3E 112
Blenheim Pde. UB10: Hil 4D 74
Blenheim Pk. Rd. CR2: S Croy 7C 168
Blenheim Pas. NW8 .... 2A 82
(not continuous)
Blenheim Pl. TW11: Tedd 5K 131
Blenheim Ri. N15 .... 4F 49
Blenheim Rd. BR1: Brom 4C 160
DA15: Sidc 1C 144
E6 .... 3B 88
E15 .... 4G 69
E17 .... 3K 49
EN5: Barn 3A 20
HA2: Harr 6F 41
NW8 .... 2A 82
SE20 .... 7J 139
SM1: Sutt 3J 165
SW20 .... 3E 152
UB5: N'olt 6F 59
W4 .... 3A 98
Blenheim Shop. Cen. SE20 .... 7J 139
Blenheim St. W1 .... 1J 11 (6F 83)
Blenheim Ter. NW8 .... 2A 82
Blenheim Way TW7: Isle 1A 114
Blenkarne Rd. SW11 .... 6D 118
Bleriot NW9 .... 2B 44
(off Belvedere Strand)
Bleriot Rd. TW5: Hest 7A 94
Blessbury Rd. HA8: Edg 1J 43
Blessington Cl. SE13 .... 3F 123
Blessington Rd. SE13 .... 3F 123
Blessing Way IG11: Bark 3C 90
Bletchingley Cl. CR7: Thor H 4B 156
Bletchley Ct. N1 .... 1E 8
(not continuous)
Bletchley St. N1 .... 1D 8 (2D 84)
Bletchmore Cl. UB3: Harl 5F 93
Bletsoe Wlk. N1 .... 2C 84
Blewbury Ho. SE2 .... 2C 108
(Tavy Bri.)
SE2 .... 2D 108
(Tilehurst Point)
Blick Ho. SE16 .... 3J 103
(off Neptune St.)
Blincoe Cl. SW19 .... 2F 135
Bliss Cres. SE13 .... 2D 122
Blissett St. SE10 .... 1E 122
Bliss Ho. EN1: Enf 1B 24
Bliss M. W10 .... 3G 81
Blisworth Cl. UB4: Yead 4C 76
Blisworth Ho. E2 .... 1G 85
(off Whiston Rd.)
Blithbury Rd. RM9: Dag 6B 72
Blithdale Rd. SE2 .... 4A 108

204 A-Z London

Blithfield St.—Bookham Ct.

Blithfield St. W8 .....3K 99
Blockley Rd. HA0: Wemb 2B 60
Bloemfontein Av. W12 .....1D 98
Bloemfontein Rd. W12 .....7D 80
Bloemfontein Way W12 .....1D 98
Blomfield Ct. *W9* *3A 4*
(off Maida Va.)
Blomfield Mans. *W12* *1E 98*
(off Stanlake Rd.)
Blomfield Rd. W9 .....5K 81
Blomfield St. EC2 .....6F 9 (5D 84)
Blomfield Vs. W2 .....5K 81
Blomville Rd. RM8: Dag 3E 72
Blondel St. SW11 .....2E 118
Blondin Av. W5 .....4C 96
Blondin St. E3 .....2C 86
Bloomburg St. SW1 .....4B 18 (4H 101)
Bloomfield Ct. N6 .....6E 46
Bloomfield Cres. IG2: Ilf 6F 53
Bloomfield Ho. *E1* *5G 85*
(off Old Montague St.)
Bloomfield Pl. W1 .....2K 11
Bloomfield Rd. BR2: Brom 5B 160
KT1: King T 4E 150
N6 .....6E 46
SE18 .....6F 107
Bloomfield Ter. SW1 .....5H 17 (5E 100)
Bloom Gro. SE27 .....3B 138
Bloomhall Rd. SE19 .....5D 138
Bloom Pk. Rd. SW6 .....7H 99
BLOOMSBURY 5E 6 (5J 83)
Bloomsbury Cl. NW7 .....7H 29
W5 .....7F 79
Bloomsbury Ct. HA5: Pinn 3D 40
TW5: Cran 1K 111
WC1 .....6F 7
Bloomsbury Ho. SW4 .....6H 119
Bloomsbury Pl. SW18 .....5A 118
WC1 .....5F 7 (5J 83)
Bloomsbury Sq. WC1 .....6F 7 (5J 83)
Bloomsbury St. WC1 .....6D 6 (5H 83)
Bloomsbury Theatre 3C 6
Bloomsbury Way WC1 .....6E 6 (5J 83)
Blore Cl. SW8 .....1H 119
Blore Ct. W1 .....1C 12
Blore Ho. *SW10* *7K 99*
(off Coleridge Gdns.)
Blossom Cl. CR2: S Croy 5F 169
RM9: Dag 1F 91
W5 .....2E 96
Blossom La. EN2: Enf 1H 23
Blossom St. E1 .....4H 9 (4E 84)
Blossom Way UB7: W Dray 4C 92
UB10: Hil 7B 56
Blossom Waye TW5: Hest 6C 94
Blount Ho. *E14* *5A 86*
(off Maroon St.)
Blount St. E14 .....6A 86
Bloxam Gdns. SE9 .....5C 124
Bloxhall Rd. E10 .....1B 68
Bloxham Cres. TW12: Hamp 7D 130
Bloxworth Cl. SM6: Wall 3G 167
Blucher Rd. SE5 .....7C 102
Blue Anchor All. TW9: Rich 4E 114
Blue Anchor La. SE16 .....4G 103
Blue Anchor Yd. E1 .....2K 15 (7G 85)
Blue Ball Yd. SW1 .....5A 12 (1G 101)
Bluebell Av. E12 .....5B 70
Blue Bell Cl. UB5: N'olt 6D 58
Bluebell Cl. BR6: Farnb 2G 173
E9 .....1J 85
RM7: Rush G 2K 73
SE26 .....4F 139
SM6: Wall 1F 167
Bluebell Way IG1: Ilf 6F 71
Blueberry Cl. IG8: Wfd G 6D 36
Bluebird La. RM10: Dag 7G 73
Bluebird Way SE28 .....2H 107
Blue Elephant Theatre *7C 102*
(off Bethwin Rd.)
Bluefield Cl. TW12: Hamp 5E 130
Bluegate M. E1 .....7H 85
Bluegates KT17: Ewe 7C 164
Bluehouse Rd. E4 .....2B 36
Blue Lion Pl. SE1 .....7G 15 (3E 102)
Blueprint Apartments *SW12* *7F 119*
(off Balham Gro.)
Blue Riband Ind. Est. CR0: Croy 2B 168
Blue Water SW18 .....4K 117
Blundell Cl. E8 .....5G 67
Blundell Rd. HA8: Edg 1K 43
Blundell St. N7 .....7J 65
Blunden Cl. RM8: Dag 1C 72
Blunt Rd. CR2: S Croy 5D 168
Blunts Av. UB7: Sip 7C 92
Blunts Rd. SE9 .....5E 124
Blurton Rd. E5 .....4J 67
Blydon Ct. *N21* *5E 22*
(off Chaseville Pk. Rd.)
Blyth Cl. E14 .....4F 105
TW1: Twick 6K 113
Blyth Ct. *BR1: Brom* *1H 159*
(off Blyth Rd.)
Blythe Cl. SE6 .....7B 122
BLYTHE HILL 7B 122
Blythe Hill BR5: St P 1K 161
SE6 .....7B 122
Blythe Hill La. SE6 .....7B 122
Blythe Hill Pl. SE23 .....7A 122
Blythe Ho. SE11 .....7J 19 (6A 102)
Blythe M. W14 .....3F 99
Blythendale Ho. *E2* *2G 85*
(off Mansford St.)
Blythe Rd. W14 .....3F 99
(not continuous)
Blythe St. E2 .....3H 85
Blythe Va. SE6 .....1B 140
Blyth Hill Pl. *SE23* *7A 122*
(off Brockley Pk.)
Blyth Rd. BR1: Brom 1H 159
E17 .....7B 50
SE28 .....7C 90
UB3: Hayes 2G 93
Blyth's Wharf E14 .....7A 86
Blythswood Rd. IG3: Ilf 1A 72
Blyth Wood Pk. BR1: Brom 1H 159
Blythwood Rd. HA5: Pinn 1B 40
N4 .....7J 47
Boades M. NW3 .....4B 64
Boadicea St. N1 .....1K 83
Boakes Cl. NW9 .....4J 43
Boardman Av. E4 .....5J 25
Boardman Cl. EN5: Barn 5B 20
Boardwalk Pl. E14 .....1E 104
Boarhound *NW9* *2B 44*
(off Further Acre)
Boarley Ho. *SE17* *4E 102*
(off Massinger St.)
Boars Head Yd. TW8: Bford 7D 96
Boathouse Cen., The *W10* *4F 81*
(off Canal Cl.)
Boathouse Wlk. SE15 .....7F 103
(not continuous)
Boat Lifter Way SE16 .....4A 104
Boat Quay E16 .....7A 88
Bob Anker Cl. E13 .....3J 87
Bobbin Cl. SW4 .....3G 119
Bobby Moore Way N11 .....7J 31
Bob Hope Theatre, The 6D 124
Bob Marley Way SE24 .....4A 120
Bockhampton Rd. KT2: King T 7F 133
Bocking St. E8 .....1H 85
Boddicott Cl. SW19 .....2G 135
Boddington Gdns. W3 .....2G 97
Boddington Ho. *SE14* *1J 121*
(off Pomeroy St.)
SW13 .....*6D 98*
(off Wyatt Dr.)
Bodeney Ho. *SE5* *1E 120*
(off Peckham Rd.)
Boden Ho. *E1* *5K 9*
(off Woodseer St.)
Bodiam Cl. EN1: Enf 2K 23
Bodiam Rd. SW16 .....7H 137
Bodicea M. TW4: Houn 6D 112
Bodington Ct. W12 .....2F 99
Bodley Cl. KT3: N Mald 5A 152
Bodley Mnr. Way SW2 .....7A 120
Bodley Rd. KT3: N Mald 6K 151
Bodmin *NW9* *2B 44*
(off Further Acre)
Bodmin Cl. HA2: Harr 3D 58
Bodmin Gro. SM4: Mord 5K 153
Bodmin St. SW18 .....1J 135
Bodnant Gdns. SW20 .....3C 152
Bodney Rd. E8 .....5H 67
Boeing Way UB2: S'hall 3K 93
Boevey Path DA17: Belv 5F 109
Bogart Ct. *E14* *7C 86*
(off Premiere Pl.)
Bogey La. BR6: Downe 7E 172
Bognor Rd. DA16: Well 1D 126
Bohemia Pl. E8 .....6J 67
Bohn Rd. E1 .....5A 86
Bohun Gro. EN4: E Barn 6H 21
Boileau Pde. *W5* *6F 79*
(off Boileau Rd.)
Boileau Rd. SW13 .....7C 98
W5 .....6F 79
Boisseau Ho. *E1* *5J 85*
(off Stepney Way)
Bolden St. SE8 .....2D 122
Boldero Pl. NW8 .....4C 4
Bolderwood Way BR4: W W'ck 2D 170
Boldmere Rd. HA5: Eastc 7A 40
Boleyn Av. EN1: Enf 1C 24
Boleyn Cl. E17 .....4C 50
Boleyn Ct. IG9: Buck H 1D 36
KT8: E Mos *4H 149*
(off Bridge Rd.)
Boleyn Dr. HA4: Ruis 2B 58
KT8: W Mole 3D 148
Boleyn Gdns. BR4: W W'ck 2D 170
RM10: Dag 7J 73
Boleyn Gro. BR4: W W'ck 2E 170
Boleyn Ho. *E16* *1J 105*
(off Southey M.)
Boleyn Rd. E6 .....2B 88
E7 .....7J 69
N16 .....5E 66
Boleyn Way EN5: New Bar 3F 21
Bolina Rd. SE16 .....5J 103
Bolingbroke Gro. SW11 .....4C 118
Bolingbroke Rd. W14 .....3F 99
Bolingbroke Wlk. SW11 .....1B 118
Bolingbroke Way UB3: Hayes 1F 93
Bolliger Ct. NW10 .....4J 79
Bollo Bri. Rd. W3 .....3H 97
Bollo Ct. *W3* *3J 97*
(off Bollo Bri. Rd.)
Bollo La. W3 .....2H 97
W4 .....4J 97
Bolney Ga. SW7 .....7C 10 (2C 100)
Bolney St. SW8 .....7K 101
Bolney Way TW13: Hanw 3C 130
Bolsover St. W1 .....4K 5 (4F 83)
Bolstead Rd. CR4: Mitc 1F 155
Bolster Gro. N22 .....7C 32
Bolt Ct. EC4 .....1K 13
Boltmore Cl. NW4 .....3F 45
Bolton Cl. KT9: Chess 6D 162
SE20 .....2G 157
Bolton Cres. SE5 .....7B 102
Bolton Dr. SM5: Cars 7A 154
Bolton Gdns. BR1: Brom 6H 141
NW10 .....2F 81
SW5 .....5K 99
TW11: Tedd 6A 132
Bolton Gdns. M. SW10 .....5A 100
Bolton Ho. *SE10* *5G 105*
(off Trafalgar Rd.)
Bolton Pl. *NW8* *1K 81*
(off Bolton Rd.)
Bolton Rd. E15 .....6H 69
HA1: Harr 4G 41
KT9: Chess 6D 162
N18 .....5A 34
NW8 .....1K 81
NW10 .....1A 80
W4 .....7J 97
Boltons, The HA0: Wemb 4K 59
IG8: Wfd G 4D 36
SW10 .....5A 100
Boltons Ct. *SW5* *5K 99*
(off Old Brompton Rd.)
Bolton's La. UB3: Harl 1E 110
Boltons Pl. SW5 .....5A 100
Bolton St. W1 .....4K 11 (1F 101)
Bolton Studios SW10 .....5A 100
Bolton Wlk. *N7* *2K 65*
(off Durham Rd.)
Bombay Ct. *SE16* *2J 103*
(off St Marychurch St.)
Bombay St. SE16 .....4H 103
Bomer Cl. UB7: Sip 7C 92
Bomore Rd. W11 .....7G 81
Bonar Pl. BR7: Chst 7C 142
Bonar Rd. SE15 .....7G 103
Bonchester Cl. BR7: Chst 7E 142
Bonchurch Cl. SM2: Sutt 7K 165
Bonchurch Rd. W10 .....5G 81
W13 .....1B 96
Bond Cl. UB7: Yiew 6B 74
Bond Ct. EC4 .....2E 14 (7D 84)
Bondfield Av. UB4: Yead 3J 75
Bondfield Rd. E6 .....5D 88
Bond Gdns. SM6: Wall 4G 167
Bond Ho. *NW6* *2H 81*
(off Rupert Rd.)
SE14 .....*7A 104*
(off Goodwood Rd.)
Bonding Yd. Wlk. SE16 .....3A 104
Bond Rd. CR4: Mitc 2C 154
KT6: Surb 2F 163
Bond St. E15 .....5G 69
W4 .....4K 97
W5 .....7D 78
Bondway SW8 .....7F 19 (6J 101)
Boneta Rd. SE18 .....3D 106
Bonfield Rd. SE13 .....4E 122
Bonham Gdns. RM8: Dag 2D 72
Bonham Rd. RM8: Dag 2D 72
SW2 .....5K 119
Bonheur Rd. W4 .....2K 97
Bonhill St. EC2 .....4F 9 (4D 84)
Boniface Gdns. HA3: Hrw W 7A 26
Boniface Rd. UB10: Ick 3D 56
Boniface Wlk. HA3: Hrw W 7A 26
Bonington Ho. EN1: Enf 5B 24
Bonita M. SE4 .....3K 121
Bon Marche Ter. M. *SE27* *4E 138*
(off Gypsy Rd.)
Bonner Hill Rd. KT1: King T 2F 151
(not continuous)
Bonner Rd. E2 .....2J 85
Bonnersfield Cl. HA1: Harr 6K 41
Bonnersfield La. HA1: Harr 6K 41
Bonner St. E2 .....2J 85
Bonneville Gdns. SW4 .....6G 119
Bonnington Ct. *UB5: N'olt* *2B 76*
(off Gallery Gdns.)
Bonnington Ho. N1 .....2K 83
Bonnington Sq. SW8 .....7G 19 (6K 101)
Bonny St. NW1 .....7G 65
Bonser Rd. TW1: Twick 2K 131
Bonsor Ho. SW8 .....1G 119
Bonsor St. SE5 .....7E 102
Bonville Gdns. NW4 .....4D 44
Bonville Rd. BR1: Brom 5H 141
Bookbinders Cott. Homes N20 .....3J 31
Booker Cl. E14 .....5B 86
Booker Rd. N18 .....5B 34
Bookham Ct. CR4: Mitc 3B 154
SW19 .....3B 154

Bredin Ho.—Bridge Rd.

Bredin Ho. *SW10* *7K* ***99***
(off Coleridge Gdns.)
Bredo Ho. IG11: Bark 3B **90**
Bredon Rd. CR0: Croy 7F **157**
Breer St. SW6 . . . . .3K **117**
Breezers Ct. *E1* *7G* ***85***
(off Highway, The)
Breezer's Hill E1 . . . . .7G **85**
Brember Rd. HA2: Harr 2G **59**
Bremer M. E17 . . . . .4D **50**
Bremner Rd. SW7 . . . . .1A **16** (3A **100**)
Brenchley Cl. BR2: Brom 6H **159**
BR7: Chst 1E **160**
Brenchley Gdns. SE23 . . . . .6J **121**
Brenchley Rd. BR5: St P 2K **161**
Brenda Rd. SW17 . . . . .2D **136**
Brende Gdns. KT8: W Mole 4F **149**
Brendon Av. NW10 . . . . .4A **62**
Brendon Cl. UB3: Harl 7E **92**
Brendon Ct. UB2: S'hall 4F **95**
Brendon Gdns. HA2: Harr 4F **59**
IG2: Ilf 5J **53**
Brendon Gro. N2 . . . . .2A **46**
Brendon Rd. RM8: Dag 1F **73**
SE9 . . . . .2H **143**
Brendon St. W1 . . . . .7D **4** (6C **82**)
Brendon Vs. N21 . . . . .1H **33**
Brendon Way EN1: Enf 7K **23**
Brenley Cl. CR4: Mitc 3E **154**
Brenley Gdns. SE9 . . . . .4B **124**
Brenley Ho. *SE1* *6E* ***14***
(off Tennis St.)
Brennand Ct. N19 . . . . .3G **65**
Brent Cl. DA5: Bexl 1E **144**
Brentcot Cl. W13 . . . . .4B **78**
Brent Ct. NW11 . . . . .7F **45**
W7 . . . . .7H **77**
Brent Cres. NW10 . . . . .2F **79**
BRENT CROSS 7E **44**
Brent Cross Fly-Over NW2 . . . . .7F **45**
NW4 . . . . .7F **45**
Brent Cross Gdns. NW4 . . . . .6F **45**
BRENT CROSS INTERCHANGE 6E **44**
Brent Cross Shop. Cen. NW4 . . . . .7E **44**
Brentfield NW10 . . . . .7H **61**
Brentfield Cl. NW10 . . . . .6K **61**
Brentfield Gdns. NW2 . . . . .7F **45**
Brentfield Ho. NW10 . . . . .7K **61**
Brentfield Rd. NW10 . . . . .6K **61**
BRENTFORD 6D **96**
Brentford Bus. Cen. TW8: Bford 7C **96**
Brentford Cl. UB4: Yead 4B **76**
BRENTFORD END 7B **96**
Brentford FC .6D **96**
Brentford Fountain Leisure Cen. 5G **97**
Brentford Ho. TW1: Twick 7B **114**
Brentford Musical Mus. 6E **96**
Brent Grn. NW4 . . . . .5E **44**
Brent Grn. Wlk. HA9: Wemb 3J **61**
Brentham Club 3C **78**
Brentham Way W5 . . . . .4D **78**
Brent Ho. *E9* *6J* ***67***
(off Frampton Pk. Rd.)
Brenthouse Rd. E9 . . . . .7J **67**
Brenthurst Rd. NW10 . . . . .6B **62**
Brent Lea TW8: Bford 7C **96**
Brentmead Cl. W7 . . . . .7J **77**
Brentmead Gdns. NW10 . . . . .2F **79**
Brentmead Pl. NW11 . . . . .6F **45**
Brent New Ent. Cen. NW10 . . . . .6B **62**
Brenton St. E14 . . . . .6A **86**
Brent Pk. Ind. Est. UB2: S'hall 3K **93**
Brent Pk. Rd. NW4 . . . . .7D **44**
NW9 . . . . .7D **44**
(not continuous)
Brent Pl. EN5: Barn 5C **20**
Brent Rd. CR2: Sels 7H **169**
E16 . . . . .6J **87**
SE18 .7F **107**
TW8: Bford 6C **96**
UB2: S'hall 3A **94**
Brent Side TW8: Bford 6C **96**
Brentside Cl. W13 . . . . .4A **78**
Brentside Executive Cen.
TW8: Bford 6B **96**
Brent St. NW4 . . . . .4E **44**
Brent Ter. NW2 . . . . .1E **62**
(not continuous)
Brent Trad. Cen. NW10 . . . . .5A **62**
Brentvale Av. HA0: Wemb 1F **79**
UB1: S'hall 1H **95**
Brent Vw. Rd. NW9 . . . . .6C **44**
Brentwaters Bus. Pk. TW8: Bford 7C **96**
Brent Way HA9: Wemb 6H **61**
N3 . . . . .6D **30**
TW8: Bford 7D **96**
Brentwick Gdns. TW8: Bford 4E **96**
Brentwood Cl. SE9 . . . . .1G **143**
Brentwood Ho. *SE18* *7B* ***106***
(off Portway Gdns.)
Brentwood Lodge *NW4* *5F* ***45***
(off Holmdale Gdns.)
Brereton Rd. N17 . . . . .7A **34**
Bressenden Pl. SW1 . . . . . . .1K **17** (3F **101**)
Bressey Av. EN1: Enf 1B **24**
Bressey Gro. E18 . . . . .2H **51**
Breton Highwalk *EC1* *5D* ***8***
(off Golden La.)
Breton Ho. EC2 . . . . .4D **8**
SE1 . . . .*7J* ***15***
(off Abbey St.)
Brett Cl. N16 .2E **66**
UB5: Yead 3B **76**
Brett Ct. N9 .2D **34**
Brett Cres. NW10 . . . . .1K **79**
Brettell St. SE17 . . . . .5D **102**
Brettenham Av. E17 . . . . .1C **50**
Brettenham Rd. E17 . . . . .2C **50**
N18 . . . . .4B **34**
Brett Gdns. RM9: Dag 7E **72**
Brett Ho. Cl. SW15 . . . . .7F **117**
Brettinghurst *SE1* *5G* ***103***
(off Avondale Sq.)
Brett Pas. E8 . . . . .5H **67**
Brett Rd. E8 .5H **67**
Brewer's Grn. SW1 . . . . .1C **18**
Brewer's Hall Gdn. *EC2* *6D* ***8***
(off London Wall)
Brewers La. TW9: Rich 5D **114**
Brewer St. W1 . . . . .2B **12** (7G **83**)
Brewery, The EC2 . . . . .5E **8** (5C **84**)
RM1: Rom 5K **55**
Brewery Cl. HA0: Wemb 5A **60**
Brewery Ind. Est., The *N1* *1D* ***8***
(off Wenlock Rd.)
Brewery La. TW1: Twick 7K **113**
Brewery M. Cen. TW7: Isle 3A **114**
Brewery Rd. BR2: Brom 1C **172**
N7 . . . . .7J **65**
SE18 .5H **107**
Brewery Sq. EC1 . . . . .3A **8** (4B **84**)
SE1 . . . . .5J **15**
Brewery Wlk. RM1: Rom 5K **55**
Brewhouse La. E1 . . . . .1H **103**
SW15 . . . . .3G **117**
Brewhouse Rd. SE18 . . . . .4D **106**
Brewhouse Wlk. SE16 . . . . .1A **104**
Brewhouse Yd. EC1 . . . . .3A **8** (4B **84**)
Brewin Ter. UB4: Yead 5A **76**
Brewood Rd. RM8: Dag 6B **72**
Brewster Gdns. W10 . . . . .5E **80**
Brewster Ho. *E14* *7B* ***86***
(off Three Colt St.)
SE1 . . . .*4F* ***103***
(off Dunton Rd.)
Brewster Rd. E10 . . . . .1D **68**
Brian Rd. RM6: Chad H 5C **54**
Briant Ho. SE1 . . . . .2J **19**
Briants Cl. HA5: Pinn 2D **40**
Briant St. SE14 . . . . .1K **121**
Briar Av. SW16 . . . . .7K **137**
Briarbank Rd. W13 . . . . .6A **78**
Briar Cl. IG9: Buck H 2G **37**
N2 . . . . .3K **45**
N13 . . . . .3H **33**
TW7: Isle 5K **113**
TW12: Hamp 5D **130**
Briar Ct. SM3: Cheam 4E **164**
SW15 . . . . .4D **116**
Briar Cres. UB5: N'olt 6F **59**
Briardale Gdns. NW3 . . . . .3J **63**
Briarfield Av. N2 . . . . .3K **45**
N3 . . . . .2K **45**
Briarfield Cl. DA7: Bex 2G **127**
Briar Gdns. BR2: Hayes 1H **171**
Briaris Cl. N17 . . . . .7C **34**
Briar La. CR0: Addtn 4D **170**
Briar Rd. DA5: Bexl 3K **145**
HA3: Kent 5C **42**
NW2 . . . . .4E **62**
SW16 .3J **155**
TW2: Twick 1J **131**
TW17: Shep 5B **146**
Briars, The WD23: Bushy 1D **26**
Briarswood Way BR6: Chels 5K **173**
Briar Wlk. HA8: Edg 7D **28**
SW15 . . . . .4D **116**
W10 . . . . .4G **81**
Briar Way UB7: W Dray 2C **92**
Briarwood Cl. NW9 . . . . .6J **43**
TW13: Felt 4G **129**
Briarwood Ct. *KT4: Wor Pk* *1C* ***164***
(off Avenue, The)
Briarwood Dr. HA6: Nwood 2J **39**
Briarwood Rd. KT17: Ewe 6C **164**
SW4 .5H **119**
Briary Cl. NW3 . . . . .7C **64**
Briary Ct. DA14: Sidc 5B **144**
E16 . . . . .6H **87**
Briary Gdns. BR1: Brom 5K **141**
Briary Gro. HA8: Edg 2H **43**
Briary La. N9 . . . . .3A **34**
Briary Lodge BR3: Beck 1E **158**
Brickbarn Cl. *SW10* *7A* ***100***
(off King's Barn)
Brick Ct. EC4 . . . . .1J **13** (6A **84**)
Brickett Cl. HA4: Ruis 5E **38**
Brick Farm Cl. TW9: Kew 1H **115**
Brickfield Cl. TW8: Bford 7C **96**
Brickfield Cotts. BR7: Chst 5E **142**
SE18 .6K **107**
Brickfield Farm Gdns. BR6: Farnb 4G **173**
Brickfield La. UB3: Harl 6F **93**
Brickfield Rd. CR7: Thor H 1B **156**
SW19 . . . . .4K **135**
Brickfields HA2: Harr 2H **59**
(not continuous)
Brickfields Way UB7: W Dray 3B **92**
Brick La. E1 . . . . .5K **9** (5F **85**)
E2 . . . . .2K **9** (3F **85**)
EN1: Enf 2C **24**
EN3: Enf H 2C **24**
HA7: Stan 7J **27**
Brick Lane Music Hall 1B **106**
BRICKLAYER'S ARMS 4D **102**
Bricklayers Arms Bus. Cen.
SE1 . . . . .4E **102**
Brick St. W1 . . . . .5J **11** (1F **101**)
Brickwall La. HA4: Ruis 1G **57**
Brickwood Cl. SE26 . . . . .3H **139**
Brickwood Rd. CR0: Croy 2E **168**
Brideale Cl. SE15 . . . . .6F **103**
Bride Ct. EC4 . . . . .1A **14**
Bride La. EC4 . . . . .1A **14** (6B **84**)
Bridel M. *N1* *1B* ***84***
(off Colebrook Row)
Brides Pl. *N1* *7E* ***66***
(off De Beauvoir Rd.)
Bride St. N7 . . . . .6K **65**
Bridewain St. SE1 . . . . .7J **15** (3F **103**)
(not continuous)
Bridewell Pl. E1 . . . . .1H **103**
EC4 . . . . .1A **14** (6B **84**)
Bridford M. W1 . . . . .5K **5** (5F **83**)
Bridge, The HA3: W'stone 4K **41**
SW8 . . . .*7F* ***101***
(off Queenstown Rd.)
Bridge App. NW1 . . . . .7E **64**
Bridge Av. W6 . . . . .4E **98**
W7 . . . . .5H **77**
Bridge Av. Mans. *W6* *5E* ***98***
(off Bridge Av.)
Bridge Bus. Cen., The
UB2: S'hall 2E **94**
Bridge Cl. EN1: Enf 2C **24**
KT12: Walt T 7H **147**
TW11: Tedd 4K **131**
W10 . . . . .6F **81**
Bridge Ct. E10 . . . . .1B **68**
E14 . . . .*7F* ***87***
(off Newport Av.)
Bridge Dr. N13 . . . . .4E **32**
Bridge End E17 . . . . .1E **50**
Bridgefield Rd. SM1: Sutt 6J **165**
Bridgefoot SE1 . . . . .6F **19** (5J **101**)
TW16: Sun 1H **147**
Bridge Gdns. KT8: E Mos 4H **149**
N16 . . . . .4D **66**
TW15: Ashf 7E **128**
Bridge Ga. N21 . . . . .7H **23**
Bridge Ho. *E9* *6K* ***67***
(off Shepherds La.)
NW3 . . . .*7E* ***64***
(off Adelaide Rd.)
NW10 . . . .*2F* ***81***
(off Chamberlayne Rd.)
SE4 .4B **122**
SM2: Sutt *6K* ***165***
(off Bridge Rd.)
SW1 . . . .*5J* ***17***
(off Ebury Bri.)
UB7: W Dray 1A **92**
W2 . . . . .6A **4**
Bridgehouse Ct. *SE1* *7A* ***14***
(off Blackfriars Rd.)
Bridge Ho. Quay E14 . . . . .1E **104**
Bridgeland Rd. E16 . . . . .7J **87**
Bridgelands Cl. BR3: Beck 7B **140**
Bridge La. NW11 . . . . .4G **45**
SW11 . . . . .1C **118**
Bridge Leisure Cen., The 4B **140**
Bridgeman Ho. *E9* *7J* ***67***
(off Frampton Pk. Rd.)
Bridgeman Rd. N1 . . . . .7K **65**
TW11: Tedd 6A **132**
Bridgeman St. NW8 . . . . .2C **82**
Bridge Mdws. SE14 . . . . .6K **103**
BRIDGEN 7E **126**
Bridgend Rd. SW18 . . . . .4A **118**
Bridgenhall Rd. EN1: Enf 1A **24**
Bridgen Ho. *E1* *6H* ***85***
(off Nelson St.)
Bridgen Rd. DA5: Bexl 7E **126**
Bridge Pde. *N21* *7H* ***23***
(off Ridge Av.)
Bridge Pk. 7H **61**
Bridgepark SW18 . . . . .5J **117**
Bridge Pl. CR0: Croy 1D **168**
SW1 . . . . .3K **17** (4F **101**)
Bridgepoint Lofts E7 . . . . .7A **70**
Bridgeport Pl. E1 . . . . .1G **103**
Bridge Rd. BR3: Beck 7B **140**
DA7: Bex 2E **126**
E6 . . . . .7D **70**
E15 . . . . .7F **69**
E17 . . . . .7B **50**
HA9: Wemb 3G **61**
KT8: E Mos 4H **149**
KT9: Chess 5E **162**
N9 . . . . .3B **34**
N22 . . . . .1J **47**
NW10 .6A **62**
SM2: Sutt 6K **165**
SM6: Wall 5F **167**

A-Z London 209

Broadgate Rd. E16 6B 88
Broadgates Av. EN4: Had W 1E 20
Broadgates Ct. *SE11* *6K 19*
(off Cleaver St.)
Broadgates Rd. SW18 1B 136
BROAD GREEN 7B 156
Broad Grn. Av. CR0: Croy 7B 156
Broadhead Strand
NW9 1B 44
Broadheath Dr. BR7: Chst 5D 142
Broadhinton Rd. SW4 3F 119
Broadhurst Av. HA8: Edg 4C 28
IG3: Ilf 4K 71
Broadhurst Cl. NW6 6A 64
TW10: Rich 5F 115
Broadhurst Gdns. HA4: Ruis 2A 58
NW6 6K 63
Broadlands E17 3A 50
TW13: Hanw 3E 130
Broadlands Av. EN3: Enf H 3C 24
SW16 2J 137
TW17: Shep 6E 146
Broadlands Cl. EN3: Enf H 3D 24
N6 7E 46
SW16 2J 137
Broadlands Ct. *TW9: Kew* *7G 97*
(off Kew Gdns. Rd.)
Broadlands Lodge N6 7D 46
Broadlands Rd. BR1: Brom 4K 141
N6 7D 46
Broadlands Way KT3: N Mald 6B 152
Broad La. EC2 5G 9 (5E 84)
N8 5K 47
N15 4F 49
TW12: Hamp 7D 130
Broad Lawn SE9 2E 142
Broadlawns Ct. HA3: Hrw W 1K 41
Broadley St. NW8 5B 4 (5B 82)
Broadley Ter. NW1 4D 4 (4C 82)
Broadmayne *SE17* *5D 102*
(off Portland St.)
Broadmead SE6 3C 140
W14 4G 99
Broadmead Av. KT4: Wor Pk 7C 152
Broadmead Cen. *IG8: Wfd G* *7F 37*
(off Navestock Cres.)
Broadmead Cl. HA5: H End 1C 40
TW12: Hamp 6E 130
Broadmead Ct. IG8: Wfd G 6D 36
Broadmead Rd. IG8: Wfd G 6D 36
(not continuous)
UB4: Yead 4C 76
UB5: N'olt 4C 76
Broad Oak IG8: Wfd G 5E 36
Broadoak TW16: Sun 6H 129
Broad Oak Cl. E4 5H 35
Broadoak Ct. SW9 3A 120
Broadoak Ho. *NW6* *1K 81*
(off Mortimer Cres.)
Broadoak Rd. DA8: Erith 7K 109
Broadoaks KT6: Surb 2H 163
Broadoaks Way BR2: Brom 5H 159
Broad Sanctuary SW1 7D 12 (2H 101)
Broadstone Ho. *SW8* *7K 101*
(off Dorset Rd.)
Broadstone Pl. W1 6G 5 (5E 82)
Broad St. RM10: Dag 7G 73
TW11: Tedd 6K 131
Broad St. Av. EC2 6G 9 (5E 84)
Broad St. Mkt. RM10: Dag 7G 73
Broad St. Pl. EC2 6F 9
Broadview NW9 6G 43
Broadview Rd. SW16 7H 137
Broad Wlk. N21 2E 32
NW1 1H 5 (1E 82)
SE3 2A 124
TW5: Hest 1B 112
TW9: Kew 7F 97
W1 3F 11 (7D 82)
Broad Wlk., The KT8: E Mos 4K 149
W8 1K 99

Broadwalk E18 3H 51
HA2: Harr 5E 40
Broadwalk, The HA6: Nwood 2E 38
Broadwalk Ct. *W8* *1J 99*
(off Palace Gdns. Ter.)
Broadwalk Ho. EC2 5G 9 (4E 84)
SW7 *2A 100*
(off Hyde Pk. Ga.)
Broad Wlk. La. NW11 7H 45
Broadwalk Shop. Cen. HA8: Edg 6C 28
Broadwall SE1 4K 13 (1A 102)
Broadwater Farm Est. N17 2D 48
Broadwater Gdns. BR6: Farnb 4F 173
Broadwater Rd. N17 1E 48
SE28 3H 107
SW17 4C 136
Broadway DA6: Bex 4E 126
(not continuous)
E13 2K 87
E15 7F 69
IG11: Bark 1G 89
SW1 7C 12 (3H 101)
W7 1J 95
W13 1A 96
Broadway, The CR0: Bedd 4J 167
E4 6A 36
HA3: W'stone 2J 41
HA6: Nwood 2J 39
HA7: Stan 5H 27
HA9: Wemb 3E 60
IG8: Wfd G 6E 36
KT7: T Ditt 7J 149
N8 6J 47
N9 3B 34
N11 5J 31
N14 *1C 32*
(off Southgate Cir.)
N22 2A 48
NW7 5F 29
NW9 6B 44
RM8: Dag 1F 73
SM1: Sutt 5A 166
SM3: Cheam 6G 165
SW13 2A 116
SW19 6H 135
UB1: S'hall 7B 76
UB6: G'frd 4G 77
W3 2G 97
W5 7D 78
Broadway Arc. *W6* *4E 98*
(off Hammersmith B'way.)
Broadway Av. CR0: Croy 5D 156
TW1: Twick 6B 114
Broadway Cen., The W6 4E 98
Broadway Chambers *W6* *4E 98*
(off Hammersmith B'way.)
Broadway Cl. IG8: Wfd G 6E 36
Broadway Ct. BR3: Beck 3E 158
SW19 6J 135
Broadway Gdns. CR4: Mitc 4C 154
IG8: Wfd G 6E 36
Broadway Ho. *BR1: Brom* *5F 141*
(off Bromley Rd.)
E8 *1H 85*
(off Ada St.)
Broadway Mkt. E8 1H 85
IG6: Ilf 2H 53
(Forest Rd.)
IG6: Ilf 2G 53
(Greystone Gdns.)
SW17 4D 136
Broadway Mkt. M. E8 1G 85
Broadway M. E5 7F 49
N13 5E 32
N21 1G 33
Broadway Pde. E4 6K 35
HA2: Harr 5F 41
N8 6J 47
UB3: Hayes 1J 93
Broadway Pl. SW19 6H 135
Broadway Retail Pk. NW2 4F 63

Broadway Shop. Cen. DA6: Bex 4G 127
Broadway Shop. Mall SW1 1C 18 (3H 101)
Broadway Sq. DA6: Bex 4G 127
Broadway Squash & Fitness Cen. *4F 99*
(off Chalk Hill Rd.)
Broadway Theatre, The
Barking 1G 89
Catford 7D 122
Broadway Wlk. E14 3C 104
Broadwell Ct. *TW5: Hest* *1B 112*
(off Springwell Rd.)
Broadwick St. W1 2B 12 (7G 83)
Broadwood Av. HA4: Ruis 6F 39
Broadwood Ter. W8 4H 99
Broad Yd. EC1 4A 8 (4B 84)
Brocas Cl. NW3 7C 64
Brockbridge Ho. SW15 6B 116
Brockdene Dr. BR2: Kes 4B 172
Brockdish Av. IG11: Bark 5K 71
Brockenhurst KT8: W Mole 5D 148
Brockenhurst Av. KT4: Wor Pk 1A 164
Brockenhurst Gdns. IG1: Ilf 5G 71
NW7 5F 29
Brockenhurst M. N18 4B 34
Brockenhurst Rd. CR0: Croy 7H 157
Brockenhurst Way SW16 2H 155
Brocket Ho. SW8 2H 119
Brockham Cl. SW19 5H 135
Brockham Cres. CR0: New Ad 7F 171
Brockham Dr. IG2: Ilf 6F 53
SW2 7K 119
Brockham Ho. *NW1* *1G 83*
(off Bayham Pl.)
SW2 *7K 119*
(off Brockham Dr.)
Brockham St. SE1 7D 14 (3C 102)
Brockhurst Cl. HA7: Stan 6E 26
Brockill Cres. SE4 4A 122
Brocklebank Ho. *E16* *1E 106*
(off Glenister St.)
Brocklebank Ind. Est. SE7 4J 105
Brocklebank Rd. SE7 4K 105
SW18 7A 118
Brocklehurst St. SE14 7K 103
Brocklesby Rd. SE25 4H 157
BROCKLEY 4K 121
Brockley Av. HA7: Stan 3K 27
Brockley Cl. HA7: Stan 4K 27
Brockley Cres. RM5: Col R 1J 55
Brockley Cross SE4 3A 122
Brockley Cross Bus. Cen.
SE4 3A 122
Brockley Footpath SE4 5A 122
(not continuous)
SE15 4J 121
Brockley Gdns. SE4 2B 122
Brockley Gro. SE4 5B 122
Brockley Hall Rd. SE4 5A 122
Brockley Hill HA7: Stan 1H 27
Brockley Jack Theatre 5A 122
Brockley M. SE4 5A 122
Brockley Pk. SE23 7A 122
Brockley Ri. SE23 1A 140
Brockley Rd. SE4 3B 122
Brockley Side HA7: Stan 4K 27
Brockley Vw. SE23 7A 122
Brockley Way SE4 5K 121
Brockman Ri. BR1: Brom 4F 141
Brockmer Ho. *E1* *7H 85*
(off Crowder St.)
Brock Pl. E3 4D 86
Brock Rd. E13 5K 87
Brocks Dr. SM3: Cheam 3G 165
Brockshot Cl. TW8: Bford 5D 96
Brock St. SE15 3J 121
Brockway Cl. E11 2G 69
Brockweir *E2* *2J 85*
(off Cyprus St.)
Brockwell Av. BR3: Beck 5D 158
Brockwell Cl. BR5: St M Cry 5K 161
Brockwell Ct. SW2 5A 120

Brockwell Ho. *SE11* *7H 19*
(off Vauxhall St.)
Brockwell Pk. 6B 120
Brockwell Pk. Gdns. SE24 7A 120
Brockwell Pk. Lido 6B 120
Brockwell Pk. Row SW2 7A 120
Brodia Rd. N16 3E 66
Brodie Ho. *SE1* *5F 103*
(off Cooper's Rd.)
Brodie Rd. E4 1K 35
EN2: Enf 1H 23
Brodie St. SE1 5F 103
Brodlove La. E1 7K 85
Brodrick Gro. SE2 4B 108
Brodrick Rd. SW17 2C 136
Brograve Gdns. BR3: Beck 2D 158
Broken Wharf EC4 2C 14 (7C 84)
Brokesley St. E3 3B 86
Broke Wlk. E8 1F 85
Bromar Rd. SE5 3E 120
Bromefield HA7: Stan 1C 42
Bromell's Rd. SW4 4G 119
Brome Rd. SE9 3D 124
Bromfelde Rd. SW4 3H 119
Bromfelde Wlk. SW4 2H 119
Bromfield St. N1 1A 84
Bromhall Rd. RM8: Dag 6B 72
Bromhead Rd. *E1* *6J 85*
(off Jubilee St.)
Bromhead St. E1 6J 85
Bromhedge SE9 3D 142
Bromholm Rd. SE2 3B 108
Bromleigh Ct. SE23 2G 139
Bromleigh Ho. *SE1* *7J 15*
(off Abbey St.)
BROMLEY
BR1 2J 159
E3 3D 86
Bromley Av. BR1: Brom 7G 141
BROMLEY COMMON 1C 172
Bromley Comn. BR2: Brom 4A 160
Bromley Cres. BR2: Brom 3H 159
HA4: Ruis 4H 57
Bromley Gdns. BR2: Brom 3H 159
Bromley Gro. BR2: Brom 2F 159
Bromley Hall Rd. E14 5E 86
Bromley High St. E3 3D 86
Bromley Hill BR1: Brom 6G 141
Bromley Ho. *BR1: Brom* *1J 159*
(off North St.)
Bromley Ind. Cen. BR1: Brom 3B 160
Bromley La. BR7: Chst 7G 143
BROMLEY PARK 1G 159
Bromley Pk. BR1: Brom 1H 159
Bromley Pl. W1 5A 6 (5G 83)
Bromley Rd. BR1: Brom 1D 140
BR2: Brom 2D 158
BR3: Beck 1D 158
BR7: Chst 1F 161
E10 6D 50
E17 3C 50
N17 1F 49
N18 3J 33
SE6 1D 140
Bromley Ski Cen. 7E 144
Bromley St. E1 5K 85
BROMPTON 2D 16 (3C 100)
Brompton Arc. SW3 7E 10
Brompton Cl. SE20 2G 157
TW4: Houn 5D 112
Brompton Cotts. *SW10* *6A 100*
(off Hollywood Rd.)
Brompton Gro. N2 4C 46
Brompton Oratory 2C 16 (3C 100)
Brompton Pk. Cres. SW6 6K 99
Brompton Pl. SW3 1D 16 (3C 100)
Brompton Rd. SW1 3C 16 (4C 100)
SW3 3C 16 (4C 100)
Brompton Sq. SW3 1C 16 (3C 100)
Brompton Ter. SE18 1D 124
Bromwich Av. N6 2E 64

Bromyard Av. W3 ... 7A **80**
Bromyard Ho. *SE15* ... *7H* ***103***
(off Commercial Way)
Bromyard Leisure Cen. ... 1A 98
Bron Ct. NW6 ... 1J **81**
BRONDESBURY ... 7H 63
Brondesbury Ct. NW2 ... 6F **63**
Brondesbury M. NW6 ... 7J **63**
BRONDESBURY PARK ... 1G 81
Brondesbury Pk. NW2 ... 6D **62**
NW6 ... 6D **62**
Brondesbury Rd. NW6 ... 2H **81**
Brondesbury Vs. NW6 ... 2H **81**
Bronhill Ter. N17 ... 1G **49**
Bronsart Rd. SW6 ... 7G **99**
Bronson Rd. SW20 ... 2F **153**
Bronte Cl. DA8: Erith ... 7H **109**
E7 ... 4J **69**
IG2: Ilf ... 4E **52**
Bronte Ct. *W14* ... *3F* ***99***
(off Girdler's Rd.)
Bronte Ho. N16 ... 5E **66**
NW6 ... 3J **81**
SW4 ... 7G **119**
Bronti Cl. SE17 ... 5C **102**
Bronwen Ct. *NW8* ... *2A* ***4***
(off Grove End Rd.)
Bronze Age Way DA8: Erith ... 2H **109**
DA17: Belv ... 2H **109**
Bronze St. SE8 ... 7C **104**
Brook Av. HA8: Edg ... 6C **28**
HA9: Wemb ... 3G **61**
RM10: Dag ... 7H **73**
Brookbank Av. W7 ... 5H **77**
Brookbank Rd. SE13 ... 3C **122**
Brook Cl. HA4: Ruis ... 7G **39**
NW7 ... 7B **30**
SW17 ... 2E **136**
SW20 ... 3D **152**
TW19: Stanw ... 7B **110**
W3 ... 1G **97**
Brook Ct. BR3: Beck ... 1B **158**
E11 ... 3G **69**
E15 ... *5D* ***68***
(off Clays La.)
E17 ... 3A **50**
HA8: Edg ... 5C **28**
IG11: Bark ... 1K **89**
SE12 ... 3A **142**
Brook Cres. E4 ... 4H **35**
N9 ... 4C **34**
Brookdale N11 ... 4B **32**
Brookdale Rd. DA5: Bexl ... 6E **126**
E17 ... 3C **50**
SE6 ... 7D **122**
(not continuous)
Brookdales NW11 ... 4G **45**
Brookdene Rd. SE18 ... 4J **107**
Brook Dr. HA1: Harr ... 4G **41**
HA4: Ruis ... 7G **39**
SE11 ... 2K **19** (3A **102**)
Brooke Av. HA2: Harr ... 3G **59**
Brooke Cl. WD23: Bush ... 1B **26**
Brooke Ho. SE14 ... 1A **122**
Brookehowse Rd. SE6 ... 2C **140**
Brookend Rd. DA15: Sidc ... 1J **143**
Brooke Rd. E5 ... 3G **67**
E17 ... 4E **50**
N16 ... 3F **67**
Brooke's Ct. EC1 ... 5J **7** (5A **84**)
Brooke's Mkt. EC1 ... 5K **7**
Brooke St. EC1 ... 6J **7** (5A **84**)
Brooke Way WD23: Bush ... 1B **26**
Brookfield N6 ... 3E **64**
Brookfield Av. E17 ... 4E **50**
NW7 ... 6J **29**
SM1: Sutt ... 4C **166**
W5 ... 4D **78**
Brookfield Cl. NW7 ... 6J **29**
Brookfield Ct. N12 ... 4E **30**
UB6: G'frd ... 3G **77**
Brookfield Cres. HA3: Kent ... 5E **42**
NW7 ... 6J **29**
Brookfield Gdns. KT10: Clay ... 6A **162**
Brookfield Pk. NW5 ... 3F **65**
Brookfield Path IG8: Wfd G ... 6B **36**
Brookfield Rd. E9 ... 6A **68**
N9 ... 3B **34**
W4 ... 2K **97**
Brookfields EN3: Pond E ... 4E **24**
Brookfields Av. CR4: Mitc ... 5C **154**
Brook Gdns. E4 ... 4J **35**
KT2: King T ... 1J **151**
SW13 ... 3B **116**
Brook Ga. W1 ... 3F **11** (7D **82**)
BROOK GREEN ... 4F 99
Brook Grn. W6 ... 3F **99**
Brook Grn. Flats *W14* ... *3F* ***99***
(off Dunsany Rd.)
Brookhill Cl. EN4: E Barn ... 5H **21**
SE18 ... 5F **107**
Brookhill Rd. EN4: E Barn ... 5H **21**
SE18 ... 6F **107**
Brook Ho. *W6* ... *4E* ***98***
(off Shepherd's Bush Rd.)
Brookhouse Gdns. E4 ... 4B **36**
Brook Ho's. *NW1* ... *2G* ***83***
(off Cranleigh St.)
Brook Ind. Est. UB4: Yead ... 1B **94**
Brooking Cl. RM8: Dag ... 3C **72**
Brooking Rd. E7 ... 5J **69**
Brookland Cl. NW11 ... 4J **45**
Brookland Gth. NW11 ... 4J **45**
Brookland Hill NW11 ... 4K **45**
Brookland Ri. NW11 ... 4J **45**
Brooklands, The TW7: Isle ... 1H **113**
Brooklands App. RM1: Rom ... 4K **55**
Brooklands Av. DA15: Sidc ... 2H **143**
SW19 ... 2K **135**
Brooklands Cl. RM7: Rom ... 4K **55**
TW16: Sun ... 1G **147**
Brooklands Ct. CR4: Mitc ... 2B **154**
KT1: King T ... *4D* ***150***
(off Surbiton Rd.)
N21 ... 5J **23**
NW6 ... 7H **63**
Brooklands Dr. UB6: G'frd ... 1C **78**
Brooklands La. RM7: Rom ... 4K **55**
(not continuous)
Brooklands Pk. SE3 ... 3J **123**
Brooklands Pas. SW8 ... 1H **119**
Brooklands Pl. TW12: Hamp H ... 5F **131**
Brooklands Rd. KT7: T Ditt ... 1A **162**
RM7: Rom ... 4K **55**
Brook La. BR1: Brom ... 6J **141**
DA5: Bexl, Bex ... 6D **126**
SE3 ... 2K **123**
Brook La. Bus. Cen. TW8: Bford ... 5D **96**
Brook La. Nth. TW8: Bford ... 5D **96**
(not continuous)
Brooklea Cl. NW9 ... 1A **44**
Brook Lodge *NW11* ... *5F* ***45***
(off Nth. Circular Rd.)
RM7: Rom ... *4K* ***55***
(off Medora Rd.)
Brooklyn SE20 ... 7G **139**
Brooklyn Av. SE25 ... 4H **157**
Brooklyn Cl. SM5: Cars ... 2C **166**
Brooklyn Gro. SE25 ... 4H **157**
Brooklyn Rd. BR2: Brom ... 5B **160**
SE25 ... 4H **157**
Brookmarsh Ind. Est. SE10 ... 7D **104**
Brook Mead KT19: Ewe ... 6A **164**
Brookmead CR0: Bedd ... 6G **155**
Brookmead Av. BR1: Brom ... 5D **160**
Brookmead Ind. Est. CR0: Bedd ... 6G **155**
Brook Mdw. N12 ... 3E **30**
Brook Mdw. Cl. IG8: Wfd G ... 6B **36**
Brookmead Rd. CR0: Croy ... 6G **155**
Brook M. WC2 ... 1D **12**
Brook M. Nth. W2 ... 2A **10** (7A **82**)
Brookmill Rd. SE8 ... 1C **122**
Brook Pde. IG7: Chig ... 3K **37**
Brook Pk. Cl. N21 ... 5G **23**
Brook Pl. EN5: Barn ... 5D **20**
Brook Ri. IG7: Chig ... 3K **37**
Brook Rd. CR7: Thor H ... 4C **156**
IG2: Ilf ... 6J **53**
IG9: Buck H, Wfd G ... 2D **36**
KT6: Surb ... 2E **162**
N2 ... 7H **31**
N8 ... 4J **47**
N22 ... 3K **47**
NW2 ... 2B **62**
TW1: Twick ... 6A **114**
Brook Rd. Sth. TW8: Bford ... 6D **96**
Brooks Av. E6 ... 4D **88**
Brooksbank St. E9 ... 6J **67**
Brooksby M. N1 ... 7A **66**
Brooksby St. N1 ... 7A **66**
Brooksby's Wlk. E9 ... 5K **67**
Brooks Cl. SE9 ... 2E **142**
Brooks Ct. SW8 ... 7G **101**
Brookscroft *E17* ... *3D* ***50***
(off Forest Rd.)
Brookscroft Rd. E17 ... 1D **50**
(not continuous)
Brooks Farm ... 7D 50
Brookshill HA3: Hrw W ... 5C **26**
Brookshill Av. HA3: Hrw W ... 5C **26**
Brookshill Dr. HA3: Hrw W ... 5C **26**
Brookside BR6: Orp ... 7K **161**
EN4: E Barn ... 6H **21**
N21 ... 6E **22**
SM5: Cars ... 5E **166**
UB10: Uxb ... 7B **56**
Brookside Cl. EN5: Barn ... 6B **20**
HA2: Harr ... 4C **58**
HA3: Kent ... 5D **42**
TW13: Felt ... 3J **129**
Brookside Cres. KT4: Wor Pk ... 1C **164**
Brookside Rd. N9 ... 4C **34**
(not continuous)
N19 ... 2G **65**
NW11 ... 6G **45**
UB4: Yead ... 7A **76**
Brookside Sth. EN4: E Barn ... 7K **21**
Brookside Wlk. N12 ... 6D **30**
NW11 ... 4G **45**
Brookside Way CR0: Croy ... 6K **157**
Brooks La. W4 ... 6G **97**
Brooks Lodge *N1* ... *2E* ***84***
(off Hoxton St.)
Brooks M. W1 ... 2J **11** (7F **83**)
Brook Sq. SE18 ... 1C **124**
Brooks Rd. E13 ... 1J **87**
W4 ... 5G **97**
Brook St. DA8: Erith ... 5H **109**
DA17: Belv, Erith ... 5H **109**
KT1: King T ... 2E **150**
N17 ... 2F **49**
W1 ... 2J **11** (7F **83**)
W2 ... 2B **10** (7B **82**)
Brooksville Av. NW6 ... 1G **81**
Brooks Wlk. N3 ... 3G **45**
Brookvale DA8: Erith ... 1H **127**
Brookview Ct. EN1: Enf ... 5K **23**
Brookview Rd. SW16 ... 5G **137**
Brookville Rd. SW6 ... 7H **99**
Brook Wlk. HA8: Edg ... 6E **28**
N2 ... 1B **46**
Brook Way IG7: Chig ... 3K **37**
Brookway SE3 ... 3J **123**
Brookwood Av. SW13 ... 2B **116**
Brookwood Cl. BR2: Brom ... 4H **159**
Brookwood Ho. *SE1* ... *7B* ***14***
(off Webber St.)
Brookwood Rd. SW18 ... 1H **135**
TW3: Houn ... 2F **113**
Broom Cl. BR2: Brom ... 6C **160**
TW11: Tedd ... 7D **132**
Broomcroft Av. UB5: Yead ... 3A **76**
Broome Rd. TW12: Hamp ... 7D **130**
Broome Way SE5 ... 7D **102**
Broomfield E17 ... 7B **50**
NW1 ... *7E* ***64***
(off Ferdinand St.)
TW16: Sun ... 1J **147**
Broomfield Av. N13 ... 5E **32**
Broomfield Ct. *SE16* ... *3G* ***103***
(off Ben Smith Way)
Broomfield Ho. *HA7: Stan* ... *3F* ***27***
(off Stanmore Hill)
SE17 ... *4E* ***102***
(off Massinger St.)
Broomfield La. N13 ... 4D **32**
Broomfield Pl. W13 ... 1B **96**
Broomfield Rd. BR3: Beck ... 3A **158**
DA6: Bex ... 5G **127**
KT5: Surb ... 1F **163**
N13 ... 5D **32**
RM6: Chad H ... 7D **54**
TW9: Kew ... 1F **115**
TW11: Tedd ... 6C **132**
W13 ... 1B **96**
Broomfield St. E14 ... 5C **86**
Broom Gdns. CR0: Croy ... 3C **170**
Broomgrove Gdns. HA8: Edg ... 1G **43**
Broomgrove Rd. SW9 ... 2K **119**
Broomhall Rd. CR2: Sand ... 7D **168**
BROOM HILL ... 7K 161
Broomhill Ct. IG8: Wfd G ... 6D **36**
Broom Hill Ri. DA6: Bex ... 5G **127**
Broomhill Rd. BR6: Orp ... 7K **161**
IG3: Ilf ... 2A **72**
IG8: Wfd G ... 6D **36**
(not continuous)
SW18 ... 5J **117**
Broomhill Wlk. IG8: Wfd G ... 6C **36**
Broomhouse La. SW6 ... 2J **117**
(not continuous)
Broomhouse Rd. SW6 ... 2J **117**
Broomleigh *BR1: Brom* ... *1J* ***159***
(off Tweedy Rd.)
Broomloan La. SM1: Sutt ... 2J **165**
Broom Lock TW11: Tedd ... 6C **132**
Broom Mead DA6: Bex ... 6G **127**
Broom Pk. TW11: Tedd ... 7D **132**
Broom Rd. CR0: Croy ... 3C **170**
TW11: Tedd ... 5B **132**
Broomsleigh Bus. Pk. SE26 ... 5B **140**
Broomsleigh St. NW6 ... 5H **63**
Broom Water TW11: Tedd ... 6C **132**
Broom Water W. TW11: Tedd ... 5C **132**
Broomwood Cl. CR0: Croy ... 5K **157**
DA5: Bexl ... 2K **145**
Broomwood Rd. SW11 ... 6D **118**
Broseley Gro. SE26 ... 5A **140**
Broster Gdns. SE25 ... 3F **157**
Brougham Rd. E8 ... 1G **85**
W3 ... 6J **79**
Brougham St. SW11 ... 2D **118**
Brough Cl. KT2: King T ... 5D **132**
SW8 ... 7J **101**
Broughton Av. N3 ... 3G **45**
TW10: Ham ... 3B **132**
Broughton Ct. W13 ... 7B **78**
Broughton Dr. SW9 ... 4A **120**
Broughton Gdns. N6 ... 6G **47**
Broughton Rd. BR6: Orp ... 2H **173**
CR7: Thor H ... 6A **156**
SW6 ... 2K **117**
W13 ... 7B **78**
Broughton St. SW8 ... 2E **118**
Broughton St. Ind. Est. SW11 ... 2E **118**
Brouncker Rd. W3 ... 2J **97**
Browells La. TW13: Felt ... 2K **129**
(not continuous)
Brown Bear Ct. TW13: Hanw ... 4B **130**
Brown Cl. SM6: Wall ... 7J **167**
Browne Ho. *SE8* ... *7C* ***104***
(off Deptford Chu. St.)
Brownfield Area E14 ... 6D **86**
Brownfield St. E14 ... 6D **86**

Burnett Rd. IG6: Ilf 7K **37**
Burney Av. KT5: Surb 5F **151**
Burney St. SE10 7E **104**
Burnfoot Av. SW6 1G **117**
Burnham NW3 7C **64**
Burnham Av. UB10: Ick 4E **56**
Burnham Cl. EN1: Enf 1K **23**
HA3: W'stone 4A **42**
NW7 7H **29**
SE1 4F **103**
Burnham Ct. *NW4* *4E **44***
(off Brent St.)
W2 *7K **81***
(off Moscow Rd.)
Burnham Cres. E11 4A **52**
Burnham Dr. KT4: Wor Pk 2F **165**
Burnham Est. *E2* *3J **85***
(off Burnham St.)
Burnham Gdns. CR0: Croy 7F **157**
TW4: Cran 1K **111**
UB3: Harl 3F **93**
Burnham Rd.
DA14: Sidc 2E **144**
E4 5G **35**
RM7: Rom 3K **55**
RM9: Dag 7B **72**
SM4: Mord 4K **153**
Burnham St. E2 3J **85**
KT2: King T 1G **151**
Burnham Way SE26 5B **140**
W13 4B **96**
Burnhill Cl. SE15 7H **103**
Burnhill Rd. BR3: Beck 2C **158**
Burnley Rd. NW10 5B **62**
SW9 2K **119**
Burnsall St. SW3 6D **16** (5C **100**)
Burns Av. DA15: Sidc 6B **126**
RM6: Chad H 7C **54**
TW14: Felt 6J **111**
UB1: S'hall 7E **76**
Burns Cl. DA16: Well 1K **125**
E17 4E **50**
SW19 6B **136**
UB4: Hayes 5H **75**
Burns Ho. *E2* *3J **85***
(off Cornwall Av.)
SE17 *5B **102***
(off Doddington Gro.)
Burnside Av. E4 6G **35**
Burnside Cl. EN5: New Bar 3D **20**
SE16 1K **103**
TW1: Twick 6A **114**
Burnside Ct. SM5: Cars 3E **166**
Burnside Cres. HA0: Wemb 1D **78**
Burnside Rd. RM8: Dag 2C **72**
Burns Rd. HA0: Wemb 2E **78**
NW10 1B **80**
SW11 2D **118**
W13 2B **96**
Burns Way TW5: Hest 2B **112**
Burnt Ash Hgts. BR1: Brom 5K **141**
Burnt Ash Hill SE12 6H **123**
(not continuous)
Burnt Ash La. BR1: Brom 7J **141**
Burnt Ash Rd. SE12 5H **123**
Burnthwaite Rd. SW6 7H **99**
BURNT OAK 2J **43**
Burnt Oak B'way. HA8: Edg 7B **28**
Burnt Oak Flds. HA8: Edg 1J **43**
Burnt Oak La. DA15: Sidc 6A **126**
Burntwood Cl. SW18 1C **136**
Burntwood Grange Rd. SW18 1B **136**
Burntwood La. SW17 3A **136**
Burntwood Vw. SE19 5F **139**
Buross St. E1 6H **85**
Burpham Cl. UB4: Yead 5B **76**
Burrage Ct. *SE16* *4K **103***
(off Worgan St.)
Burrage Gro. SE18 4G **107**
Burrage Pl. SE18 5F **107**
Burrage Rd. SE18 6G **107**
Burrard Ho. *E2* *2J **85***
(off Bishop's Way)
Burrard Rd. E16 6K **87**
NW6 5J **63**
Burr Cl. DA7: Bex 3F **127**
E1 4K **15** (1G **103**)
Burrell Cl. CR0: Croy 6A **158**
HA8: Edg 2C **28**
Burrell Row BR3: Beck 2C **158**
Burrell St. SE1 4A **14** (1B **102**)
Burrells Wharf Sq. E14 5D **104**
Burrell Towers E10 7C **50**
Burrhill Ct. *SE16* *3K **103***
(off Worgan St.)
Burritt Rd. KT1: King T 2G **151**
Burroughs, The NW4 4D **44**
Burroughs Club, The 4D **44**
Burroughs Cotts. *E14* *5A **86***
(off Halley St.)
Burroughs Gdns. NW4 4D **44**
Burroughs Pde. NW4 4D **44**
Burrow Ho. *SW9* *2A **120***
(off Stockwell Pk. Rd.)
Burrow Rd. SE22 4E **120**
Burrows M. SE1 6A **14** (2B **102**)
Burrows Rd. NW10 3E **80**
Burrow Wlk. SE21 7C **120**
Burr Rd. SW18 1J **135**
Bursar St. SE1 5G **15** (1E **102**)
Bursdon Cl. DA15: Sidc 2K **143**
Bursland Rd. EN3: Pond E 4E **24**
Burslem St. E1 6G **85**
Burstock Rd. SW15 4G **117**
Burston Rd. SW15 5F **117**
Burstow Rd. SW20 1G **153**
Burtenshaw Rd. KT7: T Ditt 7A **150**
Burtley Cl. N4 1C **66**
Burton Bank *N1* *7D **66***
(off Yeate St.)
Burton Cl. CR7: Thor H 3D **156**
KT9: Chess 7D **162**
Burton Ct. KT7: T Ditt 6A **150**
SE20 2J **157**
SW3 *5F **17***
(off Franklin's Row, not continuous)
Burton Gdns. TW5: Houn 1D **112**
Burton Gro. SE17 5D **102**
Burtonhole Cl. NW7 4A **30**
Burtonhole La. N12 4B **30**
NW7 5K **29**
Burton Ho. *SE16* *2H **103***
(off Cherry Gdn. St.)
Burton La. SW9 2A **120**
(not continuous)
Burton M. SW1 4H **17** (4E **100**)
Burton Pl. WC1 2D **6** (3H **83**)
Burton Rd. E18 3K **51**
KT2: King T 7E **132**
NW6 7H **63**
SW9 2B **120**
(Akerman Rd.)
SW9 2A **120**
(Evesham Wlk.)
Burton's Rd. TW12: Hamp H 4F **131**
Burton St. WC1 2D **6** (3H **83**)
Burtonwood Ho. N4 7D **48**
Burtop Rd. Est. SW17 3A **136**
Burt Rd. E16 1A **106**
Burtt Ho. *N1* *1G **9***
(off Aske St.)
Burtwell La. SE27 4D **138**
Burwash Ho. *SE1* *7F **15***
(off Kipling Est.)
Burwash Rd. SE18 5H **107**
Burwell *KT1: King T* *2G **151***
(off Excelsior Rd.)
Burwell Av. UB6: G'frd 6J **59**
Burwell Cl. E1 6H **85**
Burwell Rd. E10 1A **68**
Burwell Rd. Ind. Est. E10 1A **68**
Burwell Wlk. E3 4C **86**
Burwood Av. BR2: Hayes 2K **171**
HA5: Eastc 5K **39**
Burwood Cl. KT6: Surb 1G **163**
Burwood Ho. SW9 4B **120**
Burwood Pl. EN4: Had W 1F **21**
W2 7D **4** (6C **82**)
Bury Av. HA4: Ruis 6E **38**
UB4: Hayes 2G **75**
Bury Cl. SE16 1K **103**
Bury Ct. EC3 7H **9** (6E **84**)
Bury Gro. SM4: Mord 5K **153**
Bury Hall Vs.
N9 7A **24**
Bury Pl. WC1 6E **6** (5J **83**)
Bury Rd. E4 1B **36**
N22 2A **48**
RM10: Dag 5H **73**
Buryside Cl. IG2: Ilf 4K **53**
Bury St. EC3 1H **15** (6E **84**)
HA4: Ruis 5E **38**
N9 7A **24**
SW1 4B **12** (1G **101**)
Bury St. W. N9 7J **23**
Bury Wlk. SW3 4C **16** (4C **100**)
Busbridge Ho. *E14* *5C **86***
(off Brabazon St.)
Busby Ho. SW16 4G **137**
Busby M. NW5 6H **65**
Busby Pl. NW5 6H **65**
Busch Cl. TW7: Isle 1B **114**
Bushbaby Cl. SE1 3E **102**
Bushberry Rd. E9 6A **68**
Bush Cl. IG2: Ilf 5H **53**
Bush Cotts. SW18 5J **117**
Bush Ct. N14 1C **32**
W12 2F **99**
Bushell Cl. SW2 2K **137**
Bushell Grn. WD23: Bushy 2C **26**
Bushell St. E1 1G **103**
Bushell Way BR7: Chst 5E **142**
BUSHEY 1C **26**
Bushey Av. BR5: Pet W 7H **161**
E18 3H **51**
Bushey Cl. E4 3K **35**
UB10: Ick 2C **56**
Bushey Ct. SW20 3D **152**
Bushey Down SW12 2F **137**
BUSHEY HEATH 1C **26**
Bushey Hill Rd. SE5 1E **120**
Bushey La. SM1: Sutt 4J **165**
BUSHEY MEAD 2F **153**
Bushey Rd. CR0: Croy 2C **170**
E13 2A **88**
N15 6E **48**
SM1: Sutt 4J **165**
SW20 3D **152**
UB3: Harl 4G **93**
UB10: Ick 2C **56**
Bushey Way BR3: Beck 6F **159**
Bush Fair Ct. N14 6A **22**
Bushfield Cl. HA8: Edg 2C **28**
Bushfield Cres. HA8: Edg 2C **28**
Bush Gro. HA7: Stan 1D **42**
NW9 7J **43**
Bushgrove Rd. RM8: Dag 4D **72**
Bush Hill N21 7H **23**
Bush Hill Pde. EN1 7J **23**
BUSH HILL PARK 6A **24**
Bush Hill Rd. HA3: Kent 6F **43**
N21 6J **23**
Bush Ind. Est. N19 3G **65**
NW10 4K **79**
Bush La. EC4 2E **14** (7D **84**)
Bushmead Cl. N15 4F **49**
Bushmoor Cres. SE18 7F **107**
Bushnell Rd. SW17 2F **137**
Bush Rd. E8 1H **85**
E11 7H **51**
IG9: Buck H 4G **37**
SE8 *4K **103***
(off Rotherhithe New Rd.)
Bush Rd. TW9: Kew 6F **97**
TW17: Shep 5B **146**
Bush Theatre 2E **98**
Bushway RM8: Dag 4D **72**
Bushwood E11 1H **69**
Bushwood Dr. SE1 4F **103**
Bushwood Rd. TW9: Kew 6G **97**
Bushy Ct. *KT1: Hamp W* *1C **150***
(off Up. Teddington Rd.)
Bushy Lees DA15: Sidc 6K **125**
Bushy Pk. Gdns. TW11: Tedd 5H **131**
Bushy Pk. Rd. TW11: Tedd 7B **132**
(not continuous)
Bushy Rd. TW11: Tedd 6K **131**
Business Design Cen. *1A **84***
(off Upper St.)
Butcher Row E1 7K **85**
E14 7K **85**
Butchers Rd. E16 6J **87**
Bute Av. TW10: Ham 2E **132**
Bute Ct. SM6: Wall 5G **167**
Bute Gdns. SM6: Wall 5G **167**
TW10: Ham 1E **132**
W6 4F **99**
Bute Gdns. W. SM6: Wall 5G **167**
Bute M. NW11 5A **46**
Bute Rd. CR0: Croy 1A **168**
IG6: Ilf 5F **53**
SM6: Wall 4G **167**
Bute St. SW7 3A **16** (4B **100**)
Bute Wlk. N1 6D **66**
Butfield Ho. *E9* *6J **67***
(off Stevens Av.)
Butler Av. HA1: Harr 7H **41**
Butler Ct. HA0: Wemb 4A **60**
RM8: Dag *2G **73***
(off Gosfield Rd.)
Butler Ho. *E2* *3J **85***
(off Bacton St.)
E14 *6B **86***
(off Burdett St.)
SW9 *1B **120***
(off Lothian Rd.)
Butler Pl. SW1 1C **18** (3H **101**)
Butler Rd. HA1: Harr 7G **41**
NW10 7B **62**
RM8: Dag 4B **72**
Butlers & Colonial Wharf *SE1* *6K **15***
(off Shad Thames)
Butlers Cl. TW3: Houn 3D **112**
Butlers Dr. E4 1K **25**
Butler St. E2 3J **85**
UB10: Hil 4D **74**
Butlers Wharf *SE1* *6K **15***
(off Gainsford St.)
Butley Ct. *E3* *2A **86***
(off Ford St.)
Buttercup Cl. UB5: N'olt 6D **58**
Butterfield Cl. N17 6H **33**
SE16 2H **103**
TW1: Twick 6K **113**
Butterfields E17 5E **50**
Butterfield Sq. E6 6D **88**
Butterfly La. SE9 6F **125**
Butterfly Wlk. *SE5* *1D **120***
(off Denmark Hill)
Butter Hill SM5: Cars 3E **166**
SM6: Wall 3E **166**
Butteridges Cl. RM9: Dag 1F **91**
Buttermere *NW1* *1K **5***
(off Augustus St.)
Buttermere Cl. E15 4F **69**
SE1 4F **103**
SM4: Mord 6F **153**
TW14: Felt 1H **129**
Buttermere Ct. *NW8* *1B **82***
(off Boundary Rd.)
Buttermere Dr. SW15 5G **117**
Buttermere Wlk. E8 6F **67**
Butterwick W6 4F **99**
Butterworth Gdns. IG8: Wfd G 6D **36**

Calidore Cl. SW2 . . . . . 6K 119
California La. WD23: Bushy 1C 26
California Pl. *WD23: Bushy* *1C 26*
(off High Rd.)
California Rd. KT3: N Mald 4H 151
Callaby Ter. N1 . . . . . 6D 66
Callaghan Cl. SE13 . . . . . 4G 123
Callahan Cotts. *E1* *5J 85*
(off Lindley St.)
Callander Rd. SE6 . . . . . 2D 140
Callanders, The WD23: Bushy 1D 26
Callard Av. N13 . . . . . 4G 33
Callcott Ct. NW6 . . . . . 7H 63
Callcott Rd. NW6 . . . . . 7H 63
Callcott St. W8 . . . . . 1J 99
Callendar Rd. SW7 . . . . . 1A 16 (3B 100)
Callenders Cotts. DA17: Erith 2K 109
Callingham Cl. E14 . . . . . 5B 86
Callis Farm Cl. TW19: Stanw 6A 110
Callis Rd. E17 . . . . . 6B 50
Callonfield E17 . . . . . 4K 49
Callow St. SW3 . . . . . 7A 16 (6B 100)
Cally Swimming Pool 1K 83
Calmington Rd. SE5 . . . . . 6E 102
Calmont Rd. BR1: Brom 6F 141
Calne Av. IG5: Ilf 1F 53
Calonne Rd. SW19 . . . . . 4F 135
Calshot Ho. *N1* *2K 83*
(off Calshot St.)
Calshot Rd. TW6: H'row A 2C 110
(not continuous)
Calshot St. N1 . . . . . 1G 7 (2K 83)
Calshot Way EN2: Enf 3G 23
TW6: H'row A 2C 110
(not continuous)
Calstock *NW1* *1G 83*
(off Royal College St.)
Calstock Ho. SE11 . . . . . 5K 19
Calthorpe Gdns. HA8: Edg 5K 27
(not continuous)
SM1: Sutt 3A 166
Calthorpe St. WC1 . . . . . 3H 7 (4K 83)
Calton Av. SE21 . . . . . 6E 120
Calton Rd. EN5: New Bar 6F 21
Calverley Cl. BR3: Beck 6D 140
Calverley Cres. RM10: Dag 2G 73
Calverley Gdns. HA3: Kent 7D 42
Calverley Gro. N19 . . . . . 1H 65
Calverley Rd. KT17: Ewe 6C 164
Calvert Av. E2 . . . . . 2H 9 (3E 84)
Calvert Cl. DA14: Sidc 6E 144
DA17: Belv 4G 109
Calvert Dr. DA2: Bexl 2K 145
Calvert Ho. *W12* *7D 80*
(off White City Est.)
Calverton *SE5* *6E 102*
(off Albany Rd.)
Calverton Rd. E6 . . . . . 1E 88
Calvert Rd. EN5: Barn 2A 20
SE10 . . . . . 5H 105
Calvert's Bldgs. SE1 . . . . . 5E 14 (1D 102)
Calvert St. NW1 . . . . . 1E 82
Calvin St. E1 . . . . . 4J 9 (4F 85)
Calydon Rd. SE7 . . . . . 5K 105
Calypso Cres. SE15 . . . . . 7F 103
Calypso Way SE16 . . . . . 3B 104
Camac Rd. TW2: Twick 1H 131
Camarthen Grn. NW9 . . . . . 5A 44
Cambalt Rd. SW15 . . . . . 5F 117
Cambay Ho. *E1* *4A 86*
(off Harford St.)
Camber Ho. SE15 . . . . . 6J 103
Camberley Av. EN1: Enf 4K 23
SW20 . . . . . 2D 152
Camberley Cl. SM3: Cheam 3F 165
Camberley Ho. NW1 . . . . . 1K 5
Camberley Rd. TW6: H'row A 3C 110
Cambert Way SE3 . . . . . 4K 123
CAMBERWELL 1D 120
Camberwell Chu. St. SE5 . . . . . 1D 120
Camberwell Glebe SE5 . . . . . 1E 120
CAMBERWELL GREEN 1D 120
Camberwell Grn. SE5 . . . . . 1D 120
Camberwell Gro. SE5 . . . . . 1D 120
Camberwell Leisure Cen. 1D 120
Camberwell New Rd.
SE5 . . . . . 6A 102
Camberwell Pl. SE5 . . . . . 1C 120
Camberwell Rd. SE5 . . . . . 6C 102
Camberwell Sta. Rd. SE5 . . . . . 1C 120
Camberwell Trad. Est.
SE5 . . . . . 1B 120
Cambeys Rd. RM10: Dag 5H 73
Camborne Av. W13 . . . . . 2B 96
Camborne Cl. TW6: H'row A 3C 110
Camborne Cres. TW6: H'row A 3C 110
Camborne Rd. CR0: Croy 7G 157
DA14: Sidc 3C 144
DA16: Well 2J 125
SM2: Sutt 7J 165
SM4: Mord 5F 153
SW18 . . . . . 7J 117
TW6: H'row A 3C 110
Camborne Way TW5: Hest 1E 112
TW6: H'row A 3C 110
Cambourne Av. N9 . . . . . 7E 24
Cambourne M. W11 . . . . . 6G 81
Cambourne Wlk. TW10: Rich 6D 114
Cambrai Ct. N13 . . . . . 3D 32
Cambray Rd. BR6: Orp 7K 161
SW12 . . . . . 1G 137
Cambria Cl. DA15: Sidc 1H 143
TW3: Houn 4E 112
Cambria Ct. TW14: Felt 7K 111
Cambria Gdns. TW19: Stanw 7A 110
(not continuous)
Cambria Ho. *E14* *6A 86*
(off Salmon La.)
SE26 . . . . . *4G 139*
(off High Level Dr.)
Cambrian Av. IG2: Ilf 5J 53
Cambrian Cl. SE27 . . . . . 3B 138
Cambrian Grn. *NW9* *5A 44*
(off Snowden Dr.)
Cambrian Rd. E10 . . . . . 7C 50
TW10: Rich 6F 115
Cambria Rd. SE5 . . . . . 3C 120
Cambria St. SW6 . . . . . 7K 99
Cambridge Arc. *E9* *7J 67*
(off Elsdale St.)
Cambridge Av. DA16: Well 4K 125
KT3: N Mald 3A 152
(not continuous)
NW6 . . . . . 2J 81
NW10 . . . . . 3E 80
UB6: G'frd 5K 59
Cambridge Barracks Rd.
SE18 . . . . . 4D 106
Cambridge Cir. WC2 . . . . . 1D 12 (6H 83)
Cambridge Cl. E17 . . . . . 6B 50
N22 . . . . . 1A 48
NW10 . . . . . 3J 61
SW20 . . . . . 1D 152
TW4: Houn 4C 112
UB7: Harm 6A 92
Cambridge Cotts. TW9: Kew 6G 97
Cambridge Ct. *E2* *2H 85*
(off Cambridge Heath Rd.)
N16 . . . . . *7E 48*
(off Amhurst Pk.)
NW6 . . . . . 2J 81
W2 . . . . . *6C 4*
(off Edgware Rd.)
W6 . . . . . *4E 98*
(off Shepherd's Bush Rd.)
Cambridge Cres. E2 . . . . . 2H 85
TW11: Tedd 5A 132
Cambridge Dr. HA4: Ruis 2A 58
SE12 . . . . . 5J 123
Cambridge Gdns. EN1: Enf 2B 24
KT1: King T 2G 151
N10 . . . . . 1E 46
Cambridge Gdns. N17 . . . . . 7J 33
N21 . . . . . 7J 23
NW6 . . . . . 2J 81
W10 . . . . . 6F 81
Cambridge Ga. NW1 . . . . . 3J 5 (4F 83)
Cambridge Ga. M. NW1 . . . . . 3K 5 (4F 83)
Cambridge Grn. SE9 . . . . . 1F 143
Cambridge Gro. SE20 . . . . . 1H 157
W6 . . . . . 4D 98
Cambridge Gro. Rd. KT1: King T 3G 151
(not continuous)
Cambridge Heath Rd. E1 . . . . . 5H 85
Cambridge Ho. *W6* *4D 98*
(off Cambridge Gro.)
W13 . . . . . 6A 78
Cambridge Pde. EN1: Enf 1B 24
Cambridge Pk. E11 . . . . . 7J 51
TW1: Twick 6C 114
Cambridge Pk. Ct. TW1: Twick 7D 114
Cambridge Pk. Rd. *E11* *7J 51*
(off Lonsdale Rd.)
Cambridge Pl. W8 . . . . . 2K 99
Cambridge Rd. BR1: Brom 7J 141
CR4: Mitc 3G 155
DA14: Sidc 4J 143
E4 . . . . . 1A 36
E11 . . . . . 6H 51
HA2: Harr 5E 40
IG3: Ilf 1J 71
IG11: Bark 7G 71
KT1: King T 2F 151
KT3: N Mald 4K 151
KT8: W Mole 4D 148
KT12: Walt T 6K 147
NW6 . . . . . 2J 81
(not continuous)
SE20 . . . . . 3H 157
SM5: Cars 6C 166
SW11 . . . . . 1D 118
SW13 . . . . . 2B 116
SW20 . . . . . 1C 152
TW1: Twick 6D 114
TW4: Houn 4C 112
TW9: Kew 7G 97
TW11: Tedd 4K 131
TW12: Hamp 7D 130
TW15: Ashf 7E 128
UB1: S'hall 1D 94
W7 . . . . . 2K 95
Cambridge Rd. Nth. W4 . . . . . 5H 97
Cambridge Rd. Sth. W4 . . . . . 5H 97
Cambridge Row SE18 . . . . . 5F 107
Cambridge Sq. W2 . . . . . 7C 4 (6C 82)
Cambridge St. SW1 . . . . . 4K 17 (4F 101)
Cambridge Ter. N9 . . . . . 7K 23
NW1 . . . . . 2J 5 (3F 83)
Cambridge Ter. M. NW1 . . . . . 2K 5 (3F 83)
Cambridge Theatre *1E 12*
(off Earlham St.)
Cambridge Yd. W7 . . . . . 2K 95
Cambstone Cl. N11 . . . . . 2K 31
Cambus Cl. UB4: Yead 5C 76
Cambus Rd. E16 . . . . . 5J 87
Cam Ct. SE15 . . . . . 6F 103
Camdale Rd. SE18 . . . . . 7K 107
Camden Arts Cen. 5K 63
Camden Av. TW13: Felt 1A 130
UB4: Yead 7B 76
Camden Cl. BR7: Chst 1G 161
Camden Ct. DA17: Belv 5G 109
NW1 . . . . . *7G 65*
(off Rousden St.)
Camden Gdns. CR7: Thor H 3B 156
NW1 . . . . . 7F 65
SM1: Sutt 5K 165
Camden Gro. BR7: Chst 6F 143
Camden High St. NW1 . . . . . 7F 65
Camden Hill Rd. SE19 . . . . . 6E 138
Camden Ho. SE8 . . . . . 5B 104
Camdenhurst St. E14 . . . . . 6A 86
Camden La. N7 . . . . . 5H 65
Camden Lock Market *7F 65*
(off Camden Lock Pl.)
Camden Lock Pl. NW1 . . . . . 7F 65
Camden Market *1F 83*
(off Dewsbury Ter.)
Camden M. NW1 . . . . . 7G 65
Camden Pk. Rd. BR7: Chst 7D 142
NW1 . . . . . 6H 65
Camden Pas. N1 . . . . . 1B 84
(not continuous)
Camden Peoples Theatre *3A 6*
(off Hampstead Rd.)
Camden Rd. DA5: Bexl 1E 144
E11 . . . . . 6K 51
E17 . . . . . 6B 50
N7 . . . . . 4J 65
NW1 . . . . . 7G 65
SM1: Sutt 5K 165
SM5: Cars 4D 166
Camden Row HA5: Pinn 3A 40
SE3 . . . . . 2G 123
Camden Sq. NW1 . . . . . 7H 65
(not continuous)
SE15 . . . . . 1F 121
Camden St. NW1 . . . . . 7G 65
Camden Studios *NW1* *1G 83*
(off Camden St.)
Camden Ter. NW1 . . . . . 6H 65
CAMDEN TOWN 1F 83
Camden Wlk. N1 . . . . . 1B 84
(not continuous)
Camden Way BR7: Chst 7D 142
CR7: Thor H 3B 156
Cameford Ct. SW2 . . . . . 7J 119
Camelford *NW1* *1G 83*
(off Royal College St.)
Camelford Ct. W11 . . . . . 6G 81
Camelford Ho. SE1 . . . . . 5F 19 (5J 101)
Camelford Wlk. W11 . . . . . 6G 81
Camel Gro. KT2: King T 5D 132
Camellia Ho. *SE8* *7B 104*
(off Idonia St.)
Camellia Pl. TW2: Whit 7F 113
Camellia St. SW8 . . . . . 7J 101
(not continuous)
Camelot Cl. SE28 . . . . . 2H 107
SW19 . . . . . 4H 135
Camelot Ho. NW1 . . . . . 6H 65
Camel Rd. E16 . . . . . 1B 106
Camera Pl. SW10 . . . . . 7A 16 (6B 100)
Cameret Ct. *W11* *2F 99*
(off Holland Rd.)
Cameron Cl. DA5: Bexl 3K 145
N18 . . . . . 4C 34
N20 . . . . . 2G 31
Cameron Ho. *NW8* *2C 82*
(off St John's Wood Ter.)
SE5 . . . . . 7C 102
Cameron Pl. E1 . . . . . 6H 85
SW16 . . . . . 2A 138
Cameron Rd. BR2: Brom 5J 159
CR0: Croy 6B 156
IG3: Ilf 1J 71
SE6 . . . . . 2B 140
Cameron Sq. CR4: Mitc 1C 154
Cameron Ter. SE12 . . . . . 3K 141
Camerton Cl. E8 . . . . . 6F 67
Camgate Cen., The TW19: Stanw 6B 110
Camilla Cl. TW16: Sun 6H 129
Camilla Rd. SE16 . . . . . 4H 103
Camille Cl. SE25 . . . . . 3G 157
Camlan Rd. BR1: Brom 4H 141
Camlet St. E2 . . . . . 3J 9 (4F 85)
Camlet Way EN4: Barn, Had W 2D 20
Camley St. NW1 . . . . . 7H 65
Camm Gdns. KT1: King T 2F 151
KT7: T Ditt 7K 149
Camomile Av. CR4: Mitc 1D 154
Camomile Rd. RM7: Rush G 2K 73
Camomile St. EC3 . . . . . 7H 9 (6E 84)
Camomile Way UB7: Yiew 6A 74

Campana Rd. SW6 ....1J 117
Campania Bldg. *E1* 7K *85*
(off Jardine Rd.)
Campaspe Bus. Pk. TW16: Sun ...5H 147
Campbell Av. IG6: Ilf 4F 53
Campbell Cl. HA4: Ruis 6J 39
SE18 ....1E 124
SW16 ....4H 137
TW2: Twick 1H 131
Campbell Ct. N17 ....1F 49
NW9 ....6J 43
SE21 ....1G 139
SW7 ....3A 100
(off Gloucester Rd.)
Campbell Cft. HA8: Edg 5B 28
Campbell Gordon Way NW2 ......4D 62
Campbell Ho. SW1 ....6A 18
(off Churchill Gdns.)
W12 ....7D 80
(off White City Est.)
Campbell Rd. CR0: Croy 7B 156
E3 ....3C 86
E6 ....1C 88
E15 ....4H 69
E17 ....4B 50
KT8: E Mos 3J 149
N17 ....1F 49
TW2: Twick 2H 131
W7 ....7J 77
Campbell Wlk. *N1* 1J *83*
(off Outram Pl.)
Campdale Rd. N7 ....3H 65
Campden Cres. HA0: Wemb 3B 60
RM8: Dag 4B 72
Campden Gro. W8 ....2J 99
Campden Hill W8 ....2J 99
Campden Hill Ct. W8 ....2J 99
Campden Hill Gdns. W8 ....1J 99
Campden Hill Ga. W8 ....2J 99
Campden Hill Mans. W8 ....1J *99*
(off Edge St.)
Campden Hill Pl. W11 ....1H 99
Campden Hill Rd. W8 ....1J 99
Campden Hill Sq. W8 ....1H 99
Campden Ho. NW6 ....7B *64*
(off Harben Rd.)
W8 ....1J *99*
(off Sheffield Ter.)
Campden Ho. Cl. W8 ....2J 99
Campden Ho's. W8 ....1J 99
Campden Ho. Ter. W8 ....1J *99*
(off Kensington Chu. St.)
Campden Rd. CR2: S Croy 5E 168
UB10: Ick 3B 56
Campden St. W8 ....1J 99
Campe Ho. N10 ....7K 31
Campen Cl. SW19 ....2G 135
Camperdown St. E1 ......1K 15 (6F 85)
Campfield Rd. SE9 ....7B 124
Campion Cl. CR2: S Croy 4E 168
E6 ....7D 88
HA3: Kent 6F 43
RM7: Rush G 2K 73
UB8: Hil 5B 74
Campion Ct. HA0: Wemb 2E 78
Campion Gdns. IG8: Wfd G 5D 36
Campion Pl. SE28 ....1A 108
Campion Rd. SW15 ....4E 116
TW7: Isle 1K 113
Campion Ter. NW2 ....3F 63
Campion Way HA8: Edg 4D 28
Camplin Rd. HA3: Kent 5E 42
Camplin St. SE14 ....7K 103
Camp Rd. SW19 ....5D 134
(not continuous)
Campsbourne, The N8 ....4J 47
Campsbourne Ho. *N8* 4J *47*
(off Pembroke Rd.)
Campsbourne Rd. N8 ....3J 47
(not continuous)
Campsey Gdns. RM9: Dag 7B 72

Campsey Rd. RM9: Dag 7B 72
Campsfield Ho. *N8* 3J *47*
(off Campsfield Rd.)
Campsfield Rd. N8 ....3J 47
Campshill Pl. SE13 ....5E 122
Campshill Rd. SE13 ....5E 122
Campus Rd. E17 ....6B 50
Campus Way NW4 ....3D 44
Camp Vw. SW19 ....5D 134
Cam Rd. E15 ....1F 87
Camrose Av. DA8: Erith 6H 109
HA8: Edg 2F 43
TW13: Felt 4A 130
Camrose Cl. CR0: Croy 7A 158
SM4: Mord 2A 154
Camrose St. SE2 ....5A 108
Canada Av. N18 ....6H 33
Canada Cres. W3 ....5J 79
Canada Est. SE16 ....3J 103
Canada Gdns. SE13 ....5E 122
Canada Ho. *SE16* 3A *104*
(off Brunswick Quay)
Canada Memorial 6A 12
(off Green Pk.)
Canada Pl. *E14* 1D *104*
(off Up. Bank St.)
Canada Rd. W3 ....5J 79
Canada Sq. E14 ....1D 104
Canada St. SE16 ....2K 103
Canada Way W12 ....7D 80
Canada Wharf SE16 ....1B 104
Canadian Av. SE6 ....1D 140
Canal App. SE8 ....5A 104
Canal Blvd. NW1 ....6H 65
CANAL BRIDGE 6G 103
Canal Bldg. *N1* 2C *84*
(off Shepherdess Wlk.)
Canal Cl. E1 ....4A 86
W10 ....4F 81
Canal Gro. SE15 ....6H 103
Canal Mkt. *NW1* 7F *65*
(off Castlehaven Rd.)
Canal Path *E2* 1F 85
Canalside SE28 ....7D 90
Canalside Activity Cen. 4F 81
Canal St. SE5 ....6D 102
Canal Wlk. CR0 ....6E 156
N1 ....1D 84
NW10 ....7J 61
(off Westend Cl.)
SE26 ....5J 139
Canal Way W10 ....4F 81
Canal Wharf UB6: G'frd 1A 78
Canberra Cl. NW4 ....3C 44
RM10: Dag 1K 91
Canberra Cres. RM10: Dag 7K 73
Canberra Dr. UB5: Yead 3A 76
Canberra Rd. DA7: Bex 6D 108
E6 ....1D 88
SE7 ....6A 106
TW6: H'row A 3C 110
Cancell Rd. SW9 ....1A 120
Candahar Rd. SW11 ....2C 118
Candida Ct. NW1 ....7F 65
Candid Ho. *NW10* 3D *80*
(off Trenmar Gdns.)
Candle Gro. SE15 ....3H 121
Candlelight Ct. *E15* 6H *69*
(off Romford Rd.)
Candler M. TW1: Twick 7A 114
Candler St. N15 ....6D 48
Candover Cl. UB7: Harm 7A 92
Candover St. W1 ....6A 6 (5G 83)

Candy St. E3 ....1B 86
Caney M. NW2 ....2F 63
Canfield Dr. HA4: Ruis 5K 57
Canfield Gdns. NW6 ....7K 63
Canfield Ho. *N15* 6E *48*
(off Albert Rd.)
Canfield Pl. NW6 ....6A 64
Canfield Rd. IG8: Wfd G 7H 37
Canford Av. UB5: N'olt 1D 76
Canford Cl. EN2: Enf 2F 23
Canford Gdns. KT3: N Mald 6A 152
Canford Pl. TW11: Tedd 6C 132
Canford Rd. SW11 ....5E 118
Canham Rd. SE25 ....3E 156
W3 ....2A 98
Canmore Gdns. SW16 ....7G 137
CANN HALL 4G 69
Cann Hall Rd. E11 ....4G 69
Cann Ho. *W14* 3G *99*
(off Russell Rd.)
Canning Cres. N22 ....1K 47
Canning Cross SE5 ....2E 120
Canning Ho. *W12* 7D *80*
(off Australia Rd.)
Canning Pas. W8 ....3A 100
(not continuous)
Canning Pl. W8 ....3A 100
Canning Pl. M. *W8* 3A *100*
(off Canning Pl.)
Canning Rd. CR0: Croy 2F 169
E15 ....2G 87
E17 ....4A 50
HA3: W'stone 3J 41
N5 ....3B 66
Cannington Rd. RM9: Dag 6C 72
CANNING TOWN 6H 87
CANNING TOWN 6G 87
Cannizaro Rd. SW19 ....6E 134
Cannock Ho. N4 ....7C 48
Cannonbury Av. HA5: Pinn 6B 40
Cannon Cl. SW20 ....3E 152
TW12: Hamp 6F 131
Cannon Ct. *EC1* 3B *8*
(off Brewhouse Yd.)
Cannon Dr. E14 ....7C 86
Cannon Hill N14 ....3D 32
NW6 ....5J 63
Cannon Hill La. SW20 ....5F 153
Cannon Hill M. N14 ....3D 32
Cannon La. HA5: Pinn 5C 40
NW3 ....3B 64
Cannon Pl. NW3 ....3B 64
SE7 ....5C 106
Cannon Retail Pk. SE28 ....7A 90
Cannon Rd. DA7: Bex 1E 126
N14 ....3D 32
Cannons Health Club
Cannon Street 3E 14
Fulham 1F 117
Willesden Green 7E 62
Cannon St. EC4 ....1C 14 (6C 84)
Cannon St. Rd. E1 ....6H 85
Cannon Trad. Est. HA9: Wemb ...4H 61
Cannon Way KT8: W Mole 4E 148
Cannon Wharf Bus. Cen. SE8 ....4A 104
Cannon Workshops *E14* 7C *86*
(off Cannon Dr.)
Canon All. *EC4* 1C *14*
(off Queen's Head Pas.)
Canon Beck Rd. SE16 ....2J 103
Canonbie Rd. SE23 ....7J 121
CANONBURY 6C 66
Canonbury Bus. Cen. N1 ....1C 84
Canonbury Ct. *N1* 7B *66*
(off Hawes St.)
Canonbury Cres. N1 ....7C 66
Canonbury Gro. N1 ....7C 66
Canonbury Hgts. *N1* 6D *66*
(off Dove Rd.)

Canonbury La. N1 ....7B 66
Canonbury Pk. Nth. N1 ....6C 66
Canonbury Pk. Sth. N1 ....6C 66
Canonbury Pl. N1 ....6B 66
(not continuous)
Canonbury Rd. EN1: Enf 1K 23
N1 ....6B 66
Canonbury Sq. N1 ....7B 66
Canonbury St. N1 ....7C 66
Canonbury Vs. N1 ....7B 66
Canon Mohan Cl. N14 ....6K 21
Canon Rd. BR1: Brom 3A 160
Canon Row SW1 ....7E 12 (2J 101)
(not continuous)
Canons Cl. HA8: Edg 6A 28
N2 ....7B 46
Canons Cnr. HA8: Edg 4K 27
Canons Ct. E15 ....4G 69
HA8: Edg 6A 28
Canons Dr. HA8: Edg 6K 27
Canonsleigh Rd. RM9: Dag 7B 72
CANONS LEISURE Cen., The 4D 154
CANONS PARK 7J 27
Canons Pk. HA7: Stan 6J 27
Canons Pk. Cl. HA8: Edg 7K 27
Canon St. N1 ....1C 84
Canon's Wlk. CR0: Croy 3K 169
Canopus Way TW19: Stanw 7A 110
Canrobert St. E2 ....2H 85
Cantelowes Rd. NW1 ....6H 65
(not continuous)
Canterbury Av. DA15: Sidc 2B 144
IG1: Ilf 7C 52
Canterbury Cl. BR3: Beck 1D 158
E6 ....6D 88
SE5 ....2C 120
(off Lilford Rd.)
UB6: G'frd 5F 77
Canterbury Ct. NW6 ....2J *81*
(off Canterbury Rd.)
NW9 ....2A 44
SE12 ....3K 141
SW9 ....7A 102
TW15: Ashf 4B 128
Canterbury Cres. SW9 ....3A 120
Canterbury Gro. SE27 ....4A 138
Canterbury Hall KT4: Wor Pk 7D 152
Canterbury Ho. *CR0: Croy* 1D *168*
(off Sydenham Rd.)
IG11: Bark 2H *71*
(off Margaret Bondfield Av.)
SE1 ....1H 19 (3K 101)
Canterbury Ind. Pk. SE15 ....6J 103
Canterbury Pl. SE17 ....5B 102
Canterbury Rd. CR0: Croy 7K 155
E10 ....7E 50
HA1: Harr 5F 41
HA2: Harr 5F 41
NW6 ....2H 81
(not continuous)
SM4: Mord 7K 153
TW13: Hanw 2C 130
Canterbury Ter. NW6 ....2J 81
Cantium Retail Pk. SE1 ....6G 103
Cantley Gdns. IG2: Ilf 6G 53
SE19 ....1F 157
Cantley Rd. W7 ....3A 96
Canton St. E14 ....6C 86
Cantrell Rd. E3 ....4B 86
Cantwell Rd. SE18 ....7F 107
Canute Gdns.
SE16 ....4K 103
Canvey St. SE1 ....4C 14 (1C 102)
Cape Cl. IG11: Bark 7F 71
Cape Henry Ct. *E14* 7F *87*
(off Jamestown Way)
Cape Ho. *E8* 6F *67*
(off Dalston La.)
Capel Av. SM6: Wall 5K 167
Capel Cl. BR2: Brom 1C 172
N20 ....3F 31

Capel Ct.—Carmel Ct.

Capel Ct. *EC2* 1F 15
(off Bartholomew La.)
SE20 1J 157
Capel Gdns. HA5: Pinn 4D 40
IG3: Bark, Ilf 4K 71
Capel Ho. *E9* 7J 67
(off Loddiges Rd.)
Capel Rd. E7 4K 69
E12 4K 69
EN4: E Barn 6H 21
Capener's Cl. SW1 7F 11
Capern Rd. SW18 1A 136
Cape Rd. N17 3G 49
Cape Yd. E1 7G 85
Capital Bus. Cen. CR2: S Croy 7D 168
HA0: Wemb 2D 78
Capital E. Apartments *E16* 7J 87
(off Western Gateway)
Capital Ind. Est. CR4: Mitc 5D 154
DA17: Belv 3H 109
Capital Interchange Way
TW8: Bford 5G 97
Capital Wharf E1 1G 103
Capitol Ind. Pk. NW9 3J 43
Capitol Way NW9 3J 43
Capland Ho. *NW8* 3B 4
(off Capland St.)
Capland St. NW8 3B 4 (4B 82)
Caple Ho. *SW10* 7A 100
(off King's Rd.)
Caple Rd. NW10 2B 80
Capper St. WC1 4B 6 (4G 83)
Caprea Cl. UB4: Yead 5B 76
Capricorn Cen. RM8: Dag 7F 55
Capri Ho. E17 2B 50
Capri Rd. CR0: Croy 1F 169
Capstan Cl. RM6: Chad H 6B 54
Capstan Ct. *E1* 7J 85
(off Wapping Wall)
Capstan Ho. *E14* 7F 87
(off Clove Cres.)
E14 4E 104
(off Stebondale St.)
Capstan Ride EN2: Enf 2F 23
Capstan Rd. SE8 4B 104
Capstan Sq. E14 2E 104
Capstan Way SE16 1A 104
Capstone Rd. BR1: Brom 4H 141
Capthorne Av. HA2: Harr 1C 58
Capuchin Cl. HA7: Stan 6G 27
Capulet M. E16 1J 105
Capworth St. E10 1C 68
Caradoc Cl. W2 6J 81
Caradoc Evans Cl. *N11* 5A 32
(off Springfield Rd.)
Caradoc St. SE10 5G 105
Caradon Cl. E11 1G 69
Caradon Way N15 4D 48
Caramel Ct.
HA9: Wemb 2H 61
Caranday Vs. *W11* 1F 99
(off Norland Rd.)
Caravel Cl. E14 3C 104
Caravelle Gdns. UB5: N'olt 3B 76
Caravel M. SE8 6C 104
Caraway Cl. E13 5K 87
Caraway Hgts. *E14* 7E 86
(off Poplar High St.)
Caraway Pl. SM6: Wall 3F 167
Carberry Rd. SE19 6E 138
Carbery Av. W3 2F 97
Carbis Cl. E4 1A 36
Carbis Rd. E14 6B 86
Carbrooke Ho. *E9* 1J 85
(off Templecombe Rd.)
Carbuncle Pas. N17 2G 49
Carburton St. W1 5K 5 (5F 83)
Cardale St. E14 2E 104
Carden Rd. SE15 3H 121
Cardiff Ho. *SE15* 6G 103
(off Friary Est.)
Cardiff Rd. EN3: Pond E 4C 24
W7 3A 96
Cardiff St. SE18 7J 107
Cardigan Ct. *W7* 4K 77
(off Copley Cl.)
Cardigan Gdns. IG3: Ilf 2A 72
Cardigan Pl. SE3 2F 123
Cardigan Rd. E3 2B 86
SW13 2C 116
SW19 6A 136
TW10: Rich 6E 114
Cardigan St.
SE11 5J 19 (5A 102)
Cardigan Wlk. *N1* 7C 66
(off Ashby Gro.)
Cardinal Av. KT2: King T 5E 132
SM4: Mord 6G 153
Cardinal Bourne St. SE1 3D 102
Cardinal Cap All. SE1 1C 102
Cardinal Cl. BR7: Chst 1H 161
HA8: Edg 7D 28
KT4: Wor Pk 4C 164
SM4: Mord 6G 153
Cardinal Ct. *E1* 7G 85
(off Thomas More St.)
Cardinal Cres. KT3: N Mald 2J 151
Cardinal Hinsley Cl. NW10 2C 80
Cardinal Pl. SW15 4F 117
Cardinal Rd. HA4: Ruis 1B 58
TW13: Felt 1K 129
Cardinals Wlk. TW12: Hamp 7G 131
TW16: Sun 6G 129
Cardinals Way N19 1H 65
Cardinal Way HA3: W'stone 3J 41
Cardine M. SE15 7H 103
Cardington Sq. TW4: Houn 4B 112
Cardington St. NW1 1B 6 (3G 83)
Cardinham Rd. BR6: Chels 4K 173
Cardozo Rd. N7 5J 65
Cardrew Av. N12 5G 31
Cardrew Cl. N12 5H 31
Cardrew Ct. N12 5G 31
Cardross Ho. *W6* 3D 98
(off Cardross St.)
Cardross St. W6 3D 98
Cardwell Rd. N7 4J 65
Career Ct. *SE16* 2K 103
(off Christopher Cl.)
Carew Cl. N7 2K 65
Carew Ct. *SE14* 6K 103
(off Samuel Cl.)
SM2: Sutt 7K 165
Carew Manor & Dovecote 3G 167
Carew Mnr. Cotts. SM6: Bedd 3H 167
Carew Rd. CR4: Mitc 2E 154
CR7: Thor H 4B 156
N17 2G 49
SM6: Wall 6G 167
TW15: Ashf 6E 128
W13 2C 96
Carew St. SE5 2C 120
Carey Ct. DA6: Bex 5H 127
SE5 7C 102
Carey Gdns. SW8 1G 119
Carey La. EC2 7C 8 (6C 84)
Carey Mans. *SW1* 3C 18
(off Rutherford St.)
Carey Pl. SW1 4C 18 (4H 101)
Carey Rd. RM9: Dag 4E 72
Carey St. WC2 1H 13 (6K 83)
Carey Way HA9: Wemb 4H 61
Carfax Pl. SW4 4H 119
Carfax Rd. UB3: Harl 5H 93
Carfree Cl. N1 7A 66
Cargill Rd. SW18 1K 135
Cargo Point TW19: Stanw 6B 110
Cargreen Pl. SE25 4F 157
Cargreen Rd. SE25 4F 157
Cargrey Ho. HA7: Stan 5H 27
Carholme Rd. SE23 1B 140
Carillon Ct. W5 7D 78
Carinthia Ct. *SE16* 4A 104
(off Plough Way)
Carisbrook N10 2F 47
Carisbrook Cl. EN1: Enf 1A 24
Carisbrooke Av. DA5: Bexl 1D 144
Carisbrooke Cl. HA7: Stan 2D 42
Carisbrooke Ct.
SM2: Cheam 7H 165
UB5: N'olt 1D 76
(off Eskdale Av.)
W3 2J 97
(off Brouncker Rd.)
Carisbrooke Gdns. SE15 7F 103
Carisbrooke Ho. *KT2: King T* 1E 150
(off Seven Kings Way)
Carisbrooke Rd. BR2: Brom 4A 160
CR4: Mitc 4H 155
E17 4A 50
Carker's La. NW5 5F 65
Carleton Av. SM6: Wall 7H 167
Carleton Cl. KT10: Esh 7H 149
Carleton Gdns. N19 5G 65
Carleton Rd. N7 5H 65
Carleton Vs. NW5 5G 65
Carlile Cl. E3 2B 86
Carlina Gdns. IG8: Wfd G 5E 36
Carlingford Gdns.
CR4: Mitc 7D 136
Carlingford Rd. N15 3B 48
NW3 4B 64
SM4: Mord 6F 153
Carlisle Av. EC3 1J 15 (6F 85)
W3 6A 80
Carlisle Cl. HA5: Pinn 7C 40
KT2: King T 1G 151
Carlisle Gdns. HA3: Kent 7D 42
IG1: Ilf 6C 52
Carlisle La. SE1 2H 19 (3K 101)
Carlisle Mans. *SW1* 3A 18
(off Carlisle Pl.)
Carlisle M. KT2: King T 1G 151
Carlisle Pl. N11 4A 32
SW1 2A 18 (3G 101)
Carlisle Rd. E10 1C 68
N4 7A 48
NW6 1G 81
NW9 3J 43
SM1: Sutt 6H 165
TW12: Hamp 7F 131
Carlisle St. W1 1C 12 (6H 83)
Carlisle Wlk. E8 6F 67
Carlisle Way SW17 5E 136
Carlos Pl. W1 3H 11 (7E 82)
Carlow St. NW1 2G 83
Carlson Ct. SW15 4H 117
Carlton Av. CR2: S Croy 7E 168
HA3: Kent 5B 42
N14 5C 22
TW14: Felt 6A 112
UB3: Harl 4G 93
Carlton Av. E. HA9: Wemb 2D 60
Carlton Av. W. HA0: Wemb 2B 60
Carlton Cl. HA8: Edg 5B 28
KT9: Chess 6D 162
NW3 2J 63
UB5: N'olt 5G 59
Carlton Ct. IG6: Ilf 3H 53
SE20 1H 157
SW9 1B 120
UB8: Cowl 5A 74
W9 2K 81
(off Maida Va.)
Carlton Cres. SM3: Cheam 4G 165
Carlton Dr. IG6: Ilf 3H 53
SW15 5F 117
Carlton Gdns.
SW1 5C 12 (1H 101)
W5 6C 78
Carlton Grn. DA14: Sidc 4K 143
Carlton Gro. SE15 1H 121
Carlton Hill NW8 2K 81
Carlton Ho. *NW6* 2J 81
(off Canterbury Ter., not continuous)
SE16 2K 103
(off Wolfe Cres.)
TW3: Houn 6E 112
TW14: Felt 6H 111
Carlton Ho. Ter. SW1 5C 12 (1H 101)
Carlton Lodge *N4* 7A 48
(off Carlton Rd.)
Carlton Mans. N16 1F 67
NW6 7J 63
(off W. End La.)
W9 3K 81
Carlton M. *NW6* 5J 63
(off West Cotts.)
NW6 3J 81
(West Kilburn)
Carlton Pde. HA9: Wemb 2E 60
Carlton Pk. Av. SW20 2F 153
Carlton Rd. CR2: S Croy 6D 168
DA8: Erith 6H 109
DA14: Sidc 5K 143
DA16: Well 3B 126
E11 1H 69
E12 4B 70
E17 1A 50
KT3: N Mald 2A 152
KT12: Walt T 7K 147
N4 7A 48
N11 5K 31
SW14 3J 115
TW16: Sun 7H 129
W4 2K 97
W5 7C 78
Carlton Sq. E1 4K 85
(not continuous)
Carlton St. SW1 3C 12 (7H 83)
Carlton Ter. E11 5K 51
(not continuous)
N18 3J 33
SE26 3J 139
Carlton Ter. St. E7 7A 70
Carlton Twr. Pl. SW1 3D 100
Carlton Towers SM5: Cars 3D 166
Carlton Va. NW6 2H 81
Carlton Vs. SW15 5G 117
Carlwell St. SW17 5C 136
Carlyle Av. BR1: Brom 3B 160
UB1: S'hall 7D 76
Carlyle Cl. KT8: W Mole 2F 149
N2 6A 46
NW10 1K 79
Carlyle Ct. *SW6* 1K 117
(off Imperial Rd.)
SW10 1A 118
(off Chelsea Harbour Dr.)
Carlyle Gdns. UB1: S'hall 7D 76
Carlyle Ho. *KT8: W Mole* 5E 148
(off Down St.)
N16 3E 66
Carlyle M. E1 4K 85
Carlyle Pl. SW15 4F 117
Carlyle Rd. CR0: Croy 2G 169
E12 4C 70
SE28 7B 90
W5 4C 96
Carlyle's House 7C 16
Carlyle Sq. SW3 6B 16 (5B 100)
Carlyon Av. HA2: Harr 4D 58
Carlyon Cl. HA0: Wemb 1E 78
Carlyon Rd. HA0: Wemb 2E 78
UB4: Yead 5A 76
(not continuous)
Carlys Cl. BR3: Beck 2K 157
Carmalt Gdns. SW15 4E 116
Carmarthen Ct. *W7* 4K 77
(off Copley Cl.)
Carmarthen Grn. NW9 5A 44
Carmarthen Pl. SE1 6G 15 (2E 102)
Carmel Ct. *W8* 2K 99
(off Holland St.)

Cedar Ct.—Chalgrove Gdns.

Cedar Ct. SW19 3F **135**
TW8: Bford 6C **96**
Cedar Cres. BR2: Brom 3C **172**
Cedarcroft Rd. KT9: Chess 4F **163**
Cedar Dr. HA5: H End 6A **26**
N2 4C **46**
Cedar Gdns. SM2: Sutt 6A **166**
Cedar Grange EN1: Enf 5K **23**
Cedar Gro. DA5: Bexl 6D **126**
UB1: S'hall 5E **76**
W5 3E **96**
Cedar Hgts. NW2 6H **63**
TW10: Ham 1E **132**
Cedar Ho. *E14* *2E* ***104***
(off Manchester Rd.)
N22 *1A* ***48***
(off Acacia Rd.)
SE14 1K **121**
SE16 *2K* ***103***
(off Woodland Cres.)
TW9: Kew 1H **115**
TW16: Sun *7H* ***129***
(off Spelthorne Gro.)
UB4: Yead 4A **76**
W8 *3K* ***99***
(off Marloes Rd.)
Cedarhurst BR1: Brom 7G **141**
Cedarhurst Cotts. DA5: Bexl 7G **127**
Cedarhurst Dr. SE9 5A **124**
Cedarland Ter. SW20 7D **134**
Cedar Lawn Av. EN5: Barn 5B **20**
Cedar Mt. SE9 1B **142**
Cedarne Rd. SW6 7K **99**
Cedar Pk. Gdns. RM6: Chad H 7D **54**
Cedar Pk. Rd. EN2: Enf 1H **23**
Cedar Pl. SE7 5A **106**
Cedar Ri. N14 7K **21**
Cedar Rd. BR1: Brom 2A **160**
CR0: Croy 2D **168**
EN2: Enf 1G **23**
KT8: E Mos 4J **149**
N17 1F **49**
NW2 4E **62**
RM7: Rom 4J **55**
SM2: Sutt 6A **166**
TW4: Cran 2A **112**
TW11: Tedd 5A **132**
TW14: Bedf 1F **129**
Cedars, The E15 7H **69**
IG9: Buck H 1D **36**
SM6: Wall 4G **167**
TW11: Tedd 6K **131**
W13 6C **78**
Cedars Av. CR4: Mitc 4E **154**
E17 5C **50**
Cedars Cl. NW4 3F **45**
SE13 3F **123**
Cedars Ct. N9 2K **33**
Cedars Dr. UB10: Hil 2B **74**
Cedars Ho. E17 3D **50**
Cedars M. SW4 4F **119**
(not continuous)
Cedars Rd. BR3: Beck 2A **158**
CR0: Bedd 3J **167**
E15 6G **69**
KT1: Hamp W 1C **150**
N9 2B **34**
N21 2G **33**
SM4: Mord 4J **153**
SW4 3F **119**
SW13 2C **116**
W4 5J **97**
Cedar Ter. TW9: Rich 4E **114**
Cedar Tree Gro. SE27 5B **138**
Cedar Vw. *KT1: King T* *3D* ***150***
(off Milner Rd.)
Cedarville Gdns. SW16 6K **137**
Cedar Way NW1 7H **65**
TW16: Sun 7G **129**
Cedar Way Ind. Est. NW1 7H **65**
Cedra Ct. N16 1G **67**
Cedric Rd. SE9 3G **143**
Celadon Cl. EN3: Enf H 3F **25**
Celandine Cl. E14 5C **86**
Celandine Ct. E4 3J **35**
Celandine Dr. E8 7F **67**
SE28 1B **108**
Celandine Gro. N14 5B **22**
Celandine Way E15 3G **87**
Celbridge M. W2 5K **81**
Celestial Gdns. SE13 4F **123**
Celia Cres. TW15: Ashf 6A **128**
Celia Ho. *N1* *2E* ***84***
(off Arden Est.)
Celia Rd. N19 4G **65**
Celtic Av. BR2: Brom 3G **159**
Celtic St. E14 5D **86**
Cemetery La. SE7 6C **106**
TW17: Shep 7D **146**
Cemetery Rd. E7 5H **69**
N17 7K **33**
SE2 7B **108**
Cenacle Cl. NW3 3J **63**
Cenotaph 6E 12 (2J 101)
Centaur Ct. TW8: Bford 5E **96**
Centaurs Bus. Pk. TW7: Isle 6A **96**
Centaur St. SE1 1H **19** (3K **101**)
Centenary Rd. EN3: Brim 4G **25**
Centenary Trad. Est. EN3: Brim 3G **25**
Centennial Av. WD6: Els 1H **27**
Centennial Ct. WD6: Els 1H **27**
Centennial Pk. WD6: Els 1H **27**
Central Av. DA16: Well 2K **125**
E11 2F **69**
E12 3B **70**
EN1: Enf 2C **24**
HA5: Pinn 6D **40**
KT8: W Mole 4D **148**
N2 2B **46**
(Oak La.)
N2 4K **45**
(Rosemary Av.)
N9 3K **33**
SM6: Wall 5J **167**
SW11 7D **100**
TW3: Houn 4G **113**
UB3: Hayes 1H **93**
Central Bus. Cen. NW10 5A **62**
Central Church Sports Club 2K 139
Central Cir. NW4 5D **44**
Centrale Shop. Cen. CR0: Croy 2C **168**
Central Gallery *IG1: Ilf* *2F* ***71***
(in Exchange, The)
Central Gdns. SM4: Mord 5K **153**
Central Hill SE19 5C **138**
Central Ho. E15 2D **86**
IG11: Bark 7G **71**
Central Mall *SW18* *6K* ***117***
(off South Mall)
Central Mans. *NW4* *5D* ***44***
(off Watford Way)
Central Markets (Smithfield) 6A 8
Central Pde. DA15: Sidc 3A **144**
E17 4C **50**
EN3: Enf H 2D **24**
HA1: Harr 5K **41**
IG2: Ilf 6H **53**
KT6: Surb 6E **150**
KT8: W Mole 4D **148**
SE20 *7K* ***139***
(off High St.)
TW5: Hest 7D **94**
TW14: Felt 7A **112**
UB6: G'frd 3A **78**
W3 2H **97**
Central Pk. Av. RM10: Dag 3H **73**
Central Pk. Est. TW4: Houn 5B **112**
Central Pk. Rd. E6 2B **88**
Central Pl. SE25 5G **157**
Central Rd. HA0: Wemb 5B **60**
KT4: Wor Pk 1C **164**
SM4: Mord 6J **153**
Central St Martins College of Art & Design 6G 7
Central School Path
SW14 3J **115**
Central Sq. HA0: Wemb 5E **60**
NW11 6K **45**
Central St. EC1 1C **8** (3C **84**)
Central Ter. BR3: Beck 3K **157**
Central Way NW10 3J **79**
SE28 1A **108**
SM5: Cars 7C **166**
TW14: Felt 5J **111**
Central Wharf *E14* *6C* ***86***
(off Thomas Rd.)
Centre, The KT12: Walt T 7H **147**
TW3: Houn 3F **113**
TW13: Felt 2J **129**
Centre Av. N2 2C **46**
NW10 3E **80**
W3 1K **97**
Centre Comn. Rd. BR7: Chst 6G **143**
Centre Ct. Shop. Cen. SW19 6H **135**
Centre Dr. E7 4A **70**
Cen. for the Magic Arts, The *3B 6*
(off Stephenson Way)
Centre Hgts. *NW3* *7B* ***64***
(off Finchley Rd.)
Centre Point SE1 5G **103**
Centrepoint WC2 7D **6**
Centre Point Ho. *WC2* *7D* ***6***
(off St Giles High St.)
Centre Rd. E7 2J **69**
E11 2J **69**
RM10: Dag 2H **91**
Centre St. E2 2H **85**
Centre Way E17 7K **35**
IG1: Ilf 2G **71**
N9 2D **34**
Centric Cl. NW1 1E **82**
Centro Ct. E6 4D **88**
Centurion Bldg. SW8 6F **101**
Centurion Cl. N7 7K **65**
Centurion Ct. SE18 4E **106**
SM6: Wall 2F **167**
Centurion La. E3 1B **86**
Centurion Way DA18: Erith 3F **109**
Century Cl. NW4 5F **45**
Century Ho. HA9: Wemb 2F **61**
SW15 4F **117**
Century M. E5 4J **67**
Century Plaza *HA8: Edg* *6B* ***28***
(off Station Rd.)
Century Rd. E17 3A **50**
Century Yd. SE23 2J **139**
Cephas Av. E1 4J **85**
Cephas Ho. *E1* *4J* ***85***
(off Doveton St.)
Cephas St. E1 4J **85**
Ceres Rd. SE18 4K **107**
Cerise Rd. SE15 1G **121**
Cerne Cl. UB4: Yead 7A **76**
Cerne Rd. SM4: Mord 6A **154**
Cerney M. W2 2A **10** (7B **82**)
Cervantes Ct. W2 6K **81**
Cester St. E2 1G **85**
Ceylon Rd. W14 3F **99**
Chabot Dr. SE15 3H **121**
Chadacre Av. IG5: Ilf 3D **52**
Chadacre Ct. *E15* *1J* ***87***
(off Vicars Cl.)
Chadacre Ho. *SW9* *4B* ***120***
(off Loughborough Pk.)
Chadacre Rd. KT17: Ewe 6D **164**
Chadbourn St. E14 5D **86**
Chadbury Ct. NW7 1C **44**
Chad Cres. N9 3D **34**
Chadd Dr. BR1: Brom 3C **160**
Chadd Grn. E13 1J **87**
(not continuous)
Chadston Ho. *N1* *7B* ***66***
(off Halton Rd.)
Chadswell *WC1* *2F* ***7***
(off Cromer St.)
Chadview Ct. RM6: Chad H 7D **54**
Chadville Gdns. RM6: Chad H 5D **54**
Chadway RM8: Dag 1C **72**
Chadwell Av. RM6: Chad H 7B **54**
CHADWELL HEATH 7D 54
Chadwell Heath Ind. Pk. RM8: Dag 1E **72**
Chadwell Heath La. RM6: Chad H 4B **54**
Chadwell La. N8 3K **47**
Chadwell St. EC1 1K **7** (3A **84**)
Chadwick Av. E4 4A **36**
N21 5E **22**
SW19 6J **135**
Chadwick Cl. SW15 7B **116**
TW11: Tedd 6A **132**
W7 5K **77**
Chadwick M. W4 6H **97**
Chadwick Pl. KT6: Surb 7C **150**
Chadwick Rd. E11 6G **51**
IG1: Ilf 3F **71**
NW10 1B **80**
SE15 2F **121**
Chadwick St. SW1 2C **18** (3H **101**)
Chadwick Way SE28 7D **90**
Chadwin Rd. E13 5K **87**
Chadworth Ho. *EC1* *2C* ***8***
(off Lever St.)
N4 1C **66**
Chaffinch Av. CR0: Croy 6K **157**
Chaffinch Bus. Pk. BR3: Beck 4K **157**
Chaffinch Cl. CR0: Croy 5K **157**
KT6: Surb 3G **163**
N9 1E **34**
Chaffinch Rd. BR3: Beck 1A **158**
Chafford Way RM6: Chad H 4C **54**
Chagford St. NW1 4E **4** (4D **82**)
Chailey Av. EN1: Enf 2A **24**
Chailey Cl. TW5: Hest 1B **112**
Chailey Ind. Est. UB3: Hayes 2J **93**
Chailey St. E5 3J **67**
Chalbury Wlk. N1 2K **83**
Chalcombe Rd. SE2 3B **108**
Chalcot Cl. SM2: Sutt 7J **165**
Chalcot Cres. NW1 1D **82**
Chalcot Gdns. NW3 6D **64**
Chalcot M. SW16 3J **137**
Chalcot Rd. NW1 7E **64**
Chalcot Sq. NW1 7E **64**
(not continuous)
Chalcott Gdns. KT6: Surb 1C **162**
Chalcroft Rd. SE13 5G **123**
Chaldon Ct. SE19 1D **156**
Chaldon Path CR7: Thor H 4B **156**
Chaldon Rd. SW6 7G **99**
Chale Rd. SW2 6J **119**
Chalet Cl. DA5: Bexl 4K **145**
Chalet Est. NW7 4H **29**
Chalfont Av. HA9: Wemb 6H **61**
Chalfont Ct. *HA1: Harr* *6K* ***41***
(off Northwick Pk. Rd.)
NW1 *4F* ***5***
(off Baker St.)
NW9 3B **44**
Chalfont Grn. N9 3K **33**
Chalfont Ho. *SE16* *3H* ***103***
(off Keetons Rd.)
Chalfont Rd. N9 3K **33**
SE25 3F **157**
UB3: Hayes 2J **93**
Chalfont Wlk. HA5: Pinn 2A **40**
Chalfont Way W13 3B **96**
Chalford *NW3* *6A* ***64***
(off Finchley Rd.)
Chalford Cl. KT8: W Mole 4E **148**
Chalford Rd. SE21 4D **138**
Chalford Wlk. IG8: Wfd G 1B **52**
Chalgrove Av.
SM4: Mord 5J **153**
Chalgrove Cres. IG5: Ilf 2C **52**
Chalgrove Gdns. N3 3G **45**

Chalgrove Rd.—Charles Babbage Cl.

Chalgrove Rd. N17 1H 49
SM2: Sutt 7B 166
Chalice Cl. SM6: Wall 6H 167
Chalice Ct. N2 4C 46
Chalkenden Cl. SE20 7H 139
CHALKER'S CORNER 3H 115
CHALK FARM 7E 64
Chalk Farm Rd. NW1 7E 64
Chalk Hill Rd. W6 4F 99
Chalkhill Rd. HA9: Wemb 3G 61
(not continuous)
Chalklands HA9: Wemb 3J 61
Chalk La. EN4: Cockf 3J 21
Chalkley Cl. CR4: Mitc 2D 154
Chalkmill Dr. EN1: Enf 3C 24
Chalk Pit Way SM1: Sutt 6A 166
Chalk Rd. E13 5K 87
Chalkstone Cl. DA16: Well 1A 126
Chalkwell Ho. *E1* *6K 85*
(off Pitsea St.)
Chalkwell Pk. Av. EN1: Enf 4K 23
Challenge Cl. NW10 1A 80
Challenger Ho. *E14* *7A 86*
(off Victory Pl.)
Challenge Rd. TW15: Ashf 3F 129
Challice Way SW2 1K 137
Challin St. SE20 1J 157
Challis Rd. TW8: Bford 5D 96
Challoner Cl. N2 2B 46
Challoner Cres. W14 5H 99
Challoners Cl. KT8: E Mos 4H 149
Challoner St. W14 5H 99
Chalmers Ho. E17 5D 50
Chalmers Rd. TW15: Ashf 5D 128
Chalmers Rd. E. TW15: Ashf 4D 128
Chalmers Wlk. *SE17* *6B 102*
(off Hillingdon St.)
Chalmers Way TW14: Felt 5K 111
Chalsey Rd. SE4 4B 122
Chalton Dr. N2 6B 46
Chalton Ho. *NW1* *1C 6*
(off Chalton St.)
Chalton St. NW1 1C 6 (2G 83)
(not continuous)
Chamberlain Cl. SE28 3H 107
Chamberlain Cotts. SE5 1D 120
Chamberlain Cres. BR4: W W'ck 1D 170
Chamberlain Gdns. TW3: Houn 1G 113
Chamberlain Ho. *E1* *7J 85*
(off Cable St.)
NW1 1D 6
SE1 *7J 13*
(off Westminster Bri. Rd.)
Chamberlain La. HA5: Eastc 4J 39
Chamberlain Pl. E17 3A 50
Chamberlain Rd. N2 2A 46
N9 3B 34
W13 2A 96
Chamberlain St. NW1 7D 64
Chamberlain Wlk. *TW13: Hanw* *4C 130*
(off Swift Rd.)
Chamberlain Way HA5: Eastc 3K 39
KT6: Surb 7E 150
Chamberlayne Av. HA9: Wemb 3E 60
Chamberlayne Mans. *NW10* *3F 81*
(off Chamberlayne Rd.)
Chamberlayne Rd. NW10 1E 80
Chamberlens Garages *W6* *4D 98*
(off Dalling Rd.)
Chambers, The *SW10* *1A 118*
(off Chelsea Harbour Dr.)
Chambers Bus. Pk. UB7: Sip 6C 92
Chambers Gdns. N2 1B 46
Chambers La. NW10 7D 62
Chambers Pl. CR2: S Croy 7D 168
Chambers Rd. N7 4J 65
Chambers St. SE16 2G 103
Chamber St. E1 2K 15 (7F 85)
Chambers Wlk. HA7: Stan 5G 27
Chambers Wharf SE16 2G 103
Chambon Pl. W6 4C 98
Chambord St. E2 2K 9 (3F 85)
Chamomile Ct. *E17* *6C 50*
(off Yunus Khan Cl.)
Champion Cres. SE26 4A 140
Champion Gro. SE5 3D 120
Champion Hill SE5 3D 120
Champion Hill Est. SE5 3E 120
Champion Hill Stadium 4E 120
Champion Pk. SE5 2D 120
Champion Rd. SE26 4A 140
Champlain Ho. *W12* *7D 80*
(off White City Est.)
Champness Cl. SE27 4D 138
Champness Rd. IG11: Bark 6K 71
Champneys Cl. SM2: Cheam 7H 165
Chancel Ind. Est. NW10 5B 62
Chancellor Gdns. CR2: S Croy 7B 168
Chancellor Gro. SE21 2C 138
Chancellor Ho. *E1* *1H 103*
(off Green Bank)
Chancellor Pas. E14 1C 104
Chancellor Pl. NW9 2B 44
Chancellors Ct. WC1 5G 7
Chancellor's Rd. W6 5E 98
Chancellor's St. W6 5E 98
Chancellors Wharf W6 5E 98
Chancelot Rd. SE2 4B 108
Chancel St. SE1 5A 14 (1B 102)
Chancery Bldgs. *E1* *7H 85*
(off Lowood St.)
Chancery La. BR3: Beck 2D 158
WC2 6H 7 (6A 84)
Chancery M. SW17 2C 136
Chance St. E1 3J 9 (4F 85)
E2 3J 9 (4F 85)
Chanctonbury Cl. SE9 3F 143
Chanctonbury Gdns. SM2: Sutt 7K 165
Chanctonbury Way N12 4C 30
Chandaria Ct. *CR0: Croy* *2C 168*
(off Church Rd.)
Chandler Av. E16 5J 87
Chandler Cl. TW12: Hamp 1E 148
Chandler Ct. TW14: Felt 6J 111
Chandler Ho. *NW6* *1H 81*
(off Willesden La.)
WC1 *4F 7*
(off Colonnade)
Chandlers Cl. TW14: Felt 7H 111
Chandlers Ct. SE12 1K 141
Chandlers Dr. DA8: Erith 4K 109
Chandlers M. E14 2C 104
Chandler St. E1 1H 103
Chandlers Way SW2 7A 120
Chandler Way SE15 7E 102
(Innis St.)
SE15 6E 102
(St George's Way)
Chandlery, The *SE1* *1K 19*
(off Gerridge St.)
Chandlery Ho. *E1* *6G 85*
(off Bk. Church La.)
Chandon Lodge SM2: Sutt 7A 166
Chandos Av. E17 2C 50
N14 3B 32
N20 1F 31
W5 4C 96
Chandos Cl. IG9: Buck H 2E 36
Chandos Ct. HA7: Stan 6G 27
HA8: Edg 7A 28
N14 2C 32
Chandos Cres. HA8: Edg 7A 28
Chandos Pde. HA8: Edg 7A 28
Chandos Pl. WC2 3E 12 (7J 83)
Chandos Rd. E15 5F 69
HA1: Harr 5G 41
HA5: Eastc 7B 40
N2 2B 46
N17 2E 48
NW2 5E 62
NW10 4A 80
Chandos St. W1 6K 5 (5F 83)
Chandos Way NW11 1K 63
Change All. EC3 1F 15 (6D 84)
Channel Cl. TW5: Hest 1E 112
Channel Ga. Rd.
NW10 3A 80
Channel Ho. *E14* *5A 86*
(off Aston St.)
Channel Islands Est. *N1* *6C 66*
(off Guernsey Rd.)
Channelsea Path E15 1F 87
Channelsea Rd. E15 1F 87
Channon Ct. *KT6: Surb* *5E 150*
(off Maple Rd)
Chantress Cl. RM10: Dag 1J 91
Chantrey Rd. SW9 3K 119
Chantry, The E4 1K 35
UB8: Hil 3B 74
Chantry Cl. DA14: Sidc 5E 144
EN2: Enf 1H 23
HA3: Kent 5F 43
SE2 3C 108
UB7: Yiew 7A 74
W9 4J 81
Chantry Ct. SM5: Cars 3C 166
Chantry Cres. NW10 6B 62
Chantry Ho. RM13: Rain 2K 91
Chantry La. BR2: Brom 5B 160
Chantry Pl. HA3: Hrw W 1F 41
Chantry Rd. HA3: Hrw W 1F 41
KT9: Chess 5F 163
Chantry Sq. W8 3K 99
Chantry St. N1 1B 84
Chantry Way CR4: Mitc 3B 154
RM13: Rain 2K 91
Chant Sq. E15 7F 69
Chant St. E15 7F 69
Chapel Av. E12 3B 70
Chapel Cl. DA1: Cray 5K 127
NW10 5B 62
Chapel Ct. N2 3C 46
SE1 6E 14 (2D 102)
UB3: Hayes 7H 75
CHAPEL END 1D 50
Chapel Farm Rd. SE9 3D 142
Chapel Hill DA1: Cray 5K 127
N2 2C 46
Chapel Ho. St. E14 5D 104
Chapelier Ho. SW18 4J 117
Chapel La. HA5: Pinn 3B 40
RM6: Chad H 7D 54
UB8: Hil 6C 74
Chapel Mkt. N1 2A 84
Chapel M. IG8: Ilf 6K 37
Chapel Mill Rd. KT1: King T 3F 151
Chapelmount Rd. IG8: Wfd G 6J 37
Chapel of St John the Evangelist *3J 15*
(in Tower of London, The)
Chapel of St Peter & St Paul *6F 105*
(in Old Royal Naval College)
Chapel Path *E11* *6K 51*
(off Woodbine Pl.)
Chapel Pl. EC2 2G 9 (3E 84)
N1 2A 84
N17 7A 34
W1 1J 11 (6F 83)
Chapel Rd. DA7: Bex 4G 127
IG1: Ilf 3E 70
SE27 4B 138
TW1: Twick 7B 114
TW3: Houn 3F 113
W13 1B 96
Chapel Side W2 7K 81
Chapel Stones N17 1F 49
Chapel St. EN2: Enf 3H 23
NW1 6C 4 (5C 82)
SW1 1H 17 (3E 100)
Chapel Vw. CR2: Sels 6J 169
Chapel Wlk. CR0: Croy 2C 168
NW4 4D 44
(not continuous)
Chapel Way N7 3K 65
Chapel Yd. *SW18* *5K 117*
(off Wandsworth High St.)
Chaplin Cl. HA0: Wemb 6D 60
SE1 6K 13 (2A 102)
Chaplin Cres. TW16: Sun 6G 129
Chaplin Rd. E15 2H 87
HA0: Wemb 6C 60
N17 3F 49
NW2 6C 62
RM9: Dag 7E 72
Chaplin Sq. N12 7G 31
Chapman Cl. UB7: W Dray 3B 92
Chapman Cres. HA3: Kent 6E 42
Chapman Grn. N22 1A 48
Chapman Ho. *E1* *6H 85*
(off Bigland St.)
Chapman Pl. N4 2B 66
Chapman Rd. CR0: Croy 1A 168
DA17: Belv 5G 109
E9 6B 68
Chapman's La. SE2 4C 108
Chapmans Pk. Ind. Est. NW10 6B 62
Chapman Sq. SW19 2F 135
Chapman's Ter. N22 1B 48
Chapman St. E1 7H 85
Chapone Pl. W1 1C 12 (6H 83)
Chapter Chambers *SW1* *4C 18*
(off Chapter St.)
Chapter Cl. UB10: Hil 7B 56
W4 3J 97
Chapter House 1C 14 (6B 84)
Chapter Rd. NW2 5C 62
SE17 5B 102
Chapter St. SW1 4C 18 (4H 101)
Chapter Way SW19 1B 154
TW12: Hamp 4E 130
Chara Pl. W4 6K 97
Charcot Ho. SW15 6B 116
Charcroft Ct. *W14* *2F 99*
(off Minford Gdns.)
Charcroft Gdns. EN3: Pond E 4E 24
Chardin Ho. *SW9* *1A 120*
(off Gosling Way)
Chardin Rd. W4 4A 98
Chardmore Rd. N16 1G 67
Chard Rd. TW6: H'row A 2D 110
Chardwell Cl. E6 6D 88
Charecroft Way W12 2F 99
W14 2F 99
Charfield Ct. *W9* *4K 81*
(off Shirland Rd.)
Charford Rd. E16 5J 87
Chargeable La. E13 4H 87
Chargeable St. E16 4H 87
Chargrove Cl. SE16 2K 103
Charing Cl. BR6: Orp 4K 173
Charing Ct. BR2: Brom 2G 159
Charing Cross SW1 4E 12
Charing Cross Rd. WC2 7D 6 (6H 83)
Charing Cross Sports Club 6F 99
Charing Cross Underground Shop. Cen.
WC2 3E 12
Charing Ho. *SE1* *6K 13*
(off Windmill Wlk.)
Chariot Cl. E3 1C 86
Charlbert Ct. *NW8* *2C 82*
(off Charlbert St.)
Charlbert St. NW8 2C 82
Charlbury Av. HA7: Stan 5J 27
Charlbury Gdns. IG3: Ilf 2K 71
Charlbury Gro. W5 6C 78
Charlbury Rd. UB10: Ick 3B 56
Charldane Rd. SE9 3F 143
Charlecote Gro. SE26 3H 139
Charlecote Rd. RM8: Dag 3E 72
Charlemont Rd. E6 4D 88
Charles II Pl. SW3 6E 16 (5D 100)
Charles II St. SW1 4C 12 (1H 101)
Charles Auffray Ho. *E1* *5J 85*
(off Smithy St.)
Charles Babbage Cl. KT9: Chess 7C 162

Charles Barry Cl. SW4 ....3G 119
Charles Bradlaugh Ho. N17 ....7C 34
(off Haynes Cl.)
Charles Cl. DA14: Sidc 4B 144
Charles Cobb Gdns.
CR0: Wadd 5A 168
Charles Coveney Rd.
SE15 ....1F 121
Charles Cres. HA1: Harr 7H 41
(not continuous)
Charles Curran Ho. UB10: Ick 3D 56
Charles Darwin Ho. E2 ....3H 85
(off Canrobert St.)
Charles Dickens Ho. E2 ....3G 85
(off Mansford St.)
Charle Sevright Dr. NW7 ....5A 30
Charlesfield SE9 ....3A 142
Charles Flemwell M.
E16 ....1J 105
Charles Gardner Ct. N1 ....1F 9
(off Haberdasher Est.)
Charles Grinling Wlk. SE18 ....4E 106
Charles Gro. N14 ....1B 32
Charles Haller St. SW2 ....7A 120
Charles Harrod Ct. SW13 ....6E 98
(off Somerville Av.)
Charles Hocking Ho. W3 ....2J 97
(off Bollo Bri. Rd.)
Charles Ho. N17 ....7A 34
(off Love La.)
UB2: S'hall 2E 94
W14 ....4H 99
(off Kensington High St.)
Charles La. NW8 ....2C 82
Charles Lesser Ho. KT9: Chess 5D 162
Charles MacKenzie Ho. SE16 ....4G 103
(off Linsey St.)
Charlesmere Gdns.
SE28 ....2J 107
Charles Pl. NW1 ....2B 6 (3G 83)
Charles Rd. E7 ....7A 70
RM6: Chad H 6D 54
RM10: Dag 6K 73
SW19 ....1J 153
TW18: Staines 6A 128
W13 ....6A 78
Charles Rowan Ho. WC1 ....2J 7
(off Margery St.)
Charles Simmons Ho. WC1 ....2J 7
(off Margery St.)
Charles Sq. N1 ....2F 9 (3D 84)
Charles Sq. Est. N1 ....2F 9
Charles St. CR0: Croy 3C 168
E16 ....1A 106
EN1: Enf 5A 24
SW13 ....2A 116
TW3: Houn 2D 112
UB10: Hil 4D 74
W1 ....4J 11 (1F 101)
Charleston Cl. TW13: Felt 3J 129
Charleston St. SE17 ....4C 102
Charles Townsend Ho. EC1 ....3A 8
(off Skinner St.)
Charles Uton Ct. E8 ....4G 67
Charles Whincup Rd. E16 ....1K 105
Charlesworth Ho. E14 ....6B 86
(off Dod St.)
Charlesworth Pl. SW13 ....3A 116
Charleville Cir. SE26 ....5G 139
Charleville Mans. W14 ....5G 99
(off Charleville Rd.)
Charleville M. TW7: Isle 4B 114
Charleville Rd. W14 ....5G 99
CHARLIE BROWN'S RDBT. 2A 52
Charlie Chaplin Wlk. SE1 ....5H 13
(off Waterloo Rd.)
Charlieville Rd.
DA8: Erith 7J 109
Charlmont Rd. SW17 ....6C 136
Charlotte Cl. DA6: Bex 5E 126
IG6: Ilf 1G 53
Charlotte Ct. IG2: Ilf 6E 52
N8 ....6H 47
SE1 ....4E 102
(off Old Kent Rd.)
W6 ....4C 98
(off Invermead Cl.)
Charlotte Despard Av. SW11 ....1E 118
Charlotte Ho. E16 ....1K 105
(off Fairfax M.)
W6 ....5E 98
(off Queen Caroline St.)
Charlotte M. W1 ....5B 6 (5G 83)
W10 ....6F 81
W14 ....4G 99
Charlotte Pk. Av. BR1: Brom 3C 160
Charlotte Pl. NW9 ....5J 43
SW1 ....4A 18 (4G 101)
W1 ....6B 6 (5G 83)
Charlotte Rd. EC2 ....2G 9 (3E 84)
RM10: Dag 6H 73
SM6: Wall 6G 167
SW13 ....1B 116
Charlotte Row SW4 ....3G 119
Charlotte Sq. TW10: Rich 6F 115
Charlotte St. W1 ....5B 6 (5G 83)
Charlotte Ter. N1 ....1K 83
Charlow Cl. SW6 ....2A 118
CHARLTON
Shepperton 3E 146
Woolwich 7B 106
Charlton Athletic FC 5A 106
Charlton Chu. La. SE7 ....5A 106
Charlton Cl. UB10: Ick 2D 56
Charlton Ct. E2 ....1F 85
Charlton Cres. IG11: Bark 2K 89
Charlton Dene SE7 ....7A 106
Charlton Ga. Bus. Pk. SE7 ....4A 106
Charlton House 6B 106
Charlton Ho. TW8: Bford 6E 96
Charlton King's Rd. NW5 ....5H 65
Charlton La. SE7 ....4B 106
TW17: Shep 3E 146
(not continuous)
Charlton Lido 7B 106
Charlton Pk. La. SE7 ....7B 106
Charlton Pk. Rd. SE7 ....6B 106
Charlton Pl. N1 ....2B 84
Charlton Rd. HA3: Kent 4D 42
HA9: Wemb 1F 61
N9 ....1E 34
NW10 ....1A 80
SE3 ....7J 105
SE7 ....7J 105
TW17: Shep 3E 146
Charlton Way SE3 ....1G 123
Charlwood CR0: Sels 7B 170
Charlwood Cl. HA3: Hrw W 6D 26
Charlwood Ho. SW1 ....4C 18
(off Vauxhall Bri. Rd.)
TW9: Kew 7H 97
Charlwood Ho's. WC1 ....2F 7
(off Midhope St.)
Charlwood Pl. SW1 ....4B 18 (4G 101)
Charlwood Rd. SW15 ....4F 117
Charlwood St. SW1 ....6A 18 (5G 101)
(not continuous)
Charlwood Ter. SW15 ....4F 117
Charmans Ho. SW8 ....7J 101
(off Wandsworth Rd.)
Charmian Av. HA7: Stan 3D 42
Charminster Av. SW19 ....2J 153
Charminster Ct. KT6: Surb 7D 150
Charminster Rd. KT4: Wor Pk 1F 165
SE9 ....4B 142
Charmouth Ct. TW10: Rich 5F 115
Charmouth Ho. SW8 ....7K 101
Charmouth Rd. DA16: Well 1C 126
Charnock Ho. W12 ....7D 80
(off White City Est.)
Charnock Rd. E5 ....3H 67
Charnwood Av. SW19 ....2J 153
Charnwood Cl. KT3: N Mald 4A 152
Charnwood Dr. E18 ....3K 51
Charnwood Gdns. E14 ....4C 104
Charnwood Pl. N20 ....3F 31
Charnwood Rd. SE25 ....5D 156
UB10: Hil 2C 74
Charnwood St. E5 ....2H 67
Charrington Bowl 2H 163
Charrington Rd. CR0: Croy 2C 168
Charrington St. NW1 ....2H 83
Charsley Rd. SE6 ....2D 140
Chart Cl. BR2: Brom 1G 159
CR0: Croy 6J 157
CR4: Mitc 4D 154
Charter Av. IG2: Ilf 1H 71
Charter Ct. KT3: N Mald 3A 152
N4 ....1A 66
N22 ....1H 47
UB1: S'hall 1E 94
Charter Cres. TW4: Houn 4C 112
Charter Dr. DA5: Bexl 7E 126
Charterhouse 4B 8
Charter Ho. SM2: Sutt 6K 165
(off Mulgrave Rd.)
WC2 ....1F 13
(off Crown Ct.)
Charterhouse Av. HA0: Wemb 4C 60
Charterhouse Bldgs.
EC1 ....4B 8 (4C 84)
Charterhouse M. EC1 ....5B 8 (5B 84)
Charterhouse Rd. BR6: Chels 3K 173
E8 ....4G 67
Charterhouse Sq. EC1 ....5B 8 (5B 84)
Charterhouse St. EC1 ....6K 7 (5A 84)
Charteris Rd. IG8: Wfd G 7E 36
N4 ....1A 66
NW6 ....1H 81
Charter Quay KT1: King T 2D 150
(off Wadbrook St.)
Charter Rd. KT1: King T 3H 151
Charter Rd., The IG8: Wfd G 6B 36
Charters Cl. SE19 ....5E 138
Charter Sq. KT1: King T 2H 151
Charter Way N3 ....4H 45
N14 ....6B 22
Chartes Ho. SE1 ....7H 15
(off Stevens St.)
Chartfield Av. SW15 ....5D 116
Chartfield Sq. SW15 ....5F 117
Chartham Ct. SW9 ....3A 120
(off Canterbury Cres.)
Chartham Gro. SE27 ....3B 138
Chartham Ho. SE1 ....7F 15
(off Weston St.)
Chartham Rd. SE25 ....3H 157
Chart Hills Cl. SE28 ....6E 90
Chart Ho. CR4: Mitc 2D 154
E14 ....5D 104
(off Burrells Wharf Sq.)
Chartley Av. HA7: Stan 6E 26
NW2 ....3A 62
Charton Cl. DA17: Belv 6F 109
Chartres Ct. UB6: G'frd 2H 77
Chartridge SE17 ....6D 102
(off Westmoreland Rd.)
Chart St. N1 ....1F 9 (3D 84)
Chartwell Cl. CR0: Croy 1D 168
SE9 ....2H 143
UB6: G'frd 1F 77
Chartwell Ct. EN5: Barn 4B 20
IG8: Wfd G 7C 36
UB3: Hayes 7H 75
Chartwell Dr. BR6: Farnb 5H 173
Chartwell Gdns. SM3: Cheam 3G 165
Chartwell Lodge BR3: Beck 7C 140
Chartwell Pl. HA2: Harr 2H 59
SM3: Cheam 3H 165
Chartwell Way SE20 ....1H 157
Charville Ct. HA1: Harr 6K 41
Charville La. UB4: Hayes 3E 74
Charville La. W. UB10: Hil 3D 74
Charwood SW16 ....4A 138
Chase, The BR1: Brom 3K 159
DA7: Bex 3H 127
E12 ....4B 70
HA5: Eastc 6A 40
HA5: Pinn 4D 40
HA7: Stan 6F 27
HA8: Edg 1H 43
RM1: Rom 3K 55
RM6: Chad H 6E 54
RM7: Rush G 3K 73
(not continuous)
SM6: Wall 5J 167
SW4 ....3F 119
SW16 ....7K 137
SW20 ....1G 153
TW16: Sun 1K 147
UB10: Ick 5C 56
Chase Bank Ct. N14 ....6B 22
(off Avenue Rd.)
Chase Cen., The NW10 ....3K 79
Chase Ct. SW20 ....2G 153
TW7: Isle 2A 114
Chase Ct. Gdns. EN2: Enf 3H 23
Chase Cross Rd. RM5: Col R 1J 55
Chasefield Rd. SW17 ....4D 136
Chase Gdns. E4 ....4H 35
TW2: Whit 7H 113
Chase Grn. EN2: Enf 3H 23
Chase Grn. Av. EN2: Enf 2G 23
Chase Hill EN2: Enf 3H 23
Chase La. IG2: Ilf 5H 53
IG6: Ilf 5H 53
(not continuous)
Chaseley Dr. W4 ....5H 97
Chaseley St. E14 ....6A 86
Chasemore Cl. CR4: Mitc 7D 154
Chasemore Gdns. CR0: Wadd 5A 168
Chasemore Ho. SW6 ....7G 99
(off Williams Cl.)
Chase Ridings EN2: Enf 2F 23
Chase Rd. N14 ....5B 22
NW10 ....4K 79
Chase Rd. Trad. Est. NW10 ....4K 79
CHASE SIDE 2H 23
Chase Side EN2: Enf 3H 23
N14 ....5K 21
Chase Side Av. EN2: Enf 2H 23
Chaseside Av. SW20 ....1G 153
Chase Side Cres. EN2: Enf 1H 23
Chase Side Ind. Est. N14 ....7C 22
Chase Side Pl. EN2: Enf 2H 23
Chaseville Pde. N21 ....5E 22
Chaseville Pk. Rd. N21 ....5D 22
Chase Way N14 ....2A 32
Chaseways Vs. RM5: Col R 1F 55
Chasewood Av. EN2: Enf 2G 23
Chasewood Ct. NW7 ....5E 28
Chasewood Pk. HA1: Harr 3K 59
Chaston Pl. NW5 ....5E 64
(off Grafton Ter.)
Chater Ho. E2 ....3K 85
(off Roman Rd.)
Chateris Community Sports Cen.
....1J 81
Chatfield Rd. CR0: Croy 1B 168
SW11 ....3A 118
Chatham Av. BR2: Hayes 7H 159
Chatham Cl. NW11 ....5J 45
SE18 ....3F 107
SM3: Sutt 7H 153
Chatham Ho. SM6: Wall 5F 167
(off Melbourne Rd.)
Chatham Pl. E9 ....6J 67
Chatham Rd. E17 ....3A 50
E18 ....2H 51
KT1: King T 2G 151
SW11 ....6D 118
Chatham St. SE17 ....4D 102
Chatsfield Pl. W5 ....6E 78
Chats Palace Arts Cen. 5K 67

Chatsworth Av.—Cherry St.

Chatsworth Av. BR1: Brom .4K 141
DA15: Sidc .1A 144
HA9: Wemb .5F 61
NW4 .2E 44
SW20 .1G 153
Chatsworth Cl. BR4: W W'ck .2H 171
NW4 .2E 44
W4 .6J 97
Chatsworth Ct. HA7: Stan .5H 27
W8 .4J 99
(off Pembroke Rd.)
Chatsworth Cres. TW3: Houn .4H 113
Chatsworth Dr. EN1: Enf .7B 24
Chatsworth Est. E5 .4K 67
Chatsworth Gdns. HA2: Harr .1F 59
KT3: N Mald .5B 152
W3 .1H 97
Chatsworth Ho. *BR2: Brom* .4J 159
(off Westmoreland Rd.)
E16 .1K 105
(off Wesley Av.)
Chatsworth Lodge *W4* .5K 97
(off Bourne Pl.)
Chatsworth Pde. BR5: Pet W .5G 161
Chatsworth Pl. CR4: Mitc .3D 154
NW2 .6E 62
TW11: Tedd .4A 132
Chatsworth Ri. W5 .4F 79
Chatsworth Rd. CR0: Croy .4D 168
E5 .3J 67
E15 .5H 69
NW2 .6E 62
(not continuous)
SM3: Cheam .5F 165
UB4: Yead .4K 75
W4 .6J 97
W5 .4F 79
Chatsworth Way SE27 .3B 138
CHATTERN HILL .4D 128
Chattern Hill TW15: Ashf .4D 128
Chattern Rd. TW15: Ashf .4E 128
Chatterton Ct. TW9: Kew .2F 115
Chatterton M. *N4* .3B 66
(off Chatterton Rd.)
Chatterton Rd. BR2: Brom .4B 160
N4 .3B 66
Chatto Rd. SW11 .5D 118
Chaucer Av. TW4: Cran .2K 111
TW9: Rich .3G 115
UB4: Hayes .5J 75
Chaucer Cl. N11 .5B 32
Chaucer Ct. EN5: New Bar .5E 20
N16 .4E 66
Chaucer Dr. SE1 .4F 103
Chaucer Gdns. SM1: Sutt .3J 165
(not continuous)
Chaucer Grn. CR0: Croy .7H 157
Chaucer Ho. EN5: Barn .4A 20
SM1: Sutt .3J 165
(off Chaucer Gdns.)
SW1 .6A 18
(off Churchill Gdns.)
Chaucer Mans. *W14* .6G 99
(off Queen's Club Gdns.)
Chaucer Rd. DA15: Sidc .1C 144
DA16: Well .1J 125
E7 .6J 69
E11 .6J 51
E17 .2E 50
SE24 .5A 120
SM1: Sutt .4J 165
TW15: Ashf .4A 128
W3 .1J 97
Chaucer Theatre .7K 9
(off Braham St.)
Chaucer Way SW19 .5B 136
Chaulden Ho. *EC1* .2F 9
(off Cranwood St.)
Chauncey Cl. N9 .3B 34
Chaundrye Cl. SE9 .6D 124
Chauntler Cl. E16 .6K 87
Chaville Ct. N11 .4K 31
Cheadle Ct. *NW8* .3B 4
(off Henderson Dr.)
Cheadle Ho. *E14* .6B 86
(off Copenhagen Pl.)
CHEAM .6G 165
Cheam Comn. Rd. KT4: Wor Pk .2D 164
Cheam Leisure Cen. .4F 165
Cheam Mans. SM3: Cheam .7G 165
Cheam Pk. Way SM3: Cheam .6G 165
Cheam Rd. SM1: Sutt .6H 165
SM2: Cheam .7F 165
Cheam St. SE15 .3J 121
CHEAM VILLAGE .6G 165
Cheapside EC2 .1D 14 (6C 84)
N13 .4J 33
N22 .3A 48
Chearsley *SE17* .4C 102
(off Deacon Way)
Cheddar Cl. N11 .6J 31
Cheddar Waye UB4: Yead .6K 75
Cheddington Ho. *E2* .1G 85
(off Whiston Rd.)
Cheddington Rd. N18 .3K 33
Chedworth Cl. E16 .6H 87
Chedworth Ho. *N15* .4D 48
(off West Grn. Rd.)
Cheeseman Cl. TW12: Hamp .6C 130
Cheesemans Ter. W14 .5H 99
(not continuous)
Cheethams Rd. E12 .3C 70
Cheffery Ct. TW15: Ashf .6D 128
Cheldon Av. NW7 .7A 30
Chelford Rd. BR1: Brom .5F 141
Chelmer Cres. IG11: Bark .2B 90
Chelmer Rd. E9 .5K 67
Chelmsford Cl. E6 .6D 88
W6 .6F 99
Chelmsford Ct. *N14* .7C 22
(off Chelmsford Rd.)
Chelmsford Gdns. IG1: Ilf .7C 52
Chelmsford Ho. *N7* .4K 65
(off Holloway Rd.)
Chelmsford Rd. E11 .1F 69
E17 .6C 50
E18 .1H 51
N14 .7B 22
Chelmsford Sq. NW10 .1E 80
Chelmsine Ct. HA4: Ruis .5E 38
CHELSEA .6D 16 (5C 100)
Chelsea Barracks .5H 17
Chelsea Bri. SW1 .7J 17 (6F 101)
Chelsea Bri. Bus. Cen. SW8 .7F 101
Chelsea Bri. Rd.
SW1 .5G 17 (5E 100)
Chelsea Bri. Wharf
SW8 .7K 17 (6F 101)
Chelsea Cinema .5C 100
Chelsea Cloisters
SW3 .4D 16 (4C 100)
Chelsea Cl. HA8: Edg .2G 43
KT4: Wor Pk .7C 152
NW10 .1K 79
TW12: Hamp H .5G 131
Chelsea College of Art & Design
.6C 16 (5C 100)
Chelsea Ct. *BR1: Brom* .3C 160
(off Holmdene Ct.)
Chelsea Cres. NW2 .6H 63
SW10 .1A 118
Chelsea Emb. SW3 .7D 16 (6C 100)
Chelsea Farm Ho. Studios
SW10 .6B 100
(off Moravian Pl.)
Chelsea FC .7K 99
Chelsea Flds. SW19 .1B 154
Chelsea Gdns. SM3: Cheam .4G 165
SW1 .6H 17 (5E 100)
W13 .5K 77
Chelsea Ga. SW1 .6H 17
Chelsea Harbour SW10 .1A 118
Chelsea Harbour Design Cen.
SW10 .1A 118
(off Chelsea Harbour Dr.)
Chelsea Harbour Dr.
SW10 .1A 118
Chelsea Lodge *SW3* .7F 17
(off Tite St.)
Chelsea Mnr. Ct.
SW3 .7D 16 (6C 100)
Chelsea Mnr. Gdns.
SW3 .6D 16 (5C 100)
Chelsea Mnr. St.
SW3 .6D 16 (5C 100)
Chelsea Pk. Gdns.
SW3 .7A 16 (6B 100)
Chelsea Physic Garden .7E 16 (6D 100)
Chelsea Reach Twr. *SW10* .7B 100
(off Worlds End Est.)
Chelsea Sports Cen. .6D 16 (5C 100)
Chelsea Sq. SW3 .5B 16 (5B 100)
Chelsea Studios *SW6* .7K 99
(off Fulham Rd.)
Chelsea Towers SW3 .7D 16
Chelsea Village *SW6* .7K 99
(off Fulham Rd.)
Chelsea Vista SW6 .2A 118
Chelsea Wharf *SW10* .7B 100
(off Lots Rd.)
Chelsfield Av. N9 .7E 24
Chelsfield Gdns. SE26 .3J 139
Chelsfield Grn. N9 .7E 24
(not continuous)
Chelsfield Ho. *SE17* .4E 102
(off Massinger St.)
Chelsham Rd. CR2: S Croy .7D 168
SW4 .3H 119
Chelsiter Ct. DA14: Sidc .4K 143
Chelston App. HA4: Ruis .2J 57
Chelston Rd. HA4: Ruis .1J 57
Chelsworth Dr. SE18 .6H 107
Cheltenham Av. TW1: Twick .7A 114
Cheltenham Cl. KT3: N Mald .3J 151
UB5: N'olt .6F 59
Cheltenham Ct. *HA7: Stan* .5H 27
(off Marsh La.)
Cheltenham Gdns. E6 .2C 88
Cheltenham Ho. IG8: Ilf .6K 37
Cheltenham Pl. HA3: Kent .4E 42
W3 .1H 97
Cheltenham Rd. BR6: Chels .3K 173
E10 .6E 50
SE15 .4J 121
Cheltenham Ter. SW3 .5F 17 (5D 100)
Chelverton Rd. SW15 .4F 117
Chelwood N20 .2G 31
Chelwood Cl. E4 .6J 25
Chelwood Gdns. TW9: Kew .2G 115
Chelwood Gdns. Pas. TW9: Kew .2G 115
Chelwood Ho. *W2* .1B 10
(off Gloucester Sq.)
Chelwood Wlk. SE4 .4A 122
Chenappa Cl. E13 .3J 87
Chenduit Way HA7: Stan .5E 26
Cheney Ct. SE23 .1K 139
Cheney Row E17 .1B 50
Cheneys Rd. E11 .3G 69
Cheney St. HA5: Eastc .4A 40
Chenies, The BR6: Pet W .6J 161
NW1 .2H 83
(off Pancras Rd.)
Chenies Ho. *W4* .7B 98
(off Corney Reach Way)
Chenies M. WC1 .4C 6 (4H 83)
Chenies Pl. NW1 .2H 83
Chenies St. WC1 .5C 6 (5H 83)
Cheniston Gdns. W8 .3K 99
Chepstow Cl. SW15 .5G 117
Chepstow Cnr. *W2* .6J 81
(off Chepstow Pl.)
Chepstow Ct. *W11* .7J 81
(off Chepstow Vs.)
Chepstow Cres. IG3: Ilf .6J 53
W11 .7J 81
Chepstow Gdns. UB1: S'hall .6D 76
Chepstow Pl. W2 .6J 81
Chepstow Ri. CR0: Croy .3E 168
Chepstow Rd. CR0: Croy .3E 168
W2 .6J 81
W7 .3A 96
Chepstow Vs. W11 .7H 81
Chequers IG9: Buck H .1E 36
Chequers, The HA5: Pinn .3B 40
Chequers Cl. BR5: St P .4K 161
NW9 .3A 44
Chequers Ct. *EC1* .4D 8
(off Chequer St.)
Chequers Ho. *NW8* .3C 4
(off Jerome Cres.)
Chequers La. RM9: Dag .5F 91
Chequers Pde. N13 .5H 33
RM9: Dag .1F 91
SE9 .6D 124
(off Eltham High St.)
Chequer St. EC1 .4D 8 (4C 84)
(not continuous)
Chequers Way N13 .5G 33
Cherbury Cl. SE28 .6D 90
Cherbury Ct. *N1* .2D 84
(off St John's Est.)
Cherbury St. N1 .2D 84
Cherchefelle M. HA7: Stan .5G 27
Cherimoya Gdns. KT8: W Mole .3F 149
Cherington Rd. W7 .1J 95
Cheriton Av. BR2: Brom .5H 159
IG5: Ilf .2D 52
Cheriton Cl. EN4: Cockf .3J 21
W5 .5C 78
Cheriton Ct. SE12 .7J 123
Cheriton Dr. SE18 .7H 107
Cheriton Sq. SW17 .2E 136
Cherry Av. UB1: S'hall .1B 94
Cherry Blossom Cl. N13 .5G 33
Cherry Cl. E17 .5D 50
HA4: Ruis .3H 57
NW9 .2A 44
SM4: Mord .4G 153
SM5: Cars .2D 166
SW2 .7A 120
W5 .3D 96
Cherrycot Hill BR6: Farnb .4G 173
Cherrycot Ri. BR6: Farnb .4G 173
Cherry Ct. HA5: Pinn .2B 40
IG6: Ilf .3F 53
W3 .1A 98
Cherry Cres. TW8: Bford .7B 96
Cherrydown Av. E4 .3G 35
Cherrydown Cl. E4 .3H 35
Cherrydown Rd. DA14: Sidc .2D 144
Cherrydown Wlk. RM7: Mawney .2H 55
Cherry Gdn. Ho. *SE16* .2H 103
(off Cherry Gdn. St.)
Cherry Gdns. RM9: Dag .5F 73
UB5: N'olt .7F 59
Cherry Gdn. St. SE16 .2H 103
Cherry Gth. TW8: Bford .5D 96
Cherry Gro. UB3: Hayes .1K 93
UB8: Hil .5D 74
Cherry Hill EN5: New Bar .6E 20
HA3: Hrw W .6E 26
Cherry Hill Gdns. CR0: Wadd .4K 167
Cherrylands Cl. NW9 .2J 61
Cherry La. UB7: W Dray .4B 92
Cherry Laurel Wlk. SW2 .6K 119
Cherry Orchard SE7 .6A 106
UB7: W Dray .2A 92
Cherry Orchard Gdns. CR0: Croy .1D 168
KT8: W Mole .3D 148
Cherry Orchard Rd. BR2: Brom .2C 172
CR0: Croy .2D 168
KT8: W Mole .3E 148
Cherry Rd. EN3: Enf W .1D 24
Cherry St. RM7: Rom .5K 55

Cherry Tree Av.—Chevenings, The

Cherry Tree Av. UB7: Yiew 6B 74
Cherry Tree Cl. E9 1J 85
HA0: Wemb 4A 60
Cherry Tree Ct. *NW1* *7G 65*
(off Camden Rd.)
NW9 4J 43
SE7 6A 106
Cherry Tree Dr. SW16 3J 137
Cherry Tree Hill N2 5C 46
Cherry Tree Ho. N22 7D 32
Cherry Tree Ri.
IG9: Buck H 4F 37
Cherry Tree Rd. E15 5G 69
N2 4D 46
Cherry Tree Ter. *SE1* *7H 15*
(off Whites Grounds)
Cherry Tree Wlk. BR3: Beck 4B 158
BR4: W W'ck 4H 171
EC1 4D 8 (4C 84)
Cherrytree Way HA7: Stan 6G 27
Cherry Wlk. BR2: Hayes 1J 171
Cherry Way KT19: Ewe 6K 163
TW17: Shep 4F 147
Cherry Wood Cl. KT2: King T 7G 133
Cherrywood Cl. E3 3A 86
Cherrywood Ct. TW11: Tedd 5A 132
Cherrywood Dr. SW15 5F 117
Cherrywood La. SM4: Mord 4G 153
Cherry Wood Way W5 5G 79
Chertsey Bri. Rd. KT16: Chert 7A 146
Chertsey Ct. SW14 3H 115
Chertsey Dr. SM3: Cheam 2G 165
CHERTSEY MEADS 7A 146
Chertsey Rd. E11 2F 69
IG1: Ilf 4H 71
TW1: Twick 6K 113
TW2: Twick 2F 131
TW13: Felt 3G 129
TW15: Ashf 7F 129
TW16: Sun 7F 129
TW17: Shep 7A 146
Chertsey St. SW17 5E 136
Chervil Cl. TW13: Felt 3J 129
Chervil M. SE28 1B 108
Cherwell Ct. KT19: Ewe 4J 163
Cherwell Ho. NW8 4B 4
Cherwell Way HA4: Ruis 6E 38
Cheryls Cl. SW6 1K 117
Cheseman St. SE26 3H 139
Chesfield Rd. KT2: King T 7E 132
Chesham Av. BR5: Pet W 6F 161
Chesham Cl. RM7: Rom 4K 55
SW1 2G 17
Chesham Cres. SE20 1J 157
Chesham Flats *W1* *2H 11*
(off Brown Hart Gdns.)
Chesham M. SW1 1G 17
Chesham Pl. SW1 2G 17 (3E 100)
(not continuous)
Chesham Rd. KT1: King T 2G 151
SE20 2J 157
SW19 5B 136
Chesham St. NW10 3K 61
SW1 2G 17 (3E 100)
Chesham Ter. W13 2B 96
Cheshire Cl. CR4: Mitc 3J 155
E17 1D 50
SE4 2B 122
Cheshire Ct. *EC4* *1K 13*
(off Fleet St.)
Cheshire Gdns. KT9: Chess 6D 162
Cheshire Ho. N18 4C 34
SM4: Mord 7K 153
Cheshire Rd. N22 7E 32
Cheshire St. E2 3K 9 (4F 85)
Cheshir Ho. NW4 4E 44
Chesholm Rd. N16 3E 66
Cheshunt Ho. *NW6* *1K 81*
(off Mortimer Cres.)
Cheshunt Rd. DA17: Belv 5G 109
E7 6K 69
Chesil Ct. E2 2J 85
SW3 7D 16 (6C 100)
Chesilton Rd. SW6 1H 117
Chesil Way UB4: Hayes 3H 75
Chesley Gdns. E6 2B 88
Chesney Ct. *W9* *4J 81*
(off Shirland Rd.)
Chesney Cres. CR0: New Ad 7E 170
Chesney Ho. *SE13* *4F 123*
(off Mercator Rd.)
Chesney St. SW11 1E 118
Chesnut Gro. N17 3F 49
Chesnut Rd. N17 3F 49
(not continuous)
Chesnut Row N3 7D 30
Chessell Cl. CR7: Thor H 4B 156
Chessholme Ct. *TW16: Sun* *7G 129*
(off Scotts Av.)
Chessholme Rd. TW15: Ashf 6E 128
Chessing Ct. *N2* *3D 46*
(off Fortis Grn.)
CHESSINGTON 5F 163
Chessington Av. DA7: Bex 7E 108
N3 3G 45
Chessington Cl. KT19: Ewe 6J 163
Chessington Ct. HA5: Pinn 4D 40
N3 *3H 45*
(off Charter Way)
Chessington Hall Gdns.
KT9: Chess 7D 162
Chessington Hill Pk. KT9: Chess 5G 163
Chessington Ho. SW8 2H 119
Chessington Lodge N3 3H 45
Chessington Mans. E10 7C 50
E11 7G 51
Chessington Pde. KT9: Chess 6D 162
Chessington Pk. KT9: Chess 4G 163
Chessington Rd. KT17: Ewe 7B 164
KT19: Ewe 6G 163
Chessington Sports Cen. 7D 162
Chessington Way BR4: W W'ck 2D 170
Chesson Rd. W14 6H 99
Chesswood Way HA5: Pinn 2B 40
Chestbrook Ct. *EN1: Enf* *5K 23*
(off Forsyth Pl.)
Chester Av. TW2: Whit 1D 130
TW10: Rich 6F 115
Chester Cl. SM1: Sutt 2J 165
SW1 7J 11 (2F 101)
SW13 3D 116
TW10: Rich 6F 115
TW15: Ashf 5F 129
UB8: Hil 6D 74
Chester Cl. Nth. NW1 1K 5 (3F 83)
Chester Cl. Sth. NW1 2K 5 (3F 83)
Chester Cotts. SW1 4G 17
Chester Ct. *BR2: Brom* *4H 159*
(off Durham Rd.)
NW1 1K 5 (3F 83)
SE5 *7D 102*
(off Lomond Gro.)
SE8 5K 103
Chester Cres. E8 5F 67
Chester Dr. HA2: Harr 6D 40
Chesterfield Cl. SE13 2F 123
Chesterfield Ct. *KT5: Surb* *5E 150*
(off Cranes Pk.)
Chesterfield Dr. KT10: Hin W 2A 162
Chesterfield Flats *EN5: Barn* *5A 20*
(off Bells Hill)
Chesterfield Gdns. N4 5B 48
SE10 1F 123
W1 4J 11 (1F 101)
Chesterfield Gro. SE22 5F 121
Chesterfield Hill W1 4J 11 (1F 101)
Chesterfield Ho. *W1* *4H 11*
(off Chesterfield Gdns.)
Chesterfield Lodge *N21* *7E 22*
(off Church Hill)
Chesterfield M. N4 5B 48
TW15: Ashf 4A 128
Chesterfield Rd. E10 6E 50
EN5: Barn 5A 20
KT19: Ewe 7K 163
N3 6D 30
TW15: Ashf 4A 128
W4 6J 97
Chesterfield St. W1 4J 11 (1F 101)
Chesterfield Wlk. SE10 1F 123
Chesterfield Way SE15 7J 103
UB3: Hayes 2J 93
Chesterford Gdns. NW3 4K 63
Chesterford Ho. *SE18* *1B 124*
(off Tellson Av.)
Chesterford Rd. E12 5D 70
Chester Gdns. EN3: Pond E 6C 24
SM4: Mord 6A 154
W13 6B 78
Chester Ga. NW1 2J 5 (3F 83)
Chester Ho. N10 2F 47
SE8 6B 104
SW1 *3J 17*
(off Eccleston Pl.)
SW9 *7A 102*
(off Brixton Rd.)
Chesterman Ct. *W4* *7A 98*
(off Corney Reach Way)
Chester M. E17 2C 50
SW1 1J 17 (3F 101)
Chester Pl. NW1 1J 5 (3F 83)
Chester Rd. DA15: Sidc 5J 125
(not continuous)
E7 7B 70
E11 6K 51
E16 4G 87
E17 5K 49
HA6: Nwood 1H 39
IG3: Ilf 1K 71
IG7: Chig 3K 37
N9 1C 34
N17 3D 48
N19 2F 65
NW1 2H 5 (3E 82)
SW19 6E 134
TW4: Houn 3K 111
TW6: H'row A 3C 110
Chester Row SW1 4G 17 (4E 100)
Chesters, The KT3: N Mald 1A 152
Chester Sq. SW1 3H 17 (4E 100)
Chester Sq. M. SW1 2J 17
Chester St. E2 4G 85
SW1 1H 17 (3E 100)
Chester Ter. IG11: Bark 6H 71
NW1 1J 5 (3F 83)
(not continuous)
Chesterton Cl. SW18 5J 117
UB6: G'frd 2F 77
Chesterton Ct. *W3* *3H 97*
(off Bollo Bri. Rd.)
W5 5D 78
Chesterton Dr. TW19: Stanw 1B 128
Chesterton Ho. *CR0: Croy* *4D 168*
(off Heathfield Rd.)
Chesterton Rd. E13 3J 87
W10 5F 81
Chesterton Sq. W8 4J 99
Chesterton Ter. E13 3J 87
KT1: King T 2G 151
Chester Way SE11 4K 19 (4A 102)
Chesthunte Rd. N17 1C 48
Chestnut All. SW6 6H 99
Chestnut Av. BR4: W W'ck 5G 171
E7 4K 69
E12 2C 70
HA0: Wemb 5B 60
HA6: Nwood 2H 39
HA8: Edg 6K 27
IG9: Buck H 3G 37
KT8: E Mos 3K 149
KT10: Esh 7H 149
KT19: Ewe 4A 164
N8 5J 47
Chestnut Av. SW14 3K 115
TW8: Bford 4D 96
TW11: Tedd 2K 149
TW12: Hamp 7E 130
UB7: Yiew 7B 74
Chestnut Av. Nth. E17 4F 51
Chestnut Av. Sth. E17 5E 50
Chestnut Cl. BR6: Chels 5K 173
DA15: Sidc 1A 144
IG9: Buck H 3G 37
N14 5B 22
N16 2D 66
SE6 5E 140
SE14 1B 122
SM5: Cars 1D 166
SW16 4A 138
TW15: Ashf 4D 128
TW16: Sun 6H 129
UB3: Hayes 7G 75
UB7: Sip 7D 92
Chestnut Ct. *CR2: S Croy* *4C 168*
(off Bramley Hill)
N8 5J 47
SW6 6H 99
TW13: Hanw 5B 130
W8 *3K 99*
(off Abbots Wlk.)
Chestnut Dr. DA7: Bex 3D 126
E11 6J 51
HA3: Hrw W 7E 26
HA5: Pinn 6B 40
Chestnut Gro. CR2: Sels 7H 169
CR4: Mitc 5H 155
DA2: Dart 4K 145
EN4: E Barn 5J 21
HA0: Wemb 5B 60
KT3: N Mald 3K 151
SE20 7H 139
SW12 7E 118
TW7: Isle 4A 114
W5 3D 96
Chestnut Ho. *W4* *4A 98*
(off Orchard, The)
Chestnut La. N20 1B 30
Chestnut Pl. SE26 4F 139
Chestnut Ri. SE18 6H 107
WD23: Bush 1A 26
Chestnut Rd. KT2: King T 7E 132
SE27 3B 138
SW20 2F 153
TW2: Twick 2J 131
TW15: Ashf 4D 128
Chestnuts, The HA5: H End 1D 40
N5 *4C 66*
(off Highbury Grange)
UB10: Uxb 7A 56
Chestnut Ter. SM1: Sutt 4K 165
Chestnut Wlk. IG8: Wfd G 5D 36
TW17: Shep 4G 147
Chestnut Way TW13: Felt 3K 129
Cheston Av. CR0: Croy 2A 170
Chestwood Gro. UB10: Hil 7B 56
Chettle Cl. *SE1* *3D 102*
(off Spurgeon St.)
Chettle Ct. N8 6A 48
Chetwode Ho. NW8 3C 4
Chetwode Rd. SW17 3D 136
Chetwood Wlk. *E6* *5C 88*
(off Greenwich Cres.)
Chetwynd Av. EN4: E Barn 1J 31
Chetwynd Dr. UB10: Hil 2B 74
Chetwynd Rd. NW5 4F 65
Chevalier Cl. HA7: Stan 4K 27
Cheval Pl. SW7 1D 16 (3C 100)
Cheval St. E14 3C 104
Cheveney Wlk. BR2: Brom 3J 159
Chevening Rd. NW6 2F 81
SE10 5H 105
SE19 6D 138
Chevenings, The
DA14: Sidc 3C 144

Chopwell Cl.—Church Rd.

Chopwell Cl. E15 7F 69
Chorleywood Cres. BR5: St P 2K 161
Choumert Gro. SE15 2G 121
Choumert M. SE15 2G 121
Choumert Rd. SE15 3F 121
Choumert Sq. SE15 2G 121
Chow Sq. E8 5F 67
Chrisp Ho. *SE10* *6G 105* (*off Maze Hill*)
Chrisp St. E14 5D 86 (not continuous)
Christabel Cl. TW7: Isle 3J 113
Christchurch Av. DA8: Erith 6K 109
  HA0: Wemb 6E 60
  HA3: Kent, W'stone 4K 41
  N12 6F 31
  NW6 1F 81
  TW11: Tedd 5A 132
Christchurch Cl. EN2: Enf 2H 23
  N12 7G 31
  SW19 7B 136
Christ Chu. Ct. NW10 1A 80
Christchurch Ct. *EC4* *7B 8* (*off Warwick La.*)
  UB4: Yead *4A 76* (*off Dunedin Way*)
Christchurch Flats TW9: Rich 3E 114
Christchurch Gdns. HA3: W'stone 4A 42
Christchurch Grn. HA0: Wemb 6E 60
Christchurch Hill NW3 3B 64
Christchurch Ho. *SW2* *1K 137* (*off Christchurch Rd.*)
Christchurch La. EN5: Barn 2B 20
Christchurch Lodge EN4: Cockf 4J 21
Christchurch Pk. SM2: Sutt 7A 166
Christchurch Pas. EN5: Barn 2B 20
  NW3 3A 64
Christchurch Path UB3: Harl 3E 92
Christchurch Pl. SW8 2H 119
Christ Chu. Rd. BR3: Beck 2C 158
  SW14 5H 115
Christchurch Rd. DA15: Sidc 4K 143
  IG1: Ilf 1F 71
  KT5: Surb 6F 151
  N8 6J 47
  SW2 1K 137
  SW19 7B 136
  TW6: H'row A 3C 110
Christchurch Sq. E9 1J 85
Christchurch St. SW3 7E 16 (6D 100)
Christchurch Ter. SW3 7E 16
Christchurch Way SE10 5G 105
Christian Ct. SE16 1B 104
Christian Flds. SW16 7A 138
Christian Pl. *E1* *6G 85* (*off Burslem St.*)
Christian St. E1 6G 85
Christie Ct. N19 2J 65
Christie Dr. CR0: Croy 5G 157
Christie Gdns. RM6: Chad H 6B 54
Christie Ho. *SE10* *5H 105* (*off Blackwall La.*)
Christie Rd. E9 6A 68
Christina Sq. N4 1B 66
Christina St. EC2 3G 9 (4E 84)
Christine Worsley Cl. N21 1G 33
Christopher Av. W7 3A 96
Christopher Cl. DA15: Sidc 5K 125
  SE16 2K 103
Christopher Ct. TW15: Ashf 5A 128
Christopher Gdns. RM9: Dag 5D 72
Christopher Ho. *DA15: Sidc* *2A 144* (*off Station Rd.*)
Christopher Pl. NW1 1D 6 (3H 83)
Christopher Rd. UB2: S'hall 4K 93
Christophers M. W11 1G 99
Christopher St. EC2 4F 9 (4D 84)
Chryssell Rd. SW9 7A 102
Chubworthy St. SE14 6A 104
Chudleigh DA14: Sidc 4B 144
Chudleigh Cres. IG3: Ilf 4J 71
Chudleigh Gdns. SM1: Sutt 3A 166
Chudleigh Rd. NW6 7F 63
  SE4 5B 122
  TW2: Twick 6J 113 (not continuous)
Chudleigh St. E1 6K 85
Chudleigh Way HA4: Ruis 1J 57
Chulsa Rd. SE26 5H 139
Chumleigh Gdns. *SE5* *6E 102* (*off Chumleigh St.*)
Chumleigh St. SE5 6E 102
Chumleigh Wlk. KT5: Surb 4F 151
Church All. CR0: Croy 1A 168
Church App. SE21 3D 138
Church Av. BR3: Beck 1C 158
  DA14: Sidc 5A 144
  E4 6A 36 (not continuous)
  E12 3B 70
  HA4: Ruis 1F 57
  HA5: Pinn 6C 40
  N2 2B 46
  NW1 6F 65
  SW14 3K 115
  UB2: S'hall 3C 94
  UB5: N'olt 7D 58
Churchbank *E17* *4C 50* (*off Teresa M.*)
Churchbury Cl. EN1: Enf 2K 23
Churchbury La. EN1: Enf 3J 23
Churchbury Rd. EN1: Enf 2K 23
  SE9 7B 124
Church Cloisters EC3 3G 15
Church Cl. HA6: Nwood 1H 39
  HA8: Edg 5D 28
  N20 3H 31
  TW3: Houn 2C 112
  UB4: Hayes 5F 75
  UB7: W Dray 3A 92
  W8 2K 99
Church Ct. *SE16* *2B 104* (*off Rotherhithe St.*)
  TW9: Rich 5D 114
Church Cres. E9 7K 67
  N3 1H 45
  N10 4F 47
  N20 3H 31
Churchcroft Cl. SW12 7E 118
Churchdown BR1: Brom 4G 141
Church Dr. BR4: W W'ck 3G 171
  HA2: Harr 6E 40
  NW9 1K 61
Church Elm La. RM10: Dag 6G 73
CHURCH END
  Finchley 1H 45
  Willesden 6A 62
Church End E17 4D 50
  NW4 3D 44
Church Entry EC4 1B 14
Church Est. Almshouses *TW9: Rich* *4F 115* (*off Sheen Rd.*)
Church Farm House Mus. 3D 44
Church Farm La. SM3: Cheam 6G 165
Church Farm Pool 7J 21
Churchfield Av. N12 6G 31
Churchfield Cl. HA2: Harr 4G 41
  UB3: Hayes 7H 75
Churchfield Mans. *SW6* *2H 117* (*off New Kings Rd.*)
Churchfield Pl. TW17: Shep 7D 146
Churchfield Rd. DA16: Well 3A 126
  KT12: Walt T 7J 147
  W3 1J 97
  W7 2J 95
  W13 1B 96
Churchfields E18 1J 51
  KT8: W Mole 3E 148
  SE10 6E 104
Churchfields Av. TW13: Hanw 3D 130
Churchfields Rd. BR3: Beck 2K 157
Churchfield Way N12 6F 31
Church Gdns. HA0: Wemb 4A 60
  W5 2D 96
Church Gth. *N19* *2H 65* (*off St John's Gro.*)
Church Ga. SW6 3G 117
Church Grn. SW9 1A 120
  UB3: Hayes 6H 75
Church Gro. KT1: Hamp W 1C 150
  SE13 5D 122
Church Hill DA1: Cray 4K 127
  E17 4C 50
  HA1: Harr 1J 59
  N21 7E 22
  SE18 3D 106
  SM5: Cars 5D 166
  SW19 5H 135
Church Hill Rd. E17 4D 50
  EN4: E Barn 6H 21
  KT6: Surb 5E 150
  SM3: Cheam 3F 165
Church Hill Wood BR5: St M Cry 5K 161
Church Ho. *EC1* *3B 8* (*off Compton St.*)
  SW1 *1D 18* (*off Gt. Smith St.*)
Church Hyde SE18 6J 107
Churchill Av. HA3: Kent 6B 42
  UB10: Hil 3D 74
Churchill Cl. TW14: Felt 1H 129
  UB10: Hil 3D 74
Churchill Ct. BR6: Farnb 5G 173
  HA2: Harr 5F 41 (North Harrow)
  HA2: Harr 2F 59 (Roxeth)
  HA5: H End 1C 40
  N4 7A 48
  N9 1K 33
  UB5: N'olt 5E 58
  W5 4F 79
Churchill Gdns. SW1 6A 18 (5G 101)
  W3 6G 79
Churchill Gdns. Rd.
  SW1 6K 17 (5F 101)
Churchill Mus. (Cabinet War Rooms) 6D 12 (2H 101)
Churchill Pl. E14 1D 104
  HA1: Harr 4J 41
Churchill Rd. CR2: S Croy 7C 168
  E16 6A 88
  HA8: Edg 6A 28
  NW2 6D 62
  NW5 4F 65
Churchills M. IG8: Wfd G 6C 36
Churchill Ter. E4 4H 35
Churchill Theatre & Library 2J 159
Churchill Wlk. E9 5J 67
Churchill Way BR1: Brom 2J 159
  TW16: Sun 5J 129
Church La. BR2: Brom 1C 172
  BR7: Chst 1G 161
  E11 1G 69
  E17 4D 50
  EN1: Enf 3J 23
  HA3: W'stone 1K 41
  HA5: Pinn 3C 40
  KT7: T Ditt 6K 149
  KT9: Chess 6F 163
  N2 3B 46
  N8 4K 47
  N9 2B 34
  N17 1E 48
  NW9 6J 43
  RM10: Dag 7J 73
  SM6: Bedd 3H 167 (not continuous)
  SW17 5D 136
  SW19 1H 153
  TW1: Twick 1A 132
  TW10: Ham 1E 132
  TW11: Tedd 5K 131
Church La. UB3: Hayes 6G 75
  W5 2C 96
Churchley Rd. SE26 4H 139
Church Manorway DA8: Erith 4K 109
  SE2 5A 108
Churchmead *SE5* *7C 102* (*off Camberwell Rd.*)
Churchmead Cl. EN4: E Barn 6H 21
Church Mdw. KT6: Surb 2C 162
Churchmead Rd. NW10 6C 62
Churchmore Rd. SW16 1G 155
Church Mt. N2 5B 46
Chu. Paddock Ct. SM6: Bedd 3H 167
Church Pde. TW15: Ashf 4B 128
Church Pas. *EC2* *7D 8* (*off Guildhall Yd.*)
  EN5: Barn 3B 20
  KT6: Surb 5E 150
  TW1: Twick 1B 132
Church Path CR0: Croy 2C 168
  CR4: Mitc 3C 154 (not continuous)
  E11 5J 51
  E17 4D 50
  N5 5B 66
  N8 *5K 47* (*off Tottenham La.*)
  N12 3F 31 (Woodside La.)
  N12 4F 31 (Woodside Pk. Rd.)
  N17 7K 33
  NW10 7A 62
  SW14 3K 115 (not continuous)
  SW19 2H 153 (not continuous)
  UB1: S'hall 1E 94
  UB2: S'hall 3D 94 (not continuous)
  W3 2J 97 (not continuous)
Church Pl. CR4: Mitc 3C 154
  SW1 3B 12 (7G 83)
  UB10: Ick 3E 56
  W5 2D 96
Church Ri. KT9: Chess 6F 163
  SE23 2K 139
Church Rd. BR2: Brom 2J 159 (Glassmill La.)
  BR2: Brom 3G 159 (Shortlands Rd.)
  BR2: Kes 7B 172
  BR6: Farnb 5G 173
  CR0: Croy 3C 168 (not continuous)
  CR4: Mitc 1B 154
  DA7: Bex 2F 127
  DA8: Erith 5K 109
  DA14: Sidc 4A 144
  DA16: Well 2B 126
  E10 1C 68
  E12 5C 70
  E17 2A 50
  EN3: Pond E 6D 24
  HA6: Nwood 1H 39
  HA7: Stan 5G 27
  IG2: Ilf 6J 53
  IG9: Buck H 1E 36
  IG11: Bark 6G 71
  KT1: King T 2F 151
  KT4: Wor Pk 1A 164
  KT6: Surb 1C 162
  KT8: E Mos 4H 149
  KT10: Clay 7A 162
  KT19: Ewe 7K 163
  N1 6C 66
  N6 6E 46
  N17 1E 48 (not continuous)
  NW4 4D 44

Clements La. EC4 2F 15 (7D 84)
IG1: Ilf 3F 71
Clements Pl. TW8: Bford 5D 96
Clements Rd. E6 7C 70
IG1: Ilf 3F 71
SE16 3G 103
Clemson Ho. E8 1F 85
Clendon Way SE18 4H 107
Clennam St. SE1 6D 14 (2C 102)
Clensham Ct. SM1: Sutt 2J 165
Clensham La. SM1: Sutt 2J 165
Clenston M. W1 7E 4 (6D 82)
Cleopatra's Needle 3G 13 (1J 101)
Clephane Rd. N1 6C 66
Clephane Rd. Nth. N1 6C 66
Clephane Rd. Sth. N1 6D 66
Clere Pl. EC2 3F 9 (4D 84)
Clere St. EC2 3F 9 (4D 84)
Clerics Wlk. TW17: Shep 7F 147
CLERKENWELL 3J 7 (4A 84)
Clerkenwell Cl. EC1 3K 7 (4A 84)
(not continuous)
Clerkenwell Grn. EC1 4K 7 (4A 84)
Clerkenwell Rd. EC1 4J 7 (4A 84)
Clermont Rd. E9 1J 85
Clevedon Cl. N16 3F 67
Clevedon Ct. CR2: S Croy 5E 168
Clevedon Gdns. TW5: Cran 1K 111
UB3: Harl 3F 93
Clevedon Ho. SM1: Sutt 4A 166
Clevedon Mans. NW5 4E 64
Clevedon Pas. N16 2F 67
Clevedon Rd. KT1: King T 2G 151
SE20 1K 157
TW1: Twick 6D 114
(not continuous)
Cleve Ho. NW6 7K 63
Cleveland Av. SW20 2H 153
TW12: Hamp 7D 130
W4 4B 98
Cleveland Ct. W13 5B 78
Cleveland Gdns. KT4: Wor Pk 2A 164
N4 5C 48
NW2 2F 63
SW13 2B 116
W2 6A 82
Cleveland Gro. E1 4J 85
Cleveland Ho. *N2* *2B 46*
(off Grange, The)
Cleveland La. N9 7C 24
Cleveland Mans. *SW9* *7A 102*
(off Mowll St.)
W9 4J 81
Cleveland M. W1 5A 6 (5G 83)
Cleveland Pk. TW19: Stanw 6A 110
Cleveland Pk. Av. E17 4C 50
Cleveland Pk. Cres. E17 4C 50
Cleveland Pl. SW1 4B 12 (1G 101)
Cleveland Ri. SM4: Mord 7F 153
Cleveland Rd. DA16: Well 2K 125
E18 3J 51
IG1: Ilf 3F 71
KT3: N Mald 4A 152
KT4: Wor Pk 2A 164
N1 7D 66
SW13 2B 116
TW7: Isle 4A 114
W4 3J 97
W13 5A 78
Cleveland Row SW1 5A 12 (1G 101)
Clevelands, The IG11: Bark 6G 71
Cleveland Sq. W2 6A 82
Cleveland St. W1 4K 5 (4F 83)
Cleveland Ter. W2 6A 82
Cleveland Way E1 4J 85
Cleveley Cl. SE7 4B 106
Cleveley Cres. W5 2E 78
Cleveleys Rd. E5 3H 67
Cleverly Est. W12 1C 98
Cleve Rd. DA14: Sidc 3D 144
NW6 7K 63
Cleves Av. KT17: Ewe 7D 164
Cleves Ho. *E16* *1J 105*
(off Southey M.)
Cleves Rd. E6 1B 88
TW10: Ham 3C 132
Cleves Wlk. IG6: Ilf 1G 53
Cleves Way HA4: Ruis 1B 58
TW12: Hamp 7D 130
TW16: Sun 6H 129
Clewer Ct. *E10* *1C 68*
(off Leyton Grange Est.)
Clewer Cres. HA3: Hrw W 1H 41
Clewer Ho. *SE2* *2D 108*
(off Wolvercote Rd.)
Cley Ho. SE4 4K 121
Clichy Est. E1 5J 85
Clichy Ho. *E1* *5J 85*
(off Stepney Way)
Clifden Rd. E5 5J 67
TW1: Twick 1K 131
TW8: Bford 6D 96
Cliffe Ho. *SE10* *5H 105*
(off Blackwall La.)
Cliffe Rd. CR2: S Croy 5D 168
Cliffe Wlk. *SM1: Sutt* *5A 166*
(off Greyhound Rd.)
Clifford Av. BR7: Chst 6D 142
IG5: Ilf 1F 53
SM6: Wall 4G 167
SW14 3H 115
(not continuous)
Clifford Cl. UB5: N'olt 1C 76
Clifford Ct. *W2* *5K 81*
(off Westbourne Pk. Vs.)
Clifford Dr. SW9 4B 120
Clifford Gdns. NW10 2E 80
UB3: Harl 4G 93
Clifford Gro. TW15: Ashf 4C 128
Clifford Haigh Ho. SW6 7F 99
Clifford Ho. *BR3: Beck* *6D 140*
(off Calverley Cl.)
W14 *4H 99*
(off Edith Vs.)
Clifford Rd. E16 4H 87
E17 2E 50
EN5: New Bar 3E 20
HA0: Wemb 7D 60
N1 1E 84
N9 6D 24
SE25 4G 157
TW4: Houn 3B 112
TW10: Ham 2D 132
Clifford's Inn Pas. EC4 1J 13 (6A 84)
Clifford St. W1 3A 12 (7G 83)
Clifford Way NW10 4B 62
Cliff Rd. NW1 6H 65
Cliffsend Ho. *SW9* *1A 120*
(off Cowley Rd.)
Cliff Ter. SE8 2C 122
Cliffview Rd. SE13 3C 122
Cliff Vs. NW1 6H 65
Cliff Wlk. E16 5H 87
Clifton Av. E17 3K 49
HA7: Stan 2B 42
HA9: Wemb 6F 61
N3 1H 45
TW13: Felt 3A 130
W12 1B 98
Clifton Cl. BR6: Farnb 5G 173
Clifton Ct. BR3: Beck 1D 158
IG8: Wfd G 6D 36
KT5: Surb 7F 151
N4 2A 66
NW8 3A 4
SE15 7H 103
TW19: Stanw 6A 110
Clifton Cres. SE15 7H 103
Clifton Est. SE15 1H 121
Clifton Gdns. EN2: Enf 4D 22
N15 6F 49
NW11 6H 45
Clifton Gdns. UB10: Hil 2D 74
W4 4K 97
(not continuous)
W9 4A 82
Clifton Ga. SW10 6A 100
Clifton Gro. E8 6G 67
Clifton Hill NW6 2K 81
NW8 2K 81
Clifton Ho. *E2* *3J 9*
(off Club Row)
E11 2G 69
Clifton M. SE25 4E 156
Clifton Pde. TW13: Felt 3A 130
Clifton Pk. Av. SW20 2E 152
Clifton Pl. SE16 2J 103
W2 1B 10 (6B 82)
Clifton Ri. SE14 7A 104
(not continuous)
Clifton Rd. DA14: Sidc 4J 143
DA16: Well 3C 126
E7 6B 70
E16 5G 87
HA3: Kent 4F 43
IG2: Ilf 6H 53
KT2: King T 7F 133
N3 1A 46
N8 6H 47
N22 1G 47
NW10 2C 80
SE25 4E 156
SM6: Wall 5F 167
SW19 6F 135
TW7: Isle 2J 113
TW11: Tedd 4J 131
UB2: S'hall 4C 94
UB6: G'frd 4G 77
W9 3A 4 (4A 82)
Clifton St. EC2 4G 9 (4E 84)
Clifton Ter. N4 2A 66
Clifton Vs. W9 5A 82
Cliftonville Ct. SE12 1J 141
Clifton Wlk. *W6* *4D 98*
(off King St.)
Clifton Way HA0: Wemb 1E 78
SE15 7H 103
TW6: H'row A 3D 110
Climsland Ho. SE1 4K 13 (1A 102)
Clinch Ct. *E16* *5J 87*
(off Plymouth Rd.)
Cline Rd. N11 6B 32
Clinger Ct. *N1* *1E 84*
(off Hobbs Pl. Est.)
Clink Exhibition, The 4E 14
Clink St. SE1 4E 14 (1D 102)
Clink Wharf *SE1* *4E 14*
(off Clink St.)
Clinton Av. DA16: Well 4A 126
KT8: E Mos 4G 149
Clinton Ho. *KT6: Surb* *7D 150*
(off Lovelace Gdns)
Clinton Rd. E3 3A 86
E7 4J 69
N15 4D 48
Clipper Cl. SE16 2K 103
Clipper Ho. *E14* *5E 104*
(off Manchester Rd.)
Clipper Way SE13 4E 122
Clippesby Cl. KT9: Chess 6F 163
Clipstone M. W1 5A 6 (5G 83)
Clipstone Rd. TW3: Houn 3E 112
Clipstone St. W1 5K 5 (5F 83)
Clissold Cl. N2 3D 46
Clissold Ct. N4 2C 66
Clissold Cres. N16 3D 66
Clissold Leisure Cen. 3D 66
Clissold Rd. N16 3D 66
Clitheroe Av. HA2: Harr 1E 58
Clitheroe Rd. SW9 2J 119
Clitherow Av. W7 3A 96
Clitherow Ct. TW8: Bford 5C 96
Clitherow Pas. TW8: Bford 5C 96
Clitherow Rd. TW8: Bford 5B 96
Clitterhouse Cres. NW2 1E 62
Clitterhouse Rd. NW2 1E 62
Clive Av. N18 6B 34
Clive Ct. W9 4A 82
Cliveden Cl. N12 4F 31
Cliveden Ho. *E16* *1J 105*
(off Fitzwilliam M.)
Cliveden Pl. SW1 3G 17 (4E 100)
TW17: Shep 6E 146
Cliveden Rd. SW19 1H 153
Clivedon Ct. W13 5B 78
Clivedon Rd. E4 5B 36
Clive Ho. *SE10* *6E 104*
(off Haddo St.)
Clive Lloyd Ho. *N15* *5C 48*
(off Woodlands Pk. Rd.)
Clive Lodge NW4 6F 45
Clive Pas. SE21 3D 138
Clive Rd. DA17: Belv 4G 109
EN1: Enf 4B 24
SE21 3D 138
SW19 6C 136
TW1: Twick 4K 131
TW14: Felt 6J 111
Clivesdale Dr. UB3: Hayes 1K 93
Clive Way EN1: Enf 4B 24
Cloak La. EC4 2D 14 (7C 84)
Clochar Ct. NW10 1B 80
Clock Ct. E11 4K 51
Clock Ho. E3 3E 86
E17 *4F 51*
(off Wood St.)
Clockhouse, The SW19 3E 134
Clockhouse Av. IG11: Bark 1G 89
Clockhouse Cl. SW19 2E 134
Clockhouse Ct. BR3: Beck 2A 158
CLOCKHOUSE JUNC. 5E 32
Clockhouse La. RM5: Col R 1H 55
TW14: Bedf 4C 128
TW15: Ashf 4C 128
Clock Ho. Pde. E11 6K 51
Clockhouse Pde. N13 5F 33
Clockhouse Pl. SW15 6G 117
Clock Ho. Rd. BR3: Beck 3A 158
CLOCKHOUSE RDBT. 1D 128
Clock Mus., The 7D 8
Clock Pde. EN2: Enf 5J 23
Clock Pl. *SE1* *4B 102*
(off Newington Butts)
Clock Twr. Ind. Est. TW7: Isle 3K 113
Clock Twr. M. N1 1C 84
SE28 7B 90
Clock Twr. Pl. N7 6J 65
Clock Twr. Rd. TW7: Isle 3K 113
Cloister Cl. TW11: Tedd 5B 132
Cloister Gdns. HA8: Edg 5D 28
SE25 6H 157
Cloister Rd. NW2 3H 63
W3 5J 79
Cloisters, The 1E 18
Cloisters, The E1 4J 9
SW9 1A 120
TW7: Isle *3A 114*
(off Pulteney Cl.)
Cloisters Av. BR2: Brom 5D 160
Cloisters Bus. Cen.
SW8 *7F 101*
(off Battersea Pk. Rd.)
Cloisters Ct. DA7: Bex 3H 127
Cloisters Mall KT1: King T 2E 150
Clonard Way HA5: H End 6A 26
Clonbrock Rd. N16 4E 66
Cloncurry St. SW6 2F 117
Clonmel Cl. HA2: Harr 2H 59
Clonmell Rd. N17 3D 48
Clonmel Rd. SW6 7H 99
TW11: Tedd 4H 131
Clonmore St. SW18 1H 135
Cloonmore Av. BR6: Chels 4K 173
Clorane Gdns. NW3 3J 63

Colehill La.—Colthurst Dr.

Colehill La. SW6 . . . . . 1G 117
Cole Ho. SE1 . . . . . 7J 13
(off Baylis Rd.)
Coleman Cl. SE25 . . . . . 2G 157
Coleman Ct. SW18 . . . . . 7J 117
Coleman Flds. N1 . . . . . 1C 84
Coleman Mans. N8 . . . . . 7J 47
Coleman Rd. DA17: Belv 4G 109
RM9: Dag 6E 72
SE5 . . . . . 7E 102
Colemans Heath SE9 . . . . . 3E 142
Coleman St. EC2 . . . . . 7E 8 (6D 84)
Coleman St. Bldgs. EC2 . . . . . 7E 8
Colenso Dr. NW7 . . . . . 7H 29
Colenso Rd. E5 . . . . . 4J 67
IG2: Ilf 1J 71
COLE PARK 6A 114
Cole Pk. Gdns. TW1: Twick 5A 114
Cole Pk. Rd. TW1: Twick 5A 114
Cole Pk. Vw. TW1: Twick 6A 114
Colepits Wood Rd. SE9 . . . . . 5H 125
Coleraine Rd. N8 . . . . . 3A 48
SE3 . . . . . 6H 105
Coleridge Av. E12 . . . . . 6C 70
SM1: Sutt 4C 166
Coleridge Cl. SW8 . . . . . 2F 119
Coleridge Ct. EN5: New Bar 5E 20
(off Station Rd.)
W14 . . . . . 3F 99
(off Blythe Rd.)
Coleridge Gdns. NW6 . . . . . 7A 64
SW10 . . . . . 7K 99
Coleridge Ho. SE17 . . . . . 5C 102
(off Browning St.)
SW1 . . . . . 6B 18
(off Churchill Gdns.)
Coleridge La. N8 . . . . . 6J 47
Coleridge Rd. CR0: Croy 7J 157
E17 . . . . . 4B 50
N4 . . . . . 2A 66
N8 . . . . . 6H 47
N12 . . . . . 5F 31
TW15: Ashf 4A 128
Coleridge Sq. SW10 . . . . . 7A 100
(off Coleridge Gdns.)
W13 . . . . . 6A 78
Coleridge Wlk. NW11 . . . . . 4J 45
Coleridge Way UB4: Hayes 6J 75
UB7: W Dray 4A 92
Cole Rd. TW1: Twick 6A 114
Colesburg Rd. BR3: Beck 3B 158
Coles Cres. HA2: Harr 2F 59
Coles Grn. WD23: Bushy 1B 26
Coles Grn. Ct. NW2 . . . . . 2C 62
Coles Grn. Rd. NW2 . . . . . 1C 62
Coleshill Flats SW1 . . . . . 4H 17
Coleshill Rd. TW11: Tedd 6J 131
Colestown St. SW11 . . . . . 2C 118
Cole St. SE1 . . . . . 7D 14 (2C 102)
Colesworth Ho. HA8: Edg 2J 43
(off Burnt Oak B'way.)
Colet Cl. N13 . . . . . 6G 33
Colet Ct. W6 . . . . . 4F 99
(off Hammersmith Rd.)
Colet Flats E1 . . . . . 6A 86
(off Troon St.)
Colet Gdns. W14 . . . . . 4F 99
Colet Ho. SE17 . . . . . 5B 102
(off Doddington Gro.)
Colette Ct. SE16 . . . . . 2K 103
(off Eleanor Cl.)
Coley St. WC1 . . . . . 4H 7 (4K 83)
Colfe & Hatcliffe Glebe SE13 . . . . . 5D 122
(off Lewisham High St.)
Colfe Rd. SE23 . . . . . 1A 140
Colham Av. UB7: Yiew 1A 92
COLHAM GREEN 5C 74
Colham Grn. Rd. UB8: Hil 5C 74
Colham Mill Rd. UB7: W Dray 2A 92
Colham Rd. UB8: Hil 4B 74
Colham Rdbt. UB8: Hil 6C 74
Colina M. N15 . . . . . 4B 48
Colina Rd. N15 . . . . . 5B 48
Colin Cl. BR4: W W'ck 3H 171
CR0: Croy 3B 170
NW9 . . . . . 4A 44
Colin Cres. NW9 . . . . . 4B 44
COLINDALE 3K 43
Colindale Av. NW9 . . . . . 3K 43
Colindale Bus. Pk. NW9 . . . . . 3J 43
Colindeep Gdns. NW4 . . . . . 4C 44
Colindeep La. NW4 . . . . . 3A 44
NW9 . . . . . 3A 44
Colin Dr. NW9 . . . . . 5B 44
Colinette Rd. SW15 . . . . . 4E 116
Colin Gdns. NW9 . . . . . 4B 44
Colin Pde. NW9 . . . . . 4A 44
Colin Pk. Rd. NW9 . . . . . 4A 44
Colin Rd. NW10 . . . . . 6C 62
Colinton Rd. IG3: Ilf 2B 72
Colin Winter Ho. E1 . . . . . 4J 85
(off Nicholas Rd.)
Coliseum Theatre 3E 12
(off St Martin's La.)
Coliston Pas. SW18 . . . . . 7J 117
Coliston Rd. SW18 . . . . . 7J 117
Collamore Av. SW18 . . . . . 1C 136
Collapit Cl. HA1: Harr 6F 41
Collard Pl. NW1 . . . . . 7F 65
Collards Almshouses E17 . . . . . 5E 50
(off Maynard Rd.)
College App. SE10 . . . . . 6E 104
College Av. HA3: Hrw W 1J 41
College Cl. E9 . . . . . 5J 67
HA3: Hrw W 7D 26
N18 . . . . . 5A 34
TW2: Twick 1H 131
College Ct. EN3: Pond E 5D 24
NW3 . . . . . 6B 64
(off College Cres.)
SW3 . . . . . 6F 17
W5 . . . . . 7E 78
W6 . . . . . 5E 98
(off Queen Caroline St.)
College Cres. NW3 . . . . . 6A 64
College Cross N1 . . . . . 7A 66
College Dr. HA4: Ruis 7J 39
KT7: T Ditt 7J 149
College E. E1 . . . . . 6K 9 (5F 85)
College Flds. Bus. Cen.
SW19: Mitc 1C 154
College Gdns. E4 . . . . . 7J 25
EN2: Enf 1J 23
IG4: Ilf 5C 52
KT3: N Mald 5B 152
N18 . . . . . 5A 34
SE21 . . . . . 1E 138
SW17 . . . . . 2C 136
(not continuous)
College Grn. SE19 . . . . . 7E 138
College Gro. NW1 . . . . . 1G 83
College Hill EC4 . . . . . 2D 14 (7C 84)
College Hill Rd. HA3: Hrw W 7D 26
College La. NW5 . . . . . 4F 65
College Mans. NW6 . . . . . 1G 81
(off Winchester Av.)
College M. N1 . . . . . 7A 66
(off College Cross, not continuous)
SW1 . . . . . 1E 18
SW18 . . . . . 5K 117
College of Arms 2C 14
College Pde. NW6 . . . . . 1G 81
COLLEGE PARK 3D 80
College Pk. Cl. SE13 . . . . . 4F 123
College Pk. Rd. N17 . . . . . 6A 34
College Pl. E17 . . . . . 4G 51
NW1 . . . . . 1G 83
SW10 . . . . . 7A 100
College Point E15 . . . . . 6H 69
College Rd. BR1: Brom 1J 159
BR8: Swan 7K 145
CR0: Croy 2D 168
College Rd. E17 . . . . . 5E 50
EN2: Enf 2J 23
HA1: Harr 6J 41
HA3: Hrw W 1J 41
HA9: Wemb 1D 60
N17 . . . . . 6A 34
N21 . . . . . 2F 33
NW10 . . . . . 2E 80
SE19 . . . . . 4F 139
SE21 . . . . . 7E 120
SW19 . . . . . 6B 136
TW7: Isle 1K 113
W13 . . . . . 6B 78
College Rdbt. KT1: King T 3E 150
College Row E9 . . . . . 5K 67
College Slip BR1: Brom 1J 159
College St. EC4 . . . . . 2D 14 (7C 84)
College Ter. E3 . . . . . 3B 86
N3 . . . . . 2H 45
College Vw. SE9 . . . . . 1B 142
College Wlk. KT1: King T 3E 150
College Way TW15: Ashf 4B 128
UB3: Hayes 7J 75
College Yd. NW5 . . . . . 4F 65
Collent St. E9 . . . . . 6J 67
Collerston Ho. SE10 . . . . . 5H 105
(off Armitage Rd.)
Colless Rd. N15 . . . . . 5F 49
Collett Rd. SE16 . . . . . 3G 103
Collett Way UB2: S'hall 2F 95
Collier Cl. E6 . . . . . 7F 89
KT19: Ewe 6G 163
Collier Dr. HA8: Edg 2G 43
COLLIER ROW 1H 55
Collier Row La. RM5: Col R 1H 55
Collier Row Rd. RM5: Col R 1F 55
Colliers Ct. CR0: Croy 4D 168
(off St Peter's Rd.)
Colliers Shaw BR2: Kes 5B 172
Collier St. N1 . . . . . 2K 83
Colliers Water La. CR7: Thor H 5A 156
COLLIERS WOOD 7B 136
COLLIERS WOOD 7B 136
Collindale Av. DA8: Erith 7H 109
DA15: Sidc 1A 144
Collingbourne Rd. W12 . . . . . 1D 98
Collingham Gdns. SW5 . . . . . 4K 99
Collingham Pl. SW5 . . . . . 4K 99
Collingham Rd. SW5 . . . . . 4K 99
Collings Cl. N22 . . . . . 6E 32
Collington St. SE10 . . . . . 5F 105
Collingtree Rd. SE26 . . . . . 4J 139
Collingwood Av. KT5: Surb 1J 163
N10 . . . . . 3E 46
Collingwood Cl. SE20 . . . . . 1H 157
TW2: Whit 7E 112
Collingwood Ct. EN5: New Bar 5E 20
W5 . . . . . 5F 79
Collingwood Ho. E1 . . . . . 4H 85
(off Darling Row)
SE16 . . . . . 2H 103
(off Cherry Gdn. St.)
SW1 . . . . . 6C 18
(off Dolphin Sq.)
W1 . . . . . 5A 6
(off Clipstone St.)
Collingwood Rd. CR4: Mitc 3C 154
E17 . . . . . 6C 50
N15 . . . . . 4E 48
SM1: Sutt 3J 165
UB8: Hil 4D 74
Collingwood St. E1 . . . . . 4H 85
Collins Av. HA7: Stan 2E 42
Collins Ct. E8 . . . . . 6G 67
Collins Dr. HA4: Ruis 2A 58
Collins Ho. E14 . . . . . 7E 86
(off Newby Pl.)
E15 . . . . . 1H 87
(off John St.)
SE10 . . . . . 5H 105
(off Armitage Rd.)
Collinson Ct. SE1 . . . . . 7C 14
(off Gt. Suffolk St.)
Collinson Ho. SE15 . . . . . 7G 103
(off Peckham Pk. Rd.)
Collinson St. SE1 . . . . . 7C 14 (2C 102)
Collinson Wlk.
SE1 . . . . . 7C 14 (2C 102)
Collins Path TW12: Hamp 6D 130
Collins Rd. N5 . . . . . 4C 66
Collins Sq. SE3 . . . . . 2H 123
Collins St. SE3 . . . . . 2G 123
(not continuous)
Collin's Yd. N1 . . . . . 1B 84
Collinwood Av. EN3: Enf H 3D 24
Collinwood Gdns. IG5: Ilf 5D 52
Collis All. TW2: Twick 1J 131
Collison Pl. N16 . . . . . 1E 66
Coll's Rd. SE15 . . . . . 1J 121
Collyer Av. CR0: Bedd 4J 167
Collyer Pl. SE15 . . . . . 1G 121
Collyer Rd. CR0: Bedd 4J 167
Colman Ct. HA7: Stan 6G 27
N12 . . . . . 6F 31
Colman Pde. EN1: Enf 3K 23
Colman Rd. E16 . . . . . 5A 88
Colmans Wharf E14 . . . . . 5D 86
(off Morris Rd.)
Colmar Cl. E1 . . . . . 4K 85
Colmer Pl. HA3: Hrw W 7C 26
Colmer Rd. SW16 . . . . . 1J 155
Colmore M. SE15 . . . . . 1H 121
Colmore Rd. EN3: Pond E 4D 24
Colnbrook St. SE1 . . . . . 3B 102
Colne Ct. KT19: Ewe 4J 163
W7 . . . . . 6H 77
(off High La.)
Colnedale Rd. UB8: Uxb 5A 56
Colne Ho. IG11: Bark 7F 71
Colne Rd. E5 . . . . . 4A 68
N21 . . . . . 7J 23
TW1: Twick 1K 131
TW2: Twick 1J 131
Colne St. E13 . . . . . 3J 87
COLNEY HATCH 6J 31
Colney Hatch La. N10 . . . . . 6J 31
N11 . . . . . 6J 31
Cologne Rd. SW11 . . . . . 4B 118
Colombo Rd. IG1: Ilf 1G 71
Colombo St. SE1 . . . . . 5A 14 (1B 102)
Colombo Street Sports Cen. &
Community Cen. 5A 14
(off Colombo St.)
Colomb St. SE10 . . . . . 5G 105
Colonel's Wlk. EN2: Enf 3G 23
Colonial Av. TW2: Whit 6G 113
Colonial Ct. N7 . . . . . 3K 65
Colonial Dr. W4 . . . . . 4J 97
Colonial Rd. TW14: Felt 7G 111
Colonnade WC1 . . . . . 4F 7 (4J 83)
Colonnade, The SE8 . . . . . 4B 104
Colonnades, The CR0: Wadd 6A 168
W2 . . . . . 6K 81
Colonnade Wlk. SW1 . . . . . 4J 17 (4F 101)
Colosseum Ter. NW1 . . . . . 2K 5
Colour Ct. SW1 . . . . . 5B 12
Colour House Theatre 1A 154
Colroy Ct. NW11 . . . . . 5G 45
Colson Rd. CR0: Croy 2E 168
Colson Way SW16 . . . . . 4G 137
Colstead Ho. E1 . . . . . 6H 85
(off Watney Mkt.)
Colsterworth Rd.
N15 . . . . . 4F 49
(not continuous)
Colston Av. SM5: Cars 4C 166
Colston Ct. SM5: Cars 4D 166
(off West St.)
Colston Rd. E7 . . . . . 6B 70
SW14 . . . . . 4J 115
Colthurst Cres. N4 . . . . . 2B 66
Colthurst Dr. N9 . . . . . 3C 34

Court St.—Cranley Gardens

Court St. BR1: Brom 2J 159
E1 5H 85
Courtville Ho. *W10* *3G 81*
(off Third Av.)
Court Way IG6: Ilf 3G 53
IG8: Wfd G 5F 37
NW9 4A 44
TW2: Twick 7K 113
W3 5J 79
Court Wood La. CR0: Sels 7B 170
Court Yd. SE9 6D 124
Courtyard, The BR2: Kes 6C 172
E3 2C 86
EC3 *1F 15*
(in Royal Exchange)
N1 7K 65
NW1 7E 64
Courtyard Theatre, The 1F 7
(off York Way)
Cousin La. EC4 3E 14 (7D 84)
Cousins Cl. UB7: Yiew 7A 74
Couthurst Rd. SE3 6K 105
Coutts Av. KT9: Chess 5E 162
Coutt's Cres. NW5 3E 64
Couzens Ho. *E3* *5B 86*
(off Weatherley Cl.)
Coval Gdns. SW14 4H 115
Coval La. SW14 4H 115
Coval Pas. SW14 4J 115
Coval Rd. SW14 4H 115
Covelees Wall E6 6E 88
Covell Ct. *EN2: Enf* *1E 22*
(off Ridgeway, The)
SE8 7C 104
COVENT GARDEN 2F 13 (7J 83)
Covent Garden 2F 13 (7J 83)
Covent Gdn. WC2 2F 13 (7J 83)
Coventry Cl. E6 6D 88
NW6 2J 81
Coventry Cross E3 4E 86
Coventry Hall SW16 5J 137
Coventry Rd. E1 4H 85
IG1: Ilf 2F 71
SE25 4G 157
Coventry St. W1 3C 12 (7H 83)
Coverack Cl. CR0: Croy 7A 158
N14 6B 22
Coverdale Cl. HA7: Stan 5G 27
Coverdale Gdns. CR0: Croy 3F 169
Coverdale Rd. N11 6K 31
NW2 7F 63
W12 2D 98
Coverdales, The IG11: Bark 2H 89
Coverley Cl. E1 5G 85
Coverley Point SE11 4G 19
Covert, The BR6: Pet W 6J 161
HA6: Nwood 1E 38
SE19 *7F 139*
(off Fox Hill)
Coverton Rd. SW17 5C 136
Covert Way EN4: Had W 2F 21
Covet Wood Cl. BR5: St M Cry 6K 161
Covey Cl. SW19 2K 153
Covington Gdns. SW16 7B 138
Covington Way SW16 6K 137
(not continuous)
Cowan Cl. E6 5C 88
Cowan Ct. NW10 7K 61
Cowbridge La. IG11: Bark 7F 71
Cowbridge Rd. HA3: Kent 4F 43
Cowcross St. EC1 5A 8 (5B 84)
Cowdenbeath Path N1 1K 83
Cowden Rd. BR6: Orp 7K 161
Cowden St. SE6 4C 140
Cowdray Rd. UB10: Hil 1E 74
Cowdrey Cl. EN1: Enf 2K 23
Cowdrey Rd. SW19 5K 135
Cowen Av. HA2: Harr 2H 59
Cowgate Rd. UB6: G'frd 3H 77
Cowick Rd. SW17 4D 136
Cowings Mead UB5: N'olt 6C 58
Cowland Av. EN3: Pond E 4D 24
Cow La. UB6: G'frd 2H 77
Cow Leaze E6 6E 88
Cowleaze Rd. KT2: King T 1E 150
COWLEY 4A 74
Cowley La. E11 3G 69
COWLEY PEACHEY 6A 74
Cowley Pl. NW4 5E 44
Cowley Rd. E11 5K 51
IG1: Ilf 7D 52
SW9 1A 120
(not continuous)
SW14 3A 116
W3 1B 98
Cowley St. SW1 1E 18 (3J 101)
Cowling Cl. W11 1G 99
Cowper Av. E6 7C 70
SM1: Sutt 4B 166
Cowper Cl. BR2: Brom 4B 160
DA16: Well 5A 126
Cowper Gdns. N14 6A 22
SM6: Wall 6G 167
Cowper Ho. *SE17* *5C 102*
(off Browning St.)
SW1 *6C 18*
(off Aylesford St.)
Cowper Rd. BR2: Brom 4B 160
DA17: Belv 4G 109
KT2: King T 5F 133
N14 1A 32
N16 5E 66
N18 5B 34
SW19 6A 136
W3 1K 97
W7 7K 77
Cowper's Ct. *EC3* *1F 15*
(off Birchin La.)
Cowper St. EC2 3F 9 (4D 84)
Cowper Ter. W10 5F 81
Cowslip Cl. UB10: Uxb 7A 56
Cowslip Rd. E18 2K 51
Cowthorpe Rd. SW8 1H 119
Cox Ct. EN4: E Barn 4H 21
Coxe Pl. HA3: W'stone 4A 42
Cox Ho. *W6* *6G 99*
(off Field Rd.)
Cox La. KT9: Chess 4F 163
KT19: Ewe 5H 163
(not continuous)
Coxmount Rd. SE7 5B 106
Coxs Av. TW17: Shep 3G 147
Cox's Ct. E1 6J 9
Coxson Way SE1 7J 15 (2F 103)
Cox's Wlk. SE21 1G 139
Coxwell Rd. SE18 5H 107
SE19 7E 138
Coxwold Path KT9: Chess 7E 162
Crabbs Cft. Cl. BR6: Farnb 5G 173
Crab Hill BR3: Beck 7F 141
Crabtree Av. HA0: Wemb 2E 78
RM6: Chad H 4D 54
Crabtree Cl. E2 2F 85
Crabtree Ct. E15 5D 68
EN5: New Bar 4E 20
Crabtree La. SW6 7E 98
(not continuous)
Crabtree Manorway Nth.
DA17: Belv, Erith 2J 109
Crabtree Manorway Sth.
DA17: Belv 3J 109
Crabtree Wlk. CR0: Croy 1G 169
SE15 *1F 121*
(off Peckham Rd.)
Crace St. NW1 1C 6 (3H 83)
Craddock Rd. EN1: Enf 3A 24
Craddock St. NW5 6E 64
Cradley Rd. SE9 1H 143
Crafts Council & Gallery 2A 84
Cragie Ho. *SE1* *4F 103*
(off Balaclava Rd.)
Craig Dr. UB8: Hil 6D 74
Craigen Av. CR0: Croy 1H 169
Craigerne Rd. SE3 7K 105
Craig Gdns. E18 2H 51
Craigholm SE18 2E 124
Craigmore Ct. HA6: Nwood 1G 39
Craigmuir Pk. HA0: Wemb 1F 79
Craignair Rd. SW2 7A 120
Craignish Av. SW16 2K 155
Craig Pk. Rd. N18 4C 34
Craig Rd. TW10: Ham 4C 132
Craig's Ct. SW1 4E 12 (1J 101)
Craigton Rd. SE9 4D 124
Craigweil Cl. HA7: Stan 5J 27
Craigweil Dr. HA7: Stan 5J 27
Craigwell Av. TW13: Felt 3J 129
Craik Ct. *NW6* *2H 81*
(off Carlton Va.)
Crail Row SE17 4D 102
Crales Ho. SE18 3C 106
Cramer St. W1 6H 5 (5E 82)
Crammond Cl. W6 6G 99
Cramond Ct. TW14: Bedf 1G 129
Cramonde Ct. DA16: Well 2A 126
Crampton Ho. SW8 1G 119
Crampton Rd. SE20 6J 139
Crampton St. SE17 4C 102
Cranberry Cl. UB5: N'olt 2B 76
Cranberry La. E16 4G 87
Cranborne Av. KT6: Surb 3G 163
UB2: S'hall 4E 94
Cranborne Rd. IG11: Bark 1H 89
Cranborne Waye UB4: Yead 6K 75
(not continuous)
Cranbourn All. *WC2* *2D 12*
(off Cranbourn St.)
Cranbourne Av. E11 4K 51
Cranbourne Cl. SW16 3J 155
Cranbourne Dr. HA5: Pinn 5B 40
Cranbourne Gdns. IG6: Ilf 3G 53
NW11 5G 45
Cranbourne Pas. SE16 2H 103
Cranbourne Rd. E12 5C 70
E15 4E 68
HA6: Nwood 3H 39
N10 2F 47
Cranbourn Ho. *SE16* *2H 103*
(off Marigold St.)
Cranbourn St. WC2 2D 12 (7H 83)
CRANBROOK 1D 70
Cranbrook *NW1* *1G 83*
(off Camden St.)
Cranbrook Cl. BR2: Hayes 6J 159
Cranbrook Ct. TW8: Bford 6C 96
Cranbrook Dr. KT10: Esh 7G 149
TW2: Whit 1F 131
Cranbrook Est. E2 2K 85
Cranbrook La. N11 4A 32
Cranbrook M. E17 5B 50
Cranbrook Pk. N22 1A 48
Cranbrook Ri. IG1: Ilf 6D 52
Cranbrook Rd. CR7: Thor H 2C 156
DA7: Bex 1F 127
EN4: E Barn 6G 21
IG1: Ilf 7E 52
IG2: Ilf 5E 52
IG6: Ilf 5E 52
SE8 1C 122
SW19 7G 135
TW4: Houn 4D 112
W4 5A 98
Cranbrook St. E2 2K 85
Cranbury Rd. SW6 2K 117
Crandley Ct. SE8 4A 104
Crane Av. TW7: Isle 5A 114
W3 7J 79
Cranebank M. TW1: Twick 4A 114
Cranebrook TW2: Twick 2G 131
Crane Cl. HA2: Harr 3G 59
RM10: Dag 6G 73
Crane Ct. EC4 6A 84
KT19: Ewe 4J 163
Craneford Cl. TW2: Twick 7K 113
Craneford Way TW2: Twick 7J 113
Crane Gdns. UB3: Harl 4H 93
Crane Gro. N7 6A 66
Crane Ho. *E3* *2A 86*
(off Roman Rd.)
SE15 1F 121
TW13: Hanw 3E 130
Crane Lodge Rd. TW5: Cran 6K 93
Crane Mead SE16 4K 103
(not continuous)
Crane Mead Ct. TW1: Twick 7K 113
Crane Pk. Island Nature Reserve 2D 130
Crane Pk. Rd. TW2: Whit 2F 131
Crane Rd. TW2: Twick 1J 131
TW19: Stanw 6C 110
Cranesbill Cl. NW9 3K 43
Cranes Dr. KT5: Surb 4E 150
Cranes Pk. KT5: Surb 4E 150
Cranes Pk. Av. KT5: Surb 4E 150
Cranes Pk. Cres. KT5: Surb 4F 151
Crane St. SE10 5F 105
SE15 1F 121
Craneswater UB3: Harl 7H 93
Craneswater Pk. UB2: S'hall 5D 94
Crane Way TW2: Whit 7G 113
Cranfield Cl. SE27 3C 138
Cranfield Ct. W1 6D 4
Cranfield Dr. NW9 7F 29
Cranfield Ho. WC1 5E 6
Cranfield Rd. SE4 3B 122
Cranfield Rd. E. SM5: Cars 7E 166
Cranfield Rd. W. SM5: Cars 7D 166
Cranfield Row SE1 1K 19
CRANFORD 1J 111
Cranford Av. N13 5D 32
TW19: Stanw 7A 110
Cranford Cl. SW20 7D 134
TW19: Stanw 7A 110
Cranford Community College Sports Cen. 6K 93
Cranford Cotts. *E1* *7K 85*
(off Cranford St.)
Cranford Dr. UB3: Harl 4H 93
Cranford La. TW5: Cran, Hest 7K 93
TW6: Cran 6F 93
TW6: H'row A 1H 111
(Bath Rd.)
TW6: H'row A 3H 111
(Elmdon Rd.)
UB3: Harl 6F 93
Cranford Pk. Rd. UB3: Harl 4H 93
Cranford St. E1 7K 85
Cranford Way N8 4K 47
Cranhurst Rd. NW2 5E 62
Cranleigh Cl. BR6: Chels 3K 173
DA5: Bex 6H 127
SE20 2H 157
Cranleigh Ct. CR4: Mitc 3B 154
TW9: Rich 3G 115
UB1: S'hall 6D 76
Cranleigh Gdns. HA3: Kent 5E 42
IG11: Bark 7H 71
KT2: King T 6F 133
N21 5F 23
SE25 3E 156
SM1: Sutt 2K 165
UB1: S'hall 6D 76
Cranleigh Gdns. Ind. Est.
UB1: S'hall 5D 76
Cranleigh Ho's. *NW1* *2G 83*
(off Cranleigh St.)
Cranleigh M. SW11 2C 118
Cranleigh Rd. N15 5C 48
SW19 3J 153
TW13: Felt 4H 129
Cranleigh St. NW1 2G 83
Cranley Dene Ct. N10 4F 47
Cranley Dr. HA4: Ruis 2H 57
IG2: Ilf 7G 53
CRANLEY GARDENS 4F 47

Culross Bldgs.—Dagonet Gdns.

Culross Bldgs. *NW1* 2J 83
(off Battle Bri. Rd.)
Culross Cl. N15 4C 48
Culross Ho. *W10* 6F 81
(off Bridge Cl.)
Culross St. W1 3G 11 (7E 82)
Culsac Rd. KT6: Surb 2E 162
Culverden Rd. SW12 2G 137
Culver Gro. HA7: Stan 2C 42
Culverhouse *WC1* 6G 7
(off Red Lion Sq.)
Culverhouse Gdns.
SW16 3K 137
Culverlands Cl. HA7: Stan 4G 27
Culverley Rd. SE6 1D 140
Culvers Av. SM5: Cars 2D 166
Culvers Retreat SM5: Cars 1D 166
Culverstone Cl. BR2: Brom 6H 159
Culvers Way SM5: Cars 2D 166
Culvert Pl. SW11 2E 118
Culvert Rd. N15 5E 48
SW11 2D 118
Culworth Ho. *NW8* 2C 82
(off Allitsen Rd.)
Culworth St. NW8 2C 82
Culzean Cl. SE27 3B 138
Cumberland Av. DA16: Well 3J 125
NW10 3H 79
Cumberland Bus. Pk. NW10 3H 79
Cumberland Cl. E8 6F 67
IG6: Ilf 1G 53
SW20 7F 135
TW1: Twick 6B 114
Cumberland Ct. CR0: Croy 1D 168
DA16: Well 2J 125
HA1: Harr 3J 41
(off Princes Dr.)
SW1 5K 17
(off Cumberland St.)
Cumberland Cres. W14 4G 99
(not continuous)
Cumberland Dr. DA7: Bex 7E 108
KT9: Chess 3E 162
KT10: Hin W 2A 162
Cumberland Gdns. NW4 2G 45
WC1 1J 7 (3A 84)
Cumberland Ga. W1 2E 10 (7D 82)
Cumberland Ho. *E16* 1J 105
(off Wesley Av.)
KT2: King T 7H 133
N9 1D 34
(off Cumberland Rd.)
SE28 2G 107
(off Erebus Dr.)
Cumberland Mans. W1 7E 4
Cumberland Mkt. NW1 1K 5 (3F 83)
Cumberland Mills Sq. E14 5F 105
Cumberland Pk. W3 7J 79
Cumberland Pk. Ind. Est.
NW10 3C 80
Cumberland Pl. NW1 1J 5 (3F 83)
SE6 1H 141
TW16: Sun 4J 147
Cumberland Rd. BR2: Brom 4G 159
E12 4B 70
E13 5K 87
E17 2A 50
HA1: Harr 5F 41
HA7: Stan 3F 43
N9 1D 34
N22 2K 47
SE25 6H 157
SW13 1B 116
TW9: Kew 7G 97
TW15: Ashf 3A 128
W3 7J 79
W7 2K 95
Cumberland St. SW1 5K 17 (5F 101)
Cumberland Ter. NW1 1J 5 (2F 83)
Cumberland Ter. M. NW1 1J 5
(not continuous)
Cumberland Vs. *W3* 7J 79
(off Cumberland Rd.)
Cumberlow Av. SE25 3F 157
Cumbernauld Gdns.
TW16: Sun 5H 129
Cumberton Rd. N17 1D 48
Cumbrae Gdns. KT6: Surb 2D 162
Cumbrian Gdns. NW2 2F 63
Cumbrian Way UB8: Uxb 7A 56
Cuming Mus. 4C 102
(off Walworth Rd.)
Cumming St. N1 1H 7 (2K 83)
Cumnor Cl. *SW9* 2K 119
(off Robsart St.)
Cumnor Gdns. KT17: Ewe 6C 164
Cumnor Rd. SM2: Sutt 6A 166
Cunard Cres. N21 6J 23
Cunard Pl. EC3 1H 15 (6E 84)
Cunard Rd. NW10 3K 79
Cunard Wlk. SE16 4K 103
Cundy Rd. E16 6A 88
Cundy St. SW1 4H 17 (4E 100)
Cunliffe Pde. KT19: Ewe 4B 164
Cunliffe Rd. KT19: Ewe 4B 164
Cunliffe St. SW16 6G 137
Cunningham Cl. BR4: W W'ck 2D 170
RM6: Chad H 5C 54
Cunningham Ho. *SE5* 7D 102
(off Elmington Est.)
Cunningham Pk. HA1: Harr 5G 41
Cunningham Pl. NW8 3A 4 (4B 82)
Cunningham Rd. N15 4G 49
Cunnington St. W4 3J 97
Cupar Rd. SW11 1E 118
Cupola Cl. BR1: Brom 5K 141
Cureton St. SW1 4D 18 (4H 101)
Curfew Ho. IG11: Bark 1G 89
Curie Ct. HA1: Harr 7B 42
Curie Gdns. NW9 2A 44
Curlew Cl. SE28 7D 90
Curlew Ct. KT6: Surb 3G 163
W13 4K 77
Curlew Ho. EN3: Pond E 5E 24
SE4 4A 122
(off St Norbert Rd.)
SE15 1F 121
Curlew St. SE1 6K 15 (2F 103)
Curlew Way UB4: Yead 5B 76
Curness St. SE13 4E 122
Curnick's La. SE27 4C 138
Curran Av. DA15: Sidc 5K 125
SM6: Wall 3E 166
Curran Ho. *SW3* 4C 16
(off Lucan Pl.)
Currey Rd. UB6: G'frd 6H 59
Curricle St. W3 1A 98
Currie Hill Cl. SW19 4H 135
Currie Ho. *E14* 6F 87
(off Abbott Rd.)
Curry Ri. NW7 6A 30
Cursitor St. EC4 7J 7 (6A 84)
Curtain Pl. EC2 3H 9 (3E 84)
Curtain Rd. EC2 2H 9 (4E 84)
Curthwaite Gdns. EN2: Enf 4C 22
Curtis Dr. W3 6K 79
Curtis Fld. Rd. SW16 4K 137
Curtis Ho. *N11* 5B 32
(off Ladderswood Way)
SE17 5D 102
(off Morecambe St.)
Curtis La. HA0: Wemb 5E 60
Curtis Rd. KT19: Ewe 4J 163
TW4: Houn 7D 112
Curtis St. SE1 4F 103
Curtis Way SE1 4F 103
SE28 7B 90
Curtlington Ho. *HA8: Edg* 2J 43
(off Burnt Oak B'way.)
Curve, The W12 7C 80
Curwen Av. E7 4K 69
Curwen Rd. W12 2C 98
Curzon Av. EN3: Pond E 5E 24
HA7: Stan 1A 42
Curzon Cinema
Mayfair 5J 11
(off Curzon St.)
Soho 2D 12
(off Shaftesbury Av.)
Curzon Cl. BR6: Orp 4H 173
Curzon Ct. *SW6* 1A 118
(off Imperial Rd.)
Curzon Cres. IG11: Bark 2K 89
NW10 7A 62
Curzon Ga. W1 5H 11 (1E 100)
Curzon Pl. HA5: Eastc 5A 40
Curzon Rd. CR7: Thor H 6A 156
N10 2F 47
W5 4B 78
Curzon Sq. W1 5H 11 (1E 100)
Curzon St. W1 5H 11 (1E 100)
Cusack Cl. TW1: Twick 4K 131
Custance Ho. *N1* 1E 8
(off Fairbank Est.)
Custance St. N1 1E 8 (3D 84)
CUSTOM HOUSE 6A 88
Custom House 3G 15 (7E 84)
Custom Ho. Reach SE16 2B 104
Custom Ho. Wlk. EC3 3G 15 (7E 84)
Cut, The SE1 6K 13 (2A 102)
Cutbush Ho. N7 5H 65
Cutcombe Rd. SE5 2C 120
Cuthberga Cl. IG11: Bark 7G 71
Cuthbert Gdns. SE25 3E 156
Cuthbert Harrowing Ho. *EC1* 4C 8
(off Golden La. Est.)
Cuthbert Ho. *W2* 5A 4
(off Hall Pl.)
Cuthbert Rd. CR0: Croy 2B 168
E17 3E 50
N18 5B 34
Cuthbert St. W2 5A 4 (5B 82)
Cuthill Wlk. SE5 1D 120
Cutlers Gdns. EC2 6H 9
Cutlers Sq. E14 4C 104
Cutler St. E1 7H 9 (6E 84)
Cutthroat All. TW10: Ham 2C 132
Cutty Sark 6E 104
Cutty Sark Gdns. *SE10* 6E 104
(off King William Wlk.)
Cuxton BR5: Pet W 5G 161
Cuxton Cl. DA6: Bex 5E 126
Cyclamen Cl. TW12: Hamp 6E 130
Cyclamen Way KT19: Ewe 5J 163
Cyclops M. E14 4C 104
Cygnet Av. TW14: Felt 7A 112
Cygnet Cl. NW10 5K 61
Cygnet Ho. SW18 3A 118
Cygnet Ho. Nth. *E14* 6D 86
(off Chrisp St.)
Cygnet Ho. Sth. *E14* 6D 86
(off Chrisp St.)
Cygnets, The TW13: Hanw 4C 130
Cygnet St. E1 3K 9 (4F 85)
Cygnet Way UB4: Yead 5B 76
Cygnus Bus. Cen. NW10 5B 62
Cymbeline Ct. *HA1: Harr* 6K 41
(off Gayton Rd.)
Cynthia St. N1 1H 7 (2K 83)
Cyntra Pl. E8 7H 67
Cypress Av. TW2: Whit 7G 113
Cypress Ct. SM1: Sutt 5J 165
Cypress Gdns. SE4 5A 122
Cypress Ho. SE14 1K 121
SE16 2K 103
(off Woodland Cres.)
Cypress Pl. W1 4B 6 (4G 83)
Cypress Rd. HA3: Hrw W 2H 41
SE25 2E 156
Cypress Tree Cl. DA15: Sidc 1K 143
CYPRUS 7E 88
Cyprus Av. N3 2G 45
Cyprus Cl. N4 6B 48
Cyprus Gdns. N3 2G 45
Cyprus Pl. E2 2J 85
E6 7E 88
Cyprus Rd. N3 2H 45
N9 2A 34
Cyprus St. E2 2J 85
(not continuous)
Cyrena Rd. SE22 6F 121
Cyril Lodge DA14: Sidc 4A 144
Cyril Mans. SW11 1D 118
Cyril Rd. BR6: Orp 7K 161
DA7: Bex 2E 126
Cyrus Ho. EC1 3B 8
Cyrus St. EC1 3B 8
Czar St. SE8 6C 104

D

Dabbs Hill La. UB5: N'olt 6D 58
(not continuous)
Dabbs La. *EC1* 4K 7
(off Farringdon Rd.)
Dabin Cres. SE10 1E 122
Dacca St. SE8 6B 104
Dace Rd. E3 1C 86
Dacre Av. IG5: Ilf 2E 52
Dacre Cl. UB6: G'frd 2F 77
Dacre Gdns. SE13 4G 123
Dacre Ho. SW3 7B 16
Dacre Pk. SE13 3G 123
Dacre Pl. SE13 3G 123
Dacre Rd. CR0: Croy 7J 155
E11 1H 69
E13 1K 87
Dacres Est. SE23 3K 139
Dacres Ho. SW4 3F 119
Dacres Rd. SE23 2K 139
Dacre St. SW1 1C 18 (3H 101)
Dade Way UB2: S'hall 5D 94
Daerwood Cl. BR2: Brom 1D 172
Daffodil Cl. CR0: Croy 1K 169
Daffodil Gdns. IG1: Ilf 5F 71
Daffodil Pl. TW12: Hamp 6E 130
Daffodil St. W12 7B 80
Dafforne Rd. SW17 3E 136
Da Gama Pl. E14 5C 104
DAGENHAM 6G 73
Dagenham & Redbridge FC 5H 73
Dagenham Av. RM9: Dag 1E 90
(not continuous)
Dagenham Leisure Pk.
RM9: Dag 1E 90
Dagenham Rd. E10 1B 68
RM7: Rush G 7K 55
RM10: Dag, Rush G 4J 73
RM13: Rain 7K 73
Dagenham Swimming Pool 2G 73
Dagmar Av. HA9: Wemb 4F 61
Dagmar Ct. E14 3E 104
Dagmar Gdns. NW10 2F 81
Dagmar M. *UB2: S'hall* 3C 94
(off Dagmar Rd.)
Dagmar Pas. *N1* 1B 84
(off Cross St.)
Dagmar Rd. KT2: King T 1F 151
N4 7A 48
N15 4D 48
N22 1H 47
RM10: Dag 7J 73
SE5 1E 120
SE25 5E 156
UB2: S'hall 3C 94
Dagmar Ter. N1 1B 84
Dagnall Pk. SE25 6E 156
Dagnall Rd. SE25 5E 156
Dagnall St. SW11 2D 118
Dagnan Rd. SW12 7F 119
Dagobert Ho. *E1* 5J 85
(off Smithy St.)
Dagonet Gdns. BR1: Brom 3J 141

Dagonet Rd.—Darnaway Pl.

Dagonet Rd. BR1: Brom 3J **141**
Dahlia Gdns. CR4: Mitc 4H **155**
IG1: Ilf 6F **71**
Dahlia Rd. SE2 4B **108**
Dahomey Rd. SW16 6G **137**
Daimler Way SM6: Wall 7J **167**
Dain Ct. *W8* *4J 99*
(off Lexham Gdns.)
Daines Cl. E12 3D **70**
Dainford Cl. BR1: Brom 5F **141**
Dainton Cl. BR1: Brom 1K **159**
Daintry Cl. HA3: W'stone 4A **42**
Daintry Way E9 6B **68**
Dairsie Ct. BR1: Brom 1A **160**
Dairsie Rd. SE9 3E **124**
Dairy Cl. BR1: Brom 7K **141**
CR7: Thor H 2C **156**
NW10 1C **80**
Dairy La. SE18 4D **106**
Dairyman Cl. NW2 3F **63**
Dairy M. SW9 3J **119**
Dairy Wlk. SW19 4G **135**
Daisy Cl. CR0: Croy 1K **169**
Daisy Dobbings Wlk. *N19* *7J 47*
(off Jessie Blythe La.)
Daisy La. SW6 3J **117**
Daisy Rd. E16 4G **87**
E18 2K **51**
Dakin Pl. E1 5A **86**
Dakota Cl. SM6: Wall 7K **167**
Dakota Gdns. E6 4C **88**
UB5: N'olt 3C **76**
Dalberg Rd. SW2 4A **120**
(not continuous)
Dalberg Way SE2 3D **108**
Dalby Rd. SW18 4A **118**
Dalbys Cres. N17 6K **33**
Dalby St. NW5 6F **65**
Dalcross Rd. TW4: Houn 2C **112**
Dale, The BR2: Kes 4B **172**
Dale Av. HA8: Edg 1F **43**
TW4: Houn 3C **112**
Dalebury Rd. SW17 2D **136**
Dale Cl. EN5: New Bar 6E **20**
HA5: Pinn 1K **39**
SE3 3J **123**
Dale Ct. EN2: Enf 1H **23**
KT2: King T *7F 133*
(off York Rd.)
Dale Dr. UB4: Hayes 4H **75**
Dalefield *IG9: Buck H* *1F 37*
(off Roebuck La.)
Dale Gdns. IG8: Wfd G 4E **36**
Dale Grn. Rd. N11 3A **32**
Dale Gro. N12 5F **31**
Daleham Dr. UB8: Hil 6D **74**
Daleham Gdns. NW3 5B **64**
Daleham M. NW3 6B **64**
Dalehead *NW1* *1A 6*
(off Hampstead Rd.)
Dale Ho. *NW8* *1A 82*
(off Boundary Rd.)
SE4 4A **122**
Dale Lodge N6 6G **47**
Dalemain M. E16 1J **105**
Dale Pk. Av. SM5: Cars 2D **166**
Dale Pk. Rd. SE19 1C **156**
Dale Rd. KT12: Walt T 7H **147**
NW5 5E **64**
SE17 6B **102**
SM1: Sutt 4H **165**
TW16: Sun 7H **129**
UB6: G'frd 5F **77**
Dale Row W11 6G **81**
Daleside Rd. KT19: Ewe 6K **163**
SW16 5F **137**
Dale St. W4 5A **98**
Dale Vw. Av. E4 2K **35**
Dale Vw. Cres. E4 2K **35**
Dale Vw. Gdns. E4 3A **36**
Daleview Rd. N15 6E **48**
Dalewood Gdns. KT4: Wor Pk 2D **164**
Dale Wood Rd. BR6: Orp 7J **161**
Daley Ho. W12 6D **80**
Daley St. E9 6K **67**
Daley Thompson Way SW8 2F **119**
Dalgarno Gdns. W10 5E **80**
Dalgarno Way W10 4E **80**
Dalgleish St. E14 6A **86**
Daling Way E3 1A **86**
Dali Universe 6G 13 (2K 101)
Dalkeith Ct. *SW1* *3D 18*
(off Vincent St.)
Dalkeith Gro. HA7: Stan 5J **27**
Dalkeith Ho. *SW9* *1B 120*
(off Lothian Rd.)
Dalkeith Rd. IG1: Ilf 3G **71**
SE21 1C **138**
Dallas Rd. NW4 7C **44**
SE26 3H **139**
SM3: Cheam 6G **165**
W5 5F **79**
Dallas Ter. UB3: Harl 3H **93**
Dallega Cl. UB3: Hayes 7F **75**
Dallinger Rd. SE12 6H **123**
Dalling Rd. W6 4D **98**
Dallington Sq. *EC1* *3B 8*
(off Berry St.)
Dallington St. EC1 3B **8** (4B **84**)
Dallin Rd. DA6: Bex 4D **126**
SE18 7F **107**
Dalmain Rd. SE23 1K **139**
Dalmally Rd. CR0: Croy 7F **157**
Dalmany Pas. CR0: Croy 7F **157**
Dalmeny Av. N7 4H **65**
SW16 2A **156**
Dalmeny Cl. HA0: Wemb 6C **60**
Dalmeny Cres. TW3: Houn 4H **113**
Dalmeny Rd. DA8: Erith 1H **127**
EN5: New Bar 6F **21**
KT4: Wor Pk 3D **164**
N7 3H **65**
(not continuous)
SM5: Cars 7E **166**
Dalmeyer Rd. NW10 6B **62**
Dalmore Rd. SE21 2C **138**
Dalo Lodge *E3* *5C 86*
(off Gale St.)
Dalrymple Cl. N14 7C **22**
Dalrymple Rd. SE4 4A **122**
DALSTON 6F **67**
Dalston Gdns. HA7: Stan 1E **42**
Dalston La. E8 6F **67**
Dalton Av. CR4: Mitc 2C **154**
Dalton Cl. BR6: Orp 3J **173**
UB4: Hayes 4F **75**
Dalton Ho. HA7: Stan 5F **27**
SE14 *6K 103*
(off John Williams Cl.)
SW1 *5J 17*
(off Ebury Bri. Rd.)
Dalton Rd. HA3: W'stone 2H **41**
Dalton St. SE27 2B **138**
Dalwood St. SE5 1E **120**
Daly Ct. E15 5D **68**
Dalyell Rd. SW9 3K **119**
Damascene Wlk. SE21 1C **138**
Damask Ct. SM1: Sutt 1K **165**
Damask Cres. E16 4G **87**
Damer Ter. SW10 7A **100**
Dames Rd. E7 3J **69**
Dame St. N1 2C **84**
Damien Ct. *E1* *6H 85*
(off Damien St.)
Damien St. E1 6H **85**
Damon Cl. DA14: Sidc 3B **144**
Damory Ho. *SE16* *4H 103*
(off Abbeyfield Est.)
Damson Dr. UB3: Hayes 7J **75**
Damsonwood Rd. UB2: S'hall 3E **94**
Danbrook Rd. SW16 1J **155**
Danbury Cl. RM6: Chad H 3D **54**
Danbury Mans. *IG11: Bark* *7F 71*
(off Whiting Av.)
Danbury M. SM6: Wall 4F **167**
Danbury St. N1 2B **84**
Danbury Way IG8: Wfd G 6F **37**
Danby Ct. *EN2: Enf* *3H 23*
(off Horseshoe La.)
Danby Ho. *E9* *7J 67*
(off Frampton Pk. Rd.)
Danby St. SE15 3F **121**
Dancer Rd. SW6 1H **117**
TW9: Rich 3G **115**
Dando Cres. SE3 3K **123**
Dandridge Cl. SE10 5H **105**
Dandridge Ho. *E1* *5J 9*
(off Lamb St.)
Danebury CR0: New Ad 6E **170**
Danebury Av. SW15 6A **116**
(not continuous)
Daneby Rd. SE6 3D **140**
Dane Cl. BR6: Farnb 5H **173**
DA5: Bexl 7G **127**
Danecourt Gdns. CR0: Croy 3F **169**
Danecroft Rd. SE24 5C **120**
Danehill Wlk. DA14: Sidc 3A **144**
Danehurst TW8: Bford 7C **96**
Danehurst Gdns. IG4: Ilf 5C **52**
Danehurst St. SW6 1G **117**
Daneland EN4: E Barn 6J **21**
Danemead Gro. UB5: N'olt 5F **59**
Danemere St. SW15 3E **116**
Dane Pl. E3 2A **86**
Dane Rd. IG1: Ilf 5G **71**
N18 3D **34**
SW19 1A **154**
TW15: Ashf 6E **128**
UB1: S'hall 7C **76**
W13 1C **96**
Danesbury Rd. TW13: Felt 1K **129**
Danescombe SE12 1J **141**
Danes Ct. HA9: Wemb 3H **61**
NW8 *1D 82*
(off St Edmund's Ter.)
Danescourt Cres. SM1: Sutt 2A **166**
Danescroft NW4 5F **45**
Danescroft Av. NW4 5F **45**
Danescroft Gdns. NW4 5F **45**
Danesdale Rd. E9 6A **68**
Danesfield *SE5* *6E 102*
(off Albany Rd.)
Danes Ga. HA1: Harr 3J **41**
Danes Ho. *W10* *5E 80*
(off Sutton Way)
Danes Rd. RM7: Rush G 7J **55**
Dane St. WC1 6G **7** (5K **83**)
Daneswood Av. SE6 3E **140**
Danethorpe Rd. HA0: Wemb 6D **60**
Danetree Cl. KT19: Ewe 7J **163**
Danetree Rd. KT19: Ewe 7J **163**
Danette Gdns. RM10: Dag 2G **73**
Daneville Rd. SE5 1D **120**
Dangan Rd. E11 6J **51**
Daniel Bolt Cl. E14 5D **86**
Daniel Cl. N18 4D **34**
SW17 6C **136**
TW4: Houn 7D **112**
Daniel Ct. NW9 1A **44**
Daniel Gdns. SE15 7F **103**
Daniell Ho. *N1* *2D 84*
(off Cranston Est.)
Daniell Way CR0: Wadd 1J **167**
Daniel Pl. NW4 7D **44**
Daniel Rd. W5 7F **79**
Daniels Rd. SE15 3J **121**
Danleigh Ct. N14 7C **22**
Dan Leno Wlk. SW6 7K **99**
Dan Mason Dr. W4 2J **115**
Dansey Pl. W1 2C **12**
Dansington Rd. DA16: Well 4A **126**
Danson Cres. DA16: Well 3B **126**
DANSON INTERCHANGE 5D **126**
Danson La. DA16: Well 4B **126**
Danson Mead DA16: Well 3C **126**
Danson Pk. 5C 126
Danson Rd. DA5: Bexl, Bex 6C **126**
DA6: Bex 5D **126**
SE17 5B **102**
Danson Underpass DA15: Sidc 6C **126**
Danson Water Sports Cen. 4C 126
Dante Pl. SE11 4B **102**
Dante Rd. SE11 4B **102**
Danube Ct. *SE15* *7F 103*
(off Daniel Gdns.)
Danube St. SW3 5D **16** (5C **100**)
Danvers Ho. *E1* *6G 85*
(off Christian St.)
Danvers Rd. N8 4H **47**
Danvers St. SW3 7B **16** (6B **100**)
Da Palma Ct. *SW6* *6J 99*
(off Anselm Rd.)
Daphne Ct. KT4: Wor Pk 2A **164**
Daphne Gdns. E4 3K **35**
Daphne Ho. *N22* *1A 48*
(off Acacia Rd.)
Daphne St. SW18 6A **118**
Daplyn St. E1 5K **9** (5G **85**)
D'Arblay St. W1 1B **12** (6G **83**)
Darby Cres. TW16: Sun 2A **148**
Darby Gdns. TW16: Sun 2A **148**
Darcy Av. SM6: Wall 4G **167**
Darcy Cl. N20 2G **31**
D'Arcy Dr. HA3: Kent 4D **42**
Darcy Gdns. HA3: Kent 4D **42**
RM9: Dag 1F **91**
Darcy Ho. *E8* *1H 85*
(off London Flds. E. Side)
D'Arcy Pl. BR2: Brom 4J **159**
Darcy Rd. SM3: Cheam 4F **165**
SW16 2J **155**
TW7: Isle 1A **114**
Dare Ct. E10 7E **50**
Dare Gdns. RM8: Dag 3E **72**
Darell Rd. TW9: Rich 3G **115**
Darent Ho. BR1: Brom 5F **141**
NW8 *5B 4*
(off Church St. Est.)
Darenth Rd. DA16: Well 1A **126**
N16 7F **49**
Darfield *NW1* *1G 83*
(off Bayham St.)
Darfield Rd. SE4 5B **122**
Darfield Way W10 6F **81**
Darfur St. SW15 3F **117**
Dargate Cl. SE19 7F **139**
Darien Ho. *E1* *5K 85*
(off Shandy St.)
Darien Rd. SW11 3B **118**
Daring Ho. *E3* *2A 86*
(off Roman Rd.)
Dark Ho. Wlk. EC3 3G **15** (7D **84**)
Darland Lake Nature Reserve 3B 30
Darlands Dr. EN5: Barn 5A **20**
Darlan Rd. SW6 7H **99**
Darlaston Rd. SW19 7F **135**
Darley Cl. CR0: Croy 6A **158**
Darley Dr. KT3: N Mald 2K **151**
Darley Gdns. SM4: Mord 6A **154**
Darley Ho. SE11 6G **19**
Darley Rd. N9 1A **34**
SW11 6D **118**
Darling Ho. TW1: Twick 6D **114**
Darling Rd. SE4 3C **122**
Darling Row E1 4H **85**
Darlington Ct. SE6 1H **141**
Darlington Ho. *SW8* *7H 101*
(off Hemans St.)
Darlington Rd. SE27 5B **138**
Darmaine Cl. CR2: S Croy 7C **168**
Darnall Ho. *SE10* *1E 122*
(off Royal Hill)
Darnaway Pl. *E14* *5E 86*
(off Aberfeldy St.)

A-Z London 243

Darnay Ho.—Dearsley Rd.

Darnay Ho. SE16 7K 15 (3G 103)
Darndale Cl. E17 2B 50
Darnley Ho. *E14* *6A 86*
(off Camdenhurst St.)
Darnley Rd. E9 6J 67
IG8: Wfd G 1J 51
Darnley Ter. W11 1F 99
Darrell Charles Ct. UB8: Uxb 7A 56
Darrell Rd. SE22 5G 121
Darren Cl. N4 7K 47
Darren Ct. N7 4J 65
Darrick Wood Rd. BR6: Orp 2H 173
Darrick Wood School Sports Cen. 3G 173
Darrick Wood School Sports Cen.
Swimming Pool 3G 173
Darris Cl. UB4: Yead 4C 76
Darsley Dr. SW8 1H 119
Dartford Av. N9 6D 24
Dartford By-Pass DA5: Bexl, Dart 7K 127
Dartford Gdns. RM6: Chad H 5B 54
Dartford Ho. *SE1* *4F 103*
(off Longfield Est.)
Dartford Rd. DA5: Bexl 1J 145
Dartford St. SE17 6C 102
Dartington *NW1* *1G 83*
(off Plender St.)
Dartington Ho. *SW8* *2H 119*
(off Union Gro.)
W2 *5K 81*
(off Senior St.)
Dartle Ct. *SE16* *2G 103*
(off Scott Lidgett Cres.)
Dartmoor Wlk. *E14* *4C 104*
(off Charnwood Gdns.)
Dartmouth Cl. W11 6H 81
Dartmouth Ct. SE10 1E 122
Dartmouth Gro. SE10 1E 122
Dartmouth Hill SE10 1E 122
Dartmouth Ho. *KT2: King T* *1E 150*
(off Seven Kings Way)
DARTMOUTH PARK 3F 65
Dartmouth Pk. Av. NW5 3F 65
Dartmouth Pk. Hill N19 1F 65
NW5 3F 65
Dartmouth Pk. Rd. NW5 4F 65
Dartmouth Pl. SE23 2J 139
W4 6A 98
Dartmouth Rd. BR2: Hayes 7J 159
HA4: Ruis 3J 57
NW2 6F 63
NW4 6C 44
SE23 3H 139
SE26 3H 139
Dartmouth Row SE10 2E 122
Dartmouth St. SW1 7D 12 (2H 101)
Dartmouth Ter. SE10 1F 123
Dartnell Rd. CR0: Croy 7F 157
Darton Ct. W3 1J 97
Dartrey Twr. *SW10* *7A 100*
(off Worlds End Est.)
Dartrey Wlk. SW10 7A 100
Dart St. W10 3G 81
Darville Rd. N16 3F 67
Darwell Cl. E6 2E 88
Darwen Pl. E2 2H 85
Darwin Cl. BR6: Farnb 5H 173
N11 3A 32
Darwin Ct. NW1 1F 83
SE17 *4D 102*
(off Barlow St.)
Darwin Dr. UB1: S'hall 6F 77
Darwin Ho. SW1 7A 18
Darwin Rd. DA16: Well 3K 125
N22 1B 48
W5 5C 96
Darwin St. SE17 4D 102
(not continuous)
Daryngton Dr. UB6: G'frd 2H 77
Daryngton Ho. *SW8* *7J 101*
(off Hartington Rd.)
Dashwood Cl. DA6: Bex 5G 127
Dashwood Rd. N8 6K 47
Dassett Rd. SE27 5B 138
Data Point Bus. Cen. E16 4F 87
Datchelor Pl. SE5 1D 120
Datchet Ho. *NW1* *1K 5*
(off Augustus St.)
Datchet Rd. SE6 2B 140
Datchworth Ct. EN1: Enf 5K 23
Datchworth Ho. *N1* *7B 66*
(off Sutton Est., The)
Date St. SE17 5D 102
Daubeney Gdns. N17 7H 33
Daubeney Rd. E5 4A 68
N17 7H 33
Daubeney Twr. *SE8* *5B 104*
(off Bowditch)
Dault Rd. SW18 6A 118
Dauncey Ho. SE1 7A 14
Davema Cl. BR7: Chst 1E 160
Davenant Rd. CR0: Croy 4B 168
N19 2H 65
Davenant St. E1 5G 85
Davenport Cen. IG11: Bark 1B 90
Davenport Cl. TW11: Tedd 6A 132
Davenport Ho. *SE11* *3J 19*
(off Walnut Tree Wlk.)
Davenport Lodge TW5: Hest 7C 94
Davenport Rd. DA14: Sidc 2E 144
SE6 6D 122
Daventer Dr. HA7: Stan 7E 26
Daventry Av. E17 6C 50
Daventry St. NW1 5C 4 (5C 82)
Daver Ct. SW3 5D 16 (5C 100)
W5 4D 78
Davern Cl. SE10 4H 105
Davey Cl. N7 6K 65
N13 5E 32
Davey Rd. E9 7C 68
Davey's Ct. WC2 2E 12
Davey St. SE15 6F 103
David Av. UB6: G'frd 3J 77
David Cl. UB3: Harl 7G 93
David Coffer Ct. DA17: Belv 4H 109
David Ct. N20 3F 31
Davidge Ho. *SE1* *7K 13*
(off Coral St.)
Davidge St. SE1 7A 14 (2B 102)
David Ho. DA15: Sidc 3A 144
SW8 *7J 101*
(off Wyvil Rd.)
David Lee Point *E15* *1G 87*
(off Leather Gdns.)
David Lloyd Leisure
Barnet 7G 31
Cheam 7F 165
Ealing 5H 59
Enfield 2B 24
Epping Forest 1J 37
Hounslow 5A 94
Kidbrooke 4K 123
Merton 3F 153
Sidcup 5C 144
South Kensington *4K 99*
(in Point West)
David M. W1 5F 5 (5D 82)
David Rd. RM8: Dag 2E 72
David's Ct. *UB1: S'hall* *6G 77*
(off Whitecote Rd.)
Davidson Gdns. SW8 7J 101
Davidson La. HA1: Harr 7K 41
Davidson Rd. CR0: Croy 1E 168
Davidson Terraces *E7* *5K 69*
(off Claremont Rd., not continuous)
David's Rd. SE23 1J 139
David St. E15 6F 69
David Twigg Cl. KT2: King T 1E 150
Davies Cl. CR0: Croy 6G 157
Davies La. E11 2G 69
Davies M. W1 2J 11 (7F 83)
Davies St. W1 1J 11 (6F 83)
Davies Wlk. TW7: Isle 1H 113
Da Vinci Ct. *SE16* *5H 103*
(off Rossetti Rd.)
Davington Gdns. RM8: Dag 5B 72
Davington Rd. RM8: Dag 6B 72
Davinia Cl. IG8: Wfd G 6J 37
Davis Ho. *W12* *7D 80*
(off White City Est.)
Davis Rd. KT9: Chess 4G 163
W3 1B 98
Davis St. E13 2K 87
Davisville Rd. W12 2C 98
Davmor Ct. TW8: Bford 5C 96
Dawes Av. TW7: Isle 5A 114
Dawes Ho. *SE17* *4D 102*
(off Orb St.)
Dawes Rd. SW6 7G 99
UB10: Uxb 2A 74
Dawes St. SE17 5D 102
Dawley Av. UB8: Hil 5E 74
Dawley Pde. UB3: Hayes 7E 74
Dawley Pk. UB3: Hayes 2F 93
Dawley Rd. UB3: Hayes 7E 74
Dawlish Av. N13 4D 32
SW18 2K 135
UB6: G'frd 2A 78
Dawlish Dr. HA4: Ruis 2J 57
HA5: Pinn 5C 40
IG3: Ilf 4J 71
Dawlish Rd. E10 1E 68
N17 3G 49
NW2 6F 63
Dawnay Gdns. SW18 2B 136
Dawnay Rd. SW18 2A 136
Dawn Cl. TW4: Houn 3C 112
Dawn Cres. E15 1F 87
Dawpool Rd. NW2 2B 62
Daws Hill E4 2K 25
Daws La. NW7 5G 29
Dawson Av. IG11: Bark 7J 71
Dawson Cl. SE18 4G 107
UB3: Hayes 5F 75
Dawson Gdns. IG11: Bark 7K 71
Dawson Ho. *E2* *3J 85*
(off Sceptre Rd.)
Dawson Pl. W2 7J 81
Dawson Rd. KT1: King T 3F 151
NW2 5E 62
Dawson St. E2 1K 9 (2F 85)
Dawson Ter. N9 7D 24
Dax Ct. TW16: Sun 3A 148
Daybrook Rd. SW19 2K 153
Day Ho. *SE5* *7C 102*
(off Bethwin Rd.)
Daylesford Av. SW15 4C 116
Daymer Gdns. HA5: Eastc 4K 39
Daysbrook Rd. SW2 1K 137
Days La. DA15: Sidc 7J 125
Dayton Gro. SE15 1J 121
Deaconess Ct. *N15* *4F 49*
(off Tottenham Grn. E.)
Deacon Est., The E4 6G 35
Deacon Ho. *SE11* *4H 19*
(off Black Prince Rd.)
Deacon M. N1 7D 66
Deacon Rd. KT2: King T 1F 151
NW2 5C 62
Deacons Cl. HA5: Pinn 2K 39
Deacons Ct. TW1: Twick 2K 131
Deacons Leas BR6: Orp 4H 173
Deacon's Ri. N2 5B 46
Deacons Ter. *N1* *6C 66*
(off Harecourt Rd.)
Deacons Wlk. TW12: Hamp 4E 130
Deacon Way IG8: Wfd G 7J 37
SE17 4C 102
Deal Ct. *NW9* *2B 44*
(off Hazel Cl.)
UB1: S'hall *6G 77*
(off Haldane Rd.)
Deal Ho. *SE15* *6K 103*
(off Lovelinch La.)
Deal M. W5 4D 96
Deal Porters Wlk. SE16 2K 103
Deal Porters Way SE16 3J 103
Deal Rd. SW17 6E 136
Deal's Gateway SE10 1C 122
Deal St. E1 5G 85
Dealtry Rd. SW15 4E 116
Deal Wlk. SW9 7A 102
Dean Abbott Ho. *SW1* *3C 18*
(off Vincent St.)
Dean Bradley St.
SW1 2E 18 (3J 101)
Dean Cl. E9 5J 67
SE16 1K 103
UB10: Hil 7B 56
Dean Ct. HA0: Wemb 3B 60
RM7: Rom 5K 55
SW8 *7J 101*
(off Thorncroft St.)
W3 6K 79
Deancross St. E1 6J 85
Dean Dr. HA7: Stan 2E 42
Deane Av. HA4: Ruis 5A 58
Deane Ct. HA6: Nwood 1G 39
Deane Cft. Rd. HA5: Eastc 6A 40
Deanery Cl. N2 4C 46
Deanery M. W1 4H 11
Deanery Rd. E15 6G 69
Deanery St. W1 4H 11 (1E 100)
Deane Way HA4: Ruis 6K 39
Dean Farrar St. SW1 1D 18 (3H 101)
Deanfield Gdns. CR0: Croy 4D 168
Dean Gdns. E17 4F 51
Deanhill Ct. SW14 4H 115
Deanhill Rd. SW14 4H 115
Dean Ho. *E1* *6J 85*
(off Tarling St.)
SE14 *7A 104*
(off New Cross Rd.)
Dean Rd. CR0: Croy 4D 168
NW2 6E 62
SE28 1A 108
TW3: Houn 5F 113
TW12: Hamp 5E 130
Dean Ryle St. SW1 3E 18 (4J 101)
Deansbrook Cl. HA8: Edg 7D 28
Deansbrook Rd. HA8: Edg 7C 28
Dean's Bldgs. SE17 4D 102
Deans Cl. CR0: Croy 3F 169
HA8: Edg 6D 28
W4 6H 97
Deans Ct. EC4 1B 14 (6B 84)
HA8: Edg 6C 28
Deanscroft Av. NW9 1J 61
Deans Dr. HA8: Edg 5E 28
N13 6G 33
Deans Ga. Cl. SE23 3K 139
Deanshanger Ho. *SE8* *4K 103*
(off Chilton Gro.)
Deans La. HA8: Edg 6D 28
W4 *6H 97*
(off Deans Cl.)
Dean's M. W1 7K 5 (6F 83)
Deans Rd. SM1: Sutt 3K 165
W7 1K 95
Dean Stanley St. SW1 2E 18 (3J 101)
Deanston Wharf E16 2K 105
Dean St. E7 5J 69
W1 7C 6 (6H 83)
Deans Way HA8: Edg 5D 28
Deansway N2 4B 46
N9 3K 33
Deanswood N11 6C 32
Dean's Yd. SW1 1D 18
Dean Trench St. SW1 2E 18 (3J 101)
Dean Wlk. HA8: Edg 6D 28
Dean Way UB2: S'hall 2F 95
Dearne Cl. HA7: Stan 5F 27
Dearn Gdns. CR4: Mitc 3C 154
Dearsley Ho. RM13: Rain 2K 91
Dearsley Rd. EN1: Enf 3B 24

Denmark Pl. E3 ....3C **86**
  WC2 ....7D **6** (6H **83**)
Denmark Rd. BR1: Brom 1K **159**
  KT1: King T 3E **150**
  N8 ....4A **48**
  NW6 ....2H **81**
   (not continuous)
  SE5 ....1C **120**
  SE25 ....5G **157**
  SM5: Cars 3D **166**
  SW19 ....6F **135**
  TW2: Twick 3H **131**
  W13 ....7B **78**
Denmark St. E11 ....3G **69**
  E13 ....5K **87**
  N17 ....1H **49**
  WC2 ....7D **6** (6H **83**)
Denmark Ter. N2 ....3D **46**
Denmark Wlk. SE27 ....4C **138**
Denmead Ho.
  SW15 ....6B **116**
   (off Highcliffe Dr.)
Denmead Rd. CR0: Croy 1B **168**
Denmore Ct. SM6: Wall 5F **167**
Dennan Rd. KT6: Surb 1F **163**
Dennard Way BR6: Farnb 4F **173**
Denner Rd. E4 ....2H **35**
Denne Ter. E8 ....1F **85**
Dennett Rd. CR0: Croy 1A **168**
Dennett's Rd. SE14 ....1J **121**
Denning Av. CR0: Wadd 4A **168**
Denning Cl. NW8 ......1A **4** (3A **82**)
  TW12: Hamp 5D **130**
Denning Point E1 ....7K **9**
   (off Commercial St.)
Denning Rd. NW3 ....4B **64**
Dennington Cl. E5 ....2J **67**
Dennington Pk. Rd. NW6 .....6J **63**
Denningtons, The KT4: Wor Pk ..2A **164**
Dennis Av. HA9: Wemb 5F **61**
Dennis Cl. TW15: Ashf 7F **129**
Dennis Gdns. HA7: Stan 5H **27**
Dennis Ho. SM1: Sutt 4J **165**
Dennis La. HA7: Stan 3G **27**
Dennison Point E15 ....7E **68**
Dennis Pde. N14 ....1C **32**
Dennis Pk. Cres. SW20 .....1G **153**
Dennis Reeve Cl. CR4: Mitc ..1D **154**
Dennis Rd. KT8: E Mos 4G **149**
Denny Cl. E6 ....5C **88**
Denny Cres. SE11 .....5K **19** (5A **102**)
Denny Gdns. RM9: Dag 7B **72**
Denny Rd. N9 ....1C **34**
Denny St. SE11 ....5K **19** (5A **102**)
Den Rd. BR2: Brom 3F **159**
Densham Ho. NW8 ....1B **4**
   (off Cochrane St.)
Densham Rd. E15 ....1G **87**
Densole Cl. BR3: Beck 1A **158**
Denstone Ho. SE15 ....6G **103**
   (off Haymerle Rd.)
Densworth Gro. N9 ....2D **34**
Dent Ho. SE17 ....4E **102**
   (off Tatum St.)
Denton NW1 ....6E **64**
Denton Cl. BR2: Brom 7E **160**
Denton Ho. N1 ....7B **66**
   (off Halton Rd.)
Denton Rd. DA5: Bexl 2K **145**
  DA16: Well 7C **108**
  N8 ....5K **47**
  N18 ....4K **33**
  TW1: Twick 6D **114**
Denton St. SW18 ....6K **117**
Denton Ter. DA5: Bexl 2K **145**
Denton Way E5 ....3K **67**
Dents Rd. SW11 ....6D **118**
Denver Cl. BR6: Pet W 6J **161**
Denver Rd. N16 ....7E **48**
Denwood SE23 ....3K **139**
Denyer St. SW3 ......4D **16** (4C **100**)

Denys Ho. EC1 ....5J **7**
   (off Bourne Est.)
Denziloe Av. UB10: Hil 3D **74**
Denzil Rd. NW10 ....5B **62**
Deodar Rd. SW15 ....4G **117**
Deodora Cl. N20 ....3H **31**
Depot App. NW2 ....4F **63**
Depot Rd. TW3: Houn 3H **113**
  W12 ....7E **80**
Depot St. SE5 ....6D **102**
DEPTFORD 7C **104**
Deptford Bri. SE8 ....1C **122**
Deptford B'way. SE8 ....1C **122**
Deptford Bus. Pk. SE15 ....1J **103**
Deptford Chu. St. SE8 ....6C **104**
Deptford Creek Bri. SE8 .....6D **104**
   (off Creek Rd.)
Deptford Ferry Rd. E14 ......4C **104**
Deptford Grn. SE8 ....6C **104**
Deptford High St. SE8 ....6C **104**
Deptford Pk. Bus. Cen. SE8 ...5A **104**
Deptford Strand SE8 ....4B **104**
Deptford Trad. Est. SE8 ......5A **104**
Deptford Wharf SE8 ....4B **104**
De Quincey Ho. SW1 ....6A **18**
   (off Lupus St.)
De Quincey M. E16 ....1J **105**
De Quincey Rd. N17 ....1D **48**
Derby Av. HA3: Hrw W 1H **41**
  N12 ....5F **31**
  RM7: Rom 6J **55**
Derby Ga. SW1 .....6E **12** (2J **101**)
   (not continuous)
Derby Hill SE23 ....2J **139**
Derby Hill Cres. SE23 ....2J **139**
Derby Ho. HA5: Pinn 2B **40**
  SE11 ....3J **19**
Derby Lodge N3 ....2H **45**
  WC1 ....1G **7**
   (off Britannia St.)
Derby Rd. CR0: Croy 1B **168**
  E7 ....7B **70**
  E9 ....1K **85**
  E18 ....1H **51**
  EN3: Pond E 5C **24**
  KT5: Surb 1G **163**
  N18 ....5D **34**
  SM1: Sutt 6H **165**
  SW14 ....4H **115**
  SW19 ....7J **135**
  TW3: Houn 4F **113**
Derbyshire St. E2 ....3G **85**
   (not continuous)
Derby St. W1 ....5H **11** (1E **100**)
Dereham Ho. SE4 ....4K **121**
   (off Frendsbury Rd.)
Dereham Pl. EC2 .....2H **9** (3E **84**)
Dereham Rd. IG11: Bark 5K **71**
Derek Av. HA9: Wemb 7H **61**
  KT19: Ewe 6G **163**
  SM6: Wall 4F **167**
Derek Cl. KT19: Ewe 5H **163**
Derek Walcott Cl. SE24 ....5B **120**
Dericote St. E8 ....1H **85**
Deri Dene Cl. TW19: Stanw ...6A **110**
Derifall Cl. E6 ....5D **88**
Dering Pl. CR0: Croy 4C **168**
Dering Rd. CR0: Croy 4C **168**
Dering St. W1 ....1J **11** (6F **83**)
Dering Yd. W1 ......1K **11** (6F **83**)
Derinton Rd. SW17 ....4D **136**
Derley Rd. UB2: S'hall 3A **94**
Dermody Gdns. SE13 ....5F **123**
Dermody Rd. SE13 ....5F **123**
Deronda Est. SW2 ....1B **138**
Deronda Rd. SE24 ....2B **138**
Deroy Cl. SM5: Cars 6D **166**
Derrick Gdns. SE7 ....3A **106**
Derrick Rd. BR3: Beck 3B **158**
Derry Rd. CR0: Bedd 3J **167**

Derry St. W8 ....2K **99**
Dersingham Av. E12 ....4D **70**
Dersingham Rd. NW2 ....3G **63**
Derwent NW1 ....2A **6**
   (off Robert St.)
Derwent Av. EN4: E Barn 1J **31**
  N18 ....5J **33**
  NW7 ....6E **28**
  NW9 ....5A **44**
  SW15 ....4A **134**
  UB10: Ick 2C **56**
Derwent Cl. TW14: Felt 1H **129**
Derwent Ct. SE16 ....2K **103**
   (off Eleanor Cl.)
Derwent Cres. DA7: Bex 2G **127**
  HA7: Stan 2C **42**
  N20 ....3F **31**
Derwent Dr. BR5: Pet W 7H **161**
  UB4: Hayes 5G **75**
Derwent Gdns. HA9: Wemb ...7C **42**
  IG4: Ilf 4C **52**
Derwent Gro. SE22 ....4F **121**
Derwent Ho. E3 ....4B **86**
   (off Southern Gro.)
  SE20 ....2H **157**
   (off Derwent Rd.)
  SW7 ....3A **16**
   (off Cromwell Rd.)
Derwent Lodge KT4: Wor Pk ...2D **164**
  TW7: Isle 2H **113**
Derwent Ri. NW9 ....5A **44**
Derwent Rd. N13 ....4E **32**
  SE20 ....2G **157**
  SW20 ....6F **153**
  TW2: Whit 6F **113**
  UB1: S'hall 6D **76**
  W5 ....3C **96**
Derwent St. SE10 ....5G **105**
Derwent Wlk. SM6: Wall 7F **167**
Derwentwater Rd. W3 ....1J **97**
Derwent Yd. W5 ....3C **96**
   (off Derwent Rd.)
De Salis Rd. UB10: Hil 4E **74**
Desborough Cl. TW17: Shep ..7C **146**
  W2 ....5K **81**
Desborough Ho. W14 ....6H **99**
   (off Nth. End Rd.)
Desborough Sailing Club 7D **146**
Desborough St. W2 ....5K **81**
   (off Cirencester St.)
Desenfans Rd. SE21 ....6E **120**
Desford Ct. TW15: Ashf 2C **128**
Desford Rd. E16 ....4G **87**
Desford Way TW15: Ashf 2B **128**
Desmond Ho. EN4: E Barn 6H **21**
Desmond St. SE14 ....6A **104**
Desmond Tutu Dr. SE23 ......1B **140**
Despard Rd. N19 ....1G **65**
Dethick Ct. E3 ....1A **86**
Detling Ho. SE17 ....4E **102**
   (off Congreve St.)
Detling Rd. BR1: Brom 5J **141**
  DA8: Erith 7K **109**
Detmold Rd. E5 ....2J **67**
Devalls Cl. E6 ....7E **89**
Devana End SM5: Cars 3D **166**
Devas Rd. SW20 ....1E **152**
Devas St. E3 ....4D **86**
Devenay Rd. E15 ....7H **69**
Devenish Rd. SE2 ....2A **108**
Deventer Cres. SE22 ....5E **120**
Deveraux Cl. BR3: Beck 5E **158**
De Vere Cl. SM6: Wall 7J **167**
De Vere Gdns. IG1: Ilf 2D **70**
  W8 ....2A **100**
Deverell St. SE1 ....3D **102**
De Vere M. W8 ....3A **100**
   (off De Vere Gdns.)
Devereux Ct. WC2 ....1J **13**
Devereux La. SW13 ....7D **98**

Devereux Rd. SW11 ....6D **118**
Deveron Way RM1: Rom 1K **55**
Devey Cl. KT2: King T 7B **134**
Devitt Ho. E14 ....7D **86**
   (off Wade's Pl.)
Devizes St. N1 ....1D **84**
Devon Av. TW2: Twick 1G **131**
Devon Cl. IG9: Buck H 2E **36**
  N17 ....3F **49**
  UB6: G'frd 1C **78**
Devon Ct. TW12: Hamp 7E **130**
  W7 ....5K **77**
   (off Copley Cl.)
Devoncroft Gdns. TW1: Twick ..7A **114**
Devon Gdns. N4 ....6B **48**
Devon Ho. E17 ....2B **50**
Devonhurst Pl. W4 ....5K **97**
Devonia Gdns. N18 ....6H **33**
Devonia Rd. N1 ....2B **84**
Devon Mans. HA3: Kent 5C **42**
   (off Woodcock Hill)
  SE1 ....6J **15**
   (off Tooley St.)
Devon Pde. HA3: Kent 5C **42**
Devonport W2 ....1C **10** (6C **82**)
Devonport Gdns. IG1: Ilf 6D **52**
Devonport M. W12 ....2D **98**
Devonport Rd. W12 ....1D **98**
   (not continuous)
Devonport St. E1 ....6K **85**
Devon Ri. N2 ....4B **46**
Devon Rd. IG11: Bark 1J **89**
  SM2: Cheam 7G **165**
Devons Est. E3 ....3D **86**
Devonshire Av. SM2: Sutt 7A **166**
Devonshire Cl. E15 ....4G **69**
  N13 ....3F **33**
  W1 ....5J **5** (5F **83**)
Devonshire Ct. E1 ....3J **85**
   (off Bancroft Rd.)
  HA5: H End 1D **40**
  WC1 ....5F **7**
   (off Boswell St.)
Devonshire Cres. NW7 ....7A **30**
Devonshire Dr. KT6: Surb 1D **162**
  SE10 ....7D **104**
Devonshire Gdns. N17 ....6H **33**
  N21 ....7H **23**
  W4 ....7J **97**
Devonshire Gro. SE15 ....6H **103**
Devonshire Hall E9 ....6J **67**
   (off Frampton Pk. Rd.)
Devonshire Hill La. N17 ......6G **33**
   (not continuous)
Devonshire Ho. E14 ....4C **104**
   (off Westferry Rd.)
  IG8: Ilf 7K **37**
  NW6 ....6H **63**
   (off Kilburn High Rd.)
  SE1 ....3C **102**
   (off Bath Ter.)
  SM2: Sutt 7A **166**
  SW1 ....5D **18**
   (off Lindsay Sq.)
Devonshire Ho. Bus. Cen.
  BR2: Brom 4K **159**
   (off Devonshire Sq.)
Devonshire M. N13 ....4F **33**
  SW10 ....7A **16**
   (off Park Wlk.)
  W4 ....5A **98**
Devonshire M. Mth.
  W1 ....5J **5** (5F **83**)
Devonshire M. Sth. W1 ......5J **5** (5F **83**)
Devonshire M. W1 ....4H **5** (4E **82**)
Devonshire Pas. W4 ....5A **98**
Devonshire Pl. NW2 ....3J **63**
  W1 ....4H **5** (4E **82**)
  W8 ....3K **99**
Devonshire Pl. M. W1 ....4H **5** (5E **82**)

Dollar Bay Ct.—Douglas Pl.

Dollar Bay Ct. *E14* 2E 104
(off Lawn Ho. Cl.)
Dollary Pde. *KT1: King T* 3H 151
(off Kingston Rd.)
Dollis Av. N3 1H 45
Dollis Brook Wlk.
EN5: Barn 6B 20
Dollis Cres. HA4: Ruis 1A 58
Dolliscroft NW7 7B 30
DOLLIS HILL 2D 62
Dollis Hill Av. NW2 3D 62
Dollis Hill La. NW2 4B 62
Dollis M. N3 1J 45
Dollis Pk. N3 1H 45
Dollis Rd. N3 1G 45
NW7 7B 30
Dollis Valley Dr. EN5: Barn 6C 20
Dollis Valley Way EN5: Barn 6C 20
Dolman Cl. N3 2A 46
Dolman Rd. W4 4K 97
Dolman St. SW4 4K 119
Dolphin Cl. KT6: Surb 5D 150
SE16 2K 103
SE28 6D 90
Dolphin Ct. NW11 6G 45
SE8 6B 104
(off Wotton Rd.)
Dolphin Est. TW16: Sun 1G 147
Dolphin Ho. SW18 4K 117
Dolphin La. E14 7D 86
Dolphin Rd. TW16: Sun 1G 147
UB5: N'olt 2D 76
Dolphin Rd. Nth. TW16: Sun 1G 147
Dolphin Rd. Sth. TW16: Sun 1F 147
Dolphin Rd. W. TW16: Sun 1G 147
Dolphin Sq. SW1 6B 18 (5G 101)
W4 7A 98
Dolphin St. KT1: King T 2E 150
Dolphin Twr. *SE8* 6B 104
(off Abinger Gro.)
Dombey Ho. *SE1* 7K 15
(off Wolseley St.)
W11 1F 99
(off St Ann's Rd.)
Dombey St. WC1 5G 7 (5K 83)
(not continuous)
Domecq Ho. *EC1* 3B 8
(off Dallington St.)
Dome Hill Pk. SE26 4F 139
Domelton Ho. *SW18* 6K 117
(off Iron Mill Rd.)
Domett Cl. SE5 4D 120
Domfe Pl. E5 4J 67
Domingo St. EC1 3C 8 (4C 84)
Dominica Cl. E13 2B 88
Dominion Bus. Pk. N9 2E 34
Dominion Cen., The UB2: S'hall 2C 94
Dominion Cl. TW3: Houn 2H 113
Dominion Ct. *E8* 7F 67
(off Middleton Rd.)
Dominion Ho. *E14* 5D 104
(off St Davids Sq.)
Dominion Ind. Est. UB2: S'hall 2C 94
Dominion Pde. HA1: Harr 5K 41
Dominion Rd. CR0: Croy 7F 157
UB2: S'hall 2C 94
Dominion St. EC2 5F 9 (5D 84)
Dominion Theatre 7D 6
(off Tottenham Ct. Rd.)
Domonic Dr. SE9 4F 143
Domville Cl. N20 2G 31
Donald Dr. RM6: Chad H 5C 54
Donald Hunter Ho. *E7* 5K 69
(off Woodgrange Rd.)
Donald Rd. CR0: Croy 7K 155
E13 1K 87
Donaldson Rd. NW6 1H 81
SE18 1E 124
Donald Woods Gdns. KT5: Surb 2H 163
Donato Dr. SE15 6E 102
Doncaster Dr. UB5: N'olt 5D 58
Doncaster Gdns. N4 6C 48
UB5: N'olt 5D 58
Doncaster Rd. N9 7C 24
Donegal Ho. *E1* 4H 85
(off Cambridge Heath Rd.)
Donegal St. N1 2K 83
Doneraile Ho.
SW1 5J 17
(off Ebury Bri. Rd.)
Doneraile St. SW6 2F 117
Dongola Rd. E1 5A 86
E13 3K 87
N17 3E 48
Dongola Rd. W. E13 3K 87
Donington Av. IG2: Ilf 5G 53
IG6: Ilf 5G 53
Donkey All. SE22 7G 121
Donkey La. EN1: Enf 2B 24
Donkin Ho. *SE16* 4H 103
(off Rennie Est.)
Donmar Warehouse Theatre 1E 12
(off Earlham St.)
Donnatt's Rd. SE14 1B 122
Donne Ct. SE24 6C 120
Donnefield Av. HA8: Edg 7K 27
Donne Ho. *E14* 6C 86
(off Dod St.)
SE14 6K 103
(off Samuel Cl.)
Donnelly Ct. *SW6* 7G 99
(off Dawes Rd.)
Donne Pl. CR4: Mitc 4F 155
SW3 3D 16 (4C 100)
Donne Rd. RM8: Dag 2C 72
Donnington Ct. *NW1* 7F 65
(off Castlehaven Rd.)
NW10 7D 62
Donnington Mans. *NW10* 1E 80
(off Donnington Rd.)
Donnington Rd. HA3: Kent 5D 42
KT4: Wor Pk 2C 164
NW10 7D 62
Donnybrook Rd. SW16 7G 137
Donoghue Cotts. *E14* 5A 86
(off Galsworthy Av.)
Donovan Av. N10 2F 47
Donovan Ct. *SW10* 6A 16
(off Drayton Gdns.)
Donovan Ho. *E1* 7J 85
(off Cable St.)
Donovan Pl. N21 5E 22
Don Phelan Cl. SE5 1D 120
Doone Cl. TW11: Tedd 6A 132
Doon St. SE1 5J 13 (1A 102)
Dora Ho. *E14* 6B 86
(off Rhodeswell Rd.)
W11 7F 81
(off St Ann's Rd.)
Doral Way SM5: Cars 5D 166
Doran Ct. E6 2D 88
Dorando Cl. W12 7D 80
Doran Gro. SE18 7J 107
Doran Mnr. *N2* 5D 46
(off Gt. North Rd.)
Doran Wlk. E15 7E 68
Dora Rd. SW19 5J 135
Dora St. E14 6B 86
Dora Way SW9 2A 120
Dorchester Av. DA5: Bexl 1D 144
HA2: Harr 6G 41
N13 4H 33
Dorchester Cl. BR5: St P 7B 144
UB5: N'olt 5F 59
Dorchester Ct. *E18* 1H 51
(off Buckingham Rd.)
N1 7E 66
(off Englefield Rd.)
N10 3F 47
N14 7A 22
NW2 3F 63
SE24 5C 120
Dorchester Dr. SE24 5C 120
TW14: Bedf 6G 111
Dorchester Gdns. E4 4H 35
NW11 4J 45
Dorchester Gro. W4 5A 98
Dorchester Ho. TW9: Kew 7H 97
Dorchester M. KT3: N Mald 4K 151
TW1: Twick 6C 114
Dorchester Rd. KT4: Wor Pk 1E 164
SM4: Mord 7K 153
UB5: N'olt 5F 59
Dorchester Ter. *NW2* 3F 63
(off Needham Ter.)
Dorchester Way HA3: Kent 6F 43
Dorchester Waye UB4: Yead 6A 76
(Quebec Rd.)
UB4: Yead 6K 75
(Wimborne Av.)
Dorcis Av. DA7: Bex 2E 126
Dordrecht Rd. W3 1A 98
Dore Av. E12 5E 70
Doreen Av. NW9 1K 61
Doreen Capstan Ho. *E11* 3G 69
(off Apollo Pl.)
Dore Gdns. SM4: Mord 7K 153
Dorell Cl. UB1: S'hall 5D 76
Dorey Ho. *TW8: Bford* 7C 96
(off High St.)
Doria Rd. SW6 2H 117
Doric Ho. *E2* 2K 85
(off Mace St.)
Doric Way NW1 1C 6 (3H 83)
Dorie M. N12 4E 30
Dorien Rd. SW20 2F 153
Doris Av. DA8: Erith 1J 127
Doris Emmerton Ct. SW11 4A 118
Doris Rd. E7 7J 69
TW15: Ashf 6F 129
Dorking Cl. KT4: Wor Pk 2F 165
SE8 6B 104
Dorking Ct. *N17* 1G 49
(off Hampden La.)
Dorking Ho. SE1 3D 102
Dorlcote Rd. SW18 7C 118
Dorly Cl. TW17: Shep 5G 147
Dorman Pl. N9 2B 34
Dormans Cl. HA6: Nwood 1F 39
Dorman Wlk. NW10 5K 61
Dorman Way NW8 1B 82
Dorma Trad. Pk. E10 1K 67
Dormay St. SW18 5K 117
Dormer Cl. E15 6H 69
EN5: Barn 5A 20
Dormer's Av. UB1: S'hall 6E 76
Dormers Ri. UB1: S'hall 6F 77
DORMER'S WELLS 6E 76
Dormer's Wells La. UB1: S'hall 6E 76
Dormers Wells Leisure Cen. 6F 77
Dormstone Ho. *SE17* 4E 102
(off Beckway St.)
Dormywood HA4: Ruis 5H 39
Dornberg Cl. SE3 7J 105
Dornberg Rd. SE3 7K 105
Dorncliffe Rd. SW6 2G 117
Dorney NW3 7C 64
Dorney Ri. BR5: St M Cry 4K 161
Dorney Way TW4: Houn 5C 112
Dornfell St. NW6 5H 63
Dornton Rd. CR2: S Croy 6D 168
SW12 2F 137
Dorothy Av. HA0: Wemb 7E 60
Dorothy Evans Cl. DA7: Bex 4H 127
Dorothy Gdns. RM8: Dag 4B 72
Dorothy Pettingell Ho. *SM1: Sutt* 3K 165
(off Angel Hill)
Dorothy Rd. SW11 3D 118
Dorrell Pl. SW9 3A 120
Dorrien Wlk. SW16 2H 137
Dorrington Ct. SE25 2E 156
Dorrington St. EC1 5J 7 (5A 84)
Dorrington Way BR3: Beck 5E 158
Dorrit Ho. *W11* 1F 99
(off St Ann's Rd.)
Dorrit M. N18 5K 33
Dorrit St. SE1 6D 14 (2C 102)
Dorrit Way BR7: Chst 6G 143
Dorryn Ct. SE26 5K 139
Dors Cl. NW9 1K 61
Dorset Av. DA16: Well 4K 125
RM1: Rom 4K 55
UB2: S'hall 4E 94
UB4: Hayes 3G 75
Dorset Bldgs. EC4 1A 14 (6B 84)
Dorset Cl. NW1 5E 4 (5D 82)
UB4: Hayes 3G 75
Dorset Ct. HA6: Nwood 1H 39
N1 7E 66
(off Hertford Rd.)
UB5: N'olt 3C 76
W7 5K 77
(off Copley Cl.)
Dorset Dr. HA8: Edg 6A 28
Dorset Gdns. CR4: Mitc 4K 155
Dorset Ho. *NW1* 5F 5
(off Gloucester Pl.)
Dorset M. N3 1J 45
SW1 1J 17 (3F 101)
Dorset Pl. E15 6F 69
Dorset Ri. EC4 1A 14 (6B 84)
Dorset Rd. BR3: Beck 3K 157
CR4: Mitc 2C 154
E7 7A 70
HA1: Harr 6G 41
N15 4D 48
N22 1J 47
SE9 2C 142
SW8 7J 101
SW19 1J 153
TW15: Ashf 3A 128
W5 3C 96
Dorset Sq. NW1 4E 4 (4D 82)
Dorset St. W1 6F 5 (5D 82)
Dorset Way TW2: Twick 1H 131
UB10: Hil 2B 74
Dorset Waye TW5: Hest 7D 94
Dorton Cl. SE15 7E 102
Dorton Vs. UB7: Sip 7C 92
Dorville Cres. W6 3D 98
Dorville Rd. SE12 5H 123
Dothill Rd. SE18 7G 107
Douai Gro. TW12: Hamp 1G 149
Doughty Ct. *E1* 1H 103
(off Prusom St.)
Doughty Ho. *SW10* 6A 100
(off Netherton Gro.)
Doughty M. WC1 4G 7 (4K 83)
Doughty St. WC1 3G 7 (4K 83)
Douglas Av. E17 1B 50
HA0: Wemb 7E 60
KT3: N Mald 4D 152
Douglas Cl. HA7: Stan 5F 27
IG6: Ilf 7K 37
SM6: Wall 6J 167
Douglas Ct. *KT1: King T* 4E 150
(off Geneva Rd.)
NW6 7J 63
(off Quex Rd.)
Douglas Cres. UB4: Yead 4A 76
Douglas Dr. CR0: Croy 3C 170
Douglas Est. *N1* 6C 66
(off Oransay Rd.)
Douglas Eyre Sports Cen. 5K 49
Douglas Ho. KT6: Surb 1F 163
Douglas Johnstone Ho.
SW6 6H 99
(off Clem Attlee Ct.)
Douglas Mans. TW3: Houn 3F 113
Douglas M. NW2 3G 63
Douglas Path *E14* 5E 104
(off Manchester Rd.)
Douglas Pl. *SW1* 4C 18
(off Douglas St.)

Douglas Rd. DA16: Well ...1B 126
  E4 ...1B 36
  E16 ...5J 87
  IG3: Ilf ...7A 54
  KT1: King T ...2H 151
  KT6: Surb ...2F 163
  N1 ...7C 66
  N22 ...1A 48
  NW6 ...1H 81
  TW3: Houn ...3F 113
  TW19: Stanw ...6A 110
Douglas Rd. Nth. N1 ...6C 66
Douglas Rd. Sth. N1 ...6C 66
Douglas Robinson Ct. SW16 ...7J 137
  (off Streatham High Rd.)
Douglas Sq. SM4: Mord ...6J 153
Douglas St. SW1 ...4C 18 (4H 101)
Douglas Ter. E17 ...1B 50
Douglas Waite Ho. NW6 ...7J 63
Douglas Way SE8 ...7C 104
  (Octavius St.)
  SE8 ...7B 104
  (Stanley St.)
Doulton Ho. SE11 ...2H 19
Doulton M. NW6 ...6K 63
Dounesforth Gdns. SW18 ...1K 135
Douro Pl. W8 ...3K 99
Douro St. E3 ...2C 86
Douthwaite Sq. E1 ...1G 103
Dove App. E6 ...5C 88
Dove Cl. NW7 ...7G 29
  SM6: Wall ...7K 167
  UB5: N'olt ...4B 76
Dove Commercial Cen. NW5 ...5G 65
Dovecot Cl. HA5: Eastc ...5A 40
Dovecote Av. N22 ...3A 48
Dovecote Gdns. SW14 ...3K 115
Dove Ct. EC2 ...1E 14
  IG5: Ilf ...2E 52
Dovedale Av. HA3: Kent ...6C 42
  IG5: Ilf ...2E 52
Dovedale Bus. Est. SE15 ...2G 121
  (off Blenheim Gro.)
Dovedale Cl. DA16: Well ...2A 126
Dovedale Ri. CR4: Mitc ...7D 136
Dovedale Rd. SE22 ...5H 121
Dovedon Cl. N14 ...2D 32
Dovehouse Ct. UB5: N'olt ...3B 76
  (off Delta Gro.)
Dove Ho. Gdns. E4 ...2H 35
Dovehouse Mead IG11: Bark ...2H 89
Dovehouse St. SW3 ...5B 16 (5B 100)
Dove M. SW5 ...4A 100
Dove Pk. HA5: H End ...1E 40
Dover Cl. NW2 ...2F 63
  RM5: Col R ...2J 55
Dovercourt Av. CR7: Thor H ...5A 156
Dovercourt Est. N1 ...6D 66
Dovercourt Gdns. HA7: Stan ...5K 27
Dovercourt La. SM1: Sutt ...3A 166
Dovercourt Rd. SE22 ...6E 120
Doverfield Rd. SW2 ...7J 119
Dover Flats SE1 ...4E 102
Dover Gdns. SM5: Cars ...3D 166
Dover Ho. N18 ...5A 34
  SE15 ...6J 103
Dover Ho. Rd. SW15 ...4C 116
Doveridge Gdns. N13 ...4G 33
Dove Rd. N1 ...6D 66
Dove Row E2 ...1G 85
Dover Pk. Dr. SW15 ...6D 116
Dover Patrol SE3 ...2K 123
Dover Rd. E12 ...2A 70
  N9 ...2D 34
  RM6: Chad H ...6E 54
  SE19 ...6D 138
Dover St. W1 ...3K 11 (7F 83)
Dover Ter. TW9: Rich ...2F 115
  (off Sandycombe Rd.)
Dover Yd. W1 ...4A 12
Doves Cl. BR2: Brom ...2C 172
Doves Yd. N1 ...1A 84

Dovet Ct. SW9 ...1K 119
Doveton Ho. E1 ...4J 85
  (off Doveton St.)
Doveton Rd. CR2: S Croy ...5D 168
Doveton St. E1 ...4J 85
Dove Wlk. SW1 ...5G 17 (5E 100)
Dovey Lodge N1 ...7A 66
  (off Bewdley St.)
Dowanhill Rd. SE6 ...1F 141
Dowdeswell Cl. SW15 ...4A 116
Dowding Ho. N6 ...7E 46
  (off Hillcrest)
Dowding Pl. HA7: Stan ...6F 27
Dowding Rd. UB10: Uxb ...7B 56
Dowdney Cl. NW5 ...5G 65
Dowe Ho. SE3 ...3G 123
Dower Av. SM6: Wall ...7F 167
Dowes Ho. SW16 ...3J 137
Dowgate Hill EC4 ...2E 14 (7D 84)
Dowland St. W10 ...3G 81
Dowlas St. SE5 ...7E 102
Dowler Ct. KT2: King T ...1E 150
  (off Burton Rd.)
Dowler Ho. E1 ...6G 85
  (off Burslem St.)
Dowlerville Rd. BR6: Chels ...6K 173
Dowling Ho. DA17: Belv ...3F 109
Dowman Cl. SW19 ...7K 135
Downage NW4 ...3E 44
  (not continuous)
Downalong WD23: Bushy ...1C 26
Downbank Av. DA7: Bex ...1K 127
Down Barns Rd. HA4: Ruis ...3B 58
Downbury M. SW18 ...5J 117
Down Cl. UB5: Yead ...2K 75
Downderry Rd. BR1: Brom ...3F 141
Downe Cl. DA16: Well ...7C 108
Down End SE18 ...7F 107
Downend Ct. SE15 ...6E 102
  (off Longhope Cl.)
Downe Rd. BR2: Kes ...7B 172
  CR4: Mitc ...2D 154
Downer's Cott. SW4 ...4G 119
Downes Cl. TW1: Twick ...6B 114
Downes Ct. N21 ...1F 33
Downes Ho. CR0: Wadd ...4B 168
  (off Violet La.)
Downe Ter. TW10: Rich ...6E 114
Downey Ho. E1 ...4K 85
  (off Globe Rd.)
Downfield KT4: Wor Pk ...1B 164
Downfield Cl. W9 ...4K 81
Down Hall Rd. KT2: King T ...1D 150
DOWNHAM ...5F 141
Downham Cl. RM5: Col R ...1G 55
Downham Ct. N1 ...7D 66
  (off Downham Rd.)
Downham Ent. Cen. SE6 ...2H 141
Downham La. BR1: Brom ...5F 141
Downham Rd. N1 ...7D 66
Downham Way BR1: Brom ...5F 141
Downhills Av. N17 ...3D 48
Downhills Pk. Rd. N17 ...3C 48
Downhills Way N17 ...3C 48
Downhurst Av. NW7 ...5E 28
Downhurst Ct. NW4 ...3E 44
Downing Cl. HA2: Harr ...3G 41
Downing Dr. UB6: G'frd ...1H 77
Downing Rd. RM9: Dag ...7F 73
Downings E6 ...6E 88
Downing St. SW1 ...6E 12 (2J 101)
Downland Cl. N20 ...1F 31
Downleau Cl. E11 ...2G 69
Downleys Cl. SE9 ...2C 142
Downman Rd. SE9 ...3C 124
Down Pl. W6 ...4D 98
Down Rd. TW11: Tedd ...6B 132
Downs, The SW20 ...7F 135
Downs Av. BR7: Chst ...5D 142
  HA5: Pinn ...6C 40
Downsbridge Rd. BR3: Beck ...1F 159

Downs Ct. UB6: G'frd ...3A 78
Downs Ct. Pde. E8 ...5H 67
  (off Amhurst Rd.)
Downsell Rd. E15 ...4E 68
Downsfield Rd. ...6A 50
Downshall Av. IG3: Ilf ...6J 53
Downs Hill BR3: Beck ...7F 141
Downshire Hill NW3 ...4B 64
Downside TW1: Twick ...3K 131
  TW16: Sun ...1J 147
Downside Cl. SW19 ...6A 136
Downside Cres. NW3 ...5C 64
  W13 ...4A 78
Downside Rd. SM2: Sutt ...6B 166
Downside Wlk. TW8: Bford ...6D 96
  (off Windmill Rd.)
  UB5: N'olt ...3D 76
Downs La. E5 ...4H 67
Downs Pk. Rd. E5 ...5F 67
  E8 ...5F 67
Downs Rd. BR3: Beck ...2D 158
  (not continuous)
  CR7: Thor H ...1C 156
  E5 ...4G 67
  EN1: Enf ...4K 23
Down St. KT8: W Mole ...5E 148
  W1 ...5J 11 (1F 101)
Down St. M. W1 ...5J 11 (1F 101)
Downs Vw. TW7: Isle ...1K 113
Downsview Gdns. SE19 ...7B 138
Downsview Rd. SE19 ...7C 138
Downsway BR6: Orp ...5J 173
Downsway, The SM2: Sutt ...7A 166
Downton Av. SW2 ...2J 137
Downtown Rd. SE16 ...2A 104
Downway N1 ...1A 84
Dowrey St. N1 ...1A 84
Dowsett Rd. N17 ...2F 49
Dowson Cl. SE5 ...4D 120
Dowson Ho. E1 ...6K 85
  (off Bower St.)
Doyce St. SE1 ...6C 14 (2C 102)
Doyle Gdns. NW10 ...1C 80
Doyle Ho. SW13 ...7E 98
  (off Trinity Chu. Rd.)
Doyle Rd. SE25 ...4G 157
D'Oyley St. SW1 ...3G 17 (4E 100)
Doynton St. N19 ...2F 65
Draco Ga. SW15 ...3E 116
Draco St. SE17 ...6C 102
Dragonfly Cl. E13 ...3K 87
Dragon Rd. SE15 ...6E 102
Dragons Health Club
  Epsom ...4K 163
  Northolt ...1E 76
  Northwood Hills ...2G 39
  Purley ...7A 168
  St Paul's Cray ...7D 144
Dragon Yd. WC1 ...7F 7 (6J 83)
Dragoon Rd. SE8 ...5B 104
Dragor Rd. NW10 ...4J 79
Drake Cl. SE16 ...2K 103
Drake Ct. KT5: Surb ...4E 150
  (off Cranes Pk. Av.)
  SE1 ...7D 14
  (off Swan St.)
  W12 ...2E 98
  (off Scott's Rd.)
Drake Cres. SE28 ...6C 90
Drakefell Rd. SE4 ...3A 122
  SE14 ...2K 121
Drakefield Rd. SW17 ...3E 136
Drake Hall E16 ...1K 105
  (off Wesley Av.)
Drake Ho. E1 ...5J 85
  (off Stepney Way)
  E14 ...7A 86
  (off Victory Pl.)
  SW1 ...(off Dolphin Sq.)

Drakeland Ho. W9 ...4H 81
  (off Fernhead Rd.)
Drakeley Ct. N5 ...4B 66
Drake M. BR2: Brom ...4A 160
Drake Rd. CR0: Croy ...7K 155
  CR4: Mitc ...6E 154
  HA2: Harr ...2D 58
  KT9: Chess ...5G 163
  SE4 ...3C 122
Drakes Ct. SE23 ...1J 139
Drakes Courtyard NW6 ...7H 63
Drakes Dr. HA6: Nwood ...1D 38
Drake St. EN2: Enf ...1J 23
  WC1 ...6G 7 (5K 83)
Drakes Wlk. E6 ...1D 88
Drakewood Rd. SW16 ...7H 137
Draper Cl. DA17: Belv ...4F 109
  TW7: Isle ...2H 113
Draper Ct. BR1: Brom ...4C 160
Draper Ho. SE1 ...4B 102
  (off Elephant & Castle)
Draper Pl. N1 ...1B 84
  (off Dagmar Ter.)
Drapers Cott. Homes NW7 ...4H 29
  (not continuous)
Drapers Gdns. EC2 ...7F 9 (6D 84)
Drapers Rd. E15 ...4F 69
  EN2: Enf ...2G 23
  N17 ...3F 49
Drappers Way SE16 ...4G 103
Draven Cl. BR2: Hayes ...7H 159
Drawdock Rd. SE10 ...2F 105
Drawell Cl. SE18 ...5J 107
Drax Av. SW20 ...7C 134
Draxmont SW19 ...6G 135
Draycot Rd. E11 ...6K 51
  KT6: Surb ...1G 163
Draycott Av. HA3: Kent ...6B 42
  SW3 ...3D 16 (4C 100)
Draycott Cl. HA3: Kent ...6B 42
  NW2 ...3F 63
  SE5 ...7D 102
  (not continuous)
Draycott M. SW6 ...2H 117
  (off Laurel Bank Gdns.)
Draycott Pl. SW3 ...4E 16 (4D 100)
Draycott Ter. SW3 ...4F 17 (4D 100)
Drayford Cl. W9 ...4H 81
Dray Gdns. SW2 ...5K 119
Draymans M. SE15 ...2F 121
Draymans Way TW7: Isle ...3K 113
Drayside M. UB2: S'hall ...2D 94
Drayson M. W8 ...2J 99
Drayton Av. BR6: Farnb ...1F 173
  W13 ...7A 78
Drayton Bri. Rd. W7 ...7K 77
  W13 ...7K 77
Drayton Cl. IG1: Ilf ...1H 71
  TW4: Houn ...5D 112
Drayton Ct. UB7: W Dray ...4B 92
Drayton Gdns. N21 ...7G 23
  SW10 ...6A 16 (5A 100)
  UB7: W Dray ...2A 92
  W13 ...7A 78
Drayton Grn. W13 ...7A 78
Drayton Grn. Rd. W13 ...7A 78
Drayton Gro. W13 ...7A 78
Drayton Ho. E11 ...1F 69
  SE5 ...7D 102
  (off Elmington Rd.)
Drayton Pk. N5 ...4A 66
Drayton Pk. M. N5 ...5A 66
Drayton Rd. CR0: Croy ...2B 168
  E11 ...1F 69
  N17 ...2F 48
  NW10 ...1B 80
  W13 ...7A 78
Drayton Waye HA3: Kent ...6B 42
Dreadnought St. SE10 ...3G 105
Dreadnought Wharf SE10 ...6D 104
  (off Thames St.)

Dumpton Pl.—Dyson Ho.

Dumpton Pl. NW1 7E 64
Dumsey Eyot KT16: Chert 7A 146
Dunally Pk. TW17: Shep 7F 147
Dunbar Av. BR3: Beck 4A 158
RM10: Dag 3G 73
SW16 2A 156
Dunbar Cl. UB4: Hayes 6K 75
Dunbar Ct. *BR2: Brom* *3H 159*
(off Durham Rd.)
SM1: Sutt 5B 166
Dunbar Gdns. RM10: Dag 5G 73
Dunbar Rd. E7 6J 69
KT3: N Mald 4J 151
N22 1A 48
Dunbar St. SE27 3C 138
Dunbar Wharf *E14* *7B 86*
(off Narrow St.)
Dunblane Cl. HA8: Edg 2C 28
Dunblane Rd. SE9 3C 124
Dunboe Pl. TW17: Shep 7E 146
Dunboyne Rd. NW3 5D 64
Dunbridge Ho. *SW15* *6B 116*
(off Highcliffe Dr.)
Dunbridge St. E2 4G 85
Duncan Cl. EN5: New Bar 4F 21
Duncan Ct. N21 1G 33
Duncan Gro. W3 6A 80
Duncan Ho. *NW3* *7D 64*
(off Fellows Rd.)
SW1 *6B 18*
(off Dolphin Sq.)
Duncannon Ho. *SW1* *6D 18*
(off Lindsay Sq.)
Duncannon St. WC2 3E 12 (7J 83)
Duncan Rd. E8 1H 85
TW9: Rich 4E 114
Duncan St. N1 2B 84
Duncan Ter. N1 2B 84
(not continuous)
Dunch St. E1 6H 85
Duncombe Hill SE23 7A 122
Duncombe Rd. N19 1H 65
Duncrievie Rd. SE13 6F 123
Duncroft SE18 7J 107
Dundalk Ho. *E1* *6J 85*
(off Clark St.)
Dundalk Rd. SE4 3A 122
Dundas Gdns. KT8: W Mole 3F 149
Dundas Ho. *E2* *2J 85*
(off Bishop's Way)
Dundas Rd. SE15 2J 121
Dundee Ct. *E1* *1H 103*
(off Wapping High St.)
Dundee Ho. *W9* *3A 82*
(off Maida Va.)
Dundee Rd. E13 2K 87
SE25 5H 157
Dundee St. E1 1H 103
Dundee Way EN3: Brim 3F 25
Dundee Wharf E14 7B 86
Dundela Gdns. KT4: Wor Pk 4D 164
Dundonald Cl. E6 6C 88
Dundonald Ho. *E14* *2D 104*
(off Admirals Way)
Dundonald Rd. NW10 1F 81
SW19 7G 135
(not continuous)
Dundry Ho. SE26 3G 139
Dunedin Ho. *E16* *1D 106*
(off Manwood St.)
Dunedin Rd. E10 3D 68
IG1: Ilf 1G 71
Dunedin Way UB4: Yead 4A 76
Dunelm Gro. SE27 3C 138
Dunelm St. E1 6K 85
Dunfield Gdns. SE6 5D 140
Dunfield Rd. SE6 5D 140
(not continuous)
Dunford Ct. HA5: H End 1D 40
Dunford Rd. N7 4K 65
Dungarvan Av. SW15 4C 116
Dunheved Cl. CR7: Thor H 6A 156
Dunheved Rd. Nth. CR7: Thor H 6A 156
Dunheved Rd. Sth. CR7: Thor H 6A 156
Dunheved Rd. W. CR7: Thor H 6A 156
Dunhill Point SW15 1C 134
Dunholme Grn. N9 3A 34
Dunholme La. N9 3A 34
Dunholme Rd. N9 3A 34
Dunkeld Ho. *E14* *6F 87*
(off Abbott Rd.)
Dunkeld Rd. RM8: Dag 2B 72
SE25 4D 156
Dunkery Rd. SE9 4B 142
Dunkirk St. SE27 4C 138
Dunlace Rd. E5 4J 67
Dunleary Cl. TW4: Houn 7D 112
Dunley Dr. CR0: New Ad 7D 170
Dunlin Ho. *SE16* *4K 103*
(off Tawny Way)
Dunloe Av. N17 3D 48
Dunloe Ct. E2 2F 85
Dunloe St. E2 2F 85
Dunlop Pl. SE16 3F 103
Dunmore Point *E2* *2J 9*
(off Gascoigne Pl.)
Dunmore Rd. NW6 1G 81
SW20 1E 152
Dunmow Cl. RM6: Chad H 5C 54
TW13: Hanw 3C 130
Dunmow Ho. RM9: Dag 1B 90
SE11 *5H 19*
(off Newburn St.)
Dunmow Rd. E15 4F 69
Dunmow Wlk. *N1* *1C 84*
(off Popham St.)
Dunnage Cres. SE16 4A 104
(not continuous)
Dunnico Ho. *SE17* *5E 102*
(off East St.)
Dunn Mead NW9 7G 29
Dunnock Cl. N9 1E 34
Dunnock Rd. E6 6C 88
Dunn's Pas. WC1 7F 7
Dunn St. E8 5F 67
Dunollie Pl. NW5 5G 65
Dunollie Rd. NW5 5G 65
Dunoon Gdns. SE23 7K 121
Dunoon Ho. *N1* *1K 83*
(off Bemerton Est.)
Dunoon Rd. SE23 7J 121
Dunoran Home BR1: Brom 1C 160
Dunraven Dr. EN2: Enf 2F 23
Dunraven Rd. W12 1C 98
Dunraven St. W1 2F 11 (7D 82)
Dunsany Rd. W14 3F 99
Dunsfold Cl. *SM2: Sutt* *7K 165*
(off Blackbush Cl.)
Dunsfold Way CR0: New Ad 7D 170
Dunsford Way SW15 6D 116
Dunsmore Cl. UB4: Yead 4C 76
Dunsmore Rd. KT12: Walt T 6K 147
Dunsmure Rd. N16 1E 66
Dunspring La. IG5: Ilf 2F 53
Dunstable M. W1 5H 5 (5E 82)
Dunstable Rd. KT8: W Mole 4D 148
TW9: Rich 4E 114
Dunstall Rd. SW20 6D 134
Dunstall Way KT8: W Mole 3F 149
Dunstall Welling Est. DA16: Well 2B 126
Dunstan Cl. N2 3A 46
Dunstan Glade BR5: Pet W 6H 161
Dunstan Ho's. *E1* *5J 85*
(off Stepney Grn.)
Dunstan Rd. NW11 1H 63
Dunstan's Gro. SE22 6H 121
Dunstan's Rd. SE22 7G 121
Dunster Av. SM4: Mord 1F 165
Dunster Cl. EN5: Barn 4A 20
RM5: Col R 2J 55
Dunster Ct. EC3 2H 15 (7E 84)
Dunster Dr. NW9 1J 61
Dunster Gdns. NW6 7H 63
Dunster Ho. SE6 3E 140
Dunsterville Way
SE1 7F 15 (2D 102)
Dunster Way HA2: Harr 3C 58
SM6: Wall 1E 166
Dunston Rd. E8 1F 85
SW11 2E 118
Dunston St. E8 1E 84
Dunton Cl. KT6: Surb 1E 162
Dunton Ct. SE23 2H 139
Dunton Rd. E10 7D 50
RM1: Rom 4K 55
SE1 5F 103
Duntshill Rd. SW18 1K 135
Dunvegan Cl. KT8: W Mole 4F 149
Dunvegan Rd. SE9 4D 124
Dunwich Rd. DA7: Bex 1F 127
Dunworth M. W11 6H 81
Duplex Ride SW1 7F 11 (2D 100)
Dupont Rd. SW20 2F 153
Duppas Av. CR0: Wadd 4B 168
Duppas Cl. TW17: Shep 5F 147
Duppas Ct. *CR0: Croy* *3B 168*
(off Duppas Hill Ter.)
Duppas Hill La. CR0: Croy 4B 168
Duppas Hill Rd. CR0: Wadd 4A 168
Duppas Hill Ter. CR0: Croy 3B 168
Duppas Rd. CR0: Wadd 3A 168
Dupree Rd. SE7 5K 105
Duraden Cl. BR3: Beck 7D 140
Durand Cl. SM5: Cars 1D 166
Durand Gdns. SW9 1K 119
Durands Wlk. SE16 2B 104
Durand Way NW10 7J 61
Durants Pk. Av. EN3: Pond E 4E 24
Durants Rd. EN3: Pond E 4D 24
Durant St. E2 2G 85
Durban Ct. E7 7B 70
Durban Gdns. RM10: Dag 7J 73
Durban Ho. *W12* *7D 80*
(off White City Est.)
Durban Rd. BR3: Beck 2B 158
E15 3G 87
E17 1B 50
IG2: Ilf 1J 71
N17 6K 33
SE27 4C 138
Durbin Rd. KT9: Chess 4E 162
Durdan Cotts. *UB1: S'hall* *6D 76*
(off Denbigh Rd.)
Durdans Ho. *NW1* *7F 65*
(off Farrier St.)
Durdans Rd. UB1: S'hall 6D 76
Durell Gdns. RM9: Dag 5D 72
Durell Ho. *SE16* *2K 103*
(off Wolfe Cres.)
Durell Rd. RM9: Dag 5D 72
Durford Cres. SW15 1D 134
Durham Av. BR2: Brom 4H 159
IG8: Buck H, Wfd G 5G 37
TW5: Hest 5D 94
Durham Cl. SW20 2D 152
Durham Ct. *NW6* *2J 81*
(off Kilburn Pk. Rd., not continuous)
TW11: Tedd 4J 131
Durham Hill BR1: Brom 4H 141
Durham Ho. BR2: Brom 4G 159
IG11: Bark *7A 72*
(off Margaret Bondfield Av.)
RM10: Dag 5J 73
Durham Ho. St. WC2 3F 13
Durham Pl. IG1: Ilf 4G 71
SW3 6E 16 (5D 100)
Durham Ri. SE18 5G 107
Durham Rd. BR2: Brom 3H 159
DA14: Sidc 5B 144
E12 4B 70
E16 4G 87
HA1: Harr 5F 41
N2 3C 46
Durham Rd. N7 2K 65
N9 2B 34
RM10: Dag 5J 73
SW20 1D 152
TW14: Felt 7A 112
W5 3D 96
Durham Row E1 5K 85
Durham St. SE11 6G 19 (5K 101)
Durham Ter. W2 6K 81
Durham Wharf
TW8: Bford 7C 96
Durham Yd. E2 3H 85
Durley Av. HA5: Pinn 7C 40
Durley Rd. N16 7E 48
Durlston Rd. E5 2G 67
KT2: King T 6E 132
Durnford Ho. SE6 3E 140
Durnford St. N15 5E 48
SE10 6E 104
Durning Rd. SE19 5D 138
Durnsford Av. SW19 2J 135
Durnsford Rd. N11 1H 47
SW19 2J 135
Durnsford Sports Cen. 1G 47
Durrant Ct. HA3: Hrw W 2J 41
Durrant Way BR6: Farnb 5H 173
Durrell Rd. SW6 1H 117
Durrell Way
TW17: Shep 6F 147
Durrels Ho. *W14* *4H 99*
(off Warwick Gdns.)
Durrington Av. SW20 7E 134
Durrington Pk. Rd. SW20 1E 152
Durrington Rd. E5 4A 68
Durrington Twr. SW8 2G 119
Durrisdeer Ho. *NW2* *4H 63*
(off Lyndale)
Dursley Cl. SE3 2A 124
Dursley Gdns. SE3 1B 124
Dursley Rd. SE3 2A 124
Durward St. E1 5H 85
Durweston M. W1 5F 5
Durweston St. W1 6F 5 (5D 82)
Dury Falls Ct. RM5: Col R 2J 55
Dury Rd. EN5: Barn 1C 20
Dutch Barn Cl.
TW19: Stanw 6A 110
Dutch Gdns. KT2: King T 6H 133
Dutch Yd. SW18 5J 117
Dutton St. SE10 1E 122
Duxberry Av. TW13: Felt 3A 130
Duxberry Cl. BR2: Brom 5C 160
Duxford Ho. *SE2* *2D 108*
(off Wolvercote Rd.)
Dye Ho. La. E3 1C 86
Dyer Ho. TW12: Hamp 1F 149
Dyer's Bldgs. EC1 6J 7 (5A 84)
Dyers Hall Rd. E11 1G 69
Dyers Hill Rd. E11 2F 69
Dyers La. SW15 4D 116
Dykes Way BR2: Brom 3H 159
Dykewood Cl. DA5: Bexl 3K 145
Dylan Rd. DA17: Belv 3G 109
SE24 4B 120
Dylways SE5 4D 120
Dymchurch Cl. BR6: Orp 4J 173
IG5: Ilf 2E 52
Dymes Path SW19 2F 135
Dymock St. SW6 3K 117
Dyneley Rd. SE12 3A 142
Dyne Rd. NW6 7G 63
Dynevor Rd. N16 3E 66
TW10: Rich 5E 114
Dynham Rd. NW6 7J 63
Dyott St. WC1 7D 6 (6H 83)
Dysart Av. KT2: King T 5C 132
Dysart St. EC2 4G 9 (4D 84)
Dyson Ct. HA0: Wemb 4A 60
NW2 1E 62
Dyson Ho. *SE10* *5H 105*
(off Blackwall La.)

Dyson Rd. E11 6G 51
E15 6H 69
Dysons Rd. N18 5C 34

E

Eade Rd. N4 7C 48
Eagans Cl. N2 3B 46
Eagle Av. RM6: Chad H 6E 54
Eagle Cl. EN3: Pond E 4D 24
SE16 5J 103
SM6: Wall 6J 167
Eagle Ct. E11 4J 51
EC1 5A 8 (5B 84)
Eagle Dr. NW9 2A 44
Eagle Hill SE19 6D 138
Eagle Ho. *E1* *4H 85*
(off Headlam St.)
N1 *2D 84*
(off Eagle Wharf Rd.)
Eagle La. E11 4J 51
Eagle Lodge NW11 7H 45
Eagle M. N1 6E 66
Eagle Pl. SW1 3B 12
SW7 5A 100
Eagle Rd. HA0: Wemb 7D 60
TW6: H'row A 3H 111
Eaglesfield Rd. SE18 1F 125
Eagle St. WC1 6G 7 (5K 83)
Eagle Ter. IG8: Wfd G 7E 36
Eagle Trad. Est. CR4: Mitc 6D 154
Eagle Wharf Ct. *SE1* *5J 15*
(off Lafone St.)
Eagle Wharf E. *E14* *7A 86*
(off Narrow St.)
Eagle Wharf Rd. N1 2C 84
Eagle Wharf W. *E14* *7A 86*
(off Narrow St.)
Eagle Works E. E1 4K 9
Eagle Works W. E1 4J 9 (4F 85)
Ealdham Sq. SE9 4A 124
EALING 7D 78
Ealing B'way. Cen. W5 7D 78
EALING COMMON 7F 79
Ealing Grn. W5 1D 96
Ealing Pk. Gdns. W5 4C 96
Ealing Pk. Mans. *W5* *3D 96*
(off Sth. Ealing Rd.)
Ealing Rd. HA0: Wemb 6E 60
TW8: Bford 4D 96
UB5: N'olt 1E 76
Ealing Rd. Trad. Est.
TW8: Bford 5D 96
Ealing Squash & Fitness Club 6E 78
Ealing Studios 1D 96
Ealing Village W5 6E 78
Eamont Cl. HA4: Ruis 7D 38
Eamont Ct. *NW8* *2C 82*
(off Eamont St.)
Eamont St. NW8 2C 82
Eardley Cres. SW5 5J 99
Eardley Rd. DA17: Belv 5G 109
SW16 5G 137
Earhart Way TW6: Cran, H'row A 3J 111
Earl Cl. N11 5A 32
Earldom Rd. SW15 4E 116
Earle Gdns. KT2: King T 7E 132
Earlham Ct. E11 7H 51
Earlham Gro. E7 5H 69
N22 7E 32
Earlham St. WC2 1D 12 (6J 83)
Earl Ho. *NW1* *4D 4*
(off Lisson Gro.)
Earlom Ho. *WC1* *2J 7*
(off Margery St.)
Earl Ri. SE18 5H 107
Earl Rd. SW14 4J 115
EARL'S COURT 5J 99
Earls Court Exhibition Building 5J 99
Earl's Ct. Gdns. SW5 4K 99
Earls Ct. Rd. SW5 3J 99
W8 3J 99
Earl's Ct. Sq. SW5 5K 99
Earls Cres. HA1: Harr 4J 41
Earlsdown Ho. IG11: Bark 2H 89
Earlsferry Way N1 7J 65
(not continuous)
EARLSFIELD 1A 136
Earlsfield Ho.
KT2: King T *1D 150*
(off Skerne Rd.)
TW9: Kew 7H 97
Earlsfield Rd. SW18 1A 136
Earlshall Rd. SE9 4D 124
Earlsmead HA2: Harr 4D 58
Earlsmead Rd. N15 5F 49
NW10 3E 80
Earls Ter. W8 3H 99
Earlsthorpe M. SW12 6E 118
Earlsthorpe Rd. SE26 4K 139
Earlstoke St. EC1 1A 8 (3B 84)
Earlston Gro. E9 1H 85
Earl St. EC2 5G 9 (5D 84)
(not continuous)
Earls Wlk. RM8: Dag 4B 72
W8 3J 99
Earls Way BR6: Orp 2K 173
Earlswood Av. CR7: Thor H 5A 156
Earlswood Cl. SE10 6G 105
Earlswood Gdns. IG5: Ilf 3E 52
Earlswood St. SE10 5G 105
Early M. NW1 1F 83
Earnshaw St. WC2 7D 6 (6H 83)
Earsby St. W14 4G 99
(not continuous)
Easby Cres. SM4: Mord 6K 153
Easebourne Rd. RM8: Dag 5C 72
Eashing Point *SW15* *1D 134*
(off Wanborough Dr.)
Easleys M. W1 7H 5 (6E 82)
East 10 Ent. Pk. E10 1A 68
EAST ACTON 7B 80
E. Acton Arc. W3 6A 80
E. Acton Ct. W3 7A 80
E. Acton La. W3 1A 98
E. Arbour St. E1 6K 85
East Av. E12 7C 70
E17 4D 50
N2 4K 45
SM6: Wall 5K 167
UB1: S'hall 7D 76
UB3: Hayes 1H 93
East Bank N16 7E 48
Eastbank Rd. TW12: Hamp H 5G 131
EAST BARNET 6H 21
E. Barnet Rd. EN4: E Barn 4G 21
E. Beckton District Cen. E6 5D 88
EAST BEDFONT 7G 111
East Block *SE1* *6H 13*
(off York Rd.)
E. Boundary Rd. E12 3D 70
Eastbourne Av. W3 6K 79
Eastbourne Gdns. SW14 3J 115
Eastbourne M. W2 7A 4 (6A 82)
Eastbourne Rd. E6 3E 88
(not continuous)
E15 1G 87
N15 6E 48
SW17 6E 136
TW8: Bford 5C 96
TW13: Felt 2B 130
W4 6J 97
Eastbourne Ter. W2 7A 4 (6A 82)
Eastbournia Av. N9 3C 34
Eastbrook Av. N9 7D 24
RM10: Dag 4J 73
Eastbrook Dr. RM7: Rush G 3K 73
Eastbrookend Country Pk. 3K 73
Eastbrook Rd. SE3 1K 123
Eastbury Av. EN1: Enf 1A 24
IG11: Bark 1J 89
Eastbury Ct. *EN5: New Bar* *5F 21*
(off Lyonsdown Rd.)
IG11: Bark 1J 89
Eastbury Gro. W4 5A 98
Eastbury Manor House 1K 89
Eastbury Rd. BR5: Pet W 6H 161
E6 4E 88
KT2: King T 7E 132
RM7: Rom 6K 55
Eastbury Sq. IG11: Bark 1K 89
Eastbury Ter. E1 4K 85
Eastcastle St. W1 7A 6 (6G 83)
Eastcheap EC3 2G 15 (7E 84)
E. Churchfield Rd. W3 1K 97
Eastchurch Rd. TW6: H'row A 2G 111
East Cl. EN4: Cockf 4K 21
UB6: G'frd 2G 77
W5 4G 79
Eastcombe Av. SE7 6K 105
EASTCOTE 7K 39
Eastcote BR6: Orp 1K 173
Eastcote Av. HA2: Harr 2F 59
KT8: W Mole 5D 148
UB6: G'frd 5A 60
Eastcote Hockey & Badminton Club 6H 39
Eastcote Ind. Est. HA4: Ruis 7A 40
Eastcote La. HA2: Harr 4C 58
UB5: N'olt 5D 58
(not continuous)
Eastcote La. Nth. UB5: N'olt 6D 58
Eastcote Pl. HA5: Eastc 6K 39
Eastcote Rd. DA16: Well 2H 125
HA2: Harr 3G 59
HA4: Ruis 7G 39
HA5: Pinn 5B 40
Eastcote St. SW9 2K 119
Eastcote Vw. HA5: Pinn 4A 40
EASTCOTE VILLAGE 5K 39
East Ct. HA0: Wemb 2C 60
East Cres. EN1: Enf 5A 24
N11 4J 31
Eastcroft Rd. KT19: Ewe 7A 164
E. Cross Cen. E15 6C 68
E. Cross Route E3 7B 68
E9 5B 68
(Homerton)
E9 7B 68
(Old Ford)
E15 5C 68
Eastdown Ct. SE13 4F 123
Eastdown Ho. E8 4G 67
Eastdown Pk. SE13 4F 123
East Dr. SM5: Cars 7C 166
E. Duck Lees La.
EN3: Pond E 4F 25
EAST DULWICH 4F 121
E. Dulwich Gro. SE22 5E 120
E. Dulwich Rd. SE22 4F 121
(not continuous)
E. End Farm HA5: Pinn 3D 40
E. End Rd. N2 3K 45
N3 2J 45
E. End Way HA5: Pinn 3C 40
East Entrance RM10: Dag 2H 91
Eastern Av. E11 6K 51
HA5: Pinn 7B 40
IG2: Ilf 6F 53
IG4: Ilf 6B 52
RM6: Chad H 4A 54
Eastern Av. E. RM1: Rom 3K 55
Eastern Av. Retail Pk.
RM7: Rom 4J 55
Eastern Av. W. RM6: Chad H 4E 54
RM7: Chad H, Mawney, Rom 4A 54
Eastern Bus. Pk. TW6: H'row A 2G 111
Eastern Gateway E16 7A 88
Eastern Ind. Est. DA18: Erith 2G 109
Eastern Perimeter Rd.
TW6: H'row A 2H 111
Eastern Quay Apartments *E16* *1K 105*
(off Portsmouth M.)
Eastern Rd. E13 2K 87
E17 5E 50
N2 3D 46
N22 1J 47
SE4 4C 122
Eastern Rdbt. IG1: Ilf 2G 71
Easternville Gdns. IG2: Ilf 6G 53
Eastern Way DA17: Belv 2A 108
DA18: Belv, Erith 2A 108
SE2 2A 108
SE28 2A 108
E. Ferry Rd. E14 4D 104
Eastfield Gdns. RM10: Dag 4G 73
Eastfield Rd. E17 4C 50
EN3: Enf W 1E 24
N8 3J 47
RM9: Dag 4F 73
RM10: Dag 4G 73
Eastfields HA5: Eastc 5A 40
Eastfields Av. SW18 4J 117
Eastfields Rd. CR4: Mitc 2E 154
W3 5J 79
Eastfield St. E14 5A 86
EAST FINCHLEY 4C 46
East Gdns. SW17 6C 136
Eastgate Cl. SE28 6D 90
Eastglade HA5: Pinn 3D 40
EAST HAM 2D 88
E. Ham & Barking By-Pass
IG11: Bark 2J 89
Eastham Cl. EN5: Barn 5B 20
E. Ham Ind. Est. E6 4C 88
East Ham Leisure Cen. 1D 88
E. Ham Mnr. Way E6 6E 88
East Ham Nature Reserve 4D 88
E. Harding St. EC4 7K 7 (6A 84)
E. Heath Rd. NW3 3A 64
East Hill HA9: Wemb 2G 61
SW18 5K 117
Eastholm NW11 4K 45
East Holme DA8: Erith 1K 127
Eastholme UB3: Hayes 1J 93
E. India Bldgs. *E14* *7C 86*
(off Saltwell St.)
E. India Ct. *SE16* *2J 103*
(off St Marychurch St.)
E. India Dock Ho. E14 6E 86
E. India Dock Rd. E14 6C 86
E. India Way CR0: Croy 1F 169
Eastlake Ho. NW8 4B 4
Eastlake Rd. SE5 2C 120
Eastlands Cres. SE21 6F 121
East La. HA0: Wemb 3B 60
HA9: Wemb 3B 60
KT1: King T 3D 150
SE16 2G 103
(Chambers St.)
SE16 2G 103
(Scott Lidgett Cres.)
East La. Bus. Pk. HA9: Wemb 2D 60
Eastlea M. E16 4G 87
Eastleigh Av. HA2: Harr 2F 59
Eastleigh Cl. NW2 3A 62
SM2: Sutt 7K 165
Eastleigh Rd. DA7: Bex 3J 127
E17 2B 50
Eastleigh Wlk. SW15 7C 116
Eastleigh Way TW14: Felt 1J 129
East Lodge *E16* *1J 105*
(off Wesley Av.)
E. London Crematorium E13 3H 87
East London Gymnastic Cen. 6D 88
Eastman Ho. SW4 6G 119
Eastman Rd. W3 2K 97
East Mascalls SE7 6A 106
East Mead HA4: Ruis 3B 58
Eastmead Av. UB6: G'frd 3F 77
Eastmead Cl. BR1: Brom 2C 160
Eastmearn Rd. SE21 2C 138
EAST MOLESEY 4H 149
Eastmoor Pl. SE7 3B 106

Edison Dr.—Elephant Rd.

Edison Dr. HA9: Wemb 3E 60
UB1: S'hall 6F 77
Edison Gro. SE18 7K 107
Edison Ho. HA9: Wemb 3J 61
(off Barnhill Rd.)
Edison Rd. BR2: Brom 2J 159
DA16: Well 1K 125
EN3: Brim 2G 25
N8 6H 47
Edis St. NW1 1E 82
Edith Brinson Ho. E14 6F 87
(off Oban St.)
Edith Cavell Cl. N19 7J 47
Edith Cavell Way SE18 1C 124
Edith Gdns. KT5: Surb 7H 151
Edith Gro. SW10 6A 100
Edith Ho. W6 5E 98
(off Queen Caroline St.)
Edithna St. SW9 3J 119
Edith Neville Cotts. NW1 1C 6
(off Drummond Cres.)
Edith Ramsay Ho. E1 5A 86
(off Duckett St.)
Edith Rd. E6 7B 70
E15 5F 69
N11 7C 32
RM6: Chad H 7D 54
SE25 5D 156
SW19 6K 135
W14 4G 99
Edith Row SW6 1K 117
Edith St. E2 2G 85
Edith Summerskill Ho. SW6 7H 99
(off Clem Attlee Est.)
Edith Ter. SW10 7A 100
Edith Vs. W14 4H 99
Edith Yd. SW10 7A 100
Edmansons Cl. N17 1F 49
Edmeston Cl. E9 6A 68
Edmond Ct. SE14 1J 121
Edmonscote W13 5A 78
EDMONTON 3B 34
Edmonton Ct. SE16 3J 103
(off Canada Est.)
Edmonton Grn. Shop. Cen. N9 2B 34
Edmonton Leisure Cen. 3B 34
Edmund Gro. TW13: Hanw 2D 130
Edmund Halley Way SE10 2G 105
Edmund Ho. SE17 6B 102
Edmund Hurst Dr. E6 5F 89
Edmund Rd. CR4: Mitc 3C 154
DA16: Well 3A 126
Edmundsbury Ct. Est. SW9 4K 119
Edmunds Cl. UB4: Yead 5A 76
Edmund St. SE5 7D 102
Edmunds Wlk. N2 4C 46
Ednam Ho. SE15 6G 103
(off Haymerle Rd.)
Edna Rd. SW20 2F 153
Edna St. SW11 1C 118
Edred Ho. E9 4A 68
(off Lindisfarne Way)
Edrich Ho. SW4 1J 119
Edric Ho. SW1 3D 18
(off Page St.)
Edrick Rd. HA8: Edg 6D 28
Edrick Wlk. HA8: Edg 6D 28
Edric Rd. SE14 7K 103
Edridge Rd. CR0: Croy 3C 168
Edward VII Mans. NW10 3F 81
(off Chamberlayne Rd.)
Edward Av. E4 6J 35
SM4: Mord 5B 154
Edward Bond Ho. WC1 2F 7
(off Cromer St.)
Edward Cl. N9 7A 24
NW2 4F 63
TW12: Hamp H 5G 131
Edward Ct. E16 5J 87
Edward Dodd Ct. N1 1F 9
(off Haberdasher St.)
Edward Edward's Ho. SE1 5A 14
Edwardes Pl. W8 3H 99
Edwardes Sq. W8 3H 99
Edward Gro. EN4: E Barn 5G 21
Edward Ho. SE11 5H 19
Edward Mann Cl. E1 6K 85
(off Caroline St.)
Edward M. NW1 1K 5 (3F 83)
Edward Pl. SE8 6B 104
Edward Rd. BR1: Brom 7K 141
BR7: Chst 5F 143
CR0: Croy 7E 156
E17 4K 49
EN4: E Barn 5G 21
HA2: Harr 3G 41
RM6: Chad H 6E 54
SE20 7K 139
TW12: Hamp H 5G 131
TW14: Felt 5F 111
UB5: Yead 2A 76
Edward Robinson Ho. SE14 7K 103
(off Reaston St.)
Edward's Av. HA4: Ruis 6K 57
Edwards Cl. KT4: Wor Pk 2F 165
Edward's Cotts. N1 6B 66
Edwards Ct. CR2: S Croy 4E 168
(off South Pk. Hill Rd.)
Edwards Dr. N11 7C 32
Edward's La. N16 2E 66
Edwards Mans. IG11: Bark 7K 71
(off Upney La.)
Edwards M. N1 7A 66
W1 1G 11 (6E 82)
Edward Sq. N1 1K 83
SE16 1A 104
Edwards Rd. DA17: Belv 4G 109
Edward St. E16 4J 87
(not continuous)
SE8 6B 104
SE14 7A 104
Edwards Yd. HA0: Wemb 1E 78
Edward Temme Av. E15 7H 69
Edward Tyler Rd. SE12 2A 142
Edward Way TW15: Ashf 2B 128
Edwina Gdns. IG4: Ilf 5C 52
Edwin Arnold Ct. DA14: Sidc 4K 143
Edwin Av. E6 2E 88
(not continuous)
Edwin Cl. DA7: Bex 6F 109
Edwin Ho. SE15 7G 103
Edwin Pl. CR0: Croy 1E 168
(off Leslie Gro.)
Edwin Rd. HA8: Edg 6E 28
TW1: Twick 1K 131
TW2: Twick 1J 131
Edwin's Mead E9 4A 68
Edwin Stray Ho. TW13: Hanw 2E 130
Edwin St. E1 4J 85
E16 5J 87
Edwin Ware Ct. HA5: Pinn 2A 40
Edwyn Cl. EN5: Barn 6A 20
Edwyn Ho. SW18 6K 117
(off Neville Gill Cl.)
Eel Pie Island TW1: Twick 1A 132
Effie Pl. SW6 7J 99
Effie Rd. SW6 7J 99
Effingham Cl. SM2: Sutt 7K 165
Effingham Lodge KT1: King T 4D 150
Effingham Rd. CR0: Croy 7K 155
KT6: Surb 7B 150
N8 5A 48
SE12 5G 123
Effort St. SW17 5C 136
Effra Cl. SW19 6K 135
Effra Ct. SW2 5K 119
(off Brixton Hill)
Effra Pde. SW2 5A 120
Effra Rd. SW2 4A 120
SW19 6K 135
Effra Rd. Retail Pk. SW2 5A 120
Egan Way UB3: Hayes 7G 75
Egbert St. NW1 1E 82
Egbury Ho. SW15 6B 116
(off Tangley Gro.)
Egeremont Rd. SE13 2D 122
Egerton Cl. HA5: Eastc 4J 39
Egerton Ct. E11 7F 51
Egerton Cres. SW3 3D 16 (4C 100)
Egerton Dr. SE10 1D 122
Egerton Gdns. IG3: Ilf 3K 71
NW4 4D 44
NW10 1E 80
SW3 2C 16 (4C 100)
W13 6B 78
Egerton Gdns. M.
SW3 2D 16 (3C 100)
Egerton Pl. SW3 2D 16 (3C 100)
Egerton Rd. HA0: Wemb 7F 61
KT3: N Mald 4B 152
N16 7F 49
SE25 3E 156
TW2: Twick 7J 113
Egerton Ter. SW3 2D 16 (3C 100)
Egerton Way UB3: Harl 7D 92
Eggardon Ct. UB5: N'olt 6F 59
Egham Cl. SM3: Cheam 2G 165
SW19 2G 135
Egham Cres. SM3: Cheam 3G 165
Egham Rd. E13 5K 87
Eglantine Rd. SW18 5A 118
Egleston Rd. SM4: Mord 6K 153
Eglington Ct. SE17 6C 102
Eglington Rd. E4 7K 25
Eglinton Hill SE18 6F 107
Eglinton Rd. SE18 6E 106
Egliston M. SW15 3E 116
Egliston Rd. SW15 3E 116
Eglon M. NW1 7D 64
Egmont Av. KT6: Surb 1F 163
Egmont Ct. KT12: Walt T 7K 147
Egmont Rd. KT3: N Mald 4B 152
KT6: Surb 1F 163
KT12: Walt T 7K 147
SM2: Sutt 7A 166
Egmont St. SE14 7K 103
Egremont Ho. SE13 2D 122
(off Russett Way)
Egremont Rd. SE27 3A 138
Egret Ho. SE16 4K 103
(off Tawny Way)
Egret Way UB4: Yead 5B 76
Eider Cl. E7 5H 69
UB4: Yead 5B 76
Eider Ct. SE8 6B 104
(off Pilot Cl.)
Eighteenth Rd. CR4: Mitc 4J 155
Eighth Av. E12 4D 70
UB3: Hayes 1J 93
Eileen Rd. SE25 5D 156
Eindhoven Cl. SM5: Cars 1E 166
Einstein Ho. HA9: Wemb 3J 61
Eisenhower Dr. E6 5C 88
Elaine Gro. NW5 5E 64
Elam Cl. SE5 2B 120
Elam St. SE5 2B 120
Elan Ct. E1 5H 85
Eland Ho. SW1 1A 18
(off Bressenden Pl.)
Eland Pl. CR0: Wadd 3B 168
Eland Rd. CR0: Wadd 3B 168
SW11 3D 118
Elba Pl. SE17 4C 102
Elberon Av. CR0: Bedd 6G 155
Elbe St. SW6 2A 118
Elborough Rd. SE25 5G 157
Elborough St. SW18 1J 135
Elbourne Ct. SE16 3K 103
(off Worgan St.)
Elbourne Trad. Est. DA17: Belv 3H 109
Elbourn Ho. SW3 5C 16
(off Cale St.)
Elbury Dr. E16 6J 87
Elcho St. SW11 7C 100
Elcot Av. SE15 7H 103
Eldenwall Ind. Est.
RM8: Dag 1E 72
Elder Av. N8 5J 47
Elderberry Gro. SE27 4C 138
Elderberry Rd. W5 2E 96
Elderberry Way E6 3D 88
Elder Cl. DA15: Sidc 1K 143
N20 2E 30
UB7: Yiew 7A 74
Elder Ct. WD23: Bushy 2D 26
Elderfield Ho. E14 7C 86
Elderfield Pl. SW17 4F 137
Elderfield Rd. E5 4K 67
Elderfield Wlk. E11 5K 51
Elderflower Way E15 7G 69
Elder Gdns. SE27 5C 138
Elder Oak Cl. SE20 1H 157
Elder Oak Ct. SE20 1H 157
(off Anerley Ct.)
Elder Rd. SE27 4C 138
Elderslie Cl. BR3: Beck 5C 158
Elderslie Rd. SE9 5E 124
Elder St. E1 5J 9 (4F 85)
(not continuous)
Elderton Rd. SE26 4A 140
Eldertree Pl. CR4: Mitc 1G 155
Eldertree Way CR4: Mitc 1G 155
Elder Wlk. N1 1B 84
(off Popham St.)
Elderwood Pl. SE27 5C 138
Eldon Av. CR0: Croy 2J 169
TW5: Hest 7E 94
Eldon Ct. NW6 1J 81
Eldon Gro. NW3 5B 64
Eldon Pk. SE25 4H 157
Eldon Rd. E17 4B 50
N9 1D 34
N22 1B 48
W8 3K 99
Eldon St. EC2 6F 9 (5D 84)
Eldon Way NW10 3H 79
Eldred Rd. IG11: Bark 1J 89
Eldrick Ct. TW14: Bedf 1F 129
Eldridge Cl. TW14: Felt 1J 129
Eldridge Ct. SE16 3G 103
Eleanor Cl. N15 3F 49
SE16 2K 103
Eleanor Cres. NW7 5A 30
Eleanor Gdns. EN5: Barn 5A 20
RM8: Dag 2F 73
Eleanor Gro. SW13 3A 116
UB10: Ick 3D 56
Eleanor Ho. W6 5E 98
(off Queen Caroline St.)
Eleanor Rathbone Ho. N6 7H 47
(off Avenue Rd.)
Eleanor Rd. E8 6H 67
E15 6H 69
N11 6D 32
Eleanor's Station
Ruislip Lido Railway 3G 39
Eleanor St. E3 3C 86
Eleanor Wlk. SE18 4C 106
Electra Av. TW6: H'row A 3H 111
Electra Bus. Pk. E16 5F 87
Electric Av. SW9 4A 120
Electric La. SW9 4A 120
(not continuous)
Electric Pde. E18 2J 51
(off George La.)
IG3: Ilf 2J 71
KT6: Surb 6D 150
Elektron Ho. E14 7F 87
ELEPHANT & CASTLE 3B 102
Elephant & Castle SE1 4B 102
Elephant & Castle Superbowl 4C 102
(off Walworth Rd.)
Elephant La. SE16 2J 103
Elephant Rd. SE17 4C 102

Elers Rd.—Elmcroft Ter.

Elers Rd. UB3: Harl 4F **93**
W13 .... 2C **96**
Eley Rd. N18 .... 4D **34**
Eley Rd. Retail Pk. N18 .... 5D **34**
Eleys Est. N9 .... 3E **34**
N18 .... 4E **34**
(not continuous)
Elfindale Rd. SE24 .... 5C **120**
Elfin Gro. TW11: Tedd 5K **131**
Elford Cl. SE3 .... 4K **123**
Elford M. SW4 .... 5G **119**
Elfort Rd. N5 .... 4A **66**
Elfrida Cres. SE6 .... 4C **140**
Elf Row E1 .... 7J **85**
Elfwine Rd. W7 .... 5J **77**
Elgal Cl. BR6: Farnb 5F **173**
Elgar *N8* *3J* ***47***
(off Boyton Cl.)
Elgar Av. KT5: Surb 1G **163**
NW10 .... 6K **61**
(not continuous)
SW16 .... 3J **155**
W5 .... 2E **96**
Elgar Cl. E13 .... 2A **88**
IG9: Buck H 2G **37**
SE8 .... 7C **104**
UB10: Ick 2C **56**
Elgar Ct. *W14* *3G* ***99***
(off Blythe Rd.)
Elgar Ho. *NW6* *7A* ***64***
(off Fairfax Rd.)
SW1 .... *6K* ***17***
(off Churchill Gdns.)
Elgar St. SE16 .... 3A **104**
Elgin Av. HA3: Kent 2B **42**
TW15: Ashf 6E **128**
W9 .... 4H **81**
W12 .... 3D **98**
Elgin Cl. W12 .... 2D **98**
Elgin Ct. *CR2: S Croy* *4C* ***168***
(off Bramley Hill)
W9 .... 4K **81**
Elgin Cres. TW6: H'row A 2G **111**
W11 .... 7G **81**
Elgin Dr. HA6: Nwood 1G **39**
Elgin Est. *W9* *4J* ***81***
(off Elgin Av.)
Elgin Ho. *E14* *6D* ***86***
(off Ricardo St.)
Elgin Mans. W9 .... 3K **81**
Elgin M. W11 .... 6G **81**
Elgin M. Nth. W9 .... 3K **81**
Elgin M. Sth. W9 .... 3K **81**
Elgin Rd. CR0: Croy 2F **169**
IG3: Ilf 1J **71**
N22 .... 2G **47**
SM1: Sutt 3A **166**
SM6: Wall 6G **167**
Elgood Cl. W11 .... 7G **81**
Elgood Ho. *NW8* *2B* ***82***
(off Wellington Rd.)
Elham Cl. BR1: Brom 7B **142**
Elham Ho. E5 .... 5H **67**
Elia M. N1 .... 1A **8** (2B **84**)
Elias Pl. SW8 .... 6A **102**
Elia St. N1 .... 1B **8** (2B **84**)
Elibank Rd. SE9 .... 4D **124**
Elim Est. SE1 .... 7G **15** (3E **102**)
Elim St. SE1 .... 7G **15** (3D **102**)
(not continuous)
Elim Way E13 .... 3H **87**
Eliot Bank SE23 .... 2H **139**
Eliot Cotts. SE3 .... 2G **123**
Eliot Ct. SW18 .... 6K **117**
Eliot Dr. HA2: Harr 2F **59**
Eliot Gdns. SW15 .... 4C **116**
Eliot Hill SE13 .... 2E **122**
Eliot M. NW8 .... 2A **82**
Eliot Pk. SE13 .... 2E **122**
Eliot Pl. SE3 .... 2G **123**
Eliot Rd. RM9: Dag 4D **72**
Eliot Va. SE3 .... 2F **123**
Elis David Almshouses
CR0: Croy 3B **168**
Elizabethan Cl. TW19: Stanw 7A **110**
Elizabethan Way TW19: Stanw 7A **110**
Elizabeth Av. EN2: Enf 3G **23**
IG1: Ilf 2H **71**
N1 .... 1C **84**
TW18: Staines 7A **128**
Elizabeth Barnes Ct. *SW6* *2K* ***117***
(off Marinefield Rd.)
Elizabeth Blackwell Ho. *N22* *1A* ***48***
(off Progress Way)
Elizabeth Bri. SW1 .... 4J **17** (4F **101**)
Elizabeth Cl. E14 .... 6D **86**
EN5: Barn 3A **20**
RM7: Mawney 1H **55**
SM1: Sutt 4H **165**
W9 .... 4A **82**
Elizabeth Clyde Cl. N15 .... 4E **48**
Elizabeth Cotts. TW9: Kew 1F **115**
Elizabeth Ct. *BR1: Brom* *1H* ***159***
(off Highland Rd.)
E4 .... 5G **35**
IG8: Wfd G 7F **37**
KT2: King T 1E **150**
SW1 .... 2D **18**
SW10 .... *6B* ***100***
(off Milman's St.)
TW11: Tedd 5J **131**
TW16: Sun *3A* ***148***
(off Elizabeth Gdns.)
Elizabeth Fry Ho. UB3: Harl 4H **93**
Elizabeth Fry M. E8 .... 7H **67**
Elizabeth Fry Pl. SE18 .... 1C **124**
Elizabeth Gdns. HA7: Stan 6H **27**
TW7: Isle 4A **114**
TW16: Sun 3A **148**
W3 .... 1B **98**
Elizabeth Garrett Anderson Ho.
DA17: Belv *3G* ***109***
(off Ambrook Rd.)
Elizabeth Ho. *SE11* *4K* ***19***
(off Reedworth St.)
SM3: Cheam *6G* ***165***
(off Park La.)
W6 .... *5E* ***98***
(off Queen Caroline St.)
Elizabeth Ind. Est. SE14 .... 6K **103**
Elizabeth M. HA1: Harr 6J **41**
NW3 .... 6C **64**
Elizabeth Newcomen Ho. *SE1* *6E* ***14***
(off Newcomen St.)
Elizabeth Pl. N15 .... 4D **48**
Elizabeth Ride N9 .... 7C **24**
Elizabeth Rd. E6 .... 1B **88**
N15 .... 5E **48**
Elizabeth Sq. *SE16* *7A* ***86***
(off Sovereign Cres.)
Elizabeth St. SW1 .... 3H **17** (4E **100**)
Elizabeth Ter. SE9 .... 6D **124**
Elizabeth Way SE19 .... 7D **138**
TW13: Hanw 4A **130**
Elkanette M. N20 .... 2F **31**
Elkington Point SE11 .... 4J **19**
Elkington Rd. E13 .... 4K **87**
Elkstone Rd. W10 .... 5H **81**
Ella Cl. BR3: Beck 2C **158**
Ellaline Rd. W6 .... 6F **99**
Ella M. NW3 .... 4D **64**
Ellanby Cres. N18 .... 4C **34**
Elland Ho. *E14* *6B* ***86***
(off Copenhagen Pl.)
Elland Rd. SE15 .... 4J **121**
Ella Rd. N8 .... 7J **47**
Ellement Cl. HA5: Pinn 5B **40**
Ellena Ct. *N14* *3D* ***32***
(off Conway Rd.)
Ellenborough Ho. *W12* *7D* ***80***
(off White City Est.)
Ellenborough Pl. SW15 .... 4C **116**
Ellenborough Rd. DA14: Sidc 5D **144**
N22 .... 1C **48**
Ellenbridge Way CR2: Sand 7E **168**
Ellen Cl. BR1: Brom 3B **160**
Ellen Ct. *E4* *1K* ***35***
(off Ridgeway, The)
N9 .... 2D **34**
Ellen St. E1 .... 6G **85**
Ellen Terry Ct. *NW1* *7F* ***65***
(off Farrier St.)
Ellen Webb Dr. HA3: W'stone 3J **41**
Ellen Wilkinson Ho. *E2* *3K* ***85***
(off Usk St.)
RM10: Dag 3G **73**
SW6 .... *6H* ***99***
(off Clem Attlee Ct.)
Elleray Rd. TW11: Tedd 6K **131**
Ellerby St. SW6 .... 1F **117**
Ellerdale Cl. NW3 .... 4A **64**
Ellerdale Rd. NW3 .... 5A **64**
Ellerdale St. SE13 .... 4D **122**
Ellerdine Rd. TW3: Houn 4G **113**
Ellerker Gdns. TW10: Rich 6E **114**
Ellerman Av. TW2: Whit 1D **130**
Ellerslie Gdns. NW10 .... 1C **80**
Ellerslie Rd. W12 .... 1D **98**
Ellerslie Sq. Ind. Est. SW2 .... 5J **119**
Ellerton Gdns. RM9: Dag 7C **72**
Ellerton Lodge N3 .... 2J **45**
Ellerton Rd. KT6: Surb 2F **163**
RM9: Dag 7C **72**
SW13 .... 1C **116**
SW18 .... 1B **136**
SW20 .... 7C **134**
Ellery Ho. SE17 .... 4D **102**
Ellery Rd. SE19 .... 7D **138**
Ellery St. SE15 .... 2H **121**
Ellesmere Av. BR3: Beck 2D **158**
NW7 .... 3E **28**
Ellesmere Cl. E11 .... 5H **51**
HA4: Ruis 7E **38**
Ellesmere Ct. W4 .... 5K **97**
Ellesmere Gdns. IG4: Ilf 5C **52**
Ellesmere Gro. EN5: Barn 5C **20**
Ellesmere Rd. E3 .... 2A **86**
NW10 .... 5C **62**
TW1: Twick 6C **114**
UB6: G'frd 4G **77**
W4 .... 6J **97**
Ellesmere St. E14 .... 6D **86**
Ellies M. TW15: Ashf 2A **128**
Ellingfort Rd. E8 .... 7H **67**
Ellingham Rd. E15 .... 4F **69**
KT9: Chess 6D **162**
W12 .... 2C **98**
Ellington Ct. N14 .... 2C **32**
Ellington Ho. SE1 .... 3C **102**
Ellington Rd. N10 .... 4F **47**
TW3: Houn 2F **113**
TW13: Felt 4H **129**
Ellington St. N7 .... 6A **66**
Elliot Cl. E15 .... 7G **69**
Elliot Ho. *W1* *6D* ***4***
(off Cato St.)
Elliot Rd. NW4 .... 6D **44**
Elliott Av. HA4: Ruis 2K **57**
Elliott Cl. HA9: Wemb 3F **61**
Elliott Gdns. TW17: Shep 4C **146**
Elliott Rd. BR2: Brom 4B **160**
CR7: Thor H 4B **156**
HA7: Stan 6F **27**
SW9 .... 1B **120**
W4 .... 4A **98**
Elliott's Pl. N1 .... 1B **84**
Elliott Sq. NW3 .... 7C **64**
Elliotts Row SE11 .... 4B **102**
Ellis Cl. HA8: Edg 6F **29**
NW10 .... 6D **62**
SE9 .... 2G **143**
Elliscombe Mt. SE7 .... 6A **106**
Elliscombe Rd. SE7 .... 6A **106**
Ellis Ct. W7 .... 5K **77**
Ellisfield Dr. SW15 .... 7C **116**
Ellis Franklin Ct. *NW8* *2A* ***82***
(off Abbey Rd.)
Ellis Ho. *SE17* *5D* ***102***
(off Brandon St.)
Ellison Gdns. UB2: S'hall 4D **94**
Ellison Ho. *SE13* *2D* ***122***
(off Lewisham Rd.)
Ellison Rd. DA15: Sidc 1H **143**
SW13 .... 2B **116**
SW16 .... 7H **137**
Ellis Rd. CR4: Mitc 6D **154**
UB2: S'hall 1G **95**
Ellis St. SW1 .... 3F **17** (4E **100**)
Ellora Rd. SW16 .... 5H **137**
Ellswood Ct. KT6: Surb 7D **150**
Ellsworth St. E2 .... 3H **85**
Ellwood Ct. *W9* *4K* ***81***
(off Clearwell Dr.)
Elmar Rd. N15 .... 4D **48**
Elm Av. HA4: Ruis 1J **57**
TW19: Stanw 2A **128**
W5 .... 1E **96**
Elm Bank N14 .... 7D **22**
Elmbank Av. EN5: Barn 4A **20**
Elm Bank Dr. BR1: Brom 2B **160**
Elm Bank Gdns. SW13 .... 2A **116**
Elmbank Way W7 .... 5H **77**
Elmbourne Dr. DA17: Belv 4H **109**
Elmbourne Rd. SW17 .... 3F **137**
Elmbridge Av. KT5: Surb 5H **151**
Elmbridge Cl. HA4: Ruis 6J **39**
Elmbridge Dr. HA4: Ruis 5H **39**
Elmbridge Leisure Cen. 5K **147**
Elmbridge Wlk. E8 .... 7G **67**
Elmbrook Cl. TW16: Sun 1K **147**
Elmbrook Gdns. SE9 .... 4C **124**
Elmbrook Rd. SM1: Sutt 4H **165**
Elm Cl. CR2: S Croy 6E **168**
E11 .... 6K **51**
HA2: Harr 6F **41**
IG9: Buck H 2G **37**
KT5: Surb 7J **151**
N19 .... 2G **65**
NW4 .... 5F **45**
RM7: Mawney 1H **55**
SM5: Cars 1D **166**
SW20 .... 4E **152**
TW2: Twick 2F **131**
UB3: Hayes 6J **75**
Elmcote HA5: Pinn 2B **40**
Elm Cotts. CR4: Mitc 2D **154**
Elm Ct. CR4: Mitc 2D **154**
EC4 .... 1J **13**
KT8: W Mole 4F **149**
SE13 .... 3F **123**
TW16: Sun *7H* ***129***
(off Grangewood Dr.)
W9 .... *5J* ***81***
(off Admiral Wlk.)
Elmcourt Rd. SE27 .... 2B **138**
Elm Cres. KT2: King T 1E **150**
W5 .... 1E **96**
Elmcroft N6 .... 7G **47**
Elmcroft Av. DA15: Sidc 7K **125**
E11 .... 5K **51**
N9 .... 6C **24**
NW11 .... 7H **45**
Elmcroft Cl. E11 .... 4K **51**
KT9: Chess 3E **162**
N8 .... 5K **47**
TW14: Felt 6H **111**
W5 .... 6D **78**
Elmcroft Cres. HA2: Harr 3E **40**
NW11 .... 7G **45**
Elmcroft Dr. KT9: Chess 3E **162**
TW15: Ashf 5C **128**
Elmcroft Gdns. NW9 .... 4G **43**
Elmcroft St. E5 .... 4J **67**
Elmcroft Ter. UB8: Hil 6C **74**

Elmdale Rd.—Elthruda Rd.

Elmdale Rd. N13 5E 32
Elmdene KT5: Surb 1J 163
Elmdene Cl. BR3: Beck 6B 158
Elmdene Rd. SE18 5F 107
Elmdon Rd. TW4: Houn 2B 112
TW6: H'row A 3H 111
Elm Dr. HA2: Harr 6F 41
TW16: Sun 2A 148
Elmer Cl. EN2: Enf 3E 22
Elmer Gdns. HA8: Edg 7C 28
TW7: Isle 3H 113
Elmer Ho. NW1 5C 4
(off Penfold St.)
Elmer Rd. SE6 7E 122
Elmers Dr. TW11: Tedd 6B 132
ELMERS END 4K 157
Elmers End Rd.
BR3: Beck 2J 157
SE20 2J 157
Elmerside Rd. BR3: Beck 4A 158
Elmers Lodge BR3: Beck 4K 157
Elmers Rd. SE25 7G 157
Elmfield Av. CR4: Mitc 1E 154
N8 5J 47
TW11: Tedd 5K 131
Elmfield Cl. HA1: Harr 2J 59
Elmfield Ct. DA16: Well 1B 126
Elmfield Ho. N2 2B 46
(off Grange, The)
Elmfield Pk. BR1: Brom 3J 159
Elmfield Rd. BR1: Brom 2J 159
E4 2K 35
E17 6K 49
N2 3B 46
SW17 2E 136
UB2: S'hall 3C 94
Elmfield Way CR2: Sand 7F 169
W9 5J 81
Elm Friars Wlk. NW1 7H 65
Elm Gdns. CR4: Mitc 4H 155
KT10: Clay 6A 162
N2 3A 46
Elmgate Av. TW13: Felt 3K 129
Elmgate Gdns. HA8: Edg 5D 28
Elm Grn. W3 6A 80
Elmgreen Cl. E15 1G 87
Elm Gro. BR6: Orp 1K 173
DA8: Erith 7K 109
HA2: Harr 7E 40
IG8: Wfd G 5C 36
KT2: King T 1E 150
N8 6J 47
NW2 4F 63
SE15 2F 121
SM1: Sutt 4K 165
SW19 7G 135
UB7: Yiew 7B 74
Elmgrove Cres. HA1: Harr 5K 41
Elmgrove Gdns. HA1: Harr 5A 42
Elm Gro. Pde. SM6: Wall 3E 166
Elm Gro. Rd. SW13 1C 116
W5 2E 96
Elmgrove Rd. CR0: Croy 7H 157
HA1: Harr 5K 41
HA3: W'stone 5A 42
Elm Hall Gdns. E11 5K 51
(not continuous)
Elm Ho. E14 2E 104
(off E. Ferry Rd.)
KT2: King T 7F 133
(off Elm Rd.)
W10 4G 81
(off Briar Wlk.)
Elmhurst DA17: Belv 6E 108
Elmhurst Av. CR4: Mitc 7F 137
N2 3B 46
Elmhurst Ct. CR0: Croy 4D 168
Elmhurst Dr. E18 2J 51
Elmhurst Lodge
SM2: Sutt 7A 166
Elmhurst Mans. SW4 3H 119
Elmhurst Rd. E7 7K 69
N17 2F 49
SE9 2C 142
Elmhurst St. SW4 3H 119
Elmington Cl. DA5: Bexl 6H 127
Elmington Est. SE5 7D 102
Elmington Rd. SE5 7D 102
Elmira St. SE13 3D 122
Elm La. SE6 2B 140
Elm Lawn Cl. UB8: Uxb 7A 56
Elmlea Dr. UB3: Hayes 5G 75
Elm Lea Trad. Est. N17 6C 34
Elmlee Cl. BR7: Chst 6D 142
Elmley Cl. E6 5C 88
Elmley St. SE18 5H 107
(not continuous)
Elm Lodge SW6 1E 116
Elmore Cl. HA0: Wemb 2E 78
Elmore Ho. SW9 2B 120
Elmore Rd. E11 3E 68
EN3: Enf W 1E 24
Elmore St. N1 7C 66
Elm Pde. DA14: Sidc 4A 144
Elm Pk. HA7: Stan 5G 27
SW2 6K 119
Elm Pk. Av. N15 5F 49
Elm Pk. Chambers SW10 6A 16
(off Fulham Rd.)
Elm Pk. Ct. HA5: Pinn 2A 40
Elm Pk. Gdns. NW4 5F 45
SW10 6A 16 (5B 100)
Elm Pk. Ho. SW10 5B 100
Elm Pk. La. SW3 6A 16 (5B 100)
Elm Pk. Mans. SW10 7A 16
Elm Pk. Rd. E10 1A 68
HA5: Pinn 2A 40
N3 7C 30
N21 7H 23
SE25 3F 157
SW3 7A 16 (6B 100)
Elm Pas. EN5: Barn 4C 20
Elm Pl. SW7 5A 16 (5B 100)
Elm Quay Ct. SW8 7C 18 (6H 101)
Elm Rd. BR3: Beck 2B 158
BR6: Chels 7K 173
CR7: Thor H 4D 156
DA14: Sidc 4A 144
E7 6H 69
E11 2F 69
E17 5E 50
EN5: Barn 4C 20
HA9: Wemb 5E 60
KT2: King T 1F 151
KT3: N Mald 2K 151
KT9: Chess 4E 162
KT17: Ewe 6B 164
N22 1B 48
RM7: Mawney 2H 55
SM6: Wall 1E 166
SW14 3J 115
TW14: Bedf 1F 129
Elm Rd. W. SM3: Sutt 7H 153
Elm Row NW3 3A 64
Elms, The CR0: Croy 1C 168
(off Tavistock Rd.)
E12 6B 70
KT10: Clay 7A 162
SW13 3B 116
TW15: Ashf 5C 128
Elms Av. N10 3F 47
NW4 5F 45
Elmscott Gdns. N21 6H 23
Elmscott Rd. BR1: Brom 5G 141
Elms Ct. HA0: Wemb 4A 60
Elms Cres. SW4 6G 119
Elmsdale Rd. E17 4B 50
Elms Gdns. HA0: Wemb 4A 60
RM9: Dag 4F 73
Elmshaw Rd. SW15 5C 116
Elmshurst Cres. N2 4B 46
Elmside CR0: New Ad 6D 170
Elmside Rd. HA9: Wemb 3G 61
Elms La. HA0: Wemb 3A 60
Elmsleigh Av. HA3: Kent 4B 42
Elmsleigh Ct. SM1: Sutt 3K 165
Elmsleigh Ho. TW2: Twick 2H 131
(off Staines Rd.)
Elmsleigh Rd. TW2: Twick 2H 131
Elmslie Cl. IG8: Wfd G 6J 37
Elmslie Point E3 5B 86
(off Leopold St.)
Elms M. W2 2A 10 (7B 82)
Elms Pk. Av.
HA0: Wemb 4A 60
Elms Rd. HA3: Hrw W 7D 26
SW4 5G 119
ELMSTEAD 6D 142
Elmstead Av. BR7: Chst 5D 142
HA9: Wemb 1E 60
Elmstead Cl. KT19: Ewe 5A 164
N20 2D 30
Elmstead Gdns. KT4: Wor Pk 3C 164
Elmstead Glade BR7: Chst 6D 142
Elmstead La. BR7: Chst 7C 142
Elmstead Rd. DA8: Erith 1K 127
IG3: Ilf 2J 71
Elmsted Cres. DA16: Well 6C 108
Elmstone Rd. SW6 1J 117
Elm St. WC1 4H 7 (4K 83)
Elmsway TW15: Ashf 5C 128
Elmsworth Av. TW3: Houn 2F 113
Elm Ter. HA3: Hrw W 1H 41
HA7: Stan 5H 27
NW2 3J 63
NW3 4C 64
SE9 6E 124
Elmton Ct. NW8 3A 4
(off Cunningham Pl.)
Elmton Way E5 3G 67
Elm Tree Av. KT10: Esh 7H 149
Elm Tree Cl. NW8 1A 4 (3B 82)
TW15: Ashf 5D 128
UB5: N'olt 2D 76
Elm Tree Ct. NW8 1A 4
SE7 6A 106
Elm Tree Rd. NW8 1A 4 (3B 82)
Elmtree Rd. TW11: Tedd 4J 131
Elm Vw. Ct. UB2: S'hall 4E 94
Elm Vw. Ho. UB3: Harl 4F 93
Elm Wlk. BR6: Farnb 3D 172
NW3 2J 63
SW20 4E 152
Elm Way KT4: Wor Pk 3E 164
KT19: Ewe 5K 163
N11 6K 31
NW10 4A 62
Elmwood Av. HA3: Kent 5A 42
N13 5D 32
TW13: Felt 2J 129
Elmwood Cl. KT17: Ewe 7C 164
SM6: Wall 2F 167
Elmwood Ct. E10 1C 68
(off Goldsmith Rd.)
HA0: Wemb 3A 60
SW11 1F 119
Elmwood Cres. NW9 4J 43
Elmwood Dr. DA5: Bexl 7E 126
KT17: Ewe 6C 164
Elmwood Gdns. W7 6J 77
Elmwood Ho. NW10 2D 80
(off All Souls Av.)
Elmwood Rd. CR0: Croy 7B 156
CR4: Mitc 3D 154
SE24 5D 120
W4 6J 97
Elmworth Gro. SE21 2D 138
Elnathan M. W9 4K 81
Elphinstone Ct. SW16 6J 137
Elphinstone Rd. E17 2B 50
Elphinstone St. N5 4B 66
Elrington Rd. E8 6G 67
IG8: Wfd G 5D 36
Elsa Cotts. E14 5A 86
(off Halley St.)
Elsa Ct. BR3: Beck 1B 158
Elsa Rd. DA16: Well 2B 126
Elsa St. E1 5A 86
Elsdale St. E9 6J 67
Elsden M. E2 2J 85
Elsden Rd. N17 1F 49
Elsenham Rd. E12 5E 70
Elsenham St. SW18 1H 135
Elsham Rd. E11 3G 69
W14 2G 99
Elsham Ter. W14 3G 99
(off Elsham Rd.)
Elsiedene Rd. N21 7H 23
Elsie La. Ct. W2 5J 81
(off Westbourne Pk. Vs.)
Elsiemaud Rd. SE4 5B 122
Elsie Rd. SE22 4F 121
Elsinore Av. TW19: Stanw 7A 110
Elsinore Gdns. NW2 3G 63
Elsinore Ho. N1 1A 84
(off Denmark Gro.)
SE5 2C 120
(off Denmark Rd.)
W6 5F 99
(off Fulham Pal. Rd.)
Elsinore Rd. SE23 1A 140
Elsinore Way TW9: Rich 3H 115
Elsley Rd. SW11 3D 118
Elspeth Rd. HA0: Wemb 5E 60
SW11 4D 118
Elsrick Av. SM4: Mord 5J 153
Elstan Way CR0: Croy 7A 158
Elstead Ct. SM3: Sutt 1G 165
Elstead Ho. SW2 7K 119
(off Redlands Way)
Elsted St. SE17 4D 102
Elstow Cl. HA4: Ruis 7B 40
SE9 5D 124
(not continuous)
Elstow Gdns. RM9: Dag 1E 90
Elstow Grange NW6 7F 63
Elstow Rd. RM9: Dag 1E 90
Elstree Gdns. DA17: Belv 4E 108
IG1: Ilf 5G 71
N9 1C 34
Elstree Hill BR1: Brom 7G 141
Elstree Hill Sth. WD6: Els 1H 27
Elstree Rd. WD23: Bushy 1C 26
Elswick Rd. SE13 2D 122
Elswick St. SW6 2A 118
Elsworth Cl. TW14: Bedf 1G 129
Elsworthy KT7: T Ditt 6J 149
Elsworthy Ri. NW3 7C 64
Elsworthy Rd. NW3 1C 82
Elsworthy Ter. NW3 7C 64
Elsynge Rd. SW18 5B 118
ELTHAM 7B 124
Eltham Crematorium SE9 4H 125
Eltham Grn. SE9 5B 124
Eltham Grn. Rd. SE9 4A 124
Eltham High St. SE9 6D 124
Eltham Hill SE9 5B 124
Eltham Palace 7C 124
Eltham Pal. Rd. SE9 6A 124
ELTHAM PARK 4E 124
Eltham Pk. Gdns. SE9 4E 124
Eltham Pools 6C 124
Eltham Rd. SE9 5H 123
SE12 5H 123
Elthiron Rd. SW6 1J 117
Elthorne Av. W7 2K 95
Elthorne Ct. TW13: Felt 1A 130
ELTHORNE HEIGHTS 5J 77
Elthorne Pk. Rd. W7 2K 95
Elthorne Rd. N19 2H 65
NW9 7K 43
Elthorne Sports Cen. 3K 95
Elthorne Way NW9 6K 43
Elthruda Rd. SE13 6F 123

Eltisley Rd.—Epstein Rd.

Eltisley Rd. IG1: Ilf 4F **71**
Elton Av. EN5: Barn 5C **20**
HA0: Wemb 5B **60**
UB6: G'frd 6J **59**
Elton Cl. KT1: Hamp W 7C **132**
Elton Ho. *E3* *1B 86*
(off Candy St.)
Elton Pl. N16 5E **66**
Elton Rd. KT2: King T 1F **151**
Eltringham St. SW18 4A **118**
Elvaston M. SW7 2A **16** (3A **100**)
Elvaston Pl. SW7 2A **16** (3A **100**)
Elveden Ho. SE24 5B **120**
Elveden Pl. NW10 2G **79**
Elveden Rd. NW10 2G **79**
Elvedon Rd. TW13: Felt 3H **129**
Elvendon Rd. N13 6D **32**
Elver Gdns. E2 3G **85**
Elverson Rd. SE8 2D **122**
Elverton St. SW1 3C **18** (4H **101**)
Elvington Grn. BR2: Brom 5H **159**
Elvington La. NW9 1A **44**
Elvino Rd. SE26 5A **140**
Elvis Rd. NW2 6E **62**
Elwill Way BR3: Beck 4E **158**
Elwin St. E2 1K **9** (3G **85**)
Elwood St. N5 3B **66**
Elworth Ho. *SW8* *7K 101*
(off Oval Pl.)
Elwyn Gdns. SE12 7J **123**
Ely Cl. KT3: N Mald 2B **152**
Ely Cotts. SW8 7K **101**
Ely Ct. EC1 6K **7**
NW6 *2J 81*
(off Chichester Rd.)
Ely Gdns. IG1: Ilf 7C **52**
RM10: Dag 3J **73**
Ely Ho. *SE15* *7G 103*
(off Friary Est.)
Elyne Rd. N4 6A **48**
Ely Pl. EC1 6K **7** (5A **84**)
IG8: Wfd G 6K **37**
Ely Rd. CR0: Croy 5D **156**
E10 6E **50**
TW4: Houn 3A **112**
Elysian Av. BR5: St M Cry 6K **161**
Elysium Pl. *SW6* *2H 117*
(off Elysium St.)
Elysium St. SW6 2H **117**
Elystan Bus. Cen. UB4: Yead 7A **76**
Elystan Cl. SM6: Wall 7G **167**
Elystan Pl. SW3 5D **16** (5C **100**)
Elystan St. SW3 4C **16** (4C **100**)
Elystan Wlk. N1 1A **84**
Emanuel Av. W3 6J **79**
Emanuel Dr. TW12: Hamp 5D **130**
Embankment SW15 2F **117**
(not continuous)
Embankment, The TW1: Twick 1A **132**
Embankment Gdns.
SW3 7F **17** (6D **100**)
Embankment Pl. WC2 4F **13** (1J **101**)
Embassy Ct. DA14: Sidc 3B **144**
DA16: Well 3B **126**
N11 *6C 32*
(off Bounds Grn. Rd.)
NW8 1B **4**
SM6: Wall 6F **167**
W5 7F **79**
Embassy Gdns. BR3: Beck 1B **158**
Embassy Ho. NW6 7K **63**
Embassy Lodge *N3* *2H 45*
(off Cyprus Rd.)
Embassy Theatre *7B 64*
(off College Cres.)
Emba St. SE16 2G **103**
Ember Cl. BR5: Pet W 7G **161**
Ember Ct. NW9 2B **44**
Embercourt Rd. KT7: T Ditt 6J **149**
Ember Farm Av. KT8: E Mos 6H **149**
Ember Farm Way KT8: E Mos 6H **149**
Ember Gdns. KT7: T Ditt 7J **149**
Ember La. KT8: E Mos 7H **149**
KT10: Esh 7H **149**
Emberton *SE5* *6E 102*
(off Albany Rd.)
Emberton Ct. *EC1* *2A 8*
(off Tompion St.)
Embleton Rd. SE13 4D **122**
Embleton Wlk. TW12: Hamp 5D **130**
Embroidery Bus. Cen. *IG8: Wfd G* *2B 52*
(off Southend Rd.)
Embroidery World Bus. Cen.
IG8: Wfd G 2B **52**
Embry Cl. HA7: Stan 4F **27**
Embry Dr. HA7: Stan 6F **27**
Embry Way HA7: Stan 5F **27**
Emden Cl. UB7: W Dray 2C **92**
Emden St. SW6 1K **117**
Emerald Cl. E16 6B **88**
Emerald Gdns. RM8: Dag 1G **73**
Emerald Rd. NW10 1K **79**
(not continuous)
Emerald Sq. UB2: S'hall 3B **94**
Emerald St. WC1 5G **7** (5K **83**)
Emerson Apartments N8 3K **47**
Emerson Gdns. HA3: Kent 6F **43**
Emerson Rd. IG1: Ilf 7E **52**
Emerson St. SE1 4C **14** (1C **102**)
Emerton Cl. DA6: Bex 4E **126**
Emery Hill St. SW1 2B **18** (3G **101**)
Emery St. SE1 1K **19** (3A **102**)
Emery Theatre *6D 86*
(off Annabel Cl.)
Emes Rd. DA8: Erith 7J **109**
Emilia Cl. EN3: Pond E 5C **24**
Emily Pl. N7 4A **66**
Emily St. *E16* *6H 87*
(off Jude St.)
Emlyn Gdns. W12 2A **98**
Emlyn Rd. W12 2A **98**
Emmanuel Ct. E10 7D **50**
Emmanuel Ho. SE11 4J **19** (4A **102**)
Emmanuel Rd. HA6: Nwood 1H **39**
SW12 1G **137**
Emma Rd. E13 2H **87**
Emma St. E2 2H **85**
Emmaus Way IG7: Chig 5K **37**
Emmeline Ct. KT12: Walt T 7A **148**
Emminster *NW6* *1K 81*
(off Abbey Rd.)
Emmott Av. IG6: Ilf 5G **53**
Emmott Cl. E1 4A **86**
NW11 6A **46**
Emms Pas. KT1: King T 2D **150**
Emperor's Ga. SW7 3A **100**
Empingham Ho. *SE8* *4K 103*
(off Chilton Ho.)
Empire Av. N18 5H **33**
Empire Cinema *2D 12*
(off Leicester Sq.)
Empire Ct. HA9: Wemb 3H **61**
Empire Pde. HA9: Wemb 3G **61**
N18 6J **33**
Empire Rd. UB6: G'frd 1B **78**
Empire Sq. N7 3J **65**
SE20 *7K 139*
(off High St.)
Empire Way HA9: Wemb 4F **61**
Empire Wharf *E3* *1A 86*
(off Old Ford Rd.)
Empire Wharf Rd. E14 4F **105**
Empress App. SW6 5J **99**
Empress Av. E4 7J **35**
E12 2A **70**
IG1: Ilf 2D **70**
IG8: Wfd G 7C **36**
Empress Dr. BR7: Chst 6F **143**
Empress M. SE5 2C **120**
Empress Pde. E4 7H **35**
Empress Pl. SW6 5J **99**
Empress State Bldg. SW6 5J **99**
Empress St. SE17 6C **102**
Empson St. E3 4D **86**
Emsworth Cl. N9 1D **34**
Emsworth Ct. SW16 3J **137**
Emsworth Rd. IG6: Ilf 2F **53**
Emsworth St. SW2 2K **137**
Emt Ho. E6 5E **88**
Emu Rd. SW8 2F **119**
Ena Rd. SW16 3J **155**
Enbrook St. W10 3G **81**
Enclave, The SW13 2B **116**
Endale Cl. SM5: Cars 2D **166**
Endeavour Way CR0: Bedd 7J **155**
IG11: Bark 2A **90**
SW19 4K **135**
Endell St. WC2 7E **6** (6J **83**)
Enderby St. SE10 5F **105**
Enderley Cl. HA3: Hrw W 2J **41**
Enderley Rd. HA3: Hrw W 1J **41**
Endersleigh Gdns. NW4 4C **44**
Endlebury Rd. E4 2K **35**
Endlesham Rd. SW12 7E **118**
Endsleigh Gdns. IG1: Ilf 2D **70**
KT6: Surb 6C **150**
WC1 3C **6** (4H **83**)
Endsleigh Ind. Est. UB2: S'hall 4C **94**
Endsleigh Pl. WC1 3D **6** (4H **83**)
Endsleigh Rd. UB2: S'hall 4C **94**
W13 7A **78**
Endsleigh St. WC1 3D **6** (4H **83**)
Endway KT5: Surb 7H **151**
Endwell Rd. SE4 2A **122**
Endymion Rd. N4 7A **48**
SW2 6K **119**
Energen Cl. NW10 6A **62**
Energize Fitness Club *5G 99*
(in Hammersmith & West London College)
ENFIELD 3J **23**
Enfield Bus. Cen. EN3: Enf H 2D **24**
Enfield Cloisters *N1* *1G 9*
(off Fanshaw St.)
Enfield College Sports Cen. 3D **24**
ENFIELD HIGHWAY 3D **24**
Enfield Ho. *SW9* *2J 119*
(off Stockwell Rd.)
ENFIELD ISLAND VILLAGE 1H **25**
ENFIELD LOCK 1H **25**
Enfield Retail Pk. EN1: Enf 3C **24**
Enfield Rd. EN2: Enf 4C **22**
N1 7E **66**
TW6: H'row A 2G **111**
TW8: Bford 5D **96**
W3 2H **97**
ENFIELD TOWN 3J **23**
Enfield Wlk. TW8: Bford 5D **96**
Enford St. W1 5E **4** (5D **82**)
Engadine Cl. CR0: Croy 3F **169**
Engadine St. SW18 1H **135**
Engate St. SE13 4E **122**
Engel Pk. NW7 6K **29**
Engine Ct. *SW1* *5B 12*
(off Ambassador's Ct.)
Engineer Cl. SE18 6E **106**
Engineers Way HA9: Wemb 4G **61**
England's La. NW3 6D **64**
England Way KT3: N Mald 4H **151**
Englefield *NW1* *2A 6*
(off Clarence Gdns.)
Englefield Cl. BR5: St M Cry 5K **161**
CR0: Croy 6C **156**
EN2: Enf 2F **23**
Englefield Cres. BR5: St M Cry 4K **161**
Englefield Path BR5: St M Cry 4K **161**
Englefield Rd. N1 7D **66**
Engleheart Dr. TW14: Felt 6H **111**
Engleheart Rd. SE6 7D **122**
Englewood Rd. SW12 6F **119**
English Grounds SE1 5G **15** (1E **102**)
English St. E3 4B **86**
Enid St. SE16 7K **15** (3F **103**)
Enmore Av. SE25 5G **157**
Enmore Gdns. SW14 5K **115**
Enmore Rd. SE25 5G **157**
SW15 4E **116**
UB1: S'hall 4E **76**
Ennerdale *NW1* *1A 6*
(off Varndell St.)
Ennerdale Av. HA7: Stan 3C **42**
Ennerdale Cl. SM1: Sutt 4H **165**
TW14: Felt 1H **129**
Ennerdale Ct. *E11* *7J 51*
(off Cambridge Rd.)
Ennerdale Dr. NW9 5A **44**
Ennerdale Gdns. HA9: Wemb 1C **60**
Ennerdale Ho. E3 4B **86**
Ennerdale Rd. DA7: Bex 1G **127**
TW9: Rich 2F **115**
Ennersdale Rd. SE13 5F **123**
Ennis Ho. *E14* *6D 86*
(off Vesey Path)
Ennismore Av. UB6: G'frd 6J **59**
W4 4B **98**
Ennismore Gdns. KT7: T Ditt 6J **149**
SW7 7C **10** (2C **100**)
Ennismore Gdns. M.
SW7 1C **16** (3C **100**)
Ennismore M. SW7 7C **10** (3C **100**)
Ennismore St. SW7 1C **16** (3C **100**)
Ennis Rd. N4 1A **66**
SE18 6G **107**
Ennor Ct. SM3: Cheam 4E **164**
Ensbury Ho. *SW8* *7K 101*
(off Carroun Rd.)
Ensign Cl. TW6: H'row A 3G **111**
TW19: Stanw 1A **128**
Ensign Dr. N13 3H **33**
Ensign Ho. *E14* *2C 104*
(off Admirals Way)
Ensign Ind. Cen. *E1* *7G 85*
(off Ensign St.)
Ensign St. E1 7G **85**
Ensign Way SM6: Wall 7J **167**
TW19: Stanw 1A **128**
Enslin Rd. SE9 6E **124**
Ensor M. SW7 5A **16** (5B **100**)
Enstone Rd. EN3: Enf H 3F **25**
UB10: Ick 3B **56**
Enterprise Bus. Pk. E14 2D **104**
Enterprise Cen., The *BR3: Beck* *5A 140*
(off Cricket La.)
Enterprise Cl. CR0: Croy 1A **168**
Enterprise Ho. E4 7K **25**
E9 *7J 67*
(off Tudor Gro.)
E14 *5D 104*
(off St Davids Sq.)
IG11: Bark 3K **89**
KT12: Walt T 7K **147**
Enterprise Ind. Est. SE16 5J **103**
Enterprise Row N15 5F **49**
Enterprise Way NW10 3B **80**
SW18 4J **117**
TW11: Tedd 6K **131**
Enterprize Way SE8 4B **104**
Epcot M. NW10 3F **81**
Epirus M. SW6 7J **99**
Epirus Rd. SW6 7H **99**
Epping Cl. E14 4C **104**
RM7: Mawney 3H **55**
Epping Glade E4 6K **25**
Epping New Rd. IG9: Buck H 2E **36**
Epping Pl. N1 6A **66**
Epping Way E4 6J **25**
Epple Rd. SW6 1H **117**
Epsom Cl. DA7: Bex 3H **127**
UB5: N'olt 5D **58**
Epsom Rd. CR0: Wadd 4A **168**
E10 6E **50**
IG3: Ilf 6K **53**
SM3: Sutt 7H **153**
Epsom Sq. TW6: H'row A 2H **111**
Epstein Rd. SE28 1A **108**

A-Z London 257

Fitness First Health Club—Fludyer St.

Fitness First Health Club
Croydon 1B 168
Islington 1A 8 (2B 84)
Lewisham 3E 122
Tooting Bec 3E 136 (off Balham High Rd.)
Fitrooms 6H 99
Fitzalan Rd. N3 3G 45
Fitzalan St. SE11 3H 19 (4A 102)
Fitzgeorge Av. KT3: N Mald 1K 151
W14 4G 99
Fitzgerald Av. SW14 3A 116
Fitzgerald Ct. E10 1D 68 (off Leyton Grange Est.)
Fitzgerald Ho. E14 6D 86 (off E. India Dock Rd.)
SW9 2A 120
UB3: Hayes 1K 93
Fitzgerald Rd. E11 5J 51
KT7: T Ditt 6A 150
SW14 3K 115
Fitzhardinge Ho. W1 7G 5 (off Portman Sq.)
Fitzhardinge St. W1 7G 5 (6E 82)
Fitzherbert Wlk. UB1: S'hall 2H 95
Fitzhugh Gro. SW18 6B 118
Fitzjames Av. CR0: Croy 2G 169
W14 4G 99
Fitzjohn Av. EN5: Barn 5B 20
Fitzjohn's Av. NW3 4A 64
Fitzmaurice Ho. SE16 4H 103 (off Rennie Est.)
Fitzmaurice Pl. W1 4K 11 (1F 101)
Fitzneal St. W12 6B 80
FITZROVIA 5K 5
Fitzroy Cl. N6 1D 64
Fitzroy Ct. CR0: Croy 7D 156
N6 6G 47
W1 4B 6
Fitzroy Cres. W4 7K 97
Fitzroy Gdns. SE19 7E 138
Fitzroy Ho. E14 5B 86 (off Wallwood St.)
SE1 5F 103 (off Coopers La.)
Fitzroy M. W1 4A 6
Fitzroy Pk. N6 1D 64
Fitzroy Rd. NW1 1E 82
Fitzroy Sq. W1 4A 6 (4G 83)
Fitzroy St. W1 4A 6 (4G 83) (not continuous)
Fitzroy Yd. NW1 1E 82
Fitzsimmons Ct. NW10 1K 79
Fitzstephen Rd. RM8: Dag 5B 72
Fitzwarren Gdns. N19 1G 65
Fitzwilliam Av. TW9: Rich 2F 115
Fitzwilliam Hgts. SE23 2J 139
Fitzwilliam Ho. TW9: Rich 4D 114
Fitzwilliam M. E16 1J 105
Fitzwilliam Rd. SW4 3G 119
Fitzwygram Cl. TW12: Hamp H 5G 131
Five Acre NW9 2B 44
Fiveacre Cl. CR7: Thor H 6A 156
Five Bell All. E14 6B 86 (off Three Colt St.)
Five Elms Rd. BR2: Hayes 3K 171
RM9: Dag 3F 73
Fives Ct. SE11 3B 102
FIVEWAYS 2F 143
Five Ways Bus. Cen. TW13: Felt 3K 129
FIVEWAYS CORNER
Croydon 4A 168
Hendon 1C 44
Fiveways Rd. SW9 2A 120
Flack Ct. E10 7D 50
Fladbury Rd. N15 6D 48
Fladgate Rd. E11 6G 51
Flag Cl. CR0: Croy 1K 169
Flag Wlk. HA5: Eastc 6J 39
Flambard Rd. HA1: Harr 6A 42
Flamborough Ho. SE15 1G 121 (off Clayton Rd.)
Flamborough Rd. HA4: Ruis 3J 57
Flamborough St. E14 6A 86
Flamborough Wlk. E14 6A 86 (off Flamborough St.)
Flamingo Ct. SE8 7C 104 (off Hamilton St.)
Flamingo Gdns. UB5: N'olt 3C 76
Flamstead Gdns. RM9: Dag 7C 72
Flamstead Ho. SW3 5C 16 (off Cale St.)
Flamstead Rd. RM9: Dag 7C 72
Flamsted Av. HA9: Wemb 6G 61
Flamsteed Rd. SE7 5C 106
Flanchford Rd. W12 3B 98
Flanders Ct. E17 7A 50
Flanders Cres. SW17 7D 136
Flanders Mans. W4 4B 98
Flanders Rd. E6 2D 88
W4 4A 98
Flanders Way E9 6K 67 (not continuous)
Flandrian Cl. EN3: Enf L 1J 25
Flank St. E1 7G 85
Flansham Ho. E14 6B 86 (off Clemence St.)
Flask Wlk. NW3 4A 64
Flatford Ho. SE6 4E 140
Flatiron Yd. SE1 5D 14 (off Union St.)
Flavell M. SE10 5G 105
Flaxen Cl. E4 3J 35
Flaxen Rd. E4 3J 35
Flaxley Rd. SM4: Mord 7K 153
Flaxman Ct. DA17: Belv 5G 109 (off Hoddesdon Rd.)
W1 1C 12
WC1 2D 6 (off Flaxman Ter.)
Flaxman Ho. W4 5A 98 (off Devonshire St.)
Flaxman Leisure Cen. 2C 120
Flaxman Rd. SE5 3B 120
Flaxman Ter. WC1 2D 6 (3H 83)
Flaxton Rd. SE18 1H 125
Flecker Cl. HA7: Stan 5E 26
Flecker Ho. SE5 7D 102 (off Lomond Gro.)
Fleece Dr. N9 4B 34
Fleece Rd. KT6: Surb 1C 162
Fleece Wlk. N7 6J 65
Fleeming Cl. E17 2B 50
Fleeming Rd. E17 2B 50
Fleetbank Ho. EC4 1K 13 (off Salisbury Sq.)
Fleet Bldg. EC4 7A 8
Fleet Cl. HA4: Ruis 6E 38
KT8: W Mole 5D 148
Fleetfield WC1 1F 7 (off Birkenhead St.)
Fleet Ho. E14 7A 86 (off Victory Pl.)
Fleet La. KT8: W Mole 6D 148
Fleet Pl. EC4 7A 8 (6B 84) (not continuous)
Fleet Rd. NW3 5C 64
Fleetside KT8: W Mole 5D 148
Fleet Sq. WC1 2H 7 (3K 83)
Fleet St. EC4 1J 13 (6A 84)
Fleet St. Hill E1 4G 85
Fleetway WC1 1F 7 (off Birkenhead St.)
Fleetway W. Bus. Pk. UB6: G'frd 2B 78
Fleetwood Cl. CR0: Croy 3F 169
E16 5B 88
KT9: Chess 7D 162
Fleetwood Ct. E6 5D 88 (off Evelyn Dennington Rd.)
TW19: Stanw 6A 110
Fleetwood Rd. KT1: King T 3H 151
NW10 5C 62
Fleetwood Sq. KT1: King T 3H 151
Fleetwood St. N16 2E 66
Fleming N8 3J 47 (off Boyton Cl.)
Fleming Cl. W9 4J 81
Fleming Ct. CR0: Wadd 5A 168
W2 5A 4
Fleming Dr. N21 5E 22
Fleming Ho. HA9: Wemb 3J 61 (off Barnhill Rd.)
N4 1C 66
SE16 2G 103 (off George Row)
Fleming Lodge W9 5J 81 (off Admiral Wlk.)
Fleming Mead CR4: Mitc 7C 136
Fleming Rd. SE17 6B 102
UB1: S'hall 6F 77
Fleming Wlk. NW9 3A 44
Fleming Way SE28 7D 90
TW7: Isle 4K 113
Flemming Av. HA4: Ruis 1K 57
Flemming Cl. SW10 7A 16 (off Park Wlk.)
Flempton Rd. E10 1A 68
Fletcher Bldgs. WC2 1F 13 (off Martlett Ct.)
Fletcher Cl. E6 6F 89
Fletcher Ho. SE15 7J 103 (off Clifton Way)
Fletcher La. E10 7E 50
Fletcher Path SE8 7C 104
Fletcher Rd. W4 3J 97
Fletchers Cl. BR2: Brom 4K 159
Fletcher St. E1 7G 85
Fletching Rd. E5 3J 67
SE7 6A 106
Fletton Rd. N11 7D 32
Fleur-de-Lis St. E1 4H 9 (4F 85)
Fleur Gates SW19 7F 117
Flexmere Gdns. N17 1D 48
Flexmere Rd. N17 1D 48
Flight App. NW9 2B 44
Flimwell Cl. BR1: Brom 5G 141
Flinders Ho. E1 1H 103 (off Green Bank)
Flint Cl. BR6: Chels 6K 173
E15 7H 69
Flintmill Cres. SE3 2C 124 (not continuous)
Flinton St. SE17 5E 102
Flint St. SE17 4D 102
Flitcroft St. WC2 1D 12 (6H 83)
Flitton Ho. N1 7B 66 (off Sutton Est., The)
Floathaven Cl. SE28 1A 108
Flock Mill Pl. SW18 1K 135
Flockton St. SE16 2G 103
Flodden Rd. SE5 1C 120
Flood La. TW1: Twick 1A 132
Flood Pas. SE18 3C 106
Flood St. SW3 6D 16 (5C 100)
Flood Wlk. SW3 7D 16 (6C 100)
Flora Cl. E14 6D 86
Flora Gdns. RM6: Chad H 6C 54
W6 4D 98 (off Albion Gdns.)
Floral Pl. N1 5D 66
Floral St. WC2 2E 12 (7J 83)
Flora St. DA17: Belv 5F 109
Florence Av. EN2: Enf 3H 23
SM4: Mord 5A 154
Florence Cantwell Wlk. N19 7J 47 (off Jessie Blythe La.)
Florence Cl. KT12: Walt T 7K 147
Florence Ct. E5 3G 67
E11 4K 51
N1 7B 66 (off Florence St.)
SW19 6G 135
W9 3A 82 (off Maida Va.)
Florence Dr. EN2: Enf 3H 23
Florence Elson Cl. E12 4E 70
Florence Gdns. W4 6J 97
Florence Ho. KT2: King T 7F 133 (off Florence Rd)
SE16 5H 103 (off Rotherhithe New Rd.)
W11 7F 81 (off St Ann's Rd.)
Florence Mans. NW4 5D 44 (off Vivian Av.)
Florence Nightingale Mus. 7G 13 (2K 101)
Florence Rd. BR1: Brom 1J 159
BR3: Beck 2A 158
CR2: Sand 7D 168
E6 1A 88
E13 2J 87
KT2: King T 7F 133
KT12: Walt T 7K 147
N4 7K 47 (not continuous)
SE2 4D 108
SE14 1B 122
SW19 6K 135
TW13: Felt 1K 129
UB2: S'hall 4B 94
W4 3K 97
W5 7E 78
Florence St. E16 4H 87
N1 7B 66
NW4 4E 44
Florence Ter. SE14 1B 122
SW15 3A 134
Florence Way SW12 1D 136
Flores Ho. E1 5K 85 (off Shandy St.)
Florey Lodge W9 5J 81 (off Admiral Wlk.)
Florey Sq. N21 5E 22
Florfield Pas. E8 6H 67 (off Florfield Rd.)
Florfield Rd. E8 6H 67
Florian SE5 1E 120
Florian Av. SM1: Sutt 4B 166
Florian Rd. SW15 4G 117
Florida Cl. WD23: Bushy 2C 26
Florida Ct. BR2: Brom 4H 159 (off Westmoreland Rd.)
Florida Rd. CR7: Thor H 1B 156
Florida St. E2 3G 85
Florin Ct. N18 4K 33
SE1 7J 15 (off Tanner St.)
Floris Pl. SW4 3G 119
Floriston Av. UB10: Hil 7E 56
Floriston Cl. HA7: Stan 1B 42
Floriston Ct. UB5: N'olt 5F 59
Floriston Gdns. HA7: Stan 1B 42
Florys Ct. SW19 1G 135
Floss St. SW15 2E 116
Flower & Dean Wlk. E1 6K 9 (5F 85)
Flower La. NW7 5G 29
Flower M. NW11 6G 45
Flowerpot Cl. N15 6F 49
Flowers Cl. NW2 3C 62
Flowersmead SW17 2E 136
Flowers M. N19 2G 65
Flower Wlk., The SW7 6A 10 (2A 100)
Floyd Rd. SE7 5A 106
Floyer Cl. TW10: Rich 5F 115
Fludyer St. SE13 4G 123

Flynn Ct. E14 7C 86
(off Garford St.)
Foley Ho. E1 6J 85
(off Tarling St.)
Foley St. W1 6A 6 (5G 83)
Folgate St. E1 5H 9 (5E 84)
(not continuous)
Foliot Ho. N1 2K 83
(off Priory Grn. Est.)
Foliot St. W3 6B 80
Folkestone Ct. UB5: N'olt 5F 59
(off Newmarket Av.)
Folkestone Rd. E6 2E 88
E17 4D 50
N18 4B 34
Folkingham La. NW9 1K 43
Folkington Cnr. N12 5C 30
Folland NW9 2B 44
(off Hundred Acre)
Follett Ho. SW10 7B 100
(off Worlds End Est.)
Follett St. E14 6E 86
Follingham Ct. N1 1H 9
(off Drysdale Pl.)
Folly La. E17 1A 50
(not continuous)
Folly M. W11 6H 81
Folly Wall E14 2E 104
Fonda Ct. E14 7C 86
(off Premiere Pl.)
Fontaine Rd. SW16 7K 137
Fontarabia Rd. SW11 4E 118
Fontayne Av. RM1: Rom 2K 55
Fontenelle Gdns. SE5 1E 120
Fontenoy Ho. SE11 4B 102
(off Kennington La.)
Fontenoy Rd. SW12 2F 137
Fonteyne Gdns. IG8: Wfd G 2B 52
Fonthill Cl. SE20 2G 157
Fonthill M. N4 2K 65
Fonthill Rd. N4 1K 65
Font Hills N2 2A 46
Fontley Way SW15 7C 116
Fontmell Cl. TW15: Ashf 5C 128
Fontmell Pk. TW15: Ashf 5B 128
(not continuous)
Fontwell Cl. HA3: Hrw W 7D 26
UB5: N'olt 6E 58
Fontwell Dr. BR2: Brom 5E 160
Football La. HA1: Harr 1K 59
Footpath, The SW15 6C 116
FOOTS CRAY 6C 144
Foots Cray High St. DA14: Sidc 6C 144
Foots Cray La. DA14: Sidc 1C 144
Footscray Rd. SE9 6E 124
Forber Ho. E2 3J 85
(off Cornwall Av.)
Forbes Cl. NW2 3C 62
Forbes St. E1 6G 85
Forbes Way HA4: Ruis 2K 57
Forburg Rd. N16 1G 67
Fordbridge Ct. TW15: Ashf 6A 128
Fordbridge Pk. TW16: Sun 6H 147
Fordbridge Rd. TW15: Ashf 6A 128
TW16: Sun 6G 147
TW17: Shep 6G 147
FORDBRIDGE RDBT. 6A 128
Ford Cl. CR7: Thor H 5B 156
E3 2A 86
HA1: Harr 7H 41
TW15: Ashf 6A 128
TW17: Shep 4C 146
Forde Av. BR1: Brom 3A 160
Fordel Rd. SE6 1E 140
Ford End IG8: Wfd G 6E 36
Fordham KT1: King T 2G 151
(off Excelsior Cl.)
Fordham Cl. EN4: Cockf 3H 21
Fordham Rd. EN4: Cockf 3G 21
Fordham St. E1 6G 85
Fordhook Av. W5 1F 97
Ford Ho. EN5: New Bar 5E 20
Ford Ind. Pk. RM9: Dag 4H 91
Fordingley Rd. W9 3H 81
Fordington Ho. SE26 3G 139
Fordington Rd. N6 5D 46
Fordmill Rd. SE6 2C 140
Ford Rd. E3 2B 86
RM9: Dag 7F 73
TW15: Ashf 4B 128
Fords Gro. N21 1H 33
Fords Pk. Rd. E16 5J 87
Ford Sq. E1 5H 85
Ford St. E3 1A 86
E16 6H 87
Fordview Ind. Est. RM13: Rain 3K 91
Fordwich Cl. BR6: Orp 7K 161
Fordwych Rd. NW2 4G 63
Fordyce Rd. SE13 6E 122
Fordyke Rd. RM8: Dag 2F 73
Foreign St. SE5 2B 120
Foreland Ct. NW4 1F 45
Foreland Ho. W11 7G 81
(off Walmer Rd.)
Foreland St. SE18 4H 107
Foreman Ct. TW1: Twick 1K 131
Foreshore SE8 4B 104
Forest, The E11 4G 51
Forest App. E4 1B 36
IG8: Wfd G 7D 36
Forest Av. E4 1B 36
IG7: Chig 5K 37
Forest Bus. Pk. E10 7K 49
Forest Cl. BR7: Chst 1E 160
E11 5J 51
IG8: Wfd G 3E 36
N10 1F 47
Forest Ct. E4 1C 36
E11 4G 51
N12 5E 30
Forest Cft. SE23 2H 139
FORESTDALE 7B 170
Forestdale N14 4C 32
Forestdale Cen., The CR0: Sels 7B 170
Forest Dene Ct. SM2: Sutt 6A 166
Forest Dr. BR2: Kes 4C 172
E12 3B 70
IG8: Wfd G 7A 36
TW16: Sun 7H 129
Forest Dr. E. E11 7F 51
Forest Dr. W. E11 7E 50
Forest Edge IG9: Buck H 4F 37
Forester Ho. E14 7A 86
(off Victory Pl.)
Forester Rd. SE15 3H 121
Foresters Cl. SM6: Wall 7H 167
Foresters Cres. DA7: Bex 4H 127
Foresters Dr. E17 4F 51
SM6: Wall 7H 167
Forest Gdns. N17 2F 49
FOREST GATE 5J 69
Forest Ga. NW9 4A 44
Forest Ga. Retreat E7 5J 69
(off Odessa Rd.)
Forest Glade E4 4B 36
E11 6G 51
Forest Gro. E8 6F 67
Forest Hgts. IG9: Buck H 2D 36
FOREST HILL 2J 139
Forest Hill Bus. Cen. SE23 2J 139
(off Clyde Va.)
Forest Hill Ind. Est. SE23 2J 139
Forest Hill Pool 2J 139
Forest Hill Rd. SE22 5H 121
Forestholme Cl. SE23 2J 139
Forest Ind. Pk. IG6: Ilf 1J 53
Forest La. E7 5H 69
E15 5G 69
IG7: Chig 5K 37
Forest Lodge SE23 3J 139
(off Dartmouth Rd.)
Forest Mt. Rd. IG8: Wfd G 7A 36
Forest Point E7 5K 69
(off Windsor Rd.)
Fore St. EC2 6D 8 (5C 84)
HA5: Eastc 3H 39
N9 4B 34
N18 6A 34
Fore St. Av. EC2 6E 8 (5D 84)
Forest Ridge BR2: Kes 4C 172
BR3: Beck 3C 158
Forest Ri. E17 3F 51
(not continuous)
Forest Rd. E7 4J 69
E8 6F 67
E11 7F 51
E17 4J 49
IG6: Chig, Ilf 2H 53
IG8: Wfd G 3D 36
N9 1C 34
N17 4J 49
RM7: Mawney 3H 55
SM3: Sutt 1J 165
TW9: Kew 7G 97
TW13: Felt 2A 130
Forest Side E4 1C 36
E7 4K 69
IG9: Buck H 1F 37
KT4: Wor Pk 1B 164
Forest St. E7 5J 69
Forest Ter. IG7: Chig 5K 37
Forest Trad. Est. E17 3K 49
Forest Vw. E4 7K 25 & 1B 36
E11 7H 51
Forest Vw. Av. E10 5F 51
Forest Vw. Rd. E12 4C 70
E17 1E 50
Forest Wlk. N10 1F 47
Forest Way BR5: St M Cry 5K 161
DA15: Sidc 7H 125
IG8: Wfd G 4E 36
N19 2G 65
Forest Works Ind. Est. E17 3K 49
Forfar Rd. N22 1B 48
SW11 1E 118
Forge, The UB3: Harl 6F 93
Forge Cl. BR2: Hayes 1J 171
Forge Cotts. W5 1D 96
Forge Dr. KT10: Clay 7A 162
Forge La. HA6: Nwood 1G 39
SM3: Cheam 7G 165
TW13: Hanw 5C 130
TW16: Sun 3J 147
Forge M. CR0: Addtn 5C 170
Forge Pl. NW1 6E 64
Forges Rd. E12 2B 70
Forman Pl. N16 4F 67
Formation, The E16 2F 107
(off Woolwich Mnr. Way)
Formby Av. HA7: Stan 3C 42
Formby Ct. N7 5A 66
(off Morgan Rd.)
Formosa Ho. E1 4A 86
(off Ernest St.)
Formosa St. W9 4K 81
Formunt Cl. E16 5H 87
Forres Gdns. NW11 6J 45
Forrester Path SE26 4J 139
Forrest Gdns. SW16 3K 155
Forris Av. UB3: Hayes 1H 93
Forset Ct. W2 7D 4
(off Edgware Rd.)
Forset St. W1 7D 4 (6C 82)
Forstal Cl. BR2: Brom 3J 159
Forster Cl. IG8 7A 36
Forster Ho. BR1: Brom 4F 141
Forster Rd. BR3: Beck 3A 158
E17 6A 50
N17 3F 49
SW2 7J 119
Forsters Cl. RM6: Chad H 6F 55
Forsters Way UB4: Yead 6K 75
Forston St. N1 2C 84
Forsyte Cres. SE19 1E 156
Forsythe Shades Ct. BR3: Beck 1E 158
Forsyth Gdns. SE17 6B 102
Forsyth Ho. E9 7J 67
(off Frampton Pk. Rd.)
SW1 5B 18
(off Tachbrook St.)
Forsythia Cl. IG1: Ilf 5F 71
Forsyth Pl. EN1: Enf 5K 23
Forterie Gdns. IG3: Bark, Ilf 3A 72
Fortescue Av. E8 7H 67
TW2: Twick 3G 131
Fortescue Rd. HA8: Edg 1K 43
SW19 7B 136
Fortess Gro. NW5 5G 65
Fortess Rd. NW5 5F 65
Fortess Wlk. NW5 5F 65
Fortess Yd. NW5 4F 65
Forthbridge Rd. SW11 4E 118
Fortis Cl. E16 6A 88
Fortis Ct. N10 3E 46
FORTIS GREEN 4D 46
Fortis Grn. N2 4C 46
N10 4C 46
Fortis Grn. Av. N2 3D 46
Fortis Grn. Rd. N10 3E 46
Fortismere Av. N10 3E 46
Fortnam Rd. N19 2H 65
Fortnum's Acre HA7: Stan 6E 26
Fort Rd. SE1 4F 103
UB5: N'olt 7E 58
Fortrose Cl. E14 6F 87
Fortrose Gdns. SW2 1J 137
Fort St. E1 6H 9 (5E 84)
E16 1K 105
Fortuna Cl. N7 6K 65
Fortune Ct. E8 7F 67
(off Queensbridge Rd.)
IG11: Bark 2C 90
Fortunegate Rd. NW10 1A 80
FORTUNE GREEN 4J 63
Fortune Grn. Rd. NW6 4J 63
Fortune Ho. EC1 4D 8
(off Fortune St.)
SE11 4J 19
Fortunes Mead UB5: N'olt 6C 58
Fortune St. EC1 4D 8 (4C 84)
Fortune Theatre 1F 13
(off Russell St.)
Fortune Wlk. SE28 3H 107
(off Broadwater Rd.)
Fortune Way NW10 3C 80
Forty Acre La. E16 5J 87
Forty Av. HA9: Wemb 3F 61
Forty Cl. HA9: Wemb 3F 61
Forty Footpath SW14 3J 115
Forty Foot Way SE9 7G 125
FORTY HILL 1K 23
Forty Hill EN2: Enf 1K 23
Forty La. HA9: Wemb 2H 61
Forum, The KT8: W Mole 4F 149
Forum Ct. SE19 6B 138
Forum Magnum Sq. SE1 6H 13
(off York Rd.)
Forumside HA8: Edg 6B 28
Forum Way HA8: Edg 6B 28
Forval Cl. CR4: Mitc 5D 154
Forward Bus. Cen., The E16 4F 87
Forward Dr. HA3: W'stone 4K 41
Fosbrooke Ho. SW8 7J 101
(off Davidson Gdns.)
Fosbury M. W2 7K 81
Foscote Ct. W9 4J 81
(off Foscote M.)
Foscote M. W9 4J 81
Foscote Rd. NW4 6D 44
Foskett Ho. N2 2B 46
Foskett Rd. SW6 2H 117
Foss Av. CR0: Wadd 5A 168
Fossdene Rd. SE7 5K 105
Fossdyke Cl. UB4: Yead 5C 76

Fosset Lodge DA7: Bex 1J 127
Fosse Way W13 .... .5A 78
Fossil Rd. SE13 .... .3C 122
Fossington Rd.
   DA17: Belv 4D 108
Foss Rd. SW17 .... .4B 136
Fossway RM8: Dag 2C 72
Foster Ct. E16 .... .7H 87
     (off Tarling Rd.)
   NW1 .... .7G 65
     (off Royal College St.)
   NW4 .... .4E 44
Foster Ho. SE14 .... .1B 122
Foster La. EC2 .... .7C 8 (6C 84)
Foster Rd. E13 .... .4J 87
   W3 .... .7A 80
   W4 .... .5K 97
Fosters Cl. BR7: Chst 5D 142
   E18 .... .1K 51
Foster St. NW4 .... .4E 44
Foster's Way SW18 .... .1K 135
Foster Wlk. NW4 .... .4E 44
Fothergill Cl. E13 .... .2J 87
Fothergill Dr. N21 .... .5D 22
Fotheringham Rd. EN1: Enf 4A 24
     (not continuous)
Foubert's Pl. W1 .... .1A 12 (6G 83)
Foulden Rd. N16 .... .4F 67
Foulden Ter. N16 .... .4F 67
Foulis Ter. SW7 .... .5B 16 (5B 100)
Foulser Rd. SW17 .... .3D 136
Foulsham Rd. CR7: Thor H 3C 156
Founder Cl. E6 .... .6B 89
Founders Ct. EC2 .... .7E 8
Founders Gdns. SE19 .... .7C 138
Founders Ho. SW1 .... .6C 18
     (off Aylesford St.)
Foundling Ct. WC1 .... .3E 6
     (off Brunswick Cen.)
Foundry Cl. SE16 .... .1A 104
Foundry Ho. E14 .... .5D 86
     (off Morris Rd.)
Foundry M. NW1 .... .3B 6
Foundry Pl. E1 .... .5J 85
     (off Redman's Rd.)
   SW18 .... .7K 117
Fountain Cl. UB8: Hil 5E 74
Fountain Ct. DA15: Sidc 6B 126
   EC4 .... .2J 13 (7A 84)
   SE23 .... .2K 139
   SW1 .... .4J 17
     (off Buckingham Pal. Rd.)
Fountain Dr. SE19 .... .4F 139
   SM5: Cars 7D 166
Fountain Grn. Sq. SE16 .... .2G 103
Fountain Ho. CR4: Mitc 2D 154
   NW6 .... .7G 63
   W1 .... .4G 11
     (off Park St.)
Fountain M. N5 .... .4C 66
     (off Highbury Grange)
   NW3 .... .6D 64
Fountain Pl. SW9 .... .1A 120
Fountain Rdbt. CR7: Thor H 3C 156
   SW17 .... .5B 136
Fountain Rd. N3: N Mald 4A 152
Fountains, The N3 .... .7E 30
     (off Ballards La.)
Fountains Av. TW13: Hanw 3D 130
Fountains Cl. TW13: Hanw 2D 130
     (not continuous)
Fountains Cres. N14 .... .7D 22
Fountain Sq. SW1 .... .3K 17 (4F 101)
Fountayne Bus. Cen. N15 .... .4G 49
Fountayne Rd. N15 .... .4G 49
   N16 .... .2G 67
Fount St. SW8 .... .7H 101
Fouracres EN3: Enf H 1F 25
Fourland Wlk. HA8: Edg 6D 28
Fournier St. E1 .... .5J 9 (5F 85)

Fourscore Mans. E8 .... .7G 67
     (off Shrubland Rd.)
Four Seasons Cl. E3 .... .2C 86
Four Seasons Cres. SM3: Sutt 2H 165
Four Sq. Ct. TW3: Houn 6E 112
Fourth Av. E12 .... .4D 70
   RM7: Rush G 1K 73
   UB3: Hayes 1H 93
   W10 .... .4G 81
Fourth Cross Rd.
   TW2: Twick 2H 131
Fourth Way HA9: Wemb 4H 61
Four Wents, The E4 .... .1A 36
Fovant Ct. SW8 .... .2G 119
Fowey Av. IG4: Ilf 5B 52
Fowey Cl. E1 .... .1H 103
Fowey Ho. SE11 .... .5K 19
Fowler Cl. SW11 .... .3B 118
Fowler Ho. N15 .... .5D 48
     (off South Gro.)
Fowler Rd. CR4: Mitc 2E 154
   E7 .... .4J 69
   N1 .... .1B 84
Fowlers Cl. DA14: Sidc 5E 144
Fowlers M. N19 .... .2G 65
     (off Holloway Rd.)
Fowler's Wlk. W5 .... .4D 78
Fownes St. SW11 .... .3C 118
Fox & Knot St. EC1 .... .5B 8
Foxberry Rd. SE4 .... .3A 122
Foxborough Gdns. SE4 .... .5C 122
Foxbourne Rd. SW17 .... .2E 136
Foxbury Av. BR7: Chst 6H 143
Foxbury Cl. BR1: Brom 6K 141
   E16 .... .6J 141
Fox Cl. BR6: Chels 5K 173
   E1 .... .4J 85
   E16 .... .5J 87
Foxcombe CR0: New Ad 6D 170
     (not continuous)
Foxcombe Cl. E6 .... .2B 88
Foxcombe Rd. SW15 .... .1C 134
Foxcote SE5 .... .5E 102
Foxcroft WC1 .... .1H 7
     (off Penton Ri.)
Foxcroft Rd. SE18 .... .1F 125
Foxearth Spur CR2: Sels 7J 169
Foxes Dale BR2: Brom 3F 159
   SE3 .... .3J 123
Foxfield NW1 .... .1F 83
     (off Arlington Rd.)
Foxfield Rd. BR6: Orp 2H 173
Foxglove Cl. DA15: Sidc 6A 126
   N9 .... .1D 34
   UB1: S'hall 7C 76
Foxglove Ct. HA0: Wemb 2E 78
Foxglove Gdns. E11 .... .4A 52
Foxglove La. KT9: Chess 4G 163
Foxglove Path SE28 .... .1J 107
     (off Martins Pl.)
Foxglove Rd. RM7: Rush G 2K 73
Foxglove St. W12 .... .7B 80
Foxglove Way SM6: Wall 1F 167
Fox Gro. KT12: Walt T 7K 147
Foxgrove N14 .... .3D 32
Foxgrove Av. BR3: Beck 7D 140
Foxgrove Rd. BR3: Beck 7D 140
Foxham Rd. N19 .... .3H 65
Fox Hill BR2: Kes 5A 172
   SE19 .... .7F 139
Fox Hill Gdns. SE19 .... .7F 139
Foxhole Rd. SE9 .... .5C 124
Fox Hollow Cl. SE18 .... .5J 107
Fox Hollow Dr. DA7: Bex 3D 126
Foxholt Gdns. NW10 .... .7J 61
Foxhome Cl. BR7: Chst 6E 142
Fox Ho. Rd. DA17: Belv 5H 109
     (not continuous)
Foxlands Cres. RM10: Dag 5J 73
Foxlands La. RM10: Dag 5K 73
Foxlands Rd. RM10: Dag 5J 73

Fox La. BR2: Kes 5K 171
   N13 .... .2E 32
   W5 .... .4E 78
Foxlees Ct. BR1: Brom 7G 141
Foxlees HA0: Wemb 4A 60
Foxley Cl. E8 .... .5G 67
Foxley Ct. SM2: Sutt 7A 166
Foxley Rd. CR7: Thor H 4B 156
   SW9 .... .7A 102
Foxley Sq. SW9 .... .1B 120
Foxmead Cl. EN2: Enf 3E 22
Foxmore St. SW11 .... .1D 118
Fox Rd. E16 .... .5H 87
Fox's Path CR4: Mitc 2C 154
Foxton Gro. CR4: Mitc 2B 154
Foxton Ho. E16 .... .2E 106
     (off Albert Rd.)
Foxwarren KT10: Clay 7A 162
Foxwell M. SE4 .... .3A 122
Foxwell St. SE4 .... .3A 122
Foxwood Cl. NW7 .... .4F 29
   TW13: Felt 3K 129
Foxwood Grn. Cl.
   EN1: Enf 6K 23
Foxwood Rd. SE3 .... .4H 123
Foyle Rd. N17 .... .1G 49
   SE3 .... .6H 105
Framfield Cl. N12 .... .3D 30
Framfield Ct. EN1: Enf 6K 23
     (off Queen Annes Gdns.)
Framfield Rd. CR4: Mitc 7E 136
   N5 .... .5B 66
   W7 .... .6J 77
Framlingham Cl. E5 .... .2J 67
Framlingham Cres. SE9 .... .4C 142
Frampton NW1 .... .7H 65
     (off Wrotham Rd.)
Frampton Cl. SM2: Sutt 7J 165
Frampton Ct. W3 .... .2J 97
     (off Avenue Rd.)
Frampton Ho. NW8 .... .4B 4
     (off Frampton St.)
Frampton Pk. Est. E9 .... .7J 67
Frampton Pk. Rd. E9 .... .6J 67
Frampton Rd. TW4: Houn 5C 112
Frampton St. NW8 .... .4B 4 (4B 82)
Francemary Rd. SE4 .... .5C 122
Frances Ct. E17 .... .6C 50
Frances Rd. E4 .... .6H 35
Frances St. SE18 .... .3D 106
Franche Ct. RM7: Rush G 3A 136
Francis & Dick James Ct. NW7 .... .7B 30
Francis Av. DA7: Bex 2G 127
   IG1: Ilf 2H 71
   TW13: Felt 3J 129
Francis Barber Cl. SW16 .... .5K 137
Franciscan Rd. SW17 .... .5D 136
Francis Chichester Way
   SW11 .... .1E 118
   KT19: Ewe 4K 163
   TW17: Shep 4C 146
Francis Cl. EC1 .... .5A 8
   KT5: Surb 4E 150
   KT19: Ewe 4F 105
     (off Cranes Pk. Av.)
   NW7 .... .5G 29
     (off Watford Way)
   SE14 .... .6A 103
     (off Myers La.)
Francis Gro. SW19 .... .6H 135
     (not continuous)
Francis Ho. E17 .... .6B 50
   N1 .... .1E 84
     (off Colville Est.)
   SW10 .... .7K 99
     (off Coleridge Gdns.)
Francis M. SE12 .... .7J 123
Francis Rd. CR0: Croy 7B 156
   E10 .... .1E 68
   HA1: Harr 5A 42
   HA5: Eastc 5A 40

Francis Rd. IG1: Ilf 2H 71
   N2 .... .4D 46
   SM6: Wall 6G 167
   TW4: Houn 2B 112
   UB6: G'frd 2B 78
Francis St. E15 .... .5G 69
   IG1: Ilf 2H 71
   SW1 .... .3A 18 (4G 101)
Francis Ter. N19 .... .3G 65
Francis Wlk. N1 .... .1K 83
Francklyn Gdns. HA8: Edg 3B 28
Franconia Rd. SW4 .... .5H 119
Frank Bailey Wlk. E12 .... .5E 70
Frank Beswick Ho. SW6 .... .6H 99
     (off Clem Attlee Ct.)
Frank Burton Cl. SE1 .... .5K 105
Frank Dixon Cl. SE21 .... .7E 120
Frank Dixon Way SE21 .... .1E 138
Frankfurt Rd. SE24 .... .5C 120
Frank Godley Ct. DA14: Sidc 5B 144
Frankham Ho. SE8 .... .7C 104
     (off Frankham St.)
Frankham St. SE8 .... .7C 104
Frank Ho. SW8 .... .7J 101
     (off Wyvil Rd.)
Frankland Cl. IG8: Wfd G 5F 37
   SE16 .... .3H 103
Frankland Rd. E4 .... .5H 35
   SW7 .... .2A 16 (3B 100)
Franklin Bldg. E14 .... .2C 104
Franklin Cl. KT1: King T 3G 151
   N20 .... .7F 21
   SE13 .... .1D 122
   SE27 .... .3B 138
Franklin Cotts. HA7: Stan 4G 27
Franklin Cres. CR4: Mitc 4G 155
Franklin Ho. BR2: Brom 3G 159
   E1 .... .1H 103
     (off Watts St.)
Franklin Ind. Est. SE20 .... .1J 157
     (off Franklin Rd.)
Franklin Pas. SE9 .... .3C 124
Franklin Pl. SE13 .... .1D 122
Franklin Rd. DA7: Bex 1E 126
   SE20 .... .7J 139
Franklins M. HA2: Harr 2G 59
Franklin Sq. W14 .... .5H 99
Franklin's Row SW3 .... .5F 17 (5D 100)
Franklin St. E3 .... .3D 86
   N15 .... .6E 48
Franklin Way CR0: Wadd 7J 155
Franklyn Rd. KT12: Walt T 6J 147
   NW10 .... .6B 62
Franks Av. KT3: N Mald 4J 151
Frank Soskice Ho. SW6 .... .6H 99
     (off Clem Attlee Ct.)
Frank St. E13 .... .4J 87
Franks Wood Av. BR5: Pet W 5F 161
Frankswood Av. UB7: Yiew 6B 74
Frank Towell Ct. TW14: Felt 7J 111
Frank Welsh Ct. HA5: Eastc 4A 40
Frank Whymark Ho. SE16 .... .2J 103
     (off Rupack St.)
Franlaw Cres. N13 .... .4H 33
Fransfield Gro. SE26 .... .3H 139
Frans Hals Ct. E14 .... .3F 105
Frant Cl. SE20 .... .7J 139
Franthorne Way SE6 .... .2D 140
Frant Rd. CR7: Thor H 5B 156
Fraser Cl. DA5: Bexl 1J 145
   E6 .... .6C 88
Fraser Ct. E14 .... .5E 104
     (off Ferry St.)
Fraser Ho. TW8: Bford 5F 97
Fraser Rd. DA8: Erith 5K 109
   E17 .... .5D 50
   N9 .... .3C 34
   UB6: G'frd 1B 78
Fraser St. W4 .... .5A 98
Frating Cres. IG8: Wfd G 6E 36
Frazer Av. HA4: Ruis 5A 58

Frazier St.—Fulham FC

Frazier St. SE1 7J 13 (2A 102)
Frean St. SE16 3G 103
Frearson Ho. *WC1* *1H 7*
(*off Penton Ri.*)
Freda Corbet Cl. SE15 7G 103
Frederica Rd. E4 1A 36
Frederica St. N7 7K 65
Frederick Charrington Ho.
E1 *4J 85*
(*off Wickford St.*)
Frederick Cl. SM1: Sutt 4H 165
W2 2D 10 (7D 82)
Frederick Ct. *SW3* *4F 17*
(*off Duke of York Sq.*)
Frederick Cres. EN3: Enf H 2D 24
SW9 7B 102
Frederick Gdns. CR0: Croy 6B 156
SM1: Sutt 5H 165
Frederick Pl. SE18 5F 107
Frederick Rd. RM13: Rain 2K 91
SE17 6B 102
SM1: Sutt 5H 165
Fredericks Pl. EC2 1E 14 (6D 84)
N12 4F 31
Frederick Sq. *SE16* *7A 86*
(*off Sovereign Cres.*)
Frederick's Row EC1 1A 8 (3B 84)
Frederick St. WC1 2G 7 (3K 83)
Frederick Ter. E8 7F 67
Frederick Vs. *W7* *1J 95*
(*off Lwr. Boston Rd.*)
Frederic M. SW1 7F 11
Frederic St. E17 5A 50
Fredora Av. UB4: Hayes 4H 75
Fred Styles Ho. SE7 6A 106
Fred White Wlk. N7 6J 65
Freedom Cl. E17 4K 49
Freedom Rd. N17 2D 48
Freedom St. SW11 2D 118
Freegrove Rd. N7 5J 65
(not continuous)
Freehold Ind. Cen. TW4: Houn 5A 112
Freeland Ct. DA15: Sidc 3A 144
Freeland Pk. NW4 2G 45
Freeland Rd. W5 7F 79
Freelands Av. CR2: Sels 7K 169
Freelands Gro. BR1: Brom 1K 159
Freelands Rd. BR1: Brom 1K 159
Freeling Ho. *NW8* *1B 82*
(*off Dorman Way*)
Freeling St. N1 7K 65
(Carnoustie Dr.)
N1 7J 65
(Pembroke St.)
Freeman Cl. TW17: Shep 4G 147
UB5: N'olt 7C 58
Freeman Dr. KT8: W Mole 4D 148
Freeman Rd. SM4: Mord 5B 154
Freemans La. UB3: Hayes 7G 75
Freemantle Av. EN3: Pond E 5E 24
Freemantle St. SE17 5E 102
Freemasons Pl. *CR0: Croy* *1E 168*
(*off Freemasons Rd.*)
Freemasons Rd. CR0: Croy 1E 168
E16 5K 87
Freesia Cl. BR6: Chels 5K 173
Freethorpe Cl. SE19 7D 138
Free Trade Wharf E1 7K 85
Freezeland Way UB10: Hil 6D 56
Freke Rd. SW11 3E 118
Fremantle Ho. *E1* *4H 85*
(*off Somerford St.*)
Fremantle Rd. DA17: Belv 4G 109
IG6: Ilf 2F 53
Fremont St. E9 1H 85
(not continuous)
French Ordinary Ct. EC3 2H 15
French Pl. E1 2H 9 (3E 84)
French St. TW16: Sun 2A 148
Frendsbury Rd. SE4 4A 122
Frensham Cl. UB1: S'hall 4D 76
Frensham Dr. CR0: New Ad 7E 170
SW15 3B 134
(not continuous)
Frensham Rd. SE9 2H 143
Frensham St. SE15 6G 103
Frere St. SW11 2C 118
Fresham Ho. *BR2: Brom* *3H 159*
(*off Durham Rd.*)
Freshfield Av. E8 7F 67
Freshfield Cl. SE13 4F 123
Freshfield Dr. N14 7A 22
Freshfields CR0: Croy 1B 170
Freshford St. SW18 3A 136
Freshill La. UB1: S'hall 4E 76
Freshwater Cl. SW17 6E 136
Freshwater Ct. UB1: S'hall 3E 76
W1 *6D 4*
(*off Crawford St.*)
Freshwater Rd. RM8: Dag 1D 72
SW17 6E 136
Freshwell Av. RM6: Chad H 4C 54
Fresh Wharf Rd. IG11: Bark 1F 89
Freshwood Cl. BR3: Beck 1D 158
Freshwood Way SM6: Wall 7F 167
Freston Gdns. EN4: Cockf 5K 21
Freston Pk. N3 2H 45
Freston Rd. W10 7F 81
W11 7F 81
Freswick Ho. *SE8* *4K 103*
(*off Chilton Gro.*)
Freta Rd. DA6: Bex 5F 127
Freud Mus., The 6A 64
Frewell Ho. *EC1* *5J 7*
(*off Bourne Est.*)
Frewing Cl. BR7: Chst 6D 142
Frewin Rd. SW18 1B 136
Friar M. SE27 3B 138
Friar Rd. BR5: St M Cry 5K 161
UB4: Yead 4B 76
Friars Av. N20 3H 31
SW15 3B 134
Friars Cl. E4 3K 35
IG1: Ilf 1H 71
SE1 5B 14
UB5: Yead 3B 76
Friars Ct. E17 1B 50
SM6: Wall 4F 167
Friars Gdns. W3 6K 79
Friars Ga. Cl. IG8: Wfd G 4D 36
Friars La. TW9: Rich 5D 114
Friars Mead E14 3E 104
Friars M. SE9 5E 124
Friars Pl. La. W3 7K 79
Friars Rd. E6 1B 88
Friars Stile Pl. TW10: Rich 6E 114
Friars Stile Rd. TW10: Rich 6E 114
Friar St. EC4 1B 14 (6B 84)
Friars Wlk. N14 7A 22
SE2 5D 108
Friars Way W3 6K 79
Friarswood CR0: Sels 7A 170
Friary Cl. N12 5H 31
Friary Ct. SW1 5B 12
Friary Est. SE15 6G 103
(not continuous)
Friary La. IG8: Wfd G 4D 36
Friary Pk. Ct. W3 6J 79
Friary Rd. N12 4G 31
SE15 7G 103
W3 6J 79
Friary Way N12 4H 31
FRIDAY HILL 2B 36
Friday Hill E4 2B 36
Friday Hill E. E4 3B 36
(not continuous)
Friday Hill W. E4 2B 36
Friday Rd. CR4: Mitc 7D 136
DA8: Erith 5K 109
Friday St. EC4 2C 14 (7C 84)
Frideswide Pl. NW5 5G 65
Freightliners City Farm 6A 66
Friendly Pl. SE13 1D 122
Friendly St. SE8 2C 122
Friendly St. M. SE8 2C 122
Friendship Ho. *SE1* *7B 14*
(*off Belvedere Pl.*)
Friendship Wlk. UB5: N'olt 3B 76
Friendship Way E15 1E 86
Friends House 2C 6
Friends Rd. CR0: Croy 3D 168
Friend St. EC1 1A 8 (3B 84)
FRIERN BARNET 5J 31
Friern Barnet La. N11 2G 31
N20 2G 31
Friern Barnet Rd. N11 5J 31
Friern Bri. Retail Pk. N11 6A 32
Friern Ct. N20 3G 31
Friern Mt. Dr. N20 7F 21
Friern Pk. N12 5F 31
Friern Rd. SE22 7G 121
Friern Watch Av. N12 4F 31
Frigate Ho. *E14* *4E 104*
(*off Stebondale St.*)
Frigate M. SE8 6C 104
Frimley Av. SM6: Wall 5J 167
Frimley Cl. CR0: New Ad 7E 170
SW19 2G 135
Frimley Ct. DA14: Sidc 5C 144
Frimley Cres. CR0: New Ad 7E 170
Frimley Gdns. CR4: Mitc 3C 154
Frimley Rd. IG3: Ilf 3J 71
KT9: Chess 5D 162
Frimley St. *E1* *4K 85*
(*off Frimley Way*)
Frimley Way E1 4K 85
Fringewood Cl. HA6: Nwood 1D 38
Frinstead Ho. *W10* *7F 81*
(*off Freston Rd.*)
Frinsted Rd. DA8: Erith 7K 109
Frinton Ct. *W13* *5B 78*
(*off Hardwick Grn.*)
Frinton Dr. IG8: Wfd G 7A 36
Frinton M. IG2: Ilf 6E 52
Frinton Rd. DA14: Sidc 2E 144
E6 3B 88
N15 6E 48
SW17 6E 136
Friston St. SW6 2K 117
Friswell Pl. DA6: Bex 4G 127
Fritham Cl. KT3: N Mald 6A 152
Frith Ct. NW7 7B 30
Frith Ho. *NW8* *4B 4*
(*off Frampton St.*)
Frith La. NW7 7B 30
Frith Rd. CR0: Croy 2C 168
E11 4E 68
Frith St. W1 1C 12 (6H 83)
Frithville Ct. *W12* *1E 98*
(*off Frithville Gdns.*)
Frithville Gdns. W12 1E 98
Frizlands La. RM10: Dag 2H 73
Frobisher Cl. HA5: Pinn 7B 40
Frobisher Ct. NW9 2A 44
SE10 *6F 105*
(*off Old Woolwich Rd.*)
SE23 2H 139
SM3: Cheam 7G 165
W12 *2E 98*
(*off Lime Gro.*)
Frobisher Cres. *EC2* *5D 8*
(*off Beech St.*)
TW19: Stanw 7A 110
Frobisher Gdns. E10 7D 50
TW19: Stanw 7A 110
Frobisher Ho. *E1* *1H 103*
(*off Watts St.*)
SW1 *7C 18*
(*off Dolphin Sq.*)
Frobisher M. EN2: Enf 4J 23
Frobisher Pas. E14 1C 104
Frobisher Pl. Pioneer Cen.
SE15 1J 121
Frobisher Rd. E6 6D 88
N8 4A 48
Frobisher St. SE10 6G 105
Frog La. RM13: Rain 6K 91
Frogley Rd. SE22 4F 121
Frogmore SW18 5J 117
Frogmore Av. UB4: Hayes 4G 75
Frogmore Cl. SM3: Cheam 3F 165
Frogmore Ct. UB2: S'hall 4D 94
Frogmore Gdns. SM3: Cheam 4G 165
UB4: Hayes 4G 75
Frogmore Ind. Est. N5 5C 66
NW10 3J 79
UB3: Hayes 2G 93
Frognal NW3 4A 64
Frognal Av. DA14: Sidc 5A 144
HA1: Harr 4K 41
Frognal Cl. NW3 5A 64
FROGNAL CORNER 6K 143
Frognal Ct. NW3 6A 64
Frognal Gdns. NW3 4A 64
Frognal La. NW3 5K 63
Frognal Pde. NW3 6A 64
Frognal Pl. DA14: Sidc 6A 144
Frognal Ri. NW3 3A 64
Frognal Way NW3 4A 64
Froissart Rd. SE9 5B 124
Frome Ho. SE15 4H 121
Frome Rd. N22 3B 48
Frome St. N1 2C 84
Fromondes Rd. SM3: Cheam 5G 165
Frontenac NW10 7D 62
Frontier Works N17 6K 33
Frostic Wlk. E1 6K 9 (5G 85)
Froude St. SW8 2F 119
Fruen Rd. TW14: Felt 7H 111
Fruiterers Pas. *EC4* *3D 14*
(*off Queen St. Pl.*)
Fryatt Rd. N17 7J 33
(not continuous)
Fryday Gro. M. *SW12* *7G 119*
(*off Weir Rd.*)
Fryent Cl. NW9 6G 43
Fryent Country Pk. 7G 43
Fryent Cres. NW9 6A 44
Fryent Flds. NW9 6A 44
Fryent Gro. NW9 6A 44
Fryent Way NW9 5G 43
Fry Ho. E6 7A 70
Frying Pan All. E1 6J 9
Fry Rd. E6 7B 70
NW10 1B 80
Fryston Av. CR0: Croy 2G 169
Fuchsia Cl. RM7: Rush G 2K 73
Fuchsia St. SE2 5B 108
Fulbeck Dr. NW9 1A 44
Fulbeck Ho. *N7* *6K 65*
(*off Sutterton St.*)
Fulbeck Rd. N19 4G 65
Fulbeck Wlk. HA8: Edg 2C 28
Fulbeck Way HA2: Harr 2G 41
Fulbourn *KT1: King T* *2G 151*
(*off Eureka Rd.*)
Fulbourne Rd. E17 1E 50
Fulbourne St. E1 5H 85
Fulbrook M. N19 4G 65
Fulcher Ho. *N1* *1E 84*
(*off Colville Est.*)
SE8 5B 104
Fulford Ho. KT19: Ewe 7K 163
Fulford Rd. KT19: Ewe 7K 163
Fulford St. SE16 2H 103
FULHAM 2G 117
FULHAM BROADWAY 7J 99
Fulham B'way. SW6 7J 99
Fulham B'way. Shop. Cen.
SW6 *7J 99*
(*off Fulham B'way.*)
Fulham Cl. UB10: Hil 4E 74
Fulham Ct. SW6 1J 117
Fulham FC 1F 117

Gatesborough St.—Gibson Bus. Cen., The

Gatesborough St. EC2 . . . 3G 9 (4E 84)
Gates Ct. SE17 . . . 5C 102
Gatesden WC1 . . . 2G 7 (3J 83)
Gates Grn. Rd. BR2: Kes . . . 3H 171
BR4: W W'ck . . . 3H 171
Gateside Rd. SW17 . . . 3D 136
Gatestone Ct. SE19 . . . 6E 138
Gatestone Rd. SE19 . . . 6E 138
Gate St. WC2 . . . 7G 7 (6K 83)
Gate Theatre, The . . . *1J 99*
(off Pembridge Rd.)
Gateway SE17 . . . 6C 102
Gateway Arc. *N1* . . . *2B 84*
(off Upper St.)
Gateway Bus. Cen. BR3: Beck . . . 6A 140
Gateway Ho. IG11: Bark . . . 1G 89
Gateway Ind. Est. NW10 . . . 3B 80
Gateway M. E8 . . . 5F 67
Gateway Retail Pk. E6 . . . 4F 89
Gateway Rd. E10 . . . 3D 68
Gateways *KT6: Surb* . . . *5E 150*
(off Surbiton Hill Rd.)
Gateways, The SW3 . . . 4D 16
TW9: Rich . . . *4D 114*
(off Park La.)
Gateways Ct. SM6: Wall . . . 5F 167
Gatfield Gro. TW13: Hanw . . . 2E 130
Gatfield Ho. TW13: Hanw . . . 2D 130
Gathorne Rd. N22 . . . 2A 48
Gathorne St. E2 . . . 2K 85
Gatley Av. KT19: Ewe . . . 5H 163
Gatliff Cl. SW1 . . . 6H 17
Gatliff Rd. SW1 . . . 6J 17 (5F 101)
(not continuous)
Gatling Rd. SE2 . . . 5A 108
Gatonby St. SE15 . . . 1F 121
Gatting Cl. HA8: Edg . . . 7D 28
Gatting Way UB8: Uxb . . . 6A 56
Gattis Wharf *N1* . . . *2J 83*
(off New Wharf Rd.)
Gatton Rd. SW17 . . . 4C 136
Gattons Way DA14: Sidc . . . 4F 145
Gatward Cl. N21 . . . 6G 23
Gatward Grn. N9 . . . 2A 34
Gatwick Ho. *E14* . . . *6B 86*
(off Clemence St.)
Gatwick Rd. SW18 . . . 7H 117
Gauden Cl. SW4 . . . 3H 119
Gauden Rd. SW4 . . . 2H 119
Gaugin Ct. *SE16* . . . *5H 103*
(off Stubbs Dr.)
Gaumont Ter. *W12* . . . *2E 98*
(off Lime Gro.)
Gauntlet *NW9* . . . *2B 44*
(off Five Acre)
Gauntlet Cl. UB5: N'olt . . . 7C 58
Gauntlett Ct. HA0: Wemb . . . 5B 60
Gauntlett Rd. SM1: Sutt . . . 5B 166
Gaunt St. SE1 . . . 3C 102
Gautrey Rd. SE15 . . . 2J 121
Gautrey Sq. E6 . . . 6D 88
Gavel St. SE17 . . . 4D 102
Gaverick M. E14 . . . 4C 104
Gavestone Cres. SE12 . . . 7K 123
Gavestone Rd. SE12 . . . 7K 123
Gaviller Pl. E5 . . . 4H 67
Gavina Cl. SM4: Mord . . . 5C 154
Gavin Ho. SE18 . . . 4J 107
Gawain Wlk. N9 . . . 3B 34
Gawber St. E2 . . . 3J 85
Gawsworth Cl. E15 . . . 5H 69
Gawthorne Av. NW7 . . . 5B 30
Gay Cl. NW2 . . . 5D 62
Gaydon Ho. *W2* . . . *5K 81*
(off Bourne Ter.)
Gaydon La. NW9 . . . 1A 44
Gayfere Rd. IG5: Ilf . . . 3D 52
KT17: Ewe . . . 5C 164
Gayfere St. SW1 . . . 2E 18 (3J 101)
Gayford Rd. W12 . . . 2B 98
Gay Gdns. RM10: Dag . . . 4J 73
Gay Ho. N16 . . . 5E 66
Gayhurst *SE17* . . . *6D 102*
(off Hopwood Rd.)
Gayhurst Ct. UB5: Yead . . . 3A 76
Gayhurst Ho. *NW8* . . . *3C 4*
(off Mallory St.)
Gayhurst Rd. E8 . . . 7G 67
Gaylor Rd. UB5: N'olt . . . 5D 58
Gaymead *NW8* . . . *1K 81*
(off Abbey Rd.)
Gaynesford Rd. SE23 . . . 2K 139
SM5: Cars . . . 7D 166
Gaynes Hill Rd. IG8: Wfd G . . . 6H 37
Gay Rd. E15 . . . 2F 87
Gaysham Av. IG2: Ilf . . . 5E 52
Gaysham Hall IG5: Ilf . . . 3F 53
Gaysley Ho. SE11 . . . 4J 19
Gay St. SW15 . . . 3F 117
Gayton Ct. HA1: Harr . . . 6K 41
Gayton Cres. NW3 . . . 4B 64
Gayton Rd. HA1: Harr . . . 6K 41
NW3 . . . 4B 64
SE2 . . . 3C 108
Gayville Rd. SW11 . . . 6D 118
Gaywood Cl. SW2 . . . 1K 137
Gaywood Rd. E17 . . . 3C 50
Gaywood St. SE1 . . . 3B 102
Gaza St. SE17 . . . 5B 102
Gaze Ho. *E14* . . . *6F 87*
(off Blair St.)
Gean Ct. E11 . . . 4F 69
Geariesville Gdns. IG6: Ilf . . . 4F 53
Gearing Cl. SW17 . . . 4E 136
Geary Rd. NW10 . . . 5C 62
Geary St. N7 . . . 5K 65
Geddes Pl. *DA7: Bex* . . . *4G 127*
(off Arnsberga Way)
Gedeney Rd. N17 . . . 1C 48
Gedling Pl. SE1 . . . 7K 15 (3F 103)
Geere Rd. E15 . . . 1H 87
Gees Ct. W1 . . . 1H 11 (6E 82)
Gee St. EC1 . . . 3C 8 (4C 84)
Geffery's Ct. SE9 . . . 3C 142
Geffrye Ct. N1 . . . 2E 84
Geffrye Est. N1 . . . 2E 84
Geffrye Mus. . . . 1J 9
Geffrye St. E2 . . . 1J 9 (2F 85)
Geldart Rd. SE15 . . . 7H 103
Geldeston Rd. E5 . . . 2G 67
Gellatly Rd. SE14 . . . 2J 121
Gell Cl. UB10: Ick . . . 3B 56
Gelsthorpe Rd. RM5: Col R . . . 1H 55
Gemini Bus. Cen. E16 . . . 4F 87
Gemini Bus. Est. SE14 . . . 5K 103
Gemini Ct. *E1* . . . *7G 85*
(off Vaughan Way)
Gemini Gro. UB5: N'olt . . . 3C 76
General Gordon Pl. SE18 . . . 4F 107
General Wolfe Rd. SE10 . . . 1F 123
Genesis Cl. TW19: Stanw . . . 1B 128
Genesta Rd. SE18 . . . 6F 107
Geneva Cl. TW17: Shep . . . 2G 147
Geneva Ct. NW9 . . . 5B 44
Geneva Dr. SW9 . . . 4A 120
Geneva Gdns. RM6: Chad H . . . 5E 54
Geneva Rd. CR7: Thor H . . . 5C 156
KT1: King T . . . 4E 150
Genever Cl. E4 . . . 5H 35
Genista Rd. N18 . . . 5C 34
Genoa Av. SW15 . . . 5E 116
Genoa Ho. *E1* . . . *4K 85*
(off Ernest St.)
Genoa Rd. SE20 . . . 1J 157
Genotin Rd. EN1: Enf . . . 3J 23
Genotin Ter. EN1: Enf . . . 4J 23
Gentlemans Row EN2: Enf . . . 3H 23
Gentry Gdns. E13 . . . 4J 87
Geoffrey Bower Sports Cen. . . . 2D 52
Geoffrey Cl. SE5 . . . 2C 120
Geoffrey Ct. SE4 . . . 2B 122
Geoffrey Gdns. E6 . . . 2C 88
Geoffrey Ho. *SE1* . . . *7F 15*
(off Pardoner St.)
Geoffrey Jones Ct. NW10 . . . 1C 80
Geoffrey Rd. SE4 . . . 3B 122
George V Av. HA5: Pinn . . . 2D 40
George V Cl. HA5: Pinn . . . 3E 40
George V Way UB6: G'frd . . . 1B 78
George Beard Rd. SE8 . . . 4B 104
George Belt Ho. *E2* . . . *3K 85*
(off Smart St.)
George Comberton Wlk. E12 . . . 5E 70
George Ct. WC2 . . . 3F 13
George Cres. N10 . . . 7K 31
George Davies Lodge *IG6: Ilf* . . . *5G 53*
(off Veronique Gdns.)
George Downing Est. N16 . . . 2F 67
George Eliot Ho. *SW1* . . . *4B 18*
(off Vauxhall Bri. Rd.)
George Elliston Ho. *SE1* . . . *5G 103*
(off Old Kent Rd.)
George Eyre Ho. *NW8* . . . *2B 82*
(off Cochrane St.)
George Gange Way HA3: W'stone . . . 3J 41
George Gillett Ct. EC1 . . . 3D 8
George Gro. Rd. SE20 . . . 1G 157
George Inn Yd. SE1 . . . 5E 14 (1D 102)
George La. BR2: Hayes . . . 1K 171
E18 . . . 2J 51
(not continuous)
SE13 . . . 6D 122
George Lansbury Ho. *N22* . . . *1A 48*
(off Progress Way)
NW10 . . . 7A 62
George Lindgren Ho. *SW6* . . . *7H 99*
(off Clem Attlee Ct.)
George Loveless Ho. *E2* . . . *1K 9*
(off Diss St.)
George Lowe Ct. *W2* . . . *5K 81*
(off Bourne Ter.)
George Mathers Rd. SE11 . . . 4B 102
George M. *EN2: Enf* . . . *3J 23*
(off Town, The)
NW1 . . . 2B 6
George Peabody Ct. *NW1* . . . *5C 4*
(off Burne St.)
George Pl. N17 . . . 3E 48
George Potter Ho. *SW11* . . . *2B 118*
(off George Potter Way)
George Potter Way SW11 . . . 2B 118
George Rd. E4 . . . 6H 35
KT2: King T . . . 7H 133
(not continuous)
KT3: N Mald . . . 4B 152
George Row SE16 . . . 2G 103
George Sq. SW19 . . . 3J 153
George's Rd. N7 . . . 5K 65
George's Sq. *SW6* . . . *6H 99*
(off Nth. End Rd.)
George St. CR0: Croy . . . 2C 168
E16 . . . 6H 87
(not continuous)
IG11: Bark . . . 7G 71
TW3: Houn . . . 2D 112
TW9: Rich . . . 5D 114
UB2: S'hall . . . 4C 94
W1 . . . 7E 4 (6D 82)
W7 . . . 1J 95
George Tingle Ho. *SE1* . . . *3F 103*
(off Grange Wlk.)
Georgetown Cl. SE19 . . . 5E 138
Georgette Pl. SE10 . . . 7E 104
Georgeville Gdns. IG6: Ilf . . . 4F 53
George Walter Ct. *SE16* . . . *4J 103*
(off Millender Wlk.)
George Wyver Cl. SW19 . . . 7G 117
George Yd. EC3 . . . 1F 15 (6D 84)
W1 . . . 2H 11 (7E 82)
Georgiana St. NW1 . . . 1G 83
Georgian Cl. BR2: Hayes . . . 1K 171
HA7: Stan . . . 7F 27
UB10: Ick . . . 4A 56
Georgian Ct. *CR0: Croy* . . . *1D 168*
(off Cross Rd.)
E9 . . . 1J 85
EN5: New Bar . . . 4F 21
HA9: Wemb . . . 6G 61
N3 . . . 1H 45
NW4 . . . 5D 44
SW16 . . . 4J 137
Georgian Ho. *E16* . . . *1J 105*
(off Capulet M.)
Georgian Way HA1: Harr . . . 2H 59
Georgia Rd. CR7: Thor H . . . 1B 156
KT3: N Mald . . . 4J 151
Georgina Gdns. E2 . . . 1K 9 (3F 85)
Geraint Rd. BR1: Brom . . . 4J 141
Geraldine Rd. SW18 . . . 5A 118
W4 . . . 6G 97
Geraldine St. SE11 . . . 2K 19 (3B 102)
Gerald M. SW1 . . . 3H 17
Gerald Rd. E16 . . . 4H 87
RM8: Dag . . . 2F 73
SW1 . . . 3H 17 (4E 100)
Gerard Av. TW4: Houn . . . 7E 112
Gerard Gdns. RM13: Rain . . . 2K 91
Gerard Rd. HA1: Harr . . . 6A 42
SW13 . . . 1B 116
Gerards Cl. SE16 . . . 5J 103
Gerda Rd. SE9 . . . 2G 143
Germander Way E15 . . . 3G 87
Gernigan Ho. SW18 . . . 6B 118
Gernon Rd. E3 . . . 2A 86
Geron Way NW2 . . . 2D 62
Gerrard Gdns. HA5: Eastc . . . 5J 39
Gerrard Ho. *SE14* . . . *7J 103*
(off Briant St.)
Gerrard Pl. W1 . . . 2D 12 (7H 83)
Gerrard Rd. N1 . . . 2B 84
Gerrards Cl. N14 . . . 5B 22
Gerrards Ct. W5 . . . 3D 96
Gerrard St. W1 . . . 2D 12 (7H 83)
Gerridge Ct. *SE1* . . . *1K 19*
(off Gerridge St.)
Gerridge St. SE1 . . . 1K 19 (3A 102)
Gerry Raffles Sq. E15 . . . 7F 69
Gertrude Rd. DA17: Belv . . . 4G 109
Gertrude St. SW10 . . . 7A 16 (6A 100)
Gervase Cl. HA9: Wemb . . . 3J 61
Gervase Rd. HA8: Edg . . . 1J 43
Gervase St. SE15 . . . 7H 103
Gervis Ct. TW7: Isle . . . 7G 95
Ghent St. SE6 . . . 2C 140
Ghent Way E8 . . . 6F 67
Giant Arches Rd. SE24 . . . 7C 120
Giant Tree Hill
WD23: Bushy . . . 1C 26
Gibbfield Cl. RM6: Chad H . . . 3E 54
Gibbings Ho. *SE1* . . . *7B 14*
(off King James St.)
Gibbins Rd. E15 . . . 7E 68
Gibbon Ho. NW8 . . . 4B 4
Gibbon Rd. KT2: King T . . . 1E 150
SE15 . . . 2J 121
W3 . . . 7A 80
Gibbons M. NW11 . . . 5H 45
Gibbon's Rents SE1 . . . 5G 15
Gibbons Rd. NW10 . . . 6A 62
Gibbon Wlk. SW15 . . . 4C 116
Gibbs Av. SE19 . . . 5D 138
Gibbs Cl. SE19 . . . 6D 138
Gibbs Grn. HA8: Edg . . . 4D 28
W14 . . . 5H 99
(not continuous)
Gibbs Grn. Cl. W14 . . . 5H 99
Gibbs Ho. *BR1: Brom* . . . *1H 159*
(off Longfield)
Gibb's Rd. N18 . . . 4D 34
Gibbs Sq. SE19 . . . 5D 138
Gibney Ter. BR1: Brom . . . 4H 141
Gibraltar Wlk. E2 . . . 2K 9
Gibson Bus. Cen., The
N17 . . . 7A 34

Goodwin Rd. CR0: Wadd 5B 168
N9 1E 34
W12 2C 98
Goodwins Ct.
WC2 2E 12 (7J 83)
Goodwin St. N4 2A 66
Goodwood Cl. HA7: Stan 5H 27
SM4: Mord 4J 153
Goodwood Ct. *W1* *5K 5*
(off Devonshire St.)
Goodwood Dr. UB5: N'olt 6E 58
Goodwood Ho. *SE14* *1A 122*
(off Goodwood St.)
Goodwood Pde. BR3: Beck 4A 158
Goodwood Rd. SE14 7A 104
Goodwyn Av. NW7 5F 29
Goodwyns Va. N10 1E 46
Goodyear Ho. *N2* *2B 46*
(off Grange, The)
Goodyear Pl. SE5 6C 102
Goodyer Ho. *SW1* *5C 18*
(off Tachbrook St.)
Goodyers Gdns. NW4 5F 45
Goosander Way SE28 3H 107
Gooseacre La. HA3: Kent 5D 42
Goose Grn. Trad. Est. SE22 4F 121
Gooseley La. E6 4F 89
(Claps Ga. La.)
E6 3E 88
(Vicarage La.)
Goosens Cl. SM1: Sutt 5A 166
Goose Sq. E6 6D 88
Gophir La. EC4 2E 14 (7D 84)
Gopsall St. N1 1D 84
Gordon Av. E4 6B 36
HA7: Stan 7E 26
SW14 4A 116
TW1: Twick 5A 114
Gordonbrock Rd. SE4 5C 122
Gordon Cl. E17 6C 50
N19 1G 65
Gordon Ct. HA8: Edg 5A 28
W12 6E 80
Gordon Cres. CR0: Croy 1E 168
UB3: Hayes 4J 93
Gordondale Rd. SW19 2J 135
Gordon Dr. TW17: Shep 7F 147
Gordon Gdns. HA8: Edg 2H 43
Gordon Gro. SE5 2B 120
Gordon Hill EN2: Enf 1H 23
Gordon Ho. *E1* *7J 85*
(off Glamis Rd.)
SE10 *7D 104*
(off Tarves Way)
SW1 *2B 18*
(off Greencoat Pl.)
W5 3E 78
Gordon Ho. Rd. NW5 4E 64
Gordon Mans. *W14* *3F 99*
(off Addison Gdns.)
WC1 *4C 6*
(off Torrington Pl.)
Gordon Pl. W8 2J 99
Gordon Rd. BR3: Beck 3B 158
DA15: Sidc 5J 125
DA17: Belv 4J 109
E4 1B 36
E11 6J 51
E15 4E 68
E18 1K 51
EN2: Enf 1H 23
HA3: W'stone 3J 41
IG1: Ilf 3H 71
IG11: Bark 1J 89
KT2: King T 1F 151
KT5: Surb 7F 151
N3 7C 30
N9 2C 34
N11 7C 32
RM6: Chad H 6F 55
SE15 2H 121
Gordon Rd. SM5: Cars 6D 166
TW3: Houn 4G 113
TW9: Rich 2F 115
TW15: Ashf 3A 128
TW17: Shep 6F 147
UB2: S'hall 4C 94
UB7: Yiew 7A 74
W4 6H 97
W5 7B 78
W13 7B 78
Gordon Sq. WC1 3C 6 (4H 83)
Gordon St. E13 3J 87
WC1 3C 6 (4H 83)
Gordon Way BR1: Brom 1J 159
EN5: Barn 4C 20
Gore Ct. NW9 5G 43
Gorefield Ho. *NW6* *2J 81*
(off Gorefield Pl.)
Gorefield Pl. NW6 2J 81
Gore Rd. E9 1J 85
SW20 2E 152
GORESBROOK INTERCHANGE 2F 91
Goresbrook Leisure Cen. 1D 90
Goresbrook Rd. RM9: Dag 1B 90
Gore St. SW7 3A 100
Gorham Ho. *SE16* *2K 103*
(off Wolfe Cres.)
Gorham Pl. W11 7G 81
Goring Cl. RM5: Col R 1J 55
Goring Gdns. RM8: Dag 4C 72
Goring Rd. N11 6D 32
RM10: Dag 6K 73
Goring St. EC3 7H 9
Goring Way UB6: G'frd 2G 77
Gorleston Rd. N15 5D 48
Gorleston St. W14 4G 99
(not continuous)
Gorman Rd. SE18 4D 106
Gorringe Pk. Av. CR4: Mitc 7D 136
Gorse Cl. E16 6J 87
Gorsefield Ho. *E14* *7C 86*
(off E. India Dock Rd.)
Gorse Ri. SW17 5E 136
Gorse Rd. CR0: Croy 4C 170
Gorse Wlk. UB7: Yiew 6A 74
Gorseway RM7: Rush G 1K 73
Gorst Rd. NW10 4J 79
SW11 6D 118
Gorsuch Pl. E2 1J 9 (3F 85)
Gorsuch St. E2 1J 9 (2F 85)
Gosberton Rd. SW12 1D 136
Gosbury Hill KT9: Chess 4E 162
Gosfield Rd. RM8: Dag 2G 73
Gosfield St. W1 6A 6 (5G 83)
Gosford Gdns. IG4: Ilf 5D 52
Goshawk Gdns. UB4: Hayes 3G 75
Goslett Yd. WC2 1D 12 (6H 83)
Gosling Cl. UB6: G'frd 3E 76
Gosling Ho. *E1* *7J 85*
(off Sutton St.)
Gosling Way SW9 1A 120
Gospatrick Rd. N17 7H 33
GOSPEL OAK 4E 64
Gosport Rd. E17 5B 50
Gosport Wlk. N17 4H 49
Gossage Rd. SE18 5H 107
UB10: Uxb 7B 56
Gosset St. E2 1K 9 (3F 85)
Gosshill Rd. BR7: Chst 2E 160
Gossington Cl. BR7: Chst 4F 143
Gosterwood St. SE8 6A 104
Gostling Rd. TW2: Whit 1E 130
Goston Gdns. CR7: Thor H 3A 156
Goswell Pl. EC1 2B 8
Goswell Rd. EC1 1A 8 (2B 84)
Gothic Cotts. *EN2: Enf* *2H 23*
(off Chase Grn. Av.)
Gothic Ct. *SE5* *7C 102*
(off Wyndham Rd.)
UB3: Harl 6F 93
Gothic Rd. TW2: Twick 2H 131
Gottfried M. NW5 4G 65
Goudhurst Rd. BR1: Brom 5G 141
Gough Ho. *KT1: King T* *2E 150*
(off Eden St.)
N1 *1B 84*
(off Windsor St.)
Gough Rd. E15 4H 69
EN1: Enf 2C 24
Gough Sq. EC4 7K 7 (6A 84)
Gough St. WC1 3H 7 (4K 83)
Gough Wlk. E14 6C 86
Goulden Ho. SW11 2C 118
Goulden Ho. App. SW11 2C 118
Goulding Gdns. CR7: Thor H 2B 156
Gouldman Ho. *E1* *4J 85*
(off Wyllen Cl.)
Gould Rd. TW2: Twick 1J 131
TW14: Felt 7G 111
GOULDS GREEN 6D 74
Gould's Grn. UB8: Hil 7D 74
Gould Ter. E8 5H 67
Goulston St. E1 7J 9 (6F 85)
Goulton Rd. E5 4H 67
Gourley Pl. N15 5E 48
Gourley St. N15 5E 48
Gourock Rd. SE9 5E 124
Govan St. E2 1G 85
Gover Ct. SW4 2J 119
Govett Av. TW17: Shep 5E 146
Govier Cl. E15 7G 69
Gowan Av. SW6 1G 117
Gowan Ho. *E2* *2K 9*
(off Chambord St.)
Gowan Rd. NW10 6D 62
Gower Cl. SW4 6G 119
Gower Ct. WC1 3C 6 (4H 83)
Gower Ho. E17 3D 50
SE17 *5C 102*
(off Morecambe St.)
Gower M. WC1 6D 6 (5H 83)
Gower M. Mans. *WC1* *5D 6*
(off Gower M.)
Gower Pl. WC1 3B 6 (4H 83)
Gower Rd. E7 6J 69
TW7: Isle 6K 95
Gower St. WC1 3B 6 (4G 83)
Gower's Wlk. E1 6G 85
Gowland Pl. BR3: Beck 2B 158
Gowlett Rd. SE15 3G 121
Gowlland Cl. CR0: Croy 7G 157
Gowrie Rd. SW11 3E 118
Graburn Way KT8: E Mos 3H 149
Grace Av. DA7: Bex 2F 127
Grace Bus. Cen. CR4: Mitc 6D 154
Gracechurch St. EC3 2F 15 (7D 84)
Grace Cl. HA8: Edg 7D 28
SE9 3B 142
Grace Ct. *CR0: Croy* *3B 168*
(off Waddon Rd.)
SM2: Sutt 7K 165
Gracedale Rd. SW16 5F 137
Gracefield Gdns. SW16 3J 137
Gracehill *E1* *5J 85*
(off Hannibal Rd.)
Grace Ho. SE11 7H 19
Grace Jones Cl. E8 6G 67
Grace M. *SE20* *2J 157*
(off Marlow Rd.)
Grace Path SE26 4J 139
Grace Pl. E3 3D 86
Grace Rd. CR0: Croy 6C 156
Graces All. E1 7G 85
Graces M. NW8 2A 82
SE5 2D 120
Grace's Rd. SE5 2E 120
Grace St. E3 3D 86
Gradient, The SE26 4G 139
Graduate Pl. SE1 7F 15
Graeme Rd. EN1: Enf 2J 23
Graemesdyke Av.
SW14 3H 115
Grafton Cl. KT4: Wor Pk 3A 164
TW4: Houn 1C 130
W13 6A 78
Grafton Ct. TW14: Bedf 1F 129
Grafton Cres. NW1 6F 65
Grafton Gdns. N4 6C 48
RM8: Dag 2E 72
Grafton Ho. SE8 5B 104
Grafton M. W1 4A 6 (4G 83)
Grafton Pk. Rd. KT4: Wor Pk 2A 164
Grafton Pl. NW1 2D 6 (3H 83)
Grafton Rd. CR0: Croy 1A 168
EN2: Enf 3E 22
HA1: Harr 5G 41
KT3: N Mald 3A 152
KT4: Wor Pk 3K 163
NW5 5E 64
RM8: Dag 2E 72
W3 7J 79
Graftons, The NW2 3J 63
Grafton Sq. SW4 3G 119
Grafton St. W1 3K 11 (7F 83)
Grafton Ter. NW5 5D 64
Grafton Way KT8: W Mole 4D 148
W1 4A 6 (4G 83)
WC1 4B 6 (4G 83)
Grafton Yd. NW5 6F 65
Graham Av. CR4: Mitc 1E 154
W13 2B 96
Graham Cl. CR0: Croy 2C 170
Graham Ct. *SE14* *6K 103*
(off Myers La.)
UB5: N'olt 5D 58
GRAHAME PARK 1B 44
Grahame Pk. Est. NW9 1A 44
Grahame Pk. Way NW7 7G 29
NW9 2B 44
Grahame Twr. *W3* *3H 97*
(off Hanbury Rd.)
Grahame White Ho. HA3: Kent 3D 42
Graham Gdns. KT6: Surb 1E 162
Graham Ho. *N9* *1D 34*
(off Cumberland Rd.)
Graham Lodge NW4 6D 44
Graham Mans. *IG11: Bark* *7A 72*
(off Lansbury Av.)
Graham Rd. CR4: Mitc 1E 154
DA6: Bex 4F 127
E8 6G 67
E13 4J 87
HA3: W'stone 3J 41
N15 3B 48
NW4 6D 44
SW19 7H 135
TW12: Hamp H 4E 130
W4 3K 97
Graham St. N1 1B 8 (2B 84)
Graham Ter. *DA15: Sidc* *6B 126*
(off Westerham Dr.)
SW1 4G 17 (4E 100)
Grainger Cl. UB5: N'olt 5F 59
Grainger Ct. SE5 7C 102
Grainger Rd. N22 1C 48
TW7: Isle 2K 113
Gramer Cl. E11 2F 69
Gramophone La. UB3: Hayes 2G 93
Grampian Cl. BR6: St M Cry 6K 161
SM2: Sutt 7A 166
UB3: Harl 7F 93
Grampian Gdns. NW2 1G 63
Grampians, The *W6* *2F 99*
(off Shepherd's Bush Rd.)
Gramsci Way SE6 3D 140
Granada St. SW17 5D 136
Granard Av. SW15 5D 116
Granard Bus. Cen. NW7 6F 29
Granard Ho. E9 6K 67
Granard Rd. SW12 7D 118
Granary Cl. N9 7D 24
Granary Mans. *SE28* *2G 107*
(off Erebus Dr.)

Gravely Ho.—Greenham Cres.

Gravely Ho. SE8 ... 4A 104
(off Chilton Gro.)
Gravenel Gdns. SW17 ... 5C 136
(off Nutwell St.)
Graveney Gro. SE20 ... 7J 139
Graveney Rd. SW17 ... 4C 136
Gravesend Rd. W12 ... 7C 80
Gray Av. RM8: Dag ... 1F 73
Grayham Cres. KT3: N Mald ... 4K 151
Grayham Rd. KT3: N Mald ... 4K 151
Gray Ho. SE17 ... 5C 102
(off King & Queen St.)
Grayland Cl. BR1: Brom ... 1B 160
Grayling Cl. E16 ... 4G 87
Grayling Ct. W5 ... 1D 96
(off Grange Rd.)
Grayling Rd. N16 ... 2D 66
Grayling Sq. E2 ... 3G 85
(off Nelson Gdns.)
Grays Ct. RM10: Dag ... 7H 73
Grayscroft Rd. SW16 ... 7H 137
Grays Farm Production Village
BR5: St P ... 7B 144
Grays Farm Rd. BR5: St P ... 7B 144
Grayshott Rd. SW11 ... 2E 118
Gray's Inn ... 5H 7 (5K 83)
Gray's Inn Bldgs. EC1 ... 4J 7
(off Rosebery Av.)
Gray's Inn Pl. WC1 ... 6H 7 (5K 83)
Gray's Inn Rd. WC1 ... 1F 7 (3J 83)
Gray's Inn Sq. WC1 ... 5J 7 (5K 83)
Grays La. TW15: Ashf ... 4D 128
Grayson Ho. EC1 ... 2D 8
Grays Rd. UB10: Uxb ... 2A 74
Grays Ter. E7 ... 6A 70
Gray St. SE1 ... 7K 13 (2A 102)
Grayswood Gdns. SW20 ... 2D 152
Grayswood Point SW15 ... 1C 134
Gray's Yd. W1 ... 1H 11
Graywood Ct. N12 ... 7F 31
Grazebrook Rd. N16 ... 2D 66
Grazeley Cl. DA6: Bex ... 5J 127
Grazeley Ct. SE19 ... 5E 138
Gt. Acre Ct. SW4 ... 4H 119
Gt. Arthur Ho. EC1 ... 4C 8
(off Golden La. Est.)
Gt. Bell All. EC2 ... 7E 8 (6D 84)
Great Benty UB7: W Dray ... 4A 92
Great Brownings SE21 ... 4F 139
Gt. Bushey Dr. N20 ... 1E 30
Gt. Cambridge Ind. Est. EN1: Enf ... 5C 24
GREAT CAMBRIDGE JUNC. ... 4J 33
Gt. Cambridge Rd. EN1: Enf ... 4J 33
N9 ... 4J 33
N17 ... 5J 33
N18 ... 4J 33
Gt. Castle St. W1 ... 7K 5 (6F 83)
Gt. Central Av. HA4: Ruis ... 5A 58
Gt. Central St. NW1 ... 5E 4 (5D 82)
Gt. Central Way HA9: Wemb ... 4J 61
NW10 ... 4J 61
Gt. Chapel St. W1 ... 7C 6 (6H 83)
Gt. Chart St. SW11 ... 4B 118
Gt. Chertsey Rd. TW2: Twick ... 3D 130
TW13: Hanw, Twick ... 3D 130
W4 ... 2J 115
Gt. Church La. W6 ... 4F 99
Gt. College St. SW1 ... 1E 18 (3J 101)
Great Cft. WC1 ... 2F 7
(off Cromer St.)
Gt. Cross Av. SE10 ... 7F 105
(not continuous)
Gt. Cumberland M.
W1 ... 1E 10 (6D 82)
Gt. Cumberland Pl. W1 ... 7E 4 (6D 82)
Gt. Dover St. SE1 ... 7D 14 (2C 102)
Greatdown Rd. W7 ... 4K 77
Gt. Eastern Ent. Cen. E14 ... 2D 104
Gt. Eastern Rd. E15 ... 7F 69
Gt. Eastern St. EC2 ... 2G 9 (3E 84)
Gt. Eastern Wlk. EC2 ... 6H 9
Gt. Eastern Wharf
SW11 ... 7C 100
Gt. Elms Rd. BR2: Brom ... 4A 160
Great Fld. NW9 ... 1A 44
Greatfield Av. E6 ... 4D 88
Greatfield Cl. N19 ... 4G 65
SE4 ... 4C 122
Greatfields Dr. UB8: Hil ... 5C 74
Greatfields Rd. IG11: Bark ... 1H 89
Gt. Fleete Way IG11: Bark ... 2C 90
Gt. Galley Cl. IG11: Bark ... 3B 90
Gt. Gatton Cl. CR0: Croy ... 7A 158
Gt. George St. SW1 ... 7D 12 (2H 101)
Gt. Guildford Bus. Sq.
SE1 ... 5C 14 (1C 102)
Gt. Guildford St.
SE1 ... 4C 14 (1C 102)
Great Hall ... 6F 17 (5D 100)
Greatham Wlk. SW15 ... 1C 134
Gt. Harry Dr. SE9 ... 3E 142
Gt. James St. WC1 ... 5G 7 (5K 83)
Gt. Marlborough St.
W1 ... 1A 12 (6G 83)
Gt. Maze Pond SE1 ... 5F 15 (2D 102)
(not continuous)
Gt. Newport St. WC2 ... 2E 12 (7J 83)
Gt. New St. EC4 ... 7K 7 (6A 84)
Great Nth. Leisure Pk. N12 ... 7G 31
Great Nth. Rd. EN5: Barn ... 2C 20
EN5: New Bar ... 5D 20
N2 ... 5C 46
N6 ... 5C 46
Great Nth. Way NW4 ... 2D 44
Greatorex Ho. E1 ... 5G 85
(off Spelman St.)
Greatorex St. E1 ... 5G 85
Gt. Ormond St. WC1 ... 5F 7 (5J 83)
Gt. Owl Rd. IG7: Chig ... 3K 37
Gt. Percy St. WC1 ... 1H 7 (3K 83)
Gt. Peter St. SW1 ... 2C 18 (3H 101)
Gt. Portland St. W1 ... 4K 5 (4F 83)
Gt. Pulteney St. W1 ... 2B 12 (7G 83)
Gt. Queen St. WC2 ... 1F 13 (6J 83)
Gt. Russell St. WC1 ... 7D 6 (6H 83)
Gt. St Helen's EC3 ... 7G 9 (6E 84)
Gt. St Thomas Apostle
EC4 ... 2D 14 (7C 84)
Gt. Scotland Yd. SW1 ... 5E 12 (1J 101)
Gt. Smith St. SW1 ... 1D 18 (3H 101)
Great Sth. W. Rd. TW4: Houn ... 3K 111
TW14: Bedf, Felt ... 7E 110
Great Spilmans SE22 ... 5E 120
Great Strand NW9 ... 1B 44
Gt. Suffolk St. SE1 ... 5B 14 (1B 102)
Gt. Sutton St. EC1 ... 4B 8 (4B 84)
Gt. Swan All. EC2 ... 7E 8 (6D 84)
(not continuous)
Gt. Thrift BR5: Pet W ... 4G 161
Gt. Titchfield St. W1 ... 4K 5 (4F 83)
Gt. Tower St. EC3 ... 2G 15 (7E 84)
Gt. Trinity La. EC4 ... 2D 14 (7C 84)
Great Turnstile WC1 ... 6H 7 (5K 83)
Gt. Western Ind. Pk. UB2: S'hall ... 2F 95
Gt. Western Rd. W9 ... 5H 81
W11 ... 5H 81
Great W. Rd. TW5: Hest ... 2B 112
TW7: Bford, Isle ... 2B 112
TW8: Bford ... 2B 112
W4 ... 5B 98
W6 ... 5B 98
Great W. Trad. Est. TW8: Bford ... 6B 96
Gt. Winchester St. EC2 ... 7F 9 (6D 84)
Gt. Windmill St. W1 ... 2C 12 (7H 83)
Greatwood BR7: Chst ... 7E 142
Great Yd. SE1 ... 6H 15
Greaves Cl. IG11: Bark ... 7H 71
Greaves Cotts. E14 ... 5A 86
Greaves Pl. SW17 ... 4C 136
Greaves Twr. SW10 ... 7A 100
(off Worlds End Est.)
Grebe Av. UB4: Yead ... 6B 76
Grebe Cl. E7 ... 5H 69
E17 ... 7F 35
IG11: Bark ... 4A 90
Grebe Ct. E14 ... 2E 104
(off River Barge Cl.)
SE8 ... 6B 104
(off Dorking Cl.)
SM1: Sutt ... 5H 165
Grebe Ter. KT1: King T ... 3E 150
Grecian Cres. SE19 ... 6B 138
Greek Ct. W1 ... 1D 12 (6H 83)
Greek St. W1 ... 1D 12 (6H 83)
Green, The BR1: Brom ... 3J 141
(not continuous)
BR2: Hayes ... 7J 159
BR5: St P ... 7B 144
BR6: Farnb ... 4F 173
CR0: Sels ... 7B 170
DA7: Bex ... 1G 127
DA14: Sidc ... 4A 144
DA16: Well ... 4J 125
E4 ... 1K 35
E11 ... 6K 51
E15 ... 6G 69
HA0: Wemb ... 2A 60
IG8: Wfd G ... 5D 36
IG9: Buck H ... 1E 36
KT3: N Mald ... 3K 151
N9 ... 2B 34
N14 ... 2C 32
N17 ... 6H 33
N21 ... 7F 23
SM1: Sutt ... 3K 165
SM4: Mord ... 4G 153
SM5: Cars ... 4E 166
SW19 ... 5F 135
TW2: Twick ... 1J 131
TW5: Hest ... 6E 94
TW9: Rich ... 5D 114
TW13: Felt ... 2K 129
TW17: Shep ... 4G 147
UB2: S'hall ... 3C 94
UB7: W Dray ... 3A 92
UB10: Ick ... 2E 56
W3 ... 6A 80
W5 ... 1D 96
Greenacre Cl. EN5: Barn ... 1C 20
UB5: N'olt ... 5D 58
Greenacre Gdns. E17 ... 4E 50
Greenacre Pl. SM6: Wall ... 2F 167
Green Acres CR0: Croy ... 3F 169
Greenacres DA14: Sidc ... 4A 144
N3 ... 2H 45
SE9 ... 6E 124
WD23: Bushy ... 2C 26
Greenacres Av. UB10: Ick ... 3B 56
Greenacres Cl. BR6: Farnb ... 4G 173
Greenacres Dr. HA7: Stan ... 6G 27
Greenacre Sq. SE16 ... 2K 103
Greenacre Wlk. N14 ... 3C 32
Grn. Arbour Ct. EC1 ... 7A 8
(off Old Bailey)
Green Av. NW7 ... 4E 28
W13 ... 3B 96
Greenaway Av. N18 ... 6E 34
Greenaway Gdns. NW3 ... 4K 63
Greenaway Ho. NW8 ... 1A 82
(off Boundary Rd.)
WC1 ... 2J 7
(off Fernsbury St.)
Greenaway Ter. TW19: Stanw ... 1A 128
(off Victory Cl.)
Green Bank E1 ... 1H 103
Greenbank N12 ... 4E 30
Greenbank Av. HA0: Wemb ... 5A 60
Grn. Bank Cl. E4 ... 2K 35
Greenbank Cres. NW4 ... 4G 45
Greenbank Lodge BR7: Chst ... 2E 160
(off Forest Cl.)
Greenbanks HA1: Harr ... 4J 59
Greenbay Rd. SE7 ... 7B 106
Greenberry St. NW8 ... 1C 4 (2C 82)
Greenbrook Av. EN4: Had W ... 1F 21
Green Cl. BR2: Brom ... 3G 159
NW9 ... 6J 43
NW11 ... 7A 46
SM5: Cars ... 2D 166
TW13: Hanw ... 5C 130
Greencoat Mans. SW1 ... 2B 18
(off Greencoat Row)
Greencoat Pl. SW1 ... 3B 18 (4G 101)
Greencoat Row
SW1 ... 2B 18 (3G 101)
Green Ct. TW16: Sun ... 6H 129
Greencourt Av. CR0: Croy ... 2H 169
HA8: Edg ... 1H 43
Greencourt Gdns. CR0: Croy ... 1H 169
Greencourt Ho. E1 ... 4K 85
(off Mile End Rd.)
Greencourt Rd. BR5: Pet W ... 5H 161
Greencrest Pl. NW2 ... 3C 62
Greencroft HA8: Edg ... 5D 28
Greencroft Av. HA4: Ruis ... 2A 58
Greencroft Cl. E6 ... 5B 88
Greencroft Gdns. EN1: Enf ... 3K 23
NW6 ... 7K 63
Greencroft Rd. TW5: Hest ... 1D 112
Green Dale SE5 ... 4D 120
SE22 ... 5E 120
Greendale NW7 ... 4F 29
Grn. Dale Cl. SE22 ... 5E 120
Grn. Dragon Ct. SE1 ... 4E 14
Grn. Dragon La. N21 ... 5E 22
TW8: Bford ... 5E 96
Grn. Dragon Yd. E1 ... 6K 9 (5G 85)
Green Dr. UB1: S'hall ... 1E 94
Greene Ct. SE14 ... 6K 103
(off Samuel Cl.)
Greene Ho. SE1 ... 3D 102
(off Burbage Cl.)
Green End KT9: Chess ... 4E 162
N21 ... 2G 33
Greenend Rd. W4 ... 2A 98
Greener Ho. SW4 ... 3H 119
Grn. Farm Cl. BR6: Chels ... 6K 173
Greenfell Mans. SE8 ... 6D 104
Greenfield Av. KT5: Surb ... 7H 151
Greenfield Dr. BR1: Brom ... 2A 160
N2 ... 4D 46
Greenfield Gdns. BR5: Pet W ... 7H 161
NW2 ... 2G 63
RM9: Dag ... 1D 90
Greenfield Ho. SW19 ... 1F 135
Greenfield Rd. DA2: Dart ... 5K 145
E1 ... 5G 85
N15 ... 5E 48
RM9: Dag ... 7C 72
Greenfields UB1: S'hall ... 6E 76
Greenfield Way HA2: Harr ... 3F 41
GREENFORD ... 3E 76
Greenford Av. UB1: S'hall ... 7D 76
W7 ... 4J 77
Greenford Bus. Cen. UB6: G'frd ... 7H 59
Greenford Gdns. UB6: G'frd ... 3F 77
GREENFORD GREEN ... 6J 59
Greenford Ind. Est. UB6: G'frd ... 7F 59
Greenford Rd. HA1: Harr ... 7J 59
SM1: Sutt ... 4K 165
(not continuous)
UB1: S'hall ... 1G 95
UB6: G'frd ... 7G 77
GREENFORD RDBT. ... 2H 77
Greenford Sports Cen. ... 3E 76
Green Gdns. BR6: Farnb ... 5G 173
Greengate UB6: G'frd ... 6B 60
Greengate Lodge E13 ... 2K 87
(off Hollybush St.)
Greengate Pde. IG2: Ilf ... 6H 53
Greengate St. E13 ... 2K 87
Greenhalgh Wlk. N2 ... 4A 46
Greenham Cl. SE1 ... 7J 13 (2A 102)
Greenham Cres. E4 ... 6G 35

Grenville Ho. *SW1* *7C 18*
(off Dolphin Sq.)
Grenville M. N19 1J 65
SW7 4A 100
TW12: Hamp H 5F 131
Grenville Pl. NW7 5E 28
SW7 3A 100
Grenville Rd. N19 1J 65
Grenville St. WC1 4F 7 (4J 83)
Gresham Av. N20 4J 31
Gresham Cl. DA5: Bexl 6E 126
EN2: Enf 3H 23
Gresham Dr. RM6: Chad H 5B 54
Gresham Gdns. NW11 1G 63
Gresham Lodge E17 5D 50
Gresham Pl. N19 2H 65
Gresham Rd. BR3: Beck 2A 158
E6 2D 88
E16 6K 87
HA8: Edg 6A 28
NW10 5K 61
SE25 4G 157
SW9 3A 120
TW3: Houn 1G 113
TW12: Hamp 6E 130
UB10: Hil 2C 74
Gresham St. EC2 7C 8 (6C 84)
Gresham Way SW19 3K 135
Gresley Cl. E17 6A 50
N15 4D 48
Gresley Rd. N19 1G 65
Gressenhall Rd. SW18 6H 117
Gresse St. W1 6C 6 (6H 83)
Gresswell Cl. DA14: Sidc 3A 144
Greswell St. SW6 1F 117
Gretton Ho. *E2* *3J 85*
(off Globe Rd.)
Gretton Rd. N17 7A 34
Greville Cl. TW1: Twick 7B 114
Greville Ct. *E5* *4H 67*
(off Napoleon Rd.)
HA1: Harr 4J 59
Greville Hall NW6 2K 81
Greville Lodge E13 1K 87
HA8: Edg *4C 28*
(off Broadhurst Av.)
N12 5E 30
Greville M. *NW6* *1K 81*
(off Greville Rd.)
Greville Pl. NW6 2K 81
Greville Rd. E17 4E 50
NW6 2K 81
TW10: Rich 6F 115
Greville St. EC1 6J 7 (5A 84)
(not continuous)
Grey Cl. NW11 6A 46
Greycoat Gdns. *SW1* *2C 18*
(off Greycoat St.)
Greycoat Pl. SW1 2C 18 (3H 101)
Greycoat St. SW1 2C 18 (3H 101)
Greycot Rd. BR3: Beck 5C 140
Grey Eagle St. E1 4K 9 (4F 85)
Greyfell Cl. HA7: Stan 5G 27
Greyfriars *SE26* *3G 139*
(off Wells Pk. Rd.)
Greyfriars Pas. EC1 7B 8 (6B 84)
Greyhound Ct. WC2 2H 13 (7K 83)
Greyhound Hill NW4 3C 44
Greyhound La. SW16 6H 137
Greyhound Mans. *W6* *6G 99*
(off Greyhound Rd.)
Greyhound Rd. N17 3E 48
NW10 3D 80
SM1: Sutt 5A 166
W6 6F 99
W14 6F 99
Greyhound Ter. SW16 1G 155
Grey Ho. *W12* *7D 80*
(off White City Est.)
Greyladies Gdns. SE10 2E 122
Greys Pk. Cl. BR2: Kes 5B 172
Greystead Rd. SE23 7J 121
Greystoke Av. HA5: Pinn 3E 40
Greystoke Ct. W5 4E 78
Greystoke Dr. HA4: Ruis 6D 38
Greystoke Gdns. EN2: Enf 4C 22
W5 4E 78
Greystoke Ho. *SE15* *6G 103*
(off Peckham Pk. Rd.)
W5 4E 78
Greystoke Lodge *W5* *4F 79*
(off Hanger La.)
Greystoke Pk. Ter. W5 3D 78
Greystoke Pl. EC4 7J 7 (6A 84)
Greystone Gdns. HA3: Kent 6C 42
IG6: Ilf 2G 53
Greystone Path *E11* *7H 51*
(off Mornington Rd.)
Greyswood Av. N18 6E 34
Greyswood St. SW16 6F 137
Grey Turner Ho. W12 6C 80
Grierson Ho. SW16 4G 137
Grierson Rd. SE23 7K 121
Griffin Cen. TW14: Felt 5K 111
Griffin Cen., The *KT1: King T* *2D 150*
(off Market Pl.)
Griffin Cl. NW10 5D 62
Griffin Ct. TW8: Bford 6E 96
W4 5B 98
Griffin Ho. *E14* *6D 86*
(off Ricardo St.)
W6 *4F 99*
(off Hammersmith Rd.)
Griffin Mnr. Way SE28 3H 107
Griffin Pk. 6D 96
Griffin Rd. N17 2E 48
SE18 5H 107
Griffins Cl. N21 7J 23
Griffin Way TW16: Sun 2J 147
Griffith Cl. RM8: Dag 7C 54
Griffiths Cl. KT4: Wor Pk 2D 164
Griffiths Rd. SW19 7J 135
Griggs App. IG1: Ilf 2G 71
Grigg's Pl. SE1 3E 102
Griggs Rd. E10 6E 50
Grilse Cl. N9 4C 34
Grimaldi Ho. *N1* *2K 83*
(off Calshot St.)
Grimsby Gro. E16 2F 107
Grimsby St. E2 4K 9 (4F 85)
Grimsdyke Rd. HA5: H End 1D 40
Grimsel Path SE5 7B 102
Grimshaw Cl. N6 7E 46
Grimston Rd. SW6 2H 117
Grimthorpe Ho. EC1 3A 8
Grimwade Av. CR0: Croy 3G 169
Grimwade Cl. SE15 3J 121
Grimwood Rd. TW1: Twick 7K 113
Grindall Cl. CR0: Wadd 4B 168
Grindall Ho. *E1* *4H 85*
(off Darling Row)
Grindal St. SE1 7J 13 (2A 102)
Grindleford Av. N11 2K 31
Grindley Gdns. CR0: Croy 6F 157
Grindley Ho. *E3* *5B 86*
(off Leopold St.)
Grinling Pl. SE8 6C 104
Grinstead Rd. SE8 5A 104
Grisedale *NW1* *1A 6*
(off Cumberland Mkt.)
Grittleton Av. HA9: Wemb 6H 61
Grittleton Rd. W9 4J 81
Grizedale Ter. SE23 2H 139
Grocer's Hall Ct. EC2 1E 14 (6D 84)
Grocer's Hall Gdns. EC2 1E 14
Grogan Cl. TW12: Hamp 6D 130
Groombridge Cl. DA16: Well 5A 126
Groombridge Rd. E9 7K 67
Groom Cl. BR2: Brom 4K 159
Groom Cres. SW18 7B 118
Groome Ho. SE11 4H 19 (4K 101)
Groomfield Cl. SW17 4E 136
Groom Pl. SW1 1H 17 (3E 100)
Grooms Dr. HA5: Eastc 5J 39
Grosmont Rd. SE18 5K 107
Grosse Way SW15 6D 116
Grosvenor Av. HA2: Harr 6F 41
N5 5C 66
SM5: Cars 6D 166
SW14 3A 116
TW10: Rich 5E 114
UB4: Hayes 2H 75
Grosvenor Cotts.
SW1 3G 17 (4E 100)
Grosvenor Ct. E10 1D 68
N14 7B 22
NW6 1F 81
NW7 *5E 28*
(off Hale La.)
SE5 6C 102
SM2: Sutt 6K 165
SM4: Mord 4J 153
TW11: Tedd 6A 132
W3 1G 97
W5 *7E 78*
(off Grove, The)
Grosvenor Ct. Mans. *W2* *1E 10*
(off Edgware Rd.)
Grosvenor Cres. NW9 4G 43
SW1 7H 11 (2E 100)
UB10: Hil 7D 56
Grosvenor Cres. M.
SW1 7G 11 (2E 100)
Grosvenor Est. SW1 3D 18 (4H 101)
Grosvenor Gdns. E6 3B 88
IG8: Wfd G 6D 36
KT2: King T 6D 132
N10 3G 47
N14 4C 22
NW2 5E 62
NW11 6H 45
SM6: Wall 7G 167
SW1 1J 17 (3F 101)
SW14 3A 116
Grosvenor Gdns. M. E. SW1 1K 17
Grosvenor Gdns. M. Nth. SW1 2J 17
Grosvenor Gdns. M. Sth. SW1 2K 17
Grosvenor Ga. W1 3G 11 (7E 82)
Grosvenor Hill SW19 6G 135
W1 2J 11 (7F 83)
Grosvenor Hill Ct. *W1* *2J 11*
(off Bourdon St.)
Grosvenor Ho. SM1: Sutt 5K 165
Grosvenor Pde. *W5* *1G 97*
(off Uxbridge Rd.)
Grosvenor Pk. SE5 7C 102
Grosvenor Pk. Rd. E17 5C 50
Grosvenor Pl. SW1 7H 11 (2E 100)
Grosvenor Ri. E. E17 5D 50
Grosvenor Rd. BR4: W W'ck 1D 170
BR5: St M Cry 6J 161
DA6: Bex 5D 126
DA17: Belv 6G 109
E6 1B 88
E7 6K 69
E10 1E 68
E11 5K 51
IG1: Ilf 3G 71
N3 7C 30
N9 1C 34
N10 1F 47
RM7: Rush G 7K 55
RM8: Dag 1F 73
SE25 4F 157
SM6: Wall 6F 167
SW1 7J 17 (6F 101)
TW1: Twick 1A 132
TW4: Houn 3D 112
TW8: Bford 6D 96
TW10: Rich 5E 114
UB2: S'hall 3D 94
W4 5H 97
W7 1A 96
Grosvenor Sq. W1 2H 11 (7E 82)
Grosvenor St. W1 2J 11 (7F 83)
Grosvenor Ter. SE5 7C 102
Grosvenor Va. HA4: Ruis 2H 57
Grosvenor Way E5 2J 67
Grosvenor Wharf Rd. E14 4F 105
Grotes Bldgs. SE3 2G 123
Grote's Pl. SE3 2G 123
Groton Rd. SW18 2K 135
Grotto Ct. SE1 6B 14 (2B 102)
Grotto Pas. W1 5H 5 (5E 82)
Grotto Rd. TW1: Twick 2K 131
GROVE, THE 1G 139
Grove, The BR4: W W'ck 3D 170
DA6: Bex 4D 126
DA14: Sidc 5E 144
E15 6G 69
EN2: Enf 2F 23
HA7: Stan 2F 27
HA8: Edg 4C 28
KT12: Walt T 7K 147
N3 1J 45
N4 7K 47
N6 1E 64
N8 5H 47
N13 4F 33
(not continuous)
N14 5B 22
NW9 5K 43
NW11 7G 45
TW1: Twick 6B 114
TW7: Isle 1J 113
TW11: Tedd 4A 132
UB6: G'frd 6G 77
UB10: Ick 5C 56
W5 1D 96
Grove Av. HA5: Pinn 4C 40
N3 7D 30
N10 2G 47
SM1: Sutt 6J 165
TW1: Twick 1K 131
W7 6J 77
Grovebury Cl. DA8: Erith 6K 109
Grovebury Ct. DA6: Bex 5H 127
N14 7C 22
Grovebury Rd. SE2 2B 108
Grove Cl. BR2: Hayes 2J 171
KT1: King T 4F 151
N14 7B 22
SE23 1A 140
TW13: Hanw 4C 130
UB10: Ick 5C 56
Grove Cotts. SW3 7D 16
W4 6A 98
Grove Ct. *EN5: Barn* *3C 20*
(off Hadley Ridge)
KT1: King T *3E 150*
(off Grove Cres.)
KT8: E Mos 4H 149
NW8 1A 4
SW10 *6A 16*
(off Drayton Ggns.)
TW3: Houn 4E 112
W5 1E 96
Grove Cres. E18 2H 51
KT1: King T 3E 150
KT12: Walt T 7K 147
NW9 4J 43
TW13: Hanw 4C 130
Grove Cres. Rd. E15 6F 69
Grovedale Rd. N19 2H 65
Grove Dwellings E1 5J 85
Grove End E18 2H 51
NW5 4F 65
Grove End Gdns. NW8 2B 82
Grove End Ho. NW8 2A 4
Grove End La. KT10: Esh 7H 149
Grove End Rd. NW8 1A 4 (2B 82)
Grove Farm Retail Pk. RM6: Chad H 7C 54
Grovefield *N11* *4A 32*
(off Coppies Gro.)

Halton Pl.—Handen Rd.

Halton Pl. N1 1C 84
Halton Rd. N1 7B 66
Halt Robin La. DA17: Belv 4H 109
Halt Robin Rd. DA17: Belv 4G 109
(not continuous)
Halyard Ho. E14 3E 104
HAM 3C 132
Ham, The TW8: Bford 7C 96
Hamara Ghar E13 1A 88
Hambalt Rd. SW4 5G 119
Hamble Cl. HA4: Ruis 2G 57
Hambledon *SE17* 6D 102
(off Villa St.)
Hambledon Cl. UB8: Hil 4D 74
Hambledon Ct. SE22 4E 120
W5 7E 78
Hambledon Gdns. SE25 3F 157
Hambledon Pl. SE21 1E 138
Hambledon Rd. SW18 7H 117
Hambledown Rd. DA15: Sidc 7H 125
Hamblehyrst BR3: Beck 2D 158
Hamble St. SW6 3K 117
Hambleton Cl. KT4: Wor Pk 2E 164
Hamble Wlk. *UB5: N'olt* 2E 76
(off Brabazon Rd.)
Hambley Ho. *SE16* 4H 103
(off Camilla Rd.)
Hamblin Ho. *UB1: S'hall* 7C 76
(off Broadway, The)
Hambridge Way SW2 7A 120
Hambro Av. BR2: Hayes 1J 171
Hambrook Rd. SE25 3H 157
Hambro Rd. SW16 6H 137
Hambrough Ho. UB4: Yead 5A 76
Hambrough Rd. UB1: S'hall 1C 94
Ham Cl. TW10: Ham 3C 132
(not continuous)
Ham Comn. TW10: Ham 3D 132
Ham Ct. NW9 2A 44
Ham Cft. Cl. TW13: Felt 3J 129
Hamden Cres. RM10: Dag 3H 73
Hamel Cl. HA3: Kent 4D 42
Hame Way E6 4E 88
Ham Farm Rd. TW10: Ham 4D 132
Hamfrith Rd. E15 6H 69
Ham Ga. Av. TW10: Ham 3D 132
Ham House 1C 132
Hamilton Av. IG6: Ilf 4F 53
KT6: Surb 2G 163
N9 7B 24
RM1: Rom 2K 55
SM3: Cheam 2G 165
Hamilton Bldgs. EC2 4H 9
Hamilton Cl. EN4: Cockf 4H 21
HA7: Stan 2D 26
N17 3F 49
NW8 2A 4 (3B 82)
SE16 2A 104
TW13: Felt 5H 129
Hamilton Ct. CR0: Croy 1G 169
SE6 1H 141
SW15 3G 117
W5 7E 78
W9 3A 82
(off Maida Va.)
Hamilton Cres. HA2: Harr 3D 58
N13 4F 33
TW3: Houn 5F 113
Hamilton Gdns. NW8 1A 4 (3A 82)
Hamilton Ho. *E14* 5D 104
(off St Davids Sq.)
E14 7B 86
(off Victory Pl.)
NW8 1A 4
W4 6A 98
Hamilton La. N5 4B 66
Hamilton Lodge *E1* 4J 85
(off Cleveland Gro.)
Hamilton M. SW18 1J 135
SW19 7J 135
W1 6J 11 (2F 101)
Hamilton Pde. TW13: Felt 4H 129
Hamilton Pk. N5 4B 66
Hamilton Pk. W. N5 4B 66
Hamilton Pl. N19 3H 65
TW16: Sun 7K 129
W1 5H 11 (1E 100)
Hamilton Rd. CR7: Thor H 3D 156
DA7: Bex 2E 126
DA15: Sidc 4A 144
E15 3G 87
E17 2A 50
EN4: Cockf 4H 21
HA1: Harr 5J 41
IG1: Ilf 4F 71
N2 3A 46
N9 7B 24
NW10 5C 62
NW11 7F 45
SE27 4D 138
SW19 7K 135
TW2: Twick 1J 131
TW8: Bford 6D 96
TW13: Felt 4H 129
UB1: S'hall 1D 94
UB3: Hayes 7K 75
W4 2A 98
W5 7E 78
Hamilton Rd. Ind. Est. *SE27* 4D 138
(off Hamilton Rd.)
Hamilton Rd. M. SW19 7K 135
Hamilton Sq. N12 6G 31
SE1 6F 15 (2D 102)
Hamilton St. SE8 6C 104
Hamilton Ter. NW8 2A 4 (2K 81)
Hamilton Way N3 6D 30
N13 4G 33
SM6: Wall 7H 167
Ham Lands Nature Reserve 2A 132
Hamlea Cl. SE12 5J 123
Hamlet, The SE5 3D 120
Hamlet Cl. RM5: Col R 1G 55
SE13 4G 123
Hamlet Ct. EN1: Enf 5K 23
SE11 5B 102
(off Opal St.)
W6 4C 98
Hamlet Gdns. W6 4C 98
Hamlet Ind. Est. E9 7C 68
Hamlet International Ind. Est.
DA8: Erith 5K 109
Hamlet M. SE21 1D 138
Hamlet Rd. RM5: Col R 1G 55
SE19 7F 139
Hamlet Sq. NW2 3G 63
Hamlets Way E3 4B 86
Hamlet Way SE1 6F 15 (2D 102)
Hamlin Cres. HA5: Eastc 5A 40
Hamlyn Cl. HA8: Edg 3K 27
Hamlyn Gdns. SE19 7E 138
Hammelton Ct. *BR1: Brom* 1H 159
(off London Rd.)
Hammelton Grn. SW9 1B 120
Hammelton Rd. BR1: Brom 1H 159
Hammerfield Ho. *SW3* 5D 16
(off Cale St.)
Hammers La. NW7 5H 29
Hammersley Ho. *SE14* 7J 103
(off Pomeroy St.)
HAMMERSMITH 4E 98
Hammersmith Bri. W6 5D 98
Hammersmith Bri. Rd. W6 5E 98
HAMMERSMITH BROADWAY 4E 98
Hammersmith B'way. W6 4E 98
HAMMERSMITH FLYOVER 5E 98
Hammersmith Flyover W6 5E 98
Hammersmith Gro. W6 2E 98
Hammersmith Ind. Est. W6 6E 98
Hammersmith Rd. W6 4F 99
W14 4F 99
Hammersmith Ter. W6 5C 98
Hammet Cl. UB4: Yead 5B 76
Hammett St. EC3 2J 15 (7F 85)
Hammond Av. CR4: Mitc 2F 155
Hammond Cl. EN5: Barn 5B 20
TW12: Hamp 1E 148
UB6: G'frd 5H 59
Hammond Ct. *E10* 2D 68
(off Crescent Rd.)
E17 5A 50
(off Maude Rd.)
Hammond Ho. *E14* 3C 104
(off Tiller Rd.)
SE14 7J 103
(off Lubbock St.)
Hammond Lodge *W9* 5J 81
(off Admiral Wlk.)
Hammond Rd. EN1: Enf 2C 24
UB2: S'hall 3C 94
Hammonds Cl. RM8: Dag 3C 72
Hammond St. NW5 6G 65
Hammond Way SE28 7B 90
Hamond Cl. CR2: S Croy 7B 168
Hamonde Cl. HA8: Edg 2C 28
Hamond Sq. N1 2E 84
Ham Pk. Rd. E7 7H 69
E15 7H 69
Hampden Av. BR3: Beck 2A 158
Hampden Cl. NW1 2H 83
Hampden Ct. N10 7K 31
Hampden Gurney St.
W1 1E 10 (6D 82)
Hampden Ho. SW9 2A 120
Hampden La. N17 1F 49
Hampden Rd. BR3: Beck 2A 158
HA3: Hrw W 1G 41
KT1: King T 3G 151
N8 4A 48
N10 7K 31
N17 1G 49
N19 2H 65
RM5: Col R 1H 55
Hampden Sq. N14 1A 32
Hampden Way N14 1A 32
Hampshire Cl. N18 5C 34
Hampshire Hog La. W6 5D 98
Hampshire Rd. N22 7E 32
Hampshire St. NW5 6H 65
Hampson Way SW8 1K 119
HAMPSTEAD 4B 64
Hampstead Av. IG8: Wfd G 7K 37
Hampstead Cl. SE28 1B 108
Hampstead Gdns. NW11 6J 45
RM6: Chad H 5B 54
HAMPSTEAD GARDEN SUBURB 5A 46
Hampstead Grn. NW3 5C 64
Hampstead Gro. NW3 3A 64
Hampstead Heath 2B 64
Hampstead Heath Info. Cen. 4E 64
Hampstead Hgts. N2 3A 46
Hampstead High St. NW3 4B 64
Hampstead Hill Gdns. NW3 4B 64
Hampstead La. N6 1B 64
NW3 1B 64
Hampstead Mus. 4B 64
(in Burgh House)
Hampstead Rd. NW1 1A 6 (2G 83)
Hampstead Sq. NW3 3A 64
Hampstead Theatre 7B 64
Hampstead Wlk. E3 1B 86
Hampstead Way NW11 5H 45
Hampstead W. NW6 6J 63
HAMPTON 1F 149
Hampton & Richmond Borough FC 1F 149
Hampton Cl. N11 5A 32
NW6 3J 81
SW20 7E 134
HAMPTON COURT 4J 149
HAMPTON COURT 3J 149
Hampton Ct. N1 6B 66
N22 1G 47
SE16 7K 85
(off King & Queen Wharf)
Hampton Ct. Av. KT8: E Mos 6H 149
Hampton Ct. Bri. KT8: E Mos 4J 149
Hampton Ct. Cres. KT8: E Mos 3H 149
Hampton Ct. Est. KT7: E Mos 4J 149
Hampton Court Palace 4K 149
Hampton Ct. Pde. KT8: E Mos 4J 149
Hampton Ct. Rd. KT1: Hamp W 3K 149
KT8: E Mos 3K 149
TW12: Hamp 2G 149
Hampton Ct. Way KT7: T Ditt 7J 149
KT8: E Mos 7J 149
Hampton Farm Ind. Est.
TW13: Hanw 3C 130
HAMPTON HILL 5G 131
Hampton Hill Playhouse Theatre 5G 131
Hampton Ho. *DA7: Bex* 2H 127
(off Erith Rd.)
Hampton La. TW13: Hanw 4C 130
Hampton M. NW10 3K 79
Hampton Open Air Pool 7G 131
Hampton Ri. HA3: Kent 6E 42
Hampton Rd. CR0: Croy 6C 156
E4 5G 35
E7 5K 69
E11 1F 69
IG1: Ilf 4G 71
KT4: Wor Pk 2C 164
TW2: Twick 3H 131
TW11: Tedd 5H 131
TW12: Tedd 5H 131
Hampton Rd. E. TW13: Hanw 4D 130
Hampton Rd. Ind. Pk. CR0: Croy 6C 156
Hampton Rd. W. TW13: Hanw 3C 130
Hampton Sport, Arts & Fitness Cen.
5E 130
Hampton St. SE17 4B 102
HAMPTON WICK 1C 150
Hampton Youth Project 6D 130
Ham Ridings TW10: Ham 5F 133
Hamshades Cl. DA15: Sidc 3K 143
Ham St. TW10: Ham 1B 132
Ham Vw. CR0: Croy 6A 158
Ham Yd. W1 2C 12 (7H 83)
Hanah Ct. SW19 7F 135
Hanameel St. E16 1J 105
Hana M. E5 4H 67
Hanbury Cl. NW4 3E 44
Hanbury Ct. HA1: Harr 6K 41
Hanbury Dr. E11 7H 51
N21 5E 22
Hanbury Ho. *E1* 5G 85
(off Hanbury St.)
SW8 7J 101
(off Regent's Bri. Gdns.)
Hanbury M. N1 1C 84
Hanbury Rd. N17 2H 49
W3 2H 97
Hanbury St. E1 5K 9 (5F 85)
Hanbury Wlk. DA5: Bexl 3K 145
Hancock Nunn Ho. *NW3* 6D 64
(off Fellows Rd.)
Hancock Rd. E3 3E 86
SE19 6D 138
Handa Wlk. N1 6D 66
Hand Ct. WC1 6H 7 (5K 83)
Handcroft Rd. CR0: Croy 7B 156
Handel Cl. HA8: Edg 6A 28
Handel House Mus. 2J 11
(off Brook St.)
Handel Mans. SW13 7E 98
WC1 3F 7
(off Handel St.)
Handel Pde. *HA8: Edg* 7B 28
(off Whitchurch La.)
Handel Pl. NW10 6K 61
Handels Bus. Cen.
SW8 7E 18 (6J 101)
Handel St. WC1 3E 6 (4J 83)
Handel Way HA8: Edg 7B 28
Handen Rd.
SE12 5G 123

A-Z London 281

Handforth Rd. IG1: Ilf 3F 71
SW9 7A 102
Handley Gro. NW2 3F 63
Handley Page Rd. SM6: Wall 7K 167
Handley Rd. E9 7J 67
Handowe Cl. NW4 4C 44
Handside Cl. KT4: Wor Pk 1F 165
Hands Wlk. E16 6J 87
Handsworth Av. E4 6A 36
Handsworth Rd. N17 3D 48
Handtrough Way IG11: Bark 2F 89
Hanford Cl. SW18 1J 135
Hanford Row SW19 6E 134
Hanger Ct. W5 4F 79
Hanger Grn. W5 4G 79
HANGER HILL 4F 79
HANGER LANE 3E 78
Hanger La. W5 2E 78
Hanger Va. La. W5 6F 79
(not continuous)
Hanger Vw. Way W3 6G 79
Hanging Sword All. EC4 1K 13
Hankey Pl. SE1 7F 15 (2D 102)
Hankins La. NW7 2F 29
Hanley Gdns. N4 1K 65
Hanley Pl. BR3: Beck 7C 140
Hanley Rd. N4 1J 65
Hanmer Wlk. N7 2K 65
Hannah Barlow Ho. SW8 1K 119
Hannah Cl. BR3: Beck 3E 158
NW10 4J 61
Hannah Mary Way SE1 4G 103
Hannah M. SM6: Wall 7G 167
Hannay La. N8 7H 47
Hannay Wlk. SW16 2H 137
Hannell Rd. SW6 7G 99
Hannen Rd. SE27 3B 138
Hannibal Rd. E1 5J 85
TW19: Stanw 7A 110
Hannibal Way CR0: Wadd 5K 167
Hannington Rd. SW4 3F 119
Hanno Cl. SM6: Wall 7H 167
Hanover Av. E16 1J 105
TW13: Felt 1J 129
Hanover Circ. UB3: Hayes 6E 74
Hanover Cl. SM3: Cheam 4G 165
TW9: Kew 7G 97
Hanover Ct. HA4: Ruis 3J 57
NW9 3A 44
SE19 7G 139
(off Anerley Rd.)
SW15 4B 116
W12 1C 98
(off Uxbridge Rd.)
Hanover Dr. BR7: Chst 4G 143
Hanover Flats W1 2H 11
(off Binney St., not continuous)
Hanover Gdns. IG6: Ilf 1G 53
SE11 6A 102
Hanover Ga. NW1 2D 4 (3C 82)
Hanover Ga. Mans. NW1 3D 4
(off Park Rd.)
Hanover Ho. E14 1B 104
(off Westferry Cir.)
NW8 1C 4
SW9 3A 120
Hanover Mans. SW2 5A 120
(off Barnwell Rd.)
Hanover Mead NW11 5G 45
Hanover Pk. SE15 1G 121
Hanover Pl. E3 3B 86
WC2 1F 13 (6J 83)
Hanover Rd. N15 4F 49
NW10 7E 62
SW19 7A 136
Hanover Sq. W1 1K 11 (6F 83)
Hanover Steps W2 1D 10
Hanover St. CR0: Croy 3B 168
W1 1K 11 (6F 83)
Hanover Ter. NW1 2E 4 (3C 82)
TW7: Isle 1A 114
Hanover Ter. M. NW1 2D 4 (3C 82)
Hanover Trad. Est.
N7 5J 65
Hanover Way DA6: Bex 3D 126
Hanover W. Ind. Est.
NW10 3K 79
Hanover Yd. N1 2C 84
(off Noel Rd.)
Hansard M. W14 2F 99
Hansart Way EN2: Enf 1F 23
Hanscomb M. SW4 4G 119
Hans Cres. SW1 1E 16 (3D 100)
Hanselin Cl. HA7: Stan 5E 26
Hansen Dr. N21 5E 22
Hanshaw Dr. HA8: Edg 1K 43
Hansler Gro.
KT8: E Mos 4H 149
Hansler Rd. SE22 5F 121
Hansol Rd. DA6: Bex 5E 126
Hansom Ter. BR1: Brom 1K 159
(off Freelands Gro.)
Hanson Cl. BR3: Beck 6D 140
SW12 7F 119
SW14 3J 115
UB7: W Dray 3B 92
Hanson Ct. E17 6D 50
Hanson Gdns. UB1: S'hall 2C 94
Hanson St. W1 5A 6 (5G 83)
Hans Pl. SW1 1F 17 (3D 100)
Hans Rd. SW3 1E 16 (3D 100)
Hans St. SW1 2F 17 (3D 100)
Hanway Pl. W1 7C 6 (6H 83)
Hanway Rd. W7 6H 77
Hanway St. W1 7C 6 (6H 83)
HANWELL 1K 95
Hanwell Fitness Cen. 1K 95
HANWORTH 5C 130
Hanworth Ho. SE5 7B 102
(off Camberwell New Rd., not continuous)
Hanworth Rd. TW3: Houn 1C 130
TW4: Houn 1C 130
TW12: Hamp 4D 130
TW13: Felt 1K 129
TW16: Sun 7J 129
(not continuous)
Hanworth Ter. TW3: Houn 4F 113
Hanworth Trad. Est. TW13: Hanw 3C 130
Hapgood Cl. UB6: G'frd 5H 59
Harad's Pl. E1 7G 85
Harben Pde. NW3 7A 64
(off Finchley Rd.)
Harben Rd. NW6 7A 64
Harberson Rd. E15 1H 87
SW12 1F 137
Harberton Rd. N19 1G 65
Harbet Rd. E4 5F 35
N18 5F 35
W2 6B 4 (5B 82)
Harbex Cl. DA5: Bexl 7H 127
Harbinger Rd. E14 4D 104
Harbledown Ho. SE1 7E 14
(off Manciple St.)
Harbledown Rd. SW6 1J 117
Harbord Cl. SE5 2D 120
Harbord Ho. SE16 4K 103
(off Cope St.)
Harbord St. SW6 1F 117
Harborough Av. DA15: Sidc 7J 125
Harborough Rd. SW16 4K 137
Harbour Av. SW10 1A 118
Harbour Club Leisure Cen., The 2A 118
Harbour Exchange Sq. E14 2D 104
Harbour Quay E14 1E 104
Harbour Reach SW6 1A 118
Harbour Rd. SE5 3C 120
Harbour Yd. SW10 1A 118
Harbridge Av. SW15 7B 116
Harbury Rd. SM5: Cars 7C 166
Harbut Rd. SW11 4B 118
(not continuous)
Harcombe Rd. N16 3E 66
Harcourt Av. DA15: Sidc 6C 126
E12 4D 70
HA8: Edg 3D 28
SM6: Wall 4F 167
Harcourt Bldgs. EC4 2J 13
Harcourt Cl. TW7: Isle 3A 114
Harcourt Fld. SM6: Wall 4F 167
Harcourt Lodge SM6: Wall 4F 167
Harcourt Rd. CR7: Thor H 6K 155
DA6: Bex 4E 126
E15 2H 87
N22 1H 47
SE4 3B 122
SM6: Wall 4F 167
SW19 7J 135
Harcourt St. W1 6D 4 (5C 82)
Harcourt Ter. SW10 5K 99
Hardcastle Cl. CR0: Croy 6G 157
Hardcastle Ho. SE14 1A 122
(off Loring Rd.)
Hardcourts Cl. BR4: W W'ck 3D 170
Hardel Ri. SW2 1B 138
Hardel Wlk. SW2 7A 120
Harden Ct. SE7 4C 106
Harden Ho. SE5 2E 120
Harden's Manorway SE7 3B 106
(not continuous)
Harders Rd. SE15 2H 121
Hardess St. SE24 3C 120
Hardie Cl. NW10 5K 61
Hardie Rd. RM10: Dag 3J 73
Harding Cl. CR0: Croy 3F 169
SE17 6C 102
Hardinge Cl. UB8: Hil 5D 74
Hardinge Cres. SE18 3G 107
Hardinge La. E1 6J 85
(not continuous)
Hardinge Rd. N18 6K 33
NW10 1D 80
Hardinge St. E1 7J 85
(not continuous)
Harding Ho. SW13 6D 98
(off Wyatt Dr.)
UB3: Hayes 6K 75
Harding Rd. DA7: Bex 2F 127
Harding's Cl. KT2: King T 1F 151
Hardings La. SE20 6K 139
Hardington NW1 7E 64
(off Belmont St.)
Hardman Rd. KT2: King T 2E 150
SE7 5K 105
Hardwick Cl. HA7: Stan 5H 27
Hardwick Ct. DA8: Erith 6K 109
Hardwicke Av. TW5: Hest 1E 112
Hardwicke M. WC1 2H 7
Hardwicke Rd. N13 6D 32
TW10: Ham 4C 132
W4 4K 97
Hardwicke St. IG11: Bark 1G 89
Hardwick Grn. W13 5B 78
Hardwick Ho. NW8 3D 4
(off Lilestone St.)
Hardwick St. EC1 2K 7 (3A 84)
Hardwicks Way SW18 5J 117
Hardwidge St. SE1 6G 15 (2E 102)
Hardy Av. E16 1J 105
HA4: Ruis 5K 57
Hardy Cl. EN5: Barn 6B 20
HA5: Pinn 7B 40
SE16 2K 103
Hardy Cotts. SE10 6F 105
Hardy Ho. SW4 7G 119
Hardying Ho. E17 4A 50
Hardy Pas. N22 1K 47
Hardy Rd. E4 6G 35
SE3 7H 105
SW19 7K 135
Hardy's M. KT8: E Mos 4J 149
Hardy Way EN2: Enf 1F 23
Hare & Billet Rd. SE3 1F 123
Harebell Dr. E6 5E 88
Harecastle Cl. UB4: Yead 4C 76
Hare Ct. EC4 1J 13 (6A 84)
Harecourt Rd. N1 6C 66
Haredale Rd. SE24 4C 120
Haredon Cl. SE23 7K 121
HAREFIELD 1A 38
Harefield Cl. EN2: Enf 1F 23
Harefield Grn. NW7 6K 29
Harefield M. SE4 3B 122
Harefield Rd. DA14: Sidc 2D 144
N8 5H 47
SE4 3B 122
SW16 7K 137
UB8: Uxb 5A 56
Hare Marsh E2 4G 85
Hare Pl. EC4 1K 13
(off Pleydell St.)
Hare Row E2 2H 85
Haresfield Rd. RM10: Dag 6G 73
Hare St. SE18 3E 106
Hare Wlk. N1 2E 84
(not continuous)
Harewood Av. NW1 4D 4 (4C 82)
UB5: N'olt 7D 58
Harewood Cl. UB5: N'olt 7D 58
Harewood Dr. IG5: Ilf 2D 52
Harewood Pl. W1 1K 11 (6F 83)
Harewood Rd. CR2: S Croy 6E 168
SW19 6C 136
TW7: Isle 7K 95
Harewood Row NW1 5D 4 (5C 82)
Harewood Ter. UB2: S'hall 4D 94
Harfield Gdns. SE5 3E 120
Harfield Rd. TW16: Sun 2B 148
Harfleur Ct. SE11 4B 102
(off Opal St.)
Harford Cl. E4 7J 25
Harford Ho. SE5 6C 102
(off Bethwin Rd.)
W11 5H 81
Harford M. N19 3H 65
Harford Rd. E4 7J 25
Harford St. E1 4A 86
Harford Wlk. N2 4B 46
Harfst Way BR8: Swan 7J 145
Hargood Cl. HA3: Kent 6E 42
Hargood Rd. SE3 1A 124
Hargrave Mans. N19 2H 65
Hargrave Pk. N19 2G 65
Hargrave Pl. NW5 5H 65
Hargrave Rd. N19 2G 65
Hargraves Ho. W12 7D 80
(off White City Est.)
Hargwyne St. SW9 3K 119
Haringey Mus. 1E 48
Haringey Pk. N8 6J 47
Haringey Pas. N8 4A 48
Haringey Rd. N8 4J 47
Harington Ter. N9 3J 33
N18 3J 33
Harkett Cl. HA3: W'stone 2K 41
Harkett Ct. HA3: W'stone 2K 41
Harkness Ct. SM1: Sutt 1K 165
(off Cleeve Way)
Harkness Ho. E1 6G 85
(off Christian St.)
Harland Av. CR0: Croy 3F 169
DA15: Sidc 3H 143
Harland Cl. SW19 3K 153
Harland Rd. SE12 1J 141
Harlands Gro.
BR6: Farnb 4F 173
Harlech Gdns. HA5: Pinn 7B 40
TW5: Hest 6A 94
Harlech Rd. N14 3D 32
Harlech Twr. W3 2J 97
Harlequin Av. TW8: Bford 6A 96
Harlequin Cl. TW7: Isle 5J 113
UB4: Yead 5B 76
Harlequin Ct. E1 7G 85
(off Thomas More St.)

Harlequin Ct.—Hartley Rd.

Harlequin Ct. *NW10* *6K 61*
(off Mitchellbrook Way)
W5 . . . . . 7C **78**
Harlequin Ho. *DA18: Erith* *3E 108*
(off Kale Rd.)
Harlequin Rd. TW11: Tedd 7B **132**
Harlequins RUFC 7J 113
Harlescott Rd. SE15 . . . . . 4K **121**
HARLESDEN **2B 80**
Harlesden Gdns. NW10 . . . . . 1B **80**
Harlesden La. NW10 . . . . . 1C **80**
Harlesden Plaza NW10 . . . . . 2B **80**
Harlesden Rd. NW10 . . . . . 1C **80**
Harleston Cl. E5 . . . . . 2J **67**
Harley Cl. HA0: Wemb 6D **60**
Harley Ct. E11 . . . . . 7J **51**
HA1: Harr 4H **41**
N20 . . . . . 3F **31**
Harley Cres. HA1: Harr 4H **41**
Harleyford BR1: Brom 1K **159**
Harleyford Ct. SE11 . . . . . 7G **19**
Harleyford Mnr. *W3* *1J 97*
(off Edgecote Cl.)
Harleyford Rd. SE11 . . . . . 7G **19** (6K **101**)
Harleyford St. SE11 . . . . . 7J **19** (6A **102**)
Harley Gdns. BR6: Orp 4J **173**
SW10 . . . . . 5A **100**
Harley Gro. E3 . . . . . 3B **86**
Harley Ho. E11 . . . . . 7F **51**
NW1 . . . . . 4H **5**
Harley Pl. W1 . . . . . 6J **5** (5F **83**)
Harley Rd. HA1: Harr 4H **41**
NW3 . . . . . 7B **64**
NW10 . . . . . 2A **80**
Harley St. W1 . . . . . 4J **5** (4F **83**)
Harley Vs. NW10 . . . . . 2A **80**
Harling Ct. SW11 . . . . . 2D **118**
Harlinger St. SE18 . . . . . 3C **106**
HARLINGTON **6F 93**
Harlington Cl. UB3: Harl 7E **92**
HARLINGTON CORNER **1F 111**
Harlington Rd. DA7: Bex 3E **126**
UB8: Hil 3C **74**
Harlington Rd. E. TW13: Felt 7K **111**
TW14: Felt 7K **111**
Harlington Rd. W. TW14: Felt 6K **111**
Harlowe Cl. E8 . . . . . 1G **85**
Harlowe Ho. *E8* *1F 85*
(off Clarissa St.)
Harlow Mans. *IG11: Bark* *7F 71*
(off Whiting Av.)
Harlow Rd. N13 . . . . . 3J **33**
Harlyn Dr. HA5: Eastc 3K **39**
Harlynwood *SE5* *7C 102*
(off Wyndham Rd.)
Harman Av. IG8: Wfd G 6C **36**
Harman Cl. E4 . . . . . 4A **36**
NW2 . . . . . 3G **63**
SE1 . . . . . 5G **103**
Harman Dr. DA15: Sidc 6K **125**
NW2 . . . . . 3G **63**
Harman Rd. EN1: Enf 5A **24**
HARMONDSWORTH **6A 92**
Harmondsworth La. UB7: Harm, Sip . . . 6A **92**
Harmondsworth Rd. UB7: W Dray 5A **92**
Harmon Ho. SE8 . . . . . 4B **104**
Harmont Ho. *W1* *6J 5*
(off Harley St.)
Harmony Cl. NW11 . . . . . 5G **45**
SM6: Wall 7J **167**
Harmony Way BR1: Brom 2J **159**
NW4 . . . . . 4E **44**
Harmood Gro. NW1 . . . . . 7F **65**
Harmood Ho. *NW1* *7F 65*
(off Harmood St.)
Harmood Pl. NW1 . . . . . 7F **65**
Harmood St. NW1 . . . . . 6F **65**
Harmsworth M. SE11 . . . . . 2K **19** (3B **102**)
Harmsworth St. SE17 . . . . . 6K **19** (5B **102**)
Harmsworth Way N20 . . . . . 1C **30**
Harness Rd. SE28 . . . . . 2A **108**
Harold Av. DA17: Belv 5F **109**
UB3: Hayes 3H **93**
Harold Ct. *SE16* *2K 103*
(off Christopher Cl.)
Harold Est. SE1 . . . . . 3E **102**
Harold Gibbons Ct.
SE7 . . . . . 6A **106**
Harold Ho. *E2* *2K 85*
(off Mace St.)
Harold Laski Ho. *EC1* *2B 8*
(off Percival St.)
Harold Maddison Ho. *SE17* *5B 102*
(off Penton Pl.)
Harold Pl. SE11 . . . . . 6J **19** (5A **102**)
Harold Rd. E4 . . . . . 4K **35**
E11 . . . . . 1G **69**
E13 . . . . . 1K **87**
IG8: Wfd G 1J **51**
N8 . . . . . 5K **47**
N15 . . . . . 5F **49**
NW10 . . . . . 3K **79**
SE19 . . . . . 7D **138**
SM1: Sutt 4B **166**
Haroldstone Rd. E17 . . . . . 5K **49**
Harold Wilson Ho. SE28 . . . . . 1B **108**
SW6 . . . . . *6H 99*
(off Clem Attlee Ct.)
Harp All. EC4 . . . . . 7A **8** (6B **84**)
Harp Bus. Cen. *NW2* *1C 62*
(off Apsley Way)
Harp Bus. Cen., The NW2 . . . . . 2C **62**
Harpenden Rd. E12 . . . . . 2A **70**
SE27 . . . . . 3B **138**
Harpenmead Point NW2 . . . . . 2H **63**
Harper Cl. N14 . . . . . 5B **22**
Harper Ho. SW9 . . . . . 3B **120**
Harper M. SW17 . . . . . 3A **136**
Harper Rd. E6 . . . . . 6D **88**
SE1 . . . . . 7C **14** (3C **102**)
Harper's Yd. N17 . . . . . 1F **49**
Harp Island Cl. NW10 . . . . . 2K **61**
Harp La. EC3 . . . . . 3G **15** (7E **84**)
Harpley Sq. E1 . . . . . 4J **85**
Harpour Rd. IG11: Bark 6G **71**
Harp Rd. W7 . . . . . 4K **77**
Harpsden St. SW11 . . . . . 1E **118**
Harpur M. WC1 . . . . . 5G **7** (5K **83**)
Harpur St. WC1 . . . . . 5G **7** (5K **83**)
Harraden Rd. SE3 . . . . . 1A **124**
Harrier Av. E11 . . . . . 6K **51**
Harrier Ct. TW4: Houn 3C **112**
Harrier M. SE28 . . . . . 2H **107**
Harrier Rd. NW9 . . . . . 2A **44**
Harriers Cl. W5 . . . . . 7E **78**
Harrier Way E6 . . . . . 5D **88**
Harries Rd. UB4: Yead 4A **76**
Harriet Cl. E8 . . . . . 1G **85**
Harriet Gdns. CR0: Croy 2G **169**
Harriet Ho. *SW6* *7K 99*
(off Wandon Rd.)
Harriet St. SW1 . . . . . 7F **11** (2D **100**)
Harriet Tubman Cl. SW2 . . . . . 7K **119**
Harriet Wlk. SW1 . . . . . 7F **11** (2D **100**)
Harriet Way WD23: Bush 1C **26**
HARRINGAY **5B 48**
Harringay Gdns. N8 . . . . . 4B **48**
Harringay Rd. N15 . . . . . 5B **48**
(not continuous)
Harrington Cl. CR0: Bedd 2J **167**
NW10 . . . . . 3K **61**
Harrington Ct. CR0: Croy 2D **168**
W10 . . . . . 3H **81**
Harrington Gdns. SW7 . . . . . 4K **99**
Harrington Hill E5 . . . . . 1H **67**
Harrington Ho. *NW1* *1A 6*
(off Harrington St.)
UB10: Ick 4D **56**
Harrington Rd. E11 . . . . . 1G **69**
SE25 . . . . . 4G **157**
SW7 . . . . . 3A **16** (4B **100**)
Harrington Sq. NW1 . . . . . 2G **83**
Harrington St. NW1 . . . . . 1A **6** (2G **83**)
(not continuous)
Harrington Way SE18 . . . . . 3B **106**
Harriott Cl. SE10 . . . . . 4H **105**
Harriott Ho. *E1* *5J 85*
(off Jamaica St.)
Harris Bldgs. *E1* *6G 85*
(off Burslem St.)
Harris Cl. EN2: Enf 1G **23**
TW3: Houn 1E **112**
Harris Ct. HA9: Wemb 3F **61**
Harris Ho. *SW9* *3A 120*
(off St James's Cres.)
Harris Lodge SE6 . . . . . 1E **140**
Harrison Cl. N20 . . . . . 1H **31**
Harrison Ho. *SE17* *5D 102*
(off Brandon St.)
Harrison Rd. RM10: Dag 6H **73**
Harrisons Ct. *SE14* *6K 103*
(off Myers La.)
Harrison's Ri. CR0: Wadd 3B **168**
Harrison St. WC1 . . . . . 2F **7** (3J **83**)
Harrison Way TW17: Shep 5D **146**
Harris Rd. DA7: Bex 1E **126**
RM9: Dag 5F **73**
Harris St. E17 . . . . . 7B **50**
SE5 . . . . . 7D **102**
Harris Way TW16: Sun 1G **147**
Harrods 1E 16 (3D 100)
Harrogate Ct. N11 . . . . . 6K **31**
SE12 . . . . . 7J **123**
SE26 . . . . . *3G 139*
(off Droitwich Cl.)
Harrold Ho. NW3 . . . . . 7B **64**
Harrold Rd. RM8: Dag 5B **72**
Harrovian Bus. Village HA1: Harr 7J **41**
HARROW **6J 41**
Harrow Av. EN1: Enf 6A **24**
Harroway Rd. SW11 . . . . . 2B **118**
Harrow Borough FC 4E 58
Harrowby St. W1 . . . . . 7D **4** (6C **82**)
Harrow Cl. KT9: Chess 7D **162**
Harrow Club Sports Cen. 7F 81
Harrowdene Cl. HA0: Wemb 4D **60**
Harrowdene Gdns. TW11: Tedd 6A **132**
Harrowdene Rd. HA0: Wemb 3D **60**
Harrow Dr. N9 . . . . . 1A **34**
Harrowes Meade HA8: Edg 3B **28**
Harrow Flds. Gdns. HA1: Harr 3J **59**
Harrowgate Ho. E9 . . . . . 6K **67**
Harrowgate Rd. E9 . . . . . 6A **68**
Harrow Grn. E11 . . . . . 3G **69**
Harrow High School Sports Cen. 6A 42
Harrow La. E14 . . . . . 7D **86**
Harrow Leisure Cen. 3K 41
Harrow Lodge *NW8* *3A 4*
(off Northwick Ter.)
Harrow Mnr. Way SE2 . . . . . 1C **108**
SE28 . . . . . 7C **90**
Harrow Mus. & Heritage Cen. 3G 41
HARROW ON THE HILL **1J 59**
Harrow Pk. HA1: Harr 2J **59**
Harrow Pl. E1 . . . . . 7H **9** (6E **84**)
HARROW ROAD **7H 61**
Harrow Rd. E6 . . . . . 1C **88**
E11 . . . . . 3G **69**
HA0: Wemb 4K **59**
(not continuous)
HA9: Wemb 5G **61**
IG1: Ilf 4G **71**
IG11: Bark 1J **89**
NW10 . . . . . 3D **80**
SM5: Cars 6C **166**
TW14: Bedf 2C **128**
W2 . . . . . 6A **4** (5A **82**)
(not continuous)
W9 . . . . . 4F **81**
W10 . . . . . 4G **81**
Harrow Rd. Bri. W2 . . . . . 5A **82**
Harrow Safari Cinema 5K 41
Harrow St. NW1 . . . . . 5D **4**
Harrow Vw. HA1: Harr 2G **41**
HA2: Harr 2G **41**
UB3: Hayes 6J **75**
UB10: Hil 3E **74**
Harrow Vw. Rd. W5 . . . . . 4B **78**
Harrow Way TW17: Shep 2E **146**
HARROW WEALD **1J 41**
Harrow Weald Pk. HA3: Hrw W 6C **26**
Harry Hinkins Ho. *SE17* *5C 102*
(off Bronti Cl.)
Harry Lambourn Ho. *SE15* *7H 103*
(off Gervase St.)
Hartcliff Ct. W7 . . . . . 2K **95**
Hart Ct. E6 . . . . . 7E **70**
Harte Rd. TW3: Houn 2D **112**
Hartfield Av. UB5: Yead 2K **75**
Hartfield Cres. BR4: W W'ck 3J **171**
SW19 . . . . . 7H **135**
Hartfield Gro. SE20 . . . . . 1J **157**
Hartfield Ho. *UB5: Yead* *2K 75*
(off Hartfield Av.)
Hartfield Rd. BR4: W W'ck 4J **171**
KT9: Chess 5D **162**
SW19 . . . . . 7H **135**
Hartfield Ter. E3 . . . . . 2C **86**
Hartford Av. HA3: Kent 3A **42**
Hartford Rd. DA5: Bexl 6G **127**
KT19: Ewe 6H **163**
Hart Gro. UB1: S'hall 5E **76**
W5 . . . . . 1G **97**
Hart Gro. Ct. W5 . . . . . 1G **97**
Hartham Cl. N7 . . . . . 5J **65**
TW7: Isle 1A **114**
Hartham Rd. N7 . . . . . 5J **65**
N17 . . . . . 2F **49**
TW7: Isle 1K **113**
Harting Rd. SE9 . . . . . 3C **142**
Hartington Cl. BR6: Farnb 5G **173**
HA1: Harr 4J **59**
Hartington Ct. SW8 . . . . . 1J **119**
W4 . . . . . 7H **97**
Hartington Ho. *SW1* *5D 18*
(off Drummond Ga.)
Hartington Rd. E16 . . . . . 6K **87**
E17 . . . . . 6A **50**
SW8 . . . . . 1J **119**
TW1: Twick 7B **114**
UB2: S'hall 3C **94**
W4 . . . . . 7H **97**
W13 . . . . . 7B **78**
Hartismere Rd. SW6 . . . . . 7H **99**
Hartlake Rd. E9 . . . . . 6K **67**
Hartland *NW1* *1G 83*
(off Royal College St.)
Hartland Cl. HA8: Edg 2B **28**
N21 . . . . . 6H **23**
Hartland Ct. *N11* *5J 31*
(off Hartland Rd.)
Hartland Dr. HA4: Ruis 3K **57**
HA8: Edg 2B **28**
Hartland Rd. E15 . . . . . 7H **69**
N11 . . . . . 5J **31**
NW1 . . . . . 7F **65**
NW6 . . . . . 2H **81**
SM4: Mord 7J **153**
TW7: Isle 3A **114**
TW12: Hamp H 4F **131**
Hartlands, The TW5: Cran 6K **93**
Hartlands Cl. DA5: Bexl 6F **127**
Hartland Way CR0: Croy 3A **170**
SM4: Mord 7H **153**
Hartlepool Ct. E16 . . . . . 1F **107**
Hartley Av. E6 . . . . . 1C **88**
NW7 . . . . . 5G **29**
Hartley Cl. BR1: Brom 2D **160**
NW7 . . . . . 5G **29**
Hartley Ho. *SE1* *4F 103*
(off Longfield Est.)
Hartley Rd. CR0: Croy 7C **156**
DA16: Well 7C **108**
E11 . . . . . 1H **69**

High St.—Hillside La.

High St. TW3: Houn 3F 113
(not continuous)
TW5: Cran 1J 111
TW8: Bford 7C 96
TW11: Tedd 5K 131
TW12: Hamp, Hamp H 1G 149
TW13: Felt 3H 129
TW17: Shep 6D 146
TW19: Stanw 6A 110
UB1: S'hall 1D 94
UB3: Harl 6F 93
UB7: Harm 6A 92
UB7: Yiew 7A 74
UB8: Uxb 1A 74
W3 1H 97
W5 1D 96
High St. Colliers Wood SW19 7B 136
High St. Harlesden NW10 2B 80
High St. M. SW19 5G 135
High St. Nth. E6 5C 70
E12 5C 70
High St. Sth. E6 2D 88
High Timber St. EC4 2C 14 (7C 84)
High Tor Cl. BR1: Brom 7K 141
High Tor Vw. SE28 1J 107
High Trees CR0: Croy 1A 170
EN4: E Barn 5H 21
N20 3F 31
SW2 1A 138
Hightrees Ct. W7 7J 77
Hightrees Ho. SW12 6E 118
High Vw. HA5: Pinn 4A 40
Highview N6 6G 47
NW7 3E 28
UB5: N'olt 3C 76
Highview Av. HA8: Edg 4D 28
SM6: Wall 5K 167
High Vw. Cl. SE19 2F 157
High Vw. Ct. HA3: Hrw W 7D 26
Highview Gdns. HA8: Edg 4D 28
N3 3G 45
N11 5B 32
Highview Ho. RM6: Chad H 4E 54
Highview Lodge *EN2: Enf* *3G 23*
(off Ridgeway, The)
High Vw. Pde. IG4: Ilf 5D 52
High Vw. Rd. DA14: Sidc 4B 144
E18 2H 51
N2 1D 46
Highview Rd. SE19 6D 138
W13 5A 78
Highway, The E1 7G 85
HA7: Stan 1K 41
SM2: Sutt 7A 166
Highway Bus. Pk., The *E1* *7K 85*
(off Heckford St.)
Highway Trad. Cen., The *E1* *7K 85*
(off Heckford St.)
Highwood BR2: Brom 3F 159
Highwood Av. N12 4F 31
Highwood Cl. BR6: Farnb 2G 173
Highwood Ct. EN5: New Bar 5D 20
N12 3F 31
Highwood Dr. BR6: Farnb 2G 173
Highwood Gdns. IG5: Ilf 5D 52
Highwood Gro. NW7 5E 28
HIGHWOOD HILL 3G 29
Highwood Hill NW7 2G 29
Highwood Rd. N19 3J 65
High Worple HA2: Harr 7D 40
Highworth Rd. N11 6C 32
Highworth St. NW1 5D 4
Hi-Gloss Cen. SE8 5A 104
Hilary Av. CR4: Mitc 3E 154
Hilary Cl. DA8: Erith 1H 127
SW6 7K 99
Hilary Dennis Ct. E11 4J 51
Hilary Rd. W12 6B 80
(not continuous)
Hilberry Ct. WD23: Bush 1A 26
Hilbert Rd. SM3: Cheam 3F 165
Hilborough Ct. E8 7F 67
Hilborough Way BR6: Farnb 5H 173
Hilda Ct. KT6: Surb 7D 150
Hilda Rd. E6 7B 70
E16 4G 87
(not continuous)
Hilda Ter. SW9 2A 120
Hilda Va. Cl. BR6: Farnb 4F 173
Hilda Va. Rd. BR6: Farnb 4E 172
Hildenborough Gdns.
BR1: Brom 6G 141
Hildenborough Ho.
BR3: Beck *7B 140*
(off Bethersden Cl.)
Hildenlea Pl. BR2: Brom 2F 159
Hilderley Ho. *KT1: King T* *3F 151*
(off Winery La.)
Hildreth St. SW12 1F 137
Hildreth St. M. SW12 1F 137
Hildyard Rd. SW6 6J 99
Hiley Rd. NW10 3E 80
Hilgrove Rd. NW6 7A 64
Hiliary Gdns. HA7: Stan 2C 42
Hillary *N8* *3J 47*
(off Boyton Cl.)
Hillary Ct. *TW19: Stanw* *1A 128*
(off Explorer Av.)
W12 *2E 98*
(off Titmuss St.)
Hillary Cres. KT12: Walt T 7A 148
Hillary Dr. TW7: Isle 5K 113
Hillary Ri. EN5: New Bar 4D 20
Hillary Rd. UB2: S'hall 3E 94
Hillbeck Cl. SE15 7J 103
Hillbeck Ho. *SE15* *6J 103*
(off Hillbeck Cl.)
Hillbeck Way UB6: G'frd 1H 77
Hillborne Cl. UB3: Harl 5J 93
Hillboro Ct. E11 7F 51
Hillborough Cl. SW19 7A 136
Hillbrook Rd. SW17 3D 136
Hill Brow BR1: Brom 1B 160
Hillbrow KT3: N Mald 3B 152
Hill Brow Cl. DA5: Bexl 4K 145
Hillbrow Rd. BR1: Brom 7G 141
Hillbury Av. HA3: Kent 5B 42
Hillbury Rd. SW17 3F 137
Hill Cl. BR7: Chst 5F 143
HA1: Harr 3J 59
HA7: Stan 4G 27
NW2 3D 62
NW11 6J 45
Hillcote Av. SW16 7A 138
Hill Ct. EN4: E Barn 4H 21
UB5: N'olt 5E 58
W5 4F 79
Hillcourt Av. N12 6E 30
Hillcourt Est. N16 1D 66
Hillcourt Rd. SE22 6H 121
Hill Cres. DA5: Bexl 1J 145
HA1: Harr 5A 42
KT4: Wor Pk 2E 164
KT5: Surb 5F 151
N20 2E 30
Hill Crest DA15: Sidc 7A 126
KT6: Surb 7E 150
Hillcrest N6 7E 46
N21 7F 23
SE24 4D 120
Hillcrest Av. HA5: Pinn 4B 40
HA8: Edg 4C 28
NW11 5H 45
Hillcrest Cl. BR3: Beck 6B 158
SE26 4G 139
Hillcrest Ct. RM5: Col R 1K 55
SM2: Sutt *6B 166*
(off Eaton Rd.)
Hill Crest Gdns. NW2 3C 62
Hillcrest Gdns.
KT10: Hin W 3A 162
N3 4G 45
Hillcrest Rd. BR1: Brom 5J 141
BR6: Chels 2K 173
E17 2F 51
E18 2H 51
W3 1H 97
W5 5E 78
Hillcrest Vw. BR3: Beck 6B 158
Hillcroft Av. HA5: Pinn 6D 40
Hillcroft Cres. HA4: Ruis 3B 58
HA9: Wemb 4F 61
W5 6E 78
Hillcroft Rd. E6 5F 89
Hillcroome Rd. SM2: Sutt 6B 166
Hillcross Av. SM4: Mord 6F 153
Hilldale Rd. SM1: Sutt 4H 165
Hilldown Ct. SW16 7J 137
Hilldown Rd. BR2: Hayes 1G 171
SW16 7J 137
Hill Dr. NW9 1J 61
SW16 3K 155
Hilldrop Cres. N7 5H 65
Hilldrop Est. N7 5H 65
(not continuous)
Hilldrop La. N7 5H 65
Hilldrop Rd. BR1: Brom 6K 141
N7 5H 65
Hill End BR6: Orp 2K 173
Hillend SE18 1E 124
Hillersden Ho. *SW1* *5J 17*
(off Ebury Bri. Rd.)
Hillersdon Av. HA8: Edg 5A 28
SW13 2C 116
Hillery Cl. SE17 4D 102
Hill Farm Cotts. HA4: Ruis 7E 38
Hill Farm Rd. UB10: Ick 4F 57
W10 5E 80
Hillfield Av. HA0: Wemb 7E 60
N8 5J 47
NW9 5A 44
SM4: Mord 6C 154
Hillfield Cl. HA2: Harr 4G 41
Hillfield Ct. NW3 5C 64
Hillfield Ho. N5 5C 66
Hillfield M. N8 4K 47
Hillfield Pk. N10 4F 47
N21 2F 33
Hillfield Pk. M. N10 4F 47
Hill Fld. Rd. TW12: Hamp 7D 130
Hillfield Rd. NW6 5H 63
Hillfoot Av. RM5: Col R 1J 55
Hillfoot Rd. RM5: Col R 1J 55
Hillgate Pl. SW12 7F 119
W8 1J 99
Hillgate St. W8 1J 99
Hillgate Wlk. N6 6G 47
Hill Gro. RM1: Rom 3K 55
TW13: Hanw 2D 130
Hill Ho. BR2: Brom 2H 159
E5 *1H 67*
(off Harrington Hill)
SE28 1H 107
Hillhouse Av. HA7: Stan 7E 26
Hill Ho. Cl. N21 7F 23
Hill Ho. Dr. TW12: Hamp 1E 148
Hill Ho. M. BR2: Brom 2H 159
Hill Ho. Rd. SW16 5K 137
Hilliard Ho. *E1* *1H 103*
(off Prusom St.)
Hilliard Rd. HA6: Nwood 1H 39
Hilliards Ct. E1 1J 103
Hillier Cl. EN5: New Bar 6E 20
Hillier Gdns. CR0: Wadd 5A 168
Hillier Ho. *NW1* *7H 65*
(off Camden Sq.)
Hillier Lodge TW11: Tedd 5H 131
Hillier Pl. KT9: Chess 6D 162
Hillier Rd. SW11 6D 118
Hilliers Av. UB8: Hil 3C 74
Hilliers La. CR0: Bedd 3J 167
HILLINGDON 3C 74
Hillingdon Athletic Club 5F 39
Hillingdon Av. TW19: Stanw 1A 128
HILLINGDON CIRCUS 6D 56
Hillingdon Ct. HA3: Kent 4D 42
Hillingdon Cycling Circuit 1A 94
HILLINGDON HEATH 4D 74
Hillingdon Hill UB10: Hil 2A 74
Hillingdon Rd. DA7: Bex 2J 127
UB8: Uxb 1A 74
UB10: Uxb 1A 74
Hillingdon Ski Cen. 5A 56
Hillingdon St. SE17 6B 102
Hillington Gdns. IG8: Wfd G 2B 52
Hill La. HA4: Ruis 1E 56
Hillman Cl. UB8: Uxb 5A 56
Hillman Dr. W10 4E 80
Hillman St. E8 6H 67
Hillmarton Rd. N7 5J 65
Hillmead Dr. SW9 4B 120
Hillmore Ct. *SE13* *3F 123*
(off Belmont Hill)
Hillmore Gro. SE26 5A 140
Hill Path SW16 5K 137
Hillreach SE18 5D 106
Hill Ri. HA4: Ruis 1E 56
KT10: Hin W 2B 162
KT12: Walt T 7H 147
N9 6C 24
NW11 4K 45
SE23 1H 139
TW10: Rich 5D 114
UB6: G'frd 7G 59
Hillrise Mans. *N19* *7J 47*
(off Warltersville Rd.)
Hillrise Rd. N19 7J 47
Hill Rd. CR4: Mitc 1F 155
HA0: Wemb 3B 60
HA1: Harr 5A 42
HA5: Pinn 5C 40
N10 1D 46
NW8 3A 82
SM1: Sutt 5K 165
SM5: Cars 6C 166
Hillsboro' Rd. SE22 5E 120
Hillsborough Ct. *NW6* *1K 81*
(off Mortimer Cres.)
Hillsgrove Cl. DA16: Well 7C 108
HILLSIDE 4J 109
Hillside DA8: Erith 4J 109
EN5: New Bar 5F 21
N8 6H 47
NW5 3E 64
NW9 4K 43
NW10 7J 61
SE10 *7F 105*
(off Crooms Hill)
SW19 6F 135
Hillside Av. HA9: Wemb 4F 61
IG8: Wfd G 6F 37
N11 6J 31
Hillside Cl. IG8: Wfd G 5F 37
NW8 2K 81
SM4: Mord 4G 153
Hillside Cres. HA2: Harr 1G 59
HA6: Nwood 1J 39
Hillside Dr. HA8: Edg 6B 28
Hillside Est. N15 6F 49
Hillside Gdns. E17 3F 51
EN5: Barn 4B 20
HA3: Kent 7E 42
HA6: Nwood 1J 39
HA8: Edg 4A 28
N6 6F 47
N11 6B 32
SM6: Wall 7G 167
SW2 2A 138
Hillside Gro. N14 7C 22
NW7 7H 29
Hillside Ho. *CR0: Wadd* *4B 168*
(off Violet La.)
Hillside La. BR2: Hayes 2H 171
(not continuous)

Holland Cl. BR2: Hayes 2H 171
  EN5: New Bar 7G 21
  HA7: Stan 5G 27
  RM7: Rom 5J 55
Holland Ct. E17 ....4E 50
          (off Evelyn Rd.)
  KT6: Surb 7D 150
  NW7 ....6H 29
Holland Dr. SE23 ....3A 140
Holland Gdns. W14 ....3G 99
Holland Gro. SW9 ....7A 102
Holland Ho. E4 ....4A 36
  NW10 ....2D 80
          (off Holland Rd.)
HOLLAND PARK 1H 99
Holland Pk. 2H 99
HOLLAND PARK 2F 99
Holland Pk. W11 ....1G 99
Holland Pk. Av. IG3: Ilf 6J 53
  W11 ....2G 99
Holland Pk. Gdns. W14 ....2G 99
Holland Pk. M. W11 ....1G 99
Holland Pk. Rd. W14 ....3H 99
Holland Pk. Ter. W11 ....1G 99
          (off Portland Rd.)
Holland Pk. Theatre (Open Air) 2H 99
          (in Holland Pk.)
Holland Pas. N1 ....1C 84
          (off Basire St.)
Holland Pl. W8 ....2K 99
          (off Kensington Chu. St.)
Holland Pl. Chambers W8 ......2K 99
          (off Holland Pl.)
Holland Ri. Ho. SW9 ....7K 101
          (off Clapham Rd.)
Holland Rd. E6 ....1D 88
  E15 ....3G 87
  HA0: Wemb 6D 60
  NW10 ....1C 80
  SE25 ....5G 157
  W14 ....2F 99
Hollands, The KT4: Wor Pk 1B 164
  TW13: Hanw 4B 130
Holland St. SE1 ....4B 14 (1B 102)
  W8 ....2J 99
Holland Vs. Rd. W14 ....2G 99
Holland Wlk. HA7: Stan 5F 27
  N19 ....1H 65
  W8 ....1H 99
Holland Way BR2: Hayes 2H 171
Hollar Rd. N16 ....3F 67
Hollen St. W1 ....7C 6 (6H 83)
Holles Cl. TW12: Hamp 6E 130
Holles Ho. SW9 ....2A 120
Holles St. W1 ....7K 5 (6F 83)
Holley Rd. W3 ....2A 98
Hollickwood Av. N12 ....6J 31
Holliday Sq. SW11 ....3B 118
          (off Fowler Cl.)
Hollidge Way RM10: Dag 7H 73
Hollies, The E11 ....5J 51
          (off New Wanstead)
  HA3: W'stone 4A 42
  N20 ....1G 31
Hollies Av. DA15: Sidc 2K 143
Hollies Cl. SW16 ....6A 138
  TW1: Twick 2K 131
Hollies End NW7 ....5J 29
Hollies Rd. W5 ....4C 96
Hollies Way SW12 ....7E 118
Holligrave Rd. BR1: Brom 1J 159
Hollingbourne Av. DA7: Bex 1F 127
Hollingbourne Gdns. W13 ......5B 78
Hollingbourne Rd. SE24 ....5C 120
Hollingsworth Ct. KT6: Surb ...7D 150
Hollingsworth Rd. CR0: Croy ...6H 169
Hollington Cl. BR7: Chest 6F 143
Hollington Cres. KT3: N Mald ...6B 152
Hollington Rd. E6 ....3D 88
  N17 ....2G 49
Hollingworth Cl. KT8: W Mole ...4D 148

Hollingworth Rd. BR5: Pet W 6F 161
Hollins Ho. N7 ....4J 65
Hollisfield WC1 ....2F 7
          (off Cromer St.)
Hollman Gdns. SW16 ....6B 138
Hollow, The IG8: Wfd G 4C 36
HOLLOWAY 3J 65
Holloway Cl. UB7: Harm 5A 92
Holloway Ho. NW2 ....3E 62
          (off Stoll Cl.)
Holloway La. UB7: Harm, W Dray ...6A 92
Holloway Rd. E6 ....3D 88
  E11 ....3F 69
  N7 ....4K 65
  N19 ....2H 65
Holloway St. TW3: Houn 3F 113
Hollowfield Wlk. UB5: N'olt 7C 58
Hollows, The TW8: Bford 6F 97
Holly Av. HA7: Stan 2E 42
  KT12: Walt T 7B 148
Hollybank Cl. TW12: Hamp 5E 130
Hollyberry La. NW3 ....4A 64
Hollybrake Cl. BR7: Chst 7H 143
Hollybush Cl. E11 ....5J 51
  HA3: Hrw W 1J 41
Hollybush Gdns. E2 ....3H 85
Hollybush Hill E11 ....6H 51
  NW3 ....4A 64
Holly Bush La. TW12: Hamp 7D 130
Hollybush Pl. E2 ....3H 85
Hollybush Rd. KT2: King T 5E 132
Hollybush Steps NW3 ....4A 64
          (off Holly Mt.)
Hollybush St. E13 ....3K 87
Holly Bush Va. NW3 ....4A 64
Hollybush Wlk. SW9 ....4B 120
Holly Cl. BR3: Beck 4E 158
  IG9: Buck H 3G 37
  NW10 ....7A 62
  SM6: Wall 7F 167
  TW13: Hanw 5C 130
Holly Cott. M. UB8: Hil 5C 74
Holly Ct. DA14: Sidc 4B 144
          (off Sidcup Hill)
  N15 ....4E 48
  SM2: Sutt 7J 165
Holly Cres. BR3: Beck 5B 158
  IG8: Wfd G 6A 36
Hollycroft Av. HA9: Wemb 2F 61
  NW3 ....3J 63
Hollycroft Cl. CR2: S Croy 5E 168
  UB7: Sip 6C 92
Hollycroft Gdns. UB7: Sip 6C 92
Hollydale Cl. UB5: N'olt 4F 59
Hollydale Dr. BR2: Brom 3D 172
Hollydale Rd. SE15 ....1J 121
Holly Dene SE15 ....1H 121
Hollydene BR2: Brom 1H 159
          (off Beckenham La.)
Hollydown Way E11 ....3F 69
Holly Dr. E4 ....7J 25
Holly Farm Rd. UB2: S'hall 5C 94
Hollyfield Av. N11 ....5J 31
Hollyfield Rd. KT5: Surb 7F 151
Holly Gdns. DA7: Bex 4J 127
  UB7: W Dray 2B 92
Holly Gro. HA5: Pinn 1C 40
  NW9 ....7J 43
  SE15 ....2F 121
Hollygrove WD23: Bush 1C 26
Hollygrove Cl. TW3: Houn 4D 112
Holly Hedge Ter. SE13 ....5F 123
Holly Hill N21 ....6E 22
  NW3 ....4A 64
Holly Hill Rd. DA8: Erith 5H 109
  DA17: Belv, Erith 5H 109
Holly Ho. TW8: Bford 6C 96
  W10 ....4G 81
          (off Hawthorn Wlk.)
Holly Lodge HA1: Harr 5H 41

Holly Lodge Gdns. N6 ....2E 64
Holly Lodge Mans. N6 ....2E 64
Hollymead SM5: Cars 3D 166
Holly M. SW10 ....6A 16 (5A 100)
Holly Mt. NW3 ....4A 64
Hollymount Cl. SE10 ....1E 122
Holly Pk. N3 ....3H 45
  N4 ....7J 47
          (not continuous)
Holly Pk. Est. N4 ....7K 47
Holly Pk. Gdns. N3 ....3J 45
Holly Pk. Rd. N11 ....5K 31
  W7 ....1K 95
Holly Pl. NW3 ....4A 64
          (off Holly Berry La.)
Holly Rd. E11 ....7H 51
  TW1: Twick 1K 131
  TW3: Houn 4F 113
  TW12: Hamp H 6G 131
  W4 ....4K 97
Holly St. E8 ....7F 67
Holly Ter. N6 ....1E 64
  N20 ....2F 31
Holly Tree Cl. SW19 ....1F 135
Holly Tree Ho. SE4 ....3B 122
          (off Brockley Rd.)
Hollytree Pde. DA14: Sidc 6C 144
          (off Sidcup Hill)
Holly Vw. Cl. NW4 ....6C 44
Holly Village N6 ....2F 65
Holly Vs. W6 ....3D 98
          (off Wellesley Av.)
Holly Wlk. EN2: Enf 3H 23
  NW3 ....4A 64
Holly Way CR4: Mitc 4H 155
Hollywood Bowl
  Barking 3G 89
  Finchley 7G 31
  Surrey Quays 3K 103
Hollywood Ct. W5 ....7F 79
Hollywood Gdns. UB4: Yead 6K 75
Hollywood M. SW10 ....6A 100
Hollywood Rd. E4 ....5F 35
  SW10 ....6A 100
Hollywood Way IG8: Wfd G 7A 36
Holman Ct. KT17: Ewe 7C 164
Holman Ho. E2 ....3K 85
          (off Roman Rd.)
Holman Hunt Ho. W6 ....5G 99
          (off Field Rd.)
Holman Rd. KT19: Ewe 5J 163
  SW11 ....2B 118
Holmbank Dr. TW17: Shep 4G 147
Holmbridge Gdns. EN3: Pond E ...4E 24
Holmbrook NW1 ....2G 83
          (off Eversholt St.)
Holmbrook Dr. NW4 ....5F 45
Holmbury Ct. CR2: S Croy 5E 168
  SW17 ....3D 136
  SW19 ....7C 136
Holmbury Gdns. UB3: Hayes ...1H 93
Holmbury Gro. CR0: Sels 7B 170
Holmbury Ho. SE24 ....5B 120
Holmbury Mnr. DA14: Sidc 4A 144
Holmbury Pk. BR1: Brom 7C 142
Holmbury Vw. E5 ....1H 67
Holmbush Rd. SW15 ....6G 117
Holmcote Gdns. N5 ....5C 66
Holm Ct. SE12 ....3K 141
Holmcroft Ho. E17 ....4D 50
Holmcroft Way BR2: Brom 5D 160
Holmdale Gdns. NW4 ....5F 45
Holmdale Rd. BR7: Chst 5G 143
  NW6 ....5J 63
Holmdale Ter. N15 ....7E 48
Holmdene N12 ....5E 30
Holmdene Av. HA2: Harr 3F 41
  NW7 ....6H 29
  SE24 ....5C 120
Holmdene Cl. BR3: Beck 2E 158
Holmdene Ct. BR1: Brom 3C 160

Holmead Rd. SW6 ....7K 99
Holmebury Cl. WD23: Bushy 2D 26
Holme Cl. TW7: Isle 3A 114
Holme Lacey Rd. SE12 ....6H 123
Holme Rd. E6 ....1C 88
Holmes Av. E17 ....3B 50
  NW7 ....5B 30
Holmesdale Av. SW14 ....3H 115
Holmesdale Cl. SE25 ....3F 157
Holmesdale Ho. NW6 ....1J 81
          (off Kilburn Va.)
Holmesdale Rd. CR0: Croy 5D 156
  DA7: Bex 2D 126
  N6 ....7F 47
  SE25 ....5D 156
  TW9: Kew 1F 115
  TW11: Tedd 7C 132
Holmesley Rd. SE23 ....6A 122
Holmes Pl. SW10 ....6A 100
Holmes Place Health Club
  Barbican 5C 8
          (off Aldersgate St.)
  Bromley 4B 160
  Croydon 3C 168
  Hammersmith 4F 99
          (off Hammersmith Rd.)
  Merton 6A 136
  St Luke's 4E 8
Holmes Rd. NW5 ....5F 65
  SW19 ....7A 136
  TW1: Twick 2K 131
Holmes Ter. SE1 ....6J 13
Holmewood Gdns. SW2 ....6K 165
Holmewood Rd. SE25 ....3E 156
  SW2 ....7J 119
Holmfield Av. NW4 ....5F 45
Holmfield Ct. NW3 ....5C 64
Holm Gro. UB10: Hil 7C 56
Holmhurst Rd. DA17: Belv 5H 109
Holmlea Ct. CR0: Croy 4D 168
          (off Chatsworth Rd.)
Holmleigh Ct. EN3: Pond E 4D 24
Holmleigh Rd. N16 ....1E 66
Holmleigh Rd. Est. N16 ....1E 66
Holmoak Cl. SW15 ....6H 117
Holm Oak M. SW4 ....5J 119
Holmoaks Ho. BR3: Beck 2E 158
Holmsdale Ho. E14 ....7D 86
          (off Poplar High St.)
  N11 ....4A 32
          (off Coppies Gro.)
Holmshaw Cl. SE26 ....4A 140
Holmside Rd. SW12 ....6E 118
Holmsley Cl. KT3: N Mald 6B 152
Holmsley Ho. SW15 ....7B 116
          (off Tangley Gro.)
Holmstall Av. HA8: Edg 3J 43
Holmstall Pde. HA8: Edg 2J 43
Holm Wlk. SE3 ....2J 123
Holmwood Cl. HA2: Harr 3G 41
  SM2: Cheam 7F 165
  UB5: N'olt 6F 59
Holmwood Gdns. N3 ....2J 45
  SM6: Wall 6F 167
Holmwood Gro. NW7 ....5E 28
Holmwood Rd. IG3: Ilf 2J 71
  KT9: Chess 5D 162
  SM2: Cheam 7E 164
Holmwood Vs. SE7 ....5J 105
Holne Chase N2 ....6A 46
  SM4: Mord 6H 153
Holness Rd. E15 ....6H 69
Holocaust Memorial Garden 6F 11
Holroyd Rd. KT10: Clay 7A 162
  SW15 ....4E 116
Holst Ct. SE1 ....1J 19
          (off Westminster Bri. Rd.)
Holstein Way DA18: Erith 3D 108

Horniman Dr. SE23 1H 139
Horniman Mus. 1H 139
Horning Cl. SE9 4C 142
Horn La. IG8: Wfd G 6D 36
SE10 5J 105
(not continuous)
W3 7J 79
(not continuous)
Horn Link Way SE10 4J 105
HORN PARK 5K 123
Horn Pk. Cl. SE12 5K 123
Hornpark La. SE12 5K 123
Hornscroft Cl. IG11: Bark 7J 71
Horns End Pl. HA5: Eastc 4A 40
HORNSEY 4J 47
Hornsey Club, The 5H 47
Hornsey La. N6 1F 65
Hornsey La. Est. N19 7H 47
Hornsey La. Gdns. N6 7G 47
Hornsey Pk. Rd. N8 3K 47
Hornsey Ri. N19 7H 47
Hornsey Ri. Gdns. N19 7H 47
Hornsey Rd. N7 1J 65
N19 1J 65
Hornsey St. N7 5K 65
HORNSEY VALE 5K 47
Hornshay St. SE15 6J 103
Horns Rd. IG2: Ilf 5G 53
IG6: Ilf 4H 53
Hornton Ct. *W8* *2J 99*
(off Kensington High St.)
Hornton Pl. W8 2K 99
Hornton St. W8 2J 99
Horsa Rd. DA8: Erith 7H 109
SE12 7A 124
Horse & Dolphin Yd. W1 2D 12
Horsebridge Cl. RM9: Dag 1E 90
Horsecroft Rd. HA8: Edg 7E 28
Horse Fair KT1: King T 2D 150
Horseferry Pl. SE10 6E 104
Horseferry Rd. E14 7A 86
SW1 2C 18 (3H 101)
Horseferry Rd. Est. SW1 2C 18
Horseguards Av. SW1 5E 12 (1J 101)
Horse Guards Parade 5E 12 (1J 101)
Horse Guards Rd.
SW1 5D 12 (1H 101)
Horse Leaze E6 6E 88
Horsell Rd. BR5: St P 7B 144
N5 5A 66
(not continuous)
Horselydown La. SE1 6J 15 (2F 103)
Horselydown Mans. *SE1* *6J 15*
(off Lafone St.)
Horsemongers M. SE1 7D 14
Horsenden Av. UB6: G'frd 5K 59
Horsenden Cres. UB6: G'frd 5K 59
Horsenden La. Nth. UB6: G'frd 6J 59
Horsenden La. Sth. UB6: G'frd 1A 78
Horse Ride SW1 5C 12 (1G 101)
Horseshoe Cl. E14 5E 104
NW2 2D 62
Horseshoe Ct. *EC1* *3B 8*
(off Brewhouse Yd.)
Horse Shoe Cres. UB5: N'olt 2E 76
Horseshoe Dr. UB8: Hil 6C 74
Horse Shoe Grn. SM1: Sutt 2K 165
Horseshoe La. EN2: Enf 3H 23
N20 1A 30
Horseshoe Wharf *SE1* *4E 14*
(off Clink St.)
Horse Yd. *N1* *1B 84*
(off Essex Rd.)
Horsfeld Gdns. SE9 5C 124
Horsfeld Rd. SE9 5B 124
Horsfield Ho. *N1* *7C 66*
(off Northampton St.)
Horsford Rd. SW2 5K 119
Horsham Av. N12 5H 31
Horsham Ct. *N17* *1G 49*
(off Lansdowne Rd.)
Horsham Rd. DA6: Bex 5G 127
TW14: Bedf 6E 110
Horsley Dr. CR0: New Ad 7E 170
KT2: King T 5D 132
Horsley Rd. BR1: Brom 1K 159
E4 2K 35
Horsley St. SE17 6D 102
Horsman Ho. *SE5* *6C 102*
(off Bethwin Rd.)
Horsman St. SE5 6C 102
Horsmonden Cl. BR6: Orp 7K 161
Horsmonden Rd. SE4 5B 122
Hortensia Ho. *SW10* *7A 100*
(off Gunter Gro.)
Hortensia Rd. SW10 7A 100
Horticultural Pl. W4 5K 97
Horton Av. NW2 4G 63
Horton Bri. Rd. UB7: Yiew 1B 92
Horton Cl. UB7: Yiew 1C 92
Horton Ho. SE15 6J 103
SW8 7K 101
W6 *5G 99*
(off Field Rd.)
Horton Ind. Pk. UB7: Yiew 1B 92
Horton La. KT19: Eps 7H 163
Horton Pde. UB7: Yiew 1A 92
Horton Rd. E8 6H 67
UB7: Yiew 1A 92
UB11: Yiew 1A 92
Horton Rd. Ind. Est. UB7: Yiew 1B 92
Horton St. SE13 3D 122
Horton Way CR0: Croy 5K 157
Hortus Rd. E4 2K 35
UB2: S'hall 2D 94
Horwood Ho. *E2* *3H 85*
(off Pott St.)
NW8 *3D 4*
(off Paveley St.)
Hosack Rd. SW17 2E 136
Hoser Av. SE12 2J 141
Hosier La. EC1 6A 8 (5B 84)
Hoskins Cl. E16 6A 88
UB3: Harl 5H 93
Hoskins St. SE10 5F 105
Hospital Bri. Rd. TW2: Twick, Whit 7F 113
HOSPITAL BRIDGE RDBT. 2F 131
Hospital Rd. E9 5K 67
TW3: Houn 3E 112
Hospital Way SE13 6F 123
Hotham Cl. KT8: W Mole 3E 148
Hotham Rd. SW15 3E 116
SW19 7A 136
Hotham Rd. M. SW19 7A 136
Hotham St. E15 1G 87
Hothfield Pl. SE16 3J 103
Hotspur Ind. Est. N17 6C 34
Hotspur Rd. UB5: N'olt 2E 76
Hotspur St. SE11 5J 19 (4A 102)
Houblon Rd. TW10: Rich 5E 114
Houghton Cl. E8 6F 67
TW12: Hamp 6C 130
Houghton Rd. N15 4F 49
Houghton St. WC2 1H 13 (6K 83)
(not continuous)
Houlder Cres. CR0: Wadd 6B 168
Houndsden Rd. N21 6E 22
Houndsditch EC3 7H 9 (6E 84)
Houndsfield Rd. N9 7C 24
HOUNSLOW 3F 113
Hounslow Av. TW3: Houn 5F 113
Hounslow Bus. Pk. TW3: Houn 4E 112
Hounslow Cen. TW3: Houn 3F 113
Hounslow Gdns. TW3: Houn 5F 113
Hounslow Heath Nature Reserve 6B 112
Hounslow Rd. TW2: Whit 6F 113
TW13: Hanw 4B 130
TW14: Felt 1K 129
Hounslow Urban Farm 5J 111
HOUNSLOW WEST 2C 112
Houseman Way SE5 7D 102
Houses of Parliament 1F 19 (3J 101)
Houston Bus. Pk. UB4: Yead 1A 94
Houston Pl. KT10: Esh 7H 149
Houston Rd. KT6: Surb 6B 150
SE23 2A 140
Houstoun Ct.
TW5: Hest 7D 94
Hove Av. E17 5B 50
Hoveden Rd. NW2 5G 63
Hove Gdns. SM1: Sutt 1K 165
Hove St. *SE15* *7J 103*
(off Culmore Rd.)
Hoveton Rd. SE28 6C 90
Hoveton Way IG6: Ilf 1F 53
Howard Av. DA5: Bexl 1C 144
Howard Bldg. SW8 6F 101
Howard Cl. N11 2K 31
NW2 4G 63
TW12: Hamp 7G 131
TW16: Sun 6H 129
W3 6H 79
WD23: Bushy 1D 26
Howard Ct. IG11: Bark 1H 89
Howard Ho. *E16* *1K 105*
(off Wesley Av.)
SE8 *6B 104*
(off Evelyn St.)
SW1 *6B 18*
(off Dolphin Sq.)
SW9 *3B 120*
(off Barrington Rd.)
W1 *4K 5*
(off Cleveland St.)
Howard M. N5 4B 66
Howard Rd. BR1: Brom 7J 141
E6 2D 88
E11 3G 69
E17 3C 50
IG1: Ilf 4F 71
IG11: Bark 1H 89
KT3: N Mald 3A 152
KT5: Surb 6F 151
N15 6E 48
N16 4D 66
NW2 4F 63
SE20 1J 157
SE25 5G 157
TW7: Isle 3K 113
UB1: S'hall 6F 77
Howards Cl. HA5: Pinn 2K 39
Howards Crest Cl. BR3: Beck 2E 158
Howard's La. SW15 4D 116
Howards Rd. E13 3J 87
Howard St. KT7: T Ditt 7B 150
Howard Wlk. N2 4A 46
Howard Way EN5: Barn 5A 20
Howarth Ct. *E15* *5E 68*
(off Clays La.)
Howarth Rd. SE2 5A 108
Howberry Cl. HA8: Edg 6J 27
Howberry Rd. CR7: Thor H 1D 156
HA7: Stan 6J 27
HA8: Edg 6J 27
Howbury Rd. SE15 3J 121
Howcroft Cres. N3 7D 30
Howcroft La. UB6: G'frd 3H 77
Howden Cl. SE28 7D 90
Howden Rd. SE25 2F 157
Howden St. SE15 3G 121
Howe Cl. RM7: Mawney 1G 55
Howell Cl. RM6: Chad H 5D 54
Howell Ct. E10 7D 50
Howell Wlk. SE1 4B 102
Howerd Way SE18 1C 124
(not continuous)
Howes Cl. N3 3J 45
Howeth Ct. *N11* *6J 31*
(off Ribblesdale Av.)
Howfield Pl. N17 3F 49
Howgate Rd. SW14 3K 115
Howick Pl. SW1 2B 18 (3G 101)
Howie St. SW11 7C 100
Howitt Cl. N16 4E 66
NW3 6C 64
Howitt Rd. NW3 6C 64
Howland Est. SE16 3J 103
Howland Ho. SW16 3J 137
Howland M. E. W1 5B 6 (5G 83)
Howland St. W1 5A 6 (5G 83)
Howland Way SE16 2A 104
Howletts La. HA4: Ruis 5E 38
Howlett's Rd. SE24 6C 120
Howley Pl. W2 5A 4 (5A 82)
Howley Rd. CR0: Croy 3B 168
Howsman Rd. SW13 6C 98
Howson Rd. SE4 4A 122
Howson Ter. TW10: Rich 6E 114
How's St. E2 2F 85
Howton Pl. WD23: Bushy 1C 26
HOXTON 2E 84
Hoxton Hall Theatre *2E 84*
(off Hoxton Rd.)
Hoxton Mkt. N1 2G 9
Hoxton Sq. N1 2G 9 (3E 84)
Hoxton St. N1 2H 9 (1E 84)
Hoylake Cres. UB10: Ick 2C 56
Hoylake Gdns. CR4: Mitc 3G 155
HA4: Ruis 1K 57
Hoylake Rd. W3 6A 80
Hoyland Cl. SE15 7H 103
Hoyle Rd. SW17 5C 136
Hoy St. E16 6H 87
HQS Wellington 3J 13
Hubbard Ct. IG10: Lough 1H 37
Hubbard Dr. KT9: Chess 6D 162
Hubbard Rd. SE27 4C 138
Hubbards Cl. UB8: Hil 6D 74
Hubbard St. E15 1G 87
Huberd Ho. *SE1* *7F 15*
(off Manciple St.)
Hubert Cl. *SW19* *1A 154*
(off Nelson Gro. Rd.)
Hubert Gro. SW9 3J 119
Hubert Ho. *NW8* *4C 4*
(off Ashbridge St.)
Hubert Rd. E6 3B 88
Hucknall Ct. *NW8* *3A 4*
(off Cunningham Pl.)
Huddart St. E3 5B 86
(Ackroyd Dr.)
E3 5B 86
(Weatherley Cl.)
Huddleston Cl. E2 2J 85
Huddlestone Rd. E7 4H 69
NW2 6D 62
Huddleston Rd. N7 3G 65
Hudson *NW9* *1B 44*
(off Near Acre)
Hudson Apartments N8 3K 47
Hudson Cl. W12 7D 80
Hudson Ct. *E14* *5C 104*
(off Maritime Quay)
Hudson Gdns. BR6: Chels 6K 173
Hudson Pl. SE18 5G 107
Hudson Rd. DA7: Bex 2F 127
UB3: Harl 6F 93
Hudson's Pl. SW1 3A 18 (4F 101)
Hudson Way N9 3D 34
Huggin Ct. EC4 2D 14
Huggin Hill EC4 2D 14 (7C 84)
Huggins Pl. SW2 1K 137
Hughan Rd. E15 5F 69
Hugh Astor Ct. *SE1* *7B 14*
(off Keyworth St.)
Hugh Clark Ho. *W13* *1A 96*
(off Singapore Rd.)
Hugh Cubitt Ho. *N1* *2K 83*
(off Collier St.)
Hugh Dalton Av. SW6 6H 99
Hughenden Av. HA3: Kent 5B 42
Hughenden Gdns. UB5: Yead 3A 76
(not continuous)
Hughenden Ho. NW8 3C 4

Hughenden Rd.—Hyde Va.

Hughenden Rd. KT4: Wor Pk 7C 152
Hughendon EN5: New Bar 4E 20
Hughendon Ter. E15 .... 4E 68
Hughes Cl. N12 .... 5F 31
Hughes Ct. N7 .... 5H 65
Hughes Ho. *E2* *3J 85*
(off Sceptre Ho.)
SE8 .... *6C 104*
(off Benbow St.)
SE17 .... *4B 102*
(off Peacock St.)
Hughes Mans. E1 .... 4G 85
Hughes M. SW11 .... 5D 118
Hughes Rd. TW15: Ashf 6E 128
UB3: Hayes 7K 75
Hughes Ter. *E16* *5H 87*
(off Clarkson Rd.)
SW9 .... *3B 120*
(off Styles Gdns.)
Hughes Wlk. CR0: Croy 7C 156
Hugh Gaitskell Cl. SW6 .... 6H 99
Hugh Gaitskell Ho. N16 .... 2F 67
Hugh Herland Ho. KT1: King T 3E 150
Hugh M. SW1 .... 4K 17 (4F 101)
Hugh Platt Ho. *E2* *2H 85*
(off Patriot Sq.)
Hugh St. SW1 .... 4K 17 (4F 101)
Hugon Rd. SW6 .... 3K 117
Hugo Rd. N19 .... 4G 65
Huguenot Pl. E1 .... 5K 9 (5F 85)
SW18 .... 5A 118
Huguenot Sq. SE15 .... 3H 121
Hullbridge M. N1 .... 1D 84
Hull Cl. SE16 .... 2K 103
Hull Pl. E16 .... 1G 107
Hull St. EC1 .... 2C 8 (3C 84)
Hulme Pl. SE1 .... 7D 14 (2C 102)
Hulse Av. IG11: Bark 6H 71
RM7: Mawney 1H 55
Humber Cl. UB7: W Dray 1A 92
Humber Ct. *W7* *6H 77*
(off Hobbayne Rd.)
Humber Dr. W10 .... 4F 81
Humber Rd. NW2 .... 2D 62
SE3 .... 6H 105
Humberstone Rd. E13 .... 3A 88
Humberton Cl. E9 .... 5A 68
Humber Trad. Est.
NW2 .... 2D 62
Humbolt Rd. W6 .... 6G 99
Hume Ct. *N1* *7B 66*
(off Hawes St.)
Hume Ho. *W11* *1F 99*
(off Queensdale Cres.)
Humes Av. W7 .... 3J 95
Hume Ter. E16 .... 5K 87
Hume Way HA4: Ruis 6J 39
Humphrey Cl. IG5: Ilf 1D 52
Humphrey St. SE1 .... 5F 103
Humphries Cl.
RM9: Dag 4F 73
Hundred Acre NW9 .... 2B 44
Hungerdown E4 .... 1K 35
Hungerford Ho. *SW1* *7B 18*
(off Churchill Gdns.)
Hungerford La. WC2 .... 4F 13
(not continuous)
Hungerford Rd. N7 .... 6H 65
Hungerford St. E1 .... 6H 85
Hunsdon Cl. RM9: Dag 6E 72
Hunsdon Rd. SE14 .... 7K 103
Hunslett St. E2 .... 3J 85
Hunstanton Ho. *NW1* *5D 4*
(off Cosway St.)
Hunston Rd. SM4: Mord 1K 165
Hunt Cl. W11 .... 1F 99
Hunt Ct. N14 .... 7A 22
UB5: N'olt *2B 76*
(off Gallery Gdns.)
Hunter Cl. SE1 .... 3D 102
SM6: Wall 7J 167
Hunter Ho. *SE1* *7B 14*
(off Lancaster St.)
SW5 .... *5J 99*
(off Old Brompton Rd.)
SW8 .... *7H 101*
(off Fount St.)
WC1 .... *3F 7*
(off Hunter St.)
Hunterian Mus., The 7H 7
(off Portugal St.)
Hunter Lodge *W9* *5J 81*
(off Admiral Wlk.)
Hunter Rd. CR7: Thor H 3D 156
IG1: Ilf 5F 71
SW20 .... 1E 152
Hunters Cl. DA5: Bexl 3K 145
SW12 .... 1E 136
Hunters Ct. TW9: Rich 5D 114
Hunters Gro. BR6: Farnb 4G 173
HA3: Kent 4C 42
UB3: Hayes 1J 93
Hunters Hall Rd. RM10: Dag 4G 73
Hunters Hill HA4: Ruis 3A 58
Hunters Mdw. SE19 .... 4E 138
Hunter's Rd. KT9: Chess 3E 162
Hunters Sq. RM10: Dag 4G 73
Hunter St. WC1 .... 3F 7 (4J 83)
Hunters Way CR0: Croy 4E 168
EN2: Enf 1F 23
Hunter Wlk. E13 .... 2J 87
Huntingdon Cl. CR4: Mitc 3J 155
UB5: N'olt 6E 58
Huntingdon Gdns. KT4: Wor Pk 3E 164
W4 .... 7J 97
Huntingdon Rd. N2 .... 3C 46
N9 .... 2D 34
Huntingdon St. E16 .... 6H 87
N1 .... 7K 65
Huntingfield CR0: Sels 7B 170
Huntingfield Rd. SW15 .... 4C 116
Hunting Ga. Cl. EN2: Enf 3F 23
Hunting Ga. Dr. KT9: Chess 7E 162
Hunting Ga. M. SM1: Sutt 3K 165
TW2: Twick 1J 131
Huntings Farm IG1: Ilf 2J 71
Huntings Rd. RM10: Dag 6G 73
Huntley Dr. N3 .... 6D 30
Huntley St. WC1 .... 4B 6 (4G 83)
Huntley Way SW20 .... 2C 152
Huntly Rd. SE25 .... 4E 156
Hunton St. E1 .... 4K 9 (5G 85)
Hunt Rd. UB2: S'hall 3E 94
Hunt's Cl. SE3 .... 2J 123
Hunt's Ct. WC2 .... 3D 12 (7H 83)
Hunts La. E15 .... 2E 86
Huntsmans Cl. TW13: Felt 4K 129
Huntsman St. SE17 .... 4E 102
Hunts Mead EN3: Enf H 3E 24
Huntsmead Cl. BR7: Chst 7D 142
Huntsmoor Rd. KT19: Ewe 5K 163
Huntspill St. SW17 .... 3A 136
Hunts Slip Rd. SE21 .... 3E 138
Huntsworth M. NW1 .... 3E 4 (4D 82)
Hurdwick Pl. *NW1* *2G 83*
(off Hampstead Rd.)
Hurleston Ho. SE8 .... 5B 104
Hurley Ct. W5 .... 6C 78
Hurley Cres. SE16 .... 2K 103
Hurley Ho. SE11 .... 4K 19 (4B 102)
Hurley Rd. UB6: G'frd 6F 77
HURLINGHAM 3K 117
Hurlingham Bus. Pk. SW6 .... 3J 117
Hurlingham Club, The 3J 117
Hurlingham Ct. SW6 .... 3H 117
Hurlingham Gdns. SW6 .... 3H 117
Hurlingham Retail Pk. SW6 .... 3K 117
Hurlingham Rd. DA7: Bex 7F 109
SW6 .... 2H 117
Hurlingham Sq. SW6 .... 3J 117
Hurlingham Stadium 3H 117
Hurlock St. N5 .... 3B 66
Hurlstone Rd. SE25 .... 5E 156
Hurn Ct. TW4: Houn 2B 112
Hurn Ct. Rd. TW4: Houn 2B 112
Huron Cl. BR6: Chels 6J 173
Huron Rd. SW17 .... 2E 136
Huron University 1B 16 (3B 100)
Hurren Cl. SE3 .... 3G 123
Hurricane Rd. SM6: Wall 7J 167
Hurry Cl. E15 .... 7G 69
Hurst Av. E4 .... 4H 35
N6 .... 6G 47
Hurstbourne KT10: Clay 6A 162
Hurstbourne Gdns.
IG11: Bark 6J 71
Hurstbourne Ho. *SW15* *6B 116*
(off Tangley Gro.)
Hurstbourne Rd. SE23 .... 1A 140
Hurst Cl. BR2: Hayes 1H 171
E4 .... 3H 35
KT9: Chess 5G 163
NW11 .... 6K 45
UB5: N'olt 6D 58
Hurstcombe IG9: Buck H 2D 36
Hurst Ct. DA15: Sidc 2A 144
E6 .... *5B 88*
(off Tollgate Rd.)
Hurstcourt Rd. SM1: Sutt 2K 165
Hurstdene Av. BR2: Hayes 1H 171
Hurstdene Gdns. N15 .... 7E 48
Hurstfield BR2: Brom 5J 159
Hurstfield Cres. UB4: Hayes 4G 75
Hurstfield Rd. KT8: W Mole 3E 148
Hurst Gro. KT12: Walt T 7H 147
Hurst Ho. *WC1* *1H 7*
(off Penton Ri.)
Hurst La. KT8: E Mos 4G 149
SE2 .... 5D 108
Hurst La. Est. SE2 .... 5D 108
Hurstleigh Gdns. IG5: Ilf 1D 52
Hurstmead Ct. HA8: Edg 4C 28
HURST PARK 2G 149
Hurst Pl. HA6: Nwood 1D 38
Hurst Pool 3F 149
Hurst Ri. EN5: New Bar 3D 20
Hurst Rd. CR0: Croy 5D 168
DA5: Bexl 1D 144
DA8: Erith 1J 127
DA15: Bexl, Sidc 2A 144
E17 .... 3D 50
IG9: Buck H 1G 37
KT8: E Mos 3E 148
KT8: W Mole 3E 148
KT12: Walt T 5A 148
N21 .... 1F 33
Hurst Springs DA5: Bexl 1E 144
Hurst St. SE24 .... 6B 120
Hurstview Grange CR2: S Croy 7B 168
Hurst Vw. Rd. CR2: S Croy 7E 168
Hurst Way CR2: S Croy 6E 168
Hurstway Rd. W11 .... 7F 81
Hurstway Wlk. W11 .... 7F 81
Hurstwood Av. DA5: Bexl 1E 144
E18 .... 4K 51
Hurstwood Ct. N12 .... 6H 31
NW11 .... *4H 45*
(off Finchley Rd.)
Hurstwood Dr. BR1: Brom 3D 160
Hurstwood Rd. NW11 .... 4G 45
Hurtwood Rd. KT12: Walt T 7D 148
Husborne Ho. *SE8* *4A 104*
(off Chilton Gro.)
Huson Cl. NW3 .... 7C 64
Hussain Cl. HA1: Harr 4K 59
Hussars Cl. TW4: Houn 3C 112
Husseywell Cres. BR2: Hayes 1J 171
Hutchings St. E14 .... 2C 104
Hutchings Wlk. NW11 .... 4K 45
Hutchings Wharf *E14* *2C 104*
(off Hutchings St.)
Hutchins Cl. E15 .... 7E 68
Hutchinson Ct. RM6: Chad H 4D 54
Hutchinson Ho. NW3 .... 7D 64
SE14 .... 7J 103
Hutchinson Ter. HA9: Wemb 3D 60
Hutchins Rd. SE28 .... 7A 90
Hutton Cl. IG8: Wfd G 6E 36
UB6: G'frd 5H 59
Hutton Ct. *N4* *1K 65*
(off Victoria Rd.)
N9 .... *7D 24*
(off Tramway Av.)
W5 .... 5B 78
Hutton Gdns. HA3: Hrw W 7B 26
Hutton Gro. N12 .... 5E 30
Hutton La. HA3: Hrw W 7B 26
Hutton Row HA8: Edg 7D 28
Hutton St. EC4 .... 2K 13 (6B 84)
Hutton Wlk. HA3: Hrw W 7B 26
Huxbear St. SE4 .... 5B 122
Huxley Cl. UB5: N'olt 2C 76
UB8: Cowl 4A 74
Huxley Dr. RM6: Chad H 7B 54
Huxley Gdns. NW10 .... 3F 79
Huxley Ho. *NW8* *4B 4*
(off Fisherton St.)
Huxley Pde. N18 .... 5J 33
Huxley Pl. N13 .... 3G 33
Huxley Rd. DA16: Well 3K 125
E10 .... 2E 68
N18 .... 4J 33
Huxley Sayze N18 .... 5J 33
Huxley Sth. N18 .... 5J 33
Huxley St. W10 .... 3G 81
Hyacinth Cl. IG1: Ilf 6F 71
TW12: Hamp 6E 130
Hyacinth Dr. UB10: Uxb 7A 56
Hyacinth Rd. SW15 .... 1C 134
HYDE, THE 5B 44
Hyde, The NW9 .... 4A 44
(not continuous)
Hyde Cl. E13 .... 2J 87
EN5: Barn 3C 20
TW15: Ashf 6G 129
Hyde Ct. N20 .... 3G 31
Hyde Cres. NW9 .... 5A 44
Hyde Est. Rd. NW9 .... 5B 44
Hyde Farm M. SW12 .... 1H 137
Hydefield Cl. N21 .... 1J 33
Hydefield Ct. N9 .... 2K 33
Hyde Ind. Est., The NW9 .... 5B 44
Hyde La. SW11 .... 1C 118
Hyde Pk. 4D 10 (1C 100)
Hyde Pk. Av. N21 .... 2H 33
Hyde Pk. Barracks 7D 10
HYDE PARK CORNER 2F 101
Hyde Pk. Cnr. W1 .... 6H 11 (2E 100)
Hyde Pk. Cres. W2 .... 1C 10 (6C 82)
Hyde Pk. Gdns. N21 .... 1H 33
W2 .... 2B 10 (7B 82)
Hyde Pk. Gdns. M. W2 .... 2B 10 (7B 82)
(not continuous)
Hyde Pk. Ga. SW7 .... 2A 100
(not continuous)
Hyde Pk. Ga. M. SW7 .... 2A 100
Hyde Pk. Mans. *NW1* *6C 4*
(off Cabbell St., not continuous)
Hyde Pk. Pl. W2 .... 2D 10 (7C 82)
Hyde Pk. Sq. W2 .... 1C 10 (6C 82)
Hyde Pk. Sq. M. W2 .... 1C 10
Hyde Pk. St. W2 .... 1C 10 (6C 82)
Hyde Pk. Towers W2 .... 7A 82
Hyderabad Way E15 .... 7G 69
Hyde Rd. DA7: Bex 2F 127
N1 .... 1E 84
TW10: Rich 5F 115
Hydeside Gdns. N9 .... 2A 34
Hyde's Pl. N1 .... 7B 66
Hyde St. SE8 .... 6C 104
Hyde Ter. TW15: Ashf 6G 129
Hydethorpe Av. N9 .... 2A 34
Hydethorpe Rd. SW12 .... 1G 137
Hyde Va. SE10 .... 7E 104

Hyde Wlk.—Inverness M.

Hyde Wlk. SM4: Mord ... 7J 153
Hyde Way N9 ... 2A 34
UB3: Harl ... 4H 93
Hydon Ct. N11 ... 5J 31
Hydra Bldg., The
EC1 ... 2K 7
Hylands Rd. E17 ... 2F 51
Hylton St. SE18 ... 4K 107
Hyndewood SE23 ... 3K 139
Hyndman Ho. *RM10: Dag* ... *3G 73*
(off Kershaw Rd.)
Hyndman St. SE15 ... 6H 103
Hynton Rd. RM8: Dag ... 2C 72
Hyperion Ho. *E3* ... *2A 86*
(off Arbery Rd.)
SW2 ... 6K 119
Hyrstdene CR2: S Croy ... 4B 168
Hyson Rd. SE16 ... 5H 103
Hythe Av. DA7: Bex ... 7E 108
Hythe Cl. N18 ... 4B 34
Hythe Ho. *SE16* ... *2J 103*
(off Swan Rd.)
W6 ... *4E 98*
(off Shepherd's Bush Rd.)
Hythe Rd. CR7: Thor H ... 2D 156
NW10 ... 3B 80
Hythe Rd. Ind. Est. NW10 ... 3C 80

I

Ian Bowater Ct. *N1* ... *1F 9*
(off East Rd.)
Ian Ct. SE23 ... 2J 139
Ian Sq. EN3: Enf H ... 1E 24
Ibberton Ho. *SW8* ... *7K 101*
(off Meadow Rd.)
W14 ... *3G 99*
(off Russell Rd.)
Ibbotson Av. E16 ... 6H 87
Ibbott St. E1 ... 4J 85
Iberia Ho. N19 ... 7H 47
Iberian Av. SM6: Bedd ... 4H 167
Ibex Ho. *E15* ... *5G 69*
(off Forest La.)
Ibis Ct. *SE8* ... *6B 104*
(off Edward Pl.)
Ibis La. W4 ... 1J 115
Ibis Way UB4: Yead ... 6B 76
Ibrox Ct. IG9: Buck H ... 2F 37
Ibscott Cl. RM10: Dag ... 6J 73
Ibsley Gdns. SW15 ... 1C 134
Ibsley Way
EN4: Cockf ... 5H 21
ICA Cinema ... *5D 12*
(off Mall, The)
ICA Theatre ... *5D 12*
(off Mall, The)
Iceland Rd. E3 ... 1C 86
Iceni Ct. IG9: Buck H ... 1E 36
Ice Wharf Marina *N1* ... *2J 83*
(off New Wharf Rd.)
Ickburgh Est. E5 ... 2H 67
Ickburgh Rd. E5 ... 3H 67
ICKENHAM ... 3D 56
Ickenham Cl. HA4: Ruis ... 2F 57
Ickenham Grn. UB10: Ick ... 1D 56
Ickenham Rd. HA4: Ruis ... 2E 56
Ickleton Rd. SE9 ... 4C 142
Icknield Dr. IG2: Ilf ... 5F 53
Icknield Ho. *SW3* ... *5D 16*
(off Cale St.)
Ickworth Pk. Rd. E17 ... 4A 50
Icon Apartments *SE1* ... *7G 15*
(off Cluny Pl.)
Ida Rd. N15 ... 4D 48
Ida St. E14 ... 6E 86
(not continuous)
Iden Cl. BR2: Brom ... 3G 159
Idlecombe Rd.
SW17 ... 6E 136
Idmiston Rd. E15 ... 4H 69
KT4: Wor Pk ... 7B 152
SE27 ... 3C 138
Idmiston Sq.
KT4: Wor Pk ... 7B 152
Idol La. EC3 ... 3G 15 (7E 84)
Idonia St. SE8 ... 7C 104
Iffley Cl. UB8: Uxb ... 7A 56
Iffley Rd. W6 ... 3D 98
Ifield Rd. SW10 ... 6K 99
Ifor Evans Pl. E1 ... 4K 85
Ightham Ho. *BR3: Beck* ... *7B 140*
(off Bethersden Cl.)
SE17 ... *4E 102*
(off Beckway St.)
Ightham Rd. DA8: Erith ... 7G 109
Ilbert St. W10 ... 3F 81
Ilchester Gdns. W2 ... 7K 81
Ilchester Pl. W14 ... 3H 99
Ilchester Rd. RM8: Dag ... 5B 72
Ildersly Gro. SE21 ... 2D 138
Ilderton Rd. SE16 ... 5J 103
Ilderton Wharf *SE15* ... *6J 103*
(off Rollins St.)
Ilex Cl. TW16: Sun ... 2A 148
Ilex Rd. NW10 ... 6B 62
Ilex Way SW16 ... 5A 138
ILFORD ... 3F 71
Ilford Hill IG1: Ilf ... 3E 70
Ilford Ho. *N1* ... *6D 66*
(off Dove Rd.)
Ilford La. IG1: Bark, Ilf ... 3F 71
Ilford Pools ... 2J 71
Ilfracombe Flats *SE1* ... *6D 14*
(off Marshalsea Rd.)
Ilfracombe Gdns. RM6: Chad H ... 7B 54
Ilfracombe Rd. BR1: Brom ... 3H 141
Iliffe St. SE17 ... 5B 102
Iliffe Yd. *SE17* ... *5B 102*
(off Crampton St.)
Ilkeston Ct. *E5* ... *4K 67*
(off Overbury St.)
Ilkley Cl. SE19 ... 6D 138
Ilkley Rd. E16 ... 5A 88
Illingworth Cl. CR4: Mitc ... 3B 154
Illingworth Way EN1: Enf ... 5K 23
Ilmington Rd. HA3: Kent ... 6D 42
Ilminster Gdns. SW11 ... 4C 118
Ilsley Ct. SW8 ... 2G 119
Imani Mans. SW11 ... 2B 118
IMAX Cinema ... 5J 13 (1A 102)
Imber Cl. N14 ... 7B 22
Imber Ct. Trad. Est. KT8: E Mos ... 6H 149
Imber Cross KT7: T Ditt ... 6K 149
Imber Gro. KT10: Esh ... 7H 149
Imber Pk. Rd. KT10: Esh ... 7H 149
Imber St. N1 ... 1D 84
Impact Bus. Pk. UB6: G'frd ... 2B 78
Impact Ct. SE20 ... 2H 157
Imperial Av. N16 ... 4E 66
Imperial Cl. HA2: Harr ... 6E 40
Imperial College of Science,
Technology & Medicine
Imperial Coll. Rd. ... 1A 16 (3B 100)
Wilson House ... *7C 4*
(off Star La.)
Imperial Coll. Rd.
SW7 ... 2A 16 (3B 100)
Imperial Ct. HA2: Harr ... 7E 40
N6 ... 6G 47
N20 ... 3F 31
NW8 ... *2C 82*
(off Prince Albert Rd.)
SE11 ... 6J 19 (5A 102)
Imperial Dr. HA2: Harr ... 7E 40
Imperial Gdns. CR4: Mitc ... 3F 155
Imperial Ho. *E3* ... *3A 86*
(off Grove Rd.)
E14 ... *7B 86*
(off Victory Pl.)
Imperial M. E6 ... 2B 88
Imperial Pde. *EC4* ... *1A 14*
(off New Bri. St.)
Imperial Pl. BR7: Chst ... 1E 160
Imperial Rd. N22 ... 7D 32
SW6 ... 1K 117
TW14: Felt ... 7G 111
Imperial Sq. SW6 ... 1K 117
Imperial War Mus. ... 2K 19 (3A 102)
Imperial Way BR7: Chst ... 3G 143
CR0: Wadd ... 6K 167
HA3: Kent ... 6E 42
Imperial Wharf SW6 ... 2A 118
Imre Cl. W12 ... 1D 98
Inca Dr. SE9 ... 7F 125
Inca Ter. N15 ... 3B 48
Inchmery Rd. SE6 ... 2D 140
Inchwood CR0: Addtn ... 4D 170
Independent Ind. Est. UB7: Yiew ... 1A 92
Independent Pl. E8 ... 5F 67
Independents Rd. SE3 ... 3H 123
Inderwick Rd. N8 ... 5K 47
Indescon Ct. E14 ... 2C 104
India Gdns. UB5: N'olt ... 7A 58
India Pl. WC2 ... 2G 13
India St. EC3 ... 1J 15 (6F 85)
India Way W12 ... 7D 80
Indigo M. E14 ... 7E 86
N16 ... 3D 66
Indus Rd. SE7 ... 7A 106
Infirmary Ct. SW3 ... 7F 17
Ingal Rd. E13 ... 4J 87
Ingate Pl. SW8 ... 1F 119
Ingatestone Rd. E12 ... 1A 70
IG8: Wfd G ... 7E 36
SE25 ... 4H 157
Ingelow Ho. *W8* ... *2K 99*
(off Holland St.)
Ingelow Rd. SW8 ... 2F 119
Ingersoll Rd. EN3: Enf W ... 1D 24
W12 ... 1D 98
Ingestre Pl. W1 ... 1B 12 (6G 83)
Ingestre Rd. E7 ... 4J 69
NW5 ... 4F 65
Ingham Cl. CR2: Sels ... 7K 169
Ingham Rd. CR2: Sels ... 7J 169
NW6 ... 4J 63
Inglebert St. EC1 ... 1J 7 (3A 84)
Ingleborough St. SW9 ... 2A 120
Ingleby Dr. HA1: Harr ... 3H 59
Ingleby Rd. IG1: Ilf ... 1F 71
N7 ... 3J 65
RM10: Dag ... 6H 73
Ingleby Way BR7: Chst ... 5E 142
SM6: Wall ... 7H 167
Ingle Cl. HA5: Pinn ... 3C 40
Ingledew Rd. SE18 ... 5H 107
Inglefield Sq. *E1* ... *1H 103*
(off Prusom St.)
Inglehurst Gdns. IG4: Ilf ... 5D 52
Inglemere Rd. CR4: Mitc ... 7D 136
SE23 ... 3K 139
Inglesham Wlk. E9 ... 6B 68
Ingleside Cl. BR3: Beck ... 7C 140
Ingleside Gro. SE3 ... 6H 105
Inglethorpe St. SW6 ... 1F 117
Ingleton Av. DA16: Well ... 5A 126
Ingleton Rd. N18 ... 6B 34
SM5: Cars ... 7C 166
Ingleton St. SW9 ... 2A 120
Ingleway N12 ... 6G 31
Inglewood CR0: Sels ... 7A 170
Inglewood Cl. E14 ... 4C 104
Inglewood Copse BR1: Brom ... 2C 160
Inglewood M. KT6: Surb ... 1G 163
Inglewood Rd. DA7: Bex ... 4K 127
NW6 ... 5J 63
Inglis Rd. CR0: Croy ... 1F 169
W5 ... 7F 79
Inglis St. SE5 ... 1B 120
Ingoldisthorpe Gro. SE15 ... 6F 103
Ingram Av. NW11 ... 7A 46
Ingram Cl. HA7: Stan ... 5H 27
SE11 ... 3H 19 (4K 101)
Ingram Ho. E3 ... 1A 86
Ingram Rd. CR7: Thor H ... 1C 156
N2 ... 4C 46
Ingram Way UB6: G'frd ... 1H 77
Ingrave Ho. RM9: Dag ... 1B 90
Ingrave Rd. RM1: Rom ... 4K 55
Ingrave St. SW11 ... 3B 118
Ingrebourne Ct. E4 ... 3J 35
Ingrebourne Ho. *BR1: Brom* ... *5F 141*
(off Brangbourne Rd.)
NW8 ... *5B 4*
(off Broadley St.)
Ingress St. W4 ... 5A 98
Inigo Jones Rd. SE7 ... 7C 106
Inigo Pl. WC2 ... 2E 12
Inkerman Rd. NW5 ... 6F 65
Inkerman Ter. *W8* ... *3J 99*
(off Allen St.)
Inks Grn. E4 ... 5K 35
Inkwell Cl. N12 ... 3F 31
Inman Rd. NW10 ... 1A 80
SW18 ... 7A 118
Inmans Row IG8: Wfd G ... 4D 36
Inner Circ. NW1 ... 2G 5 (3E 82)
Inner Pk. Rd. SW19 ... 1F 135
Inner Ring E. TW6: H'row A ... 3D 110
Inner Ring W. TW6: H'row A ... 3C 110
Inner Temple ... 2K 13
Inner Temple Hall ... 1J 13
Inner Temple La. EC4 ... 1J 13 (6A 84)
Innes Cl. SW20 ... 2G 153
Innes Gdns. SW15 ... 6D 116
Innes Yd. CR0: Croy ... 3C 168
Innis Ho. *SE17* ... *5E 102*
(off East St.)
Inniskilling Rd. E13 ... 2A 88
Innis St. SE15 ... 7E 102
Inn of Court & City Yeomanry Mus. ... *6H 7*
(off Chancery La.)
Innova Ct. CR0: Croy ... 1E 168
Innovation Cen., The *E14* ... *2E 104*
(off Marsh Wall)
Innovation Cl. HA0: Wemb ... 1E 78
Inskip Cl. E10 ... 2D 68
Inskip Rd. RM8: Dag ... 1D 72
Institute of Archaeology ... *3C 6*
(off Gordon Sq.)
Institute of Classical Studies ... *3C 6*
(off Gordon Sq.)
Institute of Contemporary Arts ... 5D 12
Institute Pl. E8 ... 5H 67
Integer Gdns. E11 ... 7F 51
Interface Ho. *TW3: Houn* ... *3E 112*
(off Staines Rd.)
International Av. TW5: Cran ... 5A 94
International Bus. Pk. E15 ... 1F 87
International Ho. *E1* ... *3K 15*
(off St Katharine's Way)
International Trad. Est. UB2: S'hall ... 3K 93
International Way TW16: Sun ... 1G 147
Inverary Pl. SE18 ... 6H 107
Inver Cl. E5 ... 2J 67
Inverclyde Gdns. RM6: Chad H ... 4C 54
(not continuous)
Inver Ct. W2 ... 6K 81
W6 ... 3C 98
Inveresk Gdns. KT4: Wor Pk ... 3C 164
Inverforth Cl. NW3 ... 2A 64
Inverforth Rd. N11 ... 5A 32
Invergarry Ho. *NW6* ... *2K 81*
(off Carlton Va.)
Inverine Rd. SE7 ... 5K 105
Invermead Cl. W6 ... 3C 98
Invermore Pl. SE18 ... 4G 107
Inverness Av. EN1: Enf ... 1K 23
Inverness Ct. SE6 ... 1H 141
Inverness Gdns. W8 ... 1K 99
Inverness M. E16 ... 1G 107
W2 ... 7K 81

Inverness Pl.—Jamaica Rd.

Inverness Pl. W2 . . . 7K 81
Inverness Rd. KT4: Wor Pk . . . 1F 165
N18 . . . 5C 34
TW3: Houn . . . 4D 112
UB2: S'hall . . . 4C 94
Inverness St. NW1 . . . 1F 83
Inverness Ter. W2 . . . 6K 81
Inverton Rd. SE15 . . . 4K 121
Invicta Cen., The IG11: Bark . . . 1A 90
Invicta Cl. BR7: Chst . . . 5E 142
TW14: Felt . . . 1H 129
Invicta Gro. UB5: N'olt . . . 3D 76
Invicta Pde. DA14: Sidc . . . 4B 144
Invicta Plaza SE1 . . . 4A 14 (1B 102)
Invicta Rd. SE3 . . . 7J 105
Invicta Sq. E3 . . . 5C 86
Inville Rd. SE17 . . . 5D 102
Inville Wlk. SE17 . . . 5D 102
Inwen Ct. SE8 . . . 5A 104
Inwood Av. TW3: Houn . . . 3G 113
Inwood Bus. Pk. TW3: Houn . . . 4F 113
Inwood Cl. CR0: Croy . . . 2A 170
Inwood Ct. *NW1* . . . *7G 65*
(off Rochester Sq.)
Inwood Rd. TW3: Houn . . . 4F 113
Inworth St. SW11 . . . 2C 118
Inworth Wlk. *N1* . . . *1C 84*
(off Popham St.)
IO Cen. SE18 . . . 3G 107
Iona Cl. SE6 . . . 7C 122
SM4: Mord . . . 7K 153
Ion Ct. E2 . . . 2G 85
Ionian Bldg. E14 . . . 7A 86
Ionian Ho. *E1* . . . *4K 85*
(off Duckett St.)
Ion Sq. E2 . . . 2G 85
Ipsden Bldgs. SE1 . . . 5K 13
Ipswich Ho. SE4 . . . 5K 121
Ipswich Rd. SW17 . . . 6E 136
Ireland Cl. E6 . . . 5D 88
Ireland Pl. N22 . . . 7D 32
Ireland Yd. *EC4* . . . *1B 14*
(off St Andrew's Hill)
Irene M. *W7* . . . *1K 95*
(off Uxbridge Rd.)
Irene Rd. BR6: Orp . . . 7K 161
SW6 . . . 1J 117
Ireton Cl. N10 . . . 7K 31
Ireton St. E3 . . . 4C 86
Iris Av. DA5: Bexl . . . 5E 126
Iris Cl. CR0: Croy . . . 1K 169
E6 . . . 5C 88
KT6: Surb . . . 7F 151
Iris Ct. *SE14* . . . *1J 121*
(off Briant St.)
Iris Cres. DA7: Bex . . . 6F 109
Iris Rd. KT19: Ewe . . . 5H 163
Iris Wlk. HA8: Edg . . . 4D 28
Iris Way E4 . . . 6G 35
Irkdale Av. EN1: Enf . . . 1A 24
Iron Bri. Cl. NW10 . . . 5A 62
Ironbridge Cl. UB2: S'hall . . . 1G 95
Iron Bri. Ho. NW1 . . . 7D 64
Iron Bri. Rd. UB7: W Dray . . . 2C 92
UB11: W Dray, Yiew . . . 2C 92
Iron Mill Pl. SW18 . . . 6K 117
Iron Mill Rd. SW18 . . . 6K 117
Ironmonger La. EC2 . . . 1D 14 (6C 84)
Ironmonger Pas. *EC1* . . . *2D 8*
(off Ironmonger Row)
Ironmonger Row EC1 . . . 2D 8 (3C 84)
Ironmonger Row Baths . . . *2D 8*
(off Ironmonger Row)
Ironmongers Pl. E14 . . . 4C 104
Ironside Cl. SE16 . . . 2K 103
Ironside Ho. E9 . . . 4A 68
Irons Way RM5: Col R . . . 1J 55
Irvine Av. HA3: Kent . . . 3A 42
Irvine Cl. N20 . . . 2H 31
Irvine Ho. *N7* . . . *6K 65*
(off Caledonian Rd.)
Irvine Way BR6: Orp . . . 7K 161
Irving Av. UB5: N'olt . . . 1B 76
Irving Gro. SW9 . . . 2K 119
Irving Ho. *SE17* . . . *5B 102*
(off Doddington Gro.)
Irving Mans. *W14* . . . *6G 99*
(off Queen's Club Gdns.)
Irving M. N1 . . . 6C 66
Irving Rd. W14 . . . 3F 99
Irving St. WC2 . . . 3D 12 (7H 83)
Irving Way NW9 . . . 5C 44
Irwell Ct. *W7* . . . *6H 77*
(off Hobbayne Rd.)
Irwell Est. SE16 . . . 3J 103
Irwin Av. SE18 . . . 7J 107
Irwin Cl. UB10: Ick . . . 3C 56
Irwin Gdns. NW10 . . . 1D 80
Isaac Way *SE1* . . . *6D 14*
(off Lant St.)
Isabel Hill Cl. TW12: Hamp . . . 2F 149
Isabella Cl. N14 . . . 7B 22
Isabella Dr. BR6: Farnb . . . 4G 173
Isabella Ho. SE11 . . . 5K 19
W6 . . . *5E 98*
(off Queen Caroline St.)
Isabella Plantation . . . 4H 133
Isabella Rd. E9 . . . 5J 67
Isabella St. SE1 . . . 5A 14 (1B 102)
Isabel St. SW9 . . . 1K 119
Isambard M. E14 . . . 3E 104
Isambard Pl. SE16 . . . 1J 103
Isard Ho. BR2: Hayes . . . 1K 171
Isel Way SE22 . . . 5E 120
Isham Rd. SW16 . . . 2J 155
Isis Cl. HA4: Ruis . . . 6E 38
SW15 . . . 4E 116
Isis Ct. W4 . . . 7H 97
Isis Ho. N18 . . . 6A 34
NW8 . . . *4B 4*
(off Church St. Est.)
Isis Reach DA17: Belv . . . 1H 109
Isis St. SW18 . . . 2A 136
Island, The KT7: T Ditt . . . 6A 150
Island Farm Av. KT8: W Mole . . . 5D 148
Island Farm Rd. KT8: W Mole . . . 5D 148
Island Rd. CR4: Mitc . . . 7D 136
Island Row E14 . . . 6B 86
Isla Rd. SE18 . . . 6G 107
Islay Gdns. TW4: Houn . . . 5B 112
Islay Wlk. *N1* . . . *6C 66*
(off Douglas Rd. Sth.)
Isleden Ho. *N1* . . . *1C 84*
(off Prebend St.)
Isledon Rd. N7 . . . 3A 66
ISLEDON VILLAGE . . . 3A 66
Islehurst Cl. BR7: Chst . . . 1E 160
ISLEWORTH . . . 3A 114
Isleworth Bus. Complex TW7: Isle . . . 2K 113
Isleworth Prom. TW1: Twick . . . 4B 114
Isley Ct. SW8 . . . 2G 119
ISLINGTON . . . 7B 66
Islington Crematorium N2 . . . 1D 46
Islington Grn. N1 . . . 1B 84
Islington High St. N1 . . . 2A 84
(not continuous)
Islington Mus. . . . 7B 66
Islington Pk. M. N1 . . . 7B 66
Islington Pk. St. N1 . . . 7A 66
Islington Tennis Cen. . . . 6J 65
Islip Gdns. HA8: Edg . . . 7E 28
UB5: N'olt . . . 7C 58
Islip Mnr. Rd. UB5: N'olt . . . 7C 58
Islip St. NW5 . . . 5G 65
Ismailia Rd. E7 . . . 7K 69
Isobel Ho. HA1: Harr . . . 5K 41
Isom Cl. E13 . . . 3K 87
Itaska Cotts. WD23: Bushy . . . 1D 26
Ivanhoe Cl. UB8: Cowl . . . 5A 74
Ivanhoe Dr. HA3: Kent . . . 3A 42
Ivanhoe Ho. *E3* . . . *2A 86*
(off Grove Rd.)
Ivanhoe Rd. SE5 . . . 3F 121
TW4: Houn . . . 3B 112
Ivatt Pl. W14 . . . 5H 99
Ivatt Way N17 . . . 3B 48
Iveagh Av. NW10 . . . 2G 79
Iveagh Cl. E9 . . . 1K 85
HA6: Nwood . . . 1D 38
NW10 . . . 2G 79
Iveagh Ct. BR3: Beck . . . 3E 158
E1 . . . 1J 15
Iveagh Ho. SW9 . . . 2B 120
SW10 . . . *7A 100*
(off King's Rd.)
Iveagh Ter. *NW10* . . . *2G 79*
(off Iveagh Av.)
Ivedon Rd. DA16: Well . . . 2C 126
Ive Farm Cl. E10 . . . 2C 68
Ive Farm La. E10 . . . 2C 68
Iveley Rd. SW4 . . . 2G 119
Ivere Dr.
EN5: New Bar . . . 6E 20
Iverhurst Cl. DA6: Bex . . . 5D 126
Iverna Ct. W8 . . . 3J 99
Iverna Gdns.
TW14: Felt . . . 5F 111
W8 . . . 3J 99
Iverson Rd. NW6 . . . 6H 63
Ivers Way CR0: New Ad . . . 7D 170
Ives Rd. E16 . . . 5G 87
Ives St. SW3 . . . 3D 16 (4C 100)
Ivestor Ter. SE23 . . . 7J 121
Ivimey St. E2 . . . 3G 85
Ivinghoe Cl. EN1: Enf . . . 1K 23
Ivinghoe Ho. N7 . . . 5H 65
Ivinghoe Rd. RM8: Dag . . . 5B 72
Ivor Ct. N8 . . . 6J 47
NW1 . . . *3E 4*
(off Gloucester Pl.)
Ivor Gro. SE9 . . . 1F 143
Ivories, The *N1* . . . *7C 66*
(off Northampton St.)
Ivor Pl. NW1 . . . 4E 4 (4D 82)
Ivor St. NW1 . . . 7G 65
Ivory Ct. TW13: Felt . . . 2J 129
Ivorydown BR1: Brom . . . 4J 141
Ivory Ho. E1 . . . 3K 15 (1F 103)
Ivory Sq. SW11 . . . 3A 118
Ivybridge Cl. TW1: Twick . . . 7A 114
UB8: Uxb . . . 3A 74
Ivybridge Ct. *BR7: Chst* . . . *1E 160*
(off Old Hill)
NW1 . . . *7F 65*
(off Lewis St.)
Ivybridge La. WC2 . . . 3F 13 (7J 83)
Ivy Bri. Retail Pk. TW7: Isle . . . 5K 113
Ivychurch Cl. SE20 . . . 7J 139
Ivychurch La. SE17 . . . 5F 103
Ivy Cl. HA2: Harr . . . 4D 58
HA5: Eastc . . . 7A 40
TW16: Sun . . . 2A 148
Ivy Cotts. E14 . . . 7E 86
UB10: Hil . . . 3C 74
Ivy Ct. *SE16* . . . *5G 103*
(off Argyle Way)
Ivy Cres. W4 . . . 4J 97
Ivydale Rd. SE15 . . . 3K 121
SM5: Cars . . . 2D 166
Ivyday Gro. SW16 . . . 3K 137
Ivydene KT8: W Mole . . . 5D 148
Ivydene Cl. SM1: Sutt . . . 4A 166
Ivy Gdns. CR4: Mitc . . . 3H 155
N8 . . . 6J 47
Ivyhouse Rd. RM9: Dag . . . 6D 72
UB10: Ick . . . 3D 56
Ivy La. TW4: Houn . . . 4D 112
Ivymount Rd. SE27 . . . 3A 138
Ivy Rd. E16 . . . 6J 87
E17 . . . 6C 50
KT6: Surb . . . 1G 163
N14 . . . 7B 22
NW2 . . . 4E 62
Ivy Rd. SE4 . . . 4B 122
SW17 . . . 5C 136
TW3: Houn . . . 4F 113
Ivy St. N1 . . . 2E 84
Ivy Wlk. HA6: Nwood . . . 1G 39
RM9: Dag . . . 6E 72
Ixworth Pl. SW3 . . . 5C 16 (5C 100)
Izane Rd. DA6: Bex . . . 4F 127

J

Jacana Ct. *E1* . . . *3K 15*
(off Star Pl.)
Jacaranda Cl. KT3: N Mald . . . 3A 152
Jacaranda Gro. E8 . . . 7F 67
Jackass La. BR2: Kes . . . 5K 171
Jack Barnett Way N22 . . . 2K 47
Jack Clow Rd. E15 . . . 2G 87
Jack Cook Ho. IG11: Bark . . . 7F 71
Jack Cornwell St. E12 . . . 4E 70
Jack Dash Ho. *E14* . . . *2E 104*
(off Lawn Ho. Cl.)
Jack Dash Way E6 . . . 4C 88
Jackets La. HA6: Nwood . . . 1D 38
Jack Goodchild Way
KT1: King T . . . 3H 151
Jacklin Grn. IG8: Wfd G . . . 4D 36
Jackman Ho. *E1* . . . *1H 103*
(off Watts St.)
Jackman M. NW10 . . . 3A 62
Jackman St. E8 . . . 1H 85
Jackson Cl. E9 . . . 7J 67
UB10: Uxb . . . 7A 56
Jackson Ct. E7 . . . 6K 69
Jackson Ho. N11 . . . 5B 32
Jackson Rd. BR2: Brom . . . 2D 172
EN4: E Barn . . . 6H 21
IG11: Bark . . . 1H 89
N7 . . . 4K 65
UB10: Uxb . . . 7A 56
Jacksons La. N6 . . . 7E 46
Jacksons Lane Theatre . . . *6F 47*
(off Jacksons La.)
Jacksons Pl. CR0: Croy . . . 1D 168
Jackson St. SE18 . . . 6E 106
Jackson's Way CR0: Croy . . . 3C 170
Jackson Way UB2: S'hall . . . 2F 95
Jacks Pl. *E1* . . . *5J 9*
(off Corbet Pl.)
Jack Walker Ct. N5 . . . 4B 66
Jacob Ho. *DA18: Erith* . . . *2D 108*
(off Kale Rd.)
Jacobin Lodge N7 . . . 5J 65
Jacobs Cl. RM10: Dag . . . 4H 73
Jacobs Ho. *E13* . . . *3A 88*
(off New City Rd.)
Jacob St. SE1 . . . 6K 15 (2G 103)
Jacob's Well M. W1 . . . 6H 5 (5E 82)
Jacotts Ho. *W10* . . . *4E 80*
(off Sutton Way)
Jacqueline Cl. UB5: N'olt . . . 1C 76
Jacqueline Creft Ter. *N6* . . . *6E 46*
(off Grange Rd.)
Jacqueline Vs. *E17* . . . *5E 50*
(off Shernhall St.)
Jade Cl. E16 . . . 6B 88
NW2 . . . 7F 45
RM8: Dag . . . 1C 72
Jade Ter. NW6 . . . 7A 64
Jaffe Rd. IG1: Ilf . . . 1H 71
Jaffray Pl. SE27 . . . 4B 138
Jaffray Rd. BR2: Brom . . . 4B 160
Jaggard Way SW12 . . . 7D 118
Jagger Ho. *SW11* . . . *1D 118*
(off Rosenau Rd.)
Jago Cl. SE18 . . . 6G 107
Jago Wlk. SE5 . . . 7D 102
Jamaica Rd. CR7: Thor H . . . 6B 156
SE1 . . . 7K 15 (2F 103)
SE16 . . . 7K 15 (2F 103)

Jamaica St.—Joan St.

Jamaica St. E1 6J 85
James Allens School Swimming Pool 5E 120
James Anderson Ct. *E2* *2E 84*
(off Kingsland Rd.)
James Av. NW2 5E 62
RM8: Dag 1F 73
James Bedford Cl. HA5: Pinn 2A 40
James Boswell Cl. SW16 4K 137
James Brine Ho. *E2* *1K 9*
(off Ravenscroft St.)
James Campbell Ho. *E2* *2J 85*
(off Old Ford Rd.)
James Clavell Sq. *SE18* *3F 107*
(off Cartridge St.)
James Cl. E13 2J 87
NW11 6G 45
James Collins Cl. W9 4H 81
James Ct. HA6: Nwood 1H 39
N1 *1C 84*
(off Raynor Pl.)
NW9 2A 44
UB5: N'olt *2C 76*
(off Church Rd.)
James Docherty Ho. *E2* *2H 85*
(off Patriot Sq.)
James Dudson Ct. NW10 7J 61
James Est. CR4: Mitc 2D 154
James Gdns. N22 7G 33
James Hammett Ho. *E2* *1K 9*
(off Ravenscroft St.)
James Ho. *E1* *4A 86*
(off Solebay St.)
SE16 *2K 103*
(off Wolfe Cres.)
James Jeff Way SM6: Wall 7H 167
James Joyce Wlk. SE24 4B 120
James La. E10 7E 50
E11 7F 51
James Lind Ho. *SE8* *4B 104*
(off Grove St.)
James Middleton Ho. *E2* *3H 85*
(off Middleton St.)
James Newman Ct. SE9 3E 142
Jameson Cl. W3 2J 97
Jameson Ct. *E2* *2J 85*
(off Russia La.)
Jameson Ho. *SE11* *5G 19*
(off Glasshouse Wlk.)
Jameson Lodge N6 6G 47
Jameson St. W8 1J 99
James Pl. N17 1F 49
James's Cotts. TW9: Kew 7G 97
James Stewart Ho. NW6 7H 63
James St. EN1: Enf 5A 24
IG11: Bark 7G 71
TW3: Houn 3H 113
W1 1H 11 (6E 82)
WC2 1F 13 (7J 83)
James Stroud Ho. *SE17* *5C 102*
(off Bronti Cl.)
James Ter. *SW14* *3K 115*
(off Church Path)
James Terry Ct. *CR2: S Croy* *5C 168*
(off Warham Rd.)
Jamestown Rd. NW1 1F 83
Jamestown Way E14 7F 87
James Yd. E4 6A 36
Jamieson Ho. TW4: Houn 6D 112
Jamilah Ho. *E16* *7E 88*
(off University Way)
Jamuna Cl. E14 5A 86
Jane Austen Hall *E16* *1K 105*
(off Wesley Av.)
Jane Austen Ho. *SW1* *6A 18*
(off Churchill Gdns.)
Jane Seymour Ct. SE9 7H 125
Jane St. E1 6H 85
Janet Adegoke Leisure Cen. 7C 80
Janet St. E14 3C 104
Janeway Pl. SE16 2H 103
Janeway St. SE16 2G 103
Janice M. IG1: Ilf 2F 71
Jansen Wlk. SW11 3B 118
Janson Cl. E15 5G 69
NW10 3A 62
Janson Rd. E15 5G 69
Jansons Rd. N15 3E 48
Japan Cres. N4 1K 65
Japan Rd. RM6: Chad H 6D 54
Jardine Rd. E1 7K 85
Jarman Ho. *E1* *5J 85*
(off Jubilee St.)
SE16 *4K 103*
(off Hawkstone Rd.)
Jarrett Cl. SW2 1B 138
Jarrow Cl. SM4: Mord 5K 153
Jarrow Rd. N17 4H 49
RM6: Chad H 6C 54
SE16 4J 103
Jarrow Way E9 4B 68
Jarvis Cl. EN5: Barn 5A 20
IG11: Bark 1H 89
Jarvis Rd. CR2: S Croy 6D 168
SE22 4E 120
Jashoda Ho. *SE18* *5E 106*
(off Connaught M.)
Jasmin Cl. HA6: Nwood 1H 39
Jasmin Ct. SE12 6H 123
Jasmine Cl. BR6: Farnb 2F 173
IG1: Ilf 5F 71
UB1: S'hall 7C 76
Jasmine Ct. SW19 5J 135
Jasmine Gdns. CR0: Croy 3D 170
HA2: Harr 2E 58
Jasmine Gro. SE20 1H 157
Jasmine Rd. RM7: Rush G 2K 73
Jasmine Ter. UB7: W Dray 2C 92
Jasmine Way KT8: E Mos 4J 149
Jasmin Lodge *SE16* *5H 103*
(off Sherwood Gdns.)
Jasmin Rd. KT19: Ewe 5H 163
Jason Ct. *SW9* *1A 120*
(off Southey Rd.)
W1 7H 5
Jason Wlk. SE9 4E 142
Jasper Cl. EN3: Enf W 1D 24
Jasper Pas. SE19 6F 139
Jasper Rd. E16 6B 88
SE19 5F 139
Jasper Wlk. N1 3D 84
Java Wharf *SE1* *6K 15*
(off Shad Thames)
Javelin Way UB5: N'olt 3B 76
Jaycroft EN2: Enf 1F 23
Jay Gdns. BR7: Chst 4D 142
Jay M. SW7 7A 10 (2A 100)
Jazzfern Ter. HA0: Wemb 5A 60
Jean Batten Cl. SM6: Wall 7K 167
Jean Darling Ho. *SW10* *6B 100*
(off Milman's St.)
Jean Ho. SW17 5C 136
Jean Pardies Ho. *E1* *5J 85*
(off Jubilee St.)
Jebb Av. SW2 6J 119
(not continuous)
Jebb St. E3 2C 86
Jedburgh Rd. E13 3A 88
Jedburgh St. SW11 4E 118
Jeddo M. W12 2B 98
Jeddo Rd. W12 2B 98
Jefferson Bldg. E14 2C 104
Jefferson Cl. IG2: Ilf 5F 53
W13 3B 96
Jefferson Wlk. SE18 6E 106
Jeffrey Row SE12 5K 123
Jeffrey's Pl. NW1 7G 65
Jeffreys Rd. EN3: Brim 4F 25
SW4 2J 119
Jeffrey's St. NW1 7G 65
Jeffreys Walk SW4 2J 119
Jeffries Ho. NW10 7K 61
Jeffs Cl. TW12: Hamp 6F 131
Jeffs Rd. SM1: Sutt 4H 165
Jeger Av. E2 1F 85
Jeken Rd. SE9 4A 124
Jelf Rd. SW2 5A 120
Jellicoe Gdns.
HA7: Stan 6E 26
Jellicoe Ho. *E2* *2G 85*
(off Ropley St.)
NW1 4F 83
Jellicoe Rd. E13 4J 87
N17 7J 33
Jemmett Cl. KT2: King T 1H 151
Jemotts Ct. *SE14* *6K 103*
(off Myers La.)
Jem Paterson Ct.
HA1: Harr 4J 59
Jengar Cl. SM1: Sutt 4K 165
Jenkins La. IG11: Bark 2G 89
Jenkinson Ho. *E2* *3K 85*
(off Usk St.)
Jenkins Rd. E13 4K 87
Jenner Av. W3 5K 79
Jenner Cl. DA14: Sidc 4A 144
Jenner Ho. *SE3* *6G 105*
(off Restell Cl.)
WC1 *3F 7*
(off Hunter St.)
Jenner Pl. SW13 6D 98
Jenner Rd. N16 3F 67
Jennett Rd. CR0: Wadd 3A 168
Jennifer Ho. *SE11* *4K 19*
(off Reedworth St.)
Jennifer Rd. BR1: Brom 3H 141
Jenningsbury Ho. *SW3* *5D 16*
(off Cale St.)
Jennings Cl. KT6: Surb 7C 150
Jennings Ho. *SE10* *5F 105*
(off Old Woolwich Rd.)
Jennings Rd. SE22 6F 121
Jennings Way EN5: Barn 3A 20
Jenningtree Way DA17: Belv 2J 109
Jenny Hammond Cl. E11 3H 69
Jenson Way SE19 7F 139
Jenton Av. DA7: Bex 1E 126
Jephson Ct. SW4 2J 119
Jephson Ho. *SE17* *6B 102*
(off Doddington Gro.)
Jephson Rd. E7 7A 70
Jephson St. SE5 1D 120
Jephtha Rd. SW18 6J 117
Jeppesen Ct. TW19: Stanw 6A 110
Jeppos La. CR4: Mitc 4D 154
Jepson Ho. *SW6* *1K 117*
(off Pearscroft Rd.)
Jerdan Pl. SW6 7J 99
Jeremiah St. E14 6D 86
Jeremy Bentham Ho. *E2* *3G 85*
(off Mansford St.)
Jeremy's Grn. N18 4C 34
Jermyn St. SW1 4A 12 (1G 101)
Jermyn Street Theatre *3C 12*
(off Jermyn St.)
Jerningham Av. IG5: Ilf 2F 53
Jerningham Ct. SE14 1A 122
Jerningham Rd. SE14 2A 122
Jerome Cres. NW8 3C 4 (4C 82)
Jerome Ho. *KT1: Hamp W* *2D 150*
(off Old Bri. St.)
NW1 *5D 4*
(off Lisson Gro.)
SW7 *3A 16*
(off Glendower Pl.)
Jerome Pl. *KT1: King T* *2D 150*
(off Wadbrook St.)
Jerome St. E1 5J 9 (4F 85)
Jerome Twr. W3 2H 97
Jerrard St. SE13 3D 122
Jerrold St. N1 1H 9 (2E 84)
Jersey Av. HA7: Stan 2B 42
Jersey Dr. BR5: Pet W 6H 161
Jersey Ho. *EN3: Enf W* *1E 24*
(off Eastfield Rd.)
N1 6C 66
Jersey Rd. E11 1F 69
E16 6A 88
IG1: Ilf 4F 71
N1 6C 66
SW17 6F 137
TW3: Houn 1F 113
TW5: Hest 1F 113
TW7: Isle 7H 95
W7 2A 96
Jersey St. E2 3H 85
Jerusalem Pas. EC1 4A 8 (4B 84)
Jervis Bay Ho. *E14* *6F 87*
(off Blair St.)
Jervis Ct. RM10: Dag 6H 73
SE10 *1E 122*
(off Blissett St.)
W1 1K 11
Jerviston Gdns. SW16 6A 138
Jerwood Space Art Gallery 6C 14
Jesmond Av. HA9: Wemb 6F 61
Jesmond Cl. CR4: Mitc 3F 155
Jesmond Rd. CR0: Croy 7F 157
Jesmond Way HA7: Stan 5K 27
Jessam Av. E5 1H 67
Jessamine Rd. W7 1K 95
Jessel Ho. *SW1* *3D 18*
(off Page St.)
WC1 *2E 6*
(off Judd St.)
Jessel Mans. *W14* *6G 99*
(off Queen's Club Gdns.)
Jesse Rd. E10 1E 68
Jessett Cl. DA8: Erith 4K 109
Jessica Rd. SW18 6A 118
Jessie Blythe La. N19 7J 47
Jessie Duffett Ho. *SE5* *7C 102*
(off Pitman St.)
Jessie Wood Ct. *SW9* *7A 102*
(off Caldwell St.)
Jessiman Ter. TW17: Shep 5C 146
Jesson Ho. *SE17* *4D 102*
(off Orb St.)
Jessop Av. UB2: S'hall 4D 94
Jessop Ct. N1 2B 84
Jessop Rd. SE24 4B 120
Jessop Sq. *E14* *1C 104*
(off Heron Quay)
Jessops Way CR0: Bedd 6G 155
Jessup Cl. SE18 4G 107
Jetstar Way UB5: N'olt 3C 76
Jevington Way SE12 1K 141
Jewel House *3J 15*
(in Tower of London, The)
Jewel Rd. E17 3C 50
Jewel Tower *1E 18*
(off College M.)
Jewish Mus.
Camden Town 1F 83
Finchley 2K 45
Jewry St. EC3 1J 15 (6F 85)
Jew's Row SW18 4K 117
Jews' Wlk. SE26 4H 139
Jeymer Av. NW2 5D 62
Jeymer Dr. UB6: G'frd 1F 77
(not continuous)
Jeypore Pas. SW18 6A 118
Jeypore Rd. SW18 7A 118
Jillian Cl. TW12: Hamp 7E 130
Jim Bradley Cl. SE18 4E 106
Jim Griffiths Ho. *SW6* *6H 99*
(off Clem Attlee Ct.)
Joan Bicknell Cen., The 2B 136
Joan Cres. SE9 7B 124
Joan Gdns. RM8: Dag 2E 72
Joanna Ho. *W6* *5E 98*
(off Queen Caroline St.)
Joan Rd. RM8: Dag 2E 72
Joan St. SE1 5A 14 (1B 102)

298 A-Z London

Jocelin Ho.—Juniper Cres.

Jocelin Ho. *N1* 1K **83**
(off Barnsbury Est.)
Jocelyn Rd. TW9: Rich 3E **114**
Jocelyn St. SE15 1G **121**
Jockey's Flds. WC1 5H **7** (5K **83**)
Jodane St. SE8 4B **104**
Jodrell Cl. TW7: Isle 1A **114**
Jodrell Rd. E3 1B **86**
Joe Hunte Ct. SE27 5B **138**
Joel St. HA5: Eastc 3J **39**
HA6: Nwood 2J **39**
Johanna St. SE1 7J **13** (2A **102**)
John Adams Ct. N9 2A **34**
John Adam St. WC2 3F **13** (7J **83**)
John Aird Ct. W2 5A **4**
(not continuous)
John Archer Way SW18 6B **118**
John Ashby Cl. SW2 6J **119**
John Austin Cl. KT2: King T 1F **151**
John Baird Ct. SE26 4J **139**
John Barker Ct. NW6 7G **63**
John Barnes Wlk. E15 6H **69**
John Betts' Ho. W12 3B **98**
John Bradshaw Rd. N14 1C **32**
John Brent Ho. *SE8* 4K **103**
(off Bush Rd.)
John Buck Ho. NW10 1B **80**
John Burns Dr. IG11: Bark 7J **71**
John Campbell Rd. N16 5E **66**
John Carpenter St.
EC4 2A **14** (7B **84**)
John Cartwright Ho. *E2* 3H **85**
(off Old Bethnal Grn. Rd.)
John Drinkwater Cl. E11 7H **51**
John Fearon Wlk. *W10* 3G **81**
(off Dart St.)
John Felton Rd. SE16 2G **103**
John Fielden Ho. *E2* 3H **85**
(off Canrobert St.)
John Fisher St. E1 2K **15** (7G **85**)
John Goddard Way TW13: Felt 2K **129**
John Gooch Dr. EN2: Enf 1G **23**
John Harrison Way SE10 3H **105**
John Horner M. N1 2C **84**
John Islip St. SW1 5D **18** (4H **101**)
John Kane Sports Hall 7K **95**
John Kaye Ct. TW17: Shep 5C **146**
John Keats Ho. N22 7E **32**
John Kennedy Ct. *N1* 6D **66**
(off Newington Grn. Rd.)
John Kennedy Ho. *SE16* 4K **103**
(off Rotherhithe Old Rd.)
John Kirk Ho. *E6* 6E **88**
(off Pearl Cl.)
John Knight Lodge SW6 7J **99**
John Lamb Ct. HA3: W'stone 1J **41**
John McDonald Ho. *E14* 3E **104**
(off Glengall Gro.)
John McKenna Wlk. SE16 3G **103**
John Masefield Ho. *N15* 6D **48**
(off Fladbury Rd.)
John Maurice Cl. SE17 4D **102**
John Newton Ct. DA16: Well 3B **126**
John Orwell Sports Cen. 1H **103**
John Parker Cl. RM10: Dag 7H **73**
John Parker Sq. SW11 3B **118**
John Parry Ct. *N1* 2E **84**
(off Hare Wlk.)
John Penn Ho. *SE14* 7B **104**
(off Amersham Va.)
John Penn St. SE13 1D **122**
John Penrose Sports Cen. 1A **38**
John Perrin Pl. HA3: Kent 7E **42**
John Prince's St. W1 7K **5** (6F **83**)
John Pritchard Ho. *E1* 4G **85**
(off Buxton St.)
John Ratcliffe Ho. *NW6* 3J **81**
(off Chippenham Gdns.)
John Rennie Wlk. E1 7H **85**
John Roll Way SE16 3G **103**
John Ruskin St. SE5 7B **102**
John's Av. NW4 4E **44**
John's Cl. TW15: Ashf 4E **128**
John Scurr Ho. *E14* 6A **86**
(off Ratcliffe La.)
John Silkin La. SE8 5K **103**
John's La. SM4: Mord 5A **154**
John's M. WC1 4H **7** (4K **83**)
John Smith Av. SW6 7H **99**
John Smith M. E14 7F **87**
Johnson Cl. E8 1G **85**
Johnson Ho. *E2* 3G **85**
(off Roberta St.)
NW1 2G **83**
(off Cranleigh St.)
NW3 7D **64**
(off Adelaide Rd.)
SW1 4H **17**
(off Cundy St.)
SW8 7H **101**
(off Wandsworth Rd.)
Johnson Lodge *W9* 5J **81**
(off Admiral Wlk.)
Johnson Mans. *W14* 6G **99**
(off Queen's Club Gdns.)
Johnson Rd. BR2: Brom 5B **160**
CR0: Croy 7D **156**
NW10 1K **79**
TW5: Hest 7A **94**
Johnsons Cl. SM5: Cars 2D **166**
Johnson's Ct. EC4 6A **84**
Johnsons Dr. TW12: Hamp 1G **149**
Johnsons Ind. Est. UB3: Hayes 2H **93**
Johnson's Pl. SW1 6A **18** (5G **101**)
Johnson St. E1 7J **85**
UB2: S'hall 3A **94**
Johnsons Way NW10 4H **79**
John Spencer Sq. N1 6B **66**
John's Pl. E1 6H **85**
John's Ter. CR0: Croy 1E **168**
Johnston Cl. SW9 1K **119**
Johnstone Ho. *SE13* 3F **123**
(off Belmont Hill)
Johnstone Rd. E6 3D **88**
Johnston Rd. IG8: Wfd G 6D **36**
Johnston Ter. NW2 3F **63**
John Strachey Ho. *SW6* 6H **99**
(off Clem Attlee Ct.)
John St. E15 1H **87**
EN1: Enf 5A **24**
SE25 4G **157**
TW3: Houn 2C **112**
WC1 4H **7** (4K **83**)
John Strype Ct. E10 1D **68**
John Trundle Ct. EC2 5C **8**
John Trundle Highwalk *EC2* 5C **8**
(off Beech St.)
John Tucker Ho. *E14* 3C **104**
(off Mellish St.)
John Watkin Cl. KT19: Eps 7H **163**
John Wesley Ct. TW1: Twick 1A **132**
John Wesley Highwalk *EC2* 6C **8**
(off Barbican)
John Wheatley Ho. *SW6* 6H **99**
(off Clem Attlee Ct.)
John Williams Cl. KT2: King T 1D **150**
SE14 6K **103**
John Wilson St. SE18 3E **106**
John Woolley Cl. SE13 4G **123**
Joiners Arms Yd. SE5 1D **120**
Joiners Pl. N5 4D **66**
Joiner St. SE1 5F **15** (1D **102**)
Joiners Yd. *N1* 1F **7**
(off Caledonia St.)
Joint Rd. N2 1C **46**
Jollys La. HA2: Harr 1H **59**
UB4: Yead 5B **76**
Jonathan St. SE11 5G **19** (5K **101**)
Jones Ho. *E14* 6F **87**
(off Blair St.)
Jones M. SW15 4G **117**
Jones Rd. E13 4K **87**
Jones St. W1 3J **11** (7F **83**)
Jones Wlk. TW10: Rich 6F **115**
Jonquil Gdns.
TW12: Hamp 6E **130**
Jonson Cl. CR4: Mitc 4F **155**
UB4: Hayes 5J **75**
Jonson Ho. *SE1* 3D **102**
(off Burbage Cl.)
Jordan Cl. HA2: Harr 3D **58**
RM10: Dag 4H **73**
Jordan Ct. SW15 4F **117**
Jordan Ho. *N1* 1D **84**
(off Colville Est.)
SE4 4K **121**
(off St Norbert Rd.)
Jordan Rd. UB6: G'frd 1B **78**
Jordans Cl. TW7: Isle 1J **113**
Jordans Ho. NW8 3B **4**
Jordans M. TW2: Twick 2J **131**
Joscoyne Ho. *E1* 6H **85**
(off Philpot St.)
Joseph Av. W3 6K **79**
Joseph Conrad Ho. *SW1* 4B **18**
(off Tachbrook St.)
Joseph Ct. *N16* 6E **48**
(off Amhurst Pk.)
Joseph Hardcastle Cl. SE14 7K **103**
Josephine Av. SW2 5K **119**
Joseph Irwin Ho. *E14* 7B **86**
(off Gill St.)
Joseph Lister Ct. E7 7J **69**
Joseph Powell Cl. SW12 6G **119**
Joseph Priestley Ho. *E2* 3H **85**
(off Canrobert St.)
Joseph Ray Rd. E11 2G **69**
Joseph St. E3 4B **86**
Joseph Trotter Cl. EC1 2K **7**
Joshua Cl. CR2: S Croy 7B **168**
Joshua St. E14 6E **86**
Joslings Cl. W12 7C **80**
Joslyn Cl. EN3: Enf L 1H **25**
Josseline Ct. *E3* 2A **86**
(off Ford St.)
Joubert St. SW11 2D **118**
Jowett St. SE15 7F **103**
Jowitt Ho. *E2* 3K **85**
(off Morpeth St.)
Joyce Av. N18 5A **34**
Joyce Butler Ho. N22 1K **47**
Joyce Dawson Way SE28 7A **90**
Joyce Latimore Ct. *N9* 3C **34**
(off Colthurst Dr.)
Joyce Page Cl. SE7 6B **106**
Joyce Wlk. SW2 6A **120**
JOYDENS WOOD 4K **145**
Joydens Wood (Nature Reserve) 4H **145**
Joydens Wood Rd. DA5: Bexl 4K **145**
Joydon Dr. RM6: Chad H 6B **54**
Joyners Cl. RM9: Dag 4F **73**
Joystone Ct. *EN4: E Barn* 4H **21**
(off Park Rd.)
Jubb Powell Ho. N15 6E **48**
Jubilee, The SE10 7D **104**
Jubilee Av. E4 6K **35**
RM7: Rom 5H **55**
TW2: Whit 1G **131**
Jubilee Bldgs. NW8 1B **82**
Jubilee Cl. HA5: Pinn 2A **40**
KT1: Hamp W 1C **150**
NW9 6K **43**
RM7: Rom 5H **55**
Jubilee Country Pk. 4F **161**
Jubilee Ct. BR4: W W'ck 1E **170**
HA3: Kent 7E **42**
N10 3E **46**
TW3: Houn 3F **113**
(off Bristow Rd.)
Jubilee Cres. E14 3E **104**
N9 1B **34**
Jubilee Dr. HA4: Ruis 4B **58**
Jubilee Gdns. UB1: S'hall 5E **76**
Jubilee Hall Sports Cen. 2F **13**
(off Tavistock St.)
Jubilee Ho. HA7: Stan 5J **27**
SE11 4K **19**
(off Reedworth St.)
WC1 3G **7**
Jubilee La. W5 6E **78**
Jubilee Mans. *E1* 6J **85**
(off Jubilee St.)
Jubilee Mkt. IG8: Wfd G 6F **37**
WC2 2F **13**
Jubilee Pde. IG8: Wfd G 6F **37**
Jubilee Pl. SW3 5D **16** (5C **100**)
Jubilee Pl. Shop. Mall
E14 1D **104**
(off Bank St.)
Jubilee Rd. SM3: Cheam 7F **165**
UB6: G'frd 1B **78**
Jubilee Sports Cen. & Baths 3H **81**
Jubilee St. E1 6J **85**
Jubilee Vs. KT10: Esh 7H **149**
Jubilee Walkway SE1 3B **14** (7B **84**)
Jubilee Way DA14: Sidc 2A **144**
KT9: Chess 4G **163**
SW19 1K **153**
TW14: Felt 1J **129**
Jubilee Yd. SE1 6J **15**
Judd St. WC1 2E **6** (3J **83**)
Jude St. E16 6H **87**
Judge Heath La. UB3: Hayes 6E **74**
Judges Wlk. NW3 3A **64**
Juer Ho. *SW11* 7C **100**
(off Juer St.)
Juer St. SW11 7C **100**
Jules Thorn Av. EN1: Enf 4B **24**
Julia Ct. E17 5D **50**
Julia Gdns. IG11: Bark 2D **90**
Julia Garfield M. E16 1K **105**
(not continuous)
Juliana Cl. N2 2A **46**
Julian Av. W3 7H **79**
Julian Cl. EN5: New Bar 3E **20**
Julian Hill HA1: Harr 2J **59**
Julian Ho. SE21 4E **138**
Julian Pl. E14 5D **104**
Julian Tayler Path SE23 2H **139**
Julia St. NW5 4E **64**
Julien Rd. W5 3C **96**
Juliet Ho. *N1* 2E **84**
(off Arden Est.)
Juliette Rd. E13 2J **87**
Julius Nyerere Cl. *N1* 1K **83**
(off Copenhagen St.)
Junction App. SE13 3E **122**
SW11 3C **118**
Junction Av. NW10 4E **80**
Junction M. W2 7C **4** (6C **82**)
Junction Pl. W2 7B **4**
Junction Rd. CR2: S Croy 5D **168**
E13 2K **87**
HA1: Harr 6J **41**
N9 1B **34**
N17 3G **49**
N19 4G **65**
TW8: Bford 4C **96**
TW15: Ashf 5E **128**
W5 4C **96**
Junction Rd. E. RM6: Chad H 7E **54**
Junction Rd. W. RM6: Chad H 7E **54**
Juniper Cl. EN5: Barn 5A **20**
HA9: Wemb 5G **61**
KT9: Chess 5F **163**
Juniper Ct. HA3: Hrw W 1K **41**
HA6: Nwood 1J **39**
KT8: W Mole 4F **149**
RM6: Chad H 6B **54**
TW3: Houn 4F **113**
(off Grove Rd.)
W8 3K **99**
(off St Mary's Pl.)
Juniper Cres. NW1 7E **64**

Juniper Gdns.—Kenbury Mans.

Juniper Gdns. SW16 1G **155**
TW16: Sun 6H **129**
Juniper Ho. SE14 7J **103**
TW9: Kew 1H **115**
*W10 4G **81***
(off Fourth Av.)
Juniper La. E6 5C **88**
Juniper Rd. IG1: Ilf 3E **70**
Juniper St. E1 7J **85**
Juniper Way UB3: Hayes 7F **75**
Juno Ct. *SW9 7A **102***
(off Caldwell St.)
Juno Way SE14 6K **103**
Juno Way Ind. Est. SE14 6K **103**
Jupiter Ct. *SW9 7A **102***
(off Caldwell St.)
*UB5: N'olt 3B **76***
(off Seasprite Cl.)
Jupiter Hgts. UB10: Uxb 1B **74**
Jupiter Ho. *E14 5D **104***
(off St Davids Sq.)
Jupiter Way N7 6K **65**
Jupp Rd. E15 7F **69**
Jupp Rd. W. E15 1F **87**
Jura Ho. *SE16 4K **103***
(off Plough Way)
Jurston Ct. SE1 7K **13**
Justice Wlk. SW3 7C **16** (6C **100**)
Justin Cl. TW8: Bford 7D **96**
Justines Pl. E2 3K **85**
Justin Plaza CR4: Mitc 4C **154**
Justin Rd. E4 6G **35**
Jute La. EN3: Brim 2F **25**
Jutland Cl. N19 1J **65**
Jutland Ho. SE5 2C **120**
Jutland Rd. E13 4J **87**
SE6 7E **122**
Jutsums Av. RM7: Rom 6H **55**
Jutsums Ct. RM7: Rom 6H **55**
Jutsums La.
RM7: Rom, Rush G 6H **55**
Juxon Cl. HA3: Hrw W 1F **41**
Juxon Ho. *EC4 1B **14***
(off St Paul's Chyd.)
Juxon St. SE11 3H **19** (4K **101**)
JVC Bus. Pk. NW2 1C **62**

K

Kaduna Cl. HA5: Eastc 5J **39**
Kale Rd. DA18: Erith 2D **108**
Kambala Rd. SW11 3B **118**
Kangley Bri. Rd. SE26 6B **140**
Kangley Bus. Cen. SE26 5B **140**
Kaplan Dr. N21 5E **22**
Karanjia Ct. NW2 6E **62**
Kara Way NW2 4F **63**
Karen Ct. BR1: Brom 1H **159**
Karen Ter. E11 2H **69**
Kariba Cl. N9 3D **34**
Karoline Gdns. UB6: G'frd 2H **77**
Kashgar Rd. SE18 4K **107**
Kashmir Rd. SE7 7B **106**
Kassala Rd. SW11 1D **118**
Katella Trad. Est. IG11: Bark 3J **89**
Katharine Ho. *CR0: Croy 3C **168***
(off Katharine St.)
Katharine St. CR0: Croy 3C **168**
Katherine Cl. SE16 1K **103**
Katherine Ct. SE23 1H **139**
Katherine Gdns. SE9 4B **124**
Katherine Rd. E6 5A **70**
E7 5A **70**
TW1: Twick 1A **132**
Katherine Sq. W11 1G **99**
Kathleen Av. HA0: Wemb 7E **60**
W3 5J **79**
Kathleen Godfree Ct. SW19 6J **135**
Kathleen Rd. SW11 3D **118**
Kayemoor Rd. SM2: Sutt 6B **166**
Kay Rd. SW9 2J **119**
Kay St. DA16: Well 1B **126**
E2 2G **85**
E15 7F **69**
Kay Ter. E18 1H **51**
Kean Ho. SE17 6B **102**
*TW1: Twick 6D **114***
(off Arosa Rd.)
Kean St. WC2 1G **13** (6K **83**)
Keatley Grn. E4 6G **35**
Keats Av. E16 1K **105**
Keats Cl. E11 5K **51**
EN3: Pond E 5E **24**
NW3 4C **64**
SE1 4F **103**
SW19 6B **136**
UB4: Hayes 5J **75**
Keats Est. *N16 2F **67***
(off Kyverdale Rd.)
Keats Gro. NW3 4C **64**
Keats House 4C 64
Keats Ho. *E2 3J **85***
(off Roman Rd.)
*SE5 7C **102***
(off Elmington Est.)
*SW1 7B **18***
(off Churchill Gdns.)
Keats Pde. *N9 2B **34***
(off Church St.)
Keats Pl. *EC2 6E **8***
(off Moorfields)
Keats Rd. DA16: Well 1J **125**
DA17: Belv 3J **109**
Keats Way CR0: Croy 6J **157**
UB6: G'frd 5F **77**
UB7: W Dray 4B **92**
Kebbell Ter. *E7 5K **69***
(off Claremont Rd.)
Keble Cl. KT4: Wor Pk 1B **164**
UB5: N'olt 5G **59**
Keble Pl. SW13 6D **98**
Keble St. SW17 4A **136**
Kechill Gdns. BR2: Hayes 7J **159**
Kedeston Ct. SM1: Sutt 1K **165**
Kedge Ho. *E14 3C **104***
(off Tiller Rd.)
Kedleston Dr. BR5: St M Cry 6K **161**
Kedleston Wlk. E2 3H **85**
Kedyngton Ho. *HA8: Edg 2J **43***
(off Burnt Oak B'way.)
Keeble Cl. SE18 6F **107**
Keedonwood Rd. BR1: Brom 5G **141**
Keel Cl. IG11: Bark 2C **90**
SE16 1K **103**
Keel Ct. *E14 7F **87***
(off Newport Av.)
Keeley Rd. CR0: Croy 2C **168**
Keeley St. WC2 1G **13** (6K **83**)
Keeling Ho. *E2 2H **85***
(off Claredale St.)
Keeling Rd. SE9 5B **124**
Keely Cl. EN4: E Barn 5H **21**
Keemor Cl. SE18 7E **106**
Keens Cl. SW16 5H **137**
Keens Rd. CR0: Croy 4C **168**
Keen's Yd. N1 6B **66**
Keep, The KT2: King T 6F **133**
SE3 2J **123**
Keepers Ct. *CR2: S Croy 5C **168***
(off Warham Rd.)
Keepers M. TW11: Tedd 6C **132**
Keepier Wharf *E14 7K **85***
(off Narrow St.)
Keeton's Rd. SE16 3H **103**
(not continuous)
Keevil Dr. SW19 7F **117**
Keighley Cl. N7 5J **65**
Keightley Dr. SE9 1G **143**
Keilder Cl. UB10: Hil 2C **74**
Keildon Rd. SW11 4D **118**
Keir, The SW19 5E **134**
Keir Hardie Ct. NW10 7B **62**
Keir Hardie Est. E5 1H **67**
Keir Hardie Ho. N19 7H **47**
*W6 6F **99***
(off Fulham Pal. Rd.)
Keir Hardie Way IG11: Bark 7A **72**
UB4: Yead 3J **75**
Keith Connor Cl. SW8 3F **119**
Keith Gro. W12 2C **98**
Keith Ho. *NW6 2K **81***
(off Carlton Va.)
Keith Pk. Rd. UB10: Uxb 7B **56**
Keith Rd. E17 1B **50**
IG11: Bark 2H **89**
UB3: Hayes 3G **93**
Kelbrook Rd. SE3 2C **124**
Kelby Ho. *N7 6K **65***
(off Sutterton St.)
Kelby Path SE9 3F **143**
Kelceda Cl. NW2 2C **62**
Kelf Gro. UB3: Hayes 6H **75**
Kelfield Ct. W10 6F **81**
Kelfield Gdns. W10 6E **80**
Kelfield M. W10 6F **81**
Kelland Cl. N8 5H **47**
Kelland Rd. E13 4J **87**
Kellaway Rd. SE3 2B **124**
Keller Cres. E12 4B **70**
Kellerton Rd. SE13 5G **123**
Kellet Ho's. *WC1 2F **7***
(off Tankerton St.)
Kellett Ho. *N1 1E **84***
(off Colville Est.)
Kellett Rd. SW2 4A **120**
Kelling Gdns. CR0: Croy 7B **156**
Kellino St. SW17 4D **136**
Kellner Rd. SE28 3K **107**
Kellogg Twr. UB6: G'frd 5J **59**
Kellow Ho. *SE1 6E **14***
(off Tennis St.)
Kell St. SE1 7B **14** (3B **102**)
Kelly Av. SE15 7F **103**
Kelly Cl. NW10 3K **61**
TW17: Shep 2G **147**
Kelly Ct. *E14 7C **86***
(off Garford St.)
Kelly M. W9 4H **81**
Kelly Rd. NW7 6B **30**
Kelly St. NW1 6F **65**
Kelly Way RM6: Chad H 5E **54**
Kelman Cl. SW4 2H **119**
Kelmore Gro. SE22 4G **121**
Kelmscott Cl. E17 1B **50**
Kelmscott Gdns. W12 3C **98**
Kelmscott Leisure Cen. 6B 50
Kelmscott Rd. SW11 5C **118**
Kelross Pas. N5 4C **66**
Kelross Rd. N5 4C **66**
Kelsall Cl. SE3 2K **123**
Kelsey Ga. BR3: Beck 2D **158**
Kelsey La. BR3: Beck 2C **158**
Kelsey M. BR3: Beck 2C **158**
Kelsey Pk. Av. BR3: Beck 2D **158**
(not continuous)
Kelsey Pk. Rd. BR3: Beck 2C **158**
Kelsey Sq. BR3: Beck 2C **158**
Kelsey St. E2 4G **85**
Kelsey Way BR3: Beck 3C **158**
Kelson Ho. E14 3E **104**
Kelso Pl. W8 3K **99**
Kelso Rd. SM5: Cars 7A **154**
Kelston Rd. IG6: Ilf 2F **53**
Kelvedon Cl. KT2: King T 6G **133**
Kelvedon Ho. SW8 1J **119**
Kelvedon Rd. SW6 7H **99**
Kelvedon Way IG8: Wfd G 6J **37**
Kelvin Av. N13 6E **32**
TW11: Tedd 6J **131**
Kelvinbrook
KT8: W Mole 3F **149**
Kelvin Cl. KT19: Ewe 6G **163**
Kelvin Ct. SE20 1H **157**
TW7: Isle 2J **113**
W11 7J **81**
Kelvin Cres. HA3: Hrw W 7D **26**
Kelvin Dr. TW1: Twick 6B **114**
Kelvin Gdns. CR0: Wadd 7J **155**
UB1: S'hall 6E **76**
Kelvin Gro. KT9: Chess 3D **162**
SE26 3H **139**
Kelvington Cl. CR0: Croy 7A **158**
Kelvington Rd. SE15 5K **121**
Kelvin Ind. Est. UB6: G'frd 7F **59**
Kelvin Pde. BR6: Orp 1J **173**
Kelvin Rd. DA16: Well 3A **126**
N5 4C **66**
Kember St. N1 7K **65**
Kemble Dr. BR2: Brom 3C **172**
Kemble Ho. *SW9 3B **120***
(off Barrington Rd.)
Kemble Rd. CR0: Wadd 3B **168**
N17 1G **49**
SE23 1K **139**
Kemble St. WC2 1G **13** (6K **83**)
Kemerton Rd. BR3: Beck 2D **158**
CR0: Croy 7F **157**
SE5 3C **120**
Kemeys St. E9 5A **68**
Kemnal Rd. BR7: Chst 4H **143**
(not continuous)
Kemp *NW9 1B **44***
(off Concourse, The)
Kemp Ct. *SW8 7J **101***
(off Hartington Rd.)
Kempe Ho. *SE1 3D **102***
(off Burge St.)
Kempe Rd. NW6 2F **81**
Kemp Gdns. CR0: Croy 6C **156**
Kemp Ho. *E2 2K **85***
(off Sewardstone Rd.)
E6 6E **70**
*W1 2C **12***
(off Berwick St.)
Kempis Way SE22 5E **120**
Kemplay Rd. NW3 4B **64**
Kemp Rd. RM8: Dag 1D **72**
Kemps Ct. *W1 1C **12***
(off Hopkins St.)
Kemps Dr. E14 7C **86**
HA6: Nwood 1H **39**
Kempsford Gdns. SW5 5J **99**
Kempsford Rd. SE11 4K **19** (4A **102**)
(not continuous)
Kemps Gdns. SE13 5E **122**
Kempshott Rd. SW16 7H **137**
Kempson Rd. SW6 1J **117**
Kempthorne Rd. SE8 4B **104**
Kempton Av. TW16: Sun 1K **147**
UB5: N'olt 6E **58**
Kempton Cl. DA8: Erith 6J **109**
UB10: Ick 4E **56**
Kempton Ct. E1 5H **85**
TW16: Sun 1K **147**
Kempton Pk. Racecourse 7A 130
Kempton Rd. E6 1D **88**
TW12: Hamp 2D **148**
(not continuous)
Kempton Wlk. CR0: Croy 6A **158**
Kempt St. SE18 6E **106**
Kemsing Cl. BR2: Hayes 2H **171**
CR7: Thor H 4C **156**
DA5: Bexl 7E **126**
Kemsing Ho. *SE1 7F **15***
(off Long La.)
Kemsing Rd. SE10 5J **105**
Kemsley SE13 5D **122**
Kemsley Ct. W13 1C **96**
Kenbrook Ho. W14 3H **99**
Kenbury Cl. UB10: Ick 3C **56**
Kenbury Gdns. SE5 2C **120**
Kenbury Mans. *SE5 2C **120***
(off Kenbury St.)

Kenbury St. SE5 ... 2C 120
Kenchester Cl. SW8 ... 7J 101
Kencot Way DA18: Erith ... 2F 109
Kendal *NW1* ... *1K 5*
(off Augustus St.)
Kendal Av. IG11: Bark ... 1J 89
N18 ... 4J 33
W3 ... 4G 79
(not continuous)
Kendal Cl. IG8: Wfd G ... 2C 36
SW9 ... 7B 102
TW14: Felt ... 1H 129
UB4: Hayes ... 2G 75
Kendal Ct. W3 ... 5G 79
Kendale Rd. BR1: Brom ... 5G 141
Kendal Gdns. N18 ... 4J 33
SM1: Sutt ... 2A 166
Kendal Ho. E9 ... 1J 85
N1 ... *2K 83*
(off Priory Grn. Est.)
SE20 ... *2G 157*
(off Derwent Rd.)
Kendall Av. BR3: Beck ... 2A 158
CR2: Sand ... 7D 168
Kendall Ct. DA15: Sidc ... 3A 144
SW19 ... 6B 136
Kendall Lodge *BR1: Brom* ... *1K 159*
(off Willow Tree Wlk.)
Kendall Pl. W1 ... 6G 5 (5E 82)
Kendall Rd. BR3: Beck ... 2A 158
SE18 ... 1C 124
TW7: Isle ... 2A 114
Kendalmere Cl. N10 ... 1F 47
Kendal Pde. N18 ... 4J 33
Kendal Pl. SW15 ... 5H 117
Kendal Rd. NW10 ... 4C 62
Kendal Steps W2 ... 1D 10
Kendal St. W2 ... 1D 10 (6C 82)
Kender Est. *SE14* ... *1J 121*
(off Queen's Rd.)
Kender St. SE14 ... 7J 103
Kendoa Rd. SW4 ... 4H 119
Kendon Cl. E11 ... 5K 51
Kendra Hall Rd. CR2: S Croy ... 7B 168
Kendrey Gdns. TW2: Whit ... 7J 113
Kendrick Ct. *SE15* ... *1H 121*
(off Woods Rd.)
Kendrick M. SW7 ... 3A 16 (4B 100)
Kendrick Pl. SW7 ... 4A 16 (4B 100)
Kenelm Cl. HA1: Harr ... 3A 60
Kenerne Dr. EN5: Barn ... 5B 20
Kenilford Rd. SW12 ... 7F 119
Kenilworth Av. E17 ... 2C 50
HA2: Harr ... 4D 58
SW19 ... 5J 135
Kenilworth Cres. EN1: Enf ... 1K 23
Kenilworth Gdns. IG3: Ilf ... 2K 71
SE18 ... 2F 125
UB1: S'hall ... 3D 76
UB4: Hayes ... 5H 75
Kenilworth Rd. BR5: Pet W ... 6G 161
E3 ... 2A 86
HA8: Edg ... 3D 28
KT17: Ewe ... 5C 164
NW6 ... 1H 81
SE20 ... 1K 157
TW15: Ashf ... 3A 128
W5 ... 1E 96
Kenley *N17* ... *2D 48*
(off Gloucester Rd.)
Kenley Av. NW9 ... 1A 44
Kenley Cl. BR7: Chst ... 3J 161
DA5: Bexl ... 7G 127
EN4: E Barn ... 4H 21
Kenley Gdns. CR7: Thor H ... 4B 156
Kenley Rd. KT1: King T ... 2H 151
SW19 ... 2J 153
TW1: Twick ... 6B 114
Kenley Wlk. SM3: Cheam ... 4F 165
W11 ... 7G 81
Kenlor Rd. SW17 ... 5B 136

Kenmare Dr. CR4: Mitc ... 7D 136
N17 ... 2F 49
Kenmare Gdns. N13 ... 4H 33
Kenmare Rd. CR7: Thor H ... 6A 156
Kenmere Gdns.
HA0: Wemb ... 1G 79
Kenmere Rd. DA16: Well ... 2C 126
Kenmont Gdns. NW10 ... 3D 80
Kenmore Av. HA3: W'stone ... 4A 42
Kenmore Cl. TW9: Kew ... 7G 97
Kenmore Cres. UB4: Hayes ... 3H 75
Kenmore Gdns. HA8: Edg ... 2H 43
Kenmore Rd. HA3: Kent ... 3D 42
Kenmure Rd. E8 ... 5H 67
Kenmure Yd. E8 ... 5H 67
Kennacraig Cl. E16 ... 1J 105
Kennard Ho. SW11 ... 2E 118
Kennard Rd. E15 ... 7F 69
N11 ... 5J 31
Kennard St. E16 ... 1D 106
SW11 ... 1E 118
Kennedy Av. EN3: Pond E ... 6D 24
Kennedy Cl. BR5: Pet W ... 1H 173
CR4: Mitc ... 1E 154
E13 ... 2J 87
Kennedy Ct. TW15: Ashf ... 5E 128
WD23: Bushy ... 2C 26
Kennedy Cox Ho. *E16* ... *5H 87*
(off Burke St.)
Kennedy Ho. *SE11* ... *5G 19*
(off Vauxhall Wlk.)
Kennedy Path W7 ... 4K 77
Kennedy Rd. IG11: Bark ... 1J 89
W7 ... 5J 77
Kennedy Wlk. *SE17* ... *4D 102*
(off Elsted St.)
Kennet Cl. SW11 ... 4B 118
Kennet Ct. *W9* ... *5J 81*
(off Elmfield Way)
Kenneth Av. IG1: Ilf ... 4F 71
Kenneth Campbell Ho. *NW8* ... *3B 4*
(off Orchardson St.)
Kenneth Ct. SE11 ... 3K 19 (4A 102)
Kenneth Cres. NW2 ... 5D 62
Kenneth Gdns. HA7: Stan ... 6F 27
Kenneth More Rd. IG1: Ilf ... 3F 71
Kenneth More Theatre ... 3F 71
Kennet Ho. *NW8* ... *4B 4*
(off Church St. Est.)
Kenneth Rd. RM6: Chad H ... 7D 54
Kenneth Robbins Ho. N17 ... 7C 34
Kenneth Younger Ho. *SW6* ... *6H 99*
(off Clem Attlee Ct.)
Kennet Rd. TW7: Isle ... 3K 113
W9 ... 4H 81
Kennet Sq. CR4: Mitc ... 1C 154
Kennet St. E1 ... 1G 103
Kennett Ct. W4 ... 7H 97
Kennett Dr. UB4: Yead ... 5C 76
Kennett Wharf La. EC4 ... 2D 14
KENNINGHALL JUNC. ... 5D 34
Kenninghall Rd. E5 ... 3G 67
N18 ... 5D 34
Kenning Ho. *N1* ... *1E 84*
(off Colville Est.)
Kenning St. SE16 ... 2J 103
Kennings Way SE11 ... 5K 19 (5A 102)
KENNINGTON ... 7K 19 (6A 102)
Kennington Grn. SE11 ... 6J 19 (5A 102)
Kennington Gro.
SE11 ... 7H 19 (6K 101)
Kennington La. SE11 ... 6G 19 (5K 101)
KENNINGTON OVAL ... 6A 102
Kennington Oval
SE11 ... 7H 19 (6K 101)
Kennington Pal. Ct. SE11 ... 5J 19
Kennington Pk. Gdns.
SE11 ... 7K 19 (6B 102)
Kennington Pk. Ho. SE11 ... 6K 19
Kennington Pk. Pl.
SE11 ... 7K 19 (6A 102)

Kennington Pk. Rd.
SE11 ... 7K 19 (6A 102)
Kennington Rd. SE1 ... 1J 19 (3A 102)
SE11 ... 1J 19 (3A 102)
Kennistoun Ho. NW5 ... 5G 65
Kennoldes *SE21* ... *2D 138*
(off Croxted Rd.)
Kenny Dr. SM5: Cars ... 7E 166
Kennyland Ct. *NW4* ... *6D 44*
(off Hendon Way)
Kenny Rd. NW7 ... 6B 30
Kenrick Pl. W1 ... 6G 5 (5E 82)
KENSAL GREEN ... 3E 80
Kensal Ho. *W10* ... *4F 81*
(off Ladbroke Gro.)
KENSAL RISE ... 2F 81
Kensal Rd. W10 ... 4G 81
KENSAL TOWN ... 4G 81
Kensal Wharf W10 ... 4F 81
KENSINGTON ... 2K 99
Kensington Arc. *W8* ... *2K 99*
(off Kensington High St.)
Kensington Av. CR7: Thor H ... 1A 156
E12 ... 6C 70
Kensington Cen. W14 ... 4G 99
(not continuous)
Kensington Chu. Ct. W8 ... 2K 99
Kensington Chu. St. W8 ... 1J 99
Kensington Chu. Wlk. W8 ... 2K 99
(not continuous)
Kensington Cl. N11 ... 6K 31
Kensington Ct. *SE16* ... *1K 103*
(off King & Queen Wharf)
W8 ... 2K 99
Kensington Ct. Gdns. *W8* ... *3K 99*
(off Kensington Ct. Pl.)
Kensington Ct. M. *W8* ... *3K 99*
(off Kensington Ct. Pl.)
Kensington Ct. Pl. W8 ... 3K 99
Kensington Dr. IG8: Wfd G ... 2B 52
Kensington Gardens ... 5A 10 (1A 100)
Kensington Gdns. IG1: Ilf ... 1D 70
KT1: King T ... 3D 150
(not continuous)
Kensington Gdns. Sq. W2 ... 6K 81
(not continuous)
Kensington Ga. W8 ... 3A 100
Kensington Gore SW7 ... 7A 10 (2A 100)
Kensington Hall Gdns. W14 ... 5H 99
Kensington Hgts. *HA1: Harr* ... *6K 41*
(off Sheepcote Rd.)
W8 ... 1J 99
Kensington High St. W8 ... 3H 99
W14 ... 3H 99
Kensington Ho. IG8: Ilf ... 7K 37
W14 ... 2F 99
Kensington Mall W8 ... 1J 99
Kensington Mans. *SW5* ... *5J 99*
(off Trebovir Rd., not continuous)
Kensington Palace ... 2K 99
Kensington Pal. Gdns. W8 ... 1K 99
Kensington Pk. Gdns. W11 ... 7H 81
Kensington Pk. M. W11 ... 6H 81
Kensington Pk. Rd. W11 ... 6H 81
Kensington Pl. W8 ... 1J 99
Kensington Rd. RM7: Rom ... 6J 55
SW7 ... 2A 100
UB5: N'olt ... 3E 76
W8 ... 2A 100
Kensington Sports Cen. ... 7G 81
Kensington Sq. W8 ... 3K 99
Kensington Ter. CR2: S Croy ... 7D 168
Kensington Village W14 ... 4H 99
Kensington W. W14 ... 4G 99
Kensworth Ho. *EC1* ... *2F 9*
(off Cranwood St.)
Kent Av. DA16: Well ... 5K 125
RM9: Dag ... 4G 91
W13 ... 5B 78
Kent Cl. BR6: Chels ... 6J 173
CR4: Mitc ... 4J 155

Kent Ct. E2 ... 2F 85
NW9 ... 2A 44
Kent Dr. EN4: Cockf ... 4K 21
TW11: Tedd ... 5J 131
Kentford Way UB5: N'olt ... 1C 76
Kent Gdns. HA4: Ruis ... 6J 39
W13 ... 5B 78
Kent Ga. Way CR0: Addtn ... 6B 170
Kent Ho. SE1 ... 5F 103
SW1 ... *5C 18*
(off Aylesford St.)
W4 ... *5A 98*
(off Devonshire St.)
Kent Ho. App. Rd. BR3: Beck ... 1A 158
Kent Ho. La. BR3: Beck ... 6A 140
Kent Ho. Rd. BR3: Beck ... 1K 157
SE26 ... 5A 140
Kentish Bldgs. SE1 ... 5E 14 (2D 102)
Kentish Rd. DA17: Belv ... 4G 109
KENTISH TOWN ... 5F 65
Kentish Town Forum ... 5F 65
Kentish Town Ind. Est. NW5 ... 5F 65
Kentish Town Rd. NW1 ... 7F 65
NW5 ... 6F 65
Kentish Town Sports Cen. ... 6F 65
Kentish Way BR1: Brom ... 2K 159
BR2: Brom ... 2K 159
Kentlea Rd. SE28 ... 2J 107
Kentmere Ho. SE15 ... 6J 103
Kentmere Mans. W5 ... 4B 78
Kentmere Rd. SE18 ... 4J 107
KENTON ... 5C 42
Kenton Av. HA1: Harr ... 7K 41
TW16: Sun ... 2B 148
UB1: S'hall ... 7E 76
Kenton Ct. HA3: Kent ... 6B 42
SE26 ... *4A 140*
(off Adamsrill Rd.)
TW1: Twick ... 6D 114
W14 ... 3H 99
Kentone Ct. SE25 ... 4H 157
Kenton Gdns. HA3: Kent ... 5C 42
Kenton Ho. *E1* ... *4J 85*
(off Mantus Cl.)
Kenton La. HA3: Hrw W ... 6E 26
Kenton Pk. Av. HA3: Kent ... 5D 42
Kenton Pk. Cl. HA3: Kent ... 4C 42
Kenton Pk. Cres. HA3: Kent ... 4D 42
Kenton Pk. Mans. *HA3: Kent* ... *5C 42*
(off Kenton Rd.)
Kenton Pk. Pde. HA3: Kent ... 5C 42
Kenton Pk. Rd. HA3: Kent ... 4C 42
Kenton Rd. E9 ... 6K 67
HA1: Harr ... 7K 41
HA3: Kent ... 6A 42
Kenton St. WC1 ... 3E 6 (4J 83)
Kenton Way UB4: Hayes ... 3G 75
Kent Pk. Ind. Est. SE15 ... 6H 103
Kent Pas. NW1 ... 3E 4 (4D 82)
Kent Rd. BR4: W W'ck ... 1D 170
KT1: King T ... 3D 150
KT8: E Mos ... 4G 149
N21 ... 1J 33
RM10: Dag ... 5H 73
TW9: Kew ... 7G 97
W4 ... 3J 97
Kent's Pas. TW12: Hamp ... 1D 148
Kent St. E2 ... 2F 85
E13 ... 3A 88
Kent Ter. NW1 ... 2D 4 (3C 82)
Kent Vw. Gdns. IG3: Ilf ... 2J 71
Kent Wlk. SW9 ... 4B 120
Kent Way KT6: Surb ... 3E 162
Kentwell Cl. SE4 ... 4A 122
Kent Wharf *SE8* ... *7D 104*
(off Creekside)
Kentwode Grn. SW13 ... 7C 98
Kent Yd. SW7 ... 7D 10 (2C 100)
Kenver Av. N12 ... 6G 31
Kenward Rd. SE9 ... 5A 124
Kenward Way SW11 ... 2E 118

Kimbolton Ct.—Kingsland High St.

Kimbolton Ct. *SW3* *4C 16*
(off Fulham Rd.)
Kimbolton Row *SW3* *4C 16*
(off Fulham Rd.)
Kimmeridge Gdns. SE9 . . . . 4C **142**
Kimmeridge Rd. SE9 . . . . 4C **142**
Kimpton Ho. SW15 . . . . 7C **116**
Kimpton Ind. Est. SM3: Sutt 2H **165**
Kimpton Link Bus. Cen. SM3: Sutt . . 2H **165**
Kimpton Rd. SE5 . . . . 1D **120**
SM3: Sutt 2H **165**
Kimpton Trade & Bus. Cen.
SM3: Sutt 2H **165**
Kinburn St. SE16 . . . . 2K **103**
Kincaid Rd. SE15 . . . . 7H **103**
Kincardine Gdns. *W9* *4J 81*
(off Harrow Rd.)
Kincha Lodge *KT2: King T* *1F 151*
(off Elm Rd.)
Kinch Gro. HA3: Kent 7F **43**
Kinder Cl. SE28 . . . . 7D **90**
Kinder Ho. *N1* *2D 84*
(off Cranston Est.)
Kindersley Ho. *E1* *6G 85*
(off Pinchin St.)
Kinder St. E1 . . . . 6H **85**
Kinderton Cl. N14 . . . . 1B **32**
Kinefold Ho. N7 . . . . 6J **65**
Kinfauns Rd. IG3: Ilf 1A **72**
SW2 . . . . 2A **138**
King Alfred Av. SE6 . . . . 4C **140**
(not continuous)
King & Queen Cl. SE9 . . . . 4C **142**
King & Queen St. SE17 . . . . 5C **102**
King & Queen Wharf SE16 . . . . 7K **85**
King Arthur Cl. SE15 . . . . 7J **103**
King Charles I Island WC2 . . . . 4E **12**
King Charles Ct. *SE17* *6B 102*
(off Royal Rd.)
King Charles Cres. KT5: Surb 7F **151**
King Charles Ho. *SW6* *7K 99*
(off Wandon Rd.)
King Charles Rd. KT5: Surb 5F **151**
King Charles's Ct. *SE10* *6E 104*
(off Park Row)
King Charles St.
SW1 . . . . 6D **12** (2H **101**)
King Charles Ter. *E1* *7H 85*
(off Sovereign Cl.)
King Charles Wlk. SW19 . . . . 1G **135**
King Ct. E10 . . . . 7D **50**
Kingcup Cl. CR0: Croy 7K **157**
King David La. E1 . . . . 7J **85**
Kingdon Ho. *E14* *3E 104*
(off Galbraith St.)
Kingdon Rd. NW6 . . . . 6J **63**
King Edward III M. SE16 . . . . 2H **103**
King Edward Bldg. EC1 . . . . 6B **84**
King Edward Dr. KT9: Chess 3E **162**
King Edward Mans. *E8* *1H 85*
(off Mare St.)
King Edward M. SW13 . . . . 1C **116**
King Edward Rd. E10 . . . . 1E **68**
E17 . . . . 3A **50**
EN5: New Bar 4D **20**
King Edward's Gdns. W3 . . . . 1G **97**
King Edwards Gro. TW11: Tedd 6B **132**
King Edwards Mans. *SW6* *7J 99*
(off Fulham Rd.)
King Edward's Pl. W3 . . . . 1G **97**
King Edwards Rd. E9 . . . . 1H **85**
EN3: Pond E 4E **24**
HA4: Ruis 1F **57**
IG11: Bark 1H **89**
N9 . . . . 7C **24**
King Edward St. EC1 . . . . 7C **8** (6C **84**)
King Edward Wlk.
SE1 . . . . 1K **19** (3A **102**)
Kingfield Rd. W5 . . . . 4D **78**
Kingfield St. E14 . . . . 4E **104**
Kingfisher Av. E11 . . . . 6K **51**
Kingfisher Cl. HA3: Hrw W 7E **26**
HA6: Nwood 1D **38**
SE28 . . . . 7C **90**
Kingfisher Ct. *E14* *2E 104*
(off River Barge Cl.)
EN2: Enf 1E **22**
KT8: E Mos 4J **149**
SE1 . . . . *7D 14*
(off Swan St.)
SM1: Sutt 5H **165**
SW19 . . . . 2F **135**
TW3: Houn 5F **113**
Kingfisher Dr. TW10: Ham 4B **132**
Kingfisher Ho. SW18 . . . . 3A **118**
Kingfisher Leisure Cen., The 2E **150**
Kingfisher M. SE13 . . . . 4C **122**
Kingfisher Pl. N22 . . . . 2K **47**
Kingfisher Sq. *SE8* *6B 104*
(off Clyde St.)
Kingfisher St. E6 . . . . 5C **88**
Kingfisher Wlk. NW9 . . . . 2A **44**
Kingfisher Way BR3: Beck 5K **157**
NW10 . . . . 6K **61**
King Frederick IX Twr. SE16 . . . . 3B **104**
King Gdns. CR0: Wadd 5B **168**
King George IV Ct. *SE17* *5D 102*
(off Dawes St.)
King George VI Av. CR4: Mitc 4D **154**
King George VI Memorial . . . 5C **12** (1H **101**)
King George Av. E16 . . . . 6A **88**
IG2: Ilf 5H **53**
King George Cl. RM7: Mawney 3J **55**
TW16: Sun 5G **129**
King George's Dr. UB1: S'hall 5D **76**
King George Sq. TW10: Rich 6F **115**
King George's Trad. Est.
KT9: Chess 4G **163**
King George St. SE10 . . . . 7E **104**
Kingham Cl. SW18 . . . . 7A **118**
W11 . . . . 2G **99**
King Harolds Way DA7: Belv, Bex . . . 7D **108**
DA17: Belv 7D **108**
King Henry M. BR6: Chels 5K **173**
King Henry's Dr. CR0: New Ad 7D **170**
King Henry's Reach W6 . . . . 6E **98**
King Henry's Rd. KT1: King T 3H **151**
NW3 . . . . 7C **64**
King Henry's Stairs E1 . . . . 1H **103**
King Henry St. N16 . . . . 5E **66**
King Henry's Wlk. N1 . . . . 6E **66**
King Henry Ter. *E1* *7H 85*
(off Sovereign Cl.)
Kinghorn St. EC1 . . . . 6C **8** (5C **84**)
King Ho. W12 . . . . 6D **80**
King James Ct. SE1 . . . . 7B **14**
King James St. SE1 . . . . 7B **14** (2B **102**)
King John Ct. EC2 . . . . 3H **9** (4E **84**)
King John St. E1 . . . . 5K **85**
King John's Wlk. SE9 . . . . 7C **124**
(not continuous)
Kinglake Est. SE17 . . . . 5E **102**
Kinglake St. SE17 . . . . 5E **102**
(not continuous)
Kinglet Cl. E7 . . . . 6J **69**
Kingly Ct. W1 . . . . 2B **12**
Kingly St. W1 . . . . 1A **12** (6G **83**)
Kingsand Rd. SE12 . . . . 2J **141**
Kings Arbour UB2: S'hall 5C **94**
King's Arms All. TW8: Bford 6D **96**
Kings Arms Ct. E1 . . . . 5G **85**
Kings Arms Yd. EC2 . . . . 7E **8** (6D **84**)
Kingsash Dr. UB4: Yead 4C **76**
Kings Av. BR1: Brom 6H **141**
IG8: Wfd G 6E **36**
IG9: Buck H 2G **37**
(Queen's Rd.)
IG9: Buck H 6E **36**
(Station Way)
KT3: N Mald 4A **152**
N10 . . . . 3E **46**
N21 . . . . 1G **33**
Kings Av. RM6: Chad H 6F **55**
SM5: Cars 7C **166**
SW4 . . . . 7H **119**
SW12 . . . . 1H **137**
TW3: Houn 1F **113**
TW16: Sun 5H **129**
UB6: G'frd 5F **77**
W5 . . . . 6D **78**
King's Bench St. SE1 . . . . 6B **14** (2B **102**)
King's Bench Wlk. EC4 . . . . 1K **13** (6A **84**)
Kingsbridge Av. W3 . . . . 2F **97**
Kingsbridge Ct. *E14* *3C 104*
(off Dockers Tanner Rd.)
NW1 . . . . *7F 65*
(off Castlehaven Rd.)
Kingsbridge Cres. UB1: S'hall 5D **76**
Kingsbridge Dr. NW7 . . . . 7A **30**
Kingsbridge Rd. IG11: Bark 2H **89**
KT12: Walt T 7K **147**
SM4: Mord 6F **153**
UB2: S'hall 4D **94**
W10 . . . . 6E **80**
Kingsbridge Way UB4: Hayes 3G **75**
Kingsbridge Wharf IG11: Bark 3J **89**
KINGSBURY 7K **43**
Kingsbury Circ. NW9 . . . . 5G **43**
KINGSBURY GREEN 5J **43**
Kingsbury Rd. N1 . . . . 6E **66**
NW9 . . . . 5G **43**
Kingsbury Sports Cen. 4H **43**
Kingsbury Ter. N1 . . . . 6E **66**
Kingsbury Trad. Est. NW9 . . . . 6K **43**
Kings Chase KT8: E Mos 3G **149**
Kings Chase Vw. EN2: Enf 2F **23**
Kingsclere Cl. SW15 . . . . 7C **116**
Kingsclere Ct. N12 . . . . 5H **31**
Kingsclere Pl. EN2: Enf 2H **23**
Kingscliffe Gdns. SW19 . . . . 1H **135**
Kings Cl. DA1: Cray 4K **127**
E10 . . . . 7D **50**
KT7: T Ditt 6A **150**
KT12: Walt T 7K **147**
NW4 . . . . 4F **45**
TW18: Staines 7A **128**
Kings Coll. Ct. NW3 . . . . 7C **64**
Kings College London
Dental Institute 2D **120**
Hampstead Campus 4J **63**
Strand Campus 2H **13** (7K **83**)
Waterloo Campus 5J **13**
Kings Coll. Rd. HA4: Ruis 6H **39**
NW3 . . . . 7C **64**
King's College School of Medicine &
Dentistry 2C **120**
Kingscote Rd. CR0: Croy 7H **157**
KT3: N Mald 3K **151**
W4 . . . . 3K **97**
Kingscote St. EC4 . . . . 2A **14** (7B **84**)
Kings Ct. E13 . . . . 1K **87**
HA9: Wemb 2H **61**
IG9: Buck H 2G **37**
N7 . . . . *7K 65*
(off Caledonian Rd.)
NW8 . . . . *1D 82*
(off Prince Albert Rd.)
SE1 . . . . 6B **14** (2B **102**)
W6 . . . . 4C **98**
Kings Ct. M. KT8: E Mos 5H **149**
Kings Ct. Nth. SW3 . . . . 6C **16** (5C **100**)
Kingscourt Rd. SW16 . . . . 3H **137**
Kings Ct. Sth. SW3 . . . . 6C **16**
King's Cres. N4 . . . . 3C **66**
Kings Cres. Est. N4 . . . . 2C **66**
Kingscroft SW4 . . . . 6J **119**
Kingscroft Rd. NW2 . . . . 6H **63**
KING'S CROSS **2J 83**
King's Cross Bri. N1 . . . . 1F **7**
King's Cross Rd. WC1 . . . . 1G **7** (3K **83**)
Kingsdale Gdns. W11 . . . . 1F **99**
Kingsdale Rd. SE18 . . . . 7K **107**
SE20 . . . . 7K **139**
Kingsdown Av. CR2: S Croy 7C **168**
W3 . . . . 7A **80**
W13 . . . . 2B **96**
Kingsdown Cl. *SE16* *5H 103*
(off Masters Dr.)
W10 . . . . 6F **81**
Kingsdowne Rd. KT6: Surb 7E **150**
Kingsdown Ho. E8 . . . . 5G **67**
Kingsdown Rd. E11 . . . . 3G **69**
N19 . . . . 2J **65**
SM3: Cheam 5G **165**
Kingsdown Way BR2: Hayes 7J **159**
Kings Dr. HA8: Edg 4A **28**
HA9: Wemb 2H **61**
KT5: Surb 7G **151**
KT7: T Ditt 7B **150**
TW11: Tedd 5H **131**
Kingsend HA4: Ruis 1F **57**
Kingsend Ct. HA4: Ruis 1G **57**
Kings Farm E17 . . . . 1D **50**
Kings Farm Av. TW10: Rich 4G **115**
Kingsfield Av. HA2: Harr 4F **41**
Kingsfield Ho. SE9 . . . . 3B **142**
Kingsfield Rd. HA1: Harr 7H **41**
Kingsfield Ter. HA1: Harr 1H **59**
Kingsford St. NW5 . . . . 5D **64**
Kingsford Way E6 . . . . 5D **88**
Kings Gdns. IG1: Ilf 1H **71**
NW6 . . . . 7J **63**
Kings Gth. M. SE23 . . . . 2J **139**
Kingsgate HA9: Wemb 3J **61**
Kingsgate Av. N3 . . . . 3J **45**
Kingsgate Bus. Cen. *KT2: King T* *1E 150*
(off Kingsgate Rd.)
Kingsgate Cl. DA7: Bex 1E **126**
Kingsgate Est. N1 . . . . 6E **66**
Kingsgate Ho. SW9 . . . . 1A **120**
Kingsgate Mans. *WC1* *6G 7*
(off Red Lion Sq.)
Kingsgate Pde. SW1 . . . . 2B **18**
Kingsgate Pl. NW6 . . . . 7J **63**
Kingsgate Rd. KT1: King T 1E **150**
KT2: King T 1E **150**
NW6 . . . . 7J **63**
Kings Grange HA4: Ruis 1H **57**
Kingsground SE9 . . . . 7B **124**
King's Gro. SE15 . . . . 7H **103**
(not continuous)
Kings Hall Leisure Cen. 5J **67**
Kingshall M. SE13 . . . . 3E **122**
Kings Hall Rd. BR3: Beck 7A **140**
Kings Head Hill E4 . . . . 7J **25**
Kingshead Ho. NW7 . . . . 4J **29**
Kings Head Pas. *SW4* *4H 119*
(off Clapham Pk. Rd.)
Kings Head Theatre *1B 84*
(off Upper St.)
King's Head Yd. SE1 . . . . 5E **14** (1D **102**)
King's Highway SE18 . . . . 6J **107**
Kingshill *SE17* *4C 102*
(off Brandon St.)
Kingshill Av. HA3: Kent 4B **42**
KT4: Wor Pk 7C **152**
UB4: Hayes 3G **75**
UB5: Yead 3G **75**
Kingshill Cl. UB4: Hayes 3J **75**
Kingshill Ct. EN5: Barn 4B **20**
Kingshill Dr. HA3: Kent 2B **42**
Kingshold Rd. E9 . . . . 7J **67**
Kingsholm Gdns. SE9 . . . . 4B **124**
Kings Ho. *SW8* *7J 101*
(off Sth. Lambeth Rd.)
Kingshurst Rd. SE12 . . . . 7J **123**
Kingside SE18 . . . . 3C **106**
Kings Keep BR2: Brom 2G **159**
KT1: King T 4E **150**
SW15 . . . . 5F **117**
KINGSLAND 6E **66**
Kingsland NW8 . . . . 1C **82**
Kingsland Grn. E8 . . . . 6E **66**
Kingsland High St. E8 . . . . 6F **67**

A-Z London 303

Kinnaird Av.—Laburnum Gdns.

Kinnaird Av. BR1: Brom 6H 141
W4 7J 97
Kinnaird Cl. BR1: Brom 6H 141
Kinnaird Way IG8: Wfd G 6J 37
Kinnear Rd. W12 2B 98
Kinnerton Pl. Nth. SW1 7F 11
Kinnerton Pl. Sth. SW1 7F 11
Kinnerton St. SW1 7G 11 (2E 100)
Kinnerton Yd. SW1 7G 11
Kinnoul Rd. W6 6G 99
Kinross Av. KT4: Wor Pk 2C 164
Kinross Cl. HA3: Kent 5F 43
HA8: Edg 2C 28
TW16: Sun 5H 129
Kinross Ct. *BR1: Brom 1H 159*
(off Highland Rd.)
SE6 1H 141
Kinross Dr. TW16: Sun 5H 129
Kinross Ter. E17 2B 50
Kinsale Rd. SE15 3G 121
Kinsella Gdns. SW19 5D 134
Kinsham Ho. *E2 4G 85*
(off Ramsey St.)
Kintore Way SE1 4F 103
Kintyre Cl. SW16 2K 155
Kintyre Ct. SW2 7J 119
Kintyre Ho. *E14 1E 104*
(off Coldharbour)
Kinveachy Gdns. SE7 5C 106
Kinver Rd. SE26 4J 139
Kipling Ct. W7 7K 77
Kipling Dr. SW19 6B 136
Kipling Est. SE1 7F 15 (2D 102)
Kipling Ho. *E16 1K 105*
(off Southampton M.)
SE5 7D 102
(off Elmington Est.)
Kipling Pl. HA7: Stan 6E 26
Kipling Rd. DA7: Bex 1E 126
Kipling St. SE1 7F 15 (2D 102)
Kipling Ter. N9 3J 33
Kipling Twr. *W3 3J 97*
(off Palmerston Rd.)
Kippington Dr. SE9 1B 142
Kirby Cl. KT19: Ewe 5B 164
Kirby Est. SE16 3H 103
UB7: Yiew 7A 74
Kirby Gro. SE1 6G 15 (2E 102)
Kirby St. EC1 5K 7 (5A 84)
Kirby Way KT12: Walt T 6A 148
UB8: Hil 4B 74
Kirchen Rd. W13 7B 78
Kirkby Cl. N11 6K 31
Kirkdale SE26 2H 139
Kirkdale Cnr. SE26 4J 139
Kirkdale Rd. E11 1G 69
Kirkeby Ho. *EC1 5J 7*
(off Leather La.)
Kirkfield Cl. W13 1B 96
Kirkham Rd. E6 6C 88
Kirkham St. SE18 6J 107
Kirk Ho. HA9: Wemb 3E 60
Kirkland Av. IG5: Ilf 2E 52
Kirkland Cl. DA15: Sidc 6J 125
Kirkland Dr. EN2: Enf 1H 23
Kirkland Ho. *E14 5D 104*
(off St Davids Sq.)
E14 5D 104
(off Westferry Rd.)
Kirkland Ter. BR3: Beck 6C 140
Kirkland Wlk. E8 6F 67
Kirk La. SE18 6G 107
Kirkleas Rd. KT6: Surb 1E 162
Kirklees Rd. CR7: Thor H 5A 156
RM8: Dag 5C 72
Kirkley Rd. SW19 1J 153
Kirkman Pl. W1 6C 6
Kirkmichael Rd. E14 6E 86
Kirk Ri. SM1: Sutt 3K 165
Kirk Rd. E17 6B 50
Kirkside Rd. SE3 6J 105
Kirkstall Av. N17 4D 48
Kirkstall Gdns. SW2 1J 137
Kirkstall Rd. SW2 1H 137
Kirkstead Ct. E5 4K 67
Kirksted Rd. SM4: Mord 1K 165
Kirkstone *NW1 1A 6*
(off Harrington St.)
Kirkstone Way
BR1: Brom 7G 141
Kirk St. WC1 4G 7
Kirkton Rd. N15 4E 48
Kirkwall Pl. E2 3J 85
Kirkwood Pl. NW1 7E 64
Kirkwood Rd. SE15 2H 121
Kirn Rd. W13 7B 78
Kirrane Cl. KT3: N Mald 5B 152
Kirtley Ho. SW8 1G 119
Kirtley Rd. SE26 4A 140
Kirtling St. SW8 7G 101
Kirton Cl. W4 4K 97
Kirton Gdns. E2 2K 9 (3F 85)
Kirton Lodge SW18 6K 117
Kirton Rd. E13 2A 88
Kirton Wlk. HA8: Edg 7D 28
Kirwyn Way SE5 7B 102
Kitcat Ter. E3 3C 86
Kitchener Rd. CR7: Thor H 3D 156
E7 6K 69
E17 1D 50
N2 3C 46
N17 3E 48
RM10: Dag 6H 73
Kite Pl. *E2 3G 85*
(off Lampern Sq.)
Kite Yd. *SW11 1D 118*
(off Cambridge Rd.)
Kitley Gdns. SE19 1F 157
Kitson Rd. SE5 7D 102
SW13 1C 116
Kittiwake Ct. *SE1 7D 14*
(off Swan St.)
SE8 6B 104
(off Abinger Gro.)
Kittiwake Pl. SM1: Sutt 5H 165
Kittiwake Rd. UB5: N'olt 3B 76
Kittiwake Way UB4: Yead 5B 76
Kitto Rd. SE14 2K 121
Kitts End Rd. EN5: Barn 1C 20
Kiver Rd. N19 2H 65
Klea Av. SW4 6G 119
Klein's Wharf *E14 3C 104*
(off Westferry Rd.)
Knapdale Cl. SE23 2H 139
Knapmill Rd. SE6 2C 140
Knapmill Way SE6 2D 140
Knapp Cl. NW10 6A 62
Knapp Rd. E3 4C 86
TW15: Ashf 4B 128
Knapton M. SW17 6E 136
Knaresborough Dr. SW18 1K 135
Knaresborough Pl. SW5 4K 99
Knatchbull Rd. NW10 1K 79
SE5 2B 120
Knebworth Av. E17 1C 50
Knebworth Ho. SW8 2H 119
Knebworth Rd. N16 4E 66
Knee Hill SE2 4C 108
Kneehill Cres. SE2 4C 108
Kneller Gdns. TW7: Isle 6H 113
Kneller Ho. *UB5: N'olt 2B 76*
(off Academy Gdns.)
Kneller Rd. KT3: N Mald 7A 152
SE4 4A 122
TW2: Whit 6G 113
Knevett Ter. TW3: Houn 4E 112
Knight Cl. RM8: Dag 2C 72
Knight Ct. *E4 1K 35*
(off Ridgeway, The)
N15 5E 48
Knighten St. E1 1H 103
Knighthead Point E14 2C 104
Knight Ho. *SE17 4E 102*
(off Tatum St.)
Knightland Rd. E5 2H 67
Knightleas Ct. NW2 6E 62
Knightleys Ct. *E10 1A 68*
(off Wellington Rd.)
Knighton Cl. CR2: S Croy 7B 168
IG8: Wfd G 4E 36
RM7: Rom 6K 55
Knighton Dr. IG8: Wfd G 4E 36
Knighton Grn. IG9: Buck H 2E 36
Knighton La. IG9: Buck H 2E 36
Knighton Pk. Rd. SE26 5K 139
Knighton Rd. E7 3J 69
RM7: Rom 6J 55
Knightrider Ct. EC4 2B 14
Knightrider St. EC4 2B 14 (6B 84)
Knights Arc. SW1 7E 10
Knights Av. W5 2E 96
KNIGHTSBRIDGE 7E 10 (2C 100)
Knightsbridge SW1 7E 10 (2D 100)
SW7 7D 10 (2D 100)
Knightsbridge Ct. SW1 7F 11
Knightsbridge Gdns. RM7: Rom 5K 55
Knightsbridge Grn.
SW1 7E 10 (2D 100)
(not continuous)
Knights Cl. E9 5J 67
KT8: W Mole 5D 148
Knightscote Cl. UB9: Hare 2A 38
Knights Ct. BR1: Brom 3H 141
KT1: King T 3E 150
RM6: Chad H 6E 54
(off High Rd.)
Knights Hill SE27 5B 138
Knight's Hill Sq. SE27 4B 138
Knights Ho. *SW8 7J 101*
(off Sth. Lambeth Rd.)
Knights La. N9 3B 34
Knight's Pk. KT1: King T 3E 150
Knight's Pl. TW2: Twick 1J 131
Knights Rd. E16 2J 105
HA7: Stan 4H 27
Knight's Wlk. SE11 4K 19 (4B 102)
(not continuous)
Knightswood Cl. HA8: Edg 2D 28
Knightswood Ct. N6 7H 47
Knightswood Ho. N12 6F 31
Knightwood Cres. KT3: N Mald 6A 152
Knivet Rd. SW6 6J 99
Knobs Hill Rd. E15 1D 86
Knockholt Rd. SE9 5B 124
Knole, The SE9 4E 142
Knole Cl. CR0: Croy 6J 157
Knole Ct. *UB5: Yead 3A 76*
(off Broomcroft Av.)
Knole Ga. DA15: Sidc 3J 143
Knoll, The BR2: Hayes 2J 171
BR3: Beck 1D 158
W13 5C 78
Knoll Cres. HA6: Nwood 2G 39
(not continuous)
Knoll Dr. N14 7K 21
Knoll Ho. *NW8 2A 82*
(off Carlton Hill)
Knollmead KT5: Surb 1J 163
Knoll Ri. BR6: Orp 1K 173
Knoll Rd. DA5: Bexl 7G 127
DA14: Sidc 5B 144
SW18 5A 118
Knolls Cl. KT4: Wor Pk 3D 164
Knollys Cl. SW16 3A 138
Knolly's Ho. *WC1 3E 6*
(off Tavistock Pl.)
Knollys Rd. SW16 3K 137
Knottisford St. E2 3J 85
Knotts Grn. M. E10 6D 50
Knotts Grn. Rd. E10 6D 50
Knowlden Ho. *E1 7J 85*
(off Cable St.)
Knowle Av. DA7: Bex 7E 108
Knowle Cl. SW9 3A 120
Knowle Rd. BR2: Brom 2D 172
TW2: Twick 1J 131
Knowles Cl. UB7: Yiew 1A 92
Knowles Ct. *HA1: Harr 6K 41*
(off Gayton Rd.)
Knowles Hill Cres. SE13 5F 123
Knowles Ho. *SW18 6K 117*
(off Neville Gill Cl.)
Knowles Wlk. SW4 3G 119
Knowlton Grn.
BR2: Brom 5H 159
Knowlton Ho. *SW9 1A 120*
(off Cowley Rd.)
Knowsley Av. UB1: S'hall 1F 95
Knowsley Rd. SW11 2D 118
Knox Ct. SW4 2J 119
Knox Rd. E7 6H 69
Knox St. NW1 5E 4 (5D 82)
Knoyle St. SE14 6A 104
Koblenz Ho. *N8 3J 47*
(off Newland Rd.)
Kohat Rd. SW19 5K 135
Korda Cl. TW17: Shep 3B 146
Kossuth St. SE10 5G 105
Kotree Way SE1 4G 103
Kramer M. SW5 5J 99
Kreedman Wlk. E8 5G 67
Kreisel Wlk. TW9: Kew 6F 97
Kristina Ct. *SM2: Sutt 6J 165*
(off Overton Rd.)
Krupnik Pl. EC2 2H 9
Kuala Gdns. SW16 1K 155
Kubrick Bus. Est. *E7 4K 69*
(off Station App.)
Kuhn Way E7 5J 69
Kwame Ho. *E16 7F 89*
(off University Way)
Kydbrook Cl. BR5: Pet W 7G 161
Kylemore Cl. E6 2B 88
Kylemore Rd. NW6 7J 63
Kylestrome Ho. *SW1 4H 17*
(off Cundy St.)
Kymberley Rd. HA1: Harr 6J 41
Kymes Ct. HA2: Harr 2H 59
Kynance Gdns. HA7: Stan 1C 42
Kynance M. SW7 3K 99
Kynance Pl. SW7 3A 100
Kynaston Av. CR7: Thor H 5C 156
N16 3F 67
Kynaston Cl. HA3: Hrw W 7C 26
Kynaston Cres. CR7: Thor H 5C 156
Kynaston Rd. BR1: Brom 5J 141
CR7: Thor H 5C 156
EN2: Enf 1J 23
N16 3E 66
Kynaston Wood HA3: Hrw W 7C 26
Kynnersley Cl. SM5: Cars 3D 166
Kynoch Rd. N18 4D 34
Kyrle Rd. SW11 6E 118
Kyverdale Rd. N16 7F 49

L

Laburnum Av. N9 2A 34
N17 7J 33
SM1: Sutt 3C 166
UB7: Yiew 7B 74
Laburnum Cl. E4 6G 35
HA0: Wemb 1G 79
N11 6K 31
SE15 7J 103
Laburnum Ct. E2 1F 85
HA1: Harr 6F 41
HA7: Stan 4H 27
SE16 2J 103
(off Albion St.)
Laburnum Cres. TW16: Sun 1K 147
Laburnum Gdns. CR0: Croy 7K 157
N21 2H 33

Laburnum Gro. HA4: Ruis	6F **39**
KT3: N Mald	2K **151**
N21	2H **33**
NW9	7J **43**
TW3: Houn	4D **112**
UB1: S'hall	4D **76**
Laburnum Ho.	
BR2: Brom	1F **159**
Laburnum Lodge N3	2H **45**
Laburnum Pl. SE9	5E **124**
Laburnum Rd. CR4: Mitc	2E **154**
SW19	7A **136**
UB3: Harl	4H **93**
Laburnums, The E6	4C **88**
Laburnum St. E2	1F **85**
Laburnum Way BR2: Brom	1G **159**
TW19: Stanw	1B **128**
La Caye Apartments E14	4F **105**
(off Glenaffric Av.)	
Lacebark Cl. DA15: Sidc	7K **125**
Lacewing Cl. E13	3J **87**
Lacey Cl. N9	2B **34**
Lacey Dr. HA8: Edg	4A **28**
TW12: Hamp	1D **148**
Lacine Ct. SE16	2K **103**
(off Christopher Cl.)	
Lackington St. EC2	5F **9** (5D **84**)
Lackland Ho. SE1	5F **103**
(off Rowcross St.)	
Lacland Ho. SW10	7B **100**
(off Worlds End Est.)	
Lacock Cl. SW19	6A **136**
Lacock Ct. W13	1A **96**
Lacon Ho. WC1	5G **7**
(off Theobalds Rd.)	
Lacon Rd. SE22	4G **121**
Lacrosse Way E15	1H **155**
Lacy Dr. RM8: Dag	3C **72**
Lacy Rd. SW15	4F **117**
(not continuous)	
Ladas Rd. SE27	4C **138**
Ladbroke Cres. W11	6G **81**
Ladbroke Gdns. W11	7H **81**
Ladbroke Gro. W10	4F **81**
Ladbroke Gro. Ho. W11	7H **81**
(off Ladbroke Gro.)	
Ladbroke M. W11	1G **99**
Ladbroke Rd. EN1: Enf	6A **24**
W11	1H **99**
Ladbroke Sq. W11	7H **81**
Ladbroke Ter. W11	7H **81**
Ladbroke Wlk. W11	1H **99**
Ladbrook Cl. HA5: Pinn	5D **40**
Ladbrooke Cres. DA14: Sidc	3D **144**
Ladbrook Rd. SE25	4D **156**
Ladderstile Ride KT2: King T	5H **133**
Ladderswood Way N11	5B **32**
Ladlands SE22	7G **121**
Lady Aylesford Av. HA7: Stan	5F **27**
Lady Booth Rd. KT1: King T	2E **150**
Ladycroft Gdns. BR6: Farnb	5G **173**
Ladycroft Rd. SE13	3D **122**
Ladycroft Wlk. HA7: Stan	1D **42**
Ladycroft Way BR6: Farnb	5G **173**
Lady Dock Path SE16	2A **104**
Lady Elizabeth Ho. SW14	3J **115**
Ladyfern Ho. E3	5C **86**
(off Gall St.)	
Lady Forsdyke Way KT19: Eps	7G **163**
Ladygate La. HA4: Ruis	6D **38**
Lady Harewood Way KT19: Eps	7G **163**
Lady Hay KT4: Wor Pk	2B **164**
Lady Margaret Rd. N19	4G **65**
NW5	5G **65**
UB1: S'hall	7D **76**
Lady Micos Almshouses E1	6J **85**
(off Aylward St.)	
Lady Sarah Ho. N11	6J **31**
(off Asher Loftus Way)	
Lady Shaw Ct. N13	2E **32**
Ladyship Ter. SE22	7G **121**
Ladysmith Av. E6	2C **88**
IG2: Ilf	7H **53**
Ladysmith Cl. NW7	7H **29**
Ladysmith Rd. E16	3H **87**
EN1: Enf	3K **23**
(not continuous)	
HA3: W'stone	2J **41**
N17	2G **49**
N18	5C **34**
SE9	6E **124**
Lady Somerset Rd. NW5	4F **65**
LADYWELL	5D **122**
Ladywell Arena	6D **122**
Ladywell Cl. SE4	5C **122**
Ladywell Hgts. SE4	6B **122**
Ladywell Leisure Cen.	5E **122**
Ladywell Rd. SE13	5C **122**
Ladywell St. E15	1H **87**
Ladywood Av. BR5: Pet W	5J **161**
Ladywood Rd. KT6: Surb	2G **163**
LA Fitness	
Aldgate	2K **15**
(off Portsoken St.)	
Bayswater	7K **81**
(off Queen's M.)	
Bloomsbury	5G **7**
(off Conduit St.)	
Bromley	2J **159**
(off East St.)	
Covent Garden	2G **13**
Edgware	6B **28**
Finchley	3K **45**
Golders Green	7H **45**
Gospel Oak	4F **65**
Leadenhall	1H **15**
(off Billiter St.)	
London	1C **32**
Marylebone	5E **4** (5D **82**)
New Barnet	4G **21**
Old Isleworth	3B **114**
(off Swan St.)	
Piccadilly	3C **12**
(off Regent St.)	
St Pauls	6C **8**
(off King Edward St.)	
South Kensington	3C **16** (4C **100**)
Sydenham	4J **139**
Victoria	2A **18**
(off Bressenden Pl.)	
West India Quay	7C **86**
Lafone Av. TW13: Felt	2A **130**
Lafone St. SE1	6J **15** (2F **103**)
Lagado M. SE16	1K **103**
Laidlaw Dr. N21	5E **22**
Laing Dean UB5: N'olt	1A **76**
Laing Ho. SE5	7C **102**
Laings Av. CR4: Mitc	2D **154**
Lainlock Pl. TW3: Houn	1F **113**
Lainson St. SW18	7J **117**
Lairdale Cl. SE21	1C **138**
Laird Ho. SE5	7C **102**
(off Redcar St.)	
Lairs Cl. N7	5J **65**
Laitwood Rd. SW12	1F **137**
Lakanal SE5	1E **120**
(off Dalwood St.)	
Lake, The WD23: Bushy	1C **26**
Lake Av. BR1: Brom	6J **141**
Lake Bus. Cen. N17	7B **34**
Lake Cl. RM8: Dag	3D **72**
SW19	5H **135**
Lakedale Rd. SE18	6J **107**
Lake Dr. WD23: Bushy	2C **26**
Lake Farm Country Pk.	1G **93**
Lakefield Cl. SE20	7H **139**
Lakefield Rd. N22	2B **48**
Lake Footpath SE2	2D **108**
Lake Gdns. RM10: Dag	5G **73**
SM6: Wall	3F **167**
TW10: Ham	2B **132**
Lakehall Gdns. CR7: Thor H	5B **156**
Lakehall Rd. CR7: Thor H	5B **156**
Lake Ho. SE1	7C **14**
(off Southwark Bri. Rd.)	
Lake Ho. Rd. E11	3J **69**
Lakehurst Rd. KT19: Ewe	5A **164**
Lakeland Cl. HA3: Hrw W	6C **26**
Lakenheath N14	5B **22**
Laker Ct. SW4	1J **119**
Laker Ind. Est. BR3	5A **140**
(off Kent Ho. La.)	
Lake Rd. CR0: Croy	2B **170**
RM6: Chad H	4D **54**
RM9: Dag	3H **91**
SW19	5H **135**
Laker Pl. SW15	6G **117**
Lakeside BR3: Beck	3D **158**
EN2: Enf	4C **22**
KT2: King T	7H **133**
KT19: Ewe	6A **164**
N3	2K **45**
SM6: Wall	4F **167**
W13	6C **78**
Lakeside Av. IG4: Ilf	4B **52**
SE28	1A **108**
Lakeside Cl. DA15: Sidc	5C **126**
HA4: Ruis	4E **38**
SE25	2G **157**
Lakeside Cres. EN4: E Barn	5J **21**
Lakeside Dr. BR2: Brom	3C **172**
NW10	3F **79**
Lakeside Rd. N13	4E **32**
W14	3F **99**
Lakeside Station	
Ruislip Lido Railway	4F **39**
Lakeside Ter. EC2	5D **8**
Lakeside Way HA9: Wemb	4G **61**
Lakes Rd. BR2: Kes	5A **172**
Lakeswood Rd. BR5: Pet W	6F **161**
Lake Vw. HA8: Edg	5A **28**
Lake Vw. Ct. SW1	1K **17**
(off Bressenden Pl.)	
Lake Vw. Est. E3	2A **86**
Lakeview Rd. DA16: Well	4B **126**
SE27	5A **138**
Lake Vw. Ter. N18	4A **34**
(off Sweet Briar Wlk.)	
Lakis Cl. NW3	4A **64**
Laleham Av. NW7	3E **28**
Laleham Cl. SM1: Sutt	5A **166**
Laleham Ho. E2	3J **9**
(off Camlet St.)	
Laleham Rd. SE6	7E **122**
TW17: Shep	4B **146**
Lalor St. SW6	2G **117**
Lambarde Av. SE9	4E **142**
Lambard Ho. SE10	7E **104**
(off Langdale Rd.)	
Lamb Cl. UB5: N'olt	3C **76**
Lamb Ct. E14	7A **86**
(off Narrow St.)	
Lamberhurst Ho. SE15	6J **103**
Lamberhurst Rd. RM8: Dag	1F **73**
SE27	4A **138**
Lambert Av. TW9: Rich	3G **115**
Lambert Ct. DA8: Erith	6J **109**
(off Park Cres.)	
Lambert Jones M. EC2	5C **8**
Lambert Lodge TW8: Bford	5D **96**
(off Layton Rd.)	
Lambert Rd. E16	6K **87**
N12	5G **31**
SW2	5J **119**
Lambert's Pl. CR0: Croy	1D **168**
Lamberts Rd. KT5: Surb	5E **150**
Lambert St. N1	7A **66**
Lambert Wlk. HA9: Wemb	3E **60**
Lambert Way N12	5F **31**
LAMBETH	3G **19** (3K **101**)
Lambeth Bri. SE1	3F **19** (4J **101**)
Lambeth Crematorium SW17	4A **136**
Lambeth High St.	
SE1	4G **19** (4K **101**)
Lambeth Hill EC4	2C **14** (7C **84**)
Lambeth Palace	2G **19** (3K **101**)
Lambeth Pal. Rd.	
SE1	2G **19** (3K **101**)
Lambeth Rd. CR0: Croy	7A **156**
SE1	3G **19** (4K **101**)
Lambeth Towers SE11	2J **19**
Lambeth Wlk. SE11	4H **19** (4K **101**)
(not continuous)	
Lambfold Ho. N7	6J **65**
Lamb Ho. SE5	7C **102**
(off Elmington Est.)	
SE10	6E **104**
(off Haddo St.)	
Lamb La. E8	7H **67**
Lamble St. NW5	5E **64**
Lambley Rd. RM9: Dag	6B **72**
Lambolle Pl. NW3	6C **64**
Lambolle Rd. NW3	6C **64**
Lambourn Cl. CR2: S Croy	7B **168**
NW5	4G **65**
W7	2K **95**
Lambourne Av. SW19	4H **135**
Lambourne Ct. IG8: Wfd G	7F **37**
SE25	2H **35**
EN1: Enf	2A **24**
IG11: Bark	7K **71**
Lambourne Gro. SE16	5K **103**
Lambourne Ho. NW8	5B **4**
(off Broadley St.)	
SE16	4K **103**
Lambourne Pl. SE3	1K **123**
Lambourne Rd. E11	7E **50**
IG3: Ilf	2J **71**
IG11: Bark	7J **71**
Lambourn Gro. KT1: King T	2H **151**
Lambourn Rd. SW4	3F **119**
Lambrook Ho. SE15	1G **121**
Lambrook Ter. SW6	1G **117**
Lamb's Bldgs. EC1	4E **8** (4D **84**)
Lamb's Cl. N9	2B **34**
Lamb's Conduit Pas.	
WC1	5G **7** (5K **83**)
Lamb's Conduit St.	
WC1	4G **7** (4K **83**)
(not continuous)	
Lambscroft Av. SE9	3A **142**
Lambs Health & Fitness	4E **8**
Lambs Mdw. IG8: Wfd G	2B **52**
Lamb's M. N1	1B **84**
Lamb's Pas. EC1	5E **8** (4D **84**)
Lambs Ter. N9	2J **33**
Lamb St. E1	5J **9** (5F **85**)
Lamb's Wlk. EN2: Enf	2H **23**
Lambton M. N19	1J **65**
(off Lambton Rd.)	
Lambton Pl. W11	7H **81**
Lambton Rd. N19	1J **65**
SW20	1E **152**
Lamb Wlk. SE1	7G **15** (2E **102**)
LAMDA Theatre	4J **99**
(off Logan Pl.)	
Lamerock Rd. BR1: Brom	4H **141**
Lamerton Rd. IG6: Ilf	2F **53**
Lamerton St. SE8	6C **104**
Lamford Cl. N17	7J **33**
Lamington St. W6	4D **98**
Lamlash St. SE11	4B **102**
Lamley Ho. SE10	7D **104**
(off Ashburnham Pl.)	
Lammas Av. CR4: Mitc	2E **154**
Lammas Grn. SE26	3H **139**
Lammas Pk. Gdns. W5	1C **96**
Lammas Pk. Rd. W5	2D **96**
Lammas Rd. E9	7K **67**
E10	2A **68**
TW10: Ham	4C **132**
Lammermoor Rd. SW12	7F **119**
Lamont Rd. SW10	7A **16** (6B **100**)

Lamont Rd. Pas.—Langley Ct.

Lamont Rd. Pas. SW10 . . . . . 7A **16**
LAMORBEY 1K **143**
Lamorbey Cl. DA15: Sidc 1K **143**
Lamorbey Swimming Cen. 2A **144**
Lamorna Cl. BR6: Orp 7K **161**
E17 . . . . . 2E **50**
Lamorna Gro. HA7: Stan 1D **42**
Lampard Gro. N16 . . . . . 1F **67**
Lampern Sq. E2 . . . . . 3G **85**
Lampeter Cl. NW9 . . . . . 6A **44**
Lampeter Sq. W6 . . . . . 6G **99**
Lamplighter Cl. E1 . . . . . 4J **85**
Lampmead Rd. SE12 . . . . . 5H **123**
Lamp Office Ct. WC1 . . . . . 4G **7**
Lamport Cl. SE18 . . . . . 4D **106**
Lamps Ct. *SE5* *7C* ***102***
(off Thompson's Av.)
LAMPTON 1F **113**
Lampton Av. TW3: Houn 1F **113**
Lampton Ct. TW3: Houn 1F **113**
Lampton Ho. Cl. SW19 . . . . . 4F **135**
Lampton Pk. Rd. TW3: Houn 2F **113**
Lampton Rd. TW3: Houn 2F **113**
Lanacre Av. NW9 . . . . . 1K **43**
Lanain Ct. SE12 . . . . . 7H **123**
Lanark Cl. W5 . . . . . 5C **78**
Lanark Ct. *UB5: N'olt* *5E* ***58***
(off Newmarket Av.)
Lanark Ho. *SE1* *5G* ***103***
(off Old Kent Rd.)
Lanark Mans. *W9* *4A* ***82***
(off Lanark Rd.)
W12 . . . . . *2E* ***98***
(off Pennard Rd.)
Lanark M. W9 . . . . . 3A **82**
Lanark Pl. W9 . . . . . 3A **4** (4A **82**)
Lanark Rd. W9 . . . . . 2K **81**
Lanark Sq. E14 . . . . . 3D **104**
Lanata Wlk. *UB4: Yead* *4B* ***76***
(off Alba Cl.)
Lanbury Rd. SE15 . . . . . 4K **121**
Lancashire Ct. W1 . . . . . 2K **11**
Lancaster Av. CR4: Mitc 5J **155**
E18 . . . . . 4K **51**
EN4: Had W 1F **21**
IG11: Bark 7J **71**
SE27 . . . . . 2B **138**
SW19 . . . . . 5F **135**
Lancaster Cl. BR2: Brom 4H **159**
KT2: King T 5D **132**
N1 . . . . . 7E **66**
N17 . . . . . 7B **34**
NW9 . . . . . 7G **29**
TW15: Ashf 4A **128**
TW19: Stanw 6A **110**
W2 . . . . . *7K* ***81***
(off St Petersburgh Pl.)
Lancaster Cotts. TW10: Rich 6E **114**
Lancaster Ct. KT12: Walt T 7J **147**
SE27 . . . . . 2B **138**
SM2: Sutt *7J* ***165***
(off Mulgrave Rd.)
SW6 . . . . . 7H **99**
TW19: Stanw 1A **128**
W2 . . . . . *2A* ***10***
(off Lancaster Ga.)
Lancaster Dr. E14 . . . . . 1E **104**
NW3 . . . . . 6C **64**
Lancaster Gdns. BR1: Brom 5C **160**
KT2: King T 5D **132**
SW19 . . . . . 5G **135**
W13 . . . . . 2B **96**
Lancaster Ga. W2 . . . . . 2A **10** (7A **82**)
Lancaster Gro. NW3 . . . . . 6B **64**
Lancaster Hall *E16* *1J* ***105***
(off Wesley Av., not continuous)
Lancaster House 6B **12**
Lancaster Ho. EN2: Enf 1J **23**
Lancaster Lodge
W11 . . . . . *6G* ***81***
(off Lancaster Rd.)
Lancaster M. SW18 . . . . . 5K **117**
TW10: Rich 6E **114**
W2 . . . . . 2A **10** (7A **82**)
Lancaster Pk. TW10: Rich 5E **114**
Lancaster Pl. IG1: Ilf 5G **71**
SW19 . . . . . 5F **135**
TW1: Twick 6A **114**
TW4: Houn 2A **112**
WC2 . . . . . 2G **13** (7K **83**)
Lancaster Rd. E7 . . . . . 7J **69**
E11 . . . . . 2G **69**
E17 . . . . . 2K **49**
EN2: Enf 1J **23**
EN4: E Barn 5G **21**
HA2: Harr 5E **40**
N4 . . . . . 7K **47**
N11 . . . . . 6C **32**
N18 . . . . . 5A **34**
NW10 . . . . . 5C **62**
SE25 . . . . . 2F **157**
SW19 . . . . . 5F **135**
UB1: S'hall 7C **76**
UB5: N'olt 6G **59**
W11 . . . . . 6G **81**
Lancaster Rd. Ind. Est. *EN4: E Barn* . . . *5G* ***21***
(off Lancaster Rd.)
Lancaster Stables NW3 . . . . . 6C **64**
Lancaster St. SE1 . . . . . 7A **14** (2B **102**)
Lancaster Ter. W2 . . . . . 2A **10** (7B **82**)
Lancaster Wlk. UB3: Hayes 6E **74**
W2 . . . . . 3A **10** (1A **100**)
Lancaster Way KT4: Wor Pk 7D **152**
Lancastrian Rd. SM6: Wall 7J **167**
Lancefield Ct. W10 . . . . . 2G **81**
Lancefield Ho. SE15 . . . . . 4H **121**
Lancefield St. W10 . . . . . 3H **81**
Lancell St. N16 . . . . . 2F **67**
Lancelot Av. HA0: Wemb 4D **60**
Lancelot Cres. HA0: Wemb 4D **60**
Lancelot Gdns. EN4: E Barn 7K **21**
Lancelot Pl. SW7 . . . . . 7E **10** (2D **100**)
Lancelot Rd. DA16: Well 4A **126**
HA0: Wemb 4D **60**
Lance Rd. HA1: Harr 7G **41**
Lancer Sq. W8 . . . . . 2K **99**
Lancey Cl. SE7 . . . . . 4C **106**
Lanchester Ct. *W2* *1E* ***10***
(off Seymour St.)
Lanchester Rd. N6 . . . . . 5D **46**
Lancing Gdns. N9 . . . . . 1A **34**
Lancing Ho. *CR0: Croy* *4D* ***168***
(off Coombe Rd.)
Lancing Rd. CR0: Croy 7K **155**
IG2: Ilf 6H **53**
TW13: Felt 2H **129**
W13 . . . . . 7B **78**
Lancing St. NW1 . . . . . 2C **6** (3H **83**)
Lancresse Ct. *N1* *1E* ***84***
(off De Beauvoir Est.)
Landale Ho. *SE16* *3J* ***103***
(off Lower Rd.)
Landau Ct. *CR2: S Croy* *5C* ***168***
(off Warham Rd.)
Landcroft Rd. SE22 . . . . . 5F **121**
Landells Rd. SE22 . . . . . 6F **121**
Landford Rd. SW15 . . . . . 3E **116**
Landgrove Rd. SW19 . . . . . 5J **135**
Landin Ho. *E14* *6C* ***86***
(off Thomas Rd.)
Landleys Fld. *NW5* *5H* ***65***
(off Long Mdw.)
Landmann Ho. *SE16* *4H* ***103***
(off Rennie Est.)
Landmann Way SE14 . . . . . 5K **103**
Landmark Arts Cen. 5B **132**
Landmark Commercial Cen. N18 . . . . . 6K **33**
Landmark Hgts. E5 . . . . . 4A **68**
Landmark Ho. *W6* *5E* ***98***
(off Hammersmith Bri. Rd.)
Landon Pl. SW1 . . . . . 1E **16** (3D **100**)
Landon's Cl. E14 . . . . . 1E **104**
Landon Wlk. E14 . . . . . 7D **86**
Landon Way TW15: Ashf 6D **128**
Landor Ho. *SE5* *7D* ***102***
(off Elmington Est.)
Landor Rd. SW9 . . . . . 3J **119**
Landor Theatre 3J **119**
Landor Wlk. W12 . . . . . 2C **98**
Landra Gdns. N21 . . . . . 6G **23**
Landrake *NW1* *1G* ***83***
(off Plender St.)
Landridge Dr. EN1: Enf 1C **24**
Landridge Rd. SW6 . . . . . 2H **117**
Landrock Rd. N8 . . . . . 6J **47**
Landscape Rd. IG8: Wfd G 7E **36**
Landsdown Cl. EN5: New Bar 4F **21**
Landseer Av. E12 . . . . . 5E **70**
Landseer Cl. HA8: Edg 2G **43**
SW19 . . . . . 1A **154**
Landseer Ct. UB4: Hayes 2F **75**
Landseer Ho. *NW8* *3B* ***4***
(off Frampton St.)
SW1 . . . . . *4D* ***18***
(off Herrick St.)
SW11 . . . . . 1E **118**
UB5: N'olt *2B* ***76***
(off Parkfield Dr.)
Landseer Rd. EN1: Enf 5B **24**
KT3: N Mald 7K **151**
N19 . . . . . 3J **65**
(not continuous)
SM1: Sutt 6J **165**
Landstead Rd. SE18 . . . . . 7H **107**
Landulph Ho. *SE11* *5K* ***19***
(off Kennings Way)
Landward Ct. *W1* *7D* ***4***
(off Harrowby St.)
Lane, The NW8 . . . . . 2A **82**
SE3 . . . . . 3J **123**
Lane App. NW7 . . . . . 5B **30**
Lane Cl. NW2 . . . . . 3D **62**
Lane End DA7: Bex 3H **127**
SW15 . . . . . 6F **117**
Lane Gdns. WD23: Bushy 1D **26**
Lane Jane Ct. *KT2: King T* *2F* ***151***
(off London Rd.)
Lane M. E12 . . . . . 3D **70**
Lanercost Cl. SW2 . . . . . 2A **138**
Lanercost Gdns. N14 . . . . . 7D **22**
Lanercost Rd. SW2 . . . . . 2A **138**
Lanesborough Ct. *N1* *1G* ***9***
(off Fanshaw St.)
Lanesborough Pl. SW1 . . . . . 6H **11**
Laneside BR7: Chst 5F **143**
HA8: Edg 5D **28**
Laneside Av. RM8: Dag 7F **55**
Laneway SW15 . . . . . 5D **116**
Laney Ho. *EC1* *5J* ***7***
(off Leather La.)
Lanfranc Ct. HA1: Harr 3K **59**
Lanfranc Rd. E3 . . . . . 2A **86**
Lanfrey Pl. W14 . . . . . 5H **99**
Langbourne Av. N6 . . . . . 2E **64**
Langbourne Ct. E17 . . . . . 6A **50**
Langbourne Mans. N6 . . . . . 2E **64**
Langbourne Pl. E14 . . . . . 5D **104**
Langbourne Way KT10: Clay 6A **162**
Langbrook Rd. SE3 . . . . . 3B **124**
Langcroft Cl. SM5: Cars 3D **166**
Langdale *NW1* *1A* ***6***
(off Stanhope St.)
Langdale Av. CR4: Mitc 3D **154**
Langdale Cl. BR6: Farnb 3F **173**
RM8: Dag 1C **72**
SE17 . . . . . 6C **102**
SW14 . . . . . 4H **115**
Langdale Cres. DA7: Bex 7G **109**
Langdale Dr. UB4: Hayes 2G **75**
Langdale Gdns. UB6: G'frd 3B **78**
Langdale Ho. *SW1* *6A* ***18***
(off Churchill Gdns.)
Langdale Pde. CR4: Mitc 3D **154**
Langdale Rd. CR7: Thor H 4A **156**
SE10 . . . . . 7E **104**
Langdale St. E1 . . . . . 6H **85**
Langdon Ct. *EC1* *1B* ***8***
(off City Rd.)
NW10 . . . . . 1A **80**
Langdon Cres. E6 . . . . . 2E **88**
Langdon Dr. NW9 . . . . . 1J **61**
Langdon Ho. E14 . . . . . 6E **86**
Langdon Pk. TW11: Tedd 7C **132**
Langdon Pk. Rd. N6 . . . . . 7G **47**
Langdon Pl. SW14 . . . . . 3J **115**
Langdon Rd. BR2: Brom 3K **159**
E6 . . . . . 1E **88**
SM4: Mord 5A **154**
Langdons Ct. UB2: S'hall 3E **94**
Langdon Shaw DA14: Sidc 5K **143**
Langdon Wlk. SM4: Mord 5A **154**
Langdon Way SE1 . . . . . 4G **103**
Langford Cl. E8 . . . . . 5G **67**
NW8 . . . . . 2A **82**
W3 . . . . . 2H **97**
Langford Ct. *NW8* *2A* ***82***
(off Abbey Rd.)
Langford Cres. EN4: Cockf 4J **21**
Langford Grn. SE5 . . . . . 3E **120**
Langford Ho. SE8 . . . . . 6C **104**
Langford Pl. DA14: Sidc 3A **144**
NW8 . . . . . 2A **82**
Langford Rd. EN4: Cockf 4J **21**
IG8: Wfd G 6F **37**
SW6 . . . . . 2K **117**
Langfords IG9: Buck H 2G **37**
Langham Cl. *N15* *3B* ***48***
(off Langham Rd.)
Langham Ct. HA4: Ruis 5K **57**
NW4 . . . . . 5F **45**
SW20 . . . . . 2E **152**
Langham Dr. RM6: Chad H 6B **54**
Langham Gdns. HA0: Wemb 2C **60**
HA8: Edg 7D **28**
N21 . . . . . 5F **23**
TW10: Ham 4C **132**
W13 . . . . . 7B **78**
Langham Ho. Cl. TW10: Ham 4D **132**
Langham Mans. *SW5* *5K* ***99***
(off Earl's Ct. Sq.)
Langham Pk. Pl. BR2: Brom 4H **159**
Langham Pl. N15 . . . . . 3B **48**
W1 . . . . . 6K **5** (5F **83**)
W4 . . . . . 6A **98**
Langham Rd. HA8: Edg 6D **28**
N15 . . . . . 3B **48**
SW20 . . . . . 1E **152**
TW11: Tedd 5B **132**
Langham St. W1 . . . . . 6K **5** (5F **83**)
Langhedge Cl. N18 . . . . . 6A **34**
Langhedge La. N18 . . . . . 6A **34**
Langhedge La. Ind. Est. N18 . . . . . 6A **34**
Langholm Cl. SW12 . . . . . 7H **119**
Langholme WD23: Bush 1B **26**
Langhorn Dr. TW2: Twick 7J **113**
Langhorne Ct. *NW8* *7B* ***64***
(off Dorman Way)
Langhorne Rd. RM10: Dag 7G **73**
Lang Ho. *SW8* *7J* ***101***
(off Hartington Rd.)
TW19: Stanw 1A **128**
Langland Cres. HA7: Stan 2D **42**
Langland Dr. HA5: Pinn 1C **40**
Langland Gdns.
CR0: Croy 2B **170**
NW3 . . . . . 5K **63**
Langland Ho. *SE5* *7D* ***102***
(off Edmund St.)
Langler Rd.
NW10 . . . . . 2E **80**
Langley Av. HA4: Ruis 2K **57**
KT4: Wor Pk 1F **165**
KT6: Surb 1D **162**
Langley Ct. WC2 . . . . . 2E **12** (7J **83**)

A-Z London 307

Langley Cres. E11 7A **52**
HA8: Edg 3D **28**
RM9: Dag 7C **72**
UB3: Harl 7H **93**
Langley Dr. E11 7K **51**
W3 2H **97**
Langley Gdns. BR2: Brom 4A **160**
BR5: Pet W 6F **161**
RM9: Dag 7D **72**
Langley Gro. KT3: N Mald 2A **152**
Langley Ho. *W2* *5J* ***81***
(off Alfred Rd.)
Langley La. SW8 7F **19** (6K **101**)
Langley Mans. SW8 7F **19**
Langley Pk. NW7 6F **29**
Langley Pk. Girls School Sports Cen.
6E 158
Langley Pk. Rd. SM1: Sutt 5A **166**
SM2: Sutt 6A **166**
Langley Rd. BR3: Beck 4A **158**
DA16: Well 6C **108**
KT6: Surb 7E **150**
SW19 1H **153**
TW7: Isle 2K **113**
Langley Row EN5: Barn 1C **20**
Langley St. WC2 1E **12** (6J **83**)
Langley Way BR4: W W'ck 1F **171**
Langmead Dr. WD23: Bushy 1D **26**
Langmead St. SE27 4B **138**
Langmore Ct. DA6: Bex 3D **126**
Langmore Ho. *E1* *6G* ***85***
(off Stutfield St.)
Langport Ct. KT12: Walt T 7A **148**
Langport Ho. SW9 2B **120**
Langridge M. TW12: Hamp 6D **130**
Langroyd Rd. SW17 2D **136**
Langside Av. SW15 4C **116**
Langside Cres. N14 3C **32**
Langstone Way NW7 7A **30**
Langston Hughes Cl.
SE24 4B **120**
Lang St. E1 4J **85**
Langthorn Ct. EC2 7E **8** (6D **84**)
Langthorne Ct. BR1: Brom 4E **140**
Langthorne Ho. UB3: Harl 4G **93**
Langthorne Rd. E11 3E **68**
Langthorne St. SW6 7F **99**
Langton Av. E6 3E **88**
N20 7F **21**
Langton Cl. WC1 3H **7** (4K **83**)
Langton Ho. SE11 3H **19**
Langton Pl. SW18 1J **135**
Langton Ri. SE23 7H **121**
Langton Rd. HA3: Hrw W 7B **26**
KT8: W Mole 4G **149**
NW2 3E **62**
SW9 7B **102**
Langton St. SW10 6A **100**
Langton Way CR0: Croy 3E **168**
SE3 1H **123**
Langtry Pl. SW6 6J **99**
Langtry Rd. NW8 1K **81**
UB5: N'olt 2B **76**
Langtry Wlk. NW8 1K **81**
Langwood Chase
TW11: Tedd 6C **132**
Langworth Dr. UB4: Yead 6K **75**
Lanhill Rd. W9 4J **81**
Lanier Rd. SE13 6F **123**
Lanigan Dr. TW3: Houn 5F **113**
Lankaster Gdns. N2 1B **46**
Lankers Dr. HA2: Harr 6D **40**
Lankton Cl. BR3: Beck 1E **158**
Lannock Rd. UB3: Hayes 1H **93**
Lannoy Point *SW6* *7G* ***99***
(off Pellant Rd.)
Lannoy Rd. SE9 1G **143**
Lanrick Ho. *E14* *6F* ***87***
(off Lanrick Rd.)
Lanrick Rd. E14 6F **87**
Lanridge Rd. SE2 3D **108**
Lansbury Av. IG11: Bark 7A **72**
N18 5J **33**
RM6: Chad H 5E **54**
TW14: Felt 6K **111**
Lansbury Cl. NW10 5J **61**
Lansbury Ct. *SE28* *7B* ***90***
(off Saunders Way)
Lansbury Dr. UB4: Hayes 2G **75**
Lansbury Est. E14 6D **86**
Lansbury Gdns. E14 6F **87**
Lansbury Rd. EN3: Enf H 1E **24**
Lansbury Way N18 5K **33**
Lanscombe Wlk. SW8 1J **119**
Lansdell Ho. *SW2* *6A* ***120***
(off Tulse Hill)
Lansdell Rd. CR4: Mitc 2E **154**
Lansdowne Av.
BR6: Farnb 1F **173**
DA7: Bex 7D **108**
Lansdowne Cl. KT6: Surb 2H **163**
SW20 7F **135**
TW1: Twick 1K **131**
Lansdowne Ct. IG5: Ilf 3C **52**
KT4: Wor Pk 2C **164**
W11 *7G* ***81***
(off Lansdowne Ri.)
Lansdowne Cres. W11 7G **81**
Lansdowne Dr. E8 6G **67**
Lansdowne Gdns. SW8 1J **119**
Lansdowne Grn. Est. SW8 1J **119**
Lansdowne Gro. NW10 4A **62**
Lansdowne Hill SE27 3B **138**
Lansdowne La. SE7 6B **106**
Lansdowne M. SE7 5B **106**
W11 1H **99**
Lansdowne Pl. SE1 3D **102**
SE19 7F **139**
Lansdowne Ri. W11 7G **81**
Lansdowne Rd. BR1: Brom 7J **141**
CR0: Croy 2D **168**
E4 2H **35**
E11 2H **69**
E17 6C **50**
E18 3J **51**
HA1: Harr 7J **41**
HA7: Stan 6H **27**
IG3: Ilf 1K **71**
KT19: Ewe 7J **163**
N3 7D **30**
N10 2G **47**
N17 1F **49**
SW20 7E **134**
TW3: Houn 3F **113**
UB8: Hil 6E **74**
W11 7G **81**
Lansdowne Row W1 4K **11** (1F **101**)
Lansdowne Ter. WC1 4F **7** (4J **83**)
Lansdowne Wlk. W11 1H **99**
Lansdowne Way SW8 1H **119**
Lansdowne Wood Cl. SE27 3B **138**
Lansdowne Workshops SE7 5A **106**
Lansdown Rd. DA14: Sidc 3B **144**
E7 7A **70**
Lansfield Av. N18 4B **34**
Lantern Cl. HA0: Wemb 5D **60**
SW15 4C **116**
Lanterns Ct. E14 3C **104**
Lantern Way UB7: W Dray 2A **92**
Lant Ho. *SE1* *7C* ***14***
(off Toulmin St.)
Lantry Ct. W3 1H **97**
Lant St. SE1 6C **14** (2C **102**)
Lanvanor Rd. SE15 2J **121**
Lanyard Ho. SE8 4B **104**
Lapford Cl. W9 4H **81**
Lapponum Wlk. UB4: Yead 4B **76**
Lapse Wood Wlk. SE23 1H **139**
Lapstone Gdns. HA3: Kent 6C **42**
Lapwing Ct. KT6: Surb 3G **163**
SE1 *7D* ***14***
(off Swan St.)
Lapwing Twr. *SE8* *6B* ***104***
(off Taylor Cl.)
Lapwing Way UB4: Yead 6B **76**
Lapworth *N11* *4A* ***32***
(off Coppies Gro.)
Lapworth Ct. *W2* *5K* ***81***
(off Delamere Ter.)
Lara Cl. KT9: Chess 7E **162**
SE13 6E **122**
Larbert Rd. SW16 7G **137**
Larch Av. W3 1A **98**
Larch Cl. E13 4K **87**
N11 7K **31**
N19 2G **65**
SE8 6B **104**
SW12 2F **137**
Larch Ct. *SE1* *7G* ***15***
(off Royal Oak Yd.)
W9 *5J* ***81***
(off Admiral Wlk.)
Larch Cres. KT19: Ewe 6H **163**
UB4: Yead 4A **76**
Larch Dene BR6: Farnb 2E **172**
Larch Dr. W4 5G **97**
Larches, The N13 3H **33**
UB10: Hil 3D **74**
Larches Av. SW14 4K **115**
Larch Grn. NW9 1A **44**
Larch Gro. DA15: Sidc 1K **143**
Larch Ho. BR2: Brom 1G **159**
SE16 *2J* ***103***
(off Ainsty Est.)
UB4: Yead 5A **76**
W10 *4G* ***81***
(off Rowan Wlk.)
Larch Rd. E10 2C **68**
NW2 4E **62**
Larch Tree Way CR0: Croy 3C **170**
Larchvale Ct. SM2: Sutt 7K **165**
Larch Way BR2: Brom 7E **160**
Larchwood Rd. SE9 2F **143**
Larcombe Cl. CR0: Croy 4F **169**
Larcombe Ct. *SM2: Sutt* *7K* ***165***
(off Worcester Rd.)
Larcom St. SE17 4C **102**
Larden Rd. W3 1A **98**
Largewood Av. KT6: Surb 2G **163**
Larissa St. SE17 5D **102**
Larkbere Rd. SE26 4A **140**
Larken Cl. WD23: Bush 1B **26**
Larken Dr. WD23: Bush 1B **26**
Larkfield Av. HA3: Kent 3B **42**
Larkfield Cl. BR2: Hayes 2H **171**
Larkfield Rd. DA14: Sidc 3K **143**
TW9: Rich 4E **114**
Larkhall La. SW4 2H **119**
Larkhall Ri. SW4 3G **119**
(not continuous)
Larkham Cl. TW13: Felt 3G **129**
Larkhill Ter. SE18 7E **106**
Lark Row E2 1J **85**
Larksfield Gro. EN1: Enf 1C **24**
Larks Gro. IG11: Bark 7J **71**
Larkshall Ct. RM7: Mawney 2J **55**
Larkshall Cres. E4 4K **35**
Larkshall Rd. E4 5K **35**
Larkspur Cl. E6 5C **88**
HA4: Ruis 7E **38**
N17 7J **33**
NW9 5H **43**
Larkspur Gro. HA8: Edg 4D **28**
Larkspur Lodge DA14: Sidc 3B **144**
Larkspur Way KT19: Ewe 5J **163**
Larkswood Ct. E4 5A **36**
Larkswood Leisure Cen. 4K 35
Larkswood Ri. HA5: Eastc 4A **40**
Larkswood Rd. E4 4H **35**
Lark Way SM5: Cars 7C **154**
Larkway Cl. NW9 4K **43**
Larnach Rd. W6 6F **99**
Larne Rd. HA4: Ruis 7H **39**
Larpent Av. SW15 5E **116**
Larwood Cl. UB6: G'frd 5H **59**
Lascelles Av. HA1: Harr 7H **41**
Lascelles Cl. E11 2F **69**
Lascelles Ho. NW1 4D **4**
Lascotts Rd. N22 6E **32**
Laseron Ho. *N15* *4F* ***49***
(off Tottenham Grn. E.)
Lassa Rd. SE9 5C **124**
Lassell St. SE10 5F **105**
Lasseter Pl. SE3 6G **105**
Latchett Rd. E18 1K **51**
Latchingdon Ct. E17 4K **49**
Latchingdon Gdns. IG8: Wfd G 6H **37**
Latchmere Cl. TW10: Ham 5E **132**
Latchmere La. KT2: King T 6F **133**
TW10: Ham 5F **133**
Latchmere Leisure Cen. 2D 118
Latchmere Pas. SW11 2C **118**
Latchmere Rd. KT2: King T 7E **132**
SW11 2D **118**
Latchmere St. SW11 2D **118**
Lateward Rd. TW8: Bford 6D **96**
Latham Cl. E6 5C **88**
TW1: Twick 7A **114**
Latham Ct. *N11* *6D* ***32***
(off Brownlow Rd.)
SW5 *4J* ***99***
(off W. Cromwell Rd.)
UB5: N'olt *3B* ***76***
(off Seasprite Cl.)
Latham Ho. *E1* *6K* ***85***
(off Chudleigh St.)
Latham Rd. DA6: Bex 5G **127**
TW1: Twick 7K **113**
Latham's Way CR0: Wadd 1K **167**
Lathkill Cl. EN1: Enf 7B **24**
Lathkill Ct. BR3: Beck 1B **158**
Lathom Rd. E6 7C **70**
Latimer Av. E6 1D **88**
Latimer Cl. HA5: Pinn 1A **40**
KT4: Wor Pk 4D **164**
Latimer Ct. *BR2: Brom* *4H* ***159***
(off Durham Rd.)
Latimer Gdns. HA5: Pinn 1A **40**
Latimer Ho. E9 6K **67**
W11 *7H* ***81***
(off Kensington Pk. Rd.)
Latimer Ind. Est. W10 6E **80**
Latimer Pl. W10 6E **80**
Latimer Rd. CR0: Croy 3B **168**
E7 4K **69**
EN5: New Bar 3E **20**
N15 6E **48**
SW19 6K **135**
TW11: Tedd 5K **131**
W10 5E **80**
(not continuous)
Latona Ct. *SW9* *7A* ***102***
(off Caldwell St.)
Latona Rd. SE15 6G **103**
La Tourne Gdns. BR6: Farnb 3G **173**
Lattimer Pl. W4 7A **98**
Latton Cl. KT12: Walt T 7C **148**
Latymer Ct. W6 4F **99**
Latymer Gdns. N3 2G **45**
Latymer Rd. N9 1A **34**
Latymer Upper School Sports Cen. 5C 98
Latymer Way N9 2K **33**
Lauder Cl. UB5: N'olt 2B **76**
Lauder Ct. N14 7D **22**
Lauderdale Dr. TW10: Ham 3D **132**
Lauderdale House 1F 65
Lauderdale Ho. *SW9* *1A* ***120***
(off Gosling Way)
Lauderdale Mans. *W9* *3K* ***81***
(off Lauderdale Rd., not continuous)
Lauderdale Pde. W9 4K **81**
Lauderdale Pl. *EC2* *5C* ***8***
(off Beech St.)
Lauderdale Rd. W9 3K **81**

Lely Ho. UB5: N'olt 2B 76
  (off Academy Gdns.)
Leman Pas. E1 . . . .1K 15
Leman St. E1 . . . .1K 15 (6F 85)
Lemark Cl. HA7: Stan 6H 27
Le May Av. SE12 . . . .3K 141
Lemmon Rd. SE10 . . . .6G 105
Lemna Rd. E11 . . . .7H 51
Le Moal Ho. E1 . . . .5J 85
  (off Stepney Way)
Lemon Gro. TW13: Felt 1J 129
  (off Highfield Rd.)
Lemonwell Dr. SE9 . . . .5G 125
Lemsford Cl. N15 . . . .6G 49
Lemsford Ct. N4 . . . .2C 66
Lemuel St. SW18 . . . .6A 118
Lena Cres. N9 . . . .2D 34
Lena Gdns. W6 . . . .3E 98
Lena Kennedy Cl. E4 . . . .6K 35
Lenanton Steps E14 . . . .2C 104
  (off Manilla St.)
Len Clifton Ho. SE18 . . . .4D 106
  (off Cambridge Barracks Rd.)
Lendal Ter. SW4 . . . .3H 119
Lenelby Rd. KT6: Surb 1G 163
Len Freeman Pl. SW6 . . . .6H 99
Lenham Ho. SE1 . . . .7F 15
  (off Long La.)
Lenham Rd. CR7: Thor H 2D 156
  DA7: Bex 6F 109
  SE12 . . . .4H 123
  SM1: Sutt 4K 165
Lennard Av. BR4: W W'ck 2G 171
Lennard Cl. BR4: W W'ck 2G 171
Lennard Rd. BR2: Brom 1D 172
  BR3: Beck 6K 139
  CR0: Croy 1C 168
  SE20 . . . .6K 139
Lennon Rd. NW2 . . . .5E 62
Lennox Gdns. CR0: Wadd 4B 168
  IG1: Ilf 1D 70
  NW10 . . . .4B 62
  SW1 . . . .2E 16 (3D 100)
Lennox Gdns. M.
  SW1 . . . .2E 16 (3D 100)
Lennox Ho. DA17: Belv 3G 109
  (off Picardy St.)
  TW1: Twick 6D 114
  (off Clevedon Rd.)
Lennox Lewis Cen. E5 . . . .2J 67
  (off Theydon Rd.)
Lennox Rd. E17 . . . .6B 50
  N4 . . . .2K 65
Lenor Cl. DA6: Bex 4E 126
Lensbury Way SE2 . . . .3C 108
Lens Rd. E7 . . . .7A 70
Lenthall Ho. SW1 . . . .6B 18
  (off Churchill Gdns.)
Lenthall Rd. E8 . . . .7G 67
Lenthorp Rd. SE10 . . . .4H 105
Lentmead Rd. BR1: Brom 3H 141
Lenton Path SE18 . . . .6H 107
Lenton Ri. TW9: Rich 3E 114
Lenton St. SE18 . . . .4H 107
Len Williams Ct. NW6 . . . .2J 81
Leo Ct. TW8: Bford 7D 96
Leof Cres. SE6 . . . .5D 140
Leominster Rd. SM4: Mord 6A 154
Leominster Wlk. SM4: Mord 6A 154
Leonard Av. RM7: Rush G 1K 73
  SM4: Mord 5A 154
Leonard Cl. HA3: Hrw W 1J 41
  WC1 . . . .3D 6 (4H 83)
Leonard Pl. N16 . . . .4E 66
Leonard Rd. E4 . . . .6H 35
  E7 . . . .4J 69
  N9 . . . .3A 34
  SW16 . . . .1G 155
  UB2: S'hall 3D 94
Leonard Robbins Path SE28 . . . .7B 90
  (off Tawney Rd.)

Leonard St. E16 . . . .1C 106
  EC2 . . . .3F 9 (4D 84)
Leonora Ho. W9 . . . .4A 82
  (off Lanark Rd.)
Leontine Cl. SE15 . . . .7G 103
Leopards Ct. EC1 . . . .5J 7
Leopold Av. SW19 . . . .5H 135
Leopold Bldgs. E2 . . . .1J 9
  (off Columbia Rd.)
Leopold M. E9 . . . .1J 85
Leopold Rd. E17 . . . .5C 50
  N2 . . . .3B 46
  N18 . . . .5C 34
  NW10 . . . .7A 62
  SW19 . . . .4H 135
  W5 . . . .1F 97
Leopold St. E3 . . . .5B 86
Leopold Ter. SW19 . . . .5H 135
Leo St. SE15 . . . .7H 103
Leo Yd. EC1 . . . .4B 8
Leppoc Rd. SW4 . . . .5H 119
Leroy St. SE1 . . . .4E 102
Lerry Cl. W14 . . . .6H 99
Lerwick Ct. EN1: Enf 5K 23
Lescombe Cl. SE23 . . . .3A 140
Lescombe Rd. SE23 . . . .3A 140
Lesley Cl. DA5: Bexl 7H 127
Leslie Gdns. SM2: Sutt 6J 165
Leslie Gro. CR0: Croy 1E 168
Leslie Gro. Pl. CR0: Croy 1E 168
Leslie Pk. Rd. CR0: Croy 1E 168
Leslie Prince Cl. SE5 . . . .7D 102
Leslie Rd. E11 . . . .4E 68
  E16 . . . .6K 87
  N2 . . . .3B 46
Leslie Smith Sq. SE18 . . . .6E 106
Lesnes Abbey 4D 108
Lesney Farm Est. DA8: Erith 7K 109
Lesney Pk. DA8: Erith 6K 109
Lesney Pk. Rd. DA8: Erith 6K 109
Lessar Av. SW4 . . . .6G 119
Lessingham Av. IG5: Ilf 3E 52
Lessing St. SE23 . . . .7A 122
Lessington Av. RM7: Rom 6J 55
Lessness Av. DA7: Bex 7D 108
LESSNESS HEATH 5H 109
Lessness Pk. DA17: Belv 5F 109
Lessness Rd. DA17: Belv 6G 109
  SM4: Mord 6A 154
Lester Av. E15 . . . .4G 87
Lestock Cl. SE25 . . . .3G 157
  (off Manor Rd.)
Leswin Pl. N16 . . . .3F 67
Leswin Rd. N16 . . . .3F 67
Letchford Gdns. NW10 . . . .3C 80
Letchford M. NW10 . . . .3C 80
Letchford Ter. HA3: Hrw W 1F 41
Letchmore Ho. W10 . . . .4E 80
  (off Sutton Way)
Letchworth Av. TW14: Felt 7H 111
Letchworth Cl. BR2: Brom 5J 159
Letchworth Dr. BR2: Brom 5J 159
Letchworth St. SW17 . . . .4D 136
Lethbridge Cl. SE13 . . . .1E 122
Letterstone Rd. SW6 . . . .7H 99
Lettice St. SW6 . . . .1H 117
Lett Rd. E15 . . . .7F 69
Lettsom St. SE5 . . . .2E 120
Lettsom Wlk. E13 . . . .2J 87
Leucha Rd. E17 . . . .5A 50
Levana Cl. SW19 . . . .1G 135
Levant Ho. E1 . . . .4K 85
  (off Ernest St.)
Levehurst Ho. SE27 . . . .5C 138
Levendale Rd. SE23 . . . .2A 140
Levenhurst Way SW4 . . . .2J 119
Leven Rd. E14 . . . .5E 86
Leven Way UB3: Hayes 6G 75
Leverett St. SW3 . . . .3D 16 (4C 100)
Leverholme Gdns. SE9 . . . .3E 142

Leverington Pl. N1 . . . .2F 9 (3D 84)
Leverson St. SW16 . . . .6G 137
Leverstock Ho. SW3 . . . .5D 16
  (off Cale St.)
Lever St. EC1 . . . .2B 8 (3B 84)
Leverton Pl. NW5 . . . .5G 65
Leverton St. NW5 . . . .5G 65
Levett Gdns. IG3: Ilf 4K 71
Levett Rd. IG11: Bark 6J 71
Levine Gdns.
  IG11: Bark 2D 90
Levison Way N19 . . . .1H 65
Levita Ho. NW1 . . . .1D 6
  (not continuous)
Lewes Cl. UB5: N'olt 6E 58
Lewes Ct. CR4: Mitc 3D 154
  (off Chatsworth Pl.)
Lewesdon Cl. SW19 . . . .1F 135
Lewes Ho. SE1 . . . .6H 15
  (off Druid St.)
  SE15 . . . .6G 103
  (off Friary Est.)
Lewes Rd. BR1: Brom 2B 160
  N12 . . . .5H 31
Leweston Pl. N16 . . . .7F 49
Lew Evans Ho. SE22 . . . .5G 121
Lewey Ho. E3 . . . .4B 86
  (off Joseph St.)
Lewgars Av. NW9 . . . .6J 43
Lewing Cl. BR6: Orp 1J 173
Lewin Rd. DA6: Bex 5E 126
  SW14 . . . .3K 115
  SW16 . . . .6H 137
Lewis Av. E17 . . . .1C 50
Lewis Cl. N14 . . . .7B 22
Lewis Ct. SE16 . . . .5H 103
  (off Stubbs Dr.)
Lewis Cres. NW10 . . . .5A 62
Lewis Gdns. N2 . . . .2B 46
Lewis Gro. SE13 . . . .4E 122
LEWISHAM 3E 122
Lewisham Bus. Cen. SE14 . . . .6K 103
Lewisham Cen. SE13 . . . .4E 122
Lewisham Crematorium SE6 . . . .2H 141
Lewisham Hgts. SE23 . . . .1J 139
Lewisham High St. SE13 . . . .6D 122
Lewisham Hill SE13 . . . .2E 122
Lewisham Lions Cen. 5J 103
Lewisham Model Mkt. SE13 . . . .4E 122
  (off Lewisham High St.)
Lewisham Pk. SE13 . . . .5E 122
Lewisham Rd. SE13 . . . .1D 122
Lewisham St. SW1 . . . .7D 12 (2H 101)
Lewisham Way SE4 . . . .1B 122
  SE14 . . . .1B 122
Lewis Ho. E14 . . . .1E 104
  (off Coldharbour)
Lewis Pl. E8 . . . .5G 67
Lewis Rd. CR4: Mitc 2B 154
  (not continuous)
  DA14: Sidc 3C 144
  DA16: Well 3C 126
  SM1: Sutt 4K 165
  TW10: Rich 5D 114
  UB1: S'hall 2C 94
Lewis Silkin Ho. SE15 . . . .6J 103
  (off Lovelinch Cl.)
Lewis Sports and Leisure Cen. 1F 157
Lewis St. NW1 . . . .6F 65
  (not continuous)
Lewiston Cl. KT4: Wor Pk 7D 152
Lewis Way RM10: Dag 6H 73
Lexden Dr. RM6: Chad H 6B 54
Lexden Rd. CR4: Mitc 4H 155
  W3 . . . .7H 79
Lexham Gdns. W8 . . . .4J 99
Lexham Gdns. M. W8 . . . .3K 99
Lexham Ho. IG11: Bark 1H 89
  (off St Margarets)
Lexham M. W8 . . . .4J 99
Lexham Wlk. W8 . . . .3K 99

Lexington Apartments
  EC1 . . . .3F 9 (4D 84)
Lexington St. W1 . . . .2B 12 (7G 83)
Lexington Way EN5: Barn 4A 20
Lexton Gdns. SW12 . . . .1H 137
Leyborne Av. W13 . . . .2B 96
Leyborne Pk. TW9: Kew 1G 115
Leybourne Cl. BR2: Brom 6J 159
Leybourne Ho. E14 . . . .6B 86
  (off Dod St.)
  SE15 . . . .6J 103
Leybourne Rd. E11 . . . .1H 69
  NW1 . . . .7F 65
  NW9 . . . .5G 43
  UB10: Hil 1E 74
Leybourne St. NW1 . . . .7F 65
Leybridge Ct. SE12 . . . .5J 123
Leyburn Cl. E17 . . . .4D 50
Leyburn Gdns. CR0: Croy 2E 168
Leyburn Gro. N18 . . . .6B 34
Leyburn Ho. N18 . . . .6B 34
Leydenhatch La. BR8: Dart, Swan 7J 145
Leyden Mans. N19 . . . .7J 47
Leyden St. E1 . . . .6J 9 (5F 85)
Leydon Cl. SE16 . . . .1K 103
Leyes Rd. E16 . . . .7B 88
Leyfield KT4: Wor Pk 1A 164
Leyland Av. EN3: Enf H 2F 25
Leyland Gdns. IG8: Wfd G 5F 37
Leyland Ho. E14 . . . .7D 86
  (off Hale St.)
Leyland Rd. SE12 . . . .5J 123
Leylands SW18 . . . .6H 117
Leylang Rd. SE14 . . . .7K 103
Leys, The HA3: Kent 6F 43
  N2 . . . .4A 46
Leys Av. RM10: Dag 1J 91
Leys Cl. HA1: Harr 5H 41
  RM10: Dag 7J 73
Leys Ct. SW9 . . . .2A 120
Leysdown Av. DA7: Bex 4J 127
Leysdown Ho. SE17 . . . .5E 102
  (off Madron St.)
Leysdown Rd. SE9 . . . .2C 142
Leysfield Rd. W12 . . . .3C 98
Leys Gdns. EN4: Cockf 5K 21
Leyspring Rd. E11 . . . .1H 69
Leys Rd. E. EN3: Enf H 1F 25
Leys Rd. W. EN3: Enf H 1F 25
Leys Sq. N3 . . . .1K 45
Ley St. IG1: Ilf 2F 71
  IG2: Ilf 2F 71
Leyswood Dr. IG2: Ilf 5J 53
Leythe Rd. W3 . . . .2J 97
LEYTON 2E 68
Leyton Bus. Cen. E10 . . . .2C 68
Leyton Ct. SE23 . . . .1J 139
Leyton Grange Est. E10 . . . .1C 68
Leyton Grn. Rd. E10 . . . .6E 50
Leyton Grn. Twr. E10 . . . .6E 50
  (off Leyton Grn. Rd.)
Leyton Grn. Towers E10 . . . .6E 50
  (off Leyton Grn. Rd.)
Leyton Ind. Village E10 . . . .7K 49
Leyton Leisure Lagoon 7D 50
Leyton Orient FC 3D 68
Leyton Pk. Rd. E10 . . . .3E 68
Leyton Rd. E15 . . . .5E 68
  SW19 . . . .7A 136
LEYTONSTONE 3G 69
Leytonstone Ho. E11 . . . .7H 51
  (off Hanbury Dr.)
Leytonstone Rd. E15 . . . .5G 69
Leyton Way E11 . . . .7G 51
Leywick St. E15 . . . .2G 87
Lezayre Rd. BR6: Chels 6K 173
Liardet St. SE14 . . . .6A 104
Liberia Rd. N5 . . . .6B 66
Liberty Av. SW19 . . . .1B 154
Liberty Cl. N18 . . . .4A 34
Liberty Ct. IG11: Bark 2B 90

Liberty Ho. E1 7G 85
(off Ensign St.)
Liberty M. N22 1B 48
SW12 6F 119
Liberty St. SW9 1K 119
Libra Rd. E3 2B 86
E13 2J 87
Library and Lifetime Mus. 3C 168
(off High St.)
Library Ct. N17 3F 49
Library Mans. W12 2E 98
(off Pennard Rd.)
Library Pde. NW10 1A 80
(off Craven Pk. Rd.)
Library Pl. E1 7H 85
Library St. SE1 7A 14 (2B 102)
Library Way TW2: Whit 7G 113
Libro Ct. E4 4H 35
Lichfield Cl. EN4: Cockf 3J 21
Lichfield Ct. KT6: Surb 5E 150
(off Claremont Rd.)
TW9: Rich 4E 114
Lichfield Gdns. TW9: Rich 4E 114
Lichfield Gro. N3 1J 45
Lichfield Rd. E3 3A 86
E6 3B 88
HA6: Nwood 3J 39
IG8: Wfd G 4B 36
N9 2B 34
NW2 4G 63
RM8: Dag 4B 72
TW4: Houn 3A 112
TW9: Kew 1F 115
Lichfield Ter. TW9: Rich 5E 114
(off Sheen Rd.)
Lichlade Cl. BR6: Orp 4K 173
Lickey Ho. W14 6H 99
(off Nth. End Rd.)
Lidbury Rd. NW7 6B 30
Lidcote Gdns. SW9 2K 119
Liddall Way UB7: Yiew 1B 92
Liddell Cl. HA3: Kent 3D 42
Liddell Gdns. NW10 2E 80
Liddell Rd. NW6 6J 63
Lidding Rd. HA3: Kent 5D 42
Liddington Rd. E15 1H 87
Liddon Rd. BR1: Brom 3A 160
E13 3K 87
Liden Cl. E17 7B 50
Lidfield Rd. N16 4D 66
Lidgate Rd. SE15 7F 103
Lidiard Rd. SW18 2A 136
Lidlington Pl. NW1 2G 83
Lido Sq. N17 2D 48
Lidyard Rd. N19 1G 65
Liffler Rd. SE18 5J 107
Liffords Pl. SW13 2B 116
Lifford St. SW15 4F 117
Lightcliffe Rd. N13 4F 33
Lighter Cl. SE16 4A 104
Lighterman Ho. E14 7E 86
Lighterman M. E1 6K 85
Lightermans Rd. E14 2C 104
Lightermans Wlk. SW18 4J 117
Lightfoot Rd. N8 5J 47
Light Horse Ct. SW3 6G 17
Lightley Cl. HA0: Wemb 1E 78
Ligonier St. E2 3J 9 (4F 85)
Lilac Cl. E4 6G 35
Lilac Ct. E13 1A 88
TW11: Tedd 4K 131
Lilac Gdns. CR0: Croy 3C 170
RM7: Rush G 1K 73
UB3: Hayes 6G 75
W5 3D 96
Lilac Ho. SE4 3C 122
Lilac M. N22 3A 48
(off High Rd.)
Lilac Pl. SE11 4G 19 (4K 101)
UB7: Yiew 7B 74
Lilac St. W12 7C 80
Lilburne Gdns. SE9 5C 124
Lilburne Rd. SE9 5C 124
Lilburne Wlk. NW10 6J 61
Lile Cres. W7 5J 77
Lilestone Ho. NW8 3B 4
(off Frampton St.)
Lilestone St. NW8 3C 4 (4C 82)
Lilford Ho. SE5 2C 120
Lilford Rd. SE5 2B 120
Lilian Barker Cl. SE12 5J 123
Lilian Board Way UB6: G'frd 5H 59
Lilian Cl. N16 3E 66
Lilian Gdns. IG8: Wfd G 1K 51
Lilian Rd. SW16 1G 155
Lillechurch Rd. RM8: Dag 6B 72
Lilleshall Rd. SM4: Mord 6B 154
Lilley Cl. E1 1G 103
Lilley La. NW7 5E 28
Lillian Av. W3 2G 97
Lillian Rd. SW13 6C 98
Lillie Mans. SW6 6G 99
(off Lillie Rd.)
Lillie Rd. SW6 6G 99
Lillie Road Fitness Cen. 7F 99
Lillieshall Rd. SW4 3F 119
Lillie Yd. SW6 6J 99
Lillington Ho. N7 4A 66
Lillington Gdns. Est. SW1 4B 18
Lilliput Av. UB5: N'olt 1C 76
Lilliput Ct. SE12 5K 123
Lilliput Rd. RM7: Rush G 7K 55
Lily Cl. W14 4F 99
(not continuous)
Lily Gdns. HA0: Wemb 2C 78
Lily Nichols Ho. E16 1B 106
(off Connaught Rd.)
Lily Pl. EC1 5K 7 (5A 84)
Lily Rd. E17 6C 50
Lilyville Rd. SW6 1H 117
Limborough Ho. E14 5C 86
(off Thomas Rd.)
Limbourne Av. RM8: Dag 7F 55
Limburg Rd. SW11 4C 118
Lime Av. UB7: Yiew 7B 74
Limeburner La. EC4 1A 14 (6B 84)
Lime Cl. BR1: Brom 4C 160
E1 1G 103
HA3: W'stone 2A 42
HA5: Eastc 3H 39
IG9: Buck H 2G 37
RM7: Rom 4J 55
SM5: Cars 2D 166
Lime Ct. CR4: Mitc 2B 154
E11 2G 69
(off Trinity Cl.)
E17 5E 50
HA1: Harr 6K 41
SE9 2F 143
Lime Cres. TW16: Sun 2A 148
Limecroft Cl. KT19: Ewe 7K 163
Limedene Cl. HA5: Pinn 1B 40
Lime Gro. BR6: Farnb 2F 173
DA15: Sidc 6K 125
E4 6G 35
HA4: Ruis 6K 39
KT3: N Mald 3K 151
N20 1C 30
TW1: Twick 6K 113
UB3: Hayes 7F 75
W12 2E 98
Limeharbour E14 3D 104
LIMEHOUSE 6B 86
Lime Ho. TW9: Kew 1H 115
Limehouse C'way. E14 7B 86
Limehouse Ct. E14 6C 86
Limehouse Cut E14 5D 86
(off Morris Rd.)
Limehouse Flds. Est. E14 5A 86
Limehouse Link E14 6A 86
Lime Kiln Dr. SE7 6K 105
Limekiln Pl. SE19 7F 139
Lime Lodge TW16: Sun 7H 129
(off Forest Dr.)
Limerick Cl. SW12 7G 119
Lime Rd. DA18: Erith 3F 109
TW9: Rich 4F 115
Lime Row DA18: Erith 3F 109
Limerston St. SW10 7A 16 (6A 100)
Limes, The BR2: Brom 2C 172
KT8: W Mole 4F 149
SW18 6J 117
W2 7J 81
Limes Av. CR0: Wadd 3A 168
E11 4K 51
E12 3C 70
N12 4F 31
NW7 6F 29
NW11 7G 45
SE20 7H 139
SM5: Cars 1D 166
SW13 2B 116
Limes Av., The N11 5A 32
Limes Cl. N11 5B 32
TW15: Ashf 5C 128
Limes Ct. NW6 7G 63
(off Brondesbury Pk.)
Limesdale Gdns. HA8: Edg 2J 43
Limes Fld. Rd. SW14 3A 116
Limesford Rd. SE15 4K 121
Limes Gdns. SW18 6J 117
Limes Gro. SE13 4E 122
Limes Pl. CR0: Croy 7D 156
Limes Rd. BR3: Beck 2D 158
CR0: Croy 6D 156
Limes Row BR6: Farnb 5F 173
Limestone Wlk. DA18: Erith 2D 108
Lime St. E17 4A 50
EC3 2G 15 (7E 84)
Lime St. Pas. EC3 1G 15 (6E 84)
Limes Wlk. SE15 4J 121
W5 2D 96
Lime Ter. W7 7J 77
Lime Tree Av. KT10: Esh, T Ditt 7H 149
Limetree Cl. SW2 1K 137
Lime Tree Ct. CR2: S Croy 6C 168
E3 5C 86
Lime Tree Gro. CR0: Croy 3B 170
Lime Tree Pl. CR4: Mitc 1F 155
Lime Tree Rd. TW5: Hest 1F 113
Limetree Ter. DA16: Well 3A 126
SE6 1B 140
Lime Tree Wlk. BR4: W W'ck 4H 171
EN2: Enf 1H 23
WD23: Bushy 1D 26
Limetree Wlk. SW17 5E 136
Lime Wlk. E15 1G 87
KT8: E Mos 4K 149
Limewood Cl. BR3: Beck 5E 158
E17 4B 50
W13 6B 78
Limewood Ct. IG4: Ilf 5D 52
Limewood Rd. DA8: Erith 7J 109
Limpsfield Av. CR7: Thor H 5K 155
SW19 2F 135
Linacre Cl. SE15 3H 121
Linacre Ct. W6 5F 99
Linacre Rd. NW2 6D 62
Linale Ho. N1 1E 8
Linberry Wlk. SE8 4B 104
Linchmere Rd. SE12 7H 123
Lincoln Av. N14 3B 32
RM7: Rush G 2K 73
SW19 3F 135
TW2: Twick 2G 131
Lincoln Cl. HA2: Harr 5D 40
SE25 6G 157
UB6: G'frd 1G 77
Lincoln Ct. CR2: S Croy 5C 168
(off Warham Rd.)
N16 7D 48
SE12 3A 142
Lincoln Cres. EN1: Enf 5K 23
Lincoln Gdns. IG1: Ilf 7C 52
Lincoln Grn. Rd. BR5: St M Cry 5K 161
Lincoln Ho. SE5 7A 102
SW3 2D 100
Lincoln M. NW6 1H 81
SE21 2D 138
Lincoln Pde. N2 3C 46
Lincoln Rd. CR4: Mitc 5J 155
DA14: Sidc 5B 144
E7 6B 70
E13 4K 87
E18 1J 51
EN1: Enf 4K 23
EN3: Pond E 5C 24
HA0: Wemb 6D 60
HA2: Harr 5D 40
HA6: Nwood 3H 39
KT3: N Mald 3J 151
KT4: Wor Pk 1D 164
N2 3C 46
SE25 3H 157
TW13: Hanw 3D 130
Lincolns, The NW7 3G 29
Lincolns Inn Flds. WC2 7G 7 (6K 83)
Lincoln's Inn Hall 7H 7 (6K 83)
Lincoln St. E11 2G 69
SW3 4E 16 (4D 100)
Lincoln Way EN1: Enf 5C 24
TW16: Sun 1G 147
Lincombe Rd. BR1: Brom 3H 141
Lindal Cres. EN2: Enf 4D 22
Lindales, The N17 6B 34
(off Grasmere Rd.)
Lindal Rd. SE4 5B 122
Lindbergh Rd. SM6: Wall 7J 167
Linden Av. CR7: Thor H 4B 156
EN1: Enf 1B 24
HA4: Ruis 1J 57
HA9: Wemb 5F 61
NW10 2F 81
TW3: Houn 5F 113
Linden Cl. HA4: Ruis 1J 57
HA7: Stan 5G 27
KT7: T Ditt 7K 149
N14 6B 22
Linden Ct. DA14: Sidc 4J 143
W12 1E 98
Linden Cres. IG8: Wfd G 6E 36
KT1: King T 2F 151
UB6: G'frd 6K 59
Lindenfield BR7: Chst 2F 161
Linden Gdns. EN1: Enf 1B 24
W2 7J 81
W4 5A 98
Linden Gro. KT3: N Mald 3A 152
SE15 3H 121
TW11: Tedd 5K 131
Linden Ho. SE8 6B 104
(off Abinger Gro.)
TW12: Hamp 6E 130
Linden Lawns HA9: Wemb 4F 61
Linden Lea N2 5A 46
Linden Leas BR4: W W'ck 2F 171
Linden Mans. N6 1F 65
(off Hornsey La.)
Linden M. N1 5D 66
W2 7J 81
Linden Pl. CR4: Mitc 4C 154
Linden Rd. N10 4F 47
N11 2J 31
N15 4C 48
TW12: Hamp 7E 130
Lindens, The CR0: New Ad 6E 170
E17 4D 50
(off Prospect Hill)
N12 5G 31
W4 1J 115
Linden St. RM7: Rom 4K 55
Linden Wlk. N19 2G 65
Linden Way N14 6B 22
TW17: Shep 5E 146

Longville Rd. SE11 4B **102**
Long Wlk. KT3: N Mald 3J **151**
SE1 3E **102**
SE18 6F **107**
SW13 2A **116**
Longwalk Rd. UB11: Stock P 1D **92**
Long Wall E15 3F **87**
Longwater Ho. *KT1: King T* *3D* ***150***
(off Portsmouth Rd.)
Longwood Bus. Pk. TW16: Sun 5H **147**
Longwood Dr. SW15 6C **116**
Longwood Gdns. IG5: Ilf 4D **52**
IG6: Ilf 3F **53**
Longworth Cl. SE28 6D **90**
Long Yd. WC1 4G **7** (4K **83**)
Loning, The NW9 4A **44**
Lonsdale Av. E6 4B **88**
HA9: Wemb 5E **60**
RM7: Rom 6J **55**
Lonsdale Cl. E6 4C **88**
HA5: H End 1C **40**
HA8: Edg 5A **28**
SE9 3B **142**
UB8: Hil 5E **74**
Lonsdale Ct. KT6: Surb 7D **150**
Lonsdale Cres. IG2: Ilf 6F **53**
Lonsdale Dr. EN2: Enf 4C **22**
Lonsdale Dr. Nth. EN2: Enf 5D **22**
Lonsdale Gdns. CR7: Thor H 4K **155**
Lonsdale Ho. *W11* *6H* ***81***
(off Lonsdale Rd.)
Lonsdale M. TW9: Kew 1G **115**
W11 *6H* ***81***
(off Lonsdale Rd.)
Lonsdale Pl. N1 7A **66**
Lonsdale Rd. DA7: Bex 2F **127**
E11 6H **51**
NW6 1H **81**
SE25 4H **157**
SW13 1B **116**
UB2: S'hall 3B **94**
W4 4B **98**
W11 6H **81**
Lonsdale Sq. N1 7A **66**
Lonsdale Yd. W11 7J **81**
Loobert Rd. N15 3E **48**
Looe Gdns. IG6: Ilf 3F **53**
Loop Rd. BR7: Chst 6G **143**
Lopen Rd. N18 4K **33**
Lopez Ho. SW9 3J **119**
Lorac Ct. SM2: Sutt 7J **165**
Loraine Cl. EN3: Pond E 5D **24**
Loraine Cotts. N7 4K **65**
Loraine Ct. BR7: Chst 5F **143**
Loraine Ho. SM6: Wall 4F **167**
Loraine Rd. N7 4K **65**
W4 6H **97**
Lord Amory Way E14 2E **104**
Lord Av. IG5: Ilf 4D **52**
Lord Chancellor Wlk. KT2: King T 1J **151**
Lord Ct. IG5: Ilf 4D **52**
Lordell Pl. SW19 6E **134**
Lorden Wlk. E2 2K **9** (3G **85**)
Lord Gdns. IG5: Ilf 4D **52**
Lord Hills Bri. W2 5K **81**
Lord Hills Rd. W2 5K **81**
Lord Holland La. SW9 2A **120**
Lord Knyvetts Ct. TW19: Stanw 6A **110**
Lord Napier Pl. W6 5C **98**
Lord North St. SW1 2E **18** (3J **101**)
Lord Roberts M. SW6 7K **99**
Lord Robert's Ter. SE18 5E **106**
Lords Cl. SE21 2C **138**
TW13: Hanw 2C **130**
Lord's Cricket Ground
Marylebone & Middlesex County
Cricket Clubs 2B 4 (3B 82)
Lordship Gro. N16 2D **66**
Lordship La. N17 1D **48**
N22 2A **48**
SE22 4F **121**
Lordship La. Est. SE21 7G **121**
Lordship Pk. N16 2C **66**
Lordship Pk. M. N16 2C **66**
Lordship Pl. SW3 7C **16** (6C **100**)
Lordship Rd. N16 1D **66**
UB5: N'olt 7C **58**
Lordship Ter. N16 2D **66**
Lordsmead Rd. N17 1E **48**
Lord St. E16 1C **106**
Lords Vw. NW8 2C **4** (3B **82**)
Lord Warwick St. SE18 3D **106**
Lordwood Cl. DA6: Bex 5E **126**
Loreburn Ho. N7 4K **65**
Lorenzo St. WC1 1G **7** (3K **83**)
Loretto Gdns. HA3: Kent 4E **42**
Lorian Cl. N12 4E **30**
Lorimar Bus. Cen. RM13: Rain 5K **91**
Loring Rd. N20 2H **31**
SE14 1A **122**
TW7: Isle 2K **113**
Loris Rd. W6 3E **98**
Lorn Ct. SW9 2A **120**
Lorne Av. CR0: Croy 7K **157**
Lorne Cl. NW8 2D **4** (3C **82**)
Lorne Gdns. CR0: Croy 7K **157**
E11 4A **52**
W11 2F **99**
Lorne Ho. *E1* *5A* ***86***
(off Ben Jonson Rd.)
Lorne Rd. E7 4K **69**
E17 5C **50**
HA3: W'stone 2K **41**
N4 1K **65**
TW10: Rich 5F **115**
Lorne Ter. N3 2H **45**
Lorn Rd. SW9 2K **119**
Lorraine Ct. NW1 7F **65**
Lorraine Pk. HA3: Hrw W 7D **26**
Lorrimore Rd. SE17 6B **102**
Lorrimore Sq. SE17 6B **102**
Lorton Ho. *NW6* *1J* ***81***
(off Kilburn Va.)
Lothair Rd. W5 2D **96**
Lothair Rd. Nth. N4 6B **48**
Lothair Rd. Sth. N4 7A **48**
Lothbury EC2 7E **8** (6D **84**)
Lothian Av. UB4: Yead 5K **75**
Lothian Cl. HA0: Wemb 4A **60**
Lothian Rd. SW9 1B **120**
Lothrop St. W10 3G **81**
Lots Rd. SW10 7A **100**
Lotus Cl. SE21 3D **138**
Loubet St. SW17 6D **136**
Loudoun Av. IG6: Ilf 5F **53**
Loudoun Rd. NW8 1A **82**
Loudwater Cl. TW16: Sun 4J **147**
Loudwater Rd. TW16: Sun 4J **147**
Loughborough Est. SW9 3B **120**
Loughborough Pk. SW9 4B **120**
Loughborough Rd. SW9 2A **120**
Loughborough St.
SE11 5H **19** (5K **101**)
Lough Rd. N7 5K **65**
Loughton Way IG9: Buck H 1G **37**
Louisa Cl. E9 1K **85**
Louisa Ct. TW2: Twick 2J **131**
Louisa Gdns. E1 4K **85**
Louisa St. E1 4K **85**
Louise Aumonier Wlk. *N19* *7J* ***47***
(off Jessie Blythe La.)
Louise Bennett Cl. SE24 4B **120**
Louise Ct. N22 1A **48**
Louise De Marillac Ho. *E1* *5J* ***85***
(off Smithy St.)
Louise Rd. E15 6G **69**
Louise White Ho. N19 1H **65**
Louis Gdns. BR7: Chst 4D **142**
Louis M. N10 1F **47**
Louisville Rd. SW17 3E **136**
Lousada Lodge *N14* *6B* ***22***
(off Avenue Rd.)
Louvaine Rd. SW11 4B **118**
Lovage App. E6 5C **88**
Lovat Cl. NW2 3B **62**
Lovat La. EC3 2G **15** (7E **84**)
(not continuous)
Lovatt Cl. HA8: Edg 6C **28**
Lovatt Ct. SW12 1F **137**
Lovatt Dr. HA4: Ruis 5J **39**
Lovat Wlk. TW5: Hest 7C **94**
Loveday Rd. W13 2B **96**
Lovegrove St. SE1 5G **103**
Lovegrove Wlk. E14 1E **104**
Lovekyn Cl. KT2: King T 2E **150**
Lovelace Av. BR2: Brom 6E **160**
Lovelace Gdns. IG11: Bark 4A **72**
KT6: Surb 7D **150**
Lovelace Grn. SE9 3D **124**
Lovelace Ho. *E8* *1F* ***85***
(off Haggerston Rd.)
Lovelace Rd. EN4: E Barn 7H **21**
KT6: Surb 7C **150**
SE21 2C **138**
Lovelace Vs. *KT7: T Ditt* *7B* ***150***
(off Portsmouth Rd.)
Loveland Mans. *IG11: Bark* *7K* ***71***
(off Upney La.)
Love La. BR1: Brom 3K **159**
CR4: Mitc 3C **154**
(not continuous)
DA5: Bexl 6F **127**
(not continuous)
EC2 7D **8** (6C **84**)
HA5: Pinn 2B **40**
IG8: Wfd G 6J **37**
KT6: Surb 2C **162**
N17 7A **34**
SE18 4E **106**
SE25 3H **157**
(not continuous)
SM3: Cheam, Sutt 6G **165**
SM4: Mord 7J **153**
Lovel Av. DA16: Well 2A **126**
Lovelinch Cl. SE15 6J **103**
Lovell Ho. *E8* *1G* ***85***
(off Shrubland Rd.)
Lovell Pl. SE16 3A **104**
Lovell Rd. TW10: Ham 3C **132**
UB1: S'hall 6F **77**
Loveridge M. NW6 6H **63**
Loveridge Rd. NW6 6H **63**
Lovers Wlk. N3 7D **30**
(not continuous)
NW7 6C **30**
SE10 6F **105**
W1 4G **11** (1E **100**)
Lovett Dr. SM5: Cars 7A **154**
Lovett Way NW10 5J **61**
Love Wlk. SE5 2D **120**
Lovibonds Av. BR6: Farnb 4F **173**
UB7: Yiew 6B **74**
Lowbrook Rd. IG1: Ilf 4F **71**
Low Cross Wood La. SE21 3F **139**
Lowdell Cl. UB7: Yiew 6A **74**
Lowden Rd. N9 1C **34**
SE24 4B **120**
UB1: S'hall 7C **76**
Lowder Ho. *E1* *1H* ***103***
(off Wapping La.)
Lowe Av. E16 5J **87**
Lowell Ho. *SE5* *7C* ***102***
(off Wyndham Est.)
Lowell St. E14 6A **86**
Lowen Rd. RM13: Rain 2K **91**
Lwr. Addiscombe Rd. CR0: Croy 1E **168**
Lwr. Addison Gdns. W14 2G **99**
Lwr. Belgrave St.
SW1 2J **17** (3F **101**)
Lwr. Boston Rd. W7 1J **95**
Lwr. Broad St. RM10: Dag 1G **91**
Lower Camden BR7: Chst 7D **142**
Lower Chu. St. CR0: Croy 2B **168**
LOWER CLAPTON 4H **67**
Lwr. Clapton Rd. E5 3H **67**
Lwr. Clarendon Wlk. *W11* *6G* ***81***
(off Clarendon Rd.)
Lower Comn. Sth. SW15 3D **116**
Lwr. Coombe St. CR0: Croy 4C **168**
Lwr. Downs Rd. SW20 1F **153**
Lwr. Drayton Pl. CR0: Croy 2B **168**
LOWER EDMONTON 2B **34**
LOWER FELTHAM 3H **129**
Lower Fosters *NW4* *5E* ***44***
(off New Brent St.)
Lwr. George St. TW9: Rich 5D **114**
Lwr. Gravel Rd. BR2: Brom 1C **172**
Lower Grn. Gdns. KT4: Wor Pk 1C **164**
Lower Grn. W. CR4: Mitc 3C **154**
Lwr. Grosvenor Pl. SW1 1K **17** (3F **101**)
Lower Gro. Rd. TW10: Rich 6F **115**
LOWER HALLIFORD 6F **147**
Lwr. Hall La. E4 5F **35**
(not continuous)
Lwr. Hampton Rd. TW16: Sun 3A **148**
Lwr. Ham Rd. KT2: King T 5D **132**
LOWER HOLLOWAY 5K **65**
Lwr. James St. W1 2B **12** (7G **83**)
Lwr. John St. W1 2B **12** (7G **83**)
Lwr. Kenwood Av. EN2: Enf 5D **22**
Lwr. King's Rd. KT2: King T 1E **150**
Lwr. Lea Crossing E14 7G **87**
E16 7G **87**
Lwr. Maidstone Rd. N11 6B **32**
Lower Mall W6 5D **98**
Lwr. Mardyke Av. RM13: Rain 2J **91**
Lower Marsh SE1 7J **13** (2A **102**)
Lwr. Marsh La. KT1: King T 4F **151**
(not continuous)
Lwr. Merton Ri. NW3 7C **64**
Lower Mill KT17: Ewe 7B **164**
Lwr. Morden La. SM4: Mord 6E **152**
Lwr. Mortlake Rd. TW9: Rich 4E **114**
Lower Pk. Rd. DA17: Belv 4G **109**
Lower Pk. Rd. N11 5B **32**
Lower Pk. Trad. Est. W3 4J **79**
LOWER PLACE 2J **79**
Lower Pl. Bus. Cen. *NW10* *2K* ***79***
(off Steele Rd.)
Lwr. Queen's Rd. IG9: Buck H 2G **37**
Lwr. Richmond Rd. SW15 3D **116**
TW9, Rich 3G **115**
Lower Rd. DA8: Erith 3H **109**
DA17: Belv 3H **109**
HA2: Harr 1H **59**
SE1 6J **13** (2A **102**)
SE8 4K **103**
SE16 2J **103**
(not continuous)
SM1: Sutt 4A **166**
Lwr. Robert St. *WC2* *3F* ***13***
(in Robert St.)
Lwr. Sand Hills KT6: Surb 7C **150**
Lwr. Sloane St. SW1 4G **17** (4E **100**)
Lower Sq. TW7: Isle 3B **114**
Lower Sq., The SM1: Sutt 5K **165**
Lower Strand NW9 2B **44**
Lwr. Sunbury Rd. TW12: Hamp 2D **148**
LOWER SYDENHAM 4K **139**
Lwr. Sydenham Ind. Est.
SE26 5B **140**
Lwr. Teddington Rd. KT1: Hamp W 1D **150**
Lower Ter. NW3 3A **64**
SE27 *5B* ***138***
(off Woodcote Pl.)
Lwr. Thames St. EC3 3F **15** (7D **84**)
Lowerwood Ct. *W11* *6G* ***81***
(off Westbourne Pk. Rd.)
Lwr. Wood Rd. KT10: Clay 6B **162**
Lowestoft Cl. *E5* *2J* ***67***
(off Mundford Rd.)
Lowestoft M. E16 2F **107**
Loweswater Cl. HA9: Wemb 2D **60**
Loweswater Ho. E3 4B **86**

Lowfield Rd.—Lyndhurst Av.

Lowfield Rd. NW6 7J 63
W3 6H 79
Low Hall Cl. E4 7J 25
Low Hall La. E17 6A 50
Low Hall Mnr. Bus. Cen.
E17 6A 50
Lowick Rd. HA1: Harr 4J 41
Lowlands Gdns. RM7: Rom 6H 55
Lowlands Rd. HA1: Harr 6J 41
HA5: Eastc 7A 40
Lowman Rd. N7 4K 65
Lowndes Cl. SW1 2H 17 (3E 100)
Lowndes Ct. SW1 1F 17 (3D 100)
W1 1A 12
Lowndes Pl. SW1 2G 17 (3E 100)
Lowndes Sq. SW1 7F 11 (2D 100)
Lowndes St. SW1 1F 17 (3E 100)
Lownds Ct. BR1: Brom 2J 159
Lowood Ho. E1 7J 85
(off Bewley St.)
Lowood St. E1 7H 85
Lowry Cl. DA8: Erith 4K 109
Lowry Ct. SE16 5H 103
(off Stubbs Dr.)
Lowry Cres. CR4: Mitc 2C 154
Lowry Ho. N17 1F 49
(off Pembury Rd.)
Lowry Rd. RM8: Dag 5B 72
Lowshoe La. RM5: Col R 1G 55
Lowswood Cl. HA6: Nwood 1E 38
Lowther Dr. EN2: Enf 4D 22
Lowther Gdns. SW7 1B 16 (2B 100)
Lowther Hill SE23 7A 122
Lowther Ho. E8 1F 85
(off Clarissa St.)
SW1 6B 18
(off Churchill Gdns.)
Lowther Rd. E17 2A 50
HA7: Stan 3F 43
KT2: King T 1F 151
N7 5A 66
SW13 1B 116
Lowth Rd. SE5 1C 120
LOXFORD 5G 71
Loxford Av. E6 2B 88
Loxford La. IG1: Ilf 5G 71
IG3: Ilf 5G 71
Loxford Rd. IG11: Bark 6F 71
Loxford Ter. IG11: Ilf 6G 71
Loxham Rd. E4 7J 35
Loxham St. WC1 2F 7 (3J 83)
Loxley Cl. SE26 5K 139
Loxley Ho. HA9: Wemb 3E 60
Loxley Rd. SW18 1B 136
TW12: Hamp 4D 130
Loxton Rd. SE23 1K 139
Loxwood Cl. TW14: Bedf 1F 129
Loxwood Rd. N17 3E 48
Lubbock Ho. E14 7D 86
(off Poplar High St.)
Lubbock Rd. BR7: Chst 7D 142
Lubbock St. SE14 7J 103
Lucan Ho. N1 1D 84
(off Colville Est.)
Lucan Pl. SW3 4C 16 (4C 100)
Lucan Rd. EN5: Barn 3B 20
Lucas Av. E13 1K 87
HA2: Harr 2E 58
Lucas Cl. NW10 7C 62
Lucas Ct. SE26 5A 140
SW11 1E 118
Lucas Gdns. N2 2A 46
Lucas Ho. SW10 7K 99
(off Coleridge Gdns.)
Lucas Rd. SE20 6J 139
Lucas Sq. NW11 6J 45
Lucas St. SE8 1C 122
Lucerne Cl. N13 3D 32
Lucerne Ct. DA18: Erith 3E 108
Lucerne Gro. E17 4F 51
Lucerne M. W8 1J 99
Lucerne Rd. BR6: Orp 1K 173
CR7: Thor H 5B 156
N5 4B 66
Lucey Rd. SE16 3G 103
Lucey Way SE16 3G 103
Lucie Av. TW15: Ashf 6D 128
Lucien Rd. SW17 4E 136
SW19 2K 135
Lucinda Ct. EN1: Enf 4K 23
Lucknow St. SE18 7J 107
Lucorn Cl. SE12 6H 123
Luctons Av. IG9: Buck H 1F 37
Lucy Brown Ho. SE1 5D 14
Lucy Cres. W3 5J 79
Lucy Gdns. RM8: Dag 3F 73
Luddesdon Rd. DA8: Erith 7G 109
Ludford Cl. CR0: Wadd 3B 168
Ludgate B'way. EC4 1A 14 (6B 84)
Ludgate Cir. EC4 1A 14 (6B 84)
Ludgate Hill EC4 1A 14 (6B 84)
Ludgate Sq. EC4 1B 14 (6B 84)
Ludham NW5 5D 64
Ludham Cl. IG6: Ilf 1G 53
SE28 6C 90
Ludlow Cl. BR2: Brom 3J 159
HA2: Harr 4D 58
Ludlow Ct. W3 2J 97
Ludlow Rd. TW13: Felt 4J 129
W5 4C 78
Ludlow St. EC1 3C 8 (4C 84)
Ludlow Way N2 4A 46
Ludovick Wlk. SW15 4A 116
Ludwick M. SE14 7A 104
Luffield Rd. SE2 3B 108
Luffman Rd. SE12 3K 141
Lugard Ho. W12 1D 98
Lugard Rd. SE15 2H 121
Lugg App. E12 3E 70
Luke Ho. E1 6H 85
(off Tillman St.)
Luke St. EC2 3G 9 (4E 84)
Lukin Cres. E4 3A 36
Lukin St. E1 6J 85
Lullingstone Cl. BR5: St P 7B 144
Lullingstone Cres. BR5: St P 7A 144
Lullingstone Ho. SE15 6J 103
(off Lovelinch Cl.)
Lullingstone La. SE13 6F 123
Lullingstone Rd. DA17: Belv 6F 109
Lullington Gth. BR1: Brom 7G 141
N12 5C 30
Lullington Rd. RM9: Dag 7E 72
SE20 7G 139
Lulot Gdns. N19 2F 65
Lulworth NW1 7H 65
(off Wrotham Rd.)
SE17 5D 102
(off Portland St.)
Lulworth Av. HA9: Wemb 7C 42
TW5: Hest 1F 113
Lulworth Cl. HA2: Harr 3D 58
Lulworth Ct. N1 7E 66
(off St Peter's Way)
Lulworth Cres. CR4: Mitc 2C 154
Lulworth Dr. HA5: Pinn 6B 40
Lulworth Gdns. HA2: Harr 2C 58
Lulworth Ho. SW8 7K 101
Lulworth Rd. DA16: Well 2K 125
SE9 2C 142
SE15 2H 121
Lulworth Waye UB4: Yead 6K 75
Lumen Rd. HA9: Wemb 2D 60
Lumiere Bldg., The E7 5B 70
(off Romford Rd.)
Lumiere Ct. SW17 2E 136
Lumina Bldgs. E14 1E 104
(off Prestons Rd.)
Lumley Cl. DA17: Belv 5G 109
Lumley Ct. WC2 3F 13 (7J 83)
Lumley Flats SW1 5G 17
(off Holbein Pl.)
Lumley Gdns. SM3: Cheam 5G 165
Lumley Rd. SM3: Cheam 5G 165
Lumley St. W1 1H 11 (6E 82)
Lumsdon NW8 1K 81
(off Abbey Rd.)
Luna Rd. CR7: Thor H 3C 156
Lund Point E15 1E 86
Lundy Dr. UB3: Harl 4G 93
Lundy Wlk. N1 6C 66
Lunham Rd. SE19 6E 138
Luntley Pl. E1 6K 9
Lupin Cl. CR0: Croy 1K 169
RM7: Rush G 2K 73
SW2 2B 138
Lupin Cres. IG1: Ilf 6F 71
Lupino Ct. SE11 3H 19 (4K 101)
Lupin Point SE1 7K 15
Lupton Cl. SE12 3K 141
Lupton St. NW5 4G 65
(not continuous)
Lupus St. SW1 6K 17 (5F 101)
Luralda Wharf E14 5F 105
Lurgan Av. W6 6F 99
Lurline Gdns. SW11 1E 118
Luscombe Ct. BR2: Brom 2G 159
Luscombe Way SW8 7J 101
Lushington Ho. KT12: Walt T 6A 148
Lushington Rd. NW10 2D 80
SE6 4D 140
Lushington Ter. E8 5G 67
Lutea Ho. SM2: Sutt 7A 166
(off Walnut M.)
Luther Cl. HA8: Edg 2D 28
Luther King Cl. E17 6B 50
Luther M. TW11: Tedd 5K 131
Luther Rd. TW11: Tedd 5K 131
Luton Ho. E13 4J 87
(off Luton Rd.)
Luton Pl. SE10 7E 104
Luton Rd. DA14: Sidc 3C 144
E13 4J 87
E17 3B 50
Luton St. NW8 4B 4 (4B 82)
Lutton Ter. NW3 4A 64
(off Lakis Cl.)
Luttrell Av. SW15 5D 116
Lutwyche Rd. SE6 2B 140
Lutyens Ho. SW1 6A 18
(off Churchill Gdns.)
Luxborough Ho. W1 5G 5
(off Luxborough St.)
Luxborough La. IG7: Chig 3H 37
Luxborough St. W1 5G 5 (5E 82)
Luxborough Twr. W1 5G 5
Lux Cinema 2G 9
(off Hoxton Sq.)
Luxembourg M. E15 5G 69
Luxemburg Gdns. W6 4F 99
Luxfield Rd. SE9 1C 142
Luxford St. SE16 4K 103
Luxmore St. SE4 1B 122
Luxor St. SE5 3C 120
Lyall Av. SE21 4E 138
Lyall M. SW1 2G 17 (3E 100)
Lyall M. W. SW1 2G 17 (3E 100)
Lyall St. SW1 2G 17 (3E 100)
Lyal Rd. E3 2A 86
Lycett Pl. W12 2C 98
Lyceum Theatre 2G 13
Lychgate Mnr. HA1: Harr 7J 41
Lych Ga. Wlk. UB3: Hayes 7H 75
(not continuous)
Lyconby Gdns. CR0: Croy 7A 158
Lydd Cl. DA14: Sidc 3J 143
Lydden Ct. SE9 6J 125
Lydden Gro. SW18 7K 117
Lydden Rd. SW18 7K 117
Lydd Rd. DA7: Bex 7F 109
Lydeard Rd. E6 7D 70
Lyden Ho. E1 3K 85
(off Westfield Way)
Lydford NW1 1G 83
(off Royal College St.)
Lydford Cl. N16 5E 66
(off Pellerin Rd.)
Lydford Rd. N15 5D 48
NW2 6E 62
W9 4H 81
Lydhurst Av. SW2 2K 137
Lydia Ct. KT1: King T 3E 150
(off Grove Cres.)
N12 6F 31
Lydney Cl. SW19 2G 135
Lydon Rd. SW4 3G 119
Lydstep Rd. BR7: Chst 4E 142
Lyford Rd. SW18 7B 118
Lyford St. SE7 4C 106
Lygon Ho. E2 1K 9
(off Gosset St.)
SW6 1G 117
(off Fulham Pal. Rd.)
Lygon Pl. SW1 2J 17 (3F 101)
Lyham Cl. SW2 6J 119
Lyham Rd. SW2 5J 119
Lyle Cl. CR4: Mitc 7E 154
Lyle Ct. SM4: Mord 6B 154
Lyly Ho. SE1 3D 102
(off Burbage Cl.)
Lyme Farm Rd. SE12 4J 123
Lyme Gro. E9 7J 67
Lyme Gro. Ho. E9 7J 67
(off Lyme Gro.)
Lymer Av. SE19 5F 139
Lyme Rd. DA16: Well 1B 126
Lymescote Gdns.
SM1: Sutt 2J 165
Lyme St. NW1 7G 65
Lyme Ter. NW1 7G 65
Lyminge Cl. DA14: Sidc 4K 143
Lyminge Gdns. SW18 1C 136
Lymington Av. N22 2A 48
Lymington Cl. E6 5D 88
SW16 2H 155
Lymington Ct. SM1: Sutt 3K 165
Lymington Dr. HA4: Ruis 2F 57
Lymington Gdns. KT19: Ewe 5B 164
Lymington Lodge E14 3F 105
(off Schooner Cl.)
Lymington Rd. NW6 6K 63
RM8: Dag 1D 72
Lyminster Cl. UB4: Yead 5C 76
Lympne N17 2D 48
(off Gloucester Rd.)
Lympstone Gdns. SE15 7G 103
Lynbridge Gdns. N13 4G 33
Lynbrook Cl. RM13: Rain 2K 91
Lynbrook Gro. SE15 7E 102
Lynch Cl. SE3 2H 123
Lynchen Cl. TW5: Cran 1K 111
Lynch Wlk. SE8 6B 104
(off Prince St.)
Lyncott Cres. SW4 4F 119
Lyncourt SE3 2F 123
Lyncroft Av. HA5: Pinn 5C 40
Lyncroft Gdns. NW6 5J 63
TW3: Houn 5G 113
W13 2C 96
Lyncroft Mans. NW6 5J 63
Lyndale KT7: T Ditt 7J 149
NW2 4H 63
Lyndale Av. NW2 3H 63
Lyndale Cl. SE3 6H 105
Lyndean Ind. Est. SE2 3C 108
Lynde Ho. KT12: Walt T 6A 148
SW4 3H 119
Lynden Hyrst CR0: Croy 2F 169
Lyndhurst Av. HA5: Pinn 1K 39
KT5: Surb 1H 163
N12 6J 31
NW7 6F 29
SW16 2H 155
TW2: Whit 1D 130

McLeod's M.—Malmesbury Rd.

McLeod's M. SW7 .... 4K **99**
Macleod St. SE17 .... 5C **102**
Maclise Ho. *SW1* *4E 18*
(*off Marsham St.*)
Maclise Rd. W14 .... 3G **99**
Macmillan Ct. HA2: Harr 1E **58**
McMillan Ho. *SE4* *3A 122*
(*off Arica Rd.*)
SE14 .... 1A **122**
McMillan St. SE8 .... 6C **104**
Macmillan Way SW17 .... 4F **137**
McNair Rd. UB2: S'hall 3F **95**
Macnamara Ho. *SW10* *7B 100*
(*off Worlds End Est.*)
McNeil Rd. SE5 .... 2E **120**
McNicol Dr. NW10 .... 2J **79**
Macoma Rd. SE18 .... 6H **107**
Macoma Ter. SE18 .... 6H **107**
Maconochies Rd. E14 .... 5D **104**
Macquarie Way E14 .... 4D **104**
McRae La. CR4: Mitc 7D **154**
Macready Ho. *W1* *6E 4*
(*off Crawford St.*)
Macready Pl. N7 .... 4J **65**
(not continuous)
Macroom Rd. W9 .... 3H **81**
Macs Ho. E17 .... 3D **50**
Mac's Pl. EC4 .... 7J **7**
Madame Tussaud's 4G **5** (4E **82**)
Mada Rd. BR6: Farnb 3F **173**
Maddams St. E3 .... 4D **86**
Madderfields Ct. N11 .... 1H **47**
Maddison Cl. N2 .... 2A **46**
TW11: Tedd 6K **131**
Maddocks Cl. DA14: Sidc 5E **144**
Maddocks Ho. *E1* *7H 85*
(*off Cornwall St.*)
Maddock Way SE17 .... 6B **102**
Maddox St. W1 .... 2K **11** (7F **83**)
Madeira Av. BR1: Brom 7G **141**
Madeira Gro. IG8: Wfd G 6F **37**
Madeira Rd. CR4: Mitc 4D **154**
E11 .... 1F **69**
N13 .... 4G **33**
SW16 .... 5J **137**
Madeleine Cl. RM6: Chad H 6C **54**
Madeley Rd. W5 .... 6D **78**
Madeline Gro. IG1: Ilf 5H **71**
Madeline Rd. SE20 .... 7G **139**
Madge Gill Way *E6* *1C 88*
(*off High St. Nth.*)
Madge Hill W7 .... 7H **77**
Madinah Rd. E8 .... 6G **67**
Madison, The *SE1* *6E 14*
(*off Long La.*)
Madison Cres. DA7: Bex 7C **108**
Madison Gdns. BR2: Brom 3H **159**
DA7: Bex 7C **108**
Madison Ho. *E14* *7B 86*
(*off Victory Pl.*)
Madras Pl. N7 .... 6A **66**
Madras Rd. IG1: Ilf 4F **71**
Madrid Rd. SW13 .... 1C **116**
Madrigal La. SE5 .... 7B **102**
Madron St. SE17 .... 5E **102**
Mafeking Av. E6 .... 2C **88**
IG2: Ilf 7H **53**
TW8: Bford 6E **96**
Mafeking Rd. E16 .... 4H **87**
EN1: Enf 3A **24**
N17 .... 2G **49**
Magazine Ga. W2 .... 4D **10** (1C **100**)
Magdala Av. N19 .... 2G **65**
Magdala Rd. CR2: S Croy 7D **168**
TW7: Isle 3A **114**
Magdalene Cl. SE15 .... 2H **121**
Magdalene Gdns. E6 .... 4E **88**
Magdalene Rd. TW17: Shep 4B **146**
Magdalen Ho. *E16* *1K 105*
(*off Keats Av.*)
Magdalen Pas. E1 .... 2K **15** (7F **85**)
Magdalen Rd. SW18 .... 1A **136**
Magdalen St. SE1 .... 5G **15** (1E **102**)
Magee St. SE11 .... 7J **19** (6A **102**)
Magellan Ct. *NW10* *7K 61*
(*off Brentfield Rd.*)
Magellan Ho. *E1* *4K 85*
(*off Ernest St.*)
Magellan Pl. E14 .... 4C **104**
Magnaville Rd. WD23: Bushy 1D **26**
Magnet Rd. HA9: Wemb 2D **60**
Magnin Cl. E8 .... 1G **85**
Magnolia Cl. E10 .... 2C **68**
KT2: King T 6H **133**
Magnolia Ct. HA3: Kent 7F **43**
SM2: Sutt *7J 165*
(*off Grange Rd.*)
SM6: Wall 5F **167**
TW9: Kew 1H **115**
TW13: Felt *1J 129*
(*off Plum Cl.*)
UB5: N'olt 4C **76**
UB10: Hil 6D **56**
Magnolia Gdns. E10 .... 2C **68**
HA8: Edg 4D **28**
Magnolia Ho. *SE8* *6B 104*
(*off Evelyn St.*)
Magnolia Lodge E4 .... 3J **35**
W8 .... *3K 99*
(*off St Mary's Ga.*)
Magnolia Pl. SW4 .... 5J **119**
W5 .... 5D **78**
Magnolia Rd. W4 .... 6H **97**
Magnolia St. UB7: W Dray 4A **92**
Magnolia Way KT19: Ewe 5J **163**
Magpie All. EC4 .... 1K **13** (6A **84**)
Magpie Cl. E7 .... 5H **69**
EN1: Enf 1B **24**
NW9 .... 2A **44**
Magpie Hall Cl. BR2: Brom 6C **160**
Magpie Hall La. BR2: Brom 5D **160**
Magpie Hall Rd. WD23: Bushy 2D **26**
Magpie Pl. SE14 .... 6A **104**
Magri Wlk. E1 .... 5J **85**
Maguire Dr. TW10: Ham 4C **132**
Maguire St. SE1 .... 6K **15** (2F **103**)
Mahatma Gandhi Ind. Est.
SE24 .... 4B **120**
Mahlon Av. HA4: Ruis 5K **57**
Mahogany Cl. SE16 .... 1A **104**
Mahon Cl. EN1: Enf 1A **24**
Maida Av. E4 .... 7J **25**
W2 .... 4A **4** (5A **82**)
MAIDA HILL **4H 81**
Maida Rd. DA17: Belv 3G **109**
MAIDA VALE **3K 81**
Maida Va. W9 .... 3A **4** (2K **81**)
Maida Way E4 .... 7J **25**
Maiden Erlegh Av. DA5: Bexl 1E **144**
Maiden La. NW1 .... 7H **65**
SE1 .... 5D **14** (1C **102**)
WC2 .... 3F **13** (7J **83**)
Maiden Pl. NW5 .... 3G **65**
Maiden Rd. E15 .... 7G **69**
Maidenstone Hill SE10 .... 1E **122**
Maids of Honour Row TW9: Rich 5D **114**
Maidstone Av. RM5: Col R 2J **55**
Maidstone Bldgs. M.
SE1 .... 5D **14** (1C **102**)
Maidstone Ho. *E14* *6D 86*
(*off Carmen St.*)
Maidstone Rd. DA14: Sidc, Swan 6D **144**
N11 .... 6B **32**
Mail Coach Yd. E2 .... 1H **9** (3E **84**)
Main Av. EN1: Enf 5A **24**
Main Dr. HA9: Wemb 3D **60**
Mainridge Rd. BR7: Chst 4E **142**
Main Rd. DA14: Sidc 3H **143**
Main St. TW13: Hanw 5B **130**
Mainwaring Ct. CR4: Mitc 2E **154**
Mais Ho. SE26 .... 2H **139**
Maismore St. SE15 .... 6G **103**
Maisonettes, The SM1: Sutt 5H **165**
Maitland Cl. SE10 .... 7D **104**
TW4: Houn 3D **112**
Maitland Ct. *W2* *2A 10*
(*off Lancaster Ter.*)
Maitland Ho. *E2* *2J 85*
(*off Waterloo Gdns.*)
SW1 .... *7A 18*
(*off Churchill Gdns.*)
Maitland Pk. Est. NW3 .... 6D **64**
Maitland Pk. Rd. NW3 .... 6D **64**
Maitland Pk. Vs. NW3 .... 6D **64**
Maitland Pl. E5 .... 4H **67**
Maitland Rd. E15 .... 6H **69**
SE26 .... 6K **139**
Maitland Yd. W13 .... 1A **96**
Maize Row E14 .... 7B **86**
Majendie Rd. SE18 .... 5H **107**
Majestic Way CR4: Mitc 2D **154**
Major Cl. SW9 .... 3B **120**
Major Rd. E15 .... 5F **69**
SE16 .... 3G **103**
Makepeace Av. N6 .... 2E **64**
Makepeace Mans. N6 .... 2E **64**
Makepeace Rd. E11 .... 4J **51**
UB5: N'olt 2C **76**
Makinen Ho. IG9: Buck H 1F **37**
Makins St. SW3 .... 4D **16** (4C **100**)
Malabar Ct. *W12* *7D 80*
(*off India Way*)
Malabar St. E14 .... 2C **104**
Malam Ct. SE11 .... 4J **19** (4A **102**)
Malam Gdns. E14 .... 7D **86**
Malbrook Rd. SW15 .... 4D **116**
Malcolm Ct. E7 .... 6H **69**
HA7: Stan 5H **27**
NW4 .... 6C **44**
Malcolm Cres. NW4 .... 6C **44**
Malcolm Dr. KT6: Surb 1D **162**
Malcolm Ho. *N1* *2E 84*
(*off Arden Est.*)
Malcolm Pl. E2 .... 4J **85**
Malcolm Rd. E1 .... 4J **85**
SE20 .... 7J **139**
SE25 .... 6G **157**
SW19 .... 6G **135**
UB10: Ick 4B **56**
Malcolm Sargent Ho. *E16* *1K 105*
(*off Evelyn Rd.*)
Malcolmson Ho. *SW1* *6C 18*
(*off Aylesford St.*)
Malcolm Way E11 .... 5J **51**
Malden Av. SE25 .... 4H **157**
UB6: G'frd 5J **59**
Malden Cen., The 4B **152**
Malden Ct. KT3: N Mald 3D **152**
N4 .... 6C **48**
Malden Cres. NW1 .... 6E **64**
MALDEN GREEN **1C 164**
Malden Grn. Av. KT4: Wor Pk 1B **164**
Malden Hill KT3: N Mald 3B **152**
Malden Hill Gdns. KT3: N Mald 3B **152**
MALDEN JUNC. **5B 152**
Malden Pk. KT3: N Mald 6B **152**
Malden Pl. NW5 .... 5E **64**
Malden Rd. KT3: N Mald 5A **152**
KT4: Wor Pk 5A **152**
NW5 .... 5D **64**
SM3: Cheam 4F **165**
Malden Way KT3: N Mald 6K **151**
Maldon Cl. E15 .... 5G **69**
N1 .... 1C **84**
SE5 .... 3E **120**
Maldon Ct. E6 .... 1E **88**
SM6: Wall 5G **167**
Maldon Rd. N9 .... 3A **34**
RM7: Rush G 7J **55**
SM6: Wall 5F **167**
W3 .... 7J **79**
Maldon Wlk. IG8: Wfd G 6F **37**
Malet Pl. WC1 .... 4C **6** (4H **83**)
Malet St. WC1 .... 4C **6** (4H **83**)
Maley Av. SE27 .... 2B **138**
Malford Ct. E18 .... 2J **51**
Malford Gro. E18 .... 4H **51**
Malfort Rd. SE5 .... 3E **120**
Malham Cl. N11 .... 6K **31**
Malham Rd. SE23 .... 1K **139**
Malham Rd. Ind. Est.
SE23 .... 1K **139**
Malham Ter. *N18* *6C 34*
(*off Dysons Rd.*)
N18 .... 5C **34**
(Alston Rd.)
Malibu Ct. SE26 .... 3H **139**
Mall, The BR1: Brom 3J **159**
CR0: Croy 2C **168**
DA6: Bex 4G **127**
E15 .... 7F **69**
HA3: Kent 6F **43**
KT6: Surb 5D **150**
N14 .... 3D **32**
RM10: Dag 6G **73**
SW1 .... 5D **12** (2G **101**)
SW14 .... 5J **115**
TW8: Bford 6D **96**
W5 .... 7E **78**
Mallams M. SW9 .... 3B **120**
Mallard Cl. E9 .... 6B **68**
EN5: New Bar 6G **21**
NW6 .... 2J **81**
TW2: Whit 7E **112**
W7 .... 2J **95**
Mallard Ct. E17 .... 3F **51**
Mallard Ho. *NW8* *2C 82*
(*off Barrow Hill Est.*)
Mallard Path *SE28* *3H 107*
(*off Goosander Way*)
Mallard Pl. N22 .... 2K **47**
TW1: Twick 3A **132**
Mallards *E11* *7J 51*
(*off Blake Hall Rd.*)
Mallards Rd. IG8: Wfd G 7E **36**
IG11: Bark 3A **90**
Mallard Wlk. BR3: Beck 5K **157**
DA14: Sidc 6C **144**
Mallard Way NW9 .... 7J **43**
SM6: Wall 7G **167**
Mall Chambers *W8* *1J 99*
(*off Kensington Mall*)
Mallet Dr. UB5: N'olt 5D **58**
Mallet Rd. SE13 .... 6F **123**
Mall Galleries 4D **12**
Mall Gallery *WC2* *1E 12*
(*in Thomas Neals Shop. Mall*)
Malling SE13 .... 5D **122**
Malling Cl. CR0: Croy 6J **157**
Malling Gdns. SM4: Mord 6A **154**
Malling Way BR2: Hayes 7H **159**
Mallinson Rd. CR0: Bedd 3H **167**
SW11 .... 5C **118**
Mallinson Sports Cen. 7D **46**
Mallon Gdns. *E1* *7K 9*
(*off Commercial St.*)
Mallord St. SW3 .... 7B **16** (6B **100**)
Mallory Cl. SE4 .... 4A **122**
Mallory Gdns. EN4: E Barn 7K **21**
Mallory St. NW8 .... 3D **4** (4C **82**)
Mallow Cl. CR0: Croy 1K **169**
Mallow Mead NW7 .... 7B **30**
Mallows, The UB10: Ick 3D **56**
Mallow St. EC1 .... 3E **8** (4D **84**)
Mall Rd. W6 .... 5D **98**
Mall Vs. *W6* *5D 98*
(*off Mall Rd.*)
Malmains Cl. BR3: Beck 4F **159**
Malmains Way BR3: Beck 4E **158**
Malmesbury *E2* *2J 85*
(*off Cyprus St.*)
Malmesbury Cl. HA5: Eastc 4H **39**
Malmesbury Rd. E3 .... 3B **86**
E16 .... 5G **87**

Malmesbury Rd.—Manor Rd.

Malmesbury Rd. E18 ....1H 51
SM4: Mord 7A 154
Malmesbury Ter. E16 ....5H 87
Malmsey Ho. SE11 ....5H 19 (5K 101)
Malmsmead Ho. *E9* *5B 68*
(off King's Mead Way)
Malory Cl. BR3: Beck 2A 158
Malpas Dr. HA5: Pinn 5B 40
Malpas Rd. E8 ....5H 67
RM9: Dag 6D 72
SE4 ....2B 122
Malta Rd. E10 ....1C 68
Malta St. EC1 ....3A 8 (4B 84)
Maltby Cl. BR6: Orp 1K 173
Maltby Dr. EN1: Enf 1C 24
Maltby Rd. KT9: Chess 6G 163
Maltby St. SE1 ....7J 15 (2F 103)
Malthouse Dr. TW13: Hanw 5B 130
W4 ....6B 98
Malthouse Pas. *SW13* *2B 116*
(off Maltings Cl.)
Malthus Path SE28 ....1C 108
Malting Ho. *E14* *7B 86*
(off Oak La.)
Maltings W4 ....5G 97
Maltings, The BR6: Orp 1K 173
Maltings Cl. SW13 ....2B 116
Maltings Lodge *W4* *6A 98*
(off Corney Reach Way)
Maltings M. DA15: Sidc 3A 144
Maltings Pl. SE1 ....7H 15
SW6 ....1K 117
Malting Way TW7: Isle 3K 113
Malton M. SE18 ....6J 107
W10 ....6G 81
Malton Rd. W10 ....6G 81
Malton St. SE18 ....6J 107
Maltravers St. WC2 ....2H 13 (7K 83)
Malt St. SE1 ....6G 103
Malva Cl. SW18 ....5K 117
Malvern Av. DA7: Bex 7E 108
E4 ....7A 36
HA2: Harr 3C 58
Malvern Cl. CR4: Mitc 3G 155
KT6: Surb 1E 162
SE20 ....2G 157
UB10: Ick 2C 56
W10 ....5H 81
Malvern Ct. SM2: Sutt 7J 165
SW7 ....*3B 16*
(off Onslow Sq.)
W12 ....*2C 98*
(off Hadyn Pk. Rd.)
Malvern Dr. IG3: Bark, Ilf 4K 71
IG8: Wfd G 5F 37
TW13: Hanw 5B 130
Malvern Gdns. HA3: Kent 4E 42
NW2 ....2G 63
Malvern Ho. N16 ....1F 67
Malvern M. NW6 ....3J 81
Malvern Pl. NW6 ....3H 81
Malvern Rd. CR7: Thor H 4A 156
E6 ....1C 88
E8 ....7G 67
E11 ....2G 69
KT6: Surb 2E 162
N8 ....3A 48
N17 ....3G 49
NW6 ....2H 81
(not continuous)
TW12: Hamp 7E 130
UB3: Harl 7G 93
Malvern Ter. N1 ....1A 84
N9 ....1A 34
Malvern Way W13 ....5B 78
Malwood Rd. SW12 ....6F 119
Malyons, The TW17: Shep 6F 147
Malyons Rd. SE13 ....6D 122
Malyons Ter. SE13 ....5D 122
Managers St. E14 ....1E 104
Manatee Pl. SM6: Bedd 3H 167
Manaton Cl. SE15 ....3H 121
Manaton Cres. UB1: S'hall 6E 76
Manbey Gro. E15 ....6G 69
Manbey Pk. Rd. E15 ....6G 69
Manbey Rd. E15 ....6G 69
Manbey St. E15 ....6G 69
Manbre Rd. W6 ....6E 98
Manbrough Av. E6 ....3D 88
Manchester Ct. *E16* *6K 87*
(off Garvary Rd.)
Manchester Dr. W10 ....4G 81
Manchester Gro. E14 ....5E 104
Manchester Ho. SE17 ....5C 102
Manchester M. W1 ....6G 5
Manchester Rd. CR7: Thor H 3C 156
E14 ....5E 104
N15 ....6D 48
Manchester Sq. W1 ....7G 5 (6E 82)
Manchester St. W1 ....6G 5 (5E 82)
Manchester Way RM10: Dag 4H 73
Manchuria Rd. SW11 ....6E 118
Manciple St. SE1 ....7E 14 (2D 102)
Mandalay Rd. SW4 ....5G 119
Mandarin Ct. *NW10* *6K 61*
(off Mitchellbrook Way)
SE8 ....6B 104
Mandarin St. E14 ....7C 86
Mandarin Way UB4: Yead 6C 76
Mandela Cl. NW10 ....7J 61
W12 ....7D 80
Mandela Ho. *E2* *2J 9*
(off Virginia Rd.)
SE5 ....2B 120
Mandela Rd. E16 ....6J 87
Mandela St. NW1 ....1G 83
SW9 ....7A 102
(not continuous)
Mandela Way SE1 ....4E 102
Mandel Ho. SW18 ....4J 117
Mandeville Cl. SE3 ....7H 105
SW20 ....7G 135
Mandeville Ct. E4 ....5F 35
Mandeville Dr. KT6: Surb 1D 162
Mandeville Ho. *SE1* *5F 103*
(off Rolls Rd.)
SW4 ....5G 119
Mandeville M. SW4 ....4H 119
Mandeville Pl. W1 ....7H 5 (6E 82)
Mandeville Rd. N14 ....2A 32
TW7: Isle 2A 114
TW17: Shep 5C 146
UB5: N'olt 7E 58
Mandeville St. E5 ....3A 68
Mandrake Rd. SW17 ....3D 136
Mandrake Way E15 ....7G 69
Mandrell Rd. SW2 ....5J 119
Manesty Ct. *N14* *7C 22*
(off Ivy Rd.)
Manette St. W1 ....1D 12 (6H 83)
Manfred Rd. SW15 ....5H 117
Manger Rd. N7 ....6J 65
Mangold Way DA18: Erith 3D 108
Manilla St. E14 ....2C 104
Manister Rd. SE2 ....3A 108
Manitoba Ct. *SE16* *2J 103*
(off Canada Est.)
Manitoba Gdns. BR6: Chels 6K 173
Manley Ct. N16 ....3F 67
Manley Ho. SE11 ....5J 19 (4A 102)
Manley St. NW1 ....1E 82
Mann Cl. CR0: Croy 3C 168
Manneby Prior *N1* *1H 7*
(off Cumming St.)
Manning Ct. *SE28* *1B 108*
(off Titmuss Av.)
Manningford Cl. EC1 ....1A 8 (3B 84)
Manning Gdns. HA3: Kent 7D 42
Manning Pl. TW10: Rich 6F 115
Manning Rd. E17 ....5A 50
RM10: Dag 6G 73
Manningtree Cl. SW19 ....1G 135
Manningtree Rd. HA4: Ruis 4K 57
Manningtree St. E1 ....6G 85
Mannin Rd. RM6: Chad H 7B 54
Mannock M. E18 ....1A 52
Mannock Rd. N22 ....3B 48
Mann's Cl. TW7: Isle 5K 113
Manns Rd. HA8: Edg 6B 28
Manny Shinwell Ho. *SW6* *6H 99*
(off Clem Attlee Ct.)
Manoel Rd. TW2: Twick 3G 131
Manor, The SE23 ....7J 121
Manor Av. E7 ....4A 70
SE4 ....2B 122
TW4: Houn 3B 112
UB5: N'olt 7D 58
Manor Brook SE3 ....4J 123
MANOR CIRCUS 3G 115
Manor Cl. DA1: Cray 4K 127
E17 ....1A 50
EN5: Barn 4B 20
HA4: Ruis 1H 57
KT4: Wor Pk 1A 164
NW7 ....5E 28
NW9 ....5H 43
RM10: Dag 6K 73
SE28 ....7C 90
Manor Cotts. HA6: Nwood 1H 39
N2 ....*2A 46*
(off Manor Cotts. App.)
Manor Cotts. App. N2 ....2A 46
Manor Ct. BR4: W W'ck 1D 170
DA7: Bex 4H 127
E4 ....1B 36
E10 ....1D 68
HA1: Harr 6K 41
HA9: Wemb 5E 60
IG11: Bark 7K 71
KT2: King T 1G 151
KT8: W Mole 4E 148
N2 ....5D 46
N14 ....2C 32
N20 ....*3J 31*
(off York Way)
SM5: Cars 3E 166
SW2 ....5K 119
SW6 ....1K 117
SW16 ....3J 137
TW2: Twick 2G 131
W3 ....4G 97
Manor Ct. Rd. W7 ....7J 77
Manor Cres. KT5: Surb 6G 151
Manor Dene SE28 ....6C 90
Manordene Cl. KT7: T Ditt 1A 162
Manordene Rd. SE28 ....6C 90
Manor Dr. HA9: Wemb 4F 61
KT5: Surb 6F 151
KT10: Hin W 2A 162
KT19: Ewe 6A 164
N14 ....1A 32
N20 ....4J 31
NW7 ....5E 28
TW13: Hanw 5B 130
TW16: Sun 2J 147
Manor Dr., The KT4: Wor Pk 1A 164
Manor Dr. Nth. KT3: N Mald 7K 151
KT4: Wor Pk 1A 164
Manor Est. SE16 ....4H 103
Mnr. Farm Av. TW17: Shep 6D 146
Mnr. Farm Cl.
KT4: Wor Pk 1A 164
Mnr. Farm Ct. E6 ....3D 88
Mnr. Farm Dr. E4 ....3B 36
Mnr. Farm Rd. HA0: Wemb 2D 78
SW16 ....2A 156
Manorfield Cl. *N19* *4G 65*
(off Fulbrook M.)
Manor Flds. SW15 ....6F 117
Manorfields Cl. BR7: Chst 3K 161
Manor Gdns. CR2: S Croy 6F 169
HA4: Ruis 5A 58
N7 ....3J 65
Manor Gdns. *SW4* *2G 119*
(off Larkhall Ri.)
SW20 ....2H 153
TW9: Rich 4F 115
TW12: Hamp 7F 131
TW16: Sun 1J 147
W3 ....4G 97
W4 ....5A 98
Manor Ga. UB5: N'olt 7C 58
Manorgate Rd. KT2: King T 1G 151
Manor Gro. BR3: Beck 2D 158
SE15 ....6J 103
TW9: Rich 4G 115
Mnr. Hall Av. NW4 ....2F 45
Mnr. Hall Dr. NW4 ....2F 45
Manorhall Gdns. E10 ....1C 68
MANOR HOUSE 7D 48
MANOR HOUSE 7C 48
Manor Ho. *NW1* *5D 4*
(off Marylebone Rd.)
UB2: S'hall 3C 94
Manor Ho. Ct. TW17: Shep 7D 146
W9 ....*4A 82*
(off Warrington Gdns.)
Manor Ho. Dr. HA6: Nwood 1D 38
NW6 ....7F 63
Manor Ho. Est. HA7: Stan 6G 27
Mnr. House Gdn. E11 ....6K 51
Manor Ho. Way TW7: Isle 3B 114
Manor La. SE12 ....5G 123
SE13 ....5G 123
SM1: Sutt 5A 166
TW13: Felt 2J 129
TW16: Sun 2J 147
UB3: Harl 6F 93
Manor La. Ter. SE13 ....4G 123
Manor M. *NW6* *2J 81*
(off Cambridge Av.)
SE4 ....2B 122
Manor Mt. SE23 ....1J 139
Manor Pde. HA1: Harr 6K 41
N16 ....2F 67
NW10 ....*2B 80*
(off High St. Harlesden)
MANOR PARK 4B 70
Manor Pk. BR7: Chst 2H 161
SE13 ....4F 123
TW9: Rich 4F 115
TW13: Felt 2J 129
Manor Pk. Cl. BR4: W W'ck 1D 170
Manor Pk. Crematorium E7 ....4A 70
Manor Pk. Cres. HA8: Edg 6B 28
Manor Pk. Dr. HA2: Harr 3F 41
Manor Pk. Gdns. HA8: Edg 5B 28
Manor Pk. Pde. *SE13* *4F 123*
(off Lee High Rd.)
Manor Pk. Rd. BR4: W W'ck 1D 170
BR7: Chst 1G 161
E12 ....4B 70
(not continuous)
N2 ....3A 46
NW10 ....1B 80
SM1: Sutt 5A 166
Manor Pl. BR7: Chst 2H 161
CR4: Mitc 3G 155
KT12: Walt T 7J 147
SE17 ....5B 102
SM1: Sutt 4K 165
TW14: Felt 1J 129
Manor Rd. BR3: Beck 2D 158
BR4: W W'ck 2D 170
CR4: Mitc 4G 155
DA1: Cray 4K 127
DA5: Bexl 1H 145
DA15: Sidc 3K 143
E10 ....7C 50
E15 ....2G 87
E16 ....2G 87
E17 ....2A 50
EN2: Enf 2H 23
EN5: Barn 4B 20

Manor Rd.—Margaret St.

Manor Rd. HA1: Harr 6A **42**
HA4: Ruis 1F **57**
IG7: Chig 6J **37**
IG8: Wfd G 6J **37**
IG11: Bark 6K **71**
KT8: E Mos 4H **149**
KT12: Walt T 7H **147**
N16 2D **66**
N17 1G **49**
N22 6D **32**
RM6: Chad H 6D **54**
RM10: Dag 6J **73**
SE25 4G **157**
SM2: Cheam 7H **165**
SM6: Wall 4F **167**
SW20 2H **153**
TW2: Twick 2G **131**
TW9: Rich 4G **115**
TW11: Tedd 5A **132**
(not continuous)
TW15: Ashf 5B **128**
UB3: Hayes 6J **75**
W13 7A **78**
Manor Rd. Ho. HA1: Harr 6A **42**
Manor Rd. Nth. KT7: T Ditt 3A **162**
KT10: Hin W, T Ditt 3A **162**
SM6: Wall 4F **167**
Manorside EN5: Barn 4B **20**
Manorside Cl. SE2 4C **108**
Manor Sq. RM8: Dag 2C **72**
Manor Va. TW8: Bford 5C **96**
Manor Vw. N3 2K **45**
Manor Way BR2: Brom 6C **160**
BR3: Beck 2C **158**
BR5: Pet W 4G **161**
CR2: S Croy 6E **168**
CR4: Mitc 3G **155**
DA5: Bexl 1G **145**
DA7: Bex 3K **127**
E4 4A **36**
HA2: Harr 4F **41**
HA4: Ruis 7G **39**
IG8: Wfd G 5F **37**
KT4: Wor Pk 1A **164**
NW9 4A **44**
RM13: Rain 4K **91**
SE3 4H **123**
UB2: S'hall 4B **94**
Manor Way, The SM6: Wall 4F **167**
Manorway EN1: Enf 7K **23**
SE7 4B **106**
Manor Way Bus. Cen. RM13: Rain 5K **91**
Manor Waye UB8: Uxb 1A **74**
Manpreet Ct. E12 5D **70**
Manresa Rd. SW3 6C **16** (5C **100**)
Mansard Beeches
SW17 5E **136**
Mansard Cl. HA5: Pinn 3B **40**
Manse Cl. UB3: Harl 6F **93**
Mansel Gro. E17 1C **50**
Mansell Rd. UB6: G'frd 5F **77**
W3 2K **97**
Mansell St. E1 1K **15** (6F **85**)
Mansel Rd. SW19 6G **135**
Manser Ct. RM13: Rain 3K **91**
Mansergh Cl. SE18 7C **106**
Manse Rd. N16 3F **67**
Manser Rd. RM13: Rain 3K **91**
Mansfield Av. EN4: E Barn 6J **21**
HA4: Ruis 1K **57**
N15 4D **48**
Mansfield Cl. N9 6B **24**
Mansfield Ct. *E2* *1F **85***
(off Whiston Rd.)
Mansfield Dr. UB4: Hayes 4G **75**
Mansfield Hgts. N2 5C **46**
Mansfield Hill E4 7J **25**
Mansfield M. W1 6J **5** (5F **83**)
Mansfield Pl.
CR2: S Croy 6D **168**
NW3 4A **64**
Mansfield Rd. CR2: S Croy 6D **168**
E11 6K **51**
E17 4B **50**
IG1: Ilf 2E **70**
KT9: Chess 5C **162**
NW3 5D **64**
W3 4H **79**
Mansfield St. W1 6J **5** (5F **83**)
Mansford St. E2 2G **85**
Manship Rd. CR4: Mitc 7E **136**
Mansion Cl. SW9 1A **120**
(not continuous)
Mansion Cottage Vis. Info. Cen. 1C 64
Mansion Gdns. NW3 3K **63**
Mansion House 1E 14 (6D 84)
Mansion Ho. Pl. EC4 1E **14** (6D **84**)
Mansion Ho. St. EC4 1E **14**
Mansions, The SW5 5K **99**
Manson M. SW7 4A **16** (4B **100**)
Manson Pl. SW7 4A **16** (4B **100**)
Mansted Gdns.
RM6: Chad H 7C **54**
Manston *N17* *2D **48***
(off Adams Rd.)
NW1 *7G **65***
(off Agar Gro.)
Manston Av. UB2: S'hall 4E **94**
Manston Cl. SE20 1J **157**
Manstone Rd. NW2 5G **63**
Manston Gro. KT2: King T 5D **132**
Manston Ho. *W14* *3G **99***
(off Russell Rd.)
Manthorp Rd. SE18 5G **107**
Mantilla Rd. SW17 4E **136**
Mantle Ct. *SW18* *6K **117***
(off Mapleton Rd.)
Mantle Rd. SE4 3A **122**
Mantlet Cl. SW16 7G **137**
Mantle Way E15 7G **69**
Manton Av. W7 2K **95**
Manton Cl. UB3: Hayes 7G **75**
Manton Rd. EN3: Enf L 1H **25**
SE2 4A **108**
Manton Way EN3: Enf L 1J **25**
Mantua St. SW11 3B **118**
Mantus Cl. E1 4J **85**
Mantus Rd. E1 4J **85**
Manus Way N20 2F **31**
Manville Gdns. SW17 3F **137**
Manville Rd. SW17 2E **136**
Manwood Rd. SE4 5B **122**
Manwood St. E16 1D **106**
Manygate La. TW17: Shep 7E **146**
Manygate Mobile Home Est.
TW17: Shep *6F **147***
(off Mitre Cl.)
Manygates SW12 2F **137**
Mapesbury Ct. NW2 5G **63**
Mapesbury M. NW4 6C **44**
Mapesbury Rd. NW2 7G **63**
Mapeshill Pl. NW2 6E **62**
Mapes Ho. NW6 7G **63**
Mape St. E2 4H **85**
(not continuous)
Maple Av. E4 5G **35**
HA2: Harr 2F **59**
UB7: Yiew 7A **74**
W3 1A **98**
Maple Cl. BR5: Pet W 5H **161**
CR4: Mitc 1F **155**
HA4: Ruis 6K **39**
IG9: Buck H 3G **37**
N3 6D **30**
N16 6G **49**
SW4 6H **119**
TW12: Hamp 6D **130**
UB4: Yead 3B **76**
Maple Ct. *CR0: Croy* *4C **168***
(off Lwr. Coombe St.)
CR0: Croy *4C **168***
(off Waldrons, The)
Maple Ct. E6 5E **88**
KT3: N Mald 3K **151**
SE6 1D **140**
TW15: Ashf 7F **129**
Maple Cres. DA15: Sidc 6A **126**
Maplecroft Cl. E6 6B **88**
Mapledale Av. CR0: Croy 2G **169**
Mapledene BR7: Chst 5G **143**
Mapledene Est. E8 7G **67**
Mapledene Rd. E8 7F **67**
Maple Gdns. HA8: Edg 7F **29**
TW19: Stanw 2A **128**
Maple Gro. NW9 7J **43**
TW8: Bford 7B **96**
UB1: S'hall 5D **76**
W5 3D **96**
Maple Gro. Bus. Cen. TW4: Houn 4A **112**
Maple Ho. E17 3D **50**
KT1: King T *5E **150***
(off Maple Rd.)
SE8 *7B **104***
(off Idonia St.)
TW9: Kew 1H **115**
Maplehurst BR2: Brom 2G **159**
Maplehurst Cl. KT1: King T 4E **150**
Maple Ind. Est. TW13: Felt 3J **129**
Maple Leaf Dr. DA15: Sidc 1K **143**
Mapleleafe Gdns. IG6: Ilf 3F **53**
Maple Leaf Sq. SE16 2K **103**
Maple Lodge *W8* *3K **99***
(off Abbots Wlk.)
Maple M. NW6 2K **81**
SW16 5K **137**
Maple Pl. N17 7B **34**
UB7: Yiew 1A **92**
W1 5B **6** (4G **83**)
Maple Rd. E11 6G **51**
KT6: Surb 6D **150**
SE20 1H **157**
UB4: Yead 3A **76**
Maples, The KT1: Tedd 7C **132**
KT10: Clay 7A **162**
Maples Pl. E1 5H **85**
Maplestead Rd. RM9: Dag 1B **90**
SW2 7K **119**
Maple St. RM7: Rom 4J **55**
W1 5A **6** (5G **83**)
Maplethorpe Rd. CR7: Thor H 4A **156**
Mapleton Cl. BR2: Brom 6J **159**
Mapleton Cres. EN3: Enf W 1D **24**
SW18 6K **117**
Mapleton Rd. E4 3K **35**
EN1: Enf 2C **24**
SW18 6J **117**
(not continuous)
Maple Tree M. SE3 1C **124**
Maple Wlk. W10 3F **81**
Maple Way TW13: Felt 3J **129**
Maplin Cl. N21 6E **22**
Maplin Ho. *SE2* *2D **108***
(off Wolvercote Rd.)
Maplin Rd. E16 6J **87**
Maplin St. E3 3B **86**
Mapperley Cl. E11 6H **51**
Mapperley Dr. IG8: Wfd G 7B **36**
Marabou Cl. E12 5C **70**
Maran Way DA18: Erith 2D **108**
Marathon Ho. *NW1* *5E **4***
(off Marylebone Rd.)
Marathon Way SE28 2K **107**
Marban Rd. W9 3H **81**
Marble Arch 2F 11
MARBLE ARCH 7D **82**
Marble Arch W1 2E **10** (7D **82**)
Marble Arch Apartments *W1* *7E **4***
(off Harrowby St.)
Marble Cl. W3 1H **97**
Marble Dr. NW2 1F **63**
Marble Hill Cl. TW1: Twick 7B **114**
Marble Hill Gdns. TW1: Twick 7B **114**
Marble Hill House 7C 114
Marble Ho. SE18 5K **107**
W9 4H **81**
Marble Quay E1 4K **15** (1G **103**)
Marbles Ho. *SE5* *6C **102***
(off Grosvenor Ter.)
Marbrook Ct. SE12 3A **142**
Marcella Rd. SW9 2A **120**
Marcellina Way BR6: Orp 3J **173**
March *NW9* *1B **44***
(off Concourse, The)
Marchant Ct. SE1 5F **103**
Marchant Rd. E11 2F **69**
Marchant St. SE14 6A **104**
Marchbank Rd. W14 6H **99**
March Ct. SW15 4D **116**
Marchmont Gdns. TW10: Rich 5F **115**
Marchmont Rd. SM6: Wall 7G **167**
TW10: Rich 5F **115**
Marchmont St. WC1 3E **6** (4J **83**)
March Rd. TW1: Twick 7A **114**
Marchside Cl. TW5: Hest 1B **112**
Marchwood Cl. SE5 7E **102**
Marchwood Cres. W5 6C **78**
Marcia Rd. SE1 4E **102**
Marcilly Rd. SW18 5B **118**
Marcon Ct. *E8* *5H **67***
(off Amhurst Rd.)
Marconi Pl. N11 4A **32**
Marconi Rd. E10 1C **68**
Marconi Way UB1: S'hall 6F **77**
Marcon Pl. E8 6H **67**
Marco Polo Ho. SW8 7F **101**
Marco Rd. W6 3E **98**
Marcourt Lawns W5 4E **78**
Marcus Ct. E15 1G **87**
Marcus Garvey M. SE22 6H **121**
Marcus Garvey Way SE24 4A **120**
Marcus St. E15 1H **87**
SW18 6K **117**
Marcus Ter. SW18 6K **117**
Mardale Ct. NW7 7H **29**
Mardale Dr. NW9 5K **43**
Mardell Rd. CR0: Croy 5K **157**
Marden Av. BR2: Hayes 6H **159**
Marden Cres. CR0: Croy 6K **155**
DA5: Bexl 5J **127**
Marden Ho. E8 5H **67**
Marden Rd. CR0: Croy 6K **155**
N17 2E **48**
Marden Sq. SE16 3H **103**
Marder Rd. W13 2A **96**
Mardyke Cl. RM13: Rain 2J **91**
Mardyke Ho. RM13: Rain 2K **91**
SE17 *4D **102***
(off Mason St.)
Marechal Niel Av. DA15: Sidc 3H **143**
Marechal Niel Pde. *DA14: Sidc* *3H **143***
(off Main Rd.)
Maresby Ho. E4 2J **35**
Mares Fld. CR0: Croy 3E **168**
Maresfield Gdns. NW3 5A **64**
Mare St. E2 2H **85**
E8 5H **67**
Marfleet Cl. SM5: Cars 2C **166**
Margaret Av. E4 6J **25**
Margaret Bondfield Av. IG11: Bark 7A **72**
Margaret Bldgs. N16 1F **67**
Margaret Ct. EN4: E Barn 4G **21**
W1 7A **6**
Margaret Gardner Dr. SE9 2D **142**
Margaret Herbison Ho. *SW6* *6H **99***
(off Clem Attlee Ct.)
Margaret Ho. *W6* *5E **98***
(off Queen Caroline St.)
Margaret Ingram Cl. SW6 6H **99**
Margaret Lockwood Cl.
KT1: King T 4F **151**
Margaret Rd. DA5: Bexl 6D **126**
EN4: E Barn 4G **21**
N16 1F **67**
Margaret St. W1 7K **5** (6F **83**)

Margaretta Ter. SW3 7C 16 (6C 100)
Margaretting Rd. E12 1A 70
Margaret Way IG4: Ilf 6C 52
Margaret White Ho. *NW1* *1D 6*
(off Chalton St.)
Margate Rd. SW2 5J 119
Margery Fry Ct. N7 3J 65
Margery Pk. Rd. E7 6J 69
Margery Rd. RM8: Dag 3D 72
Margery St. WC1 2J 7 (3A 84)
Margery Ter. *E7* *6J 69*
(off Margery Pk. Rd.)
Margin Dr. SW19 5F 135
Margravine Gdns. W6 5F 99
Margravine Rd. W6 5F 99
Marham Dr. NW9 1A 44
Marham Gdns. SM4: Mord 6A 154
SW18 1C 136
Maria Cl. SE1 4H 103
Marian Cl. UB4: Yead 4B 76
Marian Ct. E9 5J 67
SM1: Sutt 5K 165
Marianne North Gallery 2F 115
Marian Pl. E2 2H 85
Marian Rd. SW16 1G 155
Marian St. E2 2H 85
Marian Way NW10 7B 62
Maria Ter. E1 5K 85
Maria Theresa Cl. KT3: N Mald 5K 151
Maribor *SE10* *7E 104*
(off Burney St.)
Maricas Av. HA3: Hrw W 1H 41
Marie Curie SE5 1E 120
Marie Lloyd Gdns. N19 7J 47
Marie Lloyd Ho. *N1* *1E 8*
(off Murray Gro.)
Marie Lloyd Wlk. E8 6F 67
Mariette Way SM6: Wall 7J 167
Marigold All. SE1 3A 14
Marigold Cl. UB1: S'hall 7C 76
Marigold Rd. N17 7D 34
Marigold St. SE16 2H 103
Marigold Way CR0: Croy 1K 169
Marina App. UB4: Yead 5C 76
Marina Av. KT3: N Mald 5D 152
Marina Cl. BR2: Brom 3J 159
Marina Dr. DA16: Well 2J 125
Marina Gdns. RM7: Rom 5H 55
Marina Way TW11: Tedd 7D 132
Marine Dr. IG11: Bark 4A 90
SE18 4D 106
Marinefield Rd. SW6 2K 117
Marinel Ho. SE5 7C 102
Mariner Gdns. TW10: Ham 3C 132
Mariner Rd. E12 4E 70
Mariners Cl. EN4: E Barn 5G 21
Mariners M. E14 4F 105
Marine St. SE16 3G 103
Marine Twr. *SE8* *6B 104*
(off Abinger Gro.)
Marion Av. TW17: Shep 5D 146
Marion Gro. IG8: Wfd G 5B 36
Marion Rd. CR7: Thor H 5C 156
NW7 5H 29
Marischal Rd. SE13 3F 123
Maritime Ho. SE18 4F 107
Maritime Ind. Est. SE7 4K 105
Maritime Quay E14 5C 104
Maritime St. E3 4B 86
Marius Mans. SW17 2E 136
Marius Rd. SW17 2E 136
Marjorie Gro. SW11 4D 118
Marjorie M. E1 6K 85
Mark Av. E4 6J 25
Mark Cl. DA7: Bex 1E 126
UB1: S'hall 7F 77
Marke Cl. BR2: Kes 4C 172
Market, The SM5: Sutt 1A 166
Market Cen., The UB2: S'hall 4K 93
Market Chambers *EN2: Enf* *3J 23*
(off Church St.)
Market Ct. W1 7A 6
Market Entrance
SW8 7G 101
Market Est. N7 6J 65
Market Hall N22 2A 48
Market Hill SE18 3E 106
Market La. HA8: Edg 1J 43
W12 2E 98
Market Link RM1: Rom 4K 55
Market M. W1 5J 11 (1F 101)
Market Pde. *BR1: Brom* *1J 159*
(off East St.)
DA14: Sidc 4B 144
E10 *6E 50*
(off High Rd.)
E17 *3B 50*
(off Forest Rd.)
N9 *2B 34*
(off Winchester Rd.)
N16 *1G 67*
(off Oldhill St.)
TW13: Hanw 3C 130
Market Pav. E10 3C 68
Market Pl. DA6: Bex 4G 127
EN2: Enf 3J 23
KT1: King T 2D 150
N2 3C 46
NW11 4K 45
SE16 4G 103
(not continuous)
TW8: Bford 7C 96
UB1: S'hall 1D 94
W1 7A 6 (6G 83)
W3 1J 97
Market Rd. N7 6J 65
TW9: Rich 3G 115
Market Row SW9 4A 120
Market Sq. BR1: Brom 2J 159
(not continuous)
E14 6D 86
KT1: King T *2D 150*
(off Market Pl.)
Market Sq., The *N9* *2C 34*
(off Plevna Rd.)
Market St. E6 2D 88
SE18 4E 106
Market Ter. *TW8: Bford* *6E 96*
(off Albany Rd.)
Market Trad. Est. UB2: S'hall 4K 93
Market Way E14 6D 86
HA0: Wemb 5E 60
Market Yd. M. SE1 7G 15 (2E 102)
Markfield Gdns. E4 7J 25
Markfield Rd. N15 4G 49
Markham Ho. *RM10: Dag* *3G 73*
(off Uvedale Rd.)
Markham Pl. SW3 5E 16 (5D 100)
Markham Sq. SW3 5E 16 (5D 100)
Markham St. SW3 5D 16 (5C 100)
Markhole Cl. TW12: Hamp 7D 130
Mark Ho. *E2* *2K 85*
(off Sewardstone Rd.)
Markhouse Av. E17 6A 50
Markhouse Pas. *E17* *6B 50*
(off Markhouse Rd.)
Markhouse Rd. E17 6B 50
Markland Ho. *W10* *7F 81*
(off Darfield Way)
Mark La. EC3 2H 15 (7E 84)
Mark Lodge *EN4: Cockf* *4H 21*
(off Edgeworth Rd.)
Markmanor Av. E17 7A 50
Mark Rd. N22 2B 48
Marksbury Av. TW9: Rich 3G 115
MARKS GATE 1E 54
Marks Lodge RM7: Rom 5K 55
Mark Sq. EC2 3G 9 (4E 84)
Marks Rd. RM7: Rom 5J 55
(not continuous)
Markstone Ho. *SE1* *7A 14*
(off Lancaster St.)
Mark St. E15 7G 69
EC2 3G 9 (4E 84)
Mark Wade Cl. E12 1B 70
Markway TW16: Sun 2A 148
Markwell Cl. SE26 4H 139
Markyate Ho. *W10* *4E 80*
(off Sutton Way)
Markyate Rd. RM8: Dag 5B 72
Marlands Rd. IG5: Ilf 3C 52
Marlborough *SW19* *1F 135*
(off Inner Pk. Rd.)
Marlborough Av. E8 1G 85
(not continuous)
HA4: Ruis 6E 38
HA8: Edg 3C 28
N14 3B 32
Marlborough Cl. BR6: Orp 6K 161
N20 3J 31
SE17 4C 102
SW19 6C 136
Marlborough Ct. *CR2: S Croy* *4E 168*
(off Birdhurst Rd.)
EN1: Enf 5K 23
HA1: Harr 4H 41
HA6: Nwood 1H 39
IG9: Buck H 2F 37
N17 *1G 49*
(off Kemble Rd.)
SM6: Wall 7G 167
W1 2A 12
W8 *4J 99*
(off Pembroke Rd.)
Marlborough Cres. UB3: Harl 7F 93
W4 3K 97
Marlborough Dr. IG5: Ilf 3C 52
Marlborough Flats SW3 3D 16
Marlborough Gdns. KT6: Surb 7D 150
N20 3J 31
Marlborough Gro. SE1 5G 103
Marlborough Hill HA1: Harr 4H 41
NW8 2A 82
Marlborough House 5B 12 (1G 101)
Marlborough Ho. *E16* *1J 105*
(off Hardy Av.)
NW1 *3K 5*
(off Osnaburgh St.)
Marlborough La. SE7 6A 106
Marlborough Mans. *NW6* *5K 63*
(off Canon Hill)
Marlborough M. SW2 4K 119
Marlborough Pde. *HA8: Edg* *3C 28*
(off Marlborough Av.)
UB10: Hil 4D 74
Marlborough Pk. Av. DA15: Sidc 7A 126
Marlborough Pl. NW8 2A 82
Marlborough Rd. BR2: Brom 4A 160
CR2: S Croy 7C 168
DA7: Bex 3D 126
E4 6J 35
E7 7A 70
E15 4G 69
E18 2J 51
N9 1B 34
N19 2H 65
(not continuous)
N22 7D 32
RM7: Mawney 4G 55
RM8: Dag 4B 72
SE18 3F 107
SM1: Sutt 3J 165
SW1 5B 12 (1G 101)
SW19 6C 136
TW7: Isle 1B 114
TW10: Rich 6F 115
TW12: Hamp 6E 130
TW13: Felt 2B 130
TW15: Ashf 5A 128
UB2: S'hall 3A 94
UB10: Hil 4D 74
W4 5J 97
W5 2D 96
Marlborough St. SW3 4C 16 (4C 100)
Marlborough Yd. N19 2H 65
Marlbury *NW8* *1K 81*
(off Abbey Rd.)
Marler Rd. SE23 1A 140
Marley Av. DA7: Bex 6D 108
Marley Cl. N15 4B 48
UB6: G'frd 3E 76
Marley Ho. *W11* *7F 81*
(off St Ann's Rd.)
Marley Wlk. NW2 5E 62
Marlfield Cl. KT4: Wor Pk 1C 164
Marlin Cl. TW16: Sun 6G 129
Marling Ct. TW12: Hamp 6D 130
Marlingdene Cl. TW12: Hamp 6E 130
Marlings Cl. BR7: Chst 4J 161
Marlings Pk. Av. BR7: Chst 4J 161
Marlins Cl. SM1: Sutt 5A 166
Marloes Cl. HA0: Wemb 4D 60
Marloes Rd. W8 3K 99
Marlow Cl. SE20 3H 157
Marlow Ct. N14 7B 22
NW6 7F 63
NW9 3B 44
Marlow Cres. TW1: Twick 6K 113
Marlow Dr. SM3: Cheam 2F 165
Marlowe Bus. Cen. *SE14* *7A 104*
(off Batavia Rd.)
Marlowe Cl. BR7: Chst 6H 143
IG6: Ilf 1G 53
Marlowe Ct. *SW3* *4D 16*
(off Petyward)
Marlowe Gdns. SE9 6E 124
Marlowe Ho. IG8: Wfd G 7K 37
KT1: King T *4D 150*
(off Portsmouth Rd.)
SE8 *5B 104*
(off Bowditch)
Marlowe Path SE8 6C 104
Marlowe Rd. E17 4E 50
Marlowes, The DA1: Cray 4K 127
NW8 1B 82
Marlowe Sq. CR4: Mitc 4G 155
Marlowe Way CR0: Bedd 2J 167
Marlow Gdns. UB3: Harl 3F 93
Marlow Ho. *E2* *2J 9*
(off Calvert Av.)
KT5: Surb *5E 150*
(off Cranes Pk.)
SE1 *7J 15*
(off Maltby St.)
TW11: Tedd 4A 132
W2 *6K 81*
(off Hallfield Est.)
Marlow Rd. E6 3D 88
SE20 3H 157
UB2: S'hall 3D 94
Marlow Way SE16 2K 103
Marlow Workshops *E2* *2J 9*
(off Virginia Rd.)
Marl Rd. SW18 4A 118
Marlton St. SE10 5H 105
Marlwood Cl. DA15: Sidc 2J 143
Marmadon Rd. SE18 4K 107
Marmara Apartments *E16* *7J 87*
(off Western Gateway)
Marmion App. E4 4H 35
Marmion Av. E4 4G 35
Marmion Cl. E4 4G 35
Marmion M. SW11 3E 118
Marmion Rd. SW11 4E 118
Marmont Rd. SE15 1G 121
Marmora Ho. *E1* *5A 86*
(off Ben Jonson Rd.)
Marmora Rd. SE22 6J 121
Marmot Rd. TW4: Houn 3B 112
Marne Av. DA16: Well 3A 126
N11 4A 32
Marnell Way TW4: Houn 3B 112
Marne St. W10 3G 81
Marney Rd. SW11 4E 118

Marnfield Cres. SW2 1A **138**
Marnham Av. NW2 4G **63**
Marnham Ct. HA0: Wemb 5C **60**
Marnham Cres. UB6: G'frd 3F **77**
Marnock Ho. *SE17* *5D* ***102***
(off Brandon St.)
Marnock Rd. SE4 5B **122**
Maroon Ho. E14 5A **86**
Maroon St. E14 5A **86**
Maroons Way SE6 5C **140**
Marqueen Towers
SW16 7K **137**
Marquess Rd. N1 6D **66**
Marquess Rd. Nth. N1 6D **66**
Marquess Rd. Sth. N1 6C **66**
Marquis Cl. HA0: Wemb 7F **61**
Marquis Ct. IG11: Bark 5J **71**
KT1: King T *4D* ***150***
(off Anglesea Rd.)
N4 *1K* ***65***
(off Marquis Rd.)
TW19: Stanw 1A **128**
Marquis Rd. N4 1K **65**
N22 6E **32**
NW1 6H **65**
Marrabon Cl. DA15: Sidc 1A **144**
Marrick Cl. SW15 4C **116**
Marrick Ho. *NW6* *1K* ***81***
(off Mortimer Cres.)
Marriett Ho. SE6 4E **140**
Marrilyne Av. EN3: Enf L 1G **25**
Marriner Ct. *UB3: Hayes* *7G* ***75***
(off Barra Hall Rd.)
Marriott Cl. TW14: Felt 6F **111**
Marriott Rd. E15 1G **87**
EN5: Barn 3A **20**
N4 1K **65**
N10 1D **46**
Marriotts Cl. NW9 6B **44**
Marryat Cl. TW4: Houn 4D **112**
Marryat Ho. *SW1* *6A* ***18***
(off Churchill Gdns.)
Marryat Pl. SW19 4G **135**
Marryat Rd. SW19 5F **135**
Marryat Sq. SW6 1G **117**
Marsala Rd. SE13 4D **122**
Marsden Rd. N9 2C **34**
SE15 3F **121**
Marsden St. NW5 6E **64**
(not continuous)
Marsden Way BR6: Orp 4K **173**
Marshall Cl. HA1: Harr 7H **41**
SW18 6A **118**
TW4: Houn 5D **112**
Marshall Dr. UB4: Hayes 5H **75**
Marshall Est. NW7 4H **29**
Marshall Ho. *N1* *2D* ***84***
(off Cranston Est.)
NW6 *2H* ***81***
(off Albert Rd.)
SE1 *3E* ***102***
(off Page's Wlk.)
SE17 *5D* ***102***
(off East St.)
Marshall Path SE28 7B **90**
Marshall Rd. E10 3D **68**
N17 1D **48**
Marshalls Cl. N11 4A **32**
Marshalls Dr. RM1: Rom 3K **55**
Marshalls Gro. SE18 4C **106**
Marshall's Pl. SE16 3F **103**
Marshalls Rd. RM7: Rom 4K **55**
SM1: Sutt 4K **165**
Marshall St. W1 1B **12** (6G **83**)
Marshall Street Leisure Cen. 6G 83
Marshalsea Rd. SE1 6D **14** (2C **102**)
Marsham Cl. BR7: Chst 5F **143**
Marsham Ct. SW1 3D **18** (4H **101**)
Marsham St. SW1 2D **18** (3H **101**)
Marsh Av. CR4: Mitc 2D **154**
Marshbrook Cl. SE3 3B **124**
Marsh Cen., The *E1* *7K* ***9***
(off Whitechapel High St.)
Marsh Cl. NW7 3G **29**
Marsh Ct. E8 6G **67**
SW19 1A **154**
Marsh Dr. NW9 6B **44**
Marsh Farm Rd. TW2: Twick 1K **131**
Marshfield St. E14 3E **104**
Marsh Ga. Bus. Cen. E15 1E **86**
Marshgate Cen., The
E15 1D **86**
Marshgate La. E15 7D **68**
(not continuous)
Marshgate Path SE28 3G **107**
Marshgate Sidings (Bow Depot)
E15 1D **86**
Marshgate Trad. Est. E15 7D **68**
Marsh Grn. Rd. RM10: Dag 1G **91**
Marsh Hall HA9: Wemb 3F **61**
Marsh Hill E9 5A **68**
Marsh Ho. *SW1* *6D* ***18***
(off Aylesford St.)
SW8 1G **119**
Marsh La. E10 2B **68**
HA7: Stan 5H **27**
N17 7C **34**
NW7 3F **29**
Marsh Rd. HA0: Wemb 3D **78**
HA5: Pinn 4C **40**
Marshside Cl. N9 1D **34**
Marsh St. E14 4D **104**
Marsh Wall E14 1C **104**
Marsh Way RM13: Dag, Rain 3K **91**
Marshwood Ho. *NW6* *1J* ***81***
(off Kilburn Va.)
Marsland Cl. SE17 5B **102**
Marsom Ho. *N1* *1E* ***8***
(off Fairbank Est.)
Marston Av. KT9: Chess 6E **162**
RM10: Dag 2G **73**
Marston Cl. NW6 7A **64**
RM10: Dag 3G **73**
Marston Ho. SW9 2A **120**
Marston Rd. IG5: Ilf 1C **52**
TW11: Tedd 5B **132**
Marston Way SE19 7B **138**
Marsworth Av. HA5: Pinn 1B **40**
Marsworth Cl. UB4: Yead 5C **76**
Marsworth Ho. *E2* *1G* ***85***
(off Whiston Rd.)
Martaban Rd. N16 2F **67**
Martara M. SE17 5C **102**
Martello St. E8 7H **67**
Martello Ter. E8 7H **67**
Martell Rd. SE21 3D **138**
Martel Pl. E8 6F **67**
Marten Rd. E17 2C **50**
Martens Av. DA7: Bex 4H **127**
Martens Cl. DA7: Bex 4J **127**
Martha Ct. E2 2H **85**
Martham Cl. IG6: Ilf 1F **53**
SE28 7D **90**
Martha Rd. E15 6G **69**
Martha's Bldgs. EC1 3E **8** (4D **84**)
Martha St. E1 6J **85**
Marthorne Cres. HA3: Hrw W 2H **41**
Martin Bowes Rd. SE9 3D **124**
Martinbridge Trad. Est. EN1: Enf 5B **24**
Martin Cl. N9 1E **34**
UB10: Uxb 2A **74**
Martin Ct. *CR2: S Croy* *5D* ***168***
(off Birdhurst Rd.)
E14 *2E* ***104***
(off River Barge Cl.)
Martin Cres. CR0: Croy 1A **168**
Martindale SW14 5J **115**
Martindale Av. BR6: Chels 5K **173**
E16 7J **87**
Martindale Ho. *E14* *7D* ***86***
(off Poplar High St.)
Martin Dale Ind. Est. EN1: Enf 3C **24**
Martindale Rd. SW12 7F **119**
TW4: Houn 3C **112**
Martin Dene DA6: Bex 5F **127**
Martin Dr. UB5: N'olt 5D **58**
Martineau Est. E1 7J **85**
Martineau Ho. *SW1* *6A* ***18***
(off Churchill Gdns.)
Martineau M. N5 4B **66**
Martineau Rd. N5 4B **66**
Martingale Cl. TW16: Sun 4J **147**
Martingales Cl. TW10: Ham 3D **132**
Martin Gdns. RM8: Dag 4C **72**
Martin Gro. SM4: Mord 3J **153**
Martin Ho. SE1 3C **102**
SW8 *7J* ***101***
(off Wyvil Rd.)
Martin La. EC4 2F **15** (7D **84**)
(not continuous)
Martin Pl. *SE28* *1J* ***107***
(off Martin St.)
Martin Ri. DA6: Bex 5F **127**
Martin Rd. RM8: Dag 4C **72**
Martins, The HA9: Wemb 3F **61**
Martins Cl. BR4: W W'ck 1F **171**
Martin's Mt. EN5: New Bar 4D **20**
Martin's Rd. BR2: Brom 2G **159**
Martin St. SE28 1J **107**
Martins Wlk. N10 1E **46**
N22 3A **48**
Martin Wlk. *SE28* *1J* ***107***
(off Martin St.)
Martin Way SM4: Mord 2F **153**
SW20 2F **153**
Martlesham *N17* *2E* ***48***
(off Adams Rd.)
Martlesham Wlk. *NW9* *1A* ***44***
(off Kenley Av.)
Martlet Gro. UB5: N'olt 3B **76**
Martlett Ct. WC2 1F **13** (6J **83**)
Martley Dr. IG2: Ilf 5F **53**
Martock Cl. HA3: W'stone 4A **42**
Martock Gdns. N11 5J **31**
Marton Cl. SE6 3C **140**
Marton Rd. N16 2E **66**
Martynside NW9 1B **44**
Martys Yd. NW3 4B **64**
Marvell Av. UB4: Hayes 5J **75**
Marvell Ho. *SE5* *7D* ***102***
(off Camberwell Rd.)
Marvels Cl. SE12 2K **141**
Marvels La. SE12 2K **141**
(not continuous)
Marville Rd. SW6 7H **99**
Marvin St. E8 6H **67**
Marwell Cl. BR4: W W'ck 2H **171**
Marwood Cl. DA16: Well 3B **126**
Marwood Dr. NW7 7A **30**
Mary Adelaide Cl. SW15 4A **134**
Mary Ann Gdns. SE8 6C **104**
Maryatt Av. HA2: Harr 2F **59**
Mary Bank SE18 4D **106**
Mary Cl. HA7: Stan 4F **43**
Mary Datchelor Cl. SE5 1D **120**
Maryfield Cl. DA5: Bexl 3K **145**
Mary Flux Ct. *SW5* *5K* ***99***
(off Bramham Gdns.)
Mary Grn. NW8 1K **81**
Mary Holben Ho. SW16 5G **137**
Mary Ho. *W6* *5E* ***98***
(off Queen Caroline St.)
Mary Jones Ho. *E14* *7C* ***86***
(off Garford St.)
Maryland Ind. Est. *E15* *5G* ***69***
(off Maryland Rd.)
Maryland Pk. E15 5G **69**
(not continuous)
Maryland Point *E15* *6G* ***69***
(off Grove, The)
Maryland Rd. CR7: Thor H 1B **156**
E15 5F **69**
N22 6E **32**
Maryland Sq. E15 5G **69**
Marylands Rd. W9 4J **81**
Maryland St. E15 5F **69**
Maryland Wlk. *N1* *1C* ***84***
(off Popham St.)
Maryland Way TW16: Sun 2J **147**
Mary Lawrenson Pl. SE3 7J **105**
MARYLEBONE 5H **5** (5E **82**)
Marylebone Cricket Club
Lord's Cricket Ground
1B 4 (3B 82)
MARYLEBONE FLYOVER 5B **82**
Marylebone Fly-Over
W2 6B **4** (5B **82**)
Marylebone High St.
W1 5H **5** (5E **82**)
Marylebone La. W1 6H **5** (5E **82**)
Marylebone M. W1 6J **5** (5F **83**)
Marylebone Pas. W1 7B **6** (6G **83**)
Marylebone Rd.
NW1 5D **4** (5C **82**)
Marylebone St. W1 6H **5** (5E **82**)
Marylee Way SE11 4H **19** (4K **101**)
Mary MacArthur Ho. *E2* *3K* ***85***
(off Warley St.)
RM10: Dag *3G* ***73***
(off Wythenshawe Rd.)
W6 6G **99**
Maryon Gro. SE7 4C **106**
Maryon M. NW3 4C **64**
Maryon Rd. SE7 4C **106**
SE18 4C **106**
Mary Peters Dr. UB6: N'olt 5H **59**
Mary Pl. W11 7G **81**
Mary Rose Cl.
TW12: Hamp 1E **148**
Mary Rose Mall E6 5D **88**
Mary Rose Way N20 1G **31**
Mary Seacole Cl. E8 1F **85**
Mary Smith Ct. *SW5* *4J* ***99***
(off Trebovir Rd.)
Marysmith Ho. *SW1* *5D* ***18***
(off Cureton St.)
Mary's Ter. TW1: Twick 7A **114**
(not continuous)
Mary St. E16 5H **87**
N1 1C **84**
Mary Ter. NW1 1F **83**
Maryville DA16: Well 2K **125**
Mary Wallace Theatre 1A 132
Mary Wharrie Ho. *NW3* *7D* ***64***
(off Fellows Rd.)
Marzena Ct. TW3: Houn 6G **113**
Masault Ct. *TW9: Rich* *4E* ***114***
(off Kew Foot Rd.)
Masbro' Rd. W14 3F **99**
Mascalls Ct. SE7 6A **106**
Mascalls Rd. SE7 6A **106**
Mascotte Rd. SW15 4F **117**
Mascotts Cl. NW2 3D **62**
Masefield Av. HA7: Stan 5E **26**
UB1: S'hall 7E **76**
Masefield Ct. EN5: New Bar 4F **21**
KT6: Surb 7D **150**
Masefield Cres. N14 5B **22**
Masefield Gdns. E6 4E **88**
Masefield Ho. *NW6* *3J* ***81***
(off Stafford Rd.)
Masefield La. UB4: Yead 4K **75**
Masefield Rd. TW12: Hamp 4D **130**
Masefield Vw. BR6: Farnb 3G **173**
Masefield Way
TW19: Stanw 1B **128**
Masham Ho. *DA18: Erith* *2D* ***108***
(off Kale Rd.)
Mashie Rd. W3 6A **80**
Mashiters Hill RM1: Rom 1K **55**
Maskall Cl. SW2 1A **138**
Maskani Wlk. SW16 7G **137**
Maskell Rd. SW17 3A **136**
Maskelyne Cl. SW11 1C **118**

Mason Cl. DA7: Bex	3H 127
E16	7J 87
SE16	5G 103
SW20	1F 153
TW12: Hamp	1D 148
Mason Ho. E9	7H 99
(off Frampton Pk. Rd.)	
Mason Rd. IG8: Wfd G	4B 36
SM1: Sutt	5K 165
Mason's Arms M'. W1	1K 11 (6F 83)
Masons Av. CR0: Croy	3A 168
EC2	7E 8 (6D 84)
HA3: W'stone	4K 41
Mason's Grn. La. W3	4G 79
(not continuous)	
Masons Hill BR2: Brom	3J 159
SE18	4F 107
Masons Pl. CR4: Mitc	1F 154
EC1	1B 8 (3C 84)
Mason St. SE17	4D 102
Masons Yd. EC1	1B 8 (3B 84)
SW1	4B 12 (1G 101)
SW19	5F 135
Massey Cl. N11	5A 32
Massey Ct. E6	1A 88
(off Florence Rd.)	
Massie Rd. E8	6G 67
Massingberd Way SW17	4F 137
Massinger St. SE17	4E 102
Massingham St. E1	4K 85
Masson Av. HA4: Ruis	6A 58
Mast Ct. SE16	4A 104
(off Boat Lifter Way)	
Master Gunners Pl. SE18	7C 106
Masterman Ho. SE5	7D 102
(off Elmington St.)	
Masterman Rd. E6	3C 88
Masters Cl. SW16	6G 137
Masters Dr. SE16	5H 103
Masters Lodge E1	6J 85
(off Johnson St.)	
Masters St. E1	5K 85
Mast Ho. Ter. E14	4C 104
(not continuous)	
Mastmaker Ct. E14	2C 104
Mastmaker Rd. E14	2C 104
MASWELL PARK	5G 113
Maswell Pk. Cres. TW3: Houn	5G 113
Maswell Pk. Rd. TW3: Houn	5F 113
Matcham Ct. TW1: Twick	6D 114
(off Clevedon Rd.)	
Matcham Rd. E11	3G 69
Matchless Dr. SE18	7E 106
Matfield Cl. BR2: Brom	5J 159
Matfield Rd. DA17: Belv	6G 109
Matham Gro. SE22	4F 121
Matham Rd. KT8: E Mos	5H 149
Matheson Lang Ho. SE1	7J 13
Matheson Rd. W14	4H 99
Mathews Av. E6	2E 88
Mathews Pk. Av. E15	6H 69
Mathews Yd. WC2	1E 12 (6J 83)
Mathieson Ct. SE1	7B 14
(off King James St.)	
Mathison Ho. SW10	7A 100
(off Coleridge Gdns.)	
Matilda Cl. SE19	7D 138
Matilda Ho. E1	4K 15
(off St Katherine's Way)	
Matilda St. N1	1K 83
Matins Pl. SE28	1J 107
Matisse Ct. EC1	3E 8 (4D 84)
Matlock Cl. EN5: Barn	5A 20
SE24	4C 120
Matlock Ct. SE5	4D 120
Matlock Cres. SM3: Cheam	4G 165
Matlock Gdns. SM3: Cheam	4G 165
Matlock Pl. SM3: Cheam	4G 165
Matlock Rd. E10	6E 50
Matlock St. E14	6A 86
Matlock Way KT3: N Mald	1K 151

Maton Ho. SW6	7H 99
(off Estcourt Rd.)	
Matrimony Pl. SW4	2G 119
Matson Cl. IG8: Wfd G	7B 36
Matson Ho. SE16	3H 103
Matthew Cl. W10	4F 81
Matthew Ct. CR4: Mitc	5H 155
E17	3E 50
Matthew Parker St.	
SW1	7D 12 (2H 101)
Matthews Cl. E17	1C 50
(off Chingford Rd.)	
Matthews Ho. E14	5C 86
(off Burgess St.)	
Matthews Rd. UB6: G'frd	5H 59
Matthews St. SW11	2D 118
Matthias Rd. N16	5E 66
Mattison Rd. N4	6A 48
Mattock La. W5	1B 96
W13	1B 96
Maud Cashmore Way SE18	3D 106
Maude Ho. E2	2G 85
(off Ropley St.)	
Maude Rd. E17	5A 50
SE5	1E 120
Maude Ter. E17	5A 50
Maud Gdns. E13	1H 87
IG11: Bark	2K 89
Maudlins Grn. E1	4K 15 (1G 103)
Maud Rd. E10	3E 68
E13	2H 87
Maudslay Rd. SE9	3D 124
Maudsley Ho. TW8: Bford	5E 96
Maud St. E16	5H 87
Maudsville Cotts. W7	1J 95
Maud Wilkes Cl. NW5	5G 65
Maugham Ct. W3	3J 97
(off Palmerston Rd.)	
Mauleverer Rd. SW2	5J 119
Maundeby Wlk. NW10	6A 62
Maunder Rd. W7	1K 95
Maunsel St. SW1	3C 18 (4H 101)
Maureen Campbell Ct.	
TW17: Shep	5D 146
(off Harrison Way)	
Maureen Ct. BR3: Beck	2J 157
Maurer Ct. SE10	3H 105
Mauretania Bldg. E1	7K 85
(off Jardine Rd.)	
Maurice Av. N22	2B 48
Maurice Bishop Ter. N6	6E 46
(off View Rd.)	
Maurice Brown Cl. NW7	5A 30
Maurice Ct. E1	3K 85
TW8: Bford	7D 96
Maurice Drummond Ho. SE10	1D 122
(off Catherine Gro.)	
Maurice St. W12	6D 80
Maurice Wlk. NW11	4A 46
Maurier Cl. UB5: N'olt	1A 76
Mauritius Rd. SE10	4G 105
Maury Rd. N16	2G 67
Mauveine Gdns. TW3: Houn	4E 112
Mavelstone Cl. BR1: Brom	1C 160
Mavelstone Rd. BR1: Brom	1B 160
Maverton Rd. E3	1C 86
Mavis Av. KT19: Ewe	5A 164
Mavis Cl. KT19: Ewe	5A 164
Mavis Wlk. E6	5C 88
(off Greenwich Cres.)	
Mavor Ho. N1	1K 83
(off Barnsbury Est.)	
Mawbey Ho. SE1	5F 103
Mawbey Pl. SE1	5F 103
Mawbey Rd. SE1	5F 103
Mawbey St. SW8	7J 101
Mawdley Ho. SE1	7A 14
MAWNEY	4J 55
Mawney Cl. RM7: Mawney	2H 55
Mawney Rd. RM7: Mawney	2H 55
Mawson Cl. SW20	2G 153

Mawson Ct. N1	1D 84
(off Gopsall St.)	
Mawson Ho. EC1	5J 7
(off Baldwins Gdns.)	
Mawson La. W4	6B 98
Maxden Ct. SE15	3F 121
Maxey Gdns. RM9: Dag	4E 72
Maxey Rd. RM9: Dag	5E 72
SE18	4G 107
Maxfield Cl. N20	7F 21
Maxilla Wlk. W10	6F 81
Maxim Apartments	
BR2: Brom	4K 159
(off Tiger la.)	
Maximfeldt Rd. DA8: Erith	5K 109
Maxim Rd. DA8: Erith	4K 109
N21	6F 23
Maxted Pk. HA1: Harr	7J 41
Maxted Rd. SE15	3F 121
Maxwell Cl. CR0: Wadd	1J 167
UB3: Hayes	7J 75
Maxwell Ct. SE22	1G 139
SW4	5H 119
Maxwell Gdns. BR6: Orp	3K 173
Maxwell Rd. DA16: Well	3K 125
HA6: Nwood	1F 39
SW6	7K 99
TW15: Ashf	6E 128
UB7: W Dray	4B 92
Maxwelton Av. NW7	5E 28
Maxwelton Cl. NW7	5E 28
Maya Angelou Ct. E4	4K 35
Maya Cl. SE15	2H 121
Mayall Cl. EN3: Enf L	1H 25
Mayall Rd. SE24	5B 120
Maya Pl. N11	7C 32
Maya Rd. N2	4A 46
Maybank Av. E18	2K 51
HA0: Wemb	5K 59
Maybank Gdns.	
HA5: Eastc	5J 39
Maybank Rd. E18	1K 51
May Bate Av. KT2: King T	1D 150
Maybells Commercial Est.	
IG11: Bark	2D 90
Mayberry Ct. BR3: Beck	7B 140
(off Copers Cope Rd.)	
Mayberry Pl. KT5: Surb	7F 151
Maybourne Cl. SE26	6H 139
Maybury Cl. BR5: Pet W	5F 161
EN1: Enf	1C 24
Maybury Ct. CR2: S Croy	5B 168
(off Haling Pk. Rd.)	
HA1: Harr	6H 41
W1	6H 5
(off Marylebone St.)	
Maybury Gdns. NW10	6D 62
Maybury M. N6	7G 47
Maybury Rd. E13	4A 88
IG11: Bark	2K 89
Maybury St. SW17	5C 136
Maychurch Cl. HA7: Stan	7J 27
May Cl. KT9: Chess	6F 163
Maycross Av. SM4: Mord	4H 153
Mayday Gdns. SE3	2C 124
Mayday Rd. CR7: Thor H	6B 156
Maydew Ho. SE16	4J 103
(off Abbeyfield Est.)	
Maydwell Ho. E14	5C 86
(off Thomas Rd.)	
Mayerne Rd. SE9	5B 124
Mayesbrook Pk. Arena	5A 72
Mayesbrook Rd. IG3: Ilf	3A 72
IG11: Bark	1K 89
RM8: Dag	3B 72
Mayesford Rd.	
RM6: Chad H	7C 54
Mayes Rd. N22	2K 47
Mayeswood Rd. SE12	4A 142
MAYFAIR	3J 11 (7F 83)

Mayfair Av. DA7: Bex	1D 126
IG1: Ilf	2D 70
KT4: Wor Pk	1C 164
RM6: Chad H	6D 54
TW2: Whit	7G 113
Mayfair Cl. BR3: Beck	1D 158
KT6: Surb	1E 162
Mayfair Ct. HA8: Edg	5A 28
Mayfair Gdns. IG8: Wfd G	7D 36
N17	6H 33
Mayfair M. NW1	7D 64
(off Regents Pk. Rd.)	
Mayfair Pl. W1	4K 11 (1F 101)
Mayfair Ter. N14	7C 22
Mayfield DA7: Bex	3F 127
Mayfield Av. BR6: Orp	1K 173
HA3: Kent	5B 42
IG8: Wfd G	6D 36
N12	4F 31
N14	2C 32
W4	4A 98
W13	3B 96
Mayfield Cl. E8	6F 67
KT7: T Ditt	1B 162
SE20	1H 157
SW4	5H 119
TW15: Ashf	6D 128
UB10: Hil	3D 74
Mayfield Cres. CR7: Thor H	4K 155
N9	6C 24
Mayfield Dr. HA5: Pinn	4D 40
Mayfield Gdns. NW4	6F 45
W7	6H 77
Mayfield Ho. E2	2H 85
(off Cambridge Heath Rd.)	
Mayfield Mans. SW15	5H 117
Mayfield Rd. BR1: Brom	5C 160
CR2: Sand	7D 168
CR7: Thor H	4K 155
DA17: Belv	4J 109
E4	2K 35
E8	7F 67
E13	4H 87
E17	2A 50
EN3: Enf H	2E 24
N8	5K 47
RM8: Dag	1C 72
SM2: Sutt	6B 166
SW19	1H 153
W3	7H 79
W12	2A 98
Mayfield Rd. Flats N8	6K 47
Mayfields HA9: Wemb	2G 61
Mayfields Cl. HA9: Wemb	2G 61
Mayfields Vs. HA3: Sidc	2G 61
Mayflower Cl. HA4: Ruis	6E 38
SE16	4K 103
Mayflower Ho. IG11: Bark	1H 89
(off Westbury Rd.)	
Mayflower Rd. SW9	3J 119
Mayflower St. SE16	2J 103
Mayfly Cl. HA5: Eastc	7A 40
Mayfly Gdns. UB5: N'olt	3B 76
Mayford NW1	2G 83
(not continuous)	
Mayford Cl. BR3: Beck	3K 157
SW12	7D 118
Mayford Rd. SW12	7D 118
May Gdns. HA0: Wemb	3C 78
Maygood St. N1	2A 84
Maygrove Rd. NW6	6H 63
Mayhew Cl. E4	3H 35
Mayhew Ct. SE5	4D 120
Mayhill Rd. EN5: Barn	6B 20
SE7	6K 105
Mayland Mans. IG11: Bark	6G 71
(off Whiting Av.)	
Maylands Dr. DA14: Sidc	3D 144
UB8: Uxb	7A 56
Maylands Ho. SW3	4D 16
(off Elystan St.)	

Maynard Cl. N15 5E 48
SW6 7K 99
Maynard Path E17 5E 50
Maynard Rd. E17 5E 50
Maynards Quay E1 7J 85
Mayne Ct. SE26 5H 139
Maynooth Gdns. SM5: Cars 7D 154
Mayo Ct. W13 3B 96
Mayo Ho. E1 5J 85
(off Lindley St.)
Mayola Rd. E5 4J 67
Mayo Rd. CR0: Croy 5D 156
KT12: Walt T 7J 147
NW10 6A 62
Mayow Rd. SE23 3K 139
SE26 4K 139
Mayplace Cl. DA7: Bex 3H 127
Mayplace La. SE18 6F 107
(not continuous)
Mayplace Rd. E. DA1: Cray 3J 127
DA7: Bex, Cray 3H 127
Mayplace Rd. W. DA7: Bex 4G 127
MAYPOLE 2K 145
Maypole Ct. UB2: S'hall 2D 94
(off Merrick Rd.)
May Rd. E4 6H 35
E13 2J 87
TW2: Twick 1J 131
Mayroyd Av. KT6: Surb 2G 163
May's Bldgs. M. SE10 7E 104
Mays Ct. SE10 7F 105
WC2 3E 12 (7J 83)
Mays Hill Rd. BR2: Brom 2G 159
Mays La. EN5: Ark, Barn 1H 29
Maysoule Rd. SW11 4B 118
Mays Rd. TW11: Tedd 5H 131
Mayston M. SE10 5J 105
(off Ormiston Rd.)
May St. W14 5H 99
Mayswood Gdns. RM10: Dag 6J 73
Mayton St. N7 3K 65
Maytree Cl. HA8: Edg 3D 28
Maytree Ct. CR4: Mitc 3E 154
UB5: N'olt 3C 76
Maytree Gdns. W5 2D 96
May Tree Ho. SE4 3B 122
(off Wickham Rd.)
Maytree La. HA7: Stan 7F 27
Maytree Wlk. SW2 2A 138
Mayville Est. N16 5E 66
Mayville Rd. E11 2G 69
IG1: Ilf 5F 71
May Wlk. E13 2K 87
Mayward Ho. SE5 1E 120
(off Peckham Rd.)
Maywood Cl. BR3: Beck 7D 140
May Wynne Ho. E16 7K 87
(off Murray Sq.)
Maze Hill SE3 7H 105
SE10 6G 105
Maze Hill Lodge SE10 6F 105
(off Park Vista)
Mazenod Av. NW6 7J 63
Maze Rd. TW9: Kew 7G 97
Mead, The BR3: Beck 1E 158
BR4: W W'ck 1F 171
N2 2A 46
SM6: Wall 6H 167
UB10: Ick 2C 56
W13 5B 78
Meadbank Studios SW11 7C 100
(off Parkgate Rd.)
Mead Cl. HA3: Hrw W 1H 41
NW1 6E 64
Mead Ct. NW9 5J 43
Mead Cres. E4 4K 35
SM1: Sutt 3C 166
Meadcroft Rd. SE11 7K 19 (6B 102)
(not continuous)
Meade Cl. W4 6G 97
Meader Ct. SE14 7K 103
Mead Fld. HA2: Harr 3D 58
Meadfield HA8: Edg 2C 28
(not continuous)
Meadfield Grn. HA8: Edg 2C 28
Meadfoot Rd. SW16 7G 137
Meadgate Av. IG8: Wfd G 5H 37
Mead Gro. RM6: Chad H 3D 54
Mead Ho. W11 1H 99
(off Ladbroke Rd.)
Mead Ho. La. UB4: Hayes 4F 75
Meadhurst Pk. TW16: Sun 6G 129
Meadhurst Sports Club 5H 129
Meadlands Dr. TW10: Ham 2D 132
Mead Lodge W4 2K 97
Meadow, The BR7: Chst 6G 143
N10 3E 46
Meadow Av. CR0: Croy 6K 157
Meadow Bank N21 6E 22
SE3 3H 123
Meadowbank KT5: Surb 6F 151
NW3 7D 64
Meadowbank Cl. SW6 7E 98
Meadowbank Gdns. TW5: Cran 1J 111
Meadowbank Rd. NW9 7K 43
Meadowbrook Ct. TW7: Isle 3J 113
Meadow Cl. BR7: Chst 5F 143
DA6: Bex 5F 127
E4 1J 35
EN3: Enf W 1F 25
EN5: Barn 6C 20
HA4: Ruis 6H 39
IG11: Bark 7A 72
KT10: Hin W 3A 162
SE6 5C 140
SM1: Sutt 2A 166
SW20 4E 152
TW4: Houn 6E 112
TW10: Ham 1E 132
UB5: N'olt 2E 76
Meadow Ct. N1 2E 84
TW3: Houn 6F 113
Meadowcourt Rd. SE3 4H 123
Meadowcroft BR1: Brom 3D 160
W4 5G 97
(off Brooks Rd.)
Meadowcroft Cl. N13 2F 33
Meadowcroft Rd. N13 2F 33
Meadow Dr. N10 3F 47
NW4 2E 44
Meadowford Cl. SE28 7A 90
Meadow Gdns. HA8: Edg 6C 28
Meadow Gth. NW10 6J 61
(not continuous)
Meadowgate Cl. NW7 5G 29
Meadow Hill KT3: N Mald 6A 152
Meadow La. SE12 3K 141
Meadowlea Cl. UB7: Harm 6A 92
Meadow M. SW8 6K 101
Meadow Pl. SW8 7J 101
W4 7A 98
Meadow Rd. BR2: Brom 2G 159
HA5: Pinn 4B 40
IG11: Bark 7K 71
RM7: Rush G 1J 73
RM9: Dag 6F 73
SM1: Sutt 4C 166
SW8 7H 19 (7K 101)
SW19 7A 136
TW13: Felt 2C 130
TW15: Ashf 5F 129
UB1: S'hall 7D 76
Meadow Row SE1 3C 102
Meadows Cl. E10 2C 68
Meadows Ct. DA14: Sidc 6B 144
Meadows End TW16: Sun 1J 147
Meadowside SE9 4A 124
TW1: Twick 7D 114
Meadowside Leisure Cen. 4A 124
Meadow Stile CR0: Croy 3C 168
Meadowsweet Cl. E16 5B 88
SW20 4E 152
Meadow Vw. DA15: Sidc 7B 126
HA1: Harr 1J 59
Meadow Vw. Rd. CR7: Thor H 5B 156
UB4: Hayes 4F 75
Meadowview Rd. DA5: Bexl 6E 126
KT19: Ewe 7A 164
SE6 5B 140
Meadow Wlk. E18 4J 51
KT17: Ewe 7B 164
KT19: Ewe 6A 164
(not continuous)
RM9: Dag 6F 73
SM6: Wall 3F 167
Meadow Way BR6: Farnb 3E 172
HA4: Ruis 6K 39
HA9: Wemb 4D 60
KT9: Chess 5E 162
NW9 5K 43
Meadow Way, The HA3: Hrw W 1J 41
Meadow Waye TW5: Hest 6C 94
Mead Path SW17 4A 136
Mead Pl. CR0: Croy 1C 168
E9 6J 67
Mead Plat NW10 6J 61
Mead Rd. BR7: Chst 6G 143
HA8: Edg 6B 28
TW10: Ham 3C 132
Mead Row SE1 1J 19 (3A 102)
Meads, The HA8: Edg 6E 28
SM3: Cheam 3G 165
SM4: Mord 5C 154
UB8: Cowl 4A 74
Meads Ct. E15 6H 69
Meadside Cl. BR3: Beck 1A 158
Meads La. IG3: Ilf 7J 53
Meads Rd. EN3: Enf H 1F 25
N22 2B 48
Mead Ter. HA9: Wemb 4D 60
Meadvale Rd. CR0: Croy 7F 157
W5 4B 78
Mead Way BR2: Hayes 6H 159
CR0: Croy 2A 170
HA4: Ruis 6F 39
IG8: Wfd G 5F 37
Meadway BR3: Beck 1E 158
EN5: Barn, New Bar 4D 20
IG3: Bark, Ilf 4J 71
KT5: Surb 1J 163
N14 2C 32
NW11 6J 45
SW20 4E 152
TW2: Twick 1H 131
TW15: Ashf 4C 128
Meadway, The IG9: Buck H 1G 37
SE3 2F 123
Meadway Cl. EN5: Barn 4D 20
HA5: H End 6A 26
NW11 6K 45
Meadway Ct. RM8: Dag 2F 73
TW11: Tedd 5C 132
W5 4F 79
Meadway Gdns. HA4: Ruis 6F 39
Meadway Ga. NW11 6J 45
Meaford Way SE20 7H 139
Meakin Est. SE1 3E 102
Mean Ct. TW7: Isle 2J 113
Meanley Rd. E12 4C 70
Meard St. W1 1C 12 (6H 83)
(not continuous)
Meath Ho. SE24 6B 120
(off Dulwich Rd.)
Meath Rd. E15 2H 87
IG1: Ilf 3G 71
Meath St. SW11 1F 119
Mecca Bingo
Burnt Oak 2J 43
Camden 1F 83
(off Arlington Rd.)
Chadwell Heath 7D 54
Croydon 2C 168
(off Tamworth Rd.)
Mecca Bingo
Dagenham 1E 90
Earlsfield 1K 135
East Ham 1C 88
Fulham Broadway 7J 99
(off Vanston Pl.)
Haggerston 1K 9
Hounslow 2G 113
Islington 7C 66
Kilburn 1J 81
Rosehill 7A 154
Wood Green 2A 48
(off Lordship La.)
Yeading 6K 75
Mecklenburgh Pl. WC1 3G 7 (4K 83)
Mecklenburgh Sq. WC1 3G 7 (4K 83)
Mecklenburgh St. WC1 3G 7 (4K 83)
Medburn St. NW1 2H 83
Medcroft Gdns. SW14 4J 115
Medebourne Cl. SE3 3J 123
Mede Ho. BR1: Brom 5K 141
(off Pike Cl.)
Medesenge Way N13 6G 33
Medfield St. SW15 7C 116
Medhurst Cl. E3 2A 86
(not continuous)
Median Rd. E5 5J 67
Medina Gro. N7 3A 66
Medina Rd. N7 3A 66
Medland Cl. SM6: Wall 1E 166
Medland Ho. E14 7A 86
Medlar Cl. UB5: N'olt 2B 76
Medlar Ho. DA15: Sidc 3A 144
Medlar St. SE5 1C 120
Medley Rd. NW6 6J 63
Medora Rd. RM7: Rom 4K 55
SW2 7K 119
Medusa Rd. SE6 6D 122
Medway Bldgs. E3 2A 86
(off Medway Rd.)
Medway Cl. CR0: Croy 6J 157
IG1: Ilf 5G 71
Medway Ct. NW11 6K 45
WC1 2E 6
(off Judd St.)
Medway Dr. UB6: G'frd 2K 77
Medway Gdns. HA0: Wemb 4A 60
Medway Ho. KT2: King T 1D 150
NW8 4C 4
(off Penfold St.)
SE1 7F 15
(off Hankey Pl.)
Medway M. E3 2A 86
Medway Pde. UB6: G'frd 2K 77
Medway Rd. E3 2A 86
Medway St. SW1 2D 18 (3H 101)
Medwin St. SW4 4K 119
Meerbrook Rd. SE3 3A 124
Meeson Rd. E15 7H 69
Meeson St. E5 4A 68
Meeson's Wharf E15 2E 86
Meeting Fld. Path E9 6J 67
Meeting Ho. All. E1 1H 103
Meeting Ho. La. SE15 1H 121
Megabowl
Acton 4G 79
Bexleyheath 4F 127
Croydon 2K 167
Dagenham 1H 91
Feltham 2K 129
Harrow 5F 41
Streatham Hill 2J 137
Mehetabel Rd. E9 5J 67
Meister Cl. IG1: Ilf 1H 71
Melancholy Wlk. TW10: Ham 2C 132
Melanda Cl. BR7: Chst 5D 142
Melanie Cl. DA7: Bex 1E 126
Melba Way SE13 1D 122
Melbourne Av. HA5: Pinn 3F 41
N13 6E 32
W13 1A 96

Melbourne Cl.—Merlin Ho.

Melbourne Cl. BR6: Orp ... 7J **161**
SE20 ... 7G **139**
SM6: Wall ... 5G **167**
UB10: Ick ... 4C **56**
Melbourne Ct. N10 ... 7A **32**
W9 ... 4A 82
(off Randolph Av.)
Melbourne Gdns. RM6: Chad H ... 5E **54**
Melbourne Gro. SE22 ... 4E **120**
Melbourne Ho. UB4: Yead ... 4A **76**
W8 ... 1J 99
(off Kensington Pl.)
Melbourne Mans. *W14 ... 6G 99*
(off Musard Rd.)
Melbourne M. SE6 ... 7E **122**
SW9 ... 1A **120**
Melbourne Pl. WC2 ... 1H **13** (6K **83**)
Melbourne Rd. E6 ... 2D **88**
E10 ... 7D **50**
E17 ... 4A **50**
IG1: Ilf ... 1F **71**
SM6: Wall ... 5F **167**
SW19 ... 1J **153**
TW11: Tedd ... 6C **132**
Melbourne Sq. SW9 ... 1A **120**
Melbourne Ter. *SW6 ... 7K 99*
(off Moore Pk. Rd.)
Melbourne Way EN1: Enf ... 6A **24**
Melbray M. SW6 ... 2H **117**
Melbreak Ho. SE22 ... 3E **120**
Melbury Av. UB2: S'hall ... 3F **95**
Melbury Cl. BR7: Chst ... 6C **142**
KT10: Clay ... 6B **162**
Melbury Ct. W8 ... 3H **99**
Melbury Dr. SE5 ... 7E **102**
Melbury Gdns. SW20 ... 1D **152**
Melbury Ho. *SW8 ... 7K 101*
(off Richborne Ter.)
Melbury Rd. HA3: Kent ... 5F **43**
W14 ... 3H **99**
Melbury Ter. NW1 ... 4D **4** (4C **82**)
Melchester *W11 ... 6H 81*
(off Ledbury Rd.)
Melchester Ho. *N19 ... 3H 65*
(off Wedmore St.)
Melcombe Ct. *NW1 ... 5E 4*
(off Melcombe Pl.)
Melcombe Gdns. HA3: Kent ... 6F **43**
Melcombe Ho. *SW8 ... 7K 101*
(off Dorset Rd.)
Melcombe Pl. NW1 ... 5E **4** (5D **82**)
Melcombe Regis Ct. *W1 ... 6H 5*
(off Weymouth St.)
Melcombe St. NW1 ... 4F **5** (4D **82**)
Meldex Cl. NW7 ... 6K **29**
Meldon Cl. SW6 ... 1K **117**
Meldone Cl. KT5: Surb ... 7H **151**
Meldrum Rd. IG3: Ilf ... 2A **72**
Melfield Gdns. SE6 ... 4E **140**
Melford Av. IG11: Bark ... 6J **71**
Melford Cl. KT9: Chess ... 5F **163**
Melford Ct. *SE1 ... 3E 102*
(off Fendall St.)
SE22 ... 1G **139**
(not continuous)
Melford Pas. SE22 ... 7G **121**
Melford Rd. E6 ... 4D **88**
E11 ... 2G **69**
E17 ... 4A **50**
IG1: Ilf ... 2H **71**
SE22 ... 7G **121**
Melfort Av. CR7: Thor H ... 3B **156**
Melfort Rd. CR7: Thor H ... 3B **156**
Melgund Rd. N5 ... 5A **66**
Melina Cl. UB3: Hayes ... 5F **75**
Melina Ct. SW15 ... 3C **116**
Melina Pl. NW8 ... 2A **4** (3B **82**)
Melina Rd. W12 ... 2D **98**
Melior Ct. N6 ... 6G **47**
Melior Pl. SE1 ... 6G **15** (2E **102**)
Melior St. SE1 ... 6G **15** (2E **102**)
Meliot Rd. SE6 ... 2F **141**
Meller Cl. CR0: Bedd ... 3J **167**
Melling Dr. EN1: Enf ... 1B **24**
Melling St. SE18 ... 6J **107**
Mellish Cl. IG11: Bark ... 1K **89**
Mellish Flats E10 ... 7C **50**
Mellish Gdns. IG8: Wfd G ... 5D **36**
Mellish Ho. *E1 ... 6H 85*
(off Varden St.)
Mellish Ind. Est. SE18 ... 3B **106**
Mellish St. E14 ... 3C **104**
Mellison Rd. SW17 ... 5C **136**
Melliss Av. TW9: Kew ... 1H **115**
Mellitus St. W12 ... 5B **80**
Mellor Cl. KT12: Walt T ... 7D **148**
Mellow La. E. UB4: Hayes ... 3E **74**
Mellow La. W. UB10: Hil ... 3E **74**
Mellows Rd. IG5: Ilf ... 3D **52**
SM6: Wall ... 5H **167**
Mells Cres. SE9 ... 4D **142**
Mell St. SE10 ... 5G **105**
Melody La. N5 ... 5C **66**
Melody Rd. SW18 ... 5A **118**
Melon Pl. W8 ... 2J **99**
Melon Rd. E11 ... 3G **69**
SE15 ... 1G **121**
Melrose Av. CR4: Mitc ... 7F **137**
DA1: Cray ... 7K **127**
N22 ... 1B **48**
NW2 ... 5D **62**
SW16 ... 3K **155**
SW19 ... 2H **135**
TW2: Whit ... 7F **113**
UB6: G'frd ... 2F **77**
Melrose Cl. SE12 ... 1J **141**
UB4: Hayes ... 5J **75**
UB6: G'frd ... 2F **77**
Melrose Ct. *W13 ... 1A 96*
(off Williams Rd.)
Melrose Cres. BR6: Orp ... 4H **173**
Melrose Dr. UB1: S'hall ... 1E **94**
Melrose Gdns. HA8: Edg ... 3H **43**
KT3: N Mald ... 3K **151**
W6 ... 3E **98**
Melrose Ho. *E14 ... 3D 104*
(off Lanark Sq.)
NW6 ... 3J 81
(off Carlton Va.)
Melrose Rd. HA5: Pinn ... 4D **40**
SW13 ... 2B **116**
SW18 ... 6H **117**
SW19 ... 2J **153**
W3 ... 3J **97**
Melrose Ter. W6 ... 3E **98**
Melrose Tudor *SM6: Wall ... 5J 167*
(off Plough La.)
Melsa Rd. SM4: Mord ... 6A **154**
Melthorne Dr. HA4: Ruis ... 3A **58**
Melthorpe Gdns. SE3 ... 1C **124**
Melton Cl. HA4: Ruis ... 1A **58**
Melton Ct. SM2: Sutt ... 7A **166**
SW7 ... 4B **16** (4B **100**)
(not continuous)
Melton St. NW1 ... 2B **6** (3G **83**)
Melville Av. CR2: S Croy ... 5F **169**
SW20 ... 7C **134**
UB6: G'frd ... 5K **59**
Melville Cl. UB10: Ick ... 2F **57**
Melville Ct. SE8 ... 4A **104**
W12 ... 3D 98
(off Goldhawk Rd.)
Melville Gdns. N13 ... 5G **33**
Melville Ho. EN5: New Bar ... 5G **21**
SE10 ... 1E **122**
Melville Pl. N1 ... 7C **66**
Melville Rd. DA14: Sidc ... 2C **144**
E17 ... 3B **50**
NW10 ... 7K **61**
RM5: Col R ... 1H **55**
SW13 ... 1C **116**
Melville Vs. Rd. W3 ... 1J **97**
Melvin Rd. SE20 ... 1J **157**
Melwood Ho. *E1 ... 6H 85*
(off Watney Mkt.)
Melyn Cl. N7 ... 4G **65**
Memel Ct. EC1 ... 4C **8**
Memel St. EC1 ... 4C **8** (4C **84**)
Memess Path SE18 ... 6E **106**
Memorial Av. E12 ... 2C **70**
E15 ... 3G **87**
Memorial Cl. TW5: Hest ... 6D **94**
Mendham Ho. *SE1 ... 7G 15*
(off Cluny Pl.)
Mendip Cl. KT4: Wor Pk ... 1E **164**
SE26 ... 4J **139**
UB3: Harl ... 7F **93**
Mendip Ct. *SE14 ... 6J 103*
(off Avonley Rd.)
SW11 ... 3A **118**
Mendip Dr. NW2 ... 2G **63**
Mendip Ho. *N9 ... 2B 34*
(off New Rd.)
Mendip Ho's. *E2 ... 3J 85*
(off Welwyn St.)
Mendip Rd. DA7: Bex ... 1K **127**
IG2: Ilf ... 5J **53**
SW11 ... 3A **118**
Mendora Rd. SW6 ... 7G **99**
Menelik Rd. NW2 ... 4G **63**
Menlo Gdns. SE19 ... 7D **138**
Menlo Lodge *N13 ... 3E 32*
(off Crothall Cl.)
Menon Dr. N9 ... 3C **34**
Menotti St. E2 ... 4G **85**
Menteath Ho. *E14 ... 6C 86*
(off Dod St.)
Mentmore Cl. HA3: Kent ... 6C **42**
Mentmore Ter. E8 ... 7H **67**
Meon Rd. W3 ... 2J **97**
Meopham Rd. CR4: Mitc ... 1G **155**
Mepham Cres. HA3: Hrw W ... 7B **26**
Mepham Gdns. HA3: Hrw W ... 7B **26**
Mepham St. SE1 ... 5J **13** (1A **102**)
Mera Dr. DA7: Bex ... 4G **127**
Merantun Way SW19 ... 1K **153**
Merbury Cl. SE13 ... 5E **122**
SE28 ... 1H **107**
Merbury Rd. SE28 ... 1H **107**
Mercator Pl. E14 ... 5C **104**
Mercator Rd. SE13 ... 4F **123**
Mercer Cl. KT7: T Ditt ... 7K **149**
Mercer Ho. *SW1 ... 5J 17*
(off Ebury Bri. Rd.)
Merceron Ho's. *E2 ... 3J 85*
(off Globe Rd.)
Merceron St. E1 ... 4H **85**
Mercer Pl. HA5: Pinn ... 2A **40**
Mercers Cl. SE10 ... 4H **105**
Mercer's Cotts. *E1 ... 6A 86*
(off White Horse Rd.)
Mercers M. N19 ... 3H **65**
Mercers Pl. W6 ... 4F **99**
Mercers Rd. N19 ... 3H **65**
(not continuous)
Mercer St. WC2 ... 1E **12** (6J **83**)
Merchant Ct. *E1 ... 1J 103*
(off Wapping Wall)
Merchant Ind. Ter. NW10 ... 4J **79**
Merchants Cl. SE25 ... 4G **157**
Merchants Ho. *SE10 ... 5F 105*
(off Collington St.)
Merchants Lodge *E17 ... 4C 50*
(off Westbury Rd.)
Merchants Row *SE10 ... 5F 105*
(off Hoskins St.)
Merchant St. E3 ... 3B **86**
Merchiston Rd. SE6 ... 2F **141**
Merchland Rd. SE9 ... 1G **143**
Mercia Gro. SE13 ... 4E **122**
Mercia Ho. *SE5 ... 2C 120*
(off Denmark Rd.)
Mercier Rd. SW15 ... 5G **117**
Mercury *NW9 ... 1B 44*
(off Concourse, The)
Mercury Cen. TW14: Felt ... 5J **111**
Mercury Ct. *E14 ... 4C 104*
(off Homer Dr.)
Mercury Ho. *TW8: Bford ... 6C 96*
(off Glenhurst Rd.)
W5 ... 4F **79**
Mercury Rd. TW8: Bford ... 6C **96**
Mercury Way SE14 ... 6K **103**
Mercy Ter. SE13 ... 5D **122**
Merebank La.
CR0: Wadd ... 5K **167**
Mere Cl. BR6: Farnb ... 2E **172**
SW15 ... 7F **117**
Meredith Av. NW2 ... 5E **62**
Meredith Cl. HA5: Pinn ... 1B **40**
Meredith Ho. N16 ... 5E **66**
Meredith M. SE4 ... 4B **122**
Meredith St. E13 ... 3J **87**
EC1 ... 2A **8** (3B **84**)
Meredith Twr. *W3 ... 3H 97*
(off Hanbury Rd.)
Meredyth Rd. SW13 ... 2C **116**
Mere End CR0: Croy ... 7K **157**
Mere Rd. TW17: Shep ... 6D **146**
Mere Side BR6: Farnb ... 2E **172**
Mereside Pk. TW15: Ashf ... 4E **128**
Meretone Cl. SE4 ... 4A **122**
Mereton Mans. *SE8 ... 1C 122*
(off Brookmill Rd.)
Merevale Cres. SM4: Mord ... 6A **154**
Mereway Rd. TW2: Twick ... 1H **131**
Merewood Cl. BR1: Brom ... 2E **160**
Merewood Rd. DA7: Bex ... 2J **127**
Mereworth Cl. BR2: Brom ... 5H **159**
Mereworth Dr. SE18 ... 7F **107**
Mereworth Ho. SE15 ... 6J **103**
Merganser Ct. *SE8 ... 6B 104*
(off Edward St.)
Merganser Gdns. SE28 ... 3H **107**
Meriden Cl. BR1: Brom ... 7B **142**
IG6: Ilf ... 1G **53**
Meriden Ct. SW3 ... 6C **16**
Meridian Ga. E14 ... 2D **104**
Meridian Ho. *SE10 ... 4G 105*
(off Azof St.)
SE10 ... 7E 104
(off Royal Hill)
Meridian Pl. E14 ... 2D **104**
Meridian Point SE8 ... 6D **104**
Meridian Rd. SE7 ... 7B **106**
Meridian Sq. E15 ... 7F **69**
Meridian Trad. Est. SE7 ... 4K **105**
Meridian Wlk. N17 ... 6K **33**
Meridian Way EN3: Pond E ... 7E **24**
N9 ... 4D **34**
N18 ... 5D **34**
Merifield Rd. SE9 ... 4A **124**
Merino Cl. E11 ... 4A **52**
Merino Pl. DA15: Sidc ... 6A **126**
Merioneth Ct. *W7 ... 5K 77*
(off Copley Cl.)
Merivale Rd. HA1: Harr ... 7G **41**
SW15 ... 4G **117**
Merlewood Dr. BR7: Chst ... 1D **160**
Merley Ct. NW9 ... 1J **61**
Merlin *NW9 ... 1B 44*
(off Concourse, The)
Merlin Cl. CR0: Croy ... 4E **168**
CR4: Mitc ... 3C **154**
SM6: Wall ... 6K **167**
UB5: Yead ... 3A **76**
Merlin Ct. BR2: Brom ... 3H **159**
HA4: Ruis ... 2F **57**
Merlin Cres. HA8: Edg ... 1F **43**
Merlin Gdns. BR1: Brom ... 3J **141**
Merling Cl. KT9: Chess ... 5C **162**
Merlin Gro. BR3: Beck ... 4B **158**
Merlin Ho. EN3: Pond E ... 5E **24**
SW18 ... 4A **118**

Merlin Rd.—Midland Pl.

Merlin Rd. DA16: Well 4A 126
E12 2B 70
Merlin Rd. Nth. DA16: Well 4A 126
Merlins Av. HA2: Harr 3D 58
Merlins Ct. *WC1* *2J 7*
(off Margery St.)
Merlin St. WC1 2J 7 (3A 84)
Mermaid Ct. *E8* *7F 67*
(off Celandine Dr.)
SE1 6E 14 (2D 102)
SE16 1B 104
Mermaid Ho. *E14* *7E 86*
(off Bazely St.)
Mermaid Twr. *SE8* *6B 104*
(off Abinger Gro.)
Meroe Ct. N16 2E 66
Merredene St. SW2 6K 119
Merriam Av. E9 6B 68
Merriam Cl. E4 5K 35
Merrick Rd. UB2: S'hall 2D 94
Merrick Sq. SE1 7E 14 (3D 102)
Merridene N21 6G 23
Merrielands Cres. RM9: Dag 2F 91
Merrielands Retail Pk. RM9: Dag 1F 91
Merrilands Rd. KT4: Wor Pk 1E 164
Merrilees Rd. DA15: Sidc 7J 125
Merrilyn Cl. KT10: Clay 6A 162
Merriman Rd. SE3 1A 124
Merrington Rd. SW6 6J 99
Merrion Av. HA7: Stan 5J 27
Merritt Gdns. KT9: Chess 6C 162
(not continuous)
Merritt Rd. SE4 5B 122
Merritt's Bldgs. EC2 4G 9
Merrivale N14 6C 22
NW1 *1G 83*
(off Camden St.)
Merrivale Av. IG4: Ilf 4B 52
Merrow Ct. CR4: Mitc 2B 154
Merrow Rd. SM2: Cheam 7F 165
Merrow St. SE17 5D 102
Merrow Wlk. SE17 5D 102
Merrow Way CR0: New Ad 6E 170
Merrydown Way BR7: Chst 1C 160
Merryfield SE3 2H 123
Merryfield Gdns. HA7: Stan 5H 27
Merryfield Ho. *SE9* *3A 142*
(off Grove Pk. Rd.)
Merryfields UB8: Uxb 2A 74
UB10: Uxb 2A 74
Merryfields Way SE6 7D 122
MERRY HILL 1A 26
Merryhill Cl. E4 7J 25
Merry Hill Mt. WD23: Bush 1A 26
Merry Hill Rd. WD23: Bush 1A 26
Merryhills Ct. N14 5B 22
Merryhills Dr. EN2: Enf 4C 22
Merryweather Ct. KT3: N Mald 5A 152
N19 3G 65
Mersea Ho. IG11: Bark 6F 71
Mersey Ct. KT2: King T 1D 150
Mersey Rd. E17 3B 50
Mersey Wlk. UB5: N'olt 2E 76
Mersham Dr. NW9 5G 43
Mersham Pl. *CR7: Thor H* *2D 156*
(off Livingstone Rd.)
SE20 1H 157
Mersham Rd. CR7: Thor H 3D 156
Merten Rd. RM6: Chad H 7E 54
Merthyr Ter. SW13 6D 98
MERTON 7A 136
Merton Av. UB5: N'olt 5G 59
UB10: Hil 7D 56
W4 4B 98
Merton Ct. DA16: Well 2B 126
IG1: Ilf 6C 52
Merton Gdns. BR5: Pet W 5F 161
Merton Hall Gdns. SW20 1G 153
Merton Hall Rd. SW19 7G 135
Merton High St. SW19 7K 135
Merton Ind. Pk. SW19 1K 153
Merton La. N6 2D 64
Merton Lodge EN5: New Bar 5F 21
Merton Mans. SW20 2F 153
MERTON PARK 2J 153
Merton Pk. Pde. SW19 1H 153
Merton Pl. *SW19* *1A 154*
(off Nelson Gro. Rd.)
Merton Ri. NW3 7C 64
Merton Rd. E17 5E 50
EN2: Enf 1J 23
HA2: Harr 1G 59
IG3: Ilf 7K 53
IG11: Bark 7K 71
SE25 5F 157
SW18 6J 117
SW19 7K 135
Merton Way KT8: W Mole 4F 149
UB10: Hil 7D 56
Mertoun Ter. *W1* *7E 4*
(off Seymour Pl.)
Merttins Rd. SE4 5K 121
SE15 5K 121
Meru Cl. NW5 4E 64
Mervan Rd. SW2 4A 120
Mervyn Av. SE9 3G 143
Mervyn Rd. TW17: Shep 7E 146
W13 3A 96
Messaline Av. W3 6J 79
Messent Rd. SE9 5A 124
Messeter Pl. SE9 6E 124
Messina Av. NW6 7J 63
Messiter Ho. *N1* *1K 83*
(off Barnsbury Est.)
Metcalf Rd. TW15: Ashf 5D 128
Metcalf Wlk. TW13: Hanw 4C 130
Meteor St. SW11 4E 118
Meteor Way SM6: Wall 7J 167
Methley St. SE11 6K 19 (5A 102)
Methuen Cl. HA8: Edg 7B 28
Methuen Pk. N10 3F 47
Methuen Rd. DA6: Bex 4F 127
DA17: Belv 4H 109
HA8: Edg 7B 28
Methwold Rd. W10 5F 81
Metro Bus. Cen., The SE26 6B 140
Metro Central Hgts. *SE1* *3C 102*
(off Newington C'way.)
Metro Ind. Cen. TW7: Isle 2J 113
Metropolis *SE11* *3B 102*
(off Oswin St.)
Metropolitan Bus. Cen. *N1* *7E 66*
(off Enfield Rd.)
Metropolitan Cl. E14 5C 86
Metropolitan Police Norwood Cadet
Training Cen. 1E 156
Metropolitan Sta. Bldgs. *W6* *4E 98*
(off Beadon Rd.)
Metropolitan Wharf E1 1J 103
Metro Trad. Est. HA9: Wemb 4H 61
Mews, The DA14: Sidc 4A 144
IG4: Ilf 5B 52
N1 1C 84
N8 3A 48
RM1: Rom 4K 55
SE22 5G 121
TW1: Twick 6B 114
Mews Pl. IG8: Wfd G 4D 36
Mews St. E1 4K 15 (1G 103)
Mexborough NW1 1G 83
Mexfield Rd. SW15 5H 117
Meyer Grn. EN1: Enf 1B 24
Meyer Rd. DA8: Erith 6K 109
Meymott St. SE1 5A 14 (1B 102)
Meynell Cres. E9 7K 67
Meynell Gdns. E9 7K 67
Meynell Rd. E9 7K 67
Meyrick Ho. *E14* *5C 86*
(off Burgess St.)
Meyrick Rd. NW10 6C 62
SW11 3B 118
Miah Ter. E1 1G 103
Miall Wlk. SE26 4A 140
Micawber Av. UB8: Hil 4C 74
Micawber Ct. *N1* *1D 8*
(off Windsor Ter.)
Micawber Ho. *SE16* *2G 103*
(off Llewellyn St.)
Micawber St. N1 1D 8 (3C 84)
Michael Cliffe Ho. EC1 2A 8
Michael Faraday Ho. *SE17* *5E 102*
(off Beaconsfield Rd.)
Michael Gaynor Cl. W7 1K 95
Michael Manley Ind. Est.
SW8 *2G 119*
(off Clyston St.)
Michaelmas Cl. SW20 3E 152
Michael Rd. E11 1H 69
SE25 3E 156
SW6 1K 117
Michaels Cl. SE13 4G 123
Michael Sobell Leisure Cen. 3K 65
Michael Stewart Ho. *SW6* *6H 99*
(off Clem Attlee Ct.)
Michelangelo Ct. *SE16* *5H 103*
(off Stubbs Dr.)
Micheldever Rd. SE12 6G 123
Michelham Gdns. TW1: Twick 3K 131
Michelle Ct. *BR1: Brom* *1H 159*
(off Blyth Rd.)
N12 5F 31
W3 7K 79
Michelsdale Dr. TW9: Rich 4E 114
Michelson Ho. SE11 4H 19
Michel's Row *TW9: Rich* *4E 114*
(off Michelsdale Dr.)
Michigan Av. E12 4D 70
Michigan Ho. E14 3C 104
Michleham Down N12 4C 30
Mickledore *NW1* *1B 6*
(off Ampthill Est.)
Mickleham Cl. BR5: St P 2K 161
Mickleham Gdns. SM3: Cheam 6G 165
Mickleham Rd. BR5: St P 1K 161
Mickleham Way CR0: New Ad 7F 171
Micklethwaite Rd. SW6 6J 99
Midas Bus. Cen. RM10: Dag 4H 73
Midas Metropolitan Ind. Est.
SM4: Mord 7E 152
MID BECKTON 6D 88
Midcroft HA4: Ruis 1G 57
Middle Dartrey Wlk. *SW10* *7A 100*
(off Dartrey Wlk.)
Middle Dene NW7 3E 28
Middlefield NW8 1B 82
Middlefielde W13 5B 78
Middlefield Gdns. IG2: Ilf 6F 53
Middle Grn. Cl. KT5: Surb 6F 151
Middleham Gdns. N18 6B 34
Middleham Rd. N18 6B 34
Middle La. N8 5J 47
TW11: Tedd 6K 131
Middle La. M. N8 5J 47
Middle Mill Hall KT1: King T 3F 151
Middle Pk. Av. SE9 6B 124
Middle Path HA2: Harr 1H 59
Middle Rd. E13 2J 87
EN4: E Barn 6H 21
HA2: Harr 2H 59
SW16 2H 155
Middle Row W10 4G 81
Middlesborough Rd. N18 6B 34
Middlesex Bus. Cen. UB2: S'hall 2E 94
Middlesex Cl. UB1: G'frd 4F 77
Middlesex County Cricket Club
Lord's Cricket Ground
1B 4 (3B 82)
Middlesex Ct. HA1: Harr 5K 41
W4 4B 98
Middlesex Filter Beds Nature Reserve
3K 67
Middlesex Ho. HA0: Wemb 1D 78
Middlesex Pas. EC1 6B 8
Middlesex Pl. *E9* *6J 67*
(off Elsdale St.)
Middlesex Rd.
CR4: Mitc 5J 155
Middlesex St. E1 6H 9 (5E 84)
Middlesex University
Archway Campus, The 1G 65
Cat Hill Campus 5K 21
Enfield Campus *5D 24*
(off Peerglow Est.)
Hendon Campus 4D 44
Quicksilver Place Campus 2J 47
Tottenham Campus 6K 33
Trent Pk. Campus 2B 22
Middlesex University Sports Dome *7A 34*
(off White Hart La.)
Middlesex University Swimming Pool
2K 47
Middlesex Wharf E5 2J 67
Middle St. CR0: Croy 2C 168
(not continuous)
EC1 5C 8 (5C 84)
Middle Temple 2J 13
Middle Temple Hall *2J 13*
(off Middle Temple La.)
Middle Temple La.
EC4 1J 13 (6A 84)
Middleton Av. DA14: Sidc 6B 144
E4 4G 35
UB6: G'frd 2H 77
Middleton Cl. E4 3G 35
Middleton Dr. HA5: Eastc 3J 39
SE16 2K 103
Middleton Gdns. IG2: Ilf 6F 53
Middleton Gro. N7 5J 65
Middleton Ho. E8 7G 67
SE1 *3D 102*
(off Burbage Cl.)
SW1 *4D 18*
(off Causton St.)
Middleton M. N7 5J 65
Middleton Pl. W1 6A 6
Middleton Rd. E8 7F 67
KT3: N Mald 3J 151
NW11 7J 45
SM4: Mord 6K 153
SM5: Cars 7B 154
UB3: Hayes 5F 75
Middleton St. E2 3H 85
Middleton Way SE13 4F 123
Middle Way DA18: Erith 3E 108
SW16 2H 155
UB4: Yead 4A 76
Middle Way, The HA3: W'stone 2K 41
Middleway NW11 5K 45
Middle Yd. SE1 4G 15 (1E 102)
Midfield Av. DA7: Bex 3J 127
Midfield Pde. DA7: Bex 3J 127
Midfield Way BR5: St P 7B 144
Midford Ho. *NW4* *4E 44*
(off Stratford Rd.)
Midford Pl. W1 4B 6 (4G 83)
Midholm HA9: Wemb 1G 61
Midholm Cl. NW11 4K 45
Midholm Rd. CR0: Croy 2A 170
Midhope Ho. *WC1* *2F 7*
(off Midhope St.)
Midhope St. WC1 2F 7 (3J 83)
Midhurst SE26 6J 139
Midhurst Av. CR0: Croy 7A 156
N10 3E 46
Midhurst Gdns. UB10: Hil 1E 74
Midhurst Hill DA6: Bex 6G 127
Midhurst Ho. *E14* *6B 86*
(off Salmon La.)
Midhurst Pde. *N10* *3E 46*
(off Fortis Grn.)
Midhurst Rd. W13 2A 96
Midhurst Way E5 4G 67
Midland Pde. NW6 6K 63
Midland Pl. E14 5E 104

Milton Ct. Wlk.—Monica Ct.

Milton Ct. Wlk. *EC2* *5E 8*
(off Silk St.)
Milton Cres. IG2: Ilf 7F **53**
Milton Dr. TW17: Shep 4A **146**
Milton Gdn. Est. N16 . . . . . 4D **66**
Milton Gdns.
TW19: Stanw 1B **128**
Milton Gro. N11 . . . . . 5B **32**
N16 . . . . . 4D **66**
Milton Ho. *E2* *3J 85*
(off Roman Rd.)
E17 . . . . . 4C **50**
SE5 . . . . . *7D 102*
(off Elmington Est.)
SM1: Sutt 3J **165**
Milton Lodge DA14: Sidc 4A **144**
TW2: Twick 7K **113**
Milton Mans. *W14* *6G 99*
(off Queen's Club Gdns.)
Milton Pk. N6 . . . . . 7G **47**
Milton Pl. *N7* *5A 66*
(off Eastwood Cl.)
Milton Rd. CR0: Croy 1D **168**
CR4: Mitc 7E **136**
DA16: Well 1K **125**
DA17: Belv 4G **109**
E17 . . . . . 4C **50**
HA1: Harr 4J **41**
N6 . . . . . 7G **47**
N15 . . . . . 4B **48**
NW7 . . . . . 5H **29**
NW9 . . . . . 7C **44**
SE24 . . . . . 5B **120**
SM1: Sutt 3J **165**
SM6: Wall 6G **167**
SW14 . . . . . 3K **115**
SW19 . . . . . 6A **136**
TW12: Hamp 7E **130**
UB10: Ick 4D **56**
W3 . . . . . 1K **97**
W7 . . . . . 7K **77**
Milton St. EC2 . . . . . 5E **8** (5D **84**)
Milton Way UB7: W Dray 4B **92**
Milverton Dr. UB10: Ick 4E **56**
Milverton Gdns. IG3: Ilf 2K **71**
Milverton Ho. SE6 . . . . . 3A **140**
Milverton Rd. NW6 . . . . . 7E **62**
Milverton St. SE11 . . . . . 6K **19** (5A **102**)
Milverton Way SE9 . . . . . 4E **142**
Milward St. E1 . . . . . 5H **85**
Milward Wlk. SE18 . . . . . 6E **106**
Mimosa Ho. UB4: Yead 5A **76**
Mimosa Lodge NW10 . . . . . 5B **62**
Mimosa Rd. UB4: Yead 5A **76**
Mimosa St. SW6 . . . . . 1H **117**
Minard Rd. SE6 . . . . . 7G **123**
Mina Rd. SE17 . . . . . 5E **102**
SW19 . . . . . 1J **153**
Minchenden Ct. N14 . . . . . 2C **32**
Minchenden Cres. N14 . . . . . 3B **32**
Minchin Ho. *E14* *6C 86*
(off Dod St.)
Mincing La. EC3 . . . . . 2G **15** (7E **84**)
Minden Rd. SE20 . . . . . 1H **157**
SM3: Sutt 2H **165**
Minehead Rd. HA2: Harr 3E **58**
SW16 . . . . . 5K **137**
Mineral Cl. EN5: Barn 6A **20**
Mineral St. SE18 . . . . . 4J **107**
Minera M. SW1 . . . . . 3G **17** (4E **100**)
Minerva Cl. DA14: Sidc 3J **143**
SW9 . . . . . 7A **102**
(not continuous)
Minerva Rd. E4 . . . . . 7J **35**
KT1: King T 2F **151**
NW10 . . . . . 4J **79**
Minerva St. E2 . . . . . 2H **85**
Minerva Wlk. EC1 . . . . . 7B **8** (6B **84**)
Minet Av. NW10 . . . . . 2A **80**
Minet Country Pk. 2K **93**
Minet Dr. UB3: Hayes 1J **93**
Minet Gdns. NW10 . . . . . 2A **80**
UB3: Hayes 1K **93**
Minet Rd. SW9 . . . . . 2B **120**
Minford Gdns. W14 . . . . . 2F **99**
Minford Ho. *W14* *2F 99*
(off Minford Gdns.)
Mingard Wlk. N7 . . . . . 2K **65**
Ming St. E14 . . . . . 7C **86**
Minimax Cl. TW14: Felt 6J **111**
Ministry Way SE9 . . . . . 2D **142**
Miniver Pl. EC4 . . . . . 2D **14**
Mink Ct. TW4: Houn 2A **112**
Minniedale KT5: Surb 5F **151**
Minnow St. SE17 . . . . . 4E **102**
Minnow Wlk.
SE17 . . . . . 4E **102**
Minories EC3 . . . . . 1J **15** (6F **85**)
Minshaw Ct.
DA14: Sidc 4K **143**
Minshill St. SW8 . . . . . 1H **119**
Minshull Pl. BR3: Beck 7C **140**
Minson Rd. E9 . . . . . 1K **85**
Minstead Gdns. SW15 . . . . . 7B **116**
Minstead Way
KT3: N Mald 6A **152**
Minster Av. SM1: Sutt 2J **165**
Minster Ct. EC3 . . . . . 2H **15**
W5 . . . . . 4E **78**
Minster Dr. CR0: Croy 4E **168**
Minster Gdns. KT8: W Mole 4D **148**
Minsterley Av. TW17: Shep 4G **147**
Minster Pavement *EC3* *2H 15*
(off Mincing La.)
Minster Rd. BR1: Brom 7K **141**
NW2 . . . . . 5G **63**
Minster Wlk. N8 . . . . . 4J **47**
Minstrel Gdns. KT5: Surb 4F **151**
Mint Bus. Pk. E16 . . . . . 5K **87**
Mint Cl. UB10: Hil 3D **74**
Mintern Cl. N13 . . . . . 3G **33**
Minterne Av. UB2: S'hall 4E **94**
Minterne Rd. HA3: Kent 5F **43**
Minterne Waye UB4: Yead 6A **76**
Mintern St. N1 . . . . . 2D **84**
Minton Ho. SE11 . . . . . 3J **19**
Minton M. NW6 . . . . . 6K **63**
Mint Rd. SM6: Wall 4F **167**
Mint St. SE1 . . . . . 6C **14** (2C **102**)
Mint Wlk. CR0: Croy 3C **168**
Mirabel Rd. SW6 . . . . . 7H **99**
Miranda Cl. E1 . . . . . 5J **85**
Miranda Ct. W3 . . . . . 6F **79**
Miranda Rd. N19 . . . . . 1G **65**
Mirfield St. SE7 . . . . . 4B **106**
Miriam Rd. SE18 . . . . . 5J **107**
Mirravale Trad. Est. RM8: Dag 7E **54**
Mirren Cl. HA2: Harr 4D **58**
Mirror Path SE9 . . . . . 3A **142**
Misbourne Rd. UB10: Hil 1C **74**
Missenden *SE17* *5D 102*
(off Roland Way)
Missenden Cl. TW14: Felt 1H **129**
Missenden Gdns. SM4: Mord 6A **154**
Missenden Ho. NW8 . . . . . 3C **4**
Mission, The *E14* *6B 86*
(off Commercial Rd.)
Mission Gro. E17 . . . . . 5A **50**
Mission Pl. SE15 . . . . . 1G **121**
Mission Sq. TW8: Bford 6E **96**
Missouri Ct. HA5: Eastc 6A **40**
Mistletoe Cl. CR0: Croy 1K **169**
Mistral SE5 . . . . . 1E **120**
Misty's Fld. KT12: Walt T 7A **148**
Mitali Pas. E1 . . . . . 6G **85**
(not continuous)
MITCHAM 3D **154**
Mitcham Gdn. Village CR4: Mitc 5E **154**
Mitcham Ho. SE5 . . . . . 1C **120**
Mitcham Ind. Est. CR4: Mitc 1E **154**
Mitcham La. SW16 . . . . . 6G **137**
Mitcham Pk. CR4: Mitc 4C **154**
Mitcham Rd. CR0: Croy 6J **155**
E6 . . . . . 3C **88**
IG3: Ilf 7K **53**
SW17 . . . . . 5D **136**
Mitchell *NW9* *1B 44*
(off Concourse, The)
Mitchellbrook Way NW10 . . . . . 6K **61**
Mitchell Cl. DA17: Belv 3J **109**
SE2 . . . . . 4C **108**
Mitchell Ho. *W12* *7D 80*
(off White City Est.)
Mitchell Rd. BR6: Orp 4K **173**
N13 . . . . . 5H **33**
Mitchell's Pl. *SE21* *6E 120*
(off Aysgarth Rd.)
Mitchell St. EC1 . . . . . 3C **8** (4C **84**)
(not continuous)
Mitchell Wlk. *E6* *5C 88*
(off Neats Ct. Rd.)
E6 . . . . . 5D **88**
(Elmley Cl.)
Mitchell Way BR1: Brom 1J **159**
NW10 . . . . . 6J **61**
Mitchison Rd. N1 . . . . . 6D **66**
Mitchley Rd. N17 . . . . . 3G **49**
Mitford Cl. KT9: Chess 6C **162**
Mitford Rd. N19 . . . . . 2J **65**
Mitre, The E14 . . . . . 7B **86**
Mitre Av. E17 . . . . . 3C **50**
Mitre Bri. Ind. Pk. NW10 . . . . . 4D **80**
Mitre Cl. BR2: Brom 2H **159**
SM2: Sutt 7A **166**
TW17: Shep 6F **147**
Mitre Ct. EC2 . . . . . 7D **8**
Mitre Rd. E15 . . . . . 2G **87**
SE1 . . . . . 6K **13** (2A **102**)
Mitre Sq. EC3 . . . . . 1H **15** (6E **84**)
Mitre St. EC3 . . . . . 1H **15** (6E **84**)
Mitre Way NW10 . . . . . 4D **80**
W10 . . . . . 4D **80**
Mitre Yd. SW3 . . . . . 3D **16** (4C **100**)
Moat, The KT3: N Mald 1A **152**
Moat Cl. BR6: Chels 6K **173**
Moat Ct. DA15: Sidc 3K **143**
SE9 . . . . . 6D **124**
Moat Cres. N3 . . . . . 3K **45**
Moat Cft. DA16: Well 3C **126**
Moat Dr. E13 . . . . . 2A **88**
HA1: Harr 4G **41**
HA4: Ruis 7G **39**
Moat Farm Rd. UB5: N'olt 6D **58**
Moatfield NW6 . . . . . 7G **63**
Moatlands Ho. *WC1* *2F 7*
(off Cromer St.)
Moat La. KT8: E Mos 3K **149**
Moat Pl. SW9 . . . . . 3K **119**
W3 . . . . . 6H **79**
Moat Side EN3: Pond E 4E **24**
TW13: Hanw 4A **130**
Moberley Rd. SW4 . . . . . 7H **119**
Mobil Ct. *WC2* *1H 13*
(off Clement's Inn)
MOBY DICK 4E **54**
Mocatta Ho. *E1* *4H 85*
(off Brady St.)
Modbury Gdns. NW5 . . . . . 6E **64**
Modder Pl. SW15 . . . . . 4F **117**
Model Bldgs. WC1 . . . . . 2H **7**
Model Cotts. SW14 . . . . . 4J **115**
W13 . . . . . 2B **96**
Model Farm Cl. SE9 . . . . . 3C **142**
Modern Ct. EC4 . . . . . 7A **8**
Modling Ho. *E2* *2K 85*
(off Mace St.)
Moelwyn N7 . . . . . 5H **65**
Moelyn M. HA1: Harr 5A **42**
Moffat Ct. SW19 . . . . . 5J **135**
Moffat Ho. SE5 . . . . . 7C **102**
Moffat Rd. CR7: Thor H 2C **156**
N13 . . . . . 6D **32**
SW17 . . . . . 4D **136**
Mogden La. TW7: Isle 5K **113**
Mohammedi Pk. UB5: N'olt 1E **76**
Mohawk Ho. *E3* *2A 86*
(off Gernon Rd.)
Mohmmad Khan Rd. E11 . . . . . 1H **69**
Moineau *NW9* *1B 44*
(off Concourse, The)
Moira Cl. N17 . . . . . 2E **48**
Moira Rd. SE9 . . . . . 4D **124**
Mokswell Ct. N10 . . . . . 1E **46**
Moland Mead *SE16* *5K 103*
(off Crane Mead)
Molasses Ho. *SW11* *3A 118*
(off Clove Hitch Quay)
Molasses Row SW11 . . . . . 3A **118**
Mole Abbey Gdns. KT8: W Mole 3F **149**
Mole Ct. KT19: Ewe 4J **163**
Molember Ct. KT8: E Mos 4J **149**
Molember Rd. KT8: E Mos 5J **149**
Molescroft SE9 . . . . . 3G **143**
Molesey Av. KT8: W Mole 5D **148**
Molesey Dr. SM3: Cheam 2G **165**
Molesey Pk. Av. KT8: W Mole 5F **149**
Molesey Pk. Cl. KT8: E Mos 5G **149**
Molesey Pk. Rd. KT8: E Mos 5F **149**
KT8: W Mole 5F **149**
Molesey Rd. KT8: W Mole 7C **148**
KT12: Hers, W Mole, Walt T . . . 7C **148**
Molesford Rd. SW6 . . . . . 1J **117**
Molesham Cl. KT8: W Mole 3F **149**
Molesham Way KT8: W Mole 3F **149**
Molesworth Ho. *SE17* *6B 102*
(off Brandon Est.)
Molesworth St. SE13 . . . . . 4E **122**
Moliner Ct. BR3: Beck 7C **140**
Mollis Ho. *E3* *5C 86*
(off Gale St.)
Mollison Av. EN3: Brim, Pond E 4F **25**
EN3: Enf L, Walt C 4F **25**
Mollison Dr. SM6: Wall 7H **167**
Mollison Sq. *SM6: Wall* *7H 167*
(off Mollison Dr.)
Mollison Way HA8: Edg 2F **43**
Molly Huggins Cl. SW12 . . . . . 7G **119**
Molton Ho. *N1* *1K 83*
(off Barnsbury Est.)
Molyneux Dr. SW17 . . . . . 4F **137**
Molyneux St. W1 . . . . . 6D **4** (5C **82**)
Monarch Cl. BR4: W W'ck 4H **171**
TW14: Felt 7G **111**
Monarch Ct. N2 . . . . . 5B **46**
Monarch Dr. E16 . . . . . 5B **88**
Monarch M. E17 . . . . . 6D **50**
SW16 . . . . . 5A **138**
Monarch Pde. CR4: Mitc 2D **154**
Monarch Pl. IG9: Buck H 2F **37**
Monarch Rd. DA17: Belv 3G **109**
Monarchs Way HA4: Ruis 1F **57**
Monarch Way IG2: Ilf 6H **53**
Mona Rd. SE15 . . . . . 2J **121**
Monastery Gdns. EN2: Enf 2J **23**
Mona St. E16 . . . . . 5H **87**
Monaveen Gdns. KT8: W Mole 3F **149**
Moncks Row SW18 . . . . . 6H **117**
Monck St. SW1 . . . . . 2D **18** (3H **101**)
Monclar Rd. SE5 . . . . . 4D **120**
Moncorvo Cl. SW7 . . . . . 7C **10** (2C **100**)
Moncrieff Cl. E6 . . . . . 6C **88**
Moncrieff Pl. SE15 . . . . . 2G **121**
Moncrieff St. SE15 . . . . . 2G **121**
Mondial Way UB3: Harl 7E **92**
Monega Rd. E7 . . . . . 6A **70**
E12 . . . . . 6A **70**
Monet Ct. *SE16* *5H 103*
(off Stubbs Dr.)
Moneyer Ho. *N1* *1E 8*
(off Fairbank Est.)
Money La. UB7: W Dray 3A **92**
Mongers Almshouses *E9* *7K 67*
(off Church Cres.)
Monica Ct. EN1: Enf 5K **23**

Monica James Ho. DA14: Sidc	.3A 144
Monica Shaw Ct. NW1	.1D 6
(off Purchese St., not continuous)	
Monier Rd. E3	.7C 68
Monivea Rd. BR3: Beck	.7B 140
Monk Ct. W12	.1C 98
Monk Dr. E16	.7J 87
MONKEN HADLEY	.2C 20
Monkfrith Av. N14	.6A 22
Monkfrith Cl. N14	.7A 22
Monkfrith Way N14	.7K 21
Monkham's Av. IG8: Wfd G	.5E 36
Monkham's Dr. IG8: Wfd G	.5E 36
Monkham's La. IG8: Wfd G	.5D 36
IG9: Buck H	.3E 36
Monkleigh Rd. SM4: Mord	.3G 153
Monk Pas. E16	.7J 87
(off Monk Dr.)	
Monks Av. EN5: New Bar	.6F 21
KT8: W Mole	.5D 148
Monks Cl. EN2: Enf	.2H 23
HA2: Harr	.2E 58
HA4: Ruis	.4B 58
SE2	.4D 108
Monks Cres. KT12: Walt T	.7K 147
Monksdene Gdns. SM1: Sutt	.3K 165
Monks Dr. W3	.5G 79
Monks Hill Sports Cen.	.7K 169
MONKS ORCHARD	.7A 158
Monks Orchard Rd. BR3: Beck	.1C 170
Monks Pk. HA9: Wemb	.6H 61
Monks Pk. Gdns. HA9: Wemb	.7H 61
Monks Rd. EN2: Enf	.2G 23
Monk St. SE18	.4E 106
Monks Way BR3: Beck	.6C 158
BR5: Farnb	.1G 173
NW11	.4H 45
UB7: Harm	.6A 92
Monkswood Gdns. IG5: Ilf	.3E 52
Monkton Ho. E5	.5H 67
SE16	.2K 103
(off Wolfe Cres.)	
Monkton Rd. DA16: Well	.2K 125
Monkton St. SE11	.3K 19 (4A 102)
Monkville Av. NW11	.4H 45
Monkville Ter. NW11	.4H 45
Monkwell Sq. EC2	.6D 8 (5C 84)
Monmouth Av. E18	.3K 51
KT1: Hamp W	.7C 132
Monmouth Cl. CR4: Mitc	.4J 155
DA16: Well	.4A 126
W4	.3J 97
Monmouth Ct. W7	.5K 77
(off Copley Cl.)	
Monmouth Gro. TW8	.4E 96
Monmouth Ho. W2	.6K 81
(off Monmouth Rd.)	
Monmouth Rd. E6	.3D 88
N9	.2C 34
RM9: Dag	.5F 73
UB3: Harl	.4G 93
W2	.6J 81
Monmouth St. WC2	.1E 12 (6J 83)
Monnery Rd. N19	.3G 65
Monnow Rd. SE1	.5G 103
Mono La. TW13: Felt	.2K 129
Monoux Almshouses E17	.4D 50
Monoux Gro. E17	.1C 50
Monroe Cres. EN1: Enf	.1C 24
Monroe Dr. SW14	.5H 115
Monro Gdns. HA3: Hrw W	.7D 26
Monro Way E5	.4G 67
Monsell Ct. N4	.3B 66
Monsell Rd. N4	.3A 66
Monson Rd. NW10	.2C 80
SE14	.7K 103
Mons Way BR2: Brom	.6C 160
Montacute Rd. CR0: New Ad	.7E 170
SE6	.7B 122
SM4: Mord	.6B 154
WD23: Bushy	.1E 26

Montagu Cres. N18	.4C 34
Montague Av. SE4	.4B 122
W7	.1K 95
Montague Cl. KT12: Walt T	.7K 147
SE1	.4E 14 (1D 102)
Montague Ct. DA15: Sidc	.3A 144
Montague Gdns. W3	.7G 79
Montague Ho. E16	.1K 105
(off Wesley Av.)	
Montague Pas. UB8: Uxb	.7A 56
Montague Pl. WC1	.5D 6 (5H 83)
Montague Rd. CR0: Croy	.1B 168
E8	.5G 67
E11	.2H 69
N8	.5K 47
N15	.4G 49
SW19	.7K 135
TW3: Houn	.3F 113
TW10: Rich	.6E 114
UB2: S'hall	.4C 94
UB8: Uxb	.7A 56
W7	.1K 95
W13	.6B 78
Montague Sq. SE15	.7J 103
Montague St. EC1	.6C 8 (5C 84)
WC1	.5E 6 (5J 83)
Montague Ter. BR2: Brom	.4H 159
Montague Walks HA0: Wemb	.2F 79
Montague Waye UB2: S'hall	.3C 94
Montaigne Cl. SW1	.4D 18 (4H 101)
Montalt Rd. IG8: Wfd G	.5C 36
Montana Gdns. SE26	.5B 140
SM1: Sutt	.5A 166
Montana Rd. SW17	.3E 136
SW20	.1E 152
Montbelle Rd. SE9	.3F 143
Montcalm Cl. BR2: Hayes	.6J 159
UB4: Yead	.3K 75
Montcalm Ho. E14	.4B 104
Montcalm Rd. SE7	.7B 106
Montclare St. E2	.3J 9 (4F 85)
Monteagle Av. IG11: Bark	.6G 71
Monteagle Cl. N1	.2E 84
Monteagle Way E5	.3G 67
SE15	.3H 121
Montefiore St. N16	.1F 67
Montefiore St. SW8	.2F 119
Montego Cl. SE24	.4A 120
Montem Rd. KT3: N Mald	.4A 152
SE23	.7B 122
Montem St. N4	.1K 65
Montenotte Rd. N8	.5G 47
Monterey Cl. DA5: Bexl	.2J 145
Monterey Pl. Shop. Cen. NW7	.5F 29
Montesole Cl. HA5: Pinn	.2A 40
Montesquieu Ter. E16	.6H 87
(off Clarkson Rd.)	
Montevetro SW11	.1B 118
Montford Pl. SE11	.6J 19 (5A 102)
Montford Rd. TW16: Sun	.4J 147
Montfort Pl. SW19	.1F 135
Montgolfier Wlk. UB5: N'olt	.3C 76

Montgomery Cl. CR4: Mitc	.4J 155
DA15: Sidc	.6K 125
SM2: Sutt	.7B 166
Montgomery Ct. CR2: S Croy	.5E 168
(off Birdhurst Rd.)	
W4	.7J 97
Montgomery Lodge E1	.4J 85
(off Cleveland Gro.)	
Montgomery Rd. HA8: Edg	.6A 28
W4	.4J 97
Montgomery St. E14	.1D 104
Montholme Rd. SW11	.6D 118
Monthope Rd. E1	.6K 9 (5G 85)
Montolieu Gdns. SW15	.5D 116
Montpelier Av. DA5: Bexl	.7D 126
W5	.5C 78
Montpelier Cl. UB10: Hil	.1C 74
Montpelier Ct. BR2: Brom	.4H 159
(off Westmoreland St.)	
W5	.5D 78
Montpelier Gdns. E6	.3B 88
RM6: Chad H	.7C 54
Montpelier Gro. NW5	.5G 65
Montpelier M. SW7	.1D 16 (3C 100)
Montpelier Pl. E1	.6J 85
SW7	.1D 16 (3D 100)
Montpelier Ri. HA9: Wemb	.1D 60
NW11	.7G 45
Montpelier Rd. N3	.1A 46
SE15	.1H 121
SM1: Sutt	.4A 166
W5	.5D 78
Montpelier Row SE3	.2H 123
TW1: Twick	.7C 114
Montpelier Sq. SW7	.7D 10 (2C 100)
Montpelier St. SW7	.1D 16 (3C 100)
Montpelier Ter. SW7	.7D 10 (2C 100)
Montpelier Va. SE3	.2H 123
Montpelier Wlk. SW7	.1D 16 (3C 100)
Montpelier Way NW11	.7G 45
Montrave Rd. SE20	.6J 139
Montreal Pl. WC2	.2G 13 (7K 83)
Montreal Rd. IG1: Ilf	.7G 53
Montrell Rd. SW2	.1J 137
Montrose Av. DA15: Sidc	.7A 126
DA16: Well	.3H 125
HA8: Edg	.2J 43
NW6	.2G 81
TW2: Whitt	.7F 113
Montrose Cl. DA16: Well	.3K 125
IG8: Wfd G	.4D 36
TW15: Ashf	.6E 128
Montrose Ct. HA1: Harr	.5F 41
NW9	.2J 43
NW11	.4H 45
SE6	.2H 141
SW7	.7D 10 (2B 100)
Montrose Cres. HA0: Wemb	.6E 60
N12	.6F 31
Montrose Gdns. CR4: Mitc	.2D 154
SM1: Sutt	.2K 165
Montrose Ho. E14	.3C 104
Montrose Pl. SW1	.7H 11 (2E 100)
TW14: Bedf	.6F 111
Montrose Wlk. HA7: Stan	.6G 27
Montrose Way SE23	.1K 139
Montserrat Av. IG8: Wfd G	.7A 36
Montserrat Cl. SE19	.5D 138
Montserrat Rd. SW15	.4G 117
Monument, The	.2F 15 (7D 84)
(off Monument St.)	
Monument Gdns. SE13	.5E 122
Monument St. EC3	.2F 15 (7D 84)
Monument Way N17	.3F 49
Monza St. E1	.7J 85
Moodkee St. SE16	.3J 103
Moody Rd. SE15	.1F 121
Moody St. E1	.3K 85
Moon Cl. SE12	.4J 123

Moon La. EN5: Barn	.3C 20
Moon St. N1	.1B 84
Moorcroft HA8: Edg	.1H 43
Moorcroft Gdns. BR2: Brom	.5C 160
Moorcroft La. UB8: Hil	.5C 74
Moorcroft Rd. SW16	.3J 137
Moorcroft Way HA5: Pinn	.5C 40
Moordown SE18	.7F 107
Moore Cl. CR4: Mitc	.2F 155
SW14	.3J 115
Moore Ct. N1	.1B 84
(off Gaskin St.)	
Moore Cres. RM9: Dag	.1B 90
Moorefield Rd. N17	.2F 49
Moorehead Way SE3	.3J 123
Moore Ho. E1	.7J 85
(off Cable St.)	
E2	.3J 85
(off Roman Rd.)	
N8	.4J 47
(off Pembroke Rd.)	
SE10	.5H 105
(off Armitage Rd.)	
Moorelend Rd. BR1: Brom	.7H 141
Moore Pk. Ct. SW6	.7K 99
(off Fulham Rd.)	
Moore Pk. Rd. SW6	.7J 99
Moore Rd. SE19	.6C 138
Moore St. SW3	.3E 16 (4D 100)
Moore Wlk. E7	.4J 69
Moore Way SM2: Sutt	.7J 165
Morey Cl. E15	.1H 87
Moorfield Av. W5	.4D 78
Moorfield Rd. EN3: Enf H	.1D 24
KT9: Chess	.5E 162
UB8: Cowl	.6A 74
Moorfields EC2	.6E 8 (5D 84)
Moorfields Highwalk EC2	.6E 8
(off Moorfields, not continuous)	
Moorgate EC2	.7E 8 (6D 84)
Moorgate PL. EC2	.7E 8
Moorgreen Ho. EC1	.1A 8
Moorhouse NW9	.1B 44
Moorhouse Rd. HA3: Kent	.3D 42
W2	.6J 81
Moorings, The E16	.5A 88
(off Prince Regent La.)	
Moorings Ho. TW8: Bford	.7C 96
Moorland Cl. RM5: Col R	.1H 55
TW2: Whitt	.7E 112
Moorland Rd. SW9	.4B 120
Moorlands UB5: N'olt	.1C 76
Moorlands Av. NW7	.6J 29
Moor La. EC2	.6E 8 (5D 84)
(not continuous)	
KT9: Chess	.4E 162
Moormead Dr. KT19: Ewe	.5A 164
Moor Mead Rd. TW1: Twick	.6A 114
Moor Pk. Gdns. KT2: King T	.7A 134
Moor Pl. EC2	.6E 8 (5D 84)
Moorside Rd. BR1: Brom	.3G 141
Moor St. W1	.1D 12 (6H 83)
Moot Cl. NW9	.5G 43
Moran Ho. E1	.1H 103
(off Wapping La.)	
Morant Pl. N22	.1K 47
Morant St. E14	.7C 86
Mora Rd. NW2	.4E 62
Mora St. EC1	.2D 8 (3C 84)
Morat St. SW9	.1K 119
Moravian Cl. SW10	.7A 16 (6B 100)
Moravian Pl. SE2	.2J 85
Moravian St. E2	.2J 85
Moray Av. UB3: Hayes	.1H 93
Moray Cl. HA8: Edg	.2C 28
RM1: Rom	.1K 55
Moray Ct. CR2: S Croy	.5C 168
(off Warham Rd.)	
Moray Ho. E1	.4A 86
(off Harford St.)	
Moray M. N7	.2K 65

Muncies M.—Navarino Gro.

Muncies M. SE6 2E 140
Mundania Ct. SE22 6H 121
Mundania Rd. SE22 6H 121
Munday Ho. SE1 3D 102
(off Deverell St.)
Munday Rd. E16 7J 87
Munden St. W14 4G 99
Mundford Rd. E5 2J 67
Mundon Gdns. IG1: Ilf 1H 71
Mund St. W14 5H 99
Mundy Ho. W10 3G 81
(off Dart St.)
Mundy St. N1 1G 9 (3E 84)
Mungo Pk. Cl. WD23: Bushy 2B 26
Munnery Way BR6: Farnb 3E 172
Munnings Gdns. TW7: Isle 5H 113
Munnings Ho. E16 1K 105
(off Portsmouth M.)
Munro Dr. N11 6B 32
Munro Ho. SE1 7J 13 (2A 102)
Munro M. W10 5G 81
(not continuous)
Munro Ter. SW10 7B 100
Munslow Gdns. SM1: Sutt 4B 166
Munster Av. TW4: Houn 5C 112
Munster Ct. SW6 2H 117
TW11: Tedd 6C 132
Munster Gdns. N13 4G 33
Munster M. SW6 7G 99
Munster Rd. SW6 7G 99
TW11: Tedd 6B 132
Munster Sq. NW1 2K 5 (3F 83)
Munton Rd. SE17 4C 102
Murchison Av. DA5: Bexl 1D 144
Murchison Rd. E10 2E 68
Murdoch Ho. SE16 3J 103
(off Moodkee St.)
Murdock Cl. E16 6H 87
Murdock St. SE15 6H 103
Murfett Cl. SW19 2G 135
Muriel Ct. E10 7D 50
Muriel St. N1 2K 83
(not continuous)
Murillo Rd. SE13 4F 123
Murphy Ho. SE1 7B 14
(off Borough Rd.)
Murphy St. SE1 7J 13 (2A 102)
Murray Av. BR1: Brom 3K 159
TW3: Houn 5F 113
Murray Cl. SE28 1J 107
Murray Ct. HA1: Harr 6K 41
TW2: Twick 2H 131
Murray Cres. HA5: Pinn 1B 40
Murray Gro. N1 1D 8 (2C 84)
Murray Ho. SE18 4D 106
(off Rideout St.)
Murray M. NW1 7H 65
Murray Rd. HA6: Nwood 1G 39
SW19 6F 135
TW10: Ham 2B 132
W5 4C 96
Murray Sq. E16 6J 87
Murray St. NW1 7G 65
Murrays Yd. SE18 4F 107
Murray Ter. NW3 4A 64
W5 4D 96
Mursell Est. SW8 1K 119
Musard Rd. W6 6G 99
W14 6G 99
Musbury St. E1 6J 85
Muscal W6 6G 99
(off Field Rd.)
Muscatel Pl. SE5 1E 120
Muschamp Rd. SE15 3F 121
SM5: Cars 2C 166
Muscovy Ho. DA18: Erith 2E 108
(off Kale Rd.)
Muscovy St. EC3 2H 15 (7E 84)
Museum Chambers WC1 6E 6
(off Bury Pl.)
Mus. in Docklands, The 7C 86
Museum La. SW7 2B 16 (3B 100)
Mus. of Artillery in the Rotunda
5D 106
Mus. of Classical Archaeology 3C 6
(off Gower Pl.)
Mus. of Garden History 2G 19 (3K 101)
Mus. of London 6C 8 (5C 84)
Mus. of Richmond 5D 114
(off Whittaker Av.)
Mus. of Rugby, The 6J 113
Mus. of the Order of St John, The 4A 8
(off St John's La.)
Museum Pas. E2 3J 85
Museum St. WC1 6E 6 (5J 83)
Musgrave Cl. EN4: Had W 1F 21
Musgrave Ct. SW11 1C 118
Musgrave Cres. SW6 7J 99
Musgrave Rd. TW7: Isle 1K 113
Musgrove Rd. SE14 1K 121
Musjid Rd. SW11 2B 118
Musket Cl. EN4: E Barn 6G 21
Musquash Way TW4: Houn 2A 112
Muston Rd. E5 2H 67
Mustow Pl. SW6 2H 117
Muswell Av. N10 1F 47
MUSWELL HILL 3F 47
Muswell Hill N10 3F 47
Muswell Hill B'way. N10 3F 47
Muswell Hill Pl. N10 4F 47
Muswell Hill Rd. N6 6E 46
N10 5F 47
Muswell M. N10 3F 47
Muswell Rd. N10 3F 47
Mutrix Rd. NW6 1J 81
Mutton Pl. NW1 6E 64
Muybridge Rd. KT3: N Mald 2J 151
Myatt Rd. SW9 1B 120
Myatts Flds. Sth. SW9 2A 120
(off St Lawrence Way)
Mycenae Rd. SE3 7J 105
Myddelton Av. EN1: Enf 1K 23
Myddelton Cl. EN1: Enf 1A 24
Myddelton Gdns. N21 7H 23
Myddelton Pk. N20 3G 31
Myddelton Pas. EC1 1K 7 (3A 84)
Myddelton Rd. N8 4J 47
(not continuous)
Myddelton Sq. EC1 1K 7 (3A 84)
Myddelton St. EC1 2K 7 (3A 84)
Myddleton Av. N4 2C 66
Myddleton Ho. N1 1J 7
Myddleton M. N22 7D 32
Myddleton Rd. N22 7D 32
Myers La. SE14 6K 103
Mylis Cl. SE26 4H 139
Mylius Cl. SE14 7J 103
Mylne Cl. W6 5C 98
Mylne St. EC1 1J 7 (3A 84)
Myra St. SE2 4A 108
Myrdle Ct. E1 6G 85
(off Myrdle St.)
Myrdle St. E1 5G 85
Myrna Cl. SW19 7C 136
Myron Pl. SE13 3E 122
Myrtle Av. HA4: Ruis 7J 39
TW14: Felt 5G 111
Myrtleberry Cl. E8 6F 67
(off Beechwood Rd.)
Myrtle Cl. EN4: E Barn 1J 31
UB7: W Dray 3B 92
UB8: Hil 5B 74
Myrtledene Rd. SE2 5A 108
Myrtle Gdns. W7 1J 95
Myrtle Gro. EN2: Enf 1J 23
KT3: N Mald 2J 151
Myrtle Rd. CR0: Croy 3C 170
E6 1D 88
E17 6A 50
IG1: Ilf 2F 71
N13 3H 33
SM1: Sutt 5A 166
Myrtle Rd. TW3: Houn 2G 113
TW12: Hamp H 6G 131
W3 1J 97
Myrtle Wlk. N1 1G 9 (2E 84)
Mysore Rd. SW11 3D 118
Myton Rd. SE21 3D 138
Mytton Ho. SW8 7K 101
(off St Stephens Ter.)

N

N1 Shop. Cen. N1 2A 84
N16 Fitness Cen. 4D 66
Nadine Ct. SM6: Wall 7G 167
Nadine St. SE7 5A 106
Nagasaki Wlk. SE7 3K 105
Nagle Cl. E17 2F 51
NAG'S HEAD 3J 65
Nags Head Ct. EC1 4D 8
Nags Head La. DA16: Well 3B 126
Nags Head Rd. EN3: Pond E 4D 24
Nags Head Shop. Cen.
N7 4K 65
Nainby Ho. SE11 4J 19
Nairne Gro. SE24 5D 120
Nairn Rd. HA4: Ruis 6A 58
Nairn St. E14 5E 86
Naish Ct. N1 1J 83
(not continuous)
Naldera Gdns. SE3 6J 105
Nallhead Rd. TW13: Hanw 5A 130
Namba Roy Cl. SW16 4K 137
Namton Dr. CR7: Thor H 4K 155
Nan Clark's La. NW7 2F 29
Nankin St. E14 6C 86
Nansen Ho. NW10 7K 61
(off Stonebridge Pk.)
Nansen Rd. SW11 3E 118
Nansen Village N12 4E 30
Nant Ct. NW2 2H 63
Nantes Cl. SW18 4A 118
Nantes Pas. E1 5J 9 (5F 85)
Nant Rd. NW2 2H 63
Nant St. E2 3H 85
Naoroji St. WC1 2J 7 (3A 84)
Napier NW9 1B 44
Napier Av. E14 5C 104
SW6 3H 117
Napier Cl. SE8 7B 104
UB7: W Dray 3B 92
W14 3G 99
Napier Ct. N1 2D 84
(off Cropley St.)
SE12 3K 141
SW6 3H 117
(off Ranelagh Gdns.)
UB4: Yead 4A 76
(off Dunedin Way)
Napier Gro. N1 2C 84
Napier Lodge TW15: Ashf 6F 129
Napier Pl. W14 3H 99
Napier Rd. BR2: Brom 4K 159
CR2: S Croy 7D 168
DA17: Belv 4F 109
E6 1E 88
E11 4G 69
E15 2G 87
(not continuous)
EN3: Pond E 5E 24
HA0: Wemb 6D 60
N17 3E 48
NW10 3D 80
SE25 4H 157
TW7: Isle 4A 114
TW15: Ashf 7F 129
W14 3H 99
Napier St. SE8 7B 104
(off Napier Cl.)
Napier Ter. N1 7B 66
Napier Wlk. TW15: Ashf 7F 129
Napoleon Rd. E5 3H 67
TW1: Twick 7B 114
Napton Cl. UB4: Yead 4C 76
Narbonne Av. SW4 5G 119
Narborough Cl. UB10: Ick 2E 56
Narborough St. SW6 2K 117
Narcissus Rd. NW6 5J 63
Nardini NW9 1B 44
(off Concourse, The)
Naresby Fold HA7: Stan 6H 27
Narford Rd. E5 3G 67
Narrow Boat Cl. SE28 2H 107
Narrow St. E14 7A 86
W3 1H 97
Narrow Way BR2: Brom 6C 160
Narvic Ho. SE5 2C 120
Narwhal Inuit Art Gallery 4K 97
Nascot St. W12 6E 80
Naseby Cl. NW6 7A 64
TW7: Isle 1J 113
Naseby Ct. DA14: Sidc 4K 143
Naseby Rd. IG5: Ilf 1D 52
RM10: Dag 3G 73
SE19 6D 138
NASH 6J 171
Nash Cl. SM1: Sutt 3B 166
Nash Ct. E14 1D 104
(off Nash Pl.)
HA3: Kent 6B 42
Nashe Ho. SE1 3D 102
(off Burbage Cl.)
Nash Grn. BR1: Brom 6J 141
Nash Ho. E17 3D 50
SW1 6K 17
(off Lupus St.)
Nash La. BR2: Kes 7J 171
Nash Pl. E14 1D 104
Nash Rd. N9 2D 34
RM6: Chad H 4D 54
SE4 4A 122
Nash St. NW1 1K 5 (3F 83)
Nash Way HA3: Kent 6B 42
Nasmyth St. W6 3D 98
Nassau Path SE28 1C 108
Nassau Rd. SW13 1B 116
Nassau St. W1 6A 6 (5G 83)
Nassington Rd. NW3 4D 64
Natalie Cl. TW14: Bedf 7F 111
Natalie M. TW2: Twick 3H 131
Natal Rd. CR7: Thor H 3D 156
IG1: Ilf 4F 71
N11 6D 32
SW16 6H 137
Nathan Ct. N9 7D 24
(off Causeyware Rd.)
Nathan Ho. SE11 4K 19
(off Reedworth St.)
Nathaniel Cl. E1 6K 9 (5F 85)
Nathaniel Ct. E17 7A 50
Nathans Rd. HA0: Wemb 1C 60
Nathan Way SE28 4J 107
National Army Mus. 7F 17 (6D 100)
National Film Theatre, The 4H 13
National Gallery 3D 12 (7H 83)
National Gallery (Sainsbury Wing) 3D 12
(in National Gallery)
National Maritime Mus. 6F 105
National Portrait Gallery 3D 12
National Ter. SE16 2H 103
(off Bermondsey Wall E.)
National Walks TW4: Houn 3D 112
Nation Way E4 1K 35
Natural History Mus. 2A 16 (3B 100)
Nautilus Bldg., The EC1 1K 7
(off Myddelton Pas.)
Naval Ho. E14 7F 87
(off Quixley St.)
Naval Row E14 7E 86
Naval Wlk. BR1: Brom 2J 159
(off Mitre Cl.)
Navarino Gro. E8 6G 67

A-Z London 333

Navarino Mans. E8 6G 67
Navarino Rd. E8 6G 67
Navarre Rd. E6 2C 88
Navarre St. E2 3J 9 (4F 85)
Navenby Wlk. E3 4C 86
Navestock Cl. E4 3K 35
Navestock Cres. IG8: Wfd G 7F 37
Navestock Ho. IG11: Bark 2B 90
Navigation Dr. EN3: Enf L 1H 25
Navigator Dr. UB2: S'hall 2G 95
Navigator Pk. UB2: S'hall 4A 94
Navy St. SW4 3H 119
Naxos Bldg. E14 2B 104
Nayim Pl. E8 5H 67
Nayland Ho. SE6 4E 140
Naylor Gro. EN3: Pond E 5E 24
Naylor Ho. *W10* *3G 81*
(off Dart St.)
Naylor Rd. N20 2F 31
SE15 7H 103
Nazareth Gdns. SE15 2H 121
Nazrul St. E2 1J 9 (3F 85)
Neagle Ho. *NW2* *3E 62*
(off Stoll Cl.)
Neal Av. UB1: S'hall 4D 76
Neal Cl. HA6: Nwood 1J 39
Nealden St. SW9 3K 119
Neale Cl. N2 3A 46
Neal St. WC2 1E 12 (6J 83)
Neal's Yd. WC2 1E 12 (6J 83)
Near Acre NW9 1B 44
NEASDEN 3A 62
Neasden Cl. NW10 5A 62
NEASDEN JUNC. 4A 62
Neasden La. NW10 3A 62
(not continuous)
Neasden La. Nth. NW10 3K 61
Neasham Rd. RM8: Dag 5B 72
Neate St. SE5 6E 102
(not continuous)
Neath Gdns. SM4: Mord 6A 154
Neathouse Pl. SW1 3A 18 (4G 101)
Neats Acre HA4: Ruis 7F 39
Neatscourt Rd. E6 5B 88
Nebraska St. SE1 7E 14 (2D 102)
Neckinger SE16 7K 15 (3F 103)
Neckinger Est. SE16 3F 103
Neckinger St. SE1 7K 15 (2F 103)
Nectarine Way SE13 2D 122
Needham Ho. SE11 4J 19
Needham Rd. W11 6J 81
Needham Ter. NW2 3F 63
Needleman St. SE16 2K 103
Needwood Ho. N4 1C 66
Neela Cl. UB10: Ick 4D 56
Neeld Cres. HA9: Wemb 5G 61
NW4 5D 44
Neeld Pde. HA9: Wemb 5F 61
Neil Cl. TW15: Ashf 5E 128
Neil Wates Cres. SW2 1A 138
Nelgarde Rd. SE6 7C 122
Nella Rd. W6 6F 99
Nelldale Rd. SE16 4J 103
Nellgrove Rd. UB10: Hil 4D 74
Nell Gwynne Av. TW17: Shep 6F 147
Nello James Gdns. SE27 4D 138
Nelson Cl. CR0: Croy 1B 168
KT12: Walt T 7K 147
NW6 3J 81
RM7: Mawney 1H 55
TW14: Felt 1H 129
UB10: Hil 3D 74
Nelson Ct. SE1 6B 14 (2B 102)
SE16 *1J 103*
(off Brunel Rd.)
Nelson Gdns. E2 3G 85
TW3: Houn 6E 112
Nelson Gro. Rd. SW19 1K 153
Nelson Ho. *SW1* *7B 18*
(off Dolphin Sq.)
Nelson La. UB10: Hil 3D 74
Nelson Mandela Cl. N10 2E 46
Nelson Mandela Rd. SE3 3A 124
Nelson Pas. EC1 1D 8 (3C 84)
Nelson Pl. DA14: Sidc 4A 144
N1 1B 8 (2B 84)
Nelson Rd. BR2: Brom 4A 160
DA14: Sidc 4A 144
DA17: Belv 5F 109
E4 6J 35
E11 4J 51
EN3: Pond E 6E 24
HA1: Harr 1H 59
HA7: Stan 6H 27
KT3: N Mald 5K 151
N8 5K 47
N9 2C 34
N15 4E 48
SE10 6E 104
SW19 7K 135
TW2: Whit 7F 113
TW3: Houn 6E 112
TW6: H'row A 1B 110
TW15: Ashf 5A 128
UB10: Hil 3D 74
Nelson Rd. M. SW19 7K 135
Nelson's Column 4E 12 (1J 101)
Nelson Sq. SE1 6A 14 (2B 102)
Nelson's Row SW4 4H 119
Nelson St. E1 6H 85
E6 2D 88
(not continuous)
E16 7H 87
(not continuous)
Nelsons Yd. *NW1* *2G 83*
(off Mornington Cres.)
Nelson Ter. N1 1B 8 (2B 84)
Nelson Trad. Est. SW19 1K 153
Nelson Wlk. KT19: Eps 7G 163
SE16 1A 104
Nemoure Rd. W3 7J 79
Nene Gdns. TW13: Hanw 2D 130
Nene Rd. TW6: H'row A 1D 110
Nene Rd. Rdbt. TW6: H'row A 1D 110
Nepaul Rd. SW11 2C 118
Nepean St. SW15 6C 116
Neptune Ct. *E14* *4C 104*
(off Homer Dr.)
Neptune Ho. *SE16* *3J 103*
(off Moodkee St.)
Neptune Rd. HA1: Harr 6H 41
TW6: H'row A 1E 110
Neptune St. SE16 3J 103
Neptune Wlk. DA8: Erith 4K 109
Nero Ct. TW8: Bford 7D 96
Nesbit Rd. SE9 4B 124
Nesbitt Cl. SE3 3G 123
Nesbitts All. EN5: Barn 3C 20
Nesbitt Sq. SE19 7E 138
Nesham St. E1 7G 85
Ness St. SE16 3G 103
Nesta Rd. IG8: Wfd G 6B 36
Nestles Av. UB3: Hayes 3H 93
Nestor Av. N21 6G 23
Nestor Ho. *E2* *2H 85*
(off Old Bethnal Grn. Rd.)
Netheravon Rd. W4 4B 98
W7 1K 95
Netheravon Rd. Sth. W4 5B 98
Netherbury Rd. W5 3D 96
Netherby Gdns. EN2: Enf 4D 22
Netherby Rd. SE23 7J 121
Nether Cl. N3 7D 30
Nethercourt Av. N3 6D 30
Netherfield Gdns. IG11: Bark 6H 71
Netherfield Rd. N12 5E 30
SW17 3E 136
Netherford Rd. SW4 2G 119
Netherhall Gdns. NW3 6A 64
Netherhall Way NW3 5A 64
Netherlands Rd. EN5: New Bar 6G 21
Netherleigh Cl. N6 1F 65
Nether St. N3 1J 45
N12 6E 30
Netherton Gro. SW10 6A 100
Netherton Rd. N15 6D 48
TW1: Twick 5A 114
Netherwood N2 2B 46
Netherwood Pl. *W14* *3F 99*
(off Netherwood Rd.)
Netherwood Rd. W14 3F 99
Netherwood St. NW6 7H 63
Nethewode Ct. *DA17: Belv* *3H 109*
(off Lower Pk. Rd.)
Netley *SE5* *1E 120*
(off Redbridge Gdns.)
Netley Cl. CR0: New Ad 7E 170
SM3: Cheam 5F 165
Netley Dr. KT12: Walt T 7D 148
Netley Gdns. SM4: Mord 7A 154
Netley Rd. E17 5B 50
IG2: Ilf 5H 53
SM4: Mord 7A 154
TW8: Bford 6E 96
Netley St. NW1 2A 6 (3G 83)
Nettlecombe *NW1* *7H 65*
(off Agar Gro.)
Nettleden Av. HA9: Wemb 6G 61
Nettleden Ho. *SW3* *4D 16*
(off Marlborough St.)
Nettlefold Pl. SE27 3B 138
Nettlestead Cl. BR3: Beck 7B 140
Nettleton Ct. *EC2* *6C 8*
(off London Wall)
Nettleton Rd. SE14 1K 121
TW6: H'row A 1D 110
UB10: Ick 4B 56
Nettlewood Rd. SW16 7H 137
Neuchatel Rd. SE6 2B 140
Nevada Cl. KT3: N Mald 4J 151
Nevada St. SE10 6E 104
Nevern Pl. SW5 4J 99
Nevern Rd. SW5 4J 99
Nevern Sq. SW5 4J 99
Nevil Ho. *SW9* *2B 120*
(off Loughborough Est.)
Nevill Ct. EC4 7K 7
Neville Av. KT3: N Mald 1K 151
Neville Cl. DA15: Sidc 4K 143
E11 3H 69
NW1 2H 83
NW6 2H 81
SE15 1G 121
TW3: Houn 2F 113
W3 2J 97
Neville Ct. NW8 1A 4
Neville Dr. N2 6A 46
Neville Gdns. RM8: Dag 3D 72
Neville Gill Cl. SW18 6J 117
Neville Ho. N11 4K 31
N22 *1K 47*
(off Neville Pl.)
Neville Ho. Yd. KT1: King T 2E 150
Neville Pl. N22 1K 47
Neville Rd. CR0: Croy 7D 156
E7 7J 69
IG6: Ilf 1G 53
KT1: King T 2G 151
NW6 2H 81
RM8: Dag 2D 72
TW10: Ham 3C 132
W5 4D 78
Nevilles Ct. NW2 3C 62
Neville St. SW7 5A 16 (5B 100)
Neville Ter. SW7 5A 16 (5B 100)
Neville Wlk. SM5: Cars 7C 154
Nevill Rd. N16 4E 66
Nevin Dr. E4 1J 35
Nevin Ho. UB3: Harl 3E 92
Nevinson Cl. SW18 6B 118
Nevis Rd. SW17 2E 136
Nevitt Ho. *N1* *2D 84*
(off Cranston Est.)
New Acres Rd. SE28 2J 107
(not continuous)
NEW ADDINGTON 7F 171
Newall Ho. *SE1* *3C 102*
(off Bath Ter.)
Newall Rd. TW6: H'row A 1E 110
Newark Cres. NW10 3K 79
Newarke Ho. SW9 2B 120
Newark Knok E6 6E 88
Newark Pde. NW4 3C 44
Newark Rd. CR2: S Croy 6D 168
Newark St. E1 5H 85
(not continuous)
Newark Way NW4 4C 44
New Ash Cl. N2 3B 46
New Atlas Wharf *E14* *3C 104*
(off Arnhem Pl.)
New Baltic Wharf *SE8* *5A 104*
(off Evelyn St.)
New Barn Cl. SM6: Wall 6K 167
NEW BARNET 4G 21
New Barn Rd. BR8: Swan 7K 145
New Barns Av. CR4: Mitc 4H 155
(not continuous)
New Barn St. E13 4J 87
New Barns Way IG7: Chig 3K 37
NEW BECKENHAM 6B 140
New Bentham Ct. *N1* *7C 66*
(off Ecclesbourne Rd.)
Newbery Ho. *N1* *7C 66*
(off Northampton St.)
Newbold Cotts. E1 6J 85
Newbolt Av. SM3: Cheam 5E 164
Newbolt Ho. *SE17* *5D 102*
(off Brandon St.)
Newbolt Rd. HA7: Stan 5E 26
New Bond St. W1 1J 11 (6F 83)
Newborough Grn. KT3: N Mald 4K 151
New Brent St. NW4 5E 44
Newbridge Point *SE23* *3K 139*
(off Windrush La.)
New Bri. St. EC4 1A 14 (6B 84)
New Broad St. EC2 6G 9 (5E 84)
New B'way. TW12: Hamp H 5H 131
UB10: Hil 3D 74
W5 7D 78
Newburgh Rd. W3 1J 97
Newburgh St. W1 1B 12 (6G 83)
New Burlington M. W1 2A 12 (7G 83)
New Burlington Pl. W1 2A 12 (7G 83)
New Burlington St. W1 2A 12 (7G 83)
Newburn Ho. *SE11* *5H 19*
(off Newburn St.)
Newburn St. SE11 5H 19 (5K 101)
Newbury Cl. UB5: N'olt 6D 58
Newbury Ct. DA14: Sidc 4K 143
Newbury Gdns. KT19: Ewe 4B 164
Newbury Ho. N22 1J 47
SW9 2B 120
W2 *6K 81*
(off Hallfield Est.)
Newbury M. NW5 6E 64
NEWBURY PARK 5H 53
Newbury Rd. BR2: Brom 3J 159
E4 6K 35
IG2: Ilf 6J 53
TW6: H'row A 1B 110
Newbury St. EC1 6C 8 (5C 84)
Newbury Way UB5: N'olt 6C 58
New Bus. Cen., The NW10 3B 80
New Butt La. SE8 7C 104
New Butt La. Nth. *SE8* *7C 104*
(off Hales St.)
New Broadway Bldgs. W5 7D 78
Newby *NW1* *2A 6*
(off Robert St.)
Newby Cl. EN1: Enf 2K 23
Newby Ho. *E14* *7E 86*
(off Newby Pl.)
Newby Pl. E14 7E 86
Newby St. SW8 3F 119

Newton Cl. E17 .6A **50**
HA2: Harr .2E **58**
Newton Gro. W4 .4A **98**
Newton Ho. *E1* .*7H 85*
(off Cornwall St.)
E17 .*3D 50*
(off Prospect Hill)
EN3: Enf H .3E **24**
NW8 .*1K 81*
(off Abbey Rd.)
SE20 .7K **139**
Newton Ind. Est. RM6: Chad H .4D **54**
Newton Mans. *W14* .*6G 99*
(off Queen's Club Gdns.)
Newton Pl. E14 .4C **104**
Newton Point *E16* .*6H 87*
(off Clarkson Rd.)
Newton Rd. DA16: Well .3A **126**
E15 .5F **69**
HA0: Wemb .7F **61**
HA3: Hrw W .2J **41**
N15 .5G **49**
NW2 .4E **62**
SW19 .7G **135**
TW7: Isle .2K **113**
W2 .6K **81**
Newton St. WC2 .7F **7** (6J **83**)
Newton's Yd. SW18 .5J **117**
Newton Ter. BR2: Brom .6B **160**
Newton Wlk. HA8: Edg .1H **43**
Newton Way N18 .5H **33**
New Twr. Bldgs. E1 .1H **103**
Newtown St. SW11 .1F **119**
New Trinity Rd. N2 .3B **46**
New Turnstile WC1 .6G **7**
New Union Cl. E14 .3E **104**
New Union St. EC2 .6E **8** (5D **84**)
New Wanstead E11 .6H **51**
New Way Rd. NW9 .4A **44**
New Wharf Rd. N1 .2J **83**
NEWYEARS GREEN .7B **38**
Newyears Grn. La. UB9: Hare .6A **38**
New Zealand Av. KT12: Walt T .7H **147**
New Zealand Way W12 .7D **80**
Next Generation Carlton Club .5J **81**
Nexus Ct. E11 .1G **69**
Niagara Av. W5 .4C **96**
Niagra Cl. N1 .2C **84**
Niagra Ct. *SE16* .*3J 103*
(off Canada Est.)
Nibthwaite Rd. HA1: Harr .5J **41**
Nicholas Cl. UB6: G'frd .2F **77**
Nicholas Ct. *W4* .*6A 98*
(off Corney Reach Way)
Nicholas Gdns. W5 .2D **96**
Nicholas La. EC4 .2F **15** (7D **84**)
(not continuous)
Nicholas M. W4 .6A **98**
Nicholas Pas. EC4 .1F **15**
Nicholas Rd. CR0: Bedd .4J **167**
E1 .4J **85**
RM8: Dag .2F **73**
Nicholas Stacey Ho. *SE7* .*5K 105*
(off Frank Burton Cl.)
Nicholas Way HA6: Nwood .1E **38**
Nicholay Rd. N19 .1H **65**
(not continuous)
Nichol Cl. N14 .1C **32**
Nicholes Rd. TW3: Houn .4E **112**
Nichol La. BR1: Brom .7J **141**
Nicholl Ho. N4 .1C **66**
Nicholls Av. UB8: Hil .4C **74**
Nichollsfield Wlk. N7 .5K **65**
Nicholls Point *E15* .*1J 87*
(off Park Gro.)
Nicholl St. E2 .1G **85**
Nichols Cl. KT9: Chess .6C **162**
N4 .*1A 66*
(off Osborne Rd.)
Nichols Ct. E2 .2F **85**
Nichols Grn. W5 .5E **78**
Nicholson Ct. E17 .4A **50**
N17 .3F **49**
Nicholson Ho. SE17 .5D **102**
Nicholson M. KT1: King T .4E **150**
Nicholson Rd. CR0: Croy .1F **169**
Nicholson St. SE1 .5A **14** (1B **102**)
Nickelby Cl. SE28 .6C **90**
Nickleby Cl. UB8: Hil .6D **74**
Nickleby Ho. *SE16* .*7K 15*
(off Parkers Row)
Nickols Wlk. SW18 .4K **117**
Nicola Cl. CR2: S Croy .6C **168**
HA3: Hrw W .2H **41**
Nicolas Ct. E13 .3K **87**
Nicola Ter. DA7: Bex .1E **126**
Nicol Cl. TW1: Twick .6B **114**
Nicoll Ct. N10 .7A **32**
NW10 .1A **80**
Nicoll Pl. NW4 .6D **44**
Nicoll Rd. NW10 .1A **80**
Nicolson NW9 .1A **44**
Nicolson Dr. WD23: Bushy .1B **26**
Nicosia Rd. SW18 .7C **118**
Niederwald Rd. SE26 .4A **140**
Nield Rd. UB3: Hayes .2H **93**
Nigel Cl. UB5: N'olt .1C **76**
Nigel Ct. N3 .7E **30**
Nigel Fisher Way KT9: Chess .7C **162**
Nigel Ho. *EC1* .*5J 7*
(off Portpool La.)
Nigel M. IG1: Ilf .4F **71**
Nigel Playfair Av. W6 .4D **98**
Nigel Rd. E7 .5A **70**
SE15 .3G **121**
Nigeria Rd. SE7 .7A **106**
Nighthawk NW9 .1B **44**
Nightingale Av. E4 .5B **36**
HA1: Harr .1B **60**
Nightingale Cl. E4 .4A **36**
HA5: Eastc .5A **40**
SM5: Cars .2E **166**
W4 .6J **97**
Nightingale Ct. BR2: Brom .2G **159**
E14 .*2E 104*
(off Ovex Cl.)
HA1: Harr .6K **41**
N4 .*2K 65*
(off Tollington Pk.)
SM1: Sutt .5A **166**
SW6 .*1K 117*
(off Maltings Pl.)
Nightingale Dr. KT19: Ewe .6H **163**
Nightingale Gro. SE13 .5F **123**
Nightingale Hgts. SE18 .6F **107**
Nightingale Ho. *E1* .*1G 103*
(off Thomas More St.)
E2 .*1E 84*
(off Kingsland Rd.)
SE18 .*5E 106*
(off Connaught M.)
W12 .*6E 80*
(off Du Cane Rd.)
Nightingale La. BR1: Brom .2A **160**
E11 .4K **51**
N8 .4J **47**
SW12 .7D **118**
TW10: Rich .7E **114**
Nightingale Lodge *W9* .*5J 81*
(off Admiral Wlk.)
Nightingale M. E3 .2K **85**
E11 .5J **51**
KT1: King T .*3D 150*
(off South La.)
SE11 .3K **19** (4B **102**)
Nightingale Pl. SE18 .6E **106**
SW10 .7A **16** (6A **100**)
(not continuous)
Nightingale Rd. BR5: Pet W .6G **161**
E5 .3H **67**
KT8: W Mole .5F **149**
KT12: Walt T .7A **148**
Nightingale Rd. N9 .6D **24**
N22 .1J **47**
NW10 .2B **80**
SM5: Cars .3D **166**
TW12: Hamp .5E **130**
W7 .1K **95**
Nightingales, The TW19: Stanw .1B **128**
Nightingale Sq. SW12 .7E **118**
Nightingale Va. SE18 .6E **106**
Nightingale Wlk. SW4 .6F **119**
Nightingale Way E6 .5C **88**
Nile Cl. N16 .3F **67**
Nile Dr. N9 .2D **34**
Nile Path SE18 .6E **106**
Nile Rd. E13 .2A **88**
Nile St. N1 .1D **8** (3C **84**)
Nile Ter. SE15 .5F **103**
Nimegen Way SE22 .5E **120**
Nimmo Dr. WD23: Bushy .1C **26**
Nimrod NW9 .1A **44**
Nimrod Cl. UB5: N'olt .3B **76**
Nimrod Ho. *E16* .*5K 87*
(off Vanguard Cl.)
Nimrod Pas. N1 .6E **66**
Nimrod Rd. SW16 .6F **137**
Nina Mackay Cl. E15 .1G **87**
Nine Acres Cl. E12 .5C **70**
NINE ELMS .7G **101**
Nine Elms Cl. TW14: Felt .1H **129**
Nine Elms La. SW8 .7C **18** (7G **101**)
Nineteenth Rd. CR4: Mitc .4J **155**
Ninhams Wood BR6: Farnb .4E **172**
Ninth Av. UB3: Hayes .7J **75**
Nipponzan Myohoji Peace Pagoda .6D **100**
Nirvana Apartments *N1* .*1B 84*
(off Islington Grn.)
Nisbet Ho. E9 .5K **67**
Nita Ct. SE12 .1J **141**
Nithdale Rd. SE18 .7F **107**
Nithsdale Gro. UB10: Ick .3E **56**
Niton Cl. EN5: Barn .6A **20**
Niton Rd. TW9: Rich .3G **115**
Niton St. SW6 .7F **99**
No 1 St. SE18 .3F **107**
Nobel Dr. UB3: Harl .1F **111**
Nobel Ho. SE5 .2C **120**
Nobel Rd. N18 .4D **34**
Noble Cnr. TW5: Hest .1E **112**
Noble Ct. CR4: Mitc .2B **154**
E1 .7H **85**
Noblefield Hgts. N2 .5C **46**
Noble M. *N16* .*3D 66*
(off Albion Rd.)
Noble St. EC2 .7C **8** (6C **84**)
Noel NW9 .1A **44**
Noel Ct. TW4: Houn .3D **112**
Noel Coward Ho. *SW1* .*4B 18*
(off Vauxhall Bri. Rd.)
Noel Ho. *NW6* .*7B 64*
(off Harben Rd.)
NOEL PARK .2B **48**
Noel Pk. Rd. N22 .2A **48**
Noel Rd. E6 .4C **88**
N1 .2B **84**
W3 .7G **79**
Noel Sq. RM8: Dag .4C **72**
Noel St. W1 .1B **12** (6G **83**)
Noel Ter. DA14: Sidc .4B **144**
SE23 .2J **139**
Nolan Way E5 .4G **67**
Nolton Pl. HA8: Edg .1F **43**
Nonsuch Ho. SW19 .1B **154**
Nonsuch Pl. *SM3: Cheam* .*7F 165*
(off Ewell Rd.)
Nonsuch Wlk. SM2: Cheam .7F **165**
Nora Gdns. NW4 .4F **45**
NORBITON .2G **151**
Norbiton Av. KT1: King T .1G **151**
Norbiton Comn. Rd. KT1: King T .3H **151**
Norbiton Hall KT2: King T .2F **151**
Norbiton Rd. E14 .6B **86**
Norbreck Gdns. NW10 .3F **79**
Norbreck Pde. NW10 .3E **78**
Norbroke St. W12 .7B **80**
Norburn St. W10 .5G **81**
NORBURY .2K **155**
Norbury Av. CR7: Thor H .1K **155**
SW16 .1K **155**
TW3: Houn .4H **113**
Norbury Cl. SW16 .1A **156**
Norbury Ct. Rd. SW16 .3J **155**
Norbury Cres. SW16 .1K **155**
Norbury Cross SW16 .3J **155**
Norbury Gdns. RM6: Chad H .5D **54**
Norbury Gro. NW7 .3F **29**
Norbury Hill SW16 .7A **138**
Norbury Ri. SW16 .3J **155**
Norbury Rd. CR7: Thor H .2C **156**
E4 .5H **35**
TW13: Felt .3H **129**
Norbury Trad. Est. SW16 .2K **155**
Norcombe Gdns. HA3: Kent .6C **42**
Norcombe Ho. *N19* .*3H 65*
(off Wedmore St.)
Norcott Cl. UB4: Yead .4A **76**
Norcott Rd. N16 .2G **67**
Norcroft Gdns. SE22 .7G **121**
Norcutt Rd. TW2: Twick .1J **131**
Nordenfeldt Rd. DA8: Erith .5K **109**
Norden Ho. *E2* .*3H 85*
(off Pott St.)
Norfield Rd. DA2: Dart .4J **145**
Norfolk Av. N13 .6G **33**
N15 .6F **49**
Norfolk Cl. EN4: Cockf .4K **21**
N2 .3C **46**
N13 .6G **33**
TW1: Twick .6B **114**
Norfolk Ct. EN5: Barn .4B **20**
Norfolk Cres. DA15: Sidc .7J **125**
W2 .7C **4** (6C **82**)
Norfolk Gdns. DA7: Bex .1F **127**
TW4: Houn .5D **112**
Norfolk Ho. *SE3* .*6G 105*
(off Restell Cl.)
SE8 .1C **122**
SE20 .1J **157**
SW1 .*3D 18*
(off Page St.)
Norfolk Ho. Rd. SW16 .3H **137**
Norfolk Mans. *SW11* .*1D 118*
(off Prince of Wales Dr.)
Norfolk M. *W10* .*5G 81*
(off Blagrove Rd.)
Norfolk Pl. DA16: Well .2A **126**
W2 .7B **4** (6B **82**)
(not continuous)
Norfolk Rd. CR7: Thor H .3C **156**
E6 .1D **88**
E17 .2K **49**
EN3: Pond E .6C **24**
EN5: New Bar .3D **20**
HA1: Harr .5F **41**
IG3: Ilf .1J **71**
IG11: Bark .7J **71**
NW8 .1B **82**
NW10 .7A **62**
RM7: Rom .6J **55**
RM10: Dag .5H **73**
SW19 .7C **136**
TW13: Felt .1A **130**
UB8: Uxb .6A **56**
Norfolk Row SE1 .3G **19** (4K **101**)
(not continuous)
Norfolk Sq. W2 .1B **10** (6B **82**)
Norfolk Sq. M.
W2 .1B **10**
Norfolk St. E7 .5J **69**
Norfolk Ter. W6 .5G **99**
Norgrove St. SW12 .7E **118**
Norhyrst Av. SE25 .3F **157**

Norland Ho.—Nth. Lodge Cl.

Norland Ho. *W11* 1F *99*
(off Queensdale Cres.)
Norland Pl. W11 1G 99
Norland Rd. W11 1F 99
Norlands Cres. BR7: Chst 1F 161
Norland Sq. W11 1G 99
Norland Sq. Mans.
W11 1G *99*
(off Norland Sq.)
Norley Va. SW15 1C 134
Norlington Rd. E10 1E 68
E11 1E 68
Norman Av. N22 1B 48
TW1: Twick 7C 114
TW13: Hanw 2C 130
UB1: S'hall 7C 76
Normanby Cl. SW15 5H 117
Normanby Rd. NW10 4B 62
Norman Cl. BR6: Farnb 3G 173
N22 1C 48
RM5: Col R 1H 55
Norman Ct. IG2: Ilf 7H 53
N3 1J *45*
(off Nether St.)
N4 7A 48
NW10 7C 62
W13 1B *96*
(off Kirkfield Cl.)
Norman Cres. HA5: Pinn 1A 40
TW5: Hest 7B 94
Normand Gdns. *W14* 6G *99*
(off Greyhound Rd.)
Normand M. W14 6G 99
Normand Rd. W14 6H 99
Normandy Av. EN5: Barn 5C 20
Normandy Cl. SE26 3A 140
Normandy Dr. UB3: Hayes 6E 74
Normandy Ho. *E14* 2E *104*
(off Plevna St.)
Normandy Rd. SW9 1A 120
Normandy Ter. E16 6K 87
Normandy Way DA8: Erith 1K 127
Norman Gro. E3 2A 86
Norman Hay Trad. Est., The
UB7: Sip 7B 92
Norman Ho. *SW8* 7J *101*
(off Wyvil Rd.)
TW13: Hanw 2D *130*
(off Watermill Way)
Normanhurst TW15: Ashf 5C 128
Normanhurst Av. DA7: Bex 1D 126
DA16: Well 1D 126
Normanhurst Dr. TW1: Twick 5A 114
Normanhurst Rd. SW2 2K 137
Norman Pde. DA14: Sidc 2D 144
Norman Pk. Athletics Track 6K 159
Norman Rd. CR7: Thor H 5B 156
DA17: Belv 3H 109
(not continuous)
E6 4D 88
E11 2F 69
IG1: Ilf 5F 71
N15 5F 49
SE10 7D 104
SM1: Sutt 5J 165
SW19 7A 136
TW15: Ashf 6F 129
Normans Cl. NW10 6K 61
UB8: Hil 5B 74
Normansfield Av. TW11: Tedd 7C 132
Normanshire Dr. E4 4H 35
Norman's Mead NW10 6K 61
Norman St. EC1 2D 8 (3C 84)
Normanton Av. SW19 2J 135
Normanton Pk. E4 2B 36
Normanton Rd. CR2: S Croy 5E 168
Normanton St. SE23 2K 139
Norman Way N14 2D 32
W3 5H 79
Normington Cl. SW16 5A 138
Norrice Lea N2 5B 46
Norris *NW9* 1B *44*
(off Concourse, The)
Norris Ho. *E9* 1J *85*
(off Handley Rd.)
N1 1E *84*
(off Colville Est.)
SE8 5B *104*
(off Grove St.)
Norris St. SW1 3C 12 (7H 83)
Norroy Rd. SW15 4F 117
Norry's Cl. EN4: Cockf 4J 21
Norry's Rd. EN4: Cockf 4J 21
Norseman Cl. IG3: Ilf 1B 72
Norseman Way
UB6: G'frd 1F 77
Norstead Pl. SW15 2C 134
Nth. Access Rd. E17 6K 49
North Acre NW9 1A 44
NORTH ACTON 4K 79
Nth. Acton Bus. Pk.
W3 5K 79
Nth. Acton Rd. NW10 2K 79
Northall Rd. DA7: Bex 2J 127
Northampton Gro. N1 5D 66
Northampton Pk. N1 6C 66
Northampton Rd. CR0: Croy 2G 169
EC1 3K 7 (4A 84)
EN3: Pond E 4F 25
Northampton Row EC1 3K 7
Northampton Sq. EC1 2A 8 (3B 84)
Northampton St. N1 7C 66
Northanger Rd. SW16 6J 137
Nth. Audley St. W1 1G 11 (6E 82)
North Av. HA2: Harr 6F 41
N18 4B 34
NW10 3E 80
SM5: Cars 7E 166
TW9: Kew 1G 115
UB1: S'hall 7D 76
UB3: Hayes 7J 75
W13 5B 78
North Bank NW8 2C 4 (3C 82)
Northbank Rd. E17 2E 50
NORTH BECKTON 5C 88
Nth. Birkbeck Rd. E11 3F 69
North Block *SE1* 6H *13*
(off York Rd.)
Northborough Rd. SW16 3H 155
Nth. Boundary Rd. E12 3B 70
Northbourne BR2: Hayes 7J 159
Northbourne Rd. SW4 5H 119
Nth. Branch Av. NW10 3E 80
Northbrook Dr. HA6: Nwood 1G 39
Northbrook Rd. CR0: Croy 5D 156
EN5: Barn 6B 20
IG1: Ilf 2E 70
N22 7D 32
SE13 5G 123
Northburgh St. EC1 4B 8 (4B 84)
Nth. Carriage Dr. W2 2C 10
NORTH CHEAM 3E 164
North Cheam Sports Club 3F 165
Northchurch SE17 5D 102
(not continuous)
Northchurch Rd. HA9: Wemb 6G 61
N1 7D 66
(not continuous)
Northchurch Ter. N1 7E 66
Nth. Circular Rd. E4 6G 35
E18 2A 52
IG1: Ilf 2D 70
IG11: Bark 1F 89
N3 3J 45
N12 2A 46
N13 5F 33
NW2 3A 62
NW4 7E 44
NW10 2F 79
NW11 6F 45
Northcliffe Cl. KT4: Wor Pk 3A 164
Northcliffe Dr. N20 1C 30
North Cl. DA6: Bex 4D 126
RM10: Dag 1G 91
SM4: Mord 4G 153
TW14: Bedf 6F 111
Nth. Colonnade, The E14 1C 104
North Comn. Rd. UB8: Uxb 5A 56
W5 7E 78
Northcote HA5: Pinn 2A 40
Northcote Av. KT5: Surb 7H 151
TW7: Isle 5A 114
UB1: S'hall 7C 76
W5 7E 78
Northcote M. SW11 4C 118
Northcote Rd. CR0: Croy 6D 156
DA14: Sidc 4J 143
E17 4A 50
KT3: N Mald 3J 151
NW10 7A 62
SW11 5C 118
TW1: Twick 5A 114
Northcott Av. N22 1J 47
Nth. Countess Rd. E17 2B 50
North Ct. *BR1: Brom* 1K *159*
(off Palace Gro.)
SE24 3B 120
SW1 2E *18*
(off Gt. Peter St.)
W1 5B 6 (5G 83)
NORTH CRAY 5E 144
Nth. Cray Rd. DA5: Bexl 1H 145
DA14: Sidc 6E 144
North Cray Woods 4D 144
North Cres. E16 4F 87
N3 2H 45
WC1 5C 6 (5H 83)
Northcroft Ct. W12 2C 98
Northcroft Rd. KT19: Ewe 7A 164
W13 2B 96
North Crofts SE23 1H 139
Northcroft Ter. W13 2B 96
Nth. Cross Rd. IG6: Ilf 4G 53
SE22 5F 121
Northdale Ct. SE25 3F 157
North Dene NW7 3E 28
TW3: Houn 1F 113
Northdene Gdns. N15 6F 49
Northdown Cl. HA4: Ruis 3H 57
Northdown Gdns. IG2: Ilf 5J 53
Northdown Rd. DA16: Well 2B 126
Northdown St. N1 1G 7 (2J 83)
North Dr. BR3: Beck 4D 158
BR6: Orp 4J 173
HA4: Ruis 7G 39
SW16 4G 137
TW3: Houn 2G 113
North E. Surrey Crematorium
SM4: Mord 6E 152
NORTH END 2A 64
North End CR0: Croy 2C 168
(not continuous)
IG9: Buck H 1F 37
NW3 2A 64
Nth. End Av. NW3 2A 64
(not continuous)
Nth. End Cres. W14 4H 99
Nth. End Ho. W14 4G 99
Nth. End La. BR6: Downe 7F 173
Nth. End Pde. *W14* 4G *99*
(off Nth. End Rd.)
Nth. End Rd. HA9: Wemb 3G 61
Nth. End Rd. NW11 1J 63
Nth. End Rd. W14 4G 99
Nth. End Way NW3 2A 64
Northern Av. N9 2K 33
Northernhay Wlk. SM4: Mord 4G 153
Northern Hgts. *N8* 7H *47*
(off Crescent Rd.)
Northern Perimeter Rd.
TW6: H'row A 1D 110
Northern Perimeter Rd. W.
TW6: H'row A 1A 110
Northern Rd. E13 2K 87
Northesk Ho. *E1* 4H *85*
(off Tent St.)
Nth. Eyot Gdns. W6 5B 98
Northey St. E14 7A 86
NORTH FELTHAM 6K 111
Nth. Feltham Trad. Est. TW14: Felt 5K 111
Northfield Av. HA5: Pinn 4B 40
W5 1B 96
W13 1B 96
Northfield Cl. BR1: Brom 1C 160
UB3: Harl 3H 93
Northfield Cres. SM3: Cheam 4G 165
Northfield Gdns. RM9: Dag 4F 73
Northfield Ho. SE15 6G 103
Northfield Ind. Est. NW10 3G 79
Northfield Pde. UB3: Harl 3G 93
Northfield Pk. UB3: Harl 3H 93
Northfield Path RM9: Dag 4F 73
Northfield Rd. E6 7D 70
EN3: Pond E 5C 24
EN4: Cockf 3H 21
N16 7E 48
RM9: Dag 4F 73
TW5: Hest 6B 94
W13 2B 96
NORTHFIELDS 3B 96
Northfields SW18 4J 117
Northfields Ind. Est. HA0: Wemb 1G 79
Northfields Prospect Bus. Cen.
SW18 4J 117
Northfields Rd. W3 5H 79
NORTH FINCHLEY 5F 31
Northfleet Ho. *SE1* 6E *14*
(off Tennis St.)
Nth. Flock St. SE16 2G 103
Nth. Flower Wlk. W2 3A 10
North Gdn. E14 1B 104
North Gdns. SW19 7B 136
North Ga. NW8 1C 4
Northgate HA6: Nwood 1E 38
Northgate Bus. Cen. EN1: Enf 3C 24
Northgate Dr. NW9 6A 44
Northgate Ho. *E14* 7C *86*
(off E. India Dock Rd.)
Northgate Ind. Pk. RM5: Col R 1F 55
North Gates *N12* 1A *46*
(off Bow La.)
Nth. Glade, The DA5: Bexl 7F 127
Nth. Gower St. NW1 2B 6 (3G 83)
North Grn. NW9 7F 29
North Gro. N6 7E 46
N15 5D 48
NORTH HARROW 5F 41
Nth. Hatton Rd. TW6: H'row A 1F 111
North Hill N6 6D 46
Nth. Hill Av. N6 6E 46
NORTH HILLINGDON 7E 56
North Ho. SE8 5B 104
Nth. Hyde Gdns. UB3: Harl 4J 93
UB3: Hayes 3J 93
Nth. Hyde La. TW5: Hest 5C 94
UB2: S'hall 5B 94
Nth. Hyde Rd. UB3: Harl 3G 93
Northiam N12 4D 30
(not continuous)
WC1 2F *7*
(off Cromer St.)
Northiam St. E9 1H 85
Northington St. WC1 4H 7 (4K 83)
NORTH KENSINGTON 5F 81
North Kent Indoor Bowls Club 3H 109
Northlands Av. BR6: Orp 4J 173
Northlands St. SE5 2C 120
North La. TW11: Tedd 6K 131
Northleach Ct. *SE15* 6E *102*
(off Birdlip Cl.)
North Lodge *E16* 1K *105*
(off Wesley Av.)
EN5: New Bar 5F 21
Nth. Lodge Cl. SW15 5F 117

Nth. London Bus. Pk. N11 ... 2K 31
North Mall N9 ... 2C 34
(off Plevna Rd.)
SW18 ... 5K 117
(off Buckhold Rd.)
North M. WC1 ... 4H 7 (4K 83)
North Mt. N20 ... 2F 31
(off High Rd.)
Northolm HA8: Edg ... 4E 28
Northolme Gdns. HA8: Edg ... 1G 43
Northolme Ri. BR6: Orp ... 2J 173
Northolme Rd. N5 ... 4C 66
NORTHOLT ... 7E 58
Northolt N17 ... 2E 48
(off Griffin Rd.)
Northolt Av. HA4: Ruis ... 5K 57
Northolt Gdns. UB6: G'frd ... 5K 59
Northolt Rd. HA2: Harr ... 4F 59
TW6: H'row A ... 1A 110
Northolt Swimarama ... 6E 58
Northolt Trad. Est.
UB5: N'olt ... 7F 59
Northover BR1: Brom ... 3H 141
North Pde. HA8: Edg ... 2G 43
KT9: Chess ... 5F 163
UB1: S'hall ... 6E 76
(off North Rd.)
North Pk. SE9 ... 6D 124
North Pas. SW18 ... 5J 117
North Pl. CR4: Mitc ... 7D 136
TW11: Tedd ... 6K 131
North Point N8 ... 5K 47
Northpoint Cl. SM1: Sutt ... 3A 166
Northpoint Sq. NW1 ... 6H 65
Nth. Pole La. BR2: Kes ... 6H 171
Nth. Pole Rd. W10 ... 5E 80
Northport St. N1 ... 1D 84
North Ride W2 ... 3C 10 (7C 82)
North Ri. W2 ... 1D 10 (6C 82)
North Rd. BR1: Brom ... 1K 159
BR4: W W'ck ... 1D 170
DA17: Belv ... 3H 109
HA1: Harr ... 7A 42
HA8: Edg ... 1H 43
IG3: Ilf ... 2J 71
KT6: Surb ... 6D 150
N2 ... 2C 46
N6 ... 7E 46
N7 ... 6J 65
N9 ... 1C 34
RM6: Chad H ... 5E 54
SE18 ... 4J 107
SW19 ... 6A 136
TW5: Hest ... 6A 94
TW8: Bford ... 6E 96
TW9: Kew ... 1G 115
TW9: Rich ... 3G 115
TW14: Bedf ... 6F 111
UB1: S'hall ... 6E 76
UB3: Hayes ... 5F 75
UB7: W Dray ... 3B 92
W5 ... 3D 96
Northrop Rd. TW6: H'row A ... 1G 111
North Row W1 ... 2F 11 (7D 82)
Nth. Row Bldgs. W1 ... 2G 11
(off North Row)
North Several SE3 ... 2F 123
NORTH SHEEN ... 3G 115
Northside Rd. BR1: Brom ... 1J 159
Nth. Side Wandsworth Comn.
SW18 ... 5B 118
Northspur Rd. SM1: Sutt ... 3J 165
North Sq. N9 ... 2C 34
(off Hertford Rd.)
NW11 ... 5J 45
Northstead Rd. SW2 ... 2A 138
North St. BR1: Brom ... 1J 159
DA7: Bex ... 4G 127
E13 ... 2K 87
IG11: Bark ... 6F 71
NW4 ... 5E 44
North St. RM1: Rom ... 3K 55
(not continuous)
SM5: Cars ... 3D 166
SW4 ... 3G 119
TW7: Isle ... 3A 114
North St. Pas. E13 ... 2K 87
Nth. Tenter St. E1 ... 1K 15 (6F 85)
North Ter. SW3 ... 2C 16 (3C 100)
Northumberland All.
EC3 ... 1H 15 (6E 84)
(not continuous)
Northumberland Av. DA16: Well ... 4H 125
E12 ... 1A 70
EN1: Enf ... 1C 24
TW7: Isle ... 1K 113
WC2 ... 4E 12 (1J 101)
Northumberland Cl. DA8: Erith ... 7J 109
TW19: Stanw ... 6A 110
Northumberland Cres. TW14: Felt ... 6G 111
Northumberland Gdns. BR1: Brom ... 4E 160
CR4: Mitc ... 5H 155
N9 ... 3A 34
TW7: Isle ... 7A 96
Northumberland Gro. N17 ... 7C 34
NORTHUMBERLAND HEATH ... 7J 109
Northumberland Ho. IG8: Wfd G ... 7K 37
SW1 ... 4E 12
(off Northumberland Av.)
Northumberland Pk. DA8: Erith ... 7J 109
N17 ... 7A 34
Northumberland Pk. Ind. Est.
N17 ... 7C 34
Northumberland Pk. Sports Cen. ... 7B 34
Northumberland Pl. TW10: Rich ... 5D 114
W2 ... 6J 81
Northumberland Rd. E6 ... 6C 88
E17 ... 7C 50
EN5: New Bar ... 6F 21
HA2: Harr ... 5D 40
Northumberland Row TW2: Twick ... 1J 131
Northumberland St.
WC2 ... 4E 12 (1J 101)
Northumberland Way DA8: Erith ... 1J 127
Northumbria St. E14 ... 6C 86
Nth. Verbena Gdns. W6 ... 5C 98
North Vw. HA5: Eastc ... 7A 40
SW19 ... 5E 134
W5 ... 4C 78
Northview N7 ... 3J 65
North Vw. Cvn. Site IG6: Ilf ... 1A 54
Northview Cres. NW10 ... 4B 62
North Vw. Dr. IG8: Wfd G ... 2B 52
North Vw. Rd. N8 ... 4H 47
North Vs. NW1 ... 6H 65
North Wlk. CR0: New Ad ... 6D 170
(not continuous)
W8 ... 7K 81
(off Bayswater Rd.)
North Way HA5: Pinn ... 4B 40
N9 ... 2E 34
N11 ... 6B 32
NW9 ... 3H 43
UB10: Uxb ... 7A 56
Northway NW11 ... 5K 45
SM4: Mord ... 3G 153
SM6: Wall ... 4G 167
Northway Cir. NW7 ... 4E 28
Northway Ct. NW7 ... 4F 29
Northway Cres. NW7 ... 4E 28
Northway Gdns. NW11 ... 5K 45
Northway Rd. CR0: Croy ... 6F 157
SE5 ... 3C 120
Northways Pde. NW3 ... 7B 64
(off College Cres., not continuous)
Northweald La. KT2: King T ... 5D 132
NORTH WEMBLEY ... 3D 60
Nth. Western Commercial Cen.
NW1 ... 7J 65
Northwest Pl. N1 ... 2A 84
North Wharf E14 ... 1E 104
(off Coldharbour)
Nth. Wharf Rd. W2 ... 6A 4 (5B 82)
Northwick Av. HA3: Kent ... 6A 42
Northwick Circ. HA3: Kent ... 6C 42
Northwick Cl. HA1: Harr ... 1B 60
NW8 ... 3A 4 (4B 82)
Northwick Ho. NW8 ... 3A 4
Northwick Pk. Rd. HA1: Harr ... 6K 41
Northwick Rd. HA0: Wemb ... 1D 78
Northwick Ter. NW8 ... 3A 4 (4B 82)
Northwick Wlk. HA1: Harr ... 7K 41
Northwold Dr. HA5: Pinn ... 2A 40
Northwold Rd. E5 ... 2F 67
N16 ... 2F 67
NORTHWOOD ... 1H 39
Nth. Wood Ct. SE25 ... 3G 157
Northwood Est. E5 ... 2G 67
Northwood FC ... 2H 39
Northwood Gdns. IG5: Ilf ... 4E 52
N12 ... 5G 31
UB6: G'frd ... 5K 59
Northwood Hall N6 ... 7G 47
NORTHWOOD HILLS ... 2J 39
Northwood Hills Cir. HA6: Nwood ... 1J 39
Northwood Ho. SE27 ... 4D 138
Northwood Pl. DA18: Erith ... 3F 109
Northwood Rd. CR7: Thor H ... 2B 156
N6 ... 7F 47
SE23 ... 1B 140
SM5: Cars ... 6E 166
TW6: H'row A ... 1A 110
UB9: Hare ... 1A 38
Northwood Sports Cen. ... 1K 39
Northwood Way HA6: Nwood ... 1J 39
SE19 ... 6D 138
UB9: Hare ... 1A 38
NORTH WOOLWICH ... 2E 106
North Woolwich Old Station Mus. ... 2E 106
Nth. Woolwich Rd. E16 ... 1H 105
Nth. Worple Way SW14 ... 3K 115
Norton Av. KT5: Surb ... 7H 151
Norton Cl. E4 ... 5H 35
EN1: Enf ... 2C 24
Norton Ct. BR3: Beck ... 1B 158
Norton Folgate E1 ... 5H 9 (5E 84)
Norton Folgate Ho. E1 ... 5J 9
(off Puma Ct.)
Norton Gdns. SW16 ... 2J 155
Norton Ho. E1 ... 6H 85
(off Bigland St.)
E2 ... 2K 85
(off Mace St.)
SW1 ... 2D 18
(off Arneway St.)
SW9 ... 2K 119
(off Aytoun Rd.)
Norton Rd. E10 ... 1B 68
HA0: Wemb ... 6D 60
RM10: Dag ... 6K 73
Norval Rd. HA0: Wemb ... 2B 60
Norway Ga. SE16 ... 3A 104
Norway Pl. E14 ... 6B 86
Norway St. SE10 ... 6D 104
Norway Wharf E14 ... 6B 86
(off Norway Pl.)
Norwich Ho. E14 ... 6D 86
(off Cordelia St.)
Norwich M. IG3: Ilf ... 1A 72
Norwich Pl. DA6: Bex ... 4G 127
Norwich Rd. CR7: Thor H ... 3C 156
E7 ... 5J 69
HA6: Nwood ... 3H 39
RM9: Dag ... 2G 91
UB6: G'frd ... 1F 77
Norwich St. EC4 ... 7J 7 (6A 84)
Norwich Wlk. HA8: Edg ... 7D 28
NORWOOD ... 6E 138
Norwood Av. HA0: Wemb ... 1F 79
RM7: Rush G ... 7K 55
Norwood Cl. NW2 ... 3G 63
TW2: Twick ... 2H 131
UB2: S'hall ... 4E 94
Norwood Dr. HA2: Harr ... 6D 40
Norwood Gdns. UB2: S'hall ... 4D 94
UB4: Yead ... 4A 76
NORWOOD GREEN ... 4D 94
Norwood Grn. Rd. UB2: S'hall ... 4E 94
Norwood High St. SE27 ... 3B 138
Norwood Ho. E14 ... 7D 86
(off Poplar High St.)
NORWOOD NEW TOWN ... 6C 138
Norwood Pk. Rd. SE27 ... 5C 138
Norwood Rd. SE24 ... 1B 138
SE27 ... 2B 138
UB2: S'hall ... 3C 94
Norwood Ter. UB2: S'hall ... 4F 95
Nota M. N3 ... 1J 45
Notley St. SE5 ... 7D 102
Notson Rd. SE25 ... 4H 157
Notting Barn Rd.
W10 ... 4F 81
Nottingdale Sq. W11 ... 1G 99
Nottingham Av. E16 ... 5A 88
Nottingham Ct. WC2 ... 1E 12 (6J 83)
Nottingham Ho. WC2 ... 1E 12
(off Shorts Gdns.)
Nottingham Pl. W1 ... 4G 5 (5E 82)
Nottingham Rd.
CR2: S Croy ... 4C 168
E10 ... 6E 50
SW17 ... 1D 136
TW7: Isle ... 2K 113
Nottingham St. W1 ... 5G 5 (5E 82)
Nottingham Ter. NW1 ... 4G 5
NOTTING HILL ... 7H 81
Notting Hill Ga. W11 ... 1J 99
Nottingwood Ho. W11 ... 7G 81
(off Clarendon Rd.)
Nova Bldg. E14 ... 4C 104
Nova Ct. E. E14 ... 1E 104
(off Yabsley St.)
Nova Ct. W. E14 ... 1E 104
(off Yabsley St.)
Nova M. SM3: Sutt ... 1G 165
Novar Cl. BR6: Orp ... 7K 161
Nova Rd. CR0: Croy ... 1B 168
Novar Rd. SE9 ... 1G 143
Novello St. SW6 ... 1J 117
Novel Sq. SE10 ... 3H 105
(off School Bank Rd.)
Nowell Rd. SW13 ... 6C 98
Nower Ct. HA5: Pinn ... 4D 40
Nower Hill HA5: Pinn ... 4D 40
Noyna Rd. SW17 ... 3D 136
Nubia Way BR1: Brom ... 3G 141
Nuding Cl. SE13 ... 3C 122
Nuffield Ct. TW5: Hest ... 7D 94
Nuffield Lodge N6 ... 6G 47
W9 ... 5J 81
(off Admiral Wlk.)
Nugent Rd. N19 ... 1J 65
SE25 ... 3F 157
Nugents Ct. HA5: Pinn ... 1C 40
Nugent's Pk. HA5: H End ... 1C 40
Nugent Ter. NW8 ... 2A 82
Numa Ct. TW8: Bford ... 7D 96
Nun Ct. EC2 ... 7E 8
Nuneaton Rd. RM9: Dag ... 7E 72
NUNHEAD ... 3H 121
Nunhead Cres. SE15 ... 3H 121
Nunhead Est. SE15 ... 4H 121
Nunhead Grn. SE15 ... 3H 121
Nunhead Gro. SE15 ... 3H 121
Nunhead La. SE15 ... 3H 121
Nunhead Pas. SE15 ... 3G 121
Nunnington Cl. SE9 ... 3C 142
Nunns Rd. EN2: Enf ... 2H 23
Nupton Dr. EN5: Barn ... 6A 20
Nurse Cl. HA8: Edg ... 1J 43
Nursery App. N12 ... 6H 31
Nursery Av. CR0: Croy ... 2K 169
DA7: Bex ... 3F 127
N3 ... 2A 46

Orleston Rd.—Overton Cl.

Orleston Rd. N7 . . . 6A 66
Orley Ct. HA1: Harr . . . 4K 59
Orley Farm Rd. HA1: Harr . . . 3J 59
Orlop St. SE10 . . . 5G 105
Ormanton Rd. SE26 . . . 4G 139
Orme Ct. W2 . . . 7K 81
Orme Ct. M. *W2* . . . *7K 81*
(off Orme La.)
Orme Ho. E8 . . . 1F 85
Orme La. W2 . . . 7K 81
Ormeley Rd. SW12 . . . 1F 137
Orme Rd. KT1: King T . . . 2H 151
SM1: Sutt . . . 6K 165
Ormerod Gdns. CR4: Mitc . . . 2E 154
Ormesby Cl. SE28 . . . 7D 90
Ormesby Way HA3: Kent . . . 6F 43
Orme Sq. W2 . . . 7K 81
Ormiston Gro. W12 . . . 1D 98
Ormiston Rd. SE10 . . . 5J 105
Ormond Av. TW10: Rich . . . 5D 114
TW12: Hamp . . . 1F 149
Ormond Cl. WC1 . . . 5F 7 (5J 83)
Ormond Cres.
TW12: Hamp . . . 1F 149
Ormond Dr. TW12: Hamp . . . 7F 131
Ormonde Av. BR6: Farnb . . . 2G 173
Ormonde Ct. *NW8* . . . *1D 82*
(off St Edmund's Cl.)
SW15 . . . 4E 116
Ormonde Ga. SW3 . . . 6F 17 (5D 100)
Ormonde Pl. SW1 . . . 4G 17 (4E 100)
Ormonde Ri. IG9: Buck H . . . 1F 37
Ormonde Rd. SW14 . . . 3J 115
Ormonde Ter. NW8 . . . 1D 82
Ormond Ho. N16 . . . 2D 66
Ormond M. WC1 . . . 4F 7 (4J 83)
Ormond Rd. N19 . . . 1J 65
TW10: Rich . . . 5D 114
Ormond Yd. SW1 . . . 4B 12 (1G 101)
Ormsby SM2: Sutt . . . 7K 165
Ormsby Gdns. UB6: G'frd . . . 2G 77
Ormsby Lodge W4 . . . 3A 98
Ormsby Pl. N16 . . . 3F 67
Ormsby St. E2 . . . 2F 85
Ormside St. SE15 . . . 6J 103
Ornan Rd. NW3 . . . 5C 64
Orpen Wlk. N16 . . . 3E 66
Orpheus St. SE5 . . . 1D 120
ORPINGTON . . . 2J 173
Orpington Gdns. N18 . . . 3K 33
Orpington Mans. N21 . . . 1G 33
Orpington Rd. BR7: Chst . . . 3J 161
N21 . . . 1G 33
Orpwood Cl. TW12: Hamp . . . 6D 130
Orsett M. W2 . . . 6K 81
(not continuous)
Orsett St. SE11 . . . 5H 19 (5K 101)
Orsett Ter. IG8: Wfd G . . . 7F 37
W2 . . . 6K 81
Orsman Rd. N1 . . . 1E 84
Orton St. E1 . . . 1G 103
Orville Rd. SW11 . . . 2B 118
Orwell Cl. RM13: Rain . . . 5K 91
UB3: Hayes . . . 7G 75
Orwell Ct. *E8* . . . *1G 85*
(off Pownall Rd.)
N5 . . . 4C 66
Orwell Rd. E13 . . . 2A 88
Osbaldeston Rd. N16 . . . 2G 67
Osberton Rd. SE12 . . . 5J 123
Osbert St. SW1 . . . 4C 18 (4H 101)
Osborn Cl. E8 . . . 1G 85
Osborne Av. TW19: Stanw . . . 1A 128
Osborne Cl. BR3: Beck . . . 4A 158
EN4: Cockf . . . 3J 21
TW13: Hanw . . . 5B 130
Osborne Ct. E10 . . . 7D 50
W5 . . . 5E 78
Osborne Gdns. CR7: Thor H . . . 2C 156
Osborne Gro. E17 . . . 4B 50
N4 . . . 1A 66
Osborne Ho. *E16* . . . *1J 105*
(off Wesley Av.)
Osborne M. E17 . . . 4B 50
Osborne Pl. SM1: Sutt . . . 5B 166
Osborne Rd. CR7: Thor H . . . 2C 156
DA17: Belv . . . 5F 109
E7 . . . 5K 69
E9 . . . 6B 68
E10 . . . 2D 68
EN3: Enf H . . . 2F 25
IG9: Buck H . . . 1E 36
KT2: King T . . . 7E 132
KT12: Walt T . . . 7J 147
N4 . . . 1A 66
N13 . . . 3F 33
NW2 . . . 6D 62
RM9: Dag . . . 5F 73
TW3: Houn . . . 3D 112
UB1: S'hall . . . 6G 77
W3 . . . 3H 97
Osborne Sq. RM9: Dag . . . 4F 73
Osborne Ter. *SW17* . . . *5D 136*
(off Church La.)
Osborne Way *KT9: Chess* . . . *5F 163*
(off Bridge Rd.)
Osborn Gdns. NW7 . . . 7A 30
Osborn La. SE23 . . . 7A 122
Osborn St. E1 . . . 6K 9 (5F 85)
Osborn Ter. SE3 . . . 4H 123
Osbourne Ct. HA2: Harr . . . 4F 41
Osbourne Ho. IG8: Wfd G . . . 7K 37
TW2: Twick . . . 2G 131
Oscar Faber Pl. N1 . . . 7E 66
Oscar St. SE8 . . . 2C 122
(Lewisham Way)
SE8 . . . 1C 122
(Thornville St.)
Oseney Cres. NW5 . . . 5G 65
Osgood Av. BR6: Chels . . . 5K 173
Osgood Gdns. BR6: Chels . . . 5K 173
O'Shea Gro. E3 . . . 1B 86
OSIDGE . . . 1A 32
Osidge La. N14 . . . 1K 31
Osier Ct. *E1* . . . *4K 85*
(off Osier St.)
RM7: Rom . . . 6K 55
TW8: Bford . . . *6E 96*
(off Ealing Rd.)
Osier Cres. N10 . . . 1D 46
Osier La. *SE10* . . . *3H 105*
(off School Bank Rd.)
Osier M. W4 . . . 6A 98
Osiers Ct. *KT1: King T* . . . *1D 150*
(off Steadfast Rd.)
Osiers Est., The SW18 . . . 4J 117
Osiers Rd. SW18 . . . 4J 117
Osier St. E1 . . . 4J 85
Osier Way CR4: Mitc . . . 5D 154
E10 . . . 3D 68
Oslac Rd. SE6 . . . 5D 140
Oslo Ct. *NW8* . . . *2C 82*
(off Prince Albert Rd.)
Oslo Ho. *SE5* . . . *2C 120*
(off Carew St.)
Oslo Sq. SE16 . . . 3A 104
Osman Cl. N15 . . . 6D 48
Osmani School Sports Cen. . . . 5G 85
Osman Rd. N9 . . . 3B 34
W6 . . . 3E 98
Osmington Ho. *SW8* . . . *7K 101*
(off Dorset Rd.)
Osmond Cl. HA2: Harr . . . 2G 59
Osmond Gdns. SM6: Wall . . . 5G 167
Osmund St. W12 . . . 5B 80
Osnaburgh St. NW1 . . . 4K 5 (4F 83)
(Longford St.)
NW1 . . . 2K 5
(Robert St.)
Osnaburgh Ter. NW1 . . . 3K 5 (4F 83)
Osney Ho. SE2 . . . 2D 108
Osney Wlk. SM5: Cars . . . 6B 154
Osprey NW9 . . . 1B 44
Osprey Cl. BR2: Brom . . . 1C 172
E6 . . . 5C 88
E11 . . . 4J 51
E17 . . . 7F 35
SM1: Sutt . . . 5H 165
UB7: W Dray . . . 2A 92
Osprey Ct. BR3: Beck . . . 7C 140
E1 . . . 3K 15
Osprey Est. SE16 . . . 4A 104
Osprey Ho. *E14* . . . *7A 86*
(off Victory Pl.)
Osprey M. EN3: Pond E . . . 5D 24
Ospringe Cl. SE20 . . . 7J 139
Ospringe Ct. SE9 . . . 6H 125
Ospringe Ho. *SE1* . . . *6K 13*
(off Wootton St.)
Ospringe Rd. NW5 . . . 4G 65
Osram Ct. W6 . . . 3E 98
Osram Rd. HA9: Wemb . . . 3D 60
Osric Path N1 . . . 2E 84
Ossian M. N4 . . . 7K 47
Ossian Rd. N4 . . . 7K 47
Ossie Garvin Rdbt. UB4: Yead . . . 7K 75
Ossington Bldgs. W1 . . . 5G 5 (5E 82)
Ossington Cl. W2 . . . 7J 81
Ossington St. W2 . . . 7J 81
Ossory Rd. SE1 . . . 6G 103
Ossulston St. NW1 . . . 1D 6 (2H 83)
Ossulton Pl. N2 . . . 3A 46
Ossulton Way N2 . . . 4A 46
Ostade Rd. SW2 . . . 7K 119
Ostell Cres. EN3: Enf L . . . 1H 25
Ostend Pl. SE1 . . . 4C 102
Osten M. SW7 . . . 3K 99
OSTERLEY . . . 7H 95
Osterley Av. TW7: Isle . . . 7H 95
Osterley Cl. BR5: St P . . . 1K 161
Osterley Ct. TW7: Isle . . . 1H 113
UB5: Yead . . . *3A 76*
(off Canberra Dr.)
Osterley Cres. TW7: Isle . . . 1J 113
Osterley Gdns. CR7: Thor H . . . 2C 156
UB2: S'hall . . . 2G 95
Osterley Ho. *E14* . . . *6D 86*
(off Giraud St.)
Osterley La. TW7: Isle . . . 4G 95
UB2: S'hall . . . 5E 94
(not continuous)
Osterley Lodge *TW7: Isle* . . . *7J 95*
(off Church Rd.)
Osterley Pk. . . . 6G 95
Osterley Pk. House (NT) . . . 6G 95
Osterley Pk. Rd. UB2: S'hall . . . 3D 94
Osterley Pk. Vw. Rd. W7 . . . 2J 95
Osterley Rd. N16 . . . 4E 66
TW7: Isle . . . 7J 95
Osterley Sports Club . . . 3G 95
Osterley Views UB2: S'hall . . . 1G 95
Oster Ter. E17 . . . 5K 49
Ostlers Dr. TW15: Ashf . . . 5E 128
Ostliffe Rd. N13 . . . 5H 33
Oswald Bldg. SW8 . . . 6F 101
Oswald Rd. UB1: S'hall . . . 1C 94
Oswald's Mead E9 . . . 4A 68
Oswald St. E5 . . . 3K 67
Oswald Ter. NW2 . . . 3E 62
Osward Pl. N9 . . . 2C 34
Osward Rd. SW17 . . . 2D 136
Oswell Ho. *E1* . . . *1H 103*
(off Farthing Flds.)
Oswin St. SE11 . . . 4B 102
Oswyth Rd. SE5 . . . 2E 120
Otford Cl. BR1: Brom . . . 3E 160
DA5: Bexl . . . 6H 127
SE20 . . . 1J 157
Otford Cres. SE4 . . . 6B 122
Otford Ho. *SE1* . . . *7F 15*
(off Staple St.)
SE15 . . . *6J 103*
(off Lovelinch Cl.)
Othello Cl. SE11 . . . 5K 19 (5B 102)
Other Cinema, The . . . *2C 12*
(off Rupert St.)
Otho Ct. TW8: Bford . . . 7D 96
Otis St. E3 . . . 3E 86
Otley App. IG2: Ilf . . . 6F 53
Otley Dr. IG2: Ilf . . . 5F 53
Otley Ho. N5 . . . 3A 66
Otley Rd. E16 . . . 6A 88
Otley Ter. E5 . . . 3K 67
Ottawa Gdns. RM10: Dag . . . 7K 73
Ottaway Ct. E5 . . . 3G 67
Ottaway St. E5 . . . 3G 67
Otterbourne Rd.
CR0: Croy . . . 2C 168
E4 . . . 3A 36
Otterburn Gdns. TW7: Isle . . . 7A 96
Otterburn Ho. *SE5* . . . *7C 102*
(off Sultan St.)
Otterburn St. SW17 . . . 6D 136
Otter Cl. E15 . . . 1E 86
Otterden Cl. BR6: Orp . . . 3J 173
Otterden St. SE6 . . . 4C 140
Otterfield Rd. UB7: Yiew . . . 7A 74
Otter Rd. UB6: G'frd . . . 4G 77
Otto Cl. SE26 . . . 3H 139
Otto St. SE17 . . . 6B 102
Otway Gdns. WD23: Bush . . . 1D 26
Oulton Cl. E5 . . . 2J 67
SE28 . . . 6C 90
Oulton Cres. IG11: Bark . . . 5K 71
Oulton Rd. N15 . . . 5D 48
Ouseley Rd. SW12 . . . 1D 136
Outer Circ. NW1 . . . 1D 4 & 1J 5 (2C 82)
Outgate Rd. NW10 . . . 7B 62
Outram Pl. N1 . . . 1J 83
Outram Rd. CR0: Croy . . . 2F 169
E6 . . . 1C 88
N22 . . . 1H 47
Outwich St. EC3 . . . 7H 9
Outwood Ho. *SW2* . . . *7K 119*
(off Deepdene Gdns.)
Oval, The DA15: Sidc . . . 7A 126
E2 . . . 2H 85
Oval Ct. HA8: Edg . . . 7D 28
Oval Cricket Ground, The . . . 7H 19 (6K 101)
Oval Ho. *CR0: Croy* . . . *1E 168*
(off Oval Rd.)
Oval House Theatre . . . 7J 19
Oval Mans. SE11 . . . 7H 19 (6K 101)
Oval Pl. SW8 . . . 7K 101
Oval Rd. CR0: Croy . . . 2D 168
NW1 . . . 1F 83
Oval Rd. Nth. RM10: Dag . . . 1H 91
Oval Rd. Sth. RM10: Dag . . . 2H 91
Oval Way SE11 . . . 6H 19 (5K 101)
Overbrae BR3: Beck . . . 6C 140
Overbrook Wlk. HA8: Edg . . . 7B 28
(not continuous)
Overbury Av. BR3: Beck . . . 3D 158
Overbury Rd. N15 . . . 6D 48
Overbury St. E5 . . . 4K 67
Overcliff Rd. SE13 . . . 3C 122
Overcourt Cl. DA15: Sidc . . . 6B 126
Overdale Av. KT3: N Mald . . . 2J 151
Overdale Rd. W5 . . . 3C 96
Overdown Rd. SE6 . . . 4C 140
Overhill Rd. SE22 . . . 7G 121
Overhill Way BR3: Beck . . . 5F 159
Overlea Rd. E5 . . . 7G 49
Overmead DA15: Sidc . . . 7H 125
Oversley Ho. *W2* . . . *5J 81*
(off Alfred Rd.)
Overstand Cl. BR3: Beck . . . 5C 158
Overstone Gdns. CR0: Croy . . . 7B 158
Overstone Ho. *E14* . . . *6C 86*
(off E. India Dock Rd.)
Overstone Rd. W6 . . . 3E 98
Overstrand Mans. SW11 . . . 1D 118
Overton Cl. NW10 . . . 6J 61
TW7: Isle . . . 1K 113

Palace Theatre 1D 12
(off Shaftesbury Av.)
Palace Vw. BR1: Brom 3K **159**
(not continuous)
CR0: Croy 4B **170**
SE12 . . . . . 2J **141**
Palace Vw. Rd. E4 . . . . . 5J **35**
Palace Wharf *W6* *7E 98*
(off Rainville Rd.)
Palamon Ct. *SE1* *5F 103*
(off Cooper's Rd.)
Palamos Rd. E10 . . . . . 1C **68**
Palatine Av. N16 . . . . . 4E **66**
Palatine Rd. N16 . . . . . 4E **66**
Palemead Cl. SW6 . . . . . 1F **117**
Palermo Rd. NW10 . . . . . 2C **80**
Palestine Gro. SW19 . . . . . 1B **154**
Palewell Comn. Dr. SW14 . . . . . 5K **115**
Palewell Pk. SW14 . . . . . 5K **115**
Palfrey Pl. SW8 . . . . . 7K **101**
Palgrave Av. UB1: S'hall 7E **76**
Palgrave Gdns. NW1 . . . . . 3D **4** (4C **82**)
Palgrave Ho. *SE5* *7C 102*
(off Wyndham Est.)
TW2: Whit 7G **113**
Palgrave Rd. W12 . . . . . 3B **98**
Palissy St. E2 . . . . . 2J **9** (3F **85**)
(not continuous)
Palladino Ho. *SW17* *5C 136*
(off Laurel Cl.)
Palladium Ct. *E8* *7F 67*
(off Queensbridge Rd.)
Pallant Ho. *SE1* *3D 102*
(off Tabard St.)
Pallant Way BR6: Farnb 3E **172**
Pallett Way SE18 . . . . . 1C **124**
Palliser Ct. *W14* *5G 99*
(off Palliser Rd.)
Palliser Ho. *E1* *4K 85*
(off Ernest St.)
SE10 . . . . . *6F 105*
(off Trafalgar Rd.)
Palliser Rd. W14 . . . . . 5G **99**
Pall Mall SW1 . . . . . 5B **12** (1G **101**)
Pall Mall E. SW1 . . . . . 4D **12** (1H **101**)
Pall Mall Pl. SW1 . . . . . 5B **12**
Palmar Cres. DA7: Bex 3G **127**
Palmar Rd. DA7: Bex 2G **127**
Palm Av. DA14: Sidc 6D **144**
Palm Cl. E10 . . . . . 3D **68**
Palm Ct. *SE15* *7F 103*
(off Garnies Cl.)
Palmeira Rd. DA7: Bex 3D **126**
Palmer Av. SM3: Cheam 4E **164**
Palmer Cl. BR4: W W'ck 3F **171**
TW5: Hest 1E **112**
UB5: N'olt 6C **58**
Palmer Cres. KT1: King T 3E **150**
Palmer Gdns. EN5: Barn 5A **20**
Palmer Pl. N7 . . . . . 5A **66**
Palmer Rd. E13 . . . . . 4K **87**
RM8: Dag 1D **72**
Palmer's Ct. *N11* *5B 32*
(off Palmer's Rd.)
PALMERS GREEN 3F **33**
Palmers Gro. KT8: W Mole 4E **148**
Palmers La. EN1: Enf 1C **24**
EN3: Enf H 1C **24**
Palmers Pas. *SW14* *3J 115*
(off Palmers Rd.)
Palmers Rd. E2 . . . . . 2K **85**
N11 . . . . . 5B **32**
SW14 . . . . . 3J **115**
SW16 . . . . . 2K **155**
Palmerston Cen. HA3: W'stone 3K **41**
Palmerston Ct. *E3* *2K 85*
(off Old Ford Rd.)
IG9: Buck H 1F **37**
KT6: Surb 7D **150**
Palmerston Cres. N13 . . . . . 5E **32**
SE18 . . . . . 6G **107**
Palmerston Gro. SW19 . . . . . 7J **135**
Palmerston Ho.
SE1 . . . . . *7J 13*
(off Westminster Bri. Rd.)
W8 . . . . . *1J 99*
(off Kensington Pl.)
Palmerston Mans. *W14* *6G 99*
(off Queen's Club Gdns.)
Palmerston Rd.
BR6: Farnb 4G **173**
CR0: Croy 5D **156**
E7 . . . . . 6K **69**
(not continuous)
E17 . . . . . 3B **50**
HA3: W'stone 3J **41**
IG9: Buck H 2E **36**
N22 . . . . . 7E **32**
NW6 . . . . . 7H **63**
(not continuous)
SM1: Sutt 5A **166**
SM5: Cars 4D **166**
SW14 . . . . . 4J **115**
SW19 . . . . . 7J **135**
TW2: Twick 6J **113**
TW3: Houn 1G **113**
W3 . . . . . 3J **97**
Palmerston Way SW8 . . . . . 7F **101**
Palmer St. SW1 . . . . . 1C **18** (3H **101**)
(not continuous)
Palm Gro. W5 . . . . . 3E **96**
Palm Rd. RM7: Rom 5J **55**
Palm Tree Ho. *SE14* *7K 103*
(off Barlborough St.)
Pamela Ct. N3 . . . . . 6E **30**
Pamela Gdns. HA5: Eastc 5K **39**
Pamela Ho. *E8* *1F 85*
(off Haggerston Rd.)
Pampisford Rd. CR8: Purl 7B **168**
Pams Way KT19: Ewe 5K **163**
Panama Ho. *E1* *5K 85*
(off Beaumont Sq.)
Pancras La. EC4 . . . . . 1E **14** (6C **84**)
Pancras Rd. NW1 . . . . . 1E **6** (2H **83**)
Pandian Way NW5 . . . . . 6H **65**
Pandora Rd. NW6 . . . . . 6J **63**
Panfield M. IG2: Ilf 6E **52**
Panfield Rd. SE2 . . . . . 3A **108**
Pangbourne *NW1* *2A 6*
(off Stanhope St.)
Pangbourne Av. W10 . . . . . 5E **80**
Pangbourne Dr. HA7: Stan 5J **27**
Panhard Pl. UB1: S'hall 7F **77**
Pank Av. EN5: New Bar 5F **21**
Pankhurst Av. E16 . . . . . 1K **105**
Pankhurst Cl. SE14 . . . . . 7K **103**
TW7: Isle 3K **113**
Pankhurst Rd. KT12: Walt T 7A **148**
Panmuir Rd. SW20 . . . . . 1D **152**
Panmure Cl. N5 . . . . . 4B **66**
Panmure Ct. *UB1: S'hall* *6G 77*
(off Osborne Rd.)
Panmure Rd. SE26 . . . . . 3H **139**
Panorama Ct. N6 . . . . . 6G **47**
Pansy Gdns. W12 . . . . . 7C **80**
Panther Dr. NW10 . . . . . 5K **61**
Pantiles, The BR1: Brom 3C **160**
DA7: Bex 7F **109**
NW11 . . . . . 5H **45**
WD23: Bushy 1C **26**
Pantiles Cl. N13 . . . . . 5G **33**
Panton St. SW1 . . . . . 3C **12** (7H **83**)
Paper Bldgs. EC4 . . . . . 2K **13**
Papermill Cl. SM5: Cars 4E **166**
Papillons Wlk. SE3 . . . . . 2J **123**
Papworth Gdns. N7 . . . . . 5K **65**
Papworth Way SW2 . . . . . 7A **120**
Parade, The CR0: Croy 6J **155**
KT2: King T *2E 150*
(off London Rd.)
KT4: Wor Pk 4B **164**
N4 . . . . . 1A **66**
Parade, The *SE4* *2B 122*
(off Up. Brockley Rd.)
SE26 . . . . . *3H 139*
(off Wells Pk. Rd.)
SM1: Sutt 3H **165**
SM5: Cars *5D 166*
(off Beynon Rd.)
SW11 . . . . . 7D **100**
TW12: Tedd 5H **131**
TW16: Sun 7H **129**
UB6: G'frd 5B **60**
Parade Mans. NW4 . . . . . 5D **44**
Parade M. SE27 . . . . . 2B **138**
Paradise Pas. N7 . . . . . 5A **66**
Paradise Path SE28 . . . . . 1A **108**
Paradise Pl. SE18 . . . . . 4C **106**
Paradise Rd. SW4 . . . . . 2J **119**
TW9: Rich 5D **114**
Paradise Row E2 . . . . . 3H **85**
Paradise St. SE16 . . . . . 2H **103**
Paradise Wlk. SW3 . . . . . 7F **17** (6D **100**)
Paragon, The SE3 . . . . . 2H **123**
Paragon Cl. E16 . . . . . 6J **87**
Paragon Gro. KT5: Surb 6F **151**
Paragon M. SE1 . . . . . 4D **102**
Paragon Pl. KT5: Surb 6F **151**
SE3 . . . . . 2H **123**
Paragon Rd. E9 . . . . . 6J **67**
Paramount Bldg. *EC1* *3A 8*
(off St John St.)
Paramount Ct. WC1 . . . . . 4B **6**
Parbury Ri. KT9: Chess 6E **162**
Parbury Rd. SE23 . . . . . 6A **122**
Parchmore Rd. CR7: Thor H 2B **156**
Parchmore Way CR7: Thor H 2B **156**
Pardoner Ho. *SE1* *3D 102*
(off Pardoner St.)
Pardoner St. SE1 . . . . . 3D **102**
(not continuous)
Pardon St. EC1 . . . . . 3B **8** (4B **84**)
Parent Shop. Mall *E18* *2J 51*
(off Marlborough Rd.)
Parfett St. E1 . . . . . 5G **85**
(not continuous)
Parfitt Cl. NW3 . . . . . 1A **64**
Parfrey St. W6 . . . . . 6E **98**
Pargreaves Ct. HA9: Wemb 2G **61**
Parham Dr. IG2: Ilf 6F **53**
Parham Way N10 . . . . . 2G **47**
Paris Gdn. SE1 . . . . . 4A **14** (1B **102**)
Parish Ct. KT6: Surb 5E **150**
Parish Ga. Dr. DA15: Sidc 6J **125**
Parish La. SE20 . . . . . 6K **139**
Parish M. SE20 . . . . . 7K **139**
Paris Ho. *E2* *2H 85*
(off Old Bethnal Grn. Rd.)
Parish Wharf Pl. SE18 . . . . . 4C **106**
Park, The DA14: Sidc 5A **144**
N6 . . . . . 6E **46**
NW11 . . . . . 1K **63**
SE23 . . . . . 1J **139**
SM5: Cars 5D **166**
W5 . . . . . 1D **96**
Park App. DA16: Well 4B **126**
SE16 . . . . . 3H **103**
Park Av. BR1: Brom 7H **141**
BR4: W W'ck 2E **170**
BR6: Chels 2K **173**
BR6: Farnb 3D **172**
CR4: Mitc 7F **137**
E6 . . . . . 1E **88**
E15 . . . . . 6G **69**
EN1: Enf 5J **23**
HA4: Ruis 6F **39**
IG1: Ilf 1E **70**
IG8: Wfd G 5E **36**
IG11: Bark 6G **71**
N3 . . . . . 1K **45**
N13 . . . . . 3F **33**
N18 . . . . . 4B **34**
N22 . . . . . 2J **47**
Park Av. NW2 . . . . . 5D **62**
NW10 . . . . . 2F **79**
(Alperton, not continuous)
NW10 . . . . . 5D **62**
(Dudden Hill)
NW11 . . . . . 1K **63**
SM5: Cars 6E **166**
SW14 . . . . . 4K **115**
TW3: Houn 6F **113**
TW17: Shep 3G **147**
UB1: S'hall 2D **94**
Park Av. E. KT17: Ewe 6C **164**
Park Av. M. CR4: Mitc 7F **137**
Park Av. Nth. N8 . . . . . 3H **47**
NW10 . . . . . 5D **62**
Park Av. Rd. N17 . . . . . 7C **34**
Park Av. Sth. N8 . . . . . 4H **47**
Park Av. W. KT17: Ewe 6C **164**
Park Bus. Cen. NW6 . . . . . 3J **81**
Park Chase HA9: Wemb 4F **61**
Park Cl. E9 . . . . . 1J **85**
HA3: Hrw W 1J **41**
KT2: King T 1G **151**
N12 . . . . . 3G **31**
NW2 . . . . . 3D **62**
NW10 . . . . . 3F **79**
SM5: Cars 6D **166**
SW1 . . . . . 7E **10** (2D **100**)
TW3: Houn 5G **113**
TW12: Hamp 1G **149**
W4 . . . . . 6K **97**
W14 . . . . . 3H **99**
Park Club, The 1A 98
Park Ct. *CR2: S Croy* *5C 168*
(off Warham Rd.)
E4 . . . . . 2K **35**
E17 . . . . . 5D **50**
HA3: Kent 7E **42**
HA9: Wemb 5E **60**
KT1: Hamp W 1C **150**
KT3: N Mald 4K **151**
N11 . . . . . 7C **32**
N17 . . . . . 7B **34**
SE26 . . . . . 6H **139**
SM6: Wall 5J **167**
SW11 . . . . . 1F **119**
UB8: Uxb 1A **74**
W6 . . . . . 4C **98**
Park Cres. DA8: Erith 6J **109**
EN2: Enf 4J **23**
HA3: Hrw W 1J **41**
N3 . . . . . 7F **31**
TW2: Twick 1H **131**
W1 . . . . . 4J **5** (4F **83**)
Park Cres. M. E. W1 . . . . . 4K **5** (4F **83**)
Park Cres. M. W. W1 . . . . . 4J **5** (4F **83**)
Park Cres. Rd. DA8: Erith 6K **109**
Park Cft. HA8: Edg 1J **43**
Parkcroft Rd. SE12 . . . . . 7H **123**
Parkdale N11 . . . . . 6C **32**
Parkdale Cres. KT4: Wor Pk 3K **163**
Parkdale Rd. SE18 . . . . . 5J **107**
Park Dr. HA2: Harr 7E **40**
HA3: Hrw W 6C **26**
N21 . . . . . 6H **23**
NW11 . . . . . 1K **63**
RM1: Rom 4K **55**
RM10: Dag 3J **73**
SE7 . . . . . 6C **106**
SW14 . . . . . 5K **115**
W3 . . . . . 3G **97**
Park Dwellings NW3 . . . . . 5D **64**
Park End BR1: Brom 1H **159**
NW3 . . . . . 4C **64**
Parker Cl. E16 . . . . . 1C **106**
SM5: Cars 6D **166**
Parker Ho. *E14* *2C 104*
(off Admirals Way)
Parker M. WC2 . . . . . 7F **7** (6J **83**)
Parke Rd. SW13 . . . . . 1C **116**
TW16: Sun 4J **147**

Parker Rd.—Park Towers

Parker Rd. CR0: Croy 4C 168
Parkers Row SE1 . . . . 7K 15 (2G 103)
Parker St. E16 . . . . 1C 106
WC2 . . . . 7F 7 (6J 83)
Park Farm Cl. HA5: Eastc 5K 39
N2 . . . . 3A 46
Park Farm Ct. UB3: Hayes 7G 75
Park Farm Rd. BR1: Brom 1B 160
KT2: King T 7E 132
Parkfield TW7: Isle 1J 113
Parkfield Av. HA2: Harr 2G 41
SW14 . . . . 4A 116
TW13: Felt 3J 129
UB5: N'olt 2B 76
UB10: Hil 3D 74
Parkfield Cl. HA8: Edg 6C 28
UB5: N'olt 2C 76
Parkfield Ct. SE14 . . . . 1B 122
(off Parkfield Rd.)
Parkfield Cres. HA2: Harr 2G 41
HA4: Ruis 2C 58
TW13: Felt 3J 129
Parkfield Dr. UB5: N'olt 2B 76
Parkfield Gdns. HA2: Harr 3F 41
Parkfield Ho. HA2: Harr 1F 41
Parkfield Ind. Est. SW11 . . . . 2E 118
Parkfield Pde. TW13: Felt 3J 129
Parkfield Rd. HA2: Harr 3G 59
NW10 . . . . 7D 62
SE14 . . . . 1B 122
TW13: Felt 3J 129
UB5: N'olt 2C 76
UB10: Ick 2D 56
Parkfields CR0: Croy 1B 170
SW15 . . . . 4E 116
Parkfields Av. NW9 . . . . 1K 61
SW20 . . . . 1D 152
Parkfields Cl. SM5: Cars 4E 166
Parkfields Rd. KT2: King T 5F 133
Parkfield St. N1 . . . . 2A 84
Parkfield Way BR2: Brom 6D 160
Park Gdns. DA8: Erith 4K 109
E10 . . . . 1C 68
KT2: King T 5F 133
NW9 . . . . 3H 43
Park Ga. N2 . . . . 3B 46
N21 . . . . 7E 22
SE3 . . . . 3H 123
W5 . . . . 5D 78
Parkgate Av. EN4: Had W 1F 21
Park Ga. Cl. KT2: King T 6H 133
Park Ga. Ct. TW12: Hamp H 6G 131
Parkgate Cres. EN4: Had W 1F 21
Parkgate Gdns. SW14 . . . . 5K 115
Parkgate M. N6 . . . . 7G 47
Parkgate Rd. SM6: Wall 5E 166
SW11 . . . . 7C 100
Park Gates HA2: Harr 4E 58
Park Gro. BR1: Brom 1K 159
DA7: Bex 4J 127
E15 . . . . 1J 87
HA8: Edg 5A 28
N11 . . . . 7C 32
Park Gro. Rd. E11 . . . . 2G 69
Park Hall SE10 . . . . 7F 105
(off Crooms Hill)
Park Hall Rd. SE21 . . . . 3C 138
Parkhall Rd. N2 . . . . 4C 46
Park Hall Trad. Est. SE21 . . . . 3C 138
Parkham Ct. BR2: Brom 2G 159
Parkham St. SW11 . . . . 1C 118
Park Hill BR1: Brom 4C 160
SE23 . . . . 2H 139
SM5: Cars 6C 166
SW4 . . . . 5H 119
TW10: Rich 6F 115
W5 . . . . 5D 78
Park Hill Cl. SM5: Cars 5C 166
Park Hill Ct. SW17 . . . . 3D 136
Park Hill M. CR2: S Croy 5D 168
Park Hill Ri. CR0: Croy 2E 168
Park Hill Rd. BR2: Brom 2G 159
CR0: Croy 2E 168
DA15: Sidc 3J 143
SM6: Wall 7F 167
Parkhill Rd. DA5: Bexl 7F 127
E4 . . . . 1K 35
NW3 . . . . 5D 64
Parkhill Wlk. NW3 . . . . 5D 64
Parkholme Rd. E8 . . . . 6F 67
Park Ho. E9 . . . . 7J 67
(off Shore Rd.)
N21 . . . . 7E 22
Park Ho. Gdns.
TW1: Twick 5C 114
Park Ho. Pas. N6 . . . . 7E 46
Parkhouse St. SE5 . . . . 7D 102
Parkhurst Ct. N7 . . . . 4J 65
Parkhurst Gdns. DA5: Bexl 7G 127
Parkhurst Rd. DA5: Bexl 7G 127
E12 . . . . 4E 70
E17 . . . . 4A 50
N7 . . . . 4J 65
N11 . . . . 5K 31
N17 . . . . 2G 49
N22 . . . . 6E 32
SM1: Sutt 4B 166
Parkinson Ho. E9 . . . . 7J 67
(off Frampton Pk. Rd.)
SW1 . . . . 5C 18
(off Tachbrook St.)
Parkland Ct. E15 . . . . 5G 69
(off Maryland Pk.)
Parkland Gdns. SW19 . . . . 1F 135
Parkland Gro. TW15: Ashf 4C 128
Parkland Rd. IG8: Wfd G 7E 36
N22 . . . . 2K 47
TW15: Ashf 4C 128
Parklands KT5: Surb 5F 151
N6 . . . . 7F 47
Parklands Cl. EN4: Had W 1G 21
IG2: Ilf 7G 53
SW14 . . . . 5J 115
Parklands Ct. TW5: Hest 2B 112
Parklands Dr. N3 . . . . 3G 45
Parklands Gro. TW7: Isle 1K 113
Parklands Pde. TW5: Hest 2B 112
Parklands Rd. SW16 . . . . 5F 137
Parklands Way KT4: Wor Pk 2A 164
Park La. CR0: Croy 3D 168
E15 . . . . 1F 87
HA2: Harr 3F 59
HA7: Stan 3F 27
HA9: Wemb 5E 60
N9 . . . . 3K 33
N17 . . . . 7A 34
(not continuous)
RM6: Chad H 6D 54
SM3: Cheam 6G 165
SM5: Cars 4E 166
SM6: Wall 5E 166
TW5: Cran 7J 93
TW9: Rich 4D 114
TW11: Tedd 6K 131
UB4: Hayes 5G 75
W1 . . . . 2F 11 (7D 82)
Park La. Cl. N17 . . . . 7B 34
Park La. Mans. CR0: Croy 3D 168
(off Edridge Rd.)
PARK LANGLEY 4E 158
Parklea Cl. NW9 . . . . 1A 44
Park Lee Ct. N16 . . . . 7E 48
Parkleigh Rd. SW19 . . . . 2K 153
Parkleys TW10: Ham 4D 132
Parkleys Pde. TW10: King T 4D 132
Park Lodge NW8 . . . . 7B 64
Park Lofts SW2 . . . . 5J 119
(off Mandrell Rd.)
Park Lorne NW8 . . . . 2D 4
(off Park Rd.)
Park Mnr. SM2: Sutt 7A 166
(off Christchurch Pk.)
Park Mans. NW4 . . . . 5D 44
NW8 . . . . 2C 82
(off Allitsen Rd.)
SW1 . . . . 7E 10
(off Knightsbridge)
SW8 . . . . 7F 19 (6J 101)
SW11 . . . . 1D 118
(off Prince of Wales Dr.)
Park Mead DA15: Sidc 5B 126
HA2: Harr 3F 59
Parkmead SW15 . . . . 6D 116
Parkmead Gdns.
NW7 . . . . 6G 29
Park M. BR7: Chst 6F 143
SE24 . . . . 7C 120
TW19: Stanw 7B 110
W10 . . . . 2G 81
Parkmore Cl. IG8: Wfd G 4D 36
Park Pde. NW10 . . . . 2B 80
UB3: Hayes 6G 75
W5 . . . . 3G 97
Park Pl. BR1: Brom 1K 159
(off Park Rd.)
E14 . . . . 1C 104
HA9: Wemb 4F 61
N1 . . . . 7D 66
(off Downham Rd.)
SW1 . . . . 5A 12 (1G 101)
TW12: Hamp H 6G 131
W3 . . . . 4G 97
W5 . . . . 1D 96
Park Pl. Dr. W3 . . . . 3G 97
Park Pl. Vs. W2 . . . . 5A 4 (5A 82)
Park Ridings N8 . . . . 3A 48
Park Ri. HA3: Hrw W 1J 41
SE23 . . . . 1A 140
Park Ri. Rd. SE23 . . . . 1A 140
Park Rd. BR1: Brom 1K 159
BR3: Beck 7B 140
BR7: Chst 6F 143
E6 . . . . 1A 88
E10 . . . . 1C 68
E12 . . . . 1K 69
E15 . . . . 1J 87
E17 . . . . 5B 50
EN4: E Barn 4G 21
EN5: Barn 4C 20
HA0: Wemb 6E 60
IG1: Ilf 3H 71
KT1: Hamp W 1C 150
KT2: King T 5F 133
KT3: N Mald 4K 151
KT5: Surb 6F 151
KT8: E Mos 4G 149
N2 . . . . 3B 46
N8 . . . . 4G 47
N11 . . . . 7C 32
N14 . . . . 1C 32
N15 . . . . 4B 48
N18 . . . . 4B 34
NW1 . . . . 2D 4 (3C 82)
NW4 . . . . 7C 44
NW8 . . . . 2D 4 (3C 82)
NW9 . . . . 7K 43
NW10 . . . . 1A 80
SE25 . . . . 4E 156
SM3: Cheam 6G 165
SM6: Wall 5F 167
(Clifton Rd.)
SM6: Wall 2F 167
(Elmwood Cl.)
SW19 . . . . 6B 136
TW1: Twick 6C 114
TW3: Houn 5F 113
TW7: Isle 1B 114
TW10: Rich 6F 115
TW11: Tedd 6K 131
TW12: Hamp H 4F 131
TW13: Hanw 4B 130
TW15: Ashf 5D 128
TW16: Sun 7K 129
Park Rd. UB4: Hayes 5G 75
UB8: Uxb 1A 74
W4 . . . . 7J 97
W7 . . . . 7K 77
Park Rd. E. UB10: Uxb 2A 74
W3 . . . . 2H 97
Park Rd. Ho. KT2: King T 7G 133
Park Rd. Nth. W3 . . . . 2H 97
W4 . . . . 5K 97
Park Road Swimming Pool 5H 47
Park Row SE10 . . . . 5F 105
SW2 . . . . 6A 120
PARK ROYAL 3H 79
PARK ROYAL JUNC. 1G 79
Park Royal Metro Cen.
NW10 . . . . 4H 79
Park Royal Rd. NW10 . . . . 3J 79
W3 . . . . 3J 79
Parkshot TW9: Rich 4D 114
Park Side NW2 . . . . 3C 62
Parkside DA14: Sidc 2B 144
IG9: Buck H 2E 36
N3 . . . . 1K 45
NW7 . . . . 6H 29
SE3 . . . . 7H 105
SM3: Cheam 6G 165
SW1 . . . . 6F 11
SW19 . . . . 3F 135
TW12: Hamp H 5H 131
UB3: Hayes 7G 75
W3 . . . . 1A 98
W5 . . . . 7E 78
Parkside Av. BR1: Brom 4C 160
DA7: Bex 2K 127
RM1: Rom 3K 55
SW19 . . . . 5F 135
Parkside Bus. Est. SE8 . . . . 6A 104
(Blackhorse Rd.)
SE8 . . . . 6A 104
(Childers St.)
Parkside Cl. SE20 . . . . 7J 139
Parkside Ct. E11 . . . . 6J 51
(off Wanstead Pl.)
N22 . . . . 6E 32
Parkside Cres. KT5: Surb 6J 151
N7 . . . . 3A 66
Parkside Cross DA7: Bex 2K 127
Parkside Dr. HA8: Edg 3B 28
Parkside Est. E9 . . . . 1J 85
Parkside Gdns. EN4: E Barn 1J 31
SW19 . . . . 4F 135
Parkside Ho. RM10: Dag 3J 73
Parkside Lodge DA17: Belv 5J 109
Parkside Rd. DA17: Belv 4H 109
SW11 . . . . 1E 118
TW3: Houn 5F 113
Parkside Ter. BR6: Farnb 3F 173
(off Willow Wlk.)
N18 . . . . 4J 33
Parkside Way HA2: Harr 4F 41
Park Sq. E. NW1 . . . . 3J 5 (4F 83)
Park Sq. M. NW1 . . . . 4J 5 (4E 82)
Park Sq. W. NW1 . . . . 3J 5 (4F 83)
Parkstead Rd. SW15 . . . . 5C 116
Park Steps W2 . . . . 2D 10
Parkstone Av. N18 . . . . 6A 34
Parkstone Rd. E17 . . . . 3E 50
SE15 . . . . 2G 121
Park St. CR0: Croy 2C 168
SE1 . . . . 4C 14 (1C 102)
TW11: Tedd 6J 131
W1 . . . . 2G 11 (7E 82)
Park Ter. EN3: Enf H 1F 25
KT4: Wor Pk 1C 164
SM5: Cars 3C 166
Parkthorne Cl. HA2: Harr 6F 41
Parkthorne Dr. HA2: Harr 6E 40
Parkthorne Rd.
SW12 . . . . 7H 119
Park Towers W1 . . . . 5J 11
(off Brick St.)

Pavilion M. N3 . . . . . 3J 45
Pavilion Pde. *W12* *6E 80*
(off Wood La.)
Pavilion Rd. IG1: Ilf 7D 52
SW1 . . . . . 7F 11 (3D 100)
Pavilion Sports & Fitness Club, The
. . . . . 3G 149
Pavilion Sq. SW17 . . . . . 3D 136
Pavilion St. SW1 . . . . . 2F 17 (3D 100)
Pavilion Ter. IG2: Ilf 5J 53
W12 . . . . . *6E 80*
(off Wood La.)
Pavilion Way HA4: Ruis 2A 58
HA8: Edg 7C 28
Pawleyne Cl. SE20 . . . . . 7J 139
Pawsey Cl. E13 . . . . . 1K 87
Pawsons Rd. CR0: Croy 6C 156
Paxfold HA7: Stan 5J 27
Paxford Rd. HA0: Wemb 2B 60
Paxton Cl. KT12: Walt T 7A 148
TW9: Kew 2F 115
Paxton Ct. *CR4: Mitc* *2D 154*
(off Armfield Cres.)
SE12 . . . . . 3A 142
SE26 . . . . . *4A 140*
(off Adamsrill Rd.)
Paxton Pl. SE27 . . . . . 4E 138
Paxton Rd. BR1: Brom 7J 141
N17 . . . . . 7A 34
SE23 . . . . . 3A 140
W4 . . . . . 6A 98
Paxton Ter. SW1 . . . . . 7K 17 (6F 101)
Paymal Ho. *E1* *5J 85*
(off Stepney Way)
Payne Cl. IG11: Bark 7J 71
Payne Ho. *N1* *1K 83*
(off Barnsbury Est.)
Paynell Ct. SE3 . . . . . 3G 123
Payne Rd. E3 . . . . . 2D 86
Paynesfield Av. SW14 . . . . . 3K 115
Paynesfield Rd. WD23: Bushy 1E 26
Payne St. SE8 . . . . . 7B 104
Paynes Wlk. W6 . . . . . 6G 99
Payzes Gdns. IG8: Wfd G 6C 36
Peabody Av. SW1 . . . . . 5J 17 (5F 101)
Peabody Bldgs. E1 . . . . . 2K 15
EC1 . . . . . *4D 8*
(off Roscoe St.)
SW3 . . . . . 7C 16
Peabody Cl. CR0: Croy 1J 169
SE10 . . . . . 1D 122
SW1 . . . . . 7K 17 (5F 101)
Peabody Cotts. N17 . . . . . 1E 48
Peabody Ct. *EC1* *4D 8*
(off Roscoe St.)
SE5 . . . . . *1D 120*
(off Kimpton Rd.)
Peabody Est. *E1* *7K 85*
(off Glasmis Pl.)
E2 . . . . . *2H 85*
(off Minerva St.)
EC1 . . . . . *4D 8*
(off Dufferin St., not continuous)
EC1 . . . . . *4K 7*
(off Farringdon La.)
N1 . . . . . 1C 84
SE1 . . . . . 5K 13 (1A 102)
(Duchy St.)
SE1 . . . . . 5C 14 (1C 102)
(Gt. Guildford St.)
SE1 . . . . . 6D 14
(Mint St.)
SE24 . . . . . 7B 120
SW1 . . . . . 3B 18
SW3 . . . . . 7D 16 (6C 100)
SW6 . . . . . *6J 99*
(off Lillie Rd.)
SW11 . . . . . 4C 118
W6 . . . . . 5E 98
W10 . . . . . 5E 80
Peabody Hill SE21 . . . . . 1B 138
Peabody Sq. SE1 . . . . . 7A 14 (2B 102)
(not continuous)
Peabody Ter. *EC1* *4K 7*
(off Farringdon La.)
Peabody Twr. *EC1* *4D 8*
(off Golden La.)
Peabody Trust *SE17* *4D 102*
(off Rodney Rd.)
Peabody Yd. N1 . . . . . 1C 84
Peace Cl. N14 . . . . . 5A 22
SE25 . . . . . 4E 156
UB6: G'frd 1H 77
Peace Gro. HA9: Wemb 3H 61
Peace St. SE18 . . . . . 6E 106
Peaches Cl. SM2: Cheam 7G 165
Peachey Edwards Ho. *E2* *3H 85*
(off Teesdale St.)
Peachey La. UB8: Cowl 5A 74
Peach Gro. E11 . . . . . 3F 69
Peach Rd. TW13: Felt 1J 129
W10 . . . . . 3F 81
Peach Tree Av. UB7: Yiew 6B 74
Peachum Rd. SE3 . . . . . 6H 105
Peachwalk M. E3 . . . . . 2K 85
Peachy Cl. HA8: Edg 6B 28
Peacock Av. TW14: Bedf 1F 129
Peacock Cl. RM8: Dag 1C 72
Peacock Ind. Est. N17 . . . . . 7A 34
Peacock St. SE17 . . . . . 4B 102
Peacock Theatre *1G 13*
(off Portugal St.)
Peacock Wlk. *E16* *6K 87*
(off Mortlake Rd.)
N6 . . . . . 7F 47
Peacock Yd. *SE17* *5B 102*
(off Iliffe St.)
Peak, The SE26 . . . . . 3J 139
Peaketon Av. IG4: Ilf 4B 52
Peak Fitness 2D 104
Peak Hill SE26 . . . . . 4J 139
Peak Hill Av. SE26 . . . . . 4J 139
Peak Hill Gdns. SE26 . . . . . 4J 139
Peak Ho. *N4* *1C 66*
(off Woodberry Down Est.)
Peal Gdns. W13 . . . . . 3A 78
Peall Rd. CR0: Croy 6K 155
Peall Rd. Ind. Est. CR0: Croy 6K 155
Pearce Cl. CR4: Mitc 2E 154
Pearcefield Av. SE23 . . . . . 1J 139
Pearce Rd. KT8: W Mole 3F 149
Pear Cl. NW9 . . . . . 4K 43
SE14 . . . . . 7A 104
Pear Ct. *SE15* *7F 103*
(off Thruxton Way)
Pearcroft Rd. E11 . . . . . 2F 69
Peardon St. SW8 . . . . . 2F 119
Peareswood Gdns. HA7: Stan 1D 42
Pearfield Rd. SE23 . . . . . 3A 140
Pearl Cl. E6 . . . . . 6E 88
NW2 . . . . . 7F 45
Pearl Rd. E17 . . . . . 3C 50
Pearl St. E1 . . . . . 1H 103
Pearmain Cl. TW17: Shep 5D 146
Pearman St. SE1 . . . . . 1K 19 (3A 102)
Pear Pl. SE1 . . . . . 6J 13 (2A 102)
Pear Rd. E11 . . . . . 3F 69
Pears Av. TW17: Shep 3G 147
Pearscroft Ct. SW6 . . . . . 1K 117
Pearscroft Rd. SW6 . . . . . 1K 117
Pearse St. SE15 . . . . . 6E 102
Pearson Cl. EN5: New Bar 3E 20
SE5 . . . . . *1C 120*
(off Camberwell New Rd.)
Pearson M. *SW4* *3H 119*
(off Slievemore Cl.)
Pearson's Av. SE14 . . . . . 1C 122
Pearson St. E2 . . . . . 2F 85
Pears Rd. TW3: Houn 3G 113
Peartree SE26 . . . . . 5A 140
Pear Tree Av. UB7: Yiew 6B 74
Peartree Av. SW17 . . . . . 3A 136
Pear Tree Cl. BR2: Brom 5B 160
E2 . . . . . 1F 85
KT9: Chess 5G 163
Peartree Cl. CR4: Mitc 2C 154
DA8: Erith 1K 127
Pear Tree Ct. E18 . . . . . 1K 51
EC1 . . . . . 4K 7 (4A 84)
Peartree Gdns. RM7: Mawney 2H 55
RM8: Dag 4B 72
Pear Tree Ho. SE4 . . . . . 3B 122
Peartree La. E1 . . . . . 7J 85
Pear Tree Rd. TW15: Ashf 5E 128
Peartree Rd. EN1: Enf 3K 23
Peartrees UB7: Yiew 7A 74
Pear Tree St. EC1 . . . . . 3B 8 (4C 84)
Peartree Way SE10 . . . . . 4J 105
Peary Ho. NW10 . . . . . 7K 61
Peary Pl. E2 . . . . . 3J 85
Peas Mead Ter. E4 . . . . . 4K 35
Peatfield Cl. DA15: Sidc 3J 143
Pebble Way *W3* *1H 97*
(off Steyne Rd.)
Pebworth Rd. HA1: Harr 2A 60
Peckarmans Wood SE26 . . . . . 3G 139
Peckett Sq. N5 . . . . . 4C 66
Peckford Pl. SW9 . . . . . 2A 120
PECKHAM 1G 121
Peckham Gro. SE15 . . . . . 7E 102
Peckham High St. SE15 . . . . . 1G 121
Peckham Hill St. SE15 . . . . . 7G 103
Peckham Pk. Rd. SE15 . . . . . 7G 103
Peckham Pulse Health & Leisure Cen.
. . . . . 1G 121
Peckham Rd. SE5 . . . . . 1E 120
SE15 . . . . . 1E 120
Peckham Rye SE15 . . . . . 3G 121
SE22 . . . . . 4G 121
Peckham Sq. SE15 . . . . . 1G 121
Pecks Yd. *E1* *5J 9*
(off Hanbury St.)
Peckwater St. NW5 . . . . . 5G 65
Pedlar's Wlk. N7 . . . . . 5K 65
Pedley Rd. RM8: Dag 1C 72
Pedley St. E1 . . . . . 4K 9 (4F 85)
Pedro St. E5 . . . . . 3K 67
Pedworth Gdns. SE16 . . . . . 4J 103
Peebles Ct. *UB1: S'hall* *6G 77*
(off Haldane Rd.)
Peek Cres. SW19 . . . . . 5F 135
Peel Cl. E4 . . . . . 2J 35
N9 . . . . . 3B 34
Peel Dr. IG5: Ilf 3C 52
NW9 . . . . . 3B 44
Peel Gro. E2 . . . . . 2J 85
(not continuous)
Peel Pas. W8 . . . . . 1J 99
Peel Pl. IG5: Ilf 2C 52
Peel Pct. NW6 . . . . . 2J 81
Peel Rd. BR6: Farnb 5G 173
E18 . . . . . 1H 51
HA3: W'stone 3K 41
(not continuous)
HA9: Wemb 3D 60
Peel St. W8 . . . . . 1J 99
Peel Way UB8: Hil 5A 74
Peerglow Est. EN3: Pond E 5D 24
Peerless St. EC1 . . . . . 2E 8 (3D 84)
Pegamoid Rd. N18 . . . . . 3D 34
Pegasus Cl. N16 . . . . . 4D 66
Pegasus Ct. KT1: King T 3D 150
KT10: Clay 6A 162
N21 . . . . . 7H 23
NW10 . . . . . *3D 80*
(off Trenmar Gdns.)
TW8: Bford 5F 97
W3 . . . . . *6J 79*
(off Horn La.)
Pegasus Ho. *E1* *4K 85*
(off Beaumont Sq.)
Pegasus Pl. SE11 . . . . . 7J 19 (6A 102)
SW6 . . . . . 1J 117
Pegasus Rd. CR0: Wadd 6A 168
Pegasus Way N11 . . . . . 6A 32
Peggotty Way UB8: Hil 6D 74
Pegg Rd. TW5: Hest 7B 94
Pegley Gdns. SE12 . . . . . 2J 141
Pegwell St. SE18 . . . . . 7J 107
Pekin Cl. *E14* *6C 86*
(off Pekin St.)
Pekin St. E14 . . . . . 6C 86
Pelabon Ho. *TW1: Twick* *6D 114*
(off Clevedon Rd.)
Peldon Ct. TW9: Rich 4F 115
Peldon Pas. TW10: Rich 4F 115
Peldon Wlk. *N1* *1B 84*
(off Popham St.)
Pelham Av. IG11: Bark 1K 89
Pelham Cl. SE5 . . . . . 3E 120
Pelham Cotts. DA5: Bexl 1H 145
Pelham Ct. DA14: Sidc 3A 144
SW3 . . . . . *4C 16*
(off Fulham Rd.)
Pelham Cres. SW7 . . . . . 4C 16 (4C 100)
Pelham Ho. *W14* *4H 99*
(off Mornington Av.)
Pelham Pl. SW7 . . . . . 3C 16 (4C 100)
W13 . . . . . 4K 77
Pelham Rd. BR3: Beck 2J 157
DA7: Bex 3G 127
E18 . . . . . 3K 51
IG1: Ilf 2H 71
N15 . . . . . 4F 49
N22 . . . . . 2A 48
SW19 . . . . . 7J 135
Pelham St. SW7 . . . . . 3B 16 (4B 100)
Pelican Est. SE15 . . . . . 1F 121
Pelican Ho. SE8 . . . . . 4B 104
Pelican Pas. E1 . . . . . 4J 85
Pelican Wlk. SW9 . . . . . 4B 120
Pelican Wharf *E1* *1J 103*
(off Wapping Wall)
Pelier St. SE17 . . . . . 6C 102
Pelinore Rd. SE6 . . . . . 2G 141
Pella Ho. SE11 . . . . . 5H 19 (5K 101)
Pellant Rd. SW6 . . . . . 7G 99
Pellatt Gro. N22 . . . . . 1A 48
Pellatt Rd. HA9: Wemb 2D 60
(not continuous)
SE22 . . . . . 5F 121
Pellerin Rd. N16 . . . . . 5E 66
Pellew Ho. *E1* *4H 85*
(off Somerford St.)
Pelling St. E14 . . . . . 6C 86
Pellipar Cl. N13 . . . . . 3F 33
Pellipar Gdns. SE18 . . . . . 5D 106
Pellipar Rd. SE18 . . . . . 5D 106
Pelly Rd. E13 . . . . . 1J 87
(not continuous)
Pelter St. E2 . . . . . 1J 9 (3F 85)
(not continuous)
Pelton Rd. SE10 . . . . . 5G 105
Pembar Av. E17 . . . . . 3A 50
Pemberley Chase KT19: Ewe 5H 163
Pemberley Cl. KT19: Ewe 5H 163
Pemberley Ho. *KT19: Ewe* *5H 163*
(off Pemberley Chase)
Pember Rd. NW10 . . . . . 3F 81
Pemberton Ct. *E1* *3K 85*
(off Portelet Rd.)
Pemberton Gdns. N19 . . . . . 3G 65
RM6: Chad H 5E 54
Pemberton Ho. *SE26* *4G 139*
(off High Level Dr.)
Pemberton Pl. E8 . . . . . 7H 67
Pemberton Rd. KT8: E Mos 4G 149
N4 . . . . . 5A 48
Pemberton Row EC4 . . . . . 7K 7 (6A 84)
Pemberton Ter. N19 . . . . . 3G 65
Pembridge Av. TW2: Whit 1D 130
Pembridge Cres. W11 . . . . . 7J 81
Pembridge Gdns. W2 . . . . . 7J 81
Pembridge M. W11 . . . . . 7J 81

Princelet St.—Prospect Pl.

Princelet St. E1 5K 9 (5F 85)
Prince of Orange La. SE10 7E 104
Prince of Wales Cl. NW4 4D 44
Prince of Wales Dr. SW8 7F 101
SW11 1C 118
Prince of Wales Mans. SW11 1E 118
Prince of Wales Pas. NW1 2A 6
Prince of Wales Rd. E16 6A 88
NW5 6E 64
SE3 2H 123
SM1: Sutt 2B 166
Prince of Wales Ter. W4 5A 98
W8 2K 99
Prince of Wales Theatre *3C 12*
(off Coventry St.)
Prince Regent Ct. *NW8 2C 82*
(off Avenue Rd.)
SE16 7A 86
(off Edward Sq.)
Prince Regent La. E13 3K 87
E16 3K 87
Prince Regent M. NW1 2A 6
Prince Regent Rd. TW3: Houn 3G 113
Prince Regents Ga.
NW8 3D 4 (4C 82)
Prince Rd. SE25 5E 156
Prince Rupert Rd. SE9 4D 124
Princes Arc. SW1 4B 12
Princes Av. BR5: Pet W 5J 161
IG8: Wfd G 4E 36
KT6: Surb 1G 163
N3 1J 45
N10 3F 47
N13 5F 33
N22 1H 47
NW9 4G 43
SM5: Cars 7D 166
UB6: G'frd 6F 77
W3 3G 97
Princes Cir. WC2 7E 6 (6J 83)
Princes Cl. DA14: Sidc 3D 144
HA8: Edg 5B 28
N4 1B 66
NW9 4G 43
SW4 3G 119
TW11: Tedd 4H 131
Princes Ct. HA9: Wemb 5E 60
SE16 3B 104
SW3 1E 16
(off Brompton Rd.)
Princes Ct. Bus. Cen. E1 7H 85
Princes Dr. HA1: Harr 3J 41
Princes Gdns. SW7 1B 16 (3B 100)
W3 5G 79
W5 4C 78
Prince's Ga. SW7 7B 10 (2B 100)
(not continuous)
Prince's Ga. Ct. SW7 7A 10 (2B 100)
Prince's Ga. M. SW7 1B 16 (3B 100)
Princes La. HA4: Ruis 1G 57
N10 3F 47
Princes M. TW3: Houn 4E 112
W2 7K 81
W6 5D 98
(off Down Pl.)
Princes Pde. *NW11 6G 45*
(off Golders Grn. Rd.)
Princes Pk. Av. NW11 6G 45
UB3: Hayes 7F 75
Princes Pk. Circ. UB3: Hayes 7F 75
Princes Pk. Cl. UB3: Hayes 7F 75
Princes Pk. La. UB3: Hayes 7F 75
Princes Pk. Pde. UB3: Hayes 7F 75
Princes Pl. SW1 4B 12
W11 1G 99
Prince's Plain BR2: Brom 7C 160
Prince's Ri. SE13 2E 122
Princes Riverside Rd. SE16 1K 103
Princes Rd. IG6: Ilf 4H 53
IG9: Buck H 2F 37
KT2: King T 7G 133
Princes Rd. N18 4D 34
SE20 6K 139
SW14 3K 115
SW19 6J 135
TW9: Kew 1F 115
TW10: Rich 5F 115
TW11: Tedd 4H 131
TW13: Felt 2H 129
TW15: Ashf 5B 128
W13 1B 96
Princessa Ct. EN2: Enf 5J 23
Princess Alice Ho. W10 4E 80
Princess Alice Way SE28 2H 107
Princess Av. HA9: Wemb 2E 60
Princess Cl. SE28 6D 90
Princess Ct. *KT1: King T 3F 151*
(off Horace Rd.)
N6 7G 47
W1 6E 4
(off Bryanston Pl.)
W2 7K 81
(off Queensway)
Princess Cres. N4 2B 66
Princess Louise Cl. W2 5B 4 (5B 82)
Princess Mary Ho. *SW1 3D 18*
(off Vincent St.)
Princess May Rd. N16 4E 66
Princess M. KT1: King T 3F 151
NW3 5B 64
Princess Pde. BR6: Farnb 3E 172
RM10: Dag 2G 91
Princess Pk. Mnr. N11 5K 31
Princes Sq. W2 7K 81
(not continuous)
Princess Rd. CR0: Croy 6C 156
NW1 1E 82
NW6 2J 81
Princess St. SE1 3B 102
Princes St. DA7: Bex 3F 127
EC2 1E 14 (6D 84)
N17 6K 33
SM1: Sutt 4B 166
TW9: Rich 4E 114
W1 1K 11 (6F 83)
Princes Ter. E13 1K 87
Prince's Twr. *SE16 2J 103*
(off Elephant La.)
Prince St. SE8 6B 104
Princes Way BR4: W W'ck 4H 171
CR0: Wadd 5K 167
HA4: Ruis 4C 58
IG9: Buck H 2F 37
SW19 7F 117
W3 3G 97
Prince's Yd. W11 1G 99
Princethorpe Ho. *W2 5K 81*
(off Woodchester Sq.)
Princethorpe Rd. SE26 4K 139
Princeton Ct. SW15 3F 117
Princeton M. KT2: King T 1G 151
Princeton St. WC1 6G 7 (5K 83)
Prince William Ct. *TW15: Ashf 5B 128*
(off Princes Rd.)
Principal Sq. E9 5K 67
Pringle Gdns. SW16 4G 137
(not continuous)
Printers Inn Ct. EC4 6A 84
Printers M. E3 1A 86
Printer St. EC4 7K 7 (6A 84)
Printinghouse La. UB3: Hayes 2G 93
Printing Ho. Yd. E2 1H 9 (3E 84)
Printon Ho. *E14 5B 86*
(off Wallwood St.)
Print Village SE15 2F 121
Printwork Apartments *SE1 7G 15*
(off Long La.)
Priolo Rd. SE7 5A 106
Prior Av. SM2: Sutt 7C 166
Prior Bolton St. N1 6B 66
Prioress Rd. SE27 3B 138
Prioress St. SE1 3E 102
Prior Rd. IG1: Ilf 3E 70
Priors Cft. E17 2A 50
Priors Farm La. UB5: N'olt 6C 58
Priors Fld. UB5: N'olt 6C 58
Priors Gdns. HA4: Ruis 5A 58
Priors Mead EN1: Enf 1K 23
Prior St. SE10 7E 104
Priors Wood KT10: Hin W 2A 162
Priory, The CR0: Wadd 4A 168
N8 4H 47
SE3 4H 123
Priory Apartments, The SE6 1D 140
Priory Av. BR5: Pet W 6H 161
E4 3G 35
E17 5C 50
HA0: Wemb 4K 59
N8 4H 47
SM3: Cheam 4F 165
W4 4A 98
Priory Cl. BR3: Beck 3A 158
BR7: Chst 1D 160
E4 3G 35
E18 1J 51
HA0: Wemb 4K 59
HA4: Ruis 1H 57
HA7: Stan 3E 26
N3 1H 45
N14 5A 22
N20 1C 30
SW19 1K 153
TW12: Hamp 1D 148
TW16: Sun 7J 129
UB3: Hayes 7K 75
Priory Ct. E6 1A 88
E9 5K 67
E17 2B 50
EC4 1B 14
(off Pilgrim St.)
HA0: Wemb 2E 78
KT1: King T 3E 150
(off Denmark Rd.)
KT17: Ewe 7B 164
SM3: Cheam 4G 165
SW8 1H 119
TW3: Houn 3F 113
WD23: Bush 1B 26
(off Sparrows Herne)
Priory Ct. Est. E17 2B 50
Priory Cres. HA0: Wemb 3A 60
SE19 7C 138
SM3: Cheam 4F 165
Priory Dr. HA7: Stan 3E 26
SE2 5D 108
Priory Fld. Dr. HA8: Edg 4C 28
Priory Gdns. HA0: Wemb 4A 60
N6 6F 47
NW10 3E 78
SE25 4F 157
SW13 3B 116
TW12: Hamp 7D 130
TW15: Ashf 5F 129
W4 4A 98
W5 3E 78
Priory Grange *N2 3D 46*
(off Fortis Grn.)
Priory Grn. Est. N1 2K 83
Priory Gro. EN5: Barn 5D 20
SW8 1J 119
Priory Hill HA0: Wemb 4A 60
Priory Ho. *E1 5J 9*
(off Folgate St.)
EC1 3A 8
(off Sans Wlk.)
SW1 5C 18
(off Rampayne St.)
Priory La. KT8: W Mole 4F 149
SW15 6A 116
TW9: Kew 7G 97
Priory Leas SE9 1C 142
Priory M. SW8 1J 119
Priory Pk. SE3 3H 123
Priory Pk. Rd. HA0: Wemb 4A 60
NW6 1H 81
(not continuous)
Priory Retail Pk. SW19 7B 136
Priory Rd. CR0: Croy 7A 156
E6 1B 88
IG11: Bark 7H 71
KT9: Chess 3E 162
N8 4G 47
NW6 1K 81
SM3: Cheam 4F 165
SW19 7B 136
TW3: Houn 5G 113
TW9: Kew 6G 97
TW12: Hamp 7D 130
W4 3K 97
Priory St. E3 3D 86
Priory Ter. NW6 1K 81
TW16: Sun 7J 129
Priory Vw. WD23: Bushy 1D 26
Priory Vs. *N11 6J 31*
(off Colney Hatch La.)
Priory Wlk. SW10 5A 100
Priory Way HA2: Harr 4F 41
UB2: S'hall 3B 94
UB7: Harm 6A 92
Priscilla Cl. N15 5C 48
Pritchard Ho. *E2 2H 85*
(off Ada Pl.)
Pritchard's Rd. E2 1G 85
Priter Rd. SE16 3G 103
Priter Way SE16 3G 103
Private Rd. EN1: Enf 5J 23
Probert Rd. SW2 5A 120
Probyn Ho. *SW1 3D 18*
(off Page St.)
Probyn Rd. SW2 2B 138
Procter Ho. *SE1 5G 103*
(off Avondale Sq.)
SE5 7D 102
(off Picton St.)
Procter St. WC1 6G 7 (5K 83)
Proctor Cl. CR4: Mitc 1E 154
Proctors Cl. TW14: Felt 1J 129
Progress Bus. Pk., The CR0: Wadd 2K 167
Progress Cen., The EN3: Pond E 3E 24
Progress Way CR0: Wadd 2K 167
EN1: Enf 5B 24
N22 1A 48
Project Pk. E3 4F 87
Prologis Pk. CR0: Bedd 7H 155
E16 4F 87
TW4: Houn 4A 112
Promenade, The HA8: Edg 5B 28
W4 2A 116
Promenade App. Rd. W4 7A 98
Pronto Trad. Est. UB3: Hayes 5G 75
Prospect Cl. DA17: Belv 4G 109
HA4: Ruis 7B 40
SE26 4H 139
TW3: Houn 1D 112
Prospect Cotts. SW18 4J 117
Prospect Cres. TW2: Whit 6G 113
Prospect Hill E17 4D 50
Prospect Ho. *E17 3E 50*
(off Prospect Hill)
N1 2A 84
(off Donegal St.)
SE1 3B 102
(off Gaywood St.)
W10 6F 81
(off Bridge Cl.)
Prospect Pl. BR2: Brom 3K 159
E1 1J 103
(not continuous)
N2 4B 46
N7 4J 65
N17 7K 33
NW2 3H 63
NW3 4A 64
RM5: Col R 2J 55

Q

Queen Victoria Seaman's Rest—Ramillies Rd.

Queen Victoria Seaman's Rest E14 6D 86
(off E. India Dock Rd.)
Queen Victoria St. EC4 2A 14 (7B 84)
Queen Victoria Ter. E1 7H 85
(off Sovereign Cl.)
Quemerford Rd. N7 5K 65
Quendon Ho. W10 4E 80
(off Sutton Way)
Quenington Ct. SE15 6F 103
Quentin Ho. SE1 7K 13
(off Gray St., not continuous)
Quentin Pl. SE13 3G 123
Quentin Rd. SE13 3G 123
Quernmore Cl. BR1: Brom 6J 141
Quernmore Rd. BR1: Brom 6J 141
N4 6A 48
Querrin St. SW6 2A 118
Quested Ct. E8 5H 67
(off Brett Rd.)
Questors Theatre, The 7C 78
Quex M. NW6 1J 81
Quex Rd. NW6 1J 81
Quick Rd. W4 5A 98
Quicks Rd. SW19 7K 135
Quick St. N1 2B 84
Quick St. M. N1 2B 84
Quickswood NW3 7C 64
Quiet Nook BR2: Kes 3B 172
Quill La. SW15 4F 117
Quill St. N4 3A 66
W5 3E 78
Quilp St. SE1 6C 14 (2C 102)
(not continuous)
Quilter Ho. W10 3H 81
(off Dart St.)
Quilter St. E2 1K 9 (3G 85)
SE18 5K 107
Quilting Ct. SE16 2K 103
(off Garter Way)
Quince Ho. SE13 2D 122
(off Quince Rd.)
Quinta Dr. EN5: Barn 5A 20
Quintin Av. SW20 1H 153
Quintin Cl. HA5: Eastc 4K 39
Quinton Cl. BR3: Beck 3E 158
SM6: Wall 4F 167
TW5: Cran 7K 93
Quinton Ho. SW8 7J 101
(off Wyvil Rd.)
Quinton Rd. KT7: T Ditt 1A 162
Quinton St. SW18 2A 136
Quixley St. E14 7F 87
Quorn Rd. SE22 4E 120

R

Rabbit Row W8 1J 99
Rabbits Rd. E12 4C 70
Rabournmead Dr.
UB5: N'olt 5C 58
Raby Rd. KT3: N Mald 4K 151
Raby St. E14 6A 86
Raccoon Way TW4: Houn 2A 112
Raceway, The (Go-Kart Track) 1J 83
Rachel Cl. IG6: Ilf 3H 53
Racine SE5 1E 120
(off Peckham Rd.)
Rackham Cl. DA16: Well 2B 126
Rackham M. SW16 6G 137
Rackstraw Ho. NW3 7D 64
Racquets & Fitness Spa, The 3E 130
Racton Rd. SW6 6J 99
RADA 5C 6
(off Chenies St.)
Radbourne Av. W5 4C 96
Radbourne Cl. E5 4K 67
Radbourne Ct. HA3: Kent 6B 42
Radbourne Cres. E17 2F 51
Radbourne Rd. SW12 7G 119
Radcliffe Av. EN2: Enf 1H 23
NW10 2C 80
Radcliffe Gdns. SM5: Cars 7C 166
Radcliffe Ho. SE16 4H 103
(off Anchor St.)
Radcliffe M. TW12: Hamp H 5G 131
Radcliffe Path SW8 2F 119
Radcliffe Rd. CR0: Croy 2F 169
HA3: W'stone 2A 42
N21 1G 33
SE1 3E 102
Radcliffe Sq. SW15 6F 117
Radcliffe Way UB5: Yead 3B 76
Radcot Point SE23 3K 139
Radcot St. SE11 6K 19 (5A 102)
Raddington Rd. W10 5G 81
Radfield Way DA15: Sidc 7H 125
(not continuous)
Radford Est. NW10 3A 80
Radford Ho. E14 5D 86
(off St Leonard's Rd.)
N7 5K 65
Radford Rd. SE13 6E 122
Radford Way IG11: Bark 3K 89
Radipole Rd. SW6 1H 117
Radius Pk. TW14: Felt 4H 111
Radland Rd. E16 6H 87
Radlet Av. SE26 3H 139
Radlett Cl. E7 6H 69
Radlett Pl. NW8 1C 82
Radley Av. IG3: Bark, Ilf 4A 72
Radley Cl. TW14: Felt 1H 129
Radley Ct. SE16 2K 103
Radley Gdns. HA3: Kent 4E 42
Radley Ho. NW1 3E 4
(off Gloucester Pl.)
SE2 2D 108
(off Wolvercote Rd.)
Radley M. W8 3J 99
Radley Rd. N17 2E 48
Radley's La. E18 2J 51
Radleys Mead RM10: Dag 6H 73
Radley Sq. E5 2J 67
Radley Ter. E16 5H 87
(off Hermit Rd.)
Radlix Rd. E10 1C 68
Radnor Av. DA16: Well 5B 126
HA1: Harr 5J 41
Radnor Cl. BR7: Chst 6J 143
CR4: Mitc 4J 155
Radnor Ct. HA3: Hrw W 1K 41
W7 6K 77
(off Copley Cl.)
Radnor Cres. IG4: Ilf 5D 52
SE18 7A 108
Radnor Gdns. EN1: Enf 1K 23
TW1: Twick 2K 131
Radnor Gro. UB10: Hil 2C 74
Radnor M. W2 1B 10 (6B 82)
Radnor Pl. W2 1C 10 (6C 82)
Radnor Rd. HA1: Harr 5H 41
NW6 1G 81
SE15 7G 103
TW1: Twick 1K 131
Radnor St. EC1 2D 8 (3C 84)
Radnor Ter. SM2: Sutt 7J 165
W14 4H 99
Radnor Wlk. CR0: Croy 6A 158
E14 4C 104
(off Barnsdale Av.)
SW3 6D 16 (5C 100)
Radnor Way NW10 4H 79
Radstock Av. HA3: Kent 3A 42
Radstock Cl. N11 6K 31
Radstock St. SW11 7C 100
(not continuous)
Raeburn Av. KT5: Surb 1H 163
Raeburn Cl. KT1: Hamp W 7D 132
NW11 6A 46
Raeburn Ho. UB5: N'olt 2B 76
(off Academy Gdns.)
Raeburn Rd. DA15: Sidc 6J 125
HA8: Edg 1G 43
UB4: Hayes 2F 75
Raeburn St. SW2 4J 119
Raffles Ho. NW4 4D 44
Rafford Way BR1: Brom 2K 159
RAF Museum Hendon 2C 44
RAF NORTHOLT AERODROME
6H 57
Ragged School Mus. 5A 86
Raggleswood BR7: Chst 1E 160
Raglan Cl. TW4: Houn 5D 112
Raglan Ct. CR2: S Croy 5B 168
HA9: Wemb 4F 61
SE12 5J 123
Raglan Rd. BR2: Brom 4A 160
DA17: Belv 4F 109
E17 5E 50
EN1: Enf 7A 24
SE18 5G 107
Raglan St. NW5 6F 65
Raglan Ter. HA2: Harr 4F 59
Raglan Way UB5: N'olt 6G 59
Ragley Cl. W3 2J 97
Raider Cl. RM7: Mawney 1G 55
Railey M. NW5 5G 65
Railshead Rd. TW7: Isle 4B 114
Railton Rd. SE24 4A 120
Railway App. HA3: Harr 4K 41
N4 6A 48
SE1 5F 15 (1D 102)
SM6: Wall 5F 167
TW1: Twick 7A 114
Railway Arches E2 1F 85
(off Laburnum St.)
E2 1J 9
(off Geffrye St.)
E7 4J 69
(off Winchelsea Rd.)
E8 7H 67
(off Mentmore Ter.)
E10 7D 50
(off Capworth St.)
E11 2G 69
(off Leytonstone High Rd.)
E11 1F 69
(off Sidings, The)
E17 5C 50
(off Yunus Khan Cl.)
W12 2E 98
(off Shepherd's Bush Mkt.)
Railway Av. SE16 2J 103
(not continuous)
Railway Children Wlk. BR1: Brom 2J 141
SE12 2J 141
Railway Cotts. E15 2G 87
(off Baker's Row)
SW19 4K 135
W6 2E 98
(off Sulgrave Rd.)
Railway Gro. SE14 7B 104
Railway M. E3 3C 86
(off Wellington Way)
W11 6G 81
Railway Pas. TW11: Tedd 6A 132
Railway Pl. DA17: Belv 3G 109
Railway Ri. SE22 4E 120
Railway Rd. TW11: Tedd 4J 131
Railway Side SW13 3A 116
(not continuous)
Railway St. N1 2J 83
RM6: Chad H 7C 54
Railway Ter. E17 1E 50
SE13 5D 122
TW13: Felt 1J 129
Rainborough Cl. NW10 6J 61
Rainbow Av. E14 5D 104
Rainbow Ct. SE14 6A 104
(off Chipley St.)
Rainbow Ind. Est. SW20 2D 152
UB7: Yiew 7A 74
Rainbow Quay SE16 3A 104
(not continuous)
Rainbow St. SE5 7E 102
Rainbow Theatre 2A 66
Raines Est. Ct. N16 2F 67
Raine St. E1 1H 103
Rainham Cl. SE9 6J 125
SW11 6C 118
Rainham Ho. NW1 1G 83
(off Bayham Pl.)
Rainham Rd. NW10 3E 80
Rainham Rd. Nth. RM10: Dag 2G 73
Rainham Rd. Sth. RM10: Dag 4H 73
Rainhill Way E3 3C 86
(not continuous)
Rainsborough Av. SE8 4A 104
Rainsford Cl. HA7: Stan 5H 27
Rainsford Rd. NW10 2H 79
(not continuous)
Rainsford St. W2 7C 4 (6C 82)
Rainton Rd. SE7 5J 105
Rainville Rd. W6 6E 98
Raisins Hill HA5: Eastc 3A 40
Raith Av. N14 3C 32
Raleana Rd. E14 1E 104
Raleigh Av. SM6: Bedd 4H 167
UB4: Yead 5K 75
Raleigh Cl. HA4: Ruis 2H 57
HA5: Pinn 7B 40
NW4 5E 44
Raleigh Ct. BR3: Beck 1D 158
SE16 1K 103
(off Clarence M.)
SM6: Wall 6F 167
W12 2E 98
(off Scott's Rd.)
W13 5B 78
Raleigh Dr. KT5: Surb 1J 163
N20 3H 31
Raleigh Gdns. CR4: Mitc 3D 154
(not continuous)
SW2 6K 119
Raleigh Ho. BR1: Brom 1J 159
(off Hammelton Rd.)
E14 2D 104
(off Admirals Way)
SW1 7C 18
(off Dolphin Sq.)
Raleigh M. BR6: Chels 5K 173
N1 1B 84
(off Packington St.)
Raleigh Rd. EN2: Enf 4J 23
N2 2C 46
N8 4A 48
SE20 7K 139
TW9: Rich 3F 115
TW13: Felt 3H 129
UB2: S'hall 5C 94
Raleigh St. N1 1B 84
Raleigh Way N14 1C 32
TW13: Hanw 5A 130
Ralph Brook Ct. N1 1F 9
(off Chart St.)
Ralph Ct. W2 6K 81
(off Queensway)
Ralph Perring Ct. BR3: Beck 4C 158
Ralston St. SW3 6E 16 (5D 100)
Ramac Ind. Est. SE7 4K 105
Rama Cl. SW16 7J 137
Rama Ct. HA1: Harr 2J 59
Ramac Way SE7 4K 105
Rama La. SE19 7F 139
Ramar Ho. E1 5G 85
(off Hanbury St.)
Rambler Cl. SW16 4G 137
Rame Cl. SW17 5E 136
Ramilles Cl. SW2 6J 119
Ramillies Pl. W1 1A 12 (6G 83)
Ramillies Rd. DA15: Sidc 6B 126
NW7 2F 29
W4 4K 97

Ramillies St.—Rayburne Ct.

Ramillies St. W1 1A 12 (6G 83)
Ramones Ter. CR4: Mitc 4J 155
(off Yorkshire Rd.)
Rampart St. E1 6H 85
Ram Pas. KT1: King T 2D 150
Rampayne St.
SW1 5C 18 (5H 101)
Ram Pl. E9 6J 67
Rampton Cl. E4 3H 35
Ramsay Ho. NW8 2C 82
(off Townshend Est.)
Ramsay M. SW3 7C 16 (6C 100)
Ramsay Rd. E7 4G 69
W3 3J 97
Ramscroft Cl. N9 7K 23
Ramsdale Rd. SW17 5E 136
Ramsden Dr. RM5: Col R 1G 55
Ramsden Rd. DA8: Erith 7K 109
N11 5J 31
SW12 6E 118
Ramsey Cl. NW9 6B 44
UB6: G'frd 5H 59
Ramsey Ct. CR0: Croy 2B 168
(off Church St.)
Ramsey Ho. SW9 7A 102
Ramsey Rd. CR7: Thor H 6K 155
Ramsey St. E2 4G 85
Ramsey Wlk. N1 6D 66
(off Handa Wlk.)
Ramsey Way N14 7B 22
Ramsfort Ho. SE16 4H 103
(off Camilla Rd.)
Ramsgate Cl. E16 1K 105
Ramsgate St. E8 6F 67
Ramsgill App. IG2: Ilf 4K 53
Ramsgill Dr. IG2: Ilf 5K 53
Rams Gro. RM6: Chad H 4E 54
Ram St. SW18 5K 117
Ramulis Dr. UB4: Yead 4B 76
Ramuswood Av. BR6: Chels 5J 173
Rancliffe Gdns. SE9 4C 124
Rancliffe Rd. E6 2C 88
Randall Av. NW2 2A 62
Randall Cl. DA8: Erith 6J 109
SW11 1C 118
Randall Ct. NW7 7H 29
Randall Pl. SE10 7E 104
Randall Rd. SE11 4G 19 (5K 101)
Randall Row SE11 4G 19 (4K 101)
Randalls Rents SE16 3B 104
(off Gulliver St.)
Randell's Rd. N1 1J 83
(not continuous)
Randisbourne Gdns. SE6 3D 140
Randle Rd. TW10: Ham 4C 132
Randlesdown Rd. SE6 4C 140
(not continuous)
Randolph App. E16 6A 88
Randolph Av. W9 2K 81
Randolph Cl. DA7: Bex 3J 127
KT2: King T 5J 133
Randolph Cres. W9 4A 82
Randolph Gdns. NW6 2K 81
Randolph Gro. RM6: Chad H 5C 54
Randolph M. W9 4A 82
Randolph Rd. BR2: Brom 1D 172
E17 5D 50
UB1: S'hall 2D 94
W9 4A 82
Randolph St. NW1 7G 65
Randon Cl. HA2: Harr 2F 41
Ranelagh Av. SW6 3H 117
SW13 2C 116
Ranelagh Bri. W2 5K 81
Ranelagh Cl. HA8: Edg 4B 28
Ranelagh Dr. HA8: Edg 4B 28
TW1: Twick 4B 114
Ranelagh Gdns. E11 5A 52
IG1: Ilf 1D 70
SW6 3G 117
(not continuous)
Ranelagh Gdns. W4 7J 97
W6 4B 98
Ranelagh Gdns. Mans. SW6 3G 117
(off Ranelagh Gdns.)
Ranelagh Gro. SW1 5H 17 (5E 100)
Ranelagh Ho. SW3 5E 16
(off Elystan Pl.)
Ranelagh M. W5 2D 96
Ranelagh Pl. KT3: N Mald 5A 152
Ranelagh Rd. E6 1E 88
E11 4G 69
E15 2G 87
HA0: Wemb 6D 60
N17 3E 48
N22 1K 47
NW10 2B 80
SW1 6B 18 (5G 101)
UB1: S'hall 1B 94
W5 2D 96
Ranfurly Rd. SM1: Sutt 2J 165
Rangbourne Ho. N7 5J 65
Rangefield Rd. BR1: Brom 5G 141
Rangemoor Rd. N15 5F 49
Rangers House 1F 123
Ranger's Rd. E4 1B 36
Rangers Sq. SE10 1F 123
Range Way TW17: Shep 7C 146
Rangeworth Pl. DA15: Sidc 3K 143
Rangoon St. EC3 1J 15
Rankin Cl. NW9 3A 44
Rankine Ho. SE1 3C 102
(off Bath Ter.)
Ranleigh Gdns. DA7: Bex 7F 109
Ranmere St. SW12 1F 137
Ranmoor Cl. HA1: Harr 4H 41
Ranmoor Gdns. HA1: Harr 4H 41
Ranmore Av. CR0: Croy 3F 169
Ranmore Path BR5: St M Cry 4K 161
Ranmore Rd. SM2: Cheam 7F 165
Rannoch Cl. HA8: Edg 2C 28
Rannoch Rd. W6 6E 98
Rannock Av. NW9 7K 43
Ransome's Dock Bus. Cen.
SW11 7C 100
Ransom Rd. SE7 4A 106
Ranston St. NW1 5C 4 (5C 82)
Ranulf Rd. NW2 4H 63
Ranwell Cl. E3 1B 86
Ranworth Rd. N9 2D 34
Ranyard Cl. KT9: Chess 3F 163
Raphael Ct. SE16 5H 103
(off Stubbs Dr.)
Raphael Dr. KT7: T Ditt 7K 149
Raphael St. SW7 7E 10 (2D 100)
Rapley Ho. E2 2K 9
(off Turin St.)
Raquel Ct. SE1 6G 15
(off Snowfields)
Rashleigh Ct. SW8 2F 119
Rashleigh Ho. WC1 2E 6
(off Thanet St.)
Rasper Rd. N20 2F 31
Rastell Av. SW2 2H 137
RATCLIFF 5A 86
Ratcliffe Cl. SE12 7J 123
Ratcliffe Ct. SE1 7D 14
(off Gt. Dover St.)
Ratcliffe Cross St. E1 6K 85
Ratcliffe Ho. E14 6A 86
Ratcliffe La. E14 6A 86
Ratcliffe Orchard E1 7K 85
Ratcliff Rd. E7 5A 70
Rathbone Ho. E16 6H 87
(off Rathbone St.)
NW6 1J 81
Rathbone Mkt. E16 5H 87
Rathbone Pl. W1 6C 6 (5H 83)
Rathbone Sq. CR0: Croy 4C 168
Rathbone St. E16 5H 87
W1 6B 6 (5G 83)
Rathcoole Av. N8 5K 47
Rathcoole Gdns. N8 5K 47
Rathfern Rd. SE6 1B 140
Rathgar Av. W13 1B 96
Rathgar Cl. N3 2H 45
Rathgar Rd. SW9 3B 120
Rathmell Dr. SW4 6H 119
Rathmore Rd. SE7 5K 105
Rattray Ct. SE6 2H 141
Rattray Rd. SW2 4A 120
Raul Rd. SE15 2G 121
Raveley St. NW5 4G 65
(not continuous)
Raven Cl. NW9 2A 44
Ravendale Rd. TW16: Sun 2H 147
Ravenet St. SW11 1F 119
(not continuous)
Ravenfield Rd. SW17 3D 136
Ravenhill Rd. E13 2A 88
Raven Ho. SE16 4K 103
(off Tawny Way)
Ravenings Pde. IG3: Ilf 1A 72
Ravenna Rd. SW15 5F 117
Ravenor Ct. UB6: G'frd 4F 77
Ravenor Farm 3G 77
Ravenor Pk. Rd. UB6: G'frd 3F 77
Raven Rd. E18 2A 52
Raven Row E1 5H 85
(not continuous)
Ravensbourne Av. BR2: Brom 7F 141
TW19: Stanw 1A 128
Ravensbourne Ct. SE6 7C 122
Ravensbourne Gdns. IG5: Ilf 1E 52
W13 5B 78
Ravensbourne Ho. BR1: Brom 5F 141
NW8 5C 4
(off Broadley St.)
Ravensbourne Mans. SE8 6C 104
(off Berthon St.)
Ravensbourne Pk. SE6 7C 122
Ravensbourne Pk. Cres. SE6 7B 122
Ravensbourne Pl. SE13 2D 122
Ravensbourne Rd. BR1: Brom 3J 159
SE6 7B 122
TW1: Twick 6C 114
Ravensbourne Ter. TW19: Stanw 1A 128
Ravensbury Av. SM4: Mord 5A 154
Ravensbury Ct. CR4: Mitc 4B 154
(off Ravensbury Gro.)
Ravensbury Gro. CR4: Mitc 4B 154
Ravensbury La. CR4: Mitc 4B 154
Ravensbury Path CR4: Mitc 4B 154
Ravensbury Rd. BR5: St P 3K 161
SW18 2J 135
Ravensbury Ter. SW18 2K 135
Ravenscar NW1 1G 83
(off Bayham St.)
Ravenscar Rd. BR1: Brom 4G 141
KT6: Surb 2F 163
Ravens Cl. BR2: Brom 2H 159
EN1: Enf 2K 23
KT6: Surb 6D 150
Ravens Ct. KT1: King T 5D 150
(off Uxbridge Rd.)
Ravenscourt TW16: Sun 1H 147
Ravenscourt Av. W6 4C 98
Ravenscourt Cl. HA4: Ruis 7E 38
Ravenscourt Gdns. W6 4C 98
Ravenscourt Pk. EN5: Barn 4A 20
W6 3C 98
Ravenscourt Pk. Mans. W6 3D 98
(off Paddenswick Rd.)
Ravenscourt Pl. W6 4D 98
Ravenscourt Rd. W6 4D 98
(not continuous)
Ravenscourt Sq. W6 3C 98
Ravenscraig Rd. N11 4A 32
Ravenscroft Av. HA9: Wemb 1E 60
NW11 7H 45
(not continuous)
Ravenscroft Cl. E16 5J 87
Ravenscroft Cotts. EN5: New Bar 4D 20
Ravenscroft Cres. SE9 3D 142
Ravenscroft Pk. EN5: Barn 3A 20
Ravenscroft Rd. BR3: Beck 2J 157
E16 5J 87
W4 4J 97
Ravenscroft School Sports Cen. 7C 20
Ravenscroft St. E2 1K 9 (2F 85)
Ravensdale Av. N12 4F 31
Ravensdale Gdns. SE19 7D 138
Ravensdale Mans. N8 6J 47
(off Haringey Pk.)
Ravensdale Rd. N16 7F 49
TW4: Houn 3C 112
Ravensdon St. SE11 6K 19 (5A 102)
Ravensfield Cl. RM9: Dag 4D 72
Ravensfield Gdns. KT19: Ewe 5A 164
Ravenshaw St. NW6 5H 63
Ravenshill BR7: Chst 1F 161
Ravenshurst Av. NW4 4E 44
Ravenside KT1: King T 5D 150
(off Portsmouth Rd.)
Ravenside Cl. N18 5E 34
Ravenside Retail Pk. N18 5E 34
Ravenslea Rd. SW12 7D 118
Ravensleigh Gdns. BR1: Brom 5K 141
Ravensmead Rd. BR2: Brom 7F 141
Ravensmede Way W4 4B 98
Ravens M. SE12 5J 123
Ravenstone SE17 5E 102
Ravenstone Rd. N8 3A 48
NW9 6B 44
Ravenstone St. SW12 1E 136
Ravens Way SE12 5J 123
Ravenswood DA5: Bexl 1E 144
Ravenswood Av. BR4: W W'ck 1E 170
KT6: Surb 2F 163
Ravenswood Ct. KT2: King T 6H 133
Ravenswood Cres. BR4: W W'ck 1E 170
HA2: Harr 2D 58
Ravenswood Gdns. TW7: Isle 1J 113
Ravenswood Ind. Est. E17 4E 50
Ravenswood Rd. CR0: Wadd 3B 168
E17 4E 50
SW12 7F 119
Ravensworth Ct. SW6 7J 99
(off Fulham Rd.)
Ravensworth Rd. NW10 3D 80
SE9 3D 142
Ravent Rd. SE11 3H 19 (4K 101)
Raven Wharf SE1 6J 15
(off Lafone St.)
Ravey St. EC2 3G 9 (4E 84)
Ravine Gro. SE18 6J 107
Rav Pinter Cl. N16 7E 48
Rawalpindi Ho. E16 4H 87
Rawchester Cl. SW18 1H 135
Rawlings Cl. BR3: Beck 5E 158
BR6: Chels 5K 173
Rawlings Cres. HA9: Wemb 3H 61
Rawlings St. SW3 3E 16 (4D 100)
Rawlins Cl. CR2: Sels 7A 170
N3 3G 45
Rawlinson Ct. NW2 7E 44
Rawlinson Ho. SE13 4F 123
(off Mercator Rd.)
Rawlinson Point E16 5H 87
(off Fox Rd.)
Rawnsley Av. CR4: Mitc 5B 154
Rawreth Wlk. N1 1C 84
(off Basire St.)
Rawson St. SW11 1E 118
(not continuous)
Rawsthorne Cl. E16 1D 106
Rawsthorne Ct. TW4: Houn 4D 112
Rawstone Wlk. E13 2J 87
Rawstorne Pl. EC1 1A 8 (3B 84)
Rawstorne St. EC1 1A 8 (3B 84)
(not continuous)
Raybell Ct. TW7: Isle 2K 113
Rayburne Ct. IG9: Buck H 1F 37
W14 3G 99

Ray Cl.—Red Pl.

Ray Cl. KT9: Chess 6C 162
Raydean Rd. EN5: New Bar 5E 20
Raydons Gdns. RM9: Dag 4E 72
Raydons Rd. RM9: Dag 5E 72
Raydon St. N19 2F 65
Rayfield Cl. BR2: Brom 6C 160
Rayford Av. SE12 7H 123
Ray Gdns. HA7: Stan 5G 27
IG11: Bark 2A 90
Ray Gunter Ho. *SE17* *5B 102* (off Marsland Cl.)
Ray Ho. *N1* *1E 84* (off Colville Est.)
Rayleas Cl. SE18 1F 125
Rayleigh Av. TW11: Tedd 6J 131
Rayleigh Cl. N13 3J 33
Rayleigh Ct. KT1: King T 2G 151
N22 1C 48
Rayleigh Ri. CR2: S Croy 6E 168
Rayleigh Rd. E16 1K 105
IG8: Wfd G 6F 37
N13 3H 33
SW19 1H 153
Ray Lodge Rd. IG8: Wfd G 6F 37
Ray Massey Way *E6* *1C 88* (off High St. Nth.)
Raymead Av. CR7: Thor H 5A 156
Raymead Pas. *CR7: Thor H* *5A 156* (off Raymead Av.)
Raymede Towers *W10* *5F 81* (off Treverton St.)
Raymere Gdns. SE18 7H 107
Raymond Av. E18 3H 51
W13 3A 96
Raymond Bldgs. WC1 5H 7 (5K 83)
Raymond Cl. SE26 5J 139
Raymond Ct. N10 7A 32
Raymond Postgate Ct. SE28 7B 90
Raymond Revuebar *2C 12* (off Walkers Ct.)
Raymond Rd. BR3: Beck 4A 158
E13 1A 88
IG2: Ilf 7H 53
SW19 6G 135
Raymond Way KT10: Clay 6A 162
Raymouth Ho. *SE16* *4J 103* (off Raymouth Rd.)
Raymouth Rd. SE16 4H 103
Raynald Ho. SW16 3J 137
Rayne Ct. E18 4H 51
Rayne Ho. *W9* *4K 81* (off Delaware Rd.)
Rayner Ct. *W12* *2E 98* (off Bamborough Gdns.)
Rayners Cl. HA0: Wemb 5D 60
Rayners Cres. UB5: Yead 3K 75
Rayners Gdns. UB5: Yead 2K 75
RAYNERS LANE 1D 58
Rayners La. HA2: Harr 7D 40 (not continuous)
HA5: Pinn 5D 40
Rayners Rd. SW15 5G 117
Rayner Towers *E10* *7C 50* (off Albany Rd.)
Raynes Av. E11 7A 52
RAYNES PARK 4E 152
Raynes Pk. Bri. SW20 2E 152
Raynes Pk. School Sports Cen. 3D 152
Raynham *W2* *7D 4* (off Norfolk Cres.)
Raynham Av. N18 6B 34
Raynham Ho. *E1* *4K 85* (off Harpley Sq.)
Raynham Rd. N18 5B 34
W6 4D 98
Raynham Ter. N18 5B 34
Raynor Cl. UB1: S'hall 1D 94
Raynor Pl. N1 7C 66
Raynton Cl. HA2: Harr 1C 58
UB4: Hayes 4H 75
Raynton Dr. UB4: Hayes 4H 75
Ray Rd. KT8: W Mole 5F 149
Rays Av. N18 4D 34
Rays Rd. BR4: W W'ck 7E 158
N18 4D 34
Ray St. EC1 4K 7 (4A 84)
Ray St. Bri. EC1 4K 7
Ray Wlk. N7 2K 65
Raywood Cl. UB3: Harl 7E 92
Reachview Cl. NW1 7G 65
Read Cl. KT7: T Ditt 7A 150
Read Ct. E17 6C 50
Reade Ct. *W3* *3J 97* (off Stanley Rd.)
Reade Ho. *SE10* *6F 105* (off Trafalgar Gro.)
Reade Wlk. NW10 7A 62
Read Ho. SE11 7J 19
Reading Ho. *SE15* *6G 103* (off Friary Est.)
W2 *6A 82* (off Hallfield Est.)
Reading La. E8 6H 67
Reading Rd. SM1: Sutt 5A 166
UB5: N'olt 5F 59
Reading Way NW7 5A 30
Reads Cl. IG1: Ilf 3F 71
Reapers Cl. NW1 1H 83
Reapers Way TW7: Isle 5H 113
Reardon Ct. N21 2G 33
Reardon Ho. *E1* *1H 103* (off Reardon St.)
Reardon Path E1 1H 103 (not continuous)
Reardon St. E1 1H 103
Reaston St. SE14 7K 103
Rebecca Ct. DA14: Sidc 4B 144
Reckitt Rd. W4 5A 98
Record St. SE15 6J 103
Recovery St. SW17 5C 136
Recreation Av. RM7: Rom 5J 55
Recreation Rd. BR2: Brom 2H 159
DA15: Sidc 3J 143
SE26 4K 139
UB2: S'hall 4C 94
Recreation Way CR4: Mitc 3H 155
Rector St. N1 1C 84
Rectory Bus. Cen. DA14: Sidc 4B 144
Rectory Cl. DA14: Sidc 4B 144
E4 3H 35
HA7: Stan 5G 27
KT6: Surb 1C 162
N3 1H 45
SW20 3E 152
TW17: Shep 3C 146
Rectory Ct. E18 1H 51
SM6: Wall 4G 167
TW13: Felt 4A 130
Rectory Cres. E11 6A 52 (not continuous)
Rectory Farm Rd. EN2: Enf 1E 22
Rectory Fld. Cres. SE7 7A 106
Rectory Gdns. *BR3: Beck* *1C 158* (off Rectory Rd.)
N8 4J 47
SW4 3G 119
UB5: N'olt 1D 76
Rectory Grn. BR3: Beck 1B 158
Rectory Gro. CR0: Croy 2B 168
SW4 3G 119
TW12: Hamp 4D 130
Rectory La. DA14: Sidc 4B 144
HA7: Stan 5G 27
HA8: Edg 6B 28
KT6: Surb 1B 162
SM6: Wall 4G 167
SW17 6E 136
Rectory Orchard SW19 4G 135
Rectory Pk. Av. UB5: N'olt 3D 76
Rectory Pl. SE18 4E 106
Rectory Rd. BR2: Kes 7B 172
BR3: Beck 1C 158
E12 5D 70
E17 4D 50
N16 2F 67
RM10: Dag 6H 73
SM1: Sutt 3J 165
SW13 2C 116
TW4: Cran 2A 112
UB2: S'hall 3D 94
UB3: Hayes 6J 75
W3 1H 97
Rectory Sq. E1 5K 85
Rectory Way UB10: Ick 2D 56
Reculver Ho. *SE15* *6J 103* (off Lovelinch Cl.)
Reculver M. N18 4B 34
Reculver Rd. SE16 5K 103
Red Anchor Cl. SW3 6B 100
Redan Pl. W2 6K 81
Redan St. W14 3F 99
Redan Ter. SE5 2B 120
Red Barracks Rd. SE18 4D 106
Redberry Gro. SE26 3J 139
Redbourne Av. N3 1J 45
Redbourne Dr. SE28 6D 90 (not continuous)
Redbourne Ho. *E14* *6B 86* (off Norbiton Rd.)
Redbourn Ho. *W10* *4E 80* (off Sutton Way)
REDBRIDGE 6C 52
Redbridge Ent. Cen. IG1: Ilf 2G 71
Redbridge FC 4H 53
Redbridge Foyer *IG1: Ilf* *2G 71* (off Sylvan Rd.)
Redbridge Gdns. SE5 7E 102
Redbridge La. E. IG4: Ilf 6B 52
Redbridge La. W. E11 6K 51
REDBRIDGE RDBT. 6B 52
Redbridge Sports Cen. 1H 53
Redburn St. SW3 7E 16 (6D 100)
Redburn Trad. Est. EN3: Pond E 6E 24
Redcar Cl. UB5: N'olt 5F 59
Redcar St. SE5 7C 102
Redcastle Cl. E1 7J 85
Red Cedars Rd. BR6: Orp 7J 161
Redchurch St. E2 3J 9 (4F 85)
Redcliffe Cl. *SW5* *5K 99* (off Old Brompton Rd.)
Redcliffe Ct. *E5* *3H 67* (off Napoleon Rd.)
Redcliffe Gdns. IG1: Ilf 1E 70
SW10 5K 99
W4 7H 97
Redcliffe M. SW10 5K 99
Redcliffe Pl. SW10 6A 100
Redcliffe Rd. SW10 5A 100
Redcliffe Sq. SW10 5K 99
Redcliffe St. SW10 6K 99
Redclose Av. SM4: Mord 5J 153
Redclyffe Rd. E6 1A 88
Redclyf Ho. *E1* *4J 85* (off Cephas St.)
Redcourt CR0: Croy 3E 168
Red Cow La. EC1 3C 8 (4C 84)
Redcroft Rd. UB1: S'hall 7G 77
Redcross Way SE1 6D 14 (2C 102)
Redding Ho. SE18 3C 106
Reddings, The NW7 3G 29
Reddings Cl. NW7 4G 29
Reddins Rd. SE15 6G 103
Reddons Rd. BR3: Beck 7A 140
Redenham Ho. *SW15* *7C 116* (off Ellisfield Dr.)
Rede Pl. W2 6J 81
Redesdale Gdns. TW7: Isle 7A 96
Redesdale St. SW3 7D 16 (6C 100)
Redfern Av. TW4: Houn 7E 112
Redfern Ho. *E13* *1H 87* (off Redriffe Rd.)
Redfern Rd. NW10 7A 62
SE6 7E 122
Redfield La. SW5 4J 99
Redfield M. SW5 4K 99
Redford Av. CR7: Thor H 4K 155
SM6: Wall 6J 167
Redford Cl. TW13: Felt 2H 129
Redford Ho. *W10* *3H 81* (off Dowland St.)
Redford Wlk. *N1* *1C 84* (off Popham St.)
Redgate Dr. BR2: Hayes 2K 171
Redgate Ter. SW15 6F 117
Redgrave Cl. CR0: Croy 6F 157
Redgrave Rd. SW15 3F 117
Redgrave Ter. *E2* *3G 85* (off Derbyshire St.)
Red Hill BR7: Chst 5F 143
Redhill Ct. SW2 2A 138
Redhill Dr. HA8: Edg 2H 43
Redhill St. NW1 1K 5 (2F 83)
Red House 4E 126
Red Ho. La. DA6: Bex 4D 126
Redhouse Rd. CR0: Croy 6H 155
Red Ho. Sq. N1 6C 66
Redif Ho. RM10: Dag 4H 73
Redington Gdns. NW3 4K 63
Redington Ho. *N1* *2K 83* (off Priory Grn. Est.)
Redington Rd. NW3 3K 63
Redknap Ho. TW10: Ham 3C 132
Redland Gdns. KT8: W Mole 4D 148
Redlands N15 4D 48
TW11: Tedd 6A 132
Redlands, The BR3: Beck 2D 158
Redlands Ct. BR1: Brom 7H 141
Redlands Rd. EN3: Enf H 1F 25
Redlands Way SW2 7K 119
Red La. KT10: Clay 6A 162
Redleaf Cl. DA17: Belv 6G 109
Redleaves Av. TW15: Ashf 6D 128
Redlees Cl. TW7: Isle 4A 114
Red Leys UB8: Uxb 7A 56
Red Lion Bus. Pk. KT6: Surb 3F 163
Red Lion Cl. *SE17* *6D 102* (off Red Lion Row)
Red Lion Ct. EC4 1K 13 (6A 84)
SE1 4D 14 (1C 102)
Red Lion Hill N2 2B 46
Red Lion La. SE18 7E 106
Red Lion Pde. HA5: Pinn 3C 40
Red Lion Pl. SE18 1E 124
Red Lion Rd. KT6: Surb 2F 163
Red Lion Row SE17 6C 102
Red Lion Sq. SW18 5J 117
WC1 6G 7 (5K 83)
Red Lion St. TW9: Rich 5D 114
WC1 5G 7 (5K 83)
Red Lion Yd. W1 4H 11
Red Lodge BR4: W W'ck 1E 170
Red Lodge Cres. DA5: Bexl 3K 145
Red Lodge Rd. BR4: W W'ck 1E 170
DA5: Bexl 3K 145
Redman Cl. UB5: Yead 2A 76
Redman Ho. *EC1* *5J 7* (off Bourne Est.)
SE1 *7D 14* (off Borough High St.)
Redman's Rd. E1 5J 85
Redmead La. E1 1G 103
Redmead Rd. UB3: Harl 4G 93
Redmill Ho. *E1* *4H 85* (off Headlam St.)
Redmond Ho. *N1* *1K 83* (off Barnsbury Est.)
Redmore Rd. W6 4D 98
Red Oak Cl. BR6: Farnb 3F 173
Redo Ho. *E12* *5E 70* (off Dore Av.)
Red Path E9 6A 68
Red Pl. W1 2G 11 (7E 82)

Riverside Rd. DA14: Sidc 3E 144
E15 2E 86
N15 6G 49
SW17 4K 135
TW19: Stanw 5A 110
Riverside Studios 5E 98
(off River Ter.)
Riverside Twr. SW6 2A 118
(off Boulevard, The)
Riverside Vs. KT6: Surb 6C 150
Riverside Wlk.
BR4: W W'ck 1D 170
EN5: Barn 6A 20
(not continuous)
KT1: King T 3D 150
N12 6D 30
(not continuous)
SE10 3G 105
(Morden Wharf Rd.)
SE10 2F 105
(Tunnel Av.)
SW6 3G 117
TW7: Isle 3J 113
W4 6B 98
(off Chiswick Wharf)
Riverside Works IG11: Bark 7F 71
Riverside Workshops SE1 4D 14
(off Park St.)
Riverside Yd. SW17 4A 136
Riverstone Ct. KT2: King T 1F 151
River St. EC1 1J 7 (3A 84)
River Ter. W6 5E 98
WC2 3G 13
Riverton Cl. W9 3H 81
River Vw. EN2: Enf 3H 23
Riverview Ct. E14 3B 104
River Vw. Gdns. TW1: Twick 2K 131
Riverview Gdns. SW13 6D 98
Riverview Gro. W4 6H 97
River Vw. Hgts. SE16 2G 103
(off Bermondsey Wall W.)
Riverview Pk. SE6 2C 140
Riverview Rd. KT19: Ewe 4J 163
W4 7H 97
River Wlk. KT12: Walt T 6J 147
W6 7E 98
River Way KT19: Ewe 5K 163
SE10 3H 105
TW2: Twick 2F 131
Riverway N13 5F 33
River Wharf Bus. Pk. DA17: Belv 1K 109
Riverwood La. BR7: Chst 1H 161
Rivet Ho. SE1 5F 103
(off Coopers Rd.)
Rivington Av. IG8: Wfd G 2B 52
Rivington Ct. NW10 1C 80
Rivington Cres. NW7 7G 29
Rivington Pl. EC2 2H 9 (3E 84)
Rivington St. EC2 2G 9 (3E 84)
Rivington Wlk. E8 1G 85
Rivulet Rd. N17 7H 33
Rixon Ho. SE18 6F 107
Rixon St. N7 3A 66
Rixsen Rd. E12 5C 70
Roach Rd. E3 7C 68
Roads Pl. N19 2J 65
Roan Ind. Est. CR4: Mitc 1D 154
(off Lavender Av.)
Roan St. SE10 6E 104
Robarts Cl. HA5: Eastc 5K 39
Robbins Hall EN3: Pond E 6E 24
Robb Rd. HA7: Stan 6F 27
Robert Adam St. W1 7G 5 (6E 82)
Roberta St. E2 3G 85
Robert Bell Ho. SE16 4G 103
(off Rouel Rd.)
Robert Burns Ho. N17 7C 34
(off Northumberland Pk.)
Robert Burns M. SE24 5B 120
Robert Cl. W9 4A 4 (4A 82)
Robert Dashwood Way SE17 4C 102
Robert Gentry Ho. W14 5G 99
(off Gledstanes Rd.)
Robert Jones Ho. SE16 4G 103
(off Rouel Rd.)
Robert Keen Cl. SE15 1G 121
Robert Lowe Cl. SE14 7K 103
Roberton Dr. BR1: Brom 1A 160
Robert Owen Ho. N22 1A 48
(off Progress Way)
SW6 1F 117
Robert Runcie Ct. SW2 4K 119
Roberts All. W5 2D 96
Robertsbridge Rd.
SM5: Cars 1A 166
Roberts Cl. CR7: Thor H 3D 156
SE9 1H 143
SE16 2K 103
SM3: Cheam 7F 165
UB7: Yiew 1A 92
Roberts Ct. KT9: Chess 5D 162
N1 1B 84
(off Essex Rd.)
NW10 6A 62
SE20 1J 157
(off Maple Rd.)
Roberts M. BR6: Orp 1K 173
SW1 1G 17 (3E 100)
Robertson Gro. SW17 5C 136
Robertson Rd. E15 1E 86
Robertson St. SW8 3F 119
Roberts Pl. EC1 3K 7 (4A 84)
Roberts Rd. DA17: Belv 5G 109
E17 1D 50
NW7 6B 30
Robert St. CR0: Croy 3C 168
E16 1F 107
NW1 2K 5 (3F 83)
SE18 5H 107
(not continuous)
WC2 3F 13 (7J 83)
Robert Sutton Ho. E1 6J 85
(off Tarling St.)
Robeson St. E3 5B 86
Robina Cl. DA6: Bex 4D 126
HA6: Nwood 1H 39
SE20 1G 157
(off Sycamore Gro.)
Robin Cl. NW7 3F 29
RM5: Col R 1K 55
TW12: Hamp 5C 130
Robin Ct. E14 2E 104
SE16 4G 103
SM6: Wall 5G 167
Robin Cres. E6 5B 88
Robin Gro. HA3: Kent 6F 43
N6 2E 64
TW8: Bford 6C 96
Robin Hill Dr. BR7: Chst 6C 142
ROBIN HOOD 3A 134
Robinhood Cl. CR4: Mitc 3G 155
Robin Hood Ct. EC4 7K 7
(off Shoe La.)
Robin Hood Dr. HA3: Hrw W 7E 26
Robin Hood Gdns. E14 7E 86
(off Woolmore St., not continuous)
Robin Hood Grn. BR5: St M Cry 5K 161
Robin Hood La. DA6: Bex 5E 126
E14 7E 86
SM1: Sutt 5J 165
SW15 3A 134
Robinhood La. CR4: Mitc 3G 155
Robin Hood Rd. SW19 5C 134
Robin Hood Way SW15 3A 134
SW20 3A 134
UB6: G'frd 6K 59
Robin Ho. NW8 2C 82
(off Barrow Hill Est.)
Robin Howard Dance Theatre 2D 6
(in Place, The)
Robinia Cres. E10 2D 68
Robin La. NW4 3F 45
Robins Ct. BR3: Beck 2F 159
CR2: S Croy 4E 168
(off Birdhurst Rd.)
SE12 3A 142
Robinscroft M. SE10 1E 122
Robins Gro. BR4: W W'ck 3J 171
Robinson Cl. E11 3G 69
EN2: Enf 3H 23
Robinson Ct. N1 1B 84
(off St Mary's Path)
Robinson Cres.
WD23: Bushy 1B 26
Robinson Ho. E14 5C 86
(off Selsey St.)
W10 6F 81
(off Bramley Rd.)
Robinson Rd. E2 2J 85
RM10: Dag 4G 73
SW17 6C 136
Robinson's Cl. W13 5A 78
Robinson St. SW3 7E 16 (6D 100)
Robinwood Gro. UB8: Hil 4B 74
Robinwood Pl. SW15 4K 133
Robsart St. SW9 2K 119
Robson Av. NW10 7C 62
Robson Cl. E6 6C 88
EN2: Enf 2G 23
Robson Rd. SE27 3B 138
Roby Ho. EC1 3C 8
(off Mitchell St.)
Rocastle Rd. SE4 5A 122
Roch Av. HA8: Edg 2F 43
Rochdale Rd. E17 7C 50
SE2 5B 108
Rochdale Way SE8 7C 104
(not continuous)
Roche Ho. E14 7B 86
(off Beccles St.)
Rochelle Cl. SW11 4B 118
Rochelle St. E2 2J 9 (3F 85)
(not continuous)
Rochemont Wlk. E8 1G 85
(off Pownell Rd.)
Roche Rd. SW16 1K 155
Rochester Av. BR1: Brom 2K 159
E13 1A 88
TW13: Felt 2H 129
Rochester Cl. DA15: Sidc 6B 126
EN1: Enf 1K 23
SW16 7J 137
Rochester Ct. E2 4H 85
(off Wilmot St.)
NW1 7G 65
(off Rochester Sq.)
Rochester Dr. DA5: Bexl 6F 127
HA5: Pinn 5B 40
Rochester Gdns. CR0: Croy 3E 168
IG1: Ilf 7D 52
Rochester Ho. SE1 7F 15
(off Manciple St.)
SE15 6J 103
(off Sharratt St.)
Rochester M. NW1 7G 65
W5 4C 96
Rochester Pde. TW13: Felt 2J 129
Rochester Pl. NW1 6G 65
Rochester Rd. HA6: Nwood 3H 39
NW1 6G 65
SM5: Cars 4D 166
Rochester Row SW1 3B 18 (4G 101)
Rochester Sq. NW1 7G 65
Rochester St. SW1 2C 18 (3H 101)
Rochester Ter. NW1 6G 65
Rochester Wlk. SE1 4E 14 (1D 102)
Rochester Way DA1: Dart 7K 127
SE3 1K 123
SE9 3B 124
Rochester Way Relief Rd.
SE3 1K 123
SE9 4A 124
Roche Wlk. SM5: Cars 6B 154
Rochford N17 2E 48
(off Griffin Rd.)
Rochford Av. RM6: Chad H 5C 54
Rochford Cl. E6 2B 88
Rochford Wlk. E8 7G 67
Rochford Way CR0: Croy 6J 155
Rochfort Ho. SE8 5B 104
Rock Av. SW14 3K 115
Rockbourne M. SE23 1K 139
Rockbourne Rd. SE23 1K 139
Rock Cl. CR4: Mitc 2B 154
Rockell's Pl. SE22 6H 121
Rockfield Ho. NW4 4F 45
(off Belle Vue Est.)
SE10 6E 104
(off Welland St.)
Rockford Av. UB6: G'frd 2A 78
Rock Gdns. RM10: Dag 5H 73
Rock Gro. Way SE16 4G 103
(not continuous)
Rockhall Rd. NW2 4F 63
Rockhall Way NW2 3F 63
Rockhampton Cl. SE27 4A 138
Rockhampton Rd. CR2: S Croy 6E 168
SE27 4A 138
Rock Hill SE26 4F 139
(not continuous)
Rockingham Cl. SW15 4B 116
Rockingham St. SE1 3C 102
Rockland Rd. SW15 4G 117
Rocklands Dr. HA7: Stan 2B 42
Rockley Ct. W14 2F 99
(off Rockley Rd.)
Rockley Rd. W14 2F 99
Rockmount Rd. SE18 5K 107
SE19 6D 138
Rocks La. SW13 1C 116
Rock St. N4 2A 66
Rockware Av. UB6: G'frd 1H 77
Rockware Av. Bus. Cen. UB6: G'frd 1H 77
Rockwell Gdns. SE19 5E 138
Rockwell Rd. RM10: Dag 5H 73
Rockwood Pl. W12 2E 98
Rocliffe St. N1 2B 84
Rocombe Cres. SE23 7J 121
Rocque Ho. SW6 7H 99
(off Estcourt Rd.)
Rocque La. SE3 3H 123
Rodale Mans. SW18 6K 117
Rodborough Ct. W9 4J 81
(off Hermes Cl.)
Rodborough Rd. NW11 1J 63
Rodd Est. TW17: Shep 5E 146
Roden Ct. N6 7H 47
Roden Gdns. CR0: Croy 6E 156
Rodenhurst Rd. SW4 6G 119
Roden St. IG1: Ilf 3E 70
N7 3K 65
Roden Way IG1: Ilf 3E 70
(off Roden St.)
Roderick Ho. SE16 4J 103
(off Raymouth Rd.)
Roderick Rd. NW3 4D 64
Rodgers Ho. SW4 7H 119
(off Clapham Pk. Est.)
Rodin Ct. N1 1B 84
(off Essex Rd.)
Roding Av. IG8: Wfd G 6H 37
Roding Ho. N1 1A 84
(off Barnsbury Est.)
Roding La. IG7: Chig 2K 37
IG9: Buck H 1G 37
(not continuous)
IG10: Chig 1G 37
Roding La. Nth. IG8: Wfd G 6H 37
Roding La. Sth. IG4: Ilf, Wfd G 4B 52
(not continuous)
IG8: Wfd G 3B 52
Roding M. E1 1G 103
Roding Rd. E5 4K 67
E6 5F 89

Royal Pde.—Russell Ct.

Royal Pde. BR7: Chst 7G 143
RM10: Dag 6H 73
(off Church St.)
SE3 2H 123
SW6 7G 99
TW9: Kew 1G 115
(off Layton Pl.)
W5 3E 78
Royal Pde. M. BR7: Chst 7G 143
(off Royal Pde.)
SE3 2H 123
(off Royal Pde.)
Royal Pl. SE10 7E 104
Royal Rd. DA14: Sidc 3D 144
E16 6B 88
SE17 6B 102
TW11: Tedd 5H 131
Royal Route HA9: Wemb 4F 61
Royal St. SE1 1H 19 (3K 101)
Royal Twr. Lodge E1 3K 15
(off Cartwright St.)
Royalty M. W1 1C 12 (6H 83)
Royalty Studios W11 6G 81
(off Lancaster Rd.)
Royal Veterinary College 1H 83
Royal Victoria Docks Watersports Cen. 7J 87
Royal Victoria Patriotic Bldg.
SW18 6B 118
Royal Victoria Pl. E16 1K 105
Royal Victoria Sq. E16 7K 87
Royal Victor Pl. E3 2K 85
Royal Wlk. SM6: Wall 2F 167
Royal Westminster Lodge
SW1 3C 18
(off Elverton St.)
Roycraft Av. IG11: Bark 2K 89
Roycroft Cl. E18 1K 51
SW2 1A 138
Roydene Rd. SE18 6J 107
Roydon Cl. IG10: Lough 1H 37
SW11 2D 118
(off Battersea Pk. Rd.)
Roy Gdns. IG2: Ilf 4J 53
Roy Gro. TW12: Hamp 6F 131
Royle Bldg. N1 2C 84
(off Wenlock Rd.)
Royle Cres. W13 4A 78
Roymount Ct. TW2: Twick 3J 131
Roy Rd. HA6: Nwood 1H 39
Roy Sq. E14 7A 86
Royston Av. E4 5H 35
SM1: Sutt 3B 166
SM6: Bedd 4H 167
Royston Cl. KT12: Walt T 7J 147
TW5: Cran 1K 111
Royston Ct. E13 1J 87
(off Stopford Rd.)
SE24 6C 120
TW9: Kew 1F 115
Royston Gdns. IG1: Ilf 6B 52
Royston Ho. N11 4J 31
SE15 6H 103
(off Friary Est.)
Royston Pde. IG1: Ilf 6B 52
Royston Pk. Rd. HA5: H End 5A 26
Royston Rd. SE20 1K 157
TW10: Rich 5E 114
Roystons, The KT5: Surb 5H 151
Royston St. E2 2J 85
Rozel Ct. N1 1E 84
Rozel Rd. SW4 3G 119
Rozel Ter. CR0: Croy 2C 168
(off Church Rd.)
Rq33 SW18 4J 117
Rubastic Rd. UB2: S'hall 3A 94
Rubens Gdns. SE22 7G 121
(off Lordship La.)
Rubens Pl. SW4 4J 119
Rubens Rd. UB5: N'olt 2A 76
Rubens St. SE6 2B 140
Ruby Rd. E17 3C 50
Ruby St. NW10 7K 61
SE15 6H 103
Ruby Triangle SE15 6H 103
Ruckholt Cl. E10 3D 68
Ruckholt Rd. E9 4C 68
E10 4C 68
Rucklidge Av. NW10 2B 80
Rucklidge Pas.
NW10 2B 80
(off Rucklidge Av.)
Rudall Cres. NW3 4B 64
Rudbeck Ho. SE15 7G 103
(off Peckham Pk. Rd.)
Ruddington Cl. E5 4A 68
Ruddock Cl. HA8: Edg 7D 28
Ruddstreet Cl. SE18 4F 107
Ruddy Way NW7 6G 29
Rudge Ho. SE16 3G 103
(off Jamaica Rd.)
Rudgwick Ct. SE18 4C 106
(off Woodville St., not continuous)
Rudgwick Ter. NW8 1C 82
Rudland Rd. DA7: Bex 3H 127
Rudloe Rd. SW12 7G 119
Rudolf Pl. SW8 7F 19 (6J 101)
Rudolph Rd. E13 2H 87
NW6 2J 81
Rudyard Gro. NW7 6D 28
Ruegg Ho. SE18 6E 106
(off Woolwich Comn.)
Ruffetts, The CR2: Sels 7H 169
Ruffetts Cl. CR2: Sels 7H 169
Ruffle Cl. UB7: W Dray 2A 92
Rufford Cl. HA3: Kent 6A 42
Rufford St. N1 1J 83
Rufford Twr. W3 1H 97
Rufforth Ct. NW9 1A 44
(off Pageant Av.)
Rufus Bus. Cen. SW18 2K 135
Rufus Cl. HA4: Ruis 3C 58
Rufus Ho. SE1 7K 15
(off Abbey St.)
Rufus St. N1 2G 9 (3E 84)
Rugby Av. HA0: Wemb 5B 60
N9 1A 34
UB6: G'frd 6H 59
Rugby Cl. HA1: Harr 4J 41
Rugby Gdns. RM9: Dag 6C 72
Rugby Mans. W14 4G 99
(off Bishop King's Rd.)
Rugby Rd. NW9 4H 43
RM9: Dag 6B 72
TW1: Twick 5J 113
W4 2A 98
Rugby St. WC1 4G 7 (4K 83)
Rugg St. E14 7C 86
Rugless Ho. E14 2E 104
(off E. Ferry Rd.)
Rugmere NW1 7E 64
(off Ferdinand St.)
RUISLIP 1G 57
Ruislip Cl. UB6: G'frd 4F 77
RUISLIP COMMON 4E 38
Ruislip Ct. HA4: Ruis 2H 57
RUISLIP GARDENS 3J 57
Ruislip Lido Railway 4F 39
Ruislip Local Nature Reserve 3F 39
RUISLIP MANOR 2J 57
Ruislip Rd. UB1: S'hall 2B 76
UB5: N'olt 1A 76
UB6: G'frd 3E 76
Ruislip Rd. E. UB6: G'frd 4H 77
W7 4J 77
W13 4H 77
Ruislip St. SW17 4D 136
Ruislip Woodlands Cen. 4F 39
Rumball Ho. SE5 7E 102
(off Harris St.)
Rumbold Rd. SW6 7K 99
Rum Cl. E1 7J 85
Rumford Ho. SE1 3C 102
(off Tiverton St.)
Rumney Ct. UB5: N'olt 2B 76
(off Parkfield Dr.)
Rumsey Cl.
TW12: Hamp 6D 130
Rumsey M. N4 3B 66
Rumsey Rd. SW9 3K 119
Runacres Ct. SE17 5C 102
Runbury Circ. NW9 2K 61
Runcorn Cl. N17 4H 49
Runcorn Pl. W11 7G 81
Rundell Cres. NW4 5D 44
Rundell Twr. SW8 1K 119
Runes Cl. CR4: Mitc 4B 154
Runnelfield HA1: Harr 3J 59
Running Horse Yd. TW8: Bford 6E 96
Runnymede SW19 1A 154
Runnymede Cl. TW2: Whit 6F 113
Runnymede Ct. SM6: Wall 6F 167
SW15 1C 134
Runnymede Cres. SW16 1H 155
Runnymede Gdns. TW2: Whit 6F 113
UB6: G'frd 2J 77
Runnymede Ho. E9 4A 68
Runnymede Rd. TW2: Whit 6F 113
Runway, The HA4: Ruis 5K 57
Rupack St. SE16 2J 103
Rupert Av. HA9: Wemb 5E 60
Rupert Ct. KT8: W Mole 4E 148
(off St Peters Rd.)
W1 2C 12 (7H 83)
Rupert Gdns. SW9 2B 120
Rupert Ho. SE11 4K 19 (4A 102)
Rupert Rd. N19 3H 65
(not continuous)
NW6 2H 81
W4 3A 98
Rupert St. W1 2C 12 (7H 83)
Rural Way SW16 7F 137
Rusbridge Cl. E8 5G 67
Ruscoe Rd. E16 6H 87
Ruscombe Way TW14: Felt 7H 111
Rush, The SW19 1H 153
(off Kingston Rd.)
Rusham Rd. SW12 6D 118
Rushbrook Cres. E17 1B 50
Rushbrook Rd. SE9 2G 143
Rushbury Ct. TW12: Hamp 1E 148
Rush Comn. M. SW2 7K 119
(Cotherstone Rd.)
SW2 7J 119
(New Pk. Rd.)
Rushcroft Rd. E4 7J 35
SW2 4A 120
Rushcutters Ct. SE16 4A 104
(off Boat Lifter Way)
Rushden Cl. SE19 7D 138
Rushdene SE2 3D 108
(not continuous)
Rushdene Av. EN4: E Barn 7H 21
Rushdene Cl. UB5: Yead 2A 76
Rushdene Cres. UB5: Yead 2K 75
Rushdene Rd. HA5: Eastc 6B 40
Rushden Gdns. IG5: Ilf 2E 52
NW7 6K 29
Rushen Wlk. SM5: Cars 1B 166
Rushett Cl. KT7: T Ditt 1B 162
Rushett Rd. KT7: T Ditt 7B 150
Rushey Cl. KT3: N Mald 4K 151
Rushey Grn. SE6 7D 122
Rushey Hill EN2: Enf 4E 22
Rushey Mead SE4 5C 122
Rushford Rd. SE4 6B 122
RUSH GREEN 1K 73
Rush Grn. Gdns. RM7: Rush G 1J 73
Rush Grn. Rd. RM7: Rush G 1H 73
Rushgrove Av. NW9 5A 44
Rushgrove Ct. NW9 5A 44
Rushgrove Pde. NW9 5A 44
Rushgrove St. SE18 4D 106
Rush Hill M. SW11 3E 118
(off Rush Hill Rd.)
Rush Hill Rd. SW11 3E 118
Rushley Cl. BR2: Kes 4B 172
Rushmead E2 3H 85
TW10: Ham 3B 132
Rushmead Cl. CR0: Croy 4F 169
HA8: Edg 2C 28
Rushmere Ct. KT4: Wor Pk 2C 164
Rushmere Pl. SW19 5F 135
Rushmon Pl. SM3: Cheam 6G 165
Rushmon Vs. KT3: N Mald 4B 152
Rushmoor Cl. HA5: Eastc 4K 39
Rushmore Cl. BR1: Brom 3C 160
Rushmore Cres. E5 4K 67
Rushmore Ho. SW15 7C 116
W14 3G 99
(off Russell Rd.)
Rushmore Rd. E5 4J 67
(not continuous)
Rusholme Av. RM10: Dag 3G 73
Rusholme Gro. SE19 5E 138
Rusholme Rd. SW15 6F 117
Rushout Av. HA3: Kent 6B 42
Rushton Ho. SW8 2H 119
Rushton St. N1 2D 84
Rushworth St. SE1 6B 14 (2B 102)
Rushy Mdw. La. SM5: Cars 2C 166
Ruskin Av. DA16: Well 2A 126
E12 6C 70
TW9: Kew 7G 97
(not continuous)
TW14: Felt 6H 111
Ruskin Cl. NW11 6K 45
Ruskin Ct. N21 7E 22
SE5 3D 120
(off Champion Hill)
Ruskin Dr. BR6: Orp 3J 173
DA16: Well 3A 126
KT4: Wor Pk 2D 164
Ruskin Gdns. HA3: Kent 5F 43
W5 4D 78
Ruskin Gro. DA16: Well 2A 126
Ruskin Ho. CR2: S Croy 5D 168
(off Selsdon Rd.)
SW1 4D 18
(off Herrick St.)
Ruskin Mans. W14 6G 99
(off Queen's Club Gdns.)
Ruskin Pde. CR2: S Croy 5D 168
(off Selsdon Rd.)
Ruskin Pk. Ho. SE5 3D 120
Ruskin Rd. CR0: Croy 2B 168
DA17: Belv 4G 109
N17 1F 49
SM5: Cars 5D 166
TW7: Isle 3K 113
UB1: S'hall 7C 76
Ruskin Wlk. BR2: Brom 6D 160
N9 2B 34
SE24 5C 120
Ruskin Way SW19 1B 154
Rusland Av. BR6: Orp 3H 173
Rusland Hgts. HA1: Harr 4J 41
Rusland Pk. Rd. HA1: Harr 4J 41
Rusper Cl. HA7: Stan 4H 27
NW2 3E 62
Rusper Ct. SW9 2J 119
(off Clapham Rd.)
Rusper Rd. N22 2B 48
RM9: Dag 6C 72
Russell Av. N22 2A 48
Russell Cl. BR3: Beck 3D 158
DA7: Bex 4G 127
HA4: Ruis 2A 58
NW10 7J 61
SE7 7A 106
W4 6B 98
Russell Ct. E10 7D 50
EN5: New Bar 4F 21
N14 6C 22

St Aidan's Rd.—St Francis Ho.

St Aidan's Rd. SE22 6H 121
W13 2B 96
St Albans Av. E6 3D 88
TW13: Hanw 5B 130
W4 4K 97
St Albans Cl. NW11 1J 63
St Albans Ct. EC2 6D 8
St Alban's Cres. IG8: Wfd G 7D 36
N22 1A 48
St Alban's Gdns. TW11: Tedd 5A 132
St Alban's Gro. SM5: Cars 7C 154
W8 3K 99
St Alban's La. NW11 1J 63
St Albans Mans. *W8* *3K 99*
(off Kensington Ct. Pl.)
St Alban's Pl. N1 1B 84
St Albans Rd. EN5: Barn 1A 20
IG3: Ilf 1K 71
IG8: Wfd G 7D 36
KT2: King T 6E 132
NW5 3E 64
NW10 1A 80
SM1: Sutt 4H 165
St Alban's St. SW1 3C 12 (7H 83)
(not continuous)
St Albans Studios *W8* *3K 99*
(off St Albans Gro.)
St Albans Ter. W6 6G 99
St Albans Vs. NW5 3E 64
St Alfege Pas. SE10 6E 104
St Alfege Rd. SE7 6B 106
St Alphage Gdn. EC2 6D 8 (5C 84)
St Alphage Highwalk EC2 6D 8
St Alphage Ho. EC2 6E 8
St Alphage Wlk. HA8: Edg 2J 43
St Alphege Rd. N9 7D 24
St Alphonsus Rd. SW4 4G 119
St Amunds Cl. SE6 4C 140
St Andrew's Av. HA0: Wemb 4A 60
St Andrews Chambers *W1* *6B 6*
(off Wells St.)
St Andrews Cl. HA4: Ruis 2B 58
HA7: Stan 2C 42
KT7: T Ditt 1B 162
N12 4F 31
NW2 3D 62
SE16 5H 103
SE28 6D 90
TW7: Isle 1J 113
TW17: Shep 4F 147
St Andrews Ct. E17 2A 50
SM1: Sutt 3C 166
SW18 2A 136
St Andrews Dr. HA7: Stan 1C 42
St Andrew's Gro. N16 1D 66
St Andrew's Hill EC4 2B 14 (7B 84)
(not continuous)
St Andrews Mans. *W1* *6G 5*
(off Dorset St.)
W14 *6G 99*
(off St Andrews Rd.)
St Andrews M. N16 1E 66
SE3 7J 105
SW12 1H 137
St Andrew's Pl. NW1 3K 5 (4F 83)
St Andrews Rd. CR0: Croy 4C 168
DA14: Sidc 3D 144
E11 6G 51
E12 2C 70
E13 3K 87
E17 2K 49
EN1: Enf 3J 23
IG1: Ilf 7D 52
KT6: Surb 6D 150
N9 7D 24
NW9 1K 61
NW10 6D 62
NW11 6H 45
RM7: Rom 6K 55
SM5: Cars 3C 166
UB10: Uxb 1A 74
St Andrews Rd. W3 7A 80
W7 2J 95
W14 6G 99
St Andrews Sq. KT6: Surb 6D 150
W11 6G 81
St Andrew's Twr. *UB1: S'hall* *7G 77*
(off Baird Av.)
St Andrew St. EC1 6K 7 (5A 84)
St Andrews Way E3 4D 86
St Andrew's Wharf SE1 2F 103
St Anna Rd. EN5: Barn 5A 20
St Anne's Cl. N6 3E 64
St Anne's Ct. BR4: W W'ck 4G 171
NW6 1G 81
W1 1C 12 (6H 83)
St Anne's Flats *NW1* *1C 6*
(off Doric Way)
St Anne's Gdns. NW10 3F 79
St Anne's Pas. E14 6B 86
St Anne's Rd. E11 2F 69
HA0: Wemb 5D 60
St Anne's Row E14 6B 86
St Anne's Trad. Est. *E14* *6B 86*
(off St Anne's Row)
St Anne St. E14 6B 86
St Ann's IG11: Bark 1G 89
St Ann's Ct. NW4 3D 44
St Ann's Cres. SW18 6K 117
St Ann's Gdns. NW5 6E 64
St Ann's Hill SW18 5K 117
St Ann's Ho. *WC1* *2J 7*
(off Margery St.)
St Ann's La. SW1 2D 18 (3H 101)
St Ann's Pk. Rd. SW18 6A 118
St Ann's Pas. SW13 3A 116
St Ann's Rd. HA1: Harr 6J 41
IG11: Bark 1G 89
N9 2A 34
N15 5B 48
SW13 2B 116
W11 7F 81
St Ann's Shop. Cen. HA1: Harr 6J 41
St Ann's St. SW1 1D 18 (3H 101)
St Ann's Ter. NW8 2B 82
St Ann's Vs. W11 1F 99
St Ann's Way CR2: S Croy 6B 168
St Anselm's Pl. W1 2J 11 (7F 83)
St Anselm's Rd. UB3: Hayes 2H 93
St Anthony's Av. IG8: Wfd G 6F 37
St Anthony's Cl. E1 1G 103
SW17 2C 136
St Anthony's Ct. BR6: Farnb 2F 173
SW17 2E 136
St Anthony's Flats *NW1* *1C 6*
(off Aldenham St.)
St Anthony's Way TW14: Felt 4H 111
St Antony's Rd. E7 7K 69
St Arvan's Cl. CR0: Croy 3E 168
St Asaph Rd. SE4 3K 121
St Aubins Ct. N1 1D 84
St Aubyn's Av. SW19 5H 135
TW3: Houn 5E 112
St Aubyn's Cl. BR6: Orp 3K 173
St Aubyn's Gdns. BR6: Orp 2K 173
St Aubyn's Rd. SE19 6F 139
St Audrey Av. DA7: Bex 2G 127
St Augustine's Av. BR2: Brom 5C 160
CR2: S Croy 6C 168
HA9: Wemb 3E 60
W5 2E 78
St Augustine's Ho. *NW1* *1C 6*
(off Werrington St.)
St Augustine's Mans. *SW1* *4B 18*
(off Bloomburg St.)
St Augustine's Path N5 4C 66
St Augustine's Rd. DA17: Belv 4F 109
NW1 7H 65
St Austell Cl. HA8: Edg 2F 43
St Austell Rd. SE13 2E 122
St Awdry's Rd. IG11: Bark 7H 71
St Awdry's Wlk. IG11: Bark 7G 71
St Barnabas Cl. BR3: Beck 2E 158
SE22 5E 120
St Barnabas Ct. HA3: Hrw W 1G 41
St Barnabas Gdns. KT8: W Mole 5E 148
St Barnabas Rd. CR4: Mitc 7E 136
E17 6C 50
IG8: Wfd G 1K 51
SM1: Sutt 5B 166
St Barnabas St. SW1 5H 17 (5E 100)
St Barnabas Ter. E9 5K 67
St Barnabas Vs. SW8 1J 119
St Bartholomew's Cl. SE26 4H 139
St Bartholomew's Ct. *E6* *2C 88*
(off St Bartholomew's Rd.)
St Bartholomew's Hospital Mus. 6B 8
St Bartholomew's Rd. E6 2D 88
St Benedict's Cl. SW17 5E 136
St Benet's Cl. SW17 2C 136
St Benet's Gro. SM5: Cars 7A 154
St Benet's Pl. EC3 2F 15 (7D 84)
St Bernards CR0: Croy 3E 168
St Bernard's Cl. SE27 4D 138
St Bernards Ho. *E14* *3E 104*
(off Galbraith St.)
St Bernard's Rd. E6 1B 88
St Blaise Av. BR1: Brom 2K 159
St Botolph Row EC3 1J 15 (6F 85)
St Botolph St. EC3 7J 9 (6F 85)
St Brelades Ct. N1 1E 84
St Bride's Av. EC4 1A 14
HA8: Edg 1F 43
St Brides Cl. DA18: Erith 2D 108
St Bride's Crypt Mus. *1A 14*
(in St Bride's)
St Bride's Pas. EC4 1A 14
St Bride St. EC4 7A 8 (6B 84)
St Catherines Cl. KT9: Chess 6D 162
SW17 2C 136
St Catherines Ct. TW13: Felt 1J 129
W4 3A 98
St Catherine's Dr. SE14 2K 121
St Catherine's Farm Ct. HA4: Ruis 6E 38
St Catherines M.
SW3 3E 16 (4D 100)
St Catherine's Rd. E4 2H 35
HA4: Ruis 6F 39
St Catherines Twr. E10 7D 50
St Cecilia's Cl. SM3: Sutt 1G 165
St Chads Cl. KT6: Surb 7C 150
St Chad's Gdns. RM6: Chad H 7E 54
St Chad's Pl. WC1 1F 7 (3J 83)
St Chad's Rd. RM6: Chad H 7E 54
St Chad's St. WC1 1F 7 (3J 83)
(not continuous)
St Charles Pl. W10 5G 81
St Charles Sq. W10 5F 81
St Christopher Rd. UB8: Cowl 6A 74
St Christopher's Cl. TW7: Isle 1J 113
St Christophers Dr. UB3: Hayes 7K 75
St Christopher's Gdns.
CR7: Thor H 3A 156
St Christopher's Ho. *NW1* *2G 83*
(off Bridgeway St.)
St Christopher's M. SM6: Wall 5G 167
St Christopher's Pl. W1 7H 5 (6E 82)
St Clair Cl. IG5: Ilf 2D 52
St Clair Dr. KT4: Wor Pk 3D 164
St Clair Rd. E13 2K 87
St Clair's Rd. CR0: Croy 2E 168
St Clare Bus. Pk. TW12: Hamp H 6G 131
St Clare St. EC3 1J 15 (6F 85)
St Clements Ct. EC4 2F 15
N7 6K 65
SE14 *6K 103*
(off Myers La.)
W11 *7F 81*
(off Stoneleigh St.)
St Clement's Hgts. SE26 3G 139
St Clements Ho. *E1* *6J 9*
(off Leyden St.)
St Clement's La. WC2 1H 13 (6K 83)
St Clements Mans. *SW6* *6F 99*
(off Lillie Rd.)
St Clements St. N7 6A 66
St Clements Yd. SE22 4F 121
St Cloud Rd. SE27 4C 138
St Columbas Ho. E17 4D 50
St Crispin's Cl. NW3 4C 64
UB1: S'hall 6D 76
St Cross St. EC1 5K 7 (5A 84)
St Cuthbert's Rd. NW2 6H 63
St Cyprian's St. SW17 4D 136
St Daniel Ct. *BR3: Beck* *7C 140*
(off Brackley Rd.)
St Davids Cl. BR4: W W'ck 7D 158
HA9: Wemb 3J 61
SE16 *5H 103*
(off Masters Dr.)
St Davids Ct. E17 3E 50
TW15: Ashf 2B 128
St David's Dr. HA8: Edg 1F 43
St Davids M. *E3* *3A 86*
(off Morgan St.)
St David's Pl. NW4 7D 44
St Davids Sq. E14 5D 104
St Denis Rd. SE27 4D 138
St Dionis Rd. E12 3C 70
SW6 2H 117
St Domingo Ho. *SE18* *3D 106*
(off Leda Rd.)
St Donatt's Rd. SE14 1B 122
ST DUNSTAN'S 6H 165
St Dunstan's All. EC3 2G 15
St Dunstans Av. W3 7K 79
St Dunstan's Cl. UB3: Harl 5H 93
St Dunstan's Ct. EC4 1K 13 (6A 84)
St Dunstan's Gdns. W3 7K 79
St Dunstans Hill EC3 3G 15 (7E 84)
SM1: Sutt 4G 165
St Dunstan's La. BR3: Beck 6E 158
EC3 3G 15 (7E 84)
St Dunstan's Rd. E7 6K 69
SE25 4F 157
TW4: Cran 2K 111
(not continuous)
TW13: Felt 3H 129
W6 5F 99
W7 2J 95
St Edmund's Av. HA4: Ruis 6F 39
St Edmunds Cl. DA18: Erith 2D 108
NW8 1D 82
SW17 2C 136
St Edmund's Ct. *NW8* *1D 82*
(off St Edmund's Ter.)
St Edmunds Dr. HA7: Stan 1A 42
St Edmund's La. TW2: Whit 7F 113
St Edmund's Rd. IG1: Ilf 6D 52
N9 7B 24
St Edmunds Sq. SW13 6E 98
St Edmund's Ter. NW8 1C 82
St Edward's Cl. NW11 6J 45
St Edwards Ct. E10 7D 50
NW11 6J 45
St Edwards Way RM1: Rom 5K 55
St Egberts Way E4 1K 35
St Elizabeth Ct. E10 7D 50
St Elmo Rd. W12 1B 98
(not continuous)
St Elmos Rd. SE16 2A 104
St Erkenwald M. IG11: Bark 1H 89
St Erkenwald Rd. IG11: Bark 1H 89
St Ermin's Hill SW1 1C 18
St Ervan's Rd. W10 5H 81
St Eugene Ct. *NW6* *1G 81*
(off Salusbury Rd.)
St Faith's Cl. EN2: Enf 1H 23
St Faith's Rd. SE21 1B 138
St Fidelis Rd. DA8: Erith 4K 109
St Fillans Rd. SE6 1E 140
St Francis Cl. BR5: Pet W 6J 161
St Francis' Ho. *NW1* *2H 83*
(off Bridgeway St.)

St Francis Rd. DA8: Erith 4K 109
SE22 4E 120
St Francis Twr. *E4* 6G 35
(off Burnside Av.)
St Francis Way IG1: Ilf 4H 71
St Frideswide's M.
E14 6E 86
St Gabriel's Cl. E11 2K 69
E14 5D 86
St Gabriels Mnr. *SE5* 1B 120
(off Cormont Rd.)
St Gabriels Rd. NW2 5F 63
St George's Av. E7 7K 69
N7 4H 65
NW9 4K 43
UB1: S'hall 7D 76
W5 2D 96
St George's Bldgs. *SE1* 3B 102
(off St George's Rd.)
St George's Cathedral 1K 5 (3F 83)
St George's Cir. SE1 7A 14 (3B 102)
St Georges Cl.
HA0: Wemb 3A 60
NW11 6H 45
SE28 6D 90
SW8 1G 119
St Georges Ct. E6 4D 88
E17 5F 51
EC4 7A 8 (6B 84)
HA3: Kent 6A 42
(off Kenton Rd.)
SW1 5A 18
(off St George's Dr.)
SW15 4H 117
St George's Dr. SW1 4K 17 (4F 101)
UB10: Ick 3B 56
ST GEORGE'S FIELD 7C 82
St George's Flds. W2 1D 10 (6C 82)
St George's Gdns. KT6: Surb 2H 163
St George's Gro. SW17 3B 136
St George's Ho. *NW1* 2H 83
(off Bridgeway St.)
St Georges Ind. Est. KT2: King T 5D 132
N22 7G 33
St George's La. EC3 2F 15
St George's Mans. *SW1* 5D 18
(off Causton St.)
St George's M. NW1 7D 64
SE1 1K 19
SE8 4B 104
St Georges Pde. SE6 2B 140
St George's Path *SE4* 4C 122
(off Adelaide Av.)
St George's Pl. TW1: Twick 1A 132
St George's RC Cathedral 1K 19 (3A 102)
St Georges Rd. BR1: Brom 2D 160
BR3: Beck 1D 158
BR5: Pet W 6H 161
CR4: Mitc 3F 155
DA14: Sidc 6D 144
E7 7K 69
E10 3E 68
EN1: Enf 1A 24
IG1: Ilf 7D 52
KT2: King T 7G 133
N9 3B 34
N13 3E 32
NW11 6H 45
RM9: Dag 5E 72
SE1 1K 19 (3A 102)
SM6: Wall 5F 167
SW19 7H 135
(not continuous)
TW1: Twick 5B 114
TW9: Rich 3F 115
TW13: Hanw 4B 130
W4 2K 97
W7 1K 95
St George's Rd. W. BR1: Brom 1C 160
St George's Shop. & Leisure Cen.
HA1: Harr 6J 41
St Georges Sq. E7 7K 69
E14 7A 86
KT3: N Mald 3A 152
SE8 4B 104
(not continuous)
SW1 5C 18 (5H 101)
St George's Sq. M.
SW1 6C 18 (5H 101)
St George's Ter. *E6* 3C 88
(off Masterman Rd.)
NW1 7D 64
SE15 7G 103
(off Peckham Hill St.)
St George's Theatre 4H 65
St George St. W1 1K 11 (7F 83)
St George's Wlk. CR0: Croy 3C 168
St George's Way SE15 6E 102
St George's Wharf *SE1* 6K 15
(off Shad Thames)
St George Wharf SW8 7E 18 (6J 101)
St Gerards Cl. SW4 5G 119
St German's Pl. SE3 1J 123
St German's Rd. SE23 1A 140
St Giles Av. RM10: Dag 7H 73
UB10: Ick 4E 56
St Giles Cir. W1 7D 6 (6H 83)
St Giles Cl. BR6: Farnb 5H 173
RM10: Dag 7H 73
St Giles Ct. WC2 7E 6
St Giles High St. WC2 7D 6 (6H 83)
St Giles Ho. EN5: New Bar 4F 21
St Giles Pas. WC2 1D 12
St Giles Rd. SE5 7E 102
TW5: Hest 7C 94
St Giles Ter. *EC2* 6D 8
(off Beech St.)
St Giles Twr. *SE5* 1E 120
(off Gables Cl.)
St Gilles Ho. *E2* 2K 85
(off Mace St.)
St Gothard Rd. SE27 4D 138
(not continuous)
St Gregory Cl. HA4: Ruis 4A 58
St Helena Ho. *WC1* 2J 7
(off Margery St.)
St Helena Rd. SE16 4K 103
St Helena St. WC1 2J 7 (3A 84)
St Helens KT7: T Ditt 7K 149
St Helen's Cres. SW16 1K 155
St Helen's Gdns. W10 5F 81
St Helen's Pl. EC3 7G 9 (6E 84)
St Helen's Rd. DA18: Erith 2D 108
IG1: Ilf 6D 52
SW16 1K 155
W13 1B 96
ST HELIER 7C 154
St Helier Av. SM4: Mord 7A 154
St Helier Ct. *N1* 1E 84
(off De Beauvoir Est.)
SE16 2K 103
(off Poolmans St.)
St Helier's Av. TW3: Houn 5E 112
St Helier's Rd. E10 6E 50
St Hilda's Av. TW15: Ashf 5A 128
St Hilda's Cl. NW6 7F 63
SW17 2C 136
St Hilda's Rd. SW13 6D 98
St Hilda's Wharf *E1* 1J 103
(off Wapping High St.)
St Hubert's Ho. *E14* 3C 104
(off Janet St.)
St Hughes Cl. SW17 2C 136
St Hugh's Rd. SE20 1H 157
St Ivian Ct. N10 2E 46
St James SE14 1A 122
St James Apartments *E17* 5A 50
(off High St.)
St James App. EC2 4G 9 (4E 84)
St James Av. N20 3H 31
SM1: Sutt 5J 165
W13 1A 96
St James Cl. EN4: E Barn 4G 21
HA4: Ruis 2A 58
KT3: N Mald 5B 152
N20 3H 31
SE18 5G 107
St James Ct. *E2* 3G 85
(off Bethnal Grn. Rd.)
E12 2A 70
SE3 1K 123
SW1 1B 18 (3G 101)
St James Gdns. HA0: Wemb 7D 60
RM6: Ilf 4B 54
St James Ga. IG9: Buck H 1F 37
St James Gro. SW11 2D 118
St James' Mans. *NW6* 7J 63
(off W. End La.)
St James M. E14 3E 104
E17 5A 50
(off St James's St.)
St James Residences *W1* 2C 12
(off Brewer St.)
St James Rd. CR4: Mitc 7E 136
E15 5H 69
KT6: Surb 6D 150
N9 2C 34
SM1: Sutt 5J 165
SM5: Cars 3C 166
ST JAMES'S 4C 12 (1H 101)
St James's SW1 4B 12 (1G 101)
St James's Av. BR3: Beck 3A 158
E2 2J 85
TW12: Hamp H 5G 131
St James's Chambers *SW1* 4B 12
(off Jermyn St.)
St James's Cl. *NW8* 1D 82
(off St James's Ter. M.)
SW17 2D 136
St James's Cotts. TW9: Rich 5D 114
St James's Ct. HA1: Harr 6A 42
KT1: King T 3E 150
N18 6B 34
(off Fore St.)
St James's Cres. SW9 3A 120
St James's Dr. SW17 1D 136
St James's Gdns. W11 1G 99
(not continuous)
St James's La. N10 4F 47
St James's Mkt. SW1 3C 12 (7H 83)
St James's Palace 5B 12 (2G 101)
St James's Pk. 6C 12 (2H 101)
St James's Pk. CR0: Croy 7C 156
St James's Pas. EC3 1H 15
St James's Pl. SW1 5A 12 (1G 101)
St James's Rd. CR0: Croy 7B 156
KT1: King T 2D 150
SE1 6G 103
SE16 3G 103
TW12: Hamp H 5F 131
St James's Sq. SW1 4B 12 (1G 101)
St James's St. E17 5A 50
SW1 4A 12 (1G 101)
St James's Ter. *NW8* 1D 82
(off Prince Albert Rd.)
St James's Ter. M. NW8 1D 82
St James St. W6 5E 98
St James's Wlk. EC1 3A 8 (4B 84)
St James Ter. SW12 1E 136
St James Way DA14: Sidc 5E 144
St Jeromes Gro. UB3: Hayes 6E 74
St Joan's Rd. N9 2A 34
St John Fisher Rd. DA18: Erith 3D 108
ST JOHNS 2C 122
St John's Av. N11 5J 31
NW10 1B 80
SW15 5F 117
St Johns Chu. Rd. E9 5J 67
St Johns Cl. HA9: Wemb 5E 60
N14 6B 22
N20 3F 31
(off Rasper Rd.)
SW6 7J 99
St John's Cotts. SE20 7J 139
St John's Ct. DA8: Erith 4K 109
E1 1H 103
(off Scandrett St.)
HA1: Harr 6K 41
HA6: Nwood 1G 39
(off Murray Rd.)
IG9: Buck H 1E 36
KT1: King T 4E 150
(off Beaufort Rd.)
N4 2B 66
N5 4B 66
SE13 2E 122
TW7: Isle 2K 113
W6 4D 98
(off Glenthorne Rd.)
St John's Cres. SW9 3A 120
St Johns Dr. SW18 1K 135
St John's Est. N1 2D 84
SE1 6J 15
St John's Gdns. W11 7G 81
St John's Gate 4A 8
St John's Gro. N19 2G 65
SW13 2B 116
TW9: Rich 4E 114
St John's Hill SW11 5B 118
St John's Hill Gro. SW11 4B 118
St Johns Ho. *E14* 4E 104
(off Pier St.)
SE17 6D 102
(off Lytham St.)
St John's La. EC1 4A 8 (4B 84)
St John's M. W11 6J 81
St Johns Pde. *DA14: Sidc* 4A 144
(off Sidcup High St.)
W13 1B 96
St John's Pk. SE3 7H 105
St John's Pk. Mans. N19 3G 65
St John's Pas. SW19 6G 135
St John's Path EC1 4A 8
St Johns Pathway SE23 1J 139
St John's Pl. EC1 4A 8 (4B 84)
St John's Rd. BR5: Pet W 6H 161
CR0: Croy 3B 168
DA8: Erith 5K 109
DA14: Sidc 4B 144
DA16: Well 3B 126
E4 4J 35
E6 1C 88
E16 6J 87
E17 2D 50
HA1: Harr 6K 41
HA9: Wemb 4D 60
IG2: Ilf 7H 53
IG11: Bark 1J 89
KT1: Hamp W 2C 150
KT3: N Mald 3J 151
KT8: E Mos 4H 149
N15 6E 48
NW11 6H 45
SE20 6J 139
SM1: Sutt 2K 165
SM5: Cars 3C 166
SW11 4C 118
SW19 7G 135
TW7: Isle 2K 113
TW9: Rich 4E 114
TW13: Hanw 4C 130
UB2: S'hall 3C 94
St John's Sq. EC1 4A 8 (4B 84)
St John's Ter. E7 6K 69
SE18 6G 107
SW15 3A 134
(off Kingston Va.)
W10 4F 81
St John St. EC1 1K 7 (2A 84)
St John's Va. SE8 2C 122
St John's Vs.
N11 5J 31
(off Friern Barnet Rd.)
N19 2H 65

Sandringham Ct.—School Ho.

Sandringham Ct. DA15: Sidc 6K 125
KT2: King T *1E 150*
(off Skerne Wlk.)
SE16 *1K 103*
(off King & Queen Wharf)
UB10: Hil 4E 74
W1 *1B 12*
(off Dufour's Pl.)
W9 *3A 82*
(off Maida Va.)
Sandringham Cres. HA2: Harr 2E 58
Sandringham Dr. DA2: Bexl 2K 145
DA16: Well 2J 125
TW15: Ashf 4A 128
Sandringham Flats *WC2* *2D 12*
(off Charing Cross Rd.)
Sandringham Gdns. IG6: Ilf 3G 53
KT8: W Mole 4E 148
N8 6J 47
N12 6G 31
TW5: Cran 1J 111
Sandringham Ho. *W14* *4G 99*
(off Windsor Way)
Sandringham M. TW12: Hamp 1D 148
W5 7D 78
Sandringham Rd. BR1: Brom 5J 141
CR7: Thor H 5C 156
E7 5A 70
E8 5F 67
E10 6F 51
IG11: Bark 5K 71
KT4: Wor Pk 3C 164
N22 3C 48
NW2 6D 62
NW11 7G 45
TW6: H'row A 5A 110
UB5: N'olt 7E 58
Sandrock Pl. CR0: Croy 4K 169
Sandrock Rd. SE13 3C 122
SANDS END 1A 118
Sand's End La. SW6 1K 117
Sandstone La. E16 7K 87
Sandstone Pl. N19 2F 65
Sandstone Rd. SE12 2K 141
Sands Way IG8: Wfd G 6J 37
Sandtoft Rd. SE7 6K 105
Sandwell Cres. NW6 6J 63
Sandwich Ho. *SE16* *2J 103*
(off Swan Rd.)
WC1 *2E 6*
(off Sandwich St.)
Sandwich St. WC1 2E 6 (3J 83)
Sandwick Cl. NW7 7H 29
Sandy Bury BR6: Orp 3H 173
Sandycombe Rd. TW9: Kew, Rich 3F 115
TW14: Felt 1J 129
Sandycoombe Rd. TW1: Twick 6C 114
Sandycroft SE2 6A 108
Sandy Dr. TW14: Felt 1G 129
Sandy Hill Av. SE18 5F 107
Sandy Hill Rd. SE18 4F 107
SM6: Wall 7G 167
Sandyhill Rd. IG1: Ilf 4F 71
Sandy La. BR5: St P 7D 144
BR6: Orp 7K 161
CR4: Mitc 1E 154
(not continuous)
DA14: Sidc 7D 144
HA3: Kent 6F 43
KT1: Hamp W 7A 132
KT12: Walt T 6K 147
SM2: Cheam 7G 165
SM6: Wall 6H 167
TW10: Ham 2C 132
TW11: Tedd 7A 132
Sandy La. Nth. SM6: Wall 6H 167
Sandy La. Sth. SM6: Wall 7G 167
Sandymount Av. HA7: Stan 5H 27
Sandy Ridge BR7: Chst 6E 142
Sandy Rd. NW3 2K 63
(not continuous)
Sandys Row E1 6H 9 (5E 84)
Sandy Way CR0: Croy 3B 170
KT12: Walt T 7H 147
Sanford La. N16 3F 67
Sanford St. SE14 6A 104
Sanford Ter. N16 3F 67
Sanford Wlk. N16 2F 67
SE14 6A 104
Sanger Av. KT9: Chess 5E 162
Sangley Rd. SE6 7D 122
SE25 4E 156
Sangora Rd. SW11 4B 118
Sankey Ho. *E2* *2J 85*
(off St James's Av.)
Sansom Rd. E11 2H 69
Sansom St. SE5 1D 120
Sans Wlk. EC1 3K 7 (4A 84)
Santley Ho. SE1 7K 13 (2A 102)
Santley St. SW4 4K 119
Santos Rd. SW18 5J 117
Santway, The HA7: Stan 5D 26
Sapcote Trad. Cen. NW10 6B 62
Saperton Wlk. SE11 3H 19
Saphora Cl. BR6: Farnb 5H 173
Sapperton Ct. EC1 3C 8
Sapphire Cl. E6 6E 88
RM8: Dag 1C 72
Sapphire Ct. *E1* *7G 85*
(off Cable St.)
Sapphire Rd. SE8 4A 104
Saracen Cl. CR0: Croy 6D 156
Saracens Head Yd. EC3 1J 15
Saracen St. E14 6C 86
Sarah Ct. UB5: N'olt 1D 76
Sarah Ho. *E1* *6H 85*
(off Commercial Rd.)
Sarah St. N1 1H 9 (3E 84)
Sarah Swift Ho. *SE1* *6F 15*
(off Kipling St.)
Sara La. Ct. *N1* *2E 84*
(off Stanway St.)
Saratoga Rd. E5 4J 67
Sara Turnbull Ho. SE18 4D 106
Sardinia St. WC2 1G 13 (6K 83)
Sarita Cl. HA3: Hrw W 2H 41
Sarjant Path *SW19* *2F 135*
(off Blincoe Cl.)
Sarjeant Ct. *BR4: W W'ck* *2F 171*
(off Bencurtis Pk.)
Sark Cl. TW5: Hest 7E 94
Sark Ho. EN3: Enf W 1E 24
Sark Twr. *SE28* *2G 107*
(off Erebus Dr.)
Sark Wlk. E16 6K 87
Sarnes Ct. *N11* *4A 32*
(off Oakleigh Rd. Sth.)
Sarnesfield Ho. *SE15* *6H 103*
(off Pencraig Way)
Sarnesfield Rd. EN2: Enf 4J 23
Sarratt Ho. *W10* *5E 80*
(off Sutton Way)
Sarre Rd. NW2 5H 63
Sarsen Av. TW3: Houn 2E 112
Sarsfeld Rd. SW12 1D 136
Sarsfield Rd. UB6: G'frd 2B 78
Sartor Rd. SE15 4K 121
Sarum Ter. E3 4B 86
Sassoon NW9 1B 44
Satanita Cl. E16 6B 88
Satchell Mead NW9 1B 44
Satchwell Rd. E2 2K 9 (3G 85)
Satchwell St. E2 2K 9 (3G 85)
Sattar M. *N16* *3D 66*
(off Clissold Rd.)
Saul Ct. SE15 6F 103
Sauls Grn. E11 3G 69
Saunders Cl. *E14* *7B 86*
(off Limehouse C'way.)
Saunders Ho. *SE16* *2K 103*
(off Quebec Way)
Saunders Ness Rd. E14 5E 104
Saunders Rd. SE18 5K 107
UB10: Uxb 7B 56
Saunders St. SE11 3J 19 (4A 102)
Saunders Way SE28 7B 90
Saunderton Rd. HA0: Wemb 5B 60
Saunton Av. UB3: Harl 7H 93
Saunton Ct. *UB1: S'hall* *7G 77*
(off Haldane Rd.)
Savage Gdns. E6 6D 88
EC3 2H 15 (7E 84)
(not continuous)
Savannah Cl. SE15 7F 103
Savernake Ct. HA7: Stan 6G 27
Savernake Ho. N4 7C 48
Savernake Rd. N9 6B 24
NW3 4D 64
Savery Dr. KT6: Surb 7C 150
Savile Cl. KT3: N Mald 5A 152
KT7: T Ditt 7K 149
Savile Gdns. CR0: Croy 2F 169
Savile Row W1 2A 12 (7G 83)
Saville Cres. TW15: Ashf 6F 129
Saville Rd. E16 1C 106
RM6: Chad H 6F 55
TW1: Twick 1K 131
W4 3K 97
Saville Row BR2: Hayes 1H 171
EN3: Enf H 2E 24
Savill Gdns. SW20 3C 152
Savill Ho. *E16* *1F 107*
(off Robert St.)
SW4 6H 119
Savill Row IG8: Wfd G 6C 36
Savin Lodge *SM2: Sutt* *7A 166*
(off Walnut M.)
Savona Cl. SW19 7F 135
Savona Ho. *SW8* *7G 101*
(off Savona St.)
Savona St. SW8 7G 101
Savoy Av. UB3: Harl 5G 93
Savoy Bldgs. WC2 3G 13
SAVOY CIRCUS 7B 80
Savoy Cl. E15 1G 87
HA8: Edg 5B 28
Savoy Ct. NW3 3A 64
WC2 3F 13 (7K 83)
Savoy Hill WC2 3G 13 (7K 83)
Savoy Pde. EN1: Enf 3K 23
Savoy Pl. WC2 3F 13 (7J 83)
Savoy Row WC2 2G 13
Savoy Steps WC2 3G 13
Savoy St. WC2 3G 13 (7K 83)
Savoy Theatre *3F 13*
(off Strand)
Savoy Way WC2 3G 13
Sawbill Cl. UB4: Yead 5B 76
Sawkins Cl. SW19 2G 135
Sawley Rd. W12 1C 98
Sawmill Yd. E3 1A 86
Sawtry Cl. SM5: Cars 7C 154
Sawyer Cl. N9 2B 34
Sawyer Ct. NW10 7K 61
Sawyers Cl. RM10: Dag 6J 73
Sawyer's Hill TW10: Rich 7F 115
Sawyers Lawn W13 6A 78
Sawyer St. SE1 6C 14 (2C 102)
Saxby Rd. SW2 7J 119
Saxham Rd. IG11: Bark 2J 89
Saxlingham Rd. E4 3A 36
Saxon Av. TW13: Hanw 2C 130
Saxonbury Av. TW16: Sun 3K 147
Saxonbury Cl. CR4: Mitc 3B 154
Saxonbury Ct. N7 5J 65
Saxonbury Gdns. KT6: Surb 1C 162
Saxon Bus. Cen. SW19 2A 154
Saxon Cl. E17 7C 50
KT6: Surb 6D 150
UB8: Hil 5B 74
Saxon Dr. W3 6G 79
Saxonfield Cl. SW2 1K 137
Saxon Gdns. UB1: S'hall 7C 76
Saxon Ho. *E1* *6K 9*
(off Thrawl St.)
TW13: Hanw 2D 130
Saxon Lodge *CR0: Croy* *1C 168*
(off Tavistock Rd.)
Saxon Rd. BR1: Brom 7H 141
E3 2B 86
E6 4D 88
HA9: Wemb 3J 61
IG1: Ilf 6F 71
KT2: King T 1E 150
N22 1B 48
SE25 5D 156
TW15: Ashf 6F 129
UB1: S'hall 7C 76
Saxon Ter. SE6 2B 140
Saxon Wlk. DA14: Sidc 6C 144
Saxon Way N14 6C 22
Saxony Pde. UB3: Hayes 5E 74
Saxton Cl. SE13 3F 123
Sayers Ho. *N2* *2B 46*
(off Grange, The)
Sayer's Wlk. TW10: Rich 7F 115
Sayesbury La. N18 5B 34
Sayes Ct. SE8 6B 104
Sayes Ct. St. SE8 6B 104
Scadbury Pk. Nature Reserve 7K 143
Scads Hill Cl. BR6: Pet W 6K 161
Scafell *NW1* *1A 6*
(off Stanhope St.)
Scala St. W1 5B 6 (5G 83)
Scales Rd. N17 3F 49
Scampston M. W10 6F 81
Scandrett St. E1 1H 103
Scarba Wlk. *N1* *6D 66*
(off Marquess Rd.)
Scarborough Rd. E11 1F 69
N4 1A 66
N9 7D 24
TW6: H'row A 6E 110
Scarborough St. E1 1K 15 (6F 85)
Scarbrook Rd. CR0: Croy 3C 168
Scarle Rd. HA0: Wemb 6D 60
Scarlet Rd. SE6 3G 141
Scarlette Mnr. Way SW2 7A 120
Scarsbrook Rd. SE3 3B 124
Scarsdale Pl. W8 3K 99
Scarsdale Rd. HA2: Harr 3G 59
Scarsdale Studios *W8* *3J 99*
(off Stratford Rd.)
Scarsdale Vs. W8 3J 99
Scarth Rd. SW13 3B 116
Scawen Cl. SM5: Cars 4E 166
Scawen Rd. SE8 5A 104
Scawfell St. E2 2F 85
Sceaux Gdns. SE5 1E 120
Sceptre Ct. *EC3* *3K 15*
(off Tower Hill)
Sceptre Ho. *E1* *4J 85*
(off Malcolm Rd.)
Sceptre Rd. E2 3J 85
Sceynes Link N12 4D 30
Schafer Ho. NW1 2A 6 (3G 83)
Schiller International University *5J 13*
(off Stamford St.)
Schofield Wlk. SE3 7J 105
Scholars Cl. EN5: Barn 4B 20
Scholars Pl. N16 3E 66
Scholars Rd. E4 1A 36
SW12 1G 137
Scholefield Rd. N19 2H 65
Scholey Ho. SW11 3C 118
Schomberg Ho. *SW1* *3D 18*
(off Page St.)
Schonfeld Sq. N16 2D 66
School All. TW1: Twick 1A 132
School App. E2 1H 9 (3E 84)
Schoolbank Rd. SE10 3H 105
Schoolbell M. E3 2A 86
School Ho. *SE1* *4E 102*
(off Page's Wlk.)

School Ho. La.—Selby Ho.

School Ho. La. E1 . . . . . 7K **85**
TW11: Tedd 7B **132**
School La. DA16: Well 3B **126**
HA5: Pinn 4C **40**
KT1: Hamp W 1C **150**
KT6: Surb 1G **163**
TW17: Shep 6D **146**
WD23: Bush 1A **26**
School of Hygiene & Tropical Medicine 5D 6
School of Oriental & African Studies 4D 6
School Pas.
KT1: King T 2F **151**
UB1: S'hall 7D **76**
School Rd. BR7: Chst 1G **161**
E12 . . . . . 4D **70**
KT1: Hamp W 1C **150**
KT8: E Mos 4H **149**
NW10 . . . . . 4K **79**
RM10: Dag 1G **91**
TW3: Houn 3G **113**
TW12: Hamp H 6G **131**
TW15: Ashf 6D **128**
School Rd. Av. TW12: Hamp H 6G **131**
SCHOOL ROAD JUNC. **7D 128**
School Sq. SE10 . . . . . 3H **105**
School Wlk. TW16: Sun 4H **147**
School Way N12 . . . . . 6G **31**
RM8: Dag 3C **72**
(not continuous)
Schooner Cl. E14 . . . . . 3F **105**
IG11: Bark 3B **90**
SE16 . . . . . 2K **103**
Schubert Rd. SW15 . . . . . 5H **117**
Science Mus. 2B 16 (3B 100)
Sclater St. E1 . . . . . 3J **9** (4F **85**)
Scoble Pl. N16 . . . . . 4F **67**
Scoles Cres. SW2 . . . . . 1A **138**
Scope Way KT1: King T 4E **150**
Scoresby St. SE1 . . . . . 5A **14** (1B **102**)
Scorton Av. UB6: G'frd 2A **78**
Scorton Ho. *N1* *2E 84*
(off Whitmore Est.)
Scotch Comn. W13 . . . . . 5A **78**
SCOTCH HOUSE **2D 100**
Scoter Cl. IG8: Wfd G 7E **36**
Scoter Ct. *SE8* *6B 104*
(off Abinger Gro.)
Scot Gro. HA5: Pinn 1B **40**
Scotia Bldg. *E1* *7K 85*
(off Jardine Rd.)
Scotia Ct. *SE16* *2J 103*
(off Canada Est.)
Scotia Rd. SW2 . . . . . 7A **120**
Scotland Grn. N17 . . . . . 2F **49**
Scotland Grn. Rd.
EN3: Pond E 5E **24**
Scotland Grn. Rd. Nth.
EN3: Pond E 4E **24**
Scotland Pl. SW1 . . . . . 5E **12** (1J **101**)
Scotland Rd. IG9: Buck H 1F **37**
Scotney Cl. BR6: Farnb 4E **172**
Scotney Ho. E9 . . . . . 6J **67**
Scots Cl. TW19: Stanw 1A **128**
Scotsdale Cl. BR5: Pet W 4J **161**
SM3: Cheam 7G **165**
Scotsdale Rd. SE12 . . . . . 5K **123**
Scotson Ho. SE11 . . . . . 4J **19**
Scotswood St. EC1 . . . . . 3K **7** (4A **84**)
Scotswood Wlk. N17 . . . . . 7B **34**
Scott Cl. KT19: Ewe 5J **163**
SW16 . . . . . 1K **155**
UB7: W Dray 4B **92**
Scott Ct. W3 . . . . . 2K **97**
Scott Cres. HA2: Harr 1F **59**
Scott Ellis Gdns.
NW8 . . . . . 2A **4** (3B **82**)
Scottes La. RM8: Dag 1D **72**
Scott Farm Cl. KT7: T Ditt 1B **162**
Scott Gdns. TW5: Hest 7B **94**
Scott Ho. DA17: Belv 5F **109**
E13 . . . . . *2J 87*
(off Queens Rd. W.)
E14 . . . . . *2C 104*
(off Admirals Way)
N1 . . . . . *1D 84*
(off Sherborne St.)
N7 . . . . . *6K 65*
(off Caledonian Rd.)
NW8 . . . . . *4C 4*
(off Broadley St.)
NW10 . . . . . *7K 61*
(off Kingthorpe Rd.)
Scott Lidgett Cres.
SE16 . . . . . 2G **103**
Scott Russell Pl. E14 . . . . . 5D **104**
Scotts Av. BR2: Brom 2F **159**
TW16: Sun 7G **129**
Scotts Ct. *W12* *2E 98*
(off Scott's Rd.)
Scotts Dr. TW12: Hamp 7F **131**
Scotts Farm Rd. KT19: Ewe 6J **163**
Scott's La. BR2: Brom 3F **159**
Scotts Pas. SE18 . . . . . 4F **107**
Scotts Rd. BR1: Brom 7J **141**
E10 . . . . . 1E **68**
UB2: S'hall 3A **94**
W12 . . . . . 2D **98**
Scott's Sufferance Wharf SE1 . . . . . 7K **15**
Scott St. E1 . . . . . 4H **85**
Scotts Way TW16: Sun 7G **129**
Scott's Yd. EC4 . . . . . 2E **14** (7D **84**)
Scott Trimmer Way TW3: Houn 2C **112**
Scottwell Dr. NW9 . . . . . 5B **44**
Scoulding Ho. *E14* *3C 104*
(off Mellish St.)
Scoulding Rd. E16 . . . . . 6J **87**
Scouler St. E14 . . . . . 7E **86**
Scout App. NW10 . . . . . 4A **62**
Scout La. SW4 . . . . . 3G **119**
Scout Way NW7 . . . . . 4E **28**
Scovell Cres. SE1 . . . . . 7C **14**
Scovell Rd. SE1 . . . . . 7C **14** (2C **102**)
Scrattons Ter. IG11: Bark 2D **90**
Screen on Baker Street (Cinema) *5F 5*
(off Baker St.)
Screen on the Green Cinema *1B 84*
(off Upper St.)
Screen on the Hill (Cinema)
Belsize Pk. 5C 64
Scriven Ct. E8 . . . . . 1F **85**
Scriven St. E8 . . . . . 1F **85**
Scrooby St. SE6 . . . . . 6D **122**
Scrope Ho. *EC1* *5J 7*
(off Bourne Est.)
Scrubs La. NW10 . . . . . 3C **80**
W10 . . . . . 3C **80**
Scrutton Cl. SW12 . . . . . 7H **119**
Scrutton St. EC2 . . . . . 4G **9** (4E **84**)
Scudamore La. NW9 . . . . . 4J **43**
Scutari Rd. SE22 . . . . . 5J **121**
Scylla Cres. TW6: H'row A 7D **110**
(not continuous)
Scylla Rd. SE15 . . . . . 3G **121**
(not continuous)
TW6: H'row A 6D **110**
Seabright St. E2 . . . . . 3H **85**
Seabrook Dr. BR4: W W'ck 2G **171**
Seabrook Gdns. RM7: Rush G 7G **55**
Seabrook Rd. RM8: Dag 3D **72**
Seaburn Cl. RM13: Rain 2K **91**
Seacole Cl. W3 . . . . . 6K **79**
Seacon Twr. E14 . . . . . 2B **104**
Seacourt Rd. SE2 . . . . . 2D **108**
Seafield Rd. N11 . . . . . 4C **32**
Seaford Cl. HA4: Ruis 1F **57**
Seaford Ho. *SE16* *2J 103*
(off Swan Rd.)
Seaford Rd. E17 . . . . . 3D **50**
EN1: Enf 4K **23**
N15 . . . . . 5D **48**
Seaford Rd. TW6: H'row A 5A **110**
W13 . . . . . 1B **96**
Seaford St. WC1 . . . . . 2F **7** (3K **83**)
Seaforth Av. KT3: N Mald 5D **152**
Seaforth Cres. N5 . . . . . 5C **66**
Seaforth Gdns. IG8: Wfd G 5F **37**
KT19: Ewe 4B **164**
N21 . . . . . 7E **22**
Seaforth Pl. SW1 . . . . . 1B **18**
Seagar Pl. E3 . . . . . 5B **86**
Seager Bldgs. SE8 . . . . . 1C **122**
Seagrave Cl. E1 . . . . . 5K **85**
Seagrave Lodge *SW6* *6J 99*
(off Seagrave Rd.)
Seagrave Rd. SW6 . . . . . 6J **99**
Seagry Rd. E11 . . . . . 7J **51**
Seagull Cl. IG11: Bark 3A **90**
Seagull La. E16 . . . . . 7J **87**
Sealand Rd. TW6: H'row A 6C **110**
Sealand Wlk. UB5: N'olt 3B **76**
Seal Ho. *SE1* *7F 15*
(off Pardoner St.)
Seal St. E8 . . . . . 4F **67**
Searles Cl. SW11 . . . . . 7C **100**
Searles Dr. E6 . . . . . 5F **89**
Searles Rd. SE1 . . . . . 4D **102**
Searson Ho. *SE17* *4B 102*
(off Canterbury Pl.)
Sears St. SE5 . . . . . 7D **102**
Seasons Cl. W7 . . . . . 1K **95**
Seasprite Cl. UB5: N'olt 3B **76**
Seaton Av. IG3: Ilf 5K **71**
Seaton Cl. E13 . . . . . 4J **87**
SE11 . . . . . 5K **19** (5A **102**)
SW15 . . . . . 1D **134**
TW2: Whit 6H **113**
Seaton Dr. TW15: Ashf 2A **128**
Seaton Gdns. HA4: Ruis 3H **57**
Seaton Point *E5* *4G 67*
(off Nolan Way)
Seaton Rd. CR4: Mitc 2C **154**
DA16: Well 7C **108**
HA0: Wemb 2E **78**
TW2: Whit 6G **113**
UB3: Harl 4F **93**
Seaton Sq. NW7 . . . . . 7A **30**
Seaton St. N18 . . . . . 5B **34**
Sebastian Ct. IG11: Bark 1K **89**
Sebastian Ho. *N1* *1G 9*
(off Hoxton St.)
Sebastian St. EC1 . . . . . 2B **8** (3B **84**)
Sebastopol Rd. N9 . . . . . 4B **34**
Sebbon St. N1 . . . . . 7B **66**
Sebergham Gro. NW7 . . . . . 7H **29**
Sebert Rd. E7 . . . . . 5K **69**
Sebright Ho. *E2* *2G 85*
(off Coate St.)
Sebright Pas. E2 . . . . . 2G **85**
Sebright Rd. EN5: Barn 2A **20**
Secker Cres. HA3: Hrw W 1G **41**
Secker Ho. *SW9* *2B 120*
(off Loughborough Est.)
Secker St. SE1 . . . . . 5J **13** (1A **102**)
Secombe Theatre 5K 165
Second Av. E12 . . . . . 4C **70**
E13 . . . . . 3J **87**
E17 . . . . . 5C **50**
EN1: Enf 5A **24**
HA9: Wemb 2D **60**
KT12: Walt T 6K **147**
N18 . . . . . 4D **34**
NW4 . . . . . 4F **45**
RM6: Chad H 5C **54**
RM10: Dag 1H **91**
SW14 . . . . . 3A **116**
UB3: Hayes 1H **93**
W3 . . . . . 1B **98**
W10 . . . . . 4G **81**
Second Cl. KT8: W Mole 4G **149**
Second Cross Rd. TW2: Twick 2J **131**
Second Way HA9: Wemb 4H **61**
Sedan Way SE17 . . . . . 5E **102**
Sedcombe Cl. DA14: Sidc 4B **144**
Sedcote Rd. EN3: Pond E 5D **24**
Sedding St. SW1 . . . . . 3G **17** (4E **100**)
Sedding Studios *SW1* *3G 17*
(off Sedding St.)
Seddon Highwalk *EC2* *5C 8*
(off Seddon Ho.)
Seddon Ho. EC2 . . . . . 5C **8**
Seddon Rd. SM4: Mord 5B **154**
Seddon St. WC1 . . . . . 2H **7** (3K **83**)
Sedgebrook Rd. SE3 . . . . . 2B **124**
Sedgecombe Av. HA3: Kent 5C **42**
Sedgefield Ct. *UB5: N'olt* *5F 59*
(off Newmarket Av.)
Sedgeford Rd. W12 . . . . . 1B **98**
Sedgehill Rd. SE6 . . . . . 4C **140**
Sedgemere Av. N2 . . . . . 3A **46**
Sedgemere Rd. SE2 . . . . . 3C **108**
Sedgemoor Dr. RM10: Dag 4G **73**
Sedge Rd. N17 . . . . . 7D **34**
Sedgeway SE6 . . . . . 1H **141**
Sedgewick Av. UB10: Hil 7D **56**
Sedgewood Cl. BR2: Hayes 7H **159**
Sedgmoor Pl. SE5 . . . . . 7E **102**
Sedgwick Ho. *E3* *5C 86*
(off Gale St.)
Sedgwick Rd. E10 . . . . . 2E **68**
Sedgwick St. E9 . . . . . 5K **67**
Sedleigh Rd. SW18 . . . . . 6H **117**
Sedlescombe Rd. SW6 . . . . . 6J **99**
Sedley Cl. EN1: Enf 1C **24**
Sedley Ct. SE26 . . . . . 2H **139**
Sedley Ho. *SE11* *5H 19*
(off Newburn St.)
Sedley Pl. W1 . . . . . 1J **11** (6F **83**)
Sedum Cl. NW9 . . . . . 5H **43**
Seeley Dr. SE21 . . . . . 4E **138**
Seelig Av. NW9 . . . . . 7C **44**
Seely Rd. SW17 . . . . . 6E **136**
Seething La. EC3 . . . . . 2H **15** (7E **84**)
SEETHING WELLS 6C 150
Seething Wells La. KT6: Surb 6C **150**
Sefton Av. HA3: Hrw W 2H **41**
NW7 . . . . . 5E **28**
Sefton Cl. BR5: St M Cry 4K **161**
Sefton Ct. EN2: Enf 2G **23**
TW3: Houn 1F **113**
Sefton Rd. BR5: St M Cry 4K **161**
CR0: Croy 1G **169**
Sefton St. SW15 . . . . . 3E **116**
Segal Cl. SE23 . . . . . 7A **122**
Sekforde St. EC1 . . . . . 4A **8** (4B **84**)
Sekhon Ter. TW13: Hanw 3E **130**
Selan Gdns. UB4: Yead 5K **75**
Selbie Av. NW10 . . . . . 5B **62**
Selborne Av. DA5: Bexl 1E **144**
E12 . . . . . 4E **70**
Selborne Gdns. NW4 . . . . . 4C **44**
UB6: G'frd 1A **78**
Selborne Rd. CR0: Croy 3E **168**
DA14: Sidc 4B **144**
E17 . . . . . 5B **50**
IG1: Ilf 2E **70**
KT3: N Mald 2A **152**
N14 . . . . . 3D **32**
N22 . . . . . 1K **47**
SE5 . . . . . 2D **120**
Selborne Wlk. E17 . . . . . 5B **50**
Selborne Wlk. Shop. Cen. E17 . . . . . 4B **50**
Selbourne Av. KT6: Surb 2F **163**
Selbourne Ho. SE1 . . . . . 7E **14**
Selby Cen., The 6K 33
Selby Chase HA4: Ruis 2K **57**
Selby Cl. BR7: Chst 6E **142**
E6 . . . . . 5C **88**
KT9: Chess 7E **162**
Selby Gdns. UB1: S'hall 4E **76**
Selby Grn. SM5: Cars 7C **154**
Selby Ho. *W10* *3G 81*
(off Beethoven St.)

Selby Rd.—Shafton M.

Selby Rd. E11 .3G 69
E13 .5K 87
N17 .7K 33
SE20 .2G 157
SM5: Cars .7C 154
TW15: Ashf .6E 128
W5 .4B 78
Selby St. E1 .4G 85
Selcroft Ho. SE10 .5H 105
(off Glenister Rd.)
Selden Ho. SE15 .2J 121
(off Selden Rd.)
Selden Rd. SE15 .2J 121
Selden Wlk. N7 .2K 65
Seldon Ho. SW1 .6A 18
(off Churchill Gdns.)
SW8 .7G 101
(off Stewart's Rd.)
Selfridges .1G 11
(off Oxford St.)
SELHURST .6D 156
Selhurst Cl. SW19 .1F 135
Selhurst New Rd. SE25 .6E 156
Selhurst Pk. .4E 156
Selhurst Pl. SE25: Croy, Lon .6E 156
Selhurst Rd. N9 .3J 33
SE25 .6E 156
Selina Ho. NW8 .3B 4
(off Frampton St.)
Selinas La. RM8: Dag .7E 54
Selkirk Rd. SW17 .4C 136
TW2: Twick .2G 131
Sellers Hall Cl. N3 .7D 30
Sellincourt Rd. SW17 .5C 136
Sellindge Cl. BR3: Beck .7B 140
Sellons Av. NW10 .1B 80
Sellwood Dr. EN5: Barn .5A 20
Selma Ho. W12 .6D 80
(off Du Cane Rd.)
Selman Ho. E9 .6A 68
SELSDON .7J 169
Selsdon Av. CR2: S Croy .6D 168
Selsdon Cl. KT6: Surb .5E 150
RM5: Col R .1J 55
Selsdon Ct. UB1: S'hall .6F 77
(off Dormers Ri.)
Selsdon Pk. Rd. CR0: Sels .7K 169
CR2: Sels .7K 169
Selsdon Rd. CR2: S Croy .5D 168
E11 .7J 51
E13 .1A 88
NW2 .2B 62
SE27 .3A 138
Selsdon Way E14 .3D 104
Selsea Pl. N16 .5E 66
Selsey Cres. DA16: Well .1D 126
Selsey St. E14 .5C 86
Selvage La. NW7 .5E 28
Selway Cl. HA5: Eastc .4K 39
Selway Ho. SW8 .1J 119
(off Sth. Lambeth Rd.)
Selwood Pl. SW7 .5A 16 (5B 100)
Selwood Rd. CR0: Croy .2H 169
KT9: Chess .4D 162
SM3: Sutt .1H 165
Selwoods SW2 .7A 120
Selwood Ter.
SW7 .5A 16 (5B 100)
Selworthy Cl. E11 .5J 51
Selworthy Rd. SE6 .3B 140
Selwyn Av. E4 .6K 35
IG3: Ilf .6K 53
TW9: Rich .3E 114
Selwyn Cl. TW4: Houn .4C 112
Selwyn Ct. E17 .5C 50
(off Yunus Khan Cl.)
HA8: Edg .7C 28
HA9: Wemb .3J 61
SE3 .3H 123
Selwyn Cres.
DA16: Well .3B 126
Selwyn Rd. E3 .2B 86
E13 .1K 87
KT3: N Mald .5K 151
NW10 .7K 61
Semley Ga. E9 .6B 68
Semley Ho. SW1 .4J 17
(off Semley Pl.)
Semley Pl. SW1 .4H 17 (4E 100)
Semley Rd. SW16 .2J 155
Senate St. SE15 .2J 121
Senators Lodge E3 .2A 86
(off Roman Rd.)
Senator Wlk. SE28 .3H 107
Seneca Rd. CR7: Thor H .4C 156
Sener Ct. CR2: S Croy .6C 168
Senga Rd. SM6: Wall .1E 166
Senhouse Rd. SM3: Cheam .3F 165
Senior St. W2 .5K 81
Senlac Rd. SE12 .1K 141
Sennen Rd. EN1: Enf .7A 24
Sennen Wlk. SE9 .3C 142
Senrab St. E1 .6K 85
Sentinel Cl. UB5: N'olt .4C 76
Sentinel Sq. NW4 .4E 44
September Ct. UB1: S'hall .1F 95
(off Dormer's Wells La.)
UB8: Uxb .2A 74
September Way HA7: Stan .6G 27
Septimus Pl. EN1: Enf .5B 24
Sequoia Cl. WD23: Bushy .1C 26
Sequoia Gdns. BR6: Orp .7K 161
Sequoia Pk. HA5: H End .6A 26
Seraph Ct. EC1 .1C 8
(off Moreland St.)
Serbin Cl. E10 .7E 50
Serenaders Rd. SW9 .2A 120
Sergeant Ind. Est. SW18 .6K 117
Serica Ct. SE10 .7E 104
Serjeants Inn EC4 .1K 13 (6A 84)
Serle St. WC2 .7H 7 (6K 83)
Sermon La. EC4 .1C 14
Serpentine, The .1C 100
Serpentine Gallery .6A 10 (2B 100)
Serpentine Rd. W2 .5C 10 (1C 100)
Serviden Dr. BR1: Brom .1B 160
Servite Ho. BR3: Beck .1B 158
KT4: Wor Pk .2B 164
(off Avenue, The)
Servius Ct. TW8: Bford .7D 96
Setchell Rd. SE1 .4F 103
Setchell Way SE1 .4F 103
Seth St. SE16 .2J 103
Seton Gdns. RM9: Dag .7C 72
Settle Point E13 .2J 87
(off London Rd.)
Settle Rd. E13 .2J 87
Settlers Ct. E14 .7F 87
Settles St. E1 .5G 85
Settrington Rd. SW6 .2K 117
Seven Acres SM5: Cars .2C 166
Seven Dials WC2 .1E 12 (6J 83)
Seven Dials Ct. WC2 .1E 12
(off Shorts Gdns.)
Sevenex Pde. HA9: Wemb .5E 60
Seven Islands Leisure Cen. .3J 103
SEVEN KINGS .1J 71
Seven Kings Rd. IG3: Ilf .1J 71
Seven Kings Way KT2: King T .1E 150
Sevenoaks Cl. DA7: Bex .4H 127
Sevenoaks Ct. HA6: Nwood .1E 38
Sevenoaks Rd. BR6: Chels, Orp .5K 173
BR6: Prat B .7K 173
SE4 .6A 122
Sevenoaks Way BR5: St P .7C 144
DA14: Sidc .7C 144
SEVEN SISTERS .5F 49
Seven Sisters Rd. N4 .2B 66
N7 .3K 65
N15 .7C 48
Seven Stars Cnr. W6 .3C 98
Seven Stars Yd. E1 .5K 9
Seventh Av. E12 .4D 70
UB3: Hayes .1J 93
Severnake Cl. E14 .4C 104
Severn Ct. KT2: King T .1D 150
Severn Dr. KT10: Hin W .2A 162
Severn Way NW10 .5B 62
Severus Rd. SW11 .4C 118
Seville Ho. E1 .1G 103
(off Hellings St.)
Seville M. N1 .7E 66
Seville St. SW1 .7F 11 (2D 100)
Sevington Rd. NW4 .6D 44
Sevington St. W9 .4K 81
Seward Rd. BR3: Beck .2K 157
W7 .2A 96
SEWARDSTONE .1K 25
Sewardstone Gdns. E4 .5J 25
Sewardstone Rd. E2 .2J 85
E4 .7J 25
Seward St. EC1 .3B 8 (3B 84)
Sewdley St. E5 .3K 67
Sewell Rd. SE2 .3A 108
Sewell St. E13 .3J 87
Sextant Av. E14 .4F 105
Sexton Ct. E14 .7F 87
(off Newport Av.)
Sextons Ho. SE10 .6E 104
(off Bardsley La.)
Seymer Rd. RM1: Rom .3K 55
Seymour Av. KT17: Ewe .7E 164
N17 .2G 49
SM4: Mord .7F 153
Seymour Cl. HA5: H End .1D 40
KT8: E Mos .5G 149
Seymour Ct. E4 .2C 36
N10 .2E 46
N21 .6E 22
NW2 .2D 62
Seymour Dr. BR2: Brom .1D 172
Seymour Gdns. HA4: Ruis .1B 58
IG1: Ilf .1D 70
KT5: Surb .5F 151
SE4 .3A 122
TW1: Twick .7B 114
TW13: Hanw .4A 130
Seymour Ho. E16 .1J 105
(off De Quincey M.)
NW1 .1D 6
(off Churchway)
SM2: Sutt .6K 165
(off Mulgrave Rd.)
WC1 .3E 6
(off Tavistock Pl.)
Seymour Leisure Cen. .6E 4
Seymour M. W1 .7G 5 (6E 82)
Seymour Pl. SE25 .4H 157
W1 .6E 4 (5D 82)
Seymour Rd. CR4: Mitc .7E 154
E4 .1J 35
E6 .2B 88
E10 .1B 68
KT1: Hamp W .1D 150
KT8: W Mole .5G 149
N3 .7E 30
N8 .5A 48
N9 .2C 34
SM5: Cars .5E 166
SW18 .7H 117
SW19 .3F 135
TW12: Hamp H .5G 131
W4 .4J 97
Seymour St. SE18 .3G 107
W1 .1E 10 (6D 82)
W2 .1E 10 (6D 82)
Seymour Ter. SE20 .1H 157
Seymour Vs. SE20 .1H 157
Seymour Wlk. SW10 .6A 100
Seymour Way TW16: Sun .7H 129
Seyssel St. E14 .4E 104
Shaa Rd. W3 .7K 79
Shabana Rd. W12 .1D 98
Shacklegate La. TW11: Tedd .4J 131
Shackleton Cl. SE23 .2H 139
Shackleton Ct. E14 .5C 104
(off Maritime Quay)
W12 .2D 98
Shackleton Ho. E1 .1J 103
(off Prusom St.)
NW10 .7K 61
Shackleton Rd. UB1: S'hall .7D 76
SHACKLEWELL .4F 67
Shacklewell Grn. E8 .4F 67
Shacklewell Ho. E8 .4F 67
Shacklewell La. E8 .5F 67
Shacklewell Rd. N16 .4F 67
Shacklewell Row E8 .4F 67
Shacklewell St. E2 .2K 9 (3F 85)
Shadbolt Av. E4 .5F 35
Shadbolt Cl. KT4: Wor Pk .2B 164
Shad Thames SE1 .5J 15 (1F 103)
SHADWELL .7H 85
Shadwell Ct. UB5: N'olt .2D 76
Shadwell Dr. UB5: N'olt .3D 76
Shadwell Gdns. E1 .7J 85
Shadwell Pierhead E1 .7J 85
Shadwell Pl. E1 .7J 85
(off Shadwell Gdns.)
Shady Bush Cl. WD23: Bush .1B 26
Shaef Way TW11: Tedd .7A 132
Shafter Rd. RM10: Dag .6J 73
Shaftesbury Av. EN3: Enf H .2E 24
EN5: New Bar .4F 21
HA2: Harr .1F 59
HA3: Kent .5D 42
TW14: Felt .6J 111
UB2: S'hall .4E 94
W1 .3C 12 (7H 83)
WC2 .7E 6 (6J 83)
Shaftesbury Cen. W10 .4F 81
(off Barlby Rd.)
Shaftesbury Circ. HA2: Harr .1G 59
Shaftesbury Ct. E6 .6E 88
(off Sapphire Cl.)
N1 .2D 84
(off Shaftesbury St.)
SW6 .1K 117
(off Maltings Pl.)
SW16 .3H 137
Shaftesbury Cres. TW18: Staines .7A 128
Shaftesbury Gdns. NW10 .4A 80
Shaftesbury Lodge E14 .6D 86
(off Upper Nth. St.)
Shaftesbury M. SE1 .3D 102
(off Falmouth Rd.)
SW4 .5G 119
W8 .3J 99
(off Stratford Rd.)
Shaftesbury Pde. HA2: Harr .1G 59
Shaftesbury Pl. EC2 .6C 8
(off London Wall)
W14 .4H 99
(off Warwick Rd.)
Shaftesbury Point E13 .2J 87
(off High St.)
Shaftesbury Rd. BR3: Beck .2B 158
E4 .1A 36
E7 .7A 70
E10 .1C 68
E17 .6D 50
N18 .6K 33
N19 .1J 65
SM5: Cars .7B 154
TW9: Rich .3E 114
Shaftesburys, The IG11: Bark .2G 89
Shaftesbury St. N1 .2C 84
(not continuous)
Shaftesbury Theatre .7E 6
(off Shaftesbury Av.)
Shaftesbury Way TW2: Twick .3H 131
Shaftesbury Waye UB4: Yead .5A 76
Shafto M. SW1 .2F 17 (3D 100)
Shafton M. E9 .1K 85

A-Z London 377

Shafton Rd. E9 1K 85
Shaftsbury Ct. SE5 4D 120
Shafts Ct. EC3 1G 15 (6E 84)
Shahjalal Ho. E2 2G 85
(off Pritchards Rd.)
Shakespeare Av. N11 5B 32
NW10 1K 79
TW14: Felt 6J 111
UB4: Hayes 6J 75
(not continuous)
Shakespeare Ct. EN5: New Bar 3E 20
HA3: Kent 6F 43
(not continuous)
Shakespeare Cres. E12 6D 70
NW10 1K 79
Shakespeare Dr. HA3: Kent 6F 43
Shakespeare Gdns. N2 4D 46
Shakespeare Ho. E9 7J 67
(off Lyme Gro.)
N14 2C 32
Shakespeare Rd. DA7: Bex 1E 126
E17 2K 49
N3 1J 45
NW7 4G 29
NW10 1K 79
SE24 5B 120
W3 1J 97
W7 7K 77
Shakespeare's Globe Theatre & Exhibition 3C 14 (1C 102)
Shakespeare Twr. EC2 5D 8
Shakespeare Way TW13: Hanw 4A 130
Shakspeare M. N16 4E 66
Shakspeare Wlk. N16 4E 66
Shalbourne Sq. E9 6B 68
Shalcomb St. SW10 6A 100
Shalden Ho. SW15 6B 116
Shaldon Dr. HA4: Ruis 3A 58
SM4: Mord 5G 153
Shaldon Rd. HA8: Edg 2F 43
Shalfleet Dr. W10 7F 81
Shalford Cl. BR6: Farnb 4G 173
Shalford Ct. N1 2B 84
(off Charlton Pl.)
Shalford Ho. SE1 3D 102
Shalimar Gdns. W3 7J 79
Shalimar Rd. W3 7J 79
Shallons Rd. SE9 4F 143
Shalstone Rd. SW14 3H 115
Shalston Vs. KT6: Surb 6F 151
Shamrock Rd. CR0: Croy 6K 155
Shamrock St. SW4 3H 119
Shamrock Way N14 1A 32
Shandon Rd. SW4 6G 119
Shand St. SE1 6H 15 (2E 102)
Shandy St. E1 5K 85
Shanklin Ho. E17 2B 50
Shanklin Rd. N8 5H 47
N15 4G 49
Shannon Cl. NW2 3F 63
UB2: S'hall 5B 94
Shannon Commercial Cen.
KT3: N Mald 4C 152
SHANNON CORNER 4C 152
Shannon Cnr. Retail Pk.
KT3: N Mald 4C 152
Shannon Ct. CR0: Croy 1C 168
(off Tavistock Rd.)
N16 3E 66
Shannon Gro. SW9 4K 119
Shannon Pl. NW8 2C 82
Shannon Way BR3: Beck 6D 140
Shanti Ct. SW18 1J 135
Shap Cres. SM5: Cars 1D 166
Shapland Way N13 5E 32
Shap St. E2 2F 85
Shapwick Cl. N11 5J 31
Shardcroft Av. SE24 5B 120
Shardeloes Rd. SE14 2B 122
Shard's Sq. SE15 6G 103
Sharland Cl. CR7: Thor H 6A 156
Sharman Ct. DA14: Sidc 4A 144
(off Carlton Rd.)
Sharnbrooke Cl. DA16: Well 3C 126
Sharnbrook Ho. W14 6J 99
Sharon Cl. KT6: Surb 1C 162
Sharon Ct. CR2: S Croy 5C 168
(off Warham Rd.)
Sharon Gdns. E9 1J 85
Sharon Rd. EN3: Enf H 2F 25
W4 5K 97
Sharpe Cl. W7 5K 77
Sharp Ho. SW8 3F 119
TW1: Twick 6D 114
Sharpleshall St. NW1 7D 64
Sharpness Cl. UB4: Yead 5C 76
Sharpness Ct. SE15 7F 103
(off Daniel Gdns.)
Sharp's La. HA4: Ruis 7F 39
Sharratt St. SE15 6J 103
Sharsted St. SE17 6K 19 (5B 102)
Sharvel La. UB5: N'olt 1J 75
Sharwood WC1 1H 7
(off Penton Ri.)
Shaver's Pl. SW1 3C 12
Shaw Av. IG11: Bark 2E 90
Shawbrooke Rd. SE9 5A 124
Shawbury Cl. NW9 1A 44
Shawbury Rd. SE22 5F 121
Shaw Cl. SE28 1B 108
WD23: Bushy 2D 26
Shaw Ct. W3 3J 97
(off All Saints Rd.)
Shaw Cres. E14 6A 86
Shaw Dr. KT12: Walt T 7A 148
Shawfield Ct. UB7: W Dray 3A 92
Shawfield Pk. BR1: Brom 2B 160
Shawfield St. SW3 6D 16 (5C 100)
Shawford Ct. SW15 7C 116
Shawford Rd. KT19: Ewe 6K 163
Shaw Gdns. IG11: Bark 2E 90
Shaw Ho. DA17: Belv 5F 109
E16 1E 106
(off Claremont St.)
Shaw Path BR1: Brom 3H 141
Shaw Rd. BR1: Brom 3H 141
EN3: Enf H 1E 24
SE22 4E 120
Shaws Cotts. SE23 3A 140
Shaws Path KT1: Hamp W 1C 150
(off Bennett Cl.)
Shaw Sq. E17 1A 50
Shaw Theatre 2D 6 (3H 83)
Shaw Way SM6: Wall 7J 167
Shearing Dr. SM5: Cars 7A 154
Shearling Way N7 6J 65
Shearman Rd. SE3 4H 123
SHEARS, THE 7G 129
Shears Ct. TW16: Sun 7G 129
Shears Way TW16: Sun 1G 147
Shearwater Cl. IG11: Bark 3A 90
Shearwater Ct. E1 3K 15
(off Star Pl.)
SE8 6B 104
(off Abinger Gro.)
Shearwater Rd. SM1: Sutt 5H 165
Shearwater Way UB4: Yead 6B 76
Sheath Cotts. KT7: T Ditt 6B 150
(off Ferry Rd.)
Sheaveshill Av. NW9 4A 44
Sheaveshill Ct. NW9 4K 43
Sheaveshill Pde. NW9 4A 44
(off Sheaveshill Av.)
Sheba Ct. N17 6B 34
(off Altair Cl.)
Sheba Pl. E1 4K 9 (4F 85)
Sheen Comn. Dr. TW10: Rich 4G 115
Sheen Ct. TW10: Rich 4G 115
Sheen Ct. Rd. TW10: Rich 4G 115
Sheendale Rd. TW9: Rich 4F 115
Sheenewood SE26 4H 139
Sheen Ga. Gdns. SW14 4J 115
Sheengate Mans. SW14 4K 115
Sheen Gro. N1 1A 84
Sheen La. SW14 5J 115
Sheen Pk. TW9: Rich 4F 115
Sheen Rd. BR5: St M Cry 4K 161
TW9: Rich 5E 114
TW10: Rich 5E 114
Sheen Sports & Fitness Cen. 4A 116
Sheen Way SM6: Wall 5K 167
Sheen Wood SW14 5J 115
Sheepcote Cl. TW5: Cran 7J 93
Sheepcote La. SW11 2D 118
Sheepcote Rd. HA1: Harr 6K 41
Sheepcotes Rd. RM6: Chad H 4E 54
Sheephouse Way KT3: N Mald 1K 163
Sheep La. E8 1H 85
Sheep Wlk. TW17: Shep 7B 146
Sheep Wlk. M. SW19 6F 135
Sheerness M. E16 2F 107
Sheerwater Rd. E16 5B 88
Sheffield Rd. TW6: H'row A 6E 110
Sheffield Sq. E3 3B 86
Sheffield St. WC2 1G 13 (6K 83)
Sheffield Ter. W8 1J 99
Sheffield Way TW6: H'row A 5F 111
Shelbourne Cl. HA5: Pinn 3D 40
Shelbourne Pl. BR3: Beck 7B 140
Shelbourne Rd. N17 2H 49
Shelburne Dr. TW4: Houn 6E 112
Shelburne Rd. N7 4K 65
Shelbury Cl. DA14: Sidc 3A 144
Shelbury Rd. SE22 5H 121
Sheldon Av. IG5: Ilf 2F 53
N6 7C 46
Sheldon Cl. SE12 5K 123
SE20 1H 157
Sheldon Ct. EN5: New Bar 4E 20
SW8 7J 101
(off Lansdowne Grn.)
Sheldon Ho. N1 1E 84
(off Kingsland Rd.)
Sheldon Pl. E2 2G 85
(not continuous)
Sheldon Rd. DA7: Bex 1F 127
N18 4K 33
NW2 4F 63
RM9: Dag 7E 72
Sheldon Sq. W2 6A 4 (5A 82)
Sheldon St. CR0: Croy 3C 168
Sheldrake Cl. E16 1D 106
Sheldrake Ct. E6 2C 88
(off St Bartholomew's Rd.)
Sheldrake Ho. SE16 4K 103
(off Tawny Way)
Sheldrake Pl. W8 2J 99
Sheldrick Cl. SW19 2B 154
Shelduck Cl. E15 5H 69
Shelduck Ct. SE8 6B 104
(off Pilot Cl.)
Sheldwich Ter. BR2: Brom 6C 160
Shelford KT1: King T 2G 151
Shelford Pl. N16 3D 66
Shelford Ri. SE19 7F 139
Shelford Rd. EN5: Barn 6A 20
Shelgate Rd. SW11 5C 118
Shell Cl. BR2: Brom 6C 160
Shellduck Cl. NW9 2A 44
Shelley N8 3J 47
(off Boyton Rd.)
Shelley Av. E12 6C 70
UB6: G'frd 3H 77
Shelley Cl. BR6: Orp 3J 173
HA8: Edg 4B 28
SE15 2H 121
UB4: Hayes 5J 75
UB6: G'frd 3H 77
Shelley Ct. E10 7D 50
(off Skelton's La.)
E11 4K 51
(off Makepeace Rd.)
N19 1K 65
Shelley Ct. SW3 7F 17
(off Tite St.)
Shelley Cres. TW5: Hest 1B 112
UB1: S'hall 6D 76
Shelley Dr. DA16: Well 1J 125
Shelley Gdns. HA0: Wemb 2C 60
Shelley Ho. E2 3J 85
(off Cornwall Av.)
N16 4E 66
SE17 5C 102
(off Browning St.)
SW1 7B 18
(off Churchill Gdns.)
Shelley Lodge EN2: Enf 1J 23
Shelley Rd. NW10 1K 79
Shelley Way SW19 5B 136
Shellness Rd. E5 5H 67
Shell Rd. SE13 3D 122
Shellwood Rd. SW11 2D 118
Shelmerdine Cl. E3 5C 86
Shelson Av. TW13: Felt 3H 129
Shelton Rd. SW19 1J 153
Shelton St. WC2 1E 12 (6J 83)
(not continuous)
Shene Ho. EC1 5J 7
(off Bourne Est.)
Shenfield Ho. SE18 1B 124
(off Portway Gdns.)
Shenfield Rd. IG8: Wfd G 7E 36
Shenfield St. N1 1H 9 (2E 84)
(not continuous)
Shenley Av. HA4: Ruis 2H 57
Shenley Rd. SE5 1E 120
TW5: Hest 1C 112
Shenstone W13 1C 96
Shenstone Cl. DA1: Cray 4K 127
Shenstone Ho. SW16 5G 137
Shepherd Cl. TW13: Hanw 4C 130
Shepherdess Pl. N1 1D 8 (3C 84)
Shepherdess Wlk. N1 1D 8 (2C 84)
Shepherd Ho. E14 6D 86
(off Annabel Cl.)
Shepherd Mkt. W1 4J 11 (1F 101)
SHEPHERD'S BUSH 2E 98
Shepherds Bush Empire Theatre 2E 98
Shepherd's Bush Grn. W12 2E 98
Shepherd's Bush Mkt. W12 2E 98
(not continuous)
Shepherd's Bush Pl. W12 2F 99
Shepherd's Bush Rd. W6 4E 98
Shepherds Cl. BR6: Orp 3K 173
HA7: Stan 5F 27
(not continuous)
N6 6F 47
RM6: Chad H 5D 54
TW17: Shep 6D 146
W1 2G 11
(off Lees Pl.)
Shepherds Ct. W12 2F 99
(off Shepherd's Bush Grn.)
Shepherds Grn. BR7: Chst 7H 143
Shepherd's Hill N6 6F 47
Shepherd's La. E9 6K 67
Shepherds Leas SE9 4G 125
Shepherds Ley SE28 1J 107
Shepherds Path NW3 5B 64
(off Lyndhurst Rd.)
UB5: N'olt 6C 58
(off Arnold Rd.)
Shepherds Pl. W1 2G 11 (7E 82)
Shepherd St. W1 5J 11 (1F 101)
Shepherds Wlk. NW2 2C 62
NW3 5B 64
(not continuous)
WD23: Bushy 2C 26
Shepherds Way CR2: Sels 7K 169
Shepiston La. UB3: Harl 4D 92
Shepley Cl. SM5: Cars 3E 166
Sheppard Cl. EN1: Enf 1C 24
KT1: King T 4E 150
Sheppard Dr. SE16 5H 103

Somerford Gro. Est.—South Hackney

Somerford Gro. Est. N16 4F 67
Somerford St. E1 4H 85
Somerford Way SE16 2A 104
Somerhill Av. DA15: Sidc 7B 126
Somerhill Rd. DA16: Well 2B 126
Somerleyton Pas. SW9 4B 120
Somerleyton Rd. SW9 4A 120
Somersby Gdns. IG4: Ilf 5D 52
Somers Cl. NW1 2H 83
Somers Cres. W2 1C 10 (6C 82)
Somerset Av. DA16: Well 5K 125
KT9: Chess 4D 162
SW20 2D 152
Somerset Cl. IG8: Wfd G 1J 51
KT3: N Mald 6A 152
N17 2D 48
Somerset Ct. IG9: Buck H 2F 37
W7 6K 77
(off Copley Cl.)
Somerset Est. SW11 1B 118
Somerset Gdns. N6 7E 46
N17 7K 33
SE13 2D 122
SW16 3K 155
TW11: Tedd 5J 131
Somerset Hall N17 7K 33
Somerset House 2G 13 (7K 83)
Somerset Ho. SW19 3F 135
Somerset Lodge TW8: Bford 6D 96
Somerset Rd. E17 5C 50
EN5: New Bar 5E 20
HA1: Harr 5G 41
KT1: King T 2F 151
N17 3F 49
N18 5A 34
NW4 4E 44
SW19 3F 135
TW8: Bford 6C 96
TW11: Tedd 5J 131
UB1: S'hall 5D 76
W4 3K 97
W13 1B 96
Somerset Sq. W14 2G 99
Somerset Waye TW5: Hest 6C 94
Somersham Rd. DA7: Bex 2E 126
Somers Pl. SW2 7K 119
Somers Rd. E17 4B 50
SW2 6K 119
SOMERS TOWN 1C 6 (3H 83)
Somers Town Community Sports Cen. 2H 83
Somerton Av. TW9: Rich 3H 115
Somerton Rd. NW2 3G 63
SE15 4H 121
Somertrees Av. SE12 2K 141
Somervell Rd. HA2: Harr 5D 58
Somerville Av. SW13 6D 98
Somerville Point SE16 2B 104
Somerville Rd. RM6: Chad H 6C 54
SE20 7K 139
Sonderburg Rd. N7 2K 65
Sondes St. SE17 6D 102
Songhurst Cl. CR0: Croy 6K 155
Sonia Ct. HA1: Harr 6K 41
HA8: Edg 7A 28
Sonia Gdns. N12 4F 31
NW10 4B 62
TW5: Hest 7E 94
Sonning Gdns. TW12: Hamp 6C 130
Sonning Ho. *E2* 2J 9
(off Swanfield St.)
Sonning Rd. SE25 6G 157
Sontan Ct. TW2: Twick 1H 131
Soper Cl. E4 5G 35
SE23 1K 139
Soper M. EN3: Enf L 1H 25
Sophia Cl. N7 6K 65
Sophia Ho. *W6* 5E 98
(off Queen Caroline St.)
Sophia Rd. E10 1D 68
E16 6K 87
Sophia Sq. *SE16* 7A 86
(off Sovereign Cres.)
Sopwith NW9 7G 29
Sopwith Av. KT9: Chess 5E 162
Sopwith Cl. KT2: King T 5F 133
Sopwith Rd. TW5: Hest 7A 94
Sopwith Way KT2: King T 1E 150
SW8 7J 17 (7F 101)
Sorensen Ct. *E10* 2D 68
(off Leyton Grange Est.)
Sorrel Cl. SE28 1A 108
Sorrel Gdns. E6 5C 88
Sorrel La. E14 6F 87
Sorrell Cl. SE14 7A 104
SW9 2A 120
Sorrento Rd. SM1: Sutt 3J 165
Sotheby Rd. N5 3B 66
Sotheran Cl. E8 1G 85
Sotherby Lodge *E2* 2J 85
(off Sewardstone Rd.)
Sotheron Rd. SW6 7K 99
Soudan Rd. SW11 1D 118
Souldern Rd. W14 3F 99
Sth. Access Rd. E17 7A 50
Southacre *W2* 1C 10
(off Hyde Pk. Cres.)
Southacre Way HA5: Pinn 1A 40
SOUTH ACTON 2J 97
Sth. Africa Rd. W12 1D 98
SOUTHALL 1D 94
Southall Ct. UB1: S'hall 7D 76
Southall Ent. Cen. UB2: S'hall 2E 94
SOUTHALL GREEN 3C 94
Southall La. TW5: Cran 6K 93
UB2: S'hall 6K 93
Southall Pl. SE1 7E 14 (2D 102)
Southampton Bldgs.
WC2 6J 7 (5A 84)
Southampton Gdns. CR4: Mitc 5J 155
Southampton M. E16 1K 105
Southampton Pl. WC1 6F 7 (5J 83)
Southampton Rd. NW5 5D 64
TW6: H'row A 6A 110
(not continuous)
Southampton Row WC1 5F 7 (5J 83)
Southampton St. WC2 2F 13 (7J 83)
Southampton Way SE5 7D 102
Southam St. W10 4G 81
Sth. Audley St. W1 3H 11 (7E 82)
South Av. E4 7J 25
N2 4K 45
NW10 4E 80
SM5: Cars 7E 166
TW9: Kew 2G 115
UB1: S'hall 7D 76
South Av. Gdns. UB1: S'hall 7D 76
South Bank 4H 13 (1K 101)
South Bank KT6: Surb 6E 150
Southbank KT7: T Ditt 7B 150
Sth. Bank Bus. Cen.
SW8 7D 18 (6H 101)
Sth. Bank Ter. KT6: Surb 6E 150
SOUTH BARNET 1K 31
SOUTH BEDDINGTON 6H 167
Sth. Birkbeck Rd. E11 3F 69
Sth. Black Lion La. W6 5C 98
South Block *SE1* 7G 13
(off Westminster Bri. Rd.)
Sth. Bolton Gdns. SW5 5A 100
SOUTHBOROUGH
Bromley 5D 160
Surbiton 1E 162
Southborough Cl. KT6: Surb 1D 162
Southborough Ho. *SE17* 5E 102
(off Surrey Gro.)
Southborough La. BR2: Brom 5C 160
Southborough Rd. BR1: Brom 3C 160
E9 1K 85
KT6: Surb 1E 162
Sth. Boundary Rd. E12 3D 70
Southbourne BR2: Hayes 7J 159
Southbourne Av. NW9 2J 43
Southbourne Cl. HA5: Pinn 7C 40
Southbourne Ct. NW9 2J 43
Southbourne Cres. NW4 4G 45
Southbourne Gdns.
HA4: Ruis 1K 57
IG1: Ilf 5G 71
SE12 5K 123
Sth. Branch Av. NW10 4E 80
Southbridge Pl. CR0: Croy 4C 168
Southbridge Rd. CR0: Croy 4C 168
Southbridge Way UB2: S'hall 2C 94
SOUTH BROMLEY 7E 86
Southbrook M. SE12 6H 123
Southbrook Rd. SE12 6H 123
SW16 1J 155
Southbury *NW8* 1A 82
(off Loudoun Rd.)
Southbury Av. EN1: Enf 4B 24
Southbury Leisure Cen. 3B 24
Southbury Rd. EN1: Enf 3K 23
EN3: Pond E 3A 24
Sth. Carriage Dr.
SW1 7B 10 (2D 100)
SW7 7B 10 (2B 100)
SOUTH CHINGFORD 5G 35
Southchurch Ct. *E6* 2D 88
(off High St. Sth.)
Southchurch Rd. E6 2D 88
Sth. Circular Rd. SW15 4C 116
Sth. City Ct. SE15 7E 102
South Cl. DA6: Bex 4D 126
EN5: Barn 3C 20
HA5: Pinn 7D 40
N6 6F 47
RM10: Dag 1G 91
SM4: Mord 6J 153
TW2: Twick 3E 130
UB7: W Dray 3B 92
Sth. Colonnade, The E14 1C 104
Southcombe St. W14 4G 99
South Comn. Rd. UB8: Uxb 6A 56
Southcote Av. KT5: Surb 7H 151
TW13: Felt 2H 129
Southcote Ri. HA4: Ruis 7F 39
Southcote Rd. E17 5K 49
N19 4G 65
SE25 5H 157
Southcott M. NW8 2C 82
Sth. Countess Rd. E17 3B 50
South Cres. E16 4F 87
WC1 6C 6 (5H 83)
Southcroft Av. BR4: W W'ck 2E 170
DA16: Well 3J 125
Southcroft Rd. BR6: Orp 3J 173
SW16 6E 136
SW17 6E 136
Sth. Cross Rd. IG6: Ilf 5G 53
Sth. Croxted Rd. SE21 3D 138
SOUTH CROYDON 5D 168
South Croydon Sports Club 5E 168
Southdean Gdns. SW19 2H 135
South Dene NW7 3E 28
Southdene Ct. N11 3A 32
Southdown N7 6J 65
Southdown Av. W7 3A 96
Southdown Cres. HA2: Harr 1G 59
IG2: Ilf 5J 53
Southdown Dr. SW20 7F 135
Southdown Rd. SM5: Cars 7E 166
SW20 1F 153
South Dr. BR6: Orp 5J 173
E12 3C 70
HA4: Ruis 1G 57
Sth. Ealing Rd. W5 2D 96
Sth. Eastern Av. N9 3A 34
South Eastern University 3K 65
Sth. Eaton Pl. SW1 3H 17 (4E 100)
Sth. Eden Pk. Rd. BR3: Beck 6D 158
Sth. Edwardes Sq. W8 3H 99
SOUTHEND 4F 141
South End CR0: Croy 4C 168
W8 3K 99
Sth. End Cl. NW3 4C 64
Southend Cl. SE9 6F 125
Southend Cres. SE9 6F 125
Sth. End Grn. NW3 4C 64
Southend La. SE6 4B 140
SE26 4B 140
Sth. End Rd. NW3 4C 64
Southend Rd. BR3: Beck 1C 158
E4 5F 35
E6 7D 70
E17 1D 50
E18 1J 51
IG8: Wfd G 2A 52
Sth. End Row W8 3K 99
Southern Av. SE25 3F 157
TW14: Felt 1J 129
Southerngate Way SE14 7A 104
Southern Gro. E3 3B 86
Southern Perimeter Rd.
TW6: H'row A 5A 110
TW19: Stanw 6B 110
(not continuous)
Southern Rd. E13 2K 87
N2 4D 46
Southern Row W10 4G 81
Southern St. N1 2K 83
Southern Way RM7: Rom 6G 55
SE10 4H 105
(off School Bank Rd.)
Southernwood Retail Pk. SE1 5F 103
Southerton Rd. W6 4E 98
Sth. Esk Rd. E7 6A 70
Southey Ho. *SE17* 5C 102
(off Browning St.)
Southey M. E16 1J 105
Southey Rd. N15 5E 48
SW9 1A 120
SW19 7J 135
Southey St. SE20 7K 139
Southfield EN5: Barn 6A 20
Southfield Cl. UB8: Hil 4C 74
Southfield Cotts. W7 2K 95
Southfield Ct. E11 3H 69
Southfield Gdns. TW1: Twick 4K 131
Southfield Pk. HA2: Harr 4F 41
Southfield Rd. BR7: Chst 3K 161
EN3: Pond E 6C 24
N17 2E 48
W4 2K 97
SOUTHFIELDS 1H 135
Southfields KT8: E Mos 6J 149
NW4 3D 44
Southfields Av. TW15: Ashf 6D 128
Southfields Ct. SM1: Sutt 2J 165
Southfields M. SW18 6J 117
Southfields Pas. SW18 6J 117
Southfields Rd. SW18 6J 117
Southfleet NW5 6E 64
Southfleet Rd. BR6: Orp 3J 173
South Gdns. HA9: Wemb 2G 61
SW19 7B 136
SOUTHGATE 1C 32
Southgate Av. TW13: Felt 4F 129
Southgate Cir. N14 1C 32
Southgate Ct. *N1* 7D 66
(off Downham Rd.)
Southgate Gro. N1 7D 66
Southgate Ind. Est. N14 7C 22
Southgate Leisure Cen. 7C 22
South Ga. Rd. E12 3B 70
Southgate Rd. N1 1D 84
Sth. Gipsy Rd. DA16: Well 3D 126
Sth. Glade, The DA5: Bexl 1F 145
South Grn. NW9 1A 44
South Gro. E17 5B 50
N6 1E 64
N15 5D 48
South Gro. Ho. N6 1E 64
SOUTH HACKNEY 7K 67

Stanley Cohen Ho. EC1 . . . . 4C 8
(off Golden La. Est.)
Stanley Ct. SM2: Sutt 7K 165
SM5: Cars 7E 166
W5 . . . . 5C 78
Stanley Cres. W11 . . . . 7H 81
Stanleycroft Cl. TW7: Isle 1J 113
Stanley Gdns. CR4: Mitc 6E 136
NW2 . . . . 5E 62
SM6: Wall 6G 167
W3 . . . . 2A 98
W11 . . . . 7H 81
Stanley Gdns. M. W11 . . . . 7H 81
(off Kensington Pk. Rd.)
Stanley Gdns. Rd. TW11: Tedd 5J 131
Stanley Gro. CR0: Croy 6A 156
SW8 . . . . 2E 118
Stanley Holloway Ct. E16 . . . . 6J 87
(off Coolfin Rd.)
Stanley Ho. E14 . . . . 6C 86
(off Saracen St.)
SW10 . . . . 7A 100
(off Coleridge Gdns.)
Stanley M. SW10 . . . . 7A 100
(off Coleridge Gdns.)
Stanley Pk. Dr. HA0: Wemb 1F 79
Stanley Pk. Rd. SM5: Cars 7C 166
SM6: Wall 6F 167
Stanley Picker Gallery 3E 150
(off College Wlk.)
Stanley Rd. BR2: Brom 4K 159
BR6: Orp 1K 173
CR0: Croy 7A 156
CR4: Mitc 7E 136
DA14: Sidc 3A 144
E4 . . . . 1A 36
E10 . . . . 6D 50
E12 . . . . 5C 70
E15 . . . . 1F 87
E18 . . . . 1H 51
EN1: Enf 3K 23
HA2: Harr 2G 59
HA6: Nwood 1J 39
HA9: Wemb 6F 61
IG1: Ilf 2H 71
N2 . . . . 3B 46
N9 . . . . 1A 34
N10 . . . . 7A 32
N11 . . . . 6C 32
N15 . . . . 4B 48
NW9 . . . . 7C 44
SM2: Sutt 6K 165
SM4: Mord 4J 153
SM5: Cars 7E 166
SW14 . . . . 4H 115
SW19 . . . . 6J 135
TW2: Twick 3H 131
TW3: Houn 4G 113
TW11: Tedd 4J 131
TW15: Ashf 5A 128
UB1: S'hall 7C 76
W3 . . . . 3J 97
Stanley Sq. SM5: Cars 7D 166
Stanley St. SE8 . . . . 7B 104
Stanley Ter. DA6: Bex 4G 127
N19 . . . . 2J 65
Stanmer St. SW11 . . . . 1C 118
STANMORE 5G 27
Stanmore Gdns. SM1: Sutt 3A 166
TW9: Rich 3F 115
Stanmore Hill HA7: Stan 3F 27
Stanmore Lodge HA7: Stan 4G 27
Stanmore Pl. NW1 . . . . 1F 83
Stanmore Rd. DA17: Belv 4J 109
E11 . . . . 1H 69
N15 . . . . 4B 48
TW9: Rich 3F 115
Stanmore St. N1 . . . . 1K 83
Stanmore Ter. BR3: Beck 2C 158
Stannard Cotts. E1 . . . . 4J 85
(off Fox Cl.)
Stannard M. E8 . . . . 6G 67
(off Stannard Rd.)
Stannard Rd. E8 . . . . 6G 67
Stannary Pl. SE11 . . . . 6K 19 (5A 102)
Stannary St. SE11 . . . . 7K 19 (6A 102)
Stannet Way
SM6: Wall 4G 167
Stansbury Ho. W10 . . . . 3G 81
(off Beethoven St.)
Stansfeld Rd. E6 . . . . 5B 88
E16 . . . . 5B 88
Stansfield Ho. SE1 . . . . 4F 103
(off Balaclava Rd.)
Stansfield Rd. SW9 . . . . 3K 119
TW4: Cran 2K 111
Stansgate Rd. RM10: Dag 2G 73
Stanstead Cl. BR2: Brom 5H 159
Stanstead Gro. SE6 . . . . 1B 140
Stanstead Mnr.
SM1: Sutt 6J 165
Stanstead Rd. E11 . . . . 5K 51
SE6 . . . . 1A 140
SE23 . . . . 1K 139
TW6: H'row A 6B 110
Stansted Cres. DA5: Bexl 1D 144
Stanswood Gdns. SE5 . . . . 7E 102
Stanthorpe Cl. SW16 . . . . 5J 137
Stanthorpe Rd. SW16 . . . . 5J 137
Stanton Av. TW11: Tedd 6J 131
Stanton Cl. KT4: Wor Pk 1F 165
KT19: Ewe 5H 163
Stanton Ct. CR2: S Croy 5E 168
(off Birdhurst Ri.)
Stanton Ho. SE10 . . . . 6E 104
(off Thames St.)
SE16 . . . . 2B 104
(off Rotherhithe St.)
Stanton Rd. CR0: Croy 7C 156
SE26 . . . . 4B 140
SW13 . . . . 2B 116
SW20 . . . . 1F 153
Stanton Sq. SE26 . . . . 4B 140
Stanton Way SE26 . . . . 4B 140
Stanway Ct. N1 . . . . 2E 84
(not continuous)
Stanway Gdns. HA8: Edg 5D 28
W3 . . . . 1G 97
Stanway St. N1 . . . . 2E 84
STANWELL 6A 110
Stanwell Cl. TW19: Stanw 6A 110
Stanwell Rd. TW14: Bedf 7D 110
TW15: Ashf 2A 128
Stanwick Rd. W14 . . . . 4H 99
Stanworth Ct. TW5: Hest 7D 94
Stanworth St. SE1 . . . . 7J 15 (3F 103)
Stanyhurst SE23 . . . . 1A 140
Stapenhill Rd. HA0: Wemb 3B 60
Staple Cl. DA5: Bexl 3K 145
Staplefield Cl. SW2 . . . . 1J 137
Stapleford N17 . . . . 2E 48
(off Willan Rd.)
Stapleford Av. IG2: Ilf 5J 53
Stapleford Cl. E4 . . . . 3K 35
KT1: King T 2G 151
SW19 . . . . 7G 117
Stapleford Rd. HA0: Wemb 7D 60
Stapleford Way IG11: Bark 3B 90
Staplehurst Rd. SE13 . . . . 5F 123
SM5: Cars 7C 166
Staple Inn WC1 . . . . 6J 7
Staple Inn Bldgs. WC1 . . . . 6J 7 (5A 84)
Staples Cl. SE16 . . . . 1A 104
STAPLES CORNER 1D 62
Staples Cnr. Bus. Pk. NW2 . . . . 1D 62
Staples Ho. E6 . . . . 6E 88
(off Savage Gdns.)
Staple St. SE1 . . . . 7F 15 (2D 102)
Stapleton Gdns. CR0: Wadd 5A 168
Stapleton Hall Rd. N4 . . . . 1K 65
Stapleton Ho. E2 . . . . 3H 85
(off Ellsworth St.)
Stapleton Rd. BR6: Orp 4K 173
DA7: Bex 7F 109
SW17 . . . . 3E 136
Stapleton Vs. N16 . . . . 4E 66
(off Wordsworth Rd.)
Stapley Rd. DA17: Belv 5G 109
Stapylton Rd. EN5: Barn 3B 20
Star All. EC3 . . . . 2H 15
(off Fenchurch St.)
Star & Garter Hill TW10: Rich 1E 132
Starbeck Cl. SE9 . . . . 7E 124
Starboard Way E14 . . . . 3C 104
Star Bus. Cen. RM13: Rain 5K 91
Starch Ho. La. IG6: Ilf 2H 53
Star Cl. EN3: Pond E 6D 24
Starcross St. NW1 . . . . 2B 6 (3G 83)
Starfield Rd. W12 . . . . 2C 98
Star Hill DA1: Cray 5K 127
Star La. E16 . . . . 4G 87
Starling Cl. CR0: Croy 6A 158
HA5: Pinn 3A 40
IG9: Buck H 1D 36
Starling Ho. NW8 . . . . 2C 82
(off Barrow Hill Est.)
Starling Wlk. TW12: Hamp 5C 130
Starmans Cl. RM9: Dag 1E 90
Star Path UB5: N'olt 2E 76
(off Brabazon Rd.)
Star Pl. E1 . . . . 3K 15 (7G 85)
Star Rd. TW7: Isle 2H 113
UB10: Hil 4E 74
W14 . . . . 6H 99
Star St. W2 . . . . 7B 4 (6C 82)
Starts Cl. BR6: Farnb 3E 172
Starts Hill Av. BR6: Farnb 4F 173
Starts Hill Rd. BR6: Farnb 3E 172
Starveall Cl. UB7: W Dray 3B 92
Star Yd. WC2 . . . . 7J 7 (6A 84)
State Farm Av. BR6: Farnb 4F 173
Staten Gdns. TW1: Twick 1K 131
Statham Gro. N16 . . . . 4D 66
N18 . . . . 5K 33
Statham Ho. SW8 . . . . 1G 119
(off Wadhurst Rd.)
Station App. BR1: Brom 3J 159
(off High St.)
BR2: Hayes 1J 171
BR3: Beck 1C 158
BR4: W W'ck 7E 158
BR6: Orp 2K 173
BR7: Chst 6C 142
(Elmstead La.)
BR7: Chst 1E 160
(Vale Rd.)
CR2: Sand 7D 168
DA5: Bexl 1G 145
DA7: Bex 2J 127
(Barnehurst Rd.)
DA7: Bex 2E 126
(Pickford La.)
DA16: Well 2A 126
(not continuous)
E4 . . . . 6A 36
E7 . . . . 4K 69
E11 . . . . 5J 51
E17 . . . . 5C 50
(not continuous)
E18 . . . . 2K 51
EN5: New Bar 4F 21
HA0: Wemb 6B 60
HA1: Harr 7J 41
HA4: Ruis 5K 57
(Mahlon Av.)
HA4: Ruis 1G 57
(Pembroke Rd.)
HA5: Pinn 3C 40
IG8: Wfd G 6E 36
IG9: Buck H 4G 37
KT1: King T 1G 151
KT4: Wor Pk 1C 164
KT19: Ewe 5C 164
Station App. N11 . . . . 5A 32
N12 . . . . 4E 30
NW1 . . . . 4F 5 (4D 82)
NW10 . . . . 3B 80
SE3 . . . . 3K 123
SE9 . . . . 2G 143
(Bercta Rd.)
SE9 . . . . 1D 142
(Crossmead)
SE12 . . . . 6J 123
(off Burnt Ash Hill)
SE26 . . . . 4J 139
SM2: Cheam 7G 165
SM5: Cars 4D 166
SW6 . . . . 3G 117
SW14 . . . . 3J 115
SW16 . . . . 6H 137
(Estreham Rd.)
SW16 . . . . 5H 137
(Gleneagle Rd.)
TW8: Bford 6C 96
(off Sidney Gdns.)
TW9: Kew 1G 115
TW12: Hamp 1E 148
TW15: Ashf 4B 128
TW16: Sun 1J 147
TW17: Shep 5E 146
UB3: Hayes 3H 93
UB6: G'frd 7G 59
UB7: Yiew 1A 92
W7 . . . . 1J 95
Station App. Nth. DA15: Sidc 2A 144
Station App. Rd. SE1 . . . . 7H 13 (2A 102)
W4 . . . . 7J 97
Station Arc. W1 . . . . 4K 5
(off Gt. Portland St.)
Station Av. KT3: N Mald 3A 152
KT19: Ewe 7A 164
SW9 . . . . 3B 120
TW9: Kew 1G 115
Station Bldgs. KT1: King T 2E 150
(off Fife Rd.)
Station Chambers E6 . . . . 7C 70
(off High St. Nth.)
Station Cl. N3 . . . . 1J 45
N12 . . . . 4E 30
TW12: Hamp 1F 149
Station Cotts. BR6: Orp 2K 173
Station Cres. HA0: Wemb 6B 60
N15 . . . . 4D 48
SE3 . . . . 5J 105
TW15: Ashf 3A 128
Stationer's Hall Ct.
EC4 . . . . 1B 14 (6B 84)
Station Est. BR3: Beck 3K 157
E18 . . . . 2K 51
Station Est. Rd. TW14: Felt 1K 129
Station Garage M. SW16 . . . . 6H 137
Station Gdns. W4 . . . . 7J 97
Station Gro. HA0: Wemb 6E 60
Station Hill BR2: Hayes 2J 171
Station Ho. M. N9 . . . . 4B 34
Station Pde. DA7: Bex 2E 126
(off Pickford La.)
DA15: Sidc 2A 144
E6 . . . . 7C 70
E11 . . . . 5J 51
E13 . . . . 1A 88
(off Green St.)
EN4: Cockf 4K 21
HA2: Harr 4F 59
HA3: Kent 2A 42
HA4: Ruis 2F 57
HA8: Edg 7K 27
IG9: Buck H 4G 37
IG11: Bark 7G 71
N14 . . . . 1C 32
NW2 . . . . 6E 62
RM9: Dag 6G 73
SM2: Sutt 6A 166
(off High St.)

Station Pde.—Stock Orchard Cres.

Station Pde. SW12 . . . 1E 136
TW9: Kew . . . 1G 115
TW14: Felt . . . 1K 129
TW15: Ashf . . . 4B 128
UB5: N'olt . . . 7E 58
(Court Farm Rd.)
UB5: N'olt . . . 4F 59
(Halsbury Rd. W.)
W3 . . . 6G 79
W4 . . . 7J 97
W5 . . . 1F 97
Station Pas. E18 . . . 2K 51
SE15 . . . 1J 121
Station Path E8 . . . 6H 67
(off Graham Rd.)
SW6 . . . 3H 117
Station Pl. N4 . . . 2A 66
Station Ri. SE27 . . . 2B 138
Station Rd.
BR1: Brom . . . 1J 159
BR2: Brom . . . 2G 159
BR4: W W'ck . . . 1E 170
BR6: Orp . . . 2K 173
CR0: Croy . . . 1C 168
DA7: Bex . . . 3E 126
DA15: Sidc . . . 2A 144
DA17: Belv . . . 3G 109
E4 . . . 1A 36
E7 . . . 4J 69
E12 . . . 4C 70
E17 . . . 6A 50
EN5: New Bar . . . 5E 20
HA1: Harr . . . 4K 41
HA2: Harr . . . 5F 41
HA8: Edg . . . 6B 28
IG1: Ilf . . . 3F 71
IG6: Ilf . . . 3H 53
KT1: Hamp W . . . 1C 150
KT2: King T . . . 1G 151
KT3: N Mald . . . 5D 152
KT7: T Ditt . . . 7K 149
KT9: Chess . . . 5E 162
N3 . . . 1J 45
N11 . . . 5A 32
N17 . . . 3G 49
N19 . . . 3G 65
N21 . . . 1G 33
N22 . . . 2J 47
NW4 . . . 6C 44
NW7 . . . 6F 29
NW10 . . . 2B 80
RM6: Chad H, Dag . . . 7D 54
SE13 . . . 3E 122
SE20 . . . 6J 139
SE25 . . . 4F 157
SM5: Cars . . . 4D 166
SW13 . . . 2B 116
SW19 . . . 1A 154
TW1: Twick . . . 1K 131
TW3: Houn . . . 4F 113
TW11: Tedd . . . 6A 132
TW12: Hamp . . . 1E 148
TW15: Ashf . . . 4B 128
TW16: Sun . . . 7J 129
TW17: Shep . . . 5E 146
UB3: Harl, Hayes . . . 4G 93
(not continuous)
UB7: W Dray . . . 2A 92
W5 . . . 6F 79
W7 . . . 1J 95
Station Rd. Nth.
DA17: Belv . . . 3H 109
Station Sq. BR5: Pet W . . . 5G 161
Station St. E15 . . . 7F 69
E16 . . . 1F 107
Station Ter. NW10 . . . 2F 81
SE5 . . . 1C 120
Station Ter. M. SE3 . . . 5J 105
Station Vw. UB6: G'frd . . . 1H 77
Station Wlk. IG1: Ilf . . . 2F 71
(in Exchange, The)
Station Way IG9: Buck H . . . 4F 37
SE15 . . . 2G 121
SM3: Cheam . . . 6G 165
Station Yd. TW1: Twick . . . 7A 114
Staton Ct. E10 . . . 7D 50
(off Kings Cl.)
Staunton Ho. SE17 . . . 4E 102
(off Tatum St.)
Staunton Rd. KT2: King T . . . 6E 132
Staunton St. SE8 . . . 6B 104
Staveley NW1 . . . 1A 6
(off Varndell St.)
Staveley Cl. E9 . . . 5J 67
N7 . . . 4J 65
SE15 . . . 1H 121
Staveley Ct. E11 . . . 5J 51
Staveley Gdns. W4 . . . 1K 115
Staveley Rd. TW15: Ashf . . . 6F 129
W4 . . . 6J 97
Staverton Rd. NW2 . . . 7E 62
Stave Yd. Rd. SE16 . . . 1A 104
Stavordale Rd. N5 . . . 4B 66
SM5: Cars . . . 7A 154
Stayner's Rd. E1 . . . 4K 85
Stayton Rd. SM1: Sutt . . . 3J 165
Steadfast Rd. KT1: King T . . . 1D 150
Steadman Ct. EC1 . . . 3D 8
(off Old St.)
Steadman Ho. RM10: Dag . . . 3G 73
(off Uvedale Rd.)
Stead St. SE17 . . . 4D 102
Steam Farm La. TW14: Felt . . . 4H 111
Stean St. E8 . . . 1F 85
Stebbing Ho. W11 . . . 1F 99
(off Queensdale Cres.)
Stebbing Way IG11: Bark . . . 2A 90
Stebondale St. E14 . . . 4E 104
Stedham Pl. WC1 . . . 7E 6
Stedman Cl. DA5: Bexl . . . 3K 145
UB10: Ick . . . 3C 56
Steedman St. SE17 . . . 4C 102
Steeds Rd. N10 . . . 1D 46
Steele Ho. E15 . . . 2G 87
(off Eve Rd.)
Steele Rd. E11 . . . 4G 69
N17 . . . 3E 48
NW10 . . . 2J 79
TW7: Isle . . . 4A 114
W4 . . . 3J 97
Steele's M. Nth. NW3 . . . 6D 64
Steele's M. Sth. NW3 . . . 6D 64
Steele's Rd. NW3 . . . 6D 64
Steele's Studios NW3 . . . 6D 64
Steele Wlk. DA8: Erith . . . 7H 109
Steel's La. E1 . . . 6J 85
Steelyard Pas. EC4 . . . 3E 14
Steen Way SE22 . . . 5E 120
Steep Cl. BR6: Chels . . . 6K 173
Steep Hill CR0: Croy . . . 4E 168
SW16 . . . 3H 137
Steeple Cl. SW6 . . . 2G 117
SW19 . . . 5G 135
Steeple Ct. E1 . . . 4H 85
Steeplestone Cl. N18 . . . 5H 33
Steeple Wlk. N1 . . . 1C 84
(off New Nth. Rd.)
Steerforth St. SW18 . . . 2A 136
Steering Cl. N9 . . . 1D 34
Steers Mead CR4: Mitc . . . 1D 154
Steers Way SE16 . . . 2A 104
Stelfox Ho. WC1 . . . 1H 7
(off Penton Ri.)
Stella Cl. UB8: Hil . . . 5D 74
Stellar Ho. N17 . . . 6A 34
Stella Rd. SW17 . . . 6D 136
Stelling Rd. DA8: Erith . . . 7K 109
Stellman Cl. E5 . . . 3G 67
Stembridge Rd. SE20 . . . 2H 157
Stephan Cl. E8 . . . 1G 85
Stephen Cl. BR6: Orp . . . 3K 173
Stephendale Rd. SW6 . . . 3K 117
Stephen Fox Ho. W4 . . . 5A 98
(off Chiswick La.)
Stephen M. W1 . . . 6C 6 (5H 83)
Stephen Pl. SW4 . . . 3G 119
Stephen Rd. DA7: Bex . . . 3J 127
Stephens Ct. E16 . . . 4H 87
SE4 . . . 3A 122
Stephens Lodge N12 . . . 3F 31
(off Woodside La.)
Stephenson Ct. SM2: Cheam . . . 7G 165
(off Station App.)
Stephenson Ho. SE1 . . . 3C 102
Stephenson Rd. E17 . . . 5A 50
TW2: Whit . . . 7E 112
W7 . . . 6K 77
Stephenson St. E16 . . . 4G 87
NW10 . . . 3A 80
Stephenson Way NW1 . . . 3B 6 (4G 83)
Stephen's Rd. E15 . . . 1G 87
Stephen St. W1 . . . 6C 6 (5H 83)
STEPNEY . . . 5K 85
Stepney C'way. E1 . . . 6K 85
Stepney City Apartments E1 . . . 5J 85
Stepney Grn. E1 . . . 5J 85
Stepney Grn. Ct. E1 . . . 5K 85
(off Stepney Grn.)
Stepney High St. E1 . . . 5K 85
Stepney Way E1 . . . 5H 85
Sterling Av. HA8: Edg . . . 4A 28
Sterling Cl. NW10 . . . 7C 62
Sterling Gdns. SE14 . . . 6A 104
Sterling Ho. SE3 . . . 4K 123
Sterling Ind. Est. RM10: Dag . . . 4H 73
Sterling Pl. W5 . . . 4E 96
Sterling Rd. EN2: Enf . . . 1J 23
Sterling St. SW7 . . . 1D 16 (3C 100)
Sterling Way N18 . . . 4J 33
Stern Cl. IG11: Bark . . . 2C 90
Sterndale Rd. W14 . . . 3F 99
Sterne St. W12 . . . 2F 99
Sternhall La. SE15 . . . 3G 121
Sternhold Av. SW2 . . . 2H 137
Sterry Cres. RM10: Dag . . . 5G 73
Sterry Dr. KT7: T Ditt . . . 6J 149
KT19: Ewe . . . 4A 164
Sterry Gdns. RM10: Dag . . . 6G 73
Sterry Rd. IG11: Bark . . . 1K 89
RM10: Dag . . . 4G 73
Sterry St. SE1 . . . 7E 14 (2D 102)
Steucers La. SE23 . . . 1A 140
Stevannie Ct. DA17: Belv . . . 5F 109
Steve Biko La. SE6 . . . 4C 140
Steve Biko Lodge E13 . . . 2J 87
(off London Rd.)
Steve Biko Rd. N7 . . . 3A 66
Steve Biko Way TW3: Houn . . . 3E 112
Stevedale Rd. DA16: Well . . . 2C 126
Stevedore St. E1 . . . 1H 103
Stevenage Rd. E6 . . . 6E 70
SW6 . . . 7F 99
Stevens Av. E9 . . . 6J 67
Stevens Cl. BR3: Beck . . . 6C 140
DA5: Bexl . . . 4K 145
HA5: Eastc . . . 5A 40
TW12: Hamp . . . 5C 130
Stevens Grn. WD23: Bushy . . . 1B 26
Stevens La. KT10: Clay . . . 7A 162
Stevenson Cl. EN5: New Bar . . . 7G 21
Stevenson Cres. SE16 . . . 5G 103
Stevenson Ho. NW8 . . . 1A 82
(off Boundary Rd.)
Stevens Rd. RM8: Dag . . . 3B 72
Stevens St. SE1 . . . 7H 15 (3E 102)
Steventon Rd. W12 . . . 7B 80
Stewards Holte Wlk. N11 . . . 4A 32
Steward St. E1 . . . 5H 9 (5E 84)
(not continuous)
Stewart Av. TW17: Shep . . . 4C 146
Stewart Cl. BR7: Chst . . . 5F 143
NW9 . . . 6J 43
TW12: Hamp . . . 6C 130
Stewart Quay UB3: Hayes . . . 2G 93
Stewart Rainbird Ho. E12 . . . 5E 70
(off Parkhurst Rd.)
Stewart Rd. E15 . . . 4F 69
Stewartsby Cl. N18 . . . 5H 33
Stewart's Gro. SW3 . . . 5B 16 (5B 100)
Stewart's Rd. SW8 . . . 7G 101
Stewart St. E14 . . . 2E 104
Stew La. EC4 . . . 2C 14 (7C 84)
Steyne Ho. W3 . . . 1J 97
(off Narrow St.)
Steyne Rd. W3 . . . 1H 97
Steyning Gro. SE9 . . . 4D 142
Steynings Way N12 . . . 5D 30
Steyning Way TW4: Houn . . . 4A 112
Steynton Av. DA5: Bexl . . . 2D 144
Stickland Rd. DA17: Belv . . . 4G 109
Stickleton Cl. UB6: G'frd . . . 3F 77
Stifford Ho. E1 . . . 5J 85
(off Stepney Way)
Stilecroft Gdns. HA0: Wemb . . . 3B 60
Stile Hall Gdns. W4 . . . 5G 97
Stile Hall Pde. W4: Bford . . . 5G 97
Stileman Ho. E3 . . . 5B 86
(off Ackroyd Dr.)
Stile Path TW16: Sun . . . 3J 147
Stiles Cl. BR2: Brom . . . 6D 160
DA8: Erith . . . 5H 109
Stillingfleet Rd. SW13 . . . 6C 98
Stillington St. SW1 . . . 3B 18 (4G 101)
Stillness Rd. SE23 . . . 6A 122
Stilwell Dr. UB8: Hil . . . 4B 74
Stilwell Rdbt. UB8: Hil . . . 7C 74
Stipularis Dr. UB4: Yead . . . 4B 76
Stirling Av. HA5: Pinn . . . 1B 58
SM6: Wall . . . 7J 167
TW17: Shep . . . 3G 147
Stirling Cl. DA14: Sidc . . . 4J 143
SW16 . . . 1H 155
Stirling Ct. W13 . . . 7B 78
Stirling Gro. TW3: Houn . . . 2G 113
Stirling Ho. SE18 . . . 5F 107
Stirling Rd. E13 . . . 2K 87
E17 . . . 3A 50
HA3: W'stone . . . 3K 41
N17 . . . 1G 49
N22 . . . 1B 48
SW9 . . . 2J 119
TW2: Whit . . . 7E 112
TW6: H'row A . . . 6B 110
UB3: Hayes . . . 7K 75
W3 . . . 3H 97
Stirling Rd. Path E17 . . . 3A 50
Stirling Wlk. KT5: Surb . . . 6H 151
Stirling Way CR0: Bedd . . . 7J 155
Stiven Cres. HA2: Harr . . . 3D 58
Stockbeck NW1 . . . 1B 6
(off Ampthill Est.)
Stockbury Rd. CR0: Croy . . . 6J 157
Stockdale Rd. RM8: Dag . . . 2F 73
Stockdove Way UB6: G'frd . . . 3K 77
Stocker Gdns. RM9: Dag . . . 7C 72
Stockfield Rd. SW16 . . . 3K 137
Stockford Av. NW7 . . . 7A 30
Stockholm Ho. E1 . . . 7G 85
(off Swedenborg Gdns.)
Stockholm Rd. SE16 . . . 5J 103
Stockholm Way E1 . . . 1G 103
Stockhurst Cl. SW15 . . . 2E 116
Stockingswater La. EN3: Brim . . . 2G 25
Stockland Rd. RM7: Rom . . . 6K 55
Stockleigh Hall NW8 . . . 2C 82
(off Prince Albert Rd.)
Stockley Cl. UB7: W Dray . . . 2D 92
Stockley Country Pk. . . . 7C 74
Stockley Farm Rd. UB7: W Dray . . . 3D 92
STOCKLEY PARK . . . 1D 92
Stockley Rd. UB7: W Dray . . . 4D 92
UB8: Hil . . . 6C 74
UB11: Stock P . . . 6C 74
Stock Orchard Cres. N7 . . . 5K 65

Stock Orchard St.—Strattondale St.

Stock Orchard St. N7 5K 65
Stockport Rd. SW16 1H 155
Stocksfield Rd. E17 3E 50
Stocks Pl. E14 7B 86
UB10: Hil 1C 74
Stock St. E13 2J 87
Stockton Cl. EN5: New Bar 4F 21
Stockton Gdns. N17 7H 33
NW7 3F 29
Stockton Ho. E2 3H 85
(off Ellsworth St.)
HA2: Harr 1E 58
Stockton Rd. N17 7H 33
N18 6B 34
STOCKWELL 2K 119
Stockwell Av. SW9 3K 119
Stockwell Cl. BR1: Brom 2K 159
HA8: Edg 2J 43
Stockwell Gdns. SW9 1K 119
Stockwell Gdns. Est. SW9 2J 119
Stockwell Grn. SW9 2K 119
Stockwell Grn. Ct. SW9 2K 119
Stockwell La. SW9 2K 119
Stockwell M. SW9 2K 119
Stockwell Pk. Cres. SW9 2K 119
Stockwell Pk. Est. SW9 2K 119
Stockwell Pk. Rd. SW9 1K 119
Stockwell Pk. Wlk. SW9 3A 120
Stockwell Rd. SW9 2K 119
Stockwell St. SE10 6E 104
Stockwell Ter. SW8 1K 119
Stodart Rd. SE20 1J 157
Stoddart Ho. SW8 7H 19 (6K 101)
Stofield Gdns. SE9 3B 142
Stoford Cl. SW19 7G 117
Stokenchurch St. SW6 1K 117
STOKE NEWINGTON 3F 67
Stoke Newington Chu. St. N16 3D 66
Stoke Newington Comn. N16 2F 67
Stoke Newington High St. N16 3F 67
Stoke Newington Rd. N16 5F 67
Stoke Pl. NW10 3B 80
Stoke Rd. KT2: King T 7J 133
Stokesby Rd. KT9: Chess 6F 163
Stokes Cotts. IG6: Ilf 1G 53
Stokes Ct. N2 4C 46
Stokesley St. W12 6B 80
Stokes Rd. CR0: Croy 6K 157
E6 4C 88
Stokley Ct. N8 4J 47
Stoll Cl. NW2 3E 62
Stoms Path SE6 5C 140
(off Maroons Way)
Stonard Rd. N13 3F 33
RM8: Dag 5B 72
Stondon Ho. E15 1H 87
(off John St.)
Stondon Pk. SE23 6A 122
Stondon Wlk. E6 2B 88
Stonebanks KT12: Walt T 7J 147
STONEBRIDGE 1K 79
Stonebridge Cen. N15 5F 49
Stonebridge Pk. NW10 7K 61
Stonebridge Rd. N15 5F 49
Stonebridge Shop. Cen. NW10 1K 79
Stonebridge Way HA9: Wemb 6H 61
Stone Bldgs. WC2 6H 7
Stonechat Sq. E6 5C 88
Stone Cl. RM8: Dag 2F 73
SW4 2G 119
UB7: Yiew 1B 92
Stonecot Cl. SM3: Sutt 1G 165
Stonecot Hill SM3: Sutt 1G 165
Stone Cres. TW14: Felt 7H 111
Stonecroft Rd. DA8: Erith 7J 109
Stonecroft Way CR0: Croy 7J 155
Stonecrop Cl. NW9 3K 43
Stonecutter St. EC4 7A 8 (6B 84)
Stonefield N4 2K 65
Stonefield Cl. DA7: Bex 3G 127
HA4: Ruis 5C 58
Stonefield St. N1 1A 84
Stonefield Way HA4: Ruis 4C 58
SE7 7B 106
STONEGROVE 4K 27
Stonegrove HA8: Edg 4K 27
Stone Gro. Ct. HA8: Edg 5A 28
Stonegrove Gdns.
HA8: Edg 5K 27
Stone Hall W8 3K 99
(off Stone Hall Gdns.)
Stonehall Av. IG1: Ilf 6C 52
Stone Hall Gdns. W8 3K 99
Stone Hall Pl. W8 3K 99
Stone Hall Rd. N21 7E 22
Stoneham Rd. N11 5B 32
Stonehill Bus. Pk. N18 6F 35
Stonehill Cl. SW14 5K 115
Stonehill Ct. E4 7J 25
STONEHILL GREEN 7J 145
Stone Hill Rd. W4 5G 97
Stonehill Rd. SW14 5J 115
Stonehills Ct. SE21 3E 138
Stonehill Woods Pk. DA14: Sidc 6H 145
Stonehorse Rd. EN3: Pond E 5D 24
Stonehouse NW1 1G 83
(off Plender St.)
Stone Ho. Ct. EC3 7H 9
Stone Lake Ind. Pk. SE7 4A 106
Stone Lake Retail Pk. SE7 4A 106
STONELEIGH 5C 164
Stoneleigh Av. EN1: Enf 1C 24
KT4: Wor Pk 4C 164
Stoneleigh B'way. KT17: Ewe 5C 164
Stoneleigh Ct. IG5: Ilf 3C 52
Stoneleigh Cres. KT19: Ewe 5B 164
Stoneleigh M. E3 2A 86
Stoneleigh Pk. Av. CR0: Croy 6K 157
Stoneleigh Pk. Rd. KT19: Ewe 6B 164
Stoneleigh Pl. W11 7F 81
Stoneleigh Rd. IG5: Ilf 3C 52
N17 3F 49
SM5: Cars 7C 154
Stoneleigh St. W11 7F 81
Stoneleigh Ter. N19 2F 65
Stonell's Rd. SW11 6D 118
Stonemasons Cl. N15 4D 48
Stonenest St. N4 1K 65
Stone Pk. Av. BR3: Beck 4C 158
Stone Pl. KT4: Wor Pk 2C 164
Stone Rd. BR2: Brom 5H 159
Stones End St. SE1 7C 14 (2C 102)
Stonewall E6 5E 88
Stonewold Ct. W5 6D 78
Stoney All. SE18 2E 124
Stoneyard La. E14 7D 86
Stoneycroft Cl. SE12 7H 123
Stoneycroft Rd. IG8: Wfd G 6H 37
Stoneydeep TW11: Tedd 4A 132
Stoneydown E17 4A 50
Stoneydown Av. E17 4A 50
Stoneydown Ho. E17 4A 50
(off Blackhorse Rd.)
Stoneyfields Gdns. HA8: Edg 4D 28
Stoneyfields La. HA8: Edg 5D 28
Stoney La. E1 7H 9 (6F 85)
SE19 6F 139
Stoney St. SE1 4E 14 (1D 102)
Stonhouse St. SW4 4H 119
Stonor Rd. W14 4H 99
Stonycroft Cl. EN3: Enf H 2F 25
Stoop Memorial Ground 7J 113
Stopes St. SE15 7F 103
Stopford Rd. E13 1J 87
SE17 5B 102
Stopher Ho. SE1 7B 14
(off Webber St.)
Store Rd. E16 2E 106
Storers Quay E14 4F 105
Store St. E15 5F 69
WC1 6C 6 (5H 83)
Storey Ct. NW8 2A 4
Storey Ho. E14 7D 86
(off Cottage St.)
Storey Rd. E17 4B 50
N6 6D 46
Storey's Ga. SW1 7D 12 (2H 101)
Storey St. E16 1E 106
Stories M. SE5 2E 120
Stories Rd. SE5 3E 120
Stork Rd. E7 6H 69
Storksmead Rd. HA8: Edg 7F 29
Stork's Rd. SE16 3G 103
Stormont Lawn Tennis & Squash Club
5D 46
Stormont Rd. N6 7D 46
SW11 3E 118
Stormont Way KT9: Chess 5C 162
Stormount Dr. UB3: Harl 2E 92
Storrington WC1 2F 7
(off Regent Sq.)
Storrington Rd. CR0: Croy 1F 169
Story St. N1 7K 65
Stothard Ho. E1 4J 85
(off Amiel St.)
Stothard St. E1 4J 85
Stott Cl. SW18 6B 118
Stoughton Av. SM3: Cheam 5F 165
Stoughton Cl. SE11 4H 19
SW15 1C 134
Stour Av. UB2: S'hall 3E 94
Stourcliffe Cl. W1 1E 10 (6D 82)
Stourcliffe St. W1 1E 10 (6D 82)
Stour Cl. BR2: Kes 4A 172
Stourhead Cl. SW19 7F 117
Stourhead Gdns. SW20 3C 152
Stourhead Ho. SW1 5C 18
(off Tachbrook St.)
Stour Rd. E3 7C 68
RM10: Dag 2G 73
Stourton Av. TW13: Hanw 4D 130
Stowage SE8 6C 104
Stow Cres. E17 7F 35
Stowe Cres. HA4: Ruis 6D 38
Stowe Gdns. N9 1A 34
Stowe Ho. NW11 6A 46
Stowell Ho. N8 4J 47
(off Pembroke Rd.)
Stowe Pl. N15 3E 48
Stowe Rd. W12 2D 98
Stowting Rd. BR6: Orp 4J 173
Stox Mead HA3: Hrw W 1H 41
Stracey Rd. E7 4J 69
NW10 1K 79
Strachan Pl. SW19 6E 134
Stradbroke Dr. IG7: Chig 6K 37
Stradbroke Gro. IG5: Ilf 3C 52
IG9: Buck H 1G 37
Stradbroke Pk. IG7: Chig 6K 37
Stradbroke Rd. N5 4C 66
Stradbrook Cl. HA2: Harr 3D 58
Stradella Rd. SE24 6C 120
Strafford Av. IG5: Ilf 2E 52
Strafford Ho. SE8 5B 104
(off Grove St.)
Strafford Rd. EN5: Barn 3B 20
TW1: Twick 7A 114
TW3: Houn 3D 112
W3 2J 97
Strafford St. E14 2C 104
Strahan Rd. E3 3A 86
Straight, The UB1: S'hall 2B 94
Straightsmouth SE10 7E 104
Strait Rd. E6 7C 88
Strakers Rd. SE15 4H 121
Strale Ho. N1 1E 84
(off Whitmore Est.)
Strand WC2 3F 13 (7J 83)
Strand Ct. SE18 5J 107
Strandfield Cl. SE18 5J 107
Strand Ho. SE28 1H 107
Strand La. WC2 2H 13 (7K 83)
STRAND ON THE GREEN 6G 97
Strand on the Grn. W4 6G 97
Strand Pl. N18 4K 33
Strand Theatre 2G 13
(off Aldwych)
Strang Ho. N1 1C 84
Strang Print Room 3C 6
Strangways Ter. W14 3H 99
Stranraer Way N1 7J 65
Strasburg Rd. SW11 1E 118
Strata Ct. KT12: Walt T 7H 147
Stratfield Pk. Cl. N21 7G 23
STRATFORD 7F 69
Stratford Av. UB10: Hil 2B 74
Stratford Cen., The E15 7F 69
Stratford Circus (Performing Arts Cen.)
6F 69
Stratford Cl. IG11: Bark 7A 72
RM10: Dag 7J 73
Stratford Ct. KT3: N Mald 4K 151
Stratford Gro. SW15 4F 117
Stratford Ho. Av. BR1: Brom 3C 160
STRATFORD MARSH 7D 68
STRATFORD NEW TOWN 5E 68
Stratford Office Village, The
E15 7G 69
(off Romford Rd.)
Stratford Picture House 6F 69
Stratford Pl. W1 1J 11 (6F 83)
Stratford Rd. CR7: Thor H 4A 156
E13 1H 87
(not continuous)
NW4 4F 45
TW6: H'row A 6D 110
UB2: S'hall 4C 94
UB4: Yead 4K 75
W8 3J 99
Stratford Shop. Cen. E15 7F 69
(off Stratford Cen., The)
Stratford Studios W8 3J 99
Stratford Vs. NW1 7G 65
Stratham Ct. N19 3J 65
(off Alexander Rd.)
Strathan Cl. SW18 6G 117
Strathaven Rd. SE12 6K 123
Strathblaine Rd. SW11 5B 118
Strathbrook Rd. SW16 7K 137
Strathcona Rd. HA9: Wemb 2D 60
Strathdale SW16 5K 137
Strathdon Dr. SW17 3B 136
Strathearn Av. TW2: Whit 1F 131
UB3: Harl 7H 93
Strathearn Pl. W2 1C 10 (6C 82)
Strathearn Rd. SM1: Sutt 5J 165
SW19 5J 135
Stratheden Pde. SE3 7J 105
Stratheden Rd. SE3 1J 123
Strathfield Gdns. IG11: Bark 6H 71
Strathleven Rd. SW2 5J 119
Strathmore Ct. NW8 1C 4
(off Park Rd.)
Strathmore Gdns. HA8: Edg 2H 43
N3 1K 45
W8 1J 99
Strathmore Rd. CR0: Croy 7D 156
SW19 3J 135
TW11: Tedd 4J 131
Strathnairn St. SE1 4G 103
Strathray Gdns. NW3 6C 64
Strath Ter. SW11 4C 118
Strathville Rd. SW18 2J 135
(not continuous)
Strathyre Av. SW16 3A 156
Stratton Cl. DA7: Bex 3E 126
HA8: Edg 6A 28
SW19 2J 153
TW3: Houn 1E 112
Stratton Ct. HA5: H End 1D 40
(off Devonshire Rd.)
N1 7E 66
(off Hertford Rd.)
Strattondale St. E14 3E 104

388 A-Z London

Stratton Dr.—Summerhouse Av.

Stratton Dr. IG11: Bark 5J 71
Stratton Gdns. UB1: S'hall 6D 76
Stratton Ho. *HA8: Edg* *4A 28*
(off Lacey Dr.)
Stratton Rd. DA7: Bex 3E 126
SW19 2J 153
TW16: Sun 2H 147
Stratton St. W1 4K 11 (1F 101)
Strauss Rd. W4 2K 97
STRAWBERRY HILL 3K 131
Strawberry Hill TW1: Twick 3K 131
Strawberry Hill Cl. TW1: Twick 3K 131
Strawberry Hill House 3K 131
(off Strawberry Va.)
Strawberry Hill Rd. TW1: Twick 3K 131
Strawberry La. SM5: Cars 3E 166
Strawberry Ter. N10 1D 46
Strawberry Va. N2 1B 46
TW1: Twick 3A 132
(not continuous)
Streakes Fld. Rd. NW2 2C 62
Streamdale SE2 6B 108
Stream La. HA8: Edg 5C 28
Streamline Ct. *SE22* *1G 139*
(off Streamline M.)
Streamline M. SE22 1G 139
Streamside Cl. BR2: Brom 4J 159
N9 1A 34
Stream Way DA17: Belv 6F 109
Streatfeild Av. E6 1D 88
Streatfield Rd. HA3: Kent 3C 42
STREATHAM 5J 137
Streatham Cl. SW16 2J 137
STREATHAM COMMON 6J 137
Streatham Comn. Nth. SW16 5J 137
Streatham Comn. Sth. SW16 6J 137
Streatham Ct. SW16 3J 137
Streatham High Rd. SW16 4J 137
STREATHAM HILL 2J 137
Streatham Hill SW2 2J 137
Streatham Ice Arena 5H 137
Streatham Leisure Cen. 5J 137
STREATHAM PARK 5G 137
Streatham Pl. SW2 7J 119
Streatham Rd. CR4: Mitc 1E 154
SW16 1E 154
Streatham St. WC1 7E 6 (6J 83)
STREATHAM VALE 7G 137
Streatham Va. SW16 1G 155
Streathbourne Rd. SW17 2E 136
Streatley Pl. NW3 4A 64
Streatley Rd. NW6 7H 63
Streeters La. SM6: Bedd 3H 167
Streetfield M. SE3 3J 123
Streimer Rd. E15 2E 86
Strelley Way W3 7A 80
Stretton Mans. SE8 5C 104
Stretton Rd. CR0: Croy 7E 156
TW10: Ham 2C 132
Strickland Ct. SE15 3G 121
Strickland Ho. *E2* *2K 9*
(off Chambord St.)
Strickland Row SW18 7B 118
Strickland St. SE8 2C 122
Strickland Way BR6: Orp 4K 173
Stride Rd. E13 2H 87
Strimon Cl. N9 2D 34
Stringer Ho. *N1* *1E 84*
(off Whitmore Est.)
Strode Cl. N10 7K 31
Strode Rd. E7 4J 69
N17 2E 48
NW10 6C 62
SW6 7G 99
Strome Ho. *NW6* *2K 81*
(off Carlton Va.)
Strone Rd. E7 6A 70
E12 6A 70
Strone Way UB4: Yead 4C 76
Strongbow Cres. SE9 5D 124
Strongbow Rd. SE9 5D 124
Strongbridge Cl. HA2: Harr 1E 58
Stronsa Rd. W12 2B 98
Strood Av. RM7: Rush G 1K 73
Strood Ho. *SE1* *7F 15*
(off Staple St.)
Stroud Cres. SW15 3C 134
Stroudes Cl. KT4: Wor Pk 7A 152
Stroud Fld. UB5: N'olt 6C 58
Stroud Ga. HA2: Harr 4F 59
STROUD GREEN 7K 47
Stroud Grn. Gdns. CR0: Croy 7J 157
Stroud Grn. Rd. N4 1K 65
Stroud Grn. Way CR0: Croy 7H 157
Stroudley Ho. SW8 1G 119
Stroudley Wlk. E3 3D 86
Stroud Rd. SE25 6G 157
SW19 3J 135
Stroud's Cl. RM6: Chad H 5B 54
Stroud Way TW15: Ashf 6D 128
Strouts Pl. E2 1J 9 (3F 85)
Strudwick Ct. *SW4* *1J 119*
(off Binfield Rd.)
Strutton Ground SW1 1C 18 (3H 101)
Strype St. E1 6J 9 (5F 85)
Stuart Av. BR2: Hayes 1J 171
HA2: Harr 3D 58
KT12: Walt T 7K 147
NW9 7C 44
W5 2F 97
Stuart Cl. UB10: Hil 6C 56
Stuart Ct. *CR0: Croy* *3B 168*
(off St John's Rd.)
Stuart Cres. CR0: Croy 3B 170
N22 1K 47
UB3: Hayes 6E 74
Stuart Evans Cl. DA16: Well 3C 126
Stuart Gro. TW11: Tedd 5J 131
Stuart Ho. *E16* *1K 105*
(off Beaulieu Av.)
W14 *4G 99*
(off Windsor Way)
Stuart Mantle Way DA8: Erith 7K 109
Stuart Mill Ho. *N1* *1G 7*
(off Killick St.)
Stuart Pl. CR4: Mitc 1D 154
Stuart Rd. CR7: Thor H 4C 156
DA16: Well 1B 126
EN4: E Barn 7H 21
HA3: W'stone 3K 41
IG11: Bark 7K 71
NW6 3J 81
(not continuous)
SE15 4J 121
SW19 3J 135
TW10: Ham 2B 132
W3 1J 97
Stuart Twr. *W9* *3A 82*
(off Maida Va.)
Stubbs Cl. NW9 5J 43
Stubbs Ct. *W4* *5H 97*
(off Chaseley Dr.)
Stubbs Dr. SE16 5H 103
Stubbs Ho. *E2* *3K 85*
(off Bonner St.)
SW1 *4D 18*
(off Erasmus St.)
Stubbs M. *RM8: Dag* *4B 72*
(off Marlborough Rd.)
Stubbs Point E13 4J 87
Stubbs Way SW19 1B 154
Stucley Pl. NW1 7F 65
Stucley Rd. TW5: Hest 7G 95
Studdridge St. SW6 2J 117
(not continuous)
Studd St. N1 1B 84
Studholme Ct. NW3 4J 63
Studholme St. SE15 7H 103
Studio Arts & Media Cen., The 1A 158
Studio Ct. N15 4E 48
Studio La. W5 1D 96
Studio M. NW4 4E 44
Studio Pl. SW1 7F 11
Studios Rd. TW17: Shep 3B 146
Studio Theatre 4E 166
Studland *SE17* *5D 102*
(off Portland St.)
Studland Cl. DA15: Sidc 3K 143
Studland Ho. *E14* *6A 86*
(off Aston St.)
Studland Rd.
KT2: King T 6E 132
SE26 5K 139
W7 6H 77
Studland St. W6 4D 98
Studley Av. E4 7A 36
Studley Cl. E5 5A 68
Studley Ct. DA14: Sidc 5B 144
E14 *7F 87*
(off Jamestown Way)
Studley Dr. IG4: Ilf 6B 52
Studley Est. SW4 1J 119
Studley Grange Rd. W7 2J 95
Studley Rd. E7 6K 69
RM9: Dag 7D 72
SW4 1J 119
Stukeley Rd. E7 7K 69
Stukeley St. WC2 7F 7 (6J 83)
Stumps Hill La. BR3: Beck 6C 140
Stunell Ho. *SE14* *6K 103*
(off John Williams Cl.)
Sturdee Ho. *E2* *2G 85*
(off Horatio St.)
Sturdy Ho. *E3* *2A 86*
(off Gernon Rd.)
Sturdy Rd. SE15 2H 121
Sturge Av. E17 2D 50
Sturgeon Rd. SE17 5C 102
Sturges Fld. BR7: Chst 6H 143
Sturgess Av. NW4 7D 44
Sturge St. SE1 6C 14 (2C 102)
Sturmer Way N7 5K 65
Sturminster Cl. UB4: Yead 6A 76
Sturminster Ho. *SW8* *7K 101*
(off Dorset Rd.)
Sturrock Cl. N15 4D 48
Sturry St. E14 6D 86
Sturt St. N1 1D 8 (2C 84)
Stutfield St. E1 6G 85
Styles Gdns. SW9 3B 120
Styles Ho. SE1 6A 14
Styles Way BR3: Beck 4E 158
Sudbourne Rd. SW2 5J 119
Sudbrooke Rd. SW12 6D 118
Sudbrook Gdns. TW10: Ham 3D 132
Sudbrook La. TW10: Ham 1E 132
SUDBURY 5B 60
Sudbury E6 5E 88
Sudbury Av. HA0: Wemb 3C 60
Sudbury Ct. *SW8* *1H 119*
(off Allen Edwards Dr.)
Sudbury Ct. Dr. HA1: Harr 3K 59
Sudbury Ct. Rd. HA1: Harr 3K 59
Sudbury Cres. BR1: Brom 6J 141
HA0: Wemb 5B 60
Sudbury Cft. HA0: Wemb 4K 59
Sudbury Gdns. CR0: Croy 4E 168
Sudbury Hgts. Av. UB6: G'frd 5K 59
Sudbury Hill HA1: Harr 2J 59
Sudbury Hill Cl. HA0: Wemb 4K 59
Sudbury Ho. SW18 5K 117
Sudbury Rd. IG11: Bark 5K 71
Sudeley St. N1 2B 84
Sudlow Rd. SW18 5J 117
Sudrey St. SE1 7C 14 (2C 102)
Suez Av. UB6: G'frd 2K 77
Suez Rd. EN3: Brim 4F 25
SUFFIELD HATCH 4K 35
Suffield Ho. *SE17* *5B 102*
(off Berryfield Rd.)
Suffield Rd. E4 3J 35
N15 5F 49
SE20 2J 157
Suffolk Ct. E10 7C 50
IG3: Ilf 6J 53
Suffolk Ho. *CR0: Croy* *2D 168*
(off George St.)
SE20 *1K 157*
(off Croydon Rd.)
Suffolk La. EC4 2E 14 (7D 84)
Suffolk Pk. Rd. E17 4A 50
Suffolk Pl. SW1 4D 12 (1H 101)
Suffolk Rd. DA14: Sidc 6C 144
E13 3J 87
EN3: Pond E 5C 24
HA2: Harr 6D 40
IG3: Ilf 6J 53
IG11: Bark 7H 71
KT4: Wor Pk 2B 164
N15 5D 48
NW10 7A 62
RM10: Dag 5J 73
SE25 4F 157
SW13 7B 98
Suffolk St. E7 4J 69
SW1 3D 12 (7H 83)
Sugar Bakers Ct. EC3 1H 15
Sugar Ho. La. E15 2E 86
Sugar Loaf Wlk. E2 3J 85
Sugar Quay EC3 3H 15
Sugar Quay Wlk. EC3 3H 15 (7E 84)
Sugden Rd. KT7: T Ditt 1B 162
SW11 3E 118
Sugden St. SE5 6D 102
Sugden Way IG11: Bark 2K 89
Sulby Ho. *SE4* *4A 122*
(off Turnham Rd.)
Sulgrave Gdns. W6 2E 98
Sulgrave Rd. W6 3E 98
Sulina Rd. SW2 7J 119
Sulivan Ct. SW6 2J 117
Sulivan Ent. Cen. SW6 3K 117
Sulivan Rd. SW6 3J 117
Sulkin Ho. *E2* *3K 85*
(off Knottisford St.)
Sullivan Av. E16 5B 88
Sullivan Cl. KT8: W Mole 3F 149
SW11 3C 118
UB4: Yead 5A 76
Sullivan Ct. N16 7F 49
Sullivan Cres. UB9: Hare 2A 38
Sullivan Ho. *SE11* *4H 19*
(off Vauxhall St.)
SW1 *7K 17*
(off Churchill Gdns.)
Sullivan Rd. SE11 3K 19 (4A 102)
Sullivans Reach KT12: Walt T 7H 147
Sultan Rd. E11 4K 51
Sultan St. BR3: Beck 2K 157
SE5 7C 102
Sultan Ter. N22 2A 48
Sumatra Rd. NW6 5J 63
Sumburgh Rd. SW12 6E 118
Summer Av. KT8: E Mos 5J 149
Summercourt Rd. E1 6J 85
Summer Crossing KT7: E Mos 5J 149
Summerene Cl. SW16 7G 137
Summerfield *BR1: Brom* *1K 159*
(off Freelands Rd.)
Summerfield Av. NW6 2G 81
Summerfield La. KT6: Surb 2D 162
Summerfield Rd. W5 4B 78
Summerfields Av. N12 6H 31
Summerfield St. SE12 7H 123
Summer Gdns. KT8: E Mos 5J 149
Summer Gro. BR4: W W'ck 2G 171
Summer Hill BR7: Chst 2E 160
Summerhill Cl. BR6: Orp 3J 173
Summerhill Gro. EN1: Enf 6K 23
Summerhill Rd. N15 4D 48
Summerhill Vs. *BR7: Chst* *1E 160*
(off Susan Wood)
Summerhill Way CR4: Mitc 1E 154
Summerhouse Av. TW5: Hest 1C 112

Templar Ct. NW8 2A **4**
Templar Dr. SE28 6D **90**
Templar Ho. NW2 6H **63**
RM13: Rain 2K **91**
Templar Pl. TW12: Hamp 7E **130**
Templars Av. NW11 6H **45**
Templars Cres. N3 2J **45**
Templars Dr. HA3: Hrw W 6C **26**
Templars Ho. E15 5D **68**
Templar St. SE5 2B **120**
Temple Av. CR0: Croy 2B **170**
EC4 2K **13** (7A **84**)
N20 7G **21**
RM8: Dag 1G **73**
Temple Bar 1J **13**
Temple Bar Gate *1B **14***
(off Paternoster Sq.)
Temple Chambers EC4 2K **13**
Temple Cl. E11 7G **51**
N3 2H **45**
SE28 3G **107**
Templecombe Rd. E9 1J **85**
Templecombe Way SM4: Mord 5G **153**
Temple Ct. *E1* *5K **85***
(off Rectory Sq.)
SW8 *7J **101***
(off Thorncroft St.)
Templecroft TW15: Ashf 6F **129**
Temple Dwellings *E2* *2H **85***
(off Temple St.)
TEMPLE FORTUNE 5H **45**
Temple Fortune Hill NW11 5J **45**
Temple Fortune La. NW11 6H **45**
Temple Fortune Pde. NW11 5H **45**
Temple Gdns. *EC4* *2J **13***
(off Middle Temple La.)
N21 2G **33**
NW11 6H **45**
RM8: Dag 3D **72**
Temple Gro. EN2: Enf 2G **23**
NW11 6J **45**
Temple Hall Ct. E4 2A **36**
Temple La. EC4 1K **13** (6A **84**)
Templeman Rd. W7 5K **77**
Temple Mead Cl. HA7: Stan 6G **27**
Templemead Cl. W3 6A **80**
Templemead Ho. E9 4A **68**
Temple Mill La. E10 4D **68**
(not continuous)
E15 4E **68**
TEMPLE MILLS 4D **68**
Temple Mills E10 3E **68**
Temple of Mithras (remains) *1E **14***
(off Queen Victoria St.)
Temple Pde. *EN5: New Bar* *7G **21***
(off Netherlands Rd.)
Temple Pk. UB8: Hil 3C **74**
Temple Pl. WC2 2H **13** (7K **83**)
Temple Rd. CR0: Croy 4D **168**
E6 1C **88**
N8 4K **47**
NW2 4E **62**
TW3: Houn 4F **113**
TW9: Rich 2F **115**
W4 3J **97**
W5 3D **96**
Temple Sheen SW14 4J **115**
Temple Sheen Rd. SW14 4H **115**
Temple St. E2 2H **85**
Temple Ter. *N22* *2A **48***
(off Vincent Rd.)
Templeton Av. E4 4H **35**
Templeton Cl. N15 6D **48**
N16 5E **66**
SE19 1D **156**
Templeton Ct. EN3: Enf W 1D **24**
Templeton Pl. SW5 4J **99**
Templeton Rd. N15 6D **48**
Temple Way SM1: Sutt 3B **166**
Temple W. M. SE11 3B **102**
Templewood W13 5B **78**
Templewood Av. NW3 3K **63**
Templewood Gdns.
NW3 3K **63**
Templewood Point *NW2* *2H **63***
(off Granville Rd.)
Temple Yd. *E2* *2H **85***
(off Temple St.)
Tempo Ho. UB5: N'olt 3B **76**
Tempsford Cl. EN2: Enf 4H **23**
Tempsford Ct. HA1: Harr 6K **41**
Tempus Wharf *SE16* *2G **103***
(off Bermondsey Wall W.)
Temsford Cl. HA2: Harr 2G **41**
Tenbury Cl. E7 5B **70**
Tenbury Ct. SW2 1H **137**
Tenby Av. HA3: Kent 2B **42**
Tenby Cl. N15 4F **49**
RM6: Chad H 6E **54**
Tenby Ct. E17 5A **50**
Tenby Gdns. UB5: N'olt 6E **58**
Tenby Ho. UB3: Harl 3E **92**
W2 *6A **82***
(off Hallfield Est.)
Tenby Mans. *W1* *5H **5***
(off Nottingham St.)
Tenby Rd. DA16: Well 1D **126**
E17 5A **50**
EN3: Pond E 4D **24**
HA8: Edg 1F **43**
RM6: Chad H 6E **54**
Tench St. E1 1H **103**
Tenda Rd. SE16 4H **103**
Tendring Way RM6: Chad H 5C **54**
Tenham Av. SW2 1H **137**
Tenison Ct. W1 2A **12** (7G **83**)
Tenison Way SE1 5H **13** (1K **101**)
Tenniel Cl. W2 7A **82**
Tennis Ct. La. KT8: E Mos 3K **149**
Tennison Rd. SE25 4F **157**
Tennis St. SE1 6E **14** (2D **102**)
Tenniswood Rd. EN1: Enf 1K **23**
Tennyson *N8* *3J **47***
(off Boyton Cl.)
Tennyson Av. E11 7J **51**
E12 7C **70**
KT3: N Mald 5D **152**
NW9 3J **43**
TW1: Twick 1K **131**
Tennyson Cl. DA16: Well 1J **125**
EN3: Pond E 5E **24**
TW14: Felt 6H **111**
Tennyson Ct. *SW6* *1A **118***
(off Imperial Rd.)
Tennyson Ho. DA17: Belv 5F **109**
SE17 *5C **102***
(off Browning St.)
Tennyson Mans. *W14* *6H **99***
(off Queen's Club Gdns.)
Tennyson Rd. E10 1D **68**
E15 7G **69**
E17 6B **50**
NW6 1H **81**
(not continuous)
NW7 5H **29**
SE20 7K **139**
SW19 6A **136**
TW3: Houn 2G **113**
TW15: Ashf 5A **128**
W7 7K **77**
Tennyson St. SW8 2F **119**
Tensing Ct. TW19: Stanw 1A **128**
Tensing Rd. UB2: S'hall 3E **94**
Tentelow La. UB2: S'hall 5E **94**
Tenterden Cl. NW4 3F **45**
SE9 4D **142**
Tenterden Dr. NW4 3F **45**
Tenterden Gdns. CR0: Croy 7G **157**
NW4 3F **45**
Tenterden Gro. NW4 3F **45**
Tenterden Ho. *SE17* *5E **102***
(off Surrey Gro.)
Tenterden Rd. CR0: Croy 7G **157**
N17 7A **34**
RM8: Dag 2F **73**
Tenterden St. W1 1K **11** (6F **83**)
Tenter Ground E1 6J **9** (5F **85**)
Tenter Pas. *E1* *1K **15***
(off Nth. Tenter St.)
Tent Peg La. BR5: Pet W 5G **161**
Tent St. E1 4H **85**
Terborch Way
SE22 5E **120**
Teredo St. SE16 3K **103**
Terence Ct. *DA17: Belv* *6F **109***
(off Stream Way)
Terence McMillan Stadium 4A **88**
Terence Messenger Twr. *E10* *2D **68***
(off Alpine Rd.)
Teresa M. E17 4C **50**
Teresa Wlk. N10 5F **47**
Terling Cl. E11 3H **69**
Terling Ho. *W10* *5E **80***
(off Sutton Way)
Terling Rd. RM8: Dag 2G **73**
Terling Wlk. *N1* *1C **84***
(off Popham St.)
Terminal Four Rdbt. TW6: H'row A 6E **110**
Terminal Ho. HA7: Stan 5J **27**
Terminus Pl. SW1 2K **17** (3F **101**)
Terrace, The *E2* *3J **85***
(off Old Ford Rd.)
E4 *3B **36***
(off Newgate St.)
EC4 1K **13**
IG8: Wfd G 6D **36**
N3 2H **45**
NW6 1J **81**
SE8 *4B **104***
(off Longshore)
SE23 7A **122**
SW13 2A **116**
Terrace Av. NW10 4E **80**
Terrace Gdns. SW13 2B **116**
Terrace Hill *CR0: Croy* *3B **168***
(off Hanover St.)
Terrace La. TW10: Rich 6E **114**
Terrace Rd. E9 7J **67**
E13 2J **87**
KT12: Walt T 7J **147**
Terraces, The *NW8* *2B **82***
(off Queen's Ter.)
Terrace Wlk. RM9: Dag 5E **72**
SW11 *7H **17***
(off Albert Bri. Rd.)
Terrano Ho. TW9: Kew 7H **97**
Terrapin Rd. SW17 3F **137**
Terretts Pl. *N1* *7B **66***
(off Upper St.)
Terrick Rd. N22 1J **47**
Terrick St. W12 6D **80**
Terrilands HA5: Pinn 3D **40**
Territorial Ho. SE11 4K **19**
Terront Rd. N15 4C **48**
Tersha St. TW9: Rich 4F **115**
Tessa Sanderson Pl. *SW8* *3F **119***
(off Daley Thompson Way)
Tessa Sanderson Way UB6: G'frd 5H **59**
Testerton Rd. *W11* *7F **81***
(off Hurstway Rd.)
Testerton Wlk. W11 7F **81**
Testwood Ct. W7 7J **77**
Tetbury Pl. N1 1B **84**
Tetcott Rd. SW10 7A **100**
(not continuous)
Tetherdown N10 3E **46**
Tetty Way BR2: Brom 2J **159**
Teversham La. SW8 1J **119**
Teviot Cl. DA16: Well 1B **126**
Teviot Est. E14 5D **86**
Teviot St. E14 4E **86**
Tewkesbury Av. HA5: Pinn 5C **40**
SE23 1H **139**
Tewkesbury Cl. EN4: E Barn 4G **21**
N15 6D **48**
Tewkesbury Gdns. NW9 3H **43**
Tewkesbury Rd. N15 6D **48**
SM5: Cars 1B **166**
W13 1A **96**
Tewkesbury Ter. N11 6B **32**
Tewson Rd. SE18 5J **107**
Teynham Av. EN1: Enf 6J **23**
Teynham Ct. BR3: Beck 3D **158**
Teynham Grn. BR2: Brom 5J **159**
Teynton Ter. N17 1C **48**
Thackeray Av. N17 2G **49**
Thackeray Cl. HA2: Harr 1E **58**
SW19 7F **135**
TW7: Isle 2A **114**
UB8: Hil 6D **74**
Thackeray Ct. *SW3* *5E **16***
(off Elystan Pl.)
W5 *6F **79***
(off Hanger Va. La.)
W14 *3G **99***
(off Blythe Rd.)
Thackeray Dr. RM6: Chad H 7A **54**
Thackeray Ho. WC1 3E **6**
Thackeray Lodge TW14: Bedf 6F **111**
Thackeray M. E8 6G **67**
Thackeray Rd. E6 2B **88**
SW8 2F **119**
Thackeray St. W8 3K **99**
Thackrah Cl. *N2* *2A **46***
(off Sims Gdns.)
Thakeham Cl. SE26 4H **139**
Thalia Cl. SE10 6F **105**
Thame Rd. SE16 2K **103**
Thames Av. RM9: Dag, Rain 4H **91**
SW10 1A **118**
UB6: G'frd 2K **77**
Thames Bank SW14 2J **115**
Thamesbank Pl. SE28 6C **90**
Thames Barrier Ind. Area
SE18 *3B **106***
(off Faraday Way)
Thames Barrier Vis. Cen. 3B **106**
Thamesbrook SW3 6C **16**
Thames Circ. E14 4C **104**
Thames Cl. TW12: Hamp 2F **149**
Thames Cotts. KT7: T Ditt 6B **150**
Thames Ct. KT8: W Mole 2F **149**
SE15 *7F **103***
(off Daniel Gdns.)
W7 *6J **77***
(off Hanway Rd.)
Thames Cres. W4 7A **98**
THAMES DITTON 6A **150**
Thames Ditton Miniature Railway 1A **162**
Thames Dr. HA4: Ruis 6E **38**
Thames Exchange Bldg. EC4 3D **14**
Thames Eyot TW1: Twick 1A **132**
Thamesfield Ct. TW17: Shep 7E **146**
Thamesfield M. TW17: Shep 7E **146**
Thamesgate Cl. TW10: Ham 4B **132**
Thames Gateway RM9: Dag 2F **91**
RM13: Avel, Rain, Wenn 2F **91**
Thames Gateway Pk. RM9: Dag 3F **91**
Thames Haven KT6: Surb 5D **150**
Thameshill Av. RM5: Col R 2J **55**
Thames Ho. *EC4* *2D **14***
(off Up. Thames St.)
KT1: King T *4D **150***
(off Surbiton Rd.)
SW1 *3E **18***
(off Millbank)
Thameside KT8: W Mole 3F **149**
TW11: Tedd 7D **132**
Thameside Cen. TW8: Bford 6F **97**
Thameside Community Nature Reserve
4A **90**
Thameside Ind. Est. E16 2B **106**
Thameside Leisure Cen. 7A **90**
Thameside Pk. City Farm 3A **90**

Treewall Gdns.—Trulock Ct.

Treewall Gdns. BR1: Brom 4K 141
Trefgarne Rd. RM10: Dag 2G 73
Trefil Wlk. N7 4J 65
Trefoil Ho. *DA18: Erith 2E 108*
(off Kale Rd.)
Trefoil Rd. SW18 5A 118
Trefusis Ct. TW5: Cran 1K 111
Tregaron Av. N8 6J 47
Tregaron Gdns. KT3: N Mald 4A 152
Tregarvon Rd. SW11 4E 118
Tregenna Av. HA2: Harr 4E 58
Tregenna Cl. N14 5B 22
Tregenna Ct. HA2: Harr 4E 58
Tregony Rd. BR6: Chels 4K 173
Trego Rd. E9 7C 68
Tregothnan Rd. SW9 3J 119
Tregunter Rd. SW10 6K 99
Trehearn Rd. IG6: Ilf 1H 53
Treherne Ct. SW9 1B 120
SW17 4E 136
Trehern Rd. SW14 3K 115
Trehurst St. E5 5A 68
Trelawney Est. E9 6J 67
Trelawney Ho. *SE1 6C 14*
(off Pepper St.)
Trelawney Rd. IG6: Ilf 1H 53
Trelawn Rd. E10 3E 68
SW2 5A 120
Trelawny Cl. E17 4D 50
Trellick Twr. *W10 4H 81*
(off Golborne Rd.)
Trellis Sq. E3 3B 86
Treloar Gdns. SE19 6D 138
Tremadoc Rd. SW4 4H 119
Tremaine Cl. SE4 2C 122
Tremaine Rd. SE20 2H 157
Trematon Ho. *SE11 5K 19*
(off Kennings Way)
Trematon Pl. TW11: Tedd 7C 132
Tremlett Gro. N19 3G 65
Trenance Gdns. IG3: Ilf 3A 72
Trenchard Av. HA4: Ruis 4K 57
Trenchard Cl. HA7: Stan 6F 27
NW9 1A 44
Trenchard Ct. NW4 5C 44
SM4: Mord 6J 153
Trenchard St. SE10 5F 105
Trenchold St. SW8 6J 101
Trendell Ho. *E14 6C 86*
(off Dod St.)
Trenear Cl. BR6: Chels 4K 173
Trenholme Cl. SE20 7H 139
Trenholme Rd. SE20 7H 139
Trenholme Ter. SE20 7H 139
Trenmar Gdns. NW10 3D 80
Trent Av. W5 3C 96
Trent Ct. *CR2: S Croy 5C 168*
(off Nottingham Rd.)
Trent Gdns. N14 6A 22
Trentham St. SW18 1J 135
Trent Ho. KT2: King T 1D 150
SE15 4J 121
Trent Pk. Country Pk. 1A 22
Trent Pk. Sports Cen. 4B 22
Trent Rd. IG9: Buck H 1E 36
SW2 5K 119
Trent Way KT4: Wor Pk 3E 164
UB4: Hayes 2G 75
Trentwood Side EN2: Enf 3E 22
Treport St. SW18 7K 117
Tresco Cl. BR1: Brom 6G 141
Trescoe Gdns. HA2: Harr 7C 40
Tresco Gdns. IG3: Ilf 2A 72
Tresco Ho. SE11 5J 19
Tresco Rd. SE15 4H 121
Tresham Cres. NW8 3D 4 (4C 82)
Tresham Rd. IG11: Bark 7K 71
Tresham Wlk. E9 5J 67
Tresidder Ho. SW4 7H 119
Tresilian Av. N21 5E 22
Tressell Cl. N1 7B 66
Tressillian Cres. SE4 3C 122
Tressillian Rd. SE4 4B 122
Tress Pl. SE1 4A 14
Trestis Cl. UB4: Yead 4B 76
Treswell Rd. RM9: Dag 1E 90
Tretawn Gdns. NW7 4F 29
Tretawn Pk. NW7 4F 29
Trevanion Rd. W14 4G 99
Treve Av. HA1: Harr 7H 41
Trevelyan Av. E12 4D 70
Trevelyan Cres. HA3: Kent 7D 42
Trevelyan Gdns. NW10 1E 80
Trevelyan Ho. *E2 3K 85*
(off Morpeth St.)
SE17 7B 102
(off John Ruskin St.)
Trevelyan Rd. E15 4H 69
SW17 5C 136
Trevenna Ho. *SE23 3K 139*
(off Dacres Rd.)
Trevera Ct. EN3: Pond E 4F 25
Treveris St. SE1 5B 14 (1B 102)
Treverton St. W10 4F 81
Treverton Towers *W10 5F 81*
(off Treverton St.)
Treves Cl. N21 5E 22
Treves Ho. *E1 4G 85*
(off Vallance Rd.)
Treville St. SW15 7D 116
Treviso Rd. SE23 2K 139
Trevithick Cl. TW14: Felt 1H 129
Trevithick Ho. *SE16 4H 103*
(off Rennie Est.)
Trevithick St. SE8 6C 104
Trevone Ct. *SW2 7J 119*
(off Doverfield Rd.)
Trevone Gdns. HA5: Pinn 6C 40
Trevor Cl. BR2: Hayes 7H 159
EN4: E Barn 6G 21
HA3: Hrw W 7E 26
TW7: Isle 5K 113
UB5: Yead 2A 76
Trevor Cres. HA4: Ruis 4H 57
Trevor Gdns. HA4: Ruis 4J 57
HA8: Edg 1K 43
UB5: Yead 2A 76
Trevor Pl. SW7 7D 10 (2C 100)
Trevor Rd. HA8: Edg 1K 43
IG8: Wfd G 7D 36
SW19 7G 135
UB3: Hayes 2G 93
Trevor Sq. SW7 7E 10 (2D 100)
Trevor St. SW7 7D 10 (2C 100)
Trevor Wlk. *SW7 7D 10*
(off Trevor Pl., not continuous)
Trevose Ho. *SE11 5H 19*
(off Orsett St.)
Trevose Rd. E17 1F 51
Trewenna Dr. KT9: Chess 5D 162
Trewince Rd. SW20 1E 152
Trewint St. SW18 2A 136
Trewsbury Ho. SE2 1D 108
Trewsbury Rd. SE26 5K 139
Triandra Way UB4: Yead 5B 76
Triangle, The *DA15: Sidc 7A 126*
(off Burnt Oak La.)
E8 1H 85
EC1 3B 8
IG11: Bark 6G 71
KT1: King T 2H 151
N13 4E 32
Triangle Bus. Cen., The
NW10 3B 80
Triangle Cen. UB1: S'hall 1H 95
Triangle Ct. E16 5B 88
Triangle Pas. EN4: E Barn 4F 21
Triangle Pl. SW4 4H 119
Triangle Rd. E8 1H 85
Triangle Way W3 3G 97
Trickett Ho. SM2: Sutt 7K 165
Tricorn Ho. SE28 1J 107
Tricycle Cinema *7H 63*
(in Tricycle Theatre)
Tricycle Theatre *7H 63*
(off Kilburn High Rd.)
Trident Bus. Cen. SW17 5D 136
Trident Gdns. UB5: N'olt 3B 76
Trident Ho. *E14 6E 86*
(off Blair St.)
SE28 1H 107
TW19: Stanw 7A 110
(off Clare Rd.)
Trident Pl. *SW3 7B 16*
(off Old Chu. St.)
Trident St. SE16 4K 103
Trident Way UB2: S'hall 3K 93
Trig La. EC4 2C 14 (7C 84)
Trigon Rd. SW8 7K 101
Trilby Rd. SE23 2K 139
Trillo Ct. IG2: Ilf 7J 53
Trimdon NW1 1G 83
Trimmer Wlk.
TW8: Bford 6E 96
Trim St. SE14 6B 104
Trinder Gdns. N19 1J 65
Trinder M. TW11: Tedd 5A 132
Trinder Rd. EN5: Barn 5A 20
N19 1J 65
Tring Av. HA9: Wemb 6G 61
UB1: S'hall 6D 76
W5 1F 97
Tring Cl. IG2: Ilf 5H 53
Tring Ct. TW1: Twick 4A 132
Trinidad Gdns. RM10: Dag 7K 73
Trinidad Ho. *E14 7B 86*
(off Gill St.)
Trinidad St. E14 7B 86
Trinity Av. EN1: Enf 6A 24
N2 3B 46
Trinity Buoy Wharf *E14 7G 87*
(off Orchard Pl.)
Trinity Bus. Pk. E4 6G 35
Trinity Chu. Pas.
SW13 6D 98
Trinity Chu. Rd.
SW13 6D 98
Trinity Chu. Sq. SE1 7D 14 (3C 102)
Trinity Cl. BR2: Brom 1C 172
CR2: Sand 7E 168
E8 6F 67
E11 2G 69
NW3 4B 64
SE13 4F 123
SW4 4G 119
TW4: Houn 4C 112
Trinity College of Music 6E 104
Trinity Cotts. TW9: Rich 3F 115
Trinity Ct. CR0: Croy 2C 168
EN2: Enf 2H 23
N1 1E 84
(off Downham Rd.)
NW2 5E 62
SE1 7D 14
(off Brockham St.)
SE7 4B 106
SE25 6E 156
SE26 3J 139
SW9 3K 119
W2 6A 82
(off Gloucester Ter.)
WC1 3G 7
Trinity Cres. SW17 2D 136
Trinity Dr. UB8: Hil 5E 74
Trinity Gdns. E16 5H 87
(not continuous)
SW9 4K 119
Trinity Grn. E1 4J 85
Trinity Gro. SE10 1E 122
Trinity Hospital (Almshouses)
SE10 5F 105
Trinity Ho. *SE1 3C 102*
(off Bath Ter.)
Trinity M. *E1 5J 85*
(off Redman's Rd.)
SE20 1H 157
W10 6F 81
Trinity Path SE23 3J 139
Trinity Pl. DA6: Bex 4F 127
EC3 2J 15 (7F 85)
Trinity Ri. SW2 1A 138
Trinity Rd. IG6: Ilf 3G 53
N2 3B 46
N22 7D 32
(not continuous)
SW17 4A 118
SW18 4A 118
SW19 6J 135
TW9: Rich 3F 115
UB1: S'hall 1C 94
Trinity Sq. EC3 3H 15 (7E 84)
Trinity St. E16 5H 87
EN2: Enf 2H 23
SE1 7D 14 (2C 102)
(not continuous)
Trinity Twr. *E1 7G 85*
(off Vaughan Way)
Trinity Wlk. NW3 6A 64
Trinity Way E4 6G 35
W3 7A 80
Trio Pl. SE1 7D 14 (2C 102)
Tristan Ct. *SE8 6B 104*
(off Dorking Cl.)
Tristan Sq. SE3 3G 123
Tristram Cl. E17 3F 51
Tristram Dr. N9 3B 34
Tristram Rd. BR1: Brom 4H 141
Triton Ho. *E14 4D 104*
(off Cahir St.)
Triton Sq. NW1 3A 6 (4G 83)
Tritton Av. CR0: Bedd 4J 167
Tritton Rd. SE21 3D 138
Triumph Cl. UB3: Harl 1E 110
Triumph Ho. IG11: Bark 3A 90
Triumph Rd. E6 6D 88
Triumph Trad. Est. N17 6B 34
Trocadero Cen. 3C 12 (7H 83)
Trocette Mans. *SE1 3E 102*
(off Bermondsey St.)
Trojan Ct. NW6 7G 63
Trojan Ind. Est. NW10 6B 62
Trojan Way CR0: Wadd 3K 167
Troon Cl. SE16 5H 103
SE28 6D 90
Troon Ho. *E1 6A 86*
(off White Horse Rd.)
Troon St. E1 6A 86
Tropical Ct. *W10 3F 81*
(off Kilburn La.)
Trosley Rd. DA17: Belv 6G 109
Trossachs Rd. SE22 5E 120
Trothy Rd. SE1 4G 103
Trotman Ho. *SE14 1J 121*
(off Pomeroy St.)
Trott Rd. N10 7J 31
Trott St. SW11 1C 118
Troughton Rd. SE7 5K 105
Troutbeck NW1 2K 5
Troutbeck Rd. SE14 1A 122
Trout Rd. UB7: Yiew 7A 74
Trouville Rd. SW4 6G 119
Trowbridge Rd. E9 6B 68
Trowlock Av. TW11: Tedd 6C 132
Trowlock Way TW11: Tedd 6D 132
Troy Ct. SE18 4F 107
W8 3J 99
(off Kensington High St.)
Troy Ind. Est. HA1: Harr 5K 41
Troy Rd. SE19 6D 138
Troy Town SE15 3G 121
Trubshaw Rd. UB2: S'hall 3F 95
Trueman Cl. HA8: Edg 7C 28
Truesdale Rd. E6 6D 88
Trulock Ct. N17 7B 34

Upham Pk. Rd. W4 .... 4A 98
Uphill Dr. NW7 .... 5F 29
NW9 .... 5J 43
Uphill Gro. NW7 .... 4F 29
Uphill Rd. NW7 .... 4F 29
Upland M. SE22 .... 5G 121
Upland Rd. CR2: S Croy 5D 168
DA7: Bex 3F 127
E13 .... 4J 87
SE22 .... 5G 121
SM2: Sutt 7B 166
Uplands BR3: Beck 2C 158
Uplands, The HA4: Ruis 1J 57
Uplands Av. E17 .... 2K 49
Uplands Bus. Pk. E17 .... 3K 49
Uplands Cl. SW14 .... 5H 115
Uplands Ct. N21 .... 7F 23
(off Green, The)
Uplands End IG8: Wfd G 7H 37
Uplands Pk. Rd. EN2: Enf 2F 23
Uplands Rd. EN4: E Barn 1K 31
IG8: Wfd G 7H 37
N8 .... 5K 47
RM6: Chad H 3D 54
Uplands Way N21 .... 5F 23
Upnall Ho. SE15 .... 6J 103
Upney La. IG11: Bark 6J 71
Upnor Way SE17 .... 5E 102
Uppark Dr. IG2: Ilf 6G 53
Up. Abbey Rd. DA17: Belv 4F 109
Up. Addison Gdns. W14 .... 2G 99
Up. Bank St. E14 .... 1D 104
Up. Bardsey Wlk. N1 .... 6C 66
(off Douglas Rd. Nth.)
Up. Belgrave St.
SW1 .... 1H 17 (3E 100)
Up. Berenger Wlk. SW10 .... 7B 100
(off Berenger Wlk.)
Up. Berkeley St. W1 .... 1E 10 (6D 82)
Up. Beulah Hill SE19 .... 1E 156
Up. Blantyre Wlk. SW10 .... 7B 100
(off Blantyre Wlk.)
Up. Brighton Rd. KT6: Surb 6D 150
Up. Brockley Rd. SE4 .... 3B 122
(not continuous)
Up. Brook St. W1 .... 2G 11 (7E 82)
Upper Butts TW8: Bford 6C 96
Up. Caldy Wlk. N1 .... 6C 66
(off Arran Wlk.)
Up. Camelford Wlk. W11 .... 6G 81
(off Cambourne M.)
W11 .... 6G 81
(off St Mark's Rd.)
Up. Cavendish Av. N3 .... 3J 45
Up. Cheyne Row SW3 .... 7C 16
UPPER CLAPTON 2H 67
Up. Clapton Rd. E5 .... 1H 67
Up. Clarendon Wlk. W11 .... 6G 81
(off Clarendon Rd.)
Up. Dartrey Wlk. SW10 .... 7A 100
(off Whistler Wlk.)
Up. Dengie Wlk. N1 .... 1C 84
(off Baddow Wlk.)
UPPER EDMONTON 5B 34
UPPER ELMERS END 5B 158
Up. Elmers End Rd. BR3: Beck 4A 158
Up. Farm Rd. KT8: W Mole 4D 148
Upper Feilde W1 .... 2G 11
(off Park St.)
Upper Fosters NW4 .... 4E 44
(off New Brent St.)
Upper Grn. E. CR4: Mitc 3D 154
Upper Grn. W. CR4: Mitc 2D 154
(not continuous)
Up. Grosvenor St. W1 .... 3G 11 (7E 82)
Up. Grotto Rd. TW1: Twick 2K 131
Upper Ground SE1 .... 4J 13 (1A 102)
Upper Gro. SE25 .... 4E 156
Upper Gro. Rd. DA17: Belv 6F 109
Up. Gulland Wlk. N1 .... 7C 66
(off Church Rd.)
UPPER HALLIFORD 4G 147
Up. Halliford By-Pass TW17: Shep 5G 147
Up. Halliford Grn. TW17: Shep 4G 147
Up. Halliford Rd. TW17: Shep 3G 147
Up. Hampstead Wlk. NW3 .... 4A 64
Up. Ham Rd. TW10: Ham 4D 132
Up. Handa Wlk. N1 .... 6D 66
(off Handa Wlk.)
Up. Hawkwell Wlk. N1 .... 1C 84
(off Maldon Cl.)
UPPER HOLLOWAY 2G 65
Up. Holly Hill Rd. DA17: Belv 5H 109
Up. James St. W1 .... 2B 12 (7G 83)
Up. John St. W1 .... 2B 12 (7G 83)
Up. Lismore Wlk. N1 .... 6C 66
(off Clephane Rd.)
Upper Lodge W8 .... 1K 99
(off Palace Grn.)
Upper Mall W6 .... 5C 98
(not continuous)
Upper Marsh SE1 .... 1H 19 (3K 101)
Up. Montagu St. W1 .... 5E 4 (5D 82)
Up. Mulgrave Rd. SM2: Cheam 7G 165
Upper Nth. St. E14 .... 5C 86
UPPER NORWOOD 1E 156
Upper Pk. Rd. BR1: Brom 1K 159
DA17: Belv 4H 109
KT2: King T 6G 133
N11 .... 5A 32
NW3 .... 5D 64
Up. Phillimore Gdns. W8 .... 2J 99
Up. Ramsey Wlk. N1 .... 6D 66
(off Ramsey Wlk.)
Up. Rawreth Wlk. N1 .... 1C 84
(off Basire St.)
Up. Richmond Rd. SW15 .... 4B 116
Up. Richmond Rd. W. SW14 .... 4G 115
TW10, Rich 4G 115
Upper Rd. E13 .... 3J 87
SM6: Wall 5H 167
UPPER RUXLEY 7G 145
Up. St Martin's La.
WC2 .... 2E 12 (7J 83)
Up. Selsdon Rd. CR2: Sand, Sels 7F 169
Up. Sheridan Rd. DA17: Belv 4G 109
UPPER SHIRLEY 4K 169
Up. Shirley Rd. CR0: Croy 2J 169
Upper Sq. TW7: Isle 3A 114
Upper St. N1 .... 2A 84
Up. Sunbury Rd. TW12: Hamp 1C 148
Up. Sutton La. TW5: Hest 7E 94
UPPER SYDENHAM 3H 139
Up. Tachbrook St.
SW1 .... 3B 18 (4G 101)
Up. Talbot Wlk. W11 .... 6G 81
(off Talbot Wlk.)
Up. Teddington Rd.
KT1: Hamp W 7C 132
Upper Ter. NW3 .... 3A 64
Up. Thames St. EC4 .... 2B 14 (7B 84)
Up. Tollington Pk. N4 .... 1A 66
(not continuous)
Upperton Rd. DA14: Sidc 5K 143
Upperton Rd. E. E13 .... 3A 88
Upperton Rd. W. E13 .... 3A 88
UPPER TOOTING 4D 136
Up. Tooting Pk. SW17 .... 2D 136
Up. Tooting Rd. SW17 .... 4D 136
Up. Town Rd. UB6: G'frd 4F 77
Up. Tulse Hill SW2 .... 7K 119
Up. Vernon Rd. SM1: Sutt 5B 166
UPPER WALTHAMSTOW 4F 51
Up. Walthamstow Rd. E17 .... 4E 50
Up. Whistler Wlk. SW10 .... 7A 100
(off Worlds End Est.)
Up. Wickham La.
DA16: Well 7B 108
Up. Wimpole St. W1 .... 5H 5 (5E 82)
Up. Woburn Pl. WC1 .... 2D 6 (3H 83)
Uppingham Av. HA7: Stan 1B 42
Upsdell Av. N13 .... 6F 33
Upshire Ho. E17 .... 2B 50
Upstall St. SE5 .... 1B 120
UPTON
Bexleyheath 5D 126
West Ham 7J 69
Upton Av. E7 .... 7J 69
Upton Cl. DA5: Bexl 6F 127
NW2 .... 3G 63
Upton Ct. SE20 .... 7J 139
(off Blean Gro.)
Upton Dene SM2: Sutt 7K 165
Upton Gdns. HA3: Kent 5B 42
Upton La. E7 .... 7J 69
Upton Lodge E7 .... 6J 69
Upton Lodge Cl. WD23: Bush 1B 26
UPTON PARK 1B 88
Upton Pk. Boleyn Cinema 2B 88
Upton Pk. Rd. E7 .... 7K 69
Upton Pk. 2A 88
Upton Rd. CR7: Thor H 2D 156
DA5: Bexl 4E 126
DA6: Bex 4E 126
N18 .... 5B 34
SE18 .... 6G 107
TW3: Houn 3E 112
Upton Rd. Sth. DA5: Bexl 6F 127
Upton Vs. DA6: Bex 4E 126
Upway N12 .... 6H 31
Upwey Ho. N1 .... 1E 84
Upwood Rd. SE12 .... 6J 123
SW16 .... 1J 155
Urban M. N4 .... 6B 48
Urlwin St. SE5 .... 6C 102
Urlwin Wlk. SW9 .... 1A 120
Urmston Dr. SW19 .... 1G 135
Urmston Ho. E14 .... 4E 104
(off Seyssel St.)
Urquhart Ct. BR3: Beck 7B 140
Ursula Lodges DA14: Sidc 5B 144
Ursula M. N4 .... 1C 66
Ursula St. SW11 .... 1C 118
Urswick Gdns. RM9: Dag 7E 72
Urswick Rd. E9 .... 5J 67
RM9: Dag 7D 72
Usborne M. SW8 .... 7K 101
Usher Rd. E3 .... 1B 86
Usk Rd. SW11 .... 4A 118
Usk St. E2 .... 3K 85
Utopia Village NW1 .... 7E 64
Uvedale Rd. EN2: Enf 5J 23
RM10: Dag 3G 73
Uverdale Rd. SW10 .... 7A 100
UXBRIDGE 1A 74
Uxbridge Ct. KT1: King T 5D 150
(off Uxbridge Rd.)
Uxbridge Rd. HA3: Hrw W 7A 26
HA5: H End, Pinn 2A 40
HA7: Stan 7A 26
KT1: King T 4D 150
TW12: Hamp, Hamp H 4E 130
TW13: Felt 2A 130
UB1: S'hall 1E 94
UB4: Hayes, Yead 5G 75
UB10: Hil 3C 74
W3 .... 7E 78
W5 .... 7E 78
W7 .... 1K 95
W12 .... 1C 98
W13 .... 1B 96
Uxbridge Rd. Retail Pk.
UB4: Yead 7A 76
Uxbridge St. W8 .... 1J 99
Uxendon Cres. HA9: Wemb 1E 60
Uxendon Hill HA9: Wemb 1F 61

V

Vaine Ho. E9 .... 6A 68
Vaizeys Wharf SE7 .... 3K 105
Valance Av. E4 .... 1B 36
Valan Leas BR2: Brom 3G 159
Vale, The CR0: Croy 2K 169
HA4: Ruis 4A 58
IG8: Wfd G 7D 36
N10 .... 1E 46
N14 .... 7C 22
NW11 .... 3F 63
SW3 .... 7A 16 (6B 100)
TW5: Hest 6C 94
TW14: Felt 6K 111
TW16: Sun 6J 129
W3 .... 1K 97
Vale Cl. BR6: Farnb 4E 172
N2 .... 3D 46
TW1: Twick 3A 132
W9 .... 3A 82
Vale Cotts. SW15 .... 3A 134
Vale Ct. EN5: New Bar 4E 20
W3 .... 1B 98
W9 .... 3A 82
Vale Cres. SW15 .... 4A 134
Vale Cft. HA5: Pinn 5C 40
Vale Dr. EN5: Barn 4C 20
Vale End SE22 .... 4F 121
Vale Est., The W3 .... 1A 98
Vale Farm Sports Cen. 4B 60
Vale Gro. N4 .... 7C 48
W3 .... 2K 97
Vale La. W3 .... 5G 79
Vale Lodge SE23 .... 2J 139
Valence Av. RM8: Dag 1D 72
Valence Cir. RM8: Dag 3D 72
Valence House Mus. & Gallery 3E 72
Valence Rd. DA8: Erith 7K 109
Valence Wood Rd.
RM8: Dag 3D 72
Valencia Rd. HA7: Stan 4H 27
Valentia Pl. SW9 .... 4A 120
Valentine Av. DA5: Bexl 2E 144
Valentine Ct. SE23 .... 2K 139
(not continuous)
Valentine Pl. SE1 .... 6A 14 (2B 102)
Valentine Rd. E9 .... 6K 67
HA2: Harr 3F 59
Valentine Row SE1 .... 7A 14 (2B 102)
Valentines Rd. IG1: Ilf 1F 71
Valentine's Way
RM7: Rush G 2K 73
VALE OF HEALTH 3A 64
Vale of Health NW3 .... 3B 64
Vale Pde. SW15 .... 3A 134
Valerian Way E15 .... 3G 87
Valerie Ct. SM2: Sutt 7K 165
Vale Ri. NW11 .... 1H 63
Vale Rd. BR1: Brom 1E 160
CR4: Mitc 3H 155
E7 .... 6K 69
KT4: Wor Pk 3B 164
KT19: Ewe 4B 164
N4 .... 7C 48
SM1: Sutt 4K 165
Vale Rd. Nth. KT6: Surb 2E 162
Vale Rd. Sth. KT6: Surb 2E 162
Vale Row N5 .... 3B 66
Vale Royal N7 .... 7J 65
Vale Royal Ho. WC2 .... 2D 12
(off Charing Cross Rd.)
Valery Pl. TW12: Hamp 7E 130
Valeside Ct. EN5: New Bar 4E 20
Vale St. SE27 .... 3D 138
Valeswood Rd.
BR1: Brom 5H 141
Vale Ter. N4 .... 6C 48
Valetta Gro. E13 .... 2J 87
Valetta Rd. W3 .... 2A 98
Valette Ct. N10 .... 4F 47
(off St James's La.)
Valette Ho. E9 .... 6J 67
Valette St. E9 .... 6J 67
Valiant Cl. RM7: Mawney 2H 55
UB5: N'olt 3B 76

Wakefield Rd.—Walters Ho.

Wakefield Rd. N11 . . . 5C 32
N15 . . . 5F 49
TW10: Rich . . . 5D 114
Wakefield St. E6 . . . 1B 88
N18 . . . 5B 34
WC1 . . . 2F 7 (4J 83)
Wakeford Cl. SW4 . . . 5G 119
Wakehams Hill HA5: Pinn . . . 3D 40
Wakeham St. N1 . . . 6D 66
Wakehurst Rd.
SW11 . . . 5C 118
Wakeling Rd. W7 . . . 5K 77
Wakeling St. E14 . . . 6A 86
Wakelin Ho. *N1* . . . *7B 66*
(off Sebbon St.)
SE23 . . . *7A 122*
(off Brockley Pk.)
Wakelin Rd. E15 . . . 2G 87
Wakeman Ho. *NW10* . . . *3F 81*
(off Wakeman Rd.)
Wakeman Rd. NW10 . . . 3E 80
Wakemans Hill Av. NW9 . . . 5K 43
Wakering Rd. IG11: Bark . . . 7G 71
(Barking Northern Relief Rd.)
IG11: Bark . . . 6G 71
(Church Rd.)
Wakerings, The *IG11: Bark* . . . *6G 71*
(off Wakering Rd.)
Wakerley Cl. E6 . . . 6D 88
Wakley St. EC1 . . . 1A 8 (3B 84)
Walberswick St. SW8 . . . 7J 101
Walbrook EC4 . . . 2E 14 (7D 84)
(not continuous)
Walbrook Ct. *N1* . . . *2E 84*
(off Hemsworth St.)
Walbrook Ho. *N9* . . . *2D 34*
(off Huntingdon Rd.)
Walbrook Wharf *EC4* . . . *3D 14*
(off Bell Wharf La.)
Walburgh St. E1 . . . 6H 85
Walcorde Av. SE17 . . . 4C 102
Walcot Gdns. SE11 . . . 3J 19
Walcot Rd. EN3: Brim . . . 2G 25
Walcot Sq. SE11 . . . 3K 19 (4A 102)
Walcott St. SW1 . . . 3B 18 (4G 101)
Waldair Ct. E16 . . . 2F 107
Waldeck Gro. SE27 . . . 3B 138
Waldeck Rd. N15 . . . 4B 48
SW14 . . . 3J 115
W4 . . . 6G 97
W13 . . . 6B 78
Waldeck Ter. *SW14* . . . *3J 115*
(off Waldeck Rd.)
Waldegrave Av. TW11: Tedd . . . 5K 131
Waldegrave Ct. IG11: Bark . . . 1H 89
Waldegrave Gdns. TW1: Twick . . . 2K 131
Waldegrave Pk. TW1: Twick . . . 4K 131
Waldegrave Rd. BR1: Brom . . . 4C 160
N8 . . . 3A 48
RM8: Dag . . . 2C 72
SE19 . . . 7F 139
TW1: Twick . . . 4K 131
TW11: Tedd . . . 4K 131
W5 . . . 7F 79
Waldegrove CR0: Croy . . . 3F 169
Waldemar Av. SW6 . . . 1G 117
W13 . . . 1C 96
Waldemar Rd. SW19 . . . 5J 135
Walden Av. BR7: Chst . . . 4D 142
N13 . . . 4H 33
RM13: Rain . . . 2K 91
Walden Cl. DA17: Belv . . . 5F 109
Walden Ct. SW8 . . . 1H 119
Walden Gdns. CR7: Thor H . . . 3K 155
Walden Ho. *SW1* . . . *4H 17*
(off Pimlico Rd.)
Walden Pde. BR7: Chst . . . 6D 142
(not continuous)
Walden Rd. BR7: Chst . . . 6D 142
N17 . . . 1D 48
Waldenshaw Rd. SE23 . . . 1J 139
Walden St. E1 . . . 6H 85
(not continuous)
Walden Way NW7 . . . 6A 30
Waldo Cl. SW4 . . . 5G 119
Waldo Ho. *NW10* . . . *3D 80*
(off Waldo Rd.)
Waldo Ind. Est. BR1: Brom . . . 3B 160
Waldo Pl. CR4: Mitc . . . 7C 136
Waldorf Cl. CR2: S Croy . . . 7B 168
Waldo Rd. BR1: Brom . . . 3B 160
NW10 . . . 3C 80
(not continuous)
Waldram Cres. SE23 . . . 1J 139
Waldram Pk. Rd. SE23 . . . 1K 139
Waldram Pl. SE23 . . . 1J 139
Waldrist Way DA18: Erith . . . 2F 109
Waldron Gdns. BR2: Brom . . . 3F 159
Waldronhyrst CR2: S Croy . . . 4B 168
Waldron M. SW3 . . . 7B 16 (6B 100)
Waldron Rd. HA1: Harr . . . 1J 59
HA2: Harr . . . 1J 59
SW18 . . . 3A 136
Waldrons, The CR0: Croy . . . 4B 168
Waldron's Path CR2: S Croy . . . 4C 168
Waldrons Yd. HA2: Harr . . . 2H 59
Waldstock Rd. SE28 . . . 7A 90
Waleran Cl. HA7: Stan . . . 5E 26
Walerand Rd. SE13 . . . 2E 122
Waleran Flats SE1 . . . 4E 102
Wales Av. SM5: Cars . . . 5C 166
Wales Cl. SE15 . . . 7H 103
Wales Farm Rd. W3 . . . 5K 79
Waleton Acres SM6: Wall . . . 6G 167
Waley St. E1 . . . 5A 86
Walfield Av. N20 . . . 7E 20
Walford Ho. E1 . . . 6G 85
Walford Rd. N16 . . . 4E 66
Walfrey Gdns. RM9: Dag . . . 7E 72
WALHAM GREEN . . . 1J 117
Walham Grn. Ct. *SW6* . . . *7K 99*
(off Waterford Rd.)
Walham Gro. SW6 . . . 7J 99
Walham Ri. SW19 . . . 6G 135
Walham Yd. SW6 . . . 7J 99
Walk, The *N13* . . . *3F 33*
(off Fox La.)
TW16: Sun . . . 7H 129
Walkato Lodge IG9: Buck H . . . 1F 37
Walkden Rd. BR7: Chst . . . 5E 142
Walker Cl. N11 . . . 4B 32
SE18 . . . 4G 107
TW12: Hamp . . . 6D 130
TW14: Felt . . . 7H 111
W7 . . . 1J 95
Walker Ho. NW1 . . . 1C 6 (2H 83)
Walker M. SW2 . . . 5A 120
Walker's Ct. W1 . . . 2C 12
Walkerscroft Mead SE21 . . . 1C 138
Walkers Lodge *E14* . . . *2E 104*
(off Manchester Rd.)
Walkers Pl. SW15 . . . 4G 117
Walkinshaw Ct. *N1* . . . *7C 66*
(off Rotherfield St.)
Walks, The N2 . . . 3B 46
Wallace Cl. SE28 . . . 7D 90
TW17: Shep . . . 4F 147
UB10: Uxb . . . 2A 74
Wallace Collection . . . 7H 5 (6E 82)
Wallace Ct. *NW1* . . . *6D 4*
(off Old Marylebone Rd.)
Wallace Cres. SM5: Cars . . . 5D 166
Wallace Ho. *N7* . . . *6K 65*
(off Caledonian Rd.)
Wallace Rd. N1 . . . 6C 66
Wallace Way *N19* . . . *2H 65*
(off St John's Way)
RM1: Rom . . . 1K 55
Wallasey Cres. UB10: Ick . . . 2C 56
Wallbrook Bus. Cen. TW4: Houn . . . 3K 111
Wallbutton Rd. SE4 . . . 2A 122
Wallcote Av. NW2 . . . 1F 63
Wall Ct. *N4* . . . *1K 65*
(off Stroud Grn. Rd.)
Walled Gdn. Cl. BR3: Beck . . . 4D 158
WALLEND . . . 1E 88
Wall End Ct. *E6* . . . *1E 88*
(off Wall End Rd.)
Wall End Rd. E6 . . . 7E 70
Waller Dr. HA6: Nwood . . . 2J 39
Waller Rd. SE14 . . . 1K 121
Wallers Cl. IG8: Wfd G . . . 6J 37
RM9: Dag . . . 1E 90
Waller Way SE10 . . . 7D 104
Wallflower St. W12 . . . 7B 80
Wallgrave Rd. SW5 . . . 4K 99
Wallingford Av. W10 . . . 5F 81
WALLINGTON . . . 6F 167
Wallington Cl. HA4: Ruis . . . 6E 38
Wallington Cnr. *SM6: Wall* . . . *4F 167*
(off Manor Rd. Nth.)
Wallington Ct. *SM6: Wall* . . . *6F 167*
(off Stanley Pk. Rd.)
WALLINGTON GREEN . . . 4F 167
Wallington Rd. IG3: Ilf . . . 7K 53
Wallington Sq. SM6: Wall . . . 6F 167
Wallis All. SE1 . . . 6D 14
Wallis Cl. SW11 . . . 3B 118
Wallis Ho. SE14 . . . 1A 122
Wallis M. *N8* . . . *3A 48*
(off Courcy Rd.)
Wallis Rd. E9 . . . 6B 68
UB1: S'hall . . . 6F 77
Wallis's Cotts. SW2 . . . 7J 119
Wallman Pl. N22 . . . 1K 47
Wallorton Gdns. SW14 . . . 4K 115
Wallside EC2 . . . 6D 8
Wall St. N1 . . . 6D 66
Wallwood Rd. E11 . . . 7F 51
Wallwood St. E14 . . . 5B 86
Walmar Cl. EN4: Had W . . . 1G 21
Walmer Cl. BR6: Farnb . . . 4H 173
E4 . . . 2J 35
RM7: Mawney . . . 2H 55
Walmer Ct. *KT5: Surb* . . . *5E 150*
(off Cranes Pk.)
Walmer Gdns. W13 . . . 2A 96
Walmer Ho. *W10* . . . *6F 81*
(off Bramley Rd.)
Walmer Pl. W1 . . . 5E 4
Walmer Rd. W10 . . . 6E 80
W11 . . . 7G 81
Walmer St. W1 . . . 5E 4 (5D 82)
Walmer Ter. SE18 . . . 4G 107
Walmgate Rd. UB6: G'frd . . . 1B 78
Walmington Fold N12 . . . 6D 30
Walm La. NW2 . . . 6E 62
Walney Wlk. N1 . . . 6C 66
Walnut Av. UB7: W Dray . . . 3C 92
Walnut Cl. IG6: Ilf . . . 4G 53
SE8 . . . 6B 104
SM5: Cars . . . 5D 166
UB3: Hayes . . . 7G 75
Walnut Ct. E17 . . . 4E 50
W5 . . . 2E 96
W8 . . . *3K 99*
(off St Mary's Ga.)
Walnut Flds. KT17: Ewe . . . 7B 164
Walnut Gdns. E15 . . . 5G 69
Walnut Gro. EN1: Enf . . . 5J 23
Walnut M. *N22* . . . *3A 48*
(off High Rd.)
SM2: Sutt . . . 7A 166
Walnut Rd. E10 . . . 2C 68
Walnut Tree Av. *CR4: Mitc* . . . *3C 154*
(off Dearn Gdns.)
Walnut Tree Cl. BR7: Chst . . . 1H 161
SW13 . . . 1B 116
TW17: Shep . . . 3E 146
Walnut Tree Cotts.
SW19 . . . 5G 135
Walnut Tree Ho. *SW10* . . . *6K 99*
(off Tregunter Rd.)
Walnut Tree Rd. RM8: Dag . . . 2E 72
SE10 . . . 5G 105
(not continuous)
TW5: Hest . . . 6D 94
TW8: Bford . . . 6E 96
TW17: Shep . . . 2E 146
Walnut Tree Wlk.
SE11 . . . 3J 19 (4A 102)
Walnut Way HA4: Ruis . . . 6A 58
IG9: Buck H . . . 3G 37
Walpole Av. TW9: Kew . . . 2F 115
Walpole Cl. W13 . . . 2C 96
Walpole Ct. TW2: Twick . . . 2J 131
W14 . . . *3F 99*
(off Blythe Rd.)
Walpole Cres. TW11: Tedd . . . 5K 131
Walpole Gdns. TW2: Twick . . . 2J 131
W4 . . . 5J 97
Walpole Ho. *KT8: W Mole* . . . *5E 148*
(off Approach Rd.)
SE1 . . . *7J 13*
(off Westminster Bri. Rd.)
Walpole Lodge W13 . . . 1C 96
Walpole M. NW8 . . . 1B 82
SW19 . . . 6B 136
Walpole Pk. Summer Theatre . . . 1C 96
Walpole Pl. SE18 . . . 4F 107
TW11: Tedd . . . 5K 131
Walpole Rd. BR2: Brom . . . 5B 160
CR0: Croy . . . 2D 168
E6 . . . 7A 70
E17 . . . 4A 50
E18 . . . 1H 51
KT6: Surb . . . 7E 150
N17 . . . 2C 48
(not continuous)
SW19 . . . 6B 136
TW2: Twick . . . 2J 131
TW11: Tedd . . . 5K 131
Walpole St. SW3 . . . 5E 16 (5D 100)
Walrond Av. HA9: Wemb . . . 5E 60
Walsham Cl. N16 . . . 1G 67
SE28 . . . 7D 90
Walsham Ho. SE14 . . . 2K 121
SE17 . . . *5D 102*
(off Blackwood St.)
Walsham Rd. SE14 . . . 2K 121
TW14: Felt . . . 7K 111
Walsingham NW8 . . . 1B 82
Walsingham Gdns. KT19: Ewe . . . 4A 164
Walsingham Lodge SW13 . . . 1C 116
Walsingham Mans. *SW6* . . . *7K 99*
(off Fulham Rd.)
Walsingham Pk. BR7: Chst . . . 2H 161
Walsingham Pl. SW4 . . . 6E 118
Walsingham Rd. CR4: Mitc . . . 5D 154
E5 . . . 3G 67
EN2: Enf . . . 4J 23
W13 . . . 1A 96
Walsingham Wlk. DA17: Belv . . . 6G 109
Walston Ho. *SW1* . . . *5C 18*
(off Aylesford St.)
Walter Besant Ho. *E1* . . . *3K 85*
(off Bancroft Rd.)
Walter Ct. *W3* . . . *6J 79*
(off Lynton Ter.)
Walter Grn. Ho. *SE15* . . . *1J 121*
(off Lausanne Rd.)
Walter Hurford Pde. *E12* . . . *4E 70*
(off Walton Rd.)
Walter Langley Ct. *SE16* . . . *2J 103*
(off Brunel Rd.)
Walter Rodney Cl.
E6 . . . 6D 70
Walter Savil Twr. *E17* . . . *6C 50*
(off Colchester Rd.)
Walters Cl. *SE17* . . . *4D 102*
(off Brandon St.)
UB3: Hayes . . . 2H 93
Walters Ho. *SE17* . . . *6B 102*
(off Otto St.)

Warren Farm School Sports Cen.—Water Twr. Pl.

Warren Farm School Sports Cen. 3H 95
Warren Flds. HA7: Stan 4H 27
Warren Footpath
TW1: Twick 1C 132
Warren Gdns. BR6: Chels 5K 173
E15 5F 69
Warren Ho. *N17* 3G 49
(off High Cross Rd.)
W14 4H 99
(off Beckford Cl.)
Warren La. HA7: Stan 2F 27
SE18 3F 107
Warren La. Ga. SE18 3F 107
Warren M. W1 4A 6 (4G 83)
Warren Pk. KT2: King T 6J 133
Warren Pk. Rd. SM1: Sutt 6B 166
Warren Pl. *E1* 6K 85
(off Caroline St.)
Warren Pond Rd. E4 1C 36
(not continuous)
Warren Ri. KT3: N Mald 1K 151
Warren Rd. BR2: Hayes 2J 171
BR6: Chels 5K 173
CR0: Croy 1E 168
DA6: Bex 5G 127
DA14: Sidc 3C 144
E4 2K 35
E10 3E 68
E11 6A 52
(not continuous)
IG6: Ilf 5H 53
KT2: King T 6J 133
NW2 2B 62
SW19 6C 136
TW2: Whit 6G 113
TW15: Ashf 7G 129
UB10: Ick 4A 56
WD23: Bushy 1B 26
Warren Sports Cen. 5F 55
Warrens Shawe La. HA8: Edg 2C 28
Warren St. W1 4A 6 (4G 83)
Warren Ter. RM6: Chad H 4D 54
Warren Wlk. SE7 6A 106
Warren Way NW7 6B 30
Warren Wood Cl. BR2: Hayes 2H 171
Warriner Dr. N9 3B 34
Warriner Gdns. SW11 1D 118
Warrington Ct. *CR0: Wadd* 3B 168
(off Warrington Rd.)
Warrington Cres. W9 4A 82
Warrington Gdns. W9 4A 82
Warrington Rd. CR0: Wadd 3B 168
HA1: Harr 5J 41
RM8: Dag 2D 72
TW10: Rich 5D 114
Warrington Sq. RM8: Dag 2D 72
Warrior Cl. SE28 1H 107
Warrior Sq. E12 4E 70
Warsaw Cl. HA4: Ruis 6K 57
Warspite Ho. *E14* 4D 104
(off Cahir St.)
Warspite Rd. SE18 3C 106
Warton Rd. E15 7E 68
Warwall E6 6F 89
Warwick *W14* 4H 99
(off Kensington Village)
Warwick Av. HA2: Harr 4D 58
HA8: Edg 3C 28
W2 4A 82
W9 4K 81
Warwick Bldg. SW8 6F 101
Warwick Chambers *W8* 3J 99
(off Pater St.)
Warwick Cl. DA5: Bexl 7F 127
EN4: E Barn 5G 21
TW12: Hamp 7G 131
WD23: Bushy 1D 26
Warwick Ct. BR2: Brom 2G 159
EC4 1B 14
(off Warwick La.)
Warwick Ct. *EN5: New Bar* 5E 20
(off Station Rd.)
HA3: W'stone 3J 41
N11 6C 32
UB5: N'olt 5E 58
(off Newmarket Av.)
W7 6K 77
(off Copley Cl.)
WC1 6H 7 (5K 83)
Warwick Cres. UB4: Hayes 4H 75
W2 5A 82
Warwick Dene W5 1E 96
Warwick Dr. SW15 3D 116
Warwick Est. W2 5K 81
Warwick Gdns. CR7: Thor H 3A 156
EN5: Barn 1C 20
IG1: Ilf 1F 71
KT7: T Ditt 5K 149
N4 5C 48
W14 3H 99
Warwick Gro. E5 1H 67
KT5: Surb 7F 151
Warwick Ho. *E16* 1J 105
(off Wesley Av.)
KT2: King T 1E 150
(off Acre Rd.)
SW9 2A 120
Warwick Ho. St.
SW1 4D 12 (1H 101)
Warwick La. EC4 7B 8 (6B 84)
Warwick Lodge TW2: Twick 3F 131
Warwick Pde. HA3: Kent 2B 42
Warwick Pas. *EC4* 7B 8
(off Old Bailey)
Warwick Pl. KT7: T Ditt 6A 150
W5 2D 96
W9 5A 82
Warwick Pl. Nth.
SW1 4A 18 (4G 101)
Warwick Rd. CR7: Thor H 3A 156
DA14: Sidc 5B 144
DA16: Well 3C 126
E4 5H 35
E11 5K 51
E12 5C 70
E15 6H 69
E17 1B 50
EN5: New Bar 4E 20
KT1: Hamp W 1C 150
KT3: N Mald 3J 151
KT7: T Ditt 5K 149
N11 6C 32
N18 4K 33
SE20 3H 157
SM1: Sutt 4A 166
SW5 4H 99
TW2: Twick 1J 131
TW4: Houn 3K 111
TW15: Ashf 5A 128
UB2: S'hall 3D 94
UB7: W Dray 2A 92
W5 2D 96
W14 4H 99
Warwick Row SW1 1K 17 (3F 101)
Warwickshire Path SE8 7B 104
Warwickshire Rd. N16 4E 66
Warwick Sq. EC4 7B 8 (6B 84)
SW1 5A 18 (5G 101)
(not continuous)
Warwick Sq. M. SW1 4A 18 (4G 101)
Warwick St. W1 2B 12 (7G 83)
Warwick Ter. *E17* 5F 51
(off Lea Bri. Rd.)
SE18 6H 107
Warwick Way
SW1 5J 17 (5F 101)
Warwick Yd. EC1 4D 8 (4C 84)
Washbourne Ct. *N9* 2B 34
(off Acton Cl.)
Washington Av. E12 4D 70
Washington Cl. E3 3D 86
Washington Ho. *E17* 2B 50
(off Priory Ct.)
Washington Rd. E6 7A 70
E18 2H 51
KT1: King T 2G 151
KT4: Wor Pk 2D 164
SW13 7C 98
Wastdale Rd. SE23 1K 139
Watch, The N12 4F 31
Watchfield Ct. W4 5J 97
Watcombe Cotts.
TW9: Kew 6G 97
Watcombe Pl. SE25 5H 157
Watcombe Rd. SE25 5H 157
Waterbank Rd. SE6 3D 140
Waterbeach Rd. RM9: Dag 6C 72
Water Brook La. NW4 5E 44
Watercress Pl. N1 7E 66
Waterdale Rd. SE2 6A 108
Waterden Cres. E15 5C 68
Waterden Rd. E15 5C 68
Waterer Ho. SE6 4E 140
Waterer Ri. SM6: Wall 6H 167
Waterfall Cl. N14 3B 32
Waterfall Cotts. SW19 6B 136
Waterfall Rd. N11 4A 32
N14 4A 32
SW19 6B 136
Waterfall Ter. SW17 6C 136
Waterfall Wlk. N14 1A 32
Waterfield Cl. DA17: Belv 3G 109
SE28 1B 108
Waterfield Gdns. SE25 4D 156
Waterford Ho. *W11* 7H 81
(off Kensington Pk. Rd.)
Waterford Rd. SW6 7K 99
(not continuous)
Waterford Way NW10 5D 62
Waterfront Leisure Cen. 3E 106
Waterfront Studios Bus. Cen.
E16 1J 105
(off Dock Rd.)
Water Gdns. HA7: Stan 6G 27
Water Gdns., The W2 7D 4 (6C 82)
Watergardens, The
KT2: King T 6J 133
Watergate EC4 2A 14 (7B 84)
Watergate St. SE8 6C 104
Watergate Wlk. WC2 4F 13 (1J 101)
Waterhall Av. E4 4B 36
Waterhall Cl. E17 1K 49
Waterhead *NW1* 1A 6
(off Varndell St.)
Waterhouse Cl. E16 5B 88
NW3 5B 64
W6 4F 99
Waterhouse Sq. EC1 6J 7 (5A 84)
Wateridge Cl. E14 3C 104
Water La. DA14: Sidc 2F 145
E15 6G 69
EC3 3H 15 (7E 84)
IG3: Ilf 3J 71
KT1: King T 1D 150
N9 1C 34
NW1 7F 65
SE14 7J 103
TW1: Twick 1A 132
TW9: Rich 5D 114
Water Lily Cl. UB2: S'hall 2G 95
Waterloo Bri.
SE1 3H 13 (7K 83)
Waterloo Cl. E9 5J 67
TW14: Felt 1H 129
Waterloo Gdns. E2 2J 85
RM7: Rom 6K 55
Waterloo Pas. NW6 7H 63
Waterloo Pl. *SM5: Cars* 3D 166
(off Wrythe La.)
SW1 4C 12 (1H 101)
TW9: Kew 6G 97
TW9: Rich 4E 114
Waterloo Rd. E6 7A 70
E7 5H 69
E10 7C 50
IG6: Ilf 2G 53
NW2 1C 62
RM7: Rom, Rush G 5K 55
SE1 4H 13 (1K 101)
SM1: Sutt 5B 166
Waterloo Ter. N1 7B 66
Waterlow Ct. NW11 7K 45
Waterlow Rd. N19 1G 65
Waterman Bldg. E14 2B 104
Watermans Art Cen., Cinema & Theatre
6E 96
Watermans Cl. KT2: King T 7E 132
Watermans Ct. *TW8: Bford* 6D 96
(off High St.)
Watermans M. W5 7E 78
Waterman St. SW15 3F 117
Watermans Wlk. EC4 3E 14
SE16 2A 104
Waterman Way E1 1H 103
Watermead TW14: Felt 1G 129
Watermead Ho. E9 5A 68
Watermead La. SM5: Cars 7D 154
Watermeadow La. SW6 2A 118
Watermead Rd. SE6 4E 140
Watermead Way N17 3G 49
Watermen's Sq. SE20 7J 139
Water M. SE15 4J 121
Watermill Bus. Cen. EN3: Brim 2G 25
Watermill Cl. TW10: Ham 3C 132
Water Mill Ho. TW13: Hanw 2E 130
Watermill La. N18 5K 33
Watermill Way SW19 1A 154
TW13: Hanw 2D 130
Watermint Quay N16 7G 49
Water Rd. HA0: Wemb 1F 79
Water's Edge *SW6* 1E 116
(off Palemead Cl.)
Watersedge KT19: Ewe 4J 163
Watersfield Way HA8: Edg 7J 27
Waters Gdns. RM10: Dag 5G 73
Waterside BR3: Beck 1B 158
E17 6J 49
W2 6A 4
Waterside Av. *BR3: Beck* 5E 158
(off Adamson Way)
Waterside Bus. Cen. TW7: Isle 4B 114
Waterside Cl. E3 1B 86
IG11: Bark 4A 72
KT6: Surb 2E 162
SE16 2G 103
SE28 1K 107
UB5: N'olt 3D 76
Waterside Ct. *SM5: Cars* 3E 166
(off Millpond Pl.)
Waterside Dr. KT12: Walt T 5J 147
Waterside Ho. *E14* 2D 104
(off Admirals Way)
Waterside Pl. NW1 1E 82
Waterside Point SW11 7C 100
Waterside Rd. UB2: S'hall 3E 94
Waterside Twr. *SW6* 2A 118
(off Boulevard, The)
Waterside Trad. Cen. W7 3J 95
Waterside Way SW17 4A 136
Watersmeet Way SE28 6C 90
Waterson St. E2 1H 9 (3E 84)
Waters Pl. SW15 2E 116
Watersplash Cl. KT1: King T 3E 150
Watersplash La. TW5: Cran 5K 93
UB3: Harl 4J 93
Watersplash Rd. TW17: Shep 5C 146
Waters Rd. KT1: King T 2H 151
SE6 3G 141
Waters Sq. KT1: King T 3H 151
Water St. WC2 2J 13
Water Twr. Cl. UB8: Uxb 5A 56
Water Twr. Hill CR0: Croy 4D 168
Water Twr. Pl. N1 1A 84

Wellclose St.—Wentworth Pk.

Wellclose St. E1 7G **85**
E3 2A **86**
(off Driffield Rd)
Wellcome Cen. for Medical Science 3C 6
Wellcome Mus. 7H 7
(off Portugal St.)
Well Cott. Cl. E11 6A **52**
Well Ct. EC4 1D **14** (6C **84**)
(not continuous)
Welldon Ct. HA1: Harr 5J **41**
Welldon Cres. HA1: Harr 5J **41**
Weller Ho. SE16 2G **103**
(off George Row)
Weller St. SE1 6C **14** (2C **102**)
Welles Ct. E14 7C **86**
(off Premiere Pl.)
Wellesley Av. W6 3D **98**
Wellesley Cl. SE7 5A **106**
Wellesley Ct. NW2 2C **62**
SM3: Sutt 1G **165**
W9 3A **82**
Wellesley Ct. Rd. CR0: Croy 2D **168**
Wellesley Cres. TW2: Twick 2J **131**
Wellesley Gro. CR0: Croy 2D **168**
Wellesley Ho. NW1 2D **6**
(off Wellesley Pl.)
SW1 5J **17**
(off Ebury Bri. Rd.)
Wellesley Mans. W14 5H **99**
(off Edith Vs.)
Wellesley Pde. TW2: Twick 3J **131**
Wellesley Pk. M. EN2: Enf 2G **23**
Wellesley Pas. CR0: Croy 2C **168**
Wellesley Pl. NW1 2C **6** (3H **83**)
NW5 5E **64**
Wellesley Rd. CR0: Croy 1C **168**
E11 5J **51**
E17 6C **50**
HA1: Harr 5J **41**
IG1: Ilf 2F **71**
N22 2A **48**
NW5 5E **64**
SM2: Sutt 6A **166**
(not continuous)
TW2: Twick 3H **131**
W4 5G **97**
Wellesley St. E1 5K **85**
Wellesley Ter. N1 1D **8** (3C **84**)
Wellfield Av. N10 3F **47**
Wellfield Rd. SW16 4J **137**
Wellfield Wlk. SW16 5K **137**
(not continuous)
Wellfit St. SE24 3B **120**
Wellgarth UB6: G'frd 6B **60**
Wellgarth Rd. NW11 1K **63**
Well Gro. N20 1F **31**
Well Hall Pde. SE9 4D **124**
Well Hall Rd. SE9 3C **124**
WELL HALL RDBT. 4C **124**
Wellhouse La. EN5: Barn 4A **20**
Wellhouse Rd. BR3: Beck 4C **158**
Wellhurst Cl. BR6: Chels 7K **173**
WELLING 3B **126**
Welling High St. DA16: Well 3B **126**
Wellings Ho. UB3: Hayes 1K **93**
Wellington N8 4J **47**
(not continuous)
Wellington Arch 6H 11 (2E 100)
Wellington Av. DA15: Sidc 6A **126**
E4 2H **35**
HA5: H End 1D **40**
KT4: Wor Pk 3E **164**
N9 3C **34**
N15 6F **49**
TW3: Houn 5E **112**
Wellington Bldgs.
SW1 6H **17** (5E **100**)
Wellington Cl. KT12: Walt T 7H **147**
RM10: Dag 7J **73**
SE14 1K **121**
W11 6J **81**
Wellington Ct. HA5: H End 1D **40**
(off Wellington Rd.)
NW8 2B **82**
(off Wellington Rd.)
SW1 7E **10**
(off Knightsbridge)
SW6 1K **117**
(off Maltings Pl.)
TW12: Tedd 5H **131**
TW15: Ashf 5A **128**
TW19: Stanw 7A **110**
Wellington Cres. KT3: N Mald 3J **151**
Wellington Dr. RM10: Dag 7J **73**
Wellington Gdns. SE7 6A **106**
TW2: Twick 4H **131**
Wellington Gro. SE10 7F **105**
Wellington Ho. E16 1J **105**
(off Pepys Cres.)
NW3 6D **64**
(off Eton Rd.)
UB5: N'olt 7E **58**
(off Farmlands, The)
W5 3E **78**
Wellington Mans. E10 1C **68**
Wellington M. N7 6K **65**
(off Roman Way)
SE7 6A **106**
SE22 4G **121**
SW16 3H **137**
Wellington Monument 6H 11
Wellington Mus. 6H 11 (2E 100)
Wellington Pde. DA15: Sidc 5A **126**
Wellington Pk. Est. NW2 2C **62**
Wellington Pas. E11 5J **51**
(off Wellington Rd.)
Wellington Pl. N2 5C **46**
NW8 1B **4** (3B **82**)
Wellington Rd. BR2: Brom 4A **160**
CR0: Croy 7B **156**
DA5: Bexl 5D **126**
DA17: Belv 5F **109**
E6 1D **88**
E7 4H **69**
E10 1A **68**
E11 5J **51**
E17 4A **50**
EN1: Enf 5K **23**
HA3: W'stone 3J **41**
HA5: H End 1D **40**
NW8 1B **4** (2B **82**)
NW10 3F **81**
SW19 2J **135**
TW2: Twick 5H **131**
TW12: Hamp H 5H **131**
TW14: Felt 5G **111**
TW15: Ashf 5A **128**
W5 3C **96**
Wellington Rd. Nth. TW4: Houn 3D **112**
Wellington Rd. Sth. TW4: Houn 4D **112**
Wellington Row E2 1K **9** (3F **85**)
Wellington Sq. SW3 5E **16** (5D **100**)
Wellington St. IG11: Bark 1G **89**
SE18 4E **106**
WC2 2G **13** (7K **83**)
Wellington Ter. E1 1H **103**
HA1: Harr 1H **59**
N8 3A **48**
(off Turnpike La.)
W2 7J **81**
Wellington Way E3 3C **86**
Welling United FC 3C 126
Welling Way DA16: Well 3J **125**
SE9 3G **125**
Well La. SW14 5J **115**
Wellmeadow Rd. SE13 6G **123**
(not continuous)
W7 4A **96**
Wellow Wlk. SM5: Cars 1B **166**
Well Pl. NW3 3B **64**
Well Rd. EN5: Barn 5A **20**
NW3 3B **64**
Wells, The N14 7C **22**
Wells Cl. CR2: S Croy 5E **168**
UB5: Yead 3A **76**
Wells Ct. BR2: Brom 2F **159**
NW6 2J **81**
(off Cambridge Av.)
Wells Dr. NW9 1K **61**
Wells Gdns. IG1: Ilf 7C **52**
RM10: Dag 5H **73**
Wells Ho. BR1: Brom 5K **141**
(off Pike Cl.)
EC1 1K **7**
(off Spa Grn. Est.)
IG11: Bark 7A **72**
(off Margaret Bondfield Av.)
SE16 3J **103**
(off Howland Est.)
W5 1D **96**
(off Grove Rd.)
Wells Ho. Rd. NW10 5A **80**
Wellside Cl. EN5: Barn 4A **20**
Wellside Gdns. SW14 4J **115**
Wells M. W1 6B **6** (5G **83**)
Wellsmoor Gdns. BR1: Brom 3E **160**
Wells Pk. Rd. SE26 3G **139**
Wells Path UB4: Hayes 3G **75**
Wells Pl. SW18 7A **118**
Wells Ri. NW8 1D **82**
Wells Rd. BR1: Brom 2D **160**
W12 2E **98**
Wells Sq. WC1 2G **7** (3K **83**)
Wells St. W1 6A **6** (5G **83**)
Wellstead Av. N9 7E **24**
Wellstead Rd. E6 2E **88**
Wells Ter. N4 2A **66**
Well St. E9 7J **67**
E15 6G **69**
Wells Way SE5 6D **102**
SW7 1A **16** (3B **100**)
Wells Yd. N7 5A **66**
Well Wlk. NW3 4B **64**
Wellwood Rd. IG3: Ilf 1A **72**
Welmar M. SW4 5H **119**
(off Northbourne Rd.)
Welsby Ct. W5 5C **78**
Welsford St. SE1 4G **103**
(not continuous)
Welsh Cl. E13 3J **87**
Welsh Harp Nature Reserve 1A 62
Welsh Ho. E1 1H **103**
(off Wapping La.)
Welshpool Ho. E8 1G **85**
(off Welshpool St.)
Welshpool St. E8 1G **85**
(not continuous)
Welshside NW9 6A **44**
(off Ruthin Cl.)
Welshside Wlk. NW9 6A **44**
Welstead Ho. E1 6H **85**
(off Cannon St. Rd.)
Welstead Way W4 4B **98**
Weltje Rd. W6 4C **98**
Welton Ct. SE5 1E **120**
Welton Ho. E1 5K **85**
(off Stepney Way)
Welton Rd. SE18 7J **107**
Welwyn Av. TW14: Felt 6H **111**
Welwyn St. E2 3J **85**
Welwyn Way UB4: Hayes 4G **75**
WEMBLEY 5E **60**
Wembley Arena 4G 61
Wembley Commercial Cen.
HA9: Wemb 2D **60**
Wembley Conference Cen. 4G 61
Wembley Hill Rd. HA9: Wemb 3F **61**
WEMBLEY PARK 3G **61**
Wembley Pk. Bus. Cen.
HA9: Wemb 4H **61**
Wembley Pk. Dr. HA9: Wemb 4F **61**
Wembley Retail Pk. HA9: Wemb 4H **61**
Wembley Rd. TW12: Hamp 1E **148**
Wembley Stadium 4G 61
Wembley Stadium Ind. Est.
HA9: Wemb 4H **61**
Wembley Way HA9: Wemb 6H **61**
Wemborough Rd. HA7: Stan 1B **42**
Wembury M. N6 7G **47**
Wembury Rd. N6 7F **47**
Wemyss Rd. SE3 2H **123**
Wendela Ct. HA1: Harr 2J **59**
Wendell Rd. W12 3B **98**
Wenderholme CR2: S Croy 5D **168**
(off Sth. Park Hill Rd.)
Wendle Ct. SW8 7E **18** (6J **101**)
Wendling NW5 5D **64**
Wendling Rd. SM1: Sutt 1B **166**
Wendon St. E3 1B **86**
Wendover SE17 5E **102**
(not continuous)
Wendover Cl. UB4: Yead 4C **76**
Wendover Ct. BR2: Brom 3K **159**
(off Wendover Rd.)
NW2 3J **63**
NW10 4H **79**
W1 6G **5**
(off Chiltern St.)
Wendover Dr. KT3: N Mald 6B **152**
Wendover Ho. W1 6G **5**
(off Chiltern St.)
Wendover Rd. BR2: Brom 4K **159**
NW10 2B **80**
SE9 3B **124**
Wendover Way DA16: Well 5A **126**
Wendy Cl. EN1: Enf 6A **24**
Wendy Way HA0: Wemb 1E **78**
Wenham Ho. SW8 7G **101**
Wenlake Ho. EC1 3C **8**
(off Old St.)
Wenlock Barn Est. N1 2D **84**
(off Wenlock St.)
Wenlock Ct. N1 1F **9** (2D **84**)
Wenlock Gdns. NW4 4D **44**
Wenlock Rd. HA8: Edg 7C **28**
N1 1D **8** (2C **84**)
Wenlock St. N1 1D **8** (2C **84**)
Wennington Rd. E3 2K **85**
Wensdale Ho. E5 2G **67**
Wensley Av. IG8: Wfd G 7C **36**
Wensley Cl. N11 6K **31**
SE9 6D **124**
Wensleydale Av. IG5: Ilf 2C **52**
Wensleydale Gdns. TW12: Hamp 7F **131**
Wensleydale Pas. TW12: Hamp 1E **148**
Wensleydale Rd. TW12: Hamp 6E **130**
Wensley Rd. N18 6C **34**
Wentland Cl. SE6 2F **141**
Wentland Rd. SE6 2F **141**
Wentway Ct. W13 4K **77**
(off Ruislip Rd. E.)
Wentworth Av. N3 7D **30**
Wentworth Cl. BR2: Hayes 2J **171**
BR6: Farnb 5J **173**
KT6: Surb 2D **162**
N3 7E **30**
SE28 6D **90**
SM4: Mord 7J **153**
TW15: Ashf 4D **128**
Wentworth Ct. SW18 6K **117**
(off Garratt La.)
TW2: Twick 3J **131**
W6 6G **99**
(off Paynes Wlk.)
Wentworth Cres. SE15 7G **103**
UB3: Harl 3F **93**
Wentworth Dr. HA5: Eastc 5J **39**
Wentworth Dwellings E1 7J **9**
(off Wentworth St.)
Wentworth Flds. UB4: Hayes 2F **75**
Wentworth Gdns. N13 3G **33**
Wentworth Hill HA9: Wemb 1F **61**
Wentworth M. E3 4A **86**
Wentworth Pk. N3 7D **30**

Willowdene Ct. *N20*	.7F 21

(off High Rd.)

Willow Dr. EN5: Barn 4B 20
Willow End KT6: Surb 1E 162
 N20 ....2D 30
Willowfields Cl. SE18 ....5J 107
Willow Gdns. HA4: Ruis 2H 57
 TW3: Houn 1E 112
Willow Grange DA14: Sidc 3B 144
Willow Grn. NW9 ....1A 44
Willow Gro. BR7: Chst 6E 142
 E13 ....2J 87
 HA4: Ruis 2H 57
Willowhayne Ct. KT12: Walt T 7K 147
(off Willowhayne Dr.)
Willowhayne Dr. KT12: Walt T 7K 147
Willowhayne Gdns. KT4: Wor Pk 3E 164
Willow Ho. BR2: Brom 2G 159
 W10 ....4F 81
(off Maple Wlk.)
Willow La. CR4: Mitc 5D 154
 SE18 ....4D 106
Willow Lodge SW6 ....1F 117
 TW16: Sun 7H 129
(off Forest Dr.)
Willowmead Cl. W5 ....4D 78
Willow Mt. CR0: Croy 3E 168
Willow Pl. SW1 ....3B 18 (4G 101)
Willow Rd. E12 ....3D 70
 EN1: Enf 3K 23
 KT3: N Mald 4J 151
 NW3 ....4B 64
 RM6: Chad H 6E 54
 SM6: Wall 7F 167
 W5 ....2E 96
Willows, The BR3: Beck 1C 158
 E6 ....7D 70
Willows Av. SM4: Mord 5K 153
Willows Cl. HA5: Pinn 2A 40
Willowside Ct. EN2: Enf 3G 23
Willows Ter. NW10 ....2B 80
(off Rucklidge Av.)
Willow St. E4 ....1A 36
 EC2 ....3G 9 (4E 84)
 RM7: Rom 4J 55
Willow Tree Cl. E3 ....1A 86
 SW18 ....1K 135
 UB4: Yead 4A 76
Willowtree Cl. UB10: Ick 3E 56
Willow Tree Ct. DA14: Sidc 5A 144
 HA0: Wemb 5D 60
Willow Tree La. UB4: Yead 4A 76
Willow Tree Rdbt. UB4: Yead 5B 76
Willow Tree Wlk. BR1: Brom 1K 159
Willowtree Way CR7: Thor H 1A 156
Willow Va. BR7: Chst 6F 143
 W12 ....1C 98
Willow Vw. SW19 ....1B 154
Willow Wlk. BR6: Farnb 3F 173
 E17 ....5B 50
 IG1: Ilf 2F 71
 N2 ....2B 46
 N15 ....4B 48
 N21 ....6E 22
 SE1 ....3E 102
 SM3: Sutt 3H 165
Willow Way HA0: Wemb 3A 60
 KT19: Ewe 6K 163
 N3 ....7E 30
 SE26 ....3J 139
 TW2: Twick 2F 131
 TW16: Sun 4J 147
 W11 ....7F 81
Willow Wood Cres. SE25 ....6E 156
Willow Wren Wharf UB2: S'hall 4K 93
Willrose Cres. SE2 ....5B 108
Willsbridge Ct. SE15 ....6E 102
Wills Cres. TW3: Houn 6F 113
Wills Gro. NW7 ....5H 29
(not continuous)
Wilman Gro. E8 ....7G 67

Wilmar Cl. UB4: Hayes 4F 75
Wilmar Gdns. BR4: W W'ck 1D 170
Wilmcote Ho. W2 ....5K 81
(off Woodchester Sq.)
Wilment Ct. NW2 ....3E 62
Wilmer Cl. KT2: King T 5F 133
Wilmer Cres. KT2: King T 5F 133
Wilmer Gdns. N1 ....1E 84
(not continuous)
Wilmer Lea Cl. E15 ....7E 68
Wilmer Pl. N16 ....2F 67
Wilmers Ct. NW10 ....1K 79
(off Stracey Rd.)
Wilmington Av. W4 ....7K 97
Wilmington Cl. SW16 ....7J 137
Wilmington Gdns. IG11: Bark 6H 71
Wilmington Sq. WC1 ....2J 7 (3A 84)
(not continuous)
Wilmington St. WC1 ....2J 7 (3A 84)
Wilmot Cl. N2 ....2A 46
 SE15 ....7G 103
Wilmot Pl. NW1 ....7G 65
 W7 ....1J 95
Wilmot Rd. E10 ....2D 68
 N17 ....3D 48
 SM5: Cars 5D 166
Wilmot St. E2 ....4H 85
Wilmount St. SE18 ....4F 107
Wilna Rd. SW18 ....7A 118
Wilsham St. W11 ....1F 99
Wilshaw Cl. NW4 ....3C 44
Wilshaw Ho. SE8 ....7C 104
Wilshaw St. SE14 ....1C 122
Wilsmere Dr. HA3: Hrw W 7D 26
 UB5: N'olt 5C 58
Wilson Av. CR4: Mitc 7C 136
Wilson Cl. CR2: S Croy 5D 168
 HA9: Wemb 7F 43
Wilson Dr. HA9: Wemb 7F 43
Wilson Gdns. HA1: Harr 7G 41
Wilson Gro. SE16 ....2H 103
Wilson Rd. E6 ....3B 88
 IG1: Ilf 7D 52
 KT9: Chess 6F 163
 SE5 ....1E 120
Wilson's Av. N17 ....2F 49
Wilson's Pl. E14 ....6B 86
Wilson's Rd. W6 ....5F 99
Wilson St. E17 ....5E 50
 EC2 ....5F 9 (5D 84)
 N21 ....7F 23
Wilson Wlk. W4 ....4B 98
(off Prebend Gdns.)
Wilstone Cl. UB4: Yead 4C 76
Wiltern Ct. NW2 ....6G 63
Wilthorne Gdns. RM10: Dag 7H 73
Wilton Av. W4 ....5A 98
Wilton Cl. UB7: Harm 6A 92
Wilton Ct. E1 ....6H 85
(off Cavell St.)
Wilton Cres. SW1 ....7G 11 (2E 100)
 SW19 ....7H 135
Wilton Dr. RM5: Col R 1J 55
Wilton Est. E8 ....6G 67
Wilton Gdns. KT8: W Mole 3E 148
Wilton Gro. KT3: N Mald 6B 152
 SW19 ....1H 153
Wilton Ho. CR2: S Croy 5C 168
(off Nottingham Rd.)
Wilton M. E8 ....6H 67
 SW1 ....1H 17 (3E 100)
Wilton Pde. TW13: Felt 1K 129
Wilton Pl. HA1: Harr 6K 41
 SW1 ....7G 11 (2E 100)
Wilton Rd. EN4: Cockf 4J 21
 N10 ....2E 46
 SE2 ....4C 108
 SW1 ....2A 18 (3F 101)
 SW19 ....7C 136
 TW4: Houn 3B 112

Wilton Row SW1 ....7G 11 (2E 100)
Wilton Sq. N1 ....1D 84
Wilton St. SW1 ....1J 17 (3F 101)
Wilton Ter. SW1 ....1G 17 (3E 100)
Wilton Vs. N1 ....1D 84
(off Wilton La.)
Wilton Wlk. TW13: Felt 1K 129
(off Wilton Pde.)
Wilton Way E8 ....6G 67
Wiltshire Cl. NW7 ....5G 29
 SW3 ....3E 16 (4D 100)
Wiltshire Ct.
 CR2: S Croy 5C 168
 IG1: Ilf 6G 71
 N4 ....1K 65
(off Marquis Rd.)
Wiltshire Gdns. N4 ....6C 48
 TW2: Twick 1G 131
Wiltshire La. HA5: Eastc 3H 39
Wiltshire Rd. BR6: Orp 7K 161
 CR7: Thor H 3A 156
 SW9 ....3A 120
Wiltshire Row N1 ....1D 84
Wilverley Cres. KT3: N Mald 6A 152
Wimbart Rd. SW2 ....7K 119
WIMBLEDON 6H 135
Wimbledon (All England Lawn Tennis &
 Croquet Club) 4G 135
Wimbledon Bri. SW19 ....6H 135
Wimbledon Cl. SW20 ....7F 135
Wimbledon Common 4C 134
Wimbledon Greyhound &
 Speedway Stadium 4A 136
Wimbledon Hill Rd. SW19 ....6G 135
Wimbledon Lawn Tennis Mus. 4G 135
Wimbledon Leisure Cen. 6K 135
Wimbledon Mus. of Local History 6G 135
WIMBLEDON PARK 3J 135
Wimbledon Pk. Ct. SW19 ....1H 135
Wimbledon Pk. Rd. SW18 ....1H 135
 SW19 ....2G 135
Wimbledon Pk. Side SW19 ....3F 135
Wimbledon Rd. SW17 ....4A 136
Wimbledon Stadium Bus. Cen.
 SW17 ....3K 135
Wimbledon Windmill Mus. 2D 134
Wimbolt St. E2 ....3G 85
Wimborne Av. BR5: St P 4K 161
 BR7: Chst 4K 161
 UB2: S'hall 4E 94
 UB4: Yead 6K 75
Wimborne Cl. IG9: Buck H 2E 36
 KT4: Wor Pk 1E 164
 SE12 ....5H 123
Wimborne Ct. SW12 ....3G 137
 UB5: N'olt 6E 58
Wimborne Dr. HA5: Pinn 7B 40
 NW9 ....3G 43
Wimborne Gdns. W13 ....5B 78
Wimborne Ho. E16 ....7H 87
(off Victoria Dock Rd.)
 NW1 ....4D 4
(off Harewood Av.)
 SW8 ....7K 101
(off Dorset Rd.)
 SW12 ....3G 137
Wimborne Rd. N9 ....2B 34
 N17 ....2E 48
Wimborne Way BR3: Beck 3K 157
Wimbourne Ct. N1 ....2D 84
(off Wimbourne St.)
Wimbourne St. N1 ....2D 84
Wimpole Cl. BR2: Brom 4A 160
 KT1: King T 2F 151
Wimpole M. W1 ....5J 5 (5F 83)
Wimpole Rd. UB7: Yiew 1A 92
Wimpole St. W1 ....6J 5 (5F 83)
Wimshurst Cl. CR0: Wadd 1J 167
Winans Wlk. SW9 ....2A 120
Winant Ho. E14 ....7D 86
(off Simpson's Rd.)

Wincanton Ct. N11 ....6K 31
(off Martock Gdns.)
Wincanton Cres. UB5: N'olt 5E 58
Wincanton Gdns. IG6: Ilf 3F 53
Wincanton Rd. SW18 ....7H 117
Winchcombe Rd. SM5: Cars 7B 154
Winchcomb Gdns. SE9 ....3B 124
Winchelsea Av. DA7: Bex 7F 109
Winchelsea Cl. SW15 ....5F 117
Winchelsea Cres.
 KT8: W Mole 2G 149
Winchelsea Ho. SE16 ....2J 103
(off Swan Rd.)
Winchelsea Rd. E7 ....3J 69
 N17 ....3E 48
 NW10 ....1K 79
Winchelsey Ri. CR2: S Croy 6F 169
Winchendon Rd. SW6 ....1H 117
 TW11: Tedd 4H 131
Winchester Av. NW6 ....1G 81
 NW9 ....3G 43
 TW5: Hest 6D 94
Winchester Cl. BR2: Brom 3H 159
 E6 ....6D 88
 EN1: Enf 5K 23
 KT2: King T 7H 133
 SE17 ....4B 102
Winchester Ct. W8 ....2J 99
(off Vicarage Ga.)
Winchester Dr. HA5: Pinn 5B 40
Winchester Ho. IG11: Bark 7A 72
(off Keir Hardie Way)
 SE18 ....7B 106
(off Portway Gdns.)
 SW3 ....7B 16
 SW9 ....7A 102
 W2 ....6A 82
(off Hallfield Est.)
Winchester Pk. BR2: Brom 3H 159
Winchester Pl. E8 ....5F 67
 N6 ....1F 65
Winchester Rd. BR2: Brom 3H 159
 DA7: Bex 2D 126
 E4 ....7K 35
 HA3: Kent 4E 42
 HA6: Nwood 2H 39
 IG1: Ilf 3H 71
 KT12: Walt T 7J 147
 N6 ....7F 47
 N9 ....1A 34
 NW3 ....7B 64
 TW1: Twick 6B 114
 TW13: Hanw 3D 130
 UB3: Harl 7G 93
Winchester Sq. SE1 ....4E 14
Winchester St. SW1 ....5K 17 (5F 101)
 W3 ....1J 97
Winchester Wlk. SE1 ....4E 14 (1D 102)
Winchester Wharf SE1 ....4E 14
(off Clink St.)
Winchet Wlk. CR0: Croy 6J 157
Winchfield Cl. HA3: Kent 6C 42
Winchfield Ho. SW15 ....6B 116
Winchfield Rd. SE26 ....5A 140
Winch Ho. E14 ....3D 104
(off Tiller Rd.)
 SW10 ....7A 100
(off King's Rd.)
Winchilsea Ho. NW8 ....2B 4
(off St John's Wood Rd.)
WINCHMORE HILL 7F 23
Winchmore Hill Rd. N14 ....1C 32
 N21 ....1C 32
Winchmore Vs. N21 ....7E 22
(off Winchmore Hill Rd.)
Winchstone Cl. TW17: Shep 4B 146
Winckley Cl. HA3: Kent 5F 43
Wincott St. SE11 ....4K 19 (4A 102)
Wincrofts Dr. SE9 ....4H 125
Windall Cl. SE19 ....1G 157
Windborough Rd. SM5: Cars 7E 166

HOSPITALS and HOSPICES
covered by this atlas.

N.B. Where Hospitals and Hospices are not named on the map, the reference
given is for the road in which they are situated.

ABBEY CHURCHILL LONDON, THE 3A 102 (1K 19)
22 Barkham Terrace
LONDON
SE1 7PW
Tel: 020 79285633

ASHFORD HOSPITAL 2A 128
London Road
ASHFORD
TW15 3AA
Tel: 01784 884488

ATHLONE HOUSE 1D 64
Hampstead Lane
LONDON
N6 4RX
Tel: 020 83485231

BARKING HOSPITAL 7K 71
Upney Lane
BARKING
IG11 9LX
Tel: 0208 9838000

BARNES HOSPITAL 3A 116
South Worple Way
LONDON
SW14 8SU
Tel: 020 88784981

BARNET HOSPITAL 4A 20
Wellhouse Lane
BARNET
EN5 3DJ
Tel: 020 82164000

BECKENHAM HOSPITAL 2B 158
379 Croydon Road
BECKENHAM
BR3 3QL
Tel: 01689 863000

BECONTREE DAY HOSPITAL 2E 72
508 Becontree Avenue
DAGENHAM
RM8 3HR
Tel: 0208 2767288

BELVEDERE DAY HOSPITAL 1C 80
341 Harlesden Road
LONDON
NW10 3RX
Tel: 020 84593562

BELVEDERE PRIVATE CLINIC 5C 108
Knee Hill
LONDON
SE2 0AT
Tel: 020 83114464

BETHLEM ROYAL HOSPITAL, THE 7C 158
Monks Orchard Road
BECKENHAM
BR3 3BX
Tel: 020 87776611

BLACKHEATH BMI HOSPITAL, THE 3H 123
40-42 Lee Terrace
LONDON
SE3 9UD
Tel: 020 83187722

BOLINGBROKE HOSPITAL 5C 118
Bolingbroke Grove
LONDON
SW11 6HN
Tel: 020 72237411

BRITISH HOME 5B 138
Crown Lane
LONDON
SW16 3JB
Tel: 020 86708261

BUSHEY BUPA HOSPITAL 1E 26
Heathbourne Road, Bushey Heath
BUSHEY
WD23 1RD
Tel: 020 89509090

CAMDEN MEWS DAY HOSPITAL 7G 65
1-5 Camden Mews
LONDON
NW1 9DB
Tel: 020 75304780

CARSHALTON WAR MEMORIAL HOSPITAL 6D 166
The Park
CARSHALTON
SM5 3DB
Tel: 020 86475534

CASSEL HOSPITAL, THE 4D 132
1 Ham Common
RICHMOND
TW10 7JF
Tel: 020 89408181

CASUALTY PLUS 5C 96
1010 Great West Road
BRENTFORD
TW8 9BA
Tel: 08456 777999

CENTRAL MIDDLESEX HOSPITAL 3J 79
Acton Lane
LONDON
NW10 7NS
Tel: 020 89655733

CHARING CROSS HOSPITAL 6F 99
Fulham Palace Road
LONDON
W6 8RF
Tel: 020 88461234

CHASE FARM HOSPITAL 1F 23
127 The Ridgeway
ENFIELD
EN2 8JL
Tel: 020 83666600

CHELSEA & WESTMINSTER HOSPITAL 6A 100
369 Fulham Road
LONDON
SW10 9NH
Tel: 020 87468000

CHILDREN'S HOSPITAL, THE (LEWISHAM) 5D 122
Lewisham University Hospital
Lewisham High Street
LONDON
SE13 6LH
Tel: 020 83333000

CLAYPONDS HOSPITAL 4E 96
Sterling Place
LONDON
W5 4RN
Tel: 020 85604011

CLEMENTINE CHURCHILL BMI HOSPITAL, THE 3K 59
Sudbury Hill
HARROW
HA1 3RX
Tel: 020 88723872

COLINDALE HOSPITAL 2A 44
Colindale Avenue
LONDON
NW9 5HG
Tel: 020 89522381

CROMWELL HOSPITAL, THE 4K 99
162-174 Cromwell Road
LONDON
SW5 0TU
Tel: 020 74602000

DULWICH COMMUNITY HOSPITAL 4E 120
East Dulwich Grove
LONDON
SE22 8PT
Tel: AWAITING NEW T

EALING HOSPITAL 1H 95
Uxbridge Road
SOUTHALL
UB1 3HW
Tel: 020 89675000

EASTMAN DENTAL HOSPITAL & DENTAL INSTITUTE, THE
....4K 83 (3G 7)
256 Gray's Inn Road
LONDON
WC1X 8LD
Tel: 020 79151000

EDENHALL MARIE CURIE CENTRE 5B 64
11 Lyndhurst Gardens
LONDON
NW3 5NS
Tel: 020 78533400

EDGWARE COMMUNITY HOSPITAL 7C 28
Burnt Oak Broadway
EDGWARE
HA8 0AD
Tel: 020 89522381

ELIZABETH GARRETT ANDERSON & OBSTETRIC
HOSPITAL, THE 4G 83 (4B 6)
Huntley Street
LONDON
WC1E 6DH
Tel: 020 73879300

ERITH & DISTRICT HOSPITAL 6K 109
Park Crescent, ERITH
DA8 3EE
Tel: 020 83083131

EVELINA CHILDREN'S HOSPITAL 3K 101 (1G 19)
St Thomas' Hospital, Lambeth Palace Road
LONDON
SE1 7EH
Tel: 0207 1887188

FINCHLEY MEMORIAL HOSPITAL 7F **31**
Granville Road
LONDON
N12 0JE
Tel: 020 83493121

FLORENCE NIGHTINGALE DAY HOSPITAL 5C **82** (5D **4**)
1B Harewood Row
LONDON
NW1 6SE
Tel: 020 77259940

FLORENCE NIGHTINGALE HOSPITAL 5C **82** (5D **4**)
11-19 Lisson Grove
LONDON
NW1 6SH
Tel: 020 75357700

FORDWYCH ROAD DAY HOSPITAL 5H **63**
85-87 Fordwych Road
LONDON
NW2 3TL
Tel: 020 82081612

GARDEN BMI HOSPITAL, THE 3E **44**
46-50 Sunny Gardens Road
LONDON
NW4 1RP
Tel: 020 84574500

GOODMAYES HOSPITAL 5A **54**
Barley Lane
ILFORD
IG3 8XJ
Tel: 020 89838000

GORDON HOSPITAL 4H **101** (4C **18**)
Bloomburg Street
LONDON
SW1V 2RH
Tel: 020 87468733

GREAT ORMOND STREET HOSPITAL FOR CHILDREN
.................................4J **83** (4F **7**)
Great Ormond Street
LONDON
WC1N 3JH
Tel: 020 74059200

GREENWICH & BEXLEY COTTAGE HOSPICE 5C **108**
185 Bostall Hill
LONDON
SE2 0GB
Tel: 020 83122244

GUY'S HOSPITAL 1D **102** (5F **15**)
St Thomas Street
LONDON
SE1 9RT
Tel: 020 71887188

GUY'S NUFFIELD HOUSE 2D **102** (6E **14**)
Newcomen Street
LONDON
SE1 1YR
Tel: 020 79554257

HAMMERSMITH HOSPITAL 6C **80**
Du Cane Road
LONDON
W12 0HS
Tel: 020 83831000

HARLEY STREET CLINIC, THE 5F **83** (5J **5**)
35 Weymouth Street
LONDON
W1G 8BJ
Tel: 020 79357700

HARRIS HOSPISCARE 4K **173**
Orpington Hospital,
109 Sevenoaks Road
ORPINGTON
BR6 9JX
Tel: 01689 605300

HEART HOSPITAL, THE 5E **82** (6H **5**)
16-18 Westmoreland Street
LONDON
W1G 8PH
Tel: 020 75738888

HEATHVIEW DAY CENTRE 6C **108**
Lodge Hill
LONDON
SE2 0AY
Tel: 020 83197100

HIGHGATE HOSPITAL 6D **46**
17 View Road
LONDON
N6 4DJ
Tel: 020 83414182

HILLINGDON HOSPITAL 5B **74**
Pield Heath Road
UXBRIDGE
UB8 3NN
Tel: 01895 238282

HOLLY HOUSE HOSPITAL 2E **36**
High Road
BUCKHURST HILL
IG9 5HX
Tel: 0208 5053311

HOMERTON UNIVERSITY HOSPITAL 5K **67**
Homerton Row
LONDON
E9 6SR
Tel: 020 85105555

HOSPITAL FOR TROPICAL DISEASES 4G **83** (4B **6**)
Mortimer Market, Capper Street
LONDON
WC1E 6AU
Tel: 020 7387 9300

HOSPITAL OF ST JOHN & ST ELIZABETH 2B **82**
60 Grove End Road
LONDON
NW8 9NH
Tel: 020 78064000

KING EDWARD VII'S HOSPITAL SISTER AGNES
.................................5E **82** (5H **5**)
5-10 Beaumont Street
LONDON
W1G 6AA
Tel: 020 74864411

KING GEORGE HOSPITAL 5A **54**
Barley Lane
ILFORD
IG3 8YB
Tel: 020 89838000

KING'S COLLEGE HOSPITAL 2D **120**
Denmark Hill
LONDON
SE5 9RS
Tel: 020 77374000

KING'S OAK BMI HOSPITAL, THE 1F **23**
The Ridgeway
ENFIELD
EN2 8SD
Tel: 020 83709500

KINGSBURY COMMUNITY HOSPITAL 4G **43**
Honeypot Lane
LONDON
NW9 9QY
Tel: 020 89031323

KINGSTON HOSPITAL 1H **151**
Galsworthy Road
KINGSTON UPON THAMES
KT2 7QB
Tel: 020 85467711

LAMBETH HOSPITAL 3K **119**
108 Landor Road
LONDON
SW9 9NT
Tel: 020 74116100

LATIMER DAY HOSPITAL 5G **83** (5A **6**)
40 Hanson Street
LONDON
W1W 6UL
Tel: 020 73809187

LEWISHAM UNIVERSITY HOSPITAL 5D **122**
Lewisham High Street
LONDON
SE13 6LH
Tel: 020 83333000

LISTER HOSPITAL, THE 5F **101** (6J **17**)
Chelsea Bridge Road
LONDON
SW1W 8RH
Tel: 020 77303417

LONDON BRIDGE HOSPITAL 1D **102** (4F **15**)
27 Tooley Street
LONDON
SE1 2PR
Tel: 020 74073100

LONDON CHEST HOSPITAL 2J **85**
Bonner Road
LONDON
E2 9JX
Tel: 020 73777000

LONDON CLINIC, THE 4E **82** (4H **5**)
20 Devonshire Place
LONDON
W1G 6BW
Tel: 020 79354444

LONDON FOOT HOSPITAL 4G **83** (4A **6**)
33 & 40 Fitzroy Square
LONDON
W1T 6AY
Tel: 020 75304500

LONDON INDEPENDENT BMI HOSPITAL, THE 5K **85**
1 Beaumont Square
LONDON
E1 4NL
Tel: 020 77802400

LONDON LIGHTHOUSE 6G **81**
111-117 Lancaster Road
LONDON
W11 1QT
Tel: 020 77921200

LONDON WELBECK HOSPITAL 5F **83** (6J **5**)
27 Welbeck Street
LONDON
W1G 8EN
Tel: 020 72242242

MAUDSLEY HOSPITAL, THE 2D **120**
Denmark Hill
LONDON
SE5 8AZ
Tel: 0207 7036333

MAYDAY UNIVERSITY HOSPITAL 6B **156**
Mayday Road
THORNTON HEATH
CR7 7YE
Tel: 020 84013000

MEADOW HOUSE HOSPICE 2H **95**
Ealing Hospital
Uxbridge Road
SOUTHALL
UB1 3HW
Tel: 020 8967 5179

MEMORIAL HOSPITAL 2E **124**
Shooters Hill
LONDON
SE18 3RZ
Tel: 020 88366000

MIDDLESEX HOSPITAL, THE 5G **83** (6B **6**)
Mortimer Street
LONDON
W1T 3AA
Tel: 020 76368333

MILDMAY MISSION HOSPITAL 3F **85** (2J **9**)
Hackney Road
LONDON
E2 7NA
Tel: 020 76136300

MILE END HOSPITAL 4K **85**
Bancroft Road
LONDON
E1 4DG
Tel: 020 73777000

MOLESEY HOSPITAL 5E **148**
High Street
WEST MOLESEY
KT8 2LU
Tel: 020 89414481

MOORFIELDS EYE HOSPITAL 3D **84** (2E **8**)
162 City Road
LONDON
EC1V 2PD
Tel: 020 72533411

MORLAND ROAD DAY HOSPITAL 1G **91**
Morland Road
DAGENHAM
RM10 9HU
Tel: 0208 2767933

NATIONAL HOSPITAL FOR NEUROLOGY &
              NEUROSURGERY, THE 4J **83** (4F **7**)
Queen Square
LONDON
WC1N 3BG
Tel: 020 78373611

NELSON HOSPITAL 2H **153**
Kingston Road
LONDON
SW20 8DB
Tel: 020 82962000

NEW VICTORIA HOSPITAL 1A **152**
184 Coombe Lane West
KINGSTON UPON THAMES
KT2 7EG
Tel: 020 89499000

NEWHAM GENERAL HOSPITAL 4A **88**
Glen Road
LONDON
E13 8SL
Tel: 020 74764000

NHS CENTRE (MANOR PARK) 5D **70**
30 Church Road
LONDON
E12 6AQ
Tel: 020 8553 7400

NHS WALK-IN CENTRE (BARKING & DAGENHAM) 6K **71**
Upney Lane Centre
132 Upney Lane
BARKING
IG11 9YD
Tel: 020 8924 6262

NHS WALK-IN CENTRE (CHARING CROSS) 5F **99**
Charing Cross Hospital, Fulham Palace Road
LONDON
W6 8RF
Tel: 020 8383 0904

NHS WALK-IN CENTRE (CROYDON) 3C **168**
45 High Street
CROYDON
CR0 1QD
Tel: 020 8666 0555

NHS WALK-IN CENTRE (EDGWARE) 7C **28**
Edgware Community Hospital
Burnt Oak Broadway
EDGWARE
HA8 0AD
Tel: 020 8732 6459

NHS WALK-IN CENTRE (FINCHLEY) 7F **31**
Finchley Memorial Hospital
Granville Road
LONDON
N12 0JE
Tel: 020 8349 6371

NHS WALK-IN CENTRE (HACKNEY) 5K **67**
Homerton University Hospital
Homerton Row
LONDON
E9 6SR
Tel: 020 8510 5342 / 7121

NHS WALK-IN CENTRE
             (LEYTONSTONE - WHIPPS CROSS) 5F **51**
Whipps Cross Hospital
Whipps Cross Road
LONDON
E11 1NR
Tel: 020 8558 8965 / 4229

NHS WALK-IN CENTRE
             (MIDDLESEX - NORTH) 5A **34**
North Middlesex Hospital
Sterling Way
LONDON
N18 1QX
Tel: 020 8887 2680

NHS WALK-IN CENTRE (NEW CROSS) 7A **104**
Henderson House
40 Goodwood Road
LONDON
SE14 6BL
Tel: 020 7206 3100

NHS WALK-IN CENTRE (NEWHAM) 4A **88**
Glen Road
LONDON
E13 8SH
Tel: 020 7363 9200

NHS WALK-IN CENTRE (PARSONS GREEN) 1J **117**
5-7 Parsons Green
LONDON
SW6 4UL
Tel: 020 8846 6758

NHS WALK-IN CENTRE
             (REDBRIDGE) 5A **54**
King George Hospital
Barley Lane
ILFORD
IG3 8YB
Tel: 020 8983 8000

NHS WALK-IN CENTRE (SOHO) 6H **83** (1C **12**)
1 Frith Street
LONDON
W1D 3HZ
Tel: 020 7534 6500

NHS WALK-IN CENTRE
             (TEDDINGTON) 6J **131**
Teddington Memorial Hospital
Hampton Road
TEDDINGTON
TW11 0JL
Tel: 020 8408 8232

NHS WALK-IN CENTRE (TOOTING) 5C **136**
Clare House
St. Georges Hospital, Blackshaw Road
LONDON
SW17 0QT
Tel: 020 8700 0505

NHS WALK-IN CENTRE (WHITECHAPEL) 5H **85**
174 Whitechapel Road
LONDON
E1 1BZ
Tel: 020 7943 1333

NHS WALK-IN CENTRE (WHITTINGTON) 2G **65**
Whittington Hospital, Sterling Way
LONDON
N18 1QX
Tel: 020 7288 5216

NORTH LONDON HOSPICE 3F **31**
47 Woodside Avenue
LONDON
N12 8TT
Tel: 020 83438841

NORTH LONDON NUFFIELD HOSPITAL, THE 2F **23**
Cavell Drive
ENFIELD
EN2 7PR
Tel: 020 83662122

NORTH LONDON PRIORY HOSPITAL 1D **32**
The Bourne
LONDON
N14 6RA
Tel: 020 88828191

NORTH MIDDLESEX HOSPITAL, THE 5K **33**
Sterling Way
LONDON
N18 1QX
Tel: 020 88872000

NORTHWICK PARK HOSPITAL 7A **42**
Watford Road
HARROW
HA1 3UJ
Tel: 020 88643232

NORTHWOOD & PINNER COMMUNITY HOSPITAL 1H **39**
Pinner Road
NORTHWOOD
HA6 1DE
Tel: 01923 824182

OLDCHURCH HOSPITAL 6K **55**
Oldchurch Road
ROMFORD
RM7 0BE
Tel: 01708 345533

ORPINGTON HOSPITAL 4K **173**
Sevenoaks Road
ORPINGTON
BR6 9JU
Tel: 01689 863000

PARKSIDE HOSPITAL 3F **135**
53 Parkside
LONDON
SW19 5NX
Tel: 020 89718000

PENNY SANGHAM DAY HOSPITAL 3D **94**
Osterley Park Road
SOUTHALL
UB2 4EU
Tel: 020 85719676

PLAISTOW HOSPITAL 2A **88**
Samson Street
LONDON
E13 9EH
Tel: 020 85866200

PORTLAND HOSPITAL FOR WOMEN &
CHILDREN, THE 4F **83** (4K **5**)
209 Great Portland Street
LONDON
W1W 5AH
Tel: 020 75804400

PRINCESS GRACE HOSPITAL 4E **82** (4G **5**)
42-52 Nottingham Place
LONDON
W1U 5NY
Tel: 020 74861234

PRINCESS GRACE HOSPITAL ANNEXE 5E **82** (5H **5**)
29-31 Devonshire Street
LONDON
W1G 6PU
Tel: 020 74861234

PRINCESS LOUISE DAY HOSPITAL 5F **81**
St. Quintin Avenue
LONDON
W10 6DL
Tel: 020 89690133

PRINCESS ROYAL UNIVERSITY HOSPITAL 3E **172**
Farnborough Common
ORPINGTON
BR6 8ND
Tel: 01689 814100

PRIORY HOSPITAL, HAYES GROVE, THE 2J **171**
Prestons Road
BROMLEY
BR2 7AS
Tel: 020 84627722

QUEEN CHARLOTTE'S & CHELSEA HOSPITAL 6C **80**
Du Cane Road
LONDON
W12 0HS
Tel: 020 83831111

QUEEN ELIZABETH HOSPITAL 7C **106**
Stadium Road
LONDON
SE18 4QH
Tel: 020 88366000

QUEEN MARY'S HOSPITAL 5A **144**
Frognal Avenue
SIDCUP
DA14 6LT
Tel: 020 83022678

QUEEN MARY'S HOSPITAL FOR CHILDREN 1A **166**
Wrythe Lane
CARSHALTON
SM5 1AA
Tel: 020 82962000

QUEEN MARY'S HOUSE 3A **64**
23 East Heath Road
LONDON
NW3 1DU
Tel: 020 74314111

QUEEN MARY'S UNIVERSITY HOSPITAL 6C **116**
Roehampton Lane
LONDON
SW15 5PN
Tel: 020 87896611

RAVENSCOURT PARK HOSPITAL 4C **98**
Ravenscourt Park
LONDON
W6 0NT
Tel: 020 88467777

REDFORD LODGE PSYCHIATRIC HOSPITAL 2B **34**
15 Church Street
LONDON
N9 9DY
Tel: 020 89561234

RICHARD HOUSE CHILDREN'S HOSPICE 7B **88**
Richard House Drive
LONDON
E16 3RG
Tel: 020 75110222

RICHMOND ROYAL HOSPITAL 3E **114**
Kew Foot Road
RICHMOND
TW9 2TE
Tel: 020 89403331

RODING BUPA HOSPITAL 3B **52**
Roding Lane South
ILFORD
IG4 5PZ
Tel: 020 85511100

ROEHAMPTON HUNTERCOMBE HOSPITAL 7C **116**
Holybourne Avenue
LONDON
SW15 4JL
Tel: 0208 7806155

ROEHAMPTON PRIORY HOSPITAL 4B **116**
Priory Lane
LONDON
SW15 5JJ
Tel: 020 88768261

ROYAL BROMPTON HOSPITAL 5C **100** (5C **16**)
Sydney Street
LONDON
SW3 6NP
Tel: 020 73528121

ROYAL BROMPTON HOSPITAL (ANNEXE) 5B **100** (5B **16**)
Fulham Road
LONDON
SW3 6HP
Tel: 020 73528121

ROYAL FREE HOSPITAL, THE 5C **64**
Pond Street
LONDON
NW3 2QG
Tel: 020 77940500

ROYAL HOSPITAL FOR NEURO-DISABILITY 6G **117**
West Hill
LONDON
SW15 3SW
Tel: 020 87804500

ROYAL LONDON HOMOEOPATHIC HOSPITAL, THE
.....................................5J **83** (5F **7**)
Great Ormond Street
LONDON
WC1N 3HR
Tel: 020 73918864

ROYAL LONDON HOSPITAL 5H **85**
Whitechapel Road
LONDON
E1 1BB
Tel: 020 73777000

ROYAL MARSDEN HOSPITAL (FULHAM), THE
.....................................5B **100** (5B **16**)
Fulham Road
LONDON
SW3 6JJ
Tel: 020 73528171

ROYAL NATIONAL ORTHOPAEDIC HOSPITAL 2G **27**
Brockley Hill
STANMORE
HA7 4LP
Tel: 020 89542300

ROYAL NATIONAL ORTHOPAEDIC HOSPITAL (OUTPATIENTS)
.....................................4F **83** (4K **5**)
45-51 Bolsover Street
LONDON
W1W 5AQ
Tel: 020 73875070

ROYAL NATIONAL THROAT, NOSE & EAR HOSPITAL
.....................................3C **83** (1G **7**)
330 Gray's Inn Road
LONDON
WC1X 8DA
Tel: 020 79151300

ROYAL NATIONAL THROAT, NOSE & EAR HOSPITAL -
SPEECH & LANGUAGE UNIT 5C **78**
10 Castlebar Hill
LONDON
W5 1TD
Tel: 020 89978480

ST ANDREW'S AT HARROW 2J **59**
Bowden House Clinic
London Road
HARROW
HA1 3JL
Tel: 020 89667000

ST ANDREW'S HOSPITAL 4D **86**
Devas Street
LONDON
E3 3NT
Tel: 020 74764000

ST ANN'S HOSPITAL 5C **48**
St Ann's Road
LONDON
N15 3TH
Tel: 020 84426000

ST ANTHONY'S HOSPITAL 1F **165**
London Road
SUTTON
SM3 9DW
Tel: 020 83376691

ST BARTHOLOMEW'S HOSPITAL 5B **84** (6B **8**)
West Smithfield
LONDON
EC1A 7BE
Tel: 020 73777000

ST BERNARD'S HOSPITAL 2H **95**
Uxbridge Road
SOUTHALL
UB1 3EU
Tel: 020 89675000

ST CHARLES HOSPITAL 5F **81**
Exmoor Street
LONDON
W10 6DZ
Tel: 020 89692488

ST CHRISTOPHER'S HOSPICE 5J **139**
51-59 Lawrie Park Road
LONDON
SE26 6DZ
Tel: 020 87789252

ST CLEMENT'S HOSPITAL 3B **86**
2A Bow Road
LONDON
E3 4LL
Tel: 020 73777000

ST GEORGE'S HOSPITAL (TOOTING) 5C **136**
Blackshaw Road
LONDON
SW17 0QT
Tel: 020 86721255

ST HELIER HOSPITAL 1A **166**
Wrythe Lane
CARSHALTON
SM5 1AA
Tel: 020 82962000

ST JOHN'S AND AMYAND HOUSE 7A **114**
Strafford Road
TWICKENHAM
TW1 3AD
Tel: 020 87449943

ST JOHN'S HOSPICE 2B **82** (1A **4**)
Hospital of St John & St Elizabeth, 60 Grove End Road
LONDON
NW8 9NH
Tel: 020 78064040

ST JOSEPH'S HOSPICE 1H **85**
Mare Street
LONDON
E8 4SA
Tel: 020 85256000

ST LUKE'S HOSPITAL FOR THE CLERGY 4G **83** (4A **6**)
14 Fitzroy Square
LONDON
W1T 6AH
Tel: 020 73884954

ST LUKE'S KENTON GRANGE HOSPICE 5D **42**
Kenton Grange, Kenton Road
HARROW
HA3 0YG
Tel: 020 83828000

ST LUKE'S WOODSIDE HOSPITAL 4E **46**
Woodside Avenue
LONDON
N10 3HU
Tel: 020 82191800

ST MARK'S HOSPITAL 7B **42**
Watford Road
HARROW
HA1 3UJ
Tel: 020 88643232

ST MARY'S HOSPITAL 6B **82** (7B **4**)
Praed Street
LONDON
W2 1NY
Tel: 020 77256666

ST MICHAEL'S CENTRE 1J **23**
Gater Drive
ENFIELD
EN2 0JB
Tel: 020 83669194

ST PANCRAS HOSPITAL 1H **83**
4 St Pancras Way
LONDON
NW1 0PE
Tel: 020 75303500

ST RAPHAEL'S HOSPICE 2F **165**
St. Anthony's Hospital, London Road
SUTTON
SM3 9DW
Tel: 020 83354575

ST THOMAS' HOSPITAL 3K **101** (1G **19**)
Lambeth Palace Road
LONDON
SE1 7EH
Tel: 0207 1887188

SHIRLEY OAKS BMI HOSPITAL 7J **157**
Poppy Lane
CROYDON
CR9 8AB
Tel: 020 86555500

SLOANE BMI HOSPITAL, THE 1F **159**
125-133 Albemarle Road
BECKENHAM
BR3 5HS
Tel: 020 84666911

SPRINGFIELD UNIVERSITY HOSPITAL 3C **136**
61 Glenburnie Road
LONDON
SW17 7DJ
Tel: 020 86826000

SURBITON HOSPITAL 6E **150**
Ewell Road
SURBITON
KT6 6EZ
Tel: 020 83997111

TEDDINGTON MEMORIAL HOSPITAL 6J **131**
Hampton Road
TEDDINGTON
TW11 0JL
Tel: 020 84088210

THORPE COOMBE HOSPITAL 3E **50**
714 Forest Road
LONDON
E17 3HP
Tel: 0208 5395522

TOLWORTH HOSPITAL 2G **163**
Red Lion Road
SURBITON
KT6 7QU
Tel: 020 83900102

TRINITY HOSPICE 4F **119**
30 Clapham Common North Side
LONDON
SW4 0RN
Tel: 020 77871000

UNIVERSITY COLLEGE HOSPITAL 4G **83** (3B **6**)
Gower Street
LONDON
WC1E 6AU
Tel: 020 73879300

UPTON CENTRE 4E **126**
14 Upton Road
BEXLEYHEATH
DA6 8LQ
Tel: 020 83017900

WELLINGTON HOSPITAL, THE 3B **82** (1B **4**)
8a Wellington Place
LONDON
NW8 9LE
Tel: 0207 5865959

WEMBLEY (MATS) HOSPITAL 6D **60**
116 Chaplin Road
WEMBLEY
HA0 4UZ
Tel: 020 89031323

WEST MIDDLESEX UNIVERSITY HOSPITAL 2A **114**
Twickenham Road
ISLEWORTH
TW7 6AF
Tel: 020 85602121

WESTERN EYE HOSPITAL 5D **82** (5E **4**)
171 Marylebone Road
LONDON
NW1 5QH
Tel: 020 78866666

WHIPPS CROSS UNIVERSITY HOSPITAL 6F **51**
Whipps Cross Road
LONDON
E11 1NR
Tel: 020 85395522

WHITTINGTON HOSPITAL 2G **65**
Highgate Hill
LONDON
N19 5NF
Tel: 020 72723070

WILLESDEN COMMUNITY HOSPITAL 7C **62**
Harlesden Road
LONDON
NW10 3RY
Tel: 020 84518017

RAIL, CROYDON TRAMLINK, DOCKLANDS LIGHT RAILWAY, RIVERBUS AND LONDON UNDERGROUND STATIONS

with their map square reference

A

Abbey Wood (Rail) 3C 108
Acton Central (Rail) 1K 97
Acton Main Line (Rail) 6J 79
Acton Town (Tube) 2G 97
Addington Village Stop (CT) 6C 170
Addiscombe Stop (CT) 1G 169
Albany Park (Rail) 2D 144
Aldgate East (Tube) 7K 9 (6F 85)
Aldgate (Tube) 1J 15 (6F 85)
Alexandra Palace (Rail) 2J 47
All Saints (DLR) 7D 86
Alperton (Tube) 1D 78
Ampere Way Stop (CT) 1K 167
Anerley (Rail) 1H 157
Angel (Tube) 2A 84
Angel Road (Rail) 5D 34
Archway (Tube) 2G 65
Arena Stop (CT) 5J 157
Arnos Grove (Tube) 5B 32
Arsenal (Tube) 3A 66
Ashford (Rail) 4B 128
Avenue Road Stop (CT) 2K 157

B

Baker Street (Tube) 4F 5 (4D 82)
Balham (Rail & Tube) 1F 137
Bank (Tube & DLR) 1E 14 (6D 84)
Bankside Pier (Riverbus) 3C 14 (7C 84)
Barbican (Rail & Tube) 5C 8 (5C 84)
Barking (Rail & Tube) 7G 71
Barkingside (Tube) 3H 53
Barnehurst (Rail) 2J 127
Barnes (Rail) 3C 116
Barnes Bridge (Rail) 2B 116
Barons Court (Tube) 5G 99
Battersea Park (Rail) 7F 101
Bayswater (Tube) 7K 81
Beckenham Hill (Rail) 5E 140
Beckenham Junction (Rail & CT) 1C 158
Beckenham Road Stop (CT) 1A 158
Beckton (DLR) 5E 88
Beckton Park (DLR) 7D 88
Becontree (Tube) 6D 72
Beddington Lane Stop (CT) 6G 155
Belgrave Walk Stop (CT) 4B 154
Bellingham (Rail) 3D 140
Belsize Park (Tube) 5C 64
Belvedere (Rail) 3H 109
Bermondsey (Tube) 3G 103
Berrylands (Rail) 4H 151
Bethnal Green (Rail) 4H 85
Bethnal Green (Tube) 3J 85
Bexley (Rail) 1G 145
Bexleyheath (Rail) 2E 126
Bickley (Rail) 3C 160
Birkbeck (Rail & CT) 3J 157
Blackfriars (Rail & Tube) 2A 14 (7B 84)
Blackfriars Millennium Pier (Riverbus) ...2K 13 (7A 84)
Blackheath (Rail) 3H 123
Blackhorse Lane Stop (CT) 7G 157
Blackhorse Road (Rail & Tube) 4K 49
Blackwall (DLR) 7E 86
Bond Street (Tube) 1J 11 (6F 83)
Borough (Tube) 7D 14 (2C 102)
Boston Manor (Tube) 4A 96
Bounds Green (Tube) 6C 32
Bow Church (DLR) 3C 86

Bowes Park (Rail) 7D 32
Bow Road (Tube) 3C 86
Brent Cross (Tube) 7F 45
Brentford (Rail) 6C 96
Brimsdown (Rail) 3F 25
Brixton (Rail & Tube) 4A 120
Brockley (Rail) 3A 122
Bromley-by-Bow (Tube) 3D 86
Bromley North (Rail) 1J 159
Bromley South (Rail) 3J 159
Brondesbury (Rail) 7H 63
Brondesbury Park (Rail) 1G 81
Bruce Grove (Rail) 2F 49
Buckhurst Hill (Tube) 2G 37
Burnt Oak (Tube) 1J 43
Bush Hill Park (Rail) 6A 24

C

Cadogan Pier (Riverbus) 6C 100
Caledonian Road & Barnsbury (Rail) 7K 65
Caledonian Road (Tube) 6K 65
Cambridge Heath (Rail) 2H 85
Camden Road (Rail) 7G 65
Camden Town (Tube) 1F 83
Canada Water (Tube) 2J 103
Canary Wharf (DLR) 1C 104
Canary Wharf (Tube) 1D 104
Canary Wharf Pier (Riverbus) 1B 104
Canning Town (Rail, Tube & DLR) 6G 87
Cannon Street (Rail & Tube) 2E 14 (7D 84)
Canonbury (Rail) 5C 66
Canons Park (Tube) 7K 27
Carshalton (Rail) 4D 166
Carshalton Beeches (Rail) 6D 166
Castle Bar Park (Rail) 5K 77
Catford (Rail) 7C 122
Catford Bridge (Rail) 7C 122
Chadwell Heath (Rail) 7D 54
Chalk Farm (Tube) 7E 64
Chancery Lane (Tube) 6J 7 (5A 84)
Charing Cross (Rail & Tube) 4E 12 (1J 101)
Charlton (Rail) 5A 106
Cheam (Rail) 7G 165
Chessington North (Rail) 5E 162
Chessington South (Rail) 7D 162
Chigwell (Tube) 3K 37
Chingford (Rail) 1B 36
Chislehurst (Rail) 2E 160
Chiswick (Rail) 7J 97
Chiswick Park (Tube) 4J 97
Church Street Stop (CT) 2C 168
City Thameslink (Rail)
    Holborn Viaduct 7A 8 (6B 84)
Clapham Common (Tube) 4G 119
Clapham High Street (Rail) 3H 119
Clapham Junction (Rail) 3C 118
Clapham North (Tube) 3J 119
Clapham South (Tube) 6F 119
Clapton (Rail) 2H 67
Clock House (Rail) 1A 158
Cockfosters (Tube) 4K 21
Colindale (Tube) 3A 44
Colliers Wood (Tube) 7B 136
Coombe Lane Stop (CT) 5J 169
Covent Garden (Tube) 2F 13 (7J 83)
Cricklewood (Rail) 4F 63
Crofton Park (Rail) 5B 122
Crossharbour & London Arena (DLR) 3D 104
Crouch Hill (Rail) 7K 47
Crystal Palace (Rail) 6G 139

Custom House for ExCeL (Rail & DLR) 7K 87
Cutty Sark for Maritime Greenwich (DLR) 6E 104
Cyprus (DLR) 7E 88

D

Dagenham Dock (Rail) 2F 91
Dagenham East (Rail) 5J 73
Dagenham Heathway (Tube) 6F 73
Dalston Kingsland (Rail) 5E 66
Denmark Hill (Rail) 2D 120
Deptford (Rail) 7C 104
Deptford Bridge (DLR) 1C 122
Devons Road (DLR) 4D 86
Dollis Hill (Tube) 5C 62
Drayton Green (Rail) 6K 77
Drayton Park (Rail) 4A 66
Dundonald Road Stop (CT) 7H 135

E

Ealing Broadway (Rail & Tube) 7D 78
Ealing Common (Tube) 1F 97
Earl's Court (Tube) 4K 99
Earlsfield (Rail) 1A 136
East Acton (Tube) 6B 80
Eastcote (Tube) 7A 40
East Croydon (Rail & CT) 2D 168
East Dulwich (Rail) 4E 120
East Finchley (Tube) 4C 46
East Ham (Tube) 7C 70
East India (DLR) 7F 87
East Putney (Tube) 5G 117
Eden Park (Rail) 5C 158
Edgware (Tube) 6C 28
Edgware Road (Tube) 6C 4 (5C 82)
Edmonton Green (Rail) 2B 34
Elephant & Castle (Rail & Tube) 4C 102
Elmers End (Rail & CT) 4K 157
Elmstead Woods (Rail) 6C 142
Eltham (Rail) 5D 124
Elverson Road (DLR) 2C 122
Embankment (Tube) 4F 13 (1J 101)
Embankment Pier (Riverbus) 4F 13 (1J 101)
Enfield Chase (Rail) 3H 23
Enfield Town (Rail) 3K 23
Erith (Rail) 5K 109
Essex Road (Rail) 7C 66
Euston (Rail & Tube) 2C 6 (3H 83)
Euston Square (Tube) 3B 6 (4G 83)
Ewell West (Rail) 7A 164

F

Fairlop (Tube) 1H 53
Falconwood (Rail) 4H 125
Farringdon (Rail & Tube) 5A 8 (5B 84)
Feltham (Rail) 1K 129
Fenchurch Street (Rail) 2J 15 (7F 85)
Festival Pier (Riverbus) 1K 101
Fieldway Stop (CT) 7D 170
Finchley Central (Tube) 1J 45
Finchley Road & Frognal (Rail) 5A 64
Finchley Road (Tube) 6A 64
Finsbury Park (Rail & Tube) 2A 66
Forest Gate (Rail) 5J 69
Forest Hill (Rail) 2J 139
Fulham Broadway (Tube) 7J 99
Fulwell (Rail) 4H 131